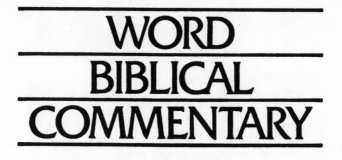

WORD

BIBLICAL

COMMENTARY

Volume 31

Hosea-Jonah

DOUGLAS STUART

THOMAS NELSON
Since 1798

NASHVILLE   DALLAS   MEXICO CITY   RIO DE JANEIRO

Word Biblical Commentary
HOSEA-JONAH
Copyright © 1987 by Thomas Nelson, Inc.

Library of Congress Cataloging-in-Publication Data
Main entry under title:

Word biblical commentary.

    Includes bibliographies.
    1. Bible—Commentaries—Collected works.
BS491.2.W67   220.7'7   81-71768
ISBN 10: 0-8499-0230-4 (vol. 31) AACR2
ISBN 13: 978-0-8499-0230-7

Printed in Mexico

The author's own translation of the text appears in italic type under the heading "Translation."

16 17 18 19 20 EPAC 15 14 13 12 11

To
Hannah
and
Maria

Hos 11:3, 4

Contents

OBADIAH

JONAH

Author's Preface

There are all sorts of biblical commentaries. Their diversity reflects a wide range of philosophies about what a commentary should be. Particularly significant is the need to choose what should be said from what could be said.

The sheer amount of information from the ancient world and from the history of scholarship on the Bible that is relevant to a biblical commentary is greater than can be included in any commentary. To include all would distort the overall picture for the reader—by mixing the truly central with the tangential. Increasingly, therefore, commentaries represent distillations rather than compendia. A commentary must be judged, then, on how well the author has selected and summarized data, and how well that selection and summary help the author illumine the meaning of the text. Does the author demonstrably understand the book/passage/sentence/phrase/term on which he or she is writing?

This is not to say that thoroughness makes no difference in the effectiveness of a commentary. It is of great help to have comprehensive bibliographical references. Length and depth are hardly irrelevant. Certainly, the choice of format is crucial to efficient exposition. And clear style obviously helps the reader. But what really counts? Is it not the fact that the commentator has convincingly understood the text?

The ultimately worthwhile commentary tends toward relentless attention to the evident themes of the text. As an example, consider Mays's scholarly commentary on Hosea. At half the length of some others, with fewer visible proofs of research, it is nonetheless more valuable. Why? Because Mays more often understands what's going on in Hosea, and he more often explains it well to the reader.

The preacher relying on Mays would probably preach most of the themes of the book accurately. I acknowledge my great indebtedness to the work of Mays, as well as that of Wolff, Freedman, and Andersen and many others, while convinced that among all the options available to date, Mays's commentary makes a special contribution simply because it most often explains Hosea best. In a related vein, I believe that Kuhnigk's realization that Hos 4 depends on Deut 32 (from which the present volume expands to detail more generally the prophetic dependence on the Mosaic covenant curses and restoration blessings) is an insight more valuable for appreciating prophetic creativity than many volumes of modern scholarly speculation have been on the subject.

Not a few lengthy commentaries take great pains to give ample space to summaries of the views of other major commentaries, with whom the author is supposedly "in dialogue." Since such dialogue is terribly difficult to carry on fairly and consistently without short-changing others' arguments, I have consciously restricted my summaries of other commentators' views, trying instead to maximize productive use of the space allotted to me by dwelling directly on explaining for the reader what I think the biblical text is saying.

As for discussions of language, text, literary form, source analysis, parallels

of likely relevance or other issues, the reader will see plenty of attention
paid to these matters in this volume. But above all else, such issues must
serve the interests of theology—the end of the process. I have made it a
commitment to discuss at whatever length necessary the essential theological
meaning of a passage as it relates to the theology of the Scriptures as a
whole. The reader deserves to see (1) directly relevant data; and (2) a convincing clarification of the data's implications for understanding the theology of
the text. All else is sauce; those things are the meat.

A related question that must be asked is: What are commentaries in practice
actually for—who uses them, and for what purpose? They should not serve
only to address topics of current interest in critical circles, nor should they
be so selective as to weight the discussion toward those issues that the commentator wants to bring to light, regardless of their theological merit. What a
commentary must do—and the only firm justification for its existence—is
constantly and carefully help its readers know what God has said and what
they are supposed to do about it.

I have kept in mind that preachers are the single biggest group of commentary buyers and users, and that they are best served by commentaries that
emphasize lasting theological concerns in proper balance with people's immediate, practical, personal or corporate questions. Whether or not I have succeeded in meeting my own standards of usefulness is a question the reader
must decide.

My warmest thanks go to the editors and publishers of the Word Biblical
Commentary, who have committed themselves to produce a series that is
bound to have wide impact and lasting usefulness. To my secretaries Tina
Howard, Carrie Powell, Barbara De Nike, and Dorrie Smith, who typed and
retyped manuscript drafts; and to my research assistants Chuck Carter, Dan
Webb, Rikki Watts, and Mark Chapman, who read and reread them, I express
my lasting appreciation.

South Hamilton, Massaschusetts   DOUGLAS STUART
November 1987

Editorial Preface

The launching of the *Word Biblical Commentary* brings to fulfillment an enterprise of several years' planning. The publishers and the members of the editorial board met in 1977 to explore the possibility of a new commentary on the books of the Bible that would incorporate several distinctive features. Prospective readers of these volumes are entitled to know what such features were intended to be; whether the aims of the commentary have been fully achieved time alone will tell.

First, we have tried to cast a wide net to include as contributors a number of scholars from around the world who not only share our aims, but are in the main engaged in the ministry of teaching in university, college, and seminary. They represent a rich diversity of denominational allegiance. The broad stance of our contributors can rightly be called evangelical, and this term is to be understood in its positive, historic sense of a commitment to scripture as divine revelation, and to the truth and power of the Christian gospel.

Then, the commentaries in our series are all commissioned and written for the purpose of inclusion in the *Word Biblical Commentary*. Unlike several of our distinguished counterparts in the field of commentary writing, there are no translated works, originally written in a non-English language. Also, our commentators were asked to prepare their own rendering of the original biblical text and to use those languages as the basis of their own comments and exegesis. What may be claimed as distinctive with this series is that it is based on the biblical languages, yet it seeks to make the technical and scholarly approach to a theological understanding of scripture understandable by— and useful to—the fledgling student, the working minister as well as to colleagues in the guild of professional scholars and teachers.

Finally, a word must be said about the format of the series. The layout in clearly defined sections has been consciously devised to assist readers at different levels. Those wishing to learn about the textual witnesses on which the translation is offered are invited to consult the section headed "Notes." If the readers' concern is with the state of modern scholarship on any given portion of scripture, then they should turn to the sections on "Bibliography" and "Form/Structure/Setting." For a clear exposition of the passage's meaning and its relevance to the ongoing biblical revelation, the "Comment" and concluding "Explanation" are designed expressly to meet that need. There is therefore something for everyone who may pick and use these volumes.

If these aims come anywhere near realization, the intention of the editors will have been met, and the labor of our team of contributors rewarded.

General Editors: *David A. Hubbard*
Glenn W. Barker †
Old Testament: *John D. W. Watts*
New Testament: *Ralph P. Martin*

Abbreviations

BANE	G. E. Wright (ed.), *The Bible and the Ancient Near East*
BAR	*Biblical Archaeologist Reader*
BASOR	*Bulletin of the American Schools of Oriental Research*
BAT	Die Botschaft des Alten Testaments
BBB	*Bibliothek van Boeken bij de Bijel*
BCSR	*Bulletin of the Council on the Study of Religion*
BDB	F. Brown, S. R. Driver, and C. A. Briggs, *Hebrew and English Lexicon of the Old Testament*
BeO	*Bibbia e oriente*
BETL	Bibliotheca ephemeridum theologicarum lovaniensium
BEvT	Beiträge zur evangelischen Theologie
BFCT	Beiträge zur Förderung christlicher Theologie
BGBE	Beiträge zur Geschichte der biblischen Exegese
BHH	B. Reicke and L. Rost (eds.), *Biblisch-Historisches Handwörterbuch*
BHK	R. Kittel, *Biblia hebraica*
BHS	*Biblia hebraica stuttgartensia*
BHT	Beiträge zur historischen Theologie
Bib	*Biblica*
BibB	Biblische Beiträge
BibIll	*Biblical Illustrator*
BibLeb	*Bibel und Leben*
BibOr	Biblica et orientalia
BibS(F)	Biblische Studien (Freiburg, 1895–)
BibS(N)	Biblische Studien (Neukirchen, 1951–)
BIES	*Bulletin of the Israel Exploration Society*
BIFAO	*Bulletin de l'institut français d'archéologie orientale*
BJRL	*Bulletin of the John Rylands University Library of Manchester*
BK	*Bibel und Kirche*
BKAT	Biblischer Kommentar: Altes Testament
BMik	*Beth Mikra*
BN	*Biblische Notizen*
BO	*Bibliotheca orientalis*
BR	*Biblical Research*
BSac	*Bibliotheca Sacra*
BSO(A)S	*Bulletin of the School of Oriental (and African) Studies*
BSS	*Bibliotheca Sanctorum*
BSt	Biblische Studien
BT	*The Bible Translator*
BTB	*Biblical Theology Bulletin*
BTS	*Bible et terre sainte*
BVC	*Bible et vie chrétienne*
BWANT	Beiträge zur Wissenschaft vom Alten und Neuen Testament
BZ	*Biblische Zeitschrift*
BZAW	Beihefte zur ZAW
CAD	*The Assyrian Dictionary of the Oriental Institute of the University of Chicago*
CAH	*Cambridge Ancient History*

CAT	Commentaire de l'Ancien Testament
CB	*Cultura bíblica*
CBQ	*Catholic Biblical Quarterly*
CBQMS	Catholic Biblical Quarterly—Monograph Series
CCath	Corpus Catholicorum
CJT	*Canadian Journal of Theology*
CleM	*Clergy Monthly*
ConB	Coniectanea biblica
COT	Commentaar op het OT
CQ	*Church Quarterly*
CQR	*Church Quarterly Review*
CRAIBL	*Comptes rendus de l'Académie des inscriptions et belles-lettres*
CSCO	Corpus scriptorum christianorum orientalium
CTA	A. Herdner, *Corpus des tablettes en cunéiformes alphabétiques*
CTM	*Concordia Theological Monthly*
CurTM	*Currents in Theology and Mission*
DACL	*Dictionnaire d'archéologie chrétienne et de liturgie*
DBSup	*Dictionnaire de la Bible, Supplément*
DD	*Dor le Dor*
DISO	C.-F. Jean and J. Hoftijzer, *Dictionnaire des inscriptions sémitiques de l'ouest*
Div	*Divinitas*
DJD	Discoveries in the Judaean Desert
DOTT	D. W. Thomas (ed.), *Documents from Old Testament Times*
DTT	*Dansk teologisk tidsskrift*
EBib	Etudes bibliques
ECarm	*Ephemerides Carmeliticae*
EHAT	Exegetisches Handbuch zum Alten Testament
EHO	Cross and Freedman, *Early Hebrew Orthography*
EI	*Ereṣ Israel*
EncJud	*Encyclopaedia judaica* (1971)
EnchBib	*Enchiridion biblicum*
EngSt	*English Studies*
EstBib	*Estudios bíblicos*
ETL	*Ephemerides theologicae lovanienses*
ETR	*Etudes théologiques et religieuses*
EuntDoc	*Euntes Docete*
EvK	Evangelische Kommentare
EvQ	*Evangelical Quarterly*
EvT	*Evangelische Theologie* (*EvTh*)
Exp	*The Expositor*
ExpTim	*Expository Times*
FRLANT	Forschungen zur Religion und Literatur des Alten und Neuen Testaments
GAG	W. von Soden, *Grundriss der akkadischen Grammatik*
GKB	Gesenius-Kautzsch-Bergsträsser, *Hebräische Grammatik*
GKC	*Gesenius' Hebrew Grammar*, ed. E. Kautzsch, tr. A. E. Cowley

HALAT	W. Baumgartner et al., *Hebräisches und aramäisches Lexikon zum Alten Testament*
HAT	Handbuch zum Alten Testament
HDR	Harvard Dissertations in Religion
HeyJ	*Heythrop Journal*
HibJ	*Hibbert Journal*
HKAT	Handkommentar zum Alten Testament
HS	*Hebrew Studies*
HSAT	*Die Heilige Schrift des Alten Testament*, 2 vols.; ed. E. Kautzsch and A. Bertholet (Tübingen: ⁴1922–23)
HSM	Harvard Semitic Monographs
HTR	*Harvard Theological Review*
HTS	Harvard Theological Studies
HUCA	*Hebrew Union College Annual*
IB	*Interpreter's Bible*
ICC	International Critical Commentary
IDB	G. A. Buttrick (ed.), *Interpreter's Dictionary of the Bible*
IDBSup	Supplementary volume to *IDB*
IEJ	*Israel Exploration Journal*
Int	*Interpretation*
ISBE	G. W. Bromiley (ed.), *International Standard Bible Encyclopedia*, 4 vols. (Grand Rapids: Eerdmans, 1979–)
ITQ	*Irish Theological Quarterly*
JA	*Journal asiatique*
JAAR	*Journal of the American Academy of Religion*
JAC	*Jahrbuch für Antike und Christentum*
JANESCU	*Journal of the Ancient Near Eastern Society of Columbia University*
JAOS	*Journal of the American Oriental Society*
JAS	*Journal of Asian Studies*
JB	A. Jones (ed.), *Jerusalem Bible*
JBC	R. E. Brown et al. (eds.), *The Jerome Biblical Commentary*
JBL	*Journal of Biblical Literature*
JBR	*Journal of Bible and Religion*
JCS	*Journal of Cuneiform Studies*
JDS	Judean Desert Studies
JEA	*Journal of Egyptian Archaeology*
JEOL	*Jaarbericht . . . ex oriente lux*
JETS	*Journal of the Evangelical Theological Society*
JJS	*Journal of Jewish Studies*
JMES	*Journal of Middle Eastern Studies*
JNES	*Journal of Near Eastern Studies*
JNSL	*Journal of Northwest Semitic Languages*
JPOS	*Journal of the Palestine Oriental Society*
JPSV	*Jewish Publication Society Version*
JQR	*Jewish Quarterly Review*
JQRMS	Jewish Quarterly Review Monograph Series
JR	*Journal of Religion*

JRAS	*Journal of the Royal Asiatic Society*
JRelS	*Journals of Religious Studies*
JSOT	*Journal for the Study of the Old Testament*
JSOTSup	Supplement to *JSOT*
JSS	*Journal of Semitic Studies*
JSSR	*Journal for the Scientific Study of Religion*
JTC	*Journal for Theology and the Church*
JTS	*Journal of Theological Studies*
Judaica	*Judaica: Beiträge zum Verständnis . . .*
KAI	H. Donner and W. Röllig. *Kanaanäische und aramäische Inschriften*
KAT	E. Sellin (ed.), Kommentar zum A.T.
KB	L. Koehler and W. Baumgartner, *Lexicon in Veteris Testamenti libros*
KD	*Kerygma und Dogma*
KJV	*King James Version*
KIT	Kleine Texte
LCC	Library of Christian Classics
LCL	Loeb Classical Library
LD	Lectio divina
Leš	*Lešonénu*
LLAVT	E. Vogt, *Lexicon linguae aramaicae Veteris Testamenti*
LQ	*Lutheran Quarterly*
LR	*Lutherische Rundschau*
LSJ	Liddell-Scott-Jones, *Greek-English Lexicon*
LTK	*Lexikon für Theologie und Kirche*
LumVit	*Lumen Vitae*
LUÅ	Lunds universitets årsskrift
MBA	Y. Aharoni and M. Ari-Yonah, *Macmillan Bible Atlas*, rev. ed. (New York: Macmillan, 1977)
MDOG	Mitteilungen der deutschen Orient-Gesellschaft
MelT	*Melita Theologica*
MGWJ	*Monatsschrift für Geschichte und Wissenschaft des Judentums*
MScRel	*Mélanges de science religieuse*
MTZ	*Münchener theologische Zeitschrift*
MVAG	Mitteilungen der vorder-asiatisch-ägyptischen Gesellschaft
NedTTs	*Nederlands theologisch tijdschrift*
NGTT	*Nederduits Gereformeerde Teologiese Tydskrif*
NHS	Nag Hammadi Studies
NICOT	New International Commentary on the Old Testament
NKZ	*Neue kirchliche Zeitschrift*
NorTT	*Norsk Teologisk Tidsskrift*
NRT	*La nouvelle revue théologique*
NSH	Kuhnigk, *Nordwestsemitische Studien zum Hoseabuch* (Rome: Biblical Institute Press, 1974)
OIP	Oriental Institute Publications
OLP	Orientalia lovaniensia periodica

OLZ	*Orientalische Literaturzeitung*
Or	*Orientalia*
OrAnt	*Oriens antiquus*
OrChr	*Oriens christianus*
OrSyr	*L'orient syrien*
OTL	Old Testament Library
OTS	*Oudtestamentische Studiën*
OTWSA	*Die Outestamentiese Werkgemeenskap in Suid-Afrika*
PAAJR	*Proceedings of the American Academy of Jewish Research*
PCB	M. Black and H. H. Rowley (eds.), *Peake's Commentary on the Bible* (London: Thomas Nelson and Sons, 1963)
PEFQS	*Palestine Exploration Fund, Quarterly Statement*
PEQ	*Palestine Exploration Quarterly*
PJ	*Palästina-Jahrbuch*
PRU	*Le Palais royal d'Ugarit*
PSTJ	*Perkins (School of Theology) Journal*
PW	Pauly-Wissowa, *Real-Encyclopädie der classischen Altertumswissenschaft*
PWSup	Supplement to PW
QDAP	*Quarterly of the Department of Antiquities in Palestine*
RA	*Revue d'assyriologie et d'archéologie orientale*
RAC	*Reallexikon für Antike und Christentum*
RArch	*Revue archéologique*
RB	*Revue biblique*
RCB	*Revista de cultura biblica*
RE	*Realencyklopädie für protestantische Theologie und Kirche*
RechBib	Recherches bibliques
REJ	*Revue des études juives*
RelS	*Religious Studies*
RelSRev	*Religious Studies Review*
RES	*Répertoire d'épigraphie sémitique*
ResQ	*Restoration Quarterly*
RevExp	*Review and Expositor*
RevistB	*Revista biblica*
RevQ	*Revue de Qumran*
RevScRel	*Revue des sciences religieuses*
RevSém	*Revue sémitique*
RGG	*Religion in Geschichte und Gegenwart*
RHPR	*Revue d'histoire et de philosophie religieuses*
RHR	*Revue de l'histoire des religions*
RivB	*Rivista biblica*
RR	*Review of Religion*
RSO	*Rivista degli studi orientali*
RSP I	*Ras Shamra Parallels I*, ed. L. R. Fisher, AnOr 49 (Rome: Pontifical Biblical Institute, 1972)
RSPT	*Revue des sciences philosophiques et théologiques*
RSR	*Recherches de science religieuse*
RTL	*Revue théologique de Louvain*

RTP	*Revue de théologie et de philosophie*
RUO	*Revue de l'université d'Ottawa*
SANT	Studien zum Alten und Neuen Testament
SAOC	Studies in Ancient Oriental Civilization
SAT	Die Schriften des Alten Testaments in Auswahl übersetzt und erklärt, ed. Herman Gunkel
SAYP	Cross and Freedman, *Studies in Ancient Yahwistic Poetry*
SB	Sources bibliques
SBB	Stuttgarter biblische Monographien
SBFLA	*Studii biblici franciscani liber annuus*
SBLASP	Society of Biblical Literature Abstracts and Seminar Papers
SBLDS	SBL Dissertation Series
SBLMasS	SBL Masoretic Studies
SBLMS	SBL Monograph Series
SBLSBS	SBL Sources for Biblical Study
SBLSCS	SBL Septuagint and Cognate Studies
SBLTT	SBL Texts and Translations
SBM	Stuttgarter biblische Monographien
SBS	Stuttgarter Bibelstudien
SBT	Studies in Biblical Theology
ScEs	*Science et esprit*
Scr	*Scripture*
ScrB	*Scripture Bulletin*
SD	Studies and Documents
SEÅ	*Svensk exegetisk årsbok*
Sef	*Sefarad*
SEHM	Stuart, *Studies in Early Hebrew Meter*
Sem	*Semitica*
SJT	*Scottish Journal of Theology*
SOTP	H. H. Rowley (ed.), *Studies in Old Testament Prophecy*
SOTSMS	Society for Old Testament Study Monograph Series
SPAW	Sitzungsberichte der preussischen Akademie der Wissenschaften
SR	*Studies in Religion / Sciences religieuses*
SSS	Semitic Study Series
ST	*Studia theologica*
STÅ	*Svensk teologisk årskrift*
STDJ	Studies on the Texts of the Desert of Judah
STK	*Svensk teologisk kvartalskrift*
StudOr	Studia orientalia
SVTP	Studia in Veteris Testamenti pseudepigrapha
TBl	*Theologische Blätter*
TBü	Theologische Bücherei
TBT	*The Bible Today*
TD	*Theology Digest*
TDOT	G. Botterweck and H. Ringgren (eds.), *Theological Dictionary of the Old Testament* (Grand Rapids: Eerdmans, 1974–)

TextsS	Texts and Studies
TF	*Theologische Forschung*
TGl	*Theologie und Glaube*
ThLife	*Theology and Life*
ThSz	*Theologiai Szemle*
TLZ	*Theologische Literaturzeitung*
TP	*Theologie und Philosophie*
TQ	*Theologische Quartalschrift*
TRev	*Theologische Revue*
TRu	*Theologische Rundschau*
TS	*Theological Studies*
TSK	*Theologische Studien und Kritiken*
TT	*Teologisk Tidsskrift*
TTKi	*Tidsskrift for Teologi og Kirke*
TTZ	*Trierer theologische Zeitschrift*
TU	Texte und Untersuchungen
TV	*Theologia Viatorum*
TWAT	G. J. Botterweck and H. Ringgren (eds.), *Theologisches Wörterbuch zum Alten Testament*
TWOT	R. L. Harris, et al. (eds.), *Theological Wordbook of the Old Testament* (Chicago, Moody Press, 1980)
TynBul	*Tyndale Bulletin*
TZ	*Theologische Zeitschrift (ThZ)*
UF	*Ugaritische Forschungen*
USQR	*Union Seminary Quarterly Review*
UT	C. H. Gordon, *Ugaritic Textbook*
UUÅ	Uppsala universitetsårsskrift
VC	*Vigiliae christianae*
VD	*Verbum domini*
VF	*Verkündigung und Forschung*
VSpir	*Vie spirituelle*
VT	*Vetus Testamentum*
VTSup	Vetus Testamentum, Supplements
WDB	*Westminster Dictionary of the Bible*
WHAB	*Westminster Historical Atlas of the Bible*
WMANT	Wissenschaftliche Monographien zum Alten und Neuen Testament
WO	*Die Welt des Orients*
WTJ	*Westminster Theological Journal*
WuD	*Wort und Dienst*
WUNT	Wissenschaftliche Untersuchungen zum Neuen Testament
WZKM	*Wiener Zeitschrift für die Kunde des Morgenlandes*
WZKSO	*Wiener Zeitschrift für die Kunde Süd- und Ostasiens*
ZA	*Zeitschrift für Assyriologie*
ZAW	*Zeitschrift für die alttestamentliche Wissenschaft*
ZDMG	*Zeitschrift der deutschen morgenländischen Gesellschaft*
ZDPV	*Zeitschrift des deutschen Palästina-Vereins*
ZEE	*Zeitschrift für evangelische Ethik*

ZKG	*Zeitschrift für Kirchengeschichte*
ZKT	*Zeitschrift für katholische Theologie*
ZRGG	*Zeitschrift für Religions- und Geistesgeschichte*
ZTK	*Zeitschrift für Theologie und Kirche*
ZWK	*Zeitschrift für wissenschaftliche Theologie*

HEBREW GRAMMAR

abs	absolute	ind	indicative
acc	accusative	inf	infinitive
act	active	juss	jussive
adv	adverb / adverbial	masc, m	masculine
aor	aorist	niph	niphal
apoc	apocopated	obj	object
c	common	pass	passive
coh	cohortative	pf	perfect
conj	conjunction	pl	plural
consec	consecutive	poss	possessive
const	construct	prep	preposition
conv	converted	pronom	pronominal
dittogr	dittography	ptcp	participle
fem, f	feminine	sg	singular
fut	future	stat	stative
gen	genitive	subj	subject / subjective
haplogr	haplography	suff	suffix
hiph	hiphil	voc	vocative
hithp	hithpael	1	first person
hoph	hophal	2	second person
impf	imperfect	3	third person
impv	imperative		

NOTE: Hebrew שׂ (*sin*) is differentiated by pointing from שׁ (*shin*) only when ambiguity might otherwise result.

TEXTUAL NOTES

Akk.	Akkadian	Heb.	Hebrew
Arab.	Arabic	Hex.	Hexapla
Aram.	Aramaic	K	Kethib (consonantal text)
Eg.	Egyptian		
Eng.	English	L	Leningrad Codex
Eth.	Ethiopic	MT	Masoretic Text
G	The Septuagint	OG	Old Greek
G[A] (etc.)	Alexandrinus Codex of the Septuagint (etc.)	OL	Old Latin
		Q	Qere (Masoretic suggested pronunciation)
Gk.	Greek		

1Q (etc.)	Manuscript from Cave 1 at Qumran (etc.)	α´	Aquila
		θ´	Theodotion
Syr	Syriac Peshitta	σ´	Symmachus
Syrh	Syrohexapla	>	mutated / transformed to
Tg	Targum		
Ug.	Ugaritic	<	from
Vg	Vulgate		

BIBLICAL AND APOCRYPHAL BOOKS

Gen	Genesis	Sir	Ecclesiasticus or The Wisdom of Jesus son of Sirach
Exod	Exodus		
Lev	Leviticus		
Num	Numbers	Matt	Matthew
Deut	Deuteronomy	John	John
Josh	Joshua	Acts	Acts
Judg	Judges	Rom	Romans
Ruth	Ruth	Phil	Philippians
1–2 Sam	1–2 Samuel	Heb	Hebrews
1–2 Kgs	1–2 Kings	Rev	Revelation
1–2 Chr	1–2 Chronicles		
Ezra	Ezra		
Neh	Nehemiah		

MISCELLANEOUS

Esth	Esther		
Job	Job	ANE	Ancient Near East
Ps(s)	Psalm(s)	AV	Authorized Version
Prov	Proverbs	b.	*breve* (metrically short poetic line)
Eccl	Ecclesiastes		
Cant	Canticles, Song of Solomon	B.C.	Before Christ
		chap(s).	chapter(s)
Isa	Isaiah	cols.	columns
Jer	Jeremiah	diss.	dissertation
Lam	Lamentations	E	Elohist (supposed biblical literary source)
Ezek	Ezekiel		
Dan	Daniel		
Hos	Hosea	ed(s).	edition; edited by; editor(s)
Joel	Joel		
Amos	Amos	esp.	especially
Obad	Obadiah	ET	English translation
Jonah	Jonah	FS	Festschrift
Mic	Micah	*hap. leg.*	*hapax legomenon*
Nah	Nahum	J	Yahwist (supposed biblical literary source)
Hab	Habakkuk		
Zeph	Zephaniah		
Hag	Haggai	JB	*Jerusalem Bible*
Zech	Zechariah	l	*longum* (metrically long poetic line)
Mal	Malachi		

lit.	literally	obv.	obverse
MS(S)	manuscript(s)	OT	Old Testament
n.	note	p.	page
NAB	*New American Bible*	Pers.	Persian
NEB	*New English Bible*	rev.	reverse
NIV	*New International Version*	RSV	*Revised Standard Version*
		tr.	translated; translator
NJV	*New Jewish Version*	UP	University Press
NT	New Testament	v(v)	verse(s)

General Bibliography

COMMENTARIES ON SEVERAL MINOR PROPHETS

(including one or more of Hosea-Jonah in combination with other books)

Allen, L. C. *The Books of Joel, Obadiah, Jonah and Micah.* NICOT. Grand Rapids: Eerdmans, 1976. **Augé, R.** *Profetes Minores.* La Bíblia, versió dels textos originals i commentari XVI. 1957. **Bergren, R. V.** *The Prophets and the Law.* Hebrew Union College Monographs 4. Cincinnati: Hebrew Union College, 1974. **Bewer, J. A.** "The Book of the Twelve Prophets." Harper Bible. New York: Harper and Row, 1949. **Bleeker, L. H. K.** and **G. Smit.** *De Kleine Propheten.* Text en Uitleg. 3 vols. Gronigen: J. B. Wolters, 1926–34. **Brockington, L. H.** "Joel," "Obadiah," "Jonah." *PCB*, 614–16, 626–29. **Cassuto, M. D.**, ed. *Sifre Ha-Miqra.* Tel Aviv: Yavneh Publishing House, 1955. **Cohen, A.** *The Twelve Prophets.* The Socino Books of the Bible. London: Socino, 1948. **Coppens, J.** *Les douze petits prophètes: Bréviare du prophétisme.* Bruges: Desclée de Brouwer; Louvain: Publications Universitaires, 1950. **Cornill, C. H.** *The Prophets of Israel.* Tr. S. F. Corkran. Chicago: Open Court, 1895. **Craghan, J.** *Esther, Judith, Tobit, Jonah, Ruth.* The Old Testament Message 16. Wilmington: Michael Glazier, 1982. **Craigie, P.** *Twelve Prophets.* Vol 1. The Daily Bible Study Series. Philadelphia: Westminster, 1984. **Deden, D.** *De Kleine Propheten.* Die Boeken van het Oude Testament 12. Roermonden: J. J. Romen and Zonen, 1953. **Deissler, A.** *Zwölf Propheten: Hosea, Joël, Amos.* 2d ed. Die Neuer Echter Bible. Würzburg: Echter Verlag, 1981. **Driver, S. R.** *The Minor Prophets.* Edinburgh: T. & T. Clark and E. J. Jack, 1906. **Duhm, B.** *The Twelve Prophets: A Version in the Various Poetical Measures of the Original Writings.* Tr. A. Duff. London: Adam and Charles Black, 1912. (= *Die zwölf Propheten, in den Vermassen der Urschrift übersetzt.* Tübingen, 1910.) **Edgar, S. L.** *The Minor Prophets.* Epworth Preacher's Commentaries. London: Epworth, 1962. **Ehrlich, A. B.** *Randglossen zur hebräischen Bibel.* Vol 5. Leipzig: 1912; 2d ed. Hildesheim: Georg Olms, 1968. **Eiselen, F. C.** "The Minor Prophets," *Whedon's Commentary.* New York: Eaton and Mains, 1907. **Ewald, H. G. A.** *Die Propheten des Alten Bundes.* Göttingen: Vandenhoeck & Ruprecht, 1867–68. **Gressmann, H.** *Die älteste Geschichtsschreibung und Prophetie Israels (von Samuel bis Amos und Hosea).* SAT 2,1. Göttingen: Vandenhoeck & Ruprecht, 1921. **Guthe, H.**, et al. *Die Heilige Schrift des Alten Testaments.* Vol 2. 4th ed. Tübingen: 1923. **Haller, M.** *Das Judentum: Geschichtsschreibung, Prophetie und Gesetzgebung nach dem Exil.* SAT 2/3. Göttingen: Vandenhoeck & Ruprecht, 1925. **Hitzig, F.**, and **H. Steiner.** *Die zwölf kleinen Propheten.* Leipzig: S. Hirzel, 1881. **Hoonacker, A. van.** *Les douze petits prophètes.* Études bibliques. Paris: J. Gabalda, 1908. **Jacob, E.**, et al. *Les petits prophètes I.* CAT 11a. Neuchâtel: Delachaux et Niestlé, 1965; 12th ed., Geneva: Labor et Fides, 1982. **Jepsen, A.** *Bibelhilfe für die Gemeinde.* Stuttgart: 1937. ———. *Das Zwölfprophetenbuch.* Leipzig and Hamburg: Gustav Schloessmanns Verlagsbuchhandlung, 1937. **Keil, C. F.** *The Twelve Minor Prophets.* Biblical Commentary on the Old Testament. Tr. J. Martin. Grand Rapids: Eerdmans, 1969. (= Biblischer Commentar über die zwölf kleinen Propheten. 3d ed., Leipzig: 1888.) **Koch, K.** *The Prophets. Volume One: The Assyrian Age.* Philadelphia: Fortress, 1982. (= *Die Propheten I. Assyrische Zeit.* Stuttgart: Kohlhammer, 1978.) ———. *The Prophets. Volume Two: The Babylonian and Persian Periods.* Philadelphia: Fortress Press, 1984. (= *Die Propheten II. Babylonisch-persische Zeit.* Stuttgart, Kohlhammer, 1980.) **Kodel, J.** *Lamentations, Haggai, Zechariah, Malachi, Obadiah, Joel, Second Zechariah, Baruch.* The Old Testament Message 14. Wilmington: Michael Glazier, 1982. **Kroeker, J.** *Die Propheten oder das Reden Gottes. Das lebendige Wort.* Giessen/Basel: 1932. **Laetsch, T.** *The Minor Prophets.* St. Louis: Concordia Publishing House, 1956. **Lehrman, S.**, et al. *The Socino Books of the Bible.* Bournemouth: Socino Press, 1952. **Lippl, J.**, et al. *Die zwölf kleinen Propheten.* 2 vols. *HSAT* 8. Bonn:

1937–38. **Marti, K.** *Das Dodekapropheton.* Kurzer Hand-Commetar zum Alten Testament. Tübingen: J. C. B. Mohr, 1904. **Mauchline, J.**, et al. *The Twelve Prophets. IB* 6. New York and Nashville: Abingdon Press, 1956. **McKeating, H.** *The Books of Amos, Hosea and Micah.* The Cambridge Bible Commentary on the New English Bible. Cambridge: Cambridge UP, 1971. **Mitchell, H. G.**, et al. *Haggai, Zechariah, Malachi, Jonah.* ICC. Edinburgh: T. & T. Clark, 1912. **Mowinckel, S.**, and **N. Messel.** *De Senere Profeter oversatt.* De Gamle Testamente. Oslo, 1944. **Nötscher, F.** *Zwölfprophetenbuch.* Echter-Bibel. Wurzburg: Echter-Verlag, 1948. **Nowack, W.** *Die kleinen Propheten.* HKAT. 3d ed. Göttingen: 1922. **Orelli, C. von.** *Die zwölf kleinen Propheten.* Kurzgefasster Kommentar zu den Heiligen Schriften. Alten und Neuen Testaments, ed. H. Strack and O. Zockler. 3d ed. Munich: Beck, 1908. **Osty, E.**, et al. *La Sainte Bible.* Paris: 1957–60. **Procksch, O.** *Die kleinen prophetischen Schriften.* Erläuterungen zum Alten Testament. 2 vols. Stuttgart: Verlag der Vereinsbuchhandlung, 1929. **Ridderbos, J.** *Korte Verklaring der Heiligen Schrift.* Kampen: Kok, 1935. **Riessler, P.** *Die kleinen Propheten.* Rottenburg: W. Bader, 1911. **Rinaldi, G.** *Profeti Minori II: Osea—Gioele—Abdia—Giona.* Torina: Marietti, 1960. **Robertson, E. H.** *Amos, Hosea, Micah, Isaiah 1–39.* Mowbray's Mini-Commentaries. Vol. 8. London: Mowbray, 1968. **Robinson, T. H.**, and **F. Horst.** *Die zwölf kleinen Propheten.* HAT 1/14. Tübingen: J. C. B. Mohr, 1964. **Schmidt, H.** *Die grossen Propheten.* SAT 2/2. Göttingen: Vandenhoeck & Ruprecht, 1923. **Schumpp, M.** *Das Buch der zwölf Propheten.* Herders Bibelkommentar 10/2. Freiburg: Herder and Co., 1950. **Sellin, E.** *Das zwölf Prophetenbuch.* KAT 12/2. 2 vols. Leipzig: A. Deichert, 1930. **Smith, G. A.** *The Book of the Twelve Prophets.* 2 vols. The Expositor's Bible. New York: A. C. Armstrong, 1899. **Smith, J. M. P.**, et al. *Micah, Zephaniah, Nahum, Habakkuk, Obadiah, and Joel.* ICC. Edinburgh: T. & T. Clark, 1911. **Unattributed** (produced by the Franciscan Biblical Institute in Japan). *Joel, Amos, Obadiah, Jonah, Micah, Nahum and Habakkuk.* Tokyo: Chuo Shuppansha, 1986. **Vawter, B.** *Amos, Hosea, Micah, with an Introduction to Classical Prophecy.* The Old Testament Message 7. Wilmington: Michael Glazier, 1981. **Vellas, B. M.** *Hermeneia Palaias Diathekes.* 5 vols. Athens: 1947–50. (Gr.) **Wade, G. W.** *Micah, Obadiah, Joel and Jonah.* London: Methuen and Co., 1925. **Watts, J. D. W.** *The Books of Joel, Obadiah, Jonah, Nahum, Habakkuk and Zephaniah.* The Cambridge Bible Commentary. Cambridge: Cambridge UP, 1975. **Weiser, A.**, and **K. Elliger.** *Das Buch der zwölf kleinen Propheten.* ATD 24–25,1. 6th ed. Göttingen: Vandenhoeck & Ruprecht, 1974. **Wellhausen, J.** *Die kleinen Propheten.* Berlin: de Gruyter, 1963.

BOOKS AND DISSERTIONS ON OR RELATING TO MORE THAN ONE MINOR PROPHET

Amsler, S. *Les actes des prophètes.* Essais bibliques 9. Geneva: Labor et Fides, 1985. **Auge, R.** *El Profetes Menors.* Montserrat: Monestir de Montserrat, 1957. **Baltzer, K.** *Die Biographie der Propheten.* Neukirchen-Vluyn: Neukirchener Verlag, 1975. **Bergren, R. V.** *The Prophets and the Law.* Monographs of the Hebrew Union College 4. Jerusalem: Hebrew Union College, 1974. **Ben-Sasson, H. H.**, ed. *History of the Jewish People.* Vol. 1: The Ancient Times. Tel Aviv: Devir, 1971. **Blenkinsopp, J. L.** *A History of Prophecy in Israel from the Settlement in the Land to the Hellenistic Period.* Philadelphia: Westminster, 1983. ———. *Prophecy and Canon.* University of Notre Dame Center for the Study of Judaism and Christianity in Antiquity 3. South Bend, IN: University of Notre Dame Press, 1977. **Brueggemann, W.** *The Prophetic Imagination.* Philadelphia: Fortress, 1978. **Buber, M.** *The Prophetic Faith.* Tr. C. Wilton-Davies. New York: Harper and Row, 1960. **Christensen, D.** *Transformations of the War Oracle in Old Testament*

Prophecy. Harvard Dissertations in Religion 3. Missoula, MT: Scholars Press, 1978. **Clakins, R.** *The Modern Message of the Minor Prophets.* New York, 1947. **Cogan, M.** *Imperialism and Religion: Assyria, Judah and Israel in the Eighth and Seventh Centuries B.C.E.* SBLMS 19. Missoula, MT: Scholars Press, 1974. **Collins, T.** *Line-Forms in Hebrew Poetry: A Grammatical Approach to the Stylistic Study of the Hebrew Prophets.* Studia Pohl, Series Major 7. Rome: Pontifical Biblical Institute Press, 1978. **Cornfeld, G.** *Archaeology of the Bible: Book by Book.* New York: Harper and Row, 1976. **Cornill, C. H.** *Der israelitische Prophetismus.* 13th ed. Berlin: de Gruyter, 1920. **Dellagiacoma, V.** *Israele spasa di Dio: Le metaphora muziale del VT.* Diss. Ateno Urbaniano de Propaganda Fide, Verona, 1961. **Duhm, B.** *Israels Propheten.* Tübingen: J. C. B. Mohr, ^{2}1922. **Eaton, J.** *Vision in Worship. The Relation of Prophecy and Liturgy in the Old Testament.* London: SPCK, 1981. **Eissfeldt, O.** *The Old Testament: An Introduction.* Tr. P. Ackroyd. New York: Harper and Row, 1965. **Ellermeier, F.** *Prophetie in Mari und Israel.* Herzberg am Harz: 1968. **Ellison, H. L.** *The Prophets of Israel: From Ahijah to Hosea.* Exeter/ Grand Rapids: Paternoster/Eerdmans, 1969. **Engnell, I.** *Critical Essays on the Old Testament.* London: SPCK, 1970. **Farrar, F. W.** *The Minor Prophets: Their Lives and Times.* Men of the Bible 14. New York: A. D. F. Randolph, 1890. **Fohrer, G.** *Die Propheten des Alten Testaments.* Vol. 6: *Die Propheten seit dem 4. Jahrhundert.* Gütersloh: Gerd Mohn, 1976. ———. *Introduction to the Old Testament.* Tr. D. E. Green. Nashville: Abingdon, 1968. ———. *History of the Israelite Religion.* Tr. D. E. Green. Nashville: Abingdon, 1972. **Fürst, J.** *Der Kanon des Alten Testaments.* Leipzig: 1868. **Gunneweg, A. H. J.** *Mündliche und schriftliche Tradition der vorexilischen Propheten.* Göttingen: Vandenhoeck & Ruprecht, 1959. **Gutierrez, R. C.** *La justicia social en los Profetas del siglo VIII: Amos, Oseas, Isaias y Miqueas.* Lizentiatsarbeit: University of Fribourg, 1970. **Hardmeier, C.** *Texttheorie und biblische Exegese: Zur rhetorischen Funktion der Trauermetaphorik in der Prophetie.* BEvT 79. Munich: Kaiser Verlag, 1978. **Harrison, R. K.** *Introduction to the Old Testament.* Grand Rapids: Eerdmans, 1969. **Hecht, F.** *Eschatologie und Ritus bei den "Reformprophetenn": Ein Beitrag zur Theologie des Altes Testament.* Pretoria Theological Studies 1. Leiden: Brill, 1971. **Herrmann, S.** *Die prophetischen Heilserwartungen im Alten Testament.* BWANT 85. Stuttgart: Kohlhammer, 1965. **Hillers, D.** *Treaty Curses and the Old Testament Prophets.* BibOr 16. Rome: Pontifical Biblical Institute, 1964. ———. *Covenant: The History of a Biblical Idea.* Baltimore: Johns Hopkins University Press, 1966. **Hunter, A. V.** *Seek the Lord! A Study of the Meaning and Function of the Exhortation in Amos, Hosea, Isaiah, Micah, and Zephaniah.* Baltimore: St. Mary's Seminary and University, 1982. **James, F.** *Personalities of the Old Testament.* New York: Scribners, 1947. **Jenni, E.** *Die politischen Voraussagen der Propheten.* ATANT 29. Zurich: Theologischen Verlag, 1956. **Kauffmann, Y.** *The Religion of Israel.* Tr. M. Greenberg. Chicago: University of Chicago Press, 1960. **Kilian, R.**, et al., eds. *Eschatologie: Bibeltheologische und philosophische Studien zum Verhältnis von Erlösungswelt und Wirklichkeitsbewältigung.* FS E. Neuhauser. St. Ottilien: Eos Verlag, 1981. **Kinet, D.** *Ba'al und Jahwe: ein Beitrag zur Theologie des Hoseabuches.* Bern: Europaische Hochschulschriften, 1977. **Kroeker, J.** *Die Propheten oder das Reden Gottes.* Das Lebendige Wort. Giessen und Basel: 1932. **Lewis, R. L.** *The Persuasive Style and Appeals of the Minor Prophets Amos, Hosea and Micah.* Ann Arbor, MI: University Microfilms IV, 1959. **Lindblom, J.** *Prophecy in Ancient Israel.* Oxford: Oxford University Press, 1962. **McCarthy, D. J.** *Old Testament Covenant: A Survey of Current Opinions.* Oxford: Blackwell, 1972. **Miller, P. D., Jr.** *Sin and Judgment in the Prophets.* SBLMS 27. Chico: Scholars Press, 1982. **Monloubon, L.** *Amos et Osée, sainteté de justice, sainteté d'amour: sous la main de Dieu 8.* Paris: Ed. Fleurus, 1964. ———. *Les prophètes de l'Ancien Testament.* Cahiers Evangile 43. Paris: Éditions du Cerf, 1983. **Montaner, L. V.** *Biblia del Mar Muerto: Profetas Minores.* Textos y Estudios "Cardinal Cisneros" de la Biblia Poliglota Matritense 29. Madrid: Instituto "Arias Montano" CSIC, 1980. **Moraldi, L.** *I manuscritti di Qumran.* Torino: Unione

Tipographicol-editrice Torinese, 1971. **Mowinckel, S.** *Prophecy and Tradition.* Oslo: 1946. ———, and **N. Messel.** *De Senere Profeter Oversatt. De Gamle Testamente.* Oslo: H. Aschehoug, 1944. **Nielsen, K.** *Yahweh as Prosecutor and Judge: An Investigation of the Prophetic Lawsuit (Rib-Pattern).* JSOTSup 9. Sheffield: UP, 1978. **Noort, E.** *Untersuchungen zum Gottesscheid in Mari: Die "Mariprophetie" in der alttestamentlichen Forschung.* Kevelaer/ Neukirchen-Vluyn: Butzon & Bercker/Neukirchener Verlag, 1977. **Noth, M.** *The History of Israel.* Tr. P. Ackroyd. New York: Harper and Row, 1960. **Oppenheimer, D.** *Status Matrimonialis Oseae ut Symb. Propheticum.* Sepher Dim Festschrift, ed. H. Bar-Deroma et al. Jerusalem: Kirjath Sepher, 1958. **Petersen, D.** *Late Israelite Prophecy: Studies in Deutero-Prophetic Literature and in Chronicles.* SBLMS 23. Missoula, MT: Scholars Press, 1977. **Rowley, H. H.** *Men of God.* London: Nelson, 1963. **Silverman, A. O.** *Behold My Messengers: The Lives and Teachings of the Prophets.* New York: Bloch, 1955. **Smith, J. M. P.** *The Prophets and Their Times.* Chicago: University of Chicago Press, 1925. **Smith, W. R.** *The Prophets of Israel.* London: 2d ed., 1895. **Smolar, L.,** and **M. Auerbach.** *Studies in Targum Jonathan to the Prophets.* Churgin, P. *Targum Jonathan to the Prophets* (combined volume). New York: KTAV, 1983. **Stuart, D.** *Favorite Old Testament Passages.* Philadelphia: Westminster, 1985. ———. *Studies in Early Hebrew Meter.* HSM 13. Missoula, MT: Scholars Press, 1976. **Thiele, E. R.** *The Mysterious Numbers of the Hebrew Kings.* Grand Rapids: Eerdmans, 1965. **Torrey, C. C.** *The Lives of the Prophets.* JBL Monographs 1. Philadelphia: Society of Biblical Literature, 1946. **Vaux, R. de.** *Ancient Israel: Its Life and Institutions.* Tr. J. McHugh. New York: McGraw-Hill, 1961. **Volz, P.** *Die vorexilische Jawehprophetie und der Messias.* Göttingen: Vandenhoeck & Ruprecht, 1897. **Vuilleumier, R.** *La tradition culturelle d'Israel dans la prophetie d'Amos et Osée.* Cahiers Theologique 45. Neuchâtel: Delachaux, 1960. **Ward, J. M.** *The Prophets.* Interpreting Biblical Texts. Nashville: Abingdon, 1982. **Warmuth, G.** *Das Mahnwort: Seine Bedeutung für die Verkundigung der vorexilixischen Propheten Amos, Hosea, Micha, Jesaja und Jeremia.* Beiträge zur biblischen Exegese und Theologie 1. Frankfurt am Main: Peter Lang, 1976. **Weippert, H.,** et al. *Beiträge zur prophetischen Bildsprache in Israel und Assyrien.* Freiburg/Göttingen: Universitätsverlag/Vandenhoeck & Ruprecht, 1985. **Winward, S.** *A Guide to the Prophets.* Atlanta: John Knox, 1976. **Wolff, H. W.** *Prophetische Alternativen: Entdeckungen des Neuen im Alten Testament.* Munich: Kaiser Verlag, 1982. ———. *Confrontations with Prophets.* Tr. Fortress Press. Philadelphia: Fortress Press, 1983. **Ziegler, J.** *Beiträge zum griechischen Dodekapropheton.* Göttingen: 1942. **Zimmerli, W.** *The Law and the Prophets.* Oxford: UP, 1965.

ARTICLES ON OR RELATING TO THE MINOR PROPHETS

Bee, R. E. "An Empirical Dating Procedure for Old Testament Prophecy." *JSOT* ll (1979) 23–35. **Boeker, H. J.** *Redeformen des Rechtsleben im Alten Testament.* WMANT 14. Neukirchen-Vluyn: Neukirchener Verlag, 1964. **Budde, K.** "Eine folgeschwere Redaktion des Zwölfprophetenbuchs." *ZAW* 39 (1921) 218–29. **Buhl, F.** "Einige text-kritische Bemerkungen zu den kleinen Propheten." *ZAW* 5 (1885) 179–84. **Davies, G. H.** "The Yahwistic Tradition in the Eighth-Century Prophets." In *Studies in Old Testament Prophecy,* H. H. Rowley, ed. Edinburgh: T. & T. Clark, 1950. 37–51. **Deroche, M.** "Yahweh's *Rib* against Israel: A Reassessment of the So-Called 'Prophetic Lawsuit' in the Preexilic Prophets." *JBL* 102 (1983) 563–74. **Driver, G. R.** Linguistic and Textual Problems: Minor Prophets II, III." *JTS* 39 (1938) 154–66; 260–73; 393–405. ———. "Notes on Hebrew Prophets and Proverbs." *JTS* 41 (1940) 162–75. **Duhm, B.** "Anmerkungen zu den zwölf kleinen Propheten." *ZAW* 31 (1911) 1–4; 81–110; 161–204. **Eakin, F. E., Jr.** "Yahwism and Baalism Before the Exile." *JBL* 84 (1965) 407–

14. **Eissfeldt, O.** "The Prophetic Literature." In *The Old Testament and Modern Study*, H. H. Rowley, ed. Oxford and New York: Oxford UP, 1951. **Engnell, I.** "Prophets and Prophetism in the Old Testament." In *Critical Essays on the Old Testament*, tr. & ed. John T. Willis. London: SPCK, 1970. 123–79. **Fohrer, G.** "Neue Literatur zur altestamentlichen Prophetie (1961–1970)." *TRu* 40 (1975) 337–77; 41 (1976) 1–12; 45 (1980) 1–39, 109–32, 193–225; 47 (1982) 105–35, 205–18. **Freehoff, S. B.** "Some Text Rearrangements in the Minor Prophets." *JQR* 32 (1941–42) 303–8. **Gaster, Th. H.** "Notes on the Minor Prophets." *JTS* 39 (1937) 163–65. **Gemser, B.** "The *Rîb* or Controversy Pattern in Hebrew Mentality." VTSup 3 (1955) 124–37. **Gerstenberger, E.** "The Woe Oracles of the Prophets." *JBL* 81 (1962) 249–63. **Ginsburg, M.** "Notes on the Minor Prophets." *Eretz-Israel* 3 (1954) 83–84. (Heb.). **Gordis, R.** *Poets, Prophets and Sages.* Bloomington: Indiana UP, 1971. **Gottwald, N. K.** "Tragedy and Comedy in the Latter Prophets." *Semeia* 32 (1984) 83–86. **Haran, M.** "From Early Classical Prophecy: Continuity and Change." *VT* 27 (1977) 385–97. **Harvey, J.** "Le *riv* pattern: Requistoire prophetique sur la rupture de l'alliance." *Bib* 43 (1962) 172–96. **Helewa, J.** "Ministère doctrinal du prêtre dans la théologie ecclésiale du prophète Osée." *ECarm* 17 (1966) 5–30. **Helfmeyer, F. J.** "Gotteserkenntnis—Liebe—Umkehr." *BK* 40 (1985) 101–107. **Hirshberg, H. H.** "Some Additional Arabic Etymologies in OT Lexicography." *VT* 11 (1967) 373–85. **Hoffman, Y.** "From Oracle to Prophecy: The Growth, Crystallization and Disintegration of a Biblical Gattung." *Journal of Northwest Semitic Languages* 10 (1982) 75–81. **Huffmon, H.** "Prophecy in the Mari Letters." *BA* 31 (1968) 101–124. ———. "The Covenant Lawsuit in the Prophets." *JBL* 78 (1959) 285–95. **Jepsen, A.** "Kleine Beiträge zum Zwölfprophetenbuch." *ZAW* 56 (1938) 85–100; 57 (1939) 242–55; 61 (1945–48) 95–114. **Kahle, P.** "Die im August 1952 entdeckte Lederrole mit dem griechischen Text der kleinen Propheten und das Problem der Septuaginta." *TLZ* 79 (1954) 81–94. **Kapelrud, A. S.** "The Spirit and the Word in the Prophets." *ASTI* 11 (1978) 40–47 **Kipper, J. B.** "A evoluçao económico-social em Israel e a pregaçao dos profetas." *RCB* 20 (1977) 309–351. **Limburg, J.** "The Prophets in Recent Study: 1967–77." *Int* 32 (1982) 56–68. **Lods, A.** "Recherches récentes sur le prophétisme israélite." *RHR* 104 (1931) 279–316. **Long, B.** "Reports of Visions among the Prophets." *JBL* 95 (1976) 353–65. **Melugin, R.** "The Typical Versus the Unique among the Hebrew Prophets." *SBL 1972 Proceedings*, 331–41. **Meyer, R.,** et al. "Propheten II." *RGG* 5:613, 633. **Moran, W. L.** "New Evidence from Mari on the History of Prophecy." *Bib* 50 (1969) 15–56. **Porteous, N. W.** "The Basis of the Ethical Teaching of the Prophets." In *Studies in Old Testament Prophecy*, H. H. Rowley, ed. Edinburgh: T. & T. Clark, 1950. **Ramsey, G. W.** "Speech-Forms in Hebrew Law and Prophetic Oracles." *JBL* 96 (1977) 45–58. **Rendtorff, R.** "Erwägungen zur Frühgeschichte des Prophetentums in Israel." *ZTK* 59 (1962) 145–67. (= "Reflections on the Early History of Prophecy in Israel." Tr. P. J. Achtemeier in *Hermeneutic, Journal for Theology and the Church*, ed. R. W. Funk and G. Ebeling [New York: Harper and Row, 1967] 4:14–34.) ———. "Prophetenspruch." *RGG* 5:635–38. **Richter, G.** "Erläuterung zu dunkeln Stellen in den kleinen Propheten." BFCT 18, 3/4 (1914). **Robinson, T. H.** "Die prophetischer Bücher im Lichte neuer Entdeckungen." *ZAW* 45 (1927) 3–9. **Rudolph, W.** "Präparierte Jungfrauen?" *ZAW* 75 (1963) 65–73. **Schoors, A.** "De vormkritische studie van de profeten." *Bijdragen* 32 (1971) 259–81. **Smalley, W. A.** "Translating 'Thus Says the Lord.' " *BT* 29 (1978) 222–24. **Stuart, D.** "The Old Testament Prophets' Self-Understanding of Their Prophecy." *Themelios* (1980/81) 9–14. **Vermeylen, J.** "Les prophètes de la conversion face aux traditions sacrales de l'Israël ancien." *RTL* 9 (1978) 5–32. **Vollers, K. A.** "Das Dodekapropheten der Alexandriner." *ZAW* 4 (1884) 1–20. **Vriezen, T. C.** "Prophecy and Eschatology." VTSup 1 (1953) 199–229. **Vuilleumier, R.** "Traditions d'Israël et liberté du prophète: Osée." *Prophètes, poètes et sages d'Israel: FS Edmond Jacob. RHPR*

59 (1979) 491–98. **Watts, J. D. W.** "Elements of OT Worship." *JBR* 26 (1958) 217–21. **Weinfeld, M.** "Ancient Near Eastern Patterns in Prophetic Literature." *VT* 27 (1977) 178–95. **Werbeck, W.** "Zwölfprophetenbuch." *RGG*³ 6, cols. 1969–70. **Wilson, R. R.** "Form-Critical Investigation of the Prophetic Literature: The Present Situation." *SBL 1973 Seminar Papers*, 100–127. **Wolfe, R. E.** "The Editing of the Book of the Twelve." *ZAW* 53 (1935) 90–130. **Wolff, H. W.** "Erkenntnis Gottes im Alten Testament." *EvT* 15 (1955) 426–31. **Ziegler, J.** "Studien zur Verwertung der Septuaginta im Zwölfprophetenbuch." *ZAW* 60 (1944) 107–31. **Zimmerli, W.** "Vom Prophetenwort zum Prophetenbuch." *TLZ* 104 (1979) 481–96.

General Introduction

Prophetic Dependency on Pentateuchal Blessings and Curses

BIBLIOGRAPHY

Baltzer, K. *Das Bundesformular.* WMANT 4. Neukirchen-Vluyn: Neukirchener Verlag, 1960. **Blank, S.** "The Curse, Blasphemy, the Spell and the Oath." *HUCA* 23 (1950–51) 73–95. **Bright, J.** *Covenant and Promise: The Prophetic Understanding of the Covenant in Pre-Exilic Israel.* Philadelphia: Westminster Press, 1975. **Dumbrell, W.** *Covenant and Creation.* New York: Thomas Nelson, 1985. **Ebeling, E.** "Sammlung von Beschwörungsformeln." *ArOr* 21 (1953) 357–423. **Fensham, F. C.** "Covenant, Promise and Expectation in the Bible." *TZ* 23 (1967) 305–22. ———. "Maledictions and Benedictions in Ancient Near Eastern Vassal-Treaties and the Old Testament." *ZAW* 74 (1962) 1–9. **Gevirtz, S.** "West-Semitic Curses and the Problem of the Origins of Hebrew Law." *VT* 11 (1961) 137–58. **Gressmann, H.** *Der Ursprung der israelitischen-jüdischen Eschatologie.* FRLANT 43. Göttingen: Vandenhoeck & Ruprecht, 1905. **Hillers, D.** *Covenant: The History of a Biblical Idea.* Baltimore: Johns Hopkins Press, 1969. ———. *Treaty-Curses and the Old Testament Prophets.* BibOr 16. Rome: Pontifical Biblical Institute, 1964. **Kline, M. G.** *Treaty of the Great King.* Grand Rapids: Eerdmans, 1963. **McCarthy, D. J.** *Old Testament Covenant: A Survey of Current Opinions.* Atlanta: John Knox, 1972. ———. *Treaty and Covenant: A Study in Form in the Ancient Oriental Documents and the O.T.* Rev. ed. AnBib 21. Rome: Pontifical Biblical Institute, 1978. **Mendenhall, G.** "Covenant Forms in Israelite Tradition." *BA* 17 (1954) 50–76. ———. *Law and Covenant in the Ancient Near East.* Pittsburgh: Biblical Colloquium, 1955. **Mercer, S. A. B.** *The Oath in Babylonian and Assyrian Literature.* Paris: P. Guenther, 1912. **Moriarty, F.** "Prophets and Covenant." *Gregorianum* 66 (1965) 817–33. **Muilenburg, J.** "The 'Office' of the Prophet in Ancient Israel." In *The Bible in Modern Scholarship,* ed. J. P. Hyatt. Nashville: Abingdon, 1965. 74–97. **Perlitt, L.** *Bundestheologie im Alten Testament.* WMANT 36. Neukirchen-Vluyn: Neukirchener Verlag, 1969. **Vogels, W.** *La promesse royale de Yahweh préparatoire à l'alliance.* Ottawa: Editions de l'Université d'Ottawa, 1970. **Wehmeir, G.** *Der Segen im Alten Testament.* Basel: Friedrich Reinhardt Kommissionsverlag, 1970.

True prophecy and true originality were mutually exclusive in ancient Israel. Understanding this fact is essential to understanding the Old Testament prophets.

Much scholarship on the Old Testament since Wellhausen's *Prolegomena to the History of Israel* (1883) has, however, been captive to the opposite view: that the OT prophets were creatively original, conceiving a perspective on history and producing interpretations of Israel's behavior largely *de novo*, without full written or oral legal-covenantal traditions as guidelines. By such a view, the prophets' legal-covenantal ideas grew up during and as a result of their creative activity, gained a decisive position in orthodox Yahwist Israelite circles, and eventuated in the composition of the deuteronomic (D) and priestly (P) law codes in the seventh and sixth-fifth centuries B.C., respectively. In other words, as preachers prior to the composition of law, the OT prophets were in effect the inventors of biblical social ethics and to some extent personal ethics as well, and the creators of most of the covenantal ideals later systematized into what is now the bulk of the Pentateuch.

The evidence does not support this view. Instead, it supports the conclusion that the OT prophets carried on their inspired ministries within a tradition that consciously and directly went back to the ancient Mosaic covenant as expressed in the Pentateuch, i.e., its first statement in Exodus-Leviticus-Numbers and its renewal in Deuteronomy. The prophets had not the slightest sense that they were creating any new doctrine but considered themselves spokespersons for Yahweh, who through them called his people *back* to obedience to the covenant he had given them many centuries before, and reminded them of its curses and blessings, which Yahweh had sworn to honor.

Throughout this volume's individual commentaries on Hosea-Jonah, therefore, regular comparison is made to the curses and blessings of the Mosaic covenant, since only thereby can what the prophets are referring to be made sense of. They invent no types of curses or blessings. They simply make reference, either literally or allusively as inspired to do so, to what is already incorporated in the Sinai covenant. The significance of this fact cannot be overstated. Nearly all of the content of the classical (writing) prophets' oracles revolve around the announcement of the near-time fulfillment of covenantal curses and the end-time fulfillment of covenantal restoration blessings. They speak of little else than these two topics: how and why God's people may expect to be punished by a variety of disasters soon, and how and why they may expect to be rescued and restored eventually.

Categorizing the curses and blessings of the prophetical books requires first categorizing the curses and blessings of the Pentateuch, for precisely there are contained all the types that eventually recur in the prophets' oracles of woe or weal. Categorization is always a somewhat subjective enterprise, and the categories we have arrived at below, referred to routinely hereafter in the commentary, represent only one of several ways that the groupings might be made. It has seemed appropriate to err on the side of more rather than fewer categories where a genuine choice has been possible. This is suggested not only by the unpredictable way that the individual curses and blessings appear (in no discernible order or hierarchy) in both the Pentateuch and the prophetical books, but also by the intrinsically wide range of issues represented among the curses and blessings. The prophets themselves probably did not see in the Pentateuch any categorization of a few, say three to five, major subject areas; instead they appear to have considered the range of curse and blessing types to have been extensive, judging from the way that they select and juxtapose what the Mosaic covenant sanctions contain.

At any rate, our count yields twenty-seven types of curses and ten types of restoration blessings. It must be noted that the prophets were not commissioned to announce any current or "first-occupation" blessings to Israel. These had been amply promised by Moses, but the time of their applicability had passed by when the writing prophets were on the scene. What God had to say to Israel was something other than immediate blessing.

A REFERENCE LIST OF COVENANT CURSES

Throughout this volume, the Pentateuchal curses will be referred to by the following categorizations, as numbered:

1. Anger / rejection from Yahweh

    Lev 26:17 "I will set my face against you . . ."
           26:24 "I myself will be hostile toward you . . ."
           26:28 "In my anger I will be hostile to you."
           26:41 ". . . made me hostile toward them . . ."
    Deut 4:24 "Yahweh your God is a consuming fire, a jealous God."
           4:25 ". . . provoking (Yahweh your God) to anger . . ."
    Deut 29:20 "Yahweh will never be willing to forgive him; his wrath and zeal will burn against that person."
           29:24 ". . . fierce, burning anger . . ."
           29:27 "Therefore Yahweh's anger (will have) burned against this land . . ."
           29:28 ". . . furious anger and great wrath . . ."
    Deut 31:17 "I will become angry with them and forsake them. I will hide my face from them . . ."
           31:17 ". . . because our God is not with us."
           31:18 "I will certainly hide my face on that day . . ."
           31:29 ". . . provoke him to anger . . ."
    Deut 32:16 ". . . angered . . ."
           32:19 "Yahweh . . . rejected them because he was angered . . ."
           32:20 "I will hide my face from them . . ."
           32:21 ". . . angered . . ."
           32:30 ". . . unless their Rock had sold them, unless Yahweh had given them up."

2. Rejection / destruction of the cult

    Lev 26:31 "I will lay waste your sanctuaries and I will take no delight in the pleasing aroma of your offerings."

3. War and its ravages

    a. General

        Lev 26:17 ". . . you will be defeated by your enemies."
             26:25 "I will bring the sword upon you . . ."
             26:25 ". . . you will be given into enemy hands."
             26:33 ". . . (I will) . . . draw out my sword and pursue you."
             26:37 "So you will not be able to stand before your enemies."
        Deut 28:25 ". . . defeated before your enemies."
             28:25 "You will come at them from one direction but flee from them in seven."
             28:49 "Yahweh will bring a nation against you from far away, from the ends of the earth, like an eagle swooping down, a nation whose language you will not understand, a fierce-looking nation without respect for the old or pity for the young."
             28:52 "Until the high fortified walls in which you trust fall down."
        Deut 32:23 "I will send my arrows against them."
             32:24 "In the street the sword will make them childless."
             32:30 ". . . one man chase a thousand, or two put ten thousand to flight . . ."
             32:41 "I will sharpen my flashing sword . . ."
             32:42 "I will make my arrows drunk with blood while my sword devours flesh."

b. Siege

Lev 26:25 "When you withdraw into your cities I will send a plague among you . . ."
26:26 "When I cut off your supply of bread . . ."
26:29 "You will eat the flesh of your sons and the flesh of your daughters."
Deut 28:52 "They will lay siege to all the cities throughout your land . . ."
28:52 "They will besiege all the cities throughout the land . . ."
28:53 ". . . the suffering your enemy will inflict on you during the siege . . ."
28:55 ". . . the suffering your enemy will inflict on you during the siege of all your cities."
28:57 ". . . during the siege and in the distress that your enemy will inflict on you in your cities."

4. Fear / terror / horror

Lev 26:16 ". . . sudden terror . . ."
26:17 ". . . you will flee even when no one is pursuing you."
26:36 ". . . I will make their hearts so fearful in the lands of their enemies that the sound of a wind-blown leaf will put them to flight."
26:36 "They will run as though fleeing from the sword, and they will fall, even though no one is pursuing them."
26:37 "They will stumble over one another as though fleeing from the sword, even though no one is pursuing them."
Deut 28:66 "You will live in constant suspense, filled with dread both night and day, never sure of your life."
28:67 "In the morning you will say 'If only it were evening!' and in the evening, 'If only it were morning!'—because of the terror that will fill your hearts . . ."
Deut 32:25 "In their homes, terror will reign."

5. Occupation and oppression by enemies / aliens

Lev 26:16 "You will plant seed in vain because your enemies will eat it."
26:17 "Those who hate you will rule over you."
26:32 "(the land) . . . your enemies who live there . . ."
Deut 28:31 "Your sheep will be given to your enemies."
28:33 ". . . nothing but cruel oppression all your days."
28:43 "The alien who lives among you will rise above you higher and higher . . ."
28:44 "He will lend to you but you will not lend to him. He will be the head but you will be the tail."
28:48 ". . . You will serve the enemies Yahweh sends against you."
28:48 "He will put an iron yoke on your neck . . ."
28:68 ". . . you will offer yourselves for sale to your enemies . . ."
Deut 32:21 "I will make them envious by those who are not a people; I will make them angry by a nation that has no understanding."

6. Agricultural disaster / unproductivity

a. Drought

Lev 26:19 "I will make the sky above you like iron and the ground beneath you like bronze."

Deut 28:22 ". . . drought . . ."

28:23 "The sky over your head will be bronze, the ground beneath you iron."

28:24 "Yahweh will turn the rain of your country into dust and powder; it will come down from the skies until you are ruined."

b. Crop pests

Deut 28:42 "Swarms of locusts will take over all your trees and the crops of your land."

28:38 ". . . locusts will devour . . ."

28:39 ". . . worms will eat (your vineyards) . . ."

c. Other

Lev 26:20 ". . . your soil will not yield its crops, nor will the trees of the land yield their fruit."

Deut 28:17 "Your basket and your kneading trough will be cursed."

28:18 "(cursed) . . . the crops of your land and the calves of your herds and the lambs of your flocks."

28:22 ". . . scorching heat . . . blight and mildew . . ."

28:40 ". . . the olives will drop off . . ."

Deut 29:23 ". . . nothing planted, nothing sprouted, no vegetation growing on it."

7. Starvation / famine

Lev 26:26 "When I cut off your supply of bread . . ."

26:26 ". . . ten women will be able to bake bread in one oven, and they will dole out the bread by weight. You will eat but not be satisfied."

26:26 "You will eat but not be satisfied."

26:29 "You will eat the flesh of your sons and the flesh of your daughters."

26:45 ". . . in hunger and thirst . . ."

Deut 28:53 ". . . you will eat the fruit of the womb, the flesh of the sons and daughters Yahweh has given you."

28:54 "Even the most gentle . . . man . . . will have no compassion on his own brother or the wife he loves or his surviving children."

28:55 "It will be all he has left . . ."

28:56 "The most gentle . . . woman . . . will begrudge the husband she loves and her own son and daughter the afterbirth from her womb and the children she bears . . ."

28:56 "She intends to eat them secretly . . ."

Deut 32:24 "I will send wasting famine against them."

8. Illness / pestilence / contamination

Lev 26:14 "wasting diseases and fever that will destroy your sight and drain away your life."

Deut 28:21 "Yahweh will plague you with diseases . . ."

28:22 ". . . wasting disease, fever, inflammation, . . . blight and mildew . . . which will plague you . . ."

28:27 ". . . the boils of Egypt, and with tumors, festering sores and the itch, from which you cannot be cured."

    28:28   ". . . blindness . . ."

    28:35   "Yahweh will afflict your knees and legs with painful boils that cannot be cured, spreading from the soles of your feet to the top of your head."

    28:59   ". . . fearful plagues on you and your descendants . . ."

    28:59   ". . . severe and lingering illnesses."

    28:60   "He will bring upon you all the diseases of Egypt that you dreaded, and they will cling to you."

    28:61   ". . . every kind of sickness . . ."

Deut 29:22   ". . . diseases with which Yahweh (will have) has afflicted it."

Deut 32:24   ". . . consuming pestilence and deadly plague."

    32:39   "I wound . . ."

9. **Desolation**

  a. **Of holy places**

    Lev 26:31   "I will . . . lay waste your sanctuaries . . ."

  b. **Of cities / towns**

    Lev 26:31   "I will turn your cities into ruins . . ."

        26:33   ". . . your cities will lie in ruins."

  c. **Of the land**

    Lev 26:32   "I will lay waste the land so that your enemies who live there will be appalled."

        26:33   "Your land will be laid waste . . ."

        26:34   ". . . the land will enjoy its sabbath years all the time it lies desolate . . ."

        26:34   ". . . the land will rest and enjoy its sabbaths."

        26:35   "see the time that it lies desolate, the land will have the rest it did not have during the sabbaths you lived in it."

        26:43   "The land will be deserted by them and will enjoy its sabbaths while it lies desolate without them."

Deut 28:51   "They will devour . . . the crops of your land."

    28:51   "They will leave you no grain, wine or oil."

Deut 29:23   "The whole land will be a burning waste of salt and sulfur . . ."

10. **Destruction by fire**

Deut 28:24   "Yahweh your God is a consuming fire . . ."

Deut 32:22   "For a fire has been kindled by my wrath, one that burns to Sheol below. It will devour the earth and its harvests and set on fire the foundations of the mountains."

11. **Harm from wild animals**

    Lev 26:22   "I will send wild animals against you . . ."

Deut 32:24   "I will send against them the fangs of wild animals; the venom of vipers that glide in the dust."

12. **Decimation / infertility**

  a. **Of family**

    Lev 26:22   ". . . (wild animals) . . . will rob you of your children . . ."

Deut 28:18   "The fruit of your womb will be cursed."

    28:59   ". . . plagues on you and your descendants . . ."

b. Of cattle

Lev 26:22   "(wild animals) . . . will destroy your cattle . . ."
Deut 28:18   ". . . the calves of your herds and the lambs of your flocks (will be cursed)."
     28:51   "They will devour the young of your livestock . . ."

c. Of population generally

Lev 26:22   "(wild animals) . . . will make you so few in number that your roads will be deserted."
     26:36   ". . . those of you who are left . . ."
Deut 4:27   ". . . only a few of you will survive among the nations to which Yahweh will drive you."
Deut 28:62   "You who were as numerous as the stars of the sky will be left but few in number."
     32:36   ". . . and no one is left, slave or free."

13. Exile / captivity

a. Of the people

Lev 26:33   "I will scatter you among the nations . . ."
     26:34   ". . . all the time . . . you are in the country of your enemies . . ."
     26:36   ". . . in the lands of their enemies . . ."
     26:38   ". . . you will perish among the nations; the land of your enemies will devour you."
     26:39   "Those of you who are left will waste away in the lands of their enemies . . ."
     26:41   ". . . I sent them into the land of their enemies . . ."
     26:44   ". . . in the land of their enemies . . ."
Deut 4:27   "Yahweh will scatter you among the peoples . . ."
      4:27   ". . . among the nations to which Yahweh will drive you."
Deut 28:36   "Yahweh will drive you . . . to a nation unknown . . ."
     28:37   ". . . all the nations where Yahweh will drive you."
     28:41   "(sons and daughters) will go into captivity . . ."
     28:63   "You will be uprooted from the land . . ."
     28:64   "Yahweh will scatter you among all nations, from one end of the earth to the other."
     28:68   "Yahweh will send you back in ships [in miseries] to Egypt . . ."
     28:68   "There you will offer yourselves for sale . . . as slaves . . ."
Deut 29:28   ". . . Yahweh (will have) uprooted them from their land and thrust them into another land . . ."
Deut 30:4   ". . . banished to the most distant land under the heavens . . ."
Deut 32:26   "I said I would scatter them . . ."

b. Of the king

Deut 28:36   "Yahweh will drive . . . the king you set over you . . . to a nation unknown . . ."

14. Forced idolatry in exile

Deut 4:28   "There you will worship man-made gods of wood and stone which cannot see or hear or eat or smell."

Deut 28:36 "You will worship other gods, gods of wood and stone."

28:64 "There you will worship other gods, gods of wood and stone which neither you nor your fathers have known."

15. Futility

Lev 26:16 "You will plant seed in vain because your enemies will eat it."

26:20 "Your strength will be spent in vain . . . (on farming)."

Deut 28:20 ". . . curses, confusion and rebuke in everything you put your hand to . . ."

28:29 "You will be unsuccessful in everything you do."

28:30 "You will be pledged to marry a woman, but another will take her and ravish her."

28:30 "You will build a house but you will not live in it."

28:30 "You will plant a vineyard but you will not even begin to enjoy its fruit."

28:31 "Your ox will be slaughtered before your eyes, but you will eat none of it."

28:33 "A people you do not know will eat what your land and labor produce."

28:38 "You will sow much seed in the field but you will harvest little."

28:39 "You will plant vineyards and cultivate them but you will not drink the wine or gather the grapes . . ."

28:40 "You will have olive trees . . . but you will not use the oil . . ."

28:41 "You will have sons and daughters but you will not keep them . . ."

16. Dishonor / degradation

Lev 26:19 "I will break down your stubborn pride."

Deut 28:20 ". . . rebuke . . ."

28:25 "You will become a thing of horror to all the kingdoms on earth."

28:37 "You will become a thing of horror, and an object of scorn and ridicule to all the nations . . ."

28:43 ". . . you will sink lower and lower."

28:44 ". . . you will be the tail . . ."

28:68 "You will offer yourselves for sale . . . as slaves but none will buy you."

17. Loss of possessions / impoverishment

Deut 28:31 "Your donkey will be forcibly taken from you and not returned."

28:31 "Your sheep will be given to your enemies and no one will rescue them."

28:31 ". . . in nakedness and dire poverty . . ."

18. Loss of family

Deut 28:30 ". . . another will take (your betrothed) and ravish her."

28:32 "Your sons and daughters will be given to another nation."

28:41 "You will have sons and daughters but you will not keep them."

Deut 32:25 ". . . the sword will make them childless."

19. Helplessness / stumbling

Lev 26:36 ". . . they will fall . . ."

26:37 ". . . they will stumble over one another . . ."

Deut 28:29 "At midday you will grope around like a blind man in the dark."

28:29 "Day after day you will be oppressed and robbed, with no one to rescue you."

28:32 ". . . powerless to lift a hand."

Deut 32:35 "In due time their foot will slip."

32:36 ". . . when . . . their strength is gone."

32:38 "Let (your gods) rise up to help you; let them give you shelter!"

32:39 ". . . no one can deliver from my hand."

20. Psychological afflictions

Deut 28:20 ". . . confusion . . ."

28:28 ". . . madness . . . and confusion of the mind . . ."

28:34 "The sights you see will drive you mad."

28:65 ". . . an anxious mind, eyes weary with longing, and a despairing heart."

28:66 ". . . you will live in constant suspense . . ."

28:67 ". . . because of the sights that your eyes will see."

21. Lack of peace / rest

Deut 28:65 "Among those nations you will find no repose, no resting place for the sole of your foot."

22. Denial of burial

Deut 28:27 "Your carcasses will be food for the birds of the air and the beasts of the earth, and there will be no one to frighten them away."

23. Becoming like the cities of the plain

Deut 29:23 "It will be like the destruction of Sodom and Gomorrah, Admah and Zeboiim, which Yahweh overthrew . . ."

24. Death / destruction

Lev 26:36 "You will perish among the nations; the land of your enemies will devour you."

26:39 "Those of you who are left will waste away . . . they will waste away."

Deut 4:26 ". . . you will quickly perish from the land . . ."

4:26 "You will not live there long but will certainly be destroyed."

Deut 28:20 ". . . destroyed and come to sudden ruin . . ."

28:21 ". . . until (Yahweh) has destroyed you from the land . . ."

28:22 ". . . until you perish . . ."

28:44 ". . . until you are destroyed . . ."

28:48 ". . . until he has destroyed you."

28:51 ". . . until you are destroyed."

28:61 ". . . until you are destroyed."

Deut 29:20 "Yahweh will blot out his name from under heaven . . ."

Deut 30:15 ". . . death and destruction."

30:18 ". . . you will surely be destroyed. You will not live long in the land . . ."

30:19 ". . . death . . ."

Deut 31:17 ". . . they will be destroyed."

Deut 32:25   "Young men and young women will perish, infants and gray-
             haired men."
    32:26   ". . . erase their memory from mankind."
    32:35   ". . . their doom rushes upon them."
    32:39   "I put to death . . ."
    32:42   ". . . the blood of the slain and the captives, the heads of
             the enemy leaders . . ."

25. General / unspecified

Deut 4:30   "When you are in distress . . ."
Deut 28:20   "Yahweh will send on you curses, confusion, rebuke in every-
             thing you put your hand to until you are destroyed and come
             to sudden ruin . . ."
    28:24   ". . . until you are ruined . . ."
    28:45   "All these curses will come upon you. They will pursue you
             and overtake you until you are destroyed . . ."
    28:59   ". . . harsh and prolonged disasters . . ."
    28:61   ". . . every kind of . . . disaster not recorded in this book
             of the Law . . ."
    28:63   ". . . it will please him to ruin and destroy you . . ."
Deut 29:19   ". . . disaster on the watered land as well as the dry."
    29:21   "Yahweh will single him out from all the tribes of Israel for
             disaster . . ."
    29:22   ". . . calamities that (will) have fallen on the land . . ."
Deut 31:17   "Many disasters and difficulties will come upon them . . ."
    31:17   ". . . these disasters have come upon us . . ."
    31:21   ". . . many disasters and difficulties . . ."
    31:29   ". . . disaster will fall upon you . . ."
Deut 32:23   "I will heap calamities upon them . . ."
    32:35   "Their day of disaster is near and their doom rushes upon
             them."

26. General punishment / curse / vengeance

Lev 26:41   ". . . they will pay for their sin . . ."
    26:43   "They will pay for their sins . . ."
Deut 28:16   "You will be cursed in the city and cursed in the country."
*Deut 29:20 "All the curses written in this book will fall upon him."
    29:21   ". . . all the curses of the covenant written in this Book of
             the Law."
    29:27   ". . . all the curses written in this book."
Deut 30:19   ". . . curses."
Deut 32:35   "It is mine to avenge; I will repay."
    32:41   "I will take vengeance on my adversaries and repay those who
             hate me."
    32:41   ". . . judgment . . ."
    32:43   "He will take vengeance on his enemies . . ."

27. Multiple punishment

Lev 26:18   "I will punish you for your sins seven times over."
    26:21   "I will multiply your afflictions seven times over."
    26:24   "I will afflict your sins seven times over."
    26:28   "I myself will punish you for your sins seven times over."

A Reference List of Covenant Restoration Blessings

Throughout this volume, the Pentateuchal restoration blessings will be referred to by the following categorizations, as numbered:

1. Renewal of Yahweh's favor / loyalty / presence

    Lev 26:42 "I will not reject them or abhor them . . ."
        26:45 ". . . to be their God."
    Deut 4:29 "You will find him if you look for him with all your heart and soul."
        4:31 "Yahweh your God is a merciful God. He will not abandon you . . ."
        30:3 ". . . Yahweh . . . will have compassion on you . . ."
        30:9 "Yahweh will again delight in you . . . just as he delighted in your fathers."

2. Renewal of the covenant

    Lev 26:42 "I will remember my covenant with Jacob . . ."
        26:44 "I will not . . . (break) my covenant with them . . ."
        26:45 "For their sake I will remember the covenant . . ."
    Deut 4:31 ". . . he will not forget the covenant with your forefathers . . ."

    [Note: Renewal of the covenant implies restoration of any of the original blessings and reversal of any of the curses.]

3. Restoration of true worship, ability to be faithful

    Deut 4:30 ". . . in the later days you will return to Yahweh your God and obey him."
        30:6 "Yahweh your God will circumcise your hearts and the hearts of all your descendants so that you may love him with all your heart . . ."
        30:8 "You will again obey Yahweh and follow all his commands . . ."

4. Population increase

    Deut 30:5 "He will make you . . . more numerous than your fathers."
        30:9 ". . . most prosperous . . . in the fruit of your womb . . ."

5. Agricultural bounty

    Lev 26:42 "I will remember the land."
    Deut 30:9 ". . . most prosperous . . . in the young of your livestock and the crops of your land."

6. Restoration of general prosperity, well-being, health

    Deut 30:3 ". . . then Yahweh your God will restore your fortunes . . ."
        30:5 "He will make you more prosperous . . . than your fathers . . ."
        30:9 "Then Yahweh your God will make you most prosperous in all the work of your hands . . ."
        30:9 "Yahweh will again . . . make you prosperous . . ."
        32:39 ". . . I will heal."

7. Return from exile / repossession of the land

> Deut 30:3　"Yahweh . . . will gather you again from all the nations where he scattered you."
>
> 　　 30:4　". . . from there Yahweh . . . will bring you back."
>
> 　　 30:5　"He will bring you to the land that belonged to your fathers and you will take possession of it."

8. Reunification

> Deut 30:3　"Yahweh will gather you again . . ."
>
> 　　 30:14　". . . from there Yahweh . . . will gather you . . ."

9. Power over enemies / aliens

> Deut 30:7　"Yahweh your God will put all these curses on your enemies . . ."

10. Freedom / restoration from death / destruction

> Lev　26:44　"I will not . . . destroy them completely . . ."
>
> Deut 30:6　". . . so that you may . . . live."
>
> 　　 32:39　". . . I bring to life . . ."

The Canonical Order of Hosea, Joel, Amos, Obadiah, and Jonah

BIBLIOGRAPHY

Audet, J.-P. "A Hebrew-Aramaic List of Books of the Old Testament in Greek Transcription." *JTS* 1 (1950) 135–54. **Beckwith, R.** *The Old Testament Canon in the New Testament Church.* Grand Rapids: Eerdmans, 1986. 450–51. **Blenkinsopp, J.** *Prophecy and Canon.* Notre Dame: University of Notre Dame Press, 1977. **Budde, K.** "Eine folgenschwere Redaction des Zwölfprophetenbuchs." *ZAW* 39 (1922) 218–29. **Childs, B.** *Introduction to the Old Testament as Scripture.* Philadelphia: Fortress, 1979. 46–106. ———. "The Canonical Shape of the Prophetic Literature." *Int* 32 (1978) 46–55. **Fürst, J.** *Der Kanon des Alten Testaments nach den Überlieferungen im Talmud und Midrasch.* Leipzig: Dörffling und Franke, 1868. **Goodblatt, D.** "Audet's 'Hebrew-Aramaic' List of the Books of the OT Revisited." *JBL* 101 (1982) 75–84. **Harris, R. L.** "Factors Promoting the Formation of the Old Testament Canon." *Bulletin of the Evangelical Theological Society* 10/1 (Winter, 1967). ———. *Inspiration and Canonicity of the Bible.* Grand Rapids: Zondervan, 1957. **Harrison, R. K.** *Introduction to the Old Testament.* Grand Rapids: Eerdmans, 1969. 260–88. **Kline, M. G.** *The Structure of Biblical Authority.* Rev. ed. Grand Rapids: Eerdmans, 1972. **Kuhl, C.** *The Old Testament: Its Origins and Composition.* Tr. C. Herriott. Richmond: John Knox, 1961. **Ryle, H. E.** *The Canon of the Old Testament.* London: Macmillan, 1892; 2d ed., 1909. **Sanders, J.** *Torah and Canon.* Philadelphia: Fortress, 1972. **Sarna, N.** "The Order of the Books." In *Studies in Jewish Bibliography, History, and Literature in Honor of J. Edward Kiev,* ed. C. Berlin. New York: KTAV, 1971. 407–413. **Tyle, R.** *The Canon of the Old Testament.* London: 1904. **Wildeboer, G.** "De vóór-Thalmudische Joodische Kanon." *Theologische Studiën* 15 (1897) 159–77; 16 (1898) 194–205; 17 (1899) 185–95. **Wolfe, R. E.** "The Editing of the Book of the Twelve." *ZAW* 53 (1935) 90–130.

An orthodox uderstanding of canonization holds that the contents of the biblical canon are a matter of divine inspiration but that the specific order of the contents may have been left in large measure to human agency.

From the human point of view, five factors—authorship, date of composition, size, style, and subject matter (including both vocabulary and themes; see below)—are the factors that may have influenced canonical order in the Old Testament. Of these, size and authorship appear to have been irrelevant in the instance of the internal ordering of the Minor Prophets (so-called from Latin *minor,* "shorter"), while style may have played a role at most in the case of one book, Jonah. Externally, i.e., taken as a group, size *was* a factor, since any of the minor prophets is shorter than any of the four longer (*major*) prophetical books, and the tendency toward a longer-to-shorter organization (as in the Pauline epistles) put the major prophets as a group before the minor prophets in the canon. Authorship was almost surely a non-issue in the ordering decisions made by a tradition whose workings we can for the most part only guess at.

This leaves date and subject matter, both of which do indeed seem to have played a significant role in the canonical ordering of the Twelve. Date of composition (and/or event in the case of Jonah) was important to the extent that a perception of a chronological order for the composition of these books may have been popularly, and perhaps accurately, widely held. In general one finds relatively early books near the beginning of the group of Minor Prophets and rather late books near the end of the group. The following table represents our own dates for the Minor Prophets relative to their order in the Hebrew Bible:

Book	Order of Composition		Order in the Hebrew Bible
Amos	1, 2, or 3	[ca. 760 B.C.]	3
Hosea	1, 2, or 3	[ca. 760–722]	1
Jonah	1, 2, or 3(?)	[ca. 760–?]	5
Micah	4	[ca. 740–700]	6
Nahum	5 or 6	[ca. 620]	7
Zephaniah	5 or 6	[ca. 620]	9
Habakkuk	7 or 8	[ca. 598–587]	8
Joel	7 or 8	[ca. 598–587]	·2
Obadiah	9	[ca. 585]	4
Haggai	10 or 11	[520]	10
Zechariah	10 or 11	[?–520–?]	11
Malachi	12	[ca. 460]	12

As this table suggests, there is a rough correspondence between canonical order and date of composition except in the case of Joel, Obadiah, and perhaps Jonah. It should be noted that the chronological placement of these three books (and some of the others as well) would be hotly debated by many scholars. Our dates for Joel, Jonah, and Obadiah might be debated, not because we have placed them too late, but in the view of a critical scholarly quasi-consensus, much too early. Nevertheless, at least nine of the twelve, 75 percent, are in approximate chronological order, suggesting that the editor(s) of the Twelve in the Hebrew Bible may consciously have sought to order the books chronologically. Of course, twelve is a very small statistical sample, and random ordering might account for some of the apparent correspondence. Moreover, the fact that certain of the books might have become habitually grouped with one another because they began circulating in writing on common scrolls about the same time might have accounted for the rest.

Helping to clarify the picture is the fact that the Septuagint order for the first six of the Twelve is different from the received Hebrew order. This alternative LXX ordering for the first six suggests strongly that they circulated independently as a collection prior to being grouped with the rest of the Twelve. It places the first six books as follows:

LXX Order	Order of Composition in the Twelve	Order of Composition in the LXX first six
Hosea	1, 2, or 3	1, 2, or 3
Amos	1, 2, or 3	1, 2, or 3
Micah	4	4
Joel	6 or 8	5
Obadiah	9	6
Jonah	1, 2, or 3(?)	1, 2, or 3(?)

In the Septuagint ordering of the first six (taken as a distinct unit that would have circulated separately) only Jonah, sixth in order but conceivably written as early as first, *might* be significantly out of correspondence to chronology. Either or both of two considerations must here come into purview: (1) The date of the composition of the story of Jonah could have been assumed to be considerably later than the events it describes, the composition of the story in its present form having been inspired as a warning to a later generation of the dangers of a narrow, particularistic Judaism. In that case the LXX order could be considered entirely chronological, according to composition rather than event. (2) Jonah, uniquely among the Prophets being a narrative rather than a collection of oracles, may simply have been put at the end of the first six, even if authored earlier than some of them, because it was obviously a somewhat different type of prophetical book. In that instance, genre / subject matter would have proved a somewhat stronger factor than date in the ordering decision, paralleling the overall tendency in the canonization of Scripture, by which books are grouped primarily by genre / subject matter, and then only secondarily, partly or largely by date within those groupings.

A good case can be made, then, for the LXX order as being chronological as long as the first six minor prophets and the second six are regarded as originally separate groupings. Only when the two groups of six (each of which groups contained within itself some relatively late and some relatively early books) were combined did the overall order of all twelve begin to appear non-chronological.

This does not explain, however, why the Hebrew Bible ordering of the Twelve, which was almost surely effected later than the beginning of the translation of LXX in the third century B.C., consciously departed from an earlier, more chronological, format. Here it is likely that the main factors were vocabulary and theme, analogous to and perhaps even partly involving the venerated ancient practice of grouping and remembering things according to "catchwords"—words, terms, and even concepts that tended to provide a ready means of data retention in a society where writing was of necessity always secondary to oral-aural learning. Much work remains to be done on this phenomenon as it pertains to the ordering of Hosea, Joel, Amos, and Obadiah in particular. In the case of Joel and Obadiah, for example, it is at least in part their oracles against foreign nations that link them with Amos. Joel ends with such oracles, Amos begins with them and ends with them, and Obadiah begins and ends with one. Jonah, whose subject is similar, fits logically after these three (cf., cautiously, R. Coote, *Amos among the Prophets*, 129–34, for a different understanding of Jonah's thematic linkage to Amos). It is important to remember that for "catchword" linkage to operate it is only necessary that any two books should share a common vocabulary / theme unit of some sort. If books A, B, and C are to be ordered by this principle, it is sufficient that A and B share something and that B and C share something *else*, and so on. A and C do not technically need to share anything at all, let alone anything in common with B. Catchword organization produces chains, not bars.

Proving our thesis that catchword-thematic linkage is the basis for the received Hebrew Bible canonical order of the minor prophets would go far beyond this introduction and is not essential for an appreciation of the content of the books under study in this volume. They are without dispute independent works, whose canonical order is a separate concern from their date and individual interpretation. The fact that the Septuagint contains the more nearly original ordering, however, and that this ordering is almost entirely chronological within the two groups of six books each, provides an initial, general perspective from which to relate these books to their historical purposes.

Hosea

Hosea

Bibliography

COMMENTARIES

Andersen, F. I. and **D. N. Freedman.** *Hosea.* AB 24. Garden City, NY: Doubleday, 1980. **Brillet, G.** *Amos et Osée.* Paris: Éditions du Cerf, 1944. **Brown, S. L.** *The Book of Hosea with Introduction and Notes.* London: Methuen, 1932. **Burroughes, J.** *An Exposition of the Prophecy of Hosea.* Edinburgh: Nichol, 1863. **Cheyne, T. K.** *Hosea with Notes and Introduction.* Cambridge: University Press, 1884. **Frey, H.** *Das Buch des Werbens Gottes um seine Kirche: Der Prophet Hosea.* Die Botschaft des Alten Testaments 23.2. Stuttgart: Calwer, 1957. **Gelderen, C. van.** and **W. H. Gispen.** *Het Boek Hosea.* COT. Kampen: Kok, 1953. **Gelin, A.** "Osee." *DBSup.* Ed. L. Pirot and F. Vigouroux. Paris: Letouzey et Ané, 1960. 6:926–40. **Ginsberg, H. L.** "Hosea." *Encyclopedia Judaica.* Vol. 8, cols. 1010–24. Jerusalem: Encyclopedia Judaica / Macmillan, 1971. **Harper, W. R.** *A Critical and Exegetical Commentary on Amos and Hosea.* ICC. New York: Scribners, 1905. **Hauret, C.** *Amos et Osée.* Verb. Sal. AT. 5. Paris: Beauchesne, 1970. **Jeremias, J.** *Der Prophet Hosea.* Göttingen: Vandenhoeck & Ruprecht, 1983. **Julianus Aeclanus: Buman, G.** *Des Julian von Aeclanum Kommentar zu den Propheten Osee, Joel und Amos.* An Bib 9. Rome: Pontifical Biblical Institute, 1958. **Kidner, D.** *Love to the Loveless. The Story and Message of Hosea.* Downers Grove, Ill: Intervarsity Press, 1981. **Knight, G. A. F.** *Hosea: Introduction and Commentary.* London: SCM Press, 1960. ———. *Hosea: God's Love.* London: SCM, 1967. **Loth, B. A.** *Osée.* Paris: 1967. **McCarthy, D. J.** "Hosea." *The Jerome Biblical Commentary,* vol. 1. Ed. R. E. Brown et al. Englewood Cliffs, NJ: Prentice Hall, 1968. 253–64. **McKeating, H.** *The Books of Amos, Hosea and Micah.* Cambridge Bible Commentary. Cambridge: UP, 1971. **MacPherson, A.** *Amos and Hosea.* Scripture Discussion Commentary. Ed. J. Bright. Chicago: ACTA Foundation, 1971. **Mays, J. L.** *Hosea.* OTL. Philadelphia: Westminster Press, 1969. **Nowack, W.** *Der Prophet Hosea erklärt.* Berlin: Mayer und Muller, 1880. **Osty, E.** *Amos, Osée.* Paris: Editions du Cerf, 1960. **Peiser, F. E.** *Hosea: Philologische Studien zum Alten Testament.* Leipzig: J. C. Hinrichs, 1914. **Pfeiffer, C. F.** "Hosea." *The Wycliffe Bible Commentary.* Ed. C. F. Pfeiffer and E. F. Harrison. Chicago: Moody Press, 1962. 801–18. **Rudolph, W.** *Hosea.* KAT 13 / 1. Gütersloh: G. Mohn, 1966. **Ryan, D.** "Hosea." *New Catholic Commentary on Holy Scripture.* London/New York: Nelson, 1969. 676–88. **Schnoller, O.** *The Book of Hosea.* Tr. J. McCurdy. New York: C. Scribners' Sons, 1902. **Scholz, A.** *Kommentar zum Buche des Propheten Hosea.* Würzburg: Woerl, 1882. **Scott, M.** *The Message of Hosea.* New York: Macmillan, 1921. **Snaith, N. H.** *Amos, Hosea and Micah.* London: Epworth, 1956. **Stramere, T.** "Osea." *BSS* 9 (1907) 1279–81. **Valeton, J. J. P.** *Amos und Hosea: Ein Kapitel aus der Geschichte der israelitische Religion.* Giessen: J. Ricker, 1898. **Vellas, B. M.** *Osee.* Hermeneia Palaias Diathekes. Athens: Aster Publishing House, 1947. **Ward, J. M.** *Hosea: A Theological Commentary.* New York: Harper and Row, 1966. **Wolff, H. W.** *A Commentary on the Book of the Prophet Hosea.* Hermeneia. Tr. G. Stansell. Ed. P. Hanson. Philadelphia: Fortress Press, 1974.

BOOKS, DISSERTATIONS AND SPECIALIZED COMMENTARIES

Adames, R. "Pecado y Conversion en Oseas: Contribucion a la Telogie Biblica del Profeta." Diss. Pontifical University Gregoriana, Rome, 1958. *Amos et Osée.* Paris: Les burgers et les mages: Éditions du Cerf, 1969. **Bitter, S.** *Die Ehe des Propheten Hosea: eine auslegungsgeschichtliche Untersuchung.* Göttinger theologische Arbeiten 3. Göttingen: Vanderhoeck und Ruprecht, 1975. **Boeker, H. J.** *Redeformen des Rechtsleben im Alten Testament.* WMANT 14. Neukirchen-Vluyn: Neukirchener Verlag, 1964. **Broughton, P. E.** "The Worship of the Northern Kingdom as Seen in the Book of Hosea." Diss. University of Melbourne, 1962. **Brueggemann, W.** *Tradition for Crisis: A Study in Hosea.* Richmond, VA: Knox, 1969. **Buck, F.** "Die Liebe Gottes beim Profeten Osee." Diss. Pontifical Biblical Institute. Rome, 1953. **Coleman, S.** *Hosea Concepts in Midrash and Talmud.* Bloemfontein: Stabilis Press, 1960. **Emmerson, G. I.** *Hosea: An Israelite Prophet in Judean Perspective.* JSOTSup 28. Sheffield: JSOT Press, 1984. **Fuhs, H. F.** *Die äthiopische Übersetzung des Propheten Hosea.* Bonn: Hanstein, 1971. **Hendriks, H. J.** "Juridical Aspects of the Marriage Metaphor in Hosea and Jeremiah." Diss. University of Stellenbosch, South Africa, n.d. **Hubbard, D. A.** *With Bands of Love: Lessons from the Book of Hosea.* Grand Rapids: Eerdmans, 1969. **Kuhnigk, W.** *Nordwestsemitische Studien zum Hoseabuch.* Rome: Biblical Institute Press, 1974. **Leeuwen, C. van.** *Hosea: Prediking van het Oude Testament.* Nijkerk: Callenbach, 1968. **Lindblom, J.** *Hosea, literarische untersucht.* Abo: Abo Akademi, 1927. **Miller, I. D.** "Other Gods and Idols in the Period of Hosea." Diss. Cambridge, 1976. **Morgan, G. C.** *Hosea: The Heart and Holiness of God.* Grand Rapids: Baker, 1964. **Ostborn, G.** *Yahweh and Baal: Studies in the Book of Hosea and Related Documents.* Lunds Universitets Arsskrift, N.F. Avd. 1. Bd. 51. 6. Lund: Gleerup, 1956. **Rand, H. B.** *Study in Hosea.* Haverhill, MA: Destiny Publishers, 1955. **Robinson, H. W.** *The Cross of Hosea.* Philadelphia: Westminster, 1949. ———. *Two Hebrew Prophets: Studies in Hosea and Ezekiel.* London: Lutterworth, 1948. **Scott, J. B.** *The Book of Hosea: A Study Manual.* SBSS. Grand Rapids: Baker, 1971. **Solari, J. K.** "Osee (Hosea)." *New Catholic Encyclopedia* 10. New York: McGraw-Hill, 1967. **Stevenson, H. I.** *Three Prophetic Voices: Studies in Joel, Amos and Hosea.* London: Marshall, Morgan and Scott, 1971. **Utzschneider, H.** *Hosea: Prophet vor dem Ende.* Orbis biblicus et orientalis 31. Fribourg, Switzerland: Universitätsverlag; Göttingen: Vandenhoeck und Ruprecht, 1980. **Vannorsdall, A. O.** "The Use of Covenant Liturgy in Hosea." Diss. Boston, 1968. **Vawter, B.** *Amos, Hosea, Micah, with an Introduction to Classical Prophecy.* OT Message 7. Dublin: Gill and MacMillan, 1981. **Vollmer, J.** *Geschichtliche Rückblicke und Motive in der Prophetie des Amos, Hosea und Jesaia.* BZAW 119. Berlin: Walter de Gruyter, 1971. **Wenham, A. E.** *Ruminations on the Book of Hosea.* Birmingham: McMichael, 1915. **White, K. O.** *Studies in the Book of Hosea: God's Incomparable Love.* Nashville: Convention Press, 1957. **Willi-Plein, I.** *Vorformen der Schriftexegese innerhalb des Alten Testaments: Untersuchungen zum literarischen Werden des auf Amos, Hosea und Micha zurückgehenden Bücher im hebräischen Zwölfprophetenbuch.* BZAW 123. Berlin: Walter de Gruyter, 1971. **Wolfe, R.** *Meet Amos and Hosea.* New York: Harper, 1945. **Wolff, H. W.** *Die Hochzeit der Hure.* Munich: Kaiser Verlag, 1979. **Wunsche, A.** *Der Prophet Hosea übersetzt und erklärt mit Benutzung der Targumim, der judischen Ausleger Raschi, aben Ezra und David Kimchi.* Leipzig: T. O. Weigel, 1868. **Ziegler, H. W.** "Das Gottesbild beim Propheten Hosea." Diss. University of Trier, 1968.

Articles

Achtemeier, E. R. "The Content of the Book of Hosea in Its Old Testament Context." *Theology in Life* 5 (1962) 125–32. **Ackroyd, P. R.** "Hosea and Jacob." *VT* 13 (1963) 245–59. **Adinolfi, M.** "Appunti sul simbolismo sponsale in Osee e Geremia." *EuntDoc* 25 (1972, ed. 1973) 126–38. **Ambanelli, I.** "Il significato dell'espressione *da⁽at ʾelohim* nel Prophela Osea." *Riv B* 21 (1973) 119–145. **Anderson, B. W.** "The Book of Hosea."

Int 8 (1954) 290–304. **Auge, R.** "Oseas." *EnchBib* 5 (1965) 125–32. **Bach, R.** "Hosea." *EKL* 2. 201–3. **Badini, G.** "La lecture des livres d'Osée et de Jonas au cours secondaire: Opportunité et méthode." *LumVit* 20 (1965) 674–90. **Batten, L. W.** "'Wissen um Gott' bei Hosea als Urform von Theologie?" *EvT* 15 (1955) 416–25. **Baumgartner, W.** "Kennen Amos und Hosea eine Heilseschatologie?" *Schweizerische Theologische Zeitschrift* 30 (1913) 30–42; 95–124; 152–70. **Beaucamp, E.** "Osee 4, 1–14, 1: Problème de la division du texte." *Div* 4 (1960) 548–60. **Behler, G. M.** "Divini Amoris Suprema Revelatio in Antiquo Foedere Data (Osee c. 11)." *Ang* 20 (1943) 102–16. **Bergren, R. V.** *The Prophets and the Law.* Monographs of Hebrew Union College 4. New York: Hebrew Union College, 1974. **Bierne, C. J.** "The Prophet in Hosea's and Our Time." *TBT* 40 (1969) 265–72. **Birkeland, H.** "Profeten Hosea's Forkynnelse." *NorTT* 38 (1937) 277–316. **Bohmer, J.** "Das Buch Hosea nach seinen Grundgedanken und Gedankengang." *Nieuwe Theologische Studien* 10 (1927) 97–104. ———. "Die Grungedanken der Predigt Hoseas." *ZWT* 44 (1902) 1–24. **Boling, R. G.** "Prodigal Sons on Trial: A Study in the Prophecy of Hosea." *McCQ* (1965) 13–27. **Buhl, F.** "Einige textkritische Bemerkungen zu den kleinen Propheten." *ZAW* 5 (1885) 179–84. ———. "Tragedy and Comedy in Hosea." *Semeia* 32 (1984) 71–82. **Buhl, M. J.** "Mari Prophecy and Hosea." *JBL* 88 (1969) 338. **Canto, R. J.** "Oseas." *CB* 22 (1965) 87–97. **Caquot, A.** "Osée et la Royauté." *RHPR* 41 (1961) 123–46. **Cherian, C. M.** "The Prophet of the Mystery of God's Love." *CleM* 22 (1958) 237–41; 317–25. **Craghan, J. F.** "An Interpretation of Hosea." *BTB* 5 (1975) 201–7. ———. "The Book of Hosea: A Survey of Recent Literature on the First of the Minor Prophets." *BTB* 1 (1971) 81–100, 145–70. **Crane, W. E.** "The Prophecy of Hosea." *Biblica Sacra* 89 (1932) 480–94. **Crotty, R.** "Hosea and the Knowledge of God." *AusBR* 19 (1971) 1–16. **Daumeste, M. L.** "Le Message du Prophète Osée." *VSpir* 75 (1946) 710–26. **Dijkema, F.** "De Profeet Hosea." *NedTTs* 14 (1925) 324–43. **Driver, G. R.** "Linguistic and Textual Problems: Minor Prophets." *JTS* 39 (1938) 154–66; 260–73; 393–405. **Duhm, B.** "Anmerkungen zu den zwölf kleinen Propheten." *ZAW* 31 (1911) 1–4; 81–110; 161–204. **Durr, L.** "Altorientalisches Recht bei den Propheten Amos und Hosea." *BZ* 23 (1935) 150–57. **Eakin, F. E., Jr.** "Yahwism and Baalism before the Exile." *JBL* 84 (1965) 407–14. **Eichrodt, W.** "The Holy One in Your Midst? The Theology of Hosea." *Int* 15 (1961) 259–73. **Elliger, K.** "Eine verkannte Kunstform bei Hosea." *ZAW* 69 (1957) 151–60. **Ellison, H. L.** "The Message of Hosea in the Light of His Marriages." *EvQ* 41 (1969) 3–9. **Engnell, I.** "Notiser till Hosea frö prof. I. Engnell's seminarium." *SEÅ* 32 (1967) 21–35. **Eszenyei, M.** "Izrael eletiviszonyai Hoseas profeta koraban." *Reformatus Szemle* (1966) 9–14. **Eybers, I. H.** "Historical References in the Preaching of the Prophet Hosea." *OTWSA.* (1975) 60–69. ———. "The Matrimonial Life of Hosea." *OTWSA* 7/8 (1964–65) 11–34. **Farr, G.** "The Concept of Grace in the Book of Hosea." *ZAW* 70 (1958) 98–107. **Feuillet, A.** "L'universalisme et l'alliance dans la religion d'Osée." *BVC* 18 (1957) 27–35. **Fohrer, G.** "Umkehr und Erlösung beim Propheten Hosea." *TZ* 11 (1955) 161–85. **Francisco, C. T.** "Evil and Suffering in the Book of Hosea." *SWJT* 5/2 (1962) 33–41. **Freehoff, S. B.** "Some Text Rearrangements in the Minor Prophets." *JQR* 32 (1941–42) 303–08. **Frey, H.** "Der Aufbau der Gedichte Hoseas." *WuD* n.f. 5 (1957) 9–103. **Gaster, T. H.** "Notes on the Minor Prophets." *JTS* 39 (1937) 163–65. **Gelston, A.** "Kingship in the Book of Hosea." *OTS* 19 (1974) 71–85. **Gemser, B.** "The Rîb or Controversy Pattern in Hebrew Mentality." *Wisdom in Israel.* VTSup 3. Leiden: E. J. Brill, 1955. 120–37. **Gerstenberger, E.** "The Woe Oracles of the Prophets." *JBL* 81 (1962) 249–63. **Giblet, J.** "De Revelatione Amoris Dei apud Oseam Prophetam." *Collectania Mechliniensia* 34 (1949) 35–39. **Gluck, J. J.** "Some Semantic Complexities in the Book of Hosea." *OTWSA* 7 (1966) 50–63. **Good, E. M.** "The Composition of Hosea." *SEÅ* 31 (1966) 21–63. ———. "Hosea and the Jacob Tradition." *VT* 16 (1966) 137–51. **Gordis, R.** "Hosea's Marriage and Message." *HUCA* 25 (1954) 9–35. **Groussouw, W. K. M.** "Un Fragment Sahidique d'Osée 2:9–5:1." *Museon* 47 (1934) 185–

204. **Gunkel, H.** "Hosea." *RGG* 2:2020–23. **Halévy, J.** "Le Livre d'Osée." *RevSem* 10 (1902) 1–12; 97–133; 193–212; 289–304. **Hall, T. O.** "Introduction to Hosea." *RevExp* 54 (1957) 501–9. **Harner, P. B.** "Nature and History in Hosea." *ThLife* 9 (1966) 308–17. **Harvey, J.** "Le Rîb Pattern: Requistoire prophétique sur la rupture de l'alliance." *Bib* 43 (1962) 172–96. **Haupt, P.** "Hosea's Erring Spouse." *JBL* 34 (1915) 41–53. **Helewa, J.** "Ministère doctrinal du prêtre dans la théologie ecclésiale du prophète Osée." *ECarm* 17(1966) 5–30. **Helfmeyer, F. J.** "Gotteserkenntnis—Liebe—Umkehr." *BK* 40 (1985) 101–7. **Hindley, J. B.** "Hosea." *NBC* (rev.). Ed. D. Guthrie et al. London / Grand Rapids: IVP / Erdmans, 1970. 703–15. **Hirshberg, H. H.** "Some Additional Arabic Etymologies in OT Lexicography." *VT* 11 (1967) 373–85. **Holt, E. K.** "*dʿt ʾlhym* und *ḥsd* im Buche Hosea." JSOT 1 (1987) 87–103. **Houtsma, M.** "Bijdrage tot de Kritiek en Verklaring van Hosea." *TT* 9 (1875) 55–75. **Huffmon, H.** "Prophecy in the Mari Letters." *BA* 31 (1968) 101–24. ———. "The Covenant Lawsuit in the Prophets." *JBL* 78 (1959) 285–95. **Humbert, P.** "Osee le prophète bedouin." *RHPR* 1 (1921) 97–118. **Jacob, E.** "Der Prophet Hosea und die Geschichte." *EvT* 24 (1964) 281–90. ———. "L'héritage cananéen dans le livre du prophète Osée." *RHPR* 43 (1963) 250–59. **Jepsen, A.** "Kleine Beiträge zum Zwölfprophetenbuch." *ZAW* 56 (1938) 85–100; 57 (1939) 242–55; 61 (1945–8) 95–114. **Johansen, J. H.** "The Prophet Hosea: His Marriage and Message." *JETS* 14 (1971) 179–84. **Kahle, P.** "Die im August 1952 entdeckte Lederrolle mit dem griechischen Text der kleinen Propheten und das Problem der Septuaginta." *TLZ* 79 (1954) 81–94. **Kapelrud, A. S.** "The Spirit and the Word in the Prophets." *ASTI* 11 (1978) 40–47. **Kelley, P. H.** "The Holy One in the Midst of Israel: Redeeming Love (Hos 11–14)." *RevExp* 72 (1975) 465–72. **Kedar-Kopfstein, B.** "Textual Gleanings from the Vulgate to Hosea." *JQR* 65 (1974) 73–97. **King, P. J.** "Hosea's Message of Hope" *BT* 33 (1982) 238–42. **Labuschagne, C. J.** "The Similes in the Book of Hosea." *OTWSA* 7 / 8 (1964 / 65) 64–76. **Lagrange, A.** "La nouvelle histoire d'Israel et le prophète Osée." *RB* 1 (1892) 203–38. **Lavani, J.** "Loci 'Clausi' in Osee." *World Congress of Jewish Studies*, vol. 1a. Jerusalem: Magnes Press, 1952. **Loewen, J. A.** "Some Figures of Speech in Hosea." *BT* 33 (1982) 238–42. **Lundbom, J.** "Poetic Structure and Prophetic Rhetoric in Hosea." *VT* 29 (1979) 300–308. **McDonald, J. R. B.** "The Marriage of Hosea." *Th* 67 (1964) 149–56. **McKenzie, J. L.** "Divine Passion in Osee." *CBQ* 17 (1955) 287–99. ———. "Knowledge of God in Hosea." *JBL* 74 (1955) 22–7. **Maley, E. H.** "Messianism in Osee." *CBQ* 19 (1957) 213–25. **May, H. G.** "An Interpretation of the Names of Hosea's Children." *JBL* 55 (1936) 285–91. ———. "The Fertility Cult in Hosea." *AJSL* 48 (1932) 73–98. **Merwe, B. J. van der.** "A Few Remarks on the Religious Terminology in Amos and Hosea." *OTWSA* 7 (1966) 143–52. ———. "Echoes from the Teaching of Hosea in Isa. 40–55." *OTWSA* 7 (1966) 20–29. **Meyer, R.,** et al. "Propheten II." *RGG* 5:613, 633. **Morag, S.** "On Semantic and Lexical Features in the Language of Hosea." *Tarbiz* 53 (1983 / 84) 489–511 (Heb.). **Morgenstern, J.** "Beena Marriage (Matriarchat) in Ancient Israel and Its Historical Implications." *ZAW* 47 (1929) 91–110. **Neef, H. D.** "Der Septuaginta-Text und der Masoreten-Text des Hoseabuches im Vergleich." *Bib* 67 (1986) 195–220. **North, F. S.** "Solution of Hosea's Marital Problems by Critical Analysis." *JNES* 15 (1957) 128–30. **Nyberg, H. S.** "Das textkritische Problem des Alten Testaments am Hoseabuch demonstriert." *ZAW* 52 (1934) 214–54. **Oort, H.** "Hosea." *TT* 24 (1890) 345–64; 480–505. **Owens, J. J.** "Exegetical Study of Hosea." *RevExp* 54 (1957) 522–43. **Paton, L. B.** "Notes on Hosea's Marriage." *JBL* 15 (1896) 9–17. **Plöger, O.** "Hosea." *RGG* 3:454. ———. "Hoseabuch." *RGG* 3:454–57. **Renaud, B.** "Fidelité humaine et fidelité de Dieu dans le livre d'Osée 1–3." *Revue de Droit Canonique* 33 (1983) 184–200. ———. "Osée 1–3: analyse diachronique et lecture synchronique, problèmes de méthode." *RevScRel* 57 (1983) 249–60. **Rendtorff, R.** "Erwägungen zur Fruhgeschichte des Prophetentums in Israel." *ZTK* 59 (1962) 145–67. ["Reflections on the Early History of Prophecy in Israel." Tr. P. J. Achtemeier, in *Hermeneutic, Journal for Theology and the Church* 4. Ed R. W. Funk and G. Ebeling. New York: Harper and Row, 1967.

14–34.] ———. "Prophetenspruch." *RGG* 5:635–38. **Roberts, J. J. M.** "Hosea and the Sacrifical Cultus." *RestQ* 15 (1972) 15–26. **Robinson, T. H.** "Die Ehe des Hosea." *TSK* 106 (1935) 301–13. **Rowley, H. H.** "The Marriage of Hosea." *BJRL* 39 (1956) 200–33. **Rudolph, W.** "Präparierte Jungfrauen?" *ZAW* 75 (1963) 65–73. **Ruppert, L.** "Hernkunft und Bedeutung der Jacob Tradition bei Hosea." *Bib* 52 (1971) 488–504. **Rust, E. C.** "The Theology of Hosea." *RevExp* 54 (1957) 510–21. **Schmidt, H.** "Die Ehe des Hosea." *ZAW* 42 (1924) 245–72. **Schreiner, J.** "Hoseas Ehe: Ein Zeichen des Gerichts." *BZ* 21 (1977) 163–83. **Schwartz, V.** "Das Gottesbild des Propheten Oseas." *BLit* 35 (1961–62) 274–79. **Sellers, O.** "Hosea's Motives." *AJSL* 41 (1924–25) 243–47. **Sellin, E.** "Die geschichtliche Orientierung der Prophetie des Hosea." *NKZ* 36 (1925) 607–58. ———. "Hosea und das Martyrium des Mose." *ZAW* 46 (1928) 26–33. **Selms, A. van.** "Hosea and Canticles." *OTSWA* 7 / 8 (1964–65) 85–89. **Soggin, J. A.** "Profezia e rivoluzione nell'Antico Testamento: L'opera di Elia di Eliseo nella volutazione di Osea." *Protestantesimo* 12 (1970) 1–14. **Stinespring, W. F.** "A Problem of Theological Ethics in Hosea." *Essays in Old Testament Ethics.* Ed. J. L. Crenshaw and J. T. Willis. New York: Ktav Publishing House, 1974. ———. "Hosea, the Prophet of Doom." *Crozier Quarterly* 27 (1950) 200–207. **Strange, J. O.** "The Broken Covenant: Bankrupt Religion (Hos 4–6)." *RevExp* 72 (1975) 437–48. **Strauss, L.** "Hosea's Love— A Modern Interpretation." *Judaism* 19 (1970) 226–33. **Szabo, A.** "Hosea's Konyvenek Problemai." *ThSz* 14 (1971) 150–56. **Tadmor, H.** "The Historical Background of Hosea's Prophecies." In *The Y. Kaufmann Jubilee Volume,* ed. M. Haran. Jerusalem: Magnes Press, 1960. **Tate, M. E.** "The Whirlwind of National Disaster: A Disorganized Society (Hos 7–10)." *RevExp* 72 (1975) 449–63. **Uffenheimer, B.** "Amos et Osée: deux modes de prophétie en Israel." In *Z. Shazar Jubilee Volume,* ed. B. Z. Luria. Jerusalem: Kirjath Sepher, 1973. **Vriezen, T. C.** "Prophecy and Eschatology." *Congress Volume, 1953.* VTSup 1. Leiden: E. J. Brill, 1953. 199–229. **Vuilleumier, R.** "Les traditions d'Israël et la liberté du prophète: Osée." *RHPR* 59 (1979) 491–98. **Ward, J. M.** "Hosea." *IDBSup* 421–22. ———. "The Message of the Prophet Hosea." *Int* 23 (1969) 387–407. **Waterman, L.** "Hosea, Chapters 1–3, in Retrospect and Prospect." *JNES* 14 (1955) 100–109. ———. "The Marriage of Hosea." *JBL* 37 (1918) 193–208. **Watson, W. G. E.** "Reflexes of Akkadian Incantation in Hosea." *VT* 34 (1984) 242–47. **Watts, J. D. W.** "Elements of OT Worship." *JBR* 26 (1958) 217–21. **Werbeck, W.** "Zwölfprophetenbuch." *RGG* 6:1969–70. **Wolfe, R. E.** "The Editing of the Book of the Twelve." *ZAW* 53 (1935) 90–130. **Wolff, H. W.** "Guilt and Salvation: A Study of the Prophecy of Hosea." *Int* 15 (1961) 274–85. ———. "'Wissen um Gott' bei Hosea als Urform von Theologie." *EvT* 12 (1952–53) 533–54. Repr. in Wolff, *Gesammelte Studien zum Alten Testament. TBü* 22. München: 1973. 182–205. ———. "Hoseas geistige Heimat." *TLZ* 81 (1956) 83–94. Repr. in Wolff, *Gesammelte Studien zum Alten Testament. TBu* 22. 232–50. ———. "Erkenntnis Gottes im Alten Testament." *EvT* 15 (1955) 426–31. **Wyrtzen, D. B.** "The Theological Centre of the Book of Hosea." *BSac* 141 (1984) 315–29. **Yaron, R.** "On Divorce in Old Testament Times." *Revue international des droits d'antiquité* 4 (1957) 117–28. **Yeivin, S.** "On the Historical Background of Hosea's Prophecy and Its Linguistic Uniqueness." *BMik* 25 (1979) 38–40. **Ziegler, J.** "Studien zur Verwertung der Septuaginta im Zwölfprophetenbuch." *ZAW* 60 (1944) 107–31.

Introduction

HOSEA AND THE COVENANT

Understanding the message of the book of Hosea depends upon understanding the Sinai covenant. The book contains a series of blessings and curses announced for Israel by God through Hosea. Each blessing or curse is based upon a corresponding type in the Mosaic law. Some blessings and curses so specifically parallel the pentateuchal formulations that they border on "citation," though citation per se was unknown in ancient legal procedure; others, more generally, merely allude to the pentateuchal wordings. Although Hosea's style was in many ways original, his message was not at all innovative. Hosea's task was simply to warn that Yahweh intended to enforce the terms of his covenant.

Because of the characteristics of (northern) Israel in the mid-eighth century B.C., God's prophetic word could hardly have been predominantly positive. Israel was continuing a history of covenant-breaking, and her Lord had determined to move against his people by unleashing the punishments specified in the law. In the short run, therefore, God's plan for his people was one that would necessarily seem to them negative. In the long run, on the other hand, God's overall plan of blessing for his chosen nation would still prevail. Accordingly, the book of Hosea now and again contains reminders to the faithful that God would one day again bring prosperity to Israel. But the vast majority of the oracles God spoke through Hosea were of woe, not weal, and they depend for their substance upon the depository of covenant curses found in Leviticus and Deuteronomy (see *General Introduction*).

THE BASIC MESSAGE OF HOSEA

Hosea contains both predictions of destruction and predictions of restoration. Punishment predominates over promise by a substantial margin. There is no particular pattern discernible in the way that the oracles of hope are distributed among the more numerous oracles of doom. The oracles of Hosea do reflect in their message the chronological presupposition found throughout the OT pre-exilic prophetic corpus: in the short run there will be woe, but later there will come a time of weal. The blessings portions of the book are therefore *eschatological* in their orientation, while the curses are more immediate. There is no hint in Hosea that Israel can actually escape from the wrath of Yahweh expressed in destruction and exile.

Deuteronomy 4:20–31 encapsulates the historical perspective of Israel's history on which Hosea's oracles are based. A total of five stages may be identified in the history of the chosen people: (1) The exodus-wilderness stage, in which the people of Israel were rescued from slavery and by God's grace gathered into a people. Hosea 2:16–17 alludes, for example, to this period in connection with a futuristic scene of blessing. (2) The making of the covenant, with its blessings and curses, by which Israel and Yahweh are bound. (3) The period of blessings, commencing with the covenant (cf. Deut 28:2–14) and continuing throughout Israel's history (e.g., Hos 2:4–15 [2–13]) until the point at which Israel's unfaithfulness is so rife that the covenant is abrogated (e.g., Hos 1:9) and the blessings are withdrawn. (4) The period of the curses. During this time Israel will undergo death, disease, destruction, deportation, etc. (Hos 3:4–5; 4:6; 5:7, 14; 7:16; 8:13–14; 9:3, 17; 10:15; 11:5–6; 13:16; etc.). Most of the book concerns predictions of the fourth state; Hosea's main task was to announce its onset. (5) The period of eschatolog-

ical blessing. After destruction and exile—and *only* thereafter—Israel will again
be restored to Yahweh and blessed. To this stage belong the seven promise
sections of the book (2:1–3 [1:10–2:1]; 2:16–25 [14–23]; 3:5; 6:1–3; 10:12;
11:8–11; 14:1–8).

It is important to understand that the promise sections do not hold out
hope for an avoidance of divine wrath, but follow Deut 4 (and Lev 26 and
Deut 30) in expecting blessing only after the curses of the covenant have
been unleashed. Once the covenant is abrogated, blessing must await the
full measure of divine punishment. The blessings are thus always eventual,
while the curses are immediate.

FORM, STRUCTURE, AND STYLE

It is not always possible to know whether or not a given oracle of Hosea
was composed for oral delivery to an audience. Though we have no choice
but to operate on the assumption that all of them were spoken before being
written, this assumption remains unproved. The metrical structure of many
of the individual poetic pericopes is either unusual, unique, or composed of
mixed types; as a result, the usual earmarks of oral composition in poetry
(lack of enjambment, use of formulae, thematic arrangement, etc.) are represented scantily. Hosea is not unique in this regard, however; the same could
be said for most of the prophetical books. Old Testament "classical" (eighth
century and later) prophecy seems generally to display certain characteristics
associated normally with oral composition and others associated with a written
style. Ultimately this uncertainty presents no great barrier to the interpretation
of Hosea's oracles—if the interpreter is willing to give content predominance
over form in analyzing the various passages of the book.

This approach is essential because "Hosea was not given to following the
structures of speech-types" (J. L. Mays, 5). In other words, typical prophetic
formal composition characteristics are either so subtly combined or so artistically modified in Hosea's oracles that one has to consider each oracle on an
ad hoc basis, i.e., on its own merits. Form criticism, by definition a comparative
enterprise, is thus less often rewarding in the exegesis of passages in Hosea
than is the case with other prophetic collections.

In addition, the editorial arranging of Hosea's oracles, whether done by
Hosea himself or someone else, is either so skillful or so nonchalant (it is
technically impossible to tell which) as to result in a relative absence of sharp
delineations between pericopes. In fact, deciding where one passage in Hosea
leaves off and another begins has been a major consideration for every commentator and critic. The results have hardly been uniform.

It is our contention that the oracles of Hosea must be seen, therefore, in
macrocosm rather than microcosm. That is, one is obliged to ignore to some
degree the rather rapid and unpredictable shifts in person, subject matter,
and tone which can occur so often from couplet to couplet and verse to
verse in a given oracle, in favor of seeing these as ultimately fitting neatly
into a coherent pericope, the point and effectiveness of which is no less comprehensible than would have been the case if the oracle displayed a more obviously
systematic pattern.

THE ISOLATION OF POETRY IN HOSEA

It is easier to differentiate poetry from prose in Hebrew when the parallelism is entirely or largely synonymous or antithetical. The differentiation of so-called synthetic parallelism from prose is much more difficult. (On the inadequacy of the category "synthetic" for Hebrew poetic parallelisms, see S. A. Geller, *Parallelism in Early Biblical Poetry*, HSM 20 [Missoula, MT: Scholars Press, 1979].) In most of Hosea's oracles, synonymous or antithetical parallelisms are represented sufficiently, and accompanied by metrical patterns obvious enough, that the identification of poetic oracles as opposed to prose oracles is not a problem. Additionally, the following clues have been used to identify the presence of poetry: (1) the relative infrequency of the article and other prosaic particles; (2) the relative frequency of *maqqeph;* (3) the relative frequency of rare vocabulary; (4) the presence of "fixed" word pairs; (5) the relative paucity of syntactical indicators; (6) the presence of laconic semantic style; (7) the presence of highly rhetorical structures that indicate the repetitiousness characteristic of poetry.

THE HISTORICAL SETTING

Hosea was called by Yahweh to prophesy the destruction and exile of Israel at a time when Israel was at the height of its prosperity. In the latter years of the reign of Jeroboam II (793–753 B.C.), probably not much earlier than 760 B.C., Hosea began his ministry through the enactment prophecy of marrying a "prostituting" Israelite and starting a family of "prostituting" Israelites, only a few years before Tiglath-Pileser III (745–728 B.C.) of Assyria changed Israel's attitudes from complacency to desperation.

The Jehu dynasty, begun in 842 B.C., came to an end with the death of Jeroboam II in 753. It was Israel's longest dynasty. Thereafter, beginning with the accession of Zechariah to the throne in Samaria in 753, attempts at dynasty proved futile. The order of the day was usurpation by assassination. Hosea eventually prophesied during the reigns of more kings than any other OT prophet. Six kings governed the north during the remaining thirty years until its fall, none of them notable for his administrative or diplomatic skills. Life in Israel became increasingly precarious; the nation's fortunes waned progressively. These developments are reflected in the book of Hosea, which appears to proceed more or less chronologically from the 750s to the 720s in the ordering of Hosea's oracles. The complacency of the early days (2:7, 10, 15 [2:5, 8, 13]) gives way to a desperation in foreign (7:8–12; 12:1) and domestic (7:3–7; 13:10–11) affairs, evidenced in the latter chapters. The Syro-Ephraimite war of 734 B.C., which ended with the capitulation of the north to Assyria after Israel was reduced to a rump state by the Assyrian conquest and by a Judean invasion (5:8–10), represented the beginning of the end for Hosea's native country.

We have no way of answering with certainty a number of key questions about the setting of Hosea's prophetic ministry. The book never states the location of any of his preaching. We may guess that he delivered oracles frequently at Samaria, and—at least prior to 734 when Bethel probably reverted to Judean control—at Bethel, as did Amos. But we have no hard evidence. None of the oracles is dated. While we may be fairly confident of the dating of some (e.g., 1:2–9; 5:5–10), and of the approximate chronological ordering of most, our analysis of setting remains ultimately speculative in any given instance. Might Hosea have had contact with Amos, his somewhat older contemporary in the north, or with any of the somewhat younger contemporary orthodox Judean prophets? We have no way of knowing.

With regard to his audience, Hosea may have enjoyed some faithful reception of his oracles among the small percentage of northerners yet concerned to keep the Mosaic covenant, but he makes no mention of this, nor do his words even hint at it. And his words surely met with both resentment and ridicule, when not utterly ignored, by the vast majority of those who heard them.

Orthodox Yahwism had become a small minority religion in Israel by Hosea's time, judging from the consistently discouraging reports of its status in the historical books and the prophets. While Judah, Canaan's "Bible-belt," had perhaps resisted the encroachment of foreign religious practices somewhat more effectively than had the north (1:7), Israel was no place for Hosea to find a sympathetic audience. The burgeoning military and economic power of the north in the days of Jeroboam II (2 Kgs 14:25–28) and the tendency of the north to have greater international contacts than the more isolated Judah resulted undoubtedly in a cosmopolitan, latitudinarian attitude religiously. Polytheistic syncretism, not monotheistic Yahwism, constituted the dominant faith.

During the many centuries that had passed between the establishment of the Mosaic covenant (on the chronological priority of the Pentateuchal law to the prophets see below, "Assumptions about Dates") and Hosea's day, the Sinai law code had fallen into a limbo of neglect. Some portions, such as the decalogue, were popularly known (cf. Hos 4:2), and most Israelites probably knew about the law in the same way that most Americans would know about the Sermon on the Mount even though they would be unable to describe its contents accurately. A prophet such as Hosea had to rely upon a common ground of awareness of the law, limited as it was, in proclaiming the enforcement of the divine covenant. The average Israelite surely recognized that the Pentateuchal law forbade idolatry and polytheism, insisted upon the worship of Yahweh at a single central sanctuary and a life of basic ethical righteousness, and provided blessings for obedience and curses for disobedience. It is this common knowledge of a few basics that affects, in part, the frequency of repetition of certain themes in the prophetic oracles. By reminding the people through his prophets that even these well-known foundational stipulations of the covenant had been violated, God gave more than sufficient notice of justification for the coming judgment. The prophets, in other words, were not moved to list for their audience every instance of Israelite infidelity to the various covenant provisions. It was enough to demonstrate major violations (idolatry, polytheism, disloyalty via foreign entanglements, multiple sanctuary worship, dishonesty, economic oppression). The presence of these violations proved that the covenant was broken; any one of them would have sufficed for that purpose (cf. Jas 2:10). Cumbersome delineations of large numbers of the 613 Pentateuchal commandments were not warranted; it is no wonder that they are not found in Hosea and the other prophets.

HOSEA THE PROPHET AND HIS FAMILY

Next to nothing can be known about Hosea and his family. Scholars have unfortunately devoted more attention to the questions of biography raised by chaps. 1 and 3 than to the rest of the book, and the results have been predictably disappointing.

The personal details Hosea gives us are so few, and those details are so inextricably linked to the message Yahweh intended—rather than having any useful interest of their own—that any attempt to write Hosea's biography on the basis of such scanty information is doomed to failure.

The identity and/or profession of the wives, or wife, of chaps. 1 and 3 has commanded the most attention. Are the two women the same woman? Was Gomer a prostitute when Hosea married her? Did she become unfaithful later, and cause him in retrospect to think of himself as having set out to marry a prostitute? Were any of the children illegitimate? Did Hosea divorce Gomer via a court proceeding which is then given an allegorical cast in chap. 2? And so on.

While these questions are not irrelevant to the understanding and appreciation of the book's message, they are definitely peripheral to it. For as the early chapters are structured, no details exist for the satisfaction of our curiosity about the people involved: all details serve the interest of the divine message of wrath and redemption and are inextricably woven into that message.

As regards chaps. 1 and 3 (chap. 2 contains no autobiographical material, even implicitly) the known biographical data can be simply listed:

Chap. 1	*Chap. 3*
Hosea's time	Fact of the marriage
Fact of the marriage	Bride price
Name of his wife (Gomer)	Non-consummation of the marriage
Sexes of the children	Previous promiscuity of the wife
Names of the children	
Order of birth of the children	

At a glance it is evident that the data furnished in chaps. 1 and 3 are inadequate for the purposes to which they have often been put, i.e., the writing of a biography of Hosea in his marriage to Gomer. There are no data in chap. 3 to prove that Gomer is to be identified with the promiscuous wife, as has so often been suggested. Nothing is ever actually stated about Gomer's profession or fidelity. And the intriguing notion that Hosea married a prostitute at God's command is blunted by the fact that the marriage remained unconsummated. Since it cannot be proved that Gomer is the same wife described in chap. 3, nothing about Gomer's marital fidelity can be learned. That she is called metaphorically an אשת זנונים "prostituting woman" in 1:2 cannot be taken as a literal statement of her profession or practice. She is merely an Israelite—all of whom are "prostitutes" as the verse implies, that is, all of whom have broken Yahweh's covenant (see *Comment* on 1:2).

Thus the frequent attempts of scholars to reconstruct the quality and / or character of Hosea's personal life are inevitably doomed. We are told only such details as happen to serve metaphorical / typological purposes. The focus of the early chapters is not on Hosea and his family but on God and Israel. Hosea marries (twice we believe) at God's command. In the first marriage he gives his children, as God commands, names with predictive significance for Israel. In the later marriage, he requires chastity of his wife as a prediction of Israel's coming confinement by Assyria. From these enactment prophecies one can learn much about God and Israel, but relatively little about Hosea's attitudes, feelings, or experiences in marriage. It would be reasonable to assume that Hosea married Gomer not later than 760 B.C. since the divine message associated with that marriage and its children predicts the downfall of Jehu's dynasty (1:4) which occurred in 753 B.C. with the death of Jeroboam II. Hosea may not have taken his second wife (chap. 3), however, until after 730 B.C., judging from the emphasis in that chapter on the impending exile and absence of kingship and cult. By this scenario, Gomer could have been dead for many years prior to the second, unconsummated marriage. No certain solution is possible.

HOSEA'S AUDIENCE

Hosea did not indicate where he preached any of his oracles. It may be assumed that several of his later oracles, reflecting the last years of the North's existence, were delivered in Samaria (i.e., the material in chaps. 10–14) but this cannot be proved. Otherwise we simply have no clear hint of any loci for his ministry.

Likewise, it cannot be determined to which group or groups Hosea actually delivered any of his prophecies. In a formal sense, Hosea certainly directed God's word to several groups. Most often, it was to Israel as a whole, indicated by "Israel," "Ephraim" or simply "you" (see 2:3, 4 [1, 2]; 4:1, 15; 5:1, 8; 6:1, 4; 9:1, 5, 7; 10:9, 12; 11:8; 12:10 [9]; 13:4, 9–13; 14:1, 8). Twice, God's word was initially directed to Hosea himself (1:2; 3:1) though this was ultimately and far more importantly destined to have its impact on the people of Israel as a whole. The priests are addressed directly twice (4:4–5; 5:1) and the royalty once (5:1). Samaria and Bethel are each addressed once (8:5 and 10:15 respectively). Judah is addressed twice in close proximity (6:4; 6:11). What we cannot tell, however, is whether these people and places were ever addressed by Hosea in their presence, or simply rhetorically. Did Hosea deliver the words of the oracle in 5:1–7 directly to an audience that contained a crowd of Israelites, including some priests and some members of the royal family as 5:1 might indicate, or was his prophesying actually seen and heard only by faithful friends and disciples—Israelites to be sure, but not necessarily including priests or royalty? Just as Israelite prophets preached oracles against foreign nations in the presence of audiences composed of Israelites rather than of the foreigners themselves, so it is not necessary to assume that a

Hoseanic oracle directed at any given Israelite group was in fact spoken in the presence of that group.

Ultimately, therefore, we can be sure only that Hosea did have an audience—whether initially or not—that included faithful Israelites who still believed the Mosaic covenant and who preserved the bare wordings of his oracles, without editorialization or transitional composition. He may have been quite unpopular in the North, and given virtually no credence until southerners, after the fall of the North, recognized his words to have been predictively true. But we simply do not know this for certain. His calling and authority came only from God, regardless of the size, composition, and receptivity of his original audience.

THE TEXT OF HOSEA

With the possible exception of the book of Job, no other OT book contains as high a proportion of textual problems as does Hosea. One can only speculate about the reasons for the poor state of the text. Its northern provenance was probably a factor. Like Job, some psalms, and some poems in the Pentateuch and former prophets, Hosea reflects the Israelite rather than the Judean dialect, and in its original form must have reflected typical Israelite orthographic practices as well. Judean copyists, into whose possession the text surely came after the fall of Samaria in 722, may have found the manuscript(s) of the book harder to deal with, or may even have given it less careful attention, than they would have with the corresponding works of a Judean prophet.

Fortunately the Septuagint of Hosea is a quite literal, nonexpansionistic rendering of the unpointed Hebrew. This allows for helpful reconstruction of the original consonantal texts at many points, even when the Septuagint translation has failed to interpret its consonantal Hebrew *Vorlage* sensibly. An attention to the Septuagint renderings is therefore reflected throughout this commentary. The Syriac, Latin, and Aramaic versions, in that order of significance, are of occasional minor value in restoring the original Hebrew text. The few lines of Hosea from chap. 2 that are preserved in the Qumran scrolls reflect the Masoretic Text in all features essential for reconstructing the autograph and are therefore helpful primarily in reinforcing the well-established observation that chap. 2 is one of the few relatively trouble-free parts of the book's text.

The single most textually problematic part of the book is perhaps 4:18–19. There, the Hebrew is exceedingly difficult to understand, and the versions appear to offer little help. In this commentary, new solutions to textually corrupt passages are proposed with some degree of enthusiasm at 4:2; 5:7; 7:12; 8:13; and 9:13, among others. A recognition that Hosea's oracles reflect often in their very wording the vocabulary of the Pentateuchal blessings and curses of Lev 26 and Deut 4, 28–32 helps determine likely original readings in several instances. Frequently the Masoretic consonantal text proves largely correct, and must simply be revocalized on the evidence of the Septuagint, with regard for the Mosaic covenant vocabulary.

UNITY AND INTEGRITY

Scholarly conclusions about the unity and / or integrity of biblical books tend to reflect basic methodological assumptions. The presence or absence of empirical data is often relegated to a secondary role. This situation is the reverse of what should prevail. In the case of Hosea, the unity of the book is demonstrable on the basis of its consistency; and its integrity, likewise, on similar grounds. The book throughout contains prophecies of weal or woe, with evidence of covenant unfaithfulness accompanying the prophecies of woe. The prophecies of the weal which will depend solely on grace do not incorporate such descriptions of Israelite behavior. The prophecies themselves, artfully and novelly composed, reflect the known covenant curse and restoration blessing types without exception. None of what is contained in present copies of the book can therefore be challenged easily in terms of authenticity, on any purely empirical grounds. One consistently finds in Hosea the sorts of things one could only expect to find as transcriptions of the preaching of an orthodox northern prophet from the latter half of the eighth century B.C.

What then of the frequent references to Judah, some of which have been judged by many scholars to be intrusive to otherwise self-contained pericopes (especially 1:7 and 6:11)? Here, several considerations are relevant. First, it must be noted that attention to Judah per se is highly reasonable, even when that attention is paid in the form of an aside (e.g., 1:7). It makes sense to conclude that both Hosea and his audience would have keen interest in the fate of Judah precisely in contrast to and separate from the fate of Israel. God's revelation of coming judgment would virtually automatically require some independent mention of Judah, however brief, in addition to Israel. Since the only two records of eighth-century northern prophetic oracles, Hosea and Amos, both contain such independent references to Judah, it is impossible, on strictly empirical grounds, to excise these sorts of Judean materials either totally or in part. The only sources for knowing what eighth-century northern prophets said or did not say are the books of Amos and Hosea. Both mention Judah, and a theory based on no evidence cannot reasonably be used to question the only evidence that exists. Theories that the addresses to Judah in Hosea 1:7 and 6:11 are late interpolations can not, therefore, be grounded in anything other than assumption.

There are, additionally, a number of references to Judah in Hosea (2:2 [1:11]; 4:15; 5:5, 10, 12, 13, 14; 6:4; 8:14; 10:11; 12:1 [11:12]; 12:3 [2]) so firmly entrenched by reason of the poetic structure that they cannot be excised without damage to the logic of the text. Most involve the use of "Judah" as a parallel to "Israel" or "Ephraim" in a synonymous poetic couplet. The presence of these references demonstrates the legitimacy of "Judean" interest within the book and raises the question: If these references to Judah are admittedly authentic, can other references to Judah be dismissed as inauthentic simply because they are not as provably locked into the flow of a passage?

Several other wordings are sometimes conjectured to be late glosses to the book (all or parts of 3:5; 4:5; 4:9; 6:10b; 14:4; 14:5; 14:10). None of these can convincingly be demonstrated as unoriginal, however (see *Comment ad loc.*) with the possible exception of 14:10. As a sort of benediction to the book, 14:10 could surely be, like 1:1, editorial in origin. Yet even in this instance a careful argument has been made in favor of authenticity (C. L. Seow, "Hosea 14:10 and the Foolish People Motif," *CBQ* 44 [1982] 212–24).

The ability to excise a portion of a text can never be considered grounds for identifying that portion as inauthentic. The situation is a bit like arguing that the ability of an individual to survive the removal of his or her gall bladder is evidence that the gall bladder is only artificially present in the human body. Virtually any piece of literature can be abridged; virtually any document has some clauses, sentences, or paragraphs relatively less crucial to, or relatively less stylistically integral to its core than others. But the portions seeming easier to excise are merely those portions someone considers peripheral or awkward. Such value judgments, not being ultimately empirically based, are always to be suspected. In the case of the book of Hosea, they cannot be sustained precisely because they are not empirically based. A cautious, non-idealistic approach to the book requires giving the benefit of the doubt to virtually the entire text, i.e., judging it to have an overall integrity. One may question various sections; but proof is lacking for a firm identification of any portion as clearly inauthentic.

ASSUMPTIONS ABOUT DATES

There is no consensus on a great many issues of dating in OT scholarship. A commentary must nevertheless adopt defensible chronologies for pertinent events, with the recognition that not all readers will find themselves in agreement.

An important assumption of this commentary is that Deuteronomy is Mosaic in origin, a product of the second millennium B.C., and not of the eighth or seventh or sixth century B.C. as has often been proposed. Deuteronomy thus antedates Hosea by centuries. This assumption rests on solid evidence, including the closer similarity of Deuteronomy to second-millennium treaty-covenants than to first-millennium treaty-covenants, as well as linguistic parallels between Deuteronomy and second-millennium Mesopotamian documents. Additionally, the reader is invited to note the evidence for the dependence of Hosea upon the blessing and curse formulations of Deuteronomy, a dependence which cannot successfully be reversed in order. This and other evidence for the early date cannot be elaborated here. The reader is referred to P. C. Craigie, *The Book of Deuteronomy*, NICOT 5 (Grand Rapids: Eerdmans, 1976) 24–29; M. Kline, *Treaty of the Great King* (Grand Rapids: Eerdmans, 1963); K. A. Kitchen, *Ancient Orient and Old Testament* (London: Tyndale, 1966) 90–102; G. Wenham, "Deuteronomy and the Central Sanctuary," *TynBul* 22 (1971) 103–18; Ch. Rabin, "Discourse Analysis and the Dating of Deuteronomy," *Interpreting the Hebrew Bible: Essays in Honor of E. I. J. Rosenthal*, ed. J. Emerton and S. Reif (Cambridge: University Press, 1982).

With regard to the reigns of the kings contemporaneous with Hosea, it is our assumption that the dates proposed by E. Thiele (*A Chronology of the Hebrew Kings* [Grand Rapids: Zondervan, 1977]) are most convincingly documented. Proposed datings for the late eighth century do not vary by more than half a decade at any rate.

SOME NOTABLE VOCABULARY

Among the many features of vocabulary that characterize the book of Hosea three groups may be mentioned as of special importance: (1) Hosea's use of the root זנה "prostitution," "to prostitute," etc.; (2) the other major theological terms, especially שוב "return," חסד "loyalty," עזב "abandon," אהב "love," and ידע "know / acknowledge"; (3) the relatively frequent mention of Egypt and Assyria in poetic parallel. It should be noted that none of these vocabulary usages is unique to Hosea, though their peculiar combination is.

Hosea employs the root זנה literally to refer to actual prostitution in only one indictment (4:13–14). Otherwise (15 times, via various forms of the verb זנה as well as the nouns זנונים and זנות) the term is used metaphorically (cf. Ezek 16, 23, etc.), after the pattern of ancient Near Eastern treaty language (cf. D. Hillers, *Treaty-Curses and the Old Testament Prophets*, BibOr 16 [Rome: Pontifical Biblical Institute, 1964] 58–60). Prostitution is scandalous unfaithfulness. Israel's prostitution was its unfaithfulness to God's covenant. Through Hosea, God denounced that promiscuity and announced the punishments it would receive accordingly.

Five other words figure especially prominently in Hosea's theological vocabulary. The word שוב ("return / turn back") is found twenty-three times in the book, in various usages. This frequency may reflect the prominence of the term in Deuteronomy, particularly chaps. 4 and 30. Twelve of these instances (2:9, 11 [7, 9]; 3:5; 5:4; 6:1; 7:10, 16; 11:5; 12:7 [6]; 14:2, 3, 8) involve the qal with the meaning of "return" to Yahweh, i.e., "repent and obey in faith." Three (8:13; 9:3; 11:5) refer to the threat of return to "Egypt" (see below). In 14:5 the verb is used in the sense of the "turning back" of Yahweh's anger; in 6:11 of the restoration of Israel's fortunes; in 5:15 of the withdrawal of Yahweh's favor from Israel; and in 4:9; 12:3 [2], 15 [14] (all hiphil) of Yahweh's repayment (punishment) of Israel for their sins. The term חסד ("loyalty") appears six times in the book (2:21 [19]; 4:1; 6:4, 6; 10:12; 12:7 [6]) with special emphasis upon Israel's need for or lack of loyalty to Yahweh and his covenant. The verb עזב ("abandon") is used only once in Hosea (4:10) though in a prominent way: it describes Israel's apostasy in abandoning Yahweh in favor of heterodox practices of various sorts. אהב ("love") is a word of obvious significance theologically (cf. Deut 6:5). Hosea employs it sixteen times. In eleven of these instances, אהב is used in some way to depict Israel's love, which is invariably portrayed as a wrong love, of things other than Yahweh (2:7, 9, 12, 14, 15 [5, 7, 10, 12, 13]; 3:1, twice; 4:18; 9:1, 10; 12:8 [7]). Usually the verb is cast in the qal active voice, but the passive is used (3:1) as well as the piel participle (chap. 2). Four times אהב is used of Yahweh's love for Israel (3:1, twice; 11:1, 4) and one time (10:11) metaphorically of Israel's early cooperative, positive spirit. The verb ידע and its noun form דעת appear eighteen times in Hosea. It refers variously to Israel's knowledge or lack of knowledge of Yahweh (2:22 [20]; 4:1, 6; 5:4; 6:3, 6; 8:2; 13:4), Israel's stupidity (2:10 [8]; 7:9 twice; 11:3), Yahweh's knowledge of Israel (5:3; 13:5), his refusal to acknowledge Israel's kings (8:4) and the knowledge / wisdom that Israel or an individual ought to have (5:9, 9:7; 14:10).

Hosea mentions Egypt thirteen times, far more proportionally than in any other prophetic book. Assyria is mentioned nine times, proportionally more than is the case in any prophet except Isaiah. Only three references to Assyria (5:13; 10:6; 14:4) are not used in parallel with Egypt. The rest (7:11; 8:9; 9:3; 11:5, 11; 12:2) link Assyria and Egypt in a way that leaves little doubt that "Egypt" can be a metonymy for foreign captivity, on the precedence of its usage in Deut 28:68. Five times (2:17 [15]; 11:1; 12:10 [9], 14 [13]; 13:4) Hosea refers to Egypt as the place from which Yahweh delivered his people, in typical allusion to the covenantal bond established by Yahweh's grace. Twice (7:11; 12:2 [1]) Egypt is mentioned in connection with the foreign political maneuvering of the late eighth-century B.C. Six times (7:16; 8:13; 9:3, 6; 11:5, 11) Egypt is symbolic of the captivity to come, which would, of course, actually be effected by Assyria and not Egypt. As "Babylon" would later signify Rome for the early Christians (e.g., 1 Pet 5:13; Rev 14:8) so "Egypt" signified the Assyrian captivity about to swallow up the decadent, disobedient nation to whom Hosea spoke God's message.

PERICOPE DIVISIONS IN HOSEA

Aside from the first and last verses of the book, which, regardless of their authorship, are clearly editorial, the vast majority of the content of Hosea may be divided roughly into three categories: evidence, curses, and blessings.

Evidence. About two-thirds of the book fits broadly within this category. Yahweh announces through Hosea neither imminent curses nor eventual blessings without first demonstrating that his covenant with Israel has indeed been broken. The book contains a variety of artfully constructed literary units, some of which are easily identified by type (e.g., the covenant lawsuits in 2:4–17 [2–15] and 4:1–19) and many of which are not (e.g., 1:2–9 or 11:1–7). But all of the literary units, except for those which are exclusively devoted to announcement of restoration blessings, contain in some form or other arguments (sections of evidence) demonstrating that Israel is guilty of covenant-breaking, i.e., of doing what the Mosaic covenant says they may not do. These evidence sections are sometimes extensive in length, uninterrupted by curse or blessing announcements (e.g., 6:6–7:11) but more often constitute only a few verses in length (as in chap. 5). The more common pattern for a full pericope is an interchange of evidence and curse, like the alternating links in a chain. In chap. 5, the pattern takes form as follows: Some evidence of covenant breaking, including the summons to hear the evidence (vv 1–2a) is followed by a curse announcement (v 2a). Then there appears more evidence of covenant-breaking (vv 3–5a), followed again by a curse announcement (vv 5b–6). Then there is more evidence (v 7a) and more curse (v 7b) and so on throughout the chapter.

Naturally, the evidence portions of the book may be introduced by summonses, challenges, or other devices, but such devices have no independent function. They exist only to contribute directly to the statement of the evidence. Moreover, the evidence statements have no independent function, either. They exist only to demonstrate that the covenant has been violated, and thus they invariably lead directly to the curses.

Curses. About one-quarter of the total proportion of the book of Hosea is devoted to curses per se. The kinds of curses Hosea announces are exactly the same kinds of curses the Mosaic covenant contains in its sanction sections (Lev 26, Deut 28–32, and in limited format, Deut 4). Hosea does not, of course, cite curses verbatim from the Pentateuch. Verbatim citation of legal passages was unknown in the ancient Near East, legal precedent being conceived of in terms of essence, and not wording. The curses come rather unpredictably except for two parameters: they always follow upon evidence (thus no pericope starts with a curse), and there is always a curse at the end of a pericope that does not make a transition to restoration blessing. Passages limited to evidence and curse always start with evidence and end with a curse, no matter how much of each element may also appear in between. Hosea announces for Israel fully twenty of the twenty-seven different covenant curse types found in the Pentateuch (see *General Introduction*).

The curses Hosea was inspired to announce were all applicable to Israel's immediate future in the eighth century B.C. Since the covenant had been abrogated by Israel's rebellions, Yahweh, the enforcer of the covenant, had no option but to unleash the stipulated covenant punishments (curses). The covenant punishments fall into many categories, some of them being quite general. Moreover, the catch-all formulae (e.g., Lev 26:43, "they will pay for their sins" or Deut 28:16, "You will be cursed in the city and cursed in the country") allow for virtually any negative, unpleasant experience that Yahweh may choose to inflict on Israel, to represent a covenant curse. Nevertheless, Hosea does not innovate curses. He announces curses only according to the categories the Pentateuch contains.

Blessings. Not more than a tenth of the book is devoted to the announcement of future blessings. No blessings are announced for Israel's present or immediate future; announcements of any such blessings would contradict the book's curse announcements. The blessings are, rather, all announced for the distant future, the era of restoration which the Mosaic Covenant promises will follow *after* the punishments for covenant-breaking have run their course (Lev 26:41–42; Deut 4:30; Deut 30:2–3).

The failure to recognize that the blessings apply to the distant future has led scholars to two equally unsatisfactory conclusions: the blessings sections, because they contradict the curses, must be inauthentic interpolations; or the blessings must be quotations of what Hosea's opponents said, rather than what Hosea himself preached (so Wolff, 109, 116–17, in the case of 6:1–3). Both approaches are obviated when it is recognized that Hosea is simply obeying Yahweh's will in announcing the restoration blessings long promised to Israel. It was Yahweh's will that Hosea's generation, like Moses' and ours, should be aware that he would never utterly abandon Israel. There would come a time when he would resurrect a remnant from exile and restore them to their homeland, once they had turned to him in their distress.

The blessings sections are seven in number. (The parenthetical blessing announced for Judah in 1:7 is not a reconstruction era blessing but applies to the immediate future, and functions by contrast to [northern] Israel's curses to heighten the impact of the judgment oracle against Israel in 1:2–9.) Three of the seven blessing announcements begin with an invitation or summons to repentance (6:1–3; 10:12; 14:1–8). The others (2:1–3 [1:10–2:1]; 2:16–

25 [14–23]; 3:5; 11:8–11) do not. At first glance, it may seem that the invitations should be considered as a separate category and not simply lumped together with the blessings. However, two considerations mitigate against this. First, the covenant restoration promises *guarantee* the repentance of a remnant of Israelites (Deut 4:30; 30:6, 8). Second, Hosea does not announce these words of invitation literally to his own generation, but rhetorically to the people of a future generation. Accordingly, the invitation portions of the blessings are probably best taken as integral introductions to the announcements themselves rather than as something more generally parallel to the evidence sections of those pericopes containing curses.

In summary, we find only three basic permutations of the contents of the pericopes in Hosea: (1) those containing an admixture of evidence and curse, never containing only one or the other, and always beginning with evidence and ending with curse; (2) those containing an admixture of evidence, curse, and blessing, in which the placements of the blessing sections vary unpredictably; and (3) those containing blessings only. While there are countless complexities and variegations to be found within the broad confines of Hosea's oracles, nearly all the oracles fall into one of these three categories.

The Title and the Time   *(1:1)*

Bibliography

Albright, W. F. "New Light from Egypt on the Chronology and History of Israel and Judah." *BASOR* 130 (1953) 4–11. **Begrich, J.** *Die Chronologie der Könige von Israel und Juda.* Tübingen: J. C. B. Mohr, 1929. Repr. Klaus, 1966. **Freedman, D. N.** "The Chronology of Israel." *The Bible and the Ancient Near East,* ed. G. E. Wright. Garden City: Doubleday, 1961. **Horn, S.** "The Chronology of King Hezekiah's Reign." *AUSS,* 2 (1964) 40–52. **Lindblom, J.** *Prophecy in Ancient Israel.* Philadelphia: Muhlenberg Press, 1962. 279–91. **McHugh, J.** "The Date of Hezekiah's Birth." *VT* 14 (1964) 446–53. **Noth, M.** *Die Israelitischen Personennamen im Rahmen der gemeinsemitischen Namengebung.* Stuttgart: 1928; repr. Hildesheim: G. Olms Verlagsbuchhandlung, 1966. **Thiele, E. R.** *A Chronology of the Hebrew Kings.* Grand Rapids: Zondervan, 1977. **Wolfe, R. E.** "The Editing of the Book of the Twelve." *ZAW* 53 (1935) 90–130.

Translation

> [1:1] *Yahweh's word which came to Hosea,[a] son of Beeri, in the time of Uzziah, Jotham, Ahaz and Hezekiah, kings of Judah; and in the time of Jeroboam, son of Joash, King of Israel.*

Notes

1.a. Or, "which Hosea received." There is no exact Eng. equivalent for the Heb. היה־אל.

Form / Structure / Setting

The superscription functions as a title for the book—there is no other. Similar titles, containing much the same wording, are found at the outset of other prophetic books: Jer 1:1–2, Ezek 1:3, Joel 1:1, Jon 1:1, Micah 1:1, Zeph 1:1, Hag 1:1, Zech 1:1, Mal 1:1. The variations among the titles are relatively insignificant, but great enough that such titles cannot be proved to be of common origin. Nothing other than the name of Hosea's father was known, or at least thought significant enough to mention.

The Judean kings, listed first, reigned between 791 B.C. (the beginning of Uzziah's reign) and 686 B.C. (the end of Hezekiah's reign); Jeroboam II reigned 793–753 B.C. Since many of Hosea's prophecies can be dated confidently after 753, during the time of no less than six other Northern kings, it would seem that the mention of a single Northern king is in fact a token. Initial date / content descriptions tend not to be comprehensive in other prophetic books as well (Isa 1:1; Ezek 1:1). The compiling of Hosea's oracles was quite probably completed after 722, for an audience of Judeans who, like all orthodox Israelites (including Hosea), recognized the sole legitimacy of the Davidic—Southern—dynasty, and had little interest in dating according to the defunct northerners. Moreover, the rapid changes in leadership in the North after Jeroboam II's death may have been confusing to many southerners of the era after Samaria's fall, and thus ignorable by the writer of 1:1.

The inclusion of Hezekiah (725–686; 715–686 as sole regent) in the southern list suggests that Hosea was, if only briefly (725–722?) a contemporary of Isaiah (cf. Isa 1:1). It must also be admitted that Hosea's prophetic ministry could have continued briefly after the death of King Hoshea and fall of the North in 722, though no specific oracle is datable to the time after 722. Hosea's interest in Judah is evident throughout the book (1:7; 2:2 [1:11]; 3:5; 4:15; 5:5, 10, 12, 13, 14; 6:4, 11; 8:14; 10:11; 12:1 [11:12]; 12:3[12:2]): all the eighth-century prophets spoke both to Judah and Israel.

Comment

The significance of the first words of the title goes beyond simply naming the book; it makes a theological statement. The book *as a whole* contains Yahweh's דבר, his word or message. The narrative portions, the prophet's words, the divine oracles, the homiletical conclusion are all Yahweh's word. In its narrowest sense, the דבר יהוה was used almost exclusively in the prophet's speech to refer to an oracle, transmitted through the prophet to the people. In the broader sense, it is the information—the prophetic message in full—that Yahweh has provided for his people.

"Hosea" (הושע) is a name formed according to the hiphil perfect (or conceivably the imperative; see Noth, *Personennamen,* 32) of ישע, meaning "(he) has rescued / delivered," the unexpressed subject being Yahweh (cf. the name הושעיה), the object being the family of the child, or perhaps Israel as a whole. Most Hebrew names implicitly, and often explicitly, follow the sentence-name pattern of the ancient Near East. The full thought upon which the name is based is: "the Lord has rescued / delivered (us)." The name is found sixteen other times in the OT: Num 13:8, 16; Deut 32:44; 2 Kgs 15:30; 17:1, 3, 4, 6; 18:1, 9, 10; 1 Chr 27:20, Neh 10:24, 12:32, and Jer 42:1, 43:2. In the latter three instances, the full form including the theophoric element is found: הושעיה, "Yah(weh) has rescued."

Hosea's father, Beeri (בארי), had a name that meant approximately "my wellspring," probably a hypocoristicon for "Yahweh is my wellspring." Wolff's suggestion that this name is "a simple expression of the parents' joy at the birth of a child" and should be translated "my Spring!" or "O Spring!" fails to recognize the sentence pattern implicit in such names.

The title of the book does not mention that Hosea is a "prophet" (נביא). Only later books (Hab 1:1, Hag 1:1, Zech 1:1) include the word נביא in the superscription.

The accession year of Hezekiah, the last mentioned in the list of Judean kings, is uncertain. 2 Kgs 18:1 suggests that the year is 729 B.C., while 2 Kgs 18:13 would seem to imply 715 B.C. Because of the possibility of a co-regency between Hezekiah and Ahaz, and because numbers are notoriously subject to corruption in textual transmission, the options for resolution are numerous. The writer of 1:1 is most likely, in our judgment, presuming an occasion at or about 725.

Explanation

God gave his word at a time and place. It was a revelation delivered in history and substantially historical in its content. It was not, however, limited solely to one time and place. Just as later Judeans, to whom Hosea did not actually preach, revered and preserved his preaching, we recognize in it God's timeless message about the sanctity of his covenant, hardly limited to the days of certain ancient kings. It is our spiritual heritage, as the church is the true Israel (Gal 3:29).

The Children's Names Presage Judgment (1:2–9)

Bibliography

Baiz, C. H. "Gomer oder die Macht der Astarte; Versuch einer feministischen Interpretation von Hos 1–4." *EvT* 42 (1982) 37–65. **Batten, L. W.** "Hosea's Message and Marriage." *JBL* 48 (1929) 257–73. **Bewer, J. A.** "The Story of Hosea's Marriage." *AJSL* 22 (1906) 120–30. **Beylin, Z.** "Studies in the Book of Hosea." *BMik* 27 (1981/82) 164–67. **Bitter, S.** *Zur Auslegungsgeschichte von Hosea 1 und 3.* Göttinger Theologische Arbeiten 3. Göttingen: Vandenhoeck und Ruprecht, 1975. **Budde, K.** "Hos 1 und 3." *TBl* 13 (1934) 337–42. **Coppens, J.** "L'histoire matrimoniale d'Osée." *BBB* 1 (1950) 38–45. **Couroyer, B.** "Corne et arc." *RB* 73 (1966) 510–21. **Dijk, H. J. van.** *Ezekiel's Prophecy on Tyre (Ez 26:1–28:19): A New Approach.* BibOr 20. Rome: Pontifical Biblical Institute, 1968. 33–36. **Ehrlich, C. S.** "The Text of Hosea 1:9." *JBL* 104 (1985) 13–19. **Gordis, R.** "Hosea's Marriage and Message." *HUCA* 25 (1954) 9–35. **Heerman, P.** "Ehe und Kinder des Propheten Hosea, eine exegetische Studie zu Hosea 1, 2–9." *ZAW* 40 (1922) 287–312. **Humbert, P.** *Les trois premiers chapîtres d'Osée.* RHR. Paris, 1918. **Isbell, C. D.** "Initial 'Alef-Yod Interchange and Selected Biblical Passages." *JNES* 37 (1978) 227–36. **Klein, H.** "Natur und Recht: Israels Umgang mit dem Hochzeitsbrauchtum seiner Umwelt." *TZ* 37 (1981) 3–18. **Kuhnigk, W.** *Nordwestsemitische Studien,* 1–5. **May, H. G.** "An Interpretation of the Names of Hosea's Children." *JBL* 55 (1936) 285–91. **McDonald, J. R. B.** "The Marriage of Hosea." *Theology* 67 (1964) 149–56. **North, F. S.** "Solution of Hosea's Marital Problems by Critical Analysis." *JNES* 16 (1957) 128–30. ———. "Hosea's Introduction to His Book." *VT* 8 (1958) 429–32. **Renaud, B.** "Le liveret d'Osée 1–3: Un travail complexe d'édition." *RevScRel* 56 (1982) 159–78. **Robinson, T. H.** "Die Ehe des Hosea." *TSK* 106 (1935) 301–13. **Rowley, H. H.** "The Marriage of Hosea." *BJRL* 39 (1956) 200–233; repr. in *Men of God: Studies in OT History and Prophecy.* NY: Nelson, 1963. **Rudolph, W.** "Präparierte Jungfrauen?" *ZAW* 75 (1963) 65–73. **Ruppert, L.** "Erwägungen zur Kompositions- und Redaktionsgeschichte von Hosea 1–3." *BZ* 26 (1982) 208–223. **Schmidt, H.** "Die Ehe des Hosea." *ZAW* 42 (1924) 245–72. **Schreiner, J.** "Hoseas Ehe, ein Zeichen des Gerichts." *BZ* 21 (1977) 163–83. **Sinclair, L. A.** "A Qumran Biblical Fragment, Hosea 4Q, XII (Hosea 1:7–2:5)." *BASOR* 239 (1980) 61–65. **Vogels, W.** "Osée-Gomer car et comme 'Yahweh-Israel': Os 1–3." *NRT* 103 (1981) 711–27. **Volz, P.** "Die Ehegeschichte Hoseas." *ZWT* (1898) 321–35. **Waldman, N. M.** "The Breaking of the Bow." *JQR* 79 (1978) 82–88. **Waterman, L.** "Hosea, Chaps. 1–3 in Retrospect and Prospect." *JNES* 14 (1955) 100–09.

Translation

²*The Beginning of Yahweh's Speaking through* [a] *Hosea.* [b]*Yahweh said to Hosea: "Marry* [c] *a prostituting woman* [d] *and (have)* [e] *prostituting children; because the*

land has gone thoroughly into prostitution, away from Yahweh." ³*He married Gomer, Diblaim's daughter.*ᵃ *She became pregnant, and bore him a son.* ⁴*Yahweh said to him: "Name him 'Jezreel,' because it will not be long before I apply the bloodshed*ᵃ *of Jezreel to the family*ᵇ *of Jehu, and then destroy*ᶜ *the kingdom of the family of Israel.* ⁵*At that time, I will smash Israel's bow in the valley of Jezreel."* ⁶*When she became pregnant again, she gave birth to a daughter. He said to him: "Name her 'No Compassion,'*ᵃ *because I will no longer have compassion on the family of Israel, since I have been utterly betrayed*ᵇ *by them.* ⁷*I will, however, have compassion on the family of Judah. I will save them by Yahweh their God, but will not save them by bow, by sword—by warfare*ᵃ—*by cavalry, by chariotry.*ᵇ ⁸*After weaning No Compassion, she became pregnant and gave birth to a son.* ⁹*He said, "Name him 'Not My People,' because you are 'Not my people'*ᵃ *and I am 'Not your Ahyeh.' "*ᵇ

Notes

2.a. The Heb. prep אל is ambiguous, and may mean either "to" or "through" in this context, as confirmed by the differing translations in the Greek manuscripts (B Q θ: ἐν; others: πρός).

2.b. The Heb.] (or]) is best left untranslated. It functions less as a true copula than as a clause marker.

2.c. Lit., "Go, take yourself a woman / wife," which is, however, not idiomatic English.

2.d. זְנוּנִים "prostitution" is an abstract noun, built on the pl pattern frequently used for abstracts as an alternative to the fem sg. אשת זנונים can hardly mean "prostitute" (זֹנָה in Heb.), and "woman / wife of prostitution" is awkward in English. "Prostituting woman" is idiomatic syntactically and sufficiently pejorative without firmly conveying the idea, contrary to fact, that Yahweh commanded Hosea to marry a professional prostitute.

2.e. The phrase "prostituting children" is also the obj of the impv קח, but in Eng. a separate helping verb is required.

3.a. בת דבלים could also mean "a (fem) citizen of Diblaim," but no such town is known, though the name of the town דְּבְלָתָיִם "Diblathaim" (Jer 48:22 and Num 33:46, 47) is similar.

4.a. דם "blood" can carry the notion of bloodshed, slaughter, violent death, or murder in much the same manner as its NT Gr. counterpart, αἷμα.

4.b. בית is here translated "family" inasmuch as "house" in this sense is quite archaic in Eng.

4.c. שבת (II) here appears to be a byform of שבת (I), and is more closely related in meaning to שבב and שבר "break" than to שבת "to rest." See Kuhnigk, *NSH*, 2–3.

6.a. In the name *Lo-ruhamah*, לא רחם is voiced in the passive. Because "compassion," the closest Eng. word to the root sense of רחם, cannot be conjugated, the name is here rendered in nominal form.

6.b. Reading with Kuhnigk (*NSH*, 4.) כִּי־נָשֹׁא אֶשָּׁא "since I have been utterly betrayed" rather than MT כִּי־נָשֹׂא אֶשָּׂא "for I will take away utterly." The root pointed by MT as if from נשא is actually נשא II, "to trick or deceive." להם then has the agentive sense, "by them." G ἀλλ' ἢ ἀντιτασσόμενος ἀντιτάξομαι αὐτροῖς appears to reflect נשא II, though imprecisely.

7.a. The word "warfare" (מלחמה), as the comprehensive center of the chiasm, is best set off in print from the two categories of weaponry on either side of it.

7.b. On the more precise meaning "charioteers" for פרשים (rather than "horsemen") see F. C. Fensham, *NGTT* 19 (1978) 195–99. The meaning in the present context is essentially "chariotry."

9.a. There appears to be little merit in the suggestion of Kuhnigk (*NSH*, 4–5) that a play on words is involved between עַמִּי, "my people" and עִמָּי, "with me." Although the consonantal MT is certainly ambiguous, the pronunciation would hardly have been uncertain.

9.b. *Ahyeh* (אהיה) is the 1 c sg form of the divine name Yahweh. See *Comment*.

Form / Structure / Setting

1:2b–9 is clearly a literary unit. The passage records four separate commands given by Yahweh to Hosea. The commands are stylistically similar;

each begins with an imperative and is followed by כי ("because"). In the case of the latter three commands, the style is quite precise. The command, קרא שם ("name . . .") is followed by כי ("because") and an explanatory clause which identifies the reason for the naming with a judgment warning, of which the name is symbolic. Vv 5 and 7 represent expansions on the basic pattern, with v 7, the promise to Judah, being somewhat parenthetical to the main concerns of the passage, though neither irrelevant nor disruptive. Such asides, part of skillful preaching to general audiences, are found throughout the prophetic books.

Vv 5 and 7 express an important aspect of Hosea's inspired message: Israel, for its rebellion against Yahweh, must be conquered (by the Assyrians) whereas Judah will escape military conquest by grace of Yahweh's intervention. The basic historical pattern of the sequence of Yahweh's judgment is thus established. Israel, more thoroughly corrupted by syncretism, will fall first. And Judah? For the time being, Judah is safe from such severe punishment, though nevertheless dependent on Yahweh's grace for deliverance. Nothing is implied about the distant future of Judah (cf. 6:11). Judah is *not* here called unequivocally pleasing to Yahweh; she is merely not at the moment the object of Yahweh's wrath.

The pericope ends at v 9. The following pericope, beginning at 2:1 [1:10], deals with new concerns: the restoration of Israel, cleansed from sin and reunited.

The form of such a passage as 1:2–9 is not easy to classify exactly. It functions metaphorically / allegorically since its ultimate focus is the relationship of Yahweh to Israel, not Hosea to Gomer and her children. But it is genuine history (*memorabile*, as Wolff [10–11] terms it).

Dramatic prophetic activities of this type are not uncommon in the OT (cf. Isa 8:1–4; Jer 27). Divine command to perform a symbolic act is followed by divine explanation of the act's symbolic importance. The act itself is then done in obedience to the command and in service of the symbolism. In the case of 1:2–9, the marriage account has all three of these: command, explanation, act. The three other instances, i.e., the naming of the children, are technically elliptical in that no mention of the fulfillment of the act itself is given. This is simply assumed, since naming a child is so easily accomplished that describing the process would add no impact and indeed, be needlessly redundant.

A progression of sorts is evident in these verses. The formal structure is built from four separate sequences of the pattern: (a) "(Yahweh) said . . ."; (b) "Go name . . ."; (c) "Because (*kî*) . . ."; (d) the interpretation. It has often been argued that each successive use of the pattern (v 4, v 6, v 9) is increasingly stylized and brief ("economical in expression" in the words of Mays, 22) in comparison to its predecessor. This is not an entirely satisfactory description of the data, especially because it assumes that vv 5 and 7 are unoriginal to the context, an assumption we doubt (see above). Moreover, it would be a mistake to substitute quantity for quality, ignoring the reality of ellipsis (that which is unexpressed can be as significant as that which is said, especially in the context of a repetitive pattern). Finally, one must note that the hearts of two of the patterns (the command and the interpretation) are roughly of equal length in the case of the marriage and the naming of "Not My People" (Lo-Ammi). Even v 9, which at first glance seems to constitute a noticeably shorter instance of the basic four-part pattern, is not really different. Here the relative brevity is mainly a function of the particular parallelistic turn of phrase employed by Hosea. What could be added to increase the clarity or force of the statement, "You are not mine / my people; I am not your 'Ahyeh' / 'Yahweh' "?

In the case of the marriage to Gomer, the symbolism is of necessity spelled out. The naming of Jezreel is structured likewise. The naming sequence of "No Compassion" (Lo-Ruhamah) could also be ambiguous; the focus of the lack of mercy must be made clear. But "Not My People" is virtually free of ambiguity. The name requires by way of interpretation only the wording in the name itself.

The four instances of the pattern do not so much constitute a progression in a particular direction or of a particular style, as they are repetitive of a single direction and style. The issue in each is a broken relationship; Yahweh and his people are at odds, estranged.

The entire pericope is prose. There is no full poetry in these verses, though a few elements that could be called "poetical" are present: occasional parallelisms, paronomasia and *figura etymologica,* chiasm (v 7). Otherwise the language is patently prosaic, as the difficulty in arranging the verses stichometrically in both *BHK* and *BHS* illustrates. There is enjambment, uneven line-length between supposedly parallel lines, little economy of expression, no syntactical reversals, and no parallelism between entire lines (cola or hemistichs). Hosea, like the prophets in general, is capable of elegant prose or poetry; this is the former.

It is possible, though ultimately unprovable, that 1:2–9 describes events that took place at the outset of Hosea's prophetic ministry. His marriage to Gomer may have coincided with the first occasion of his appearance as a prophet of Yahweh. It is entirely possible that these events transpired in the last years of the reign of Jeroboam II, who died in 753 B.C. The six-month reign of his son and successor Zechariah (d. 752 B.C.), technically the last scion of the Jehu dynasty, would represent a *terminus ad quem* for the naming of Jezreel, the first child, since by any later date the dynasty would already have ceased to exist and the prediction of its destruction at "Jezreel" would be meaningless.

At least five or six years would have been required for all the events described in 1:2–9. The marriage and the three pregnancies, at least one of which followed a weaning—which in ancient times was at age two or three (see v 8, *Comment*)—would require such an interval. We therefore suggest an approximate date of ca. 760 B.C. for the marriage. Assuming that the children were born in fairly prompt sequence, Not My People would have been born by about 754. The lack of any reference at all to an interval of time between Jezreel and No Compassion, however, means that our dates must remain speculative.

It is not possible to determine whether Hosea is himself the author of the narrative in 1:2–9 (compare typical third-person autobiography in Ezra, Nehemiah, Acts, etc.; see Allwohn, *Die Ehe des propheten Hosea in psychoanalyti-*

schen Beleuchteung [Giessen: Topelmann, 1926]) or whether it is biographical, written by a disciple or other editor. Likewise, the date of composition is not surely ascertainable. There is nothing to prevent the conclusion that it was composed rather soon after the birth of Not My People; but it could as well be "conscious retrospect of the past years" (Wolff, 11).

Comment

1:2 "The Beginning of Yahweh's Speaking through Hosea" (תחלת דבר יהוה בהושע) is probably a title for the entire pericope, 1:2–9, not simply an introduction to v 2. It would be incorrect to understand the title in the sense "When Yahweh first spoke through Hosea (he said) . . ." since this would imply that the first command, to marry a "prostituting" woman, is the "beginning" spoken of. Rather, the marriage, the birth, and the naming of the three children are all aspects of the single symbolic story of unfaithfulness and rejection that 1:2–9, as a unit, tells.

תחלת is in construct to a verbal clause ("Yahweh's speaking through Hosea"). This clause functions in the construct chain exactly as would a noun in the same position. Because a noun is more common in the second, "governing" position of a construct, the G translators read the unpointed דבר as דָבָר ("word of"; Greek λόγου) rather than MT's almost certainly original דַּבְּרֹ. On the alternative pointing of the infinitive construct, cf. GKC § 52*o*.

The preposition ב before Hosea (הושע) is important. It means neither "to" nor "with," but "through." Hosea is not the primary audience for the lesson taught. Rather, the marriage and its children's names are a way for Yahweh to use Hosea's circumstances so that *through* them the terrible truth of Israel's corruption and coming destruction is revealed to all.

There is nothing to indicate that the inspired author has read back into the events of the marriage a symbolism later discovered. It was from "the beginning" that God's command functioned as a lesson rather than in Hosea's hindsight. The introduction states simply that the marriage and the naming of the children were the first public prophetic acts God asked of Hosea.

The term אשת זנונים cannot mean "a prostitute" or "a prostitute for a wife." "Prostitute" would appear in Hebrew as either זונה or אשה זונה (cf. Josh 2:1; Judg 11:1; etc.). Instead זנונים as a plural abstract refers more to a trait than a profession. The entire sequence of events in chaps. 1–3 demonstrates nothing about Gomer's marital faithfulness. There is no evidence that she was adulterous and none that she was a practicing prostitute.

Hosea's later use of the term זנונים helps fix the definition, particularly as the word is used in the phrase רוח זנונים "spirit of prostitution" or "prostituting spirit" in 4:12 and 5:4. There, the clear referent is the inclinations of Israel, whose "cohabitations" with all sorts of syncretistic and heterodox doctrines and practices are metaphorically depicted as analogous to the promiscuity of a common prostitute. Israel's waywardness and infidelity constitute a national "prostitution"; Gomer, as a citizen of that thoroughly wayward nation is described, just as any Israelite woman could be, as an אשת זנונים precisely because she is a *typical* Israelite, and this is an indictment in itself. God has commanded Hosea to marry a woman who by reason of being involved in the endemic Israelite national unfaithfulness is "prostituting." To marry any Israelite woman was to marry a "prostituting woman," so rife was the religious promiscuity of Hosea's day.

The clause קַח לְךָ "take for yourself" ("marry and have") has a double object, the wife *and* the children. Marriage is the focus, rather than concubinage, a normal family growth being envisioned.

Hosea's "prostituting children" (יַלְדֵי זְנוּנִים) were so called because, like their mother, they would be part of the corrupt, faithless nation. No suggestion is made that the children were: 1) born in adultery to Gomer before she married Hosea; 2) automatically inclined to inherit their mother's tendency to promiscuity; 3) not Hosea's own natural offspring. Rather, precisely because the "(whole) land has gone thoroughly into prostitution away from Yahweh" they are here linked with זָנֹה "prostitution." Indeed, according to the prevailing metaphor at this point in the pericope, it would have been conceivable for Yahweh to have described even Hosea as an אִישׁ זְנוּנִים, "a prostituting man," or for Hosea to have replied, à la Isa 6:5, "Woe is me, for I am a prostituting man, living among prostituting people." Prostitution is Hosea's most common metaphor for the covenant infidelity that provoked Yahweh's wrath against Israel, and the term is used in that sense throughout the book.

With regard to the woman Hosea later married (chap. 3), זְנוּנִים is not mentioned and nothing in 1:2–9 involves her. Chap. 1 is best understood as independent of chap. 3.

In using זָנֹה as metaphorically indicative of the nation's covenant disloyalty, Hosea, like other prophets (most notably Ezekiel), follows a long established literary pattern. Allusions to covenant disloyalty as "prostitution" are also found in treaty documents of the first millennium B.C. (see Hillers, *Treaty-Curses*, 58–60). In Israel's own literary history one notes the early covenantal metaphorical language of Exod 34:15, 16 and Deut 31:16, where to "prostitute (זָנֹה) after other gods" means to break the first of the Ten Commandments and thus to violate the national covenant with Yahweh.

3 Gomer, Diblaim's daughter, is unknown outside the book. Much ultimately useless effort has been expended seeking some sort of symbolic value for her name, or the name Diblaim. The symbolism is in Gomer's title, "prostituting woman," rather than in her name. Technically, גֹּמֶר is probably a theophoric hypocoristicon: a short form (even nickname) of a sentence name whose full form might have been something like "Yahweh has completed our family." Rudolph (50) suggests that the *o-e* vowel combination could be the result of a scribal employment of the vowels from the word בֹּשֶׁת "shame," an unprovable conjecture.

"Gomer became pregnant and bore him a son" (וַתֵּלֶד לוֹ בֵּן). The prepositional לוֹ "him / to him" is not present in the parallel statements of the birth of the other two children, vv 6 and 8. But it is not possible to press the grammar to the point of concluding that Jezreel was legitimate (born to *"him"*) while No Compassion and Not My People were not. Hebrew has no such fixed syntactical patterns for discriminating between legitimate and illegitimate children. The general movement toward brevity of expression as successive children are born, evidenced even in the lack of identification of Yahweh as the speaker in vv 6 and 9, means that nothing certain can be made of the presence or absence of לו in those verses. Indeed, several manuscripts omit לו at all three points.

Note how matter of fact all of v 3 is. Nothing extraneous, elegant, or dramatic is included. The first two verbs (וילך ויקח) simply pick up the verbs of the command in v 2 (קח, לך, "marry"). That command has thus been obeyed, Gomer being identified as the person Hosea married. The second part of the command, to have children, is then fulfilled initially by the first pregnancy and birth.

4 The new child was linked by his name with the prophetic message from Yahweh. The command is exactly the same as it would be in the case of No Compassion and Not My People: קרא שם "name (him)." The names are message names, as also are borne by the children of Isaiah (7:3; 8:3–4), the Messiah in Isaiah's prophecy (7:14 and 9:5 [9:4]) and numerous other entities (e.g., Oholah and Oholibah in Ezek 23). This particular message-name, Jezreel, is on the surface ambiguous. It must have been, therefore, effective in conveying Yahweh's message in those days when Jezreel was growing up. That is, his name served as a constant reminder of Yahweh's message through Hosea, since routine questions from friends and acquaintances about the meaning of the child's ambiguous name would eventually lead to a "hearing" of the message of judgment it implied. The name, composed of the imperfect of זרע "to sow" and the divine element אל "God," would mean "God sows / has sown / planted." But the name is also that of the proper noun Jezreel, a locality. In the latter sense it could refer to something about Jezreel as a place, in terms of God's plan. Moreover, there were at least two possible referents for Jezreel: the valley-plain stretching between the Samaria highlands and the Galilee highlands; and the town (modern Zerʿin) near Mount Gilboa, at the eastern edge of the highlands near the *Nahr Jalud* valley which leads ultimately to the Jordan. The town had been a second royal residence, in addition to Samaria, for the Omri dynasty kings (1 Kgs 18:45–46; 21:1, 23; 2 Kgs 8:29). The reference to Jezreel was noncommittal. "God sows / will sow" could be positive—a word of hope. Conversely, the name could refer to the past, a reminder of judgment, recalling the brutal slaughter at Jezreel which brought Jehu, the first king of the dynasty of which Jeroboam II was a scion, to power (2 Kgs 9–10).

The remainder of the verse shows which options in each case are significant. Hosea was told from the beginning exactly what the message of the name was about. It was the *town* that provided the relevant historical focus, harking back to Jehu's bloody massacre. In contrast to 2:2, there is no hint here of promise in the Lord's explanation for the name; no symbolic, hopeful value of "God sows." Rather, just as Jehu's actions at Jezreel eliminated the Omri dynasty, so now Yahweh will eliminate the Jehu dynasty, and, depending on how the word ממלכות is to be taken, perhaps eventually the entire kingship of the North. There will be "another Jezreel"—another massacre. This one will "apply the bloodshed of Jezreel to the family of Jehu." Such a punishment announcement, with its continuation in v 5, reflects the covenant curses of war (type 3; Lev 26:17; Deut 28:25, et al.), the captivity of the king (Deut 28:36 and 31:4), and death and destruction (type 24; Lev 26:38, etc.).

The phrase עוד מעט "it will not be long" sets an approximate time frame for the execution of the judgment sentence. The judgment sentence is here pronounced, but its execution will take place only according to Yahweh's timing. (On delayed executions of judgement sentences, cf. Gen 2:17; 4:15; Deut 30:17–18; John 16:11; Rev 20; etc.) The Jehu dynasty collapsed with the death of Zechariah in 752 B.C. The literal fulfillment of the עוד מעט as regards the Jehu dynasty kings was swift. Less than forty years would be needed for the Northern Kingdom itself to come to an end. After the death of Jeroboam II in 753, only one of his six successors died a natural death, such was the level of intrigue and instability preceding the fall of the North in 722. In that sense the time was indeed "soon."

In the statement "I shall apply the bloodshed of Jezreel to the family of Jehu," דמי can mean the "bloodshed" or "bloodguilt" associated with murder (Exod 22:1, 2 Sam 16:7, etc.). The vocabulary here may be influenced by Deut 32:43. At any rate, a violent death is implied. Though Jezreel's history as a city was a somewhat bloody one, including the murder of Naboth by Ahab (and Jezebel) of the Omri dynasty (1 Kgs 21), the primary reference here must be to Jehu's slaughter of both the Omrides and the Judean Davidides.

It should be noted that the present oracle does not per se condemn Jehu's coup at Jezreel, called for by Elisha (2 Kgs 9:1–10). דמי יזרעאל *could* mean "bloodguilt of Jezreel" in the sense of a wrong needing requital, but it more likely means only "massacre at Jezreel" in the sense of a great, decisive slaughter. The former connotation, "bloodguilt," is found for דמים in Lev 20:9, Deut 19:10, 2 Sam 21:1, etc. But the connotation "killing" or "bloodshed" is also well attested, as in דמי מלחמה "bloodshed of battle" (1 Kgs 2:5) or דמי חנם, "unnecessary bloodshed" (1 Kgs 2:31), etc. Recognition of the use of פקד in the context, so often associated with requital of justice in the OT, should not lead to the conclusion that Hosea is condemning Jehu for fulfilling God's command. Instead, Yahweh now announces that he will turn the tables on the house of Jehu because of the real issue, i.e., *what has happened in the meantime*. In the same way that Jehu in 842 had annihilated a dynasty famed for its long history of oppression and apostasy, so Yahweh himself will now put an end to the Jehu dynasty because it, in turn, has grown hopelessly corrupt.

The term ממלכות may mean "kingship" or "kingdom," in the context of v 4. If "kingship" is understood, it could be argued that Hosea is here told only that the Jehu dynasty is to be destroyed with nothing about its successors being revealed. On the other hand, if "kingdom" is meant, the verse must be taken to include a prediction of the destruction of the Northern Kingdom per se. Even the vocalization is uncertain. In the eighth century the consonantal text would not have distinguished between ממלכת (*maml*e*kat*), "kingdom of" and ממלכת (*maml*e*kūt*), "kingship of." Moreover, there is doubt as to whether a real semantic distinction can be forced between ממלכות and ממלכת. The two words may have functioned in some contexts virtually as synonyms.

5 This verse mentions "Jezreel" no longer as the city, but now as the valley (cf. 2:2, 24). The Jezreel valley (עמק יזרעאל) was the site of the North's loss of independence at the hands of the Assyrians. In 733 B.C. Tiglath-Pileser's armies captured the valley in the Assyrian campaign launched to quell rebellion in Syria-Palestine. Tiglath-Pileser incorporated much of the North into As-

syrian administrative districts, with the exception of Ephraim and some parts
of other historic tribal boundaries. The broad valley area was by Hosea's
day already famous as a great, historic battlefield, the scene of several decisive
battles in Israel's past (Deborah and Barak's defeat of the Canaanites, Judg
4–5; Gideon's defeat of the Midianites, Judg 6–8; the Philistine defeat of
Israel under Saul, 1 Sam 29–31; the Egyptian defeat of Judah under Josiah,
2 Kgs 23:29–30). The proximity of the large gateway city of Megiddo, on
the southern edge of the valley, led to its later identification as the site of
these battles, so that the Jezreel valley is called also the "plain of Megiddo"
(בקעת מגדון) as in Zech 12:11. Armageddon ('Αρμαγεδών) in Rev 16:16 is
a Greek transliteration of either the Hebrew הר מגדון "hill of Megiddo" or
the Aramaic ארץ מגדון "land of Megiddo," linked because of its historic
role as a battlefield with the fate of Zion in Zech 12:11.

Thus "Jezreel" became in Israel a kind of byword for "decisive battle"
alongside "Midian" in Isa 9:3 [4] and 10:26 and Ps 83:10 [9]. The fact that
the great defeat of Midian by Gideon took place at Jezreel (the valley) reinforces
the similarity in usage of the two words.

There is no explicit referent for ביום ההוא "at that time." These words
constitute an introductory cliché that alerts the hearer / reader to the fact that
the following oracle concerns the future. The meaning could well be paraphrased "in the future." ביום ההוא is one of several terms (e.g., באחרית
הימים "at a later time"; באים הימים "the time is coming") which all refer
to an indefinite point sometime in the future, the exact timing of which is
known only to God.

It has sometimes been suggested that the use of "Israel" in this verse
instead of בית ישראל "house / family of Israel" signals that the verse is an
interpolation, even if of genuine Hoseanic material. The fact, however, that
the word "Israel" occurs alone thirty-one times in the book, as opposed to
only five occurrences of "family of Israel," makes this view suspect.

For קשת "bow" as a metaphor of military strength, see Gen 49:24; 1 Sam
2:4; 2 Sam 1:18; 2 Kgs 13:15–16; Ps 7:13 [12]; Ezek 39:3; etc. The plain
reference of the verse is to Tiglath-Pileser's utter defeat of Israel in 733 and
the resulting Galilean subjugation. To "break the bow" is typical treaty curse
language, symbolic of total defeat (cf. 1 Sam 2:4). Hillers (*Treaty-Curses*, 60)
cites several parallels from Syria-Palestine and Mesopotamia.

6 The repetition in form of the naming of the second child and the
explanation for the name leave no doubt that the focus of interest is the
symbolic message-name and its meaning. In the explanation of the meaning
of "Jezreel," a transition from concern for the dynasty to concern for the
northern nation as a whole was evident. Now that transition is complete
and it is exclusively the fate of the Northern nation that is of concern. God
has decided to withdraw his compassion from Israel. On the omission of לו
"to him" from the naming pattern, see above, v 3.

The name of the daughter, "No Compassion" (לא רחמה, *Lo-Ruhamah*),
is a message-name different in format from "Jezreel." While לא in MT sometimes represents the non-homologous homophone *lō* (Canaanite *lū) meaning
"indeed" or "surely," there is virtually no likelihood of confusion here, since
we have no comparable example of a proper name composed with *lū as an

element. The *lōʾ* clearly signals a negative name in contrast to the general practice of giving children positive names in ancient Israel. Exceptions to that practice were very few, the most notable being אִי כָבוֹד (*Ichabod*, 1 Sam 4:21), which meant something like "Lack of Glory." For a child to be called "No Compassion" or "Unpitied" must have been very striking—indeed, an outrageous name for a daughter. Those who must have asked about it and heard the explanation Hosea gave could readily recognize allusion to the traditional covenant curses of divine rejection and wrath (type 1; Deut 31:17; 32:19, 20, et al.).

The verb in the name רֻחָם is from a root originally meaning "womb" and referring to tender (motherly) love and compassion. In this case the form is best understood as a pual perfect, not a participle; the full name would literally mean "She has not been shown compassion."

The announcement of the name signifies a change of status for Israel. God's compassion had been extended repeatedly to a wayward people. They had benefited in spite of their disloyalty, but this would now cease. Disloyalty must earn its true reward, rejection. The root is employed again in 2:6 [4] ("I will have no compassion . . .") and in the reversal (2:25 [23]) where Yahweh graciously promises for the future: "I will have compassion on No Compassion." The phrase "family of Israel" (בֵית יִשׂרָאֵל), used a total of five times by Hosea, obviously contrasts with בֵית יֵהוּא "family of Jehu" in 1:4, further reinforcing the shift of emphasis from the dynasty to the whole nation.

MT's pointing interpreted the verb of the final clause of this verse ("since I have been utterly betrayed by them") as נשׁא. Kuhnigk suggests, however, that it must rather be the verb נשׁא "reject," in the passive voice, which would look exactly like נשׁא in the original unpointed text (*NSH*, 4). The notion of betrayal / rejection is exactly what we would expect in the context.

7 Many commentators regard v 7 as an interpolation. The commonly cited reasons are: (1) it interrupts the flow of the section by introducing the issue of the fate of Judah, otherwise not of concern here; (2) it is expansionistic, not paralleled in vv 4 and 9; and (3) the phrase בְּיהוה אלהיהם, "by Yahweh their God" is disruptive, third-person speech in a context where Yahweh himself is the speaker. In favor of the authenticity of the verse, however, it must be noted that (1) the verse is not in fact awkward, and not stylistically different from other Hoseanic material; (2) the elegant chiasm at the end of the verse bespeaks the same sort of compositional quality already evident in 1:2–9 itself; (3) the verse deals directly with issues raised initially in v 6, picking up directly language used in v 6 (. . . אֲרֵחם אֶת־בֵית, "I will not have compassion on the family of . . ."); and (4) the natural interest of readers / hearers of the prophecy, both Northerners and later Southerners, would involve the fate of Judah. Compartmentalization of such a concern was not as acceptable to OT prophets as it is to some modern-day scholars.

God made explicit promises regarding Judah. They would ultimately escape the Assyrian onslaught, because he would have compassion on them (אֲרֵחם), and because he would save / deliver them (אֹושׁיעם and הוֹשַׁעתים). But what specifically is the chronology of this arrangement for Judah? Was Judah to be exempt from Assyrian intervention in the period from 733–722 B.C. during which the North died an agonizing death? Or was Judah being promised deliverance only from actual *destruction* by Assyria? The latter option is the most realistic, especially in light of the promise of the miraculous nature of deliverance. In effect, Judah is promised: "I will keep Assyria from destroying you, though they will surely destroy the family of Israel."

The most dramatic occasion of Yahweh's saving intervention for Judah during the entire neo-Assyrian period came in 701, when Sennacherib's armies invested Jerusalem. Alone among the great cities of Syria-Palestine, Jerusalem did not fall, but was delivered by the divine rout of the Assyrians (2 Kgs 19:32–37). The central referent of the promise to save the Judeans without resort to military prowess may thus be the 701 B.C. deliverance. But the promise was not a blanket guarantee for all ages, as the fall of Judah in 587 to the Babylonians demonstrated.

The last five word-groups of the verse contain a chiasm. It centers on the third element, במלחמה "by warfare." The first two elements, בקשת "by bow," and בחרב "by sword," are parallel, being the common weaponry carried by footsoldiers. The fourth and fifth elements, בסוסים "by cavalry" (lit., "horses"), and בפרשים "by chariotry" (lit., "charioteers") are again synonymously parallel, indicating the common mounted combatants. By this literary device, Yahweh assures the deliverance of Judah without troops either on foot or mounted; that is, without any *warfare*. Judah is to be spared for the time being for reasons unspecified in the oracle, though possibly related to its relatively greater orthodoxy.

The intervention of Yahweh in political and military crises on behalf of his people is a virtually pan-biblical theme (cf. Exod 15:1–18; Deut 33:2–5; Judg 5:2–5; Ezek 39:1–10; Joel 2:30–32; Zech 14:1–5). The older notion that such a concept was "characteristically late" in date (Harper, 213) is without justification.

8 The verse follows the established laconic pattern of reporting the barest facts. From the verb "she weaned" (ותגמל) we have some idea of the time that elapsed between the birth of the first and third children since children were probably nursed until about age three in ancient times (2 Macc 7:27; the Egyptian "Instructions of Ani," *ANET*, 420; 1 Sam 1:23). Perhaps five or six years is a reasonable guess for the actual interval from the birth of Jezreel to the birth of No Compassion.

Why would Hosea or a narrator take the trouble to add this bit of chronological detail? Perhaps it emphasizes the *durative* value of the prophet's message. That is, several years after the revelation that Yahweh has withdrawn his compassion from Israel, another revelation comes to say that Yahweh has now actually "divorced" himself from being his people's God. Things have not solved themselves or gotten better in the three- or four-year interim; if anything they are much worse. Time has not healed this wound but enlarged it.

9 The vocabulary is that of the Mosaic covenant, formulated in terms of "my people . . . your God" (Exod 6:7; Lev 26:12; Deut 27:9), and reflected often in the prophets (cf. Jer 7:23; 11:4). Hosea is reminded in these familial terms of the fact that, for Israel, dissolution of their personal relationship with God is the necessary result of rebellion. Obedience led to kinship; disobedience must lead to being disowned / divorced. Thus this message-name, Not

My People, and the divine explanation in the rest of the verse, are unmistakable in their assertion that the covenant is now broken. Since Israel's very identity was that of a covenant people, they are now formally cut adrift.

This does not mean that Yahweh has permanently abandoned his people. In 2:1–3 [1:10–2:1] the fact that the abandonment will eventually be reversed is made clear, in conformity with the schema laid out in Deut 4:25–31 et al.

The message of the verse is dramatic. Yahweh's union with his people is dissolved. The first message-name, לא עמי "Not My People," could hardly have been ambiguous to its hearers. Since Yahweh was the speaker, Israel must be the referent.

The second name, לא־אהיה לכם, has the *maqqeph* between לא and אהיה, demonstrating that the Masoretes, at least, considered the two words linked as a unit, i.e., without a sentence relationship between them. The thought parallelism supports this interpretation, and extends it to include the verse's final word, לכם.

Following the Hebrew word order, we may schematize this portion of the verse as follows:

For	You	Not	People	My
(Connective)	(Pronoun)	(Negative)	(Noun)	(Possessive)

And	I	Not	*Ahyeh*	Your
(Connective)	(Pronoun)	(Negative)	(Noun)	(Possessive)

The elements of each sentence are fully parallel. The use of לכם *lakem* "your" after אהיה is merely a normal grammatical alternative to the use of the suffixed possessive pronoun.

The word we have translated as Ahyeh (אהיה) was vocalized by the Masoretes as אֶהְיֶה *ʾehyeh*. This comports with the Masoretic decision to vocalize the divine name in the form of the qal present / future in Exod 3:14 also. Apparently they, too, recognized at this point that אהיה in this verse was not a simple verb "I will be," but a repetition of the divine name "Yahweh," revealed to Moses in Yahweh's first person speech in Exod 3 as אהיה rather than יהוה. The Greek, also, indicates that אהיה is a name, by capitalizing the first letter: Ἐιμι. Though the consonants of אהיה are undoubtedly rightly recognized as an alternate form of the tetragrammaton, the Masoretic vocalization of them is suspect.

The divine name in Exod 3:14 and Hos 1:9 is better vocalized אַהְיֶה *ʾahyeh*, the Canaanite / Hebrew causative of the verb היה (*hyh*) / הוה (*hwh*) "to be." In other words, *ʾahyeh* is merely the first person form of the third-person name *yahweh*. The y / w interchange (ahyeh / yahweh) is well known in Northwest Semitic. The name Yahweh, then, means "He who causes to be / creates."

Yahweh himself reverts here to the first person form of the name, harking back to the ancient original use of the first person form in Exod 3:14. Why? Because the first person form was that associated with the tradition of the initiation of the covenant. Yahweh was withdrawing the very covenant he so dramatically initiated via the revelation of his name and is using the same form of the name he used to Moses. Thus the passage contains four symbolic names in all: the names of Hosea's three children and Yahweh's new name Not Your Ahyeh / Yahweh, indicating his rejection of Israel.

To this point in their history, Israel's identity had been understood in terms of a special relationship, that of a people (עַם), and a God (אהיה / יהוה). Both elements are now negated. The עַם has become לֹא עַם and אהיה has become לֹא אהיה. The curse type is no. 1, rejection, as evidenced in Deut 31:17, 18; 32:30, et al.

Explanation

The central focus of 1:2–9 is the symbolically significant, message-bearing names. Actions (getting married, having children) are not themselves directly significant to the revelation Yahweh provides, but function as precursors. Of course Hosea must marry and have children in order for the revelation mediated by the naming of the children to take place.

Because Hosea's wife and children will be Israelites, they will automatically be exposed to and entangled by זנונים "prostitution," syncretism / disloyalty to Yahweh. The presumption of the passage is that any Israelite woman Hosea married and any children he had would automatically be tainted by this "prostitution," so great was Israel's corruption and religious unfaithfulness at the time.

The children's names tell the story as regards Israel's fate. Names had significance in the ancient biblical world beyond anything most modern Westerners are used to. Children's names were not necessarily chosen prior to the birth. The naming of a child was often, if not usually, based upon events or circumstances which accompanied its birth in some way, although on the principle of homophony. That is, the name would often reflect an event or issue that happened or was current in the mind of the family at birth (Gen 21:3–7; 25:26; 29:32; etc.; cf. Stuart, *ISBE* 3:483–88).

Positive names were the rule. Reflecting this desire toward the positive, the Sumerian / Babylonian goddess Nin-tu is recorded in one ancient text describing herself as ". . . the good midwife of the gods. I say only pleasant things at the time of birth." Yet in Hos 1:4–9, three negative names are given (Jezreel, technically an ambiguous name, is immediately explained as negative): No Compassion (Lo-Ruhamah), Not My People (Lo-Ammi) and Not Your Ahyeh (אהיה) (Lo-Ahyeh-Lakem) are all bluntly negative.

The collective impact of these four names embodies the message of 1:2–9: Israel's apostasy had become so great that Yahweh could no longer put up with them. He had to abandon them, divorce them.

What of Hosea's role in 1:2–9? It is hardly central, to be sure. He is mentioned by name for the first time in the book in 1:1, and for the last time in 1:2. But he is simply not the one on whom these verses are focused. The focus is upon Yahweh and what he will do in Israel (and parenthetically, to Judah). Hos 1:2–9 is also unconcerned with Hosea's home life. Hosea is *not* paralleled with God, except in the obvious and superficial sense that aspects of his marriage and family are invested with theologically significant overtones. He does not, however, suffer here as Yahweh has suffered. There is no hint in 1:2–9 that he is rejected or defrauded by his family as Yahweh was by his "family." His children's *names*, not their identity or behavior, speak prophetically: they do not rebel against him as Yahweh's children do. Accordingly, interpretations that link Hosea and his family psychologically to Yahweh and Israel founder for lack of evidence in the text.

Hos 1:2–9 functions as a summarizing preface to the entire book. It presents an overview, in stark and moving terms, of the prophet's proportionately dominant message: God has given up his people. The theme of restoration *after* this judgment then follows immediately in 2:1–3 [1:10–2:1].

Israel's Restoration in Jezreel's Great Day (2:1–3 [1:10–2:1])

Bibliography

Albright, W. F. "The Refrain 'And God Saw Ki Tob.'" *Mélanges . . . A. Robert.* Paris: Bloud et Gay, 1957. **Gorgulho, L.** "A Perspectiva Ecumenica de Oseias 2, 1–3." *Revista Ecclesiastica Brasilieira* 22 (1962) 607–15. **Kugel, J. L.** "The Adverbial Use of KÎ TÔB." *JBL* 99 (1980) 433–35. **Renaud, B.** "Genèse et unité rédactionelle de Os 2." *RevScRel* 54 (1980) 1–20. ———. "Osée ii:2: ʿlh mn hʾrṣ: essai d'interprétation." *VT* 33 (1983) 495–500. **Stuart, D. K.** "The Sovereign's Day of Conquest." *BASOR* 221 (1976) 159–64. **Wolff, H. W.** "Der grosse Jesreeltag (Hosea 2, 1–3)" *EvT* 12 (1952–53) 78–104; repr. in *Gesammelte Studien zum Alten Testament*, 151–181.

Translation

2:1 [1:10]*The children of Israel will become[a] in number like the sand of the sea, which can neither be measured nor counted. Where[b] they were called[c] "You are 'Not My People,'" they will be called "Children of the Living God."*

2 [1:11]*The Judahites and the Israelites will unite.[a] They will appoint themselves a single leader, and will come up from the land / be resurrected.[b] How great[c] the day of Jezreel will be!*

3 [1]*Call your brothers[a] "My People," and your sisters[a] "Shown Compassion."*

Notes

*(Hebrew verse number 2:1 equals 1:10 in the English translations, where chap. 2 starts at Hebrew 2:3. The numbers below, as do those in all *Notes* of this volume, follow the Hebrew.)

1.a. For MT והיה "will become," G reads καὶ ἦν "(the number of the children of Israel) was . . . ," which would either reflect an original Heb. ויהי, or else an assumption on the part of the G translators that 2:1 was so closely linked to 1:9 as to require a past sense. (והיה is translated καὶ ἔσται in v 1b and thereafter, as expected.) The original wording of v 1 may have been an impf, יהיה, subsequently corrupted in transmission to והיה. The context would seem unquestionably to require a fut form of the verb. α′ and σ′ support MT's והיה, as expected in Hosea.

1.b. במקום אשר must mean "in the place where," or just "where." It is not a synonym for תחת אשר "instead of," and refers, then, to new people in locations or contexts to which God's people did not extend in Hosea's day.

1.c. Or, "Where it was said to them. . . ." Only the portion "Not My People" is the name, rather than the entire quoted sentence.

2.a. Or ". . . will be gathered together" or the like.

2.b. Kuhnigk's suggestion (*NSH*, 8–10) following Dahood, that ועלו מן־הארץ, lit." and will come up from the land", is resurrection language is appealing. But the return from the land (ארץ) of exile to the land of promise is so clearly an expectation of restoration passages in the Pentateuch that we opt for the dual wording to help convey the ambiguity of the Heb.

2.c. The clause . . . כי גדול is grammatically ambiguous. כי may parallel its usage in 1:4–9 ("for / because") or may be an intensifying element, here where "explanations" are no longer part of the structure. On the intensifying כי, see Albright, *Mélanges . . . A. Robert* and Kugel *JBL* 99 (1980) 433–35.

3.a. G reads singulars (אחיך, "your brother"; אחותך, "your sister"), unlikely unless the Heb. *Vorlage* had singulars or unless יזרעאל "Jezreel," 2:2, is construed as a voc, leading to an inner-Heb. text correction or G translation decision to take the sg forms of "brother" and "sister." Context and logic demand pl suff for the Heb.

Form / Structure / Setting

This oracle contrasts sharply in tone with the severe punishment predicted for the North in 1:2–9. Here we read of a radically new era, "Jezreel's day," in which a reunited Israel will be restored to its familial relationship with God, under a single leader, reborn to the status originally envisioned for it in Yahweh's promises to Abraham.

Aside from the contrast in tone and the fact that the passage describes an obviously distant era, the linkages with 1:2–9 are very strong. Indeed, it is obvious that the most appropriate place for the oracle in the overall structure of the book is immediately after 1:2–9, with which it shares so many affinities in structure, vocabulary, and historical-theological outlook.

These affinities are at least seven in number:

1. The concern for the fate of Israel vis-à-vis the fate of Judah is addressed in vv 1 and 2, and possibly even in v 3. The reference is implicit in the way that ישראל "Israel" is now used to designate the united people in v 1, is explicit in v 2, and may be reflected in the plural suffixal forms in v 3 (see *Comment*).

2. Each of the four figures named in 1:2–9, Jezreel, No Compassion (Lo-Ruhamah), Not My People (Lo-Ammi), and Not Your Ahyeh (Lo-Ahyeh), is alluded to in a new way in this passage.

3. The same ultimate concern for the fate of God's covenant people is addressed. The time frame has shifted to the eschatological, answering the question of the ultimate fate of (northern) Israel in history, as opposed to the immediate fate of Israel in the eighth century B.C.

4. The scope is again major, involving the nation per se, and describing dramatic decisive action on Yahweh's part in relation to Israel as a corporate entity.

5. The passage is again prose. V 3, prose yet parallelistic, both concludes the prior prose passage, and serves as a transition to the poetry which begins with 2:4.

6. Familial language and the language of God's possession of his people ("children of the living God") recall the similar metaphors in 1:2–9.

7. There is a structural progression from longer, compound-complex sen-

tences to short, pithy, "bare bones" expressions in the passage, paralleling the increasingly laconic speech noticeable in 1:4–9 (if not 1:2–9).

The passage may be identified as Hoseanic in style rather than "late non-Hoseanic" as was once thought likely. Certain of the key words in the passage are known from other sections of the book: בני ישראל "Israelites" (3:1, 4, 5); קבץ "unite" (8:10, 9:6); כ as introducing a comparison (2:5, 2:17, 3:1, 4:9, 4:16, 5:10, 5:12, 5:14, 6:4). (Wolff [*Hosea*, 25] has argued that ראש "leader" and בני אל חי "children of the living God" are more natural to Hosea's day than to a later, exilic period of authorship.) Other linguistic features, such as the presence of passive verb forms and the lack of first person speech on the part of Yahweh, do not constitute adequate criteria for evaluating the authenticity of the passage. Some of those who have correctly taken ועלו מן־הארץ "they will come up from the land" in v 2 as referring to a return from exile have dated the passage as exilic, but on the basis of a bias against the authenticity of predictive prophecy.

A precise dating within the years of Hosea's ministry is not possible to suggest. None of the seven restoration passages in the book can be dated, simply by reason of their eschatological subject matter.

What of the fact that 2:1–3 is an oracle of eschatological salvation whereas 1:2–9 is an oracle of judgment? This contrast is exactly what the covenant juxtaposition of pre-exilic curses and post-exilic restoration promises would dictate (cf. Lev 26:33–45; Deut 4:25–31, et al.). Israel's history had an immediate direction (destruction and exile) and an ultimate direction (deliverance and restoration). The pattern of 1:2–9 and 2:1–3 in tandem fits the predictions of the covenant sanctions. Moreover, the tendency of the entire book is to alternate salvation oracles with judgment oracles unpredictably and without editorial transition.

Does 2:3, a semi-parallelistic "couplet" whose concern is exhortation, belong with 2:1–2, a prose salvation oracle? The answer is in the affirmative, precisely because of the semantic content of the exhortation itself. The vast population of the eschatologically restored Israel, construed logically in the plural (thus "your brothers," "your sisters") are now in a position to participate in a joyous renaming. They will rename themselves, reversing the impact of the two names in 1:4–9 which referred to the whole nation (in negative terms), now announcing that a new covenantal relationship has replaced the one formerly broken. Thus 2:3 is a fitting climax to 2:1–2; the new names are a capstone to the oracle of salvation, which in toto provides complements for all the names given in 1:4–9.

Comment

2:1 [1:10] The day is coming when Israel's population will be immeasurably expanded, partly by the inclusion of people not originally Israelite.

From the figures given in 2 Kgs 15:19–20, it would appear that there were approximately 60,000 free landholders in northern Israel in Hosea's day. The total population, including non-landholders and their families, might have reached 400,000 or more. Judah would have been perhaps half as populous (cf. 2 Chr 13:3), or about 200,000 in number. All Israel, then, would not likely have exceeded two-thirds of a million persons. Other sources of partial population figures, such as Sargon II's claim to have exiled 27,290 persons from Samaria in 722 B.C. comport with this rough estimate. Israel was a small nation. Assyria, with a population in excess of 120,000 just within its sometimes capital [sic] Nineveh (Jonah 4:11), outnumbered Israel and Judah enormously.

The emphasis of the verse is not, however, on numerical growth per se, but on the fulfillment of the expansion promises to the patriarchs, and on the reunification of Israel with Judah, both of which developments would overturn the defeat and humiliation predicted in 1:4–9 and actually experienced in the Assyrian decimation of 722.

The motif of an eventual innumerable progeny is central to the patriarchal promise accounts in Genesis (13:16; 15:5; 22:17; 26:24, 28:14, 32:12) and to the covenantal restoration of those promises in the sanctions passages (Lev 26:9, 45; Deut 30:5; i.e., number 4 in our categorization). The new age that Yahweh announces through Hosea is thus related to the most ancient traditions. These traditions do not concern themselves with a divided nation, and considering the proximity of the explicit promise of reunification in the following verse, it would seem that בני ישראל "Israelites" is intended in this context to refer to all Israel, North and South combined, even though בני ישראל can refer to the North alone in Hosea (4:1). At any rate, it is evident from the passage as a whole that the North will not be restored and numerically expanded apart from reunification with the South and the inclusion of other peoples as well, who will share the same benefits and eschatological blessing (cf. 3:5; Exod 12:38).

The wording of the growth promise, including the phrase כחול הים "like the sand of the sea" is almost identical to the wording in Gen 32:12, but the description of Israel's population in such terms is hardly limited to patriarchal contexts. The phrase itself is a cliché for innumerability, and is applied in the OT to countless numbers of Canaanites (Josh 11:4), Amalekites / Midianites (Judg 7:12), Philistines (1 Sam 13:15), quail in the wilderness (Ps 78:27), grain supplies (Gen 41:49), thoughts of God (Ps 139:18), troubles of Job (Job 6:3), widows in conquered Israel (Jer 15:8), etc. There are occasions when historical Israel is described as being as numerous *already* as the sand of the sea: 2 Sam 17:11 (Israel mustered for battle); 1 Kgs 4:20 (Judah and Israel in Solomon's time; see also Isa 10:22 and 48:19). Jer 33:22, on the other hand, parallels very closely the eschatological emphasis of the term in Hosea.

The phrase בני אל חי "children of the living God" is a combination known only from Hosea. The expression אל חי "living God" is otherwise attested only in Josh 3:10, Ps 42:3 [2] and Ps 84:3 [2]. Compare Isaiah's so-called "idol passages" (mainly Isa 40:18–20; 41:5–7; 44:9–20; and 46:5–11) emphasizing the contrast between dumb, motionless idols and the living God, though אל חי itself does not occur in Isaiah.

2 [1:11] Three dramatic reversals will constitute Jezreel's great new day. These are the unification of Israel and Judah under a single leader, their return from exile, and their revival (restoration blessing types 7, 8, and 10).

Kuhnigk (*NSH*, 5–6) identifies here a balanced poetic couplet:

וְנִקְבְּצוּ בְּנֵי־יְהוּדָה 9
וּבְנֵי־יִשְׂרָאֵל יַחְדָּו 9

If MT יחדו is construed as a verb, an apparently chiastic structure emerges:

And gathered will be the Judahites
And the Israelites will be united.

More likely, however, is that the verse is prose and the "even" syllable count accidental. The adverb *yhdw* "together" is frequently found at the end of clauses or lines of poetry (e.g. Amos 1:15), and its placement is no problem.

The use of שים ל "to appoint" has its linguistic parallel in 1 Sam 8:5 where the Israelites ask Samuel for a King (שימה לנו מלך "appoint us a King . . ."). Hosea predicts here that they will appoint themselves a single *leader*. The avoidance of the word מלך in the context is probably due to the eschatological cast of the oracles (cf. Ezek 40–48, passim). The word ראש "head" is more commonly associated with times prior to the institution of the monarchy (cf. Num 14:4; Judg 11:8), times which for Hosea constitute in part a paradigm for the age of restoration. The choosing of kings by Israel and Judah had been part of a history of strife, warfare, disobedience and apostasy. A "leader," unlike the apostate eighth-century Israelite kings, would be appointed to rule in the new age.

The clause ועלו מן־הארץ "and will come up from the land / be resurrected" provides the most dramatic wording of the verse, one that may well have dual connotations: both return from exile and resurrection from "death." The terminology is quite appropriate to the situation. Israel has been cast off, is no longer Yahweh's covenant people, and (eventually along with Judah, though this was not stated anywhere in 1:2–9) will be destroyed as an independent people. For them to make such a comeback as is envisaged in 2:1–3 requires a reversal of great magnitude. And what more appropriate terminology to employ for this reversal than words which can be construed to imply rejuvenation-resurrection, along with return from exile?

ארץ is employed here perhaps both in the sense of the land of exile (cf. Deut 4:27–30 et al.) and the earth which surrounds the grave. Kuhnigk (*NSH*, 8–10) translates ארץ by *Unterwelt*, "nether world," a sense it has in OT poetical contexts (e.g., Pss 71:20, 95:4; Isa 43:6, Jer 15:7), and notes along with other commentators the close connection with the resurrection language found in Ezek 37:12–14:

Behold, I will open your graves and raise you from your graves, O my people; and I will bring you home into the land of Israel. And you shall know that I am Yahweh, when I open your graves and raise you from your graves, O my people. And I will put my spirit in you, and you shall come alive. . . .

It is in this context that the great day of Jezreel takes on meaning. It does not refer merely to a day of increased agricultural fertility or a day when the town of Jezreel will become a positive rather than a negative memory in Israel. Rather it is a day of eschatological deliverance from the covenant

curses of national death and deportation. Jezreel, like "Gettysburg" or "Pearl
Harbor" in American history, was a name fraught with emotive overtones
in ancient Israel. Now a new, decisive day is at hand—and Jezreel becomes
a paradigm or symbol for Israel as a whole.

The construction "day of X" can refer to a decisive battle, either literally
or figuratively; cf. the "day of Midian" in Isa 9:4 [3], and the "day of Yahweh"
elsewhere in the prophets.

3 [1]   The plural imperative אמרו "say" has an unspecified subject, though
there can be little doubt that the people of the future, reunited Israel and
Judah, are those who are to speak these words to one another. The command
also serves as a present word of comfort, in that it contains a proleptic guarantee
of the eventual unity of God's people. The "brothers" and "sisters" are fellow
Israelites, including Judeans, if 2:1-2 is taken seriously. The time will come,
after the fullness of punishment is complete, that Israelites will call their fellow
citizens, brothers and sisters, "My People" and "Shown Compassion." It is
inevitable that there will be a day when Yahweh will gather them together
under a single leader.

Among other options, it is possible that 2:1-3 reflects the years immediately
following the Syro-Ephraimite war, i.e., after 733 B.C., in which Israel and
Judah, with their Syrian and Assyrian allies respectively, were bitter enemies.
Hosea now can assure those enemies of eventual reconciliation to one another
and to Yahweh their God; and can invite them to anticipate this great future
day by their speech.

Explanation

The passage's central thrust is encouragement. The future is both glorious
and secure. It is not even possible for the Israel of Hosea's day to do anything
either to accomplish or prevent the reunification and expansion predicted.
God will bring these changes about on behalf of Israel and Judah and a
"people" not yet imagined, in an eschatological setting, far beyond Hosea's
day.

A day of salvation is coming. It will involve (1) a vast numerical increase
for God's people, (2) reunification under a single leader, and (3) return from
exile and rejuvenation / resurrection. These promises address the current situation of Hosea's time: population decimation due to war; national division;
divided and unstable monarchies; the impending Assyrian exile; spiritual /
covenantal deadness.

There is no indication in the passage that what is contemplated is merely
a restoration of the old tribal league system that existed in the days of the
Judges and until the kingship of Saul. Those were hardly times of numerical
greatness or true unity (cf. Judg 18-21). Rather, only in a radically different
future age will all that a righteous Israelite hoped for be brought to pass.

This era of blessing must be preceded by a time of wrath, however, as
1:2-9 precedes 2:1-3. The promise of numerical growth cannot be fulfilled
until after Yahweh's judgment causes Israel's growth to cease because of
their sin (cf. 4:9-10; 9:11-14, 16; 14:1 [13:16]). The promise of reunification
must await the judgment of further strife and division. The promise of a

single leader under which the united people can prosper will not be realized until God has judged corrupt disloyal kings (7:7; 8:4; 10:7; 10:15; 13:10–11). Resurrection follows death and destruction, which must first be endured (4:3, 6; 5:9–10; 8:8; 9:6; 11:6; 13:1–3; 14:1 [13:16]; cf. Deut 30:1–3). Thus the passage conveys throughout a strong contrast to the situation of Hosea's present and near future.

From the vantage point of the new covenant, it is clear that the final fulfillment of all this comes via the work of Christ. How does Christ's work represent the referent of this salvation oracle? First, it is the church, Christ's body, who constitute the innumerable people whom the living God has made his children (Rom 9:24–26). Those who are in Christ constitute Abraham's seed, of whom this prediction of great growth was made; and the church inherits what God had prepared for Abraham's seed, thereby fulfilling God's promise (Gal 3:29).

By democratizing God's people, shifting the membership potential from Israel to all nations, Jesus initiated the great day of Jezreel. In his work a special value was added to the sense of 2:1 [1:10]. It becomes abundantly clear that it refers not just to Israelites being restored to God, but to the fact that people who never could have made such a claim, now, by reason of Christ's sacrifice for the whole world, have the potential of joining with God's people. Hosea could hardly have foreseen exactly how dramatically and on what a great scale God would eventually fulfill these words of salvation—nor, entirely, can we. As Wolff (29) points out, "This is not yet completed with respect to Israel (Rom 10:1; 11:26) or the nations (Rev 7:9 ff)."

Divorce Proceedings with a Surprise Ending   (2:4–17 [2–15])

Bibliography

Allegro, J. M. "A Recently Discovered Fragment of a Commentary on Hosea from Qumran's Fourth Cave." *JBL* 78 (1959) 142–48. **Barth, C.** "Zur Bedeutung der Wustentradition." *Congress Volume.* VTSup 15. Leiden: E. J. Brill, 1966. 14–23. **Baumgärtel, F.** "Die Formel *ne'um-jahweh*." *ZAW* 73 (1961) 277–90. **Brongers, H. A.** "Bemerkungen zum Gebrauch der adverbialen *we'attāh* im Alten Testament." *VT* 15 (1965) 289–99. **Cassuto, U.** "The Second Chapter of the Book of Hosea." *Biblical and Oriental Studies.* Vol. 1. Tr. I. Abrahams. Jerusalem: Magnes Press, 1973. 101–40. **Clines, D. J.** "Hosea 2: Structure and Interpretation." *Studia Biblica 1978. I. Papers on Old Testament and Related Themes,* ed. E. A. Livingstone. JSOTSup 11. Sheffield: JSOT Press, 1979. 83–103. ———. "Story and Poem: The Old Testament as Literature and as Scripture." *Int* 34 (1980) 115–27. **Deem, A.** "The Goddess Anath and Some Biblical Hebrew Cruces." *JSS* 23 (1978) 25–30. **Freedman, D. N.** "*Pŝṭy* in Hos 2:7." *JBL* 74 (1955) 275. **Friedman, M. A.** "Israel's Response in Hosea 2:17b: 'You are my Husband.'" *JBL* 99 (1980) 199–204. **Galbiati, E.** "La struttura sintetica di Osea 2." *Studi sull'Oriente e la Bibbia offerti a Giovanni Rinaldi,* ed. G. Buccellati et al. Genoa: Editrice Studio e

Vita, 1967. **Geller, M. J.** "The Elephantine Papyri and Hosea 2, 3: Evidence for the Form of the Early Jewish Divorce Writ." *JSJ* 8 (1977) 139–48. **Holladay, W. L.** "ERES—Underworld: Two More Suggestions." *VT* 19 (1969) 123–24. **Humbert, P.** "La formule hebraïque en *hineni* suivi d'un participe." *REJ* 97 (1934) 58–64. Repr. in *Opuscules d'un hebraïsant.* Memoires de l'Universite de Neuchatel 26. Neuchatel: Sécretariat de l'Université, 1958. 54–59. **Jongeling, B.** "Lākēn dans l'Ancien Testament." *Remembering All The Way.* Oudtestamentische Studien 21. Leiden: E. J. Brill, 1981. **Krszyna, H.** "Literarische Struktur von Os 2, 4–17." *BZ* 13 (1969) 41–59. **Kruger, P. A.** "Israel, the Harlot (Hos 2:4–9)." *JNSL* 11 (1983) 107–116. **Limburg, J.** "The Root ריב and the Prophetic Lawsuit Speeches." *JBL* 88 (1969) 291–304. **Lys, D.** "J'ai deux amours, ou l'amant jugé: Exercise sur Ósée 2, 4–25." *ETR* 51 (1976) 59–77. **Nielsen, K.** *Yahweh as Prosecutor and Judge: An Investigation of the Prophetic Lawsuit.* Tr. F. Cryer. JSOTSup 9. Sheffield: JSOT Press, 1978. **North, F. S.** "The Expression 'The Oracle of Yahweh' as an Aid to Critical Analysis." *JBL* 71 (1952) x. **Riemann, P. A.** "Desert and Return to Desert in the Pre-exilic Prophets." Unpublished Ph.D. Dissertation, Harvard University, 1964. **Tangberg, K. A.** "A Note on *pištî* in Hosea II 7, 11." *VT* 27 (1977) 222–24. **Thompson, J. A.** "Israel's 'Lovers.'" *VT* 27 (1977) 475–81. **Tsimaryon, Ts.** "I Will Go and Return to My First Husband (Hos. 2:9)." *BMik* 31 (1985/86) 293–97. [Heb.] **Turner, P. D. M.** "'Anoikodomein and Intra-Septuagintal Borrowing." *VT* 27 (1977) 492–93. **Würthwein, E.** "Der Ursprung der prophetischen Gerichtsrede." *ZTK* 49 (1952) 1–16. **Yeivin, I.** "Assimilation of *Nûn* at the End of a Word." *Leshonenu* 42 (1977) 73–4 (Hebrew). **Young, D. W.** "Notes on the Root *ntn* in Biblical Hebrew." *VT* 10 (1960) 457–59.

Translation

Yahweh introduces the evidence against Israel

2:4 [2] *Make an accusation against your mother.*
Make the accusation that[a] *she is not my wife, and I am not her husband*

And that she must remove her signs of prostitution from her face,
And her signs of adultery from between her breasts.

Adumbration of judgment

5 [3] *Or else I will strip her naked*
And leave her like she was the day she was born.

I will make[a] *her like the wilderness,*
I will make[a] *her like the parched land,*
I will cause her to die of thirst.

Additional evidence

6 [4] *I can have no compassion on her children*
Because they are prostituting[a] *children;*

7 [5] *Because their mother has practiced prostitution;*
She who conceived them has been a disgrace.

Because she said:
'I will follow my lovers,
Those who gave me food and water,
Wool and flax, oil[a] *and drink.'*[b]

The first judgment sentence

8 [6] *Therefore:*
> *I am going to block her* a *way with thorns,*
> *And I will put up a wall for her* b
> *So that she cannot find her paths;*

9 [7] *So that when she pursues her lovers,*
> *She will not catch up with them*
> *And when she seeks them, she will not find them.* a

> *She will say:*
> *'Let me go back to my first husband, because things*
> *were better for me then than they are now.'*

Additional evidence

10 [8] *She does not know that it was I who gave her the grain, fruit-of-the vine,* a
> *and olive oil; and supplied her in abundance with silver, and provided* b
> *her with gold—not Baal!* c

The second judgment sentence

11 [9] *Therefore:*
> *I will take back my grain at its time,*
> *And my fruit-of-the-vine at its season.*

> *And I will snatch away my wool and flax,*
> *Used to cover* a *her nakedness.*

12 [10] *Now I will expose her shamefulness* a *in front of her lovers,*
> *And no one can rescue her from me.*
13 [11] *I will put an end to all her rejoicing—*
> *Her feats,* a *her new moon celebrations, her sabbaths—all her special days.*

14 [12] *I will turn them into a forest,* a
> *I will demolish her vines and fig trees, of which she said,*
> *'They are the payment my lovers gave me.'*

> *Or wild animals* b *will eat them up.*

15 [13] *I will take her to task for the days devoted to the Baals,*
> *On which she has been burning offerings* a *to them.*

Additional evidence

> *She dressed up with her rings and her jewelry*
> *And followed her lovers, but forgot me.*
> *—Oracle of Yahweh.* b

The third judgment sentence—a surprise verdict

16 [14] *Therefore:*
> *I am going to seduce her.*
> *I will bring* a *her into the wilderness*
> *And I will romance her.*

17 [15]   *I will give her the vineyards ª from there*
And the Achor Valley as a gateway of hope.

She will respond there as she did when she was young.
As when she went up from the land of Egypt.

Notes

4.a. Taking כי "that" as a relative particle, the content of the accusation is thus initially identified in this verse: it is an accusation of unfaithfulness in a divorce proceeding.

5.a. The verb שׁית is a common synonym for שׂים and its most usual parallel in poetic couplets; thus the word "make" is used here for both Heb. words.

6.a. Cf. n. 1:2.

7.a. The term שׁמן here refers to processed oil, as opposed to the יצהר (raw olive oil) of v 10.

7.b. The suffs of לחמי "food," מימי "water," etc., are dative in force rather than merely possessive suffs. See Kuhnigk, *NSH*, 10–13.

8.a. The context demands "*her* way" rather than "your (fem sg) way" as MT has it. It is possible, as Kuhnigk suggests (*NSH*, 14–15) that the MT consonants דרכך are to be vocalized דָּרְדְּ־כִי, with emphatic כי, "(her) very way." G and Syr have the 3 fem sg suff, "her way." G's rendering the difficult שׂ (the governing verb, here translated "block") by ἀνοικοδομήσω "I will wall up" is possibly secondary to Lam 3:9 (Turner, "Anoikodomein," *VT* 27 [1977] 492–93).

8.b. Reading the suff in a dative as opposed to a poss sense. See 7.b above.

9.a. G actually adds αὐτούς "them," reflecting its usual practice of supplying pronom obj for verbs. In Vg, however, where it might be expected, no pronoun appears.

10.a. Heb. תירושׁ does not mean "new wine" but is an archaic poetic word for "wine." Thus we use this archaic poetic English term "fruit-of-the-vine."

10.b. Reading the inf abs, MT עָשׂוּ would appear to indicate morphologically the 3 m pl qal pf ind, "they made." Syntactically, however, this is most difficult. It is far preferable to take עָשׂוּ as an inf abs, either in the *qātul* pattern (for examples see Kuhnigk, *NSH*, 20) or repointed to עָשׂוֹ, the alternate to עָשׂה.

10.c. MT לבעל is best read *lō baʿal*, "not Baal," involving a somewhat anomalous orthography by reason of the omission of ʾaleph. See van Dijk, *Ezekiel's Prophecy on Tyre* (Rome: Pont. Bib. Inst., 1968), 105, and Kuhnigk, *NSH*, 19–20.

11.a. לכסות is considered by G a purpose clause and is thus negated (μὴ καλύπτειν "so as not to cover") as if the *lamedh* stood for *lōʾ*. We take it as a relative clause, "used to cover." An alternate possibility is to assume the presence of the piel *privatum*, and translate "so as to expose. . . ."

12.a. נבלתה "her shamefulness" is often translated "her genitals," but there is no actual lexical evidence for such a meaning. The use of euphemisms is so common in biblical Heb., however, that this term may be intended to imply the parts of the female body normally covered out of propriety.

13.a. With G and some modern translations, the sgs here are to be understood in a collective sense, and best translated as pls.

14.a. G μαρτύριον "witness" reflects a corruption: עיד rather than יער "forest."

14.b. G adds "birds of the sky and reptiles of the earth"; it is possible that this is not merely an expansion, but a reflection of haplogr in MT.

15.a. The exact meaning of קטר is still debated. An alternate translation is "burning incense."

15.b. On the options for translating the expression נאם יהוה see Baumgärtel, *ZAW* 73 (1961) 277–90.

16.a. G has καὶ τάξω "and I shall make, appoint," almost surely an inner-Greek corruption of καὶ κατάξω "and I shall lead."

17.a. G has τὰ κτήματα αὐτῆς "her possessions" conceivably reflecting a different Heb. original. σ´, however, has τοὺς ἀμπελῶνας αὐτῆς "her vineyards," reflecting MT.

Form / Structure / Setting

The general form of the sayings in 2:4–17 is that of the lawsuit or legal accusation (*rîb*). A favorite and effective device of the prophets was to portray Yahweh as a prosecutor undertaking a court case against his lawbreaking people, Israel. In this passage the dominant metaphorical representation of Israel is Yahweh's wife, whose unfaithfulness is the cause for him (it seems at first) to sue her for divorce by accusing her of adultery. She is the defendant—and yet it becomes increasingly clear that he still loves her. He is the plaintiff, her wronged husband. But he is also the prosecuting attorney, the judge, the jury, and even the police officer who will carry out the court's judgment. The "corespondents"—to use modern divorce terminology—are her lovers, the Baals. With them she has been unfaithful against her husband, Yahweh. Three kinds of punishments, each introduced by לכן, "therefore," (vv 8, 11, 16) will result.

Both the beginning and end of this court case have surprising twists. At the beginning (v 4), the children of Israel are asked to help support Yahweh's evidence against his wife by offering their testimony as part of the accusation, an unusual and striking opening for the case. At the end (vv 16–17), Yahweh announces a third "punishment" which does not fit the crime, but will fit His loving grace. He announces that, having firmly punished Israel for her infidelity, and having thereby reduced her to dependency, he will romance her again, to reestablish a loving relationship with her. Throughout, the parallels to a similar though nonlegal allegory in Ezek 16 are prominent. These parallels are noted in the verse-by-verse comments.

Vv 4–17 constitute a self-contained unit. The court metaphor is absent in 2:1–3, and the following pericope clearly refers to Israel as Yahweh's wife without any further connection to the court metaphor and with a new kind of introductory formula, והיה ביום ההוא "in that day . . .". This sets it apart formally from vv 4–17, where the unfaithful wife is always referred to in the third person, and where legal issues predominate.

The basic structure reflects the alternation of evidence and predictions of punishment, as found throughout the book. The specific features of the passage may be summarized as follows:

4a	Yahweh's call to court (accusation and evidence)
4b	His desire for Israel (the cessation of her promiscuity)
5	The first mention of punishment (Israel has committed a capital crime)
6–7	Evidence against Israel
8–9	The first judgment sentence of Yahweh (capture and confinement) and its hoped-for result: repentance
10	Evidence against Israel
11–15a	The second judgment sentence of Yahweh (various desolations)
15b	Evidence against Israel
16–17	The final, surprise "judgment" sentence of Yahweh

Most of the passage is free verse, containing a high percentage of irregular, synthetic parallelisms, and unbalanced meter. One section appears to be traditionally metrical (vv 4–7a); and one section is probably metrical (vv 6–7a).

If the sections are adjusted for the variability of copula, with prosaic accretions deleted, and vocalized according to eighth-century speech, the parallelism and syllabic meter (see Stuart, *Studies in Early Hebrew Meter*) may be summarized as follows:

Vv 4–7:

4a	Triplet	Synthetic	6:7:7	1:1:1
4b	Couplet	Synonymous	10:10	1:1
5a	Couplet	Synonymous	8:9	1:1
5b	Triplet	Synonymous	7:7:7	1:1:1
6	Couplet	Synthetic	8:8	1:1:1
7a	Couplet	Synonymous	6:6	1:1

Vv 16–17:

16	Triplet	Synthetic	7:7:7	1:1:1
17a	Couplet	Synthetic	10:8	1:1
17b	Couplet	Synonymous	11:11	1:1

(In 16a it is assumed that לכן הנה is introductory to the poetic portion and thus an anacrusis which should not be counted metrically.)

There is no significance to the fact that three times a triplet is followed by two couplets in these verses. Triplets and couplets vary freely and unpredictably in Hebrew poetry; the particular pattern discernible here is coincidental.

The passage reflects an economic prosperity in Israel, as future deprivation is contrasted to present abundance (vv 5, 7, 10, 11, 15). It also presupposes the existence of a thriving Baalist fertility cult (vv 7, 10, 15) alongside the official Yahwistic cult with its holy days widely observed (vv 13, 15). The passage mentions no threats to peace and prosperity either internally from civil strife, or externally from Assyria or other foreign powers.

These conditions would perhaps coincide with the early period of Hosea's ministry, in the final "golden" years of the reign of Jeroboam II (i.e., about 760–755 B.C.) prior to the economic and political reversals brought on by the first western campaign of the Assyrians under Tiglath-Pileser III. The affinities between the imagery of this passage, which speaks of the breaking of the covenant in terms of divorce, and the imagery of 1:2–9, where the covenant is portrayed as broken in the various names, may also be considered evidence of the relatively early date.

The passage is not easily divisible into smaller units, since these would be fragmentary and dependent on the overall context for their meaning. It is not impossible that some material from what were once separate oracles were combined by Hosea to make the single unified allegorical passage. It would be difficult to imagine, however, that the passage could be non-Hoseanic. It is unlikely that an editor could have been responsible for so complex and interwoven an allegory, with its many subtle connections to other parts of the book.

Comment

4 [2] The court scene opens with the aggrieved husband and father (Yahweh) speaking as plaintiff before the court at first addressing his children.

His remarks move from accusation to admonition. He asks the children to bring the accusation against their mother in support of his own lawsuit against her. This device of artistic license in the allegory requires the reader / hearer to understand a distinction between corporate Israel as the prostituting wife, and at least certain of her children, or citizens.

The bluntness and repetition of the imperative (ריבו "make an accusation") suggest that the children are "hostile witnesses." The allegory does not concern itself with exceptions to the general wickedness. The picture described is not that of good children voluntarily siding with their wronged father against their unfaithful mother; children and mother are one, and their own individual actions and attitudes, ranging from complacency (v 10) to idolatry (v 15), will constitute damning testimony as they speak.

Würthwein has demonstrated that a basic meaning of ריב is to accuse (*ZTK* 49 [1952] 4). Its use here with the preposition ב "against" surely conforms to this basic sense. The specific content of the legal accusation made via the children is that the marriage between the plaintiff (Yahweh) and his wife (Israel) is nullified. Many commentators have taken the words "She is not my wife and I am not her husband" to represent some sort of Israelite legal divorce formula. There is, however, no sure evidence to support this otherwise reasonable conjecture. The issue of divorce is at any rate secondary to the main point of the allegory. This is more a trial for adultery than divorce. As the passage continues it will be obvious that divorce is merely one of the punishments that the unfaithful Israel must endure, and is not the sole purpose of the lawsuit. The purpose of the legal action is both corrective and restorative. Ultimately, the plaintiff does not so much seek a divorce as a chastened wife. It is in this more general sense that the children's testimony makes sense. Their accusation relates to a *fait accompli:* Israel's unfaithfulness has wrought havoc with the covenant. The essence of the legal case is Israel's adulterous "prostitution" which is in evidence already in v 4 [2].

In the admonition of v 4b [2b] the plaintiff wants his wife to take the first, most basic step of reform—to change her outward appearance. The words זנוניה and נאפופיה, being abstract plurals, are ambiguous. They could mean simply "her prostituting" and "her adultery" respectively, but the context suggests that they refer also to the makeup and / or jewelry worn on face and torso by a prostitute. The possibility that these terms have their referent in the amulets worn by women in Baal worship is intriguing, though we have no actual confirmation of such worship attire.

The husband speaks of his wife only in the third person. This need not reflect enmity per se, but is probably an aspect of the legal style, in which the court and the witnesses are addressed, but not the defendant.

5 [3] From accusation and admonition the discourse now moves directly to a threat, a legal ultimatum. Yahweh's role is now that of judge, with power to carry out the foregone sentence of "guilty." If Israel will not remove her outward signs of unfaithfulness, he will remove her clothing, food and water so that she dies exposed. In the first half of the verse Israel was the wife; now she is the land (not merely a people who will be brought back into the wilderness, *contra* Freedman and Andersen, 226).

It was the legal responsibility of a husband to provide food, clothing and marital rights for his wife (Exod 21:10). Israel's unfaithfulness has violated the responsibility for the marital rights; now even the food and clothing will be taken away. Here the parallels to Ezek 16 are strong. At birth, Israel was a helpless abandoned infant, on whom Yahweh graciously bestowed his loving protection. Now in her maturity, she has forgotten his love and openly cheated on him. But though she does not realize it, she has been utterly dependent on him all along, and he can quickly return her to helplessness by abandoning her (cf. vv 6 [4], 8 [6], 10–14 [8–12]).

The threat to strip Israel naked (v 5a [3a], גלה, cf. v 12 [10]) recalls the curse language of a number of ancient Near Eastern treaties, wherein to be stripped naked like a prostitute is one metaphor of the punishment for breaking a treaty covenant (cf. Hillers, *Treaty Curses,* 58–59). Beyond this, the language may also derive from a purposeful ironical use of some of the elements of the Baal cult. The Canaanites and their many Israelite converts regarded the land as the female, which was fertilized by the rain (sperm) of Baal, who as the god of weather was *par excellence* the god of fertility. Hosea turns this imagery against the Israelite Baalists. The land in fact owes its fertility only to Yahweh. Baal is sterile!

The normal punishment for adultery in ancient Israel was either burning (Gen 38:24; Lev 21:9) or stoning (Deut 22:23–24). These are not mentioned at all in the passage, because the several punishments that are described relate primarily to Israel as a land: exile (curse type 13); desolation (type 9c); drought (type 6a); and death (type 24).

6 [4] The judge, Yahweh, cannot hold the children, Israel's citizenry, guiltless. They, too, are prostituting. The term בני זנונים "prostituting children" is parallel to the ילדי זנונים of 1:2 which it recalls. It does not mean that they are the "offspring of a prostitute," but that they share the promiscuous unfaithfulness of a prostitute.

The children, like the mother, are now referred to in the third person and are thus included in the indictment. They have no more testimony to give. The testimony or evidence is now directed against them.

Yahweh's judgment recalls the threat of 1:6 employing the same imperfect verb form, ארחם "have compassion," further evidence of how closely chaps. 1 and 2 are interdependent. Withdrawal of compassion is a punishment based on curse type 1 (anger / rejection; cf. Lev 26:24, Deut 32:19).

7 [5] Now the mother again represents the nation, and her own words, quoted as testimony, condemn her. She determinedly "chased" (אלכה, cohortative) her lovers rather than waiting for them to come to her as a prostitute normally would (Gen 38:14–18; Jer 3:2).

Her "lovers" (מאהבי) are, of course, the Baals. While perhaps not officially sanctioned by Jeroboam II, Baal worship was freely tolerated so that it flourished among the populace in a syncretism with Yahwism. Israel's calling the Baals "lovers" is a metaphor first attested in Hosea, and otherwise only in Jeremiah and Ezekiel, where it also refers to rivals of Yahweh for Israel's allegiance. The piel participle מאהבים is probably not indicative of an especially passionate sense (*contra* Wolff, 35) but represents only a synonymous alternative to the qal. Attraction to "lovers" (other gods) directly parallels the notion of political / military attraction to other national powers (*pace* Thompson, *VT* 27 [1977] 475–81).

The metaphor shifts again to represent the wife / mother as the people of the nation, whose agricultural bounty constitutes the prostitute's wages. The parallel terms employed include main areas of life: bread and water; wool and flax; oil and drink. In Ugaritic poetry, similarly, *lḥm* "bread" is often paired with *šqy* "drink"; *mym* "water" with *šmn* "oil" (cf. Kuhningk, *NSH* 11–13). The pairings in Hosea need not be understood to break up and recreate traditional fixed pairs (so Kuhningk) but rather may reflect an alternative tradition.

Israel's covenant prostitution (זנתה) is shameful (הבישה). Verse 7 [5] thus prepares the way for the punishment announced in v 8 [6].

8 [6] "Therefore" (לכן), often used by the prophets to introduce imminent divine actions, here signals the first of three formal sentences that Yahweh, the judge, hands down against Israel for her prostituting adultery.

The next word, הנני, is coupled with a participle, as here, 124 other times in the OT. In 117 such combinations the speaker is God, announcing a threat or promise. Hosea's audience could thus probably anticipate what was coming: God's response to Israel's sin.

By another shift of metaphor, the punishment will be that applied to a dumb animal who tends to wander off from its owner (cf. 4:16; 8:9; Jer 2:23–25). Israel will be restrained like a cow, sheep or donkey—hedged and walled in—so that she cannot find the paths she was accustomed to taking. Such a picture of a rebellious animal also parallels Deut 32:15 and Hos 4:16 (and cf. the motif of restraint in 3:3–4). The increasing Assyrian domination of the north following Tiglath-Pileser's first western campaign in 748 B.C., the destruction of Samaria in 722, the exile, and the subsequent subjugation to other nations thereafter all in part fulfill this prediction of restraint.

Confinement might seem a merciful punishment, but the real point of the allegory is a prediction of captivity and exile (curse type 13; cf. Lev 26:33–34 et al), the fate of a defeated, decimated nation (Deut 28:62–68).

9 [7] Though determinedly seeking (רדף) the Baals, the promiscuous wife Israel will be consistently thwarted. Only then will she recognize that her only hope is Yahweh. The verb שוב "return" here expresses repentance, hence conversion (cf. Amos 4:6, et al; Isa 21:12; Zech 1:3; etc.). It is also the standard verb for return from exile (Jer 30:3, 10; Amos 9:14; Isa 10:21, 22; etc.), and that sense may also be present, as in Deut 4:29–30, where רדף and שוב similarly occur together.

In her own words (cf. v 7 [5]) Israel predicts her future actions. She will decide to return to אישי הראשון "my first man / husband." This does not necessarily imply that she has actually divorced her husband and married someone else. Remarriage to her first husband would have been a violation of the covenant (Deut 24:1–3). Rather, she is to be reconciled to her "original husband" after being denied access to those with whom she had her affairs. "Then" (אז) when "things were better for me" can only refer to Israel's early, formative days, including the wilderness period following the exile (cf. 11:1–3). The intimacy Yahweh and his people knew can be restored as it was before the arrival in Canaan.

The Israelites felt no urgency to return to Yahweh as long as he blessed them with plenty. So he must deprive them severely. They will be driven by their loneliness and misery back to him (Deut 4:30). With its quotation of Israel's future attitude, v 9 [7] provides the first clear evidence in the passage that Yahweh's covenant lawsuit will succeed not only in its proximate goal of punishment, but in its ultimate goal of reconciliation.

10 [8] More evidence against the unfaithful wife is revealed: she is foolish, thoughtless, and forgetful. She forgets what her divine husband has provided her with, and manages in her twisted reasoning to attribute his provisions to Baal.

To deny that the yearly harvests were a gift of Yahweh (cf. the confession in Deut 26:5–10) was to deny that Yahweh was still Israel's God—a rejection of Yahweh's lordship, an implicit violation of the decalogue's first commandment.

The covenant allusions of the verse are evidenced in the use of the three words דָּגָן, תִּירוֹשׁ, and יִצְהָר, "grain, wine, and olive oil." These three words occur in Deut 7:13; 11:14; 12:17; 14:23; 18:4; and 28:51 (cf. the Ugaritic text Keret C, iii) as a synecdoche for the full range of agricultural blessings given by Yahweh. The forgetful wife, Israel, is attributing the plenteous harvests of the final years of Jeroboam II's reign directly to the powers of the fertility god, Baal.

And she goes further. She credits Baal with the general commercial prosperity of those days, as symbolized in the "silver and gold" which flowed to the coffers of the upper classes—the nobility, royalty, urban bourgeoisie—who since the time of Solomon had most embraced Canaanite Baal religion (cf. Bright, *History of Israel*, 241–48). Baalism was not protective of social justice as was Yahwism. Thus once the greedy had embraced Baal worship, wealth was easier to attain.

Precious metals came as the influx mainly from trading and tariffs rather than mining *per se*, and were used (עָשׂוּ) selfishly to buy the kind of luxuries Israel's neighbors had: fine houses, large land holdings, etc. Yahweh had generously bestowed true wealth on an undeserving nation as evidence of his grace (Deut 28:1–12), and the adulterous nation, finding her lovers so much more attractive than Yahweh, had credited it to their account rather than his.

11 [9] The second judgment sentence, characterized by reversals, begins here and continues through v 15a [13a] with first-person verbs expressing the judge's decisions. What Israel had in abundance will be snatched away; her relationship to her lovers will change from delight to shame; her festivities will cease; her arable lands will be overgrown. V 11 [9] deals specifically with grain and wine, wool and flax, in the reverse order of their appearance in the foregoing verses (grain and wine in v 10 [8]; wool and flax in v 7 [5]). Yahweh gave those things, and Israel sinned the more. Now he will withdraw them, fulfilling curse types 6 and 7 (agricultural disaster and famine). The Baal fertility cult is thereby implicitly excoriated, for it in fact cannot bring fertility or prevent infertility. The "time" and "season" refer to the point of ripeness, when everyone anxiously awaits the approaching harvest. But the harvest was to be disastrous. The Northern Kingdom's fortunes rapidly deteriorated in the chaotic years after 748 B.C. Especially after the Assyrian conquests of 722, Israel found itself in full economic distress. Foreign military and economic conquest so disrupted the agrarian economy that there could be no bounteous harvest for a long time (cf. Lev 26:34).

Ancient Near Eastern marriage laws provided that an unfaithful wife could be cast out of the house by her husband, without support (cf. Code of Hammurabi, 141). This was Yahweh's intent toward Israel. He was no longer obligated by the duty to feed and clothe his wife ("cover her nakedness"), because she had shown herself no longer worthy of decent treatment.

12 [10] The metaphor shifts from land to wife: stripping the land is stripping the wife. Yahweh is completely in charge: the naked wife will get no protection from the former lovers, who have no ability to help her, she now will learn. Her lovers can only stand and gawk at her—intervention against Yahweh is impossible. The proclamation "No one can rescue her from me" (אִישׁ לֹא יַצִּילֶנָּה מִיָּדִי) reflects the language of judgment in the covenant curses of Deut 32:39: "no one can rescue from me" (אֵין מִיָּדִי מַצִּיל).

Her "folly" (נַבְלוּתָה) is a metonymy for her nakedness, and perhaps even genitalia. Israel will be shamed and disgraced openly. The use of the verb גלה, with its dual meaning of "reveal" and "exile," suggest the coming time when Israel, forsaken by Yahweh, will be gawked at as she is led to exile, her people naked in the manner of exiles, all because of disloyalty to Yahweh's covenant (cf. the captivity / exile curses in Lev 26:33, Deut 4:27; 28:36, et al).

13 [11] The metaphor now shifts to the festivals. These were a source of Israel's rejoicing, basic to the nation's sense of identity in the prosperous last days of the Jehu dynasty. The use of the feminine singular possessive suffix with each of the nouns referring to festivals may be a means of stressing that these were *Israel's*, but that Yahweh had nothing to do with them.

The holidays, listed in ascending order of frequency but descending order of importance, were especially disgusting because they provided the occasion for the bulk of the Baal worship. The "feast" (חג) was any of the three yearly agricultural / historical festivals characterized by nationwide visitation of the sanctuary for worship (Exod 23:14–17; 34:18–23). The "new moon" (חדש; Num 28:11–15) was probably an occasion of fertility practices though there is no direct evidence for this. It at least involved worship and prophetic consultations (cf. H. H. Rowley, *Worship in Ancient Israel* [London: SPCK, 1967] 90–91). The Sabbath (שבת) was originally simply the day of rest (Exod 23:12; 34:21) but from Amos 8:5 we learn that in the time of Jeroboam II it was apparently included as a feast day, like the new moon (cf. Isa 1:13; 2 Kgs 4:23).

Though these holidays were in their origin legitimate, they had been turned into "days of Baal" (v 15 [13]) by Israel, thus syncretistic in nature. Accordingly Yahweh announces that he will destroy the covenant calendar he himself had revealed. What could interrupt such traditions? The end of the nation as a sovereign state, off its land and in bondage. The covenantal curse predicting the rejection of the cult (Lev 26:31) was now to be enforced.

14 [12] V 14 [12] follows logically on v 13 [11], inasmuch as figs and grapes (wine) figured prominently as festivals food. These crops were often grown together (cf. Luke 13:6) and harvested at about the same time (Mic 7:1) in the early fall, prior to the feast of Tabernacles. The agricultural curse that

". . . your soil will not yield its crops, nor will the trees of the land yield their fruits" (Lev 26:20; cf. Deut 28:39, 40) most closely describes the fate Hosea presents poetically here. Without wine and figs there could be neither festivals (especially Tabernacles) nor prosperity of the kind enjoyed during Jeroboam II's reign.

A prostitute's fee was אתנן. Hosea uses אתנה, possibly an invented term intended as an anagram of תאנה "fig tree." A prostitute's fee could not pay a vow at the temple, being money earned from a detestable practice (Deut 23:19 [18]). The verse thus implies that the produce from the vines and fig trees was tainted wealth, because it came via the generosity of Baals as Israel saw it and thus was the result of "prostitution."

What Israel believed to represent the gifts of her lovers will now be turned to wilderness or devoured—displaying again the impotence of the Baals and fulfilling both the desolation curses (type 9c) and the wild animal curses (type 11) of the Sinai covenant.

15a [13a] The second judgment sentence concludes with a summary of Israel's punishment, the sweeping "general" curses (type 26; cf. Lev 26:41; et al.) and the cause—Baal worship.

The use of פקד, here "take to task" with its object "the days of the Baals," recalls its use with the object "the bloodshed of Jezreel" in 1:3. Events so heinous require severe punishment.

In its most basic sense, the word בעל meant simply "lord," i.e., the lord or deity of any of a number of local cults attested in the OT: Baal / Lord of Peor (Num 25:3), Baal / Lord of Hermon (Judg 3:3), Baal / Lord-Berith or Baal / Lord of the Covenant (Judg 8:33), Baal / Lord of Samaria (1 Kgs 16:32), Baal / Lord of Carmel (1 Kgs 18:19–40), Baal / Lord of Ekron (2 Kgs 1:2–4), etc. Here, however, Hosea uses בעלים "Baals" in the plural (cf. 2:18 [16]; 11:2).

The picture of Baalism here comports with that of the Ugaritic myths, which portray a variety of characteristics, sometimes conflicting, within one deity. The Canaanites and their many Israelite converts may have held a variety of theologies, but all recognized the two essential functions of Baal: divine lordship and production of fertility. When various "lovers" at a plurality of shrines were envisaged, "the Baals" were spoken of. Otherwise, the singular, "Baal," was routinely employed.

The "days of the Baals" are the same festival days described in v 13 [11]. Hosea uses the verb קטר, hiphil, here even though the piel is more often used in reference to pagan burnt offerings. Nevertheless, Hosea's meaning is entirely clear: Israel was engaged in *pagan* worship.

15b [13b] Now resumes the metaphor of the promiscuous prostitute, bedecked for seduction, chasing after lovers (see vv 4 [2] and 7–8 [5–6]), her stubborn attitude a complement to her behavior.

The reference to rings and jewelry may indicate cultic practice. Exod 32:2 ff. specifically mentions the נזם "earring" in connection with the golden calf worship, and the חליה "jewelry" may also have recalled some aspect of Baal worship.

Israel forgot Yahweh: that is the essence of the indictment. How can she remain his wife if she doesn't even remember that she is married to him? In 4:6 and 13:4–6 שכח "to forget" functions as a precise antonym of the covenantally important verb יָדַע "to know." Thus Israel's forgetting placed her outside the covenant.

"Oracle of Yahweh" (נְאֻם יְהוָה) identifies that Yahweh is being quoted by the passage but does not necessarily mark the end of a section; it can in fact introduce an oracle (2:18 [16]) or occur somewhat unpredictably in the middle of an oracle (2:23 [21]) (cf. North, *JBL* 71 [1952] x, and Baumgärtel, *ZAW* 73 [1961] 277–90).

16 [14] A third and final time, לָכֵן "therefore" introduces the judge's sentence. Surprisingly, it is restoration!

Yahweh has decided to appeal anew to his wayward bride, starting over with her in response to her willingness to return (v 9 [7]; cf. Deut 30:2, 3). The wilderness was where she was dependent on and relatively faithful to him after they were newly "married" in the covenant at Sinai (cf. 13:4–6) so there they will return, symbolically.

The language is passionate. "Seduce" (מְפַתֶּיהָ) means to romance, entice, allure (cf. Exod 22:5 [16]; Hos 7:11). To "romance her" (דִּבֶּר עַל לִבָּהּ) is a tender expression, used of courtship (Gen 34:3) and winning back love (Judg 19:3), and also kind, considerate favor not necessarily involving romantic intentions (Ruth 2:13).

Logically, this new relationship initiated by Yahweh in vv 16–17 reflects a time *after* the substantial punishments represented in the previous verses are complete. The focus is eschatological. After destruction and exile, a remnant of northern Israel will still have a future. The wronged husband never had in mind utterly, permanently, to abandon his wife. After she has learned her lesson, he will love her again as the covenant promises (Deut 4:31).

17 [15] From the pattern of other speeches in this passage, we might expect the wife's response to be given in her own words (cf. vv 7 [5], 9 [7], 13 [11]). Instead, the passage ends with Yahweh's own prediction of Israel's response. In the restoration, he will transform her into the kind of wife she had failed to be in the past (cf. Deut 30:6).

The final verse recalls in detail the original wilderness and conquest experience that constituted the basic foundational experience of Israel. Two themes from Israel's wilderness experience are selected to represent the recollection of those days. (1) The gift of the land is alluded to in the promise to give Israel back "her vineyards from there" (cf. Josh 24:13). (2) "Trouble Valley" (the Valley of Achor), the notorious site of holy war disobedience (Josh 7, esp. v 24), was probably the plain leading into the central hill country from the Jordan lowlands southwest of Jericho. (See F. M. Cross and J. T. Milik, "Explorations in the Judean Buqe'ah," *BASOR* 142 [1956] 5–17. The exact location is still disputed; see Wolff, 42–43.) This valley, a source of disappointment early in the conquest, would now be a gateway of hope.

Israel will now "respond" (עָנָה) just as she did the first time. עָנָה sums up the range of positive relationships and actions (see vv 23–24 [21–22]) which follow God's salvation. Things will thus be as they were during the exodus from Egypt, the original situation being repeated in the eschatological situation. Israel had foolishly chosen to depend upon the Baals; now she will learn to depend only on Yahweh, and the Baals will be nothing to her— as it was before she ever knew them. The Pentateuchal restoration promise that eschatological Israel would again benefit from the blessings given that

first generation in the original Sinai covenant (Lev 26:45), including "ownership" by Yahweh ("I will be their God"), will be fulfilled

Explanation

The betrayed husband will punish his wife for her infidelity with lovers
whose powers of fertility are an illusion. But after punishing her, he will
restore her to himself, for he has never ceased to love her. Thus are woven
together a warning and an appeal, law and gospel, in an invitation to the
nation of Israel viewed as a continuum in history. Yahweh calls his wayward
people eventually back to himself, to things as they were centuries prior.

Though the passage is an allegory, its portrayal of God as other than
cold and dispassionate is surely a biblical theme. God's attitude toward his
people and his world in both testaments is love—which though surely a matter
of behavior and relationship, still involves the essence of an emotion. The
Bible never attributes to God an emotionalism or the sort of passions that
could be called human, but in God's compassionate *agape* for this lost world
(John 3:16), there is the presence of what, in human terms and on human
analogy, at least, is an emotional fervor.

If God were to become a man, would he be rigid, unmoved, dispassionate,
ever "proper" and distant? The answer to that question is already known.
Hosea thus presents a metaphorical picture that has some referents in Christ
himself.

Later in the book, God asks, "What will I do with you, Ephraim?" (6:4).
Hos 2:4–17 [2–15] may in one sense be considered an answer to that question.
The answer takes two forms—one proximate, the other ultimate.

The proximate result of Israel's promiscuity will be punishment fitting
the crime—rejection, deprivation, and exile. The ultimate result, on the other
hand, is reconciliation. The key to a proper appreciation of the relationship
of these two results is to see them in their logical or chronological order. It
is not until Israel has learned her lesson—been taken to task—that she will
be able to respond properly to her Lord's alluring love. Not until she has
suffered for her double iniquity (10:10; cf. Isa 40:2) can pardon, closeness,
and the original relationship be restored.

In this allegory, Yahweh "courts" Israel in two senses. He takes Israel to
court in the accusation of a crime—adultery. But as the passage unfolds, it
is clear virtually from the outset (v 5 [3]) that the actual purpose will be to
"court" Israel in the sense of inviting her back to faithfulness after she has
done penance for her sin. Yahweh will never lose his beloved nation. He
will renew it. Playing all the decisive roles, judge, jury, prosecutor, police,
he can put an end to her promiscuity by seeing that Israel, collectively and
individually, is taken from her lovers and made chaste again. The legal metaphor thus stands alongside the love parable. Yahweh will indict and convict
as the evidence dictates. But after serving her sentence, Israel has hope for
the distant future even more glorious than was the distant past. That future
is not to be fulfilled until after a sentence of exile and debasement. It will
be truly fulfilled only in a new age, one we know to have been ushered in
by Christ (Rom 11:28–32).

Images of Restoration   (2:18–25 [16–23])

Bibliography

Albright, W. F. *Yahweh and the Gods of Canaan.* Garden City, NY: Doubleday, 1968.
Baumgartner, W. "Kennen Amos und Hosea eine Heilseschatologie?" *Schweizerische Theologische Zeitschrift* 30 (1913) 40–42, 95–124, 152–70. Bright, J. "The Future in the Theology of Eighth-Century Prophets: The Beginnings of Eschatology." Chap. 3 in *Covenant and Promise.* Philadelphia: Westminster Press, 1976. Childs, B. S. *Memory and Tradition in Israel.* SBT 37. Naperville, IL: Allenson, 1962. Devescovi, U. "La nuova alleanza in Osea." BibOr 1 (1959) 172–78. Driver, G. R. "Problems and Solutions." VT 4 (1954) 225–45. Huffmon, H. "The Treaty Background of Hebrew YĀDAᶜ." *BASOR* 181 (1966) 131–77.

Translation

18 [16] *In that day* [a] *(oracle of Yahweh),*
    You will call me [b] *"my husband."*
    You will no longer call me [a] *"my Baal."* [b]

19 [17] *I will remove the names of the Baals from her mouth.*
    They will no longer be mentioned by name. [a]

20 [18] *I will make a covenant for them in that day,*
    With the animals of the field, with the birds of the sky, and the creeping things on the ground.

    Bow, sword—warfare [a] *—I will destroy from the earth,*
    And I will settle them securely.

21 [19] *I will betroth you to me forever.*
    I will betroth you to me with rightness, with justice, with loyalty, and with compassion.

22 [20] *I will betroth you to me with faithfulness, and you will know* [a] *Yahweh.*

23 [21] *In that day, I will respond* [a] *(oracle of Yahweh).*
    I will respond to the sky, and it will respond to the earth.

24 [22] *The earth will respond to the grain, the fruit-of-the-vine, and the olive oil;*
    And they will respond to Jezreel.

25 [23] *I will sow her* [a] *for me in the land,*
    I will have compassion on No Compassion,

    I will say to Not My People, "You are my people,"
    And he will say "My God." [b]

Notes

18.a. Or "In the future. . . ." ביום ההוא contrasts to the common היום הזה / ב "today / now." As Hosea uses the expression it can refer to the proximate future (1:5) or the eschatological future (2:18, 20, 23).
18.b. G has καλέσει (3 sg) "she will call," as do Syr and Vg. α′ σ′ θ′ show harmonization toward the MT. It is impossible to decide whether the 2 f sg or 3 f sg is original. The suff of

the MT may reflect an original object suff, which in poetry can (rarely) take the form of the poss suff: "She will call me." At any rate, "me" is understood, whether explicit or not.

18.b. Or "my husband/lord." בעל is triply ambiguous, and this ambiguity is played on here. G has the pl transliteration (βααλιμ), presumably a harmonization with 2:15 and 2:19, but disruptive of the parallelism.

19.a. Lit., "their name." G has "their names" (τὰ ὀνόματα αὐτῶν), a simple translational accommodation.

20.a. Warfare (מלחמה) is the general term, encompassing and summarizing the prior two. Here only the first three elements of the chiasm are retained from 1:7. It is not a metonymy for "weapons of war" contra Wolff, Mays, et al.

22.a. Vg, many MT MSS, and Cyril of Alexandria read כי אני יהוה, "(you will know) that I am Yahweh." This is at least plausible in the context, as the MT could have been affected by haplogr, but does violence to the probable metaphor intended. See Comment.

23.a. Or "sing / answer / speak up"; see Explanation. G uses ἐπακούω "listen / respond / obey" for ענה here, a word it does not otherwise use to translate ענה. The exceptional translation is entirely justified by the context, however, where ענה means other than simply "answer."

25.a. It is not clear what "her" refers to. If it refers narrowly to Jezreel, the immediate antecedent, an emendation to "him" (זה־) would be required by precise grammar.

25.b. G reads κύριος ὁ θεός μου εἶ σύ "you are Yahweh my God." This is probably an expansion, but the MT may also be haplographic.

Form / Structure / Setting

While 2:4–25 constitutes a relatively unified, compound-complex oracle, vv 18–25 may be treated as a separate pericope, a series of sayings, in free verse, which elaborate on the nature of the faithful relationship between Israel and Yahweh in the restoration. This same period is described in 2:17, and the verb ענה "respond" again expresses the relationships of Yahweh, Israel and the land (vv 23–24), unmistakably reminiscent of the bride's response (וענתה) in v 17.

The primary basis for separating vv 18–25 from vv 4–17 is that the court lawsuit form is no longer in evidence. Nevertheless, the passage mirrors closely the words and themes of the preceding pericopes in the book. Specifically, vv 18–25 may be considered an expansion on the "ultimate judgment" expressed in the previous passage. Orthodoxy, security, an eternal relationship unmarred by faithlessness, agricultural bounty, general harmony, and the direct attention of God will constitute the conditions of the restoration.

Though the scenes shift rapidly, the subject matter itself remains the same: images of restoration. The pronouns used to refer to Israel also shift rather rapidly (you [fem sg], v 18; her, v 19; them [masc / fem pl] v 20; you [fem sg], vv 21–22; her, v 23), but Yahweh is always the speaker. As in vv 4–17, he dominates the action, removing heterodoxy, instituting his new covenant, betrothing Israel to himself, ensuring fertility, welcoming the prodigal home— all according to the predictions of the new age in the Mosaic covenantal sanctions. The consistency of Yahweh as speaker and the repetition of "in that day" (ביום ההוא) provide a structural unity for the passage.

The names of Hosea's children are skillfully woven into the end of the passage to form its climax. This is the third time they appear. The pivotal agent of the various responses is "Jezreel." By means of "sowing" (both "Jezreel" and "I will sow" are based on the root זרע) Yahweh will restore compassion to No Compassion and peoplehood to Not My People.

Because chap. 3, a prose narrative following up the first marriage of 1:2–3, is unrelated, the terminus of the pericope under consideration must be v 25.

It is difficult to specify a setting for this passage, a salvation oracle, since such oracles can rarely be related to specific events or circumstances. In that the passage contains the names of Hosea's children in a new light, its composition must have followed the original naming. If, as we have argued, the births recorded in chap. 1 took place over a period of at least five years, this prophecy must have followed the onset of Hosea's public ministry by at least that period. A considerably later date is not required in light of the close connections with 2:4–17. The covenantal pattern of sin-punishment-restoration was already set at Sinai (Deut 4:25–31) and thus somewhat "timeless." If, however, this oracle was composed as a comfort to the orthodox among Hosea's audience, a timing around 733 B.C. is possible to imagine. Then, Tiglath-Pileser III had defeated the northern kingdom in settling the Syro-Ephraimite war, and had annexed most of the north except for the Ephraimite hill country. The kind of agricultural prosperity gloriously portrayed in vv 18–25 is only a memory.

But all of this is merely speculation. God knew Israel's immediate and ultimate future. Exactly when he chose to reveal through Hosea the truths contained in 2:4–25 is not clear. However, the close connections of the vocabulary and, in general, the subject matter of these verses with so many other parts of the book disallows any attempt to deny them to Hosea as genuine.

Comment

18 [16]   The formula ביום ההוא (lit., "in that day"; cf. 1:5; 2:20 [18], 23 [21]) is eschatological, not synonymous with the "Day of the Lord" (יום יהוה) concept attested in Amos, Joel, Zechariah and others of the prophets. As Hosea uses it, it is a synonym for "in the future" (1:5) or "in the coming new age" (here and 2:20 [18], 23 [21]). There is no hint that it describes a period of change to be expected in the lifetime of Hosea's audience.

"Oracle of Yahweh" (נאם יהוה) is used here, as elsewhere, essentially parenthetically, to inform the reader/hearer that God is being quoted directly (cf. 2:15 [13]; 11:11), thus emphasizing the authority behind the prophet's words.

This verse describes a future time when Israel, Yahweh's bride, will call him only איש and never again בעל. Both of these words can mean "husband," איש referring to husband as "man" in the sense of marriage partner, and בעל connoting more the lordship, ownership, and legal right of the husband in relation to a wife ("master"). The point of this oracle is based, however, not on that distinction, but on the fact that בעל means "Baal," the god, as well as "husband, lord, master." Israelites in the new age of restoration will simply never use the word בעל in *any* of its meanings. Baal worship will not exist, *a fortiore*, because even the very word בעל will be unknown (v 19 [17]).

It is not necessary to presuppose as referent for those words a syncretism in which Yahweh was worshiped as Baal and thus called "Baal." Such a Yahweh-Baal syncretism may or may not have existed (cf. Wolff, 49–50). The fact is that the words בעל and יהוה are frequently found in juxtaposition in OT names. The Samaria Ostraca may reflect the old neutral meaning of בעל as "lord." Thus a name like בעליה, Baaliah (1 Chr 12:6) could mean simply "Yahweh is lord" rather than "Baal-Yahweh" or "Yahweh is Baal." In the new age as described by our passage, however, the very idea of a Baal-Yahweh syncretism would be impossible. The divine establishment of religious purity into the soul of the nation will represent a fulfillment of the renewal blessings of the Sinai covenant (Deut 4:30; 30:6, 8; type 3), as also widely reflected elsewhere in the prophets (e.g. Jer 31:33–34; Zeph 3:9).

19 [17] Though Israel is now spoken of in the third person, the speaker is still Yahweh and the subject matter is the same. They (the pronoun refers to the Baals, not unnamed Israelites) will not be mentioned any more. The second sentence could as well be translated: "Their names will no longer be remembered." The verb זכר "remember, mention" in the qal / niphal has the sort of ambiguity favored by Hosea. At once, the prophecy describes the elimination of invocation of the Baals, and the act of forgetting all about them. The more common term for invoking a god, קרא בשם "call on the name of" lacks the rich ambiguity so useful in the present metaphor.

Thus will come to pass the uncompromising worship of Yahweh wherein only *his* name is mentioned / invoked in worship. This in fact had always been required of Israel as Exod 23:13b specifies: "You shall not mention / invoke (זכר, hiphil) the names of other gods. They shall not be heard from your mouth." To "mention" (qal) or "invoke" (hiphil) the name of a god was to worship or summon the god for some religious purpose. When the Baal cult has been eliminated from Israel (2:8–9 [6–7], 13–15 [11–13]) and forgotten, only Yahweh's name will be involved in worship, and the restoration of the true covenant relationship will have taken place.

20 [18] The oracle predicts two parallel restoration blessings: freedom from harm via the animal kingdom because of Yahweh's covenant with fauna, and freedom from harm via humans as exemplified by a secure life free from any threat of war. Both blessings are reversals of curses (types 11 and 3 respectively) and are manifestations of the general restoration blessing of covenant renewal (type 2, as in Lev 26:45 and Deut 4:31). The term ביום ההוא "in that day" again emphasizes that the events described are eschatological.

"To make a covenant" (כרת ברית) is usually understood in terms of international treaty-covenants, and this usage does occur in 10:4 and 12:2 [1]. Here, however, the covenant is not made with other nations, but with other aspects of creation. The threats of 2:4–17 [2–15] no longer will apply in the new age. Wild animals, birds, and insects will not devour the vineyards or crops (2:14 [12]); and exile and deprivation (via, e.g., war) will not threaten the populace (cf. 2:5 [3], 15 [13]). The covenant is thus not made *with* God's people, but is imposed *on behalf of* God's people on all living creatures, with peace as a purpose. In all likelihood, a people more numerous than ethnic Israel per se is envisioned as benefiting from this covenant, as the contextual ambiguity of the word להם "for them" suggests. Hosea has already prophesied the existence of a new kind of Israel, very different from the one he knew in the eighth century B.C. (2:1–3 [1:10–2:1]).

The three groups of living creatures are given in their precise order from the Gen 1 creation account (Gen 1:30). Ezekiel (38:20) also employs this particular Genesis account language, in the context (38:17–23) of a threat to all creation (cf. also Jer 15:3). Here it is the *absence* of such a threat that is predicted.

In ancient Near Eastern treaties, attacks from wild animals and destruction from war were two prominent motifs employed in the curse-threats appended to the treaty stipulations (see D. R. Hillers, *Treaty-Curses*, 54–56). Such curse-threats are now removed.

21–22 [19–20] These two verses form a unit, the verse division being an obtrusive one. As Yahweh addresses his beloved directly, the metaphor shifts to marriage betrothal, bringing full circle the allegorical theme begun in 2:4. The emphasis is now not merely reconciliation but restoration. The old marriage has been annulled. The new marriage will have the qualities the old lacked: fairness, justice, loyalty, mercy, honesty and above all, permanence (לְעוֹלָם "forever").

The betrothal metaphor is expressed dramatically via the decisive threefold repetition of the verb אָרַשׂ "to betroth" in the first person common singular form. Such repetition, even in this free verse context, recalls ancient premonarchic poetic style (see W. F. Albright, *Yahweh and the Gods of Canaan*, 1–52).

The verb אָרַשׂ (piel) refers to the ancient Israelite practice of settling the marriage contractually by the groom's payment of the bride-price to the bride's father. This was the final step in the courtship process, virtually equivalent in legal status to the wedding ceremony. After the betrothal, cohabitation would follow at an arranged time.

Several OT legal texts imply that a woman betrothed was as good as married in the eyes of the law (e.g., Deut 20:7; 22:23–29; Exod 22:16–17). David's betrothal to Michal is equated in his speech to marriage (2 Sam 3:14; cf. 1 Sam 18:25).

A rich ambiguity attends the five occurrences of the preposition with the descriptions of the qualities the marriage will have. The words of Yahweh can mean that he will betroth Israel to him *with* or *by means of* rightness, justice, etc., in the sense that these qualities can denote the bride price of this marriage. David betrothed Michal *with* (בְּ) promises of blessing. Playing a dual role, Yahweh pays *himself* the bride price, as Israel's husband and father.

On the other hand, בְּ can also indicate accompaniment: i.e., these blessings will accompany the marriage, characterizing both Israel's and Yahweh's response. In terms of the ongoing marriage relationship, the latter value of בְּ is undoubtedly the more prominent, though both senses are probably to be understood in these verses. The six terms that characterize the new marriage covenant reflect the deep sense of social justice that set orthodox Israel apart from its less socially-concerned neighbors in the ancient world.

The marriage will be permanent. לְעוֹלָם "forever" implies indefinite duration in the sense of a practically, though not technically infinite, permanence. The hope of the original covenant was for a faithful relationship between Yahweh and his people for all time (Deut 4:40) and this hope is reflected here in terms of the restoration of the true covenant. "Rightness" (צֶדֶק) includes both salvation / deliverance and fairness / equity. "Justice (מִשְׁפָּט) is the action and relationship whereby equity and fairness are established. "Loyalty" (חסד) is the unfailing, binding devotion that keeps a covenant relationship alive and well. "Compassion" (רחמים), once denied to Israel as a judgment (1:6), is the parental attentiveness which includes protective love and forgiveness, as well as concern for the person in need. "Faithfulness" (אמונה) includes truth as "troth"—reliability, honesty, believability, dependability. Both partners will display these six qualities, their tone being set by Yahweh's generous initiative, to which Israel need only respond.

As a result, the bride will "know" (ידע) Yahweh. The textual variants which expand the wording to "know that I am Yahweh" are unlikely to represent the original. Rather, since Hebrew ידע is the most common OT euphemism for cohabitation, i.e., the consummation of the marriage in this case (e.g., Gen 4:1; Num 31:18; 1 Kgs 1:4), Yahweh and the new Israel will this time live together as man and wife. While the term can have sexual overtones, its use here suggests not sex but metaphorically "intimacy" in a covenant sense. Eschatological Israel will know Yahweh, but not other lovers, in the intimacy of a consummated marriage of permanent faithfulness. She will "know" Yahweh as her ally (see Huffmon, *BASOR* 181 [1966] 31–37), will "know" him as his loyal vassal (cf. Exod 1:8; Deut 13:3; Amos 3:2). Yahweh will see to it that this marriage alliance lasts. He will initiate and uphold it via his new covenant stipulations.

23–24 [21–22]   An arbitrary verse division again separates a unified saying. As a result of the new marriage, Yahweh will respond (ענה) in a beneficent manner for the benefit of Israel, who had learned to respond (ענה) to him as she should have from the beginning (v 17 [15]).

Once more we are reminded by the use of ביום ההוא "in that day" that the setting is eschatological. Yahweh is still the speaker, as the final parenthetical notation נאם יהוה "oracle of Yahweh" reemphasizes for the reader/hearer. The first verb of these verses, אענה "I will respond / sing," is omitted in G and Syr. On the uncertain assumption that the MT is correct, the repetition of the verb constitutes a stylistic emphasis. The first occasion, "I will respond / sing" is the essence of the promise (cf. v 17 [15]). An interpretative paraphrase would be "I will do what is required."

The second mention of ענה introduces the actual means of response: "I will respond to the sky . . ." Yahweh claims the weather / storm god Baal's supposed speciality, control of the elements whereby rain waters the earth as the key element of the fertility cycle.

ענה, in addition to its meaning "respond," can mean "answer" in that Yahweh's granting fertility to the earth can be considered an answer to prayer. But it also can mean "speak up" and "sing" with connotations both of acting by divine decree and creating cosmically harmonious "music of the skies."

A full agricultural cycle is here described. The sky waters the earth, which responds with grain, wine, and oil, those elements Yahweh once had to withhold (v 10 [8]) to teach Israel a hard lesson. These, harvested by the people in a restored Jezreel, the traditional "breadbasket" of the north, provide the resurgence of bounty from which the nation will be fed.

No longer is "Jezreel" a code word for doom, particularly that of the Jehu dynasty. It is now a glorious name, full of its most basic sense: "God sows /

plants." Yahweh will superintend all fertility in the new age. His judgment will be lifted, the covenant restoration blessing of agricultural bounty (type 5; Lev 26:42 and Deut 30:9) fulfilled.

25 [23] The final word of v 24 [22], יזרעאל "Jezreel," and the first word of v 25 [23], וזרעתיה "I will sow her," share the root זרע "to sow / plant." The two verses are also connected by the continuing theme of the names of Hosea's children. No Compassion (Lo-Ruhamah) and Not My People (Lo-Ammi) are used as vehicles for the transformation of the messages once conveyed by these names. Thus "Agricultural Bounty," "Compassion" and "Peoplehood" are returned to the nation from which they had been withdrawn. To the new Israel, Yahweh newly becomes "my God." The old curse of rejection (type 1) is withdrawn. The new blessing of Yahweh's favor (type 1; cf. Lev 26:45 "I will be their God") replaces it.

The entire oracle of salvation closes fittingly at this point. The doom and destruction guaranteed in 1:4–9 and 2:4–15 [2–13] will have come to pass, yielding to a future in which such harsh judgment never again need be feared.

The clarity of the verse at first blush seems threatened by syntactical ambiguity in the lack of a sure referent for the third person feminine singular object suffix (ה-on וזרעתיה "I will sow her"). Wolff and others have speculated that v 25a [23a] must be the apodosis of a sentence which "perhaps mentioned Jezreel's mother" (Wolff, 54). Wolff asks, however, "What would be the meaning of sowing 'the mother of Jezreel'?", a question which obviates that proposal.

Clearly, the referent has to be the land of Israel. Jezreel, otherwise masculine, is construed as feminine in a synecdoche, the emphasis being upon Jezreel as the crop center of the north, standing for *all* Israel agriculturally. The third person feminine singular object suffix thus refers implicitly to ארץ ישראל "the land of Israel," mediated indirectly through the reference to Jezreel at the end of v 24 [22].

Explanation

The passage has two complementary foci: the reestablishment of orthodoxy and attendant agricultural abundance. Both are eschatological themes in the prophets and both characterize the pentateuchal promises of restoration in the new covenant age. Presupposed is the punishment of the north, involving exile and deprivation. As with the salvation oracle in 2:1–3 [1:10–2:1], the events described seem to be in the distant future, not to be expected by Hosea's immediate audience per se. To describe things yet unseen, in a distant time and circumstance, requires the language of human analogy. Descriptions of heaven, for example, in the Bible are based on the analogy of human society. We must therefore recognize the kind of language employed in Hosea and other prophetical writings to describe the new covenant age, appreciating its substantially figurative nature. Both the material blessings and the religious purity predicted here, according to the covenant, constitute aspects of the salvation / deliverance accomplished solely by God, who establishes them on behalf of his new "wife." The age described can only be the church age. The co-heirs of Christ are the heirs of this promise (Gal 3:29).

In Deut 31:21, which introduces the poem of chap. 32, Yahweh tells Moses

that "when many disasters and difficulties come upon them, this song (i.e.,
chap. 32) will answer / speak up / sing / respond / testify (ענה) against them."
Here is a possible antecedent for ענה in Hos 2:23–24 [21–22] (and perhaps
in v 17b [15b] as well). Because ענה can connote "sing" (especially "sing anti-
phonally") and was the verb used to signify the famous national song of curse
(Deut 32), it could be employed appropriately here by Hosea's audience in
a description of eschatological blessing rather than curse. With ענה in vv
23–25 [21–23] Hosea thus heightens the aspect of reversal of the covenant
curses in the restoration period. Yahweh had to teach Israel, through Moses,
a curse song in Deut 32. Now, according to Hosea, he will one day be able
to respond / sing to Israel with a new song, one of blessing.

Israel Loved and Therefore Chastened   (3:1–5)

Bibliography

Atten, L. W. "Hosea's Message and Marriage." *JBL* 48 (1929) 257–73. **Borbone,
P. G.** "Il capitolo terzo di osea." *Henoch* 2 (1980) 257–66. ———. "Il terro incomodo:
L'interpretatione del testo masoretico di Osea 3, 1." *Henoch* 7 (1985) 151–60. **Eybers,
I. H.** "The Matrimonial Life of Hosea." *Die Oud Testamentiese Werkgemeenskap in Suid-
Afrika* 7 / 8 (1964–65) 11–34. **Fox, M.** "TÔB as Covenant Terminology." *BASOR* 209
(1973) 41–42. **Fück, J.** "Hosea Kapitel 3." *ZAW* 39 (1929) 283–90. **Ginsberg, H. L.**
"Studies in Hosea 1–3." *Yehezkel Kaufman Jubilee Volume.* Ed. M. Haran. Jerusalem:
Magnes, 1960. **Gordis, R.** "Hosea's Marriage and Message: A new Approach." *HUCA*
25 (1954) 9–40. ———. "Some Hitherto Unrecognized Meanings of the Verb שוב."
JBL 52 (1933) 153–62. **Gordon, C. H.** *Homer and the Bible.* Ventnor, NJ: Ventnor
Publishers, 1967. **Haupt, P.** "Hosea's Erring Spouse." *JBL* 34 (1915) 41–53. **Hillers,
D.** "A Note on Some Treaty Terminology in the Old Testament." *BASOR* 176 (1964)
46–47. **Malamat, A.** "Origins of Statecraft in the Israelite Monarchy." *BA* 28 (1965)
34–65. **Moran, W. L.** "The Ancient Near Eastern Background of the Love of God
in Deuteronomy." *CBQ* 25 (1963) 77–87. ———. "A Note on the Treaty Terminology
of the Sefire Stelas." *JNES* 22 (1963) 173–76. **Mutingh, L. M.** "Married Life in Israel
According to the Book of Hosea." *Die Oud Testamentiese Werkgemeenskap in Suid-Afrika*
7 / 8 (1964–65) 77–84. **Tushingham, A. D.** "A Reconsideration of Hosea, chapters
1–3." *JNES* 12 (1953) 150–59. **Yaron, R.** "Aramaic Marriage Contracts from Elephantine." *JSS* 3 (1958) 1–39.

Translation

[1] *Yahweh said to me again:* [a]
   "Show love [b] *to a woman who loves evil* [c] *and commits adultery, just as Yahweh
shows love to the Israelites though they turn to other gods and love raisin cakes."*
[2] *I bought her for myself with fifteen shekels* [a] *of silver, a homer of barley,* [b] *and a
jug of wine.* [c]

³*I said to her:*

*"For a long time you will remain mine. You will not engage in prostitution, and no one will have you. I myself ⟨will have no sex⟩*ᵃ *with you.* ⁴*Because for a long time the Israelites will remain without king, without official, without sacrifice, without pillar, without ephod or teraphim.* ⁵*Afterwards the Israelites will return to seek Yahweh their God and David their king. They will turn in fear*ᵃ *to Yahweh and his goodness in the end times."*

Notes

1.a. עוֹד "again" may be construed also with לֵךְ אֱהַב "love again . . . ," though this appears less likely.

1.b. In consideration of idiomatic Eng., the Heb. לֵךְ "go" is omitted in translation.

1.c. Reading the act ptcp, with G and vocalizing רֵעַ rather than רָע. Alternatively, "one who is loved by a companion" or "one who loves a companion."

2.a. The text lacks the word "shekel," though this is the clear meaning.

2.b. MT reads "a homer of barley and a lethech of barley." It is not known for certain what a lethech was, if there was such a thing (i.e., if the text is not corrupt). Suggestions that it was a measure equal to half a homer are only speculation.

2.c. G reads νέβελ οἴνου "a jug of wine" instead of לֶתֶךְ שְׂעֹרִים "a lethech of barley." This is probably more original than MT, likely the result of a corruption. לֶתֶךְ occurs only here in the entire OT.

3.a. It appears that a verb (probably אֵלֵךְ "I will go") and a negative particle (לֹא) have been lost. Otherwise the text makes no discernible sense. הָלַךְ אֶל "go into" means to "have sex with."

5.a. Cf. Jer 36:16 for this sense of פָּחַד אֶל "turn in fear."

Form / Structure / Setting

The form of the passage is close to that of 1:2–9. It is a prophetic autobiographical recollection, perhaps best called *memorabile*. A few specific events are recalled from the prophet's life in a bare, even laconic manner. Yahweh's words make clear that the prophet is acting typologically. In addition, and in contrast to 1:2–9, Hosea's own words, rather than God's, establish the typological significance of some of the actions (especially vv 3–5). Here again a real marriage illustrates the situation prevailing in the metaphorical marriage between Yahweh and Israel.

Because 2:25 [23] so clearly ends the salvation oracle of 2:18–25 [16–23], and 4:1 so clearly begins a covenant lawsuit form, 3:1–5 is set apart as a unit of its own. It is prose throughout.

The five verses make up a unit following the pattern: command, action, interpretation. However, the order of the pattern is slightly adjusted: in v 1 Yahweh interprets his command, prior to Hosea's action in v 2. Also, in v 3 Hosea himself gives a command and predicts the action that will result from it. The interpretation then follows, as expected. There is a strong connection between the two commands, which are, in effect, one. Yahweh's command to Hosea is to "show love" (v 1). His interpretation is that such love will parallel his own for Israel (v 1). Hosea's buying "her" (v 2) is the action fulfilling the command. Hosea then specifies that the woman he has "bought" must remain chaste (v 3). Similarly, Yahweh will put a stop to Israel's wicked behavior by chastening the Israelites (vv 4, 5). This, perhaps even ironically, interprets the first command to "love." The structure may be represented as follows:

> v 1   Command: Show love to an evil woman.
> v 1   Interpretation: I show love to Israel though
>   they are evil.
> v 2   Action: Hosea acquires the woman.
> v 3   Command: Hosea chastens his wife (future).
> v 4   Action: Israel is chastened (future).   ⎫ Second inter-
> v 5   Interpretation: Chastening will lead to   ⎬ pretation of
>   obedience.   ⎭ "love" in v 1.

Thus Yahweh's love involves chastening, which in turn produces obedience: a basic covenantal theme (cf. Deut 30:1–10).

After chap. 1, we heard nothing more of Gomer. She was not mentioned in 2:4, for that "woman" was a "wife" and "mother" only allegorically. The present passage probably speaks of another woman. Hosea married her, too, at God's command. She was an adulteress, and conceivably even a prostitute (cf. Gordon, *Homer,* 21; Ginsberg, "Studies"). Gomer's prostitution, by contrast, was metaphorical. This woman is warned against the actual practice of prostitution (3:3), and forcibly kept from it (v 4).

Since the passage's purpose is not to give a chronology of Hosea's personal life, we can only speculate when he married his second wife. Such details would have no kerygmatic significance, and would only distract from the book's message. We suggest a moderately late date for the marriage, however, for two reasons.

First, the placement of chap. 3 after chap. 2 can hardly be accidental since chap. 3 depends on chap. 2 generally for certain of its implications. For example, 2:4–17 [2–15] describes the inevitable deprivation that must come to Yahweh's bride, Israel, before she will be ready to be wooed anew by him; similarly, 3:1–5 describes the deprivation that the Israelites must experience before they will turn to him in fear. Both passages demonstrate that God's justice is not incompatible with his love, but rather is a major aspect thereof. Both begin with Israel's infidelity and end with a prediction of a future period when fidelity will be the norm. Both describe a restoration in the eschatological future. Both implicitly set the restoration at a time beyond the age of Hosea. Chap. 3 does so explicitly with its repetition of ימים רבים "a long time" (lit., "many days") and its closing adverbial phrase באחרית הימים "in the end times." The full sense of the brief chap. 3 comes out, thus, only after the longer and more detailed chap. 2, just as chap. 2, in which the three children of Gomer and Hosea are grown (2:24–25 [22–23]) presupposes chap. 1. Accordingly, *prima facie*, chap. 3 can be considered to describe a second marriage many years after the first. There is no hint of any kind in chap. 3 that Hosea is buying back his first wife.

Second, there is an overtone throughout the book that the *next* major event to come in Israel's history is the removal of the nation's independence. Most of chap. 2 still presupposes prosperity (see 2:7 [5], 10 [8], 11 [9], etc.) prior to disaster. In chap. 3 not only is no evidence of prosperity forthcoming;

vv 4 and 5 could be understood to imply that the North is about to or has already fallen, since they emphasize the long time that Israel will endure without its former institutions.

We suggest therefore a date at least as late as the reign of Hoshea (732–722 B.C.), and possibly as late as 722, when the North fell to Assyria, for the marriage described in this chapter. There can be no objection that Hosea married this late either on the ground that he was too old or that the times were too insecure for marriage. This is not a normal but a symbolic marriage. Hosea will have no sex with this wife, the marriage remaining unconsummated (v 3). Prophets were, of course, on other occasions called upon to engage in dealings that the times made to seem inappropriate (e.g., Jeremiah; Jer 32:6–15).

There is no reason to suggest in the case of a chapter so thoroughly autobiographical that anyone other than Hosea is its author. (For a contrary view see Atten, *JBL* 48 (1929) 257–73).

Comment

1 The verb אהב "to love / show love" occurs four times in the verse, dominating its vocabulary. Hebrew אהב has a wider range of meaning than does the English verb "to love." It includes the English senses of "love romantically," "prefer / like" but also "do acts of love for," "be loyal / compassionate towards" and even "be allied with." It includes divine love (Gr. ἀγάπη), parental love (στοργή), general human social love (φίλος), and romantic love (ἔρος). Hosea is to "show love for" a new wife in the sense of caring for her and protecting her. The adulteress, by contrast, "loves" evil, in the sense of "take delight in / prefer / like." Yahweh loves Israel in that he is loyal to her as a nation (cf. Deut 4:37; 23:5; et al.). This "love" is a technical, covenantal term for a relationship of loyalty. Israel "takes delight in / prefers / likes" raisin cakes.

Yahweh's love for Israel is noble, unselfish, generous, protective. Israel's love for its raisin cakes and the adulteress's love for evil are selfish, indulgent, pleasure-oriented. Since the verbal root is the same in each case, the contrast between those two types of love is always implicit, but no less striking. Hosea's new wife does not deserve his love, but she will receive it. Israel does not deserve Yahweh's love, but he has been showing it to her all along—and will continue to do so both during and by means of the long season of disruption he will impose on her.

The woman Hosea marries is an actual adulteress (אהבת רע ומנאפת "who loves evil and commits adultery"). His command to her concerning "prostitution" (v 3) suggests that she was indeed a professional prostitute. Hosea is no longer using זנה metaphorically as was the case in chaps. 1 and 2.

The actions of Israelites directly parallel those of the adulteress. She commits adultery; they turn to other gods (spiritual adultery). She loves evil; they love raisin cakes, a synecdoche for heterodox indulgence. Raisin cakes (אשישי ענבים), sweets made from pressed and dried grapes, were prized as a delicacy (cf. Cant 2:5; 2 Sam 6:19). By Hosea's time they were probably routinely associated with cultic worship, the fitting metaphorical food of the religious nymphomaniac who seeks spiritual and material gratification from other gods than Yahweh.

2 Hosea paid a bride-price for his second wife, in parallel to the figurative bride-price Yahweh had paid for his "new" wife (2:21–22 [19–20]). Since Yahweh's new wife, Israel, in chap. 2 was also his *former* wife, now chastened and repentant, some interpreters have suggested that Hosea is buying back Gomer. In 2:21–22 [19–20], however, Yahweh does not buy back the same old Israel, but a new Israel, a remnant transformed eschatologically, an Israel he had not yet married, as it were. To assume that Gomer left and that he then bought her back from her father or someone she had married or a house of prostitution, still in her defiant adulterous state (3:1), hardly comports with the picture given in 2:18–25 [16–23].

Mention of the bride price makes clear one of the points of the passage: the wife is Hosea's property. She is paid for, and under Israelite law, he owns her and can do with her as he wishes. He can now *enforce* chastity, keeping her at home, allowing her to be intimate with no one, not even himself.

The bride-price was in money, grain and wine. The barley was equal to a homer, i.e., about five bushels. Neither the barley, an inexpensive grain, nor the jug of wine were expensive. And fifteen shekels of silver would weigh only about four-tenths of an ounce. Thus the total price was not excessive. A female slave would cost more: thirty shekels (Exod 21:32; cf. the same price for a woman devoted by vow to a sanctuary, Lev 27:4).

Partly by cash, partly by payment "in kind," Hosea bought a wife. He clearly owned her because he clearly bought her. That is the point of the "itemized bill" in v 2.

3 Hosea gave four instructions to his new wife, each more restrictive than the preceding one. First, she must live / stay / remain (ישב) with him for a long time (ימים רבים "many days"). This otherwise reasonable restriction must have seemed to a professional prostitute unexpected. A prostitute might expect to be resold eventually, or shared with other men, or soon abandoned. But Hosea tells her she will stay with him at length.

The second instruction precludes her practicing prostitution (her prior profession?). She has been bought; her sinful life is now over. The third instruction makes clear that she will not have relations with anybody else. Hosea has bought her and she had no choice in the matter. The fourth instruction may well have been a complete surprise. She is told that even her husband has no intention of having sex with her. This is clearly the sense of the instruction, textual problems notwithstanding. She has been brought from adultery and prostitution to chastity in a sexless marriage, taken from one extreme and made to conform to another. The reader / hearer is already beginning to see what is in store for Israel. A different kind of life is ahead.

We must keep in mind that these restrictions fulfill the command to "show love." They are not so much intended to harm, as to protect. As Yahweh is a "jealous" God, and as he wishes to prohibit Israel from sinning further for her own good, so Hosea acts restrictively toward the new wife. He has bought her not for his own pleasure, but in order to reform her.

4 In parallel to Hosea's command that his wife will remain (ישׁב) with him for a long time, he now states that "the Israelites will remain (ישׁב) a long time. . . ." Hosea is no longer speaking to his wife. He is now addressing the hearer / reader with the hard word of Yahweh for Israel, as the introductory כי, so typically used to presage divine discourse, suggests.

A series of five negations leaves no doubt that Israel's basic institutions will be taken away, implying that her national sovereignty and social infrastructure will be eliminated. Israel will have no king (curse type 136; cf. Deut 28:36; 31:4). Since kingship was integral to the nation's identity, its end would mean a different kind of existence. Israel will also be without an official (שׂר). Instead of allowing for a lesser form of government, this presages the final end of Israel's self-rule. In Hosea's time the implication was quite clear: another nation (surely the powerful Assyria) would rule Israel.

Sacrifice (זבח) and pillar (מצבה), prominent signs of the official Northern Yahwistic cultus, will also be taken away (curse type 2; Lev 26:31). The mention of pillar is significant. The pillar was a large stone erected at a shrine, and probably symbolic of deity, especially in idolatrous worship. Such pillars were outlawed in Israel (Deut 16:22) under the Mosaic covenant now ignored in the north.

The ephod was a garment worn by a priest in the practice of divination (mechanistic discernment of the divine will). It contained a pocket in which the *Urim* and *Thummim* (alternately light and dark-sided dice thrown for combinations that would reveal "yes" and "no" answers) were kept (Exod 28:30). Teraphim, household idols, could also be consulted (Ezek 21:26 [21]; Zech 10:2) in pagan divination.

The sacrificial system and the ephod were orthodox. The pillar and the teraphim were abominably pagan. Israel, in its syncretism, had mixed the holy with the forbidden—had adulterated its religion. So, orthodox and heterodox features *alike* would now be taken away. Neither leadership, nor worship, nor divination would any longer be available to Israel's citizens.

5 The ultimate outcome will be positive, deprivation, not harm. The root אחר "to follow, come after" at the beginning and end of this verse emphasizes the long time of deprivation before Israel's restoration (cf. the sequence of deprivation / restoration in 2:4–25 [2–23], and in Lev 26, Deut 4 and Deut 30).

Paronomasia may be present in the verb יָשֻׁבוּ "will return" in comparison to the previous יָשְׁבוּ "will remain" (v 4). The Israelites will certainly return geographically from exile (restoration blessing type 7; Deut 30:3–5). Additionally, however, שׁוב "return" can have the sense of coming back in true faith to Yahweh (e.g., Deut 4:30) in contrast to "turning to other gods," a necessary precursor to the return from exile.

The oracle also predicts that Israel will "seek" (בקשׁ) Yahweh, i.e., come to God to know him and to do his will (cf. Zeph 2:3; Zech 8:22; Mal 3:1; etc.). Yahweh, the text says, will be "their God" once again, in the language of the first of the covenant restoration promises (Lev 26:44–45).

And David will be their king. With this theme 2:1–3 [1:10–2:1] is closely connected. The prophets looked forward to a day when Israel, north and south, would be reunited (e.g., Jer 31; Ezek 37; cf. Deut 30:3, 4; eschatological blessing type 8). The various successive dynasties that populated the northern monarchy were hardly the ideal—the Davidic dynasty alone remained chosen (1 Kgs 11:13). The mention of David is not therefore to be regarded as an interpolation. It is another way of speaking of the "one leader" predicted in 2:2 [1:11]; i.e., a member of Davidic line. This is but a hint of the sort of messianic eschatology that will be more strongly manifest in later prophets (cf. Jer 30:9).

In describing the return to Yahweh as a "turning in fear" (פחד אל־) the oracle makes clear that the Israelites will have learned a lesson prior to their return (cf. Deut 4:30; and the frequent use of פחד in Deut 28). But their God will not be cruel or vindictive. When they approach him they will find "his goodness" (טובו). On the parallel of 2:18–25 [16–23], the days of return are proclaimed as good times.

The oracle concludes with the adverbial phrase "in the end times" (באחרית הימים), sometimes treated as an addition to the original text by those who excise, where possible, Judean references in Hosea, since the phrase is associated with oracles of southern prophets (Isa 2:2; Mic 4:1; etc.). However, its occurrences in Gen 49:1, Num 24:14 and Deut 4:30 make the suspicion unnecessary. The term is merely further evidence of the close connection of Hosea with the covenant sanctions (specifically, Deut 4:30). The "end times" are the eschatological age (cf. Isa 2:2; Jer 49:39; Ezek 38:8, 16; Dan 10:14; Mic 4:1), and thus the chapter predicts events that are part of the restoration era, in accord with the eschatology long revealed to Israel (Lev 26; Deut 4 and 30). Its major elements (return and blessing after deprivation; restoration of Davidic rule; reunification of North and South, etc.) would have been recognizable to the Israelites of Hosea's day, whether or not they respected the covenant in which those elements were contained.

Explanation

In chap. 1, Hosea married Gomer, who was *figuratively* a prostitute. In chap. 3, he obediently chooses a wife who was at least sexually promiscuous, and perhaps a professional prostitute. The allegorical parallel is the same in both cases: Israel's unfaithfulness to Yahweh is like the unfaithfulness of a loose woman.

At this point, however, the emphases of the two chapters diverge. In chap. 3, Hosea is to have no sex with the former adulteress. In decisively restraining her previous habits, he mirrors God and Israel. God will restrain Israel's promiscuity in a drastic way—by dissolving it as a nation, leaving it fatally deprived of basic national institutions of government, worship, divination, etc. The message of chap. 1, by contrast, had been revealed not through any actions of Hosea in respect to Gomer, but via the names of the children and Yahweh's changed name.

Ethical issues must not overshadow the intent of the chapter. It does not address the question of how God could command (or appear to command) something otherwise forbidden by the law (marrying an adulteress or prostitute). Nor is it (a story of) a teleological suspension of the ethical, whereby at God's command, Hosea does something otherwise wrong, but now right because it is done at God's behest. The details are sparse, and do not describe any legal-moral violation by Hosea.

His new wife has done wrong, but the marriage actually stops this. The Mosaic law prevented only priests from marrying someone formerly immoral (Lev 21:7). Whether she was divorced or never married, Hosea could legally marry this woman. Further, his refusal to consummate the marriage removes any doubt as to the morality of the action, and obviates the possibility of moral compromise. Hosea interpreted Yahweh's command in keeping with the law.

God's love can be both punitive and restorative. This is the essence of the chapter's message. When punishment is deserved, it will be given. Love demands this—not the indulgent love of the adulteress-prostitute Israel for the cultic raisin cakes, but the firm, gracious love of God for his wayward people. Since the people of Israel could not find any "good" apart from Yahweh, he must of necessity teach them that lesson.

Such a promise must have given substantial comfort to those of the north (and later of the south) who still sought to obey Yahweh and to understand their history according to his Word. Their exile, subjugation and humiliation had a purpose. The original promises of God would not be forgotten. The covenant predictions for Israel would be followed precisely. The chastity of Hosea's second marriage was, therefore, a sign to be remembered in the centuries of deprivation. God always had loved them, even when they had loved others. One day he would again restore them to himself, in good circumstances, with his chosen leader appointed for them.

The "end times" thus described have their ultimate fulfillment in the new covenant in Christ. Christ is David's son, who rules his people as their head. His goodness includes the fruit of the Spirit (Gal 5:22–23), which renders unnecessary the old law. In him are crucified the passions of the flesh (Gal 5:24), the forbidden sort of love. His kind of love has as its ultimate goal God's true goodness.

Yahweh's Case against Israel (4:1–19)

Bibliography

Aartun, K. "Textüberlieferung und vermeintliche Belege der Konjunktion *P* in Alten Testament." *UF* 10 (1978) 1–13. **Albright, W. F.** "The High Place in Ancient Palestine." *Congress Volume*. VTSup 4. Leiden: E. J. Brill, 1957. 242–58. **Ambanelli, I.** "Il significato dell'espressione *da*ᶜ*at* ʾ*elōhîm* nel profeta Osea." *RevistB* 21 (1973) 119–45. **Andre, G.** *Determining the Destiny, PQD in the Old Testament.* ConB, OT Series 19. Lund: Gleerup, 1980. **Balz-Cochois, H.** *Gomer, der Hoehenkult Israels im Selbstferstaendnis der Volksfroemmigkeit; Untersuchungen zu Hosea 4, 1–5, 7.* Europäische Hochschulschriften 23 / 191. Bern: Universitaires Européenes, 1982. **Brueggemann, W.** "On Land-losing and Land-receiving." *Crux* 19 (1980) 166–73. **Budde, K.** "Zu Text und Auslegung des Buches Hosea." *JBL* 45 (1926) 280–97. **Cardinelli, I.** "Hosea 4, 1–3, eine Strukturanalyse." *Festschrift G. J. Botterweck.* Ed. H. J. Fabry. Köln / Bonn: Hanstein, 1977. **DeRoche, M.** "The Reversal of Creation in Hosea." *VT* 31 (1981) 400–409. ———. "Structure, Rhetoric and Meaning in Hosea iv:4–10." *VT* 33 (1983) 185–98. **Dion, P. E.** "Did

Cultic Prostitution Fall into Oblivion During the Postexilic Era?" *CBQ* 43 (1981) 41–48. **Gemser, B.** "The *Rib* or Controversy Pattern in Hebrew Mentality." *Wisdom in Israel: FS H. H. Rowley.* VTSup 3. Leiden: E. J. Brill, 1955. 124–37. **Harrelson, W.** "Knowledge of God in the Church." *Int* 30 (1976) 12–17. **Holladay, W. L.** "On Every High Hill and under Every Green Tree." *VT* 11 (1961) 170–76. **Huffmon, H. B.** "The Treaty Background of Hebrew *YADAᶜ*." *BASOR* 181 (1966) 131–77. **Junker, H.** "Textkritische-, formkritische-, und traditionsgeschichtliche Untersuchung zu Os 4:1–10." *BZ* N.F. 4 (1960) 165–73. **Klein, H.** "Natur und Recht: Israels Umgang mit dem Hochzeitsbrauchtum seiner Welt." *TZ* 37 (1981) 3–18. **Knauf, E. A.** "Beth Aven." *Bib* 65 (1984) 251–53. **Laney, J. C.** "The Role of the Prophets in God's Case against Israel." *B Sac* 138 (1981) 313–25. **Leskow, T.** "Die dreistufige Tora: Beobachtungen zu einer Form." *ZAW* 82 (1970) 362–79. **Lohfink, N.** "Zu Text und Form von Os 4:4–6," *Bib* 42 (1961) 303–32. **Lundbom, J. R.** "The Contentious Priests and Contentious People in Hosea iv: 1–10." *VT* 36 (1986) 52–70. **Malamat, A.** "UMMATUM in Old Babylonian Texts and Its Ugaritic and Biblical Counterparts." *UF* 11 (1979) 527–36. **McMillion, P.** "An Exegesis of Hos 4:1–5:7." *RestQ* 17 (1974) 236–481. **Nielsen, K.** *Yahweh as Prosecutor and Judge: An Investigation of the Prophetic Lawsuit (Rib-pattern).* JSOTSup 9. Winnona Lake, IN: Eisenbrauns, 1978. **Price, B. F.** "Questions and Answers." *BT* 16 (1965) 123–27. **Rabin, C.** "Etymological Miscellanea." *Scripta Heirosolumitana* 8 (1961) 384–400. **Rost, L.** "Erwägungen zu Hos 4:13f." In *FS Alfred Bertholet,* ed. W. Baumgartner et al. Tübingen: Mohr, 1950. 451–60. **Rudolph, W.** "Hosea 4, 15–19." In *Gottes Wort und Gottes Land: FS H. Witterzberg,* ed. H. G. Reventlow. Göttingen: Vandenhoeck und Ruprecht, 1965. ———. "Präparierte Jungfrauen?" *ZAW* 75 (1963) 65–73. **Wieder, A. A.** "Ugaritic-Hebrew Lexicographical Notes." *JBL* 84 (1965) 160–64. **Zolli, J.** "Hosea 4:17–18." *ZAW* 56 (1938) 175.

Translation

The accusation against the land

[1] *Listen to the word of Yahweh, Israelites! For Yahweh has an accusation against the whole land, because there is no faithfulness, no loyalty and no knowledge of God in the land.* [2] *Cursing, lying, murder, stealing, and adultery break forth*[a] *⟨in the land⟩,*[b] *and the idols*[c] *crowd against*[d] *one another!* [3] *Therefore the land will dry up*[a] *and all who live in it will become barren, along with the wild animals*[b] *and the birds of the sky. Even the fish of the sea will be taken away!*

The accusation against the priesthood

[4] *Surely God*[a] *has an accusation against a particular person.*
God[a] *intends to reprove an individual—*
And it is you—yes, you[b]*—priest, against whom I make the accusation!*

[5] *You will stumble by day and the prophet will stumble with you at night.*
You will perish in terror [6]*when*[a] *my people perish from lack of knowledge.*

Because you have rejected knowledge,
I will also reject you as my priest.

You have forgotten the law of your God,
so I in turn will forget your children.

[7] *The richer*[a] *they became, the more they sinned against me;*
their Glory they traded for[b] *disgrace.*

⁸ *They feed on the sin of my people;*
they live off their iniquity.

⁹ *So it will be like people like priest.*
I will punish him for his ways,
I will repay him for his deeds.

¹⁰ *They will eat but not be satisfied;*
they will practice prostitution but not break forth,
because they have abandoned Yahweh, to revere prostitution.[a]

The accusation against the false cult

¹¹ *Wine and the fruit-of-the-vine*[a] *dulls the mind of my people!*[b]
¹² *He consults his wood!*
His staff advises him!

For a prostituting spirit has led them astray,
And they are prostituting themselves away from their God.

¹³ *On the mountain tops they make sacrifices;*
On the hills they burn offerings

Under oak and poplar
And under terebinth, for their[a] *shade is nice.*

Therefore your daughters turn to prostitution,
And your daughters-in-law commit adultery.

¹⁴ *Shall I not punish your daughters, since they turn to prostitution?*
And your daughters-in-law, since they commit adultery?

Indeed, the men[a] *make offerings*[b] *with the prostitutes,*
And sacrifice with the cult prostitutes!
A people that lacks understanding must be ruined because it turns to prostitution.[c]

The fall of the false cult

¹⁵ *As for you, Israel, do not incur guilt ⟨from Yahweh.⟩*[a]
Do not enter Gilgal;
Do not go up to Beth-Awen;
Do not swear "As Yahweh lives. . . ."

¹⁶ *Since like a stubborn cow,*
Israel is stubborn,

Then Yahweh will pasture them
Like a lamb in the Expanse.[a]

¹⁷ *Ephraim is in league with idols.*
Leave him to himself![a]

¹⁸ *When their drinking is finished,*
They take their fill of prostitution.
They really love the shame of insolence![ab]

¹⁹ *A wind has wrapped them*[a] *in its wings,*
And they will come to shame because of their sacrifices.[b]

Notes

2.a. The verb פרץ is here translated in conformity to the pun intended in v 10.

2.b. Restoring בארץ with G ἐπὶ τῆς γῆς "in the land." Its loss was probably the result of haplogr via homoiotel.

2.c. דמים "bloodshed" and דמים "idols" are non-homologous homographs. For the reasons we have translated "idols" see *Comment* on v 2.

2.d. Lit., "touch" or "overtake."

3.a. Reading אבל II "dry up" rather than אבל I "to mourn."

3.b. G appears to be expanding from 2:20 [18], by adding καὶ σὺν τοῖς ἑρπετοῖς τῆς γῆς "and with the creeping things of the ground" (= וברמש האדמה).

4.a. Revocalizing MT אַל "not" to אֶל "God."

4.b. Reading the MT consonants with the following vocalization: כִּימָּךְ רִיבִי כֹהֵן וְעַמְּךָ (כִּימָה is the emphatic כִּי with enclitic mem appended). See Kuhnigk, *NSH*, 30–31.

6.a. Reading the MT consonants with the following vocalization: כִּי נִדְמוּ [or] וְדָמִיתָ אֻמֶּה כָּ Cf. Kuhnigk, *NSH*, 30–32. The unlikely reference to "mother" is thus obviated.

7.a. Hebrew רבב can mean either to "be rich" (see M. Dahood, *Psalms I*, AB 16 [Garden City, NY: Doubleday, 1966] 99, 299 and *Psalms II*, AB 17 [1968] 293) or to "increase."

7.b. The 3 m pl reading fits the context much better. MT אָמִיר "I traded" (BDB, 558) should be revocalized אָמִירוּ "they traded" (so Kuhnigk, *NSH*, 39–45), or corrected to הֵמִירוּ "they traded" (with the Masoretic scribal correction *tiqqun sōpherîm*, and Syr, Tg).

10.a. The first word of v 11, זנות "prostitution," goes with v 10.

11.a. יין "wine" and תירוש "fruit-of the vine" are taken together as a collective (although it would also be possible to vocalize יקב as a pl). On the parallelism of "wine" and "fruit-of-the-vine" see Kuhnigk, *NSH*, 45–46 (*contra* Wolff, 72, note o / p); cf. *Comment*.

11.b. The first word of v 12, עמי "my people," goes with v 11.

13.a. Lit., "its."

14.a. The text has the 3 m pl ind pronoun הם. To avoid ambiguity in Eng., "they" is translated here "the men."

14.b. Heb. פרד, piel, is more likely cognate to Ugaritic *brd* "to make an offering" than a synonym of פרד, niphal, "to separate / go aside with." The parallelism with זבח in the following line confirms this translation. Cf. Wieder, *JBL* 84 (1965) 163–64. Heb. פרד "make an offering" may be a derivative from the sense "divide" inherent in פרד / *brd*.

14.c. We follow G, which construes אם זנה "if a prostitute" μετὰ [*sic*] πόρνης with v 14 (i.e., perhaps עם זנונים "with prostitution") and reads Σὺ δὲ Ἰσραὴλ μὴ ἀγνόει "but you, Israel, do not be ignorant," i.e., ואתה ישראל אל תאשם. The text of vv 15–19 is highly problematic, and this "solution" is only tentative.

15.a. MT and the versions read יהודה "Judah." This is grammatically awkward, even if logically possible in the context. We suggest that MT resulted from a corruption of something akin to מיהוה "from Yahweh" and reclaim a מ from assimilation with the מ of יאשם immediately preceding.

16.a. "Expanse" (מרחב) is probably a poetic euphemism for the netherworld, Sheol, etc. See Kuhnigk, *NSH*, 50–52.

17–18.a-a. The text of vv 17b–18 is very problematic. Any translation involves conjecture. See, e.g., Wolff, 72–73, notes y-dd.

18.b. Reading מְגִנָּהּ "insolence" rather than MT מָגִנֶּיהָ "her shields."

19.a. Reading אותם "them," with many commentators.

19.b. The MT form (from a sg) זבחה [?] is unusual. It may be dialectical. Alternatively, read מזבחותם, pl from מזבח "altar," thus "their altars (shall come to shame)" or, "(they shall come to shame) because [supplying a lost מ] of their altars."

Form / Structure / Setting

Chap. 4 is composed of four sections, each with a degree of unity and individuality, and all functioning under the general form of the prophetic lawsuit and one of its sub-categories, the "court speech" (cf. C. Westermann,

Basic Forms of Prophetic Speech [Philadelphia: Westminster, 1967] 199 ff.).
Vv 1–3 introduce the lawsuit in general terms. The case is called in the
language of a "court speech," the accusation is made, the evidence (or "complaint") is provided, the judgment sentence is pronounced: the land, utterly
corrupt, will dry up and its inhabitants—man, animal, and even fish—will
die. This all-encompassing oracle of judgment serves as a prose introduction
to the oracles that follow. Yahweh is again (cf. 2:4–18 [2–16]) both prosecutor
(vv 1a–2) and judge (v 3).

Vv 4–10 contain a specification of certain charges, evidence, and the judgment. Here Israel's priests are singled out for arrogance, profiteering, heterodoxy, and misleading the people. Their judgment, in line with the general
pattern established in vv 1–3, will be famine and deprivation, standard covenant curse punishments.

The next section, vv 11–14, attacks the northern cult itself. It is a cult of
debauchery, a "prostitution" of the true religion (accusation) characterized
by multiple sanctuaries and actual cult prostitution (evidence). This sort of
abomination must be destroyed (judgment sentence).

Some portions of the final section, vv 15–19, are almost impossible to
translate because of the state of the text (esp. vv 17b–19). Nevertheless, it
clearly contains the language of warning, evidence, and judgment.

If these four sections once existed independently, Hosea later wove them
into a single unified oracle. The resulting unit has an overall consistency
(the theme of accountability) and a clear logical progression. Transitional
elements link the four sections, if not to all of the others, certainly to the
prior and/or subsequent sections.

Because the first section is the most general and is prose, many suggest it
should be separated from the others. Three things argue against this, however:
the strong connection forged by the repetition of the root ריב (v 4), the
connecting particle אך "surely", and the expected progression of any lawsuit
from the general (as vv 1–3) to the specific (vv 4–19).

The structure may be schematized as follows:

1–3	Accusation against the land	
	1a	Prophetic summons / "proclamation formula"
	1b, c	Accusation
	2	Evidence
	3	Judgment sentence (curse)
4–10	Accusation against the priesthood	
	4	Accusation
	5–10	Judgment sentences (curses) alternated with citations of evidence
11–14	Accusation against the false cult	
	11–12a	Evidence
	12b	Accusation

13	Evidence
14	Judgment sentence (curse)

15–19   Fall of the false cult

15	Warning
16–17	Evidence alternating with judgment sentences (two of each)
18	Evidence
19	Judgment sentence (curse)

A number of transitions occur in the passage between persons. For example, in vv 4–6 the priest (singular) is directly addressed in an excoriation of the corrupt priesthood. But we also hear about the sins of some individuals, in the third person singular (vv 12, 14, 16) and groups, in the third person plural (vv 7, 10, 12, 13, 14, 18). Yahweh himself is either speaking directly in the first person (vv 4–9, 12, 14) or is spoken of in the third person (vv 10, 12, 15, 16).

Analyzing rhetorically the changes or transitions in the audience / speaker throughout the oracle provides no evidence that the passage should be delineated into smaller units than the four we suggest. None of the four sections contains the kind of grouping of persons, issues or styles that would be true earmarks of independence. Rather, the lawsuit format itself allows for many transitions. Yahweh is both Prosecutor and Judge, and thus speaks in different ways. Moreover, this lawsuit has a variety of "counts," defendants, and evidence, and thus follows a compound-complex pattern. It nevertheless functions for a unified purpose—to call Israel to task for its corrupt institutions of cult and priesthood, and to stress the fact that Yahweh will demand accountability for the abuse of his law.

There are several useful clues in the chapter to its provenance. Hoseanic authorship cannot be questioned on other than presuppositional grounds. As to date, we suggest a time still within the kingship of Jeroboam II. There are no indications of political instability. Prosperity seems the norm at least among the classes who enjoy the debauchery provided for in the cult (vv 7, 8, 11, 18) and the times appear to manifest a conspicuous sort of complacent self-indulgence of the kind associated with the days prior to 745 B.C. Moreover, Hosea's early prophecies tend to contain the word "prostitution" more often than do the later prophecies [the root זנה is not used at all after 9:1, while appearing in chaps. 2–6 frequently].

The emphasis upon the ignoring of the word of God by the priests and the cult would seem to imply that 1) the priests in question know Yahweh's law but have purposely forgotten it (v 6); and 2) the cult in question was once Yahwistic but has now become syncretistic and involves cult prostitutes (vv 12–14). This would suggest Bethel, rather than Samaria or another *originally* heterodox site as the setting of the chapter. It is especially the Bethel altars or sacrifices (v 19) that will bring this people to shame.

Most of the chapter is composed in free verse. There is some possibility that certain portions are metrical poetry (esp. vv 4–10, 13–16) since they exhibit a rough correspondence in syllable count and contain synonymous parallelisms.

Comment

1 The command "Listen to the word of Yahweh, Israelites" launches the second major section of the book (4:1–9:9). It reminds the hearer/reader that the word is from Yahweh (cf. 1:1–2) and that Hosea is a legitimate prophet who speaks with divine authority. It is made clear that the message concerns the nation as a whole, the breadth of the audience underscored both by the mention of "those who live in the land," and by the hyperbolic prediction of destruction for all animal life in v 3. Yahweh is taking his people to court to answer for their crimes. Israel's offenses are summarized in three general sins of omission in covenantal terms (v 1) followed by six more specific sins (v 2).

The first of the sins of omission is lack of faithfulness (אמת, "truthfulness," "fidelity," etc.). Though אמת is a synonym for אמונה (2:22 [20]), it occurs only here in Hosea. It connotes decent, responsible relations between one person and another (cf. Gen 24:49; 47:29; Exod 18:21; Josh 2:12, 14; 1 Sam 12:24, etc.) and thus among the citizens of a society. "Loyalty" (חסד, also "devotion," "covenant faithfulness," etc.; see N. Glueck, *Hesed in the Bible,* tr. A. Gottschalk [Cincinnati: Hebrew Union College, 1967], and K. D. Sackenfeld, *The Meaning of Hesed in the Hebrew Bible,* 1977) suggests the bond of reciprocity that must characterize a true, ongoing personal relationship, such as the loyal grace that Yahweh's covenant generously provides to Israel (Exod 34:6; 2 Sam 15:20; Ps 36:8; Jer 9:23). The "knowledge of God" (דעת אלהים), an important concept in Hosea, is particularly significant here, standing in parallelism with and summarizing the two sins of omission preceding it. It also points to the six sins of commission following. The use of דעת אלהים elsewhere in Hosea (6:6), along with other expressions of knowing God based upon the root ידע (2:22 [20]; 4:6; 5:4; 8:2; 13:4; etc.) demonstrates how in Hosea the term represents the essence of the covenant relationship between God and his people (cf. Ambanelli, *RevistB* 21 [1973] 119–45; Harrelson, *Int* 30 [1976] 12–17). Therefore when there is *no* knowledge of God in the land, the covenant has obviously been abrogated. This knowledge is more important than sacrifice (6:6); was the basis for Yahweh's deliverance of Israel in the exodus (13:4); constitutes the essence of the eschatological blessings (2:22 [20]); and its absence will mean destruction for the nation (v 6). The term derives in part from the language of ancient Near Eastern treaties, where ידע represents the acknowledgment of the binding relationship between the parties, especially the loyalty of the vassal to the suzerain (Huffmon, *BASOR* 181 [1966] 131–77). Hosea thus accuses the Israelites of a contempt for God. This is central to the evidence against them.

2 In support of the accusation that Israel has broken the covenant, Hosea now cites six crimes from the apodictic decalogue list (Exod 20:1–17; Deut 5:6–21), the very heart of the covenant stipulations.

The six laws are cited in summary fashion, not in their decalogue order, the first five each via a single word, in the infinitive absolute ("cursing," "lying," etc.), and the last of the six in a clause of its own ("the idols crowd against one another"). Structurally, the verse takes the form of a poetic triplet of which the final clause constitutes the third line perhaps because idolatry is the most blatant, obvious proof that the first and most programmatic of the commandments ("you must have no other gods before / besides me") has been broken.

The six covenant crimes compare to the decalogue as follows:

אלה "cursing": No. 3, "Do not use Yahweh's name wrongly . . ." (Exod
   20:7; Deut 5:11).
כחש "lying": No. 9, "Do not give any dishonest testimony . . ." (Exod
   20:16; Deut 5:20).
רצח "murder": No. 6, "Do not murder" (Exod 20:13; Deut 5:17).
גנב "stealing": No. 8, "Do not steal" (Exod 20:15; Deut 5:19).
נאף "adultery": No. 7, "Do not commit adultery" (Exod 20:14; Deut 5:18).
דמים "idols . . .": No. 2, "Do not make any image or likeness . . ." (Exod
   20:4–6; Deut 5:8–10).

Three of the six commandment violations are given in the exact root vocabulary of the decalogue (רצח "murder"; גנב "stealing"; נאף "adultery"), from the commandments containing only a single verb form and the negative לא "not". The other three citations are summaries, using vocabulary that does not precisely repeat the wordings to which they refer. "Cursing" (אלה) means denouncing or wishing evil against someone, or else sealing a private covenant, by invoking Yahweh's name (e.g., Judg 17:2), and does not refer to what is commonly called "swearing." "Lying" (כחש) denotes dishonesty in interpersonal relations, the most grievous examples of which are dishonest legal testimony (Exod 23:1) and dishonest business dealings (Deut 25:13–16).

The reference to multiple idols (lit., "the idols touch the idols") employs the noun דָּמִים (or דְּמִים; the original vocalization is uncertain) from the root דמה, used several times by Hosea (דמה I in 12:11 [10]; דמה II "perish" in 4:5, 6; 10:7, 15). דמה (I) means to "be like" or to "resemble" (see Dahood, *Psalms I*, 31–32, 163; *Psalms II*, 39; *Psalms III*, 297; and J. Holman, "Analysis of the Text of Ps 139," *BZ* 14 [1970] 216–17). A related word, דְּמוּת is found (cf. צלם, "image") four times in the Syrian Aramaic inscription from Tell Fekheriyeh, in the sense of "image" or "likeness" (A. Millard and P. Bordreuil, "A Statue from Syria with Assyrian and Aramaic Inscriptions," *BA* 45 [1982] 135–42; A. Abou-Assaf, A. Bordreuil, A. Millard, *La Statue de Tell Fekherye et son inscription bilingue assyro-araméenne*, Paris, 1982). This word summarizes the terms employed in the second commandment, פסל "image" and תמונה "likeness", as a synonym of both. Israel's idolatry undoubtedly involved Baal and Asherah worship, but may also have extended to worship of Yahweh via idols, given the appeal of idolatry as a worship aid in ancient times.

3 Flagrant violation of the covenant by Israel (under the all-encompassing term "land") demands swift retribution, in the form of a massive drought (curse type 6a as in Lev 26:19; Deut 28:22–24), conveying hyperbolically the full range of curses (cf. Deut 28:15–19; Deut 32:23–27) rather than only a literal drought.

The verse describes, then, a catastrophe which results in a land devoid of life. This judgment is, typically, introduced by על־כן, a synonym of לכן (2:8, 11, 16) "therefore." The first verb (אבל) describes the withering of vegetation (cf. its use in Amos 1:2; Jer 4:28; 12:4; Joel 1:10). The second verb (אמל) in the pual can refer to barrenness in child-bearing (e.g., Jer 15:9) or of agriculture (Isa 16:8; 33:9; Joel 1:10, 12; Nah 1:4). The "drought" will be so severe that even the sea will become dry, its fish "taken away." The verb used in this case (אסף, Niphal), a common expression for "passing away" or "being buried" (e.g., Gen 25:8; 35:29; 49:33; etc.), is a circumlocution for "to die" (cf. its curse context use in Lev. 26:25).

4 God now stands as the prosecutor to specify the charges. The first couplet resumes the theme of the lawsuit.

אך "surely" begins the specification. The language is still in the third person, and God is referred to as אֵל (correcting MT אַל־ "not"; cf. 2:1; 11:9; and 12:1). In the synonymous parallelism of the couplet, אִישׁ ("person," "somebody," etc.) is placed chiastically at the beginning and end to stress the particularity of the charge. The lawsuit narrows to apply to an individual, the priest, as representing a category, all priests (and prophets; see below).

The direct address of God begins. It may be that God, as prosecutor, imagined as speaking among elders and spectators at the trial (cf. Ruth 4:11), suddenly turns and points to the priest present announcing: "It is you—yes, you—priest, against whom I am making the accusation." There is, in other words, a surprise element possibly implied by the stress on "you" in the wording. In this sentence, the consonants must be revocalized with Kuhnigk (*NSH*, 31–32) as follows: וְעַמְּךָ כִּימָה רִיבִי כֹהֵן with the second word, כִּימָה intensifying the suffix ךָ "you."

Though it is conceivable that vv 4–10 constitute an attack on a particular priest (compare Amos 7:10–17), it is far more likely that the singular כהן "priest" is meant to apply generally to the priesthood, the institution which was supposed to mediate faithfully between God and his people.

5 Indeed, the clergy in general have led Israel astray and distorted the cult, for priest and prophet are paralleled in this verse.

The verb כשל "stumble" is cast in the converted perfect tense which would seem to imply a future judgment. The judgment of "stumbling" as a means of destruction recalls Deut 32:35 (". . . in due time their foot will slip . . .") as well as the curses of Deut 28:28–29 (blindness, groping about, helplessness). But the most direct connection with the covenant curses is found in Lev 26:37: "They will stumble, a man with/against his brother . . ." (וכשלו איש באחיו; curse type 19; cf. Hos 5:5; 14:2 [1]).

Priest (and prophet) will be punished by stumbling in the daytime (reading כָּשַׁלְתָּה יוֹמָם as opposed to MT כָשַׁלְתָּ הַיּוֹם when stumbling is abnormal, as well as at night, when it might be more expected. This plays effectively on the practice by the false prophets of seeking nighttime revelations (H. W. Wolff, *TLZ* 81 [1956] 83–90).

The mention of "prophet" here has troubled some commentators since elsewhere, it is alleged, Hosea speaks only in glowing terms of the prophets (6:5; 9:7–9; 12:10, 13). This view, however, probably misunderstands 9:7–9 (see *Comment*) and ignores the fact that at the Jerusalem temple prophets served the cult along with the priests (Isa 28:7; Jer 2:8; 4:9; 5:31; 6:13; 8:10; 14:18; 18:18; 23:11; Mic 3:11). It is unlikely that the well-attested southern practice of priest-prophet cooperation was unknown in the north.

The consonants of the final two words of the verse and the first word of v 6 are best vocalized as follows (with Kuhnigk, *NSH*, 30–31); וְדָמִית אֵמָה כְּנִדְמוּ "You will perish in terror, when [my people] perish . . . ," with אמה "terror" functioning adverbially. This reading is consistent with the curse language of Deut 32:25 ("in their homes terror [אמה] will reign . . . ") and Deut 28:65–67, where a day-and-night fear (פחד) afflicts covenant breakers (curse type 4). Moreover, destruction ("you will perish"; curse type 24) is the ultimate result of covenant breaking, the end to which most of the curses point (e.g., Deut 28:45).

6 The traditional division between v 5 and v 6 falls in the middle of a sentence that includes the last two words of v 5 and reads, "You will perish in terror when my people perish from lack of knowledge." This declaration shows how closely linked vv 4–10 are to vv 1–3. It brings into the picture the destruction of the whole nation (עמי "my people") of which the destruction of the priests is only one aspect. The drought/famine language of v 3 is recalled, in that "perishing from" (דמה) often connotes death resulting from a lack of food and water. Here, however, we learn that the real "drought" is otherwise, a lack of knowledge (דעת), the same shortcoming that constituted the essential break of the covenant described in v 1.

In terms that sound almost lamentative, God describes the tragic loss of covenant knowledge experienced by "my people," a term of covenant relationship in Hosea (cf. 2:3, 25; 4:8, 12; 6:11; 11:7). Israel had full covenant knowledge of its God, being bound to him by the Sinai relationship. Israel has now consciously rejected that "knowledge" relationship. And just as the priest rejected the knowledge, God will reject him from being priest (כהן, piel). Just as the priest has (consciously) forgotten the law of his God, God will forget the priest's children.

The covenant involved protection in return for loyalty and knowledge. Now will come the opposite: instead of protection, perishing (type 24), instead of loyalty, rejection (type 1), instead of knowledge, forgetting (type 1). Via these polar opposites God turns the tables against the priests for their abuse of the covenant stipulations.

Forgetting God's תורה "law" is an elaboration of the concept of rejecting God's covenant knowledge. In Hosea, "forget" functions as the opposite of "know" and can mean "disobey." Knowledge (דעת) involves a constant awareness of and obedience to the covenant relationship. Within this relationship, the תורה is the content of the actual requirements of the covenant "contract." The clergy were supposed to support this תורה, not merely by obeying it themselves, but also by instructing the people in its demands (Deut 31:9–13). Prophets like Hosea would not have needed to call people back to the covenant if the priests had done so.

Since the priesthood was hereditary, God announces that he will "forget" the priests' children. This is not merely a way of saying that the priesthood will be cut off but is rather the language of the curses of childlessness and/or bereavement (Deut 32:25; 28:18, 32, 41, 53–54; type 12a), here applied specifically to the priests.

7 This verse reveals three conditions of the northern priesthood. It was wealthy (כרבם "the richer they became"); heterodox (חטאו "they sinned");

and degenerate (. . . "their glory [כבודם] they traded . . ."). The priests—
not their children—are now referred to in the third person plural.

The prosperity that characterized the long reign of Jeroboam II also benefited the clergy. Their uncritical support of the upper classes and indulgence
of syncretism and materialism earned them (and probably the cult prophets)
wealth and prestige from a grateful populace, via tithes and donations. The
religious festivals, though compromising the true faith (v 13) were well attended and central to the nation's sense of identity (2:13). The clergy surely
regarded their own "success" as part of the general divine blessing (2:4–18)
and thus continued and expanded their sin against God, exchanging glory
for shame.

The words of the verse reflect Deut 32:15–16 closely. Abundance produces
an accrued wealth, which in turn results in false security and the temptation
to abandon God for some competing divinity. The resulting religion is degenerate.

Their "Glory" (כבודם), a proper name, is Yahweh (see Dahood, *Psalms I*,
99, 299; *Psalms II*, 293; van Dijk, *Tyre*, 23, 99; and in similar fashion Jer
2:11, ". . . my people have changed their Glory for worthless idols"). Thus
"disgrace" (קלון) may be taken as a metonymy for "idolatry," "false gods"
or the like. Israel's own priests actually abetted Israel's drift from Yahwism
to pagan polytheism.

8 Instead of teaching the people the nature of righteousness and motivat-
ing them to seek it, the priests are prospering via the OT equivalent of
selling indulgences. The priest who officiated at a sacrifice had the right to
a portion of the sacrificed animal (Lev 7:28–38). But the northern priests
were presumably exacting sin offerings (Lev 4) from the people in return
for declaring them forgiven. The Hebrew for "sin offering" is simply חטאת
(e.g., Lev 4:25; 16:27; etc.), the same word used for "sin." Thus the first
word of v 8 is the basis of a play on words: as the priests eat the "sin offering"
they are being nourished by the "sin" of the people. The second half of the
synonymous couplet makes this clear: they (the priests) live off the people's
iniquity.

God rejects this cult. It maintains in some ways the form he desires, but
it is loathsome in its hypocrisy (cf. Amos 4:4–5). Profit has become the interest
of the priesthood rather than service to God, and indulgence has become
the posture of the nation rather than purity in worship and deeds. The
priests' true duty was to encourage knowledge of and obedience to God (vv
6, 7). Instead, they encouraged sin and benefited from the multitude of sin
offerings.

9 In this verse and the beginning of the next the judgment sentence is
pronounced upon the priests. They will suffer the same fate as the rest of
the nation (cf. vv 5–6 where prophet, priest, and people perish together).

The idea that the priests' sin would be closely connected to the people's
sin is not a new one (Lev 4:3). The saying "like people, like priest" has the
ring of an epigram. It may have been a saying current among the priests,
with a positive sense originally. If so, its words are given a new meaning by
the oracle of judgment.

God declares that he will punish "his ways" and "his deeds." In light of

the shift back to the singular כהן "priest" in v 9a, we should take "his" as
referring to the clergy, not the people (עם). The punishment will be appropriate to the crimes. The evildoers will get exactly what they deserve, although
specific punishments are not enumerated (curse type 26; cf. the use of פקד
"repay" in Deut 5:9; Lev 26:16).

10 "Eating" (אכל), the central metaphor describing the priests' sin in v
8, will be a vehicle for their punishment; likewise "prostitution," referring
back further to 1:2 and 2:4–6 [2–4]. The priests are now again referred to
in the third person plural.

A synonymous couplet begins the judgment sentence. The punishments—
hunger and infertility (cf. types 7 and 12c)—are part of the stock of covenant
curses (Deut 28:17–18; 32:24–28). The curse style is that of the unfulfilled
expectation, or "futility curse" (see Hillers, *Treaty Curses*, 28 ff.), i.e., type
15, in which the guilty party's plans are dashed by God's withholding of
blessing (cf. Deut 28:30–33, 38–41; Hos 8:7; 9:12, 16; Amos 5:11; Mic 6:14–
15; etc.). For the opposite, blessing via benefit from the plans of others, see,
e.g., Josh 24:13.

The couplet has both literal and metaphorical levels. Literally, whatever
they may find to eat will not be enough to satisfy (שׂבע), and cultic ritual
sex, "prostitution" (הזנו), will, by reason of their infertility, prohibit their
"breaking forth" (יפרצו). פרץ, used to indicate childbirth (e.g., Gen 38:29;
here in the negative), implies lack of conception, or fetal death. Their generation is fated to die off.

Metaphorically, the priests' "devouring" of the people will not succeed
because God will punish them and take away their prosperity. Their "prostitution," idolatry and participation in the Baal fertility cult, will yield no increase
numerically or in terms of honor, prestige, or wealth.

The verse concludes this section on the priests (vv 4–10) with a statement
summarizing their sinful activity as prostitution. כי "because" introduces the
reason for their punishment: they had abandoned (עזב) Yahweh in favor
of "prostitution" (זנות), i.e., Baal worship. The verbs עזב and זנה appear
together in Deut 31:16 in a similar sense. Besides זנה in verbal and nominal
forms, Hosea uses קלון "disgrace" in 4:7, אויב "enemy" in 8:3, and מאהבים
"lovers" in 2:12–15 [10–13] as metonymies for the Baals.

The verb שׁמר ("revere," "keep," "attend to," etc.) is widely used in the
OT in the sense of revering / keeping the commandments of the Mosaic law.
It also can be used, however, as here, in connection with reverence for (i.e.,
worship of) idols, as in Ps 31:7 [6] (and Jonah 2:9), or more neutrally to
denote any worship of a god (Prov 27:18).

11 The hearer / reader is now introduced to a new section of the lawsuit
in which more evidence against Israel is presented. The corrupt cult, and
the relation of the citizenry to it, becomes the subject of vv 11–14. That it is
a cult of debauchery and self-indulgence is clear from God's initial characterization of its association with drunken folly: "wine and the fruit-of-the-vine
dulls the mind of my people." Here "wine" (יין) and "fruit-of-the-vine" (תירוש)
are associated closely as a compound subject in hendiadys, the verb used
with both (יקח) thus being singular. These terms for wine both refer to
processed, fermented wine, יין being the current Hebrew term in Hosea's
day, and תירוש the archaic term used almost exclusively in poetic parallelisms

(*pace* Wolff, 83). They occur together, for example, in synonymous parallelism in the Ugaritic poetical text 2 Aqhat VI (7–8). תירוש appears six times in Deuteronomy including 28:51 and 33:28. The close affinity of Hosea with these chapters of Deuteronomy may account partly for his frequent use of this otherwise archaic word either along with or instead of יין.

In Hosea "mind" (לב) is the center of analytical or reflective thought (7:2; cf. 7:11; 13:6, 8). Drunkenness interferes with the intellectual faculties of the people, literally "taking away" their mind. This idiom for dulling the intelligence occurs once elsewhere in the OT, in Job 15:12. It recalls the theme of lack of knowledge from 4:1, 6, but with a different emphasis. The alcoholic intoxication allowed by and incorporated into the cult revelry stands as a paradigm of their folly generally. For the people's mind to be dulled is to make it impossible for Yahweh to deal intelligently with them.

The verse division should be construed so as to exclude זנות "prostitution," which must go with v 10, and to include עמי "my people," which is traditionally part of v 12.

12 Divine speech continues to portray vividly the utter folly of the northern cult. Idolatry is mocked, and the cult denounced again as "prostitution."

Demented people! Israel inquires of and is advised by (synonymous terms) his "wood" (עץ) and his "staff" (מקל). It is not certain exactly which of several kinds of divination is intended here. The "wood" could refer to an idol of wood (cf. עץ in Deut 4:28; 28:36; 29:16). In Sumerian mythology wood was called "the flesh of the gods" because idols were so commonly crafted of it (cf. Jer 10:3; Isa 44:9–20; Hab 2:18–19). The Asherah pole used to represent the goddess Asherah (Deut 16:21; Judg 6:25f) is another possible referent for עץ. "Great trees" mentioned in connection with cults or prophets (Gen 12:6; Deut 11:30; Judg 4:5, etc.) may have been sources of divine oracles. Consultation of "wood" and "staff" most probably, however, denoted rhabdomancy—the determination of divine will by the examination of which way a stick (or sticks) falls (see Ezek 21:21).

A tragic futility is portrayed in these depraved cultic rituals thought somehow to be better than true knowledge via Yahweh's law. Such a conscious abandonment of the covenant can only anger God (cf. Deut 32:21, 28). The people are thus "led astray" by their "spirit of prostitution" (רוח זנונים) or "prostituting spirit." This spirit is either their own traitorous attitude, or else the power of unfaithfulness itself which sweeps them along in disobedience and error (cf. "spirit of confusion," רוח עועים, Isa 19:14). It is not an independent spirit-being, but a powerful, habituating devotion to heterodoxy.

The final clause, "they are prostituting themselves away from their God," recalls 1:2, "the land has gone thoroughly into prostitution away from (מאחרי) Yahweh." Here "away from" (מתחת) has the sense of getting "out from under" (cf. Exod 6:7, "out from under the yoke of the Egyptians"; 2 Kgs 8:20, 22, ". . . revolted out from under . . ."). God accuses Israel of finding his strict, moral monotheism oppressive, something that the indulgent Baal cult appeared to give freedom from. This is the force of the "prostituting spirit"— it is the spirit of selfish freedom, unfaithfulness to the "straight and narrow" life demanded by Yahweh, who is, whether they know it or not, "their God" (אלהיהם).

13 The "prostitution" of the false cult, described in terms of its debauchery and folly in vv 11–12, is displayed evidentially in the multiplicity of its shrines and altars (13a, b). The "mountain tops" (ראשי ההרים) and "hills" (הגבעות) are synonyms for the illegal shrines or "high places" (במות; cf. 10:8). On the basis of scattered OT accounts and archaeological recovery it is clear that such altar-shrines were simple arrangements, consisting at most of a small altar, a grove of trees, an idol of some kind, and a מצבה "stone pillar" representing either Yahweh, or Baal. Such altar-shrines, easy to erect, dotted the landscape and are referred to via the standard expression "on every high hill and under every green tree" (Deut 12:2; 1 Kgs 14:23; 2 Kgs 17:10; Jer 2:20, etc.; cf. Holladay, *VT* 11 [1961] 170–76). They served the decentralized Canaanite religion flourishing when the Israelites conquered the promised land, and their antiquity probably helped give them an aura of authenticity. The original practice of centralized worship at the official sanctuaries at Bethel and Dan (1 Kgs 12:26–33) had gradually become only one option among many.

Many of the sacrifices offered at these "high places" were probably dedicated syncretistically to Yahweh, whatever other Baal-Asherah overtones may have attended the worship. Hosea, like Amos, does not attack the concept itself of offering sacrifices. Rather, the heterodoxy of the worship site and procedure are unacceptable.

The people "made sacrifices" (יזבחו) and "burned offerings" (יקטרו) as a habitual practice (thus the imperfects). Listing three types of large trees suggests how generalized the practice was. In their "nice" shade worshipers would comfortably gather to cook and eat the sacrificial meal. The Mosaic law restricted this practice of worshipers eating part of the sacrifice they had offered to certain kinds of offerings (Lev 7:12–35). Most offerings could be eaten in part by the priests (Lev 7:28–35; 10:12–15; Num 18:8–19) except for those wholly dedicated to Yahweh (Lev 6:23). Further, the eating of sacrifices anywhere but Jerusalem was expressly forbidden (Deut 12:5–7, 15–27).

The synonymous couplet which concludes the verse at first glance appears to be a judgment sentence, introduced as it is by על־כן "therefore," a typical indicator of judgment clauses in the *rîb* (law-suit) pattern (cf. 2:4–17 [2–15]). But vv 13b–14 contain elements of "evidence" rather than predictions of punishment. Thus the admittedly ambiguous Hebrew imperfect verbs presumably are not statements of what God will do to the women of Israel (punishment), but descriptions of what Israelite women are doing against God (evidence). Beyond על־כן, the parallelism is precise: the daughters "turn to prostitution" (תזנינה) and the daughters-in-law to "adultery" (תנאפנה). As נאף functions simply as a synonym, part of a fixed pair with זנה, so "daughters" (בנות) and "daughters-in-law" (כלות) constitute a fixed pair referring generally to females in the population (see Kuhnigk, *NSH*, 49–50) and not to any special sub-group. Vv 13b and 14a present a vivid description of the sins of the women, complemented in v 14b by an excoriation against the sins of the men.

There is no evidence in these charges that the women are participating in fertility cult rituals, such as the ritual deflowering of virgins via intercourse with their fathers-in-law at shrines; or via intercourse with strangers in the

name of a god or goddess (see Wolff, 86–87; L. Rost, *FS Alfred Bertholet,*
451–60; W. Rudolph, *ZAW* 75 [1963] 65–73; H. Klein, *TZ* 37 [1981] 3–18;
et al). Such a reconstruction of the situation is problematic for two reasons.
First, there is no actual reference to such a practice in the OT. If something
so abominable as a ritual loss of virginity really took place routinely in the
north, one would expect at least one of the biblical writers to condemn it
clearly, as they do with a great variety of other sins.

Second, the reconstruction ignores the legal context of זנה "prostitute" as
a treaty / covenant term. In Exod 34:15–16, for example, women who worship
other gods "prostitute themselves to their gods," and "lead your sons to do
the same." This language closely parallels Hos 4:13b–14a, and illumines it.
It is the women's theological heterodoxy that constitutes their "prostitution."

14 Many translations interpret v 14a as an indicative statement, as if
God exonerated the women of Israel because their guilt was not entirely
voluntary. More likely, however, v 14a is a question (cf. H. Nyberg, *Studien
zum Hoseabuch,* ad loc. [Uppsala: Lundequistska, 1935]), one that may even
extend as far as the end of v 14 (i.e., "Shall I not punish . . . even the men
who . . ."), though this is less certain. The women's guilt is surely punishable.
How would God punish "land" and "people" yet exempt the women?

V 14 reinforces by repetition the situation described in v 13, and adds
the promise of punishment as a judgment sentence. The evidence is clear.
"Shall I not punish" accordingly? God asks.

God's concern is hardly limited to Israel's women, however. How can he
ignore the evidence of the literal, physical prostitution that "they" (הם), the
men, are involved with? The divine judge/prosecutor turns now to the men,
to recount *their* crimes prior to announcing their judgment. Here in v 14b
occurs a rare non-metaphorical use of זנה in Hosea. "Prostitutes" (הזנות) is
from the singular זנה, the common Hebrew term for "prostitute" in the
literal sense of a woman who sells sex.

Since הזנות is paralleled here by הקדשות "the cult prostitutes," it is likely
that the "dividing" (יפרדו) is related to, or is an aspect of, the sacrificing
(יזבחו) which the men do with these prostitutes. The cult prostitutes functioned as official participants at the altar-shrine sacrifices. Israelite men would
bring their sacrifices to the shrine, prepare these and offer (פרד) the portions
with the cult prostitutes (פרד, piel, probably has this sense rather than the
supposed "go off"). Then they would have intercourse with the cult prostitutes,
as a ritual act of "sympathetic magic," designed to stimulate the god(s) of
fertility to fertilize the land. For homosexuals, homosexual prostitutes were
provided (1 Kgs 14:24; 15:12; 22:46; 2 Kgs 23:7).

Such a custom was widespread in the ancient Near East and is documented
both from the OT (Gen 38:21, 22; Deut 23:17) and from texts from Syria,
Phoenicia, Egypt, and Mesopotamia (see Code of Hammurabi, laws 110, 127,
178–82; the text cited by Harper, 261–62; Middle Assyrian Laws No. 40 [T.
Meek, *ANET,* 183]; W. F. Albright, *Archaeology and the Religion of Israel* [Balti-
more: Johns Hopkins, 1956] 75 f., 158 f.; E. A. Speiser, *Genesis,* AB 1 [Garden
City, NY: Doubleday, 1964] 299 n. 21; M. Pope, *Song of Songs,* AB 7c [Garden
City, NY: Doubleday, 1977] 214–29).

The men's and women's prostitution having been presented as damning evidence, the hearer / reader now learns the resultant fate of the nation, rendered in an epigrammatic judgment sentence (curse): "A people that lacks understanding must be ruined because it turns to prostitution" (זֹנֶה, masc sg qal act ptcp).

Prostitution leads to ruin! (Cf. Prov 10:8, 10 for ילבט as "will be ruined.") Thus the entire oracular section (vv 11–14) comes to a logical conclusion: A dull-minded people (v 11), led astray by a "prostituting spirit" (v 12), engage in a variety of sinful cultic practices (vv 13–14b) which constitute a prostitution that will ruin them (v. 14b). This reflects curse type 24 (cf. Deut 28:20, et al).

In the "people that lacks understanding" (עם לא יבין) we hear the echo of the people who are "destroyed for lack of knowledge" (v 6) because "there is no knowledge of God in the land" (v 1). The themes of "lack of knowledge" and "prostitution" are thus interwoven in the section, as depictions of the epidemic sinfulness of the northern kingdom.

15 The final section (vv 15–19) of the lawsuit begins with a fourfold imperative warning Israel against further guilt via worship at two major northern sanctuary centers, Gilgal and Bethel. The verse is unusual for its hortatory style, for its apparent reference to Judah (but see below) and for its rather close connection to Amos 5:5. Our reconstruction eliminates the reference to Judah (see *Translation* and *Notes*) in addition to reading MT's אם זנה with v 14 as "to prostitution."

The verse is loosely chiastic, with its first and fourth elements relatively synonymous (". . . do not incur guilt from Yahweh"; "Do not swear, 'As Yahweh lives' "), and second and third elements comparable likewise ("Do not enter Gilgal"; "Do not go up to Beth-Awen"). These prohibitions are not permanent (which would be expressed by לא plus the imperfect) but temporal warnings about the false religion practiced at those particular sites (perhaps among others).

The limited correspondence of vocabulary between Hos 4:15 and Amos 5:5 is probably coincidental, the same subject matter merely occasioning a slight overlap in vocabulary from two prophets whose ministry was so complementary.

Hosea 4:15 reads:	ואל־תבאו הגלגל ואל־תעלה בית־און
	"Do not enter Gilgal; do not go up to Beth-Awen"
Amos 5:5 reads:	ואל־תדרשו בית־אל והגלגל לא תבאו
	"Do not seek Bethel; do not enter Gilgal"

Aside from the fact that they both prohibit worship at Bethel (בית־אל in Amos; בית־און "Beth-Awen" in Hosea) and Gilgal, the oracles are divergent.

The essence of the verse's message is found in the first imperative אל־תאשמו "do not incur guilt" (cf. 10:2; 13:1; 14:1 [13:16]), the subsequent prohibitions identifying practices that would result in guilt, i.e., pilgrimages to Gilgal and Bethel. Gilgal, the site at which the Israelites encamped after crossing the Jordan (Josh 4:19), became a major sanctuary, degenerating into a center of heterodox worship (9:15; 12:11). "Beth-Awen" ("House of Trouble"), a sarcastic metonymy for Bethel, "House of God," (5:8; 10:5) and reminiscent of Amos 5:5, ". . . Bethel will come to trouble (לאון)," was the leading northern shrine (1 Kgs 12:28–30; Amos 7:13). Swearing at these false sanctuaries with the oath "as Yahweh lives . . ." mocked the true faith, and violated the third commandment (Exod 20:7; Deut 5:11; cf. Hos 4:2).

This oath was traditional in covenants or vows (Deut 6:13; 10:20; Judg 8:19; Ruth 3:13; 1 Sam 14:39; Jer 23:7; Amos 8:14; etc.; cf. Ugaritic *ḥy ʾaliyn bˤl*, "As the valiant Baal lives . . .") and was entirely orthodox. In Jer 4:2; 5:2 the oath is actually enjoined, as long as it follows upon the rejection of idolatry and is sworn "in a truthful, just, and righteous way." Why does Hosea prohibit it? Because when Yahweh's name was invoked in Bethel or Gilgal, idolatry was *not* rejected, and the oath therefore *not* righteous, but rather "in vain" (לשוא, Exod 20:7). Yahweh will not honor the form of the oath if the circumstances of its utterance are sinful.

16 The judgment on unfaithful Israel will be death (curse type 24). Hosea summarizes the damning evidence, using the metaphor of a stubborn cow to depict Israel's unfaithfulness. He then announces the judgment, depicting her fate via the metaphor of shepherding a lamb in the underworld. כי "since" introduces the protasis of the conditional sentence, highly assonant via the repetition of *k*, *r*, and *s*: *kî kᵉparāh sorērāh sārar yiśraʾēl* "Since like a stubborn cow Israel is stubborn."

Israel refuses to obey Yahweh. What he wants them to do, they balk at. The metaphor recalls the earlier figure of an animal with a propensity to wander off, who must be fenced in (2:8 [6]). This time, however, the context is not one of the generous patience and grace of Yahweh.

The sentence of judgment constitutes the apodosis, introduced by עתה "then": "then Yahweh will pasture them like a lamb in the Expanse." A shift of metaphor transforms Israel into a lamb (כבש), smaller, more docile than a cow. Israel will be "a different kind of animal," when Yahweh is through with it. The promise that Yahweh will "pasture them" (ירעם) is very different from the images in a poem like Ps 23. No "green pastures" or "still waters" for this lamb! Its habitat will be the "Expanse" (מרחב), a synecdoche for the "afterworld," Sheol (cf. Ps 49:15 [14]: "Like sheep they will be settled in Sheol; death will pasture them"). The word מרחב can refer to the vast expanses of the nether world (Pss 18:20 [19] [=2 Sam 22:20] and 31:9 [8]), and in Job 38:17, 18 an alternate noun form from the same root (רחב) is used in the expression רחבי־ארץ "expanses of the underworld" in parallelism with שערי־מות ("gates of Death") and שערי־צלמות ("gates of Gloom"). See further Kuhnigk, *NSH*, 50–52.

The vivid metaphor makes clear that Israel's sins are mortal ones.

17 The statement that Ephraim is in league with / bound to idols is a way of giving evidence that Israel is no longer part of the covenant with Yahweh. Here occurs the first of thirty-six times that "Ephraim" functions as a metonymy for Israel (see 5:3–4; 11:8 for Israel and Ephraim in parallelism), a practice also of Isaiah, Ezekiel, Jeremiah, Obadiah and Zechariah. Ephraim constituted the bulk of the shrunken northern kingdom after the Assyrian campaign in 733 B.C. Because this passage, among others mentioning Ephraim, is probably earlier in date than 733, the use of the term cannot result merely from historical circumstances. Amos does not use the term. Hosea may have been inspired to coin it because he preached almost exclusively in Ephraimite territory. It became particularly appropriate after 733, of course.

חבור "in league with" reflects the language of covenant alliance (cf. Gen 14:3), now with idols—calf idols (cf. 8:4–5; 13:2; 14:9 [8]) and possibly also Asherah poles (4:12) and teraphim (3:4; cf. דמים "idols" 4:2). Idolatry is a paramount evidence of covenantal violation (cf. Deut 4:25 et al.).

Is there any hope for this confederate of idols? No. הנח־לו "Leave him to himself!" is the judgment sentence for the idolater, i.e., abandon-ment / rejection (type 1; cf. Deut 31:18; 32:20). Mocking the impotence of idols and the foolishness of those who trust them for deliverance is well attested in the prophets (Isa 45:20; 46:7; Jer 2:28; cf. Hos 14:4 [3]). Israel / Ephraim, abandoned by Yahweh, is now left to the nothings that he has been depending on.

18 The verse poses so many textual problems that any reconstruction must be highly speculative. G varies from MT substantially, and there is little basis for choice between them. One can be fairly sure from the context that the topic is Israel's continuing degeneration toward inevitable destruction. The reference to hard drinking (סבא) seems consistent with the context, and Hosea's common theme word זנה "prostitution" is expected if the verse contains reference to covenant-breaking practices perhaps including the wor-ship-sex of the fertility cult mentioned in v 14. The connection of drinking and ritual sex has documentation (M. Pope, *Song of Songs* 214–29; 374).

"Prostitution" (זנה) is expressed via the infinitive absolute plus finite verb, thus we translate "take their fill of prostitution." Then the "shame of insolence" (קלון מגנה) is described as something that the Israelites "really love," again with the absolute infinitive construction, if we may trust the text.

Israel's cult is degenerate, depraved, debauched. In light of such evidence, Yahweh must bring judgment.

19 The "wind" (רוח) that has bound Israel and sweeps them along is probably a play on the prostituting "spirit" (רוח) of v 12. It is also possible that it functions here with a double meaning. The wings of this wind / spirit can wrap (צרר) Israel, suggestive of its power to control. But v 19a is not simply another statement of evidence but a part of the sentence of judgment. Destruction by wind is well attested in judgment contexts (Job 1:19; Pss 1:4; 35:5; Prov 11:29; Isa 11:15; 57:13; Jer 22:22; Ezek 27:26; etc) and is a variation on the death / destruction curses (type 24). Shame, rather than pros-perity, will be Israel's earnings from its sacrifices.

Explanation

God's covenant people are called to court, found to be in violation of the stipulations of his covenant, and sentenced to destruction.

The passage details a long series of crimes against the divine law, all related to the catalog of blessings and curses found in Deut 28–33. The sins of omission and commission pictured so relentlessly throughout the chapter make up a remarkably complete picture of the depths of Israel's apostasy.

It is essential to realize that priesthood and cult were not merely two institu-tions among many in Israel, but were the very fabric of that society. The religion of the people was more determinative of the destiny of the nation even than the actions of the government. Israel's bond to Yahweh was a matter of religious observance, which civil and international affairs could only mirror, not determine.

By supplementing their religious base of Yahwism with other forms of worship (vv 2, 12, 13, 17, 18) apparently effective for their Canaanite neighbors and the nations surrounding them, the Israelites assumed that they had hit upon a formula for abundance. A syncretistic religion was not only more enjoyable, in terms of the practices it allowed and / or prescribed (vv 14, 18), but it also seemed to bring better results. The last years of Jeroboam were prosperous. Surely this "blessing" was proof of righteousness, and the narrow standards of fundamentalistic Yahwism were now shown to have been needless and oppressive strictures!

But the manifold covenant violations cited repeatedly throughout the lawsuit were evidence that the people and their cult were so wrongly oriented that they did not know God at all! Their "success religion" was a travesty of true religion, that must be punished by destruction (vv 3, 5, 9, 16, 19). It was not "truth" (v 2) or "glory" (v 7) but "prostitution" (vv 10, 11, 12, 14, 15, 18). They were receiving no guidance from their ridiculous divination (v 11) or idols (vv 2, 17), but were being swept relentlessly to folly by a prostituting spirit (v 12). The end of all this could only be the destruction of the land itself (v 3), as Israel would be exiled and its territory blighted.

The priesthood is denounced not because there is something intrinsically wrong with it as an institution, but because it is not doing what it was instituted by Yahweh to do. When the priests, charged to see that the law is known and kept by the people (Deut 31:9–13) fail in their solemn responsibility, then a prophet must call them to task. By embracing the multiple countersanctuaries (v 15), approving heterodox religious practices characterized by debauchery (vv 11, 14, 18) and by neglecting their basic duty under the covenant (vv 6, 7) the priesthood earned the same fate as the people (v 9).

The covenant was to be "daily life" to Israel (Deut 32:47). They were a "kingdom of priests" (Exod 19:6). Now neither that priestly kingdom nor the official priests (or prophets) within it were keeping the covenant.

As God had predicted to an earlier generation of Israelites through Moses: ". . . because this people abandoned the covenant of Yahweh . . . and went off and worshipped other gods . . . therefore Yahweh's anger burned against this land, so that he brought on it all the curses written in this book" (Deut 29:25–27), so Hosea confirmed, "Therefore, the land will dry up, and all who live in it will become barren" (v 3), and "they will come to shame" (v 19).

An Unclean People Summoned to Judgment (5:1–7)

Bibliography

Budde, K. "Zu Text und Auslegung des Buches Hosea (5:1–6:6)." *JPOS* 14 (1934) 1–41. **Elliger, K.** "Eine verkannte Kunstform bei Hosea." *ZAW* 69 (1957) 151–60. **Held, M.** "The Action-Result (Factitive-Passive) Sequence of Identical Verbs in Biblical

Hebrew and Ugaritic." *JBL* 84 (1965) 272–82. **Muilenburg, J.** "Mizpah." *IDB* 3:407–9. **Muraoka, T.** "Hosea V in the Septuagint Version." *Abr-Nahrain* 24 (1986) 120–38. **Noth, M.** "Beiträge zur Geschichte des Ostjordanlandes III." *ZDPV* 68 (1951) 49–50. **Weiss, R.** "A Note on אתה in Exodus 10, 11." *ZAW* 76 (1964) 188.

Translation

Summons to Israel's leadership

5:1 *Hear this, priests!*
Pay attention, family of Israel!
Listen, family of the king!
Because the judgment is yours. [a]

Prediction of captivity

Since you have been a trap for Mizpah,
A net spread over Tabor,
2 *A ⟨pit⟩* [a] *dug* [b] *at Shittim,* [c]
Then I will be shackles [d] *for all of you.* [e]

Evidence against Israel

3 *I know Ephraim;*
Israel is not hidden from me;

Now that Ephraim practices prostitution, [a]
Israel is unclean.

4 *They will not give up* [a] *their deeds*
to return to their God.

For a prostituting spirit is in their midst, [b]
so that they do not know Yahweh.
5 *Israel's pride testifies against him.*

Judgment against them

As for Israel—that is, Ephraim—they will stumble because of their guilt;
Judah, too, will stumble with them.

6 *With their flocks and herds they will go to seek Yahweh,*
But they will not find him. He will have withdrawn from them.

7 *They have betrayed Yahweh;*
Indeed, they are children born [a] *illegitimate,* [b]
So now a new people [c] *will eat their portions!*

Notes

1.a. The Heb. is a purposeful double-entendre. Grammatically it can mean either "this judgment is against you" or "to you justice is entrusted."

2.a. Reading שחת "pit" instead of MT שחט "corruption." The ה goes with "Shittim."

2.b. Lit., "(which) they dug."

2.c. The place name (ה)שטים "Shittim" (Num 25:1) belongs in the context in parallel to Mizpah and Tabor (v 1). MT's vocalization is unlikely.

2.d. MT מוּסָר is ambiguous. It can mean "shackle," from אסר as here translated. The more common vocalization is מוֹסֵר, but Job 12:18 has the present vocalization. It can also mean "instruction" or "correction" from יסר. G (Vg) has παιδευτής "teacher," presupposing מְיַסֵּר or the like.

2.e. Following G instead of MT (כלם "all of you").

3.a. Following G Syr Tg, with the 3 pers form of the verb.

4.a. The Heb. is ambiguous as to whether the subject of יתנו "they will give up" is "Israel" (unexpressed) or "their deeds." In the latter case, translate "their deeds do not permit ⟨them⟩ (יתנו-(ם)), assuming either haplogr of the ם or a "shared" ם with מעלליהם "their deeds" (see Kuhnigk, *NSH*, 59–66).

4.b. Or, "within them." The NIV translation "in their heart" is only interpretive.

7.a. Reading either יֻלְדוּ (qal, passive) or יֻלְדוּ (pual) with G.

7.b. Heb. זָרִים can also mean "loathsome" (from זור II).

7.c. MT as it stands makes little sense (". . . a new moon will eat them, their fields"). G substitutes ἡ ἐρυσίβη (החסיל) "the locust" for חדש "new moon" which probably reflects a scribal change made sometime earlier in the Heb. text tradition used by G. Our emendation is simpler than others proposed thus far (see Harper, 268; Wolff, 95, n. m), assuming haplogr of only a single letter, ע, thus: יאכל (ע)ם חדש "a new people will eat" (see *Comment*).

Form / Structure / Setting

A triple imperative in v 1 announces a summons to the Israelite leadership. Thereafter comes a denunciation of Israel's rebelliousness, and a judgment prediction (v 7). A break with the *rîb* (lawsuit) of 4:1–19 is evident at the outset of the passage. The address to the priests (in the plural) while reminiscent of the lawsuit against the priesthood (כהן, singular) in 4:4–10 is hardly indicative of formal continuity with chap. 4. Nevertheless, this reminiscence may explain why the two passages were juxtaposed editorially. Verse 8 begins a different imperative, a war summons related to another historical situation.

The passage divides into two units, each somewhat independent of the other. Vv 1–2 contain a divine summons to attention, like a judge's summary of the evidence against a guilty defendant, and a judgment sentence: ". . . I will be shackles for all of you." First-person divine speech continues in v 3, leading to the concluding section (4–7), in which Yahweh is spoken of in the third person. The second unit, vv 3–7, is similar to vv 1–2 in that it also summarizes the evidence against Israel and ends with a judgment sentence, ". . . a new people will eat their share!"

We can discern in vv 1–7 a disputation, without the full features of the *rîb* pattern (cf. 2:4–17 [2–15]; 4:1–19). Wolff (95) considers the passage a messenger speech in combination with a disputation. Whatever its formal designation, the passage clearly condemns Israel's sin and announces Yahweh's judgment thereon.

The presence or absence of uniformity in such matters as speaker, addressee, poetic parallelism, or other formal features is relatively insignificant in Hosea (cf. 2:4–7 [2–5]). The unity of a passage is evident far more in subject matter, theological categories, tone, and general logic—things which by their very nature cannot be quantified. The passage is poetic. Two synonymous triplets comprise the bulk of vv 1–2, which also display external parallelism and a closely balanced meter in exquisite structure. V 3 is also synonymous in parallelism, befitting its close connection to vv 1–2 (see above). Vv 4–7 are synthetic in their parallelism, and therefore relatively unbalanced metrically, but clearly poetic as evidenced in their style, syntax, and vocabulary.

There is some evidence that all three localities mentioned in vv 1–2 (Mizpah,

Tabor, Shittim) may have been annexed by Tiglath-Pileser after the completion of the Syro-Ephraimite war in 733 B.C. (cf. A. Alt, "Hosea 5:8–6:6," *Kleine Schriften* [Munich: C. H. Beck'sche, 1953] 2:187, n.1). That date would then become the *terminus ad quem* of the prophecy. How much earlier the passage can be fixed in time is more difficult to assess.

The circle of addressees presupposed in 5:1–7 is not ultimately different from those of 4:1–19, since in one way or another all of Israel is called to task in each passage. That the royal family is addressed directly suggests that this oracle could have been spoken at Samaria. With regard to the cities mentioned, we note that in 4:15 Bethel and Gilgal, major northern cult centers located only fifteen miles apart, would have been, from the point of view of Hosea's audience, "local" sanctuaries. Tabor, Mizpah, and Shittim (5:1–2), however, were relatively more distant sites, and not necessarily "cult centers," suggesting that the conscious geographical scope of 5:1–7 is just as broad as in 4:1–19.

Otherwise, several continuities between 4:1–19 and 5:1–7 would suggest a similar setting for 5:1–7, perhaps late in the reign of Jeroboam II or shortly thereafter. At least in terms of shared vocabulary the similarities are strong: זנה, 4:10, 18 and 5:3; רוח זנונים, 4:12 and 5:4; אין דעת אלהים, 4:1 (cf. also 4:6) and ידעו לא יהוה, 5:4; כשל, 4:5 and 5:5.

Comment

1–2 The formal structure may be diagrammed as follows:

> v 1   Imperative: Hear (שמעו)   Addressee: priests
> Imperative: Pay attention (הקשיבו)   Addressee: family of Israel.
> Addressee: family of the king   Imperative: Listen (האזינו)
> Reason for summons: Because the judgment is yours.
> Evidence: Since you have been a trap (*pah*) at Mizpah (*ph//ph*)
> Evidence: A net spread (*rešet pᵉrûśāh*) over Tabor (*tpr//tbr*)
> v 2   Evidence: A pit (*šahătāh*) dug at Shittim (*šht//štt*)
> Judgment sentence: Then I will be shackles for all of you.

Each unit has four major elements. In the first there are three imperatives and a judgment sentence. In the second unit, there are three accusations connected with three scattered sites, also followed by a judgment statement.

The first unit contains a three-element, somewhat chiastic address. Two particular terms of Israelite leadership (priests, royalty) surround the more general inclusive term for leadership (family of Israel; cf. 1:7). Secondly, the third line reverses the order from imperative-addressee to addressee-imperative, forming thus a chiasm of word order. The fourth line then contains a purposeful ambiguity, saying either that Israel's leadership has the responsibility for "justice" or that they are about to receive "judgment." Both meanings can be understood.

In the second unit, paronomasia is employed. In the first three lines three types of hunting traps recall certain consonantal sounds (see above) in the names of three Israelite localities, probably chosen primarily for their sound, not because they were parallel to Bethel and Gilgal. The fourth line again contains a purposeful ambiguity in that מוסר can mean either "instruction / chastisement" or "shackles." The entire sequence is a divine saying with a certain unity of its own, yet appropriate as an introduction to the larger unit of which it is a part, vv 1–7.

The triple summons with which the passage begins is reminiscent of the triple summons of Jacob to his children in Gen 49:1–2. There, the imperatives are, respectively, האספו "gather," הקבצו "approach," and שמעו "hear," the latter being the key imperative. (See D. Stuart, *Studies in Early Hebrew Meter,* 139.) Of the three imperatives in the present passage, שמעו "hear" is also the key; הקשיבו "pay attention" and האזינו "listen" are from roots that occur as synonymous fixed pairings with שמע rather often (הקשיב // שמע Job 13:6; 33:31; Prov 4:1; 7:24; Isa 28:23; 49:1; Mic 1:2; האזין // שמע Gen 4:23; Deut 32:1; Judg 5:3; Job 34:2; Ps 49:2; Isa 1:2,10; 28:23; 32:9; Jer 13:15; Joel 1:2). Since most of these passages are not covenant lawsuits, but "summonses" to hear the word of God, the present summons need not be understood as a courtroom speech. It may be construed as more general legal teaching. As Wolff (97) points out, when a prophet speaks as a law teacher, "it is not always possible to distinguish between him and the plaintiff." Here, however, the likelihood is that the legal teacher/prosecutor is Yahweh.

None of the groups addressed can escape judgment. Indeed, the "family of Israel" (בית ישראל), i.e., its leadership collectively, is due for judgment. Suggestions to emend "family of Israel" to "elders of the family of Israel" (e.g., Rudolph) are advanced only when the chiasm (priests: people: royalty) is missed. An attack on the royal family already appeared in 1:4; the priesthood came under judgment in 4:4–10. The people / nation as a whole heard its doom predicted in each of the chapters thus far, with responsibility being placed on the leadership. The verse, then, does not introduce anything new but reemphasizes the fact that while all segments of the society will come under judgment (vv 3–7), the leadership particularly has failed in its sacred responsibilities to Yahweh.

By the juxtaposition of three types of hunting traps with three localities (including Shittim in v 2a) the oracle continues God's excoriation of the leadership, royalty and priesthood. The three sites mentioned are significant more for their randomness than for any special characteristics that they share in common. The sense of the accusation is: "to places like . . . you have become like. . . ." All over Israel, political and religious oppression keeps the people from the freedom that they would have via a true knowledge of Yahweh (v 4). The nation's government and religion were established by God to protect and benefit his people. Instead, they have preyed upon the people, like snares to trap and imprison rather than to support and protect.

There were several cities named Mizpah in ancient Israel (cf. Muilenburg, *IDB* 3:407–9). The best known is Mizpah of Benjamin, where Samuel served as judge (1 Sam 7:6, 16) and Saul was anointed king (1 Sam 10:17). Any one, however, would do for the purposes of the oracle, in which randomness rather than specificity is the key. Shittim (v 2a), known from the Baal-Peor story (Num 25:1–2; cf. Hos 9:10), was originally a Moabite city but was clearly part of Israelite territory during the reign of Jeroboam II and briefly thereafter (M. Noth, *ZDPV* 68 [1951] 49–50). Tabor, the mountain, called today *jebel et-tor,* is a 1500 ft. peak north of the Jezreel valley and was the meeting point of the common boundaries of Issachar, Naphtali, and Zebulun (Josh 19:12, 22, 34). Thus via examples from city and country alike, Deut 28:16 is recalled: "You will be cursed in the city and cursed in the country."

The fact that Mizpah, Tabor, and Shittim can be proved to have been some sort of cult centers (see Wolff, 98–99 for the evidence) is hardly the point: the cult was so diversified that *any* locality probably had an active shrine (cf. 4:13). The point is rather that the leadership is corrupting the people everywhere.

2 One of the curses for covenant infidelity was that of oppression by enemies (type 5). The final sentence of v 2 reflects this. God announces that he will place all of them in shackles (lit., "be shackles for all of you"). This prediction has two close parallels in Deuteronomy, the "iron yoke" of 28:48, and the "slavery" of 28:68. Ezek 20:37 contains another close parallel, likewise in a judgment context, using a cognate of מוסר: "I will bring you in with the shackles (מסרת) of the covenant." The traps the leaders have set to imprison Israel's innocent will be nothing compared to the chains and fetters in which Yahweh will lead them to exile and slavery in a foreign nation. The force of the word כלם "all of them," is simply to convey that the captivity will involve all Israel—not just its leadership.

3 Vv 3–7 continue the theme of judgment as a result of unfaithfulness. The emphasis now shifts from the leadership to the people as a whole. In v 3 the point that Yahweh was not fooled by what was going on in Ephraim / Israel is hammered home by two externally parallel synonymous couplets.

Yahweh's continued first person speech provides a connection with the close of v 2. The verse does not introduce a new concept, i.e., the omniscience of God, but emphasizes God's cognition of Israel's sin *in contrast to* the deception that the people themselves have been trapped into (vv 1–2). Since Israel has engaged in "prostitution" ([ה]הזנ), covenant infidelity, it is "unclean" (נטמא). The verb טמא occurs again in 6:10 and 9:4 where, as here, it is employed as a description of guilt. To be "clean" or "unclean" (טמא) was an important distinction in Israel and became a common metaphor, used by the prophets to portray defilement vis-à-vis the covenant (see especially Ezekiel, Haggai, and Amos 7:17). Certain kinds of uncleanness were considered so offensive as to be grounds for banishment (Lev 7:19–21).

It was the function of the priests to distinguish between clean and unclean (Lev 10:10) so that worship and cultic life could be properly conducted. Obviously the priests had failed (v 1) and Israel had become loathsome to Yahweh just as if actual prostitution were being allowed to defile the sanctuary.

4 The description of Israel's waywardness continues. The national misbehavior is deliberate. Whether one translates "they will not give up their deeds" or "their deeds do not permit them" the message conveyed is the same: Yahweh's covenant people have removed themselves from him.

The stylistic shift to the third person plural is probably occasioned partly by logic. A description of the deeds of the *people* (pl) is more appropriate here where the emphasis is upon voluntary participation in the false cult. In vv 1–2 the role of the citizenry was (implicitly) passive. Here, however, Israel's citizens are kept away from Yahweh by their own deeds. In Hosea, "deeds" (מעללים) seem to mean in effect *evil* deeds (cf. 4:9; 7:2; 9:15; 12:3 [2]), both cultic and social. (Cf. Deut 28:20, where רע מעלליך "your evil deeds" constitute the basis for the covenant curses.) Such evil deeds amount to "forsaking" (עזב) Yahweh (Deut 28:20; also Deut 29:24; 31:16, 17; Hos 4:10).

The "prostituting spirit" (רוח זנונים) in their midst is an orientation that prevails among the people, rather than something that possesses them individually (cf. 1:2; 4:12). By reason of this orientation, they are unable to know Yahweh.

V 4b reflects much of the sense of chap. 4, especially the verb ידע "know" and the theme, "lack of knowledge."

5 Israel, on the witness stand, is unable to avoid condemning himself by reason of his pride. Although G translates ταπεινωθήσεται "shall be humbled" for ענה (II), thus construing the verse as a judgment sentence (cf. 7:10) it is more likely that ענה ב should be taken in its usual idiomatic sense of "testify against," as in Deut 31:21 (cf. Exod 20:16; Num 35:30; 1 Sam 12:3; 2 Sam 1:16; Job 32:12; Mic 6:3). Legal terminology is employed only here and in v 1, though the legal nature of the entire passage is implicit throughout.

The "pride of Israel" (גאון־ישראל) refers to the arrogant rebellion of the people against Yahweh's law by their false cult and social injustice. Both actions show a disdain for the strictures of the Mosaic code—such things are beneath them. Abandonment of single-minded loyalty to Yahweh has permitted a life of self-indulgence.

The juxtaposition of ישראל "Israel" and אפרים "Ephraim" as subjects of the plural verb יכשלו "they stumble" probably reflects either hendiadys or apposition, the ו preceding אפרים meaning "even," "indeed," "that is," "namely," etc. (cf. 2 Sam 1:23; Amos 4:10; 1 Chr 21:12). At any rate, the verb in the plural is not surprising (cf. the similar shift to the plural in 7:10, where "Israel" is first construed as a singular, then as a plural).

The reference to Judah in 5bβ is often taken as a gloss on the assumption that references to Judah represent the concern of a Judean redactor. כשל גם יהודה עמם "Judah, too, will stumble with them" is alleged to lack poetic coordination with the foregoing material. As Kuhnigk has pointed out, however (*NSH*, 66–67), the two forms of כשל "stumble" (niphal in 5bα; qal in 5bβ) which link the Judah "gloss" to the rest of v 5 reflect a widely attested pattern of parallelism in Hebrew and Ugaritic (see M. Held, *JBL* 84 [1965] 272–82 and 8:11). The supposed gloss would appear, then, to coordinate nicely with the rest of v 5, and may be retained as genuine. The reference to Judah informs Hosea's audience that Judah can fall by pride just as easily as can Israel. Hosea uses כשל a total of six times (4:5; 5:5; 14:2 [1]; 14:10 [9]), each indicating judgment for sin. The metaphor of stumbling is a covenant curse term (type 19, e.g., Deut 32:35) denoting coming into trouble generally as a result of disobedience (cf. 4:5).

6 The sacrificial system that flourished in the north was illegal because it was not limited to a single sanctuary (Jerusalem) and incorporated proce-

dures and beliefs from the Canaanite cult (Deut 12:1–14; 31a). Following
the approach of their neighbors, the Israelites concluded that the sheer volume
of their sacrifices would placate Yahweh (4:13; cf. 2 Kgs 3:27). They now
are told that their sacrifices will be of no avail and too late (cf. Amos 8:11–
12). Yahweh will have "withdrawn" (חלץ) from them (cf. 5:15) when they
arrive at the shrines with their sacrificial animals to "seek" him (בקש); cf.
3:5; 5:15). After the people find themselves "stumbling" (v 5), they will realize
their mistake and attempt to turn to their God with their sacrifices. This
situation recalls 1 Sam 15:7–35, the tragic story of Saul's belated attempt at
repentance after violating the ban provisions of holy war. Samuel's reply to
Saul ("Does Yahweh take pleasure in burnt offerings and sacrifices as in
obeying the voice of Yahweh? To obey is better than sacrifice . . .") develops
a similar theme: sacrifice itself is not wrong; but sacrifice unaccompanied by
proper faith and works is useless. The situation is similar: Saul too late tried
to win back Yahweh's favor (1 Sam 15:24–29). Yahweh "is not a human
being that he should change his mind" (v 29).

Yahweh's "withdrawal" is not an act of capriciousness. The people themselves have long since withdrawn themselves from him (v 4). His rejection
(curse type 1) recalls the curses of Deut 31:18 and 32:20 ("I will hide my
face") and the tragic lament of the cursed Israelites in Deut 31:17, "our
God is not with us."

7   "They have betrayed (בגדו ב) Yahweh." Here בגד denotes unfaithfulness in the sense of defrauding someone (cf. Exod 21:8).

On the assumption that ילד is passive rather than active-transitive (note
7.a), the proper sense of בנים זרים is "illegitimate children," not illegitimate
by being born after ritual sex at the many shrines, but by being the nation's
citizenry *in toto*. They have no right to inherit the land. Only proper children
have inheritance rights. For the meaning זר as "illegitimate," "unauthorized,"
see Exod 30:33; Lev 10:1; 22:10; Num 1:51; Ps 44:21; Isa 17:10. Dahood's
suggestion that זרים derives from זור II "to be loathsome" is an option
grammatically, but the resultant translation, "They have been faithless to
Yahweh because they were born loathsome children" (M. Dahood, *Psalms
II*, 59) hardly improves upon the sense.

V 7b in MT is questionable and has occasioned conjectural emendations,
without which the sense is elusive ("Now a new moon will devour them with
(?) their portions"). The most commonly proposed emendations for חדש
are חסיל "locust" and מחשית "destroyer", neither of which is very convincing.

It is clear that v 7b must represent a legal threat / judgment sentence of
some sort. We propose restoration of the consonant ע (יאכל עם חדש "a
new people will eat") based upon the following curse warnings: "(The produce
of your land and the labor) *a people you do not know will eat* . . ." (. . .
יאכל עם אשר לא ידעת); "They *will eat* (ואכל) the produce of your livestock
and the produce of your land . . ." (Deut 28:33, 51).

Both curses employ the futility motif (type 15) in which earnest intentions
never come to fruition because punishment interrupts their fulfillment (cf.
Hos 5:6). Both employ the verb אכל as does Hos 5:7. Our emendation assumes
that 5:7 originally read יאכל עם, just as in Deut 28:33, rather than יאכלם
as now in MT and the other versions. חדש is to be vocalized חָדָשׁ "new"

rather than the questionable חֹדֶשׁ "new moon" of MT. Then, עַם חָדָשׁ "a new people" is simply the equivalent in prophetic verse of עַם אֲשֶׁר לֹא יָדַעְתָּ "a people you do not know" in Deut 28:33.

Israel will lose its land. It will be taken captive (curse type 13 implicitly; cf. Deut 28:36, 41, 49–52,64–68). The destruction of the nation and the exile of its people are Yahweh's judgment sentence on the illegitimate children who have betrayed his covenant with them. The Assyrian conquest and captivity of Israel in 722 B.C. constitute the ultimate fulfillment of this prediction.

Explanation

For Israel, religion and state were as two sides of a coin. Royal family and the priestly family both inherited their authority and exercised their leadership responsibilities in spheres that, although distinct, complemented one another. The priesthood served the interests of the monarchy by adapting the religious demands upon the people to fit the materialistic, nationalistic interests of the kingship. The fertility cult was an important adjunct to the royalty's concern to promote prosperity, especially among the upper classes. The greater the fertility, the greater the harvests. The greater the harvests, the larger the tithes and taxes. In turn, the monarchy could give official support and subsidy to the false cult (cf. 1 Kgs 18:19) so as to establish it throughout the land. After all, the northern cult got its start at Bethel, Dan, and the multiple high places via the monarchy (1 Kgs 12:26–33). It was therefore to the advantage of the priesthood and monarchy to work together.

For this passage (5:1–7) to commence with a summons to Israel in terms of priests and royalty—Israelite leadership—is appropriate. The priests must be held accountable because they are the teachers of the law and the directors of the religious practices of the people. The monarchy is held accountable because it has the ultimate authority to control or replace the priesthood (cf. 1 Kgs 2:26–27, 35; 12:31; 2 Kgs 10:11; 12:7–8; 16:15–16; 23:8) and because it benefits from the support of the priests, who legitimize the kingship (cf. 2 Sam 19:11–12) in the eyes of the citizenry. This nefarious symbiosis must now be punished by captivity.

A corollary of captivity (v 2b) is foreign domination, including exile (v 7b). Complementing the nation's leadership (vv 1–2) is its population as a whole (vv 3–7), already introduced in the inclusive terms בֵּית יִשְׂרָאֵל "family of Israel" in v 1a and כֻּלָּם "all of you" in v 2b. How foolish the nation is to think that somehow what it does could escape Yahweh's notice (v 4)! So influenced are they by the prostituting spirit that they do not know Yahweh anymore (v 4b); he has withdrawn himself from them. As bastard children who have betrayed him, they deserve the coming disasters.

We know already on the basis of the covenant formulations (e.g., Deut 4:25–31) and the hopeful passages in Hos 1–3 that the ultimate plan of God was to create a new people, restored to him in a new covenant. That new covenant, too, has its warnings about illegitimacy (Heb 12:8).

The passage reminds us that people can become so habituated to sin and specific sinful practices (v 4a) that reconciliation to God becomes exceedingly difficult. Israel was in the grip of a paralysis of sorts. They had forgotten

what it was even to know Yahweh any more. Their depravity caused his
withdrawal from them. Paul's description of the habituation to sin (Rom
6:15–23) as a slavery is not far different from the description of Israel's
situation here. The description of people trying to come too late to him
with their sacrifices is analogous to Jesus' awesome forecast of rejection of
those who tried too late to gain the Kingdom (Matt 7:21–23).

Wrath, Return, Restoration   (5:8–7:1aγ)

Bibliography

Alt, A. "Hosea 5:8–6:6. Ein Krieg und seine Folgen in prophetischer Beleuchtung."
Kleine Schriften zur Geschichte des Volkes Israel. 2:163–87. **Ambanelli, I.** "Il significato
dell'espressione *daʿat ʾelohim* nel profeta Osea." *RivB* 21 (1973) 119–45. **Barré,
M. L.** "Bulluṭsa-rabi's Hymn to Bula and Hosea 6:1–2." *Or* 50 (1981) 241–45.
———. "New Light on the Interpretation of Hos 6:2." *VT* 28 (1978) 129–41. **Bauer,
J. B.** "Bundestreue will ich, nicht Opfer (Hos 6:6)." *BK* 23 (1968) 131–32. **Baumgartner,
W.** "Der Auferstehungsglaube im Alten Orient." *ZMR* 48 (1933) 193–214. **Begrich,
J.** "Das Priestliche Hielsorakel." *ZAW* 52 (1934) 81–92; also in *Gesammelte Studien
zum Alten Testament*, ed. W. Zimmerli. TBü 21. München: Chr. Kaiser Verlag, 1964.
217–31. **Behrens, E.** ". . . Like Those Who Remove the Landmark (Hosea 5:10a)."
Studia Biblica et Theologica 1 (1971) 1–5. **Ben-Yehudah, B.** "The Logical Precision of
Biblical Language." *BMik* 24 (1979) 149–60 (Heb.). **Berghe, P. van den.** "Repentir
et fidélité (OS 6)." *Assemblées du Seigneur* 41 (1971) 4–81. **Borbone, P. G.** "L'uccisione
dei profeti (Osea 6,5)." *Hen* 6 (1984) 271–92. **Brawer, A. J.** "The Root of the Word
שַׁעֲרוּרִיָה." *BMik* 13 (1968) 114–15 (Heb.). **Budde, K.** "Zu Text und Auslegung des
Buches Hosea (6:7–7:2)." *JBL* 53 (1934) 118–32. **Caquot, A.** "Osée et la Royauté." *RHPR*
41 (1961) 123–46. **Dahood, M.** "Some Northwest Semitic Words in Job." *Bib* 38 (1957)
306–20. **Day, J.** "עַל אֲרוֹת" in Isaiah 26:19." *ZAW* 90 (1978) 265–69. ———. "Pre-Deuter-
onomic Allusions to the Covenant in Hosea and Psalm LXXVII." *VT* 36 (1986) 1–12.
Driver, G. R. "Hosea 6:5." *VT* 1 (1951) 246. **Farr, G.** "The Concept of Grace in the
Book of Hosea." *ZAW* 70 (1958) 98–107. **Fitzmyer, J. A.** *The Aramaic Inscriptions of
Sefire.* BibOr 19. Rome: Pontifical Biblical Institute, 1967. **Foresti, F.** " 'Morte'e Risurre-
zione' in contesto di Alleanza: Interpretazione di Os 6,2." *ECarm* 27 (1976) 3–51.
Gevirtz, S. *Patterns in the Early Poetry of Israel.* SAOC 32. Chicago: University of Chicago
Press, 1963. **Good, E. M.** "Hosea 5⁸–6⁶: An Alternative to Alt." *JBL* 85 (1966) 273–
86. **Hill, D.** "On the Use and Meanings of Hosea 6:1 in Mt's Gospel." *NTS* 24 (1977–
78) 107–19. **König, F.** "Die Auferstehungshoffnung bei Osee 6:1–3." *ZTK* 70 (1948)
94–100. **Lind, M. C.** "Hosea 5:8–6:6." *Int* 38 (1984) 398–403. **Loretz, O.** "Neues
Verständnis einiger Schriftstellen mit Hilfe des Ugaritischen." *BZ* 2 (1958) 287–91.
———. "Tod und Leben nach altorientalischer und kanaanäischbiblischer Anschauung
in Hos 6, 1–3." *BN* 17 (1982) 37–42. **Mansoor, M.** "The Thanksgiving Hymns and
the Massoretic Text." *RevQ* 3 (1961) 259–66, 387–94. **McArthur, H. K.** "On the
Third Day." *NTS* 18 (1971–72) 81–86. **McCasland, S.** "The Scripture Basis of 'On
the Third Day.' " *JBL* 48 (1929) 124–37. **Moor, J. C. de.** "Ugaritic *hm*—Never 'Behold.' "
UF 1 (1969) 201–2. **Nötscher, F.** "Zur Auferstehung nach drei Tagen." *Bib* 35 (1954)
313–19. **Schildenberger, J.** " 'Dass wir leben vor seinem Antlitz' (Os 5, 15–6, 6)." *Am*

Tische des Wortes 2 (1965) 28–36. **Schmidt, H.** "Hosea 6:1–6." In *FS E. Sellin,* ed. A. Jirku. Leipzig: 1927. 111–26. **Spiegel, S.** "A Prophetic Attestation on the Decalogue: Hosea 6:5 with Some Observations on Psalms 15 and 24." *HTR* 27 (1934) 105–44. **Stamm, J. J.** "Eine Erwägung zu Hosea 6:1–2." *ZAW* 57 (1939) 266–68. **Stuart, D.** "The Sovereign's Day of Conquest." *BASOR* 221 (1976) 159–64. **Torczyner, H.** "Gilead, a City of Them That Work Iniquity." *Bulletin of the Jewish Palestine Exploration Society* 11 (1944) 9–16. ———. (Tur-Sinai) "After You, Benjamin." *BMik* 1 (1956) 19–20 (Heb.). **Whitley, C. F.** "Has the Particle םע an Asseverative Force?" *Bib* 55 (1974) 304–08. ———. "The Semantic Range of *Hesed.*" *Bib* 62 (1981) 519–26. **Wijngaards, J.** "Death and Resurrection in Covenant Context (Hos 6:2)." *VT* 17 (1967) 226–39. **Wright, G. E.** *Shechem.* New York: McGraw-Hill, 1965. **Zolli, J.** "Hosea 6:5." *ZAW* 57 (1939) 288. ———. "Note on Hosea 6:5." *JQR* 31 (1940–41) 79–82.

Translation

The watchman sounds the alarm

5:8 *Blow the horn in Gibeah, the trumpet in Ramah!*
Shout the alarm in Beth-Awen, descendants [a] *of Benjamin!*
9 *Ephraim will be destroyed on the day of punishment.*
Among the tribes of Israel I proclaim what is certain.
10 *The officials of Judah have become like those who shift boundary markers.* [a]
I will pour out my wrath on them like water.
11 *Ephraim is oppressed, crushed in judgment,*
Because he decided [a] *to follow a blah.* [b]

God's harm to Ephraim and Judah

12 *I am like pus to Ephraim,*
and like infection to the family of Judah.

13 *When Ephraim saw his illness,*
and Judah his sores,

Ephraim went to Assyria,
and sent to the great king. [a]

But he cannot heal you
or cure your sores.

14 *It is I who am like a lion to Ephraim*
and like a young lion to the family of Judah.

I—yes I—will tear apart and withdraw,
I will carry away so that no one can rescue.

15 *I will go back to my place*
until they suffer for their guilt [a] *and seek me.*
When in trouble, they will search me out.

Restoration promised

6:1 *Let us return to Yahweh.*
For he has torn us [a] *apart, yet he will heal us;*
he has attacked us, [a] *yet he will bandage us.*

² *He will bring us to life after two days,*
on the third day resurrect us,
that we may live in his presence ³ *and know him.*^a

Let us strive to know Yahweh.
As sure as the sunrise is his coming forth.
He will come to us like rain,
like spring showers renewing^b *the land.*

The disloyalty of Ephraim and Judah

⁴ *What should I do with you, Ephraim?*
What should I do with you, Judah?

Your loyalty is like morning mist,
like the dew which goes away early in the day.

⁵ *Therefore I have cut them*^a *up*^b *in accordance with my fearsome speech.*^c
I have killed them in accordance with the words of my mouth.
And my justice comes forth like light.^d

⁶ *For I am pleased by loyalty—not sacrifice,*
and knowing God rather than burnt offerings.

⁷ *But look*^a—*they have walked on*^b *my covenant like it was dirt,*^c
see,^d *they have betrayed me!*

⁸ *Gilead is a city of evildoers,*
whose footprints are bloody.^a

⁹ *Like a waiting bandit*
is the guild of the priests.

They murder on the road to Shechem,
what premeditated evil^a *they do!*

¹⁰ *Within the family of Israel*
I have seen terrible things.

See^a *Ephraim's prostitution—*
Israel is unclean.

A restoration promise to Judah and Israel

¹¹ *Also, Judah:*
I am setting^a *a harvest for you,*

When I restore^b *my people,*
^{7:1a} *When I heal Israel,*

And Ephraim's iniquity will disappear,^a
As will Samaria's evil.^b

Notes

8.a. Reading אחרי כי for MT אחריך "after you." אחרים "descendants" is perhaps found in constr form along with the intensive כי also in Judg 5:14a, where we find a parallelism between אחר and שרש "root/lineage". See Kuhnigk, *NSH*, 72–73; cf. Tur-Sinai, *BMik* 1 (1956) 19–20. Intensive כי in constr chains occurs also in 2:8 and 8:5.

10.a. גבול has the sense of boundary stone or boundary marker in addition to simply "boundary."

11.a. For the hiphil of יאל other nuances are possible: "resolved to," "persisted in," etc. The asyndetic juxtaposition of הואיל and הלך "go, follow" has parallels in 9:9, Deut 1:5, 1 Sam 2:3, etc.

11.b. The meaning of צו is uncertain. In Isa 28:10, 13 it is used in repetition to mean something like "Blah blah blah. . . ." The word is often emended to צר "foe" or צרו "his foe." A more neutral translation might be: "he insisted on following a *nothing.*"

13.a. Reading מַלְכִּי־רָב, a construction perhaps modeled after the Assyrian *šarru rabû* "great king." The title *mlk rb* is known from Sefire 1 (cf. Fitzmyer, *Sefire,* 61). It probably represents *malkᵉ rab,* the *i* in Heb. being an anaptytic, intermediate helping vowel facilitating the pronunciation of the consonantal clusters of the construct, as also in Assyrian, Phoenician, Punic, etc.

15.a. G ἀφανισθῶσιν "they will be reduced to nothing" reads יִשַּׁמּוּ or יִשֹּׁמּוּ, from שמם rather than אשם (cf. 10:2; 14:1), whereas α′ σ′ θ′ presuppose אשם. It is possible that אשם in Hosea has the nuance "to be punishable / punished" (Wolff, 105, n. i).

6:1.a. The suffs in each half of the verse do double duty.

3.a. "Him" is reflected in the double-duty suff of לפניו "in his presence." Alternatively, vocalize נֵדְעָהוּ.

3.b. MT יוֹרֶה "early rain" is redundant, and thus less likely than יָרְוֶה (from רוה) "renew."

5.a. "Them" is supplied from the 3 m pl suff in the second half of the sentence.

5.b. MT חצב (usually "to hew / cut up") may actually reflect Ug. ḥṣb "to smite / fight." The parallel, "kill" (הרג) pairs easily with either option.

5.c. Reading בְּנִבִּי אֶיסִ "with my fearsome speech," with M. Dahood, "Hebrew-Ugaritic Lexicography VI," *Bib* 49 (1968) 362. Cf. Kuhnigk, *NSH,* 81. The synonymous parallelism with "words of my mouth" makes the translation "prophets" questionable here.

5.d. Reading מִשְׁפָּטִי כָאוֹר "my justice like light" with G Syr Tg. כאור may also be translated "like the sun" (Kuhnigk, *NSH,* 81).

7.a. Either הֵם or הֵמָּה can have the sense of "look," "behold." See Kuhnigk, *NSH,* 82–85. Cf. M. Dahood, Psalms I, 288, 291. For a contrary view, cf. de Moor, *UF* 1 (1969) 201–2.

7.b. Reading עבר as "walk over, tread on," the sense it has in, e.g., Isa 51:23 (Kuhnigk, *NSH,* 83).

7.c. The idea that an obscure Israelite city, Adam, would figure so prominently in the passage is obviated by the simple recognition that אדם can mean "dirt" (cf. Kuhnigk, *NSH,* 82–85).

7.d. For שם as "see, look behold" (parallel to הֵמָּה / הִגָּה) see Kuhnigk, *NSH,* 82–85.

8.a. Reading עִקְּבֵיהֶם דָּם "their footprints are bloody" as opposed to MT's vocalization ("tracked with blood").

9.a. כי has here the exclamatory sense "what / how!" זִמָּה connotes mischief that is planned or devised carefully.

10.a. See n. 7.d.

11.a. The pass ptcp (שִׁית) is perhaps to be read here. Alternatively, read "he has set." "I am setting" takes the verb as the act ptcp and assumes that the 1st pers pronouns of the context are adequate to clarify the subj here.

11.b. Although שבות (from שבה) normally means "captivity" or "imprisonment," the translation of שבות in combination with שוב (both from שוב) as "turn one's fortune" or "bring about a restoration" is advisable here. On the expression, see S. Mowinckel, *The Psalms in Israel's Worship II* (New York: Abingdon, 1962) 249–50, n. xxvii.

7:1.a. The verb גלה can mean "disappear," "vanish," "go away" in *both* the niphal (Isa 38:12) and the qal (Isa 24:11; Prov 27:25).

1.b. Reading the sg, רעת "evil," with G Syr Vg and in obvious synonymous parallelism with עון "iniquity."

Form / Structure / Setting

The cry of warning that summons the Benjaminites to war, with its triple imperative ("blow the horn . . . the trumpet . . . shout"), begins a new section of prophetic revelation. Its focus is war, its language associated with the Day of Yahweh.

The next clear break comes at 7:16. Meanwhile, the material located between 5:8 and 7:16 is so closely related that it is not impossible to regard it as a single "transmission unit" (cf. Wolff, 108–10).

We judge, however, that the last word of 7:1aδ marks a new beginning ("How deceitfully they act!" . . .) and that the subject matter and particular vocabulary of 7:1b–16 are further evidence of a new pericope. With regard to the possibility of a break after 6:10, it is awkward to connect 6:11b with the bulk of chap. 7 in which no mention of hope or restoration is to be found. The translation of שבות עמי שובי בשובי (6:11b) as "Whenever I wanted to restore the fortunes of my people . . . ," while technically a grammatical possibility, is only that. Verse 6:11b thus connects far more easily with 6:11a. Those commentators who excise the reference to Judah on tendentious grounds reject a natural connection in favor of a more awkward one. Since they reason that a prediction of restoration cannot follow directly 6:10, their only option is to recast 6:11 as an expression of conditionality, contrary to fact, and link it to what follows.

The present passage contains five discernible sub-units: a summons to war (5:8–11); a depiction of God's harm to Ephraim and Judah in which God is portrayed metaphorically as infection and a lion (5:12–15); an invitation to restoration and return to Yahweh via a penitential song (6:1–3); a description of the disloyalty of Ephraim and Judah in contrast to God's justice (6:4–10); and a restoration promise to Judah and Israel proclaiming hope in the distant future (6:11–7:1a). These five sub-units are linked together more by logic than style. One stylistic linkage which does appear is the Ephraim : Judah :: Judah : Ephraim parallelism between 5:12, 13 (et al.) and 6:11–7:1a. The five all relate directly or indirectly to the circumstances of the Syro-Ephraimite war, 735–732 B.C.

The passage contains elements of both hope and doom reflecting in microcosm the overall structure of the book. In the present passage the alternation may well represent the existential situation of 735–732: disaster seemed to be falling on the nation, yet the crisis might represent an opening toward a new age.

There are three expressions of hope. The first comes in a transitional verse, 5:15. God, portrayed to this point as a destructive lion, now changes to a God who hides himself from Israel with the purpose of shocking the people into returning to him. The second and most substantial word of hope follows immediately in 6:1–3. The prophet, by a penitential song, invites the people to repentance. Finally, after condemning both Israel and Judah for their covenant-breaking crimes, God addresses both with a brief, simple word of consolation, promising them a "harvest," (6:11–7:1a) characterized by restoration of prosperity and healing.

The entire passage takes the form of a series of divine speeches, with the single exception of 6:1–3. In terms of the prosodic structure, synthetic parallelism does not predominate as might be expected. Rather, there is a surprising concentration of synonymous parallelism (5:8; 5:12–15; 6:1–3; 6:4–7). Because synonymous parallelism ends at 6:7 and synthetic parallelism continues (vv 8–10), 6:4–10 may be structurally bifid. More likely, however, the change signals the corresponding logical shift from a general description of the two nations' sins to specific examples of priestly infidelity in the north. That 6:7

goes with 6:4–6 is evident structurally, though many commentators have presumed the "song" to end at v 4 (especially when אדם in v 7 is taken as a place name).

While some textual corruption is evident (see notes), the passage's intent and compositional characteristics can be discerned. Couplets and triplets vary unpredictably, as is normal in Hebrew poetry especially of the earlier periods. In 6:1–3a an elegantly simple structure is observed in the penitential song. The first cohortative line ("Let us return to Yahweh") and the second cohortative line ("Let us strive to know Yahweh") are in effect the corresponding members of a split couplet. Each, however, introduces a description of healing after harm based on the surety of Yahweh's consistency. 6:1–3 is thus an artfully crafted song containing two couplets (one split) and two triplets.

Ephraim predominates in the passage as the name of the north (eight times). Israel is mentioned three times, only once (6:10) independently of a parallelism in which it complements Ephraim. Judah appears by name six times, usually in parallelism with Ephraim, so that north and south together are the subject of the oracle. Only in the restoration promise at the end of the passage does Judah occupy the initial, "prominent" position in the parallelism, and there probably in chiastic reversal, in parallel with 5:12,13 et al.

The presence of Ephraim and Judah together centrally in the passage indicates a new situation. In most or all of the oracles from 1:2 through 5:7, the setting was the prosperous, complacent, indulgent period of the latter years of Jeroboam's reign (i.e., up to 753 B.C.). Now we hear a cry of alarm to prepare for war (5:8). Yahweh is tearing apart his people (5:12–14), and both north and south are suffering (5:13, 14; 6:1–2). Urgent appeal is made to Assyria (5:13). The events depicted in 5:8–14 and the events mentioned in the past tense in 6:1–2 must be assigned to the period of the Syro-Ephraimite war (A. Alt, *Kleine Schriften* 2:163–87). This conflict did immense harm to both kingdoms, pitting them against one another and providing the occasion for Assyrian encroachment, the very thing the war started by Pekah and Rezin was designed to prevent.

The Syro-Ephraimite war is described briefly in 2 Kgs 16:5–9 and 2 Chr 28:5–23 (cf. A. L. Oppenheim, "Tiglath-Pileser III: Campaigns against Syria and Palestine," *ANET* 283–84; J. Bright, *A History of Israel* [Philadelphia: Westminster, 1960] 256–57; M. Noth, *The History of Israel*, tr. S. Godman [London: Black, 1960] 257–61). Threatened by conquest from the expanding Assyrian empire under Tiglath-Pileser III, Israel's king Pekah (2 Kgs 15:17–31; 740[?]– 732 B.C.) and Syria's king Rezin formed a coalition against Assyria. They proposed to King Jotham of Judah (750–735) that he join them. When he refused they attacked Judah, fearing that Judah would side with Assyria, even if only passively. Jotham died in 735 and his successor, Ahaz (735– 715), appealed directly to Assyria (2 Kgs 16:7–8). Tiglath-Pileser complied by attacking Damascus, Syria's capital, thereby immediately lifting the pressure from Judah. After conquering Damascus (and other cities in the region), Tiglath-Pileser systematically took Gilead, Galilee, and the Jezreel plain, including Megiddo. Much of Israel's population was deported (6:11b), and most of the north was made part of Assyria's collection of imperial provinces. Only the territory of Ephraim and Benjamin (thus the emphasis upon Benjamin in 5:8) remained independent.

After this destructive invasion (5:11) Pekah was assassinated by Hoshea (732–723) who quickly appealed for peace, making Israel a vassal of Assyria (5:13). It would appear to be precisely at this point—just after the invasion of Tiglath-Pileser had ended the war, Pekah had died, and Hoshea had appealed to Assyria—that our passage should be dated, i.e., 732. Though not every part of the passage can be proved to date to this period (e.g., 6:8–10), the overall unity leads to no other conclusion. As Wolff says (of all of 5:8–7:16, in fact): ". . . all redactional formulas are absent. These sayings have been combined without any seams." Though we separate 7:1b–16, the argument applies *mutatis mutandis* to the present passage.

Why, then, does God speak of a future judgment on Israel (5:9) if the invasion is over? Simply because the north's punishment has only begun. The covenant remains broken (6:4, 7, 10) and its stipulations continue to be violated (5:10, in ref. to Judah; 6:8–10 in ref. to Israel). The devastation the people have just seen is only the beginning. God will punish Ephraim further (5:9, 12–15; 6:11); though Judah, which escaped relatively unscathed, is invited to concentrate not on the punishment it is due (5:10, 12–15) but on its future restoration (6:11).

The passage thus reflects much of what has happened as of 732 B.C., and much of what is yet to come. The greater devastation of 722, wrought by Shalmaneser V (726–722) and his successor Sargon II (722–705) is probably the referent for 5:15. The investing of Jerusalem in 701 by Sennacherib (705–681) may represent an aspect of the fulfillment of the "harvest" set for Judah (6:11).

Comment

5:8   The hearer/reader is invited by Hosea's words to imagine a scene well-understood in ancient Israel. A watchman from his vantage point atop a hill or watchtower sees in the distance an advancing army. Immediately the war alarm is sounded by ram's horn and trumpet, and by the shouting of heralds. War and its ravages constitute a major covenantal curse type (3; cf. Deut 28:25, et al.).

This verse describes an invasion of the territory of Benjamin from the south, i.e., from Judah. The enemy is portrayed as advancing along the main mountain road from Jerusalem through Bethel and thereafter into the heart of Ephraim. Gibeah, only three miles north of Jerusalem, is the first to be attacked; then Ramah, five miles north of Jerusalem; and finally Bethel, eleven miles north of Jerusalem, on the northern border of Benjamin. (Beth-Awen is a derogatory substitute name for Bethel; see 4:15.) Along this route, in the opposite direction (Judg 20:18, 19) Israelite troops had once attacked Gibeah in response to a heinous crime committed in that city during the days of the judges (Judg 19–20).

The three cities mentioned had originally been northern territory (Josh 18:21–23). Abijah had captured them for Judah early in the ninth century (2 Chr 13:19), but their ownership seesawed thereafter (1 Kgs 15:16–22). They apparently reverted to Israelite control either during the reign of Jehoash (798–782 B.C.; cf. 2 Kgs 14:11–14), or during the Syro-Ephraimite war (2 Kgs 16:5; cf. Isa 7:6).

After Assyria responded to Ahaz's plea and attacked the North, Pekah probably withdrew most of his troops from the southern portion of his shrinking kingdom. Left relatively undefended, Benjamin was a first target for military vengeance by Ahaz. We have no record of what military action Ahaz actually took. In light of v 10, it is evident that he did at least push the boundary further north so that Judah encompassed much or most of Benjamin once again. The present warning is much more than a prediction that only three cities would fall, but rather a general call for the entire territory to expect invasion. The "descendants of Benjamin" (*in toto*) are addressed. This is emphasized by the emphatic כי which is infixed between אחרי "descendants of" and בנימין "Benjamin." (The most common mid-construct use of the emphatic כי is before proper nouns, as here.)

9 "Ephraim" may indicate the North as a whole, including Benjamin (cf. 4:17). The counter-invasion from Judah is probably not envisaged here, but rather more of the devastating Assyrian expansion. Contemporaneously, Isaiah prophesied that the Assyrians would not be satisfied with only part of the Northern Kingdom, but would eventually take all the North and attack the South as well (Isa 7:1–8:8). He urged the Judeans to depend on Yahweh for deliverance (Isa 8:9–15) knowing that Assyria would ultimately become an oppressor, rather than remain an ally. Hosea's words in v 9 come at just such a point. He "proclaims" (present) what will be (תהיה, imperfect). There still is a Northern Kingdom, though reduced in size. Pekah has been, or is about to be, overthrown by Hoshea. Can Ephraim assume that the worst is over, and thus rest and rebuild? No, it can only wait for its doom. It will be "destroyed" (לשמה תהיה; curse type 24; cf. שמם in Lev 26:22, 31–34) according to Hosea's message preached throughout "the tribes of Israel," i.e., to tribal territories now subjugated by Assyria (cf. Isa 9:1), and even to Judah. The watchman's cry has shifted metaphorically to a proclamation of God's word by his prophet to all of Israel. (The referent of "I" in v 9b is ambiguous. Either Yahweh, Hosea, or the watchman could be the speaker.)

The frantic plotting and shifting of alliances under kings like Pekah and Hoshea were useless. The wars they embarked upon could only hasten the inevitable downfall of the North, which finally came in 722 B.C. What they (and Judah) had seen so far was only the beginning.

The "day of punishment" (יום תוכחה) may be a metonymy for the "day of the Lord" (יום יהוה) (cf. L. Koehler, *Old Testament Theology* [London: Lutterworth, 1957] 221–25) much as Ps 149:7 uses תוכחה in connection with calamitous historical judgment from Yahweh. "Punishment" (retribution for sins) constituted a covenantal curse (type 26: cf. Lev 26:41, 43; Deut 32:35 et al.).

The proclamation of destruction was נאמנה "certain / sure / set / trustworthy." The sins of Ephraim had led God to unleash against them Assyria, whose expanding empire would inevitably reduce Ephraim to a "ruin / thing destroyed." Even the invitation to be "healed" by Yahweh (6:1–3) presupposed the certainty of the coming destruction.

10 From Benjamin (v 8) to Ephraim (v 9) to Judah (v 10) to Ephraim (v 11) an alternating ABAB pattern is discernible in the present subsection.

In this verse, Judah comes under attack to an extent not hitherto found in the book. The full judgment saying includes both accusation (boundary changing) and sentence (wrath). The "officials of Judah" (שׂרי יהודה) included probably the military commanders as well as the royalty and other high government leadership.

A well-known covenant curse prohibited the moving of a boundary marker (Deut 27:17) because of the sacredness of the tribal and personal land allotments (Deut 19:14). Judah's re-annexation of Benjaminite territory violated the terms of the covenant vis-à-vis the tribal allotments. Such encroachment, no matter how justified it may have seemed to Judeans after the northern coalition's perfidy, represented oppression of a portion of God's people (Prov 23:10–11; cf. Job 24:2–4). Boundaries, set by God so that each tribe or family would be protected from economic vicissitudes, were considered permanent. On the tribal scale, Benjamin could hardly occupy its divinely appointed place among the tribes if its territory was subjugated by Judah. Judah's action could thus not be excused simply because it came in response to an illegal attack from Ephraim and Syria. Yahweh did not favor Judah over Israel in the conflict.

Hosea's authority was by no means limited to Israelite matters. The prophets represented Yahweh to a variety of peoples, since his covenant lordship extended to all nations (cf. Amos 1:3–2:16; Jer 1:5; Isa 2:4; Jonah 3:4, et al), so a judgment sentence against Judah was appropriate to Hosea's message.

God will pour out his "wrath like water." "Wrath" (עברה, cf. 13:11) is both a punishment consequent to and a synonym for anger; it can indicate action and/or attitude. Both עברה and שׁפך "pouring out" appear in contexts of divine destruction (e.g., Zeph 1:14–18). The intent of these words is clear: Judah, like Israel, faces God's fury (curse type 1; Deut 29:24, 27, 28, et al.) and can expect no special dispensation from the covenant's sanctions.

11 The focus returns to Israel's present condition in the aftermath of Tiglath-Pileser's conquest. Ephraim, unlike Judah thus far, had *already* experienced the covenant-enforcing wrath of God. עשׁוק "oppressed" is part of the language of the covenant curses (Deut 28:29, 33; cf. Lev 19:13; Deut 24:14; Hos 12:8) as is רצוץ "crushed" (Deut 28:33; cf. Amos 4:1). These terms relate Israel's fate to curse type 19 (helplessness) and to curse type 5 (oppression by enemies). The mention of משׁפט "judgment" identifies the trials of the Northern Kingdom as punishment for covenant violation (see Deut 32:41). Like v 10, v 11 contains both an accusation and a "judgment saying." Here, both are in the past tense. The accusation is stated in v 11b, introduced by כי (cf. 1:3, 6, 9; etc.): "he insisted on following a blah (צו)." If our translation of צו is correct, and the word is not merely the remainder of some other word such as צרו "his foe," there are at least two possible meanings for the accusation. "Following idolatry" is one, since the nothingness and worthlessness of idols is frequently stressed by the prophets. The same expression "to follow" (הלך אחרי) is used in covenant-enforcement contexts in connection with Israel's following gods other than Yahweh (Deut 28:14; cf. Deut 6:14; 8:19; 11:28; 13:3; Judg 2:12, etc.). Another possible meaning is "following Aram" (the Syrian kingdom of Damascus, under Rezin, its king). Alliance with nations like Assyria (v 13) or Egypt (7:11, 16), normally mentioned explicitly, is probably not in view. However, Aram / Syria is never mentioned explicitly in Hosea either, and this expression of contempt may be the equivalent of an overt citation by name. It is indeed theoretically possible that the text in MT, אחרי־צו is to be restored to either ⟨ר⟩צו⟨ן⟩ אחר or ⟨ר⟩צ⟨י⟩ן אחר, i.e., "after Rezin."

In any event, Ephraim is being punished for a lack of faithfulness. By desperate alliance with Damascus against Assyria, the Israelites showed themselves not to trust the basic covenant promise that "Yahweh will grant that the enemies who rise up against you will be defeated before you. They will come at you from one direction but flee from you in seven" (Deut 28:7).

12 God speaks, in a simile, of the process by which he brings covenant punishment to North and South. He weakens his people. The verse expresses via its simple synonymous parallelism that God's unleashing of warfare on the area functioned like "pus" (עש) or "infection" (רקב; the word can also refer generally to any sort of decay; cf. Job 13:28). The people's misery is and will be God's doing, not that of Tiglath-Pileser, and was not merely a temporary, incidental misfortune.

God does not hold back from graphic language or imagery in expressing the miseries attendant to covenant breaking (cf. Deut 28:53–57; Ezek 16). Sickness is prominent among the covenant curses (type 8; Deut 28:21–22, 27, 35, 59–61; 32:24) and the similes and metaphors of sickness in vv 13–14 bear implicit reference to the broken covenant.

13 The figure of the sick person continues to describe Israel and Judah, metaphorically. Both "illness" (חלי; Deut 28:59, 61) and its parallel "sores" (מזור) represent covenant plagues (see v 12), and can connote miseries afflicted by an enemy, rather than merely human illnesses (cf. Isa 1:5–6; Jer 30:12–13).

Ignoring the possibility that their miseries were the result of Yahweh's disfavor, Israel and Judah sought relief of their symptoms instead of a real cure. Judah had appealed to Assyria after the Syro-Ephraimite coalition attacked in 734 B.C. Now in 732 the young king Hoshea, presiding over a nation that had already lost the coastal plain, Galilee, and the Transjordan to Assyria, sued for peace to Tiglath-Pileser III following the precedent of Menahem in 738 (*ANET*, 283a). The direct address of v 13b seems to include both Israel and Judah. Neither Samaria nor Judah will be helped by appeal to Assyria. Assyria's ultimate policy toward Israel, either north or south, was unpredictable, and trusting it to help was folly (cf. 2 Chr 28:16–21).

The plural suffixes in v 13b (כם־ "you") probably refer to both Israel and Judah. Eventually, both will suffer at the hands of the Assyrians as vv 14 and 15 make evident.

14 Continuing the pattern of the Ephraim / Judah synonymous parallelisms, God now identifies himself as their real foe, in the simile and then metaphor of a lion who will further harm them. What illness may have spared, the beast's injury will now destroy. The syntax emphasizes that God is the lion. "It is *I*" (כי אנכי) and "I-yes I" (אני אני) begin each half of the verse, respectively. The people must understand why and from whom their continuing suffering comes, so that they may repent and turn to him for healing (5:15–6:3).

"Lion" (שחל) and "young lion" (כפיר) are a standard fixed pair in poetry. The covenant curses concerning harm from wild animals (type 11; Deut

32:24; 28:26) are recalled by this theriomorphism (cf. 13:7). A judgment is
coming, far more severe than they have experienced thus far. And Israel's
own God, Yahweh, is the real source of danger, not Assyria. In the second
couplet, simile has shifted to metaphor, and three "promises" are made: destruction, withdrawal and inescapable capture (curse types 24, 1 and 5 respectively). This is almost a precise capsulization of the message of vv 12–15.
The final clause, "so that no one can rescue" (מציל ואין), like the similar
wording in 2:12b, reflects and reinforces the point made in Deut 32:39:
Israel is entirely Yahweh's property to punish, and is capable of receiving
help from no other god.

15 Continuing briefly the lion metaphor (אלך "I will go" reflecting the
אלך of v 14) God promises that as the lion goes back to "his place" God will
go away from his people, leaving them torn apart (cf. 2 Kgs 17:23). The
withdrawal has a beneficent intent, however, to force the people to consider
their guilt so that they will be moved to return to him.

The verse provides a carefully constructed transition from the judgments
of 5:8–14 to the invitation to repentance of 6:1–3. Following initially the
metaphorical format of vv 12–14, and generally the judgment format of
5:8–14, it leads to the glimmer of hope for restoration in the invitation song
of 6:1–3. By describing Yahweh as a God willing to wait for his people's
repentance, the theme of the penitential song in 6:1–3 is adumbrated. Since
that song represents a response to the judgment portrayed in 5:10–14, v 15
becomes a bridge from judgment to penitence and restoration.

The threat of divine absence is a basic covenant curse motif (type 1). Those
who have abandoned their sovereign will learn what it is to be abandoned
by him. Yahweh's withdrawal will last "until" (עד אשר) the people "suffer
for their guilt" (יאשמו). The verb אשם appears five times in Hosea. It can
mean either to "incur guilt" (4:15; 13:1) or, as here, to "suffer for guilt,"
i.e., suffer the consequences of wrongdoing (10:2; 14:1 [13:16]). Both Israel
and Judah will have to undergo the destructive calamities attendant to covenant
breaking. Only then will come the opportunity to return to their Lord (cf.
2:4–17; 3:1–5).

After their punishment, they will "seek me" (יבקשו פני) says God, using
the covenant terminology of invitation to blessing after national destruction
and exile. Deut 4:25–31 announces this same theme: covenant disloyalty (v
25) will result in destruction and humiliating exile (vv 26–28); but such dire
circumstances will be a door to renewal of the relationship with Yahweh if
Israel will again seek (בקש) him (vv 29–31).

The final clause of v 15, בצר להם ישחרנני "When in trouble, they will
search me out," reflects the language of Deut 4:30 (בצר ל), describing the
circumstances antecedent to Israel's finding God. שחר, here parallel to בקש,
can connote an intense seeking of Yahweh by one in great affliction (Pss
63:2 [1]; 78:34; Isa 26:9), in addition to "being intent" on doing something,
or "looking hard" to find something. It is strongly implied that because of
God's mercy, such diligent searching will succeed (cf. Deut 4:29).

6:1–3 These three verses comprise a distinct section of the full passage.
Hosea presents on behalf of Israel a song, of the type called "penitential"
(e.g., Pss 6; 32; 38; 51; 102; 130; cf. H. Gunkel, J. Begrich, *Einleitung in*

die Psalmen [Göttingen: Vandenhoeck & Ruprecht, 1937], and S. Mowinckel, *The Psalms in Israel's Worship I*, tr. D. R. Ap-Thomas [Oxford: B. Blackwell, 1962] 193–246). Some scholars have speculated this song was independently composed, perhaps by northern (Bethel) priests for temple worship after the Assyrian campaign in 733 B.C., and inserted in its present context by an editor. By this theory, the song does not reflect Hosea's doom-oriented outlook elsewhere in the passage or book. After all, why would Hosea reassure Israel (and presumably Judah) that Yahweh would "in two or three days" (v 2) heal his people when he had told them that Yahweh was withdrawing from them for a long time (5:15) and was generally disgusted with them (5:8–14; 6:4–10)? Alternatively, some have considered the song a parody of the national attitude composed by Hosea as a foil against which to preach the true word of doom; others take it as a priestly composition created precisely as a rejoinder to Hosea's doom-saying.

Such views are unnecessary. The song is Hoseanic in style and not disruptive of the context. Its placement follows the alternating doom-hope pattern that characterizes the entire book. It represents a faithful presentation of covenant teaching, because its orientation is eschatological, not immediate.

The song is structured so that two cohortative invitations to the people ("Let us return to Yahweh," v 1; "Let us strive to know Yahweh," v 3a) are followed by assertions that Yahweh is faithful to heal and restore. The song's main concerns, that the people "return" to Yahweh and "know" him, are central themes of the inspired message Hosea preached (for שׁוב "return," cf. 2:9 [7], 11 [9]; 3:5; 7:10; 14:2 [1]; for ידע "know," cf. 2:22 [20]; 4:6; 5:4; 6:6; 8:2; 13:4).

The time frame is intended to be future, following a neutral time-sequence patterning characteristic of covenants. All generations are "you," whether past, present or future (cf. Deut 4:25–31; 30:1–10; Lev 26:14–39; Josh 24, *passim*, etc.). The nation is a continuum. Particular individuals and groups may come and go in the continuum, but they are all part of the corporate identity which is the "nation" per se. The song of 6:1–3 is thus eschatological, relating to a nation that is a continuum throughout history. Hosea's contemporaries would themselves no more see the healing of Israel than Moses' contemporaries saw the exile predicted for them as "you" in Deut 4.

1 The helping verb לכו "come" is used idiomatically in hendiadys with נשׁובה "let us return," and is best left unexpressed in translation. It adds clarity to the cohortative form of the verb, by stressing the imperative aspect. The prophet pleads with his own nation (perhaps including Judah) to return to Yahweh.

כי הוא is probably intensive, "For *he* is the one who has . . . ." Grammatically it is identical to the emphatic construction in 5:14a. It emphasizes that the present distress is punishment directly from Yahweh, not a situation Yahweh has simply allowed. And though Yahweh has "torn us apart" and "attacked us" (the 1 com sg suffixes being implicit to טרף and י; see notes), he will also "heal us" and "bandage us."

It must be remembered, however, that the song is an expression of hope. Israel does not control Yahweh. The song praises his consistency and dependability, but *when* and *how* he would eventually heal and bandage are not specified.

Israel's hope is based on covenant promise. Hosea knows that Yahweh will never utterly reject his people. He may heal and bandage a people quite distant in time, only a "remnant" of the present nation, but such a return *will* surely take place. The fulfillment of the song is thus implicitly reserved for another generation than that which heard Hosea sing it. Its confidence is based partly on the awesome boast of Yahweh in Deut 32:39: "I put to death and bring to life; I wound and I heal" (i.e. restoration blessing type 6).

2–3aα The first two lines of the triplet in vv 2–3aα form a chiasm (bring to life : two days :: third day : resurrect). As chiasms occur almost exclusively in synonymous parallelisms, there can be little doubt that "two days" and "third day" constitute a poetic numerical figure of the n:n+1 sort (see S. Gervirtz, *Patterns in the Early Poetry of Israel*, [Chicago: U. of Chicago Press, 1963] 18–22; W. F. Albright, "Some Canaanite-Phoenician Sources of Hebrew Wisdom," *Wisdom in Israel: FS H. H. Rowley*, VTSup 3 [Leiden: E. J. Brill, 1955] 1–15). The poetic figure should not be taken literalistically (in two or three days, all would be well) or to mean "soon" (even in a relative sense; cf. Loretz, *BZ* 2 [1958] 290). Its intent is more likely that after "a set time" Yahweh would again visit his people in mercy; thus he would not, in effect, forget them (cf. 3:4, 5).

The first two verbs (חיה, piel, and קום, hiphil) here in chiastic parallel, clearly denote coming back to life from the dead, a theme already expressed in 2:2, and analogous (as in 2:1–3) to Ezek 37:6, 10, 12–14. The attempts of Wolff (117–18) and others to eliminate the concept of resurrection from the verse are unsuccessful.

Two important NT references to the resurrection of Jesus "on the third day" (1 Cor 15:4; Luke 24:7) share the wording of G for v 2b: . . . ἐν τῇ ἡμέρᾳ τῇ τρίτῃ ἀναστησόμεθα καὶ ζησόμεθα ἐνώπιον αὐτοῦ . . . ". . . on the third day we will be resurrected and will live in his presence." (Cf. McArthur, *NTS* 18 [1971–72] 81–86.) It is not clear from either NT context that Hos 6:2 is considered to be an actual prediction of Jesus' resurrection (the sense of Paul's "according to the Scriptures" is that of analogy).

The basic promise of the verse is that Israel can definitely expect Yahweh to renew his people. But this is not a promise without conditions. Rather, it will require "living in his presence" and "knowing him." These two conditions are one and the same. Israel must and will again become the special possession of Yahweh, fully loyal to him and under his authority (thus in the language of covenant, "knowing" him; blessing type 3) when the healing and bandaging occur.

3 Complementing the initial invitation of v 1, "Let us return to Yahweh," is the song's second invitation, "Let us strive to know Yahweh." The two invitations appear to constitute a split couplet. The first invitation, to "return," was followed by an expression of confidence that return would one day be possible. The second invitation, to "know," is followed by an expression of the reliability of Yahweh, certifying that he is indeed knowable. To know Yahweh means to accept his covenant lordship (see 4:1). A daily event, the appearance of the sun at morning, and a yearly event, the spring rains, are two kinds of phenomena that are predictable and certain. To these are compared via similies Yahweh's "going forth" (מוֹצָא) and his "coming" (lit., "he will come," יָבוֹא). Their implication is that as Yahweh has in the past, he will continue in the future to make himself available to be known (restoration blessing type 1; cf. Deut 4:29).

His "going forth" will end the withdrawal from Israel described in 5:15— and thus by implication will follow Israel's recognizing Yahweh. Hosea's message is a summons to faithful orthodoxy in a national crisis of indefinite duration. Knowing Yahweh in a restored covenant relationship will refresh and renew Israel as rain refreshes dry land. Though comparison of Yahweh's blessing to rain has often been thought to border on Canaanite religious thinking, where the function of the gods was closely associated with the weather, the simile contains no hint of this. Orthodox Yahwists could talk about the weather without converting to Baalism. Yahweh controlled the elements too, after all (cf. 1 Kgs 17:1; 18:1, 45). The wording of the triplet may have been influenced by Deut 32:2, though a direct connection cannot be proved.

4 Like a parent whose love requires that he or she punish a disobedient child, God struggles within himself (cf. 11:8–9). The plaintive question he asks reflects the hopelessness of the present situation. Every tactic used so far to reform his people has failed. In prosperity, they ignored him (4:10b); in calamity they turned elsewhere for help (5:11). Whether he promised hope (cf. 2:23–25 [21–23]) or threatened wrath (cf. 5:1–7) the results were the same. The question God asks is genuine, yet in the final analysis, rhetorical.

The covenant loyalty of both Israel and Judah was fleeting. Where it had existed it had been unstable. He now must act, and asks himself what to do. The repetition of the same words ("What should I do with you" מָה אֶעֱשֶׂה לָךְ) follows the style of repetitive parallelism known especially from older OT poetry (cf. W. F. Albright, *Yahweh and the Gods of Canaan*, 1–28). The emphasis inherent in repetition helps depict the severity of the agony of the situation. God must harm those he has loved and chosen. Ephraim and Judah have sinned greatly, and the coming Assyrian conquest will harm both greatly.

The central problem is disloyalty. By violating the covenant stipulations via heterodoxy and (implicitly) social injustice Israel has shown that its חֶסֶד, loyalty to the covenant relationship, is thin and temporary. A genuine חֶסֶד of sorts may once have existed but the *sine qua non* of loyalty is that it must *continue* (cf. Glueck, *Hesed;* Sackenfeld, *Hesed;* and Whitley, *Bib* 62 [1981] 519–26). A loyalty that is temporary or that evaporates like ground fog or dew is no loyalty at all. These similes of Israel's unreliability contrast sharply with the picture of Yahweh's absolute reliability in vv 1–3.

5 This verse in triplet form tells what Yahweh has done already to Ephraim and Judah, and why he has done it, in effect answering the question posed in v 4. When the spurious MT vocalization בַּנְּבִיאִים "with prophets" is properly reconstrued as בְּנִבְאֵי אִים or the like ("in accordance with my fearsome speech"; n. 5.c), the awkward problem of "striking down with prophets" vanishes.

Though it gives him no pleasure to harm his people, God *has done* this to them, and justly. They are said to have been cut up (חָצַב) i.e., decimated, and slain (הָרַג) "in accordance with" what he has spoken to them (אִמְרֵי־פִי "words of my mouth"). These words reflect the curses of the Mosaic covenant, through catchword connections with Deut 33 and 32. In Deut 33:9, אמרה "word" is used in parallel to ברית "covenant." The covenant blessings and curses presented by Moses in poetic form in Deut 32 are called אמרי־פי "words of my mouth," v 1, and אמרתי "my speech / words," v 2. The punishment of being "killed" (הרג) is a covenant judgment (Amos 4:10; 9:1, 4), though the notion of killing is expressed via other vocabulary in Deut 28 and 32 (curse type 24).

The destruction that Israel has experienced is Yahweh's "justice" (משפט; cf. Deut 32:4), inevitable, and all-encompassing. It functions like (sun) light, appearing daily and exposing what had been hidden. Yahweh thus declares that Israel's miseries were unavoidable. Israel had broken his covenant, and his justice had to "come forth" (cf. v 3), decimating the nation during the war of 735–732 B.C.

6 God's oft-quoted prioritizing of covenant requirements does not actually reject the sacrificial system. The people have understood worship as their Canaanite neighbors understood it, as limited to ritual acts of sacrifice (including the communal meal and its attendant indulgences). One showed devotion to the gods by sacrificing to them regularly. In turn, the gods did their part by benefiting their supplicants.

But Yahweh's relationship to Israel was not just another religion. The Canaanites might be free to oppress their neighbors, flirt with other gods via the rampant syncretism of the day, or live self-centered lives in which personal passions could claim the highest priority. But Israel's covenant with Yahweh had stipulations that went far beyond prescriptions for ritual. These are summarized as חסד "(covenant) loyalty," and דעת־אלהים "knowing God."

In 4:1 these two basic categories of covenant fulfillment were supplemented by a third, אמת "honesty." The poetic structure of v 6, however, in which the common pair זבח "sacrifice" and עולות "burnt offerings" are juxtaposed contrastingly with the two more general terms, does not lend itself to the inclusion of אמת.

Yahweh's words here amount to a rejection of the cult itself (curse type 2; cf. Lev 26:31) because it had become so unbalanced. The tendency to settle for a mechanistic, ritual-dependent religion of "motions" rather than of godly actions must again and again be attacked: compare Amos 5:21–24; Isa 1:12–17; Micah 6:6–8; Ps 51:16–17; Matt 9:13; 12:7 (cf. Hos 4:8, 13; 8:13). Declaring the sacrificial system meritless *except* as an adjunct to the "weightier matters of the law" was in effect the suzerain's declaration to his vassal how the covenant was to be kept, and what its essential—as opposed to peripheral—demands were. Israel had been mauled in war. They were desperate for relief. Now they needed to hear how misplaced their efforts and priorities were. In specifying what he took pleasure in, Yahweh also set before his people a program for the future. If they wished in a future generation to please him, they would have to seek "loyalty" and a "knowledge of God." Otherwise, it may be inferred, more of the same miseries, and perhaps worse, awaited them. The verse thus provides a justification of Yahweh's past wrath as well as an indication of what will be required to prevent further wrath in the future.

7 The start of a new section of the passage has been sometimes construed here (so Mays, 99), because of the supposed geographical reference via emendation to "in Adam," parallel to Gilead (v 8) and Shechem (v 9). But v 7 is as closely connected to the thought expressed in vv 4–6 as it is to what follows, and especially relates to v 4b as a general statement of Israel's infidelity. The verses that follow give specific, selected evidence of that infidelity; thus v 7 provides a transition from vv 4–6 to vv 8–10. The fact that God speaks about Israel rather than to them indicates no shift; third-person reference began already in v 5.

Four words have meanings different from what might seem their most obvious renderings: המה here means "look" (*pace* de Moor, *UF* 1 [1969] 201–2); אדם is far more likely a variant of אדמה "dirt" than the E. Jordan city of Adam (Josh 3:16); עבר probably means "walk on" rather than the more abstract "transgress"; and שם has the sense "see" as also in v 10b (notes 7.a–d).

The concern of this statement is not how the covenant was broken "there at Adam," but that by treating the covenant "like dirt," the nation has betrayed (בגד) Yahweh himself. Here in Hosea ברית "covenant" appears only for the second time. In 2:20 [18] the term denoted the future universal covenant. In the present passage the Mosaic covenant is clearly at issue. Its stipulations were Israel's law; when broken wholesale, the covenant was negated and Israel brought under its curses (cf. 4:1–2; 4:6; 8:12). The people were guilty of treason.

8 The powerful could not legally oppress the weak (Lev 19:9–18), and certainly not violently (Exod 20:13; 21:12–35; Num 35:16–21, 31–33; Deut 19:11–13). "Bloodshed pollutes the land" (Num 35:33).

Though "Gilead" usually refers to the northern Transjordan, rather than a city, the city of Ramoth-Gilead (*Khirbet jelʿad*) is probably meant here. The mention in a Ugaritic text (UT 170:2) of *bnš gt glʿd*, "people of Gat-Gilead," ("Winepress of Gilead") in parallel to other cities, supports the MT reading; no emendation is justified.

Gilead is a city of פעלי־און ("evildoers"). This term occurs widely in the Psalms to indicate the enemies of the righteous and of Yahweh. They are here accused of manslaughter, but no further specifics are given (cf. 12:12 [11]). The assassination of Pekahiah in 740 B.C. by Pekah and "fifty men of Gilead" (2 Kgs 15:25) may have been the referent. Shedding blood in peacetime was onerous (e.g., 1 Kgs 2:5). Some brutal uprising must lie behind the accusation against Gilead.

9 The scene shifts to "the road to Shechem." (On the interruption of the construct chain by the verb, see Freedman, "The Broken Construct Chain," *Bib* 53 [1972] 536.) Shechem was a major religious (Deut 27:4, 12–14; Josh 8:30; 24:1, 25) and political (Josh 20:7; Judg 9:1; 1 Kgs 12:1, 25) center, important since patriarchal times (Gen 33:18–20). Bands of priests are here excoriated for committing premeditated murder there. The accusation may be metaphorical, connoting the "murder" of orthodoxy. Or a variety of despicable acts current in Hosea's day may be in focus. Perhaps a struggle among branches of the priesthood occasioned these words. It is also possible that the "murder on the road to Shechem" referred to the ambushing of pilgrims, refugees, or even Shechemite priests by illegitimate priests from the government-sanctioned cult. Ultimately, we cannot be certain what this "murder" was.

It is not certain that MT חבר "guild" is original. G reads ἔκρυψαν, which would reflect חבאו "are hidden" or the like. If חבר is correct, a pun on the alternative meaning of the word ("exorcism, spell") may be intended: חבר כהנים could mean "(magic) spells of the priests."

10 The scene shifts again to the entire "family of Israel" rather than any specific locale. The sometimes-proposed emendation of בית ישראל to בית־אל is unwarranted. The two citations of outrageous sins—presumably well known to Hosea's audience—in vv 8 and 9 are but examples of generalized corruption (cf. v 7). God sees "a terrible thing" (שעוריה, Qere), Ephraim's "prostitution" (זנות) and the fact that Israel is "unclean" (נטמא), all terms associated with covenant infidelity. (For שערירית in a context of covenant-breaking, cf. Jer 18:13–17.) V 10b is virtually equivalent to 5:3b, where Ephraim's "prostitution" and Israel's uncleanness are likewise set in synonymous parallelism. The idea that Israelite covenant-breaking was openly visible prepares the way for the descriptions of "open" sin in 7:1–2, but is also a conclusion based on the incriminating evidence presented in vv 4–9.

6:11–7:1a The corollary concern for the status of Judah and Israel in the restoration period now receives attention (cf. 1:7; 3:5; 4:15; 5:5). The foregoing accusations against Ephraim, apart from the particular citations in vv 8–9, must be understood as applying to Judah as well. But Hosea's message follows the covenantal sanctions with predictions of restoration after punishment. So for the third time in the passage (cf. 5:5; 6:1–3) the reader/hearer receives a reminder that God will never finally abandon his people (cf. Lev 26:44).

The coming restoration is described as a "harvest" (קציר). This term is occasionally symbolic of either reward or punishment in the OT and can function metaphorically to describe a decisive intervention of God (Joel 4:13 [3:13], the nations; Jer 51:33, Babylon). In light of the pentateuchal blessings in which abundant harvests are a sign of God's favor (Deut 30:9; cf. 28:4–5, 11), it is likely that קציר here has positive rather than negative connotations (i.e., restoration blessing type 5).

The second couplet of the promise emphasizes restoration of prosperity (שוב שבות; cf. Deut 30:3) and "healing" (רפא; cf. Deut 32:9). The nation—North and South—will be strong and well (blessing type 6). Such a promise has already been substantially represented in Hosea (2:1–3 [1:10–2:1]; 2:16–25 [14–23]; 3:5; 6:1–3), including the concept that the restoration must await Judah's punishment.

The third couplet promises divinely effectuated righteousness (blessing type 3; cf. Deut 30:6 et al.). The couplet pairs Ephraim and Samaria synonymously: the whole nation, capital and countryside, will be healed. This prediction of the future ability to be faithful is central to Hosea's restoration forecasts (2:17–19 [15–17], 21–22 [19–20]; 10:12; 11:11; 14:1–4 [13:16–14:3], 8 [7]; cf. Zeph 3:9–13). The many sins for which the northern kingdom was so guilty will simply disappear (גלה, niphal; see note 7.c). Just as Yahweh purified Israel during the forty years in the wilderness (Num 14:27–35), he will eventually purify Israel (Hos 6:10) via destruction and exile (cf. Deut 4:27; Amos

9:8–10). Then an obedient remnant, forcibly but happily conformed to the covenant (cf. Deut 30:6–8) will reap the blessings of the restoration age.

Explanation

Matt 9:13 records Jesus' challenge to the Pharisees to learn the real meaning of the statement in Hos 6:6, "I desire compassion, not sacrifice." Jesus linked this prophetic word with his own ministry, suggesting that if the Pharisees could understand and practice Hosea's words they would not only support his work of compassion, but do likewise. The Pharisees made a mistake similar to that made by the Israelites, 750 years earlier, in the assumption that a formal, ritualistic religion would please God, regardless of their mode of life or condition of heart (a mentality that plagues God's people still). Such an approach to pleasing God is illusory (6:4).

Central to the entire passage is the hurtful, angry proclamation by God in 6:6–7. God rejected Israel's partial fulfillment of the covenant as no fulfillment at all. By concentrating only on the rituals, the people treated the covenant like "dirt" (6:7). It was covenantal treason (6:7) to permit disloyalty to God both politically (5:13) and ethically (6:8–9). Part of the law could not be obeyed to the exclusion of the rest.

War provided the proximate punishment in this case for the guilty nation. The entire passage reflects in one way or another the "infection" and "mauling" of the Syro-Ephraimite war. The outrageous crimes in cities on both sides of the Jordan (6:4–10) may all have been related, directly or indirectly, to the circumstances of the war and its aftermath. But these bitter times in turn set the stage for the mention of a day of restoration, indefinite as to its timing, but certain to come because of Yahweh's unfailing love for his people (6:1–3; 6:11–7:1a).

The passage is thus a forceful statement of divine rejection of Israel, mollified by intrusions of hope. Israel's infidelity, summarized as so often in Hosea by the curse term זנות "prostitution" (6:10), meant that the nation was defiled. God would no longer protect Israel, but would withdraw from them. In trouble and having no hope in any other, they would then finally come to their senses and return to him (cf. 2:9 [7]; 3:5).

No other passage so thoroughly involves Israel and Judah in tandem. Their interrelationship in the war occasions their close connection but is not the sole explanation for it. Here especially Judah's sinfulness is at issue. In contrast to the occasions where Judah's relative righteousness is compared with Israel's corruption (e.g., 4:15) or Judah's deliverance is vouchsafed as against Israel's destruction (1:7), the equally damning evidence against both Judah and Israel is now stressed. This is not a new theme here (cf. 5:5), but is somewhat unique in its pervasiveness.

The Syro-Ephraimite war brought out the worst in both Israel and Judah. Neither would escape Yahweh's wrath. But neither would miss Yahweh's future blessings. Eventually North and South alike would "seek" Yahweh (בקש, 5:15; cf. Deut 4:29), seek the "face" (פני, 5:5) he had hidden from them (Deut 32:30). Their sickness and sores (5:13) could then be healed (7:1). Their iniquity could then disappear (7:1).

Ephraim Mixed Up among the Nations (7:1aδ–16)

Bibliography

Budde, K. "Hosea 7:12." *ZAW* 26 (1912) 30–32. ———. "Zu Text und Auslegung des Buches Hosea (6:7–7:2)." *JBL* 53 (1934) 118–33. **Dahood, M.** "The Conjunction *pa* in Hosea 7:1." *Bib* 57 (1976) 247–48. ———. "Ugaritic and the Old Testament." *ETL* 44 (1968) 35–54. ———. "Ugaritic-Hebrew Lexicography XI." *Bib* 54 (1973) 351–66. **Driver, G. R.** "Problems of the Hebrew Text and Language." In *Alttestamentliche Studien: FS F. Nötscher*, ed. H. Junker and J. Botterweck. Bonn: P. Hanstein, 1950. 46–61. **Gaster, T. H.** "Zu Hosea 7:3–6, 8–9." *VT* 4 (1954) 78–79. **Halevi, B.** "Sexual and Fire Metaphors in Hosea." *BMik* 22 (1977) 473–76 (Heb.). **Hvidberg, F. F.** *Weeping and Laughter in the Old Testament: A Study of Canaanite-Israelite Religion.* Leiden: E. J. Brill, 1962. **Paul, S. M.** "The Image of the Oven and the Cake in Hosea VII 4–10." *VT* 18 (1968) 114–20. **Rubin, P.** "Hos 7:1–7." *AJSL* 52 (1936) 34–40.

Translation

Crime is widespread in Israel (general wickedness)

7:1aδ *How deceitfully they act!*
 The thief breaks in [a]
 the bandits roam [b] *outside!*

2 *They do not think*
 that I take note of all their evil.

 Now their transgressions surround them;
 they are right in front of me.

The corruption of the government (domestic politics)

3 *The kings rejoice* [a] *in their evil,*
 the officials in their lies.

4 *They are all adulterers;*
 they are like a burning oven
 whose baker [a] *can stop stirring the fire*
 from the kneading of the dough until it is leavened.

5 *Daily the kings are sick,* [a]
 the officials feverish [b] *from wine,*
 extending the hand even [c] *to infidels.*

6 *Indeed, they are inflamed* [a] *like an oven,*
 their heart burns within them. [b]

 All night their fury [c] *slumbers;*
 in the morning it blazes up like a roaring fire.

[7] *All of them are as hot as an oven;*
they devour their rulers,[a]
all their kings fall.
Not one of them calls on me.

Israel's unfaithful diplomacy (international politics) and its result

[8] *Ephraim is among the nations;*
he is mixed up.[a]

Ephraim has been a flat loaf
that has not been turned over.

[9] *Foreigners have devoured his strength,*
but he does not know it.

Even mold[a] *has crept in*[b] *upon him,*
but he does not know it.

[10] *Israel's pride testifies against him.*
They will not return to Yahweh their God;
they will not seek him in spite of all this.

[11] *Israel has become like a pigeon—*
gullible and brainless.

They call to Egypt,
they send to Assyria.

[12] *As they go,*
I will throw my net over them.

I will bring them down like the birds of the sky,
I will punish[a] *them sevenfold*[b] *for their evil.*[c]

Punishment is inevitable (governmental and national destruction)

[13] *Woe to them, because they have fled from me!*
Destruction to them, because they have rebelled against me!

How can I redeem them
when they speak lies about me?

[14] *But they do not cry to me from their heart*
when they wail on their beds (and)
for the sake of grain and fruit-of-the-vine[a] *slash themselves.*[b]

They are stubborn[c] *against me*
[15] *though I trained*[a] *them.*

I strengthened their arms,
but they plot evil against me.

[16] *They shall return to*[a] *the yoke;*
they shall become like a slack bow.[b]

Their officials will fall by the sword
because of their denouncing tongues.

This will be mockery on them
in[c] *the land of Egypt.*

Notes

1.a. G adds πρὸς αὐτόν "into it" reflecting perhaps עליו or אליו (?). The term "breaks in" expresses idiomatically in Eng. what a thief does to a house.

1.b. The MT consonantal text may be read either פָּשַׁט or פְּשַׁט, the latter being the conjunction פְּ "and" + the ptcp of שׁוּט. The translation is not necessarily affected.

3.a. Reading the pl מלכים on the basis of G and the other pls in the verse. "Kings" and "officials" are the subjs, not the objs, of the verbs, which must be vocalized in the qal, rather than MT's piel.

4.a. Reading בְּעֵר הֵם instead of MT's confused בְּעֵרָה מ and vocalizing אֹפֵהוּ for MT אֹפֶה.

5.a. We read יום / יומם מלכין החלו "daily the kings are sick" (cf. Kuhnigk, *NSH*, 90–92). The versions differ greatly, reflecting the poor state of the text. Emendation to sgs (מלך "king" and החלה "he is sick") is unwarranted (cf. n.3.a). החלו is the hiph intransitive of חלה "to be sick."

5.b. Reading חֲמַת rather than MT חֲמָת. Cf. Kuhnigk, *NSH*, 90–92.

5.c. The best reading of the consonants of MT would seem to be מָשַׁךְ יָד וַאֶת־, i.e., the inf abs plus the sg "hand" + the *waw* intensive ("even"). See Kuhnigk, *NSH*, 90–92.

6.a. G (ἀνεκαύθησαν "they were inflamed") reflects קדחו or the like. Kuhnigk (*NSH*) retains MT קֵרְבוּ as a piel denominative from קֶרֶב "heart". MT literally would mean something like "(He has extended his hand with infidels) when they approach."

6.b. Reading בער בם for MT בארבם "their intrigue."

6.c. MT אֹפֵהֶם means "their baker" (?). אַפֵּהֶם, our reading, follows Syr, Tg.

7.a. In poetic parallelism with מלך "king," שׁפט has the same meaning as it has in the book of Judges, i.e., "ruler, governor," so also in Ug. Cf. M. Dahood, "Ugaritic-Hebrew Parallel Pairs," *RSP I*, 267–68.

8.a. "Mixed up" is precisely the meaning of יתבולל here. The root בלל means "mix" and / or "confuse."

9.a. Or "gray hair." Cf. Freedman and Andersen, 467.

9.b. The proper sense of זרק here is debated. A cognate to colloquial Arab. *zrq* "sneak upon" seems more likely in the context than does זרק II "to shine / glitter."

12.a. Vocalizing MT as אֲיַסְּרֵם. Otherwise, the text might represent a corruption of סם אָאֱסָרֵם "I will bind / imprison them," since the context treats of entrapment.

12.b. The emendation of שמע "report" to שבע "sevenfold" rests on the parallel in Lev 26:28 ויסרתי אתכם אף־אני שבע על־חטאתיכם "*I* will punish you sevenfold for your sins"; cf. Lev 26:18, 21, 24. This covenant curse has been corrupted in MT and the versions first by misreading שבע as שמע, and possibly also by the addition of כ (which may, however, reflect metrical demands).

12.c. MT לעדתם "to their congregation" is a misreading and jumbling of לרעתם or על־רעתם "for their evil." Cf. G τῆς θλίψεως. This part of the sentence also parallels Lev 26:28.

14.a. The Heb. term תירוש is archaic, thus the archaic translation. Cf. 2:10.

14.b. Reading יתגדדו with G. Cf. 1 Kgs 18:28.

14.c. G (ἐπαιδεύθησαν "they were taught") reflects יִסָּרוּ or the like. We revocalize MT to יֻסָּרוּ, from סרר "train."

15.a. Or "punished." The verb has the sense both of "punish" and "instruct." See *Comment*.

16.a. MT לֹא "not" is a corruption of ל or אֶל־ "to." Being put "to the yoke" is a covenant curse (Deut 28:48; cf. Lev 26:13 where freedom from the yoke is a covenant blessing).

16.b. On the meaning "slack" for רמיה see Driver, *Alttestamentliche Studien*, 53–54.

16.c. Kuhnigk (*NSH*, 96, 101) suggests taking ב as "from / since" so that the entire line reads: "Das ist ihr Spotten seit dem Ägypterland [That is their mockery since the land of Egypt]." See *Comment*.

Form / Structure / Setting

Within 7:1 a new section begins. The next clear break comes with the call to alarm in 8:1. The chapter is unified around a common theme: the frantic, hopeless political intrigue of Ephraim, centered at Samaria. The general faithlessness of Israel, their personal debauchery, passion for political intrigue, vulnerability in international affairs, and ultimate destruction are all described here. Most, if not all, of the accusations are made against decisions and practices that originate in the city of Samaria. The chapter catalogs the evils of the Northern capital, and thus follows naturally from the mention of Samaria at the end of the previous pericope.

The structure may be summarized as follows:

  a. Lament over the general wickedness of the nation   vv 1–2
  b. Lament over Samaritan domestic politics   vv 3–7
  c. Lament over Israel's folly in foreign affairs, and a
      judgment sentence (v 12)   vv 8–12
  d. Lament over doom for Israel's rebellion   vv 13–16

The pattern of the laments is somewhat chiastic, i.e., general sins : domestic sins :: international sins : general destruction.

Several catchwords provide links between the subsections of the full passage: רעה "evil / wickedness" in vv 2, 3, 12 (cf. also in 7:1a); גדד "slash" in vv 1 (as גדוד "robbers"), 14; שר "official" in vv 3, 5, 16; יסר "punish / instruct" in vv 12, 15, etc. Others relate to previous pericopes: e.g., גדוד in 7:1 and 6:9; and the entire clause of 7:10a (to 5:5a).

The passage consists of divine speech in the form of (accusatory) "personal laments." Verse 10b should be considered part of that speech. (Yahweh speaks of himself in the third person at many points in Hosea.) Israel is consistently in the third person, as if Yahweh were addressing someone concerning them, as witness in a covenant lawsuit.

The predominating prosodic pattern is synonymous parallelism (all or parts of vv 1–3, 5–11, 13, 15). A bit of antithetical parallelism (vv 14a, 15) is present in the remainder, which is otherwise synthetic. Metrical patterns vary freely, as typically elsewhere.

The setting of the passage is best related to the political instability in Samaria after 733 B.C. (for a contrary view see H. Tadmor, "The Historical Background of Hosea's Prophecies," *Yehezkel Kaufman Jubilee Volume,* ed. M. Haran [Jerusalem, 1960] 84–88). Vv 3–7, in particular, via the metaphor of the superheated baker's oven depict the kind of passion involved in the assassination of Pekah. But those verses may also recall frantic political changes of the north's last days. Since the fall of the Jehu dynasty in 752 B.C. with the assassination of Zechariah, three more kings (Shallum, Pekahiah, and Pekah) had been murdered (2 Kgs 15:8–26). By the time Pekah, who had ruled since 740, was assassinated by Hoshea (732–723) in the aftermath of the Syro-Ephraimite war (2 Kgs 15:27–30), the faultlines in the north's political infrastructure had widened irrevocably.

Vv 8–12 would appear to refer to Hoshea's desperate, inconsistent attempts at foreign alliances. He came to power submitting to Assyrian hegemony, paying tribute, and thus preserving the central-southern portions of the nation not yet controlled by Assyria. Within a few years (i.e., sometime in the mid-720s) he stopped tribute payments to Assyria and appealed for support to a temporarily resurgent Egypt (1 Kgs 17:2–4). This was the "mixed up" foreign policy "among the nations" (v 8) of a dying people (v 9).

Yahweh then announces woe to Israel (vv 13–16). Such "pigeon-headed" (cf. v 11) policies as those pursued after 733 B.C. were merely further evidence of disobedience. While the Egyptians laugh at Israel, the Assyrians will take them into captivity (v 16). And so it happened. Shalmaneser (727–722) took Hoshea prisoner in 723. Samaria, "like a slack bow," then fell in 722 to the Assyrians led by the new king Sargon II (722–705). Sargon claimed to have taken captive 27,290 Israelites (Pritchard, *ANET,* 284–85; cf. H. Tadmor, *JCS* 12 [1958] 22–41, 77–101). God's word that Israel's "officials will fall by the sword" was accomplished.

Comment

1aδ   After שׁמרן "Samaria," which ends the previous passage, the remainder of the first verse constitutes a triplet. Its opening line ("How deceitfully they act!") states the general situation of Israel's wickedness, and the following two lines illustrate this deceit, Israel's unfaithfulness to the covenant while thinking to honor Yahweh via outward religious practices. The twin crimes of breaking and entering, and banditry, are cited in evidence, emphasizing the blatant nature of the violations. (To take שׁקר as "idol" rather than "deceit" [Freedman and Andersen, 432] will not fit the context.) The two crimes are a synecdoche for civil and social injustices in general. God is not lamenting the government's failure to put more police on the streets, but rather the society's toleration of open evils of all sorts, while hypocritically maintaining its religious rituals.

2   The stress continues upon the openness of the nation's sins. Ephraim's guilt is not hidden; God has watched it all. The first half of the initial couplet (ובל־יאמרו ללבבם) means simply "they do not think." No emphasis is placed on introspection or indecision. זכרתי can mean "I remember," "I notice," or even "I know," usually in the sense of "keeping track of." It is commonly used in connection with remembering the covenant (cf. Lev 26:42; Ps 105:8; Amos 1:9). The fact that Israel is blissfully unaware of its behavior reflects the influence of Canaanite religion on Israelite thought patterns. The Canaanite approach emphasized cyclical mythology and ritual re-enactment (see G. E. Wright, *The Old Testament Against Its Environment* [London: SCM, 1950]; W. F. Albright, *Yahweh and the Gods of Canaan* [Garden City: Doubleday, 1968]). It tended to ignore the divine rule over history, and thus allowed for a personally indulgent ethical system.

But even if Israel did not remember God's revelation, he remembered their sin. "Now" (עתה) introduces the conclusion to vv 1–2 (cf. 5:3). Their "transgressions" (מעלליהם) connote general covenant unfaithfulness rather than political intrigue per se. מעל consistently has the sense of failure to live up to expected responsibilities, i.e., "undutifulness," specifically against God. These evil ways now are so rife as to surround Israel, the people's iniquity being "right in front of me" (נגד פני). As Yahweh looks at Israel he sees not people but sins—filling his field of vision, as it were. "When I look at them all I can see is their sins" is the sense of the second couplet.

3   Attention centers now on the political leadership: royalty, appointed officials, and presumably also influential nobility. Though there is no formal break between vv 2 and 3, the subject is more specific, i.e., the kings and those with influence in the affairs of the royal court. "Their evil" is both the context of and the motivation for their rejoicing. Since the subjects of the verb are "kings" and "officials" it is unnecessary to emend יְשַׂמְּחוּ "they delight" to יִמְשְׁחוּ "they anoint," as is often done. MT's awkwardly singular "king," מֶלֶךְ, would require an unexpressed subject, "they" for יְשַׂמְּחוּ. The verb must apply to שָׂרִים "officials" as well, and since the "anointing" of the officials is unlikely historically, the plural "kings," מְלָכִים/ן, with G, is to be preferred.

The sort of "evil" and "lies" the verse addresses are those of political conspirators, whose plotting has brought kings, and therefore their chosen officials, to power. The description may have included all the kings who came to power via usurpation after 752 B.C., but surely included Hoshea ben Elah (732–723). Hoshea and his minions disregarded Yahweh's sovereignty in assuming power violently, as may be reflected in the verb "rejoice," a word used twice in the OT (1 Sam 11:15; 2 Kgs 11:14) to express the joy at a royal coronation, and often to express ceremonial celebration (e.g., Ezra 3:12, 13). The context, however, does not appear to make reference to the installations per se of Hoshea (732 B.C.) or any other kings.

4 The catchword "adulterers" (מְנָאֲפִים), used before to express covenant infidelity (2:4; 4:13, 14; cf. Jer 9:2; 23:10) is here also a pun on אָפָה "to bake," v 4, and אַנֵּף "anger," v 6, words which sound rather similar to it. The passion of the king, his court officials, and the influential nobility is likened to a baker's oven so hot that the baker need not tend the fire during the entire baking process. The heat of their treachery and transgression drives them to take matters into their own hands, ignoring Yahweh in their maneuvering.

The bake-oven (תַּנּוּר) serves as the basis for the simile that continues through v 7, and relates to the simile of the unturned flat loaf in v 8b. It was a round, domed, beehive structure made from fired clay with floor-level apertures and a large door on top. It usually had a stone floor. A roaring fire was built inside and allowed to burn until the interior was glowing hot. The coals were left, not swept out as with more modern brick ovens. The bread loaves were then pressed onto the oven walls, or laid among the coals. The door at the top of the oven was sealed, and the bread was left to bake in the retained heat, which would not dissipate for hours, providing that the oven had been adequately fired. The oven envisioned here may be the large-capacity oven of a royal baker or the like since בֹּעֵר "baker" is a masculine term. Women in ancient Israel did most of the baking, it is assumed, since virtually every house had an oven (cf. Lev 26:26). But professional bakers could be either women (1 Sam 8:13) or men (Jer 37:21), operating in baker's districts in the cities (Jer 37:21; Neh 3:11). Their professional-size ovens, small volcanoes of flame when first lit because the fire roared out of the door at the top, were surely well known to the citizens of Samaria. The figure of v 4 depicts a super-heated oven, built with a great fire that would continue from the time the dough was kneaded with yeast until it had risen, (an hour or two, depending on the amount of dough prepared) to be put into the oven later when the coals were red hot and the walls were glowing.

So were Samaria's leaders. They had come to power, by the heat of treachery (v 6) and violent usurpation (v 7)—but certainly not by Yahweh's will.

5 The kings and officials are now depicted as feverishly hot from drunken-

ness, thus eagerly friendly (?) even to those who scoff at religious faith (לצים
"infidels"). Fueled by alcohol, the brain can better suppress conscience and
entertain wickedness, depravity, and conspiring with scoffers. It is not completely clear what MT consonantal משך יד means; "extending the hand" is
a likely translation (cf. Kuhnigk, *NSH*, 92). Presumably the drunken officials
either *welcome* infidels, *drink* with infidels, or *cooperate* with infidels. Alternatively, the term may have something to do with acts of violence (cf. Freedman
and Andersen, 458). The expression is unique in the OT, thus not easily
solved.

6 The two synonymous couplets comprising v 6 reinforce the point of
the metaphor operative in vv 4–7: the governmental leaders are utterly consumed by their desire for power. Asleep or awake, they are never free from
the flame of passion for intrigue. The horrible, destructive force of this passion
drives them even to the assassination of royalty (v 7), who represent Yahweh
(see De Vaux, *Ancient Israel*, 100–113). The second couplet (6b, i.e., "All
night . . . roaring fire") continues the oven analogy. The oven was not fired
up at night, of course, but the coals were kept alive in the oven so that a
newly laid fire would catch and reheat the oven the next morning. Samaria's
leaders are likened to that fire: only when they are asleep (ישן) does the
fury of their emotional frenzy abate. Their waking hours, however, are devoted
to mischief against Yahweh's will.

7 The oven simile reaches its climax in a verse structured by external
chiasm. The first and fourth lines form a synthetically parallel couplet; the
second and third lines, a synonymously parallel couplet. Like v 4, v 7 begins
with "all of them" (כלם) as its subject, and thus the entire government and
those with political influence are condemned. The verb יחמו "are hot" is
merely a stylistic alternative to the other terms for heat used in vv 4–7. The
point of the frequent mention of the fury of the government's leaders is
now revealed explicitly: they have come to power by "devouring" (cf. 2:14 [12];
13:18), i.e., killing off kings ("rulers" is a poetic synonym for "kings;" cf. n.
1). No single assassination is in view. But then, only one king, Menahem,
had *not* been assassinated since the death of Jeroboam II.

The intrigue of Northern politics in Israel's last days was marked by its
fierce intensity. Speaking of these self-appointed rulers and their cohorts by
third person forms ("all of them"; "they"; etc.), Yahweh disassociates himself
from their machinations. Israelite affairs of state have been carried along by
the fever of a selfish, godless lust for national control. "Like every revolutionary
state that has no faith in anything beyond itself, Israel was burning up in its
own anger" (Mays, 106–7). The nation's self-centeredness is painfully evident
in the final statement. The lament of Israel's only true sovereign is both
plaintive and bitter: "Not one of them calls on me." If they had only sought
Yahweh, he would have gladly helped them; but so arrogant and egotistical
were they that they paid no attention.

8 Two apothegms describe Ephraim's weakness and vulnerability. The
nation is mixed up and half-baked. These sentences are reminiscent of the
style of tribal blessings (cf. Gen 49:3–22; Deut 33:2–29) though it is impossible
to be sure that this portion of the prophecy is ironically styled on that model.
The verb form יתבולל, the hithpolel of בלל, means "is mixed up," and is

purposefully ambiguous. It can mean mixed up, as in the ingredients in bread (continuing the baking metaphor), or confused (cf. בלל, qal, Gen 11:7, 9). In the literal sense, Ephraim was intermixed among the "nations" (בעמים). Israel's struggle for survival in its last two decades, in the face of increasing Assyrian power, was characterized by frantic foreign policy shifts, particularly between successive alliances with Assyria and Egypt, but also vis-à-vis Syria-Damascus and Philistia. All of this represented a failure to trust in Yahweh (cf. v 7) and an unwillingness to return to him (v 10). Hoshea's lurching foreign policy is illustrative. In 732 B.C., Hoshea, after killing Pekah, suddenly shifted from alliance with Egypt, Philistia, and Aram-Damascus to alliance with Assyria. A few years later he broke that alliance, and coming virtually full circle, again sought alliance with Egypt. These confused policies are caricatured in the figurative sense of "mixed up."

As a result Israel became like a flat loaf (עגה) not turned over. According to the usual explanation, the bread loaves pressed onto the hot oven walls or laid among the coals needed turning after a time. If left unturned, they would be half-baked; crusty or burnt on one side yet still doughy on the other. Similarly, Ephraim was rigid and crusty toward Yahweh. But its soft underbelly was exposed to the nations. Like an unturned loaf it lacked both the strength and consistency to survive. However, no evidence exists to suggest a turning process was ever used in baking bread. More likely, the "turning" refers to doubling the dough over for strength and compactness as opposed to weakness from thinness. At any rate, poor quality would result from failure to turn the loaf in either case, and poor quality is what Ephraim was now characterized by.

9 Both couplets of the verse end identically: "but he does not know it." Personified now in the masculine singular, Israel does not know how weak and vulnerable he has become. The first line of v 9a, אכלו זרים כחו "foreigners have devoured his strength," is the determining statement. The first half of 9b ("even mold [or gray hair] has crept in upon him") reinforces, by an image associated with decay, the point that Israel would soon find its viability endangered.

Israel, now debilitated with age, was in its last decade of existence. But who were the "foreigners" who had sapped Israel's vitality? Most likely they must be identified with all the nations Israel "mixed with" in the years after 745: Assyria, Egypt, Syria-Damascus, Philistia, and even Judah (5:8–10). War and its aftermath left the nation reduced in population, territory, and economic vitality. Many Israelite territories were now Assyrian provinces. Heavy Assyrian tribute as well as, presumably, gifts to Egypt, and the taxes imposed to provide them, had drained the wealth of the royalty, the temple, and the citizenry alike. In the late 730s and early 720s the North was dying—and yet its own people did not know it. The once great nation was like a ruined loaf, fit only for casting aside.

10 The verse begins with a saying also used in 5:5a ("Israel's pride testifies against him"). The similar contexts occasion the identical saying which is probably original in both locations. Just as in 5:4–6, now Israel, mixed up and half-baked, also refuses to return (שוב) to God, or to seek (בקש) "Yahweh their God" (יהוה אלהיהם, v 10). It is too late for Israel—their death is near (v 9). Israel's pride has bred a stubbornness that cuts them off from Yahweh's blessing. Here Yahweh speaks of himself in the third person (cf. 2:22 [20]; 4:7, 10; 6:6; 8:13; 11:10; 12:1 [11:12] as a means of contrast to Israel's faith in everything *but* Yahweh. The subject, Israel, is now plural instead of singular (cf. such shifting in 2:4–17 [2–15]). The Israelites habitually trust in other sources of potential relief than their own God. They are like moldy bread; or perhaps an old man, blissfully ignorant of how decrepit he has become. "Who needs Yahweh?" says Israel, in effect. "Why turn to him? Our greatness will see us through once again!" In spite of "all this" (בכל־זאת) i.e., the serious deterioration of Israel's position among the nations (vv 8, 9), Israel stubbornly keeps independent of its covenant Lord.

11   In Hosea's day Israel's foreign policy flipflopped between loyalties to Assyria and Egypt. God likens them to a pigeon (dove), a bird not known for its wit (cf. Matt 10:16). Menahem (752–742 B.C.) had submitted to Assyria, paying Tiglath-Pileser III ("Pul") substantial tribute (2 Kgs 15:19–20). When Pekah (740–732) assassinated Menahem's son Pekahiah, he opposed Assyria, in league with Syria-Damascus (2 Kgs 16:5). Then overtures to Egypt were probably made, though the brief accounts in Kings and Chronicles do not mention Egypt in this connection. After the Assyrians had captured much of the North in response to the Syro-Ephraimite invasion of Judah (2 Kgs 16:5–9; 15:29) Hoshea (732–723) first shifted the nation back to submission to Assyria, but later stopped payment of tribute, and sought alliance with Egypt (2 Kgs 17:3–4). What a pigeon Israel was! Tricked, deceived, gullible (פותה), brainless (אֵין לב)—an easy mark for the nations to devour (v 9), and ripe for punishment from Yahweh (v 12). Egypt and Assyria could not possibly help the covenant people when the real source of their malady was their guilt before Yahweh (cf. 5:13–15).

12   The bird metaphor leads into a description of the judgment Yahweh will bring upon Israel. With his bird-hunting net (cf. 5:1) he will catch Israel winging its way to foreign nations for help. The resulting captivity (curse type 13) will represent Israel's own downfall as a nation, i.e., destruction (v 13). The text of v 12b may be restored on the basis of the covenant curse formula in Lev 26:28 (and 26:18, 21, 24; see n. 12.b). In Lev 26:18, 19 God promises: "I will punish you sevenfold for your sins. I will break down your stubborn pride (גאון) . . . ." In Hos 7, the pride (גאון) of Israel has led to that very sevenfold (כש(ב)ע) punishment (איסרם). Israel's evil (רעתם; cf. vv 1, 2, 3; note 12.c) is, of course, the illegality of refusing to be loyal in all ways to its covenant Lord. The multiple-punishment curse (type 27) will be well-deserved.

13   The divine saying now openly becomes a cry of woe (אוי), a predictive sort of funerary lament announcing destruction (cf. 9:12). In ancient Israel אוי was originally a mournful cry at the death of a loved one, or lamentively, about oneself in a situation of mortal peril (1 Sam 4:7; Isa 6:5). The prophets used it as a means of signaling disaster for Israel (Isa 3:11; Jer 13:27; Lam 5:16) or another nation (Num 21:29; Jer 48:46; Ezek 24:6, 9). It implies the inevitability of calamity; and it is appropriate to situations where one's doom is certain (cf. the parallel שד "destruction").

Upon Israel this woe was now pronounced, because it had fled (נדד) from and rebelled (פשע) against Yahweh. The latter term implies revolt against authority, as in a revolution against a king or empire (1 Kgs 12:19; 2 Kgs 3:7; 8:20; 2 Chr 21:8). In 8:1, פשע is used of rebellion against Yahweh's law (תורה), clarifying the present usage. Because Israel had transgressed the divine law, the Lord must punish the rebellious nation as the law specified. In verse 13b Yahweh expresses his lack of options in a conditional (. . . ו . . . ו) interrogative: "How can I redeem them (ואנכי אפדם) when they speak lies (כזבים) about me?" "Redeem" (פדה) is originally a financial term meaning simply to "buy back." It was used in certain legal situations where an individual could pay a fee to buy back property that would otherwise have been condemned to death (including one's first-born; Lev 27:27–31). Yahweh could buy back his people from their mortal fate only if they were worthy of redemption. The term was often used of Israel's redemption from bondage (Exod 13:13; Deut 7:8; 9:26), but redemption was not Yahweh's plan in this case. Only after his people had been delivered to their substantial destruction (curse type 24; cf. Deut 28:20 et al.) could there be hope of re-demption (cf. 13:14).

The "lies" Israel had spoken about Yahweh are to be identified with the broken promises to keep the covenant. Israel's oaths of fidelity during the yearly festivals were proved false by their reliance on superpowers. Their loyalty to Yahweh proved fleeting (cf. 6:4).

14a The bulk of verse 14 is a triplet of ten syllables to each line, describing how the Israelites cry out in the course of their sacrifices, but without true loyalty. The expression "from their heart" (בלבם) probably has the same sense as the Assyrian treaty expression *ana gamurti libbi*, which means "with one's whole heart" (W. von Soden, *AHW*, 279–80). The crying out (זעק), wailing (ילל, hiphil) and slashing (גדד, hithpael) were all aspects of the Canaan-ite style of worship employed by the Israelites. The North was now in difficult straits, not the least agriculturally. For the sake of grain and wine (cf. 2:10 [8]) they appealed to Yahweh (though on other occasions probably to Baal as well) in this pagan manner (cf. 1 Kgs 18:26–29) forbidden in Israel (cf. Lev 19:28; Deut 14:1). "Their beds" (משכבותם) is probably not, as has sometimes been suggested, a copy error for "their altars" (מזבחותם). Canaanite worship involved a sacrificial meal, eaten at leisure while reclining on cushions beside the altar (Amos 2:8; Isa 57:7–12, esp. v 7). Upon these "beds" the Israelites cried out, wailed, and even slashed themselves in a sincere but covenantally worthless attempt to invoke Yahweh's aid in these hard times.

14b–15 The final two words of v 14 (יסורו בי "they are stubborn against me") begin a synthetic couplet, which is completed by the first two words of v 15 (ואני יסרתי "though I instructed them"). The remainder of v 15 consti-tutes a synthetic couplet which has a similar meaning ("I strengthened their arms, but they plot evil against me"). Together, the four lines of the two couplets form a chiasm in which "they are stubborn against me" parallels "they plot evil against me" and "I instructed them" parallels "I strengthened their arms." These couplets both lament and condemn at the same time.

God raised Israel (cf. 11:1). He taught and strengthened them. They had his protection and guidance (11:1–4; 13:4–5), yet rebelled. In contrast to "a stubborn cow" (4:16) Israel is now likened, in effect, to a stubborn child (cf.

Isa 30:1, הוי בנים סוררים "Woe to the stubborn children"), a rebellious, wanton child, impossible to discipline, as in Deut 21:18–20 (בן סורר). The punishment for such a child was death. Israel's stubbornness manifested itself in plotting against Yahweh, i.e., being disobedient to him by attaching themselves instead to Egypt and Assyria. It may also be that this general reference to their plotting evil against him (אלי יחשבו־רע) would include the disloyalty of the illegal Bethel cult and the Baal cults, which characterized the North's religion.

16 The lament concludes with a description of the punishment Israel will receive for its rebellion against Yahweh: captivity, helplessness and death in war (curse types 13, 19, 3). Again the Samaritan leadership is particularly—though not exclusively—in focus. The prediction of return to the yoke (see n. 16a) is a prediction of subjugation to a foreign people, i.e., captivity, which brings about the end of the nation. Deut 28:47–48 predicts: "Because you did not serve Yahweh . . . you will serve the enemies Yahweh sends against you. He will put an iron yoke (על ברזל) on your neck until he has destroyed you." Israel would not return to Yahweh, so they must return to the yoke, i.e., the sort of bondage they had once known in Egypt. The "slack bow" (קשת רמיה) provides an analogy of weakness and ineffectiveness (cf. Ps 78:56–57); the bow is unstrung or has no tension, so that no arrow can be shot from it (cf. G. R. Driver, "Problems," 53). For all its frantic attempts at shoring up its position militarily and politically, Israel is deathly weak and exposed helplessly among the nations (vv 8, 9, 11), ripe for the plucking by Assyria, whose practices of subjugation, captivity, and deportation were well known to Hosea's northern audience, as well as to his southern readership. Neither hearer nor reader could fail to miss the point of these words.

The officials (שרים) would be killed by the sword, a frequent covenant curse motif (cf. Lev 26; Deut 28:32; passim), i.e., in military action (by the Assyrians in 722 b.c.) because their tongues had spoken denunciation (זעם). זעם functions here as a synonym for ליץ, polel (to "scoff," "mock," "act as an infidel"; cf. the participle in v 5), since the object is the same: the word of Yahweh. Whether this word is the Mosaic covenant itself (most likely) or the warnings of the prophet(s) (less likely), it represents a defiance of Yahweh himself. "This" (זו) refers to the events predicted in the entire verse, not simply the death of the officials. Thus the general destruction and subjugation of Israel will constitute the source of the Egyptian mockery (לעג) against Israel. They will take delight in seeing a fickle, unreliable ally done in by the very nation it sought help from in preference to Egypt. Such a prediction would be especially appropriate at a time when Israel was once again contemplating turning to Egypt, i.e., the early 720s (2 Kgs 17:3–4). Not only will the Egyptians not be able to help Israel, they will end up laughing at them; thereby fulfilling the curse of Deut 28:37, "you will become . . . an object of scorn and ridicule to all the nations where Yahweh will drive you."

Explanation

Yahweh expresses his bitter disappointment with Israel by four laments that together comprise a single lengthy personal lament of accusation against

Israel. Personal laments, as known especially from the Psalms, normally contain most or all of the following six elements: (1) an address to God; (2) the complaint; (3) an expression of trust in God; (4) a plea for deliverance; (5) an expression of assurance in God's faithfulness; and (6) a word of praise to God. Because Yahweh himself is the speaker here, elements 3, 5, and 6 are of course inappropriate. Element 1, the address, is made to all who will listen. Element 2, the complaint, comprises the bulk of the chapter. Element 4, the plea for deliverance, is transformed in this chapter to a prediction of destruction.

Behind the lament lies the tragic fact of Israel's conduct in its final years. Both in domestic (7:3–7) and in foreign (8–11) policy Israel's successive leaders had scrambled to secure their power. Driven by a lust for success, they neglected the one thing that would really have secured peace, blessing and hope: a return to Yahweh and obedience to his covenant. They repeatedly ignored opportunities to return to him (vv 7, 10, 14) and instead showed themselves thoroughly reprobate (vv 1–2), hot-headed (vv 4–7), weak (vv 8–9), proud (v 10), gullible (v 11), rebellious (vv 13, 15) and misled (v 14). Thus they deserved destruction (vv 12, 13) and captivity (v 16) according to the covenant curses of Lev 26 and Deut 28–32.

The essence of God's complaint is the rebellion of his people. "Not one of them calls on me" (v 7); "They will not return . . . they will not seek" (v 10); "they have fled from me . . . they have rebelled against me!" (v 13); "they are stubborn . . . they plot evil against me" (v 15).

By its transgression, Israel has become known as an open, flagrant covenant violator (vv 1–2). Their crimes block a proper relationship with Yahweh, their God. It can only be restored by a penitent return (cf. 6:1–3) but their actions take them in every direction (e.g., v 12) other than toward their God. Thus the sin remains, the transgressions pile up so as to surround the people (v 2), filling Yahweh's field of vision.

Israel's infidelity was manifest internationally in two ways. First, they lurched turbulently between Egypt and Assyria (v 11) ultimately unfaithful therefore to both, and thus odious to both—the one becoming their captor, the other their heckler (v 16). Second, their infidelity was far more significantly directed at Yahweh, whose covenant would have protected them from their steady degeneration (vv 8–9), and their final downfall (v 12) at his hands. And all the while they acted as if he did not notice (v 2). Their habitual practices and attitudes contrary to God's will cut them off from his blessing. Persisting in sin has severe consequences under the new covenant as well (Gal 5:17).

Israel Reaps the Storm for Its Sin
(8:1–14)

Bibliography

Ahlström, G. W. "Oral and Written Transmission: Some Considerations." *HTR* 59 (1966) 69–81. **Cazelles, H.** "The Problem of the Kings in Os 8:4." *CBQ* 11 (1949) 14–25. **Dahood, M.** "עלׁ שׁיר 'to sing before.' " *Bib* 54 (1973) 354. ———. "Ugaritic Lexicography." *Mélanges Eugène Tisserant I,* itta del Vaticano, 1964. 81–104. ———. "Ugaritic and the Old Testament." *ETL* 44 (1968) 35–54. **Emmerson, G. I.** "The Structure and Meaning of Hos 8, 1–3." *VT* 25 (1975) 200–210. **Freedman, D. N.** "The Broken Construct Chain." *Bib* 53 (1972) 534–36. **Gnuse, R.** "Calf, Cult and King: The Unity of Hosea 8:1–13." *BZ* 26 (1982) 83–92. **Lundbom, J. R.** "Double-duty Subject in Hos 8, 5." *VT* 25 (1975) 228–30. **Nicholson, E. W.** "Problems in Hos 8, 13." *VT* 16 (1966) 355–58. **Thompson, J. A.** "Israel's 'Lovers.' " *VT* 27 (1977) 475–81. **Torczyner, H.** "Dunkle Bibelstellen." In *Vom Alten Testament: FS K. Marti.* BZAW 41. Giessen: Töpelmann, 1925. 277–78.

Translation

Punishment for transgression and rejection

8:1 *God[a] waits[b] like a young lion[c]*
Yahweh, like an eagle over the house,[d]

Because they have transgressed my covenant,
And rebelled against my law.

2 *Let them call out to me: "O God of*
Israel,[a] we know you."

3 *Israel has rejected the Good One.[a]*
The enemy will pursue him.

Political and religious disobedience

4 *They[a] have made kings,*
But not by my will.

They have deposed[b] them
But I have not acknowledged[c] it.

With their silver and gold,
they made idols for themselves;
as a result, they will be destroyed.[d]

5 *I reject[a] the bull[b] of Samaria;*
I am furious at them.
How long will 6 *the Israelites[a] be incapable of innocence?*

As for it,[b] a craftsman made it;
it is not God!

So, the bull of Samaria
will go up in flames.[c]

Coming agricultural disaster

7 *Though they sow with a wind,*
they will reap in a storm.[a]

Grain without a head
will produce no flour.[b]

Even if it does produce,
foreigners will devour it.

8 *Israel is devoured;*
now they are among the nations
like something[a] *nobody wants.*

Israel in Assyria and Egypt (vv 9–13)

9 *For behold they have gone up to Assyria—*
A wild donkey off by itself is Ephraim;
lovers[a] *have hired*[b] *it.*

10 *Even though they have been hired*[a] *by the nations,*
now I will gather them.

And they will cease for a while
from anointing[b] *king or officials.*

The corruption of the cult

11 *Though Ephraim has made many altars to take away sin*[a]
they have become for him altars for committing sin!

12 *I wrote for him my many laws;*[a]
they are considered as something foreign.

13 *They offer sacrifices as my gifts,*
and they eat the meat,
(but) Yahweh is not pleased with them.

Now he will remember their guiltiness,
and he will punish their sins.
Behold they will return to Egypt.[a]

Destruction by fire

14 *Israel forgot his maker,*
Judah built temples / palaces,[a]
He fortified many cities.

But I will send fire into his cities,
and it will consume his fortresses.

Notes

1.a. The Heb. text is difficult to comprehend as it stands in MT ("To your palate a trumpet, like the eagle over the house of Yahweh"). The versions confirm that the text was corrupted early in its transmission. In the first half of the couplet, G reads εἰς κόλπον αὐτῶν ὡς γῆ "to their bosoms like the earth," reflecting a *Vorlage* which read אל חק כעפר. G apparently supplied the αὐτῶν "their" simply from the context. Andersen and Freedman (485–86) propose identifying the verse as a chiasm אל חך : כשפר :: על בית יהוה : כנשר, a suggestion which moves toward a solution, though resulting still in an unsatisfactory translation: "Like a horn to the mouth! / Like an eagle over Yahweh's house." If the verse, however, is understood to reflect the covenant curses of harm from wild animals (type 11) and to contain a chiasm of a different sort אל : חכה כ(כ)פר :: כנשר על בית : יהוה it reads more convincingly. MT אֶל "to" must then be revocalized to אֵל, "God."

1.b. The ך of MT חכך "your palate" belongs with the following word, in parallel to כנשר "like an eagle." The remaining form חך is best vocalized as the act ptcp of חכה "to wait" (qal, Isa 30:18; piel, Hos 6:9), written defectively or apocopated by corruption.

1.c. MT שפר could reflect some sort of animal (Akk. *šapparu*, "wild goat" has been suggested; "stag" or "antlered stag" [cf. Gen 49:21] has also been proposed). G's reading γῆ "earth" (=עפר) makes doubtful the first consonant of MT שפר, although, following G one could posit עפֶר "fawn" as the animal intended; the fawn seems unlikely as a threatening animal, however. I propose therefore reading כ(כ)פר *kepîr* "lion," already employed by Hosea in a similar context in 5:14, and highly appropriate to the threat intended in the present verse.

1.d. Reading בֵּית for MT's construct בֵּית.

2.a. The construct "God of Israel," אֱלֹהֵי ישראל (MT, אֱלֹהַי) is split by ידענוך "we know you" for metrical reasons (7:8 syllable count). Composite names and other stereotyped phrases are especially subject to such splitting in the OT. Cf. Kuhnigk, *NSH*, 102–4; Dahood, *Psalms III*, 480; and Freedman, *Bib* 53 (1972) 534–36. Several unusual translations have resulted here from the failure to recognize this phenomenon.

3.a. On טוב as "the Good One" see Dahood, *ETL* 44 (1968) 52.

4.a. Kuhnigk (*NSH*, 104–5) places הם with v 3 and vocalizes: אויב ירדפו הֵם "they have pursued the Enemy" (i.e., Baal). While it is possible to approach the scansion this way, or to identify הֵם as a dittogr from the first two consonants of המליכו "they have made kings," the better approach is to recognize that the couplet is balanced (8:8 syllables) only with the inclusion of הֵם.

4.b. The verb is less likely שרר "to rule" than שור, a simple biform of סור, hiph, meaning "remove / get rid of / depose." Kuhnigk (*NSH*, 105) suggests a double-entendre from both verbs: "they have deposed them / set up officials." There is no certainty that שרר, hiph, would mean "set up officials," however.

4.c. On this meaning of ידע see Gen 18:19; 39:6; 2 Sam 7:20; etc.

4.d. Reading the pl יכרתו with G Syr Tg.

5.a. Instead of MT זָנַח "he has cast away," read either זָנֹח (inf abs in place of the finite verb, "I have cast away/am casting away") or זֹנֵח (act pres ptcp, "I am casting away); so H. J. van Dijk, *Ezekiel's Prophecy on Tyre*, 70. A form with the pronoun "I" is avoided *metri causa* in this 6:5 couplet.

5.b. Reading עֶגְלְ־כִי, the intensive, instead of MT עֶגְלֵך "your bull"; so Kuhnigk, *NSH*, 106; cf. Hos 2:8, *darkᵉ-kî*. On the meaning "bull" rather than "calf" for עגל, see W. F. Albright, *From the Stone Age to Christianity* (Garden City, NY: Doubleday, 1957) 300–301.

6.a. MT כי מישראל "indeed from Israel" is illogical. The emendation to בני ישראל "Israelites," though speculative, at least makes the line intelligible.

6.b. MT והוא "as for it" is resumptive logically of עגל שמרון "bull of Samaria."

6.c. שבבים occurs only here in the OT. It may mean "flames" (שבב; Aramaic and Job 18:5, etc.) or perhaps "bits / splinters" (Ug. *tbb*); or it may be the result of a textual corruption.

7.a. There is no evidence that סופה means "whirlwind."

7.b. Wolff and Mays translate "bread," a non-literal translation sometimes thought appropriate to the supposed rhyme of MT צֶמַח "head" and קֶמַח "flour." The rhyme was possible only in medieval Heb., however, and not during Hosea's time. See *Comment*.

8.a. The usual translation ("vessel / utensil") for כלי is not idiomatic in English; cf. כלי חמדה "precious thing" in 13:15.

9.a. Vocalizing אֹהֲבִים "lovers" for MT אֲהָבִים "gifts of love."

9.b. The verb תנה "to hire / pay for a prostitute" is a speculation, but seems to fit the context.

10.a. The vocalization of חנה, here passive, should be יֻתֶּנּוּ or the like.

10.b. Reading with G ויחדלו "they will cease" and ממשח "from anointing."

11.a. The piel *privatum* לְחַטֵּא "to take away sin" is more likely than MT's לַחֲטֹא "to sin." Cf. Kuhnigk, *NSH*, 107–8.

12.a. K רבו may reflect an archaic case ending with רב "many, multitude"; with G Syr read תורתי "my laws."

13.a. G adds καὶ ἐν Ἀσσυρίοις ἀκάθαρτα φάγονται "and among the Assyrians they will eat unclean things," probably an expansion from 9:3b in the G *Vorlage*, which sought a complementary line to finish the couplet. In fact, v 13b is itself the complementary line to v 9a.

14.a. Since היכל means both "palace" and "temple," it is impossible to differentiate between them in translation; both senses may be intended. We take "Judah" as the subject of "built temples," the ו preceding יהודה being secondary (or possibly a poss suff to go with היכלות, thus "his temples"). In the synonymous parallelism of the triplet, the sense would be "Israel and Judah both forgot their maker and built . . . and fortified. . . ."

Form / Structure / Setting

A new section of oracles begins at 8:1 with the theme of rejection and transgression, and including a general description of Israel's sin (vv 1b–3; cf. 7:1–2) as an introduction to a catena of evidences and curses. The passage ends at v 14, with a description of the judgment of fire that will befall Israel (and Judah).

Three types of sayings predominate. Most are predictions of punishment for Israel based on the Pentateuchal covenant curses. Interspersed among these are laments over Israel's rebellion (parts of vv 3–4; 8–9; 11–13), i.e. evidence that the covenant has been broken. Wolff (135, 142) considers the sayings in v 7 to be sapiental. They are, in fact, more probably straightforward futility curses (type 15).

The general structure may be summarized as follows:

Prediction of punishment for Israel's covenant transgressions and rejection of Yahweh	vv 1–3
Condemnation of political intrigue and religious idolatry	vv 4–6
An agricultural futility curse and its implication for Israel	vv 7–8
Description of Israel's plight internationally	vv 9–10
Condemnation of the corrupt cult	vv 11–13
The futility of defense against destruction by fire	v 14

Two "broken" structures are evident. The splitting of "God of Israel" (see note 2.a) is paralleled on a much larger scale by the splitting of a couplet as an inclusio, i.e., vv 9–13:

For behold (המה) they have gone up to Assyria—
Behold (המה) they will return to Egypt.

That vv 9–13 were thus framed by a split couplet was first noticed by D. N. Freedman (*Prolegomenon* to G. B. Gray, *The Forms of Hebrew Poetry* [New York: Ktav, 1972] xxxvi–xxxvii) and has been described at length by J. Lundbom ("Poetic Structure and Prophetic Rhetoric in Hosea," *VT* 29 [1979] 300–308). The couplet is completely parallel, repeating one word (הֵמָּה, MT הֵמָּה, "behold"); pairing a perfect and an imperfect in typical poetic style (עלו "they have gone up" and ישובו "they will return"); and using אשור "Assyria" and מצרים "Egypt" as a fixed pair (cf. 7:11; 9:3; 11:5, 11; 12:2 [1]). Similar examples occur in Hos 4:11–13 (q.v.) and Jer 51:20–23. By delaying the conclusion of a couplet, a prophet can create suspense. Here, the sins of international political unfaithfulness and heterodox religious practices are detailed until the suspense builds to a single option for Yahweh: to send Israel back into bondage. In Hosea as in other prophetical books, "Egypt" can equal captivity and exile in the tradition of Deut 28:68. A secondary unifying factor of the section thus created (vv 9–13) is that of the subject of "Ephraim" (vv 9, 11) in contrast to "Israel" elsewhere in the chapter.

Most of the parallelisms are synthetic. Synonymous parallelisms are found in vv 4, 13b, 9aα and 13bγ, and 14. Antithetical parallelisms occur in vv 7 and 11. There are several triplets interspersed among the sayings. The varieties of parallelisms and the variations of couplets with triplets are unpredictable, as is virtually always the case in Hebrew poetry.

With respect to the setting, the juxtaposition of 8:1–14 and the post-733 B.C. oracles in 5:8–7:16 can hardly have been accidental. The mention of enemy pursuit (v 3) recalls 5:8. The aftermath of the Syro-Ephraimite War is the most likely setting for these oracles. Israel's deteriorating international position is described in vv 8–10 (cf. 7:8–9); its internal political instability, in v 4 (cf. 7:3–7). Hoshea's initial desperate appeal to Assyria (v 9; cf. 7:11–12) had already taken place, as had perhaps also his sudden reversal and appeal to Egypt. The "bull of Samaria" (vv 5–6) is singular, the one at Dan probably having been destroyed or captured when the Assyrians invaded in 733 (cf. 1 Kgs 12:29 and Hos 7:1–16, *Form / Structure / Setting*). There is a possibility that the term "bull of Samaria" is employed because "bull of Bethel" would be impossible since Bethel reverted to Judahite control in 732 (see 5:8–10, *Comment*). This would fix the passage after 732 without doubt. However, the term "Samaria" may have been as much a metonymy for the Northern Kingdom as a whole as it was a city name. The mention of Samaria does not mean that these words were preached in that city; such an assumption is based on the awkward and therefore questionable MT rendering of v 5, עגלך שמרון "your bull, O Samaria," which is obviated by our revocalization (see n. 5.b).

We date the passage, then, tentatively in the reign of Hoshea, probably sometime between 731 and 725.

Comment

1 Hosea's Israel is heading for destruction. The "young lion" (see n. 1.c) and the eagle, killers, wait for prey. Yahweh will kill Israel, via the enemy (v 3) in war. Deut 28:49 provides a partial backdrop ("Yahweh will bring a nation against you from far away, like an eagle swooping down . . .") for the imagery. The concept of Yahweh's attacking Israel like a wild animal (curse type 11) has, of course, a close parallel in 5:14, where כפיר "young lion" is also found as a simile for Yahweh.

The reason for the coming attack is stated in the explicitly convenantal language of the second couplet. Israel has violated the covenant and disobeyed the Mosaic law. The enemy in terms of the war alarm is Assyria, but Israel's ultimate enemy is Yahweh (cf. 5:13–16; 6:1; 7:3–16). Troubles stem from unfaithfulness to him, political and economic difficulties being simply a manifestation of his disfavor. Israel deserves, indeed requires, that disfavor because of their disobedience to the covenant.

The terms תורה "law" and ברית "covenant" occur three and five times, respectively in Hosea, but are paired synonymously only here. In each use of תורת (construct singular or plural) MT construes the singular, though the consonants may be vocalized either as plural or singular. As in 4:6, the law is the full body of the covenant stipulations delivered both to the Levites (Deut 31:26) and the populace as a whole (Deut 32:46–47). These individual *laws* comprising the *law* are written (8:12) and therefore open before all. Disobeying the law was therefore a conscious, willful act against Yahweh who calls the law "*my* law," and the covenant "*my* covenant."

2 Israel attempted to offset their disobedience by intensified worship. The verb זעק "call out" carries the connotation of calling for help (Judg 12:2; 2 Sam 19:29). In distress, needing food and security after the disastrous events of 733 B.C., Israel appealed formally to its national God while still flirting with other gods (vv 3, 4–6) and heterodox practices (v 11). This recalls the wailing appeals to Yahweh described in 7:14.

The present urgent plea uses covenantally related language: "O God of Israel, we know you" (ידענוך). On the split construct ישׂראל . . . אלהי "God of Israel" see n. 2.a. Both parts of the appeal (the name and the assertion of knowledge) are attempts to remind Yahweh of his connection with his people. The phrase "God of Israel," often preceded by "Yahweh" or "Yahweh of Hosts," is common throughout the OT. The Israelites assumed that this connection between Yahweh and Israel was irrevocable: he was and therefore would always remain their God regardless of their behavior. Moreover, they presumed to "know" him, i.e., be allies of his, and counted upon that alliance (but cf. 4:1). God cites their appeal in outrage. A paraphrase would be: "And they have the gall to call to me . . . !" Their claim is hypocritical, belied by their deeds of disloyalty (v 3, etc.).

3 Israel has consciously "rejected" (זנח) the "Good One" (טוב) i.e., Yahweh, thereby violating the covenant. Their punishment will come according to a well-known curse. The "enemy" (אויב) will "pursue him" (ירדפו). This wording is most closely paralleled by Deut 28:22, 45, but reflects a theme (curse type 3) mentioned repeatedly in Lev 26 and Deut 28–32. To be pursued, in the terminology of the covenant curses, is a way of expressing that one will be on the losing side in a war (compare Deut 28:7 with 28:25; cf. Lev 26:7). Israel may expect to be conquered by Assyria (cf. v 4).

4 With v 4 begins a specification of Israel's sins in rejecting the "Good One." First described are crimes against the covenant in the areas of the governance of the nation, and its cult. The Israelites have arrogated to themselves the right to install or depose kings (cf. 7:3–7). Yahweh *alone* determines who can be king either by charismatic gifts or by direct revelation through a prophet. He *gives* kings to the nations (e.g., 1 Kgs 19:15–16); they do not decide who their kings will be. The phrase translated "by my will" (ממני) means literally "by me" or "from me." The king was Yahweh's representative or regent, not the people's choice. As in 7:3–7, the volatile internal maneuverings after 748 B.C. which produced a rapid-fire succession of Northern kings, most assuming power by assassination (2 Kgs 15:8–30), is the referent for these words. Nothing in these words suggests that the Northern kingship per se was illegal (cf. 1 Kgs 11:11; 2 Kgs 9:1–3); it was the way that kings were imposed and deposed that God rejected.

The second half of the verse attacks the false cult's practice of idolatry. As v 5 makes clear, the bull-idol of gold was the most obvious (and official) manifestation of these "idols" (עצבים). But there were others. As the Israelites in their syncretism had adulterated Yahwism with many of the features of other religions, idolatry had naturally proliferated (1 Kgs 11:4–10; Hos 4:17; 13:2, etc.).

The final clause, "as a result, they will be destroyed" (‹ו›למען יכרת), states tersely the result of idolatry according to the covenant. The verb כרת, niphal "be destroyed," is commonly used in judgment oracles by the prophets (cf. Lev 26:22, 30 hiphil). Even more akin is the formula in the "Holiness Code" of Lev 17–26 (often elsewhere as well) about the fate of the one defiled by sin: "that soul shall be destroyed from among his people" (e.g., Lev 17:4; 18:29). The word למען, translated here "as a result," can indicate either purpose ("so that") or result ("so"). It is thus possible to construe the entire sentence which constitutes v 4b as follows: "With their silver and their gold, they make their own idols so that they will be destroyed!" The sense would be that the Israelites invite their own doom by their outrageously foolish disobedience.

5 As Israel has "rejected" (זנח) Yahweh (v 3), so now Yahweh has rejected (זנח) the bull of Samaria. The context suggests the reading of a first-person form ("I reject") rather than the preterite as in MT or the imperative as in G (see n. 5.c). The "bull of Samaria" (n. 5.b) since its public establishment in duplicate by Jeroboam II (1 Kgs 12:26–30) on the model of the golden bull manufactured by Aaron (Exod 32) had been the centerpiece of the Northern counter-cultus.

It is often argued that the golden bull was not intended to be an idol representing a deity, but rather simply a platform, akin to the ark, for Yahweh to stand on. So concludes W. F. Albright (*From the Stone Age to Christianity* [2d ed., Baltimore: Johns Hopkins, 1957] 299): "Among Canaanites, Aramaeans, and Hittites we find the gods nearly always represented as standing on the back of an animal or as seated on a throne borne by animals—but never as themselves in animal form." The biblical accounts do not in fact support this view, however. In the earliest confessions about the bull (Exod 32:4; 1 Kgs 12:28) it was obviously regarded as a deity. Even if a pedestal for Yahweh, it was much more than simply pious artwork. As Albright admits, "It is true that the Hurrians considered the two bulls Sheri and Khurri, who supported the throne of the storm-god Teshub, as minor deities . . . ," adding "but they were not identified with the great storm-god!" As Pope has shown, the Ugaritic iconography represented the god El precisely as a bull (M. Pope, *El in the Ugaritic Texts,* VTSup 2 [Leiden: E. J. Brill, 1955]).

The Israelites considered the עגל "bull" an idol representing a deity. Most may have originally considered that deity Yahweh. Others may have kept the bull neutral in their minds. But with the advent of Canaanite ways of worship, the distinction had apparently blurred: the bull was itself thought a god, as the denial in v 6 makes obvious. Use of the bull-idol was therefore idolatry, attacked by the prophets as a betrayal of the essence of the covenant (cf. Exod 20:3–4). Because of this, Yahweh is "furious" at Israel. He can be a "jealous God" (Exod 20:5) in opposition to idolatry, and his fury is aroused on those occasions when Israel turns to idolatry thereafter (Num 25:3; cf. Deut 11:16, 17; 29:25–28; Josh 23:16; etc.).

Yahweh then asks a bitter question: "How long will the Israelites (n. 6.a) be incapable of innocence?" The interrogative "how long" (עד־מתי) is a rhetorical way of expressing the yearning of an unfulfilled hope (cf. Pss 6:4; 74:10; 90:13; Jer 12:4; Zech 1:12). But it can also express, as here, the impatience with an annoying situation (Jer 4:14; Hab 2:6). Israel could not seem to avoid guilt. "Innocence" (נקיץ) was beyond their ability (לא יוכלו; cf. 5:13). Holding steadfastly to worship of the bull-idol, they guaranteed that Yahweh could not accept their appeals (v 13).

6 That which a craftsman has manufactured can hardly be a god, yet the Israelites believed it so. As a background to the phrase לא אלהים "not God" see Deut 32:21 (לא אל). The idol worshiped was probably a small statue of a young bull (עגל). Other shapes are possible, such as a staff with a small bull-figure at the top (so O. Eissfeldt, "Lade and Stierbild," *ZAW* 58 [1940 / 41] 190–215) or even a human figure with a bull's head (cf. K. Galling, "Das Stierbild von tell-el-aschᶜari," *ZDPV* 69 [1953] 186–87). But a bull-like statue is most likely. It was almost surely carved of wood, because it could "go up in flames" (שבבים; cf. Exod 32:20), and overlaid with a thin skin of gold leaf. Many ancient idols were likewise made of a wooden core. The Sumerians even called wood "the flesh of the gods" because of its common use in idols.

The folly of worshiping something made by human hands is a typical theme in the prophets (e.g., Isa 2:8, 20; 40:18–20; 44:9–20; Jer 10:1–16, etc.). Yet the incongruity of worshiping a statue was shunted aside in favor of the standard system used by all the other nations. Israel could not stand alone even in this most basic feature of its covenant with Yahweh—the exclusive worship of an invisible God.

The bull of Samaria will be put to the fire, a standard form of covenant punishment (Lev 20:14; 21:9; Num 11:1; Deut 32:22; type 10) especially suitable for idols (Deut 7:5, 25). Since Israel had not destroyed their idols as the law required, Yahweh will now do it for them.

7 And he will hardly stop with the bull-idol; the people themselves must be punished. V 7 contains three brief futility curses, in which expectations are thwarted before they can be realized (type 15; cf. Deut 28:30–42). The first two of these curses have sometimes been identified as "wisdom sayings" because they supposedly reveal an epigrammatic sapiental style. There is, however, no proof of this. The first saying, indeed, simply reflects the futility curse of Deut 28:38: "You will sow much seed in the field, but you will reap little." In ancient times sowers would throw their seed with a gentle wind, which helped scatter it evenly on a tilled field; רוח has thus an adverbial sense, i.e., "with a wind," without symbolic overtones. The disaster which brings to nought the planning and effort of the sower is seen in the storm disintegrating and scattering the heads of grain before they can be harvested. "Storm" is adverbial, because of its locative ending (סופתה). Bad weather, the bane of farmers, will function as the proximate agent of Yahweh's judgment on Israel (curse type 6c).

There is a possibility, moreover, that the entire saying is a double-entendre, since רוח "wind" is often used as a metonymy for foolish, worthless behavior or goals (Eccl 1:14, 17; Prov 11:29; Job 7:7) and appears in Hosea in connection with the driving force of the "prostituting spirit" (4:12, 19; 5:4). The saying follows a sowing-reaping format otherwise well known (Prov 11:18; 22:8; Job 4:8; cf. Gal 6:7), i.e., "what you sow you will reap," or "what you sow you will reap many times over." The latter sense could apply here. What Israel has sown (רוח, "worthlessness," direct object) it will reap in a storm (סופתה, adverb).

The second saying also employs the futility curse format, and may even be built upon the first. That "grain without a head will produce no flour" is hardly a new revelation but it makes a serious point. If Yahweh causes the stalks to yield no grain, or if the yield is destroyed, famine (curse type 7) will result. Wolff (132, n. 1) assumes that צֶמַח "bud," "head" was rhymed by קֶמַח "flour." This could be so only in medieval Hebrew, however. In the eighth century B.C. צמח was pronounced ṣimḥ and קמח was pronounced qamḥ. The couplet is balanced metrically (5:5) but not rhymed. The third futility curse describes how foreigners will devour what Israelites had planted (curse type 5). This motif follows almost exactly the Mosaic covenant curses (Lev 26:16; Deut 28:33, 51; cf. Deut 32:21b). The enemy (v 3) will get what Israel had worked for, and Israel's dependence on the fertility cult will have proved a tragic mistake.

8 This verse may well recall the motif of the eagle in v 1, a bird of prey about to devour. Israel's international entanglements are likened to the sort of miserable existence they will have when scattered among the nations for their infidelity (curse type 13). Compare Lev 26:38, "the land of your enemies will consume (אכל) you"; Lam 2:5, "Yahweh is like an enemy; he has devoured (בלע) Israel." Their scattering among the nations is, metaphorically, a devouring of Israel (cf. Lev 26:33; Deut 28:64–65; 32:26). Thus Israel was already beginning to experience the enforcement of these curses. They were, according to v 8, "among the nations" (בגוים) and unwanted. Their own flip-flop foreign policy (cf. *Comment* on 7:3–4) had been a major factor leading to their current dilemma. Once Israel was great; "now" (עתה) it was helplessly foundering among those from whom it desperately but futilely sought aid. The term "something nobody wants" (כלי אין חפץ בו) appears in Jer 22:28 to describe the sad status of the deposed King Jehoiachin in exile and in Jer 48:38 to describe a defeated, doomed Moab. These parallels are instructive. Israel was defeated and doomed; even more distress would follow (vv 10, 13, 14). That this plight represented the abandonment of Israel to Yahweh is evident from what follows.

9 Israel's national disloyalty was manifest most dramatically in its appeal to Assyria. The verse begins with half of a split couplet ("For behold they have gone up to Assyria—") which finds its completion in the last sentence of v 13 ("Behold they will return to Egypt"). Between are framed descriptions of Israel's sin and its result—international rejection and Yahweh's coming punishment. The appeal to Assyria was presumably that made by Hoshea in 732 B.C., upon assuming power, in order to stop total conquest of Israel by Tiglath-Pileser III (cf. 7:8–12).

The first half of the following couplet constitutes a metaphorical castigation

of Israel's degenerate status among the nations. Ephraim is called a פרא
that is "off by itself." The פרא was either a wild donkey, onager, or zebra.
Though these animals travel in herds, they have little contact with humans
or other animals (cf. Job 24:5; Ps 104:11). The word פרא makes a visual
pun with אפרים "Ephraim," though whether such a pun could be distinguished
aurally is questionable. פרא may recall the poetic promise of God to Ishmael
in Gen 16:12, where פרא conveys the sense of one isolated, and at enmity
with others.

The second half of the couplet ("lovers have hired it") finds a striking
parallel in Jer 2:23–25, which is set in the midst of a series of metaphors
describing Israel's unfaithfulness: ". . . you are . . . a wild donkey accustomed
to the wilderness . . . in her heart who can restrain her? Any males that
pursue her need not tire themselves; at mating time they will find her. . . .
For you said, 'I love foreign gods; I must follow them!' " In Hos 8:9, the
nation is in danger from its foes, easy prey for those who have the resources
to hire (i.e., demand) its love—whether Egypt, or, at the point this prophecy
was delivered, Assyria.

10 The first couplet of the verse portrays the Israelites as dispersed (at
least metaphorically) through seeking help from foreign alliances. "Gather"
(קבץ; piel) can describe the gathering of the exiles back to the promised
land in blessing (Deut 30:3; Ezek 20:41); or a gathering up for judgment of
the accursed (Joel 4:2 [3:2]; Zeph 3:8; cf. Hos 9:6). The latter meaning is
obviously intended here. "Wherever they are, wherever they have sold themselves, I will gather them for punishment" is the sense.

The second couplet echoes the theme of 3:4 and speaks implicitly of the
coming exile. The partially corrupt text, when emended (nn. 10a, b), predicts
one of the features of the judgment Israel will receive at the hand of its
God. The nation's independence will be taken away, its own rulers deposed,
and it will be subject to the dominion of its enemies as specified in the covenant
curses (type 5 and probably type 13b; cf. Deut 28:36). This will endure for
a "while" (מעט), i.e., not indefinitely and certainly not permanently (cf. 2:1–
3; Lev 26:40–45; Deut 4:29–31; 30:1–9).

11 The aberrations and distortions of orthodoxy in the Northern cult
also displeased Yahweh. Multiple altars (v 11), disregard for the laws (v 12),
and love of sacrifice-feasts (v 13) are reproached. The system of multiple
altars was an inheritance from the Canaanite system (see 4:13), and a violation
of the covenant stipulation of a single sanctuary (Deut 12). The Ephraimites
had built and rebuilt altars all over their territory, for the purpose of expiation
of sin (לַחֲטֹא, piel *privatum*). But their altars became in fact a means for sin
(לַחֲטֹא).

Without an altar there was hardly a means of worship under the old covenant. Knowing this full well, Jeroboam I had instituted the beginnings of
the multiple-altar system in the North immediately upon taking the throne
(1 Kgs 12:26–33, esp. v 31). This approach to worship became so ingrained
in the Israelite consciousness that even a reform as drastic as Jehu's (2 Kgs
9–10) left the multiple sanctuaries virtually unaffected (2 Kgs 10:29). The
Northern priests may even have looked back to the patriarchal period, when
multiple altars were normal and proper (Gen 12:7; 13:8; 22:9; 26:25; 33:20,
etc.) for their justification, as if no Mosaic law (cf. v 12) had intervened.

The Northern altars were, however, sites of false worship. Altar-based practices, including gluttony and drunkenness, were part of a system wherein the sacrifice-feast had become the focus of the activity rather than the symbol of fellowship; priests proliferated as formalism replaced covenant obedience (4:7–9). These altars, then, became places to sin rather than places to be forgiven.

12 Yahweh declares that the Israelites are ignoring his laws. From the point of view of historical interest, the verse makes several assertions about the Sinai law: (1) A large number of individual laws were known. "Many" (MT רבו, vocalize רֹבּוֹ or רֹב) reflects and parallels הרבה ("made many") in v 11, describing the large number of sanctuaries in the North. (2) The Sinai commandments were regarded as life guidelines or commands, as תורה means. (3) The laws existed in written form, although this hardly precludes the probability that the largely illiterate populace heard rather than read the laws. (4) Yahweh himself was the author of the laws. Even the mediation of Moses need not be mentioned, so direct was the revelation. (5) The laws were widely ignored, or scoffed at ("considered as something foreign"). "Foreign" (זר) often has the sense of "off-limits," "improper," or "illegitimate" (Lev 10:1; Num 3:4; Prov 2:16).

The "laws" mentioned are surely the Mosaic laws. The problem for Israel was not that they lacked the Sinai code, but that they flagrantly disregarded it (cf. 4:2). The contents of an old Solomonic-era copy of the Pentateuch or one of its books such as Deuteronomy shocked Josiah when it was actually read to him (2 Kgs 22:11–13). People tend to learn society's laws more by osmosis than by careful study. Most people live under laws they have never actually seen in print. In Israel during Hosea's day, however, since priest and prophet were negligent in publicizing the law among the people (cf. 4:5, 6) it became, in fact, a "foreign" thing to the citizenry. In Deut 32:16 it was false gods and idols that were defined as זר "foreign." But now Yahweh's own written law was "foreign" to Israel, and they were only too familiar with false gods and idols (vv 4–6).

13 This verse concludes the subsection that indicts the cult. It speaks of God's displeasure with Israel's sacrifice-feast system, which had become virtually an end in itself rather than a renewal of communion with Yahweh. If the MT text is accurate or nearly so, the verse takes the form of a triplet. Its first line is unusual grammatically, in the interest of the common poetic device of assonance: זִבְחֵי הַבְהָבַי יִזְבָּחוּ lit., "the sacrifices, my gifts, they sacrificed." The construct זִבְחֵי הַבְהבי is analogous in form to the expression בַּת צִיּוֹן ("daughter Zion," not "daughter of Zion"; cf. Isa 37:22, etc.) and means simply "sacrifices as my gifts." When the verb form יזבחו is added, the assonance of *b, h, y* and *z* sounds is unmistakable.

Though Israel went through the proper motions, devotedly, Yahweh was still displeased. Their confidence rested not in him but in the offering system, which they believed sure to work if attended to diligently. In their arrogance learned during the years of prosperity before 745 B.C. when multiple sacrifices seemed to work to produce material blessings (cf. 2:8), they applied the "proper" procedures to get the desired results. But their sacrifices could never be acceptable because they were offered by unrepentant people corrupted by "their guiltiness" (עֲוֹנָם) and "their sins" (חַטֹּאותָם). Hosea's Israel seems not to have understood this concept. If an Israelite was ritually unclean, he or she could not rightly appear at Yahweh's altar to sacrifice. Here, as in Hos 5:3 and 6:10, Israel is (implicitly) unclean not from contact with something dead or diseased (e.g. Num 19:14–16) but from sin. They might bring their sacrifice and eat its meat, but it would not be efficacious.

He would, therefore, now remember their guiltiness and punish their sin. "Now" (עַתָּה) introduces a judgment sentence (cf. 2:12 [10]; 4:16; 5:7). Its claim is stated in fully synonymous parallelism: Yahweh will "remember" (יִזְכֹּר) Israel's guiltiness and "punish" (יִפְקֹד) their sins (curse type 26). Both verbs can have the sense of "paying attention to," or "acting upon" and both are found in OT contexts dealing with legal matters (זכר: Gen 40:14; Lev 26:45; Amos 1:9; פקד: Exod 32:34; Lev 18:25; Isa 13:11; cf. Hos 1:4; 9:9b).

The nature of Yahweh's punishment is made explicit in the prediction "Behold they will return to Egypt," the concluding line of the split couplet begun in v 9a. Why should this judgment be expressed in terms of a return to Egypt? Certainly, there may have occurred a token fulfillment in that after Hoshea had sent to Egypt for help in about 726 B.C. (2 Kgs 17:4) some Northerners may have sought exile in Egypt rather than captivity in Assyria (cf. Jer 43). But the basis for this wording is the curse language of Deut 28:68, clearly figurative and hyperbolic: Israel will return "with lamentations" (MT erroneously: "in ships") "to Egypt" and offer themselves as slaves, "but no one will buy you." Egypt was simply a metonymy for "captivity / exile" (curse type 13) which was the fate awaiting Israel for their callous disregard for the "many laws" of their God.

14 The verse is a covenant judgment in brief. It contains an indictment (the triplet comprising v 14a) and a judgment sentence of punishment (the couplet comprising v 14b). The first line of the triplet, "Israel forgot (שָׁכַח) his maker (עֹשֵׂהוּ)" closely reflects vv 15–18 of the covenant curse poem contained in Deut 32, in which Israel "forgot (שָׁכַח) the God who gave you birth" (v 18) and abandoned "God who made him (עֹשֵׂהוּ)"; cf. Hosea's use of שׁכח in 2:15 [13]; 4:6; 13:6 to indicate covenant infidelity. The remainder of v 14a speaks of the vast building of sanctuaries (and perhaps, royal domiciles), and fortifying of cities throughout the North and South. In these things Israel (and Judah) trusted for spiritual and political-military security. This appears to be a way of summarizing what Deut 32:15–18 predicts in essence: the people of Israel will turn from Yahweh to rely upon their own devices, confident in their own accomplishments. Such behavior went hand in hand with negligence of the covenant and thus is condemned. In turn, fortifications and sanctuaries cannot save a disobedient nation, and will be destroyed.

Destruction by fire (cf. Deut 32:22) symbolizes divine wrath (as already in Hos 8:6). The image of fire devouring cities and fortresses appears as well, repeatedly, in Amos 1:4–2:5. Both prophets incorporate the motif from the Pentateuchal covenant curses (type 10). The proximate origin of the fire will be enemy troops, burning everything in the cities that will burn. The ultimate origin, however, is Yahweh, who judges by fire, among other things (cf. Lev 20:14; 21:9; Num 11:1. On the use of fire to finalize conquest in war, see Josh 6:24; 7:15; 11:11; Judg 20:48; etc.). The reference to Judah in v 14a is "worked into" the verse not as an afterthought but as a typical prophetic reminder that the South was guilty, too. The mention of Judah as a builder of temples / palaces (1 Kgs 6:1–7:12) is not praise, but condemnation.

Explanation

Though the Israelites desperately hoped for deliverance from the increasingly threatening Assyrian territorial gains, they would instead be punished. Because they had broken the covenant (vv 1, 12, 14, *et passim*) they were now subject to its penalties, including death. Their enemies like a vulture waited to devour them. Despised on the international level (v 8), the pawns of other nations (v 9), they were heading inexorably toward captivity.

As is the case throughout the book, the predictions of punishment in chap. 8 follow the categories of the Mosaic covenant. Pursuit by enemies (v 3), destruction (v 4), judgment by fire (vv 5, 14), agricultural disaster (v 7a), loss to others of the fruit of one's labor (v 7b), loss of nationhood (v 10) and return to "Egypt" (v 13) all mirror Lev 26 and Deut 28–32.

What in fact has Israel done? Five sorts of sins are specifically cited: (1) the refusal to acknowledge Yahweh's right of divine ordination of the king (v 4); (2) idolatry (vv 4b–6); (3) dependence on international allies rather than on Yahweh (vv 9–10); (4) a corrupt cult (vv 5, 6, 11, 13); and (5) arrogant disregard for the law of their God (vv 1, 2–3a, 5b, 12, 14). Because both sovereign and vassal were bound to the terms of the covenant, Yahweh must punish Israel for their manifold disobedience.

The passage portrays vividly the nearness of destruction. From the image of the lion and eagle (v 1) to the image of fire raging through the country's cities and forts, the imminence of war overshadows the North. Against this, Israel's trust is foolishly misplaced. Their hope in their defensive preparations (v 14), their intense religious ritual (v 13) and their various allies (vv 9–10) cannot be rewarded. The enemy will devour and consume them.

From Festival Days to Punishment Days (9:1–9)

Bibliography

Auerbach, E. "Die Feste in Alten Israel." *VT* 8 (1958) 1–18. **Dahood, M.** "Hebrew-Ugaritic Lexicography IX." *Bib* 52 (1971) 337–56. **Dobbie, R.** "The Text of Hosea 9:8." *VT* 5 (1955) 199–203. **Driver, G. R.** "Difficult Words in the Hebrew Prophets." *Studies in Old Testament Prophecy,* ed. H. H. Rowley. Edinburgh: T. and T. Clark, 1950. **Harvey, D. W.** "Rejoice Not, O Israel." In *Israel's Prophetic Heritage: Essays in Honor of J. Muilenberg.* New York: Harper and Row, 1962. 116–27. **Humbert, P.** "Laetari et exultare dans le vocabulaire religieux de l'Ancien Testament." *RHPR* 22

(1942) 185–214. **Kutsch, E.** "Erwägungen zur Geschichte der Passafeier und des Massotfestes." *ZTK* 55 (1958) 31–32. **Kraus, H.-J.** "Zur Geschichte des Passah-Massot-Festes." *EvT* 18 (1958) 47–67. **Vaux, R. de.** "Death and Funeral Rites." *Ancient Israel,* pt. 1, chap. 6. New York: McGraw-Hill, 1961. **Weiden, W. A. van der.** "Radix hebraica עיב." *Verbum Domini* 44 (1966) 97–104.

Translation

"Prostitution" at the festivals will produce famine and captivity

9:1 *Do not rejoice, Israel!*
Do not shout for joy, my people![a]

For you have prostituted yourself away from your God.
You love the prostitute's fee at every grain[b] *threshing floor.*

2 *The threshing floor and press*[a] *will not feed them;*[b]
the fruit-of-the-vine[c] *will fail*[d] *them.*[e]

3 *They will not stay in Yahweh's land,*
but Ephraim will return to Egypt,
and in Assyria they will eat unclean food.

4 *They will not pour out wine to Yahweh,*
nor will they offer[a] *their sacrifices to him.*

(That will be) like mourners' bread[b] *for them.*
All who eat it will be defiled.

Indeed, their bread[b] *will be for their own throats;*[c]
it[d] *will not enter Yahweh's house.*

No feasting in captivity and desolation

5 *What will you do on the assembly day,*
on the day of Yahweh's feast?

6 *Even if*[a] *they walk away from destruction,*
Egypt will gather them,
Memphis will bury them.

The weed will covet[b] *their wealth;*
the thorn will dispossess[c] *them from their tents.*[d]

Punishment for deep corruption

7 *The days of punishment have come;*
the days of retribution have come.[a]

Israel ⟨cries out⟩[b]*:*
"Stupid is the prophet!
Crazy is the man of the spirit!",
because your sins are so many,
your hostility so great.[c]

8 *Is Ephraim a watchman?*[a]
Is God's people[b] *a prophet?*[a]

A fowler's snare is on all of his paths,
hostility in the house of his God.
⁹*They have deeply corrupted*ᵃ *themselves,*
as in the days of Gibeah.

He will remember their guilt,
he will punish their sins.

Notes

1.a. The MT consonantal text is best redivided and vocalized as follows: אַל־גִּילְךָ עַמִּי־ם "do not shout for joy, my people." The complete parallelism is evident thereby, and a variety of proposed emendations are obviated. See Kuhnigk, *NSH*, 109–111.

1.b. Syr omits דָגָן "grain," probably via simple haplogr.

2.a. The "press" can be used for both wine and oil.

2.b. G οὐκ ἔγνω αὐτούς "did not know them" reflects ידע "know." The ר / ד misconstrual with ידע / ירע occurs also in Prov 13:20 (G). The other versions support MT.

2.c. Again we represent the archaic-poetic Hebrew term with an archaic-poetic English term.

2.d. On this meaning of כחש cf. Hab 3:17; Zech 13:4.

2.e. With the versions and several MSS, בָם is to be read here.

4.a. On this meaning of ערב, see G. R. Driver, *Studies*, 64–66. The vocalization may be יֶעֱרְבוּ rather than MT יַעַרְבוּ.

4.b. Or "food."

4.c. While נפש can commonly mean "self," it also often carries its most basic meaning of "throat," as in Jonah 2:6[5]; Hab 2:5, etc.

4.d. It is possible that the verb was originally pl, יבאו "they will (not) enter," the consonants being reversed in transmission to יבוא "it will (not) enter." See *Comment*.

6.a. On the use of הנה to introduce a conditional clause, cf. 1 Sam 9:7 and see Lambdin, 168–71.

6.b. Vocalizing מְחַמֵּד, piel ptcp. Its subj is קמוש "weed." The direct obj (כספם "their money") is introduced in this case by ל, as in Gen 1:5; Jer 40:2; 1 Chr 16:37, etc.

6.c. "Dispossess" is a common meaning of ירש. The subj of this clause is חוח "thorn."

6.d. באהליהם means *"from* their tents," ב commonly meaning "from" (cf. Deut 1:44, etc.).

7.a. It is not necessary to emend the second באו in the interests of poetics, as so commonly is done. See Kuhnigk, *NSH*, 115–116.

7.b. G κακωθήσεται presupposes יֵרְעוּ (niph) from רעע "be corrupted" (cf. Prov 11:15; 13:20). The original vocalization, however, was more probably יָרִיעוּ, the hiph of רוע "shout."

7.c. The vocalization הַמַּשְׂטֵמָה ר'ב is perhaps preferable to MT.

8.a. The context suggests that each line of the first couplet in v 8 is either sarcasm or an ironic question.

8.b. The parallelism is surely Ephraim // God's people; we read therefore עַם "people" for MT עִם "with" and אֱלֹהִים (with G) for MT אֱלֹהָי.

9.a. Or, "corrupted themselves to the depths." The two verbs שחת and עמק are used in asyndetic hendiadys.

Form / Structure / Setting

Chap. 8 ended with a prediction of judgment based on a description of Israel's sins. Chap. 9 begins a new scene, as evidenced by the direct address in v 1 (and also v 5) and the emphasis upon a nation optimistically celebrating festival days. The passage proceeds immediately to, and ends with, predictions of punishment; v 10 introduces a new passage, sweepingly retrospective in style, a divine speech in the first person, not connected closely to 9:1–9.

In contrast to the prevailing form of chap. 8, 9:1–9 is not a divine speech (though the prophet's words are always implicitly Yahweh's words). "My people" in v 1 can mean Hosea's people. And while Yahweh often speaks about himself in the third person in Hosea, here speech about Yahweh is the uniform pattern (i.e., "your God," v 1; "Yahweh's land," v 3; "to Yahweh," v 4; etc.). The form is that of the covenant enforcement warning (*Drohwort*). The prediction of a variety of punishments constitutes the main content of the passage.

Vv 1–4 attack specifically the confidence of Israel in its (fall) festivals and vv 5–9 describe more broadly the present degeneration and future suffering of the nation. Both parts are introduced by direct address to the people at the time of the Succoth (Booths, Tabernacles) harvest holiday. The overall structure of the passage may be represented as follows:

Vv 1–4   Direct address at festival, calling Israel to task, and description of future troubles, emphasizing the end of religious rituals and exile

Vv 5–6   Direct address at festival, calling Israel to task, and predicting captivity and desolation

Vv 7–9   Israel's arrogant degeneracy and Yahweh's punishment

The original setting of these words may have been a fall harvest celebration sometime during the 720s, in what Mays (125) calls "The breathing space in the years after the crisis of 733." Any such festival would have been religious, dedicated to Yahweh, and technically a fulfillment of the covenant's command for a feast at the end of the agricultural year (Exod 23:16; Deut 16:13–17). The command to associate this festival closely with the Exodus (Lev 23:33–43) was largely ignored, however, in both Israel and Judah until the restoration period (Neh 8:17; cf. Judg 21:19–21). The festivals were characterized by joyous rituals, sacrifices, and appeals to Yahweh. Where Baalism coexisted with Yahwism, they were probably syncretistic. Where Yahweh alone was worshiped (e.g., Bethel?) the ceremonies were performed with the mechanistic expectations typical of Canaanite religion (i.e., that regardless of personal behavior, proper worship automatically produces blessing; cf. 4:13; 5:6–7; 7:14; 8:11–13).

The passage predicts exile (vv 3, 6), deprivation (vv 2, 6b–7) and the destruction of what the nation had trusted in (vv 1–2, 4, 6b, 7–8). Those punishments appear inevitable and imminent: "The days of punishment have come" (v 7). Israel's days were not merely numbered; they were at an end. The same people now enjoying the fruits of harvest and dedicating a portion of them to their God would soon find themselves without such agricultural blessings (v 2), unable to celebrate the festivals (vv 4–5) because they had fallen under the oppression of another nation. The present passage may be among the last oracles delivered by Hosea before the fall of the North in 722 B.C.

Because synonymous parallelism predominates slightly in the passage, the meter is for the most part balanced or nearly balanced syllabically. A sprinkling of synthetic parallelism (parts of vv 1, 4, 6–9) and one instance of antithetical parallelism (v 3) complete the picture. Three triplets (in vv 3, 6, 7) complement the more usual couplets.

Comment

1 Addressing Israel, "my people" (עמי), on behalf of Yahweh, the prophet calls for a cessation of celebration. They are to stop their "rejoicing" (שמח) and "shouting for joy" (גיל), a standard fixed pair of terms denoting the fall harvest festival revelries of dancing, singing, shouting, etc. both for the benefit and enjoyment of the people, and as an act of devotion to Yahweh (Exod 23:16; Deut 16:13–17; Lev 23:33–43). By the 720s when these words were first spoken much of the north was in Assyrian hands. In those parts still independent, however ("Ephraim"), agricultural concerns remained foremost in the economy. The people obviously considered their celebration of Yahweh's blessing in harvest a proper act of devotion. Hosea accuses them, however, of being covenant breakers whose celebration is evidence of their infidelity to Yahweh! Employing the prostitution metaphor for the last time, Hosea accuses Israel of prostitution "away from" (מעל) its God (cf. 1:2 מאחרי "away from" and 4:12 מתחת "away from, out from under").

According to v 1b, Israel—the prostitute—loves receiving the אתנן (the fee paid to a prostitute, here presumably the grain; cf. also Deut 23:18; Mic 1:7). How has Israel prostituted itself? It celebrated the harvest as the result of the successful application of the mechanisms of the fertility cult. At least three sorts of sins were involved: (1) treating Yahweh as if he were Baal, they assumed that faithful service to the cultic rituals had required him to respond by blessing the harvest; (2) the direct worship of Baal was allowed to prosper alongside Yahwism; (3) they carried out their worship at multiple sanctuaries, all of which were illegal (cf. 4:13). Thus the stipulations of the covenant were broken. Israel was unfaithful to her husband, and became a "prostitute."

The prostitute's fee is said to be earned at the "grain threshing floors" (גרנות דגן), which were spacious, flat, open areas used not only for threshing wheat and barley, but also as assembly areas for religious or civil ceremonies (e.g. 1 Kgs 22:10), or more general harvest festivities (Ruth 3:2–14). Israel loved what happened at the threshing floors, and what they thought they earned there, more than they loved Yahweh.

2 As a result of their prostitution, the Lord of the covenant must enforce its sanctions. These include, of course, the deprivation of grain, oil, and wine (Deut 28:51; cf. Hos 2:11[9], etc.) so that hunger ensues. Hosea depicts the loss of those three staples artistically, using גרן "threshing floor" as a kind of synecdoche for "grain" and יקב "press" for oil. The יקב, a double cistern carved from rock, in which the juice pooled in the lower cistern, was used for either wine or oil production (cf. Joel 2:24). Instead of the two actual products, the prophet cites the places they are produced, and says that these will "not feed them" (לא ירעם). In the second line of the couplet תירוש, the archaic poetic term for "wine" is used, and it is stated simply that this will "fail them" (יכחש בם). Although כחש (piel) can mean "lie, trick, deceive" it is not likely that a pun or double-entendre is intended, as crop "failure" is a common, normal sense of כחש (cf. כחש in Hab 3:17). Note that the basic agricultural products processed in the fall festival were grain, wine, and oil (the barley harvest having occured earlier, followed immediately by the summer "Weeks" or "Pentecost" festival). These three crop products were not to be enjoyed much longer in Israel, since the people themselves were about to be deported (v 3). The threat of v 2, because it is expressed in general terms, is neither exclusively a threat of harvest failure, nor a threat of futility (that others will eat what the Israelites had labored to produce or that it will be destroyed by nature [cf. Deut 28:30, 38, 42]). Either or both can be meant (*pace* Wolff, 154); i.e., curse types 6 (agricultural disaster), 7 (famine), and 15 (futility) may all be involved. The point is that Israel will soon experience severe deprivation.

3 A more explicit prediction of exile could hardly be imagined. The Israelites are told that they will be leaving their land to live under foreign domination. They can no longer remain in "Yahweh's land" (אֶרֶץ יהוה), a term parallel to "Yahweh's house" (8:1). The prophet's words suggest first that the land was not Israel's and certainly not Baal's. Baal could do nothing to stop Yahweh from punishing Israel (cf. Deut 32:37–39). The people had mistakenly presumed that once they possessed the land, it was theirs forever and they could choose which gods to serve in it. But title to the land had never been conveyed from Yahweh to Israel. Second, as continuing property owner (cf. Lev 25:23), Yahweh had the right to remove undesirable tenants from his land, cutting off its produce. When Israel was denied further access to the promised land, the blessings of the covenant were also abrogated.

The ancient curses expressed in several variations the threat of exile (type 13; Lev 26:33, 38; Deut 4:26–27; 28:21, 36, 64, etc.). In the remainder of v 3, Hosea's words recall specific aspects of these exile curses: the return to "Egypt" (a metonymy for exile; Deut 28:68; cf. Hos 7:16; 8:13; 11:5, 11) and eating unclean food in Assyria (a way of saying that they would no longer be independent, but would be subject to other nations' rules and habits; cf. Deut 4:28: "There you will worship man-made gods of wood and stone . . ."; cf. also Deut 28:36, 64; Ezek 4:13; Amos 7:17).

Those who have not returned to Yahweh (cf. 2:9[7]; 3:5; 6:1; 7:10; 14:2[1]) must therefore return to "Egypt." The gift of deliverance from Egypt and the gift of the promised land are thus rescinded. Ephraim will be in slavery in a foreign land, as they were at their origins. "Egypt" and "Assyria" are mentioned in synonymous parallelism as often in Hosea (7:11; 8:9–13; 11:5, 11; 12:2[1]).

4 V 4 builds on the theme of life in an unclean land. In exile, Israel will no longer be able to carry out its covenant obligations of sacrificial ritual, structured around food (worship and eating went together in the ancient world). Food language thus dominates the verse. In the first couplet the cessation of the libation and other offerings is predicted. The libation was an offering of wine, poured out symbolically to Yahweh upon the altar (Num 15:5–12; Exod 29:38–41; Lev 23:12–13). But in captivity there will be no Yahwistic worship center, whether legitimate (i.e., Jerusalem) or illegitimate (the various northern sanctuaries) where such libations or other sacrifices (זִבְחֵיהֶם) may be offered.

The second and third couplets of the verse describe how the exiled Israelites' bread will be as unclean as that of mourners. The mention of bread may be occasioned by the linkage of bread with wine in legal passages about the

libation (see Exod 29:40; Lev 23:14; Num 15:4, 6, 9). According to the Pentateuchal laws about uncleanness (e.g., Num 19:11–22) mourners, because they
were in contact with a dead body, were "ritually excluded" from the sanctuary
and anything they touched became unclean. The "bread of mourners"
(לחם אונים; cf. Ezek 24:17, G) is bread suitable only for their own throats
(לנפשם) to swallow, and cannot come into the temple (although בית יהוה
may refer more generally to Israel; cf. 8:1). Jeremiah, in a prediction of
exile and captivity for Judah (Jer 16:1–13) mentions the practice of the mourners' funeral meal (vv 5–7) as an evidence of divine judgment. This notion
is probably also to be understood in Hos 9:4. That is, people will be eating
the bread of mourners rather than the bread of sacrifices because when Hosea's
inspired words are fulfilled, cultic celebration will have given way to disease
and death (i.e., curse type 24; Lev 26:16, etc.). Additionally, the "defilement"
(טמא, niphal) of the people may imply the fulfillment of the covenant curse
of forced idolatry in exile (type 14; Deut 4:28, et al.).

5   The prophet again questions his audience directly (cf. v 1), as a prelude
to the remainder of the judgments announced in the passage. His rhetorical
question implies that soon there will be no "assembly day" (יום מועד), i.e.,
no "day of Yahweh's feast" (יום חג־יהוה). The two terms are synonymous.
The people will be able neither to enjoy their harvest festivals nor worship
Yahweh when deported to Assyria. The form of the question "What will
you do . . ." is intended to contrast to what the Israelites were then doing,
that is, rejoicing. It picks up the theme of v 1, and likewise calls Israel to
halt its complacent celebration. The "feast of Yahweh" (חג־יהוה; cf. Lev
23:39; Judg 21:19) would appear to refer specifically to the autumn feast of
Tabernacles, also called סכות "booths / tabernacles" or אסיף "ingathering /
harvest." The festival at which and about which Hosea spoke these words
was established by Jeroboam I about 930 B.C. as a Northern counterpart to
the one celebrated in Judah, though held in the eighth rather than the seventh
month (1 Kgs 12:32). The Northern festival was *ipso facto* improper, and
obviously a suitable locus for attack upon the multiple covenant violations
constituting Israel's "prostitution." Celebration at harvest time serves ironically
as the setting for a threat of mourning in deprivation.

6   V 6 takes in part the form of the futility curse (type 15). Carefully
laid plans and earnest efforts will be of no avail when Yahweh's punishment
is unleashed; the Israelites will be taken captive (curse type 13) and killed
(curse type 24) and their precious possessions taken over by weeds and thorns
(the curse of desolation, type 9). The logic follows very closely the covenant
curses of Lev 26 and Deut 28–32, where various forms of devastation and
destruction both precede and follow upon capture and deportation. Those
who escape death from disease, famine, war, etc. go into exile where some
of these same miseries, and others such as religious intolerance, await them.
Two kinds of futility are expressed: the futility of attempting to escape from
destruction (שד) and the futility of amassing personal property only to have
it decay in isolation while its owners are captive elsewhere.

The first half of the verse reflects the theme of v 3, the return to "Egypt."
The pairing of מצרים "Egypt" and מף "Memphis" appears to be occasioned
by traditional synonymous poetic practice as well as a certain degree of asso-

nance: *mṣrym tqbṣm // mp tqbrm*. Even if the people slated for Yahweh's judgment should happen to survive ("walk away from," הלכו) the conquest of their land, the enemy would "gather" (קבץ) and "bury" (קבר) them. The verb אסף "gather," a close synonym of קבץ, can be a technical term for burial (2 Kgs 22:20; Ps 26:9). It may be that קבץ should be understood here as having a similar value (cf. Ezek 22:30–31) particularly because it is paralleled by קבר (cf. Jer 8:2; 25:33). At any rate, the idea of collecting or gathering for mass burial is clear. God had once gathered his people for deliverance *from* Egypt; now they will be gathered for destruction *by* "Egypt." The great cemetery of Memphis and the ancient pyramid tombs there may have made the allusion all the more forceful in the minds of the listeners.

The people's wealth will be "coveted" (חמד) by weeds, and their tents dispossessed (ירש) by thorns. Such images often portray judgment on enemy lands (e.g., Isa 34:13) but may also be used of Israel's fate (Isa 5:6; 7:23–25). There is no indication here that "their wealth" (כספם) should be taken to refer to the money / silver used for idolatry (cf. 8:4b) or that "their tents" (אהליהם) should be construed as the tents "of the pilgrims attending the festival" (Wolff, 156). The simple general sense of wealth and personal possessions is more likely the referent of these words.

7 The first part of v 7 is a summary statement concluding the catena of punishments begun in v 6. The imminence of punishment (פקדה) and retribution (שלם), both terms probably reflecting the covenant curse of general punishment / vengeance (type 26), is stressed by the repetition of the perfect verb "have come" (באו). The verb is less likely a prophetic perfect tense predicting the future than a true historical perfect emphasizing the fact that the troubles which began after 748 B.C. and intensified after 733 represented the beginning of the end for Israel. The prophets may use "day" (יום; cf. Amos 3:14); "time / season" (עת; cf. Jer 8:12) or "year" (שנה; cf. Jer 11:23) to indicate that there is coming an appointed, fixed date of sure divine judgment. The use of "days" (ימי) here, however, may imply that the punishments of divine covenant enforcement will endure for an indefinitely long time (cf. Lev 26:34, 35 and Deut 28:29, 33). In the words of Deut 31:29, ". . . In future days (ימים) disaster will come upon you because you will do evil in the sight of Yahweh and provoke him to anger by what your hands have made." Hosea has been inspired to warn the people that they have indeed entered those "days."

With the words "Israel cries out" (יריעו ישראל; see n. 7.b) and continuing through v 9a, the prophet scathingly denounces Israel for its arrogance and degeneracy. The first charge is that the Israelites are so sinful they even mock God's prophet(s), presuming to know that his/their words are fake. Probably the words "prophet" and "man of the spirit" are to be taken to indicate the class, rather than a single prophet, though the words as Hosea heard them undoubtedly applied to him. The prophet is said to be אויל "stupid, a fool," one whose words cannot be taken seriously (cf. Prov 10:8, 10). In the parallel line of the same couplet, the prophet is called a "man of the spirit" (איש הרוח), a term otherwise unknown in the OT, and possibly a derogatory coinage of the people, perhaps built on the pattern of איש אלהים "man of God"; cf. 1 Sam 10:6; 1 Kgs 18:12; 22:21–22; 2 Kgs 2:9, 16. The word משגע "crazy" connotes especially nonsensical babbling (cf. Jer 29:26). Implicit in the people's language is that Hosea himself is not to be believed; his message is of no merit; the woe he predicts is insane nonsense. They do not wish to let it interrupt their enjoyment of the harvest festivities. Their callous derision is rooted in the magnitude of their sins / guiltiness and their "hostility" (משטמה). The latter term occurs in the OT only in this and the following verse. It derives presumably from שטם "to bear a grudge / harbor animosity," and seems to denote stubborn antagonism to a person or principle (cf. L. Koehler, W. Baumgartner, *Supplement ad Lexicon in Veteris Testament: Libros* [Leiden: E. J. Brill, 1958] 169). But it is not simply Hosea at whom the people's opposition is directed. It is ultimately God and his law which they reject, thus incurring עון "guilt / sin." It is this very עון that God promises in v 9 to remember.

8 As vocalized in MT, v 8 begins with a couplet whose meaning is obscure. Merely with the revocalization of MT עם "with" to עם "people," the correction of אלהי "God of" to אלהים "God" (following G) and realization that the couplet can be interrogative, a sense appropriate to the context emerges. Hosea turns the tables on the people's cynical derision of prophets. Their mockery assumes that they know more than the inspired prophet(s), so Hosea asks ironically, "Is Ephraim a watchman? Is God's people a prophet?" The answer, obviously, is "No!" "Watchman" (צפה), a lookout from an early-warning outpost, is applied metaphorically to prophets several times in the OT (Isa 56:10; Jer 6:17; Ezek 3:17; 33:2, 6, 7), emphasizing their role in warning of approaching danger (cf. Ezek 33:7–20). In the synonymous parallelism of the first couplet of v 8 it is thus paired with נביא "prophet." So Hosea, in effect, mocks the people who mocked him. If Ephraim really is a watchman, a prophet, he ought to be able to see the severity of his plight: snares everywhere he turns, hostility in his own country.

"Snare" (פח) is used in the OT almost exclusively as a figure for trouble or enmity, whether past / present (Ps 91:3; 124:7; Jer 18:22) or in warnings of future danger (Josh 23:13; Ps 11:6; Isa 24:17, 18). Here it is used in parallelism with משטמה "hostility," either to connote the hostility that Israel will receive in their own country (on בית אלהיו "house of his God," cf. 8:1; 9:3; 9:15), or to describe the people's hostility; i.e., the snares are present *because of* the people's continuing hostility to God. Of these options, the former is the more likely. Ephraim, the arrogant, complacent rejecter of prophets cannot see what the prophets see: danger and divine hostility (curse types 19 and 1). Their land is Yahweh's "house," and he is preparing to eject them from it (cf. v 15).

9 Israel's sin is so extensive that it demands punishment. Hosea's words were not simply a warning of what might happen if Israel did not eventually change. The violation of the covenant was already absolute: Israel was a "prostitute" (v 1) and the time for its retribution had already come (v 7). Israel was as bad, in fact, as Gibeah in the days of the Judges, whose outrageous sinfulness is described in the Deuteronomic history (Judg 19–21) as a prime example of degradation. By the juxtaposition of two relatively synonymous verbs (העמיקו שחתו) without a copula, Hosea gives added emphasis to Israel's depravity ("they have deeply corrupted themselves"). The verb שחת, also used by Hosea in a different sense ("destroy") in 11:9 and 13:9, recalls the usages in Deut 4:25; 31:29; and 32:5, all of which predict the sort of corruption that will nullify the covenant. It appears from the metrical structure that the two verbs constitute a genuine hendiadys, rather than representing variant wordings for the couplet (cf. Stuart, *SEHM*, 89 n. 15; Cross and Freedman, *SAYP*, 17, n. h).

In the same way that Yahweh firmly judged Gibeah he will "remember (Israel's) guilt" and "punish their sins" (curse type 26). In the Judges episode, the tribes united to punish Benjamin at Yahweh's command. Now Yahweh himself will mete out the punishment. The fact that Hosea includes verbatim the verdict already used in 8:13, where exile was explicitly mentioned as the main form of punishment, suggests that this is also the actual mechanism by which Yahweh would "remember" (יזכר) and "punish" (יפקוד). Thus v 9 serves as a conclusion to the explicit predictions of exile in vv 3–6. The "sins" and "guilt" refer to the various covenant violations otherwise mentioned or implied in the book. The "punishment" they may expect is exile to Assyria.

Explanation

People often find it hard to believe the worst about their own future, even when all signs point increasingly to danger. After the tentative withdrawal of the bulk of Assyrian forces from most of the North by 732 B.C., most people apparently adjusted to their new status and resumed their old way of life. God in his common grace provided a bountiful fall harvest. Some Israelites attributed this bounty to Yahweh's renewed approval, some to Baal's, some to both, others to their own faithfulness to the rituals they presumed to guarantee the fertility of the land. Enjoying a fine time of religious celebration, who wanted to listen to the doomsaying of a narrow, negative prophet?

To his unappreciative audience Hosea proclaimed God's imminent wrath (vv 7, 9) and was called a lunatic (v 7). He called them to sobriety (v 1) in the face of impending destruction (v 6), exile to "Egypt" (Assyria) (vv 3, 6) and the various miseries (vv 2–6) of captivity. Because they had knowingly prostituted the sacred covenant (v 1) so blatantly as to rival the historic outrages of Gibeah (v 9) they must now learn that the coming times will bring them not more rejoicing (v 5) but hostility, entrapment (v 8) and punishment appropriate to their depravity (v 9).

The passage rings with contrasts: Israel's current rejoicing as against the deprivations they will endure; the food they joyously partake of in abundance now contrasted to the bread of mourning they will soon enough eat; their religious sacrifices vs. their coming exilic religious bondage; their arrogant rejection of the prophet's authority vs. their own misreading of the times and lack of discernment; their complacency vs. the promise that God will "remember their guilt and punish their sins."

For the last time in the book, Hosea invokes the ancient treaty-covenant curse term זנה "to engage in prostitution" in description of Israel's covenant breaking. This passage as much as any other in the book gives definition to that metaphorical term. Israel loves other gods than Yahweh, and / or other things than his commands. Their faithfulness, such as it is, is limited to procedures and rituals selfishly trusted to produce personal benefit. They have separated themselves from him by reason of promiscuous sins and attitudes.

It should not be surprising that Hosea's message fell mostly upon deaf ears. Such a response is predictable when hard words from God are proclaimed where they have not been invited. For the Christian, to whom Christ promises special help in the face of hostility, the preaching of the divine message may result in far worse distress than being mocked (cf. Luke 21:12–17). Few Israelites stood with Hosea against the prevailing injustices and degradations. He at least stood firm even when his very sanity was questioned. Only by likewise standing firm with Christ may Christians expect to be delivered by God from the punishments prescribed by the new covenant's curses (Luke 21:18–19).

Ephraim Rejected, Exiled, Unloved (9:10–17)

Bibliography

Braun, H. " 'Der Fahrende.' " *ZTK* 48 (1951) 32–38. **Bright, J.** "The Future in the Theology of the Eighth-Century Prophets: The Beginnings of Eschatology." Chap. 3 in *Covenant and Promise*. Philadelphia: Westminster Press, 1976. **Dahood, M.** "Hebrew-Ugaritic Lexicography I." *Bib* 44 (1963) 289–303. ———. "Hebrew-Ugaritic Lexicography XI." *Bib* 54 (1973) 351–66. **Henke, O.** "Zur Lage von Beth Peor." *ZDPV* 75 (1959) 155–63. **Kraus, H.-J.** "Gilgal: Ein Beitrag zur Kultusgeschichte Israels." *VT* 1 (1951) 191–99. **Lohfink, N.** "Hate and Love in Osee 9:15." *CBQ* 25 (1963) 417. **Muilenburg, J.** "The Site of Ancient Gilgal." *BASOR* 140 (1955) 11–27.

Translation

Sin at Baal-Peor

9:10 *Like grapes in the wilderness*
I found Israel.

Like the first fruit on the fig tree, at its beginning, [a]
I took notice of their [b] *ancestors.*

But [c] *they came to Baal-Peor,*
consecrated themselves to "Shame," [d]
and became detestable [e] *like their lover.* [f]

Coming punishments

11 *"Ephraim!* [a] *Their honor will fly away like a bird—without birth, without pregnancy, and without conception.* 12 *Even if they should raise their children, I will make them bereft, without a person left.* [a] *And woe also to them* [b], *when I depart from them!* 13 *Ephraim will be like a man who ⟨sees⟩* [a] *a siege* [b] *set* [c] *for him* [d] *and his children, and* [e] *brings out* [f] *his children to slaughter* [g].

Prophetic interjection

¹⁴*Give them, Yahweh.—What should you give them?—Give them a miscarrying womb and shriveled breasts!*

Sin at Gilgal

¹⁵*Their every evil is at Gilgal*
Indeed, I have hated them there.

Coming punishments

Because of their evil deeds
I will drive them from my house

I will no longer love them
*(since) all their officials are rebellious.*ᵃ

¹⁶*Ephraim is beaten down,*
their root is dried up,
they cannot produce fruit.

Even if they bear children,
*I will kill their precious offspring.*ᵃ

Prophetic interjection

¹⁷*Let God*ᵃ *reject them*
*for they have not listened*ᵇ *to him;*
let them become wanderers among the nations.

Notes

10.a. "At its beginning," MT בראשיתה, appears to modify תאנה "fig tree." It may refer to the first fruit-bearing season of the fig tree or the very beginning of the appearance of the fruit. If translated more neutrally or emended to בראשית, it could mean simply "at first." Syr omits this phrase, and it has often been suspected as a gloss. Against this suspicion, one notes that virtually all its consonant and vowel sounds comport perfectly with the alliteration of the couplet.

10.b. G (αὐτῶν "their") presupposes אבותיהם rather than MT "*your* fathers / ancestors."

10.c. The contrast potentially present in הם "behold," rather than "they," is best rendered idiomatically by "but."

10.d. MT בּשֶׁת "shame" is a metonymy for "Baal," whether original with Hosea or the result of pious replacement later.

10.e. Lit., "detestable things."

10.f. Vocalizing the MT consonants as אֹהֲבָם.

11.a. The first couplet of v 11 says, lit., "Ephraim is like a bird; their honor flies away," which is awkward according to Eng. syntax but acceptable in Heb.

12.a. Lit., "without a human/man."

12.b. I.e., the people themselves rather than merely their offspring.

13.a. Revocalizing and emending MT to כְּאִישׁ רֹאֶה "like a man who sees" instead of כַּאֲשֶׁר רָאִיתִי "as what I see," which appears nonsensical in the context. This and other readings in v 13 are based on the recognition that the miseries of siege, as described especially in Deut 28, constitute the figurative repertoire for this prediction. For details, see *Comment.*

13.b. Taking צוּר as the inf of צור "to besiege." "Rock" (צוּר), "Tyre" (צֹר), "Prey" (צַיִד) etc., are not appropriate to the context.

13.c. Reading שָׁתוּ; lit., "they (indefinite) set."

13.d. Reading לה as "for him." MT שׁתוּלה "planted" is illogical in the context.

13.e. The second "Ephraim" would appear to be dittogr. See also n. 13.f.

13.f. It is likely that a helping verb of some sort, perhaps "will hasten" (יִמְחַר or יָחוּשׁ) or the like, has been lost before לְהוֹצִיא.

13.g. Reading הֶרֶג "slaughter" instead of MT הֹרֵג "killer / butcher." But cf. Ezek. 21:16.

15.a. Or "stubborn."

16.a. Lit., "the coveted of their womb."

17.a. Reading with G ὁ θεός "God"; cf. 9:8.

17.b. Or "obeyed."

Form / Structure / Setting

With this passage a new section of the book begins. Two new features differentiate 9:10–17 (and many of the successive passages) from the previous material. One difference is the emphasis upon historical retrospective (e.g., vv 10 and 15a) especially in metaphorical cast. Such retrospective has occurred only once before (9:9, which functions in effect as a transition to the present section) but now it becomes far more common, and obviously prominent. The second difference is that now a reflective manner or mood becomes considerably more evident than was the case in 4:1–9:9. Only in 2:4–17[2–15] is such a reflective manner of speech paralleled. The present passage concludes with v 17. Chap. 10 begins a new pericope, on a new subject, introduced again by historical retrospective in metaphorical cast.

The passage is predominantly divine speech, containing predictions of doom and misery according to the covenant curse categories. Two interjections of prophetic speech (vv 14, 17) bring to an end each of the major divisions of the oracle. The structure may be summarized as follows:

v 10　　Poetic retrospective on the distant past (how Israel, once Yahweh's delight, became detestable to Yahweh at Baal-Peor).

vv 11–14　Prose series of curses ending with a prophetic interjection (v 14).

v 15a　　Poetic retrospective on the immediate past up to the present (how Israel is still detestable to Yahweh, Gilgal being an antitype of Baal-Peor).

vv 15b–17　Poetic series of curses ending with a prophetic interjection (v 17).

The meter is surprisingly regular with syllabically balanced couplets and triplets predominating. Vv 11–14 are in all likelihood prose. Three triplets are found (vv 10b, 16a, 17), as usual in no predictable order. The parallelism is largely synonymous though vv 16b–17 are synthetic.

While nothing in the passage unambiguously fixes its date, it seems to reflect the mid-720s, very close to or at the beginning of the fall of the North. That fall is a foregone conclusion, something that Hosea is expecting and even inviting (vv 14, 17). His statement "for they have not listened to him" appears appropriate to a time when the prophet has, as it were, given Israel up as a lost cause. The emphasis in vv 12–14 upon the miseries of a time of siege, particularly as it distorts the normal relationships between parents and children, seems appropriate to a time when a siege, i.e., that of the Assyrians in 725–722 B.C., is imminent. The divine historical retrospective and reflective mood also would fit such a stage in Israel's history, when as it draws to a close, Yahweh reviews his relationship with his people, reaffirming the fact that he has no option but to destroy them. He will, therefore, soon "drive them from my house" and "no longer love them" (v 15).

Comment

10 Yahweh, speaking as if to an unidentified third party about Israel, describes the time he first took Israel to himself. The emphasis is upon rarity, not upon serendipity (cf. Deut 7:7–8; 9:1–6). With a striking metaphor, quite possibly influenced by the vocabulary of Deut. 32:10 (see Kuhnigk, *NSH*, 35–39), Yahweh likens himself to a traveller in the barren wastes of the wilderness (מדבר) suddenly coming upon a bearing grapevine, which, of course, would be a stunningly rare event. So was his relationship with Israel at its beginning in Egypt and at Sinai. Israel was a rare and unparalleled thing—his own special people. Israel was attractive to Yahweh only when she was faithful to the Sinai covenant. When she neglected it, she prostituted herself. Only by coming back to it could she come back to Yahweh (2:18, 19[16,17]; cf. Lev 26:40–45; Deut 4:29–31; 30:1–10; 32:36). The emphasis on a unique (but not perfect) young Israel in Hosea does not contradict the Pentateuch account, which contains frequent examples of unfaithfulness (Exod 32) during the wilderness period. The theme elsewhere in Hosea that the formation of Israel took place in Egypt (2:17[15]; 11:1; 12:10[9], 14[13]; 13:4) suggests that this metaphor is not describing the wilderness per se. That is, Israel is likened to "grapes in the wilderness," not "Israel" to grapes and "wilderness" to the Sinai experience. Israel here can only mean all the tribes of God, rather than "Ephraim," in contrast to Judah.

The second couplet is externally parallel to the first. The Israelite ancestors of Hosea's age (lit., "your fathers") Yahweh noticed / discovered / sighted as one might early figs. The term בכורה refers to the late May / early June fig which ripens on the previous year's sprouts, and is tender for eating far in advance of the תאנה, the late summer fig from new growth. There are only a few בכורות to a tree—thus they are a rarity, like grapes in the wilderness. The oft-cited usage of בכורה in Isa 28:4 describes *not* the desirability of the first figs, but their fragility and vulnerability. Likewise, v 10 does not assert Israel's intrinsic excellence, but rather the uniqueness of Yahweh's choice of her as his people (cf. Deut 7:7–8).

A terrible turning point in Israel's relationship to her God occurred at Baal-Peor (Num 25:1–5). There, large numbers of Israelite men engaged with Moabite and Midianite women in sexual rites, presumably partly in the hope of ensuring agricultural fertility upon entering Canaan. This constituted a consecration (נזר) to Baal, whom Yahweh here calls by the pejorative בשת "shame." The later practice of substituting בשת "shame" for בעל "Baal" by pious OT copyists may have been begun on the precedent of this verse. The Baal-Peor incident represented a rejection of Yahwism in favor of idolatrous Baal worship, accompanied by marriage infidelity, in defiance of the Sinai covenant. This automatically broke the covenant with Yahweh (Exod 23:32–33; Deut 17:2, etc.) as the golden bull incident of Exod 32 almost did. Thereafter, from Yahweh's point of view, Israel was a changed people. Their entire history, including the whole time of their occupation of the promised land, was, on balance, one of rebellion and sin. In spite of individual exceptions, the post-conquest nation generally was composed of people who were to Yahweh שקוצים "detestable things." This word, used most often of idols in the OT (e.g. 2 Kgs 23:13; Ezek 5:11; Dan 11:31) also describes Baal, "their lover" (אהבם). Israel has become as odious to Yahweh as Baal, a false nothing of a "god." Yahweh looks back reflectively on the history of his own chosen people. What he sees disgusts him.

11   Ephraim had, for a time, honor, moments of national greatness. Such honor would include their part in the exodus from Egypt and the conquest of Canaan, the political, military, and economic greatness of the united monarchy, the relative power under great, though evil, kings such as Ahab and Jeroboam II, etc. For much of their history the North was more prominent than the South, dominating client-states such as Ammon and Moab repeatedly, and enjoying relative military success (even against Assyria at Qarqar in 853 B.C.). But whatever their glory, like a bird it will now fly off (עוף, hithpael; no connection to flightiness in foreign alliances [7:11, 12] is intended). In place of the honor comes a curse of infertility (type 12); cf. "The fruit of your womb will be cursed . . ." (Deut 28:18). The general curses of decimation and disease (e.g. Deut 28:61–62) may also form the background for the prediction of lack of reproduction. What a tragic sham the fertility cult, enticing to so many Israelites throughout their history, will turn out to have been! V 11 begins a prose section of curses that concludes with Hosea's own imprecation in v 14. The alternation of prose with poetry in prophetic contexts, within unified passages, is well attested in OT prophetic literature, and is part of the inspired artistry of a prophet like Hosea.

12   A fertility curse whose focus is the death of offspring (i.e. curse types 12 and / or 18) extends the cycle of death from conception and pregnancy (v 11) through adulthood. The term אדם "person" can refer to a human of any age, including, as here, one raised from childhood to adulthood. Israelite children will not live out normal lives. The manner of God's bringing about this bereavement (שכל) is not specified, but only the timing, "when I depart (בשורי) from them."

Of the various bereavement curse formulations, Deut 28:41 ("You will have sons and daughters but you will not keep them, because they will go into captivity") is perhaps the closest to that of v 12, though Deut 32:25 specifically employs the verb שכל "to bereave/make childless." The latter part of v 12 predicts the withdrawal of God from his people, beginning the process of punishment for covenant violations (curse type 1; cf. Lev 26:17a; Deut 32:20; 31:17–18).

13   The text of v 13 in MT is corrupt. By comparing G and by recognizing that the language should likely conform to that of the covenant curses, a reconstruction, though tentative, is possible. The theme of bereavement, set in v 12, must be the main subject of the verse. The statement "Woe to *them*" in v 12 introduces the focus: something is now to be said about the miseries of parents losing children (curse type 18). The pivotal word is צור, which we judge to be either the infinitive of the verb "to besiege" (i.e., צור), or perhaps a corruption of the noun מצור "siege." Several curses are devoted to the miseries that will prevail during the time that the unfaithful Israelites will be besieged by their enemies as a result of breaking the covenant with Yahweh. Generally, covenant-breaking produces terror in one's home (Deut.

32:35) and conditions so horrible that "the sights you see will drive you mad" (Deut 28:34). More specifically, a time of siege produces desperate starvation resulting in cannibalism, portrayed in Deut 28:53–57 in graphic detail even more shocking than that found in similar ancient Near Eastern treaty-curses (curse type 3; cf. Hillers, *Treaty Curses,* 62–63). People who have otherwise been loving parents will kill and eat their own children (cf. Lev 26:29). If the famine of siege is indeed the subject of the verse, the action of a parent bringing a child out of the house to be slaughtered for eating fits the category of Deut 28:53–57. (Slaughtering would not likely occur indoors.)

14 Hosea himself now speaks, breaking forth into imprecatory prayer against faithless Israel, continuing the theme of parental miseries. As v 13 focused on a father's perspective, v 14 now sees the horror from a mother's viewpoint. It is hard to imagine that this prayer could be an intercessory prayer of the prophet, who asks God that no more children be born, since barrenness in the coming days would be a relative blessing (so Mays, 134–35 and Wolff, 166–67). A comparison with the non-Israelite treaty curses which mention especially the miseries of "dry breasts" (Hillers, *Treaty Curses,* 61–62) shows that the language is certainly curse language.

Hosea prays for something that he surely knows God already is planning to bring about: the reversal of Israel's famous fertility blessings (Deut 28:4, 11; Exod 23:36). The pairing of "womb" (רחם) and "breasts" (שדים) in the present imprecation recalls ironically the happy language of Gen 49:25, "blessings of breasts and womb." These, Hosea prays, are no longer to be Israel's.

15 Divine speech resumes, now in poetic form again. V 15a, corresponding to vv 11–14, constitutes a second section of retrospective. The time frame is now the same as that of Hosea's audience: instead of evidence from a past site of sin, Baal-Peor, a present site of sin is mentioned, i.e., Gilgal. Because of the sort of thing that goes on at Gilgal, Yahweh (still) hates Israel (שׂנא, perfect, with present sense). Nothing has improved since the heinous infidelity at Baal-Peor. Where is Gilgal? Right across the Jordan River from Baal-Peor. Where are the Israelites? Right where they were all along—never far distant from their illegitimate lovers like Baal, and at best in a state of lukewarm and wavering allegiance to Yahweh's covenant.

There are two reasons for this attack on Gilgal. It was an ancient cult center from the very beginning of the conquest (Josh 4:19–5:12) which remained prominent throughout the North's history, thus becoming a heterodox worship center (Deut 12). In light of the attacks on it by Amos (4:4; 5:5) and Hosea (4:15; 12:12[11]), it must have been a center at least for aberrant, heterodox Yahwism, if not outright syncretism. As such, Yahweh would have no choice but to hate Israel because of it (curse type 1). The verb שׂנא "hate" reflects covenant terminology. It could as well be translated "reject" or "oppose," in contrast to אהב which means "be allied with" as often as "love" in such contexts. Personal emotions are beside the point. The wrath of the covenant God is the predominating issue. A second reason for the attack on Gilgal might be its connections with the Northern monarchy, which Hosea elsewhere denounces as a leading agent of Israel's sinfulness (7:3–7; 10:7, 15). Gilgal was the site of the inauguration of Saul (1 Sam 11:15) and already in

Saul's time a place where covenant-breaking religious rites could occur (1 Sam 15:21–23).

"Gilgal" was also probably a synecdoche for Israel as a whole. Their deeds may be described in a blanket manner, as "evil." Yahweh will "drive" them (גרש) "from my house" (מביתי), just as Pharaoh has driven out (גרש) Israel from Egypt (cf. Exod 11:1) and Yahweh had driven out (גרש) the Canaanites (Exod 34:11; Josh 24:12, 18). Yahweh's "house" is Israel's land (cf. 8:1). The covenant (indeed the decalogue itself, Exod 20:12; Deut 5:16) provides that the people may not remain on the land if they break the covenant (i.e., curse type 13; Lev 26:32–35, 38; Deut 28:21, 36, 63–64, etc.)

Thus his covenant "love" will stop (לא אוסף אהבתם "I will no longer love them"). The effects of this declaration, reminiscent of 1:6, will be felt by the whole nation. But the rebellious officials (שריהם סררים) will be especially involved. As in 1:4–7, the sequence of rejection logically describes the downfall of the government before the defeat and capture of the people. Moreover, Israel's leaders seemed intimately involved in helping the nation to sin, and their stubbornness/rebelliousness made it impossible for Yahweh to influence them for good (cf. 4:16). Such stiff-necked resistance to the sovereign's authority will bring the end of the resisting officials themselves (cf. 3:4).

16 V 16a presents the tragic state of the dying nation via the metaphor of a plant which has been struck down, dried up and unable to bear fruit. Since the sound of the word for "fruit," פרי, is vaguely reflected in the word Ephraim (אפרים) it is possible that a sort of pun is present. Ephraim the "doubly fruitful" (cf. Gen 41:52) is now Ephraim the completely fruitless. The metaphor reflects the actualization of those curses against the people which promise barrenness to their land (Lev 26:20, 32–35; Deut 28:17–18, 21–24, 38–40; 32:32–33; etc., i.e., curse type 9c) and impotence, defeat and destruction to themselves (cf. Lev 26:31, 36, 39; Deut 28:20; 32:30; etc.). In v 16b the metaphor yields to a very plain curse-threat, continuing the theme of deprivation of children from vv 11–14, but with an even greater specificity: it is Yahweh himself who will "kill their precious offspring." This specificity demonstrates that the prophetic interjection of v 14 is less likely intercession than imprecation. Yahweh's personal involvement in the process of bereavement is consonant with the theme of the covenant curses: they do not just happen; Yahweh causes them (e.g., Deut 28:20–25: "Yahweh will send . . . Yahweh will plague . . . Yahweh will turn . . . Yahweh will cause . . ." etc.; and Deut 32:39, "I put to death and I bring to life . . . and no one can deliver from my hand"). Whatever fertility Israel may happen to experience will not last—Yahweh will prevent Israel's offspring from growing up (curse type 12c). The nation will yield no "fruit."

17 The second section of divine curses is now concluded by a second inspired imprecation by Hosea, who asks that God turn the tables on Israel. As they rejected him (cf. מאס in Lev 26:43; 1 Sam 8:7) he should now reject them (ימאסם cf. 4:6; 1 Sam 15:23; curse type 1). God's covenant promises to scatter the unfaithful "among the nations" (גוים, Lev 26:33) so that they will perish "among the nations" (Lev 26:38) or to scatter them "among all the nations (בכל־העמים) from one end of the earth to the other" (type 13) include the punishments Hosea now calls forth against his own people.

How has Ephraim failed God? By their disobedience, not "listening to him." Obedience to the terms of the covenant, not frenzied acts of formalized devotion or ritual worship (cf. 7:14; 8:11, 13; 9:1, 5), is what Yahweh demands of Israel. It has been their identity that they were the nation which Yahweh had chosen, rescued, and settled miraculously in Canaan, a land not originally theirs. Now each aspect of this identity will be nullified. They will be rejected, unprotected, and homeless, "consumed off the land" (Deut 28:21). Theirs is the fate of the wandering refugee, in effect the curse of Cain (Gen 4:12).

Explanation

Divine speech and prophetic speech combine in this passage to pronounce upon the disobedient Israelites the fulfillment of the curses for disobedience contained in the Mosaic covenant. Here for the first time Hosea himself calls down the wrath of God upon his own compatriots (vv 14, 17). He is thus both announcer and imprecator of punishment.

What Israel will receive is well-earned, since she has consistently disobeyed Yahweh's commands. From its occasion of flagrant disloyalty in the pagan consecration at Baal-Peor (v 10) to its present syncretism across the river at Gilgal (v 15), Israel's record has been negative rather than positive. Their predisposition to sin while yet presuming upon Yahweh's constant forgiveness has made them become to Yahweh "as detestable as their lover," i.e., Baal, "shame." As Gilgal is not far distant from Baal-Peor, so Israel's behavior is not far distant from what it had been when they engaged in forbidden sexual fertility rites with foreign women at Baal-Peor. They had not moved much, either geographically or religiously.

The passage treats especially Israel's uniqueness—not intrinsically (cf. Deut 7:7–8) but in terms of being specially chosen by Yahweh (v 10). Once so special, Israel will now become nothing. Its honor will fly away like a bird (v 11). The people miraculously rescued and settled in a new land will become a dispersed people, worthless as a dead plant (v 16), on the run among the nations, without a land (v 17).

Two kinds of punishment dominate the passage: bereavement / infertility (vv 11–14, 16–17) and expulsion / exile (vv 15, 17). These punishments come from a God whose patience is exhausted by the people's "evil deeds" (v 15). Israel is now hated, no longer loved (v 15). Has Yahweh changed, become less tolerant, more hasty to impose judgment? Not at all. Israel is simply and finally getting what it has long deserved but been spared by reason of the patience of God. Their coming calamities are their own fault. If they had not been blatantly unfaithful, even in their worship (vv 10, 15), if their deeds had not been evil (v 15), or their officials not rebellious (v 15), if they had not refused to listen to Yahweh when he called them to repentance (v 17), the situation could have been different. But they must now know rejection (v 17), separation (v 12), horrible miseries of bereavement (vv 11–14, 16), infertility (v 15), and exile (v 17). Yahweh's house is no longer home to Israel.

The End of Cult, King, and Capital (10:1–8)

Bibliography

Albright, W. F. "The High Place in Ancient Palestine." *Congress Volume.* VTSup 4. Leiden: E. J. Brill, 1957. 242–58. **Dahood, M.** *Psalms I.* Anchor Bible 16. Garden City, NY: Doubleday, 1966. 35–36. **Driver, G. R.** "Problems of the Hebrew Text and Language." In *Alttestamentliche Studien: FS F. Nötscher,* ed. H. Junker and J. Botterweck. Bonn: P. Hanstein Verlag, 1950. 46–61. **Fohrer, G.** "Der Vertrag zwischen König und Volk in Israel." *ZAW* 71 (1959) 1–22. **Torczyner, H.** "Dunkle Bibelstellen." In *Vom Alten Testament,* ed. K. Budde. BZAW 41. Giessen: Töpelmann, 1925. 274–80. **Tromp, N. J.** *Primitive Conceptions of Death and the Nether World in the Old Testament.* BibOr 21. Rome: Pontifical Biblical Institute, 1969. 11–12, 83–84.

Translation

Rejection of the cult and kingship

10:1 *Israel is a spreading / barren[a] vine;*
he yields / used to yield plenty[b] of fruit.[c]

The more his fruit,
the more altars he made.

The finer his land,
the finer sacred stones were made.[d]

2 *Their heart is deceptive.[a]*
Now they incur guilt.[b]

He himself will break the necks[c] of their altars,
he will destroy their sacred stones.

3 *Indeed, now they will say: "We have no king*
Because we did not fear Yahweh.
And the king—what did he ever[a] do for us?"

Royal and religious sin and its punishment

4 *Speaking[a] words, swearing emptily, making covenants—*
while justice has sprouted like poisonous plants along the furrows of the field.

5 *At the bull of Beth-Awen,*
the inhabitants of Samaria tremble.

Indeed, its people will mourn[a] over it,
and its priests (will mourn)[b] over it,

who shout for joy about its glory,
for it 'has gone into exile' for them.[c]

6 *It, too, shall be taken[a] to Assyria,*
as a gift for the great king.[b]

Israel's disobedience and its punishment

> *Ephraim disgraces himself,*
> *Israel is shamed by his disobedience.*[c]

> [7] *Samaria will be destroyed;*
> *its king will be like a twig on the water.*

> [8] *Destroyed will be the evil high places,*[a]
> *the sins* [b] *of Israel.*

> *Thorns and thistles will grow up*
> *over their altars.*

> *They will say to the mountains, "Cover us!"*
> *and to the hills, "Fall on us!"*

Notes

1.a. The translation of MT בּוֹקֵק is disputed. The often-suggested meaning "luxuriant" is based primarily on the Arab. cognate *baqqa*, and the G translation. Kuhnigk (*NSH*, 117) suggests reading בּוֹקַק, a poal pf from בוק, i.e., "watered." We judge that the simple qal ptcp of בקק, i.e., as pointed in MT, is the likely original form and that the word is used by Hosea with both its meanings, as a purposeful double-entendre. Even for the meaning "barren," the active ptcp is appropriate, since the vine "produces barrenness," i.e., yields no grapes, or causes no grapes to grow. The verb is masc because it functions as an attributive governed by the gender of Israel, which is personified in the masc sg throughout [*sic*] v 1.

1.b. The impf connotes here either past durative or present action, and is probably also a purposeful double-entendre. שוה, piel, means basically to make something come up to par, to the level or standard it ought to meet. G reads fem forms in v 1a; this is unlikely to be original.

1.c. The line literally means: "he used to produce up to his (לוֹ) standard (i.e., plenty) of fruit."

1.d. Kuhnigk's suggestion (*NSH*, 117) to revocalize MT to הֵיטִיב וּמַצֵּבוֹת, i.e., a 3 m sg pf verb, with *waw*-intensive before מצבות "sacred stones" is convincing, and produces a grammatical symmetry otherwise obscured (see *Form / Structure / Setting*). G maintains the sg verb throughout the verse as well.

2.a, b. For this couplet, in light of the possibility that חלק may also mean "to die" and אשם may possibly mean "to perish," Kuhnigk (*NSH*, 119–20) translates "Their heart is dead; now they may perish." Such a translation cannot be ruled out, especially in light of the frequent double-entendres elsewhere in the book; cf. Dahood, *Psalms I*, 35–36, and Tromp, *Primitive Conceptions*, 11–12, 83–84.

2.c. The meaning of ערף is specifically and only "to break the neck."

3.a. Translating the impf by its past durative aspect.

4.a. G (λαλῶν) reads דֹּבֵר (ptcp); in light of the parallelism with the other infs, we vocalize דַּבֵּר, the piel inf constr. MT "they spoke" is not impossible, however.

5.a. The translation of the pf verbs אבל "mourn" and גלה "shout" is governed by the impfs in the verse.

5.b. The verb אבל "mourn" obviously does double duty in v 5a.

5.c. Here עם "people" is construed in the sg; thus the 3 m sg suffixal ending.

6.a. On the basis of G Syr Tg, read the hiph, יוּבִילוֹ (but see Kuhnigk, *NSH*, 120–21). The passive translation reflects the fact that the subj is indefinite.

6.b. Vocalizing מַלְכִּי־רָב "the great king" (cf. 5:13). Good (*JBL* 85 [1966] 273–86) and Ginsburg (*EncJud* 8:1010–24) retain the vocalization רָב partly on the grounds that the same "mistake" would not be made twice in the book. Ginsburg translates מלך ירב as "patron king."

6.c. There is little merit in emending עצתו "his disobedience" to עצבו "his idol," though it has been done widely since Wellhausen. The identification of עֵצָה as "disobedience" originated with Kennicott and was again advanced by G. R. Driver with additional evidence (*Alttestamentliche Studien*, 54).

8.a. Or, במות־און may conceivably mean "high places of (Beth)-Awen," though such an obscure means of allusion would probably have been lost on Hosea's audience, and thus seems unlikely.

8.b. Reading the pl constr "sins of" (חטאתי) with G, in conformity with the pl במות "high places."

Form / Structure / Setting

The shift of designation from "Ephraim" to "Israel" as the dominant subject and the exclusive use of third-person speech are two formal indications of a new literary unit beginning with 10:1. Yahweh does not here speak in the first person, nor is Israel addressed directly. The theme shifts to announcement specifically of the fate of the nation's cultic symbols (altars, idols, sacred stones, high places) and its political symbol, the king. The mood is again reflective and retrospective, typical of the passages positioned after 9:10. In light of the third-person reference to Yahweh (v 2) it is likely that Hosea is the speaker.

The unity of the passage is evidenced by its structural logic, which may be summarized as follows:

vv 1–2a   Israel's increasing cultic sin
   vv 2b–3   Punishment: destruction of altars and kingship
vv 4–5a   Royal and religious sin
   vv 5b–6a   Punishment: exile
vv 6b   Israel's disgraceful disobedience
   vv 7–8   Punishment: destruction, desolation, death.

Note also that in each of the portions that describe coming punishment, Hosea alludes to the people's speech. In vv 3 ("we have no king," etc.) and 8 ("Cover us!" etc.), a direct quote is the mode of citation. In v 5 the mourning of people and priest is described, though no words are quoted; rather, mention is made of wailing and weeping (cf. 7:14).

The meter is problematic, except in vv 1–2 and 8b, where rather normal synonymous parallelism predominates and meter is thus quite balanced. The couplet (5 : 6 :: 5 : 6 syllable count) in v 1b is elegantly structured, in an almost epigrammatic fashion. As Kuhnigk (NSH, 117–19) demonstrates, the precise staccato style helps lead to the correction of the misdivided MT consonants in the fourth line of the double couplet:

כְּרֹב לְפִרְיוֹ	kᵉrōb lᵉpiryô	5 syllables	"The more his fruit,
הִרְבָּה לַמִּזְבְּחוֹת	hirbā lamizbᵉḥōt	6 syllables	the more altars he made.
כְּטוֹב לְאַרְצוֹ	kᵉṭōb lᵉʾarṣō	5 syllables	The finer his land,
הֵיטִיב וּמַצֵּבוֹת	hêṭîb ûmaṣṣēbōt	6 syllables	the finer sacred stones were made."

All of vv 3–8a could be considered prose, with occasional parallelistic (i.e., semi-poetic or rhetorically stylized) portions such as 6b. Alternatively, we have reconstructed the passage as parallelistic synthetic verse, but since there are no evident caesurae in any couplets, it may be as close to prose as to typical poetry.

The date of the passage is possible to discern only in general terms. It appears that the Northern cult, with its various heterodox aberrations, was flourishing at the time of this speech. Sacred cult objects were numerous, and predictions of distress for king and people are still placed in the present / future tense. These factors reflect generally the same sort of conditions evident in 9:1–9 (and 9:10–17), thus probably fixing the date sometime during the reign of Hoshea (732–723 B.C.).

Comment

1 Hosea's words are both ironic and reflective. On the assumption that his audience knew both meanings of בקק (see nn. 1.a, b), the metaphor of Israel as a vine would at once address two considerations: Israel's prosperity, a gift from Yahweh (cf. 2:10 [8], and Israel's misuse of her blessing from Yahweh (cf. 2:7 [5]). The first sense of the double-entendre in גפן בוקק "spreading vine" might have reminded Hosea's audience of the metaphorical comparison of people to flora or fauna in tribal blessings such as Gen 49 and Deut 33 (e.g., Gen 49:21, "Naphtali is a spreading terebinth"). This first meaning would convey the fact that Yahweh had abundantly prospered Israel, as a basis for the following words about what Israel did with her prosperity (1b). The other sense of גפן בוקק "barren vine" would serve to adumbrate Israel's coming fate. A barren vine is good for nothing and must be destroyed (cf. Matt 7:19). This "vine" has not fulfilled its purpose, which was to serve its role as Yahweh's faithful people (cf. Isa 5:1–7; Jer 2:21).

The second line of the initial couplet emphasizes the remarkable fruitfulness of the vine. "Israel" is the subject rather than "Ephraim" because the history of that prosperity begins with the united people's conquest of the promised land. Unfortunately, Israel presumptuously abused its divine blessing. Assuming that its prosperity was the result of formal religious practices, the people multiplied altars and lavishly adorned the sacred stones of the fertility cult in expectation of ever more agricultural abundance, but in violation of the divine law (Deut 12:1–14; Exod 23:24). This "Canaanite" mechanistic approach to religion benefitted priests (cf. 4:7–13) and people alike. Israelites could enjoy the pleasures of debauchery forbidden by orthodox Yahwism (4:14) and live selfish, materialistic lives (5:4–5) yet think themselves religiously exemplary by reason of faithfulness to the cult. Such violation of the covenant's stipulations was prostitution (9:1–2). The altars and sacred stones had become rivals to true devotion to Yahweh. As such, they would be destroyed (v 2b). Yahweh himself had given Israel her plenty and she had misused it. Throughout the book this emphasis prevails often in connection with the roots רבב and רבה ("to be great," "to multiply"). Israel had ignored Yahweh in trusting upon such things as her agricultural bounty (2:7–13 [5–11]; 9:1), wealth in precious things (2:15 [13]; 8:4; 9:6), a large priesthood (4:7), many fortifications (8:14), multiple altars (4:13; 8:11), a large army (10:13), etc. The very success of the nation Yahweh chose and blessed had led to unfaithfulness.

2 In multiplying altars and sacred stones the Israelites had shown themselves a deceitful people. Their heart, which was supposed to be exclusively devoted to Yahweh's sovereignty (Deut 6:5), was divided (cf. 7:14). The Israelites had often conjoined worship of Yahweh with that of Baal and Asherah, and had added idolatry and other illegal worship accoutrements to their religion. They had been forewarned: "Make sure that there is no man or woman, clan or tribe . . . whose heart (לב) turns away from Yahweh . . . to worship the gods of those nations" (Deut 29:18). But Israel's לב had indeed turned away from Yahweh, and thus they were guilty.

God must then do to Israel's altars and sacred stones what they were supposed to have done to those of the Canaanites (Deut 12:3; cf. Exod 23:14; 32:13). He himself will "break the neck" (ערף) of the altars. Elsewhere, ערף is used mainly of breaking the necks of sacrificial animals before slaughtering them. The similar prediction in Amos 3:14 ("the horns of the altar will be cut off and fall to the ground") confirms what is simply logical: to destroy an altar one begins at the top and works down. The similarity of this to slaughtering animals provides a striking metaphor, appropriate to the natural close association of altars and slaughter. Yahweh will also "destroy" (ישדד) the sacred stones. The verb שדד reflects the use of שד "destruction / devastation / annihilation" in 7:13; 9:6; and 10:14. The verb may connote especially the kind of destruction that war produces. Nothing will be left of Israel's once proud cult (cf. 9:4–5), not even the physical symbols of worship. Yahweh has rejected it, according to the ancient curses (cf. Lev 26:31; type 2).

3 The first judgment sentence of the book contained an announcement of the end of Israel's kingship (1:4). V 3 returns to this theme once again. The word עתה "now" coupled with the imperfect verb functions to introduce the judgment sentence (cf. 2:12 [10] and 8:10) and need not be linked to the present. Hosea cites proleptically the speech of the Israelites after the destruction of their nation: "We have no king." Hoshea (732–23 B.C.), Israel's king at the time this oracle was delivered, would be its last. Frequently in Hosea the kingship is portrayed as a key element in the overall covenant infidelity that characterizes Israel (1:4; 7:3–7; 8:4; 10:3; 13:10, 11), and just as frequently Hosea announces the demise (often via exile) of the kingship (1:4; 3:4; 10:3, 7, 15; 13:10, 11; i.e., curse type 13b). This is not an "anti-monarchy" stance but a statement of judgment against the monarchy. It is also a way of describing the end of the nation itself (cf. the curse in Deut 28:36: "Yahweh will drive you and the king you set over you to a nation unknown to you or your fathers"). The impotence of the king to resist this deportation (cf. 10:7) parallels that of the people. Their mutual fate will be horror, scorn, and ridicule (Deut 28:37). Then the people will recognize and confess (10:3) that their loss of the kingship is a punishment, because they did not "fear" (ירא) Yahweh. As a covenant term, "fear" means in effect to "obey" in the sense of giving exclusive, diligent honor and worship to a sovereign.

The final statement, "and the king—what did he ever do for us?" could theoretically be the words of either the people or the prophet. But nowhere else does the prophet associate himself with Israel. He speaks words given him from Yahweh, so Israel is normally "you" or "they." On this basis we assign the statement to the people rather than to Hosea.

Their complaint is ironic. 1 Sam 8 records the Israelites' initial demand for a king to lead them into battle and protect them from their enemies. Once Yahweh has, however, caused their enemies to defeat them and they find themselves in exile under the oppression of the "great king" of Assyria (8:10), their own king would be useless to them. What could he do indeed? What value is a former king to a former nation?

4 The things Israel's kings did are now tersely summarized by a series of infinitive clauses (cf. 4:2). The time frame is brought back to the present from the future quotation of v 3 and Hosea is the speaker. Israel's experience with its kings has not been exemplary; their trust in the king and in the institution of kingship has been betrayed. They wanted from the king leadership, protection, justice. What they got was a sham. The king talked a lot ("speaking words"), made many pledges ("swearing emptily"), and concluded international treaties ("making covenants"), but none of this really helped Israel. The "justice" (מִשְׁפָּט "order, equity, judgment") which the king was supposed to have provided had in fact turned out to be treachery, "poisonous plants" (רֹאשׁ) in a food-producing field. While it has often been argued that Hosea borrowed and reworked the metaphorical connection of "justice" and "poison" from Amos (cf. Amos 5:7; 6:12), it is more likely that both prophets simply reflect covenantal curse language in their metaphors. Deut 29:17b links רֹאשׁ "poison" and לַעֲנָה "bitterness" in a dire warning: "make sure there is no root among you that produces poisonous and bitter fruit." Deut 32:32–33 contains a similar metaphor using רֹאשׁ: "Their grapes are filled with poison . . . their wine is . . . the poison of cobras." In each of these cases, the unfaithfulness that the Israelites show to Yahweh is likened to unexpected deadly foulness instead of something edible. Hosea thus reports scathingly that where good food was sought, poison was found. The justice that should have grown with good leadership has been choked out. That which was hurtful has prevailed. Note that v 4b is not therefore directed exclusively at the king. Injustice, including covenant disloyalty of all sorts, pervades the nation. The king does not by himself produce all the injustice. His neglect, rather, allows the sinful human nature of the people (cf. 4:12) to seek its natural end: a society that is corrupt.

5 Israel's corruption manifests itself specifically in their idolatry. Deut 29:17 makes a similar connection: turning from Yahweh is what allows the poison to develop from the roots of the "plant." The centerpiece of the cult was the gold-leaved bull statue (cf. 8:5) at Bethel, called Beth-Awen here again by the scornful nickname perhaps originated by Amos (5:5). The sins of the royalty in v 4 are paralleled in this verse by the sins of the royal city, Samaria.

There, the bull, perhaps understood by some as merely a platform for Yahweh, though by others as either an actual representation of Yahweh or even a god in its own right, was a symbol of rebellion, violating the prohibition against graven images (Exod 20:4–5). That commandment specifically forbade "bowing down to" or "worshiping" such an image, yet Samaria's citizenry "trembled" (גּוּר) in fear at the bull. (On גּוּר as "worship, reverence" cf. Ps 22:24.) This statue they so revered, to which they made pilgrimages, and whose pagan priests (כֹּמֶר refers to idol priests in the OT) shouted ecstatically over it in the course of the Bethel cult worship rites, was quickly to become an object to be mourned over. "Mourning" (אָבַל) connotes the practice of lamentation for the dead or lost, as well as the more general expression of woe in the midst of various sorts of miseries. Here again the mourning is future (cf. v 3). The people will express their distress when their central religious symbol goes into exile (גלה). In saying "its people" (עמו) Hosea identifies Israel as the people of the golden bull rather than the people of Yahweh. Rejecting Yahweh and his demands for social justice (4b) they chose whom they would serve (Josh 24:15), an impotent god (Deut 32:37–38), a bauble Yahweh would exile along with his former covenant people (i.e., curse types 2 and 13). The idol they kissed and sacrificed to (13:2), their "glory" (כבוד), they will bewail as it goes to the hands of their captors. Yahweh's ability to dispose of Israel's idols is proof of his sovereignty (cf. Isa 10:10–11), and proof that Israel made the wrong choice in rejecting him and his covenantal demands. "It 'has gone into exile' from them" mirrors the statement of Phinehas' wife upon hearing of the capture of Israel's original religious symbol, the ark, by the Philistines: "The glory (כבוד) has departed / gone into exile (גלה) from Israel" (1 Sam 4:21–22). As reused by Hosea, the verb גלה, here translated by the past tense, is a predictive perfect. The capture of the bull idol, like the ancient capture of the ark, spells doom for its people.

6   V 6a concludes the prediction of the fate of the bull. It will become simply an item of booty carried by the conquering Assyrians back to their king (מלכי־רב "great king"). Although יבל "take" and מנחה "gift" can both be used in connection with the payment of tribute by a weak nation to a more powerful one, the bull idol in this case is more likely to be part of the plunder of war. In other words, this prediction expects that Israel will be conquered and its possessions taken as prizes of war (curse types 3 and / or 6). Alternatively, it may envision that tribute will be paid by Hoshea to Tiglath-Pileser III (745–728 B.C.) or Shalmaneser V (727–722) in order to avoid destruction. At any rate, Israel's false security will be unmasked, and rejoicing will turn to mourning (v 5).

V 6b does not connect directly to v 6a, as if to say that the deportation of the bull were a cause for shame. Rather, it introduces the final of the passage's three listings of Israel's unfaithfulness. Hosea sums up Israel's situation: they are a people characterized by a "disobedience" (עצה; see note 6.c) which brings them disgrace and shame. In light of the use of עצה (the homonym meaning "counsel," "plan") in Deut 32:28 in connection with Israel's foolishness as a nation, it is possible that Hosea again employs a double-entendre: at once Israel is a people (1) devoid of sense and, accordingly, (2) disobedient to Yahweh. Israel is to blame. However one takes עצה, these words do not mean that Israel, through no fault of its own, lacks discernment (cf. the context of Deut 32:28–29) but that Israel, and specifically its capital, Samaria, has purposely decided to disobey the covenant.

7   The three centers of authority in the North were king, cult, and capital city. The final two verses of the passage announce the fulfillment of covenant sanctions against each of these, beginning in v 7a with the capital. Hosea states simply that it will be "destroyed" (נדמה). It is likely that the destruction of all the cities of the North is thereby adumbrated, on the assumption that the capital functions as a synecdoche for Israel in general, and its remaining cities in particular. Specific curses foretelling the siege and destruction of the cities of the rebellious nation abound in the Pentateuchal curse corpus (type 9a; Lev 26:25, 31, 33; Deut 28:16, 52, 55, 57; cf. Deut 32:25). Samaria fulfilled its destiny of destruction in 722 B.C. (2 Kgs 17:5–6), after which it was never rebuilt.

A graphic description of the helplessness of the king completes the verse. He will be carried off, powerless to resist, like a twig or chip of wood is born along on water (curse type 13b). Already in v 3 the theme of the impotence of the king was introduced. Again the utter folly of the people's looking to the king for deliverance, rather than to Yahweh, is emphasized. In times of international crisis people usually rally around their national leader. But Israel's real national leader, according to the Mosaic covenant, was Yahweh, not the king the people chose (1 Sam 12:12; cf. Ps 93:1; 96:10; 97:1; 99:1, etc.). Thus their hope for rescue was misplaced. Just as the bull idol which they worshiped and the city in which they felt secure were to fall to their enemies, so the king himself would be taken captive. This covenant curse (cf. Deut 28:36) was, of course, fulfilled in the capture and imprisonment of King Hoshea in 723 B.C. (2 Kgs 17:4).

8 Hosea's announcement of divine retribution ends with a description of the devastation of Israel's many shrines and altars, as well as the people who worshiped there. V 8 heralds the fulfillment of the threefold curse on high places (במות), altars (מזבחות), and people in imagery similar to that of the curses in Leviticus (e.g., Lev 26:30; i.e., curse type 9a). In direct violation of the covenant (Deut 12:2–14), Israel had borrowed from the Canaanites the במה "high place" system, and had in many cases simply taken over the formerly pagan high places themselves. Virtually any town or village might have one or more high places, shrines set on hills, usually with trees (sometimes the grove was designated as a spot for the worship of the fertility goddess Asherah) and a מצבה "sacred stone," and always a sacrificial altar. Hundreds of high places dotted the landscape (1 Kgs 14:23; cf. Hos 4:13). These high places are called here (if the text is not corrupt) "high places of evil," and this phrase is set in opposition to "the sins of Israel" as if the high places are the, or a, central aspect of Israel's sin. The presence of the high place system was proof that Israel was a heterodox people (cf. Deut 12:2). If they had never adopted that blatant, systematic betrayal of Yahweh, their fate as a nation might have been different. Now their evil high places would be destroyed and fall into ruins. The mention of "thorns and thistles" is a common poetic way of describing an untended, uninhabited waste (e.g., Isa 32:13; Jer 12:13) which in this case represents the fulfillment of a variety of curses of devastation (type 9a) in Lev 26 and Deut 28–32. Lev 26:31 (". . . I will lay waste your sanctuaries") is particularly closely related to the present verse.

The passage closes by quoting the cry of those who will be alive at the time these calamities will occur. Their cry for death is not a response simply to the destruction of the cult, but is intended to represent a summation of woes. Implicit in the various predictions of destruction of cult centers is that such devastation will be merely one part of the generalized calamity which will affect the whole nation. War, disease, famine, natural catastrophes, and any other sorts of miseries may potentially be part of the punishment process. The miseries endured will be so great that people will cry desperately for relief—in effect for sudden death and burial under the land's hills (the very places the high places were set on) from earthquakes or the like. In that time of awesome divine vengeance, "the sights you see will drive you mad"

(Deut 28:34). Death will become preferable to life, so great will be the horror (cf. Lev 26:16; Deut 28:67; i.e., curse type 4).

Explanation

The highly structured oracle of Hos 10:1–8 follows a pattern common throughout the book. Citations of evidence of covenant transgressions are followed immediately by announcements of implementation of the covenant's curses. The passage emphasizes the sin of Israel's cult which by its very nature corrupted the relationship of the people with their God. How could Yahweh ignore the many worship sites and altars, sacred stones, and reverence of the golden bull? How could he continue to bless a land that consistently violated the covenant he had graciously bestowed on his chosen people—and turned away from him all the more as he blessed them all the more?

Yahweh had prospered Israel for a long time. Now he would desolate it. The contrast between the picture of Israel's bountiful past agricultural productivity in v 1 and the coming of wild, unchecked overgrowth after a time of awful defeat and destruction could not be more stark. The desolation will include the capture of the bull idol by Israel's dreaded enemies, the Assyrians. It will also involve the end of the kingship as a natural consequence of the end of national independence. The hilltop shrines found throughout that land—and, of course, the people who worshiped at them—will also be destroyed.

The theme of loss of confidence or protection runs as an undercurrent throughout the passage. The cult, the bull idol, the land and powerful king were things in which the Israelites trusted. The fact that all of these would come to an end, and that Israel would be left, as it were, naked and exposed without the major visible symbols of its religion and government, heightens the misery the people are to expect when the covenant punishments begin in earnest. Because they "did not fear Yahweh" (v 3) they foolishly honored an unjust king and worshiped an idol whose only power was in their own minds. Such people were plainly disloyal to their original commitment to the covenant. Their hearts were "deceptive" (v 2) and thus they incurred guilt and its natural consequence, wrath.

Israel both worshiped other gods and also worshiped Yahweh in ways of their own making. Israel rejected their God (cf. Deut 32:15) and so their God rejected them (Deut 32:19).

Hosea prophesies that people who have rejected Yahweh will call for hill and mountain to fall on them (v 8b). This saying Jesus applies anew to those who reject him, when destruction comes at the end of the current age (Luke 23:30). What Hosea—and Jesus—expect is not simply a hiding from divine wrath (as e.g., Isa 2:10, 21) but woes so great that death will be preferred to life (as e.g., Jer 8:3). The wrath Hosea predicted has already come. The wrath Jesus predicted with Hosea's words is yet to come (Rev 6:16; 9:6). The prescription for avoiding that wrath is essentially unchanged: faithfulness to God and his covenant. For those who accept the lordship of the sovereign of the new covenant, and show their loyalty by obedience to his commands, that time of wrath will hold no lasting pain (Rev 7:9–17).

War against the Wicked Ones (10:9–15)

Bibliography

Astour, M. C. "841 B.C.: The First Assyrian Invasion of Israel." *JAOS* 91 (1971) 383–89. **Dahood, M.** "Ugaritic *drkt* and Biblical *derek*." *TS* 15 (1954) 627–31. **Farr, G.** "The Concept of Grace in the Book of Hosea." *ZAW* 70 (1958) 98–107. **Goshen-Gottstein, M. H.** " 'Ephraim Is a Well-Trained Heifer' and Ugaritic *mdl*." *Bib* 41 (1960) 64–66. **Kölichen, J. C. von.** "Der 'Lehrer der Gerechtigkeit' und Hos 10:12 in einer rabbinischen Handschrift des Mittelalters." *ZAW* 74 (1962) 324–27. **Robertson, E.** "Textual Criticism of Hos 10:11." *Transact. Glasgow U. Or. Soc.* 8 (1938) 16–17. **Stuart, D.** "The Sovereign's Day of Conquest." *BASOR* 221 (1976) 159–64. **Westermann, C.** "Die Begriffe für Fragen und Suchen im Alten Testament." *KD* 6 (1960) 2–30. **Zirker, H.** "דרך = *potentia?*" *BZ* 2 (1958) 291–94.

Translation

War as a punishment

10:9 *Since the days of Gibeah, Israel has sinned.*[a] *There they have stayed.*[b] *Will not*[c] *war overtake*[d] *them in Gibeah*[e] *because of the wicked ones?*[f]

10 ⟨*I am coming*⟩[a] *to punish them.*[b] *Nations will assemble against them when they are punished*[c] *for their double inquity.*[d]

Israel's original potential

11 *Ephraim was a young cow,*
trained,
liking to thresh.

I put on (her) yoke,[a]
her good neck I harnessed.[b]

Ephraim would plow,[c]
Judah would harrow.

O Jacob,[d]

Israel's future potential

12 *Sow for yourselves righteousness,*
reap the ⟨*fruit*⟩[a] *of loyalty,*
break up for yourselves the new ground of ⟨*knowledge*⟩.[b]

Indeed,[c] *seek Yahweh until he comes,*
and waters[d] *you with justness.*[e]

Israel's misplaced potential

13 *You have plowed evil,*
you have reaped wickedness,
you have eaten the fruit of dishonesty.

Because you have trusted in your ⟨*chariotry*⟩,[a]
in the number of your soldiers,

¹⁴*the tumult will rise against*[a] *your people,*
  and all your fortifications will be destroyed.

Destruction via war

  Like Shalman's destruction of Beth-Arbel on the day of battle (mothers[b] *were bashed*[c] *to death along with*[d] *their children),* ¹⁵ *so I will do*[a] *to you, family of Israel,*[b] *because your evil is evil indeed.*[c] *At dawn the King of Israel shall be silenced for good.*

Notes

(The text of vv 9–12 is notably difficult, and at points insolubly corrupt.)

9.a. Reading חטא "he sinned" with G ἥμαρτεν and Vg *peccavit.*

9.b. Or, conceivably, "there they took a stand (to do battle)," or the like.

9.c. MT לא cannot be the simple negative particle, unless the sentence is construed as an interrogative. Equally possible would be the reading of לֹי / לֹו, the asseverative particle.

9.d. The imperfect of נשג may conceivably be construed in the past tense, i.e., "Did not war overtake them in Gibeah . . . ?"

9.e. It is also possible that בגבעה here is a play upon הגבעה "Gibeah" in v 9a; if the sentence is construed with a fut verb, the specification of the city of Gibeah appears less likely than a general statement about war "in the hills" throughout Israel. See *Comment.*

9.f. MT עָלָוה appears to be a metathesis of עולה "wicked ones," perhaps a historical development in Heb. speech, but more likely a copy error.

10.a. Reading בָאתִי "I am coming" with most G MSS ἦλθον for MT בְאַוָּתִי, "As / when I please. . . ."

10.b. With G παιδεῦσαι αὐτούς "to punish them," read איסרם; either a typical form of יסר or perhaps a mutation thereof which obscures the *yodh* is required.

10.c. G Syr Vg read pass infs (either niph or pual, presumably). Could a bi-form of יסר exist in Hosea's Northern dialect? Consonantal MT is identical to v 10a (see n.10.b.); "I punish them" is therefore a possible reading.

10.d. Reading with Q, following G Syr Vg. K, "before both their eyes," is unlikely.

11.a. Instead of MT עָבַרְתִּי "I passed / traveled through," read עֲבַרְתִּי "I put on." MT עַל "on" must also be revocalized to עֹל / עֹ'ל "yoke."

11.b. Lit., "the fairness of her neck I caused to be mounted (with yoking)." The impf אַרְכִיב is used in parallelism with the pf עברתי and thus indicates past action. See Kuhnigk, *NSH,* 121–23.

11.c. The impf verb יחרוש (like ישׂדד, following) is used for past durative action; its subj is אפרים "Ephraim," not יהודה "Judah." See below, *Form / Structure / Setting.*

11.d. With Kuhnigk, *NSH,* 121–23, we read ליעקב "O Jacob," instead of לי יעקב.

12.a. Reading with G (εἰς καρπὸν ζωῆς) פרי "fruit" for MT פי "mouth / edge"; though G was hardly privy to a pristine text itself (reading, e.g., חיים "life" for MT חסד "loyalty"?).

12.b. MT ועת "and time" (followed by G^L Syr Vg) appears less likely in the context than דעת "knowledge" (so G: γνώσεως).

12.c. MT לדרוש "to seek" is better revocalized: לֹו דָרוש, "indeed, seek . . ." G ἐκζητήσατε "seek out" may or may not reflect דָרוש.

12.d. Of the various options for translating or emending ירה, the hiph of ירה II "to water, give to drink" is most appropriate in light of the agricultural metaphors of the context.

12.e. Or "justice," "right," "equity," etc. Kuhnigk's alternative translation, "at the right time" (*NSH,* 123) is possible but less than convincing, without the benefit of a preposition (cf. לצדקה, Joel 2:23, "at the right time").

13.a. With G, read בְּרִכְבָּך "in your chariotry" for MT בְּדַרְכְּךָ "in your way."

14.a. Or "among." In such a context, either meaning for ב is possible.

14.b. The sgs (אם "mother," רטשה "bashed") are best conveyed idiomatically via pls.

14.c. Or "smashed," "beaten down" or the like.

14.d. Or "upon, on top of."

15.a. With G ποιήσω "I will do" we read אעשה; יֵעָשֶׂה (3 m sg niph) is found also in some MSS.

15.b. Reading בית ישראל "family of Israel" with G, instead of MT "Bethel," especially since "Bethel" is usually called Beth-Awen in Hosea (4:15; 5:8; 10:5; 12:5 [4], G).

15.c. Lit., "because of the evil of your evil;" if the "double iniquity" of v 10 is in view, this unusual superlative construction may be retained. It may also be the result of dittogr.

Form / Structure / Setting

Whereas 10:1–8 did not portray Yahweh as speaking directly to Israel, in 10:9–15 he himself brings both an indictment and a judgment verdict to his wayward people. The preceding passage, 10:1–8, concludes forcefully at 10:8; chap. 11 begins a different theme, based on a historical retrospective unlike that of the present passage. The dual prose threats of war in vv 9–10 and 14–15 form an inclusio for the entire passage, marking it off as a unit.

Once again, a contemplative mood (especially in vv 11–13a) accompanied by historical retrospective characterizes the divine speech. Further evidence of the unity of the passage comes from two catchwords. "War" (מלחמה) occurs in vv 9 and 14, identifying the specific form Yahweh's punishment will take. "Wickedness" (עולה) occurs in vv 9 and 13a, in connection with Israel's character and behavior. Three other words, close synonyms, are also used in a distribution which helps link the passage together thematically: "iniquity / guiltiness" (עון; v 10); "evil" (רשע; v 13); and "evil" (רעה; v 15). If the text of v 15 is reliable, the double use of רעה may well represent an artful direct connection with שתי עונתם "their double iniquity" in v 10. These synonyms are not, strictly speaking, catchwords, but they function in virtually the same manner, providing a logical-semantic thread which runs the length of the passage.

A transition from describing Israel in the third person to using direct address occurs in v 11b. However, a decision to accept the MT reading in v 9 ("you have sinned" rather than "has sinned"; see n. 9.a) or to accept MT's לו יעקב "for himself Jacob" without revocalization to ליעקב "O Jacob" in v 11b would alter this analysis. The single reference to Yahweh in the third person (". . . seek Yahweh until he comes," v 12b) is included so inextricably in a direct address to Israel that it can hardly be viewed as evidence of an interjection of the prophet, or some other party.

The basic structure of the passage may be represented as follows:

I.	Prose announcement of war punishment for iniquity	vv 9–10
II.	Poetic indictment of Israel	vv 11–14a
	A. Israel's calling (early potential)	v 11
	B. Israel's challenge (future potential)	v 12
	C. Israel's misuse of its calling (present and past abuse of potential)	v 13
	D. Resulting punishment	v 14a
III.	Prose announcement of war punishment of cult and king	vv 14b–15

The poetic structure of vv 11–14a eludes easy description. Its metrical structure is complicated, perhaps because of textual corruptions. Several triplets are found (vv 11, 12, 13). The vocative interjection "O Jacob" (v 11b) appears not to fit the surrounding metrical patterns (or parallelism) and must therefore be considered an instance of anacrusis. One couplet, at least, exhibits metrical balance. It is v 14a, which concludes the poetic section of the passage. Vocalized according to the pronunciation of the eighth century B.C. in the Northern dialect (see Stuart, *SEHM*, 24–28), the couplet appears thus:

וְקָאם שָׁאוֹן בַּעֲמֶּךָ	waqā³m šā³ôn baʿammekā	8 syllables	"the tumult will rise against your people,
וְכָל־מִבְצָרֶיךָ יוּשַּׁד	wakol mibṣarēkā yūššad	8 syllables	and all your fortifications will be destroyed."

Elsewhere, metrical regularity is more difficult to detect, if it exists at all.

It is difficult to assign a date or provenance to the passage with certainty. As in most of the oracles found in the book after 9:9, Israel appears to be enjoying a brief reprieve from misery. Evidently they are not at the moment in a state of war, since war is described as a future event (vv 9, 10, 14, 15). The king is still in power, since his deposing is yet to come (v 15). Bethel is still the center of the Northern heterodox cult (if MT's reading is kept in v 15) and Israel's manifold iniquitous practices are presumably still in full swing (vv 9, 10, 13, 15). The nation has plenty of men in arms, and a system of fortifications still intact (vv 13, 14a). The early 720s, in the most stable of King Hoshea's years, would constitute a likely time for the original delivery of these words. But virtually no time in Hosea's prophetic ministry can be ruled out by any of the factors adduced above. There is no firm evidence to tell us where in Israel Hosea might have spoken these words of Yahweh. Only if MT's "Bethel" is retained in v 15 can a provenance be identified.

Comment

9 The "days of Gibeah" again constitute a paradigm of the depth to which Israel is capable of sinking morally and religiously, as in 9:9 (cf. Isa 1:10). "There they have stayed" (שׁם עמדו) provides a link with the third sentence of the verse. Israel—the whole nation—is still at Gibeah (Judg 19) so war (Judg 20) will soon overtake them *at Gibeah,* i.e., still in their sins. It is also possible that the imperfect verb תשׂיגם is to be construed in the past tense (so Andersen and Freedman, 560, 565; cf. n. 9.d), i.e., "Did not war overtake them in Gibeah . . . ?" The point then would be: "If God punished Israel by war that time, will he not do it again?" In any case, the verse unquestionably implies that Israel's punishment will come via a destructive war, "because of the wicked ones"(על־בני עולה). The phrase is probably intended not only to recall the perverse cruelty of the homosexual rapists of Gibeah (Judg 19:30) but to apply as a characterization of the Israel of Hosea's time as well. The coming war (curse type 3) will involve all the North, not just Gibeah, the Judean-captured Benjaminite border town just north of Judah (cf. 5:8–10), here a synecdoche for sinful Israel. Alternatively, one might regard בגבעה as a double-entendre, and translate "in the hills," or the like, as a way of describing warfare "everywhere."

10 In spite of the several textual uncertainties, the gist of the verse is clear: Yahweh is preparing to requite Israel for its sinfulness by means of the nations he will assemble against them in war. The prediction of punishment for covenant violations at the hand of the enemy nation(s)—often just "enemies"—is the single most frequent type of curse in the covenant sanctions.

Here, Yahweh promises to come (בּאתי; see n. 10.a) and to punish (n. 10.b) via "nations," עמים, the plural being the form most often seen in Hosea (cf. 7:8; 9:1) as opposed to the usual singular form of the covenant curses (but cf. Deut 28:37 and 64). The verse continues the reference to the original incident at Gibeah. The nations—plural—now gather against Israel just as the tribes gathered against Benjamin (cf. אסף in Judg 20:11, 14). Then, the tribes fulfilled their obligations under the Israelite covenant, to enforce Yahweh's law. Now the nations, also subject to Yahweh's law, will perform his bidding against the rebels.

Again, as in v 9, the reason for the punishment comes at the end, as a reminder of guilt. The warfare will ensue to put an end to Israel's "double iniquity" (שׁתי עונתם). This phrase could connote the "then and now" aspect of Israel's continuing to sin as at Gibeah, or could simply state metaphorically that Israel's wickedness was extreme. The present text may also represent a corruption of an original expression that Israel will suffer double for her sins (cf. Isa 40:2) on the analogy of the covenant curse, "I will punish you for your sins seven times over" (i.e., curse type 27; Lev 26:18).

11 The poetic portion of the passage (11–14a) begins with picturesque metaphors used to describe Israel's election. In contrast to the "Israel" of vv 9, 10, the term used to denote the Northern Kingdom is now "Ephraim," the term favored in the poetry of Hosea beginning in chap. 5. The metaphorical poem speaks in historical retrospect of Israel's original state. She was like a young cow trained to thresh. This threshing was probably not that of an animal yoked, pulling around a threshing sledge, but the relatively pleasant job (cf. Isa 50:11) of walking around the threshing floor over the harvested stalks until the grain was separated from the ears. The cow could even eat while working (Deut 25:4). So was the condition of Israel in her early years when Yahweh called her (cf. 11:1). But he had a further, more significant purpose in mind—to plow his land. In parallel to "Ephraim would plow" we read "Judah would harrow." The mention of Judah is not as disruptive as might be thought. Throughout Hosea, as in the other eighth-century prophets, the essential unity of the nation is almost always presupposed. Ephraim and Judah are Yahweh's people, not his "peoples."

Together, they were to do his work in his land. Israel had a "good neck" (טוב צוארה)—not a good-looking neck, but a strong neck. It was her master's right to expect faithful service. Her "field" was obedience to the covenant—that was the "yoke" Yahweh placed on her (on על "yoke" as a sovereign's demands on his people, cf. 1 Kgs 12:4–14).

The last phrase in MT, לו יעקב "for himself Jacob," is best revocalized to read "O Jacob" (ליעקב; see n. 11.d), a vocative. The mention of Jacob completes a transition from "Ephraim" alone to "Ephraim and Judah," to "Jacob," a term used uniquely here to indicate the nation as a whole, particularly as it was in its early days. "Jacob" preceded "Israel." The young cow preceded the present Ephraim and Judah who have abused their calling (v 13). In addressing them as "Jacob" he is, almost wistfully, reminding them of the original purpose and call he tendered them. The retrospective depiction of Jacob as a chosen patriarch in chap. 12 is likewise used as a device to contrast the modern, rebellious nation to its faithful ancestor (12:2–6; 12–14).

12 At the close of v 11 direct divine address to Israel, now in the second person plural, began. All the people, collectively and individually, are given a challenge: Israel's election cannot be understood as simply the fulfillment of an agricultural function in Canaan, but rather pleasing Yahweh by living lives faithful to his covenant and therefore upright and unselfish.

In all likelihood, the exhortation of v 12a (the triplet) is prospective and retrospective, a restatement of Yahweh's historical expectations—past and especially future—for Israel. Their response is described in v 13—they did just the opposite of what he asked. Since the invitation is simply quoted as a present imperative, there is no grammatical necessity to assume that the words cite the historic invitation; but in the context of the entire poem, the movement from past election (v 11) to challenge (v 12) to disobedience (v 13) to punishment (v 14) seems clear enough, and this order suggests that the present words of invitation represent the *original* rather than a new exhortation, i.e., a call to eschatological restoration of a status that should have existed all along (cf. Deut 4:31; Lev 26:45).

The triplet asks, via agricultural metaphors related to crop farming, for three qualities to be manifest in "Jacob": "righteousness" (צדקה), "loyalty" (חסד) and "knowledge" (דעת; see n. 12.b). The first two of these terms are preceded by a *lamedh* (ל), which may function virtually as a direct object marker (cf. Gen 1:5; Jer 40:2; 1 Chr 16:37). In other places in the book, other groupings of qualities expected from the covenant are mentioned (e.g., 2:21–22 [19–20]; 4:1; 12:7 [6]). חסד "loyalty" is common to all the groups, as befits its basic meaning of *covenant* loyalty, i.e., obedience to the terms of the revealed contract. The other terms specify what true חסד should produce. "Righteousness" (צדקה) is proper, equitable behavior under the covenant. "Knowledge" (דעת) means in Hosea a right, obedient relationship with Yahweh, including faithful allegiance to him. Had Israel manifested such qualities, the indictment of v 13 and punishments of vv 14–15 would never have needed mention.

The verse ends with a couplet (essentially v 12b) citing the invitation to "seek" (דרש) Yahweh, implying turning to God in times of distress (cf. C. Westermann, *KD* 6 [1960] 2–30) rather than simply routine prayer. The final couplet may then represent a program for rescue *after* the destruction of war has come (cf. דרש in Deut 4:29–31): if the people turn to Yahweh he stands ready to deliver them and restore them to himself. The agricultural metaphor extends even to this promise, given on the analogy of the welcome rain which ends droughts and causes crops to grow. Yahweh promises to water (or "rain upon") his people with "justness" (צדק). Probably this refers to both how he will refresh them (justly) and what he will impart to them (just behavior). The term can even connote "rescue," in that "justness" removes people from unjust situations.

13 The "challenge" of the present is not an invitation but a denunciation.

The triplet (13a) reviews Israel's actual record as compared with its calling. Instead of righteousness, loyalty, and knowledge, Israel has plowed, reaped, and eaten "evil" (רשע), "wickedness" (עולה), and "dishonesty" (כחש). Collectively and individually, these terms are the opposite of the three positive terms in v 12a. "Evil" is the opposite of righteousness. "Wickedness" is the opposite of loyalty, connoting an attitude of rebellion. "Dishonesty" as used in this context refers not to one's social relationships (4:2; 7:3) but to allegiance to Yahweh under the covenant. The original challenge is thus utterly unfulfilled; Israel consistently chose to do what was forbidden.

The couplet (v 13b) introduces overtly the theme of war, which is to be the proximate means of punishment, as the covenant curses predict. Instead of trusting in God Israel has trusted in its military machine. "Chariotry" and "soldiers" suggest military might in general (cf. 1:7b). Chariots were especially feared as weapons of war. Israel had 2000 of them in the days of Ahab (Oppenheim, *ANET*, 287–88), more than any of their neighbors. Even after the defeat of Samaria, Sargon II of Assyria pressed fifty captured Israelite chariots into use in his own army (*ANET*, 284). Israel's trust (בטח), however, was sadly misplaced, and in terms reminiscent of Deut 28:52 ("They will lay siege to your cities . . . until the high fortified walls in which you trust [בטח] fall down . . .") this couplet and its companion in v 14a reveal the utter folly of that misdirected confidence.

14–15 The first couplet (14a) concludes the poetic portion of the passage. The "tumult" (שאון) is the roaring, generally terrifying din of ancient combat (cf. Isa 13:4; Jer 51:55). The battle shout itself (cf. Judg 7:18, 20; 2 Chr 13:15) would constitute part of the noise as well. No city will escape destruction. The thick, high walls surrounding the Israelite cities will not withstand the enemy's onslaught. These walls are described as "fortified" (בצרות) in Deut 28:52; here the cognate term "fortifications" (מבצרים) is employed. These will be "destroyed" (יושד), in keeping with the several predictions of destruction (שד) in Hosea (7:13; 9:6; 10:2; 12:2 [1]), i.e., curse type 24.

The passage then reverts (14a-15) to prose, continuing on the theme of Israel's destruction in war. The second half of v 14 and v 15a together form a complete sentence, which likens the destruction of the North to the destruction of Beth-Arbel. Evidently this event was universally known in Israel, and notorious for its brutality, but no other reference to it or to "Shalman" is known. Partly with G, some scholars have proposed emending the text to read "As Shallum destroyed the house of Jeroboam" (כשד שלם בית ירבעם), yet no violent battle is mentioned in connection with that usurpation (2 Kgs 15:10). Others, notably Astour (*JAOS* 91 [1971] 383–89), suggest reading "Shalmaneser" (I) whose invasion of Israel in the first years of the Jehu dynasty may have provided a fitting symbol of judgment, as that dynasty had since fallen and the nation itself was now in danger of collapse. Yet others suggest reading "Shalmaneser" (V), 727–722 b.c., who perhaps destroyed a "Beth-Arbel" (usually thought to be the site of *Irbid* in Gilead) on his way to destroy Samaria. This identification is possible only if the passage is to be dated in 722, just before the fall of Samaria. Another candidate for "Shalman" is Salmanu (Assyrian "Salamani"), a Moabite king mentioned in a tribute list of Tiglath-Pileser III (Oppenheim, *ANET*, 282; cf. Amos 1:11–2:3), the bashing of mothers and children at Beth-Arbel being something a Moabite king would be remembered for. The point of the statement is at any rate clear: in the manner of battles fought to exterminate a population (2 Kgs 8:12; Isa 13:16; Nah 3:10; Ps 137:9; cf. Hos 13:16), Israel itself would experience numbing brutality. Thus would be fulfilled in part the predictions in the covenant itself of the horrors of the war Yahweh would use to punish his rebellious people (see esp. Deut 32:25; 28:34, 53–57; Lev 26:37).

This kind of calamity will come to Israel itself. Lev 26:33 predicts: "Your land will be laid waste and your cities will lie in ruins." Now Yahweh announces directly to the "house," or family (בית) of Israel, that because their evil is so great, they must reap what they have sown (cf. vv 12–13) as the covenant demands. They will receive the Beth-Arbel treatment, as it were. The king himself, as leader of the family of Israel, will suffer annihilation. It will not be only women and children or some particular class who will be brutalized. The OT prophets, in connection with the notion of the "day of Yahweh," follow the ancient pattern of expression that a great sovereign's wars are over in a day (Stuart, *BASOR* 221 [1976] 159–64). Here Yahweh announces that Israel's king—the key prize in the war of conquest—will be taken captive and deposed ("silenced for good," נדמה נדמה) right away, at dawn (בשחר) on that day of conquest. In point of fact, this seemingly hyperbolic statement was conservative. King Hoshea was captured and imprisoned by the Assyrians under Shalmaneser V even before the siege of Samaria got underway (2 Kgs 17:4).

Explanation

In Gal 5 Paul contrasts the fruit of the spiritual life (vv 22–23) with the behavior that is produced by a sinful nature (vv 19–21). To the former he encourages conformity. Of the latter he warns that such behavior characteristically leads to exclusion from God's kingdom. This new covenant challenge parallels remarkably Israel's challenge under the old covenant. God set forth an expectation. In the allegory of the central poetic section of the passage, that expectation entailed the service of the young cow Israel in doing the labor which under Yahweh's guidance ("yoke") would yield the fruit of obedience. Israel chose, however, the "acts of the sinful nature" (Gal 5:19). Israel's behavior broke the covenant and set into motion its curse provisions, the most prominent of which was destruction in war.

War is the dominant warning of the passage: nations massing to attack (v 10); the destruction of fortifications (v 14a); brutal killing (v 14b); the silencing of the king (v 15), etc. Tragically, however, Hosea's audience in the 720s was apparently still complacent, presuming that their king and military would somehow stand against the Assyrians they had been powerless to resist a few years earlier. Perhaps the death of Tiglath-Pileser III in 728 B.C. had emboldened them. Through Hosea, God assured them otherwise. Just as Israel suffered in the covenant war after the incident at Gibeah—in the days of the Judges (v 9), so they would now have a "new" Gibeah—their own total defeat. Divine action and the brutal Assyrian military conquest were in this case one and the same.

Paul's list of deeds produced by the sinful nature (Gal 5:19–21) is rather lengthy. Immorality may take a great many forms. Note, by way of comparison, how many terms to evidence Israel's evil behavior are used in the present passage: "sin," "wicked ones" (v 9); "double iniquity" (v 10); "evil," "wickedness," "dishonesty" (v 13); "evil . . . evil" (v 15). Finding enough English terms to translate the Hebrew words is not easy. The inference is evident: Israel has run the gamut of sins. The original challenge to right behavior has been reversed into a consistent misbehavior. The fate of Beth-Arbel must now become the fate of Beth-Israel.

Israel in and out of Egypt   (11:1–11)

Bibliography

Bartina, S. "Y desde Egipto lo he proclamado hijo mio." *EstBib* 22 (1970) 157–60. **Bjornard, R. B.** "Hosea 11:8–9, God's Word or Man's Insight?" *BR* 27 (1982) 16–25. **Bruggemann, W.** "A Shape for OT Theology II: Embrace of Pain." *CBQ* 47 (1985) 395–415. **Bussche, H. van den.** "Ballade der miskende liefde (Os 11)." *Collationes Brugenses et Gandavenses* 4 (1958) 434–66. ———. "La ballade de l'amour méconnu: Commentaire d'Osee 11:1–10." *BVC* 41 (1961) 18–34. **Driver, G. R.** "Problems of the Hebrew Text and Language." In *Alttestamentliche Studien: FS F. Nötscher,* ed. H. Junker and J. Botterweck. Bonn: P. Hanstein Verlag, 1950. 46–61. **Glanzman, G. S.** "Two Notes: Amos 3,15 and Osee 11,8–9." *CBQ* 23 (1961) 227–33. **Goldman, M.D.** "The Real Interpretation of Os 11,3." *AusBR* 4 (1954–55) 91–92. **Gross, H.** "Das Hohelied der Liebe Gottes: Zur Theologie von Hosea 11." In *Mysterium der Gnade: FS J. Auer,* ed. H. Rossman et al. Regensburg: Pustet, 1975. 83–91. **Hirschberg, H.** "Some Additional Arabic Etymologies in Old Testament Lexicography." *VT* 11 (1961) 373–85. **Israel, F.** "Una varieta di gazzella menzionata in Osea 11,8." *BeO* 18 (1976) 61–64. **Janzen, J. G.** "Metaphor and Reality in Hosea 11." *SBL 1976 Seminar Papers,* ed. G. MacRae. Missoula, MT: Scholars Press, 1976. 413–45. **Kraus, H.-J.** "Hosea 11:1–9." *Göttinger Predigtmeditationen* (1952–53) 33–38. **Lindars, B.** "Rachel Weeping for Her Children—Jeremiah 31:15–22." *JSOT* 12 (1979) 47–62. **Lods, A.** "Une tablette inédite de Mari, intéressante pour l'histoire ancienne du prophétisme sémitique." In *Studies in Old Testament Prophecy,* ed. H. H. Rowley. Edinburgh: T. and T. Clark, 1950. **Lohfink, N.** "Hos xi 5 als Bezugtext von Dtn. xvii 16." *VT* 31 (1981) 226–28. **Long, B. O.** "The Divine Funeral Lament." *JBL* 85 (1966) 85–86. **Mays, J. L.** "Response to Janzen, 'Metaphor and Reality in Hosea 11.'" *Semeia* 24 (1982) 45–51. **McKenzie, J. L.** "Divine Passion in Osee." *CBQ* 17 (1955) 287–99. **Rabin, Ch.** "Hebrew *baddîm,* 'power.'" *JSS* 18 (1973) 57–58. **Ritschl, D.** "God's Conversation: An Exposition of Hosea 11." *Int* 15 (1961) 286–303. **Schüngel-Straumann, H.** "Gott als Mutter in Hosea 11." *TQ* 166 (1986) 119–34. **Soggin, J. A.** "Hosea 11,5 (cf. 10,9b?): Emphatic *Lamed?*" *Old Testament and Oriental Studies.* BibOr 29. Rome: Pontifical Biblical Institute, 1975. 223. **Sprye, T.** "*tybwt*' (Syriac)—מֹשַׁבָה." *VT* 7 (1957) 408–10. **Zenger, E.** "'Durch Menschen zog ich sie . . .' (Hos 11, 4); Beobachtungen zum Verstandnis des prophetischen Amtes im Hoseabuch." In *Künder des Wortes: FS T. Schreiner,* ed. L. Ruppert et al. Württemberg: Echter, 1982. 183–201.

Translation

The Past

11:1 *When Israel was a child*[a] *I loved him;*
Out of Egypt I called my son.[b]

² *When* [a] *I had called them,*
then they left me. [b]

They sacrified to the Baals,
they burned offerings to the idols.

³ *I was the one who taught* [a] *Ephraim to walk,*
taking them by the arms [b];
but they were not aware that I restored them to health.

⁴ *I used to pull them with human* [a] *cords,*
with ropes of love.

I was to them like one [b] *who lifted*
the yoke [c] *from off* [d] *their jaws,*
And I reached out to him [e] *and fed* ⁵ *him.* [a]

The immediate future and the present

He will return [b] *to the land* [c] *of Egypt,*
Assyria will be [d] *his king,*
because they refuse to return. [e]

⁶ *The sword will be loosed* [a] *in his cities,*
and will consume his false prophets,
and devour them because of their counsels.

⁷ *My people are stubborn* [a] *in turning away from me* [b];
It is Baal [c] *on whom they call,*
All together they exalt him. [d]

The eschatological future

⁸ *How can I give you up,* [a] *Ephraim?*
hand you over, Israel?

How can I give you up [a] *like Admah,*
treat you like Zeboim?

I have had a change of mind;
I am altogether moved by a change of heart.

⁹ *I will not carry out my fierce anger,*
I will not again destroy Ephraim.

For I am God and not a man in your midst, [a]
the Holy One, and I will not come in wrath. [b]

¹⁰ *They will go after Yahweh.*
He will roar like a lion;

When he will roar,
the children will hurry [a] *from the sea;* [b]

¹¹ *They will hurry like a bird from Egypt,*
and like a dove from the land of Assyria,
and I will return [a] *them to their homes.*
               —Oracle of Yahweh

Notes

1.a. Or "lad," "boy," "young man."

1.b. G (τὰ τέκνα αὐτοῦ) reads בניו "his sons," probably a harmonization already in the Heb. *Vorlage* to connect the sg "Israel" with the pls in vv 2–7.

2.a. Reading כ)קראי("when I had called" on the basis of G (καθὼς μετεκάλεσα) and Syr.

2.b. MT מפניהם "from them" must be divided into מפני "from me" and הם "they."

3.a. תרלתי is an unusual form (a "tiphel"?) but obviously is equivalent to הרגלתי, the normal hiph of רגל.

3.b. Or, MT זרועתיו may be the result of זרועתי "my arms" and the ו "but" of the following line, written again accidentally. If so, a translation such as "and I held them in my arms" would be conceivable.

4.a. On the possibility that אדם here means "leather" see Hirschberg, *VT* 11 (1961) 373–85; cf. P. Saydon, "The Maltese Translation of the Bible," *Melita Theologica* 16 (1965) 4.

4.b. Reading כְּמָרִימֵי (sg) instead of MT; see Kuhnigk, *NSH*, 126, 133.

4.c. The frequently proposed emendation of על "yoke" to עֻל "infant" is hardly advisable. See *Comment*.

4.d. On this meaning of על, for which there is ample evidence, see Kuhnigk, *NSH*, 133.

4.e. It is not impossible that MT ואט represents a contraction of ואעט "and I clothed (him)."

5.a. Revocalizing (with G) לו "him" for MT לא.

5.b. G incorrectly vocalized יָשֻׁב (κατῴκησεν) as in 9:3. G obviously had a text whose orthography was *defectivo* rather than *plene* in this case.

5.c. Instead of אל־ארץ "to the land of," G inexplicably reads אפרים "Ephraim."

5.d. The transitional הוא can function predicatively in the future tense as well as in the present or past tenses.

5.e. Or, "repent."

6.a. The most likely vocalization is וְחִלָּה from חלל "to let loose" (cf. Kuhnigk, *NSH*, 134–35). Also possible is חִלָּה (piel) "wound," as in Deut 29:21.

7.a. Here vocalize *tillā'-ū-m* תִלְאֻם (from לאי / לאו "to be strong / solid" etc.); Kuhnigk, *NSH*, 134–45.

7.b. G reads "him," i.e., the 3 masc sg suffix rather than "me," probably from a dittographic conjoining of the ו from the next word.

7.c. Emending על "yoke" to ב)על("Baal" in light of the specific mention of Baal worship in v 2.

7.d. Vocalizing לו "him" for MT לא "not."

8.a. Or "How gladly I will give you up," etc. (cf. Glanzman, *CBQ* 23 [1961] 227–33).

9.a. Note that "in your midst" (בקרבך) belongs here and not in the next line.

9.b. Or, the same words can be translated "I will not come against any city."

10.a. The common translation "come trembling" for חרד may be inappropriate in such a context. The basic sense of חרד is to "jump" or "shake," which can then apply to either fearful trembling, or, as here, quick movement.

10.b. Or, "west."

11.a. Vocalize וַהֲשִׁיבוֹתִים with G. MT ("I will cause them to live," from ישב) is not impossible, however.

Form / Structure / Setting

The passage at its outset has similarities to the form of the legal complaint made by parents against a rebellious child (Deut 21:18–21; cf. Isa 1:2–20 where hope is held out that the child [Israel] may yet repent and receive compassion rather than death). Though Hos 11:1–11 is less obviously structured as a legal complaint than the Isaiah oracle, "historical-theological accusation" (so Wolff, 193) is a possible designation for it. It contains a statement (as if to the court) of evidence about the child's rebellion in the face of loving care, a sentence of judgment, but then a surprise (vv 8–11): the plaintiff

Yahweh, addressing the defendant Israel, changes his mind (v 8) and decides not to destroy Israel utterly (the punishment for a rebellious child in Deut 21 is death) but to restore him. This surprise verdict parallels that of 2:16–17 [14–15]. Complaint yields to punishment, then to hope.

The passage is entirely divine speech, including, probably, v 10, which refers to Yahweh in the third person. God who refers metaphorically to himself as "pus" and "infection" (5:12) would hardly avoid comparing himself in first-person speech to a lion. Israel is referred to in the third person singular (vv 1, 4, 5, 6), the third person plural (vv 2–5, 7, 10, 11), and the second person singular (vv 8, 9). The variation of the persons and their pronouns is somewhat unpredictable, but by no means illogical or confusing. To Hosea's audience it would have been accepted as typical. The suggestion that v 10 is a late Judean gloss is obviated by the fact that nothing in it specifically addresses Judean interests.

Chap. 11 appears to be a distinct entity. Like 10:9–15 it contains a historical reflection on Israel's past and changes to direct address later in the passage. But otherwise it shows no sign of being directly connected. A new passage begins with 12:1 [11:12], where Ephraim/Israel/Judah are the subjects, and the new theme (trickery, lies, violence, etc.) does not follow closely chap. 11.

The passage changes somewhat at v. 8. Here Ephraim (paralleled by Israel) is addressed directly as the dominant subject as opposed to "Israel" in v 1 and "Ephraim" in v 3, each spoken of in the third person. The spirit of the passage shifts to hope and a promise of restoration. This follows the basic pattern expressed in the Mosaic covenant (blessing and restoration following destruction and exile; cf. Lev 26:38–45, et al.). The passage's logic presents to us a loving God who reaches out to a child in mercy. For Yahweh to show his mercy once again by bringing his "children" back from exile is simply a turn full circle to a new benefaction, as was the theme of 2:4–17 [2–15], 18–25 [16–23] and chap. 3. Moreover, if a sense of the court proceeding is to be understood throughout, the decision to show mercy as expressed in vv 8–11 is not so much a contradiction as a development. The plaintiff may choose not to exercise his right to demand utter destruction of the rebel(s), and the judge (also Yahweh, of course) may partially suspend the capital aspect of the punishment sentence in keeping with the covenant promises of restoration for a remnant (e.g., Deut 4:27).

In structure, the passage shifts from past to present to immediate future, to eschatological future, as follows:

A. Past: God's calling and Israel's rebellion (vv 1–4)
B. Present and future: immediate threat to Israel for their continuing rebellion (vv 5–7). [Note that in each of these verses Israel's current attitude and future punishment are described.]
C. Eschatological future: refusal to destroy utterly, and promise of restoration (vv 8–11).

There are other, more subtle patterns within the passage. For example, v 1, which speaks of Israel in the third person singular as Yahweh's son, and v 4b ("And I reached out to him and fed him"), which does the same, may be considered to form a sort of inclusio around the intervening material (vv 2–4a) in which Israel is "they" or "them." Moreover, certain key words tend to reappear in contrasting usages: "call" (קרא; twice in vv 1–2, of Yahweh's call to the people, once in v 7 of the people's calling upon Baal); the repetition of יחד as "all together" and "altogether" in vv 7, 8; the verb שוב "return" in vv 5, 7, 11 used in a different form and sense in each case; אכל "eat/ devour" in v 4 of Yahweh's feeding the child Israel and in v 6 of the sword devouring the false prophets; the rescue from Egypt originally (v 1) and eschatologically (v 11); the beloved child (בן, v 1) and the forgiven, rebellious "children" (בנים; v 10), etc. Such catchwords tend to demonstrate the unity of the passage at least on the level of its vocabulary.

This oracle, like those after 9:9, may be dated near the end of Hoshea's reign, i.e., around 727–723 B.C. The Baal cult continues to flourish (v 7) but its end seems near (v 6). Hoshea incurred the wrath of Shalmaneser V (727–722) by cutting off tribute payments to Assyria and seeking an alliance of some sort with Egypt (2 Kgs 17:4). Assyria then became the implacable enemy of Israel, and it could only be a matter of time before the wrath of God, through Assyria, struck in war (vv 5–6). It cannot be inferred from v 11 ("they will hurry from Egypt . . .") that there are already refugees in Egypt in anticipation of an Assyrian conquest. The language of return to bondage in "Egypt" is stereotyped covenant terminology (e.g., Deut 28:68; cf. Hos 7:16); the real place of exile will be Assyria, which in its position in the "B" lines of the parallelisms in vv 5 and 11 is actually an explication of the typological term "Egypt."

Comment

1 Again, in retrospective language God describes his people in terms of their origins (cf. 9:10; 10:1; 10:9, 11). Here, the allegory chosen to convey this mood is close to the heart: Israel is a son.

The concept of Yahweh as a father is well attested elsewhere in the OT, e.g., Deuteronomy (14:1; 32:6), Isaiah (1:2–20; 3:9), and Jeremiah (3:19, 22; 4:22; 31:9, 20). Though in ancient texts kings are often referred to as the children of the gods (e.g., Azitawaddu of Karatepe: see Rosenthal, *ANET* Sup, 218; and Zimrilim of Mari: see A. Lods, *Studies*) and the Davidic king is possibly called "son" in Ps 2:7 (the text is in question), these appellations hardly provide meaningful parallels for the biblical metaphor of Israel as a son. Yahweh's words in Hos 11:1 are best understood in light of Exod 4:22–23, the commission from Yahweh to Moses at the very beginning of his journey to Egypt to lead the exodus: "Israel is my firstborn son . . . Let my son go. . . ." Hosea and Exodus both link the adoption of Israel to sonship with the liberation from Egypt, the emphasis being placed on the very first encounter of Yahweh with his infant nation. Other references to early Israel from the surrounding context (9:10; 10:1, etc.) presupposed this earliest encounter, but did not mention it directly. The distant past functions now again as a point of comparison with the present (cf. 2:14–15 [16–17] and even the future (vv 8–11).

Israel is called a נער ("child," "young man," "lad," etc.) whom Yahweh "loved" (ואהבהו). The use of אהב is closely connected with covenantal fidelity in Deuteronomy (6:5; 7:8, 13; 10:15; 23:6 [5]), and it is virtually a double-entendre in its employment here. It means to have deep affection for, but also to be "loyal to," as in the Amarna letters where "love" is proclaimed for the Pharaoh by his vassal kings and vice versa (e.g., the letters of Tušratta to Amenophis III). Hosea's covenantal concerns and use of language similar to Deuteronomy make it probable that אהב in v 1 carries this sense as well.

Yahweh says that he called his son out of Egypt. "Call" (קרא) is used in a variety of senses in the OT, as in modern English. Here the emphasis is only partly upon "election" / "adoption." The context suggests that "summon" or "gather" is also intended, and the statement must be seen in the light of divine guidance and protection. It is in this latter sense that v 1a functions as a Messianic prophecy. A second special exodus from Egypt, that of the child Jesus after the death of Herod (Matt 2:15), comports precisely with the wording Hosea was inspired to use, and which therefore does double-duty. It has its own meaning in Hos 11:1, in a context which does not concern itself with the Messiah. It has as well a *sensus plenior,* deriving from the double potential of the specific wording chosen. Events in Jesus' life thus *fulfill* (i.e., complete the potential meanings of) the wording of v 1b, while not constituting its sole referent.

2 The essence of Israel's rebellion is expressed here in two ways: (a) they refused to respond to Yahweh's call (both election and guidance); (b) they showed this refusal by worshiping the Baals and other false gods specifically forbidden to them in the law. Thus Israel committed sins both of omission and commission. Leaving undone what they should have done, and doing what they should not, Israel showed themselves incorrigibly rebellious (cf. Deut 21:18).

V 2 thus contrasts sharply with v 1. Yahweh mercifully loved his son Israel and helped him leave Egypt. Israel responds by rebellion. There is no corresponding attitude or action on Israel's part to the attitude and action of his loving father Yahweh. In the metaphor of a NT story, the son has, as it were, left home and spent his fortune on riotous living with the Baals (cf. Luke 15:13). (On the identification of the "Baals," the various manifestations of Baal, see *Comment* on 2:15 [13], 18 [16]). Israel "chose new gods" (cf. Josh 24:15; Judg 5:8), thereby breaking the most basic rule of the covenant, "You will have no other gods besides me" (Exod 20:3). They violated the covenant in making "idols" (פסלים) of these gods (cf. Exod 20:23; 34:17) and in sacrificing (זבח, קטר) to them (cf. Exod 22:20). Could the case against Israel as a rebellious child be any more damning?

3 The fault was in no way Yahweh's. Using the image of the tender, patient parent training a child to walk, he proclaims his own innocence. There is both irony and pathos in these words. He had held little Ephraim's hands as Ephraim took his first hesitant steps, and cared for him when he was sick ("restored them to health," רפאתים; cf. 5:13; 6:1; 7:1 and especially Exod 15:26). Yet Ephraim did not even acknowledge this compassionate attention (לא ידעו). The one who tenderly cared for and raised the child may be guiltless before the law if the child is incorrigible (Deut 21:21), but still hurt by the child's rejection. Israel could not see that Yahweh had been the key to their well-being as he "taught them to walk" (תרגל) through their history, holding them by the hand. Upon reaching adolescence, they showed themselves to be ingrates, unconcerned to fulfill their calling to sonship. Though he had guided them out of Egypt and through the wilderness (Num 9:18, "At Yahweh's command the Israelites set out, and at his command they encamped"; cf. Exod 40:36–38), faithfully healing their afflictions (Exod 15:26, "I am Yahweh who heals you"), his loving care had gone for nought.

4 The text of v 4 is corrupt, but its gist is discernible. While most of the verse seems to shift to the metaphor of the unyoked beast of burden, the final line (including the first word of v 5) may revert to the sonship metaphor of the first three verses. This impression depends mostly on the singular pronouns referring to Ephraim. If they were plural ("I reached out to them and fed them") this line, too, would universally be accepted as continuing the animal metaphor. In light of the many shifts of person, number, and gender that are noted throughout the book in its many and varied metaphorical descriptions of Israel (and Yahweh), the most likely interpretation is that the entire verse does represent a metaphorical shift, in which Yahweh's love for Israel is paralleled now to concern for a dependent beast rather than for a dependent child. He leads the animal gently, with "human" (אדם) cords and ropes of love (אהבה) just as he taught the child to walk, taking him by the arms. He makes the animal more comfortable by graciously removing the yoke, just as he eased the child's misery by healing him.

This imagery illustrates further the beneficence of God toward Israel in the exodus and in the wilderness. The yoke (על) is the symbol of oppression and / or servitude in the covenant vocabulary (Lev 26:13; Deut 28:48; cf. 1 Kgs 12:4–14). Israel's rescue from the house of bondage is like the lifting of the yoke from (or "over" depending on how one translates על) the jaw of an animal. The reference to reaching out and feeding the animal probably symbolizes the constant presence of Yahweh with Israel, and his feeding them, even miraculously, as in Exod 16:4–35 and Num 11:4–34. The verse, in sum, is a masterful illustration of divine grace and condescension.

5 Suddenly the extended metaphors of past history stop, and Hosea's audience hears their coming punishment. The blunt historical reality of exile and servitude is brought home to them. Israel will return (שוב) to Egypt. This reflects the covenantal curse language (e.g., Deut 28:68) in which "Egypt" stands as a metonymy for the land of the conquering enemy (cf. 7:13; 8:16; 9:3, 6) and return thereto is the beginning of exile and a reentrance into bondage (i.e., curse type 13). In the second line of the triplet that comprises v 5, "Assyria" is specified as the nation who will dominate the captured and exiled Israelites. The parallelism of Egypt and Assyria is thus a true synonymous parallelism in which the second line is more "prosaically" precise than the first (cf. Deut 32:18 as compared to Deut 32:15b). Assyria is called here Israel's (future) מלך "king." Though tersely worded, this surely implies the end of the kingship and national sovereignty in Israel (cf. 3:4; 7:7; 10:3, 7, 15; 13:11). The king of Assyria was called obliquely the "great king" (מלכי־רב) in 5:13 and 10:6; now the Assyrian nation itself is identified as Israel's coming king. In contrast to the days when Israel was cared for tenderly by their father / master, the coming days will bring the fulfillment of his promised wrath. Their flagrant apostasy (v 2) is summarized in a reference to their stubbornness: "They refuse to return" (מאנו לשוב) not to "Egypt," about which they will have no choice, but to Yahweh, from whom they have apostasized (cf. 3:5; 5:4; 6:1; 7:10; 12:7 [6]; 14:2 [1], 3 [2]). That is the irony of the covenant curse in Deut 28:68 upon which this verse is partly based. What Yahweh rescued his people from (slavery), he will return them to, because of their disloyalty to his covenant. For the third time in the passage (cf. v 2, v 3b) we read a description of how Yahweh's love (also expressed three times, in vv 1, 3, 4 respectively) is spurned. This time, that love has reached its limits (cf. 1:6).

6 The Israelites will become subject to Assyria by being conquered in a bloody war. The three lines of the triplet make three statements. First, warfare (the "sword," חרב) will occur in the various cities. In times of war, people gathered from the countryside into the cities which were surrounded by high, thick walls topped with fortified battle stations (cf. 10:14). For Yahweh to announce through Hosea that the battle would reach to the inside of the cities was a way of saying that the Assyrians would breach the Israelite fortifications, enter the cities, and kill their inhabitants (curse type 3). The "sword" (חרב) is identified most often as the means of destruction for covenant infidelity (Lev 26:25, 33, 36, 37; Deut 28:22; 32:24, 41, 42). Note that the enemy's sword, as it inflicts punishment on the rebels, becomes in effect Yahweh's sword (Deut 32:41; cf. 33:29). (On "city" as a major term in the curse contexts, cf. Lev 26:25, 31, 33; Deut 28:52, 55, 57; cf. 32:25.)

The second line singles out the false prophets (here בד V, as in Isa 44:25 and Jer 50:36) for destruction. The sword will "consume" them (כלה piel; cf. Lev 26:44; Deut 28:21; Josh 24:20). The third line is partly synonymous ("devour," אכל: cf. Lev 26:38; Deut 31:17; 32:22; esp. Deut 32:42, "my sword devours flesh") and partly "synthetic" ("because of their counsels"). Such counsels (מעצות) were probably of two natures. The false prophets were essentially diviners and predicters who foresaw good things for Israel instead of the destruction that was in fact at hand (cf. Jer 6:14; 11:8; 1 Kgs 22:1–28; J. P. Sisson, "Jeremiah and the Jerusalem Conception of Peace," *JBL* 105 [1986] 429–42). Their words in these days undoubtedly contrasted sharply with those of Hosea. In addition, it is quite possible that Hoshea's naïve foreign policy, which incurred the wrath of Shalmaneser V, was supported in part by divination from the בדים "false prophets." More significantly, however, they gave leadership to Israel's apostasy, encouraging the nation by favorable predictions and by heterodox religious indoctrination so that there was no sense of urgency to abandon Baalism, idolatry, multiple shrines, and other covenant violations. Therefore, when the sword comes, they must be killed.

7 Our reconstruction of the text understands the verse to bring to a conclusion the protestation of Yahweh against his obstreperous people, though it is possible that it should be considered the third and final summary of Israel's unfaithfulness (with v 2 and v 3). It restates the utter infidelity of the nation, and their unified (יחד "all together") apostasy from Yahweh in favor of Baal.

With few alterations to the MT text (and / or revocalizations), however, one could read the words of the verse in the following way:

> Then my people will tire of turning away from me;
> and on the Most High they will call;
> all together they will surely exalt him.

The sense which results from this construction is different: the verse becomes a transition toward the expectation of renewal to the covenant (see below, vv 8–11). It envisons a time when the Israelites, weary of their suffering under Assyria, will once again turn to Yahweh and seek his lordship. Given the present state of the text it cannot be determined which of these options is correct.

8 A sudden shift provides hope for Israel. *After* Israel's full punishment for disloyalty has taken place (through Assyria's conquest and exile of Israel), Yahweh will restore his people. This follows the pattern of events predicted in Deut 4:25–31.

In exile, Israel will turn back to Yahweh. On the basis of this repentance, Yahweh will restore the nation: "Yahweh your God is a merciful God. He will not abandon or destroy you, or forget the covenant with your forefathers, which he confirmed to them by oath" (v 31). Hos 11:8–11 poetically renews this promise. As a nation in the land of Canaan, Israel was finished. But in terms of God's plans for the world, his people's history had just entered its second stage. The sayings which follow must be understood in this light.

As Kuhnigk (*NSH,* 139) has shown, v 8a, the interrogative quatrain, is cast in perfectly balanced 7:7, 7:7 meter. The plaintiff, instead of demanding that the rebellious child be punished by death, has decided instead to limit its punishment. He could never finally "give up" (נתן) or "hand over" (מגן) Ephraim/Israel. He will not do to his own people what he did to Admah and Zeboim. These cities were obliterated along with Sodom and Gomorrah (Gen 10:19; 14:2–8) in a sudden destruction of divine wrath. The covenant curses mention these four cities (Deut 29:23; curse type 23) as paradigms for what could happen to Israel if it disobeyed the covenant. Israel's destruction would leave behind only waste as a reminder of what happens to nations who defy God.

But now God says that he will not take his punishment to such an extreme. Why? His heart ("mind," לב) has changed, and his "change of heart" (נחומים) moves him to mercy. Here again (v 8b) the second line of the couplet explicates the first line. Yahweh's change of mind (the idiom is virtually identical to the English idiom) is a product not of whim or circumstance, but of his eternally consistent nature. He is a compassionate God whose basic desire toward his people is to win them back to himself (2:3 [1], 16–17 [14–15]; cf. 1 Kgs 18:37).

9 Though Yahweh has every right under the covenant to eliminate Israel from the earth, as the fourfold use of לא "not" in the verse indicates, he will not. He would be justified in carrying out his "fierce anger" (חרון אפי), "destroying" (שחת) Ephraim and coming at them "in wrath" (בעיר). These three phrases describe Israel's potential ultimate judgment, a combination of types 1 (rejection) and 24 (destruction). Yahweh now announces that he will restore Israel because his character includes grace. He is not one of the Israelites ("a man in your midst") whose emotions might reflect arbitrary passions and whose wrath might be vindictive rather than equitable. He is

God, the Holy One (קדוש). To be "holy" (קדש) is to be set apart from typical human things so as to reflect Godlikeness. Of course, God himself is the essence of Godlikeness. From a human point of view, however, his holiness embodies all that makes him different from humans, and especially the qualities that elevate his thinking and moral behavior above their usually petty standards.

From a historical perspective, the second line of the first couplet is crucial. "I will not *again* (לא אשוב) destroy Ephraim" makes no sense if the change of heart applies to the destruction of the nation in 722 B.C. by Assyria (cf. Wolff's [202] unsuccessful attempts to interpret שוב without understanding that the context is eschatological). Indeed, the very term "fierce anger" (חרון אפי) was used in 8:5 to express Yahweh's wrath against Samaria, culminating in its overthrow by Assyria. Once divine wrath has struck, Yahweh will thereafter begin the process of renewing his people. They need never fear that he will repeat the punishment (cf. Gen 8:21; Isa 40:2). Those who will survive that catastrophe may look forward to a time of deliverance. Such a hope is part of the expectation of the covenant itself (Deut 4:29–31; 32:43; cf. Hos 6:1–3) and of the preexilic prophets. This is not a promise of mercy for those alive in Hosea's day, but for their descendants, the remnant that will follow. To righteous followers of the covenant, those who heeded Hosea's message, it would nevertheless be a source of great encouragement.

10 One day, Israel will return to Yahweh and then be able to return from exile. Their punishment will end, as promised through Moses. The message of v 10 is that Yahweh himself will announce this return, upon their conversion. In Hosea 5:14 and 13:7 the terms שחל and כפיר are used to portray Yahweh as a "lion"; here אריה, the great maned African lion, is used, as elsewhere in the Prophets, to carry a more positive connotation. The roaring (שאג) of Yahweh like a lion (Amos 1:2; 3:8; Joel 4:16 [3:16]; Jer 25:30) seems to function as a symbolic representation of his calling people to hear his judgment. When the great lion Yahweh will roar, no one will fail to hear, and the restoration of Israel will be at hand (cf. Joel 4:16 [3:16]). Here that roaring is emphasized by the repetition of the verb (ישאג). Hosea's audience presumably understood this cliché as a signal of the new age for Israel (cf. 2:18–25 [16–23]; 3:5). But the restoration promised here will apply to reconverted Israelites only (cf. Deut 4:29). Thus first the condition is stated: "After Yahweh they shall go." The new Israel will be characterized by righteous behavior and true faith (cf. Zeph 3:12–13).

These "children" (בנים) will receive the blessing which could not be given to the obstreperous "child" (בן) of vv 1–3. They will "hurry" (חרד; not "tremble"; see n. 10.a) from the "sea" or "west" (ים). This formulation implies that the exile will be extensive, and that the eschatological roar of return will be heard by people in a variety of locations including the "sea" (cf. "distant coasts of the sea," Isa 11:1).

11 Israel will hurry home. Much of the language of v 11 reflects vocabulary already employed in the book (חרד "to hurry," in the verse above; יונה "dove" in 7:11; the pairing of Egypt and Assyria in 7:11; 8:8–9; 9:3; the verb שוב "to return," *passim*), yet the promise in the verse is nevertheless electrifying. The "bird" (צפור) and "dove" (יונה) are here employed not as animals that "tremble" or animals that "follow" but as "A" and "B" words respectively for animals that can fly, i.e., move swiftly. When the return commences, nothing can stop it. The faithful will "fly" back, not merely to the land as sojourners or the like, but to their "homes," an indication of true resettling in possession of original inheritances. Throughout Israel's history, residence in the land was a central blessing of their covenant with Yahweh (cf. 2:18 [16], 20 [18]). Now would be fulfilled the promise of 2:25 [23], "I will plant her for myself in the land." The covenant restoration blessing of return from exile and repossession of the land (type 7) will come to pass for Israel.

Explanation

Chap. 11 reveals God's profound love for Israel as strongly as any passage in the book. Yahweh tells of his love for the "child" Israel, the child's rebellion against him, and the punishment that must inevitably follow. But the punishment will not be mortal. The second half of the chapter reveals God's love in an especially passionate way. He will not do that which according to legalistic human logic he ought—annihilate Israel. Rather he will make provision for their return from exile, their resettlement in peace after punishment. Though the metaphor of Israel as the rebellious child does not dominate the chapter, occurring overtly only in vv 1–6, it provides the entire passage with the flavor of a legal proceeding. Thus the accusation against the child and protestation of the parent's innocence (vv 1–4, 7) is followed by the severe though limited punishment (vv 5–6) and then by a "change of heart" on the part of the plaintiff who not only declines to press the charges to their legal punishment limit, but determines to bring the child back home. Three times the sins of the nation are described and three times the loving care and upbringing of the father are contrasted to them, even before the announcement of return from exile completes the picture of divine mercy.

The concept of return expressed by the verb שוב is a central thematic element. The verb is used in four ways. The return to Egypt as punishment is expressed in v 5a. Then, Israel's refusal to return to Yahweh (v 5b) is described. Third, Israel's turning away from Yahweh in apostasy (משובה) is mentioned (v 7). Fourth is Yahweh's returning the Israelites to their homes (v 11). Added to this is the general concept of the return from Egypt/Assyria, though in this latter connection the emphasis upon haste occasions the use twice of חרד "to hurry."

The passage throughout contrasts Yahweh's sovereign holiness, and the grace it allows him to exercise, with Ephraim's stubborn rebellion and selfishness. Yahweh is free to be "himself"—to exercise his own eternally consistent motives of compassion and protection, and to spare Israel rather than obliterate them. They deserve the fate of Admah and Zeboim (v 8), but will instead be able to turn to Yahweh in exile, and be brought home to resettle the promised land (vv 10–11). This is because Yahweh is not a human, but God; not a sinful Israelite, but the Holy One. His ways are above their ways. He will rescue them in spite of themselves.

The promise of Deut 4:30 (and parallels in Lev 26 and Deut 30) that

Yahweh "cannot forget the covenant" is two-sided. The covenant is restorable, but only on the grounds of the fidelity of both parties. When Israel once again fulfills its obligations, the covenant and its blessings may be quickly renewed. The joint return of Israel's remnant began in a literal sense during the Persian regime under Cyrus (539 B.C.). In the broader sense Israel's real restoration began only in Christ, the author and finisher of the new covenant.

Thus in 11:11 the New Testament evangelist Matthew is inspired to recognize an adumbration of the return of God's son Jesus in his early youth from Egypt (Matt 2:15; see *Comment*). God's full, complete plan for Israel was not revealed even in the remarkably sweeping predictions of Deut 4:20–31. It could be finally understood, in its most complete sense, only in the life and work of the Messiah. The passage is a story of how divine disappointment is overcome by divine determination to restore a people to faith. Jesus the Christ accomplished this.

Israel a Deceiver   *(12:1 [11:12]–13:1)*

Bibliography

Abrahamson, S. "The Historical Dictionary." *Leš* 42 (1977) 9–16 [Heb.] **Ackroyd, P. R.** "Hosea and Jacob." *VT* 13 (1963) 245–59. **Bentzen, A.** "The Weeping of Jacob, Hos 12:5a." *VT* 1 (1951) 58–59. **Coote, R. B.** "Hosea xii." *VT* 21 (1971) 389–402. **Cornill, D.** "Hosea 12:1." *ZAW* 7 (1887) 285–89. **Dahood, M.** "Hebrew-Ugaritic Lexicography IX." *Bib* 52 (1971) 337–56; X: *Bib* 53 (1972) 386–403; XI: *Bib* 54 (1973) 351–66. ———. *Ugaritic-Hebrew Philology.* Rome: Pontifical Biblical Institute, 1965. **Deller, K.** "*šmn bll* (Hos 12, 2): Additional Evidence." *Bib* 46 (1965) 349–52. **Dumbrell, W. J.** "The Role of Bethel in the Biblical Narratives from Jacob to Jeroboam I." *AJBA* 2 (1974–75) 65–76. **Diedrich, F.** *Die Anspielungen auf die Jakob-Tradition in Hosea 12, 1–13, 3: Ein literaturwissenschaftlicher Beitrag zur Exegese früher Prophetentexte.* Forschung zur Bibel 27. Würzburg: Echter Verlag, 1977. **Eitam, D.** "Olive Presses of the Israelite Period." *Tel Aviv* 6 (1979) 146–55. **Elliger, K.** "Der Jakobs Kampf am Jabbok: Gen. 32, 23 ff. als hermeneutishes Problem." *ZTK* 48 (1951) 1–31. **Eslinger, L. M.** "Hosea 12:5a and Genesis 32:29: A Study in Inner Biblical Exegesis." *JSOT* 18 (1980) 91–99. **Gertner, M.** "The Masorah and the Levites: Appendix on Hosea XII." *VT* 10 (1960) 241–84. **Ginsburg, H. L.** "Hosea's Ephraim, More Fool than Knave: A New Interpretation of Hosea 12:1–14." *JBL* 80 (1961) 339–47. **Good, E.** "Hosea and the Jacob Tradition," *VT* 16 (1966) 137–51. **Grimm, D.** "Erwägungen zu Hosea 12.12 'in Gilgal opfern sie Stiere.'" *ZAW* 85 (1973) 339–47. **Holladay, W. L.** "Chiasms, the Key to Hosea 12, 3–6." *VT* 16 (1966) 53–64. **Jacob, E.** "La Femme et le prophète: À propos d'Osée 12:13–14." *Hommage à W. Vischer.* Montpellier: Causse Graille Castelman, 1960. 83–87. **McCarthy, D.** "Hosea XII 2: Covenant by Oil." *VT* 14 (1964) 215–21. **McKenzie, S. L.** "The Jacob Tradition in Hosea xii:4–5." *VT* 36 (1986) 311–22. **Reines, C.** "Hosea 12:1." *JJS* 2 (1950–51) 156–57. **Sellin, E.** "Hosea und das Martyrium des Mose." *ZAW* 46 (1928) 26–33. **Suzuki, Y.** "Eschatological Negation of the Prophet Hosea in Terms of the Traditions of Jacob in Hos 12." *Seisho-Gaku Ronshu* 18 (1983) 5–52. [Japanese]. **Tournay, R.** "Quelques relectures bibliques antisamaritaines." *RB* 71 (1965) 504–36. **Vriezen, Th.** "Hosea 12." *Nieuwe Theologische Studien* 25 (1941) 144–49. ———. "La tradition de Jacob dans Osée 12." *OTS* 1 (1942) 64–78. **Zolli, E.** "Il significato de רד e רתח in Osea 12:1 e 13:1." *RSO* 32 (1957) 371–74.

Translation

Israel a deceiver

12:1 [11:12] *"Ephraim has surrounded me with deceit,*
and the family of Israel with fraud."

And Judah[a] *remains unruly*[b] *against God,*
even[c] *against the faithful Holy one.*[d]

2 [1] *Ephraim associates himself*[a] *with the wind,*
he pursues the east wind all day.

He multiplies lying and destruction;[b]
they make a covenant with Assyria,
and deliver[c] *oil to Egypt.*

Announcement of the lawsuit

3 [2] *Yahweh has a lawsuit against Judah*[a]
and a plan[b] *to punish Jacob according to his ways;*
according to his deeds he will repay him.

Yahweh's faithfulness

4 [3] *In the womb he grasped his brother's heel;*[a]
When he was powerful,[b] *he struggled with God,*
5 [4] *He struggled with an angel and endured,*[a]
he wept and pleaded with him for favor.

At Bethel[b] *he found him,*
there he spoke with him.[c]

6 [5] *It was*[a] *Yahweh, God of the armies;*
Yahweh is his renowned name.

7 [6] *As for you, return to your God;*
maintain loyalty and justice,
and wait constantly on your God.

Israel like Canaan a deceiver

8 [7] *Canaan*[a]—*in his hand are fraudulent scales;*
he loves to exploit.

9 [8] *And Ephraim said, "How rich I am!*
I have found power[a] *for myself!"*

[b] *All ⟨his⟩ profits will not suffice ⟨him⟩*
⟨because of⟩ the iniquity he has committed.[b]

Yahweh's faithfulness

10 [9] *"I am Yahweh your God*[a]
from the land of Egypt.

I will make you dwell in tents again
as on the assembly days.

11 (10) *I spoke through* [a] *the prophets,*
I gave them many revelations
and by the prophets I gave parables."

Examples of deceit: Gilead and Gilgal

12 [11] *If Gilead is evil,*
what worthlessness they are! [a]

In Gilgal they sacrifice bulls; [b]
moreover their altars are like stone-heaps
along the furrows of the field.

Yahweh's faithfulness

13 [12] *Jacob fled to the fields of Aram;* [a]
Israel was a servant in exchange for a wife,
in exchange for a wife he kept (sheep).

14 [13] *By a prophet Yahweh brought up Israel*
from Egypt, and by a prophet he was kept. [a]

Judgment to come

15 [14] *Israel has provoked him* [a] *bitterly*
His Lord will leave his blood-guilt on him,
and will repay him for his contempt.

13:1 *Truly* [a] *he has spoken terror* [b] *against* [c] *Ephraim,*
he has raised his voice [d] *against Israel:*
"[Because] [e] *he has incurred guilt with Baal,* [f] *he must die."* [g]

Notes

1.a. There is no textual evidence to support the deletion of יהודה "Judah," though it is often suggested.

1.b. The text of v 1b is probably corrupt. MT רד is uncertain as to meaning, though it appears in some contexts to mean "roam" or the like. "Unruly" is a conjecture.

1.c. The *waw* is used intensively here and in v 6a.

1.d. Reading consonantal MT as קדוש־ם נאמן.

2.a. Or, possibly "feeds on," from רעה I.

2.b. G μάταια "vain things" appears to have read שוא rather than שד "destruction / plunder." Kuhnigk (*NSH*) suggests reading שֵׁד "demon," though the context seems not to support the revocalization.

2.c. In light of the parallelism, the verb is probably a transitive pl, i.e., יובלו. The final *waw* should come from the beginning of v 3, where it is awkward. Cf. Syr.

3.a. "Israel" is commonly substituted here, on the theory that "Judah" must represent a later Judean redaction, because it is inappropriate to Hosea's interests. But we are dealing here with a passage more concerned than most with *all* Israel; and the parallelism may be seen either as analogous to the n : n + 1 sort in which a lesser (Judah) is then paralleled by a greater (Jacob) or as an example of "broken" pairs ("Ephraim" in v 2 is paralleled by "Judah" here).

3.b. Thus expressing the ל which in this case shows purpose or intent.

4.a. Or "tricked his brother." עקב is a double-entendre. See *Comment.*

4.b. Or "in his adulthood" or "when he had become wealthy." The term באון has potentially all these values.

5.a. The impf can also mean "so that he might win" or the like, but יכל does not necessarily connote victory, as much as it connotes not losing. There is no reason to assume that Jacob is not still the subj of the verbs in v 5a.

5.b. G reads οἴκῳ Ὠν, i.e., בֵּית־אָוֶן "Beth-Awen" as in 4:15; 5:8; 10:5, 8. But the reference is to Jacob's Bethel, not Hosea's critical nickname; so MT may be the more original, and G a harmonization.

5.c. MT עִמָּנוּ reflects an alternate 3 m sg suff to the usual pattern: עִמּוֹ.

6.a. The *waw* intensive is here rendered by "it was."

8.a. Since כְּנַעַן "Canaan" also means "merchant," a double-entendre is probably to be discerned here.

9.a. Or "wealth" or the like.

9.b-b. G πάντες οἱ πόνοι αὐτοῦ οὐχ εὑρεθήσονται αὐτῷ, δι᾽ ἀδικίας ἃς ἥμαρτεν suggest the original text to have been: כָּל־יְגִיעָיו לֹא יִמָּצְאוּ לוֹ עַל־אָוֶן אֲשֶׁר חָטָא "all his profits will not suffice him, because of the iniquity he has committed." (MT is somewhat nonsensical.) On the niph of מצא with ל as "to suffice / be enough for" cf. Josh 17:16.

10.a. G adds ἀνήγαγόν σε, i.e., הוֹצֵאתִיךְ "who / I brought you out" or הֶעֱלִיתִיךְ "who / I brought you up." The emphasis on the *name* here rather than the action suggests that the verb may be unoriginal in G, however.

11.a. Here דבר על occurs as "speak through," a different sense from its use in 2:16 [14] and 7:13.

12.a. The text of v 12a is suspect; the Heb. as it stands is very awkward.

12.b. G ἄρχοντες misread שָׂרִים "officials."

13.a. The lack of the usual prep מן "from" with ברח "to flee" is not surprising in poetry especially in the context of a locality. Note that Jacob did flee (ברח) *to* Aram (Gen 27:43), there to find a wife (Gen 28:1–29:30), as well as *from* Aram (31:22, 27).

14.a. Or "shepherded" or "watched over." The root שׁמר is used here in an echo of its use in v 13.

15.a. No object is expressed for the verb הכעיס, but clearly the angered party is Yahweh. "Israel has aroused bitter anger" would be an alternate translation.

13:1.a. MT כ should most likely be vocalized כִּי (cf. Andersen and Freedman, *Hosea,* 629).

1.b. G read תֹּרֹת "laws" (δικαιώματα), but otherwise α' σ' θ' and Vg read MT רְתֵת "terror," a rare word attested otherwise only in 1QH4, 33.

1.c. The ב before יִשְׂרָאֵל "Israel" in the second line of the tricolon does double duty here as well.

1.d. See 1.b.

1.e. The *waw* introduces the protasis of a conditional sentence.

1.f. While it is possible to translate "at Baal (-Peor)" (cf. 9:10), the rendering "with / by Baal" better fits the usual grammatical sense of ב, as well as the context.

1.g. Vocalizing וַיָּמֻת rather than the *waw* conversive. The use of ו twice suggests a conditional meaning (*Because* he has . . . *then* he . . .). The line is vocalized by MT as if prose, though it is surely poetry, i.e., the third line of the tricolon.

Form / Stru·ture / Setting

In 12:1 [1.:12]–13:1 a new literary unit introduces a somewhat new theme: a deceitful nation defrauds Yahweh by cheating on his covenant. Chapter 11 ends with the promise of return and resettlement. Now there is no promise but only threat. Accusations against Israel for its trickery abound. The passage concludes with a prediction of retribution for Israel's crimes.

The unity of the passage is not obvious at first blush. Topics shift often, and do not follow each other predictably. There is no evidence, however, of a break in the passage before 13:1. The many accusations may logically be expected to culminate in a word of judgment, according to the pattern which predominates in Hosea and other prophetical books. Although short judgment sentences appear at vv 9–10 [8–9], it is the lengthy judgment sentence of 12:5 [4]–13:1 that evidently concludes the passage. In 13:2 begins a different accusation, focusing on the durative aspect of Israel's sin.

The form may generally be described as the "lawsuit" (ריב). The term itself occurs in v 3 and the accusations and judgment sentence contribute to the pattern. However, there are present elements not usually associated with the lawsuit pattern: historical digressions into Jacob's life (vv 4–5 [3–4]; v 13 [12]), and the fact that the prophet speaks rather than Yahweh (except in vv 1 [11:12] and 10–11 [9–10], where Hosea appears to be citing Yahweh's words in the first person as a basis for his message).

The passage is at least in part retrospective and reflective, as each passage after 9:9 has been. Israel-Judah are seen partly through and partly in contrast to their origins, as a device for presenting the evidence against them. The collage of evidential accusations and reflections leaves with the reader/hearer an impression which unifies the passage: the covenant nation has been cheating on its God.

The following outline captures the passage's salient subject matter, showing especially the theme that Israel should turn to Yahweh, the only God who has historically benefited Israel and revealed himself to them.

Introduction: Israel a deceiver (vv 1–2 [11:12–12:1])
Announcement of the lawsuit (v 3 [2])
   Yahweh: the God of Jacob's renaming at Peniel and Bethel (vv 4–6 [3–5])
Invitation to return to Yahweh (v 7 [6])
Israel's deceit like that of "Canaan" (vv 8–9 [7–8])
   Yahweh: Israel's benefactor, judge, and revealer (vv 10–11 [9–10])
Examples of deceit: Gilead and Gilgal (v 12 [11])
   Yahweh: benefactor of Jacob/Israel on the move (vv 13–14 [12–13])
Announcement of judgment (12:15 [14]–13:1)

The central themes of the passage therefore are (1) Israel's deceitfulness: the nation cheats on its God by breaking his covenant; (2) the identity of Yahweh: he is Israel's only proper God; (3) Israel's refusal to return to Yahweh: it must be punished.

The sayings in the passage are mostly formulated as the words of the prophet. Yahweh is spoken of in the third person, except in vv 1 [11:12] and 10–11 [9–10] where he is quoted directly. It has sometimes been suggested that in v 1a [11:12a] we should understand the "me" as Hosea, expressing his frustration with the lack of receptivity to his divinely appointed message. This is possible, though the book contains so little first-person reference to Hosea (3:1 and possibly 9:17 if MT is followed) that such an identification must be made with great caution. Indeed, if the parallelism in v 1 [11:12a] is correctly rendered by our translation of the problematic text, "me" finds its counterpart in v 1b [11:12b] in "God," and this obviates the issue of who the speaker is.

There is little in the text by which to fix its original setting. The reference in a single parallelism to Israel's alliances with Assyria and Egypt suggests a date during Hoshea's kingship, after the beginning of Shalmaneser V's reign, when Hoshea sent for help to Egypt (2 Kgs 17:3–4). During the relatively peaceful years of the mid-720s B.C., we may assume that Israel's prosperity returned in some measure, though much of its former territory was in Assyrian hands. The references in this passage to national abundance (vv 8–9 [7–8] and 12 [11]) tend to confirm a date in the "breathing space" before Shalmaneser's attack in 723.

Comment

12:1 [11:12] In v 1a [11:12a] Yahweh laments that he is besieged by the treachery of his people. Ephraim / Israel has encircled (סבב) their own God as an army encircles a city. Their weapons are "deceit" (כחש; cf. 7:3; 10:13) and "fraud" (מרמה). The complaint of Yahweh (probably not the prophet, *pace* Wolff, 208–10) parallels those in lament psalms concerning the encirclement of the enemy (e.g., Pss 22:13, 17; 88:18; 118:10–12; cf. Deut 32:10). Both כחש and מרמה are mentioned often in such psalms as characteristic of the behavior of the psalmists' oppressing enemies. Israel's "deceit" and "fraud" are found in their cheating on the covenant. Verse 2b [1b] mentions one example, foreign covenants without Yahweh's permission. Their deceit and fraud also include dishonesty and abuse of others ("violence") in v 2b [1b]; greedy materialism (v 9 [8]); heterodox religious practices (v 12 [11]) and other capital crimes (v 15 [14]). Though enamored of Baal and Asherah, Ephraim still pledged allegiance to its national God, Yahweh, while ignoring his covenant. Their actions showed that they were deceivers.

1b [11:12b] undoubtedly became corrupted early in the history of its transmission, judging from the divergent readings of the ancient versions. If our speculative reconstruction (cf. NIV) is correct, the couplet accuses Judah also of unfaithfulness to God (אל), "the Holy One" (קדוש; cf. 11:9). In effect, then, wherever Yahweh looked he was surrounded by cheaters. Even Judah, with its legal central sanctuary, Davidic kingship, and legitimate priesthood (cf. 2 Chr 13:5–11) had steadily corrupted itself and become "unruly" (though there is no clarity about the definition of רד). Yahweh alone was faithful / honest (נאמן) to the covenant, while Ephraim and Judah only pretended to be. The mention of Judah is unintrusive here, and not merely because Hosea's audience would naturally be concerned about the south and its fate. The chapter is interested in the whole people of God (thus the emphasis on the pre-division Jacob traditions).

2 [1] It was folly for Ephraim to look for security from any other source than Yahweh. Yahweh promised in his covenant to protect Israel from all dangers if they would remain loyal but guaranteed trouble if they sought alliances elsewhere (cf. Isa 30:1–5; 31:1–3; Jer 2:16–19; 37:7–10; Ezek 17:15). Israel was not expected to be isolated from its political environment, but to be isolationist as regards the concluding of covenants with other nations. Their only proper covenant had been given them on Mt. Sinai (cf. v 14 [13]).

Ephraim the alliance seeker was therefore Ephraim the idiot, out running around chasing the wind, trying to catch it. He was attempting something impossible. The verse is comprised of a metaphor (virtually a parable) and its interpretation. The wind is that which is illusory, impossible to grasp (cf. 8:7; Eccl, *passim*). The east wind (קדים) is the intensely hot dry desert wind that is miserable to endure (cf. 13:15) and sought ("pursued," רדף) only by a suicidal fool. Thus is Ephraim portrayed. The wind was the security Ephraim sought from Assyria and Egypt in turn; it was illusory. The pursuit of the wind was the covenant-making itself and the gift-giving that went with it, i.e., "oil to Egypt." Others suggest that "oil" may allude to the practice of examining patterns of oil on water as a kind of ancient lie detector test to ensure that parties to an oath were pledging loyalty honestly. In this interpretation MT יובל is considered a form of בלל "to mix," and the clause reads: "Oil is mixed with Egypt." (Cf. McCarthy, *VT* 14 [1964] 215–21, and Deller, *Bib* 46 [1965] 349–52.)

At any rate, the whole process of international entanglements was bound to fail. Hoshea pledged his faithfulness in a vassal treaty to Assyria (2 Kgs 17:3); then, when he thought the times favored his plans, broke that treaty and sent messengers to Egypt for help in throwing off Assyrian domination (2 Kgs 17:4). By such actions Israel demonstrated their treachery against Yahweh, showing themselves in the process to be a people who multiply (ירבה) "lying" (כזב) and "destruction" (שד). In internal matters, the nation's multiple immorality was well documented; it can be no surprise therefore that in external matters of diplomacy, their pattern of treachery continued true to form.

3 [2] The lawsuit against Israel includes Judah, because it is against the whole people, not merely the rump state of Ephraim. Thus the parallel for "Judah" is "Jacob" (3b [2b]) in ascending parallelism. Smaller-to-larger progressions in fixed pairs are well known in numerical parallelisms (see S. Gevirtz, *Patterns in the Early Poetry of Israel*, 15–24, *et passim*). Here, one may also note Amos 1:3–2:16, where Israel is the "featured" nation, yet Judah comes first in order.

The court, in which Yahweh is both prosecutor and judge as well as plaintiff (cf. 4:1–19) will hear evidence against Israel leading to well-deserved judgment according to Israel's "ways" (דרכיו) and "deeds" (מעלליו). A review of Israel's origins and past deeds, in the person of Jacob (vv 4–5 [3–4], 13 [12]) serves as a foil against which the namesake nation of Hosea's day may be measured.

There is no indication here that God is displeased with the patriarch Jacob. While the verse uses "Jacob" ambiguously, it is the evolved *national* Jacob, not the patriarch, that is on trial.

Here alone Hosea reaches back beyond the Exodus to the patriarchal period as described in Genesis for examples of the original relationship between God and "Israel." Israel is not a "chip off the old block" but a nation *unlike* its eponymous ancestor, in that it refuses to acknowledge Yahweh as its sole God. The original purpose of the lawsuit is stated here only as punishment; later it will become evident (vv 7 [6], 10 [9]) that Yahweh also has plans for blessing Israel, through their turning back to him because of his wrath (cf. 2:4–17 [2–15]).

4 [3] A single couplet, mentioning two key events in the patriarch's life, constitutes the first half of a quatrain which concludes in v 5a [4a]. Its purpose is to remind the nation who their ancestor was, and how he got both his names. The couplet is introductory to the verses which follow and encapsulates the two naming stories. Like the original stories in Genesis, it casts no aspersion on Jacob. The story of the birth name "Jacob" comes from Gen 25:21–26, where יעקוב is chosen to reflect עקב "to grasp by the heel." The name "Jacob" was given the child on the basis of the birth omen of his hand grasping his brother's heel—*not* because the true etymology is to be found therein (see *ISBE*, rev. ed. 3:483–88). "Jacob" is attested in ancient Semitic onomastica, and derives probably from *yahkub-ʾil* "may God protect" (M. Noth, "Mari und Israel," in *Festschrift Alt*, ed. W. Zimmerli, Tübingen: Mohr, 1953). Ancient names were commonly given on the basis of sounds heard or thought of in connection with the birth event (i.e., as non-homologous homophones) rather than on the basis of genuine etymology (cf. 1:6, *Comment*). Later in the Genesis story, Esau accuses Jacob of deception / trickery using the verb עקב (27:36), which can also have the meaning "to deceive," though likely from a different original root than עקב "to grasp the heel." In Hos 12:4 [3] the stress is placed upon the situation at birth (בבטן "in the womb"). The second sense of עקב "to deceive," may be *suggested* simply by mention of the verb itself (as "Jacob" in v 3 [2] suggests *both* patriarch and nation) but there is no warrant for translating the verb as "deceived" in the way Hosea has contextualized it.

Likewise, the second line of the couplet (v 4b [3b]) is essentially positive in what it says about Jacob's encounter with God when he was a person of "power" (און). This line refers to Jacob's wrestling with the angel of God at Peniel (Gen 32:22–31), a story which records that God, speaking through the angel, renamed him "Israel," a name based loosely (not strictly etymologically) on the verb שרה piel, "to struggle/contend." The renaming is a key aspect of the background of the nation. The verse as a whole is part of a progression which continues in v 5 [4] toward the climax in v 6 [5], where the object of this struggle is identified as the revelation of *Yahweh* to Jacob. The naming of Jacob / Israel and its implications fades in significance compared to Yahweh's name and the implications that name (Yahweh's) held for Jacob and for the whole history of Israel.

5 [4] Verse 5a [4a] completes the quatrain begun in v 4 [3]. The first line ("he struggled . . . endured") is resumptive of v 4b [3b], which it parallels synonymously. It adds to the terse poetic summary of Gen 32:22–32 the detail that Jacob's wrestling with God was actually a wrestling with an angel of God (the Genesis account reads "man," though it is obvious that Jacob regards his opponent as more than a mere man) and that Jacob could not be defeated by the angel—both effective capsulizations of the Genesis account. The second line summarizes Jacob's appeal for a blessing (Gen 32:26) after having his thigh/hip injured by the angel. The verb בכה "he wept" does not appear in the Genesis account, but here, with חנן, describes the earnest appeal for favor from the angel, the two verbs probably tending to occur together in hendiadys (cf. Esth 8:3) in normal speech.

Genesis 35:1–10 relates how Jacob again encountered God in Bethel, where he confirmed the angel's renaming Jacob "Israel." These events are summarized in v 5a [4a] ("At Bethel he found him . . ."). The subject of the two verbs "found" and "spoke" is probably in this case God, though it could be Jacob as well. Since Gen 35:13 and 15 both mention Bethel as the place where *God* spoke to Jacob, it is reasonable to assume that Hosea's poetic recitation of this event probably intends to phrase it similarly.

6 [5] Now comes the point which the retelling of Jacob's encounters with Yahweh is intended to lead up to. His renaming was the consequence of a revelation. Jacob had been met by the God who was beginning the process of the election of Israel. His renaming via these special revelatory events was symbolic of his new relationship; Jacob was becoming a servant of Yahweh, and Yahweh was revealing to him the divine plan for a special "nation, community of nations, and kings" of whom he would be the ancestor, and also "a land" that Yahweh promised "to give to you and to your descendants after you" (Gen 35:11–12). By language that has the ring of a liturgical formulation,

Hosea thus reminds the Israel of his day who their God is. He is "Yahweh,
God of the armies; *Yahweh* is his renowned name" (זכרו; cf. Exod 3:15; Pss
102:13 [12]; 135:13). The implication for Israel is clear. They are nothing
without Yahweh, just as Jacob was nothing without Yahweh. But God had
graciously and repeatedly revealed himself specially to Jacob, occasioning a
change in his name as evidence of his being specially chosen. Jacob's election
to become the man "Israel" was the start of a process that culminated in the
election of a gang of slaves in Egypt to become the nation "Israel." By being
reminded of its origins (i.e. origins that Yahweh initiated) via stories about
its namesake, Israel is therefore reminded of its identity and obligations. By
definition, if your name is "Israel," Yahweh is your God.

7 [6]   Thus Hosea immediately calls the nation to return to Yahweh. Israel
can find identity, purpose—and survival—only in Yahweh. By implication,
the worship of other gods, or illegitimate non-covenantal "worship" of Yahweh
(vv 12–13 [11–12]), or foreign alliances (v 2 [1]) will be useless to them. Their
only hope is a true "return" (שׁוב; cf. 5:4; 6:1; 7:10; 11:5; 14:2 [2], 3 [2], 8 [7])
to Yahweh and the behavior his covenant prescribes: the practice of חסד
"covenant loyalty" and משׁפט "justice," according to the consistant faithfulness
that Jacob displayed ("wait constantly on your God"). Hosea is not here advising
the nation how to be spared destruction, but reassuring those who believe
Yahweh's word that the nation would always live on in the form of a repentant
remnant even though individual citizens would be born, die, and suffer their
own personal fates. The national continuum "you" (ואתה; cf. Deut 4:25–
31) can escape the general fate of the eighth-century Israelites, if they will
wait upon Yahweh for his deliverance and protection. Some of the "you"
will survive the siege and the killing to remain alive into the time of exile
(Deut 4:27), from which they personally or in the form of their descendants
will experience return and restoration. Thus Hosea holds out a real hope
and a real challenge to his audience. Simply because the general direction
of the fate of the nation *qua* nation is already fixed does not imply that
it is futile to be obedient to Yahweh. Returning to Yahweh always has
benefit, though its formal outworking in national restoration must be eschatological.

8 [7]   8 [7] has a format similar to certain ancient tribal "blessings" (cf.
e.g. Gen 49:13, 16, 19, 20, 21, 27). The name appears in the initial position
of the sentence, and a metaphorical description follows. Here, as in some
other "blessings," the description is hardly flattering (cf. Gen 49:5–7, 17, 27).
"Canaan" would appear to be a derogatory double entendre for Ephraim.
"Canaanite" could mean not only an inhabitant of the promised land ("Canaan"
derives originally from the name of the Phoenician coast) but also a "trader"
or a "merchant" (cf. Job 40:30; Prov 31:24; Ezek 17:4; Zeph 1:11) as the
Phoenicians were associated with long-distance commercial trade. By this metaphor, Hosea declares Ephraim to be a greedy merchant, and at the same
time no better than the Canaanites whose immoral culture deserved extinction
(cf. Gen 15:16). Amos portrays the north similarly (Amos 8:4–6). Ephraim's
control of key north-south trade routes and its agricultural productivity (cf.
2:10 [8]) gave it a prosperity, but one enjoyed only by the upper classes.
The poor failed to share in the wealth.

"Fraudulent scales" (מאזני מרמה) were a dishonest merchant's key tools.

They became symbolic in OT literature of unscrupulous dealings (Deut 25:13; Prov 11:1; 20:23; cf. Mic 6:11). "Canaan" is thus one who loves to "oppress" (עשק). Hosea employed עשק in 5:11 to foretell in accordance with the covenant curse predictions (Deut 28:29, 33) that Ephraim would be "oppressed." Here, however, the verb is used to help portray before the court, as part of the covenant lawsuit, the despicable character of the nation deserving such a fate. The term is used especially to signify keeping the downtrodden and poor in their place by force (Amos 4:1; Mal 3:5; etc.). In Israel, the justice of the Law ("You shall not oppress your neighbor," Lev 19:13) was being ignored.

9 [8] Ephraim is revealed to be the unjust merchant, "Canaan," by his boast that he is rich and powerful. Thus his own testimony confirming his observed behavior becomes evidence against him in the lawsuit (cf. 8:2 and 10:3 for other examples of speech by the personified nation). His words are simple. They state his attitude of self-security. Ephraim rejoices in his wealth, with confidence that it was worth the oppression of others, the immorality, the religious infidelity, and with confidence also that it made him a secure nation.

But it is worthless. The prophet, perhaps quoting the words of the divine prosecutor of the lawsuit, announces the folly of Ephraim's misplaced trust. His "gains" (יגיעי) will do him no good. How can they help him when he faces Yahweh's wrath? Ephraim is doomed and doesn't know it (cf. Amos 6:1–7; Zeph 1:11–13). He will not be able to buy his way out of the coming punishment; wealth will not "suffice" (מצא, niphal; curse type 15, futility). In gaining his obscene profits, Ephraim has "committed iniquity" (חטא . . . עון), i.e., shown himself to be a sinner. It is possible that assonance is to be noticed in the words מצא (twice), עון / און and לא / לו / לי as they are found in v 9a [8a] and 9b [8b] respectively, though this may be accidental rather than purposeful.

10 [9] Ephraim is again reminded of who his real God is, and where his real trust should have been. Ephraim had not become "powerful" on his own. Any good he had received was from Yahweh, always his only benefactor. He was the God who made Israel's national history happen, from its very origins in slavery in Egypt. This Ephraim must and will know: Yahweh is *"your"* God. Because Ephraim did not heed Yahweh, he now receives a word of judgment.

The great wealth of Ephraim, with its splendid houses and symbols of luxury enjoyed especially by the upper classes, will not only not "suffice" (v 9 [8]); it will be taken away. The rich nation will be made to live once again in nomad's tents, their homes during the exodus and wilderness years. This is no happy promise as some commentators have thought, but a word of judgment. To be stripped of wealth and housed in tents is to be disciplined. Yahweh will reduce Israel's standard of living to the barest (cf. Lev 26:30–35; Deut 28:30, 52, 65: Hos 2:4 [2], 11–14 [9–12]). Leviticus 23:43 describes the exodus accomodations in language very similar: ". . . I made the Israelites dwell in huts (סכות) when I brought them out of Egypt. I am Yahweh your God." Perhaps Hosea draws here upon that ancient formulation, reversing the wording and the import for Israel. Instead of dwelling in huts as a memorial of their deliverance, they will dwell in tents as a punishment for their misuse of the resources Yahweh has granted them. Their towns and cities, in other words, will lie desolate (curse type 9b).

The "assembly days" (יְמֵי מוֹעֵד; cf. 9:5) included especially the Feast of Tabernacles ("Huts," סֻכּוֹת) which the Israelites were familiar with, even though this particular festival was not much observed in Hosea's time (cf. Neh 8:17). They knew from those days the relative primitiveness and inconvenience of tent dwelling. An undesirable fate awaited them.

11 [10] Yahweh reminds Israel that they are without excuse in their rejection of his covenant. He consistently revealed his expectations for them, just as he had revealed himself repeatedly to Jacob. Their only true God since their beginnings (v 10 [9]), he continually reminded the people of their obligations "through the prophets" (עַל־הַנְּבִיאִים). The triplet that constitutes v 11 [10] is not designed to laud the prophets, but to remind the nation of his means of warning them when they persisted in ignoring the covenant.

Moses was the OT prophet *par excellence*, the paradigm for all the other true prophets, whose ministry was based on the original revelation mediated through Moses (cf. v 14 [13]). The true orthodox prophets were Yahweh's spokespersons to call successive generations back to covenant fidelity. They did not, of course, recite covenant stipulations word for word, any more than a modern preacher merely recites biblical passages word for word. They were inspired to use a variety of innovative and memorable techniques to draw people's attention to Yahweh's Word. Thus God "spoke" (דָּבַר) through them, gave "revelations" (on this meaning of חָזוֹן, which in prophetic speech rarely means "vision," cf. 2 Chr 32:32; Prov 29:18; 2 Sam 7:17) and "parables" (דָּמָה). The message was not the prophets' to do with what they wished (cf. Amos 3:7, 8; Jer 20:9); it was Yahweh's, and they were messengers sent to deliver it. Israel was guilty by their refusal to obey repeated warnings and invitations from Yahweh, delivered in a variety of formats, all intended to restore the nation to its essential responsibilities.

12 [11] The first half-dozen words (אִם . . . . הָיוּ) read awkwardly, suggesting textual corruption. In light of the mention of Gilgal it is probable that "Gilead" is an original reading. The inclusion of these two cities appears at first to represent a *non sequitur* from 11 [10]. In the overall context of the lawsuit, however, it is appropriate. The *rîb* (lawsuit) pattern generally provides for an interspersing of accusation, evidence, and judgment sentences. V 12 [11] appears to be an accusation, presenting evidence to the divine court, giving two "counts" of covenant crimes. The more general mention of Gilead's "evil" (אָוֶן) and "worthlessness" (שָׁוְא), if the text is correct, was apparently enough to remind Hosea's audience of the city's bloody reputation (cf. 6:8). The cult center Gilgal is cited for its multiple altars, every one illegal according to the covenant (cf. 2:8 [6], 9 [7]; 4:19; 8:13; 9:6; 10:8). Gilgal also enjoyed a reputation for iniquity, openly excoriated in 9:15 and presumed in 4:15.

It is possible that Hosea lists these two cities for the special kind of cult-associated or cult-condoned criminality which they represented in his day. Gilead was apparently known for some sort of murder, literal or figurative, in which its priests had a part (6:8–9). Gilgal was a place where virtually any sort of cultic worship might be engaged in—except perhaps orthodox worship—depending on one's preference. The fact that the names of both cities began with the same sound also fit the prophetic sense of assonance (cf. Amos 5:5) as Hosea strove to frame Yahweh's word in ways memorable to his audience. It is also possible that Gilead was already destroyed by the armies of Tiglath-Pileser III (thus it had become "worthlessness") and that Hosea wished to imply the same fate for Gilgal. The text as we have translated it, however, would not support the latter interpretation.

13–14 [12–13] The multiple meanings of the verb שמר "to shepherd," "to keep," "to watch over," provide a kind of mnemonic word play by which Israel's obligation to the Law is underscored. Vv 13 [12] and 14 [13] form a historically oriented meditation on שמר. Resuming reference to Jacob, the prophet now reminds his audience of another aspect of Jacob's story. V 13 [12] is a triplet in partly synonymous and partly synthetic parallelism, with a progression toward the key point, that Jacob "was a shepherd" (שמר), i.e., a "keeper" of sheep. This assertion is intended to provide the first aspect of the comparison completed by the couplet in v 14, namely, that just as Jacob was a "keeper," so was Moses, the one whom Yahweh chose to bring his people out of Egypt. Hosea's implication is clear: the sheep have strayed from their shepherd's keeping (cf. Isa 53:6). The person, Israel, kept (שמר) sheep. The nation Israel was kept (שמר) by the prophet Moses who remains their keeper through the covenant he mediated. On the basis of this catchword Hosea builds not a syllogism but a simple reminder: Israel disobeyed the keeper by not keeping the covenant.

13 [12] Jacob's "flight" (ויברח) to Paddan-Aram (here the "fields of Aram") was undertaken on the instruction of his father (Gen 28:5). He served (עבד; Gen 29:20, 30) his Uncle Laban for Rachel and Leah as his wives (באשה). In Genesis 30:31 the verb שמר is used of Jacob's job, keeping sheep. The details of the trip to Aram, the work and the wives are not in themselves particularly significant. They are included as necessary story line components to the catchword שמר.

14 [13] The term בנביא "by a prophet," used twice in the verse with obvious reference to Moses, picks up the aural rhythm of באשה "for a wife," used twice at the end of v 13 [12]. The original Israel "kept" בְּ ("for") a wife. The corporate Israel left Egypt and "was kept" בְּ ("by") a prophet. Inasmuch as שמר is the verb most associated with keeping the commandments / covenant of Yahweh in the OT, occurring scores of times in that sense, the mere mention of שמר as what Moses did for Israel—on the analogy of what Jacob did for sheep—must have been intended as a subtle reminder of Israel's central task. They must allow that same covenant to keep them again.

15 [14] The lawsuit concludes (12:15 [14]–13:1) with a judgment sentence, worded as a prediction of how Yahweh will respond to being so angered by his covenant nation. Three of the key terms of v 15 [14] are found also in Deut 32. The first of these, כעס (to "provoke" someone to an angry reaction; Deut 32:16; cf. the noun in Deut 32:19), is used in the OT most often to indicate the arousal of Yahweh's punishing wrath by the worship of other gods. Deut 4:25–26 is, however, the *locus classicus* of כעס in the manner it is used in v 15 [14]: ". . . If you act corruptly . . . by doing what is evil in the sight of Yahweh your God (cf. Hos 12:7 [6], 10 [9]), so as to provoke him, I call heaven and earth to witness against you this day, that you soon

. . . will be utterly destroyed." In Deut 32:21 Yahweh promises to "provoke" Israel in retaliation for being provoked by the fact that they have slighted him in favor of other gods. He will slight them, making them insignificant in comparison to their enemies who will conquer them. This prediction is what v 15b [14b] is about.

To "leave" (נטשׁ) is used here in a somewhat different sense from its use in Deut 32:15 since its object is the "blood-guilt" (דם) of Israel. "Blood-guilt" is a term denoting a level of guilt so great, for an offense so severe, that capital punishment is required. Known most from its usage in Leviticus (e.g., Lev 20) it is used also in a similar context in Deut 32:43 (cf. 32:14, 42). Accidental blood-guilt could be removed (e.g., Josh 20:1–9). But there was no accident to Israel's blood-guilt. It would be left, and Israel would die (curse type 24). The promise to "repay (שׁוב, hiphil) picks up v 3b [2b] and at the same time recalls Deut 32:41 and 43 where it is נקם "vengeance" which Yahweh will repay to the covenant rebels. Israel's "contempt" (חרפה) is a contempt for the divine law. The use of אדניו "his lord" only here in Hosea is perhaps due to the implicit emphasis upon offense against the covenant sovereign; "contempt" tends to connote a personal insult rather than a general attitude. The evil nation has not learned from the example of its eponymous ancestor Jacob, from Moses, or from Hosea or other covenant prophets. It despises Yahweh, and must be paid back (curse type 26) for such a capital offense.

13:1 The final verse of the passage furnishes the judgment sentence from Yahweh, whom Israel has so "bitterly provoked" (12:15 [14]). Yahweh, speaking directly a final time (cf. 12:1 [11:12], 10–11 [9–10]), finds Israel guilty ("he has incurred guilt with Baal") and specifies the punishment ("he must die," curse type 24). This divine speech in the third line of the triplet is introduced by two lines of synonymous parallelism in which the prophet reports that the verdict has gone against Israel. The syncretistic allegiance to Baal which on balance had characterized Israel's faith more often than not, was a crime which necessitated the unleashing of the curses. The God who had revealed himself to and through Jacob (vv 3–6 [2–5]; 13 [12]) and Moses (v 14 [13]) must repay such blood-guilt by the only appropriate punishment, death. On the connection of national guilt (אשׁם) with capital punishment cf. Ezek 25:12–14.

Commentators have usually placed 13:1 with the remainder of chap. 13. Andersen and Freedman (624), whose translation of the verse is insightful, follow suit, though admitting (pp. 628–29) the uncertainties. The verse is best understood as a fitting conclusion to the lawsuit (cf. ריב; v 3 [2]), however. It conjoins cleanly with v 15 [14] of chap. 12, and has no obvious organic relation to the new theme of continuing sin introduced by "now" (ועתה) in 13:2. The death of Israel is a foregone conclusion in the lawsuit: "according to his deeds he will repay him" (v 3 [2]).

Explanation

Israel's guilt is forcefully exposed to the divine court in the lawsuit form followed generally in 12:1 [11:12]–13:1. Even Judah is mentioned as having the same sort of rebellious attitude that is about to result in Ephraim's destruction. Evidence of Ephraim's covenant-breaking is presented in the form of their deceit and fraud (12:1 [11:12]), lying and destruction (v 2 [1]), exploitations (v 8 [7]), excessive profits and iniquity (v 9 [8]), evil, worthlessness and heterodox religion (vv 12–13 [11–12]), provocations, capital crimes, and contempt (v 15 [14]).

Having forgotten who they are, the Israelites have ignored both their election as the people of one God, Yahweh, and their covenant responsibilities. For this reason their history is once again laid before them, particularly in the person of Jacob by whose God-given name, Israel, they are known and whose faithful response to God's election is contrasted to their rejection.

Most commentators have judged that chap. 12 (13:1 excluded from the passage) portrays Jacob as a deceiver in order to provide an example of what Israel has also become. Such an interpretation falls short on two accounts. First, it is out of character for Hosea's historical retrospectives. The other true retrospectives in the book (9:10, for example, would not be such) present Israel's history prior to the conquest as a time of relative closeness to Yahweh (2:17 [15]; 9:10; 10:11, etc.), when the nation had not yet wholly departed from its obligations. Hosea holds the exodus-wilderness period before the people in contrast to their behavior in his own day. For the Jacob stories then to portray a pre-Sinai sinfulness would be highly unlikely. Second, the statements made about Jacob in chap. 12 are either neutral or positive, but not negative. If Hosea had wished to select stories about Jacob which would mirror Israel's sin (i.e., his deceit of Esau and Laban; Gen 27:31), he could easily have done so. Instead, the stories he selects either contrast with Israel's infidelity, or serve a linguistic-mnemonic purpose in making a point about Israel's covenant obligations (v 13 [12], שמר).

And as Jacob was a sheep "keeper," so Moses and the covenant mediated through him were to keep Israel in right relationship to Yahweh (vv 13–14 [12–13]). The passage twice dwells upon the name of Yahweh (vv 6 [5], 10 [9]). The one who revealed himself to Jacob is the one Israel has ignored; the one who brought them from Egypt is the one who will impoverish them again (v 10 [9]). Cities like Gilgal and Gilead mirror the national rebelliousness that leaves Yahweh no choice but to destroy his nation (12:15 [14]–13:1).

The passage also looks to the future, as with most of the reflective passages after 9:9. The future holds punishment for Israel (vv 3 [2], 9 [8], 10 [9], 15 [14]; 13:1), with a single exception. V 7 [6] leaves some hope for that remnant who by reason of repentance may escape the worst of Yahweh's judgment wrath (cf. Lev 26:44; Deut 4:20; 30:3). So it is the case with the Christian in the new covenant era. Those who repent and turn to Christ, fulfilling his covenant, will be rescued from the coming wrath of God (1 Thess 1:10) though not without experiencing trials (Mark 13:13). Though like the Israel of Hosea's day, we have all surrounded God with our deceit and fraud and thus deserve "by nature" wrath (Eph 2:3), our blood-guilt is not held against us. His blood has paid our penalty. He will not raise his voice against us, but in our defense.

"I Will Destroy You, Israel"
(13:2–14:1 [13:16])

Bibliography

Bailey, L. R. "The Golden Calf." *HUCA* 42 (1971) 97–115. **Dahood, M.** "Hebrew Ugaritic Lexicography." I:*Bib* 44 (1963) 289–303; XII:*Bib* 55 (1974) 381–93. ———. "Interrogative *kî* in Psalm 90, 11; Isaiah 36, 19 and Hosea 13, 9." *Bib* 60 (1979) 573–74. ———. "Ugaritic and Phoenician or Qumran and the Versions." *AOAT* 22 (1973) 53–58. **Day, J.** "A Case of Inner Scriptural Interpretation." *JTS* 31 (1980) 309–19. **Gray J.** "The Kingship of God in the Prophets and Psalms." *VT* 11 (1961) 1–29. **Harrelson, W.** "About to Be Born." *Andover Newton Quarterly* 11 (1970) 56–61. **Huffmon, H. B.** "The Treaty Background of Hebrew *YĀDAʿ*." *BASOR* 181 (1966) 31–37. **Hvidberg, O.** "Die Vernichtung des goldenen Kalbes und der ugaritische Ernteritus." *AcOr* 33 (1971) 5–46. **Manross, L. N.** "*Beth Essentiae*." *JBL* 73 (1954) 238–39. **May, H. G.** "The Fertility Cult in Hosea." *AJSL* 48 (1932) 76–98. **Vuilleumier-Bessard, R.** "Osée 13:2 et les manuscrits." *RevQ* 1 (1958/59) 281–82. **Wittstruck, T.** "The Influence of Treaty Imagery on the Beast Imagery of Daniel 7." *JBL* 97 (1978) 100–102.

Translation

Prophetic speech: judgment for idolatry

13:2 *Even now they continue to sin!*
They have made for themselves cast images,
Idols from silver according to their own skill.[a]
All of it is the work of craftsmen.

To these[b] *they sacrifice*[c] *lambs,*[d]
human beings[e] *kiss bulls!*[f]

3 *Therefore they shall be like morning mist,*
like dew which goes away early,
like chaff blown[a] *from a threshing floor,*
like smoke out a window.

Divine speech: judgment for polytheism

4 *But I, Yahweh, have been your God*[a]
since the land of Egypt.

You were to know no god beside me;
there is no savior except me.

5 *I fed*[a] *you in the wilderness,*
in a parched land.

6 *When I fed them, they were satisfied;*
they were satisfied, and so became arrogant.
Therefore they forgot me.

7 *So I will become to them like a lion,*
like a leopard by the road I will watch.[a]

⁸*I will attack them like a bear robbed of her cubs,*[a]
I will rip open their insides.[b]

Whatever comes along[c] *will devour them there,*
wild animals will pull them apart.

⁹*I*[a] *will destroy you, Israel.*
Who[b] *then will be your helper?*

¹⁰*Where*[a] *is your king*
that he may help you in all your cities?[b]

And your rulers, of whom you said,
"Give me a king and officials"?

¹¹*I gave you a king in my anger,*
and I took him away in my fury.

¹²*Ephraim's iniquity is wrapped up,*
his sin is stored up.

¹³*The pangs of a woman in childbirth will come for him,*
but he is an unwise child.

When it is time, he will not be present[a]
at the opening of the womb.[b]

¹⁴*From Sheol shall I ransom them?*[a]
From death shall I redeem them?[a]

Where[b] *are your plagues,*[c] *death?*[a]
Where[b] *is your scourge, Sheol?*[a]
Pity is hidden from me!

Prophetic speech: drought and war as punishments

¹⁵*Though he flourish among the marshes,*[a]
Yahweh will bring up an east wind,
coming up out of the wilderness.

His water source will dry up,[b]
his spring will become dry.

He[c] *will strip the storehouse*
[a]*of every desirable thing.*

14:1 [13:16] *Samaria will be desolated*[b]
because she rebelled against her God.

They will fall by the sword;
their little children will be smashed down,
their[c] *pregnant women will be ripped open.*

Notes

2.a. G κατ᾽ εἰκόνα and Vg *quasi similitudinem* read כתבנית "by a design," which is equally as plausible as MT (cf. Isa 44:13). The spelling תבונם is unique and may be a miswriting of תבונתם "their skill," the more expected form.

2.b. MT הם may also conceivably reflect *himmu* "behold." Cf. המה in 9:10, etc.

2.c. Kuhnigk (*NSH*, 149) following Dahood, corrects MT אֹמְרִים זֹבְחֵי "saying, sacrificing" to אִמְּרֵי־ם זֹבְחֵי "sacrificial lambs" on the analogy of Ug. *imr dbḥ*. With G (θύσατε) and Vg (*immolate*), however, a correction to זבחו (3 pl pf) "they sacrifice" is required.

2.d. MT should be vocalized אִמְּרִים "lambs" (cf. Ug. *imr*) in parallel with עגלים "calves."

2.e. On the use of אדם with a pl verb, cf., e.g., Jer 47:2.

2.f. It might also be possible to translate; "to the bulls human beings bring drink (offerings)," reading the verb שקה, *hiph*, rather than MT נשק "kiss." The drink offering, as expressed in שקה "to give/back drink to" might complete the parallelism with זבח "sacrifice." In light of the known practice of kissing idols in worship (1 Kgs 19:18; see *Comment*) the verb נשק, with MT is to be prefered.

3.a. The pual (יְסֹעַר) is required since מץ "chaff" is the subj.

4.a. Here G contains what appears to be an insertion, though it may conceivably reflect the original text: στερεῶν οὐρανὸν καὶ κτίζων γῆν, οὗ αἱ χεῖρες ἔκτισαν πᾶσαν τὴν στρατιὰν τοῦ οὐρανοῦ, καὶ οὐ παρέδειξά σοι αὐτὰ τοῦ πορεύεσθαι ὀπίσω αὐτῶν · καὶ ἐγὼ ἀνήγαγόν σε "who establishes heaven and creates earth, whose hands have framed the whole host of heaven; but I have not revealed to you that you should follow them. And I brought you up." MT could easily be the result of a haplogr.

5.a. Following G (ἐποίμαινόν σε) Syr, which read רעיתיך, a likely kind of *lectio difficilior* in the context.

7.a. Here G Syr misread "Assyria" (i.e., אשׁור).

8.a. Lit., "childless, bereaved."

8.b. Lit., "the lining of their heart."

8.c. Reading with Kuhnigk (*NSH*, 180) כל־בא for MT כלביא "like a lion."

9.a. Vocalizing consonantal MT as שַׁחְתִּיךְ is far more likely than the 3 m sg.

9.b. MT "for against me, against your helper" is evidently garbled. In light of the questions that follow, an interrogative such as that of G (Syr), τίς "who," is appropriate here. We therefore emend MT כי to מי.

10.a. G Vg Tg all attest the interrogative "where?" In light of its established use 3x in the passage, אֱהִי should probably be understood as a northern dialectical form for "where?" rather than being emended to אַיֵּה.

10.b. The possibility of emending עֶזְרֶךָ to צָרֶיךָ (". . . help you from all your *foes*") is also attractive, but see *Comment*.

13.a. Lit., "will not stand / station himself."

13.b. Lit., "at the breaking-forth place of children."

14.a. The context would appear to favor the interpretation of these clauses as questions.

14.b. See above, n. 10.a.

14.c. G reads δίκη, usually understood as "judgment / punishment / penalty." Exactly how this would reflect MT דבר, or mutate to νῖκος "victory" (a corruption of νεῖκος?) in 1 Cor 15:55 remains problematic. Was G's *Vorlage* רִיבֶיךָ rather than דְּבָרֶיךָ?

15.a. The plural of אחו with בן yields "among the marshes." Cf. Gen 41:2, 18; Job 8:11 and Ug *'aḥ*. MT "among the brothers" is less likely in light of the floral context.

15.b. MT "(he) will be ashamed" is far less likely than וְיָבֵשׁ "will dry up."

15.c. The subject is Yahweh, who is the referent for the pronoun הוא "he."

14:1.a. Heb. 14:1 = Eng 13:16, Heb. 14:2 = Eng 14:1, etc.

1.b. Or, possibly, "must bear her guilt" (with MT). G (ἀφανισθήσεται) confirms תֶּאְשַׁם "will be desolated."

1.c. Lit., "its pregnant women," the reference being to Samaria in v 1a [13:16a].

Form / Structure / Setting

As often in Hosea's prophecies, past and present combine to explain the future. Israel's continuing (present) sinful arrogance (vv 2, 6, 15) contrasted to Yahweh's constant (past) faithfulness (vv 4–6) mean that Israel's (future) death is certain (vv 3, 7–14). In this passage Hosea brings to a close via climactic crescendo the predictions and warnings that comprise the bulk of the book. "Even now" (ועתה) in v 2 provides the transition from the lawsuit passage of 12:1 [11:12]–13:1. No special connection stylistically can be drawn between 12:1 [11:12]–13:1 and 13:2–14:1 [13:16], though they obviously function simi-

larly to indict and doom Israel. A new passage begins again in 14:2 [1], where
the remnant of Israel is invited to return to Yahweh after having been duly
punished.

Cohesive and balanced, the passage should be considered a literary unit.
The prophet speaks in vv 2–3, Yahweh in vv 4–14, and the prophet again
in 13:15–14:1 [13:16]. The emphasis rests upon the proximate destruction
of the nation for its sins: idolatry and polytheism, violating the first two
commandments of the decalogue. Vv 2 and 3 express the punishment for
idolatry-annihilation. V 4 reminds Israel of who their only God was supposed
to be. The imperfect תדע should probably be read, "(You) were to know,"
i.e., as a past durative expressing the general sense "should" or "ought."
The remainder of the passage builds a picture of Israel's arrogant refusal to
serve Yahweh alone, in spite of his unilateral covenant mercies to them,
and the necessary result of such refusal: destruction.

The overall progression may be schematized as follows:

> Judgment for idolatry (vv 2–3; the prophet is the speaker)
> > Evidence of idolatry (v 2)
> > Resultant punishment of annihilation (v 3)
> Judgment for polytheism
> > Yahweh speaks (vv 4–14)
> > > The covenant obligation of sole loyalty to Yahweh (v 4)
> > > Israel's refusal to remain loyal (vv 5–6)
> > > Punishment by wild animals (vv 7–8)
> > > Punishment by loss of the king (vv 9–11)
> > > Inevitability of the punishment (vv 12–13)
> > > Punishment via Sheol (v 14)
> > Hosea speaks (13:15–14:1 [13:16])
> > > Punishment via drought (v 15)
> > > Punishment via the horrors of war in the cities (14:1 [13:16])

The metrical structure of the passage is complex. Synonymous parallelism
may be discerned in all or part of the following verses: 2, 3, 4, 7, 8, 10, 11, 14,
15, 14:1 [13:16], a greater proportion than found in the book as a whole.
Two quatrains are present. V 3 is a clearly indissoluble quatrain, rather than
merely four poetic lines for which placement of the caesura is difficult. V
2a, though difficult to categorize, also appears to be a quatrain, in synthetic
parallelism. Unless a substantial haplography has altered the parallelism in
the text of v 14b, the statement "Pity is hidden from me!" (נחם יסתר מעיני)
forms an ejaculatory conclusion to the prediction of consignment to Sheol
reminiscent of the naming of Hosea's second child (לא רחמה "No Compassion"). This single statement encapsulates the message of the passage, that
there is no longer any chance of repentance / pity / changing of Yahweh's
mind (all nuances of נחם).

Accordingly, the setting would appear to be the final years of the Northern
Kingdom. It is likely that vv 9–11 refer to the capture of Hoshea (733–723
B.C.), an event which left Israel without a king, defenseless before the Assyrians
(cf. 2 Kgs 17:4). It is also possible in light of v 14 that Israel's capital city
Samaria was actually now besieged by the Assyrian armies as they began to

occupy the remainder of the northern kingdom. The references to Israel's prosperity during its often glorious history (vv 2, 10, 15) do not mean that the nation was still prosperous. 725 or 724 B.C. are likely dates for the original delivery of this punishment oracle. It is not possible to say if these words were delivered in or near Samaria. By this time Hosea could even have taken up residence in Judah, preaching the severity of the punishments beginning to fall on Judah's northern brother state.

Comment

2 Even though Israel had been reduced to a small area whose capital was perhaps already besieged, the Israelites doggedly maintained their idolatry. The verb יוֹסִפוּ "they continue" can connote an increase in sinful activity (e.g., "they sin all the more") as well as its continuation or repetition. Israel had adopted the religious practices of their neighbors, and viewed the Sinai covenant as a quaint historical fact, not a living relationship. The word used for "cast image" (מַסֵּכָה) is the same word used for the golden bull in Exod 32:4, 8 and Deut 9:16. Presumably the bull worship mentioned in v 2b as well as in 8:5–6 and 10:5–6 is the specific focus of Hosea's inspired invective. The covenant did not allow Yahweh (or any other god) to be worshiped by means of a manufactured image (Deut 5:8–9; Exod 20:4–5; 34:17). But the Israelites continued to manufacture a variety of idols, including probably Baal, Asherah, and miniature copies of the bull idol. As in 8:5, the irony that people worshiped what they themselves had made constitutes the focus of the indictment. Idols were mere products of their own skill. All of "it" (the 3 masc sg suffix is masculine in agreement with מַעֲשֵׂה "work") was human invention, yet human beings worshipped it as something divine! Hosea thus mocks the absurdity of humans trying to create gods.

The text of v 2b is suspect, and MT cannot be translated intelligibly as pointed. Our minor emendation has the advantage of restoring a logical parallelism to the couplet. The prophet's outrage at the folly of idol worship is expressed by two illustrations of practices common in the northern cult. First, the people sacrificed animals (e.g., אֲמָרִים "lambs") to things that craftsmen had made, i.e. the golden bulls. Second, they kissed the golden bulls as part of their evidence of devotion to them (cf. 1 Kgs 19:18). This Hosea mocks via the ambiguity of the poetic phraseology. The words יִשָּׁקוּן אָדָם עֲגָלִים can mean "the people kiss the bulls" but also "humans kiss bulls!" with the sense "How ridiculous!" implied.

3 "Therefore" (לָכֵן) introduces the punishment (as in 2:8 [6], 11 [9], etc.) appropriate to Israel's continuing sin. Four similes, each describing commonly observable phenomena whereby something essentially transitory disappears (cf. 6:4), are used to depict Israel's coming "disappearance." The verse is unusual metrically in that it is a true quatrain, not easily divisible into couplets. The four examples of disappearance—mist, dew, chaff, smoke—combine to emphasize how utterly Israel's destruction will be accomplished by her avenging God. The nation will vanish from the world scene, no longer to occupy the promised land, and no longer to exist as an independent entity among the community of nations.

In vv 2–3 evidence of idolatry is followed by the promise of rapid extinction. This follows a pattern in the Mosaic covenant, as found, for example, in Deut 4:25–26: ". . . if you then become corrupt and make any kind of idol . . . you will quickly (מהר) perish from the land. . . ." This longstanding warning has begun to be fulfilled. When mist, dew, chaff, and smoke vanish the result is nothingness. Israel will similarly disappear and become desolate (cf. Lev 26:31–35; Deut 28, 29). Compare also Deut 32:26: "I said I would scatter them and erase their memory from mankind . . ." in which the themes of dispersal (curse type 13) and death (type 24) are both reflected, as in the present verse. In the context of Deut 32 the threat is softened by the promise that not all the people would actually be killed. But the corporate entity, Israel, would cease to exist. That is what Hosea's words mean.

4 Yahweh begins to speak in the first person. The topic of the remaining portion of the passage, through 14:1 [13:16], is polytheism. Israel's divided loyalty to Yahweh was no true loyalty at all. The divine speech begins with a reminder of the original covenant obligation of Israel to know no God but Yahweh. The first commandment of the decalogue is the paramount stipulation. Their survival depended upon keeping it, as the verse implies. Unless Yahweh was their only God, they would have no salvation, since "there is no savior" (מושיע אין) apart from him.

In effect the Sinai covenant's preamble (identification of Yahweh as the sovereign), prologue (recitation of his benevolence toward his people) and central stipulation (the first commandment) are all restated in this verse. Yahweh's own covenant identity as Israel's God (cf. 11:1; 12:9 [8]) was what the nation's idolatry and polytheism implicitly denied. "Know" (ידע) as it is used in connection with the prohibition of "knowing" any god but Yahweh connotes "having a / any relationship with" (cf. Deut 11:28; 32:17; Jer 9:2; 31:34). For Yahweh to say "You were to know no god beside me" is to say "You were to have a relationship exclusively with me." The language of the verse, like that of the first commandment, is idiomatic and does *not* acknowledge that there are real gods other than Yahweh (cf. Isa 43:11; 45:5, 21). In Amos 3:2 ידע is likewise employed in the sense of covenantal relationship.

5 Here the reflective, retrospective mood is manifest clearly. The wilderness period demonstrated the same act of salvation (cf. מושיע, v 4) as did the exodus. Yahweh had abundantly fulfilled his covenant responsibilities to provide for the nation (cf., e.g., Lev 26:3–5, 9–13). In a barren land, miraculously, they had manna and quail (Exod 16, Num 11:4–34). In a parched land they were provided water, also miraculously (Exod 17:1–7; Num 20:2–13). MT's ידעתיך "I knew you" is likely a corruption of רעיתיך "I fed you" (see note 5.a) in light of the continuing theme of feeding in v 6. Without Yahweh, the infant nation would have died in the Sinai peninsula. They owe their very lives to him, and always have.

6 A progression of events and attitudes is described in this triplet. God generously met the needs of his people in the wilderness. But instead of gratefulness, and a recognition of their dependency on Yahweh, the Israelites took the occasion of their being replete or "satisfied" (שבע) to forget (שכח) their God (cf. 2:15 [13]). Such rebellion following God's provision for them represented nothing surprising. Israel had shown this tendency since the exodus itself. The verse reflects the prediction of Deut 31:2, for example: "When I have brought them into the land . . . and they have eaten and become full (שבע) . . . they will turn to other gods . . . and despise me and break my covenant." The warning that Israel should not become arrogant (lit., "lift up [רום] the heart [לב]") so as to forget (שכח) Yahweh is also well known from Deut 8:14. Hos 13:4–6 may well be based partly on Deut 8:11–15 in light of the close thematic and vocabulary connections between the two passages. However, other passages in Deuteronomy also reflect the danger of arrogance and rebellion after receiving the fullness of the covenantal material blessings (e.g., 6:11–14; 11:15–16).

7–8 Vv 7 and 8 detail a single theme via three couplets. Yahweh's destruction of his people for their disobedience to the covenant is likened both in metaphor and simile to the attack of wild animals on the populace (curse type 11). Thereby Yahweh stresses the severity—i.e., violence—of the coming destruction. In vv 7 and 8a, the lion (שחל), leopard (נמר) and bear (דב) typify devouring animals (cf. 1 Sam 17:34–37). The attack of wild animals was a common curse motif in ancient Near Eastern covenant sactions (Hillers, *Treaty Curses and the Old Testament Prophets*, 54–56). Lev 26:22 ("I will send wild animals against you . . .") and Deut 32:24 ("The teeth of animals I will send upon them; with the venom of creatures that crawl in the dust . . .") present this motif in the Sinai covenant (cf. Lam 3:10–11; Isa 5:29–30; 7:18; 14:29; 15:9; 56:9; Jer 2:14–15; 4:7; 12:9; 48:40; 49:22; 50:44; Hos 5:14; Hab 1:8). In these references the lion is described most often, though a variety of animals from bees to wolves are also mentioned as animal agents symbolic of divine wrath.

7 Yahweh's action will be deliberate and precise. At a time not predictable by the Israelites, perhaps at a time they least expect trouble, he will attack. He is waiting for them ("watch," שור in Jer 5:26 describes the patient waiting of the fowler) and will soon spring upon them. The language is metaphorical, as in the curses. The actual vehicle of the attack would be Assyria, whose armies were probably already poised against Samaria.

8 The attack of the "animals" will kill, not merely maim. No help will be given (cf. v 9b). The she-bear robbed of her cubs (cf. Prov 17:12; 2 Sam 17:8) provides a vivid image of destructive rage. "Wild animals" (חית השדה) employed in synonymous parallelism to "whatever comes along" (כל בא) simply reinforces the point that the unleashing of covenant sanctions will be severe.

9 Just as wild animals brutally destroy, so Yahweh has determined to destroy (שחת) Israel (cf. Lam 2:8). Jeremiah 4:7 describes the "lion" as the "destroyer (שחת) of nations," i.e., Babylon. Here the destroyer is portrayed as Yahweh himself, though Hosea's audience would understand that the Assyrian army would accomplish his destruction.

God addresses Israel directly only in this verse and the two which follow (if our vocalization of the text is correct). The verse reflects the statement in v 4 that "there is no savior except me." Yahweh has arranged Israel's circumstances so that they are totally dependent on him. Having foolishly forsaken that dependence, they will have no recourse when their own God turns against them in wrath. "Who then will be your helper?" is a rhetorical question to which the answer can only be "No one." The question reflects the helplessness curses (type 19). The Israelites undoubtedly continued to hope that they might somehow be rescued from the Assyrians, and they sacrificed to their idols intensely, appealing to that end (v 1). But woe to this people who has abandoned its only savior! The covenant curses found in poetic form in Deut 32:28–42 state the theme on which this woe is based, e.g., "Then he will say, "Where are their gods/ the rock in which they took refuge/ who ate the fat of their sacrifices/ and drank the wine of their libation?/ Let them rise up and help (עזר) you/ let them be your protection!'" (Deut 32:37–38).

The covenant promise to an obedient Israel included help (עזר) against its enemies (cf. Deut 33:7, 26, 29). The covenant curse to the apostate nation substitutes wrath for that help. It must be remembered, however, that the divine promise to destory (שחת, piel, i.e., curse type 24) in v 9 is not a promise to destroy completely. The latter (expressed sometimes by שחת, hiphil) is guaranteed by the covenant *not* to happen: "For Yahweh your God is a merciful God. He will not . . . wipe you out (שחת, hiphil) . . ." (Deut 4:31). The difference is seen between the nation as historical continuum and the particular nation of Hosea's time. The former would never cease to exist. The latter was already being destroyed.

10   The divine taunt continues, focusing on Israel's governmental disarray. We are probably at the point in Hosea's ministry (725 B.C. or later) when Shalmaneser V had already taken Hoshea captive (2 Kgs 17:4). The Assyrians probably also imprisoned the royal family, and most of the significant military-governmental leaders.

What the people had demanded originally from God (1 Sam 8) they received, i.e., "kings and officials." Samuel had not acceded to the demand gladly (1 Sam 8:6–7) as v 11 of the present passage reiterates. The king had represented three advantages to Israel: (a) stable, continuous government; (b) equity with other nations, as the international system of that day was royal in structure; (c) leadership in war (cf. 1 Sam 8:5, 19, 20). After Hoshea was deposed, Israel lost what (often inept) help it had in these areas and stood naked before its adversaries.

The mention that the king might give help "in all your cities" reflects the prominent role cities play in curse descriptions of military siege. The original conquest of Israel under Joshua was a city-by-city military operation. The conquest of Israel would be similar, simply because most Israelites lived in or associated themselves with a city. The miseries expressed in terms of the cities (Lev 26:25, 31, 33; Deut 28:16, 52–57; 32:25) thus complement the miseries expressed in terms of crops, herds, etc. The king might not defend the countryside but would be expected to defend the cities. Without a king, or even a government, what could Israel do against the Assyrians whom Yahweh had set upon them? Nowhere in Hosea is the kingship portrayed in a particularly positive light (1:4; 7:3–7; 8:4–10; 10:3–4, 7, 15), and here the lack of a kingship is no benefit, either. The loss of the kingship (and the royal governmental structure) is a covenant punishment (type 13a; cf. 3:4).

11   God had granted Israel a king in the days of Samuel, even though their demand represented a rejection of the theocracy that had prevailed since the patriarchs. God had "given them a king in his anger" i.e., the problematic Saul, partly as a means of teaching Israel a lesson. The Northern kingship which began with Saul (1 Sam 10–11) in about 1031 B.C. came to an end with the removal of Hoshea from the throne in 725 B.C. Twenty-three kings had ruled over the north but David alone had kept the national covenant inviolable. Every one of the twenty kings of Israel after Solomon "did what Yahweh considered evil" (1 and 2 Kings, *passim*). The whole history of the kingship had been a manifestation of God's anger / fury. Israel's kings had been chosen without God's consent (cf. 8:4) and the kingship itself had now been abolished by God as a portent of the coming national disaster (cf. Deut 28:36).

12 Two things about Ephraim, the rump state of Israel, are stated by this synonymous couplet: (1) it is guilty as charged of covenant transgressions; (2) this sin has been noted and will not be forgotten or forgiven until punished. Appreciating the verse requires the background which vv 2–11 provide, because it resumes the reference to Israel's idolatry and polytheism made in vv 2 and 6. The declaration that Ephraim's iniquity (עֲוֹן) and sin (חַטָּאת) are wrapped up (צְרוּר) and stored up (צְפוּנָה) represents no comfort for Hosea's audience. It means that the loss of the kingship, the reduction of the land and the investing of Samaria are only the beginnings of the full punishments known from Lev 26, Deut 4 and Deut 28–32. The worst is still to come, since the payback of the long history of Israel's disloyalty is still "on hold," as it were.

The covenant curses in Lev 26 predict awesome punishments precisely for these two terms, "iniquity" (עֲוֹן; cf. Lev 26:39–43) and "sin" (חַטָּאת; cf. Lev 26:18, 21, 24, 28). Other terms (not "obeying," שׁמע ב; and not "observing," שׁמר, etc.) are more common to the Deuteronomic curses. The verb צרר (hiphil) is used in Deut 28:52 in its sense of "besiege," but otherwise neither צרר nor צפן figure in the covenant curse vocabulary. The covenant language, in other words, does not suggest that there is a grace period during which Israel may sin without immediately being punished. No covenant would ever contain such a stipulation. Nevertheless Israel had benefited throughout its history from Yahweh's reluctance to impose deserved wrath upon them. The people indeed assumed that he would not ever punish them (cf. 5:4). Hosea's word now announces that the destructive punishments, so long delayed, are yet coming.

13 Israel's plight at a crisis time in its history is likened metaphorically to the plight of a fetus malpositioned in the womb and thus unable to be born. In ancient times, a child would die if it failed to achieve a "presentation" position so as to fit through the cervix (מִשְׁבַּר בָּנִים). The mother would also die unless the dead fetus would eventually "present" properly. This agonizingly tragic image depicts Israel as a nation whose potential will be snuffed out in judgment, because it is an "unwise" (לֹא חָכָם) child. At this point the metaphor obviously leaves aside technical accuracy, since an unborn child is not capable of wisdom as the OT knows it. Rather, the metaphor concentrates here on Israel's lack of wisdom (ability to make godly choices) which will cause it to lose its life, on the basis of Deut 32:28–29 ("They are a nation without sense [תְבוּנָה]; if only they were wise—[חָכְמ] . . .").

The verbs of the verse (יבֹאוּ‎ ‎יָ, יַעְמֹד‎) are imperfects which should probably be translated in the future tense. Though the labor pains of childbirth are employed by other prophets in describing the agony of the nation under divine punishment (e.g., Jer 6:24; 13:21; 22:23; Isa 13:8; 26:17–18) in such cases the focus is upon the writhing pain of the mother. Here, uniquely, the unborn child is the subject. It is a child which cannot be born and therefore must surely die. There is no hint of any hopefulness in these words (*contra* Wolff, 228: "Behind the metaphor stands the certainty that Yahweh . . . is to bring Israel new life").

14 The understanding of the couplet and triplet which comprise v 14 hinges on how one interprets ambiguous Hebrew clauses. If the first four are declarative statements (and אֱהִי‎ is translated "I shall be" or the like), there is some cause to consider the verse partly a promise rather than a threat. In light of the fifth clause, however ("Pity is hidden from me"), the first four would seem best translated as questions (see note 14.a). Yet even נֹחַם‎ (here "pity") might mean "a change of heart" (cf. the verb נֹחַם‎, Niphal in 1 Sam 15:11, 35). The noun occurs in the OT only here, and is thus not definable with certainty. The context, nevertheless, is one of judgment, and it is therefore hard to attribute a hopefulness to these words. The "plagues" (דְּבָרִים‎) and "scourge" (קֶטֶב‎) reflect the language of Deut 32:24 (cf. קֶטֶב‎ // דֶּבֶר‎ in Psa 91:6, i.e., curse type 8), and hardly seem to contribute to any hope for Israel.

G, however, appears to translate the first couplet as if a promise ("I will deliver them from the power of Hades, and will redeem them from death") and thus the rhetorical questions of the triplet (in G, "Where is your penalty, death; where is your sting, Hades?") might be considered hopeful assertions, in effect that the penalty of death and sting of hell are now so distant from Ephraim that they cannot be found. Nevertheless, the questions to death and Hades are actually presented quite neutrally and literally in G, as is the following clause ("Comfort / compassion is hidden from my eyes"). This part of v 14 in G therefore cannot be assumed to represent a hopeful promise. G normally translates Hosea clause by clause, as literally as possible, without much regard for the sweep of the logic.

In 1 Cor 15:55, Paul cites the first two lines of v 14b either periphrastically or from a G text containing νίκη "victory" for δίκη "penalty" and θάνατε "death" twice instead of once in parallel with ᾅδη "Hades." He also uses these lines "neutrally" so that it is impossible to judge from the context of 1 Cor 15 whether the questions are meant to represent the well-deserved punishment which Christ has delivered us from, or whether they are meant to suggest the absence (via distance) of such punishments from the believer.

For Hosea's audience, these words were probably unambiguous in light of the inflections in Hosea's delivery which would have clarified the meaning. We judge *that* meaning to have included only the negative guarantee of punishment, so that "Where are your plagues / scourge?" is in fact a divine summons for the covenant punishments to commence. Sheol, the place of the dead, will overtake Israel, in fulfillment of the covenant warnings to the disobedient (Deut 4:26, etc.; i.e. curse type 24).

15 This relatively long verse, composed of a triplet and two couplets, uses two metaphors to describe the coming desolation. Israel is envisioned as a plant that will die for lack of water. The divine storehouse is then depicted as a place of blessings for Israel ("desirable things") which will be stripped bare of all that it once held. Both images reflect the Pentateuchal curses. The warnings that the land will become unproductive because of drought (curse type 6a) are found mainly in Lev 26:19–20, 32,35; and Deut 28:22–24; 29:23. The denuding of the "storehouse" (אוצר) is an image probably most directly occasioned by the presence of this word in Deut 28:12 and 32:34. It is therefore unlikely that the reading in G (καταξηρανεῖ τὴν γῆν αὐτοῦ καί, i.e., "he will dry up his land [ארצו for אוצר] and . . .") is the more original, since MT preserves the word which the prophet presumably intended. The "storehouse" or "reserve" refers to a heavenly repository of rain in Deut 28:12 (though of wrath in Deut 32:34). In the present context, the term is not a metaphor for Israel, but for the heavenly treasury of agricultural benefits and blessings, the place from which God pours out bounty on his people. This will now be stripped of its contents with the result that the sky will become like bronze (Deut 28:23). It will yield no rain, no sun in proper measure with darkness, etc. Each desirable thing (כל חמדה) which Yahweh had heretofore heaped upon his people's land will now be eliminated.

The former prosperity of Israel is now passing away. The east wind, off the desert (מדבר) may even represent Assyria metaphorically. Sheol and death (v 14) will come via Assyrian armies, leaving only desolation in their wake.

14:1 [13:16]   The focus narrows to the besieged capital Samaria, the only major reminder of the once successful, influential Northern Kingdom. Samaria naturally was the prime target of the Assyrian assault, as the headquarters of the rebel Hoshea. The covenant curses predict doom for countryside and city alike. Here the city curses (type 9b) are described as imminently fulfilled. The initial couplet states the reason for the punishment: rebellion against Yahweh. The concluding triplet describes the punishment itself. The punishment is military (the "sword," curse type 3); and it will be merciless, extending even the the brutal slaughter of infants and pregnant women.

The curses of Lev 26 are the backdrop for the prediction of Samaria's desolation (שמם) in v 1a. The verb שמם occurs no less than seven times in Lev 26 (vv 22, 31, 32 (twice), 34, 35, 43). Leviticus 26:25–31 describes the miseries of the city under siege and then captured, with an aftermath of awful slaughter, as a punishment for covenant infidelity. The background for v 1b may also be Lev 26, at least in part, since the latter refers to destruction by the sword (v 25) and the violent death of children (v 29; cf. v 22; Deut 28:52–57; 32:25). The practice of slitting open pregnant women in war as punishment for rebellion is attested also in 2 Kgs 15:16 and Amos 1:13.

The siege of Samaria (2 Kgs 17:15) lasted three years—more than enough time for the desperate sorts of acts of starving people described in Deut 28:52–57 to take place. The city undoubtedly suffered greatly. When it fell, the Assyrians ended its history as a capital, making it temporarily a desolate place. According to his annals, Sargon II, who came to power in Assyria just as the siege was coming to an end, took captive 27,290 Israelites from Samaria. The cultivation of the farming districts around the city probably ceased thereupon, so that lions and other wild animals literally moved into the countryside (2 Kgs 17:25) in fulfillment of vv 7–8. The city was occupied on a limited scale through NT times, though only a minority of its inhabitants were ethnic Israelites, since the Assyrians imported a diverse collection of peoples to settle the region (2 Kgs 17:29; cf. Jer 41:5).

Explanation

The wrath of God against the people who have broken his covenant is here portrayed with intensity unmatched elsewhere in Hosea. This passage constitutes the climax of the punishment message which began in chap. 1. Though frequently interrupted by reminders of hope for the eventual future, the dominant message of Hosea is that the Northern Kingdom must come to a miserable end because it has violated its solemn contract with Yahweh.

Hosea preached these words close to the end of Israel's existence as an independent nation. The northern counter-cultus (v 2) established by Jeroboam I had prevailed through the North's entire history (2 Kgs 17:22–23). This open violation of the covenant's first and second commandments (Exod 20:3–4; Deut 5:7–8) was by itself sufficient cause for the invocation of divine sanctions. Because Israel had persisted to the last in this sin, no mere token punishment was to be expected. Israel would be swept away into oblivion (v 3), violently decimated (vv 7–8); helpless before the enemy Yahweh had ordained to destroy them (vv 10–13) and slated for certain death (vv 14–14:1 [13:16]).

The Israelites had violated the essence of the covenant by rejecting the exclusive status of its giver, Yahweh. The result meant disaster. V 4 provides a précis. Israel was commanded to acknowledge Yahweh alone. The command's corollary was that unless Israel did so, they would lose the protection that Yahweh alone could give. By detaching themselves from their only real source of life, the Israelites guaranteed their own death as a nation.

Yahweh summons death and Sheol to overtake the covenant people, assuring them that pity will not deter him from acting against them (v 14). The sovereign's patience cannot wait forever while the vassal revels in disobedience. Israel, the "unwise child" (v 13) has missed the opportunity to be a great nation, blessed of God. They have forgotten him (v 6). So he will withhold from them his covenant blessings (v 14b). As due reward for their iniquity / sin (v 12) the nation and its capital must die in war. The word that Hosea began to announce in the latter years of the Jehu dynasty (1:2–9) was coming to pass in the remainder state already crippled by the capture of its king and key government leaders (vv 10–11).

Israel got what it deserved as the wage of its sin: death (Rom 6:23). But v 14 of this very passage is excerpted by Paul in 1 Cor 15:15 to remind the believer that God's free gift (Rom 6:23b) has reversed the usual pattern. A wording that heralded the onset of punishment for the offenders in Hos 13 is reused to remind followers of Christ that although the old covenant (νόμος "law") guaranteed death to the rebel (1 Cor 15:56) the new covenant in Christ provides victory over death. Christ has met once for all the full force of the covenant curses and by his own satisfaction of the law through payment of its penalty has rendered the power of the plagues of the old covenant ineffective against the Christian. The reward of resurrection of the believers to live eternally with God will replace in the new covenant the punishment of death and destruction which applied to Israel in the old covenant. For this all who are in Christ can say with Paul, "Thanks be to God" (1 Cor 15:57).

A Promise for the Remnant That Will Return   (14:2–9 [1–8])

Bibliography

Coote, R. "Hos 14:8: 'They Who Are Filled with Grain Shall Live.'" *JBL* 93 (1974) 161–73. **Driver, G. R.** "Difficult Words in the Hebrew Prophets." In *Studies in Old Testament Prophecy*, ed. H. H. Rowley. Edinburgh: T. and T. Clark, 1950. **Feuillet, A.** "'S'asseoir à l'ombre' de l'époux." *RB* 78 (1971) 391–405. **Gordis, R.** "The Text and Meaning of Hosea 14:3." *VT* 5 (1955) 88–90. **Kidner, D.** "The Way Home: An Exposition of Hosea 14." *Themelios* 1 (1975–76) 34–36. **Müller, H. P.** "Imperativ und Verheissung im AT: Drei Beispiele." *EvT* 28 (1968) 557–71. **Testuz, M.** "Deux fragments inédits des manuscrits de la Mer Morte." *Sem* 5 (1955) 38–39. **Wetenholz, J.** and **A.** "Help for Rejected Suitors: The Old Akkadian Love Incantation MAD V8." *Or* 46 (1977) 198–219.

Translation

The prophet gives Israel its future prayer of repentance

14:2 [1] *Return, Israel, to Yahweh your God, for you stumbled in your iniquity.* 3 [2] *Take words with you and return to Yahweh. Say to him: "Completely*[a] *forgive our*[b] *iniquity. We will take*[c] *what is good, and we will fully repay the fruit of our lips.* 4 [3] *Assyria cannot save us. We cannot ride on horses.*[a] *And we cannot again say 'Our god'*[b] *to the product of our hands. Blessed*[c] *is the orphan who*[d] *finds compassion*[e] *in you."*

Yahweh's promise to answer the people's prayer

5 [4] *I will heal their apostasy*[a]
   I will love them voluntarily,
      for my anger will have turned from him.

6 [5] *I will be like dew to Israel,*
   he will sprout like the crocus,
      he will strike his roots as if in Lebanon.[a]

7 [6] *His shoots will go forth,*
   his splendor will be like the olive tree,
      his scent like that of Lebanon.[a]

8 [7] *Those who dwell in his shade will return;* [a]
they will revive as [b] *grain and will sprout.*

Like the vine will be his renown,
like the wine of Lebanon.

9 [8] *What will Ephraim* [a] *have to do any more with idols?*
I will have responded [b] *and I will bless* [c] *him.*

I am like a luxuriant fir tree,
On me your [d] *fruit is found.*

Notes

3.a. On this meaning of כל cf. 2 Sam 1:9; Job 27:3; Ezek 11:15, etc.

3.b. We judge that the 1 c pl suffs apply implicitly here also.

3.c. Reading the 1 c pl with Tg. G has the 2 m pl. The sg of MT is hardly impossible, however.

4.a. See 3.b.

4.b. With G, the word could also be translated as a pl, i.e., "our gods."

4.c. Vocalizing consonantal MT as אֲשֻׁרַי. Also possible is "because" (cf. Gen 30:18; 1 Kgs 3:19, etc.).

4.d. On the relative clause without a relative particle after אשרי "Blessed," cf. Prov. 8:32.

4.e. G reads ירחם as a piel rather than a pual; Q ירוחם, however, confirms the pual of MT.

5.a. G τὰς κατοικίας αὐτῶν "their dwellings" for משובתם "their apostasy," though not entirely impossible ("I will restore their dwellings") is contextually unlikely.

6.a. Lit., "like Lebanon." The Heb. phrase is elliptical, conveying a comparison of circumstances rather than individual plants. The Lebanon "crocus" (Andersen and Freedman, 646), or "forest" may also be intended in the elliptical wording. The common emendation to לִבְנֶה "poplar" is theoretically possible, since the mutation of לבנה to לבנן "Lebanon" could have occurred under the influence of לבנן in v 8.

7.a. See 6.a.

8.a. Or "They will again dwell. . . ." See *Comment.*

8.b. The comparative is implicit; additionally, the כ of כגפן "like the vine" may do double duty in the verse.

9.a. Following G, which reads לו "to him" for MT לי "to me." Kuhnigk (*NSH,* 156) interprets MT לי as a 3 m sg form, for which several analogies exist.

9.b. G ἐταπείνωσα "I have humbled" takes the verb as ענה II; cf. 2:17 [15]; 5:5; 7:10. The sense would then be: "I have humbled him but (now) I will bless him."

9.c. For MT אֲשׁוּרֶנּוּ several roots (שור, שרר, אשר, etc.) and corresponding pointings have been proposed since "I will watch him" seems illogical. The versions differ substantially. We read אֲאַשְּׁרֶנּוּ (cf. Mays, 184; KB, 957).

9.d. The versions uniformly attest to the 2 masc sg suff. The shift to direct address is problematic at first glance, but parallels the similar shift in v 4b [36].

Form / Structure / Setting

In 14:2–9 [1–8] Hosea has coupled his own inspired prophetic exhortation to Israel (vv 2–4 [1–3]) with God's promise of restoration (vv 5–9 [4–8]). It is the future Israel which is envisioned here. They are invited, urged, and implored to turn back to Yahweh from their situation of punishment. If they honestly express their penitence to him, he will in turn respond mercifully to them, restoring the abundance he had withdrawn because of their infidelity (13:15–14:1 [13:16]).

The combination of exhortation and divine speech recalls the penitential psalms. Indeed, Westermann (*The Praise of God in the Psalms* [Atlanta: John Knox Press, 1965] 61–62) identifies the present passage with such psalms. The people are urged to pray for Yahweh's forgiveness, and the divine promise of forgiveness is given. The passage is not, however, a liturgy for a worship service of repentance. First, the covenant sanctions which Hosea's prophecies follow envision an opportunity for repentance and restoration for Israel only after its unfaithfulness has been fully punished. Second, there is no hint here that a spontaneous revival of orthodoxy in worship is expected. Yahweh will hardly grant Israel the promised blessing until after the national remnant shows true, substantial, change. Israel's repentance was, of course, nowhere yet on the horizon. They continued to sin (13:2).

The passage's structure may be summarized as follows:

A program for repentance	(vv 2–4 [1–3])
Invitation to return to Yahweh	(v 2 [1])
The suggested prayer of repentance,	
including vow of penitence and	
confession of trust	(vv 3–4 [2–3])
A divine promise of restoration	(vv 5–9 [4–8])
Healing will replace divine anger	(v 5 [4])
Israel's future prosperity in Yahweh	(vv 6–9 [5–8])

The prophetic summons in vv 2–4 [1–3] appears to be prose. It lacks the parallelisms and typical meter expected in poetry. A fully poetic structure might reflect an outline for a service of penitential worship. The presence of prose materials mitigates against this. In vv 5–9 [4–8], however, the poetic structure is evident, and synonymous parallelisms dominate. Only in v 9a [8a] is synthetic parallelism clearly present. The stichometry of v 8 [7] is not agreed upon; for a different division of the lines, cf. Wolff (232) or Andersen and Freedman (642). The presence of three triplets in a row (vv 5 [4], 6 [5], 7 [6]) is noteworthy. The remainder of the poem is in couplet form.

Nothing in the passage explicitly provides us with its date, though this program of repentance has the ring of a parting word of hope to a people heading into exile and death—a word for them to take with them and to communicate to their children (cf. Deut 30:2, 6) so that the nation will remember that their God has not forever abandoned them (Lev 26:44).

These verses appear, therefore, to presuppose the destruction, past or imminent, of Samaria (cf. 13:2–14:1 [13:16]). Perhaps they were spoken in the last months of the siege, in 722 B.C. or thereabouts, and they may even have followed the fall of the Northern Kingdom. The suggested wording of the prayer of penitence in v 4 [3] ("Assyria cannot save us. We cannot ride on horses") may presume a situation in which neither political nor military maneuvering has validity any longer.

Comment

2 [1] The passage begins with an imperative to return (שׁוּב) to Yahweh. Implicitly, this imperative is addressed to the future nation in exile, who will finally be willing to return to their God, having learned from their manifold miseries (cf. Lev 26:40–45; Deut 4:29–31; 30:1–10). The covenant verb שוב "return" is of course a central word in Hosea's hortatory vocabulary (cf. 2:9 [7], 11 [9]; 3:5; 6:1; 7:10, 16; 12:7 [6]; 14:2 [1]) reflecting its use seven times in Deut 30:1–10 (cf. Deut 4:30).

Israel's iniquity (עון; cf. 4:8; 5:5; 7:1; 8:13; 9:7, 9; 13:12) has caused them to stumble (כשל; cf. 4:5; 5:5; 14:10 and Lev 26:37). Both עון and כשל are part of the vocabulary of the covenant curses; the verse links Israel's stumbling (curse type 19, as punishment already under way) with its past sin (disloyalty to the divine covenant). Israel's downfall has begun and will run its course before the return can be accomplished. The hope of return is no pipedream but a divine guarantee for a righteous remnant (Deut 4:29–31, et al; cf. Hos 3:1–5). The invitation to return is thus a real word of hope for the nation as a continuum, though not a prediction of blessing for the same generation who first heard these words from Hosea's lips.

3 [2] For the future, repentant remnant Hosea provides the wording of a petition for forgiveness and a vow of penitence. It is not likely that we have here an exact formula for the people's prayer, but rather a kind of précis of their appeal. An Israelite who appeared before Yahweh was supposed to bring a sacrificial offering to guarantee his or her vow (Exod 23:15; 34:20). It is instructive to note, then, that the prophet does not advise the future Israelites to take "sacrifices" to their covenant Lord. Sacrifices are worthless without obedience (cf. 4:8; 5:6; 6:6; 8:13). They are rather to take "words" (דברים) and "what is good" (טוב), i.e., their confession and vow of promise, accompanied by right actions which will fulfill that promise. The suggestion that טוב here means "word" (R. Gordis, *VT* 5 [1955] 88–90) is appealing philologically but ultimately unlikely in light of the context. To "repay the fruit of our lips" (cf. Prov 13:2) means here to fulfill the vow of repentance by good deeds which conform to the covenant's demands.

Because it is a promise in the covenant, the forgiveness of Yahweh is something that Israel will in the future be able boldly to request. Yahweh is willing to grant a petition to "completely forgive our iniquity." This is not an arrogant or presumptuous expectation. It is a hope for which the grace of God allows. (On the phrase נשא עון "forgive iniquity" see Exod 34:7; Mic 7:18, etc.)

As Andersen and Freedman point out (645), the wording of the people's speech to Yahweh has in total seven statements: three positive (v 3b), three negative (v 4a), and the conclusion (v 4b). The three positive elements, i.e., the imperative (". . . forgive . . .") and the two promises ("we will take . . . ; . . . we will repay . . .") complete the first half of the penitence speech.

4 [3] The penitence speech continues with three brief statements cast in the negative, each of which is a confession of failure and inability, and thus by implication a confession that Yahweh alone has the power to save and benefit his people. The people admit that there is no hope in "Assyria," "horses," or idols (synecdoches for political entanglements, military might, and heterodox worship, respectively). By disavowing these previous objects of trust, Israel implicitly renews its original covenant trust in Yahweh. Israel had repeatedly, though inconsistently, hoped in Hosea's time for deliverance from Assyria (5:13; 8:9) as a solution to its international problems. It had also trusted repeatedly in its horses, including the chariotry, central to Israel's military. This was a direct violation of the famous covenant "horse" stipulation of Deut 17:6a, which probably determined Hosea's vocabulary in this instance (cf. Isa 30:16; 31:3; 36:8). Moreover, since Israel depended upon Egypt for its supply of horses, the reference may also imply a dependence on Egypt, parallel to dependence on Assyria (Deut 17:6b). But the most galling trust was Israel's stubborn confidence in its idols, right to the end of its nationhood (cf. 13:2). The "work of our hands," the golden bulls and other idols were the creation of people who themselves were the creation of God, thus obviously without saving power (cf. 8:6; 13:2). This most basic unfaithfulness to the covenant the future Israel must and will repudiate.

The threefold confession of v 4a [3a], when added to the threefold expression of devotion in v 3b [2b], anticipates strict loyalty to Yahweh, and utter dependence upon him. Will Israel's radical reaffirmation of the original national commitment to Yahweh alone (cf. 2:9b [7b]) be rewarded? It will indeed, because Yahweh is a God of compassion, who has shown himself ready to forgive and restore his people (Lev 26:42–45; Deut 4:31; 30:2–9; Hos 2:1–3 [1:10–2:1], 18–25 [16–23]; 3:5; 6:1–3; 11:8–11). This assurance, as often in the penitential psalms, is here expressed metaphorically by the image of the orphan finding compassion in Yahweh. Whether one takes MT אשׁר as "because" or "blessed" the point of the expression of trust remains the same: Yahweh is ever willing to "show compassion" (רחם) to the needy (cf. 1:6, 7; 2:3 [1]). Just as an adult takes in an orphan and loves it as his own child, so God promises to receive Israel again. The orphan in ancient Israelite society was desolate and helpless, unable to survive on its own. Yahweh promised to be the orphan's protector in the covenant (Exod 22:22). On this compassion the future Israel could rest its hope.

5 [4]   Now Yahweh begins to speak. His speech, cast in poetry, is full of promise. He assures Israel that he will one day heal the breach of the covenant that has brought their punishment, that he will then love them freely and generously, and that they will need no longer fear his anger, for the time is coming when it will be gone. Israel is referred to by both "them" and "him," the easy change of pronoun being well attested throughout Hosea. In this case the shift to "him" has the advantage of providing a bridge to the prevailing metaphor of vv 6–9 in which Israel is likened to a (singular) luxuriant tree.

The very apostasy (משׁובתם) which characterized Israel in the past (cf. 5:4; 7:2; 11:5) is what Yahweh promises to heal (רפא). The term משׁובה is used only in the books of Hosea (here and 11:7), Proverbs (once) and Jeremiah (nine times) in the OT, though its meaning is perfectly clear. The connection of רפא "heal" with a form of שׁוב "return" is paralleled by the use of these terms together in Isa 6:10. In the vocabulary of the covenant curses, רפא appears in Deut 28:27 and 35, where there are mentioned respectively the itch and the sore which cannot be healed as punishments for disloyalty. But now healing is promised for the repentant nation in the future, whereas no healing was possible in the past. The promise of generous love utilizes a primary covenant term אהב ("love"; cf. Deut 4:37), in its technical sense found in treaties expressing the notion "be loyal to, show faithfulness to," etc., as well as in its more common connotation of emotional closeness. This is a love which will not be earned—what could Israel possibly present to Yahweh as an acceptable payment? Rather, as reflected by the sense of נדבה as "voluntary offering" or "offering made out of generosity" Yahweh's love will again give blessing to his people. The "anger" (אף) of God, also a technical covenant term, is the precurser to his covenant punishments (Deut 29:19, 22,-23, 26, 27; 31:17; 32:22). To predict that his anger will turn (שוב) is to predict that the punishments will cease for good. The love and anger are not indication of emotional vicissitude, but covenantally expressed descriptions of the process of punishment and forgiveness. Yahweh's anger will be appeased (cf. 11:9) only by his own grace (cf. 2:16, 17 [14, 15]). Israel remains as undeserving of this merciful forgiveness as she was of her initial election. She will, in the eschaton, receive the blessing of being made faithful (restoration blessing type 3; cf. Deut 30:6).

6 [5] V 6 [5], a triplet, begins the metaphorical part of the poem in vv 5–9 [4–8]. Three similes make up the verse: Yahweh likens himself to dew (or "moisture," the water that a plant requires to flourish); Israel's future abundant splendor is likened to the crocus (or more loosely, "lily"); and Israel's future stability to the rootedness of the vast Lebanon forest. Prosperity is associated with or expressed via abundant plant life especially in three OT loci: in the covenant restoration blessings (e.g., Deut 30:9), in the wisdom literature (e.g., Song of Solomon) and in a host of prophetic predictions of restored covenantal blessings (e.g., Amos 9:13–14; Mic 7:14; Isa 55:13). Yahweh's promise to be like dew (טל) to Israel, and thereby to cause her to flourish, is reminiscent not only of the blessing promises in Deut 33:13 and 28 (cf. also Deut 32:2) but also of some of the styles of the love language of the Song of Solomon (cf. also Isa 26:19). The allusion to Lebanon's glory and beauty has abundant parallels both in the Song and in prophetic blessing predictions (e.g., Isa 35:2; 60:13). Lebanon's slopes, moistened almost continuously by dew, were places of lush growth year round. The crocus, known for its rapid growth and proliferation early in the spring, is another appropriate image to convey Israel's coming prosperity. Hosea's use of פרח "to sprout" here contrasts to 10:4, where royal, corrupt "justice" sprouted in a very different way. The notion of blossoming / sprouting is thematic of the new age (cf. Isa 35:1, 2). The use of שרש "root" is also different from its previous use in 9:16 ("Their root has dried up"; cf. Deut 29:18). Here, as in Isa 37:31 and 53:2, the "root" describes the fixedness and security of the eschatological nation blessed and made prosperous by its God. Israel's fleeting loyalty was previously described by Hosea in terms of dew (6:4; 13:3). Now Yahweh's steadfast loyalty is described in part by the same word. When his covenant is once again kept, his instruction will "fall like rain, and my words descend like dew, like showers on new grass, like abundant rain on tender plants" (Deut 32:2).

7 [6] The poem's third triplet continues directly the metaphor developed in v 6. It even ends similarly, with a reference to the Lebanon forest, famed for its plant life in a region of the world where barrenness is the rule rather than the exception. This is in effect what Yahweh promises Israel: what has been exceptional before (lush agricultural bounty), which Israel prostituted herself to Baal in order to obtain (cf. 2:10 [8]), Yahweh will in the future give in such generosity that Israel will not even seem like the same land. The language of the verse is purposely hyperbolic, like the "milk and honey" language of the promises which encouraged the band of former slaves as they undertook the conquest of Canaan under Joshua (Josh 5:6: cf. Exod 3:8; Lev 20:24; Num 16:13, 14; Deut 6:3; 31:20; Jer 11:5; 32:22; Ezek 20:6, 15). The three lines of the triplet allude to three aspects of Israel's future status: stability ("his shoots"), visibility ("his splendor"), and desirability ("his scent"; cf. the parallels adduced in Westenholz, J. and A., *Or* 46 [1977] 198–219). In light of the reference to "shoots" (ינקותיו), the metaphor is apparently describing a tree (Ezek 17:22) or vine (Ps 80:12). The comparison of Israel's future beauty to that of the olive tree (cf. Jer 16:11) and scent to that of the (cedar) forests of Lebanon (cf. Cant 4:11) is simply one more variation on the theme of covenant blessing as mediated through agricultural bounty commonly expressed in the prophets on the basis of the language of the covenant itself (e.g., Deut 33:13–16; 30:9–10; Jer 33:13; Amos 9:13–14; Joel 3:17, etc.).

8 [7]   The two couplets of v 8 [7] predict three restoration blessings for Israel: return (type 7), revival in numbers (type 4), and flourishing (type 6), all of which will make Israel famous for its desirability. The mention of dwelling "in his shade" is not entirely clear as to its referent. Is it Israel's shade or Yahweh's shade which is to protect and benefit the dwellers? A frequently proposed emendation substitutes בצלי "in my shade" for MT בצלל "in his shade" though without support from the versions, on the theory that surely Yahweh must be the one who gives the shade (cf. Pss 17:8; 36:8; 91:1, etc.). Moreover, in v 9 [8], Yahweh likens himself to a luxuriant fir tree. But already in vv 6 [5] and 7 [6] Israel was likened to a tree, and that metaphor-simile would seem to carry on through v 8 [7] as well. Accordingly, it is most likely that "those who dwell in his shade" are those who maintain their connection with and identity in the umbrella or "shade" of the national covenant.

The "return" (שׁוב) can refer either to a return to Yahweh or return from exile. The latter is obviously dependent on the former, and so both senses may be intended. An explicit promise of return from exile was already given through Hosea (11:11) so that no objection can be raised to this interpretation on the ground that the prophet's future hope was a vague one. Upon their return the people will again enjoy Yahweh's provision of abundance. Israel will become a place once again with a wide, positive reputation (זכר). Again פרח "sprout" is used, and "Lebanon" for the third time appears at the end of a verse as a virtual epiphora, to provide a comparison—this time in connection with its fabled wine. The "milk and honey" existence Israel sought will finally be given by Yahweh's grace. It will the the equivalent of a coming back to life (יחיו) for the formerly disobedient nation. Israel was once like a vine in the wilderness (10:1) to Yahweh. Now it will become like a vine among the nations—the seat of plenty.

9 [8]   Since Ephraim was the remainder state of the north in Hosea's day, the mention of the name "Ephraim" was probably intended partly to return the focus to the contemporary period from the future where it had been set in vv 5–8 [4–7] (if not as a split word pairing with Israel in v 6 [5]).

These words give no hint that the nation of Hosea's day might expect to escape punishment by ceasing idolatry. Rather, God wished current Ephraim to know that his future promise included them just as much as any other element in the historical nation. The very ones who so diligently neglect him at present (14:1 [13:16]) will nevertheless be eligible for his blessing. Ephraim's name is mentioned first in the sentence, virtually in a *casus pendens* ("As for Ephraim, . . .") in the style of some of the tribal blessings (Gen 49:3, 8; Judg 5:17; cf. Deut 33:7, 8, 13, 18, etc.). Via a rhetorical question God appeals for Ephraim to abandon its idolatry, the implication being that until the idolatry ceases there can be no hope for restoration (cf. Deut 4:28–30 where the turn from idolatry in exile to covenant faithfulness provides the prerequisite for rescue). In 4:17 Hosea had excoriated Ephraim for being allied with idols (cf. also 8:4; 13:2). Now Ephraim is challenged to break that bond which keeps it from Yahweh's blessing.

Yahweh promises to respond (ענה) as in the magnificent poem of 2:23–25 [21–23] where the response likewise is symbolized in luxuriant growth and agricultural bounty. He will make even Ephraim blessed, becoming for them like a fir tree (ברוש). The "fir" can signify any of a variety of coniferous trees, perhaps including the Phoenician juniper. Though fir trees have no fruit, this is hardly a barrier to the metaphorical promise, "On me your fruit is found." Even possible is oblique allusion to the notion of the tree of life (Gen 3:22 and Rev 22:2), itself a fruit tree. The fir's year-round greenness makes it a suitable symbol for the tree of life, the resultant freedom from any danger of death being one type (10) of restoration blessing. But the fruit is Yahweh's own gift. He is to Israel an always-producing fruit tree. The fruit (פרי) may again be part of a word play with Ephraim (אפרים) as in 9:16. The message of this word of God through Hosea is thus consistent with the overall message: Yahweh and Yahweh alone is Israel's benefactor.

Explanation

A simplified pattern of the chronology of covenant predictions for the history of Israel might read: blessing, curse, blessing. (Cf. Deut 4, where the blessings of obedience are foretold in vv 1–14, warning is given via the curses of punishment for disloyalty in vv 15–28, and then promise is made of restoration blessing following punishment in vv 29–31. See also the chronological pattern in Lev 26 and Deut 30:1–10.) Hosea follows the pattern implicitly, though with an important exception: there could be no prediction of blessing for obedience to the corrupt contemporary Israel. The time for that was long past. Hosea's inspired message therefore concentrates on the warning of punishment, followed by the promise of restoration; i.e., curse, blessing, in that chronological order. A majority of the oracles in the book are devoted to adumbrations of punishment. But frequently Hosea was called to deliver reminders of the hope of future restoration according to the ancient divine promise (2:1–3 [1:10–2:1], 16–25 [14–23]; 3:5; 6:1–3; 10:12b; 11:8–11). Hos 14:2–9 [1–8] is the final such passage, fittingly the capstone to his collection of oracles. It is a word of promise for those of faith among his contemporaries, even if one they could not expect to be fulfilled in their own lifetimes. The time frame for Israel's restoration in the OT is just as indefinite as is the time frame for the return of Christ in the NT. To the person of faith, this indefiniteness is not a major problem. It is enough to know that God's gracious plan will ultimately prevail and that his people will one day be fully united with him. One can hope that the restoration may come soon, and one should be prepared for it by maintaining loyalty to the divine commands, but no one can presume that it will arrive during his or her lifetime.

The orthodox in late eighth-century Israel did not need by this point (if the dating of 14:2–9 [1–8] in the last days of Samaria's existence is correct) any further certainty that severe times were ahead, or that the miseries of those times were well deserved. They could rejoice to know, however, that the decimation of the nation politically, militarily, economically, and socially did not represent the end of the Israel of God. A time would come when repentance would bring abundant blessing, when the tragedies of the past would be only a memory.

God promises that he will once again love Israel "voluntarily" (נדבה) and that his anger will be turned away from his people (v 5 [4]). For this to happen, the future Israel would need to repent and seek their only true God (vv 2–4 [1–3]). But they would not need to buy the divine favor in the manner of the materialistic idolatrous fertility cult. Their only offering need be sincere words, their promise to repay the fruit of their lips, i.e., to keep the vow of repentance made to Yahweh. Yahweh had once adopted the orphan Israel as his people. After their present rejection he will again take them back, and they will again be blessed. He will show his compassion again (v 4b [3b]). The nation's apostasy will be cured (v 5 [4]) and its prosperity restored (vv 6–9 [5–8]) by Yahweh himself.

The future age for the repentant people will be free from the idolatry (v 9a [8a]) so abhorrent to God, that exemplified Israel's unfaithfulness to the covenant. Fittingly, one last time the prophet's words remind the people that closeness to Yahweh means distance from idolatry and divine help in keeping the covenant (Deut 30:6). If only they could have learned that lesson before the covenant curses were unleashed upon them, rather than after!

The new age will be an age of abundant life. God himself will be the sustenance of Israel. After they turn to him, the tree of life will ever blossom and bear fruit for the people of God. The Israel which has seen this promise as it has begun ultimately to be fulfilled is the church of Christ. The church has inherited the restoration promises of Hosea and the rest of the OT (Gal 3:29). We look forward to an eternal sustenance, and to the final abolition of any threat of covenant curse (Rev 22:2–3).

Challenge to the Wise Reader (*14:10* [*9*])

Bibliography

Budde, K. "Der Schluss des Buches Hosea." In *Studies Presented to C. H. Toy.* New York: Macmillan, 1912. 205–11. **Seow, C.** "Hosea 14:10 and the Foolish People Motif." *CBQ* 44(1982) 212–24.

Translation

14:10 [9] *Who is wise? Let him understand these things.*
Intelligent? [a] *Let him know them.*

For the ways of Yahweh are right;
so the righteous will [b] *walk in them,*
but those who rebel [c] *will stumble in them.*

Notes

10.a. The מִי "who?" does double duty both for חכם "wise" and נבון "intelligent."

10.b. Or, "should, must," etc. On the (unlikely) possibility that ילכו "walk" does double duty, see Andersen and Freedman, 648.

10.c. Or, "the rebels," "the revolters," "the transgressors," "the disobedient," etc.

Form / Structure / Setting

Verse 10 [9] is a self-contained, individually composed poem whose focus is the whole book of Hosea. It is composed of a couplet, which contains a dual question and a dual challenge; and a triplet, which decribes briefly the different relationship to the ways (or paths) of Yahweh on the part of those who keep the covenant and then those who do not. The couplet is synonymous in its parallelism. The triplet is synthetic-antithetic. Both parallelisms are typical of what is loosely called "wisdom." The first line ("Who is wise? Let him understand these things") is rather similar to Ps 107:43, a kind of coda to a long psalm recounting God's redemptive acts among his people, and to Jer 9:11, where the context is covenant obedience / disobedience, similar to the concern of the triplet in v 10b [9b]. The contrasting of the fates of the "righteous" (צדקים) and the "disobedient" (פשעים) in v 10b [9b] has numerous parallels in the antitheses of the Proverbs (e.g. 10:24, 29, 30; 11:3; 12:3, 5, 7, etc.).

There is no warrant to dismiss the poem as non-Hoseanic (cf. Seow, *CBQ* 44 [1982] 212–24) though no proof that it comes from the prophet himself, either. A dating of such "wisdom" elements as the poem contains is not possible. Moreover, the question may be posed as to whether or not anything in the poem is to be strictly linked to wisdom circles. The language is as much Deuteronomic as proverbial. The "ways of Yahweh" (דרכי יהוה) are in fact the covenant stipulations of the Pentateuch. For the righteous to "walk" (הלך) in them is nothing other than for them to *keep* them (Deut 8:6; 10:12; 11:22, 28; 19:9; 26:17; 28:9; 30:16; 31:29; cf. Judg 2:22). In wisdom language, the "righteous" are usually antithesized by the "wicked" (רשעים). Here, however, the antithesis is "rebels" or "disobedient" (פשעים), the participle of a verb especially appropriate in connection with covenant violations (cf. Amos 1:3, 6, 9, etc. and 3:14; 5:12). Hosea has already used פשע in 7:13 and 8:1 (q.v.). Moreover, the verb כשל "to stumble" is a covenant curse term (Lev 26:37) employed otherwise five times in Hosea (curse type 19, cf. 4:5 twice; 5:5 twice; 14:2).

Comment

14:10 [9] The final verse challenges the reader to both proper attitudes and proper actions in connection with the prophecies of Hosea. The attitude of the reader should be that of a disciple. Here are words to be learned if one is truly wise. By implication, only a fool would ignore their great value. The message of the poem hinges on the categorical assertion that "the ways of Yahweh are right" (v 10b [9b]). This principle is the governing basis for both knowledge and behavior. The wise persons will know that they are right; the righteous persons will obey them because they are right (cf. Ps 18:22, 23). Those who choose to disobey will land in trouble. Violating the covenant cannot but cause a person to stumble, i.e., run afoul of the covenant curses (cf. Mal 2:8).

Explanation

The words of v 10 [9] serve as a reminder to readers of all generations that Hosea's message continues as a message for them. The words are not simply directed to his contemporaries, thus being of no more than arcane interest to us. Rather, the "ways of Yahweh" are a guide to the righteous, and a source of understanding to the intelligent of all successive periods. The reader has a basic choice to make. Will he / she choose to obey Yahweh's law, the only "right" way? Or will he / she rebel against it? To do the latter is to disenfranchise oneself from the covenant blessings which attend Yahweh's favor.

The poem does not attempt to delineate the ways in which Hosea's message remains instructive beyond the fall of the North in 722 b.c. That is the proper task of the wise reader. But it does assert that Hosea faithfully represented Yahweh's word and that the wise of any generation could only regard the words of the book as Yahweh's own words. They are right words, a knowledge of which and an obedience to which, as is the case with the rest of Yahweh's words, is essential to walking in a right direction in life.

Joel

Joel

Bibliography

BOOKS AND COMMENTARIES

Ahlström, G. *Joel and the Temple Cult of Jerusalem.* SVTP 21. Leiden: E. J. Brill, 1971. **Allen, L.** *The Books of Joel, Obadiah, Jonah and Micah.* NICOT. Grand Rapids: Eerdmans, 1976. **Amon, G.** *Die Abfassungszeit des Buches Joel.* Diss. Würzburg, 1942. **Bellinger, W. H.** *Psalmody and Prophecy.* JSOTSup 27. Sheffield: JSOT Press, 1984. **Besnard, A.-M.** *Le Mystère du nom: Quiconque invoquera le nom du Seigneur sera sauvé.* LD 35. Paris, 1962. **Bewer, J. A.** *A Critical and Exegetical Commentary on Obadiah and Joel.* ICC. Edinburgh: T. & T. Clark, 1911. **Bič, M.** *Das Buch Joel.* Berlin: Evangelische-Verlagsanstalt, 1960. **Birkeland, H.** *Zum hebräischen Traditionswesen: Die Komposition der prophetischen Bücher des Alten Testaments.* Avhandlinger utgitt ar Det Norske Vindenskaps-Akademi i Oslo 2/1, 1938. **Brockington, L. H.** "Joel." In *PCB.* London: Thomas Nelson and Sons, 1963. **Butterworth, G.** *The Date of the Book of Joel.* Diss. Nottingham, 1970/71. **Chary, T.** *Les prophètes et le culte à partir de l'exile autour du second Temple. L'idéal cultuel des prophètes exiliens et post-exiliens.* Bibliothèque de Théologie 3/3. Tournai: Desclée, 1955. **Cole, R.** "Joel." In *The New Bible Commentary Revised* ed. D. Guthrie and J. Moyter. Grand Rapids: Eerdmans, 1970. 716–25. **Condamin, A.** *Poèmes de la Bible.* Paris, 1933. 97–103. **Couve de Murville, M.** "Joel." In *A New Catholic Commentary on Holy Scripture,* ed. R. Fulter et al. London: Thomas Nelson and Sons, 1969. **Credner, K.** *Der Prophet Joel übersetzt und erklärt.* Halle, 1831. **Driver, S. R.** *The Books of Joel and Amos.* The Cambridge Bible for Schools and Colleges. Cambridge, 1897; 2d ed., 1915. **Edgar, S. L.** *The Minor Prophets (excluding Amos, Hosea, and Micah).* Epworth Preacher's Commentaries. London: Epworth, 1962. **Fohrer, G.** *Die Propheten des Alten Testaments. Band 6: Die Propheten seit dem 4 Jahrhundert.* Gütersloh: Gerd Mohn, 1976. **Frey, H.** *Das Buch der Kirche in der Weltwende: Die Kleinen nachexilischen Propheten.* BAT 24. Stuttgart: Calwer, 1957. 203–49. **Gangi, M. di.** *The Book of Joel.* Shield Bible Study Series. Grand Rapids: Baker Book House, 1970. **Grätz, H.** *Der einheitliche Charakter der Prophetie Joels und die künstliche Gliederung ihrer Teile.* Breslau: Skutsch, 1873. **Gressmann, H.** *Der Messias.* Göttingen, 1929. **Haldar, A.** *The Nature of the Desert in Sumero-Accadian and West-Semitic Religions.* UUA 1950/3. Uppsala: A. B. Lundequist, 1960. 56–59. **Haller, M.** *Das Judentum, Geschichtsschreibung Prophetie und Gesetzgebung nach dem Exil.* SAT 2/3. Göttingen, 1925. **How, J. C. H.** *Joel and Amos.* Smaller Cambridge Bible for Schools. Cambridge, 1910. **Jones, D.** *Isaiah 56–66 and Joel: Introduction and Commentary.* Torch Bible Commentaries. London: SCM, 1964. **Kapelrud, A. S.** *Joel Studies.* UUÅ 4. Uppsala: A. B. Lundequist, 1948. **Keller, C.** "Joel." In *Osée, Joël, Amos, Abadias, Jonas.* Commentaire de l'Ancien Testament 11a. Neuchâtel: Delachaux and Niestlé, 1965. 99–155. **Kennedy, J. H.** "Joel." In The Broadman Bible Commentary, vol. 7 (*Hosea-Malachi*), ed. C. Allen. Nashville: Broadman, 1972. **Kessner, G.** *Das Zeitalter des Propheten Joel.* Leipzig: Grimme & Trömel, 1888. **Knieschke, W.** *Die Eschatologie des Joel in ihrer historisch-geographischen Bestimmtheit.* Naumburg, 1912. **Koch, K.** *The Prophets. Vol. 1, The Assyrian Age.* Philadelphia: Fortress, 1982. **Kritzinger, J.** *Die Profesie van Joël.* Amsterdam: Swetsen Zeitlinger, 1945. **Kutal, B.** *Liber Prophetae Joelis.* Commentarii in Prophetas Minores 2. Olmütz, 1932. **Lattimore, R.** *The Date of Joel.* Diss. Southern Baptist Theological Seminary, 1951. **Marti, K.** "Der Prophet Joel." In *Der heilige Schrift des Alten Testament,* ed. E. Kautzsch and A. Bertholet. Vol. 2. Tübingen, 1923. 23–29. **Medd, E.** *A Historical and Exegetical Study on the "Day of the Lord" in the Old Testament, with Special Reference to the Book of Joel.* Diss. St. Andrews

University, 1968 / 69. **Merx, E. O. A.** *Die Prophetie des Joel und ihre Ausleger von den ältesten Zeiten bis zu den Reformatoren: Eine exegetisch-kritische und hermeneutisch-dogmengeschtliche Studie.* Halle, 1879. **Montet, E.** *De recentissimis disputationibus de Joelis aetate.* Diss. Genf, 1880. **Murphy, R.** "The Book of Joel." In *The Interpreter's One-Volume Commentary on the Bible,* ed. C. Layman. Nashville: Abingdon, 1971. 461–64. **Myers, J.** *Hosea, Joel, Amos, Obadiah, and Jonah.* The Layman's Bible Commentary, vol. 14. Atlanta: John Knox, 1959. **Plöger, O.** *Theocracy and Eschatology.* Tr. S. Rudman. Richmond: John Knox, 1968. 96–105. **Preuss, G.** *Die Prophetie Joels unter besonderer Berücksichtigung der Zeitfrage.* Diss. Halle, 1889. **Price, W.** *The Prophet Joel and the Day of the Lord.* Chicago: Moody Press, 1976. **Rinaldi, G. M.** *Il libro di Joele.* Rapallo, 1938. **Rudolph, W.** *Joel-Amos-Obadja-Jonah.* KAT 13/2. Gütersloh: Gütersloher Verlagshaus, 1971. **Scheepers, J.** *Die gees van god en die gees van die mens in die OT.* Utrecht, 1960. **Schmalohr, J.** *Das Buch des Propheten Joel, übersetzt und erklärt.* ATAbh 7/4. Münster, 1922. **Scholz, A.** *Kommentar zum Buche des Propheten Joel.* Würzburg, 1885. **Theis, J.** *"Der Prophet Joel."* In *Die Zwölf Kleinen Propheten.* vol. 1, ed. J. Lippl and J. Theis. Bonn, 1937. **Thompson, J. A.** *The Book of Joel: Introduction and Exegesis.* IB 6:729–38. **Thurre, E.** *Dieu et son peuple selon le livre de Joël.* Diss. Lic. Fribonig, 1975 / 76. **Trinquet, J.** *Habaquq, Abadias, Joël. SBJ.* Paris: Éditions du Cerf, 1959. **Wade, G.** *The Books of the Prophets Micah, Obadiah, Joel and Jonah.* Westminster Commentaries. London, 1925. **Watts, J. D. W.** *The Books of Joel, Obadiah, Jonah, Nahum, Habakkuk and Zephaniah.* The Cambridge Bible Commentary on the New English Bible. Cambridge: Cambridge UP, 1975. **Welchbillig, H.** *Studie zur Formgeschichte des Buches Joel.* Diss. Lic. Trier, 1967. **Widmer, G.** *Die Kommentare von Raschi, Ibn Esra, Radaq zu Joel.* Basel: Volksdruckerie, 1945. **Williams, A. L.** *Joel and Amos.* The Minor Prophets Unfolded. London, 1918. **Wolff, H. W.** *Die Botschaft des Buches Joel.* München: Kaiser, 1963. ———. *Joel and Amos.* Hermeneia. Philadelphia: Fortress Press, 1977. **Wood, G.** "Joel." In The Jerome Biblical Commentary, ed. R. Brown et al. Englewood Cliffs, NJ: Prentice-Hall, 1968. **Wunsche, A.** *Die Weissagung des Propheten Joel übersetzt und erklärt.* Leipzig, 1872.

ARTICLES

Baumgartner, W. "Joel 1 und 2." In *Karl Budde zum siebztigen Geburtstag,* ed. K. Marti. BZAW 34. Giessen: Topelmann, 1920. 10–19. **Blois, K. de.** "Metaphor in Common Language Translations of Joel."*BT* 36 (1985) 208–16. **Bourke, G.** *"Le Jour de Yahvé dans Joël."* RB 66 (1959) 5–31, 191–212. **Cannon, W.** "The Day of the Lord in Joel." *CQR* 103 (1927) 32–63. **Childs, B.** "The Enemy from the North and the Chaos Tradition." *JBL* 68 (1959) 187–98. **Dahood, M.** "The Minor Prophets and Ebla." In *The Word of the Lord Shall Go Forth: Essays in Honor of David Noel Freedman in Celebration of His Sixtieth Birthday,* ed. C. Meyers and M. O'Connor. Winona Lake, IN: Eisenbrauns, 1983. 46–67. **Deden, D.** "Joel—de Pinksterprofeet." *Verbum* 25 (1958) 197–205. **Delcor, M.** "Joel." *Catholicisme* 6 (1965) 913–15. **Dennefeld, L.** "Les Problèmes du livre de Joël." *RSR* 4 (1924) 555–75; 5 (1925) 35–57, 591–608; 6 (1926) 26–49. **Engnell, I.** "Joel's bok." In *Svenskt Bibliskt Uppslagsverk,* ed. I. Engnell et al. Vol. 1. Gävle: Skolförlaget, 1948. 1075–77. **Garrett, D. A.** "The Structure of Joel." *JETS* 28 (1985) 289–97. **Good, R. M.** "The Just War in Ancient Israel." *JBL* 104 (1985) 385–400. **Görg, M.** "Eine formelhalfte Metapher bei Joel und Nahum," *BN* 6 (1978) 12–14. **Gray, G. B.** "The Parallel Passages in Joel in Their Bearing on the Question of Date." *Exp* 4/8 (1893) 208–25. **Greenwood, D.** "On Jewish Hope for a Restored Northern Kingdom." *ZAW* 88 (1976) 376–85. **Holzinger, H.** "Sprachcharakter und Abfassungszeit des Buches Joel," *ZAW* 9 (1889) 89–131. **Hoop, S. De.** "Is Joël een Apocalypticus van't jaar 400 vor C?" *TT* (1885) 571–95. **Hosch, H.** "The Concept of Prophetic Time in the Book of Joel." *JETS* 15 (1972) 31–38. **Janzen, W.** "War in the Old Testament." *Mennonite Quarterly Review* 46 (1962) 155–66. **Jensen, K.** "Indledningsspørgsmall i Joels Bog." *DTT* 4 (1941) 98–112. **Jepsen, A. S.** "Kleine Beiträge zum Zwölfpropheten-buch I. Joel." *ZAW* 58 (1938) 85–96. **Kapelrud, A.** "Joel" and "Joelbuch." *BHH* 2:869–70. **Kutsch, E.** "Heuschreckenplage und Tag Jahwes in Joel 1 und 2." *TZ* 18 (1962) 81–89. **Maries, L.** "À propos de récentes études sur Joël." *RSR* 37 (1950) 121–24. **Marti, K.** "Der Prophet Joel" in *HSAT* 2. **Matthes, J.** "Het book Joël." *TT* (1885) 34–66. ———. "Nieuwe Joël-Studien." *TT* (1887) 357–81. **Mikre-Selassie, G. A.** "Repe-titions and Synonyms in the Translation of Joel—With Special Reference to the Amharic Language." *BT* 36 (1985) 230–37. **Möller, W.** "Die Bedeutung Joels in der Schriftpro-phetie." In *Nach dem Gesetz und Zeugnis*. Halle, 1931. 1–104. **Müller, H.-P.** "Prophetie und Apokalyptik bei Joel." *TV* 10 (1966) 231–52. **Myers, J.** "Some Considerations Bearing on the Date of Joel." *ZAW* 74 (1962) 177–95. **Neil, W.** "Joel." *IDB* 2:926–29. **Nestle, E.** "Zur Kapiteleinleitung in Joel." *ZAW* 24 (1904) 122–27. **Nola, A. di.** "Gioele." *Libro di Enc. Rel.* 3 (1971) 254–55. **Pantrel, R.** "Joel." DBSup 4 (1948) 1098–1104. **Plath, M.** "Joel, Prophet." RGG² 3:311–13. **Prinsloo, W.** "Die boek Joël: verleentheid of geleentheid?" *NGTT* 24 (1983) 255–63. **Rad, G. von.** "The Origin of the Concept of the Day of Yahweh." *JSS* 4 (1959) 97–108. **Rahmer, M.** "Der hebräischen Traditionen in den Werken des Hieronymus: Die Commentarien zu den XII kleinen Propheten, II. Joel." *MGWJ* 41 (1897) 625–39, 691–92. **Redditt, P. D.** "The Book of Joel and Peripheral Prophecy." *CBQ* 48 (1986) 225–240. **Reicke, B.** "Joel und seine Zeit." In *Wort-Gebot-Glaube: Beiträge zur Theologie des Alten Testaments: FS Walther Eichrodt zum 80. Geburtstag*, ed. H. Stoebe. ATANT 59. Zurich: Zwingli, 1970. 133–41. **Rimbach, J. A.** "Those Lively Prophets—Joel Ben Pethuel." *CurTM* 8 (1981) 302–4. **Rinaldi, G.** "Gioele e il Salmo 65." BibOr 10 (1968) 113–22. **Rudolph, W.** "Ein Beitrag zum hebräischen Lexikon aus dem Joelbuch." VTSup 16 (1967) 244–50. ———. "Wann wirkte Joel?" In *Das ferne und nahe Wort: FS Leonhard Rost*, ed. F. Maass. BZAW 105. Berlin: A. Töpelmann, 1967. 193–98. **Sievers, E.** "Alttestamentliche Miscellen VI: Joel." In *Berichte über die Verhandlungen der Königlich Sächsischen Gesellschaft der Wissen-schaften zu Leipzig. Philologisch-historische Klasse* 59 (1907) 3–37. **Sisti, A.** "Gioele: Bibliotheca Santorum." *Lateranense* 6 (1965) 486–89. **Stephenson, F. R.** "The Date of the Book of Joel." *VT* 19 (1969) 224–29. **Stocks, H.** "Der 'Nordliche' und die Komposition des Buches Joel." *NKZ* 19 (1908) 725–50. **Thompson, J.** "The Date of Joel." In *A Light Unto My Path: Old Testament Studies in Honor of Jacob M. Myers*, ed. H. Bream et al. Gettysburg Theological Studies 4. Philadelphia: Temple University, 1974. 453–64. ———. "The Use of Repetition in the Prophecy of Joel." In *On Language, Culture and Religion: in Honor of Eugene A. Nida*, ed. M. Black and W. Smalley. The Hague: Mouton and Co., 1974. 101–10. **Tobias, H.** "Joel: His Life and Times." *BibIll* 12 (1986) 56–59. **Treves, M.** "The Date of Joel." *VT* 7 (1957) 149–56. **Visser, J. Th. de.** "Nieuwe poging tot oplossing van het Joël-vraagstuk. *Theologische Studien.* Utrecht, 1887. 301–327. **Volck, W.** "Joel, der Prophet." *Realencyklopädie für protestantische Theolo-gie und Kirche*. 3d ed. Leipzig, 1896–1913. 9:234–37. **Weise, M.** "Joelbuch." *RGG³* 3:800–802. **Welch, A.** "Joel and the Post-exilic Community." *Exp* 8 (1920) 161–80.

Introduction

JOEL'S ERA

Nothing personal is known about the man Joel, and considerable debate exists as to the date of his prophecy. Jewish tradition placed Joel between Hosea and Amos, though the reasons for this location are debated. On the ordering of the Minor Prophets in general and the relationships of canonical order to relative chronology in the Minor Prophets, see *General Introduction,* pp. xlii–xlv.

Since Joel mentions Judah and Jerusalem routinely, but never Israel or Samaria, it has usually been assumed that he spoke his oracles after 722 B.C. when the Assyrians destroyed Samaria and completed their annexation of the northern tribal territories. (This is, of course, only an argument from silence.) And since he portrays an active temple worship in chaps. 1 and 2, the period between the first and second temples (586–516 B.C.) could hardly be the date of the book—or at least most of it.

For these and the following additional reasons, Joel is typically dated during the postexilic, second temple era. His apocalyptic perspective is thought to have more affinities with late OT apocalyptic as identified especially in Daniel, Zechariah, and parts of Isaiah, as opposed to the earlier apocalyptic of Isaiah and Ezekiel. The references in chap. 4 to Phoenicia and Philistia and their dealing with Greece are thought to reflect conditions in the Persian era, typically the fourth century B.C. The lack of any mention of a king, compared to most other pre-exilic prophetic books, also seems reason to avoid a pre-exilic dating. And the perspective of foreign occupation (2:20; 4:3 [3:3]) and diaspora (2:26; 4:6 [3:6]) seems consistent with a postexilic date.

These arguments, however, are not as convincing as they once may have seemed. Apocalyptic has its provable origins at least as early as the beginning of the seventh century B.C. (Isa 13). Moreover, Joel's type of apocalyptic is not so easily classified. Is the invader of Joel 2 a distantly future cosmic army, or is it the Assyrians or Babylonians in embellished language (as with the Babylonians in Nah 2 or Hab 1 or Jer 6)? The fact that 2:1–11, normally acknowledged as genuine, has so many close comparisons with Isa 13 suggests that Joel's apocalyptic style may well be earlier than that of, say, Zech 1–8. As to the role of Phoenicia and Philistia in chap. 4, Amos 1:6–10 is so remarkably similar as to suggest that Joel's references are here not merely earlier than the Exile, but perhaps even of a traditional sort, reflecting long-held antipathies from practices in existence prior even to Amos' day.

The lack of reference to a kingship in Jerusalem is merely another argument from silence. Joel is a small book. Suppose one had only Amos 1–4 (without the superscription) or Mic 5–7, comparably large blocks of material but without explicit reference to kingship? We know otherwise, however, that these prophets knew a monarchy in Israel and Judah. Here, too, Nahum may be mentioned, decidedly preexilic yet without a hint that Judah has a monarchy. Thus it is wrong to assume, even in chap. 1 where so many societal leaders are mentioned, that no reference to a king means no king was in existence. Prophets are not mentioned either, even in chap. 3, but they surely existed in Joel's era, whenever it was. Additionally, of course, there is the possibility that the book dates from 587–86, when the monarchy had already fallen captive but Jerusalem was still secure (2 Kgs 25:4–8).

On the matter of foreign occupation and diaspora, a change of perspective in this regard is now advisable. As S. Stohlmann has argued at length ("The Judean Exile after 701 B.C.E.," in *Scripture in Context* 2, ed. W. Hallo et al. [Winona Lake, IN: Eisenbrauns, 1983] 147–75), an awareness of exile, deportation, etc., was not something limited to the period after the Babylonian exile of 586, but was a natural byproduct of a policy of population shifting and depletion carried out routinely by the Assyrians and others in the ancient Near East during and after the eighth century. In other words, there had been many exiles prior to the Exile, and a prophetic reference to Israelites in exile (as Joel 4:7) need not refer to something as late as the sixth century. Moreover, exile was one of the expected punishments of war according to ancient Near Eastern traditions attested at least as early as Hammurabi's Code (xxvii, 22–23, 74), ca. 1700 B.C., and repeatedly thereafter, so that its presence in Joel must be understood as a reflection of a reality routinely understood as a dire fate in ancient times.

Ultimately, however, any dating of the book of Joel can be only inferential and speculative. It is on the basis of the sorts of conditions apparently reflected in the prophecy that one assigns a tentative date. As argued in more detail below, our assumption is that Joel is a unified work composed under the circumstances of an invasion against the city of Jerusalem (and thus, of course, Judah) by Mesopotamian enemy forces, either Assyria or Babylonia. If this admittedly speculative assessment is correct, the words of the book would likely have been spoken on one of these occasions: the Assyrian invasion of 701 B.C., the Babylonian invasion of 598, or the Babylonian invasion of 588.

There is reason to think, therefore, that the book's content and perspective are preexilic rather than postexilic. But such a dating is not essential to the appreciation of the book's message. Here is a book that in its first half describes present distress and in its second half describes future deliverance. Since it is possible to appreciate the general character of both the distress (invasion, drought, desolation) and the deliverance (return from exile, defeat of enemies, final judgment of the nations), the impact of the book remains unabated even when the precise date of the invasion or Joel's era cannot be determined.

STRUCTURE

The book divides into four pericopes, the first two of which describe an enemy's invasion of Jerusalem and Judah and concomitant conditions. Thereafter come two pericopes of hope, the first of which emphasizes prosperity, safety, and the outpouring of God's spirit, the second emphasizing the defeat and judgment of all hostile powers and the restoration of Jerusalem and Judah.

Schematically the structure may be represented as follows:

1:1	Title	
1:2–20	Pericope I	
	vv 2–7	Description of invasion, including locust metaphor
	vv 8–20	Calls to lamentation and further descriptions, including drought and desolation
2:1–17	Pericope II	
	vv 1–11	Description of invasion, with call for alarm (v 1) and identification of foe (v 11)
	vv 12–17	Call to repentance, including call for special time of fasting (vv 15–17)
2:18–3:5	Pericope III	

[2:18–32]	2:18–27	Dual promise of removal of foe and restoration of agricultural bounty
	3:1–5	Special promise of the new age of the Spirit
	[2:28–32]	
4:1–21	Pericope IV	
[3:1–21]	vv 1–16	Eventual military defeat and divine judgment for the nations
	vv 17–21	Peace and abundance in Jerusalem and Judah

Joel shares its simple woe-then-weal overall structure with a majority of the prophetic books, in contrast to Isaiah and Hosea, for example, where an alternating distribution of woe / weal / woe / weal, etc. is found. Joel is also somewhat more tightly organized than many of the prophetic books, with such a degree of thematic and vocabulary linkage among the pericopes, and a logical progression from one pericope to the next, that it is reasonable to conclude that Joel's message was originally composed and delivered either at one time or in a relatively short span of time (perhaps a week or a month).

STYLE

Joel's four oracles, averaging 18 verses, are remarkably consistent in length. Many OT prophetic oracles are shorter (as typically in Amos and Hosea) and many are longer (as often in Ezekiel and Isaiah). Joel's medium-sized oracles are long enough to allow for repetitious continuity, i.e., the elaboration of a theme through a group of similar subsections, yet short enough to concentrate on one or at the most two themes without becoming tedious or running short of arresting vocabulary, parallelisms, etc.

Joel's style is especially characterized, then, by variations on a theme. In chap. 1, for example, he effectively portrays the need for universal lamentation by demanding consideration of this action from a series of disparate types, including, on the one hand, drunks (1:5, an imaginative way to begin a lament call) and, on the other, temple priests (1:13). Or in his awesome portrait of Yahweh's invading army (2:1–11), the constant, unstoppable progress of the enemy toward and against Jerusalem courses along in a series of images from that of specks of movement visible on the crests of faraway hills (v 2) to the feel and sound of the foe right on top of the defenders (vv 9–11). Likewise, Joel's description of the democratization of the Holy Spirit (3:1–5 [2:28–32]) is perhaps the most comprehensive elaboration of this doctrine anywhere in Scripture. And his vision of the valley of judgment (4:1–16) is one of the OT's most graphic assurances of the eventual defeat of the enemies of God's people, portrayed via a thorough, repetitious attention to the "nations" and their just desert.

Joel is an apocalypticist but not strictly a visionary, somewhat in the manner of Isaiah. Nowhere is his affinity to Isaiah's apocalyptic style more evident than in 2:1–11, which compares strikingly with Isa 13, with which it shares some vocabulary, thematic emphasis, the general perspective on an invading foe, and the issue of invasion as punishment from Yahweh. Since the latter issue is Pentateuchal in origin (e.g., Lev 26:17, 25, 33, 37; Deut 28:25, 49;

32:23, 24) and the basis for the former factors in comparison, it is not necessary to posit a copying of Isaiah on Joel's part or vice versa. However, the affinities between the two passages should give pause to those who find an early date for Joel unlikely.

JOEL'S MESSAGE

Joel and the Covenant

Like all the canonical prophets, Joel depended on the Mosaic covenant of the Pentateuch for the basic points of his message: the covenant's curses must come as a result of national disobedience; but after a period of chastisement, God will restore his people and bless them in ways they had not yet experienced.

The correspondences do not stop at this general level. In many particulars Joel 1 and 2 reflect both structurally and thematically what is found especially in Deut 32. The nonimperative verbs in Joel 1 are predominantly preterite, while the nonimperative verbs in chap. 2 are predominantly present-future. Interestingly, Deut 32 displays a similar shift in preferred tenses, as the song shifts largely from what has happened (vv 1–21a) to what is coming (vv 21b–43). When the thematic correspondences are added, the result is a high degree of comparability as evidenced in the following listing of key features.

	Deut 32	Joel 1:1–2:17
Call to attention	vv 1–2	1:2–3
Justness of Yahweh	vv 3–4	2:13–14
Appeal to remember the past	v 7	1:2
Israel Yahweh's special people	vv 8–12	1:17
Past agricultural bounty	vv 13–14	1:5–20; 2:3
Yahweh's rejection	vv 19–21	1:15; 2:11, 17
Destructive fire	v 22	2:3, 5
Harm	v 23	2:13
Arrows	v 23	2:8
Famine	v 24	1:4–20
Harmful animals	v 24	1:4, 6
Invasion	v 25	1:6; 2:1–11
Taunt of the enemy	v 27	2:17
Yahweh's rejection	vv 26–30	1:15; 2:11, 17
Judgment day	vv 34–35	1:15; 2:1, 2, 11
Rescue and forgiveness	vv 36–38	2:12–14, 17
Deliverance from Israel's enemies	vv 39–43	2:20–27
Recompense of the land	v 43	2:18–27

By no means do we wish to suggest that Joel is a reworking of Deut 32. Rather, the listing above shows that both Joel 1:1–2:27 and Deut 32 agree in reflecting the basic covenantal themes of curse and restoration in many of their varieties of expression, and shows also Joel's dependence, like that of the other prophets, on covenantal sanctions established already in the Mosaic era. Thus Joel's message was not really new or unique. It was, rather, a variation on a perspective on history and a way of portraying key events in that history long known to orthodox Israelites.

Joel and Yahweh's Sovereignty

Joel's depiction of the absolute authority of Yahweh over all the peoples of the earth is among the strongest in the Old Testament. Parts of Isaiah, Daniel, and the Psalter are well known for their universal monotheism, and to this list could be added at least Amos 1–2 and those portions of the various prophetic books that contain oracles against foreign nations, since the mere presence of such oracles implies at least a measure of universal divine sovereignty. But Joel is notable for (1) its routine, generalized reference to "the nations" (1:6; 2:17, 19; 4:2, 9, 11, 12 [3:2, 9, 11, 12]; only Obadiah has proportionately as many references), especially in contexts of Yahweh's judgment against them; (2) its extensive prediction that all the nations will be required to assemble for a final, decisive, cosmic battle of judgment in which Yahweh will punish the nations "all around" (3:12 [4:12]); and (3) its insistence that even the invader threatening Judah and Jerusalem is Yahweh's own army, moving at his command (2:11, 25) in fulfillment of the punishment due his people via the Day of Yahweh.

Judah and Jerusalem

In addition to referring implicitly to Jerusalem (via the "temple" in 1:13–16 and the "city" in 2:9, etc.) and Judah (via the "land" in 1:2; 2:1; etc.), Joel mentions by name Zion seven times, Jerusalem six times (three of these in parallel with Zion), and Judah six times (three in parallel with Jerusalem). The present distress and future rescue of these places, capital and country, constitutes one of the book's central foci. Even the famous prediction of the outpouring of God's Spirit (3:1–5 [2:28–32]) concludes with mention of the site of the coming deliverance as Zion / Jerusalem.

Such attention to Judean and Jerusalemite interests comports with the theory that Joel's prophecy was delivered inside Jerusalem to inhabitants of a city secured against an invader and fearful for its survival and the survival of its environs. Joel's care in reassuring the local population of their long-term future does not exclude in any way God's people elsewhere or at other times (cf. 4:6, 7), but it emphasizes the long-established covenantal centrality of Jerusalem (Deut 12) while at the same time reflecting the political reality that Judah was in Joel's day the remainder state of a once much larger nation.

The Democratization of the Spirit

The presence and power of the Spirit of God in prophecy is a typical OT theme, but Joel 3:1–5 [2:28–32] takes this doctrine a step further. In the OT one normally expects to find reference to God's Spirit being present or falling on (על) selected individuals, such as prophets or kings, but not on everyone. Indeed, a basic assumption may have prevailed in Israelite culture to the effect that it would not be appropriate for everyone to possess the Spirit (Num 11:26–28).

Joel contains no mention of prophets (נביאים), whether positive or negative, an absence shared with Obadiah, Jonah, and Nahum. Instead, the book calls attention to a different mode of fulfilling prophetic functions: in the coming age all of God's people will possess and act via the empowering of the Spirit. (No longer will this important function, revelatory speech or activity, be limited to specially called or trained individuals.)

It has often been suggested that 3:1–5 [2:28–32] implies some sort of anti-prophetic stance on Joel's part. But for this there is no real support in the text. Rather, in the same way that Moses saw that a democratization of the Spirit of God could only represent an improvement over the prevailing selectivity (Num 11:29), Joel foresaw a time when the limits of intermediation in knowing God's will would be removed by gracious divine action, and everyone would experience what Joel himself presumably understood, i.e., the beneficial nature of direct encounter and interaction with a living God. The initial fulfillment of Joel's words about the Spirit came at the occasion of the apostles' Pentecost experience (Acts 2:1–41), which had the effect of markedly stimulating the growth of the fledgling church (Acts 2:41–47) and which emphasized commonality (v 44) and equality of spiritual access to God (vv 38–39).

The General Nature of the Distress

Three distinct crises facing Judah and Jerusalem can be discerned in 1:1–2:17. The most obvious is an invasion, whether of locusts literally or of an actual army compared metaphorically to locusts. (On this issue, see below.) A second crisis is that of drought, as evidenced in the descriptions of general herbal dryness, shriveling of crops, lack of water supply, etc. (e.g., 1:10, 12, 17–18, 20) and in the descriptions of relief therefrom in the restoration-promise portion of the book (e.g., 2:22–23). A third is desolation. This desolation may in part have been the result of the drought (as perhaps in 1:11–12) but is connected more closely to the invasion itself, the aftermath of which was a parched, ruined, even burned-over land (1:9, 16, 19–20; 2:3, 5). (On desolation as a result of divinely ordained enemy invasion, cf. Exod 23:29; Isa 27:10; Jer 4:27; 33:10; Ezek 6:14; 26:19; Mic 7:13; etc.) From the point of view of the curses, invasion, drought, and desolation are, of course, major punishments for infidelity to the Mosaic covenant. (See Hosea *Introduction*.) Their presence implies general national disobedience to Yahweh, regardless of whatever particular sets of violations may have been foremost in Joel's day.

The Day of Yahweh

While many OT prophets incorporated predictions of the Day of Yahweh among their oracles, this concept is so prominent in Joel that it may be likened to an engine driving the prophecy.

The term יום יהוה occurs five times (1:15; 2:1, 11; 3:4; 4:14) in a distribution that involves each of the four major subsections of the book. In one oracle it is positionally initial (2:1), in three medial, and in one, virtually final (3:4). In this way the concept of the Day of Yahweh permeates the book, leaving the hearer / reader with little doubt as to its significance for Joel's message.

The Day of Yahweh is best understood as having its origins in Israelite Holy War (G. von Rad, "The Origin of the Concept of the Day of Yahweh," *JSS* 4 [1959] 97–108) and particularly in the cultural expectation that a true sovereign could complete a war of conquest in a single day, whether he chose to intervene in an existing battle or to attack a foe *de novo* (D. K. Stuart, *BASOR* 221 [1976] 159–64). And a war of conquest is surely central to Joel. The great conquest of Judah and Jerusalem, unparalleled in other eras (1:2), turns out to be a Day of Yahweh (1:15; 2:1, 11) in which the enemy forces are in fact Yahweh's own army (2:25). In addition, the great final war of judgment against all the nations of chap. 4 [3] is also a Day of Yahweh (4:14 [3:14]), when he will intervene to protect and benefit his people and suppress their enemies. In this regard it would be technically accurate to note that Joel sees two Days of Yahweh: the one underway, described in 1:1–2:17, and the one coming in the future, as described in 2:18–4:21 [3:21]. Both Days are "near" (קרוב; 1:15; 4:14 [3:14]), the imminence of the Day being a standard prophetic theme, but the actual timing of the two events will be separated by an uncertain span.

Eschatology and Silence on Judah's Sins

Joel does not identify any covenant violations on the part of his nation. Nowhere does he specify exactly what Judah and Jerusalem have done to deserve the distress they now face. This has sometimes been taken as evidence for a late date for the book, on the grounds that pre-exilic prophets tend to indict Israel and / or Judah for particular kinds of crimes, while postexilic prophets tend to see the aftermath of those crimes, i.e., punishment, as complete or nearly so, and look to a future redemption rather than to present faults.

In fact, the pattern is mixed. Some pre-exilic prophets such as Nahum and Habakkuk do not say what Judah has done to deserve the oppression of the Assyrians or Babylonians, while some postexilic prophets, such as Haggai, Zechariah, and Malachi, make a point of excoriating Judeans for their postexilic disobedience. (R. Pierce, "A Thematic Development of the Haggai / Zechariah / Malachi Corpus," *JETS* 27 [1984] 401–11.)

It is probably the strong eschatological perspective of Joel that accounts most for its silence on covenant violations per se. The end of things as they now exist constitutes an overriding interest of the book. Judah and Jerusalem are presently facing an end, being overrun by an enemy who may well terminate their existence as independent entities. Agricultural productivity has been brought to a halt, and even temple worship is at least temporarily at a sort of end because of the desolation of the land (1:9, 13, 16). Beyond this is a more distant end—an end of enemy oppression (chap. 4 [3]), of distance from Yahweh (chap. 3 [2:28–32]), of the land's desolation itself (2:18–27), and of the shame of God's people (2:26–27). These interests apparently outweighed any concern to attack the Judeans for their disobedience to Yahweh.

The Identity of the Invaders

It is widely held that the invasion Joel portrayed in chaps 1 and 2 was simply that of locusts, and that Joel saw in the resultant temporary disruption of life in Jerusalem and its environs evidence of the wrath of God that would eventually come in full at the approaching Day of Yahweh. The enumeration of locust terms in 1:4 and 2:25, the apparent connection between these terms and Yahweh's "great army" in 2:25, and the several descriptions of the invasion that seem more suited to insects than to humans (stripping trees, 1:7; devastating herbage, 2:3; running on walls, 2:8; darkening the sky, 2:10) would tend to favor this interpretation.

But there are reservations that may be held against this view. First, Joel's language seems to suggest, with wording as strong as any used in the OT to imply uniqueness, that the invasion he describes was without precedent and would not be replicated (1:2–3). Yet in the Near East, locust plagues tended to occur every few decades, even in southern Palestine, and were therefore hardly unparalleled. It is surely the case that a locust plague can be a devastating event. Some locust swarms are small and localized (i.e., less than a square mile in dimension), but others may be scores of square miles in size and sweep over country after country. In 1869, remnants of desert swarms from West Africa migrated all the way to England before dying off. The Palestinian locust plague of 1915 was particularly devastating. But recovery can also be rapid. For example, wine prices in Jerusalem merely doubled after the 1915 locust plague (J. Thompson, *IB* 6:738), hardly suggesting agricultural ruin. And the 1968 Ethiopian locust plague is considered only a minor problem in that country's recent agricultural history. Locust damage, in other words, tends to be temporary rather than permanent, extensive though it may be at the height of the infestation. Proof of the transient nature of the inconvenience of a locust plague may be seen implicitly in Exod 10:20 and Amos 4:9, where locusts failed to produce a lasting fear of Yahweh, but were apparently seen simply as a temporary natural difficulty. Nah 3:17 even compares Nineveh's transientness to the brief, unenduring visit of locusts. A final consideration with regard to locust invasions is that they have historically come into Palestine from the south and east, rather than from the north (cf. 2:20).

Additionally, one cannot ignore the fact that, in the OT, human armies are sometimes compared to locusts via either simile or metaphor (Judg 6:5; 7:12; Nah 3:15–16; Jer 46:23) and that human weakness—not merely strength—can also be described by comparison to these insects (Num 13:33; Ps 109:23). Locusts are part of the OT's stereotypical imagery of judgment (Deut 28:38; 1 Kgs 8:37; Amos 7:1; etc.) to the extent that their mention in contexts of distress, actual or potential, may well have had for Joel's audience the same effect that "approaching hoofbeats" or "the sound of the trumpet" might have for a modern Christian audience.

A second consideration must be that of the prophetic practice of synecdochic allusion to the covenant sanctions. No prophet ever mentions all of the types of covenant curses or blessings, though among the prophets all the types known from the Pentateuch do receive mention. Instead, the prophets allude to the full range of punishments or rewards by merely mentioning one or some. A careful reading of Lev 26, Deut 4, and Deut 28–32 reveals that the ultimate national fate for a disobedient Israel will be defeat in war, capture, and exile. Most of the covenant curses revolve around or lead up to that fate, and most of the covenant restoration blessings involve restoration from it. The sanctions are implicitly a package. They all go together (Deut 28:15, 45); mentioning any one is a way of alluding to all. Accordingly, "locust," like "sword" or "famine" or "plague," individually or together (cf. Jer 24:10; Ezek 6:11), can function virtually as a code word for "covenant curses." As Joel uses his references to locusts, they blend into the broader picture of enemy invasion, which, as the progress of chaps. 1 and 2 shows, is the ultimate threat facing Jerusalem and Judah. Drought and devastation are employed similarly in chaps. 1 and 2 as samples or paradigms of divine judgment, distressing in their own right, but also serving as reminders that God's full judgment against his unfaithful nation is coming.

Affinities to Joel's style and language in describing the invasion of his land are found elsewhere in the prophets, in contexts that do not involve locusts but clearly do involve enemy forces. These also tend to confirm that the threat portrayed in Joel 1 and 2 is a human army. For example, in Hab 3:16–17 reference is made to fig trees not budding, grapeless vines, lack of an olive crop, fields that produce no food, lack of sheep and cattle—all as the result of an invasion of an enemy nation. The parallels to Joel 1:14–20 are strong, yet humans, not locusts, have caused the devastation. Several passages in Jeremiah describe invasions with imagery and terminology parallel to that of Joel 1–2:17. Jer 50:41–46, for example, describes an invading army from the north, well armed, making a loud noise, invading in formation, causing fear to grip those invaded, destroying pastureland, causing the earth to quake, etc. Jer 51:27–33 features an alarm to battle, locust-like invaders, quaking earth, desolation, fire, etc. (cf. also Jer 4:5–29; 6:22–24; 49:19–22). In Isa 24:1–3, in addition to the evident parallel in chap. 13, the prophet describes an invasion in terms of wasting the land, a devastated cross section of citizenry, drought, withering of plant life, a cutting off of wine, the city broken into, etc. (cf. Isa 63:13–14; 64:1–6; etc.). Nah 2:1–10 portrays an advancing attack, wasted land, impressive, unstoppable troops invading the city, the fall of the city, etc. From these and other passages it is evident that the kind of language and imagery used in Joel 1:1–2:17 is language tradition-ally appropriate to the description of invading human armies, and hardly characteristic of locusts per se. In other words, if the two references to locusts in the book, 1:4 and 2:25, are understood as metaphorical rather than literal, the rest of the imagery fits perfectly well with the scenario of a Babylonian or Assyrian invasion.

To this it may be objected that nowhere else in the Bible are invaders compared to locusts metaphorically, but only in simile. The weakness of this objection, however, is twofold. First, it makes an artificial distinction between simile and metaphor not native to biblical modes of comparison. That human armies are compared to locusts (Judg 6:5; 7:12; Nah 3:15–16; cf. *CTA* 14:192–94), whether by simile or metaphor, is the relevant consideration. Second, it ignores the parallel in Isa 7:18 where Egypt and Assyria are compared, respectively, to flies and bees by metaphor. Prophets made such comparisons (cf. also Ezek 19; 29:3–5; Hos 10:1; etc.) as a routine aspect of their artistry.

Neither is the lack of a calling of warriors to arms in 1:1–2:17 a valid objection to the passage's portraying a human invasion. Not all prophetic calls-to-alarm invasion descriptions contain such an element, though, of course, Joel 4:9–11 has one in connection with the final divine war of judgment. The well-known alarm pericopes in Isa 13 and Hos 5:8–10, for example, omit mention of resistance to the invasion.

Finally, it might be argued that Joel's language in 1:2 concerning the uniqueness of the invasion probably reflects Exod 10:6, 14, and that since the Exodus passage involves a literal locust plague, it is therefore most likely that Joel also has in mind a literal plague. But there is reason to think otherwise. It must be kept in mind that the locust plague in Exodus has virtually no significance in isolation but functions as part of the story of divine victory over the most powerful nation of the period. The exodus was a Day of Yahweh. It was a time of the sovereign's intervention against his disobedient vassal, as Pharaoh's words in Exod 10:16–17 acknowledge. For elements of the Exod 10 story to be reused in the case of a Mesopotamian army's invasion of Judah is therefore entirely appropriate. Comparable elements of reused exodus motifs are known to us from Isa 13, 19, 40, 52; Jer 43; Hos 2; Mic 6; Hab 3; et al. And for a poetic comparison of an army of divine judgment to a locust plague, what better allusion could Joel make than to the locust plague of Exod 10?

THE TEXT OF JOEL

The book is relatively free of major textual difficulties, except for 2:23, where the notorious "teacher of righteousness" language originated from a textual corruption (q.v.) and later played a role in the Qumran community's understanding of its leadership. Minor textual complications emerge at 1:9, 4:8, and 4:21. The Septuagint is often a reliable basis for establishment of the text. The Syriac and Vulgate are rarely useful, while the Targum is both expansionistic and eccentric.

PREVIOUS SCHOLARSHIP IN JOEL

Through most of the nineteenth century, the unity and authenticity of the book of Joel remained largely unchallenged, partly because of the support of scholars like E. W. Hengstenberg, C. F. Keil, and A. Merx. Early in the present century, B. Duhm, whose approach was partly anticipated by G. A. Smith and followed eventually by J. Bewer and T. H. Robinson, posited a division in the book, chaps. 1 and 2 being analyzed as reflecting a local locust plague in Joel's time, while chaps. 3 [2:28–32] and 4 [3] were considered to be second-century Maccabean eschatology. Duhm also identified late interpolations within chaps. 1 and 2 (1:15; 2:1–2, 10–11). Scholars who have accepted Duhm's general approach have also tended to dismiss the authentic Joel as merely an uninteresting Persian-era cult prophet with little social concern or theological acuity, whose only real interest was to promote faithful worship so that the nation might prosper agriculturally. In the latter assessment they are joined more recently by Kapelrud and Rudolph, both of whom regard Joel as a pre-exilic prophet who was otherwise a cult functionary—a prophet who, according to Kapelrud, was liturgically preoccupied, and whose confidence in Israel's ultimate total deliverance without judgment for her disobedience contrasts with the balanced perspective of other pre-exilic prophets.

Jepsen, Eissfeldt, and recently, Wolff, were more inclined to see the book as unified, though a product of the Persian, second-temple, period. Weiser posited a two-stage composition by a single author. Eissfeldt has attempted to redeem respect for Joel by stressing the nobility of his interest in the difficulties of everyday life, though chap. 4, particularly, cannot be fitted convincingly within such a perspective. Wolff seeks to rehabilitate Joel rather by pointing to his creative transformation of the Day of Yahweh concept in the fourth century into an effective invitation to repentance in the light of the developing apocalyptic sense of coming judgment for Israel, and to his supposed anti-prophetic outlook in chap. 3, which Wolff seems to applaud.

At present, then, virtually no consensus can be claimed for scholarship on Joel, whether as to date, or unity, or theological perspective, or even the literalness of the imagery. Noticeably missing from recent scholarship on Joel has been attention to his dependence on covenantal ideas and structures, particularly those of the Mosaic covenant sanctions.

A Simple Title   (1:1)

Translation

1:1 *Yahweh's word, that came to Joel son of Pethuel*[a]

Notes

1.a. Since G (βαθουήλ) Syr L all render this name exactly as they render the name of Rebekah's father Bethuel (Gen 22:23, etc.; cf. the name in Josh 19:4; 1 Chr 4:30), there is some possibility that MT's Pethuel (supported by G[86], Tg Vg) is secondary.

Comment

Of the various formats for titles of prophetical books, this is one of the shortest and simplest, comparing closely with Jonah 1:1 in limiting the author's identification to his own and his father's name. Otherwise, cf. Hos 1:1; Mic 1:1; Zeph 1:1 and the G version of Jer 1:1, all of which start similarly but add more material.

Joel is a common Old Testament name, occurring both early (1 Sam 8:2) and late (Neh 11:9). It means "Yahweh is God." Historically, the phonology began with *yahw'-ēl* (the apocopated form of *Yahweh* plus *'ēl*) and progressed as follows: *yahw'ēl* → *yaw'ēl* → *yō'ēl*.

A Call to Lament   (1:2–20)

Bibliography

Baumgartner, W. "Joel 1 und 2." In *Karl Budde zum siebzigsten Geburtstag,* ed. K. Marti. BZAW 34. Giessen: Topelmann, 1920. 10–19. **Dressler, H.** "Ugaritic *uzr* und Joel 1:13." *UF* 7 (1975) 221–25. **Frankfort, T.** "Le יפ de Joël 1:12." *VT* 10 (1960) 445–48. **Kutsch, E.** "Heuschreckenplage und Tag Jahwes in Joel 1 und 2." *TZ* 18 (1962) 81–94. **Mallon, E.** "A Stylistic Analysis of Joel 1:10–12." *CBQ* 45 (1983) 537–48. **Plath, M.** "Joel 1:15–20." *ZAW* 47 (1929) 159–60. **Sellers, O.** "Stages of Locust in Joel." *AJSL* 52 (1935–36) 81–85. **Sprengling, M.** "Joel 1:17." *JBL* 38 (1919) 129–41. **Stephenson, F.** "The Date of the Book of Joel." *VT* 19 (1969) 224–29. **Thompson, J. A.** "Joel's Locusts in the Light of Ancient Near Eastern Parallels." *JNES* 14 (1955) 52–55. **Treves, M.** "The Date of Joel." *VT* 7 (1957) 149–56.

Translation

1:2 *Listen to this, leaders;*[a]
Pay attention, everyone who lives in the land.

Has this happened (before) in your lifetime?
Or in the lifetimes of your ancestors?

³*Tell about it to your children,*
And your children^a *to their children*
And their children^a *to yet a further generation.*

⁴*What the nearly full-grown locust*^a *left, the adult locust*^b *ate.*
What the adult locust left, the infant locust^c *ate.*
What the infant locust left, the young locust^d *ate.*

⁵*Wake up, drunks,*^a *and cry!*
Wail, all you wine drinkers!
Because of the juice of the grape,^b *for it is cut off from your mouths.*

⁶*Because a nation has invaded*^a *my land,*
Strong and innumerable.

Its teeth are lion's teeth,
Its jaws those of a lioness.

⁷*It has made my vine a waste,*
And my fig tree a stump.

It has completely stripped it and thrown it away,
Its branches show a bare white.^a

⁸*Wail like*^a *a virgin with sackcloth around her*
(Wails) over the husband she was betrothed to.^b

⁹*The meal offerings and drink offerings are cut off from Yahweh's house.*
The priests, the ministers of the altar,^a *are in mourning.*

^{10 a}*The fields are desolate,*
The land has withered.

Indeed, the grain is desolate,
The fruit of the vine has wilted,
The olive oil has run dry.

¹¹*Wilt, farmers. Wail, vinedressers,*
Over the wheat and the barley,
Because the harvest of the field has perished.

¹²*The grapevine has wilted, the fig tree has dried up,*
The pomegranate, as well as the date palm and the apple.

All the trees on the landscape have wilted away.
Indeed the joy has wilted^a *from the human beings.*

¹³*Change clothing*^a *and lament, priests.*
Wail, you who minister at the altar.

Come, spend the night in sackcloth,
Ministers of God.^b

For the cereal offerings and libations
Have been held back from your God's house.

¹⁴*Schedule a fast! Announce a cessation of work!*
Gather the leaders; all those who live in the land,
At the house of Yahweh Your God,
And cry out to Yahweh.

15a *Woe* [b] *for the day!*
For Yahweh's Day is near.
It comes as a mighty ruin from the Almighty. [c]

16 *Is not the food cut off before our eyes,*
Joy and rejoicing from our God's house?

17 *The figs have dried out under their casings,* [a]
The storehouses are ruined,

The granaries are broken down,
Because the grain has shriveled.

18 *How the animals groan,* [a]
The herds of cattle wander around, [b]
Because they have no pasturage;
The flocks also are desolate. [c]

19 *I call to you, Yahweh,*
Because fire has devoured the wilderness pasture land,
And flame has ignited all the trees on the landscape.

20 *The wild animals, as well, pant after* [a] *you,*
Because the streams of water have dried up,
And fire has devoured the wilderness pasture land.

Notes

2.a. Heb. זקנים "leaders" designates community / religious leaders and has little to do with chronological age.

3.a-a. On the basis of mechanistic theories of prosody, some commentators have proposed eliminating ובניכם לבניהם "and your children to their children," thus gutting the triplet of both its structure and some of its emphasis.

4.a, b, c, d. These designations for the different forms of the locust, though still speculative, are much more specific to the hearer / reader than the usual "jumper," "creeper," "hopper," etc.

5.a. Here G adds ἐξ οἴνου αὐτῶν, "from their wine," after μεθύοντες "drunken") perhaps because μεθύοντες by itself was thought to be ambiguous, since it can mean "drenched," or "stupefied," in addition to "intoxicated."

5.b. G takes על עסיס, "because of the juice of the grape," with the end of the previous line to produce οἱ πίνοντες οἶνον εἰς μέθην, "(You) who drink wine unto intoxication."

5.c. The reading of G described in 5.b. removes a clear subject from the final clause of the verse (for it . . . mouths) for which G compensates with the words εὐφροσύνη καὶ χαρά, "gladness and rejoicing," apparently borrowed from v 16.

6.a. Lit., "come up against" (עלה על), a military term.

7.a. Here G (ἐλεύκανε) has taken the enemy to be the subject of הלבינ(ו), perhaps because the final waw was not present in G's Vorlage, or perhaps just parallelistically, since "it" (the enemy) is the subject of the other clauses in the verse.

8.a. G (θρήνησον πρός μὲ ὑπὲρ νύμφην, "wail to me more than a virgin") suggests a G Vorlage of something like היליל אלי מן בתולה. But no convincing reconstruction of 8.a. has been forthcoming, as Wolff's lengthy but inconclusive discussion of the text (*Joel*, 18) demonstrates.

8.b. As G's translation (τὸν ἄνδρα αὐτῆς τὸν παρθενικόν, "the husband of her virginity") indicates, בעל נעורים means "the husband one was betrothed to" and has little to do with the age at which a woman was married.

9.a. Reading with G, θυσιαστηρίῳ, "altar," rather than יהוה, "Yahweh" in MT.

10.a. Since G begins the verse with ὅτι (= כִּי, "Because") the text from which G worked may have contained כִּי. On the inconclusiveness of this fact textually, however, see Cross and Freedman, *SAYP*, 161–68.

12.a. G (ἤσχυσαν) treats the Hebrew form as if from בוש, "to be ashamed," but thereby also confirms MT.

13.a. Lit., "gird yourselves," the point being to change into sackcloth.

13.b. Reading with G (θεῷ) which would reflect אלהים, "God," not "my God."

15.a. It is possible that "woe for the day," etc. is what the priests are to call out (v 14); Syr takes vv 15–20 as the words of lament by introducing them with the imperative wᵉmrw, "and say."

15.b. The versions repeat the equivalent of "woe" twice (Syr) or three times (G, L), suggesting that MT may be shorter than the original here because of haplogr via homoiotel.

15.c. Heb. שֹׁד מִשַּׁדַּי an alliteration, lit., "ruin from the Mountain One."

17.a. This first clause in the verse is not really understood, as the vast and sometimes hilarious differences among ancient and modern translations demonstrate. It is likely that G, for example ("the heifers have jumped at their mangers"), or Vg ("the work animals are rotting in their muck") are guessing just as much as we are at the meaning.

18.a. Some G MSS (τί ἀποθήσομεν ἐν αὐτοῖς, "What will we store in them?") obviously reflect MT in spite of their misconstrual.

18.b. G (ἔκλαυσαν, "cried") also reflects MT.

18.c. The word in MT (נֶאְשְׁמוּ) is probably a biform of שׁמם "to be desolate" rather than a form of אשׁם "to be guilty, subject to punishment."

20.a. Or possibly, "cry to," in light of the parallelism with v 19a; cf. Arabic *ajja*, "cry out."

Form / Structure / Setting

Joel 1:2–20, in the whole or in part, has sometimes been identified with either the Old Testament communal laments (cf. Baumgartner, BZAW 34: *Karl Budde*, 10–19; C. Westermann, "Struktur and Geschichte der Klage im Alten Testament," *ZAW* 66 [1954] 44–80) or more recently with a separate form, the "Call to Communal Lamentation" (Wolff, 21–24). It is not in fact a communal lament, since such songs feature a structure centering on six elements (address to God, complaint, expression of trust, plea for deliverance, word of assurance, expression of praise) as evidenced in the communal laments of the Psalter (cf. B. W. Anderson, *Out of the Depths*, 2d ed. [Philadelphia: Westminster, 1983] 63–92). Moreover, communal laments lack the sort of emphasis found here on direct address to various members of the community, summoning them to mourning and/or to reflection (leaders, v 1; farmers, v 11; priests, v 13; etc.). It is best identified as a call to communal lament.

A call to communal lament is not always easily distinguished from an elegy or funerary lament. Both contain frequent imperatives (usually plural) requesting a cessation of normal activities and a turning of attention to mourning; both contain descriptions of the tragedy; both call for reflection / reaction; both contain direct address to the "fallen." (On this format see Amos 5:1–17; in Joel 1:2–20 the direct address to the "fallen" naturally involves the victims themselves.) Thus a call to lament and an elegy are somewhat different expressions of the same essential form.

The present passage adds an element of appeal to God (vv 19–20) on the part of both prophet (v 19) and animals (v 20), followed in each verse by continuing descriptions of the tragedy. The overall structure may be portrayed as follows:

Call to reflection / reaction   vv 2–3
Description of tragedy   v 4
Call to mourning (drunkards) and further description   vv 5–7
Call to mourning (general) and further description   vv 8–10
Call to mourning (farmers) and further description   vv 11–12
Call to mourning (priests) and further description   vv 13–18
Appeal to Yahweh and further description   vv 19–20

Wolff (*Hosea*, 20) sees in v 2a "Listen . . . pay attention" wisdom language. In fact, this formulation is merely a standard poetic attention imperative without specifically wisdom overtones (cf. Gen 4:23; Num 23:18; Judg 5:3; Isa 1:2; 1:10; 28:23; 32:9; Jer 13:15; Hos 5:1; etc.).

The authorship of 1:2–20 is routinely attributed to Joel himself, who may be assumed to be the speaker. In vv 6 and 7 the first-person usages (my land, my vine, etc.) represent simply a personification of the nation (cf. Lam 1:15) rather than Yahweh's land or Joel's land, etc. The frequency of interchange between prophetic speech and divine speech, however, was so normal in ancient Israel that the need to make a distinction as to speaker would probably not have occurred to anyone in Joel's audience. Elsewhere the pronouns show Joel clearly to be speaking (vv 16, 19) and Yahweh to be the hearer (vv 19, 20).

There is nothing in the passage to fix its date precisely. The frequent mention of a functioning temple (vv 9, 13, 14, 16) and living in the land (v 2) suggest a time other than the exile (586–516 B.C.). The language in v 3 about the need to keep alive the knowledge of the present event reflects the early monarchical-era wording of Ps 78:3–8, though that does not automatically exclude its being much later in date. The emphasis on the uniqueness of the disaster (v 2b) suggests a pre-exilic date, since thereafter the fall of Judah and the exile seem to dominate prophetic writings as *the* disaster in Israel's history. The nearness of Yahweh's Day (v 15) is a pre-exilic theme, but also a post-exilic and even New Testament theme, thus useless for dating *per se*. It has sometimes been thought that the mention in vv 9 and 13 of מנחה and נסך, cereal offerings and drink offerings, in combination, reflects a late date (post-exilic), but this would even be of interest only if one dated virtually all specific temple sacrifice language late (as is sometimes unconvincingly done) and only if the combination of the two terms could be proved an exilic / post-exilic neologism, which it cannot.

Joel's home is unknown. The common suggestion that he was a Jerusalemite in light of his frequent references to Judah's capital has no more merit than would an identification of Amos as a northerner because of his frequent mention of Bethel and Samaria.

On the likely dating of the book as a whole, and therefore by implication v 1, to either 701 or 597 / 588 B.C.; see Joel, *Introduction*.

Synonymous parallelism predominates in the pericope. There is a high percentage of triplets (vv 3, 4, 5, 10b, 11, 19, 20) and two quatrains (vv 14, 18). Connections to the Pentateuchal sanctions passages abound, as would be expected in any prophetic corpus, but especially to the Song of Moses, Deut 32:1–43, a covenant curse poem. These connections are noted in the *Comment* below.

Comment

1:2 The call to lament begins with imperative verbs of hearing (שמעו
. . . האזינו, "Listen . . . pay attention") as do Deut 32:1 (same verbs, reverse
order) and many other such songs (in the Prophets, cf. Isa 1:10; 28:23; Hos
5:1; Mic 1:2; 3:1). The call is general, to leaders (זקנים; cf. 1:14; 2:16; 3:1
[2:28]) first, but to all the population of Judah as well. The event that has
occasioned Joel's call to the nation is unparalleled, even in "the lifetime of
your ancestors." This may be hyperbole (cf., however, 2:2) but it may also
signal an event of no prior comparable severity such as the Babylonian invasion
of January 588 (see J. Bright, *History of Israel*, 308–9). Suggestions that the
reference to זקנים (elders / leaders) in 2a points to a post-exilic date are obviated by the mention of the term in Deut 32:7. Joel consciously alludes to
the Song of Moses routinely.

3 Again with allusion to Deut 32:7 ("days of old . . . generations long
past . . .") and in parallel to similar imperatives (Exod 12:26; Deut 4:9; 6:7;
Ps 78:4–6, et al.) the Israelites are advised that this event is so important
that it must be made a national memory.

4 The invasion is compared to various kinds of locusts that have devoured
everything edible. The picture given is highly figurative, rather than literal,
since all the stages of locusts do not work together at once. The repetitious
pattern of the verse is highly stylized, lit.,

> What was left (יתר) of *a, b* ate;
> What was left of *b, c* ate;
> What was left of *c, d* ate.

This pattern seems borrowed almost exactly from the Egyptian locust plague
account in Exod 10:5, 15.

Excursus: Literal or Figurative Locusts?

From time to time commentators have tried valiantly to identify with precision
the four terms used here for locust stages (at least we assume that they indicate
locust stages). Wolff (*Joel*, 27–28) provides an excellent review of the options and
concludes, properly, that "the usage of the designations [for stages of locusts]
varies in the Old Testament." In other words, our translations ("nearly full-grown
locust" for גזם; "adult locust" for ארבה; "infant locust" for ילק; "young locust"
for חסיל) are ultimately speculative. Indeed, entomologists identify six rather than
four separate stages for the desert locust (B. P. Uvarov, *Locusts and Grasshoppers*
[London: Imperial Bureau of Entomology, 1928] 250–61), and the Talmud uses
more than twenty different names for locusts (L. Lewysohn, *Die Zoologie des Talmuds*
[Frankfurt: Joseph Baer, 1858] 286–97). Technically, locusts are merely grasshoppers that hatched under perfect rainfall conditions and multiplied accordingly.
At any rate, Joel is not giving his hearers / readers a lesson in entomology; he is
emphasizing in a dramatic way the fact that the land of Judah has been thoroughly
desolated.

It has been argued that neither in the Bible nor in other ancient Near Eastern literature are locusts ever *symbols* for human invaders, even though in Ugaritic, Egyptian, and Assyrian literature human armies are frequently compared to locusts in terms of number and designation (see J. A. Thompson, *JNES* 14 [1955] 52–55 for a review of the evidence).

Against this view it must be recognized that Joel, like other Old Testament prophets, is consciously attentive to Pentateuchal curse language, which is highly symbolic and metaphorical. Locusts *per se* are mentioned in Deut 28:38, 42 precisely in the context of defeat by enemies and exile. (And we should be reminded that the curses of Lev 26 and Deut 28–32 are a package, referring to a single era of judgment.) Moreover, Joel's extensive metaphorical comparison of the invading armies to a locust plague, unparalleled as it is for length, is still a *comparison*, in the manner of much other ancient literature (see the summary in W. E. Staples, "An Inscribed Scaraboid from Megiddo," *New Light from Armageddon*, OIP 9 [Chicago: University of Chicago Press, 1931] 60–63). The fact that Joel's comparison is mainly metaphorical while other attested comparisons are mainly similitudinous can hardly be determinative for one interpretation or the other. Finally, the factor of Joel's extreme language, hyperbolic though it is, cannot be ignored. Joel treats this event, which dominates chaps. 1 and 2, as being of far greater significance than any of the relatively frequent locust plagues would deserve (see esp. 1:11, 17; 2:20, 25; cf. 4:17 [3:17]).

The "locusts" of 1:4 and 2:25, then (and these are the only places where locusts are actually mentioned in the book), must be understood as figurative, symbols for the invading Babylonian armies. More than just one plague among many (cf. Exod 10:1–18), this was *the* plague par excellence, the destructive, unstoppable invasion unleashed to consume Israel as locusts consume a field.

5 Here begins the call for response, the description of the tragedy having been concluded for the moment at v 4. There is probably a degree of intentional shock value in issuing to drunks (שכורים) the first imperatives to action: "wake up" (הקיצו) and "cry" (בכו). It is drunks and "drinkers of wine" who represent a heedless, incautious attitude; they are people capable of being unaware of what is happening around them. This sort of complacency is what Joel is attacking. The invasion has disrupted Jerusalem's way of life, and people cannot simply go about business as usual. One of the major crops used for wine, grape juice (עסיס), has been ruined. From the point of view of a literal locust plague, the connection is obvious: stripped grape vines can't produce. (Thompson [*IB* 6:738] reports a doubling of wine prices after the famous 1915 locust plague in Palestine—an inconvenience, though hardly a calamity.) But from the point of view of the Babylonian invasion, the countryside has fallen to the enemy, who have taken the fruit of the vine for themselves (cf. curse type 15, esp. Deut 28:30, 33).

6 Here the "locusts" are actually called a (foreign) nation (גוי) with the devouring ability of a lion (curse types 5 and 11, respectively). The jaws / teeth . . . lion / lioness parallelism is of a standard synonymous type (cf. Job 29:17; Ps 58:6; Prov 30:14) and says nothing *per se* about locusts, but it does suggest the enemy's strength and devastation (cf. Jer 4:6–7).

Does "my land" (ארצי) imply that Yahweh is being quoted directly, at least at this point? In light of Ezek 38:16, where Gog comes up against "my people . . . my land," the answer would seem to be yes.

7 Grape vines and fig trees have been stripped in Yahweh's ("my") land by the invaders. That the one is "thrown away" (השליך) and the other cut down to a stump (קצפה) represents figurative language, since locusts cannot cut trees to stumps or throw them away—and locust activity is the prevailing metaphor. It may also, however, indicate subtly a more literal fact: the invaders are a human army that has purposely undone years of careful agricultural preparation (cf. Hab 3:17; Deut 28:39; 32:32; etc.; curse type 6, agricultural disaster, is in view here).

8 "Wail" (אלי) is a feminine singular imperative, indicating that some female group or feminine thing is being addressed (ארץ "land," v 6?; אדמה "land," v 10?; or more likely גפן "vine" and תאנה "fig tree," together personified, since these are the more immediate feminine singular referents). Betrothals in ancient Israel long preceded marriage. They might take place even before persons were born: parents could betroth a potential male child to a potential female child of another family. נעורים, the masculine plural abstract, indicates "youth" in the sense of the age prior to marriage (see esp. Wolff, *Joel*, 29–30). Thus, here the wailing is to resemble the sort of bitter disappointment experienced by a woman who had long expected marriage to the one she now mourns. Such futility reflects curse type 15 especially. Sackcloth (שק) is a coarse animal-hair fabric used as a self-abnegating body covering in mourning (cf. Gen 37:34; 2 Sam 21:10; 1 Kgs 21:27; Jonah 3:5, 6; *IDB* 4:147).

9 The focus of disappointment shifts to the temple. The agricultural devastation caused by the invasion means that there is no longer adequate wine, flour, and oil for the twice-daily cereal and drink offerings (Lev 2:6; Exod 29:38–41; etc.). Animal offerings would be a problem only if much more time had gone by. Pasturage is affected, of course, as v 18 clearly indicates; but in the short run, lack of feed would result in more slaughtering, not less. Nevertheless, the verse seems to indicate that the invasion is a recent thing—days or, at most, weeks in the past—so that cattle gathered into the besieged city have not yet died off.

The priests "are in mourning" (אבלו) for two reasons: they lament the interruption of sacrifices (cf. vv 13, 16), and they themselves are hungry because the sharing of sacrifices provides their own food supply (Lev 2:3, 10, etc.).

10 The Pentateuchal curses predicting desolation of fields and land (שדה, אדמה; e.g. Deut 28:33, 42; etc.) and the loss to enemies of grain, wine, and oil (דגן, תירוש, יצהר; e.g., Deut 28:51) are now being fulfilled. God is punishing his nation for its sins. יצהר is simply a poetic, nonprose word for wine, thus translated "fruit of the vine." It does not indicate any special sort of wine (cf. Hos 2:8).

11 Now it is the producers of the crops who are called to mourning. אכרים "dirt farmers" and כרמים "vine dressers" also occur in parallel in 2 Chr 26:10 and Isa 61:5 as terms suggesting all crop workers. "Wilt" (הביש) is a sort of pun here. It usually refers to drying out, as in a drought (e.g., Gen 8:14; Ps 90:6; Hos 9:16; Joel 1:12, 20), but can also be used of people's despair (e.g., 2 Sam 19:6; Hos 2:7). Drought imagery seems to be prominent at this point in the passage, and this is probably an indication of an actual drought that followed the invasion. It is also an example of the rapid shift

of metaphor typical of virtually all OT poetry. The ancient hearer / reader
would have no trouble understanding all of the passage as describing the
aftermath of an invasion.

12 By mentioning five types of fruit vines / trees and then "all the trees"
(cf. Neh 13:15), Joel effectively drums in the extent of the devastation of
the crop lands. Then, by metaphorically treating joy (ששון) as a fruit and
human beings (בני אדם) as its "tree," he brings home the disaster in a striking,
personal sort of way. (On the routine grouping of grapevines, fig trees, and
pomegranates, cf. Num 20:5; Deut 8:8; on the devastation of fruit in general
as a curse, cf. Lev 26:20; Deut 28:40.)

13 V 13 is an elaboration of the theme already introduced in v 9, now
in direct address format, so that the priests are specifically called to don the
uncomfortable grieving garb of sackcloth (cf. v 8; 2 Sam 12:16; 1 Kgs 21:27)
and participate in the mourning process. The starvation / famine curses (type
7; cf. Lev 26:26; Deut 32:24) are thus fulfilled even in regard to worship
per se.

14 The priests (who are still being addressed) are instructed to schedule
(קדש, literally, "set aside") a fast day so that everyone, including the nation's
leadership, can cry out (זעק) together to Yahweh for help (cf. Judg 6:7; Jer
11:11; 1 Sam 7:8). A typical one-day fast is probably envisioned (Judg 20:26;
1 Sam 14:24; Isa 58:3–5; Jer 36:6–9), involving cessation of routine activity,
no eating, and special prayer. Fasting is a form of self-denial which, like
wearing sackcloth, is intended to heighten the seriousness of one's appeal to
God.

15 At this point the dominant theme of the book—the Day of the Lord—
appears, as an explanation and justification for all that has been said so far.
"Woe for the day!" (אהה ליום) in a certain sense says it all, though the specificity of "Yahweh's Day" (יום יהוה) and the ominously alliterative *šōd miššaday*
("a mighty ruin from the Almighty") leave no possibility of doubt that Joel's
call for mourning concerns much more than any mere locust plague or
drought. The enemy invasion represents God's judgment against His people,
the great king's decisive one-day intervention against the disobedient vassal
state (cf. D. Stuart, *BASOR* 221 [1976] 159–64). Joel's "Alas for the Day!"
compares to Amos' "Woe to you who desire the Day . . ." (Amos 5:18).
Both announce unmistakably that Yahweh's intervention will not occur on
behalf of, but in judgment of, Israel. Day of Yahweh language, occurring
sixteen times in the OT prophets, represents a fulfillment of curse type 1
(rejection by Yahweh; cf. Lev 26:17, 28; Deut 29:27, 28; Deut 31:17, 18, etc.)
as well as of curse type 3 (war; cf. Lev 26:25, 33; Deut 28:49; 32:23, 41).

16 Reversion to the theme of food deprivation (curse type 7), this time
via a rhetorical question, reinforces the point just made. We can all see (". . .
before our eyes," נגד עינינו), can we not, says Joel, that the judgment of
famine is already upon us, and thus our previous ability to rejoice in worship
is also gone.

17 Since the harvests have been taken by invaders (cf. Judg 6:3–6, 11)
there has been no attention paid to grain storehouses. As a result, they are
falling apart from lack of repair. Instead of the sight of full granaries, people
are seeing empty, broken-down ones—visible reminders that the drought

already mentioned (vv 10–12; curse type 6a) has ruined the potential harvest.

18 Verses 18–20 are concerned mainly with descriptions of starving, thirsty cattle, and large mammals. Humankind's closest associates in creation are, of course, large land mammals (Gen 1:24–26); people and cattle or other larger land animals are routinely mentioned together in the Old Testament (e.g., Jonah 4:11). Thus the illustrations of agricultural disaster which began with humans, then progressed to plant life, now conclude with cattle and wild animals.

19 After calling all others to appeal in mourning to Yahweh, the prophet himself joins in. In vv 19 and 20 the metaphor of destructive fire predominates. This represents an allusion to curse type 10, as in Deut 28:22, where Yahweh himself is the punishing fire, and Deut 32:22, which identifies destructive fire as an instrument of Yahweh's wrath, to "devour the earth and its harvests."

The appeal, therefore, must be made directly to Yahweh, because he is the ultimate source of the devastation the land has experienced, through the proximate agency of the enemy.

20 A locust plague *per se* could not cause the drying up of "streams of water" (אֲפִיקֵי מִים); this is stereotypical drought language (curse type 6a), possibly reflecting, however, the common practice in ancient Near Eastern warfare of attempting to weaken the enemy by diverting, blocking, or filling in their water supplies (cf., e.g., Gen 26:18; 2 Kgs 3:19, 25; 2 Chr 32:4). As in v 19, it is wild animals that are mentioned as being most immediately affected by the "fire." The final line of v 20, "fire . . . pasture land," is virtually identical to the middle line of v 19. Is this evidence that one or both triplets are corrupt? Hardly. Rather, the repetition is designed to emphasize the extent of the disaster as divine wrath: "God has burned over our whole country" would be a précis of these verses.

Explanation

In this lengthy call to communal lamentation to Yahweh, three metaphors are employed prominently to describe the extent ·of a devastation that has befallen Judah. The metaphors are a locust invasion (v 4 and in part vv 5–7), a famine-producing drought (vv 9–12, 16–18), and judgment fire (vv 19–20).

The three metaphors do not point literally to locusts, drought, and fire, but serve as vehicles for a poetic literary artistry designed to depict the investing of the land of Judah and the encirclement of Jerusalem by an invading Mesopotamian army (v 6a). If this army can be identified with the Assyrians, the time of which Joel speaks is probably 701 B.C., when Sennacherib's forces surrounded Jerusalem. If the army is Babylonian, the time would be either 597 B.C., the occasion of the first great Babylonian invasion of Nebuchadnezzar, or 588–587 B.C., during the final siege of Jerusalem before its great destruction and the exile of 586 (see *Introduction*).

Much like Lamentations, which via its acrostic format relentlessly rolls through instance after instance of the miseries resulting from invasion, Joel 1 describes similar distresses from many angles. What has happened? Yahweh has unleashed the curses promised by his covenant for the disobedient nation: invasion by an enemy and its attendant pains. This is no mere locust plague, distressing as such could be. This is a harbinger of the Day of Yahweh itself (v 15), an event of moment for the nation's whole history (vv 1–2), a time to call out for mercy from Yahweh.

Sounding the Alarm in Zion　(2:1–17)

Bibliography

Bach, R. *Die Aufforderungen zur Flucht und zum Kampf im alttestamentlichen Prophetenspruch.* WMANT 9. Neukirchen: Neukirchener Verlag, 1962. **Bourke, J.** "Le jour de Yahvé dans Joël." *RB* 66 (1959) 5–31, 191–212. **Carroll, R.** "Eschatological Delay in the Prophetic Tradition?" *ZAW* 94 (1982) 47–58. **Görg, M.** "Eine formelhafte Metapher bei Joel und Nahum." *BN* 6 (1978) 12–14. **Kutsch, E.** "Heuschreckenplage und Tag Jahwes in Joel 1 und 2." *TZ* 18 (1962) 81–94. **Leibel, D.** "On *ye'abbetûn* (Joel 2:7)." *Leš* 24 (1959–60) 253 [Heb.]. **Loewenstamm, S.** *"y'btûn = ye'awwetûn?" Leš* 24 (1959–60) 107–8 [Heb.]. ———. *"ûb'ad haššelah yippōlû"* (Joel 2:8b)." *Leš* 26 (1961–62) 62. [Heb.]. **Whitley, C.** *"'bt* in Joel 2:7." *Bib* 65 (1984) 101–2.

Translation

The attack

2:1 *Blow the horn in Zion,*
Sound the alarm on my holy mountain.

Let everyone that lives in the land tremble,
Because the Day of Yahweh is coming, because it is near,[a]

2 *The day of darkness and gloom,*
The day of clouds and blackness.

Like the dawn spreading across the hills is the populous, strong nation.
Nothing like it has existed from ancient times,
Nor will it again for generation after generation.

3 *In front of it fire devours;*
Behind it flame blazes

Like the Garden of Eden is the land in front of it,
But behind it, a desolate wilderness.
There is simply no escape from it.

4 *Its appearance is like that of horses.*
They[a] *run as cavalry do.*

5 *Like the sound of chariots pounding across the mountaintops,*
Like the sound of a flaming fire devouring stubble,
Like a strong nation lined up for battle.

6 *Nations writhe in agony at the sight of it.*
Everyone's face becomes flushed.[a]

⁷*They run like soldiers,*
They scale a wall like warriors.

They proceed each on his course,
They don't deviate[a] *from their paths.*

⁸*They don't interfere with each other.*
Everyone[a] *goes on his way.*[b]
They dodge[c] *the arrows—they don't quit.*

⁹*They mass against the city*
They run at the wall,
They climb up into the houses

In through the windows
They enter like a thief

¹⁰*Before it the earth shakes,*
The sky quakes.

Sun and moon darken,
And the stars withhold their light.

¹¹*Yahweh has raised his voice before his army!*
How very great is his encampment!
How strong[a] *are those who carry out his words!*[a]

How great is the Day of Yahweh,
And very fearful! Who can endure it?

The call to repentance

¹²*Even now (oracle of Yahweh)*[a]
Return to me with all your heart,
With fasting, weeping, and mourning.

¹³*Tear your heart—not your clothes!*
Return to Yahweh your God,

For he is gracious and compassionate,
Patient and fully loyal—
One who changes his mind about doing harm.

¹⁴*Who knows? He may turn and show compassion*
And may cause blessing to remain after this.[a]
Meal offerings and drink offerings belong to Yahweh your God!

¹⁵*Blow the horn in Zion!*
Schedule a fast!
Announce a cessation of work!

¹⁶*Assemble the people,*
Schedule an assembly,
Gather the elders,

Assemble the children,
Even those nursing at the breast!

Let the bridegroom come out of his bedroom,
And the bride from her chamber.

¹⁷ Let the priests, the ministers of Yahweh, weep
Between the porch and the altar.

Let them say: Have mercy on your people, Yahweh,
Don't let your possession become an object of scorn,
Ruled over ᵃ by foreigners.

Why should it be said among the nations,
"Where is their God?"

Notes

1.a. כי קרוב "for it is near" fits the meter's syllable count and is hardly redundant, as is sometimes argued.

4.a. The enemy has been "it" (3d masc sg) and is now "they" (3d masc pl); the abrupt pronom shift is typical of Hebrew poetry.

6.a. G (ὡς πρόσκαυμα χύτρας "like the blackness of a cauldron") was perhaps reading something like כבצו פרור, lit., "like the silt of a pot," assuming the waw on כבץ to be an anticipatory suff. Vg (ollam, "pot") also confused פארור "glowing heat" with פרור "pot."

7.a. As the articles by Leibel and Loewenstamm indicate, the exact meaning of עבט is debatable.

8.a,b. Here G (καταβαρυνόμενοι ἐν τοῖς ὅπλοις αὐτῶν "weighed down with their arms . . .") probably got "weighed down" from a Vorlage having כבד "heavy" or גבד instead of גבר "strong," and stumbled contextually through במסלתו to get "from (מ or ב) their weapons."

8.c. Here G (πεσοῦνται "they fall") more literally attests to MT, while Tg (ולאתר דאינון) שליחין אזלין קטלין "where they are sent they go and kill") probably supports the entire line except for יפלו לא.

11.a-a. G (ἔργα λόγων αυτοῦ "the deeds of his words") reflects a Vorlage such as עשי דבריו, to which Tg and σ', by translating with pls, also attest. Syr L and Vg basically agree, so MT's wording is likely not original.

12.a. G adds ὁ θεὸς ὑμῶν "[Yahweh] your God," a probable expansion based on vv 13, 14.

14.a. Lit., "after it," i.e., the invasion. Cf. n. 4.a.

17.a. The straightforward meaning of ב משל is "rule over," not "mock."

Form / Structure / Setting

2:1–17 continues closely on chap. 1, to which it is related, and from which it may be separated only somewhat artificially. It is recognized as a separate section by its initial command to alarm the citizenry, something much more dramatic than the call to lament of chap 1, and the fact that at 2:18 the shift to restoration promises launches a new pericope.

Nevertheless, the similarity to 1:1–20 is unmistakable. Both passages describe an invasion along with attendant disasters, and call for an appeal to Yahweh for relief. In 1:1–20 the invasion / disaster descriptions are interspersed with various summonses to lament. In 2:1–17, however, the invasion / disaster descriptions come all at the outset (vv 1–11) with the call for return to Yahweh (including lamentation) following in vv 12–17.

Three known forms are combined in the passage: (1) an invasion alarm (vv 1–2a; cf. Hos 5:8–10; 8:1; Jer 4:5–6; 6:1–4); (2) a description of the invading enemy (vv 2b-11; cf. Jer 4:5–16; 46:3–24; 47:2–6; 49:19–22; Ezek 38:4–9, 15–22; Mic 1:3–4; Nah 2:1–10); and (3) a call to repentance / lamentation (vv 12–17; cf. 1:2–20; Isa 23:1–14; Jer 4:8; 25:34–38; Ezek 30:2). Note that Jer 4:5–17 also combines these three elements.

The continuing descriptions of desolation, defoliation, and drought in this chapter echo such descriptions in chap. 1. Particularly striking is the irony that Yahweh serves both as the commander of the enemy forces (v 11) and the ally to whom the people must turn for help (v 12). Without Yahweh the people might not experience the coming national destruction, but without him they could also not have rescue.

V 11 is central and pivotal to the passage. In vv 1–10, the elaborate description of the unstoppable invading force builds steadily, from the first alarm and distant appearance of the foe on the mountain crests (v 2) to their relentless march across the intervening terrain (vv 3–5), to the point where the quality of their battle formation is clearly visible at near range (vv 6–8), to the point where they are finally at and into the city, causing chaos (vv 9–10). Who is this as yet technically unidentified horde? V 11 tells us that it is none other than Yahweh's army! And what is the implication? Jerusalem and its people are not merely experiencing war, but are receiving God's judgment.

After v 11, then, the passage reverts to the kind of call to repentance / mourning that dominated chap. 1. Included is the linkage of horn-alarm in v 15 with the call to repentance / mourning, which makes clear that the real task of the people is not to prepare for war against Yahweh's army, since that would be futile, but to let the current invasion serve to impel them to cast themselves on Yahweh's mercy (vv 13–14, et al.).

The overall structure may thus be diagrammed:

Alarm and progressing invasion	vv 1–10
Identification of enemy and implication	v 11
Summons to repent / mourn	vv 12–17

The call to repentance / mourning (vv 12–17) involves in vv 16 and 17 many of the same constituencies within the population that are also mentioned in chap. 1:

2:16	people	1:14
	assembly	1:14
	elders	1:2, 14
	children	1:3
	bridegroom	(1:8)
	bride	(1:8)
2:17	priests	1:9, 13

What is missing from the longer summons in chap. 1 is any reference to farmers and cattle (1:11, 18, 20) and, of course, the drunks (1:5).

The passage contains a remarkably high ratio of triplets (12) to couplets (17), with mostly "synthetic" parallelism in each case. A few triplets (vv 9, 15, 16) and couplets (vv 9, 10, 16) are cast in short (*breve*) meter, partly reflective of the sense of rapidity with which the enemy is portrayed as advancing.

V 9 takes the invasion beyond that of a siege to include an overrunning of Jerusalem, the enemy having scaled the walls and entered the city's houses. Those who take the passage as depicting locusts hopping and flying into the city consider such a completion of conquest as unremarkable. Unremarkable it is indeed—for what damage can locusts do to a city other than to annoy people briefly by reason of their sheer numbers? But if the description is intended to indicate an occupation by human enemies (curse type 5) and the horror of war brought home (type 4; cf. Deut 32:25, "In their homes, terror will reign . . ."), then its impact as fulfilling predictions of the Day of Yahweh (v 11) is understandable.

Accordingly, v 9 must be understood as the ultimate expectation of the invasion underway—the conquest by an enemy that will eventually bring an end to Jerusalem. Such a conquest occurred, of course, in 586 B.C. The fact that it could have been foreseen explicitly as early as 701, thus suggesting the earliest date for the present passage, is impossible to deny in light of Amos's, Hosea's, Isaiah's, and Micah's own expectations of the eventual capture of Judah.

Comment

1 The call to alarm takes place in Jerusalem, identified by the parallelism "Zion . . . my holy mountain" (cf. Jer 26:18; Isa 2:3; Mic 3:12; Zech 8:3; *CTA* 3.3.26–28) and sounded by the שׁופר, ram's horn, the standard signal for almost any sort of alarm or general summons in Israel (e.g., Exod 19:16, 19; Judg 3:27; 1 Sam 13:3; 2 Sam 2:28; Jer 6:1; Hos 5:8; Zeph 1:16; etc.; cf. 1 Thess 4:16). Jerusalem, like nearly all ancient cities, had watchmen stationed on its walls to give early warning of danger (cf. Ezek 33:2–4). Here Yahweh is the watchmen's commander ("*my* holy mountain" cannot point to Joel) ordering them to blow the alarm so that the population of the city will realize its danger. That danger is the long-awaited great Day of Yahweh, when he will intervene not on behalf of, but *against* Israel. On the ram's horn alarm and the Day, cf. esp. Zeph 1:16 and Zech 9:14, the latter portraying Yahweh as sounding the horn himself, rather than simply ordering it sounded.

2 The darkness and gloom language is intended to portray coming judgment and destruction (2:10; 3:4; Isa 8:22; 13:10; Ezek 34:12; 38:9; Amos 5:18, 20; Zeph 1:15) for people who still might have naively thought that Yahweh's intervention would represent deliverance (cf. Amos 5:18–20). The foe is awesome (v 26; cf. 1:2, 3), a massive empire army so great that its like cannot be imagined past or future. The vast armies of the Assyrians under Sennacherib in 701 or the Babylonians under Nebuchadnezzar in the 590s and 580s would both fit this only partly grandiloquent description.

3 The invaders devastate the land much as wildfire would. This language is not so much literal as metaphorical. Fire symbolizes divine judgment in the covenant curses (type 11; cf. Deut 32:22) and here produces desolation of the land, also a curse category (type 10; cf. Lev 26:33; Deut 29:22–23). Fire often signifies divine presence or arrival as well (Exod 24:17; Num 9:15–

16; Deut 4:11–12; 5:22–26; Ps 97:3) and specifically conveys this in Zeph 1:18 relative to the Day of Yahweh.

Ezekiel also adopts the Garden of Eden / desolation contrast (Ezek 28:13–19; note the fire in v 18; 31:16–18; and 36:35, where Eden follows desolation in a promise oracle).

No "escape" (פליטה) adds here the emphasis of inevitability to the Day's judgment, illustrated in Amos 5:9 as well as Zeph 1:2–3.

4 As a suggestion of an enemy's overwhelming strength and swiftness, horses and horse-weaponry provided a most fearsome metaphor in ancient times (e.g., Exod 15:1, 19; Deut 20:1; Josh 11:4; Job 39:9; cf. Isa 31:1). Israel, with its rugged terrain, never relied on mounted warfare to the extent that other nations did. Thus horses are especially associated with the coming of the eschatological foreign enemy here and in Jeremiah (6:23) and Ezekiel (38:4).

5 Appealing to the senses, this triplet gives an impression of both the sound and the sight of the enemy—a great din in the distance, a wide wall of advancing warriors. The description of the eschatological locust plague of Rev 9:1–11, alluding in part to Joel, contains similar elements, including the comparison in v 9 of the sound of the locusts to "horses and chariots rushing into battle." Yahweh's divine army of conquest is thus here and in the following verses (6–9) loosely compared, now and again, to locusts on the march in a more or less conscious sense, though other metaphors coexist with the locust comparison.

6 Emphasis shifts briefly to the action of those who see the great fierce-looking (cf. Deut 28:49) enemy force in the distance. Obviously mere locusts are not the real topic. The reaction of writhing (cf. Ps. 96:9; Jer 5:22) and flushed faces in hot panic (cf. Isa 13:8) on the part of entire nations (עמים) conveys the fear of seeing a conquering military horde led by Yahweh.

7 These two couplets seem to portray the foe in a manner appropriate in part to locusts and in part to a human army. They are *like* (. . . כ . . . . כ) soldiers / warriors, and yet obviously also constitute an army intent on conquest—disciplined, organized, and not stoppable by ordinary defense barriers like walls (cf. Deut 28:52).

8 A balance between cooperation and independence (indicated by איש "each," and גבר, here "every one") characterizes this perfect fighting force. Arrows shot at them make no difference—they just keep coming (cf. Lev 26:17, 37; Deut 28:25).

9 The enemy finally arrives at, and in, the city. All defensive efforts have failed, and the populace is overwhelmed by invaders who overrun everything, penetrating every house. The conquest is complete. One may think of two levels of invasion imagined concurrently: symbolically, the locusts, and literally, the divine army. Mention of the invasion of houses may be understood as alluding to the divine judgment plague on the Egyptians in Exodus, in which locusts "filled" the Egyptian houses (Exod 10:6). On the military level, however, capture and destruction of houses brings to completion the conquest of a city (cf. Deut 28:30; 32:25; 2 Kgs 25:9; Neh 7:4). The curses of war and its ravages (type 3) are fulfilled.

10 That the Day of Yahweh will be characterized in part by tremors and darkness is a common prophetic theme (cf. 2:2; 3:4). This association of quaking and darkness with catastrophe is a natural one: stable ground and light during the daytime represent security; their absence reflects disaster. The covenant curses already anticipate this sort of reversal of natural security (Deut 28:29, "At midday you will grope around like a blind man in the dark; type 19; cf. the fear / terror / horror curses of type 4) but do not identify either darkness or earthquake as curses per se. They are, rather, signs of theophany (cf. Hab 3:6, 10; 1 Kgs 19:11; Ezek 32:7, 8) that the Day of Yahweh involves.

11 Suddenly the identity and purpose of the enemy are entirely clear, as three כי clauses ("because / how") are employed. The enemy attack because they belong to Yahweh and are doing his bidding. The triplet (11a) is partly chiastic: sandwiched between mention of Yahweh's shouting (נתן קולו) his command and the army's obedience to that word is a final, climactic ejaculation about the strength of the foe, already portrayed variously in vv 2–10. And lest any hearer / reader should fail to make the connection, the following couplet (11b) leaves no doubt that the invasion represents the Day of Yahweh— great (גדול; cf. Zeph 1:14), fearful (נורא; cf. Mal 3:23), and unendurable (מי יכילנו; cf. Mal 3:2) to his foes, i.e., the inhabitants of Judah and Jerusalem.

12 Here begins the call for repentance. Return (שבו) is the first imperative since v 1. (On the theological importance of שוב "return," cf. Hos 14:1, 2 et passim and Holladay, The Root ŠUBH. . . .) The call to "return . . . with all your heart" reflects Deuteronomy, especially Deut 4:29, 30; 30:2. It is followed by the specific call for fasting, weeping, and mourning, which are not really three things, but one—the visible part of the process of repentance (cf. Jonah 3:5–9; Esth 4:3; Ezra 10:1–6; Neh 8:9, 10).

13 "Tear your heart (קרעו לבבכם)—not your clothes" is reminiscent of Hos 14:2 ("Take words with you" [as your offering, instead of food]) or Amos 5:4 ("Seek me . . . do not seek Bethel . . .") or Amos 5:21–24 ("I hate . . . your feasts . . . But let justice roll . . ."). In each of these instances, the fuller context shows no prophetic disdain for the sacrificial system per se. They call instead for more than mere ritual or mere outward piety. Formal mourning was easy. True conversion to a godly life was not. Here, "heart" means essentially "mind" or "will," which needs to be reshaped to faithful obedience.

The triplet (13b) repeats the old Mosaic revealed formulation about Yahweh's character (Exod 34:6–7, repeated essentially with various wordings; see the listing at Jonah 4:2, Comment). In effect Joel is reminding his hearers / readers that they aren't dealing with just any God, but with Yahweh, whose very name has always been associated with his compassion and willingness, in response to human contrition (e.g., Jonah 4:2), to forestall the harm he would otherwise have brought.

14 The rhetorical "Who knows . . . show compassion" is a terse formulation (מי יודע ישוב ונחם) perhaps widely used (e.g., Jonah 3:9) to indicate the freedom and sovereignty of God (cf. 2 Sam 12:22). Human repentance does not control God. People cannot force God to show them his forgiveness. They can only appeal to him for mercy in not meting out against them what they very well deserve. They may hope for his compassion, but they cannot command it (Zeph 2:3; Lam 3:29).

"After this" (אחריו, lit., "after it") at the end of the second line of the triplet probably refers to "after the invasion," though it could also indicate "behind Yahweh," i.e., as a result of his intervention.

The final line of the triplet, somewhat laconic in phrasing, appears to say that offerings are rightfully Yahweh's (on the grammar, compare Ps 3:9 [8]; Jonah 3:10) and by implication makes an interesting prediction. The time is coming when, it may be hoped in faith, meal offerings (מנחה) and drink offerings (נסך), in contrast to the present dearth (1:9, 13), will again be available to give to Yahweh. As a hint of restoration blessing, this would represent type 5, agricultural bounty. At any rate, repentance involves the faithful keeping of the covenant in order to enjoy its blessings (cf. Hos 3:5).

15 This second call for the horn to be sounded in Zion and for fasting and work cessation is a combination of imperatives from 2:1 and 1:14 *verbatim*. Ancient hearers / readers would not discern in this recombination an uninventive borrowing, but would rather be powerfully reminded of the linkage of two themes that run throughout the first half of the book (1:1–2:17): invasion and the need for repentance, the first serving to heighten the urgency of the second.

16 The three imperatives of v 15 are followed here by four more, as well as a jussive, יצא "Let . . . come out." The metrical units flow rapidly in quite terse (*breve*) staccato metrical fashion so that vv 15 and 16 in the Hebrew give to the ear the impression of a long series of quickly shouted commands, as if to say, "Stop everything! Waste no time! Do this!"

When even infants (יונקי שדים) and elders (זקנים) are to join the fast / mourning, and when newlyweds cannot even consummate their marriage, the situation must be critical indeed. The bridegroom and bride are not in different rooms, but together. חדר "bedroom" and חפה "chamber" are both used for the inner room of a house where the married couple go (Judg 15:1; 2 Sam 13:10; Ps 19:6 [5]) and here are used together to imply one room, according to the synonymous parallelism.

17 The priests, whose special province is intermediation between God and people, are commanded to take their stand at the traditional spot for priestly intercession in the temple complex (cf. 1 Kgs 8:22; Ezek 8:16), and Joel even gives them the essential wording of their lament. They are to appeal to Yahweh's sense of humiliation in two ways: that his personal property (נחלה, cf. Deut 9:26, 29; Ps 74:2) not be given away to strangers, and that his power to help his people not be challenged (cf. similar appeals in Pss 42:3, 10; 44:11–14; 79:10; 115:2; Mic 7:10).

The fear expressed is that of permanent captivity (curse type 13). The hope of their lament is for return / repossession (restoration blessing type 7) which will eliminate their—and in the "argument" of the appeal, Yahweh's—shame. They cannot hope that Yahweh will forget all about the invasion by ignoring the enforcing of his covenant. Their punishment is a foregone conclusion; they can only hope that his mercy will restore them soon (Deut 32:36, 43; Lam 3:31–32, 40–50).

Explanation

The proper response to the unstoppable invasion is unstinting repentance. There is a great sense of urgency here as exemplified in the two calls for alarm (vv 1, 15) and the rapid-fire imperatives of vv 15–16. Yahweh's people, cooped up hopelessly in Jerusalem as the overwhelming army (Yahweh's own!) relentlessly approaches, must realize that their only hope to escape extinction is an all-out appeal by the total populace. Their sins may have been great, but so is Yahweh's mercy. Indeed, he is by nature a forgiving God who can change his intent (נחם, v 14).

But the repentance must be absolutely genuine. It should involve the proper formal actions (here fasting, open sorrow, concerted prayer) but must also involve a true change of the will / mind (v 13) and a turning (שוב, v 13) away from disobedience to firm loyalty to Yahweh. Even then, the nation's fate is not certain (v 14). But restoration becomes a true possibility if the people evidence true conversion.

And, of course, part of Yahweh's nature is compassion on the sinful. He does not have to forgive, but he does. From the point of view of the New Covenant, he did not have to give his only son for the sins of the world, but he did. And on the basis of the one who became sin for us (2 Cor 5:21), the father's compassion is always assured to the truly penitent (1 John 1:9).

Restoration and the Outpouring of the Spirit (2:18–3:5 [2:18–32])

Bibliography

Ahlström, G. *"Hammōreh liṣdāqāh* in Joël 2:23."* Congress Volume. VTSup 17. Leiden: E. J. Brill, 1969. 25–36. **Besnard, A.** *Le mystère du nom: Quiconque invoquera le nom du seigneur sera sauvé.* LD 35. Paris: Éditions du Cerf, 1962. **Budde, K.** "Der Umschwung in Joel 2." *OLZ* 22 (1919) 104–10. ———. " 'Der von Norden' in Joel 2:20." *OLZ* 22 (1919) 1–5. **Childs, B.** "The Enemy from the North and the Chaos Tradition." *JBL* 78 (1959) 187–98. **Dahood, M.** "Four Cardinal Points in Psalm 75:7 and Joel 2:20." *Bib* 52 (1975) 397. ———. "Hebrew *tamrûrîm* and *tîmārôt.*" *Or* 46 (1977) 385. **Gelin, A.** "L'annonce de la Pentecôte (Joël 3:1–5)." *BVC* 27 (1959) 15–19. **Kaiser, W.** "The Promise of God and the Outpouring of the Holy Spirit: Joel 2:28–32 and Acts 2:16–21." *The Living and Active Word of God: Essays in Honor of Samuel J. Shultz.* Ed. M. Inch and R. Youngblood. Winona Lake, IN: Eisenbrauns, 1983. 109–22. **Kerrigan, A.** "The 'sensus plenior' of Joel 3:1–5 in Acts 2:14–36." *Sacra Pagina: Miscellanea Biblica, Congressus Internationalis Catholici de Re Biblica,* vol. 2. Ed. J. Coppens et al. BETL 12–13. Paris: Librairie Lecoffre, J. Gabalda, 1959. 295–313. **Kunstmann, W.** "O Derramamento do Espíritu Santo e Sinais do Dia do Senhor Segundo o Profeta Joel 2:28–32." *Igreja Luterana* 26 (1965) 128–34. **Meiden, L. van der.** "De vertaling van het woord מורה in Joel 2:23." *GTT* 51 (1951) 136–39. **O'Toole, R.** "Acts 2:30 and the Davidic Covenant of Pentecost." *JBL* 102 (1982) 245–58. **Roth, C.** "The Teacher of Righteousness and the Prophecy of Joel." *VT* 13 (1963) 91–95. **Sellers, O.** "A Possible Old Testament Reference to the Teacher of Righteousness (Joel 2:23)." *IEJ* (1955) 93–101. **Sheppard, G.** "Canonization: Hearing the Voice of the Same God through Historically Dissimilar Traditions." *Int* 36 (1982) 21–33.

Translation

Yahweh's blessing of land and people

2:18 *But*[a] *Yahweh has become*[b] *jealous for his land*
And has taken[b] *pity on his people.*

19 *Yahweh spoke up and said to his people: I am going to send you grain, fruit of the vine, and olive oil, so that you will have plenty of them.*[a] *I will no longer give you over to shame*[b] *among the nations.* 20 *I will drive the northerners*[a] *far away from you, and will force them into a barren, desolate*[b] *land, their*[c] *vanguard*[d] *into*[e] *the eastern sea and their rear guard into the western sea.*

Their smell will rise,
Their stench will go up.[f]

Miraculous bounty from Yahweh

[g] *Surely he has done something great!*[g]
21 *Do not be afraid, land,*[a]
Rejoice and be glad,
Because Yahweh has done something great!

22 *Do not be afraid, wild animals,*[a]
Because the wilderness pasturelands have become green,
Because the trees have borne their fruit,
The fig tree and the grapevine have given their multitude.[b]

23 *Children of Zion, rejoice and be glad in Yahweh your God,*
Because he has given you food[a] *according to (his) righteousness,*[b]
And has rained on you autumn rain[c] *and spring rain, as before.*[d]

24 *The threshing floors will be full of grain.*
The vats will overflow with the fruit of the vine and olive oil.

25 *I will restore to you twofold*[a]
What the adult locust,[b] *the infant locust,*[c] *the young locust,*[d] *and the nearly full-grown locust*[e] *ate,*
My great army[f] *which I sent among you.*

26 *You will eat until you are full,*
And you will praise the name of Yahweh your God,

Who has done miraculous things[a] *for you;*
[b] *And never again will my people be put to shame.*[b]

27 *You will know that I am in the midst of Israel,*
That I, Yahweh, am your God and there is no other,
And never again[a] *will my people be put to shame.*

The outpouring of Yahweh's spirit

3:1 *Afterward I will pour out my spirit on all flesh.*

Your sons and daughters will prophesy,
Your old men will have[a] *dreams,*
Your young men will see visions.[b]

² *Also on the* ᵃ *male slaves and female slaves*
I will pour out my Spirit at that time. ᵇ

³ *I will put signs* ᵃ *in the sky and on the earth,* ᵃ
Blood, fire, and plumes ᵇ *of smoke.*

⁴ *The sun will be turned into darkness*
And the moon into blood
Before ᵃ *the coming of the Day of Yahweh,*
Great ᵇ *and fearful.* ᵇ

⁵ *And everyone who calls on the name of Yahweh will be saved, because there*
will be escape in Mount Zion, that is, ᵃ *Jerusalem, just as Yahweh said,*
among the survivors, ᵇ *whom Yahweh will call.* ᶜ

Notes

18.a. "But" is simply the contrastive equivalent of "and" as a translation for Heb. ו. "Then," frequently used, is needlessly interpretive.

18.b. The past tense in Eng. reflects the Heb. proleptic conv impf, which some strands in the G tradition (ζηλώσει, φείσεται) erroneously take as volitive (juss).

19.a. Lit., "of it," collective.

19.b. Here Tg adds כפנא [the shame of] "hunger" interpretively and too narrowly.

20.a. Or "northerner," collective.

20.b. For MT שממה "desolate / desolation," G has ἀφανιῶ "I will hide / obliterate" [his face .], perhaps reading אשממה (!) and assuming it to be a coh.

20.c. Lit., "his."

20.d. Lit., "face."

20.e. Or simply "toward" (אל).

20.f. The verb (עלה) is the same root as that of "rise." Our translation renders the tense change by the purposeful variation in language.

20.g-g. As the versification demonstrates, "Surely . . . great" might apply to the "northerner," as G and Tg assume. Tg even adds ביש "[Surely he has done many] evil things," ruling out Yahweh as the subj. But it is more likely that the contrast of Yahweh with the northerners begins here, in light of v 21 bβ.

21.a. This is אדמה "earth, dirt, land," not "nation."

22.a. "Wild animals" is more idiomatic for בהמות שדה than the usual "beasts of the field."

22.b. Heb. חיל, the same term used, contrastively, again in 25b ("army").

23.a. MT המורה "the teacher" is supported by Tg Vg σ´ and was perhaps a proof text for the Teacher of Righteousness at Qumran. This reading is surely secondary, however, to G (τὰ βρώματα "the food"), supported by Syr and L. The original was probably either האכל or המאכל, with המורה representing a dittographic replacement.

23.b. Or "in a righteous way" or the like.

23.c. Here the many Hebrew MSS containing יורה "autumn rain" are preferable to those containing מורה "teacher."

23.d. MT בראשון might mean "in the first [month]," i.e., springtime (cf. Tg בירח ניסן "in the month of Nisan"), whereas G Syr Vg and one Heb. MS read more convincingly כראשון "as before."

25.a. Reading with the sometimes proposed emendation to שנים את, or even את שנים, involving no consonantal alterations. See *Comment.*

25.b,c,d,e. See 1:4, nn. a, b, c, d. Tg (עממיה ולישניא שלטוניא ומלכותא) ignores the literal reading to interpret figuratively: "peoples, language groups, powers, and kingdoms."

25.f. See note 22.b.

26.a. Or "has acted miraculously . . . ," the inf functioning adverbially.

26.b-b. On the genuineness of this line, see below, *Form / Structure / Setting.*

27.a. The somewhat more elaborate לעולם . . . עוד אין (cf. v. 26b) still means "never again. . . ."

3:1.a. "Dream dreams" prevails in many English translations, though idiomatically unjustified.

1.b. Or "revelations." חזון is a message, not merely a sight.

2.a. Some (late) G texts followed by L insert μου "my" [male slaves]. Tg shows no definiteness (עבדי . . . אמהן), though this might be simply idiomatic translation.

2.b. Lit., "in those days."

3.a. The wording of Acts 2:19 reflects slightly expansive late G texts, reading οὐρανῷ ἄνω καὶ σημεῖα ἐπὶ τῆς γῆς κάτω . . . "heaven above, and signs on the earth below."

3.b. The exact meaning of תימרה is uncertain. Also possible are "billows," "columns," etc.

4.a. Or "in the presence of."

4.b. Grammatically, "great" and "fearful" may modify either "Day" or "Yahweh."

5.a. Or "and," if Zion and (greater) Jerusalem are thought separate entities.

5.b. Here G (εὐαγγελιζόμενοι) had בשרים or the like in its *Vorlage* instead of בשרידים. The awkwardness of the Heb. syntax affected Syr (lmšwzb "to those who survive").

5.c. Or "is calling."

Form / Structure / Setting

At 2:18 the prophecy of Joel shifts from woe to weal. The remainder of the book deals with predictions of benefit for God's people and the subjugation of their enemies—i.e., restoration blessings. In the sixty-odd lament psalms in the psalter (for a cautious listing see B. Anderson, *Out of the Depths*, 2d ed. [Philadelphia: Westminster Press, 1983] 235–36), a sudden shift from the plea for deliverance to the "oracle of assurance" is routinely observed. In Joel, the assurance material beginning with 2:18 similarly follows a plea for deliverance (2:17; cf. 1:19, etc.), and this has led Wolff, for example (*Joel*, 57–58), to identify the form of 2:18–3:5 as an "assurance oracle following a plea."

The context of the form is even broader, however, being rooted in the old Mosaic covenantal expectation of a turning of Israel's fortunes, upon their conversion, from woe to weal in a coming grand era (Lev 26:40–45; Deut 4:29–31; 30:1–10). Thus while the prophets may occasionally employ elements of style associated with lament psalm assurance oracles in announcing the coming restoration blessings (cf. Isa 41:10–16; 43:1–5; Jer 31:3–6; Mic 5:2–6), it is not those psalms *per se* that determine the weal formulations.

Considerable debate exists about the integration of 3:1–5 [2:28–32] with the rest of the promise oracles. Its evident close relation to 2:18–27 caused Jerome to include it with chap. 2 in the Vulgate, a chapter schema adopted thereafter in G and by modern versions as well. Yet chap. 3 [2:28–32] is clearly somewhat special by reason by its concentration on the age of the Spirit, a theme otherwise not represented in Joel. However, as a way of portraying one of the ten types of restoration blessings (no. 3, restoration of orthodoxy) it functions quite integrally and can hardly be better placed anywhere in or after chap. 4 [3].

Structurally, 2:18–3:5 [2:32] may be divided into three major units:

(1) 2:18–20, in which restoration of the land from desolation and drought is paralleled by deliverance of God's people from their invaders. Here prose narrative (the "prophetic perfect") predominates, surrounded by two poetic couplets.

(2) 2:20βγ-27, a delightful prediction of the restoration of agricultural bounty, all in poetic form. Repetitive parallelism begins and concludes

this section (". . . has done something great" in vv 20 and 21; "And never again . . . shame" in vv 26, 27).

(3) 3:1–5 [2:28–32], perhaps the most striking linkage of salvation with spirituality in the OT. This section begins and ends with non-narrative prose statements and is otherwise poetic.

In the poetic sections, synonymous parallelisms are evident in somewhat less than half of the couplets. The four triplets are not especially remarkable. The translation of v 25 only *seems* to suggest an overlong second line. Each section is set off by *inclusios;* and the chiastic quatrain at the outset of the second section (20βγ-21) reflects the *inclusio* pattern as well. No short (*breve*) meter is found in the passage.

Nothing in the pericope gives the slightest hint as to date. The idea that 3:1–5 reflects some sort of late post-exilic pro-prophet, anti-priest mentality by reason of its emphasis on widespread charismata is questionable at best. The gift of God's Spirit is a concern widely represented at various points in the OT (e.g., Exod 31:3; Num 11:26–29; Judg 14:6; 1 Sam 10:10; Isa 11:2; Ezek 37:14) and in no way can such a concern be proved a criticism of the priesthood, let alone a datable one. The supposed partial quotes of Obad 17 by Joel 3:5, or Isa 44:8; 45:14 by Joel 2:27, more likely reflect a common prophetic linguistic repertoire. For that matter, one could theoretically reverse the chronological order, taking Joel as the source of the other two.

Comment

18 Here begin the promises of future restoration from Yahweh. His land (אַרְצוֹ) will be freed from its drought and desolation. His people (עַמּוֹ) will be freed from their invaders. Drought, desolation, and invasion were the dominant curse metaphors of the book to this point, and the theme of rescue from them continues to be important hereafter. In the parallelism, קִנֵּא, piel, "has become jealous" indicates possessive intervention (cf. Deut 32:21; note the narrative tenses) while its complement, חָמַל "has taken pity," shows that this intervention is compassionate rather than judgmental. The narrative tenses (perfects and converted imperfects) begin here and continue prominently through v 24 in the manner of the prophetic perfect: the prophet has seen the future and is reporting on what he saw happen.

19 The land / people balance of v 18 is reflected in v 19's prose promise that Yahweh will send plenty of grain, wine, and oil (דָּגָן, תִּירוֹשׁ, יִצְהָר), three standard poetic and prose terms for agricultural staples (cf. Hos 2:8, etc.), and that he will rescue his people from the shame of being subjugated to their enemies. Thus the curses of starvation / famine (type 7) and occupation / oppression by enemies (type 5) are reversed by restoration blessings of agricultural bounty (type 5; cf. Lev 26:42; Deut 30:9) and power over enemies (type 9; cf. Deut 30:7).

20 Because of the desert to the east and the Mediterranean to the west, most invasions of Palestine came from the north. Certainly the captivity invasions of the Assyrians and Babylonians did. Thus "northerner" (צְפוֹנִי) indicates the "invaders" that have been such a threat to Judah and Jerusalem to this point in the book. In the grand language of this prediction, the invaders will be (a) removed far away, (b) split apart, and (c) drowned. In other words, three types of curses reserved for unfaithful Israel will be applied to her enemies in the eschaton (restoration blessing type 9). Removal represents the curse of exile (cf. Deut 30:4, ". . . banished to the most distant land . . ."). Being split apart represents one aspect of the curse of defeat in war (cf. Deut 28:25, "You will come at them from one direction but flee from them in seven"). Being drowned represents the death / destruction curses (e.g., Deut 28:20, ". . . destroyed and come to sudden ruin . . .") but may also hint at the curse of denial of burial (Deut 28:27), especially in light of the concluding reference to the "smell and stench" of the dead bodies.

20βγ-21 A chiastic quatrain, whose first and fourth lines are highly repetitive, launches the second section of the present pericope by an encouraging word spoken directly to the land (אדמה) from which the plants grow. The resulting emphasis upon the ability to rejoice because Yahweh has "done something great" (הגדיל לעשות) signals that the present troubles will not just gradually disappear, but that a dramatic reversal of fortunes is in store for the future repentant people, as the covenant guarantees (e.g., Deut 4:29; cf. Isa 40:1). Thus will be fulfilled the promise, "I will remember the land" of Lev 26:42.

Though the land itself was not overtly summoned to mourn in chap. 1, the verbs of mourning / drying up (הוביש, etc., in 1:10 et al.) that are applied to the land in effect brought the land in on the process, which is now reversed by the imperatives in the internally parallel second and third lines of the quatrain.

22 The wild animals, who were previously described as suffering so from the drought (1:20 now directly parallel to "land," v 21, and "children of Zion," v 23), are not to be afraid (cf. v 21) because bounteous agricultural productivity is again in store. The verse moves from wild animals (בהמות שדה) and their wilderness pasturelands (נאות מדבר) in the first couplet to cultivated fruit trees, including fig tree and grapevine, in the second. Thus all nature is to spring forth for the benefit of both animals *and* humans.

23 Just as "do not be afraid" from the inner couplet of v 21 was reused in v 22, now its parallel line, "rejoice and be glad" (גילו ושמחו), is reused in the direct address to the "children of Zion" (בני ציון) "citizens of Jerusalem"). They are to rejoice that the drought is over: the yearly cycle of rainy periods will resume, and thus Yahweh will give his people food (Lev 26:3). This happens "according to (his) righteousness" (לצדקה), a term synecdochically indicating here *generosity* (cf. Hos 10:12 and δικαιοσύνη as "charity" in Matt 6:1), one prominent aspect of true righteousness. MT's corrupt text מורה לצדקה was taken woodenly at Qumran to mean "a teacher of righteousness" without much regard for the present context.

24 Two examples of agricultural abundance, in the hyperbolic language typical of restoration blessings, are given (Lev 26:5; Amos 9:13; Mal 3:10). The three classic raw harvest staples—grain, grape juice, and olive oil—appear here once again (cf. v 19), except that בר "grain" replaces its synonym דגן in this grouping.

25 Multiple punishment is one of the curse types (no. 27; cf. Lev 26:18,

21, 24, 28). A "double" restoration is likewise one means of portraying the complete compensation that Yahweh will give to his people. Isa 40:2 contains a related notion: Jerusalem will be fully compensated, having paid doubly for her sins (cf. Jer 16:18; 17:18). Double reward figures prominently also in Isa 61:7 ("double portion") and Zech 9:12 ("I will restore to you twofold").

Here it is again evident (cf. 2:11) that the invasion of locusts (whether literal or figurative) was Yahweh's doing, and the invaders were his army (חיל, used in contrast to its contextually more positive meaning of "multitude" in v 22).

26 Having enough to eat will result in the praise of God, and God's miraculous liberation and restoration of his people (cf. Ezek 37) will result in the confidence that they may dwell in safety, fearing no full-scale punishment again (Lev 26:5, 6; Isa 45:17; Zeph 3:15). A literal locust plague would hardly have resulted in international "shame" (בוש). Rather, defeat and exile at the hands of their enemies constituted Judah's "shame" (Jer 12:13; Ezek 16:52, 54, 61; Isa 54:4; Hos 4:19; etc.).

The last line of the second couplet is repeated as the last line of v 27. It is also possible that these identical lines should be understood as opening and closing a quatrain, in which the couplet "You will know . . . is no other" is chiastically positioned, similarly to the pattern in 20βγ-21 that opened this section of the oracle.

27 Yahweh's deliverance of his people from their shame among the nations (exile) will cause them finally to realize (cf 3:17) two things they had been depriving themselves of by their disobedience: (1) that he would again be in their midst (בקרב, Exod 8:22; 17:7; Num 11:20–21; Deut 17:20) and (2) that he alone would be their God (Isa 45:5–6, 18, 22; 46:9). Both are constituents of the basic covenantal relationship that will be properly reestablished in the future. If they will be covenant people they can again enjoy his sovereign power among and over them (restoration blessing type 1, Lev 26:42, 45). This is the point of בקרב, here "in the midst of" (see Exod 8:22 and 33:5). They must also obey the first commandment to have no gods other than him (Exod 20:3), which amounts to a corollary of the third type of restoration blessing—restoration of true obedience (Deut 4:30; 30:6, 8).

3:1 Once this true restoration of covenant relationship has been achieved ("afterward," אחרי־כן) and the people have fully turned back to Yahweh, he can bless them with a renewal of his favor (restoration blessing type 1), manifested particularly by his own spirit being given to them in abundance.

There are two special emphases in this promise: the fullness of the Spirit ("pour out," שפך) and the democratization of the Spirit ("all flesh," כל־בשר). The first is addressed by the verbs in the verse ("prophesy," "have dreams," "see visions"), all of which describe revelatory functions associated with the fullness of God's Spirit (on the "fullness" of the Spirit as a heightening of obedience and revelatory powers, cf. Deut 34:9; Acts 7:55; 11:24; Eph 5:18–20). The second is addressed by the noun subjects (sons and daughters, old men, young men).

In the new age *all* of God's people will have *all* they need of God's Spirit. The old era was characterized by the Spirit's selective, limited influence on *some* individuals: certain prophets, kings, etc. But through Joel the people are hearing of a new way of living, in which everybody can have the Spirit. On this spiritual bounty compare Ezek 36:26–29; Hos 14:4–8; Micah 7:19; Zeph 3:9–13; Zech 8:16, 22.

2 Even slaves will partake, on a par with the free, in the blessing of the Spirit's outpouring, no societal restrictions being able to limit the power of God to give himself to his people. The wording "at that time," literally, "in those days" (בימים ההמה), is one of the standard ways of describing the indefinitely future timing of the restoration era (Jer 31:29, 33; 33:15, 16; Joel 4:1; Zech 8:23; etc.). Most common is the singular "at that time," literally, "in that day" (ביום ההוא; Isa 11:10, etc.).

3, 4 A chiastic structure (I: sky: earth // earth portents: sky portents: Yahweh) serves to create the impression that when Yahweh comes, everything will break loose at once. These "signs" (מופתים; cf. Exod 4:21; 7:3, 9; Deut 4:34; 34:11; Isa 8:18) are not just indicators but fully supernatural portents associated with the intervention of Yahweh to or on behalf of his people (e.g., blood: Exod 7:17–21; fire and smoke: Exod 19:18; darkness: Exod 10:21; Deut 4:11).

The synonymous parallelism of the initial couplet of v 4 (sun . . . darkness, moon . . . blood) does not focus on the sun and moon separately, as if there were to be daytime and nighttime signs in the sky, but merely pairs moon with sun, the sign being darkness during the daytime (cf. 1:2; Josh 10:12–14).

All of this dramatic and cataclysmic action heralds Yahweh's coming to deliver the righteous and dispense with the wicked, the intended activity of the sovereign's day of conquest.

5 The prose conclusion to the oracle provides a simple, direct answer to the invasion. Its message is that there is coming a time when salvation will be readily available to the people of Jerusalem, but only if they return faithfully to Yahweh. Its focus is eschatological, yet as a prediction of what will someday happen to Israel, viewed as a continuum, it would have constituted a great encouragement to the believers among Joel's audience.

To "call on the name of Yahweh" (קרא בשם יהוה) means not merely to pray to him, but to worship him consistently and presumably exclusively (Gen 4:26; 12:8; 13:4; 1 Kgs 18:24; Ps 116:17; Zeph 3:9); the expression can also indicate open acknowledgment of one's faith in the midst of a hostile environment (Ps 105:1; Isa 12:4; Zech 13:9).

The "survivors" (שרידים) are almost certainly those who will have managed to live through the destruction and exile of Yahweh's judgment (either the Assyrian or Babylonian exile; see *Introduction*) and who are alive when he calls his people out of exile to restoration (Lev 26:40–45; Deut 4:27–31; 30:2–10; 32:36–43). The timing of the restoration cannot be controlled by the remnant. Yahweh will act when he chooses to. Moreover, any restoration will be predicated on conversion. People must call on Yahweh if they expect to escape from their judgment fate.

In quoting this verse at Pentecost, Peter is recorded as emphasizing the initial clause (Acts 2:21) and the final clause (Acts 2:39) even though he spoke in Jerusalem, the dominant subject of the remainder of the verse. This emphasis, however, is faithful to the impact of the verse in its context.

Though spoken to encourage Jerusalemites at a time when the holy city was under attack, its real concern is future deliverance for a covenant people. "Everyone who calls" and the "survivors whom Yahweh will call" are one and the same—a broad constituency not limited to a single locale, by reason of the spirit and language of the oracle as a whole.

Explanation

After a lengthy description of an enemy invasion and call for repentance, Joel's inspired message shifts to a joyous promise of relief, compensation, and blessing. Of the ten types of restoration blessings that could have been used to depict the coming era of renewal as described in 2:18–3:5, six are attested here (renewal of divine favor and presence, renewal of the covenant, restoration of orthodoxy, agricultural bounty, power over enemies, freedom from death / destruction). Two (agricultural bounty, renewal of divine favor and presence) predominate. God's people may expect that the time will come when he already will have (in the spirit of the narrative tenses employed) given them more food production than they or the animals can eat, and that he will be with them—all of them—in a new and special way via the outpouring and filling of his Spirit.

Thus the passage looks happily to an era in which both the physical and spiritual needs of God's people will be fully met. Particularly rousing are the promises of 3:1–5 [2:28–32], which are quoted to one extent or another in nine different NT contexts (Matt 24:29; Mark 13:24–25; Luke 21:25; Acts 2:17–21, 39; 21:9; 22:16; Rom 10:13; Titus 3:6; Rev 6:12). For in the new age, salvation will not only be available to all who turn in faith to the true God, but there will be no distinction of spirituality on the basis of age, gender, or social status. God's spirit will be available to both young and old, to both male and female, and to both slave and free.

For Christians the significance of this expectation should be clear. Those who live in the age of the Spirit cannot expect God to restrict any ministry of the Spirit from anyone simply because he or she is old or young, male or female, or of high or low standing socially. Where churches attempt to do this, they risk missing the fullness of God's blessing.

Judgment against Israel's Enemies (4:1–21 [3:1–21])

Bibliography

Freund, Y. "Multitudes, Multitudes in the Valley of Decision (A Study in the Book of Joel)." *BMik* 21 (1975s) 271–77; 315. [Heb.] **Homerski, J.** "Sad nod Narodami w Eschatologicznej wizji Joela (Jl 4:1–21)." *Roczniki Teol.-Kanoniczne* 28 (1981) 35–47. **Luria, B.** "And a Fountain Shall Come Forth from the House of the Lord." *DD* 10 (1981) 45–48. ———. ". . . מעין ומבית ה' יצא (Joel 4:18)." *BMik* 15, 1 (1969–70)

3–13. [Heb.] **Milik, J.** "Notes d'epigraphie et de topographie palestiniennes." *RB* 66 (1959) 553–55. **Miller, P.** "The Divine Council and the Prophetic Call to War." *VT* 18 (1968) 100–107. **Myers, J.** "Some Considerations Bearing on the Date of Joel." *ZAW* 74 (1962) 177–95. **Oca, E. Dell.** "El valle de Josafat: ¿nombre simbólico o topográfico?" *RB* 28 (1966) 169–70. **Ogden, G.** "Joel 4 and Prophetic Responses to National Laments." *JSOT* 26 (1983) 97–106. **Tournay, R.** "Relectures bibliques concernant la vie future et l'eschatologie." *RB* 69 (1962) 481–505. **Treves, M.** "The Date of Joel." *VT* 7 (1957) 149–56. **Weiss, M.** "In the Footsteps of One Biblical Metaphor." *Tarbiz* 34 (1964–65) 107–28. [Heb.] ———. "On the Traces of a Biblical Metaphor II." *Tarbiz* 34 (1964–65) 211–23, 303–18. [Heb.]

Translation

Nations summoned to the valley of judgment

4:1 *Indeed, in those days, at that time* [a] *when I will restore the fortunes* [b] *of Judah and Jerusalem,*

2 *I will gather all the nations*
And bring them down to the valley of Jehoshaphat [a]
And enter into judgment with them there

On behalf [b] *of my people, my possession, Israel,*
Whom they scattered among the nations.

They divided up my land
3 *And cast lots for my people.*

They traded boys for prostitutes [a]
And sold girls for wine that they drank.

4 *Also, what were your intentions toward me,* [a] *Tyre, Sidon, and all the districts of Philistia? Were you paying me back for something or doing something against me? Quickly, rapidly I will return on your own heads what you were doing* 5 *because you took my silver and gold and brought my fine treasures into your temples,* 6 *and sold the Judeans and Jerusalemites to the Greeks in order to get them far away from their own territory.* 7 *Well, I am going to rouse* [a] *them from the place to which you have sold them and return on your own heads what you were doing.* 8 *I will sell your sons and daughters by the Judeans. They will sell them into captivity,* [a] *to a faraway nation. For Yahweh has spoken.*

9 *Announce this among the nations:*
Prepare yourselves religiously [a] *for war.*

Rouse the warriors, let them approach.
Let all the men of war advance for attack.

10 *Beat your plowshares into swords*
And your pruning knives into spears.
The weakling must say "I am a soldier." [a]

11 *Hurry!* [a] *Come, all nations around.*
Gather [b] *there!* [c] *He who is frightened must be a soldier.* [c]

12 *Let the nations be roused and advance for attack*
Into the valley of Jehoshaphat, [a]

For there I will sit down to judge
All the nations around.

13 Let loose the sickle, for the harvest is ripe.
Come and tread, for the winepress is full.
The vats overflow, for their wickedness is great.

14 Mêlée!ª Mêlée in the valley of the verdict!ᵇ
For the Day of Yahweh is near in the valley of the verdict.ᵇ

15 The sun and moon have darkened,
The stars have stopped their shining.

16 Yahweh roars from Zion,
He raises his voiceª from Jerusalem
So thatᵇ the sky and the earth shake.

But Yahweh is a refuge for his people,
A stronghold for the Israelites.

The restored Jerusalem

17 You will know that ªI, Yahweh your God,
Am dwellingª on Zion, my holy mountain.

Jerusalem will be a holy place
And foreigners will not travelᵇ through it again.

18 At that time,
The mountains will drip grape juice,
The hills will run with milk,
And all the ravines of Judah will run with water.
A fountain will come out from Yahweh's house
And will water the streambed of the acacias.

19 Egypt will become a desolation,
Edom will become a desolate wilderness,

Because of their violence to the Judeans,
In whose land they shed innocent blood.

20 Judah will be settled forever,
And Jerusalem from generation to generation.
21 ªWill I leave their bloodshed unpunished?ª I will not leave it unpunished!

Yahweh dwells in Zion!

Notes

1.a. Or "At that time, that point in time."
1.b. Or "reverse the captivity." השיב שבות is a somewhat ambiguous expression and the ancient versions tended to see in it a reference to ending the exile.
2.a. Tg (פילוג דינה) "decision of judgment"; cf. also v 12) and θ' (κρίσεως "judgment") seem not to have read Jehoshaphat, יהושפט, but משפט or שפטים, "judgment." Could a term such as משפט עמק "valleys of judgment" have produced עמק יהושפט "Valley of Jehoshaphat"?
2.b. Or "on account of" (על).
3.a. G (πορναῖς "to prostitutes") followed by L and Vg, misunderstands the force of ב מכר "trade for" and makes it "give to" as if for ownership or marriage.

4.a. Or "What did you have against me?" or "What are you to me?" The Heb. ‫מה‬ . . . ‫לי‬ is ambiguous.

7.a. Tg inexplicably translates ‫בגלי‬ . . . ‫מיתי‬, "to bring (back) in captivity."

8.a. Reading with G (εἰς αἰχμαλωσίαν "into captivity"). ‫לשבאים‬ is likely a corruption of ‫לשבי‬ "into captivity."

9.a. Or "sanctify (yourselves) with regard to war" or "sanctify a war."

10.a. G ἰσχύω "strong" nevertheless reflects ‫גבור‬ "soldier" (cf. Isa 5:22).

11.a. Assuming MT to be cognate to Arabic *ğšš*. G Syr Tg translate the equivalent of "assemble," perhaps reflecting ‫גושו‬ or the like in their *Vorlagen*.

11.b. Only Tg has a jussive (‫יתקרבון‬ "let [them] gather") among the versions; G Vg Syr have the imperative. Thus ‫הקבצו‬ "gather" may have been the original wording.

11.c-c. MT "Bring down, Yahweh, your soldiers," a sudden prayer for holy war help (?), interrupts the context. G ὁ πραΰς ἔστω μαχητής "Let the weakling become a soldier" reflects an original ‫הנחת יהי גבור‬ "he who is frightened must become a soldier," ‫הנחת‬ being the niph ptcp of ‫חתת‬. Once ‫יהי‬ "let become" became corrupted to ‫יהוה‬ "Yahweh," the suffix to ‫גבור‬ was added ("your soldiers") to make sense. Tg and Vg reflect in part the more corrupt later MT reading.

12.a. See n. 2.a.

14.a. Or "Noise!" or "Multitude!" or the like.

14.b. Here Tg reads exactly as with ‫עמק יהושפט‬ "Valley of Jehoshaphat" in vv 2, 12.

16.a. Or "thunders."

16.b. Here the *waw* appears to introduce a result clause.

17.a-a. Or "I am Yahweh your God, who dwells. . . ."

17.b. Here Syr (*yᶜmrwn*) reads "dwell" instead of "pass through," perhaps to contrast directly with ‫ישב‬ "dwelling" above.

21.a-a. Taking the first clause as a question, the interrogative particle being typically omitted after a conjunction. On the grammar, cf. Jer 25:29. Other translations or emendations are legion, but the overall point is clear: Yahweh's (and Israel's) enemies, signified by Egypt and Edom in v 19, will not get away with the evil they have done.

Form / Structure / Setting

Chap. 4 consists of a group of restoration promises, all of which in one way or another give reassurance that Israel's enemies will be dispensed with so that Israel (Judah and Jerusalem) may have peace. In a general sense, then, the form is that of the oracle against foreign nations found so routinely in the prophetic books. But this type of oracle functions here especially in fulfillment of the restoration blessing of power over enemies (type 9) and has a distinctly eschatological ring throughout.

That the chapter is a new pericope follows both from its elaborate introductory formula ("In those days, at that time") and its shift of topic from spiritual filling (3:1–5 [2:28–32]) to the unstoppable process of judging Israel's foes (from 4:2 [3:2] to 4:21 [3:21]).

Two subsections are evident (vv 1–16: judgment in the Valley of Jehoshaphat / verdict; and vv 17–21: re-inhabited, happy Jerusalem), but beyond these the overall integration of themes and wordings that characterizes the book as a whole prevents further delineation. Vv 4–8, because they are prose and mention by name certain foreign regions / peoples (Tyre, Sidon, Philistia, Greece, Sabeans [but see note 8.a]), are often identified as a separate oracle, though needlessly. The poetry-prose-poetry format of vv 1–16 has parallels both within the book (2:18 ff.) and outside of it (e.g., Amos 7). Moreover, 4:2–3 concerns itself with trading in captured, enslaved Israelites, which is exactly what vv 4–8 is responding to and embellishing.

Since 1:1–2:17 presented such a detailed picture of invasion, drought, and desolation, it is entirely understandable that the reversal of these three conditions should continue to occupy attention in the book's concluding pericope. Not only are Israel's enemies removed and judged, but the drought that had afflicted Judah and Jerusalem is now banished forever by means of a fountain (4:18 [3:18]), and the desolation is shifted to Egypt and Edom (et al.) away from the newly verdant Judah (4:18–20 [3:18–20]).

Divine speech dominates chap. 4[3], though typical unpredictable shifts to third-person references to Yahweh occur as well. Somewhat over a third of the poetic portion (vv 1–3, 9–21) contains synonymous parallelism. Six triplets are interspersed among seventeen couplets, an average ratio for prophetic material.

Vocabulary and thematic connections with earlier chapters abound. 4: 9–14 [3:9–14] corresponds closely to 2:1–9. In 4:15–16 [3:15–16], 2:10 recurs verbatim. In 4:16 [3:16], Yahweh's "voice" is heard again as it was in 2:11. Mention of the "children of Judah" in 4:19 echoes the "children of Zion" in 2:23. The formula בימים ההמה "at that time" (lit., "in those days") of 4:1 [3:1] is a calque of 3:2. Other notable vocabulary sharings include עסיס "grape juice" (4:18; 1:5); אפיק "torrent" (4:18 [3:18]; 1:20); מדבר שממה "desolate wilderness" (4:19 [3:19]; 2:3); דור ודור "from generation to generation" (4:20 [3:20]; 2:2); etc.

Nothing in chap. 4[3], provides independent evidence for the date of the book. The mention of commerce with Tyre / Sidon / Philistia (v 4) could be contemporaneous with Amos (1:6–10) or even earlier, but could be later as well. Egypt and Edom (v 19) were both chronic foes of Israel during virtually the entire period of the monarchy (1031–586 B.C.). The absence of reference to the north is uniform throughout the book and tends to date it after 722 B.C., though how much after is only speculative.

Comment

4:1 [3:1] Verse 1 is a prose introduction to the chapter, which begins with a standard restoration promise formula (בימים ההמה "in those days"; cf. 3:2) and then adds the synonymous clause בעת ההיא "at that time" (cf. also Jer 33:15; 50:4, 20) so as to emphasize from 2:18 on the linkage that exists with everything that has gone before. In all their Old Testament contexts, the phrases are associated with future blessings promised as consolation for God's people.

It is Judah and Jerusalem that are currently threatened by the invasion, drought, and devastation, and therefore they are mentioned together at the outset (as also in vv 6, 20) as candidates for a "restoring of fortunes" (אשיב שבות; cf. Deut 30:3 and frequently in the prophets).

2a,b This triplet and couplet appear poetic but may be merely parallelistic prose. Their concern is the righteous, legal punishment of Israel's enemies in vindication of God's holy nation "whom they scattered" (פזר, piel; cf. Jer 50:17; Esth 3:8), i.e., exiled / deported. Was the offense committed via one of the Mesopotamian deportations (722? 701? 598? 586 B.C.?) or the sort of smaller deportation following the capture of Judean troops in border wars (as reflected in Amos 1:9)? Or was it a combination, involving forays by Judah's or Israel's neighbors to capture slave-market spoil once the Assyrians or Babylonians had decimated the resistance? Here, at least, no answer is given.

Part of the reason may be the general nature of the punishment gathering: "all the nations" (כל־הגוים) must appear before Yahweh in the valley. In effect, this is a description of a kind of great, final judgment. For God's people to be safe and free forever, all enemies—past, present, and potential—must be reined in.

It is impossible to locate the Valley of Jehoshaphat (עמק יהושפט). An עמק "valley" is a broad floor among mountains, but no עמק by this name is cited elsewhere in the OT. Nothing about Jehoshaphat *per se* tells us where such a valley would be. Perhaps the only solution open to us is to regard "Jehoshaphat" as merely a symbol since the name literally means "Yahweh has judged." (See also n. 2.a).

However, the word following יהושפט "Jehoshaphat" is ונשפטתי "I will enter into judgment," the niphal of שפט "to judge." Could יהושפט represent a corruption of the niphal infinitive absolute השפט? A more metrically balanced line would result. In the final analysis, fortunately, the location of the judgment plays no role at all in the interpretation of the passage, which assures that a final, authoritative judgment on a world-wide scale will occur at Yahweh's demand, for the benefit of his people and for the detriment of his and their foes.

2bδ-3 These two couplets describe poetically an enemy's capture of Israelite land and deportation of people for sale as slaves, curse types 5 and 13 (cf. Deut 28:41). On "casting lots" (נדה גורל) for the captured land, cf. Obad 11; Nah 3:10; Num 33:54; etc. Kidnapping someone for sale as a slave was punishable by death in the Sinai covenant (Exod 21:16). Deut 21:14, moreover, prohibits the sale of prisoners of war. Not only had Israel's enemies done this sort of thing, they had done it purely for materialistic advantage—for money then spent in casual, wasteful self-indulgence (cf. Amos 1:8; 2:6). "Prostitution and wine drinking" were a stock pair of terms indicating debauchery (Hos 4:11). Later, buying Israelites back from slavery became a complicated business (Neh 5:8).

4 A rhetorical challenge to coastal Phoenicia (Tyre, Sidon) and coastal Palestine ("the districts of Philistia"; cf. Josh 13:2) launches the main prose section of the passage. People of these regions were seafaring traders whose markets for slaves around the Mediterranean fueled their interest in both buying captured Israelite prisoners of war and capturing some themselves for sale elsewhere, especially to the Greeks along the northern Mediterranean coast. Prior to Amos's time, both groups had sold Israelite captives to Edom (Amos 1:6, 9). By Ezekiel's day, at least, Tyre's slave trade with Greece was well established (Ezek 27:13). Thus a late date for this section (vv 4–8), i.e., in the Persian period, need not be posited on the basis of the sea trade of slaves described.

The point of asking "were you paying me back. . . . ?" (הגמול אתם משלמים עלי), for which there could be no positive answer, is to demonstrate the lack of justification for these crimes against Israel and / or Judah.

Thus vindication is promised soon ("quickly, rapidly"). Indeed, whether the "invasion" of which Joel speaks was Assyrian or Babylonian (598 / 588–586 B.C.) in origin, Phoenicia and Philistia did indeed suffer significantly in both. Thus their evil was returned to them already "on their heads" (cf. Ps 7:16; Esth 9:25; Jer 23:19). On Yahweh's vengeance on behalf of his people, cf. Isa 34:8; against the Philistines, cf. Ezek 25:15–17; against Tyre, Ezek 26.

5–6 The land's silver and gold are Yahweh's possession (cf. Hag 2:8) as surely as are Judah's citizens. The reference to appropriating Yahweh's treasures for "your temples" (or possibly "palaces"), היכליכם, indicates concerted national effort, not isolated individual theft. It may refer to cooperative involvement in looting the Jerusalem temple (2 Kgs 24:13–14) in the first great Babylonian exile (598 B.C.) with deals having been struck with the Babylonians for purchase of some furnishings, but more likely it refers to the plunder from the border wars of various occasions. Selling captured people as slaves to the Greeks not only violated God's law (see 4:3 [3:3]) but also removed those who were sold from beyond the practical help of Judah so that they could not be bought back.

7–8 Those wronged, both Yahweh and his people, turn the tables on their unprincipled foes. Yahweh will bring his exiled people back (Deut 30: 3–5) into action ("rouse," רוע, hiphil) and through the agency of their fellow Judeans, sell the notorious people-sellers themselves into captivity.

This curse of exile upon the Phoenicians and Philistines is exactly the sort of ironic reversal specified in Deut 30:7 as a restoration blessing for Israel: "Yahweh . . . will put all these curses on your enemies. . . ." No historical record exists of Judeans trading in Phoenician or Philistine slaves during or after the exile. Some Judeans may well have purchased slaves from among the Sidonians who were sold into slavery by Artaxerxes III in 345 B.C., or the citizens of Tyre and Gaza who were sold into slavery by Alexander the Great in 332 B.C., but even that is only speculation. Accordingly, this curse on Israel's enemies may be as much stereotyped ("a taste of your own medicine") as literal.

"For Yahweh has spoken" (כי יהוה דבר) is a common prophetic reminder of the divine origin of an oracle's words (Isa 1:2; etc.).

9 At the outset of this second poetic section it becomes clear that the "judgment" in the valley of Jehoshaphat first alluded to in v 2 (also in v 12) is no benign civil court case, but a war of destruction on "the nations" (בגוים).

Messengers must "rouse" (רוע, hiphil; see v 7) everyone—"all the men of war"—to line up ready for battle (עלה carries here the sense of "advance for attack"). This will be a divine international holy war, and all the nations must "prepare religiously" (קדש, piel; cf. Jer 6:4) for it. Holy war in the Old Testament (Deut 20) was a total war of annihilation against God's enemies. The implication is clear: the nations must fight, but they cannot win. Their defeat and destruction are assured because their adversary is Yahweh. For similar summonses of the nations to battle, see Isa 8:9–10; Jer 46:3–4, 9; Ezek 38:7–8; cf. Zeph 2:1.

10 After a standard challenge to prepare for war by converting iron farming implements into weapons (cf. Isa 2:4; Micah 4:3) comes a requirement that goes beyond typical holy war regulations which provided that only volunteers need fight (Deut 20:5–9). In the coming great war of judgment, even the weakling (החלש) will have to declare himself a soldier (גבור). This synecdochic formulation is a way of saying that all the enemy population will be judged.

11 V 11 summarizes three themes already stated (all nations must come, everyone has to fight, they must gather *"there,"* שמה, i.e., the Valley of Jehoshaphat) and introduces one new kind of emphasis: the initial imperative Hurry! (עושו). Not only must the judgment battle come to pass, its coming cannot be delayed. Swiftness of justice for those long oppressed, and against the oppressors, is a natural, important interest in both judgment and restoration oracles (cf. Deut 32:35; Zeph 1:14; Isa 49:17; 60:22; Rev 22:20).

12 For the third time in the passage the theme word עור (hiphil, "rouse") appears (also vv 7, 9). Otherwise v 12 is largely a variation on what v 2 states. "I will sit down to judge" (אשב לשפט) in no way implies relaxation, i.e., that Yahweh has decided against war. The setting suggests the authority of the throne. Yahweh will be entirely in charge, disposing of the enemy nations by defeating them in war or by any means he chooses.

13 Three metaphors comparing the enemy to crop materials portray complete readiness for a full, decisive dealing with God's enemies. The grain, grape, and olive harvest, Israel's three main crops (cf. 1:10; 2:24), here symbolize that all have gathered (קבץ, v 11; cf. Gen 41:35, 38) and are ready to be "cut down" or "trampled," as it were, in judgment. Harvest-judgment imagery is well represented elsewhere in the Old Testament (Isa 17:4–6; 63:3; Hos 6:11; Mic 4:13) and in the New Testament as well (Mark 4:29; Matt 13:39–40; Rev 14:20).

14 The scene is pitched battle. המונים, here translated "mêlée," connotes the roar of a mass of people, or the like, as in the sound of any army fighting (Isa 13:4; 29:5–8). Both המונים and עמק החרוץ "valley of the verdict" are repeated in the verse, the effect being emotive: War! There! "The Day of Yahweh" (יום יהוה), described as "near" (קרוב) in 1:15, "coming" and "close" in 2:1, "great" in 2:11, "fearful" in 3:4 [2:31], is now again "near" (קרוב), the descriptive language having come full circle.

15 The Day of Yahweh has clearly begun, because the darkness associated with it (2:2; 3:4 [2:31]; cf. Amos 5:18, etc.) has descended on all the sky's sources of light. In Hebrew poetic practice, moon and stars serve as parallels to sun. The ancient hearer / speaker would not tend to think because of this language that the night would be unusually dark, too, but would see the whole verse as stressing the total darkness of the fateful day. On such darkness as curse fulfillment, see Deut 28:29.

16 In the Old Testament, at least, and perhaps in the New Testament also, all detailed statements regarding God's voice describe it as thunderous to the hearer (on 1 Kgs 19:12, see J. Lust, *VT* 25 [1975] 111–15). It is enough to mention the roar of the all-powerful supreme commander to affirm that he has won the battle. Jer 25:30 similarly portrays Yahweh as shouting his judgment against humankind, and Amos 1:2a shares verbatim the wording of the first line of this verse's triplet. Ps 29 describes Yahweh's voice like a thunderstorm sweeping inland from the Mediterranean coast. Symbolically he dwells in Jerusalem (v 27; cf 1 Kgs 8:27–30), so in this shift of metaphor he roars from Jerusalem rather than from the valley. He is also the universal sovereign (Pss 2; 24; 29; etc.), so his roar shakes everything in earth and sky.

He will not, however, roar against Israel anymore. In the restoration era he will be both מחסה "refuge" and מעוז "stronghold" to his people (on this parallelism cf. Isa 25:4 and Ps 146:2; Ps 146 shares several themes with Joel 4 [3]). The restoration blessing comports with type 10, freedom from destruction, as in Lev 26:44; Deut 30:6.

17 Zion, i.e., Jerusalem, figures prominently is so many restoration oracles because the restoration blessings presume its continued existence in several areas: (1) blessing type 1, renewal of Yahweh's presence, involves Jerusalem implicitly as his dwelling place (see v 16 above); (2) blessing types 2 and 3, renewal of the covenant and restoration of orthodoxy, both assume the Sinai covenant's designation of Jerusalem as worship center (Deut 12); and (3) blessing types 7 and 8, repossession of the land and reunification, both imply Jerusalem's historic centrality in governmental administration.

V 17 adds as well the promise of freedom from destruction (blessing type 10) in the promise that "foreigners will not travel through it again," i.e., that foreign invaders will never again invest the city.

18 Agricultural bounty (restoration blessing type 5) rarely fails to make an appearance in full restoration oracles. Almost everyone was a farmer of some sort in the agrarian society of moisture-marginal ancient Israel / Judah, and promises of abundant crops and water had a powerful impact as a source of hope. Most of Joel's language here parallels what is found elsewhere in the Old Testament and represents a full reversal of the agricultural disaster of chaps. 1 and 2. Indeed, people of the ancient Near East in general thought in such terms poetically: "The skies rain oil, the wadis run honey" (*CTA* 6.3.6–7). On mountains dripping juice, cf. Amos 9:13; for the land running with milk, Exod 3:8; on ravines running with water, Isa 30:25; on a fountain from Yahweh's house, Ezek 47:1–12 (and Rev 22:1–2).

The "streambed of acacias" (נחל השטים) is unique and perhaps represents a known, especially dry wadi near Jerusalem. (Acacias can grow in remarkably dry, barren places.)

19 Egypt and Edom will be desolated (curse type 9) as historic enemies (e.g., 1 Kgs 14:25–26; Obad 9–14) that must now endure what they once wished for Israel (restoration blessing type 9; cf. 2:3). These two sections stand as paradigms for "the nations" (vv 2, 9, 11, 12) just as Phoenicia and Philistia do in v 4. Egypt and Edom are attacked routinely in prophetic oracles against foreign nations (including Balaam's—Num 24:8, 18), but they are employed as a parallel poetic pair only here.

20 The result will be permanent freedom and security, i.e., a reversal of all that the invasion described in chaps. 1 and 2 was bringing to Joel's audience. Dwelling with Yahweh (vv 17, 18, 21) means "dwelling" (ישב) in peace.

21 "Their bloodshed" (דמם) is the history of injury, oppression, exile, etc., done to the Israelites by their foes among "the nations." As Deut 30:7 promises, what Israel's enemy has done it will not get away with, but will have done to it. Joel's audience could take some comfort in knowing that Israel would, on the Day, be vindicated. Vengeance on Yahweh's enemies (Deut 32:41–42) is not a matter of pettily getting even, but of covenantal justice, as in Amos 1–2.

The closing cry, "Yahweh dwells in Zion," is here a kind of promise to the presently afflicted (cf. Ps 9:11–12). Jerusalem, under attack by an unstoppable enemy, has been, is, and will be not just any city, but Yahweh's dwelling place. From that fact all righteous hearers / readers of Joel's prophecy can take heart.

Explanation

From the perspective of the covenant, God's prophets proclaimed a foreseeable but indefinitely scheduled future. Joel 4 addresses an important interest of the people of Jerusalem, threatened by an invasion and perhaps a siege. What was the ultimate fate that they, their city, and their country would meet? Would the enemy prevail, destroy them, annex their territory, and exile them forever? Would their various enemies, past and present, end up having succeeded at international lawlessness, while the remainder of Israel— Judah and Jerusalem—disappeared as an entity in the community of nations? Would Yahweh ever again be worshiped on Mount Zion? Were the invasion, drought, and desolation so graphically described in chaps. 1 and 2 the beginning of the end of a city, state, and people? Where was Yahweh? Would his Day of rescue ever come?

The chapter provides a reassuring answer to these questions. A great final judgment will take place, one that will vindicate those faithful to Yahweh and punish those opposed to his purposes and his people. He will establish himself forever in his people's capital with all they need to live securely and joyously.

Joel 4 is also Christian eschatology. The Day it describes is one we await as well (Acts 17:31; 1 Thess 5:2). The final eternal era will be unmarred by opposition to God's purposes or people. He will be everywhere supreme and will reign from his holy city (Rev 21:1–3). Its river will give life (Rev 22:1–2), all as Joel foretold.

The guarantee of eventual vindication is a great sustenance to God's people to remain faithful and to continue to trust. This is the contextual, practical function of Joel 4.

Amos

Amos

Bibliography

COMMENTARIES

Amsler, S. "Amos." In E. Jacob, C. Keller, and S. Amsler, *Osée, Joël, Abadias, Jonas.* Commentaire de l'Ancien Testament 11a. Neuchâtel: Delachaux & Niestlé, 1965. 157–291. **Baur, G.** *Der Prophet Amos erklärt.* Giessen, 1847. **Bič, M.** *Das Buch Amos.* Berlin: Evangelische-Verlagsanstalt, 1969. **Blechmann, M.** *Das Buch Amos in Talmud und Midrasch.* Leipzig, 1937. **Burrons, W.** *Amos.* 1898. **Canney, M.** "Amos." *A Commentary on the Bible*, ed. A. S. Peake. New York, 1920. 547–54. **Cohen, G.** *Amos.* Everyman's Bible Commentary. Chicago: Moody Press, 1971. **Cripps, R.** *A Critical and Exegetical Commentary on the Book of Amos.* London: SPCK, 1929. **Deissler, A.** *Zwölf Propheten: Hosea, Joël, Amos.* Die Neue Echter Bibel. Würzburg: Echter Verlag, 1981. **Delcor, M.** "Amos." La Sainte Bible. Paris, 1961. **Driver, S. R.** *The Books of Joel and Amos.* The Cambridge Bible for Schools and Colleges. Cambridge: Cambridge University Press, 1897; 2d ed., 1915. **Edghill, E. A.**, and **G. A. Cooke.** *The Book of Amos.* Westminster Commentaries. London: Methuen, 1914; 2d ed., 1926. **Elhorst, H. J.** *De profetie van Amos.* Leiden, 1900. **Fosbroke, H. E. W.** "The Book of Amos: Introduction and Exegesis." *IB* 6:761–853. **Frey, H.** *Das Buch des Ringens Gottes um seine Kirche: Der Prophet Amos.* Die Botschaft des Alten Testaments 23 / 1. Stuttgart: Calwer, 1958; 2d ed., 1965. **Gelderen, C. van.** *Het boek Amos.* Commentaar op het Oude Testament. Kampen, 1933. **Gressmann, H.** *Die älteste Geschichtsschreibung und Prophetie Israels.* SAT 3 / 1. Göttingen, 1910; 2d ed., 1921. **Guthe, H.** "Der Prophet Amos." *HSAT* 2:30–47. **Hammershaimb, E.** *The Book of Amos: A Commentary.* Tr. J. Sturdy. Oxford: Basil Blackwell, 1970. **Harper, W. R.** *A Critical and Exegetical Commentary on Amos and Hosea.* ICC. Edinburgh: T. & T. Clark, 1905. **Hauret, C.** *Amos et Osée.* Verbum Salutis. Ancien Testament 5. Paris: Beauchesne, 1970. **Hitzig, F.**, and **H. Steiner.** *Amos.* Kurzgefasstes exegetisches Handbuch zum Alten Testament. Leipzig, 1881. **Honeycutt, R. L.** *Amos and His Message: An Expository Commentary.* Nashville: Broadman Press, 1963. **Hoonacker, A. van.** *Amos.* Études bibliques. Paris, 1908. **How, J. C. H.** *Joel and Amos.* Smaller Cambridge Bible for Schools. Cambridge: Cambridge UP, 1910. **Howard, J.** *Among the Prophets.* London: Pickering and Inglis, 1967. **Hyatt, J. P.** "Amos." *PCB.* London: Thomas Nelson and Sons, 1963. 617–25. **Keil, C. F.** "Amos." In C. F. Keil and F. Delitzsch, *Biblical Commentary.* Edinburgh, 1868. **King, P.** "Amos." *JBC* 1:245–52. **Kraft, C.** "The Book of Amos." In C. Laymon, ed., *The Interpreter's One-Volume Commentary on the Bible.* Nashville: Abingdon, 1971. 465–76. **Kutal, B.** *Libri Prophetarum Amos et Abdiae.* Commentarii in Prophetas Minores 3. Olmütz, 1933. **Lüthi, W.** *In the Time of the Earthquake: An Exposition of the Book of the Prophet Amos.* Tr. J. Haire and I. Henderson. London: Hodder and Stoughton, 1940. **Marsh, J.** *Amos and Micah: Introduction and Commentary.* Torch Bible Commentaries. London: SCM, 1959. **McKeating, H.** *The Books of Amos, Hosea and Micah.* The Cambridge Bible Commentary on the New English Bible. Cambridge: Cambridge UP, 1971. **Martin-Achard, R.**, and **S. P. Re'emi.** *Amos & Lamentations: God's People in Crisis.* International Theological Commentary. Grand Rapids: Eerdmans, 1984. **Mays, J. L.** *Amos: A Commentary.* OTL. Philadelphia: Westminster, 1969. **Motyer, J. A.** "Amos." *The New Bible Commentary Revised*, ed. D. Guthrie et al. London: Intervarsity, 1970. 726–41. ———. *The Day of the Lion.* Downers Grove, IL: Intervarsity, 1974. **Osty, E.** *Amos, Osée.* La Sainte Bible. Paris: Éditions du Cerf, 1952. **Proksch, O.** *Die kleinen prophetischen Schriften vor dem Exil.*

Erläuterungen zum Alten Testament 3. Stuttgart: Calwer, 1910. **Robinson, T. H.** "Amos." HAT. Tübingen, 1964. **Routtenberg, H.** *Amos of Tekoa: A Study in Interpretation.* New York: Vantage, 1971. **Rudolph, W.** *Joel-Amos-Obadja-Jona.* KAT 13 / 2. Gütersloh: Gütersloher Verlagshaus / Gerhad Mohn, 1971. **Ryan, D.** "Amos." R. Fuller et al., eds., *A New Catholic Commentary on Holy Scripture.* London: Thomas Nelson and Sons, 1969. 693–701. **Sellin, E.** *Amos.* KAT. Leipzig / Gütersloh, 1923. **Smith, G. A.** *Amos.* The Expositor's Bible. London and New York, 1896; 2d ed., 1928. **Smith, R.** "Amos." Broadman Bible Commentary. Nashville: Broadman, 1972. 7:81–141. **Snaith, N.** *Amos, Hosea and Micah.* Epworth Preachers Commentaries. London: Epworth, 1945–46. ———. *The Book of Amos.* 2 vols. London: Epworth, 1945–46. **Steinle, W.** *Amos, Prophet in der Stunde der Krise.* Stuttgart: J. F. Steinkopf, 1979. **Sutcliffe, T. H.** *The Book of Amos.* Biblical Handbooks. London, 1939. **Tatford, F.** *Prophet of Social Injustice: An Exposition of Amos.* Eastbourne: Prophetic Witness, 1974. **Vawter, B.** *Amos, Hosea, Micah: With an Introduction to Classical Prophecy.* The Old Testament Message. Wilmington: Michael Glazier, 1981. **Ward, J. M.** *Amos, Hosea.* Knox Preaching Guides 7. Atlanta: John Knox, 1981. **Werner, H.** *Amos.* Exempla Biblica 4. Göttingen: Vandenhoeck & Ruprecht, 1969. **Williams, A. L.** *Joel and Amos.* The Minor Prophets Unfolded. London, 1918. **Wolff, H. W.** *Joel and Amos.* Hermeneia. Philadelphia: Fortress, 1977.

BOOKS AND DISSERTATIONS

Arieti, J. A. *A Study of the Septuagint of the Book of Amos.* Diss. Stanford, 1972. **Balla, E.** *Die Droh- und Scheltworte des Amos.* Leipzig, 1926. **Barstad, H.** *The Religious Polemics of Amos.* SVTP. Leiden: E. J. Brill, 1984. **Bartczyk, G.** *Die Visionsberichte des Amos: Literarische Analyse und Thologische Interpretation.* Diss. Münster, 1977. **Barton, J.** *Amos' Oracles Against the Nations.* Cambridge: Cambridge UP, 1980. **Baumann, E.** *Der Aufbau der Amosreden.* BZAW 7. Giessen, 1907. **Baumgartner, W.** *Kennen Amos und Hosea eine Heilseschatologie?* Diss. Zürich, 1913. **Beek, M. A.** *Amos: Een inleiding tot het verstaan der profeten van het O.T.* Lochem, 1947. **Berg, W.** *Die sogenannte Hymnen fragmente im Amosbuch.* Europäische Hochschulschriften 23 / 45. Bern: Herbert Lang; Frankfurt: Peter Lang, 1974. **Bjørndalen, A. J.** *Untersuchungen zur allegorischen Rede der Propheten Amos und Jesaja.* Berlin: DeGruyter, 1985. **Brillet, G.** *Amos et Osée.* Paris: Éditions du Cerf, 1944. **Christensen, D.** *Transformations of the War Oracle in the Old Testament.* Missoula, MT: Scholars Press, 1975. **Cleary, F. X.** *The Interpretation of Suffering according to Amos and Hosea: The Origins of Redemptive Suffering.* Diss. Pontifical Gregorian University, 1978. **Cooper, J. S.** *The Curse of Agade.* Baltimore: Johns Hopkins Press, 1983. 239–40. **Coote, R.** *Amos among the Prophets.* Philadelphia: Fortress Press, 1981. **Copass, B. A.** *Amos.* Nashville, 1939. **Cramer, K.** *Amos: Versuch einer theologischen Interpretation.* BWANT 51. Stuttgart, 1930. **Crenshaw, J.** *Hymnic Affirmation of Divine Justice: The Doxologies of Amos and Related Texts in the Old Testament.* SBLDS 24. Missoula, MT: Scholars Press, 1975. **Csekey, S.** *Amos: Próféta könyve forditotta és magyarázta.* Budapest, 1939. **Curtis, J. J.** *An Application of the Syntax of the Hebrew Verbs to the Writings of Amos.* Diss. Southern Baptist Seminary, 1949. **Dannell, G. A.** *Studies in the Name Israel in the Old Testament.* Uppsala: Appelbergs Boktrykeri, 1946. 110–36. **Elhorst, H. J.** *De profetie van Amos.* Leiden, 1900. **Eybers, I. H.**, et al. *Studies in the Books of Hosea and Amos.* OTWSA. Potchefstroom: Rege-Pers Beperk, 1965. **Fohrer, G.** *Die Propheten des Alten Testaments.* Vol. 1: *Die Propheten des 8. Jahrhunderts.* Gütersloh: Gütersloher Verlagshaus / Gerhard Mohn, 1974. 22–55. **Gordis, R.** *Poets, Prophets and Sages.* Bloomington, IN: Indiana UP, 1971. **Gressmann, H.** *Die älteste Geschichtsschreibung und Prophe-*

tie Israels. SAT 3 / 1. Göttingen, 1910; 2d ed., 1921. **Grosch, H.** *Der Prophet Amos.* Handbücherei für den Religionsunterricht 6. Gütersloh: Gütersloher Verlagshaus / Gerhard Mohn, 1969. **Gunning, J. H.** *De Godspraken van Amos.* Leiden, 1885. **Harper, W. R.** *The Utterances of Amos Arranged Strophically.* Chicago, 1900 [= series in *The Biblical World,* Aug.–Nov. 1898; 86–89, 179–82, 251–56, 333–38.] **Hartung, K.** *Der Prophet Amos, nach dem Grundtext erklärt.* BibS(F). Freiburg, 1898. **Herntrich, V.** *Amos, der Prophet Gottes.* Wege in die Bibel 4. Göttingen, 1941. **Holwerda, B.** . . . *Begonnen hebbende van Mozes* . . . Terneuzen: D. H. Littoij, 1953. 31–47. **Hunter, A. V.** *Seek the Lord! A Study of the Meaning and Function of the Exhortation in Amos, Hosea, Isaiah, Micah and Zephaniah.* Baltimore: St. Mary's Seminary and University, 1982. **Ingleheart, J. H.** *Education and Culture in the Book of Amos: A Reevaluation.* Diss. University of Kentucky, 1964. **Janzen, W.** *Mourning Cry and Woe Oracle.* BZAW 125. Berlin / New York: DeGruyter, 1972. **Jiménez, M.** *Relecturas de Amós-Isaias.* Diss. Franciscan Biblical Institute, 1973. **Johnson, S. E.** *The Septuagint of Amos.* Chicago: University of Chicago Press, 1936. **Kahlert, H.** *Zur Frage nach der geistigen Heimat des Amos.* Eine Prüfung des These von H. W. Wolff. Dielheimer Blätter zum AT 4. Dielheim, 1973. **Kapelrud, A. S.** *Central Ideas in Amos.* Skrifter utgitt av Det Norske Videnskaps-Akademi i Oslo, II. Hist.-Filos. Klasse 2. Oslo: H. Aschenhoug, 1956. Repr. Oslo: Oslo University, 1961. **Kelley, P.** *Amos: Prophet of Social Justice.* Grand Rapids: Baker Book House, 1972. **Koch, K., H. J. Kraus,** et al. *Amos: Untersucht mit den Methoden einer strukturalen Formgeschichte.* Kevelaer: Butzon & Butzon / Neukirch: Neukirchener Verlag, 1976. **König, A.** *Die Profeet Amos.* Koort Verklarings oor die Ou Testament. Kaaptud / Pretoria: Kerk Uitgewers, 1974. **Krause, M.** *Das Verhältnis von sozialer Kritik und kommende Katastrophe in den Unheilsprophezeiungen des Amos.* Diss. Hamburg, 1972. **Kroeker, J.** *Die Propheten oder das Reden Gottes (vorexilisch): Amos und Hosea.* Das lebendige Wort 4. Giessen, 1932. **Kuntz, M.** *Ein Element der alten Theophanieüberlieferung und seine Rolle in der Prophetie des Amos.* Diss. Tübingen, 1968. **Lemcke, G.** *Die Prophetensprüche des Amos und Jesaja metrisch-stilistisch und literar-ästhetisch betrachtet.* Breslau, 1914. **Lindblom, J.** *Die literarische Gattung der prophetischen Literatur. Eine literargeschichtliche Untersuchung zum Alten Testament.* UUÅ 1924. Uppsala, 1924. 66–97. **Lohr, M.** *Untersuchungen zum Buch Amos.* BZAW 4. Giessen, 1901. **Maag, V.** *Text, Wortschatz und Begriffswelt des Buches Amos.* Leiden: E. J. Brill, 1951. **Markert, L.** *Struktur und Bezeichnung des Scheltwortes—eine gattungsgeschichtliche Studie an Hand des Amosbuches.* Diss. Erlangen / Nürnberg, 1974. BZAW 140. **McFayden, J. E.** *A Cry for Justice: A Study in Amos.* New York, 1912. **Meinhold, J.,** and **H. Lietzmann.** *Der Prophet Amos, Hebräische und Griechisch.* Kleine Texte fur theologische Vorlesungen und Übungen 15 / 16. Bonn, 1905. **Mitchell, H. G.** *Amos: An Essay in Exegesis.* Boston, 1900. **Naastepad, T. J. M.** *Amos: Verklaring van een bijbelgedeelte.* Kampen, 1976. **Neher, A.** *Amos: Contribution à l'étude du prophétisme.* Paris: J. Vrin, 1950. **Oesterly, W. O. E.** *Studies in the Greek and Latin Versions of the Book of Amos.* Cambridge: Cambridge UP, 1902. **Oettli, S.** *Amos und Hosea: Zwei Zeugen gegen die Anwendung der Evolutionstheorie auf die Religion Israels.* BFCT 5 / 4. Gütersloh, 1901. **Ogden, D.** *A Geography of Amos.* Diss. University of Utah, 1982. **Osswald, E.** *Urform und Auslegung im masoretischen Amos-text.* Diss. Jena, 1951. **Prado, J.** *Amos, el Profeta Pastor.* Madrid: El Perpetuo Socorro, 1950. **Praetorius, F.** *Die Gedichte des Amos.* Halle, 1924. **Proksch, O.** *Die Geschichtsbetrachtung bei Amos, Hosea und Jeremiah.* Königsberg, 1901. ———. *Textkritische Bemerkungen zum Buche Amos.* Sitzungsberichte der Preussischen Akademie der Wissenschaften zu Berlin, Philologische-Historische Klasse. Berlin, 1918. 1248–62. **Queen Southerland, K. M.** *The Futility Curse in the Old Testament.* Diss. Southern Baptist Seminary, 1982. **Reventlow, H. G.** *Das Amt des Propheten bei Amos.* FRLANT 80. Göttingen: Vandenhoeck & Ruprecht, 1962. **Riedel, W.** *Altestamentliche Untersuchungen I.* Leipzig, 1902. 29–36. **Rieger, J.** *Die Bedeutung der Geschichte für die Verkündigung des Amos und Hosea.* Giessen, 1929.

Robinson, T. H. *The Book of Amos: Hebrew Text.* London, 1923. **Rusche, H.** *Das Buch Amos erläutert.* Geistliche Schriftslesung AT 4. Düsseldorf: Patmos, 1975. **Schmidt, H.** *Der Prophet Amos.* Tübingen, 1917. **Schrade, H.** *Der verborgene Gott: Gottesbild und Gottesvorstellung in Israel und im alten Orient.* Stuttgart: W. Kohlhammer, 1949. 157– 63. **Seesemann, O.** *Israel und Juda bei Amos und Hosea.* Leipzig, 1898. **Seierstad, I.** *Die Offenbarungserlebnisse der Propheten Amos, Jesaja und Jeremia.* Oslo: J. Dybwad, 1946; 2d ed., 1965. **Shoot, W. B.** *The Fertility Religions in the Thought of Amos and Micah.* Diss. USC, 1951. **Sievers, E.,** and **H. Guthe.** *Amos, metrische bearbeitet.* Abhandlung der Sächsischen Gesellschaft der Wissenschaften 23 / 3. Leipzig, 1907. **Snaith, N.** *Notes on the Hebrew Text of Amos.* London: Epworth, 1945–46. **Steenbergen, V.** *Motivation in Relation to the Message of Amos.* Diss. USC, 1953. **Stuart, D.** *Studies in Early Hebrew Meter.* HSM 13. Missoula, MT: Scholars Press, 1976. 197–213. **Sutcliffe, T. H.** *The Book of Amos.* Biblical Handbooks. London, 1939. **Thorogood, B.** *Guide to the Book of Amos with Theme Discussions on Judgement, Social Justice, Priest, and Prophet.* London: Theological Education Fund, 1971. **Tourn, G.,** and **J. A. Soggin.** *Amos, profeta de la justicia.* Barcelona: Tierra Nueva, 1978. **Touzard, J.** *Le livre d'Amos.* Paris, 1908. **Tuschen, W.** *Die historischen Angaben im Buche des Propheten Amos.* Diss. Freiburg, 1951. **Tweedie, A.** *A Sketch of Amos and Hosea.* Edinburgh / London, 1916. **Valeton, J. J.** *Amos und Hosea: Ein Kapitel aus der Geschichte der israelitischen Religion.* Tr. K. Echternacht. Giessen, 1898. **Varadi, M** *Il Profeta Amos.* 1947. **Veldkamp, H.** *Paraphrase van het boek van den profeet Amos en van het boek van den profeet Obadjah.* 1940. **Vienney, A.** *Amos de Tekoa, son époque et son livre.* Montauban, 1899. **Vollmer, J.** *Geschichtliche Rückblicke und Motive in der Prophetie des Amos, Hosea, und Jesaja.* BZAW 119. Berlin: DeGruyter, 1971. **Vuilleumier-Bessard, R.** *La tradition culturelle d'Israel dans la prophétie d'Amos et d'Osée.* Cahiers Théologique 45. Neuchâtel: Delachaux & Niestlé, 1960. **Waller, H. S.** *The Unity of the Book of Amos.* Diss. Southern Baptist Seminary, 1948. **Ward, J.** *Amos and Isaiah: Prophets of the Word of God.* Nashville: Abingdon, 1969. **Warmuth, G.** *Das Mahnwort: Seine Bedeutung für die Verkündigung der vorexilischen Propheten Amos, Hosea, Micha, Jesaja und Jeremia.* Beiträge zur biblischen Exegese und Theologie 1. Frankfurt am Main, 1976. **Watts, J. D. W.** *Vision and Prophecy in Amos.* Grand Rapids: Eerdmans, 1958. **Weiser, A.** *Die Prophetie des Amos.* BZAW 53. Giessen: Töpelmann, 1929. **Werner, H.** *Amos.* Exempla Biblica 4. Göttingen: Vandenhoeck & Ruprecht, 1969. **Whitesides, R. A. D.** *The Gospel according to Amos.* Diss. Princeton Theological Seminary, 1952. **Willi-Plein, I.** *Verformen der Schriftexegese innerhalb des Alten Testaments: Untersuchen zum literarischen Werden der auf Amos, Hosea und Micha zurückgehenden Bücher im hebräischen Zwölf prophetenbuch.* BZAW 123. Berlin: DeGruyter, 1971. **Wolfe, R. E.** *Meet Amos and Hosea, the Prophets of Israel.* New York: Harper, 1945. **Wolff, H. W.** *Amos the Prophet: The Man and His Background.* Tr. F. R. McCurley. Philadelphia: Fortress, 1973. ———. *Die Stunde des Amos: Prophetie und Protest.* Munich: Chr. Kaiser Verlag, 1969.

ARTICLES

Albert, E. "Einige Bemerkungen zu Amos." *ZAW* 33 (1913) 265–71. **Alger, B.** "The Theology and Social Ethics of Amos." *Scr* 17 (1965) 109–16. **Allen, L. C.** "Amos, Prophet of Solidarity." *Vox Evangelica* 6 (1969) 42–53. **Alonso Díaz, J.** "El nuevo tipo de profecía que inicia Amós." *CB* 23 (1966) 36–42. **Amsler, S.** "Amos, prophète de la onzième heure." *ThZ* 21 (1965) 318–28. **Andrews, M.** "Hesiod and Amos." *JR* 23 (1943) 194–205. **Arieti, J. A.** "The Vocabulary of Septuagint Amos." *JBL* 93 (1974) 338–47. **Ashbel, D.** *"ha‘arot lenebo᾿ot ‘amos."* *BMik* 1 (1966) 103–7. **Bach, R.** "Gottesrecht und weltliches Recht in der Verkündigung des Propheten Amos." In *FS Gunther Dehn*, ed. W. Schneemelcher. Neukirchen: Verlag der Buchhandlung des Erziehungsvereins, 1957. 23–34. **Bailey, J. G.** "Amos: Preacher of Social Reform." *TBT* 19 (1981) 306–13. **Baumann, E.** "Eine Einzelheit." *ZAW* 64 (1952) 62. **Benson, A.** "'From the Mouth of the Lion.' The Messianism of Amos." *CBQ* 19 (1957) 199–212. **Berridge, J. M.** "Jeremia und die Prophetie des Amos." *TZ* 35 (1979) 321–41. **Boehmer, J.** "Die Eigenart der prophetischen Heilspredigt des Amos." *TSK* 76 (1903) 35–47. **Bohlen, R.** "Zur Sozialkritik des Propheten Amos." *TTZ* 95 (1986) 282–301. **Bonora, A.** "Amos defensore del diritto e della guistizia." *Testimonium Christi: Scritti in onore de Jacques Dupont*. Brescia: Paideia, 1985. 69–90. **Botterweck, G. J.** "'Sie verkaufen den Unschuldigen um Geld.' Zur sozialen Kritik des Propheten Amos." *BibLeb* 12 (1971) 215–31. ———. "Zur Authentizät des Buches Amos." *BZ* N. F. 2 (1958) 176–89. **Braslavi, Y.** "*'ariyot midbar-tekoaᶜ beseper ᶜamos.*" *BMik* 13, 1 (1967–68) 56–64. **Bratisiôtis, P. I.** "*'Amos.*" ThreskEthEnk 2 (1963) 447–49. **Braun, M. A.** "James' Use of Amos at the Jerusalem Council: Steps toward a Possible Solution of the Textual and Theological Problems." *JETS* 20 (1977) 113–21. **Bruston, E.** "Messages prophétiques: I. Le Message d'Amos." *ETR* 7 (1932) 158–72. **Budde, K.** "Zur Geschichte des Buches Amos." In *Studien zur semitischen Philologie und Religionsgeschichte: FS Julius Wellhausen*, ed. K. Marti. BZAW 27. Giessen, 1914. 63–77. ———. "Zu Text und Auslegung des Buches Amos." *JBL* 43 (1924) 46–131; 44 (1925) 62–122. **Carlson, A.** "Profeten Amos och Davidriket." *Religion och Bibel* 25 (1966) 57–58. **Caspari, W.** "Wer hat die Aussprüche des Propheten Amos gesammelt?" *NKZ* 25 (1914) 701–15. **Cherian, C. M.** "The Message of Amos the Pioneer Prophet." *CleM* 22 (1958) 81–91. **Cohen, S.** "The Political Background of the Words of Amos." *HUCA* 36 (1965) 153–60. **Collins, J.** "History and Tradition in the Prophet Amos." *ITQ* 41 (1974) 120–33. **Condamin, A.** "Les chants lyriques des prophètes." *RB* 10 (1901) 352–76. **Coote, R.** "Ripe Words for Preaching: Connotative Diction in Amos." *Pacific Theological Review* 8 (1976) 13–19. **Coulot, C.** "Propositions pour une structuration du livre d'Amos au niveau rédactionnel." *RevScRel* 51 (1977) 169–86. **Craghan, J.** "The Prophet Amos in Recent Literature." *BTB* 2 (1972) 242–61. ———. "Tradition and Techniques in the Prophet Amos." *TBT* 60 (1972) 782–86. **Crenshaw, J.** "A Liturgy of Wasted Opportunity." *Semitics* 1 (1970) 27–36. ———. "Amos and the Theophanic Tradition." *ZAW* 80 (1968) 203–15. ———. "The Influence of the Wise on Amos." *ZAW* 79 (1967) 42–51. **Crook, M.** "Did Amos and Micah Know Isaiah 9:2–7 and 11:1–9?" *JBL* 73 (1954) 144–51. **Crüsemann, F.** "Kritik an Amos im deuteronomistichen Geschichtswerk." In *Probleme biblischer Theologie: FS G. Von Rad*, ed. H. W. Wolff. Munich: Chr. Kaiser, 1971. 57–63. **Danell, G. A.** "Var Amos verkligen en nabi?" *SEÅ* 16 (1951) 7–20. **Davies, G. H.** "Amos—The Prophet of Re-Union." *ExpTim* 92 (1981) 196–99. **Desnoyers, L.** "Le prophète Amos." *RB* 26 (1917) 218–46. **Devescovi, U.** "Camminare sulle alture." *RivB* 9 (1969) 235–42. **DeWaard, J.** "Translation Techniques Used by the Greek Translators of Amos." *Bib* 59 (1978) 339–50. **Dijkema, F.** "Le fond des prophéties d'Amos." *OTS* 2. Leiden: E. J. Brill, 1943. 18–34. **Dines, J.** "Reading the Book of Amos." *ScrB* 16 (1986) 26–32. **Dion, P.** "Le message moral du prophète Amos s'inspirait-il du 'droit de l'alliance'?" *ScEs* 27 (1975) 5–34. **Döller, J.** "Vom 'Uberschüssigen' bei Amos." *Studien und Mitteilingen aus dem "Benedictiner-und Cistercienserorden* 28 (1907) 413–15. **Driver, G. R.** "A Hebrew Burial Custom." *ZAW* 66 (1966) 314–15. ———. "Difficult Words in the Hebrew Prophets." In *Studies in Old Testament Prophecy Presented to H. Wheeler Robinson*, ed. H. H. Rowley. Edinburgh: T. & T. Clark, 1950. 52–72. ———. "Two Astronomical Passages in the Old Testament." *JTS* n.s. 4 (1953) 208–12. **Dumeste, M.** "La spiritualité des prophètes d'Israël (Le message du prophète Amos)." *VSpir* 74 (1946) 834–52; 75 (1946) 424–37. **Dürr, L.** Altorientalisches Recht bei den Propheten Amos und Hosea." *BZ* 23 (1935) 150–57. **Eissfeldt, O.** "Amos und Jona in volkstumlicher Überlieferung." *Kleine Schriften* 4 (1968) 137–42. **Engnell, I.** "Amos"; "Amos' bok." In *Svenskt Bibliskt Uppslagsverk*, ed. 1. Engnell et al. Gävle:Skolförlaget, 1948. 1:59–61, 61–63. **Fang, C.** "Universalism and the Prophet Amos." *ColcT Fujen* 5.20 (1974) 165–71. **Farr, G.** "The Language of Amos, Popular or Cultic?" *VT* 16 (1966) 312–24. **Fendler, M.** "Zur sozialkritik des Amos: Versuch einer wirtschafts- und sozialgeschichtlichen Interpretation alttestamentlicher Texte." *EvT* 33 (1973) 32–53. **Fensham, F. C.** "A Possible Origin of the Concept of the Day of the Lord." *OTWSA* 7–8 (1966) 90–97. ———. "Common Trends in Curses of the Near Eastern Treaties and *kudurru*-Inscriptions compared with Maledictions of Amos and Isaiah." *ZAW* 75 (1963) 155–75. ———. "The Treaty between the Israelites and the Tyrians." *VTSup* 17 (1968) 71–87. ———. "Widow, Orphan and the Poor in Ancient Near Eastern Legal and Wisdom Literature." *JNES* 21 (1962) 129–39. **Feuillet, A.** "L'universalisme et l'alliance dans la religion d'Amos." *BVC* 17 (1957) 17–29. **Finley, T.** "The Waw-Consecutive with 'Imperfect' in Biblical Hebrew: Theoretical Studies and Its Use in Amos." In *Tradition and Testament: Essays in Honor of Charles Lee Feinberg*, ed. J. S. Feinberg and P. D. Feinberg. Chicago: Moody Press, 1981. **Frost, S. B.** "Asseverations by Thanksgiving." *VT* 8 (1958) 380–90. **Garrett, D.** "The Structure of Amos as a Testimony to Its Integrity." *JETS* 27 (1984) 275–76. **Gaster, T. H.** "An Ancient Hymn in the Prophecies of Amos." *Journal of the Manchester Egyptian and Oriental Society* 19 (1935) 23–36. **Gemser, B.** "Die Godsgetuienis van Amos." *Hervormde Teologiese Studies* 1 (1943–44) 9–21. **Gese, H.** "Kleine Beiträge zum Verständnis des Amosbuches." *VT* 12 (1962) 417–38. **Glück, J. J.** "*Nagid*—Shepherd." *VT* 13 (1963) 144–50. ———. "Three Notes on the Book of Amos." *Studies on the Books of Hosea and Amos.* OTWSA 7–8 (1965) 115–21. **Gordis, R.** "The Composition and Structure of Amos." *HTR* 33 (1940) 239–51. **Gottlieb, H.** "Amos og Kulten." *DTT* 30 (1967) 65–101. ———. "Amos und Jerusalem." *VT* 17 (1967) 430–63. **Gray, J.** "The Day of Yahweh." *SEÅ* 39 (1974) 5–37. **Gunneweg, A.** "Religion oder Offenbarung: Zum hermeneutischen Problem des Alten Testaments." *ZTK* 74 (1977) 151–78. **Guthe, H.** "Der Prophet Amos." *HSAT* 2:30–47. **Halévy, J.** "Recherches bibliques—le livre d'Amos." *RevSém* 11 (1903) 11–31, 97–121, 193–209, 289–300; 12 (1904) 11–18. **Hallo, W. W.** "From Qarqar to Carchemish: Assyria and Israel in the Light of New Discoveries." *BAR* 2. Garden City: Doubleday, 1964. 152–90. **Haran, M.** "The Rise and Fall of the Empire of Jeroboam II." *Zion* 31 (1966) 18–38. ———. "The Rise and Decline of the Empire of Jeroboam ben Joash." *VT* 17 (1967) 266–97. **Harper, W. R.** "The Utterances of Amos Arranged Strophically." *Biblical World* (Aug.–Nov. 1898) 86–89, 179–82, 251–56, 333–38. [As book, Chicago, 1900.] **Heicksen, H.** "Tekoa: Historical and Cultural Profile." *JETS* 13 (1970) 81–89. **Herntrich, V.** "Das Berufungsbewusstsein des Amos." *Christentum und Wissenschaft* 9 (1933) 161–76. **Hillers, D.** "A Note on Some Treaty Terminology in the Old Testament." *BASOR* 176 (1964) 46–47. **Hirscht, A.** "Textkritische Untersuchungen über das Buch Amos." *ZWT* 44 (1903) 11–73. **Hoffman, G.** "Versuch zu Amos." *ZAW* 3 (1883) 110–11. **Hoffman, H.** "Form—Funktion—Intention." *ZAW* 82 (1970) 341–46. **Hoffman, Y.** "The Day of the Lord as a Concept and a Term in the Prophetic Literature." *ZAW* 93 (1981) 37–50. **Hogg, H.** "The Starting-Point of the Religious Message of Amos." *Transactions of the Third International Congress for the History of Religions* 1. Oxford, 1908. 325–27. **Honeycutt, R.** "The Lion Has Roared." *Southwestern Journal of Theology* 9 (1960) 25–35. **Hoonacker, A. van.** "Notes d'exégèse sur quelques passages difficiles d'Amos." *RB* 14 (1905) 163–87. **Horst, F.** "Die Doxologien im Amosbuch." *ZAW* 47 (1929) 45–54. **Howard, G.** "Revision toward the Hebrew in the Septuagint Text of Amos." *EI* 16 (1982) 125–33. ———. "Some Notes on the Septuagint of Amos." *VT* 20 (1970) 108–12. **Howie, C.** "Expressly for Our Time: The Theology of Amos." *Int* 13 (1959) 273–85. **Huey, F.** "The Ethical Teaching of Amos: Its Content and Relevance." *Southwestern Journal of Theology* 9 (1966) 57–67. **Huffmon, H. B.**

"The Social Role of Amos' Message." In *The Quest for the Kingdom of God: Studies in Honor of George E. Mendenhall*, ed. H. B. Huffmon et al. Winona Lake, IN: Eisenbrauns, 1983. 109–16. **Humbert, P.** "Un heraut de la justice, Amos." *RTP* n.s. 5 (1917) 5–35. **Hyatt, J.** "The Book of Amos." *Int* 3 (1949) 338–49. ――――. "The Deity Bethel and the Old Testament." *JAOS* 59 (1939) 81–89. **Irwin, W. A.** "The Thinking of Amos." *AJSL* 49 (1932–33) 102–14. **Johnson, A.** "Amos—The Prophet of Reunion." *ExpT* 92 (1981) 196–200. **Jozaki, S.** "The Secondary Passages in the Book of Amos." *Kwansei Gakuin University Annual Studies* 4 (1956) 25–100. **Junker, H.** "Amos, der Mann, den Gott mit unwiderstehlicher Gewalt zum Propheten machte." *TTZ* 65 (1956) 321–28. ――――. "Amos und die 'Opferlose Mosezeit.'" *TGI* 27 (1935) 686–95. **Kaiser, W.** "The Davidic Promise and the Inclusion of the Gentiles." *JETS* 20 (1977) 97–111. **Kallikuzhuppil, J.** "Liberation in Amos and Micah." *Bible Bhashyam* 11 (1985) 215–23. **Kapelrud, A.** "Amos og hans omgivelser." *NorTT* 84 (1983) 157–66. ――――. "Amosbuch." *BHH* 1:85–87. ――――. "Central Ideas in Amos." *Skrifter utgitt av Det Norske Videnskaps-Akademi i Oslo* II 1956 / 4. Oslo: H. Ascheboug, 1961. 54–59. ――――. "God as Destroyer in the Preaching of Amos and in the Ancient Near East." *JBL* 71 (1952) 33–38. ――――. "New Ideas in Amos." *VTSup* 15 (1966) 193–206. ――――. "Propheten Amos og hans yrke." *NorTT* 59 (1958) 76–79. **Kaupel, H.** "Gibt es opferfeindliche Stellen im Alten Testament?" *TGl* 17 (1925) 172–78. **Keller, C.** "Notes bibliques de prédication sur les textes du prophète Amos." *VCaro* 60 (1961) 390–98. **Kelley, P.** "Contemporary Study of Amos and Prophetism." *RevExp* 63 (1966) 375–85. **Klein, R. W.** "The Day of the Lord." *CTM* 39 (1968) 517–25. **Koch, K.** "Die Rolle der hymnischen Abschnitte in der Komposition des Amos-Buches." *ZAW* 86 (1976) 504–37. **Koehler, L.** "Amos." *Schweizerische Theologische Zeitschrift* 34 (1917) 10–21, 68–79, 145–57, 190–208. ――――. "Amos-Forschungen von 1917 bis 1932." *TRev* n.f. (1932) 195–213. **Kohata, F.** "A Stylistic Study on the Metaphors of Amos." In *FS M. Sekine*, ed. S. Arai et al. Tokyo: Yamamoto Shoten, 1972. 147–61. [Japanese.] **Krause, H.** "Die Gerichtsprophet Amos, ein Vorläufer des Deuteronomisten." *ZAW* 50 (1932) 221–39. **Labuschagne, C.** "Amos' Conception of God and the Popular Theology of the Time." *OTWSA* 75 (1966) 122–33. **Lang, B.** "The Social Organization of Peasant Poverty in Biblical Israel." *JSOT* 24 (1982) 47–63. **Laridon, V.** "Amos, genuinae religionis defensor ac propheta iustitiae socialis." *Collationes Brugenses* 47 (1951) 405–10; 48 (1952) 3–7, 27–31. **Lattes, D.** "Amos, prophète de la justice." *Madregoth* 1 (1946) 23–31. **Leahy, M.** "The Popular Idea of God in Amos." *ITQ* 22 (1955) 68–73. **Lehming, S.** "Erwägungen zu Amos." *ZTK* 55 (1958) 145–69. **Lewis, R.** "Four Preaching Aims of Amos." *Asbury Seminary Review* 21 (1967) 14–18. **Lohman, P.** "Einige Textkonjekturen zu Amos." *ZAW* 32 (1912) 274–77. **Luria, B. Z.** Amos—Prophet and Worldly Man." *DD* 10 (1982) 183–86. **Maag, V.** "Amos"; "Amosbuch." *RGG* 1:328–30, 330–31. **Maclean, H.** "Amos and Israel." *Reformed Theological Review* 18 (1959) 1–6. **Maigret, J.** "Amos et le sanctuaire de Bethel." *BTS* 47 (1962) 5–6. **Malamat, A.** "Origins of Statecraft in the Israelite Monarchy." *BA* 28 (1965) 34–65. **Mamie, P.** "Le livre d'Amos: Les châtiments et le 'reste d'Israël.'" *Nova et Vera* 37 (1962) 217–23. **Martin-Achard, R.** "La prédication d'Amos: Remarques exégétiques et homilétiques." *ETR* 41 (1966) 13–19. **Mauchline, J.** "Implicit Signs of a Persistent Belief in the Davidic Empire." *VT* 20 (1970) 287–303. **Mays, J. L.** "Words about the Words of Amos: Recent Study of the Book of Amos." *Int* 13 (1959) 259–72. **McCollough, W.** "Some Suggestions about Amos." *JBL* 72 (1953) 247–54. **Melugin, R.** "The Formation of Amos: An Analysis of Exegetical Method." *SBL 1978 Seminar Papers*. Missoula, MT: Scholars Press, 1978. 369–91. **Miller, C.** "Amos and Faith Structures: A New Approach." *TBT* 19 (1981) 314–19. **Monloubou, L.** "Amos." *DBSup* 8 (1969) 706–24. **Montgomery, J.** "Notes on Amos." *JBL* 23 (1904) 94–96. **Moreno, C.** "Amos." *Theologia y Vida* 4 (1964) 23–35. **Morgenstern, J.** "Amos Studies I." *HUCA* 11 (1936) 19–140. ――――. "Amos Studies II." *HUCA* 12–13 (1937–38) 1–53. ――――. "Amos

Studies III." *HUCA* 15 (1940) 59–304. ———. "Amos Studies IV." *HUCA* 32 (1961) 295–350. ———. "The Univeralism of Amos." In *Essays Presented to Leo Baeck on the Occasion of his Eightieth Birthday.* London: East and West Library, 1954. 106–26. **Moriarty, F.** "Preacher and Prophet." *Way* 20 (1980) 3–14. **Mousset, P.** "La pédagogie d'un prophète: Amos." *Catéchistes* 27 (1956) 267–73. **Neuberg, F.** "An Unrecognized Meaning of Hebrew DOR." *JNES* 9 (1950) 215–17. **Oettli, S.** "Die Kultus bei Amos und Hosea." *Griefswalder Studien. Theologische Abhandlungen. FS Hermann Cremer.* Gütersloh, 1895. 1–34. **Oort, H.** "De profeet Amos." *TT* 14 (1880) 114–58. ———. "Het Vaderland van Amos." *TT* 25 (1891) 121–26. **Otzen, B.** "Amos og afguderne." *NorTT* 84 (1983) 167–85. **Overholt, T.** "Commanding the Prophets: Amos and the Problem of Prophetic Authority." *CBQ* 41 (1979) 517–32. **Paton, L. B.** "Did Amos Approve the Calf-Worship at Bethel?" *JBL* 13 (1894) 80–91. **Peifer, C.** "Amos the Prophet: The Man and His Book." *TBT* 19 (1981) 295–300. **Praetorius, F.** "Bemerkungen zu Amos." *ZAW* 35 (1915) 12–25. ———. "Zum Texte des Amos." *ZAW* 34 (1914) 42–44. **Prager, M.** "Amos, der Hirte aus Teqoa." *BLit* 36 (1962–63) 84–96, 164–72, 243–55, 295–308. **Preus, H.** "'. . . ich will mit dir sein.'" *ZAW* 80 (1968) 139–73. **Rad, G. von.** "The Origin of the Concept of the Day of Yahweh." *JSS* 4 (1959) 97–108. **Rahmer, M.** "Die hebräischen Traditionen in den Werken des Hieronymus." *MGWJ* 42 (1898) 1–61, 97–107. **Raitt, T. M.** "The Prophetic Summons to Repentance." *ZAW* 83 (1971) 30–49. **Randellini, L.** "Il profeta Amos, difensore del poveri." *Bollettino del-l'Amicizia Ebraico-Cristiana di Firenze* 6 (1971) 35–43. ———. "Ricchi e Poveri nel libro del profeta Amos." *Studii Biblici Franciscani* 2 (1952) 5–86. **Reventlow, H. B. von.** "Das Amt des Propheten bei Amos." FRLANT 80. Göttingen: Vandenhoeck & Ruprecht, 1962. 90–110. **Roberts, J. J.** "Recent Trends in the Study of Amos." *ResQ* 13 (1970) 1–16. **Robscheit, H.** "Die thora bei Amos und Hosea." *EvT* 10 (1950–51) 26–38. **Rosenbaum, S.** "Northern Amos Revisited: Two Philological Suggestions." *HS* 18 (1977) 132–48. **Rothstein, G.** "Amos und seine Stellung innerhalb des Prophetismus." *TSK* 78 (1905) 323–58. **Rudolph, W.** "Gott und Mensch bei Amos." In *Imago Dei: FS für Gustav Krüger,* ed. H. Bornkamm. Giessen, 1932. 19–31. ———. "Schwierige Amosstellen." In *Wort und Geschichte: FS für Karl Elliger zum 70. Geburtstag,* ed. H. Gese and H. P. Rüger. Kevelaer / Neukirchen-Vluyn: Butzon & Bercker / Neukirchener Verlag, 1973. 157–62. **Sansoni, C.** "Amos, uomo del suo tempo." *BibOr* 10 (1968) 253–65. **Sant, V.** "Religious Worship in the Book of Amos." *MelT* 3 (1950) 75–92; 4 (1951) 34–47. **Sauermann, O.** "Der Prophet der sozialen Gerechtigkeit." *Der Seelsorger* 24 (1954) 229–35, 273–78. **Schenker, A.** "Gerichtsverkündigung und Verblendung bei den vorexilischen Propheten." *RB* 93 (1986) 563–80. **Schmid, H.** "Amos. Zur Frage nach der 'geistigen Heimat' des Propheten." *WuD* 10 (1969) 85–103. ———. "Hauptprobleme der neueren Prophetforschung." *Schweizer Theologische Umschau* 35 (1965) 3–11. **Schmidt, H.** "Die Herkunft des Propheten Amos." In *FS Karl Budde zum siebsigsten Geburtstag,* ed. K. Marti. BZAW 34. Giessen, 1920. 158–71. **Schmidt, W.** "Die deuteronomistische Redaktion des Amosbuches: Zu den theologischen Unterschieden zwischen dem Prophetenwort und seinem Sammler." *ZAW* 77 (1965) 168–93. **Schottroff, W.** "Amos—Das Porträt eines Propheten (I-V)." *Stimme der Gemeinde* 24 (1972) 113–15, 145–46, 193–96, 225–27, 289–92. ———. "Warum Amos kein Gehör fand." *Stimme der Gemeinde* 24 (1972) 225–27. **Seierstad, I.** "Amosprophetien i ljoset av nyare gransking." *TTKi* 2 (1931) 111–27. ———. "Erlebnis und Gehorsam bei Propheten Amos." *ZAW* 52 (1934) 22–41. **Seilhamer, F.** "The Role of Covenant in the Mission and Message of Amos." In *A Light Unto My Path: Old Testament Studies in Honor of Jacob M. Myers,* ed. H. N. Bream et al. Philadelphia: Temple UP, 1974. 435–51. **Sinclair, L.** "The Courtroom Motif in the Book of Amos." *JBL* 85 (1966) 351–53. **Smalley, W.** "Recursion Patterns and the Sectioning of Amos." *BT* 30 (1979) 118–27. **Smart, J. D.** "Amos." *IDB* 1:116–21. **Smend, R.** "Das Nein des Amos." *EvT* 23 (1963) 404–23. **Smith, G. V.** "The Concept of God / The Gods as King in the Ancient Near East and the Bible." *Trinity Journal* 3 (1982) 18–38. **Smith, R.** "The Theological Implications of the Prophecy of Amos." *Southwestern Journal of Theology* 9 (1966) 49–56. **Snyder, G.** "The Law and Covenant in Amos." *ResQ* 25 (1982) 158–66. **Sowada, J.** "Let Justice Surge Like Water." *TBT* 19 (1981) 301–5. **Speier, S.** "Bemerkungen zu Amos." *VT* 3 (1953) 305–10. ———. "Bemerkungen zu Amos, II." *Homenaje a Millás-Vallicrosa.* Barcelona: Consejo Superior de Investigaciones Científicas, 1956. 2:365–72. **Speiser, E.** "Of Shoes and Shekels." In *Oriental and Biblical Studies,* ed. J. J. Finkelstein and M. Greenberg. Philadelphia: University of Pennsylvania Press, 1967. 151–59. **Stamm, J. J.** "Der Name des Propheten Amos und sein sprachlicher Hintergrund." In *Prophecy: Essays Presented to G. Fohrer on His Sixty-fifth Birthday,* ed. J. A. Emerton. Berlin: De-Gruyter, 1980. 137–42. **Staples, W.** "Epic Motives in Amos." *JNES* 25 (1966) 106–12. **Stephany, A.** "Charackter und zeitliche Aufeinanderfolge der Drohsprüche in der Prophetie des Amos." *Christentum und Wissenschaft* 7 (1931) 281–89. **Stoebe, H. J.** "Der Prophet Amos und sein bürgerlicher Beruf." *WuD* n.f. 5 (1957) 160–81. ———. "Überlegungen zu den geistlichen Voraussetzungen der Prophetie des Amos." In *Wort—Gebot—Glaube. Beiträge zur Theologie des Alten Testaments. Festschrift Walther Eichrodt zum 80. Geburtstag,* ed. H. J. Stoebe. Zürich: Zwingli, 1970. 209–25. **Story, C.** "Amos—Prophet of Praise." *VT* 30 (1980) 67–80. **Stuhlmueller, C.** "Amos, Desert-Trained Prophet." *TBT* 1 (1962–63) 224–30. **Super, A.** "Figures of Comparison in the Book of Amos." *Semitics* 3 (1973) 67–80. **Szabo, A.** "Textual Problems in Amos and Hosea." *VT* 25 (1975) 500–524. **Talmon, S.** "The Gezer Calendar and the Seasonal Cycle of Ancient Canaan." *JAOS* 83 (1963) 177–87. **Terrien, S.** "Amos and Wisdom." In *Israel's Prophetic Heritage: Essays in Honor of James Muilenburg,* ed. B. W. Anderson and W. Harrelson. New York: Harper and Brothers, 1962. 108–15. **Tietsch, A.** "Die Botschaft des Amos." *Zeichen der Zeit* (1972) 211–17. **Torczyner, H.** "Dunkle Bibelstellen." In *Vom Alten Testament: Karl Marti zum siebstigen Geburtstag,* ed. K. Budde. BZAW 41. Giessen, 1925. 274–80. **Torrey, C. C.** "Notes on Am 2:7; 6:10; 8:3; 9:8–10." *JBL* 15 (1896) 151–54. ———. "On the Text of AM 5:25; 6:1, 2; 7:2." *JBL* 13 (1894) 63. **Trapiello, J.** "Situacíon histórica del profeta Amós." *EstBib* 26 (1967) 249–74. **Tromp, N.** "Amos—profetie als kritische funktie." *Ons Geestelijk Erf.* 48 (1971) 294–302. **Tucker, G.** "Prophetic Superscriptions and the Growth of a Canon." In *Canon and Authority,* ed. G. W. Coats and B. O. Long. Philadelphia: Fortress Press, 1977. 56–70. **Waard, J. de.** "Translation Techniques Used by the Greek Translators of Amos." *Bib* 59 (1978) 339–50. **Wagner, S.** "Überlegungen zur Frage nach den Beziehungen des Propheten Amos zum Südreich." *TLZ* 96 (1971) 653–70. **Wal, A. van der.** "The Structure of Amos." *JSOT* 26 (1983) 107–13. **Walker, J.** "The Language of Amos." *Southwestern Journal of Theology* 9 (1966–67) 37–48. **Ward, J. M.** "Amos." *IDBSup.* 21–23. **Watts, J. D. W.** "Amos, the Man." *RevExp* 63 (1966) 387–92. ———. "Amos—the Man and his Message." *Southwestern Journal of Theology* 9 (1966) 21–26. ———. "The Origin of the Book of Amos." *ExpTim* 66 (1954–55) 109–12. **Weiser, A.** "Die Berufung des Amos." *TBl* 7 (1928) 177–82. **Weisman, Z.** "Stylistic Parallels in Amos and Jeremiah: Their Implications for the Composition of Amos." *Shnaton* 1 (1975) 129–49. **Weiss, M.** "The Origin of the Day of Yahweh Reconsidered." *HUCA* 37 (1966) 29–72. **Wer, A. van der.** "The Structure of Amos." *JSOT* 26 (1983) 107–13. **Whitford, J.** "The Vision of Amos." *BSac* 70 (1913) 109–22. **Williams, D.** "The Theology of Amos." *RevExp* 63 (1966) 393–403. **Winter, A.** "Analyse des Buches Amos." *TSK* (83 (1910) 323–74. **Wolff, H. W.** "The Irresistible Word (Amos)." *CurTM* 10 (1983) 4–13. **Woude, A. S. van der.** "Three Classical Prophets: Amos, Hosea and Micah." In *Israel's Prophetic Tradition. Essays in Honour of Peter Ackroyd,* ed. R. Coggins et al. Cambridge / London / New York: Cambridge University Press, 1982. **Würthwein, E.** "Amos-Studien." *ZAW* 62 (1950) 10–52. **Yoshida, H.** "Prophecy and Salvation—in the Case of Amos—." *Kiyo* (The Bulletin of Christian Research Institute, Meiji Gakuin University) 14 (1981) 27–47. [Japanese.] **Zyl, A. van.** "Die Zonderbesef by Amos." *NGTT* 9 (1968) 69–82.

Introduction

AMOS' ERA

Amos' travels from his native Judah into Israel took place in the first half of the eighth century B.C., when Jeroboam II (786–746 B.C.) was Israel's king. The book's introduction (1:1) confirms this dating as does the account of Amos' encounter with Jeroboam's chief priest at Bethel, Amaziah (7:10–17). The king of Judah during Amos' ministry was Uzziah (1:1), who lived until 742 but brought his son, Jotham, into coregency with him in 750. The absence of any mention of a successor to Jeroboam or Uzziah in 1:1 suggests that Amos was not active as a prophet beyond the 750s. How early he began to prophesy, however, and for how long, cannot be determined. It would appear that the start of his career preceded that of his close contemporary Hosea by not more than half a decade. It is possible that their preaching overlapped in the 750s, although neither mentions the other nor is mentioned outside their respective books.

Jeroboam II was the last king in the North's longest dynasty—that of Jehu, founded in 842. Egypt, Assyria, and Babylon were all relatively weak during Jeroboam's reign (cf. Jonah, *Introduction*). He had succeeded in subduing the Arameans, Israel's most powerful nearby enemy (2 Kgs 14:25–28). A considerable factor in this was the partial revival of Assyrian strength under Adad-Nirari III (806–783), whose conquest of Damascus in 801 B.C. and subsequent imposition of substantial military and economic authority over Syria gave respite to the Israelites, with whom Adad-Nirari had no direct concern. Moreover, there was no Israelite-Judean war during Jeroboam's reign. In the final half of his tenure (i.e., the 760s and 750s), Israel reached what was probably its height in terms of economic prosperity. Agriculture flourished in spite of occasional crop failures (4:6–9). International peace, in contrast to the frequent wars of the previous century (1:3–2:3), allowed Israel to gain wealth via international trade. Large-scale urbanization followed the new economic order, since those whose profit came from trade (3:15; 4:1; 6:1–6; 8:5) and those who benefited from slave labor (2:6; 8:6) or usury (2:8; 5:10–12) were no longer bound to the land as their farmer ancestors had been. Those with the means to buy up food in the countryside and resell it to a captive audience in the cities could make enormous profits if they were greedy enough, as many were (8:4–6).

Excessive wealth led to the creation of a leisured upper class who increasingly adopted a decadent lifestyle (2:8; 4:1; 6:1–6). But other forms of unfaithfulness to the covenant were rampant as well, including sexual immorality (2:7) and idolatry (8:14). These were hardly limited to any socioeconomic class. Nevertheless, it was the exploitation of the poor and defenseless by the rich and powerful that God particularly exposed through Amos' oracles and which constitutes a remarkably frequent theme in the book. In light of the overt references to judicial corruption as well (2:7; 5:10–12), it is evident that a genuine breakdown in the delivery of justice to the citizenry had occurred in Israel in Amos' day.

Toward the midpoint of the eighth century, Israel enjoyed peace, prosperity, and a measure of international prestige. A confident nation (6:8) took comfort in its military prowess (6:13) and ignored its exploitation of the needy and the growing disparity between privilege and poverty. Religion per se was enthusiastically practiced (2:8; 5:21–23) but by a people whose fidelity to the covenant was a sham. The nation was characterized by religious hypocrisy. Israel was a people often orthodox in style of worship but disobedient in personal and social behavior.

THE MAN AMOS

To such a people the prophet Amos was sent by Yahweh away from his native Judah (1:1, 2; 7:12) and north to Israel, where his preaching brought him official opposition (7:10–13). We know nothing of his personal history aside from the book. His age, life span, family life, etc. are all untold. Except for the fact that he preached at least once at Bethel, the North's main sanctuary (7:13), we do not even know where he did most of his preaching, or how often, or over what exact span of time.

Amos was from Tekoa in Judah, about 10 miles south of Jerusalem, where he was a sheep-breeder (1:1; 7:14) and sycamore-fig cultivator (7:14). Both jobs could have involved him in extensive travel as an agricultural specialist, perhaps frequently into the North. But exactly why and how God called him to preach across national boundaries is simply not knowable on the evidence.

Amos was certainly a prophet. His disclaimer to the priest Amaziah (7:14–17) stressed that he did not train to be a prophet but was called specially by God from his usual employment (somewhat on the analogy of Elisha, 1 Kgs 19:19–21). Amos is an illustration of the biblical principle that spiritual gifts are more important than academic training for ministry, for his oracles are fully as powerful and compelling as any in the OT (contra Jerome, who for some reason was inclined to denigrate Amos' preaching style). If his travels afforded him an opportunity to see firsthand the inequities of Israel's economic and legal systems, and if his own prominence in the small-town environment of Tekoa gave him firsthand experience as a jurist in court cases—as have been frequently suggested—those opportunities were still quite secondary to the revelatory power of God in making Amos his mouthpiece.

In ancient Israel prophets were compensated by donations (2 Kgs 5:16–23) and in some instances by the government (1 Kgs 18:19). Amaziah apparently thought Amos was, in part, preaching in Bethel because the money was better there than in Judah (7:12). Amos' rejoinder makes it clear that he had no interest in a profession but had left (presumably temporarily) a successful business career in obedience to Yahweh who "took him" from it. Nevertheless, he must have appeared to be a professional prophet to those who did not know his background (7:10–17).

There is some possibility that Amos' prophecies were all delivered within a short time—i.e., less than a single year. If the statement "that which he saw concerning Israel two years before the earthquake" is taken in its most literal sense (but compare, for example, the "Judah and Jerusalem" restriction of Isa 1:1), it could imply that he "saw" all his oracles in the twelve-month period that preceded the (undatable) earthquake. It is also possible that Amaziah somehow succeeded in enforcing his banishment decree against Amos (7:12–13) although Amos' response (7:16–17) hardly represents acquiescence. For a book of its relative length, however, Amos shows surprisingly little evidence of historical development. In contrast to the book of Hosea, where dates from the 750s (1:4) to the 720s (13:10) are easily discernable, nothing in Amos can be securely dated earlier or later than anything else therein.

Because he mentions Samaria and / or some of its leading citizens several times (3:9, 12; 4:1; 6:1; 8:14), it seems reasonable enough to assume that some of Amos' preaching took place in Samaria. But it is also conceivable that a preacher at Bethel would see so many Samaritans visiting the official sanctuary there (7:14–15; 5:5) that he need not have set foot in Samaria to address good numbers of them. What little we know of Amos, then, we know mainly through his message. His words from God, not his person, were the concern of those who preserved his oracles.

Amos' Style

Amos employs a considerable variety of compositional techniques in conveying the revelations God had given him. While no technique is absolutely unique, some are used in a way that produces a finished product without parallel in other OT prophecy. If Amos was not a professionally trained prophet, this certainly did not detract from his ability to deliver powerful, moving oracles whose impact cut to the very heart of a wayward nation's responsibilities before God.

Amos routinely employs what are commonly called messenger formulae (כה אמר יהוה "This is what Yahweh said"; אמר יהוה "Yahweh said"; נאם יהוה "Oracle of Yahweh"; etc.) to provide a very close identification of his speeches with Yahweh's authorship. Three times he recounts an oath of Yahweh with the words "Yahweh has sworn" (4:2; 6:8; 8:7), suggesting that he has been an auditor of the divine council in which such an oath would presumably have been announced. Amos also employs a summoning formula ("Listen to this . . .") in 3:1; 4:1; 5:1; 8:4, suggestive of the function of a herald who gathers people to hear an official proclamation. In each instance the effect is to subordinate his own creativity to the revelation of God.

Amos effectively uses the device of summary quotation, capturing the essence of an attitude or a pattern of behavior by citing some sort of characteristic language. In 4:1, for example, he quotes the callous demands of idle rich women; in 6:13, the boastful language of a people exulting in their military prowess; in 8:5, the greedy merchants; and in 9:10, the speech of a complacent populace.

Perhaps especially noteworthy is Amos' use of climactic patterns. A number of his oracles build steadily to a high point, where the essence of the message is emphasized dramatically. In the compound oracle of 1:3–2:16, bordering nations around the points of the compass are identified as enemies of Yahweh. At the last, Israel itself is treated as a foreign nation, whose crimes against the covenant have made it, too, an enemy of its own God. In 3:3–8, instance after instance of naturally bound events is cited to lead to the inevitability of the prophet's preaching what God has spoken to him. In the four visions of 7:1–8:3, threats of doom that are rescinded give way to announcements of unavoidable destruction. The elaborately chiastic funerary lament of 5:1–17 evidences another kind of patterning, one in which the careful balance of a large-scale chiasm is mingled with the characteristic language and content of a funeral elegy.

Amos masterfully employs other speech forms as well: the n : n + 1 numerical parallelisms favored in ancient Near Eastern synonymous poetry (1:3, 6, etc.); woe / funerary oracles (5:18–27; 6:1–7); wisdom argumentation (3:2–8; 6:12); curse formulae (7:17); etc. Like most OT prophets, his preaching is full of incisive simile and metaphor; like all, he uses synecdoche and metonymy often.

Perhaps unique to Amos (though some scholars would posit the same process in connection with the "servant songs" in Isaiah) is his excerpting of a well-known hymn at three points (4:13; 5:8; 9:5–6) as a means of contact with his audience's understanding of the power of Yahweh to enforce his will. This most effective strategy is analogous to Amos' quoting people in such a way that their own words condemn them. Their old favorite hymn itself shows them a Yahweh of judgment and power, a God enforcing his commands in all the earth, rather than the pliable, placatable God they thought they were dealing with (5:16–17).

Amos' oracles vary considerably in length. The longest (1:3–2:16) contains 390 word units in the written Hebrew. The shortest (1:2) contains only 12. The average oracle is about 110 word units (8 or 9 verses) long and might have taken less than two minutes to recite or sing, barring repetitions or special pauses. Most of Amos' oracles are poetic, though some are a mix of prose and poetry (e.g., 3:1–2; 5:1–17; 6:8–14; 9:11–15), as is typical in the prophetic books.

Though the book contains five visions (7:1–9; 8:1–3; 9:1–6), these are hardly prominent compared to the nonvisionary material and are the sorts of visions that emphasize audition to the virtual exclusion of "vision." It is thus reasonable to say that Amos was not to any significant degree a visionary—compared to, say, Ezekiel. But as the first of the writing prophets, his involvement in visions (compared to Hosea or Micah, for example) is noteworthy.

THE STRUCTURE OF THE BOOK

Five major categories of material may be identified in the book of Amos. They are, in order of quantity: (1) sayings spoken by the prophet himself; (2) first-person accounts of visions; (3) a third-person account of opposition Amos experienced at Bethel; (4) excerpts from an old Yahwistic hymn; (5) the title.

The book begins with the title (1:1) and moves immediately to a large block of prophetic sayings of various types (1:2–6:14) in which two of the hymnic fragments are inserted (4:13; 5:8), in both instances as a means of strengthening the impact of the respective oracles into which they are inserted. In chap. 7 the vision accounts begin. The first three of these (vv 1–3; 4–6; 7–9), closely connected in structure, are followed by the sole third-person narrative about Amos, apparently because the wording of the visions—specifically the third vision—strongly related to the reaction of Amaziah the priest of Bethel and may indeed have partly occasioned his reaction. The fourth vision account (8:1–3), structurally similar to the first three, demonstrates rather graphically by its placement that Amos' preaching of doom had not really been stopped.

Thereafter, sayings resume until 9:1–6, which contains a fifth and final vision account, in format different from the previous four and not nearly so pictorially oriented. Though technically a vision, it is in function virtually another of the sayings. This account concludes with the third and final hymnic fragment (9:5–6) again employed to intensify the audience impact of the oracle. A final segment of sayings (9:7–15) completes the book.

From one point of view, then, the book's structure is a relatively simple one. When it is recognized that the hymnic fragments are not functionally independent, even though distinctly recognizable in genre, and that the title is the barest sort of introduction, the book has a structure that may be outlined broadly in three parts:

1. First group of oracles, 1:2–6:14
2. Visions, with related narrative, 7:1–8:3
3. Final group of oracles, 8:4–9:15

This very basic structure was probably the convenient design of contemporaries concerned that Amos' inspired message not be lost, i.e., colleagues or disciples of the prophet. Or, Amos may himself have organized his oracles this way for preservation. The close connection between the four vision accounts in 7:1–9, 8:1–3 and the Amos-Amaziah encounter in 7:10–17 has implications for the placement of that entire block (7:1–8:3) where it now stands. It is quite likely that when Amaziah talks of "all his words" (7:10) in his message to Jeroboam II he has in mind much more than the three vision accounts found in 7:1–9, even though these vision accounts may have been the most galling of "all" Amos' preaching. In other words, Amaziah's remark suggests that prior to the events described in 7:10–17 Amos had done plenty of preaching in Israel. And it is also likely that, in light of Amos' strong reply (7:14–17) and the additional judgment vision of 8:1–3, Amaziah's warning did not succeed in silencing Amos. Thus his delivery of oracles on Yahweh's behalf likely continued for some time. From this it may be inferred that the relative placement of 7:1–8:3 is not so much thematic as chronological. This material constituted neither the beginning nor the end of Amos' preaching.

Beyond this it is not possible to infer either a strictly chronological or a strictly thematic ordering for most of the oracles. The placement of the restoration promise oracles (9:11–15) at the end of the book, however, is probably thematic. The outlook of such oracles, following the Mosaic covenant order, is more distant in the future than that of any of the judgment oracles: national restoration follows national punishment. Thus often in the ordering of prophetic books, judgment oracles are placed toward the front and restoration promise oracles are placed toward the end. The orthodox sense of historical development made such an ordering so appropriate as to become quite common.

The structuring of material in the first six chapters shows no special organizing principle. After a brief oracle demonstrating Yahweh's power (1:2), the compound oracle against foreign nations ensues (1:3–2:16). But that oracle is also an oracle against Israel (2:6–16) and Judah (2:4–5), who, in the context, are treated to the same fate as if they were enemy nations. It is therefore inappropriate to see some special concern in the book's beginning with foreign nation oracles as opposed to oracles about Israel.

The brief oracle in 3:1–2 ("You only have I chosen . . . will punish . . .") and the oracle that follows it about the necessity of prophesying (3:3–8) function at least in part as a transition to a focus virtually exclusively on Israel, with the remaining oracles of chaps. 3–6 devoted to judgments against Israel. In each of these oracles evidence of covenant breaking is accompanied by prediction of punishment. Several of these oracles begin with an imperative ("Listen," "Proclaim," "Go," etc.) and two with "Woe" (5:18; 6:1).

After the quartet of visions in 7:1–8:3, judgment oracles of the general type observed in chaps. 3–6 resume, continuing through 9:10 (the "vision" in 9:1–6 being only minimally a vision). Then the two restoration promises of 9:11–15 complete the collection.

Tenuous reconstruction of the history of Israelite / Judean religion notwithstanding, there is no firm evidential basis for identifying Judean influence on the formation of the book. Quite conceivably Amos' oracles were gathered and published in response to the threat to Israelite orthodoxy posed by the Assyrian incursions during the second half of the eighth century. On the other hand, it was in Judah that the book was probably preserved as well as read most, after the fall of Samaria in 722.

AMOS' MESSAGE

Amos and the Covenant

Whatever one may wish to say about his style, Amos' message was essentially unoriginal on two counts: it was God's word, not his, and it conformed closely to the already long-revealed Mosaic covenant. The covenantal perspective governs the content to a substantial degree. The crimes Amos identifies are those the Sinai covenant defines as crimes (e.g., oppression of the poor, denial of inheritance rights, failure to observe sabbatical and jubilee laws, etc.). Moreover, the punishments Amos predicts for Israel all fit the curse categories established in the Pentateuch (see *General Introduction*). The restoration promises also comport closely with the paradigm statement of those promises in Leviticus and Deuteronomy (see also Hosea, *Introduction*). Thus, while certain of the particulars of the message God gave to Amos may be of intense interest, it must be remembered that his message was not essentially new: God, the sovereign enforcer of his covenant, would severely punish its violators but would not destroy them completely; consequently a remnant could one day again be his people and do his will. In a Pentateuchal passage as compact as Deut 4:21–31, the characteristic emphases of Amos' message are already set out. Amos therefore functions not as an innovator but as one called by God to remind and / or inform his generation of old truths. Israel was a covenant people (as were her neighbors, though perhaps implicitly, 1:3–2:5) whose God was determined to exercise his responsibilities in accordance with the covenant that bound Israel to him.

History in Amos

Klaus Koch (*The Prophets*, vol. 1; *The Assyrian Period*, tr. M. Kohl [Philadelphia: Fortress Press, 1983]) has called Israel's prophets "moral futurists," that is, people concerned with how moral behavior affects what happens subsequently in the world. Koch also places much of Amos' proclamation in the category of metahistory, "a theory about the cohesion of all reality as a single . . . complex process, in which Israel and Yahweh form the two essential poles" (p. 73). These observations, neither of which is entirely new or limited to Amos, provide useful perspectives on the book's content. God's message to Israel and to us through Amos especially emphasizes the relationship of morality to the course of history, and does indeed envision specific events against the backdrop of the full salvation history from creation to the eschaton—and particularly from Israel's creation to its restoration after exile.

As regards the near future, Amos prophesies mainly doom. The entire book, with the exception of 9:11–15, i.e., sixteen separate oracles including even the biographical account of 7:10–17, has as its focus the fact that Israel (and in the case of 1:3–2:5 Judah and other [*sic*] foreign nations) will be punished by some combination of defeat in war, disaster, capture, exile, and population decimation. As regards the more distant future, after the enforcement of the covenant curses against disobedient peoples, Yahweh will elevate his people, a *new* Israel, to a position of prominence in the world (9:11–15). The past also plays a significant role in Amos' message, though not to the same extent that prevails, for example, in Isaiah or Hosea. The recent past (from as early as perhaps 900 B.C. onward) was the era of the trans-Israelite border wars and their attendant atrocities condemned in 1:3–2:3. Israel had been hurt (2:13) but had also benefited in such wars (6:13). More distantly located in the past was the exodus from Egypt, the wilderness travels, and the conquest (2:9–10; 5:25; 9:7), as well as the general history of Israel's progressive corruption in the promised land (2:4–5; 2:11–12; 4:4; 5:5; 8:14). References to the past in Amos serve mainly to show that the present state of unfaithfulness to God's covenant is not a novelty, although they also demonstrate his sovereignty over Israel (2:10; 9:7). Amos does not, however, speak of the past for its own sake. His focus is set on what is coming and why. The past is part of this "why."

Amos and Yahweh's Sovereignty

Amos portrays Yahweh as sovereign not only over (northern) Israel, but over all nations of the earth, over all creation, and over all individuals, including specifically Amos himself. Twice in address to Israel, Yahweh is called אלהיך "your God" (4:12; 9:15). But Yahweh is also God of all nations (1:3–2:3; see also below, "The Foreign Nations"). As יהוה צבאות "Yahweh of the Armies" (3:13, etc.), he is supreme in heaven. As creator and sustainer of the physical world (cf. especially the hymn fragments in 4:13; 5:8; and 9:5–6), he has control over all territories and, by implication, their populations. His very voice withers vegetation (1:2). He is sovereign over the individual, such as Amaziah and his family (7:17), and over Amos himself whose call to prophesy was, in terms of his career, unexpected (7:14–15) but irresistible (3:8). He can depose kings (7:9) and can destroy even his own people (e.g., 8:1–3).

Even from a minimalist point of view, Amos reflects an essential mono-theism, i.e., the view that Yahweh is supreme and all-powerful God, whether or not other lesser "gods" may exist. Beyond this, however, the consistent outlook of the book is in fact straightforwardly monotheistic, in contrast to the prevailing polytheistic theologies of Amos' day, even in his native Judah and in Israel.

The Foreign Nations

In Amos, reference to foreign nations is concentrated in 1:3–2:16. There the systematic excoriation of the repeated שלשה . . . ארבעה ("three . . . four") covenant violations of Israel's neighbors, including Judah, yields in like manner to a lengthy denunciation of Israel's sins, demonstrating that Israel itself has become, in effect, a nation foreign to Yahweh. This rejection of Israel at the outset of the book (curse type 1; cf. *General Introduction*) reminds one of the opening oracles in Hosea, where the theme of Israel's no longer being Yahweh's people and he no longer their God has a similar function—to establish the proposition that the divine covenant has finally been abrogated.

Significant about the oracles against foreign nations is their unmistakable implication that Israel's God has a covenant relationship with nations other than Israel: Yahweh is the punisher of the sins of Aram, Moab, etc. Their "gods" have no role in this. Moreover, the punishments predicted and the sins described in these oracles reflect quite directly the Sinai covenant sanc-tions categories. It is not new, however, to read of Yahweh controlling the des-tiny of foreign kings (1:8, 15; note the references to "royal fortifications"—ארמנות—through 2:5). Already in the previous century the prophet Elisha had served as a herald of the assassination and succession of Ben-Hadad by Hazael in Aram (2 Kgs 8:7–15). But the intense portrayal of Yahweh's control over foreign nations (cf. also 3:9; 4:10; 6:14; 9:7) is noteworthy in Amos, the earliest of the "writing" prophets.

Amos the Geographer

As a dealer in large quantities of livestock, Amos may have traveled exten-sively in Israel and its environs (cf. P. C. Craigie, "Amos the *nōqēd* in the Light of Ugaritic," *SR* 11 [1982] 29–33). However, one must assume that the places mentioned in the book were generally known to Amos' audience if the oracles were to make any sense. Thus it is common knowledge, not special geographical expertise, that is reflected in Amos' words. Nevertheless, the attention paid to geographical issues and affinities is intense.

The complex oracle against foreign nations (1:1–2:16) is carefully organized so that the points of the compass are touched in polar order: Aram to the northwest (1:3–5), Philistia to the southwest (1:6–8), Tyre to the northwest (1:9–10), and Edom to the southeast (1:11–12), with Israel itself being finally centered on. In each instance, the capital or leading cities of a nation are carefully identified. Indeed, Damascus' relative position is further fixed by mention of its relative location (1:5).

Amos' frequent attention to Samaria is well known (3:9, 12; 4:1; 6:1; 8:14), as is his concern for the covenant disobedience at Bethel (3:14; 4:4; 5:5–6; 7:10, 13). Other Israelite-Judean sites figure prominently as well: Carmel (1:2; 9:3), Gilgal (4:4), Beersheba (5:5; 8:14), Lo Debar (6:13), Karnaim (6:13), and Dan (8:14). Particularly striking is the emphasis on the transjordan city of Succoth (9:11), whose rebuilding symbolizes the restoration of the Davidic empire's prestige and power. Amos' oracles also contain references to non-Israelite locales such as Damascus (5:27), Lebo-Hamath (6:14), Calneh, Hamath, and Gath (6:2), Crete (9:7), Kir (1:5; 9:7), Edom (9:12), and, of course, Egypt (2:10; 3:1; 3:9; 4:10; 8:8; 9:5, 7). This frequent representation of geographical data has two effects: it gives the hearer / reader a concrete sense of the involvement of God in the human sphere, and it reinforces the sense that Yahweh is sovereign over all peoples and places. Yahweh's control and his implicit covenant extend everywhere.

Amos and Economics

Yahweh's concern for the plight of the poor and the decadence of the rich pervades the book. The misuse and abuse of economically weak people by those with economic power is condemned from the outset—in connection with the slave sales following the border wars mentioned in 1:3–2:16 (esp. 1:6, 9) and quite forcefully in the initial portrayal of oppression within Israel itself (2:6–8). Samaria was obviously a center of economic discrimination (3:9, 10; 4:1), although such practices generally existed throughout the nation as well (5:12; 8:4–6). While idle, rich living virtually depends on the exploitation of others, this fact is not overtly mentioned at several points where high living is condemned. As Jesus taught (Matt 6:24; cf. 1 Tim 6:10), the danger of materialism is not only in its unfairness to others but in the godless self-centeredness that corrupts an individual. It is that very godlessness—without mention of oppression per se—that is depicted in some of the oracles against the idle rich (3:15; 6:1–6; 6:8). Amos portrays Yahweh as offended both by exploitation and by "conspicuous consumption."

Judicial Corruption

Juries of community elders probably decided most civil and criminal court cases in the Israel of Amos' day. Many of their decisions reflected an apparently prevailing attitude that the Mosaic covenant protections against the loss of inherited land were archaic and needlessly restrictive. They felt free to preside over case after case in which heavily indebted farmers had their property confiscated as payment to lenders (2:6, 8; 3:10 [?]; 5:12), and they paid no heed to dishonesty in the marketplace (5:11; 8:5–6). No other prophet was inspired to give such a proportion of scrutiny to the justice system of Israel. The courts, or the justice process, are explicitly described in 2:7, 8; 5:10, 12, 15, and the general state of national injustice in 3:10; 5:7–24; and 6:12. Israel in the part and the whole was guilty of an absence of what is "right" (צדק, צדקה) and thus what is of "justice" (משפט). The court process at the city gates throughout the land should have vindicated the needy against the exploiters. Instead it handed them over, "turning aside" (סר) the justice due them (2:7). The "needy" (אביונים, 2:6; 4:1; 5:12; 8:4, 6), the "poor" (דלים, 2:7; 4:1; 5:11; 8:6) and the "oppressed" (ענוים, 2:7; 8:4) are in Amos also the "righteous" (צדיקים, 2:6; 5:12). Their innocence, however, was not protected by Israel's legal practices. This structural, endemic violation of the covenant at the very point where people were seeking recourse for their difficulties constituted indisputable evidence that Israel deserved the covenant's punishments. The injustice passages are thus all linked to predictions of destruction and exile. A nation that no longer has even the decency to maintain a fair and disinterested legal system is a nation deserving destruction.

Idolatry and Immorality

On God's behalf Amos denounced Israel's idolatry, not simply because idolatry was a fraudulent means of worship, but also because it was a system of life which in contrast to covenant religion required no personal ethics, thus allowing its practitioners to exploit others for their own gain. Idolatry was rampant in Israel, a condition reflected by the wide distribution of attacks on it throughout the book. Judah's idolatry is a central factor in its apostasy (2:4) as is Israel's (2:8—note the language אלהיהם "their god"). The opposition to orthodoxy reflected in 2:12 may also reflect the acceptance of an alternative system, which in some cases may have been essentially Yahwistic, either exclusively or predominantly, but because it was carried on in clear contradiction to the Mosaic covenant (Deut 12:1–19) it was idolatrous, a rival religion. Consequently, the heterodox worship at Bethel and/or other covenantally illegal cult sites such as Gilgal and Beersheba is categorically condemned (3:14; 4:4–5; 5:4–5; cf. 7:10–13).

At 5:26 and 8:14 explicit mention is made of idolatry. The virtually universal assumption of the ancient world, that representations of gods and goddesses made present their essence and aid, had been welcomed more and more into Israel. Though the excesses of Ahab's day (874–853 B.C.), when Yahwistic religion was all but expunged from the north (1 Kgs 18, 19), were not repeated in Jeroboam's reign, the witness of Amos and Hosea to idolatry, as also attested in 2 Kgs 14:24, confirms the adulteration of Israelite religion. Amos mentions both Bethel (e.g., 4:4) and Dan (8:14), the centers where the golden bull-idols were worshiped. Samaria also appears to have had its idol (8:14), but whether this was associated with Yahweh or not cannot easily be determined.

Amos' oracles reflect the presence of plenty of regular, heartfelt worship experiences in the lives of the people (5:21–28; 8:3). But in the absence of orthodox, covenantal religion and in the presence of idolatry and personal/social immorality, this religion was hateful to God (5:21). Amos makes no attacks on either priests or prophets as a class, as, for example, Hosea does (Hos 4:4–9; 5:1–3). Prophets are mentioned positively (2:12; 3:8), perhaps according to the view that only true prophets of Yahweh are legitimately prophets at all.

The Unity of North and South

Throughout the OT God's people are viewed as an essential unity in spite of the permanent political division that tore Israel from Judah upon the death of Solomon in 931 B.C. Amos reflects this presumption of unity in two ways. First, certain oracles either link Israel and Judah closely (e.g., 6:1, "complacent in Zion . . . secure in Mount Samaria") or speak of the "family of Israel" (בית ישראל, 5:25), "Jacob" (6:8), the "entire family" (3:1), "Israel . . . from Egypt" (9:7), etc. in a context that leaves no doubt that the entire nation is being considered, even if the actual audience may have been northern. Second, the restoration promises of 9:11–15 reflect the common prophetic (cf. Isa. 11:10–16; Jer 33:7–24; Ezek 37:15–28; etc.) expectation of reunification under a new David (9:11) with the original full benefit of occupying the promised land (9:14–15). Thus Amos, by no means uniquely, portrays Israel and Judah as awaiting the same general future by reason of their sameness under the divine covenant. Attempts to differentiate a later, pseudepigraphic Judean corpus from Amos' "original" oracles have always run afoul of this reality in one way or another (see below).

Exile

Amos never mentions Assyria, the nation that eventually conquered Israel and deported many of its citizens. In the era of Amos' prophetic activity (ca. 760 B.C.) this is to be expected. Assyria was a dormant power, beset by border wars and internal strife (cf. the commentary on Jonah) and hardly a threat to Israel. How could Amos' audience, then, make sense of his words about exile?

The answer is that they had, in fact, ample precedent for understanding such practice. The precedents are threefold. (1) The "literary" precedent— that of the covenant—would have served adequately as a clarification for those who still knew and/or respected what the covenant taught about the danger of exile as a result of disobedience (e.g., Lev 26:33; Deut 28:64–68; cf. Exod 20:12). (2) Informed Israelites would be well aware that for at least a century prior to Amos' day the practice of deporting and resettling conquered populations had been carried out by Assyria and the kingdom of Urartu. Indeed, as A. Goetze points out (*Kleinasien: Kulturgeschichte des Alten Orients,* 2d ed. [Munich: C. H. Beck, 1957] 196–97), Urartu managed the deportation of 50,000 captives after one of its conquests. There is reason to believe that Assyria may also have taken captives from Damascus after the subjugation of Ben-Hadad by Adad-Nirari III in 800 B.C. (cf. 2 Kgs 13:5). (3) In the border wars of the ninth and eighth centuries among the nations surrounding Israel and/or these nations and Israel itself, captives were taken to be resold as slaves en masse to other localities (1:6; 1:9). While these deportations were apparently undertaken more for profit than for purposes of political suppression, each was nevertheless termed a גלות "exile" by Amos.

Finally, as to the concept of becoming captives in a foreign land, nothing was more strongly etched in the national historical memory of Israelites than their sometime sojourn in Egypt, from which miraculous rescue had been necessary. The Israelites identified themselves as a people redeemed from slavery and given a land not originally their own. The prediction of removal from that very land to an existence of—at least virtual—slavery once again (cf. Deut 28:68) must have been a hateful, though fully comprehensible, message to hear.

PREVIOUS RESEARCH ON AMOS

Until modern critical biblical scholarship became widespread in the early part of the last century, the book of Amos was usually considered a theologically unified collection from the hand of Amos himself. The biographical account of 7:10–17 was most often assumed to be the composition of a disciple, though a few scholars also attributed this portion of the book to Amos, assuming that he was writing about himself in the third person.

Since that time, however, Amos has only rarely been considered a book whose parts were all genuinely the product of their reputed author.

An assumption on the part of many scholars engaged in literary criticism has been that scripture is neither univocal nor consistent. This has produced a tendency toward atomism in the analysis of collections of prophetic oracles. As a result one sees in the case of the book of Amos a history of attempts (1) to isolate distinct units at the smallest levels, i.e., to consider the book a compendium of many distinct, originally unrelated elements combined editorially into longer oracles whose unity is evident only at a surface level; and to (2) discern various layers of development historically and / or theologically, so that the book is judged to be the product of centuries of development from an original core of genuine materials.

In the 1960s and 1970s OT scholarship began gradually to move away from atomism and to be willing to recognize larger—sometimes multichapter—units of prophetic composition. This trend was to some extent influenced by the rise of rhetorical criticism in the 1960s, with its emphasis on literary wholes, and also by so-called canonical criticism, with its emphasis on the unity of the finished scripture as more important than the supposed compositional stages (see B. Childs, *Introduction to the Old Testament as Scripture* [Philadelphia: Fortress Press, 1979]). But it occurred also partly as the result of a simple reaction against atomism, which had yielded few useful results theologically. Nevertheless, the book of Amos has continued to be subject to atomistic analysis and to the assumption that if a portion of a book might have been of particular interest in a given era, it was likely composed in that era.

For example, Rudolph (*Joel, Amos, Obadja, Jonah*. KAT 13 / 2 [Gütersloh: G. Mohn, 1971]) devotes at least 10 percent of his introductory section on the structure of Amos to a discussion of how the superscription (1:1) is composite, consisting of an early core from Amos' circle ("the words of Amos . . . earthquake"), supplemented later from a Judean source by the remainder of v 1, in order to fix the date for Judean readers of another century. Or, for example, J. L. Mays (*Amos*, OTL [Philadelphia: Westminster, 1969]), who attributes "the large part of the material . . . with confidence to Amos," nevertheless follows strongly entrenched scholarly tradition in identifying the oracles against Tyre (1:9–10), Edom (1:11–12), and Judah (2:4–5) as secondary, from the exilic period, as are also parts or all of 1:1–2; 3:7; 4:13; 5:8–9; 8:8; 9:5–6. H. W. Wolff's commentary on Amos (*Joel, Amos,* Hermeneia [Philadelphia: Fortress, 1977]), followed to some extent by Coote (*Amos Among the Prophets* [Philadelphia, Fortress, 1981]), employs straightforwardly circular reasoning to identify a core of genuine sayings from Amos, supplemented successively by (1) additions from a circle of eighth-century disciples; (2) additions made during the late seventh-century reign of Josiah in Judah; (3) a Deuteronomistic redaction sometime thereafter (cf. W. H. Schmidt, *ZAW* 77 [1965] 163–93); and (4) a postexilic optimistic supplement (9:11–15).

Form-critical studies of Amos have for the most part proved useful to its interpretation. Gunkel's students H. Gressmann (*Amos,* SAT [Göttingen: Vandenhoeck & Ruprecht, 1910]) and E. Balla (*Die Droh- und Scheltworte des Amos* [Leipzig: A. Edelmann, 1926]) developed with regard to Amos their teacher's identifications of *threats* and *rebukes* as basic prophetic oracular types. The "threats" may now be understood as covenant curse-fulfillment announcements and the "rebukes" as presentations of evidence that the covenant was indeed violated.

Analyses of Amos by proponents of a "myth and ritual" approach, following Mowinckel (e.g., H. H. Rowley, "Was Amos a Nabi?" in *FS O. Eissfeldt* [Halle: Niemeyer, Studien," *ZAW* 62 [1950] 10–52), have not proved very useful. This school views Amos as a cultic prophet, a position for which evidence could not be more lacking. Likewise, support for Amos as a regular in Israelite wisdom circles (S. Terrien, "Amos and Wisdom," *Israel's Prophetic Heritage* [New York: Harper, 1962] 108–15; and Wolff, *Amos,* Hermeneia, 1977) is minimal. Of recent works on Amos, the commentary by J. L. Mays and the essays by J. D. W. Watts (*Vision and Prophecy in Amos* [Grand Rapids: Eerdmans, 1958]) are especially noteworthy for their cautious, empirical approach which explores data in and about the book while generally avoiding inventive theorization.

The Title and Time (1:1)

Bibliography

Bič, M. "Der Prophet Amos—ein Haepatoskopos." *VT* 1 (1951) 293–96. **Budde, K.** "Die Überschrift des Buches Amos und des Propheten Heimat." In *Semitic Studies in Memory of Rev. Dr. Alexander Kohut,* ed. G. A. Kohut. Berlin, 1897. 106–110. **Craigie, P. C.** "Amos the *nōqēd* in the Light of Ugaritic." *SR* 11 (1982) 29–33. **Fuhs, H. F.** "Amos 1:1: Erwägungen zur Tradition und Redaktion des Amosbuches." *FS G. J. Botterweck.* Ed. H. J. Fabry. Köln / Bonn: Hanstein, 1977. 271–89. **Gilead, C.** "Amos— From the Herdsmen in Tekoa." *BMik* 18 (1972) 375–81. [Heb.] **Isbell, C. D.** "A Note on Amos 1:1." *JNES* 36 (1977) 213–14. **Murtonen, A. E.** "The Prophet Amos— a Hepatoscoper?" *VT* 2 (1952) 170–71. **Peiser, F. E.** *"Šenatayim lipne hara'aš:* Eine philologische Studie." *ZAW* 36 (1916) 218–24. **Segert, S.** "Zur Bedeutung des Wortes *nōqēd.*" VT Sup 16. Leiden: E. J. Brill, 1967. 279–83. **Soggin, J. A.** "Das Erdbeben von Amos 1:1 und die Chronologie der Könige Ussia und Jotham von Juda." *ZAW* 82 (1970) 117–21. **Stoebe, H. J.** "Der Prophet Amos und sein bürgerlicher Beruf." *WuD* n.f. 5 (1957) 160–81. **Waitz, Y.** "Amos: Sheep Breeder, Cattle Breeder, and Sycamore Fig Slitter." *BMik* 13 (1968) 141–44. [Heb.] **Wright, J.** "Did Amos Inspect Livers?" *AusBR* 23 (1975) 3–11. **Yadin, Y.,** et al. *Hazor II: An Account of the Second Season of Excavations, 1956.* Jerusalem: Magnes Press, 1960.

Translation

[1] *The words of Amos, one of*[a] *the sheep breeders*[b] *of*[c] *Tekoa, which he saw concerning Israel*[d] *in the time of Uzziah king of Judah, and Jeroboam, son of Joash king of Israel, two years before the earthquake.*

Notes

1.a. G (οἱ ἐγένοντο) would reflect a plural verbal clause, אשר היו "which took place . . ." with the sense that the *words* took place among the sheep breeders in Tekoa, as if Amos preached there first. However, the singular of MT אשר היה, lit., "who was," is followed by Vg and Tg.

1.b. G has νακκαρίμ (G[A]: Ἀκκαρείμ), mistaking the *daleth* of נקדים "sheep breeders" for a *resh* and taking the word as a place name or technical name. The word נקד was obviously unknown to some of the ancient translators, judging from their varied renderings (θ': *nocedim;* Lucian and the Catena: Καριαθιαρειμ ("Kirjath-jearim"). Otherwise, α' σ' Vg Tg all reflect MT. Bič's suggestion (*VT* 1 [1951] 293–96) that נקד means "hepatoscoper" (one who divines the future by examining animal livers) has proved more amusing than convincing.

1.c. Several G MSS read here ἐν θεκουε "in Tekoa," which may reflect a Heb. *Vorlage* of בתקוע, though it may also be due either to an inner-Greek corruption (ἐν for ἐκ) or an anomalous but acceptable idiomatic translation of MT.

1.d. Surprisingly, G has Ἰερουσαλήμ "Jerusalem" instead of Ἰσραήλ "Israel." Could the change be purely accidental, or based somehow on the format in Isa 1:1? W. R. Harper's suggestion (*Amos and Hosea,* ICC 2 [Edinburgh: T. & T. Clark, 1905]) that the confusion resulted from similar abbreviations remains unprovable.

Form / Structure / Setting

This editorial title to the book of Amos has a form not significantly different from that of the titles of several prophetic books (cf. Isa 1:1; Hos 1:1; Mic 1:1; Zeph 1:1, and especially Jer 1:1–3) which similarly list a prophet's lineage and the king(s) contemporaneous with him. The introductory phrase (דברי עמוס) is modified in this case by two relative clauses, one identifying Amos' profession and home territory, the other identifying the words' object, i.e., Israel. The title also contains two dating phrases, one identifying the two kings during whose reign Amos prophesied (Uzziah and Jeroboam [II]) and the other identifying the year he preached—or began to preach—as "two years before the earthquake."

Aside from the highly specific dates in Haggai and the beginning of Zechariah, this fixing of Amos' prophetic activity to a single year is largely unparalleled. The dates of Uzziah's reign (791–740; until 767 as coregent) and Jeroboam II's reign (793–753) are well known; the time of the earthquake is another matter. Famous as a catastrophe in Israelite history (cf. Zech 14:5), it cannot otherwise be dated with certainty. Yadin (*Hazor II*, 24–37) dated the earthquake to about 760 B.C. on the basis of destruction levels at Hazor and elsewhere, but that dating is subject to an error of a decade or two in either direction. The superscription cannot be taken to indicate that Jeroboam II was still alive when Amos finished his ministry. As the attention paid to Southern rather than Northern kings in Hos 1:1 also demonstrates, the Southern audience for whom these titles were written did not know the confusing shifts in the monarchy of the Northern Kingdom after the death of Jeroboam II well enough for the editor (whether prophet, disciple, or later compiler) to bother listing the Northern kings other than Jeroboam II. Thus Zechariah, Shallum, Menahem, Pekahiah, and possibly Pekah, who were also contemporaneous with Uzziah (i.e., between 753 and 740 B.C.), are omitted, and Uzziah the Judean is listed before Jeroboam the Israelite. Because the listing of kings is slanted toward the interests of the Judeans, and is selective, we therefore have no way of knowing whether or not the common assumption that Amos preceded Hosea is correct. However, Amos' oracles surely preceded Hosea's *later* oracles, since Hosea's work is dated considerably beyond the death of Uzziah in 740 B.C.

Although the latest data for Amos' prophetic activity is 740, the earliest reasonable date would probably not precede 767, the year King Amaziah died and Uzziah became sole monarch rather than simply coregent. This conclusion rests on an ultimately unsupportable argument from silence: the editor would have mentioned Amaziah in 1:1 had Amos' ministry begun while the older king was still alive, and Zech 14:5 would have mentioned Amaziah rather than simply Uzziah in connection with the earthquake if it had happened earlier than 767. Thus the title is probably enough evidence to fix Amos' preaching not earlier than 767. And the latest date would be 742, since the latest date for the earthquake would have been 740, the end of Uzziah's reign, and Amos' words preceded it by two years.

Comment

"Words" (דברי) is here a technical term, which denotes Amos' sayings, i.e., oracles (cf. Job 31:40; Eccl 1:1; Neh 1:1), thus emphasizing not the individual words so much as their grouping into units of prophetic message for Israel. While most other prophetic collections begin with singulars such as "word" (דבר; e.g., Hos 1:1; Joel 1:1; Mic 1:1) or "revelation" (חזון; e.g., Isa 1:1; Obad 1) or "pronouncement" (משא; e.g., Nah 1:1; Hab 1:1), the use of the plural here and in Jer 1:1 hardly can be seen as differentiating these books' contents from the others. Rather, it is evidence that the superscriptions to the prophetic books, which include other formats as well, were probably produced and fixed independently of one another. What they share, as one would expect, is a concern to identify briefly the contents of the books they head; the fact that they are by no means all precisely alike betrays the variations that different authors, editors, or compilers would naturally produce.

The name of the prophet, Amos, is almost certainly a hypocoristicon of the fuller form, Amasiah (עמסיה), as found in 2 Chr 17:16. Among the other prophetic books, only the superscription to Jeremiah (1:1) also mentions the employment and hometown of the prophet. Brief as it is, the superscription to Amos is one of the most detailed in the OT prophetic corpus. Amos is called a נקד, which judging from its use in 2 Kgs 3:4 and in Ugaritic (IAB, Col 6) probably means small cattle raiser / breeder rather than merely "shepherd." It is interesting to note that Amos identifies himself as a בקר, a "(large) cattle breeder," in 7:14, suggesting that he may have dealt in sheep, goats, cows, and oxen. Whether he was the owner of such a business, or merely an employee, cannot be known. But it would be a mistake to assume on the basis of his oracles against the rich (e.g., 4:1–2; 5:11–12; 8:4–6) that Amos himself was a poor man.

Tekoa, Amos' hometown, is mentioned several other times in the OT (2 Sam 14:2, 4, 9; 2 Chr 11:6; 20:20; Jer 6:1). It was located about six miles south of Jerusalem. Amos was thus a Judean, as 7:12 confirms, whose "words" were nevertheless directed to the Northern Kingdom (על ישראל).

The use of חזה "saw" with דברי "words . . ." is not unusual in Hebrew in spite of its seeming illogic in English translation. The verb חזה can have the sense of "perceive a revelation" and is sometimes used with revelations that are purely verbal, having no hint of visual content (cf. Isa 2:1; 13:1; Ezek 13:8). The name "Yahweh" is not mentioned in the title, but the wording clearly implies that Amos' words were not his own.

Amos' words are here dated *in some measure* to a year which preceded the famous earthquake (Zech 14:5) in Uzziah's reign. It cannot be concluded from the phrasing of the title, however, that all of his oracles were received and delivered in that one year. Just as the book's content is described restrictively (as "concerning Israel," when in fact he preached about several other nations, including Judah, cf. Isa 1:1), so the wording of the dating may be restrictive, and thus no proof of a brief tenure in the North. Internal factors elsewhere in the book do suggest for Amos, however, a length of prophetic activity considerably shorter than that of his contemporary Hosea.

Explanation

The concerns of the superscription are three: to inform the reader of the identity, origin, and era of the author; to identify the book as divine prophecy; and to link at least some of the oracles to a period preceding a famous earthquake.

Who Amos is (a sheep breeder conveying prophetic oracles), where he came from (a Southerner preaching to Northerners), and when he preached (in the latter days of the reign of Jeroboam II—days notorious for greed, corruption, and apostasy) are of genuine interest to the readers of the book. Samaria fell to the Assyrians in 722 b.c., within a few decades of Amos' preaching. The main audience for the book was to be those who would read it in Judah in the decades and centuries that followed. It was for this audience that the Judean-oriented superscription was composed. Amos' oracles, no matter how early they may have been collected and written, probably had little popularity in the North. By their nature they were hardly calculated to be popular with the people of the disobedient nation to whom Amos was especially sent by Yahweh. But in the South, where orthodoxy, if not orthopraxy, still had its adherents in large numbers, Amos' words were surely taken as a kind of warning by analogy. The doom he had predicted for the North had actually transpired because Israel was, as he had said, a sinful nation which had broken the divine covenant. And, therefore, what of Judah?

Amos prophesied *before* the great earthquake. Some of his sayings appear to predict an earthquake as a vehicle for carrying out the covenant destruction / death curses (3:14–15; 6:11; 9:1, 9), and part of his fame in Judah as a true prophet may have derived from this perception. As Zech 14:5 makes clear, the earthquake was seen as a divine punishment. That Amos should have announced its coming is proof that he did not invent his words, but "saw" them. The origin of the book's message is Yahweh himself.

Yahweh the Lion Sends Desolation   (1:2)

Bibliography

Bertholet, A. "Zu Amos 1:2." *FS G. N. Bonwetsch.* Leipzig, 1918. 1–12. **Budde, K.** "Amos 1:2." *ZAW* 30 (1910) 37–41. **Hillers, D.** *Treaty-Curses and the Old Testament Prophets. BeO* 16. Rome: Pontifical Biblical Institute, 1964. 54–56. **Lust, J.** "A Gentle Breeze or a Roaring Thunderous Sound? Elijah at Horeb: 1 Kings xix 12." *VT* 25 (1975) 111–15. **Weiss, M.** "In the Footsteps of One Biblical Metaphor." *Tarbiz* 34 (1964–65) 107–28. (Heb.).

Translation

1:2 *Yahweh will roar from Zion;*
He will raise his voice from Jerusalem.

ª *The shepherds' pastures will dry up;*
Even ᵇ *the top of Carmel will wither.* ªᶜᵈ

Notes

2.a-a. Tg apparently interprets רעים "shepherds" as symbolic of "kings" and rewords the couplet accordingly: ויצדון מדורי מלכיא ויחרב תקוף כרכיהון "(And) the dwellings of the kings will become desolate, and the fortification of their castles will become a waste."

2.b. The *waw* that initiates this line of the couplet is required by the sense and thus must be retained in the meter (7 syllables).

2.c. The second couplet is clearly the result of the first and could even be considered the apodosis of a conditional sentence comprising the verse. The simple juxtaposition of the couplets indicates adequately in English both the resultative and the conditional.

2.d. The impf verbs have usually been translated as present tense; but the future tense is more appropriate to a curse / punishment announcement.

Form / Structure / Setting

Amos 1:2 is sometimes linked to 1:1, sometimes to 1:3–2:16, and sometimes treated as an independent pericope. There is nothing about the grammatical structure of the verse that decides which of these options is best. Hundreds of independent passages and, indeed, several entire OT books begin with converted imperfect forms analogous to the phrase ויאמר "[And] he said" which begins 1:2. Moreover, the phrase כה אמר יהוה "This is what Yahweh says" does not necessarily indicate the beginning of a new pericope; it is used both medially and terminally, as well as initially, in OT prophetic passages. So the question of the interrelationship of 1:2 to what precedes it and what follows it must be decided strictly on the grounds of form and content.

The form of the verse is that of the curse announcement, i.e., the announcement that a curse (or curses) of the Mosaic covenant is now about to be enforced by Yahweh via the type of punishment that the curse calls for. Since the poetic announcement of punishment in 1:2 mentions only Israel and not the surrounding nations otherwise excoriated in the poem in 1:3–2:16, it is not likely that 1:2 was intended to serve as an introduction specifically to the latter pericope. Moreover, its meter (7:7, 7:7 in the vocalization of the eighth century B.C.) has no parallel in 2:3–16, and certainly not in the prose title or superscription of 1:1. And the speaker in 1:2 is someone other than Yahweh, whereas in 2:3–16 it is Yahweh himself. Accordingly, the two-couplet poem is best considered an independent unit. Functionally, it is a thematic prelude to the whole message of Amos in somewhat the same way that the vision of Yahweh's chariot in Ezek 1 captures the essence of the message of judgment and restoration that Ezekiel will proclaim.

Amos 1:2 cannot be dated relative to the rest of the book. There is no way to determine if it was originally independent or part of a larger oracle and selected as a thematic introduction to the book by Amos or another compiler, or even if it was perhaps the very first oracle Amos proclaimed.

Comment

The two poetic couplets that constitute v 2 stand as an introduction to the entire book. By means of two simple synonymous parallelisms found also in Joel 4:16 (cf. also Jer 25:30 and Isa 66:6), Amos announced that Yahweh's word to Israel was a word of judgment, that he intended to enforce the curses of his covenant against his disobedient vassals, and that destruction would be the result.

The first couplet speaks of Yahweh as "roaring" (שאג), thereby implicitly comparing him metaphorically to a lion. Much in the manner of Hos 5:14

("I am like a lion to Ephraim . . ."), this usage suggests that the covenant curse of harm from wild animals (cf. Lev 26:22 and Deut 32:24) was to be carried out by Yahweh himself. Like a lion roaring its intention to leave its home to seek prey, Yahweh's voice, as mediated through his prophet Amos, announces death to his enemies. The carefully crafted poem is typically elliptical in that the full process whereby the announcement of a curse fulfillment eventuates in disaster for Israel is left unspecified. But the net effect is very clear: judgment is to fall upon Israel. The more explicit parallel in Jer 25:30 leaves no doubt that the language employed is that of curse.

The poem identifies Yahweh's proper earthly dwelling place as Jerusalem. The Northern cult, with its main sanctuaries at Bethel and Dan and its subsidiary sanctuaries dotting the landscape, was an illegal cult (Deut 12). From the one place he had legitimately caused his name to dwell, Jerusalem (cf. 9:11), Yahweh's voice (קול)—his word—had come forth as a precursor to devastation.

Relevant to its use in Amos 1:2, the word קול has a special meaning in the OT beyond its common meanings of "voice" and "sound." The plural, קולות, is often translated "thunder" (e.g., Exod 9:23 et passim; 19:16). The combination נתן קולות, lit., "to produce sounds," normally means "to thunder." In Job 37:2, 4, 5 and 1 Sam 7:10, קול in the singular carries the sense of "thunder." The קול יהוה "voice of Yahweh" in Ps 29:3, 4, 5, 7, 8, 9 is obviously theophanic thunder (cf. also Ps 18:14[13]; 46:7[6]; and 68:34[33], where נתן קול means "to thunder"). It is therefore likely that יתן קולי as Amos uses it here could have connoted thundering. Indeed, throughout the Bible the voice of God is described as thunderous (not the "still small voice" of mistranslation; see J. Lust, "A Gentle Breeze or a Roaring Thunderous Sound?" *VT* 25 [1975] 111–15 on 1 Kgs 19:12). If so, there may be the hint of a futility curse in the poem. Thunder is usually associated with rain, and therefore with agricultural fertility, as is the case in the allegorical Ps 29. But the thunder Yahweh produces from Jerusalem will have the opposite effect—instead of the hoped for rain, it will produce drought. The second couplet of the verse vividly depicts a disastrous drought, one so severe it wilts even the high hillside pasturelands—indeed, even the very top of the lofty Carmel range, a lush area where plenty of water could still be found after three years of drought in the time of Elijah (1 Kgs 18:33–35). A drought so total as 1:2 depicts represents a horrific fulfillment of the Pentateuchal drought curses (Lev 26:19; Deut 28:22–24) and could result, naturally, in a whole gamut of agricultural disasters including the general desolation of the land.

Implicitly the poem declares that the covenant has been violated and that Yahweh must enforce its punishment provisions. Like a predatory lion, his voice "thunders"—not a thunder producing rain, but a thunder producing devastation.

Explanation

The encapsulation of three types of curses (wild animals, futility, drought) in a single, two-couplet poem is powerfully suggestive of the full range of divine wrath which the God of Zion will bring against his wayward people, Israel. The mere mention of Zion and Jerusalem as the origin of Yahweh's word and / or destructive action is a tacit condemnation of the false, degenerate Northern cult that the Southern farmer Amos was called by God to condemn.

Judgment was of necessity his primary message. The punishments specified by the Pentateuchal curses had to be unleashed. And in addition to the three mentioned above, would not the destructive earthquake that followed two years later also serve to confirm the effects of Yahweh's "thunder" against the North? Israel's fate was to be death and destruction, adumbrated in a variety of ways in this little poem of ominous language. The immediate future as God announced it through Amos was a future of punishment for a guilty nation.

Judgment for International and Israelite Atrocities (1:3–2:16)

Bibliography

Bach, R. "Gottesrecht und weltliches Recht in der Verkündigung des Propheten Amos." In *FS Günther Dehn*, ed. W. Schneemelcher. Neukirchen: Verlag der Buchhandlung des Erziehungsvereins, 1957. 23–34. **Barré, M.** "Amos 1:11 Reconsidered." *CBQ* 47 (1985) 420–27. ———. "The Meaning of *P ʾšbynw* in Amos 1:3–2:6." *JBL* 105 (1986) 611–31. **Bartlett, J. R.** "The Brotherhood of Edom." *JSOT* 2 (1977) 2–27. **Barton, J.** *Amos's Oracles against the Nations: A Study of Amos 1.3–2.5.* SOTSMS 6. Cambridge: Cambridge University Press, 1980. **Beaucamp, E.** "Amos 1–2: Le *pèshaʿ* d'Israel et celui des nations." *ScEs* 21 (1969) 435–41. **Beek, M. A.** "The Religious Background of Amos 2:6–8." *OTS* 5 (1948) 132–41. **Bentzen, A.** "The Ritual Background of Amos 1:2–2:16." *OTS* 8 (1950) 85–99. **Bewer, J. A.** "Critical Notes on Amos 2:7 and 8:4." *AJSL* 19 (1903) 116–17. **Blenkinsopp, J.** "The Prophetic Reproach." *JBL* 90 (1971) 267–78. **Botterweck, G. J.** "Zur Authentizität des Buches Amos." *BZ* 2 (1958) 176–89. **Bronznick, N.** "More on *hlk ʿl.*" *VT* 35 (1985) 98–99. **Christensen, D. L.** "The Prosodic Structure of Amos 1–2." *HTR* 67 (1974) 427–36. ———. *Transformations of the War Oracle in OT Prophecy: Studies in the Oracles Against the Nations.* HDR 3. Missoula, MT: Scholars Press, 1975. **Coote, R. B.** "Amos 1:11: *rhmyw.*" *JBL* 90 (1971) 206. **Dahood, M.** "Hebrew-Ugaritic Lexicography VIII." *Bib* 51 (1970) 391–404. ———. "To Pawn One's Cloak." *Bib* 42 (1961) 359–66. ———. "Ugaritic and the Old Testament." *ETL* 44 (1968) 35–54. **Diez Macho, A.** "Fragmente de Amos 1, 8–3, 7 en hebreo y targum babilonias." *EstBib* 19 (1960) 91–95. **Fishbane, M.** "Additional Remarks on *Rhmyw* (Amos 1:11)." *JBL* 91 (1972) 391–93. ———. "The Treaty Background of Amos 1:11 and Related Matters." *JBL* 89 (1970) 313–18. **Grether, H. G.** "Some Problems of Equivalence in Amos 1:3." *BT* 22 (1971) 116–17. **Grintz, J. M.** "*ʿl hglwtm glwt slmh lhsgyr lʾdwm.*" *BMik* 13, 1 (32) (1967–68) 24–26. **Happel, O.** "Am 2:6–16 in der Urgestalt." *BZ* 3 (1905) 355–67. **Haran, M.** "Some Problems of the Historical Background of 'Prophecies of the Nations' in the Book of Amos." *Yediot* 30 (1966) 56–69. [Heb.] ———. "Observations on the Historical Background of Amos 1:2–2:16." *IEJ* 18 (1968) 201–12. ———. "The Rise and Decline of the Empire of Jeroboam ben Joash." *VT* 17 (1967) 266–97. **Hayes, J. H.** "The Usage of Oracles Against Foreign Nations in

Israel." *JBL* 87 (1968) 81–92. **Held, M.** "Studies in Biblical Homonyms in the Light of Accadian." *JANESCU* 3 (1970) 46–55. **Hobbs, T. R.** "Amos 3:1b and 2:10." *ZAW* 81 (1969) 384–87. **Höffken, Peter.** "Zu den Heilzusätzen in der Völkerorakelsammlung des Jeremiabuches." *VT* 27 (1977) 398–412. **Knierim, R. P.** " 'I will not cause it to return.' in Amos 1 and 2." *Canon and Authority.* ed. G. W. Coats and B. O. Long. Philadelphia: Fortress Press, 1977. 163–75. **Lehming, S.** "Erwägungen zu Amos." *ZTK* 55 (1958) 145–69. **Lewis, J.** "An Asseverative לא in Psalm 100:3?" *JBL* 86 (1967) 216. **Lurie, B. Z.** "The Prophecies unto the Nations in the Book of Amos from the Point of View of History." *BMik* 54 (1972–73) 285–301. **Malamat, A.** "Amos 1:5 in the Light of the Til Barsip Inscriptions." *BASOR* 129 (1953) 25–26. **McAlpine, T. H.** "The Word against the Nations." *SBT* 5 (1975) 3–14. **Marti, K.** "Zur Komposition von Amos 1:3–2:3." In *Abhandlung zur semitischen Religionskunde und Sprachwissenschaft: Wolf Wilhelm Grafen von Baudissin zum 26. September 1917,* ed. W. Frankenberg and F. Küchler. BZAW 33. Giessen, 1918. 323–30. **Moran, W. L.** "A Note on the Treaty Terminology of the Sefire Stelas." *JNES* 22 (1963) 173–76. **Morgenstern, J.** "Amos Studies 1." *HUCA* 11 (1936) 130–40. **Müller, H-P.** "Die Wurzeln ʿyq, yʿq und ʿwq." *VT* 21 (1971) 556–64. ———. "Phönizien und Juda in exilisch-nachexilischer Zeit." *WO* 6 (1971) 189–204. **Muntingh, L. M.** "Political and International Relations of Israel's Neighboring Peoples according to the Oracles of Amos." *OTWSA* 75 (1966) 134–42. **Paul, S. P.** "Amos 1:3–2:3: A Concatenous Literary Pattern." *JBL* 90 (1971) 397–403. **Pfeifer, G.** "Denkformenanalyse als exegetische Methode, erläutert an Amos, 1, 2–2, 16." *ZAW* 88 (1976) 56–71. **Priest, J.** "The Covenant of Brothers." *JBL* 84 (1965) 400–406. **Puech, E.** "Milkom, le dieu ammonite, en Amos, 1:15." *VT* 27 (1977) 117–25. **Reider, J.** "Contributions to the Scripture Text." *HUCA* 24 (1952–53) 85–106. ———. "Etymological Studies in Biblical Hebrew." *VT* 4 (1954) 276–95. **Rendtorff, R.** "Zu Amos 2:14–16." *ZAW* 85 (1973) 226–27. **Richardson, H. N.** "Amos 2:13–16: Its Structure and Function." *SBL 1978 Seminar Papers.* Missoula, MT: Scholars Press, 1978, 361–67. **Roth, W. M. W.** "The Numerical Sequence x / x + 1 in the Old Testament." *VT* 12 (1962) 300–311. **Rudolph, W.** "Die angefochtenen Völkersprüche in Amos 1–2." In *Schalom: Studien zu Glaube und Geschichte Israels. FS A. Jepsen,* ed. K.-H. Bernhardt. Stuttgart: Calwer, 1971. 45–49. **Schoville, K. N.** "A Note on the Oracles of Amos Against Gaza, Tyre, and Edom." *Studies in Prophecy.* VTSup 26. Leiden: E. J. Brill, 1974. 55–63. **Schwantes, M.** "Profecia e Organização: Anotações à luz de um texto (Am 2, 6–16)." *EstBib* 5 (1985) 26–39. **Segert, S.** "A Controlling Device for Copying Stereotype Passages? (Amos i 3–ii 8, vi 1–6)." *VT* 34 (1984) 481–82. **Soper, B. K.** "For Three Transgressions and for Four: A New Interpretation of Amos 1:3, etc." *ExpTim* 71 (1959–60) 86–87. **Speiser, E. A.** "Of Shoes and Shekels." *BASOR* 77 (1940) 15–20. **Torrey, C. C.** "Notes on Am 2:7; 6:10; 8:3; 9:8–10." *JBL* 15 (1896) 151–54. **Ulrichsen, J. H.** "Oraklene i Amos 1, 3 ff." *NorTT* 85 (1984) 39–54. **Waard, J. de.** "A Greek Translation—Technical Treatment of Amos 1:15." *On Language, Culture and Religion: In Honor of Eugene A. Nida.* Ed. M. Black and W. Smalley. The Hague: Mouton, 1974. 111–18. **Weiss, M.** "Methodologisches über die Behandlung der Metaphor dargelegt an Am. 1, 2." *TZ* 23 (1967) 1–25. ———. "The Pattern of Numerical Sequence in Amos 1–2." *JBL* 86 (1967) 416–23. **Zolli, I.** "Note Esegetiche (Amos 2:7a)." *RSO* 16 (1936) 178–83.

Translation

Aram

1:3 *This is what Yahweh said:* [a]

Because of the multiple crimes [b] *of Damascus,*
I will not restore it, [c]

Because they threshed the pregnant women[d] *of Gilead*
With iron threshing sledges.

4   *I will send fire on Hazael's palace*
And it will consume Ben-Hadad's[a] *royal fortifications.*

5   *I will break the gate-bar of Damascus*
And will cut off him who reigns[a] *in the Valley of Aven,*[b]
And him who holds the scepter, from Beth-eden.[c]
The people of Aram will be exiled to Kir,[d]
                  Yahweh said.

Philistia

6 *This is what Yahweh said:*

Because of the multiple crimes of Gaza,
I will not restore it;

Because they exiled an entire[a] *population,*[b]
Handing them over to Edom.

7   *I will send fire on the wall of Gaza*
That will consume its royal fortifications.

8   *I will cut off him who reigns from Ashdod*
And him who holds the sceptre from Ashkelon.

I will turn my hand against Ekron,
Until the last of the Philistines perish,
              the Lord[a] *Yahweh said.*

Tyre

9 *This is what Yahweh said:*

Because of the multiple crimes of Tyre,
I will not restore it;

Because they handed over an entire population[a] *to Edom,*
And did not honor a brotherhood treaty.[b]

10   *I will send fire on the wall of Tyre*
That will consume its royal fortifications.

Edom

11 *This is what Yahweh said:*

Because of the multiple crimes of Edom,
I will not restore it;

Because he pursued his brother with the sword
And suppressed his compassion.[a]

His anger has been always[b] *alert*[c]
And his wrath on guard continually.

12   *I will send fire on Teman*
That will consume the royal fortifications of Bozrah.

Ammon

¹³ *This is what Yahweh said:*

> *Because of the multiple crimes of the Ammonites,*
> *I will not restore it;*
>
> *Because they tore open the pregnant women of Gilead*
> *In order to enlarge their own borders.*

¹⁴   *I will set fire to the wall of Rabbah*
> *That will consume its royal fortifications,*
>
> *Amid the war cry on the day of battle,*
> *Amid the raging wind* ᵃ *on the day of the storm.* ᵇ

¹⁵   *Their king* ᵃ *will go into exile,*
> *He* ᵇ *and his officials together,*
> > > *Yahweh said.*

Moab

²:¹ *This is what Yahweh said:*

> *Because of the multiple crimes of Moab,*
> *I will not restore it;*
>
> *Because he burned the bones*
> *Of the King of Edom to lime.*

²   *I will send fire on Moab*
> *That will devour the royal fortifications of Kerioth.*
>
> *Moab will die amid tumult,*
> *Amid the war cry and the sounding of the horn.*

³   *I will cut off the ruler from his midst,* ᵃ
> *And all his officials* ᵇ *I will kill along with him,*
> > > *Yahweh said.*

Judah

⁴ *This is what Yahweh said:*

> *Because of the multiple crimes of Judah,*
> *I will not restore it;*
>
> *Because they have rejected Yahweh's law,*
> *And have not kept his statutes.*
>
> *Their fakes* ᵃ *have led them astray,*
> *The ones their ancestors followed.*

⁵   *I will send fire on Judah*
> *That will consume the royal fortifications of Jerusalem.*

Israel: internal crimes

⁶ *This is what Yahweh said:*

> *Because of the multiple crimes of Israel,*
> *I will not restore it;*

Because they have sold the righteous for money,
And the needy in exchange for a pair of sandals.

7   *They trample* [a] *the heads of the poor into the dust of the earth,* [b]
     And they keep the oppressed from getting anywhere. [c]

     Father and son have sex with the same girl,
     Thereby profaning my holy name.

8   *They stretch out on clothes taken as collateral,*
     Beside every altar.

     They drink wine given to pay a fine,
     At the house of their god.

A long history of disobedience

9   *I am the one who destroyed the Amorite before them,*
     Whose height was as great as that of the cedars,
     And who was as strong as the oaks.
     I destroyed his fruit above and his root below.

10   *I am the one who brought you up from the land of Egypt.*
     I led you in the wilderness forty years,
     To take possession of the Amorite's land.

11   *I appointed some of your children* [a] *prophets*
     And some of your young people Nazirites. [b]
     Is that not so, Israelites? (Oracle of Yahweh)

12   *But you made the Nazirites drink wine,*
     And you commanded the prophets, "Do not prophesy."

The judgment sentence

13   *So I will make you bog down,* [a]
     As a cart bogs down
     When it is loaded with sheaves.

14   *The swift person will lose his ability to flee;*
     The strong person will have no strength.
     The soldier will not save himself;

15   *The archer will not stand his ground.*
     The fast runner will not escape; [a]
     The horse rider will not save himself.

16   *The very bravest* [a] *of the soldiers*
     Will flee naked on that day. (Oracle of Yahweh)

Notes

3.a. G has the past tense here, but the future tense (λέγει) for *'amar* elsewhere in the passage.
3.b. Lit., "three crimes . . . and four," a typical n : n + 1 numerical parallelism.
3.c. The options for translating אשיבנו are many. The verb שוב has perhaps the broadest,

most complex field of meaning of any Heb. verb (see W. L. Holladay, *The Root ŠÛBH in the Old Testament* [Leiden: E. J. Brill, 1958]). Here, the 3 m sg object suffix may well connote Yahweh's will or decision to punish (lit., "I will not revoke it"), though alternatives such as "I will not hold it (i.e., fire) back" or "Indeed (taking לא as an asseverative) I will pay it (i.e., my revenge / punishment) back," are quite possible. Our translation follows Barré, "The Meaning of *lᵉ ʾšybnw*."

3.d. Reading with G, L, and 5QAm. Tg reads "Those who dwell in the land of Gilead," while σ' and Vg have been conformed to MT's haplographic text. MT is metrically too short as it stands. Amos' frequent use of stock phrases in the passage argues against assuming a conflation from v 13. The prosaic את־ of MT is probably the corrupted remnant of an original הרות.

4.a. G (ᶜΑδερ) mistook *resh* for *daleth*.

5.a. G's κατοικοῦντας "inhabitants" supports MT, being merely an alternate translation.

5.b. MT's vocalization leads to the meaning "Evil Valley." G's vocalization of און, Ὤν, shows that the original vocalization may not have had the theological meaning that MT seems to give it. Amos' audience probably inferred no symbolic intent here.

5.c. Beth-eden means literally "place of pleasantness," but there is no reason to believe that Amos intends anything other than the simple geographical name, *contra* Wolff, 129 ("House of Pleasure") or M. Buber and F. Rosenzweig (*Bücher der Kündung* [Köln: Jakob Hegner, 1958] 633, "House of Lust").

5.d. G reads קריא ἐπίκλητος. Its *Vorlage* may have added the א of אמר to קר.

6.a. G τοῦ Σαλωμων misread שלמה as Solomon.

6.b. Or, "entire (local) populations."

8.a. אדני "Lord" is not reflected in G and may be secondary here, although it is attested widely in the other versions.

9.a. See n. 6.b.

9.b. Or, "friendship treaty."

11.a. Gʷ and *Hier* took *rḥm* literally to mean "womb," and Gᴮ took it more figuratively as "mother." G adds ἐπὶ γῆς "on the ground," but perhaps only to fill out the sense of שחת "suppressed."

11.b. For לעד G read εἰς μαρτύριον, i.e., לְעֵד "for a witness."

11.c. Reading, with Syr and Vg, ויטר from נטר in light of the clear parallelism with שמר "to keep."

14.a. G took סער as a verb καὶ σεισθήσεται "will be tossed about."

14.b. G interpreted סופה as συντελείας αὐτῆς "her end."

15.a. Gᴸ, α', σ', Vg read Milcom, the god. G otherwise reads οἱ βασιλεῖς αυτῆς, i.e., *mᵉlākêha*, "her kings," an inexplicable corruption.

15.b. For הוא "he," the G *Vorlage* read apparently כהניו, judging from the G rendering οἱ ἱερεῖς αὐτῶν "their priests."

2:3.a. Vocalizing מקרבה *miqqirboh* "from his midst," the rarer orthography of the 3 m sg suffix being preserved.

3.b. Reading שריו "his officials" instead of שרים "officials" with Gᴸ.

4.a. I.e., false gods. כזבים usually means "lies," but the context indicates idol worship.

7.a. Reading השפים "they trample" with G, from שוף I, otherwise attested solely in Gen 3:15.

7.b. על־עפר־ארץ "into the dust of the earth," widely questioned as cumbersome, is actually necessary metrically. G ἐκονδύλιζον "they strike (the heads of the poor)" appears to have been supplying a verb for a sense it assumed.

7.c. Lit. "turn aside the oppressed's road," i.e., keeping them from making progress or finding justice.

11.a. The usual translation "sons" is inaccurately narrow.

11.b. G ἁγιασμόν "holiness" either read only נֶזֶר or took נזרים as an abstract pl.

13.a. Since מעיק (עוק) "bog down" is a *hapax legomenon*, its meaning is hard to pinpoint. The versions vary greatly, but the following picture portrays people unable to move enough to escape destruction. A heavy-laden cart, stuck, is a perfect metaphor for the plight predicted.

15.a. Assuming the niph of מלט "escape" following the passive in G.

16.a. G's *Vorlage* apparently had metathesized אמץ to מצא "find" (εὑρήσει) which required the rest of the clause in G to become distorted ("will not take heart in power"), specifically taking גבורים "soldiers" as "power," a pl abstract.

Form / Structure / Setting

Eight individual oracles against Syro-Palestinian nations are woven inextricably into the compound oracle constituted by 1:3–2:16. The general form of each oracle is that usually identified as the messenger speech, in which the prophet delivers to his audience the message he has been given from God, quoting God verbatim in the first person and overtly identifying his words as a repetition of the divine speech. Since orthodox prophecy in general reports the words of the Lord and eschews theological creativity (see D. K. Stuart, "The Old Testament Prophets' Self Understanding of Their Prophecy," *Themelios* 1 [1980] 9–14), the messenger speech can hardly be seen as unusual by reason of its claim to represent Yahweh's message. Rather, the messenger speech form is notable only in that it (1) overtly calls special attention to the fact that the prophet is functioning as nothing but a carrier of information, and (2) implicitly attributes external authority to the word spoken, since messengers in ancient times were normally at the disposal primarily of influential persons. The arrival of a messenger at any location was undoubtedly always a subject of interest, even though such arrivals might have occurred fairly frequently in some locations. Building upon this well-known feature of ancient life, the prophets sometimes presented their oracles as messages bringing a statement directly from a sovereign. The specific content did not necessarily vary appreciably from what one would find in a woe oracle, or a lawsuit oracle, etc. The form employed, however, provided an option for variety and hinted at an urgency, and thus became one option for casting oracles among the prophets (cf. Isa 7:7; Jer 2:1–2; 10:1–2; Ezek 3:10–11; etc.). Examples of messenger speeches elsewhere in the OT include Gen 32:3–4; Judg 11:14–15; 2 Kgs 18:19; 19:6.

But these eight oracles are only incidentally messenger speeches, in comparison to their primary category: i.e., oracles against foreign nations. Predictions of judgment against foreign nations are found, in one form or another, in every prophetic book. In some instances, only the "nations" in general are mentioned (e.g., Joel 3:1–3; Hag 2:22), but more often, specific foreign nations are named as slated for divine wrath. The eight oracles in Amos 1:3–2:16 are of the latter variety and, in fact, constitute the longest catena of oracles against foreign nations among the Minor Prophets. All such oracles rest on a shared theological assumption: there is one God, Yahweh, who has power over the whole earth, and whose righteousness will not tolerate unrighteousness on the part of any nation. In other words, Yahweh is not merely the God of Israel or Judah, but has an implicit covenantal relationship with all nations, through which he expects obedience to a basic sort of "international law" and in recognition of which he will enforce that covenant's sanctions against those who rebel against it.

In Amos 1 and 2 the general format of a given oracle is:

1. The messenger introduction (כה אמר יהוה "This is what Yahweh said").
2. Certainty of deserved punishment.

3. Evidence (specification of crimes).
4. Announcement of curse (punishment).
5. A concluding formula (אמר יהוה "Yahweh said"; or נאם יהוה "oracle of Yah-weh").

The fifth element is omitted in the instance of the Tyre, Edom, and Judah oracles, and the formula נאם יהוה "oracle of Yahweh" appears once more than is absolutely necessary, i.e., at the end of 2:11, in the Israel oracle. Other-wise the eight oracles are remarkably uniform. The oracle against Israel is longer and more detailed than any of the others because it constitutes the climax to the entire group of oracles (Israel, being the most guilty of the group, has become in effect a foreign nation to Yahweh). Thus four oracles (Tyre, Edom, Judah, Israel) exhibit minor individual peculiarities, and four (Aram, Philistia, Ammon, Moab) are quite uniform. Many scholars have at-tempted to deny the authenticity of those oracles, or parts of them, that exhibit any individuality. This tyranny of the minority (for, indeed, the Aram, Philistia, Ammon, and Moab oracles together constitute less than 50 percent of the bulk of the whole) has no merit. Variations of style and structure are so common among individual oracles of given prophets that the attempt to impose a monolithic, subjectively induced norm upon all eight of the oracles in Amos 1:3–2:16 necessarily fails. To make Amos so ponderously uncreative and conformist that each of his oracles against foreign nations must be a precise calque of the others is needlessly anti-empirical. Thus we may conclude from the overall similarities and from the absence of any reliable data to the contrary that all the eight oracles in 1:3–2:16 comprise an original unit.

The parallelism employed in the passage is mostly synthetic, although synonymous parallelism is found scattered throughout, most notably in the n : n + 1 parallelisms (see below, on 1:3). Thus the meter is largely unbalanced (though often surprisingly regular) as is expected wherever synthetic parallel-ism prevails.

Exactly when during his ministry or where in Israel Amos delivered this compound oracle cannot be determined. It has always seemed reasonable to conclude that he may have found the most needy and appropriate audience for most of his oracles at either Bethel or Samaria, but one can hardly insist on either of these as the site of the delivery of the oracle. As always, the possibility that Amos preached this word from God repeatedly at various locations over a period of time must be reckoned with.

The atrocities mentioned in the various individual oracles appear to have been committed in connection with border wars that may have occurred almost any time from the late years of Solomon's reign, 940 B.C. or thereabouts, to Amos' own day, in the mid-eighth century. Attempts to show that international developments in the experiential memory of Amos' own contemporaries are the backdrop for the catalog of crimes are ill-founded. We simply do not have enough data to document externally these charges of brutality, or to fix them within a narrow time limit. In regard to his covenant, Yahweh takes, as it were, the long view. Sins committed centuries prior can still consti-tute the effective basis for unleashing the covenant's punishments at a given point in history (cf. 2 Kgs 17:21, 22; 1 Kgs 14:16).

Comment

1:3 Aram, the city-state in eastern Syria bordering Israel's northeast, was Israel's most constant and most potent foe during the border wars that broke out frequently in the ninth and eighth centuries. The Arameans had been subdued by David (2 Sam 8:6) but had broken free late in Solomon's reign (1 Kgs 11:23–25) and troubled Israel frequently thereafter. Damascus, its capital, governed a conglomeration of Syrian cities and their districts, for whom the territory to the south, the transjordan Israelite region of Gilead, was geographically inviting real estate into which to expand.

Amos announces that God will punish Aram-Damascus for its multiple crimes, lit. "three crimes and four." This n : n + 1 formulation is a standard type of numerical synonymous parallelism reflected frequently in the OT in various combinations (see S. Gevirtz, *Patterns in the Early Poetry of Israel* [Chicago: University of Chicago Press, 1963], 15–30; W. M. Roth, "The Numerical Sequence x / x + 1 in the Old Testament," *VT* 12 [1962] 300–311). It cannot be taken literally to indicate a precise number of crimes, but it does connote multiplicity. This is no isolated incident that Yahweh denounces, but a pattern of brutality attested repeatedly. The "crimes" (פשעים) are violations of the implicit world-wide covenant, i.e., rebelliousness against Yahweh's sovereign law.

The reference to threshing pregnant women appears to be a hyperbole, the intention of which is to summarize all sorts of gruesome treatment inflicted on the Gileadites by invading Aramean soldiers (cf. 2 Kgs 8:12, and below, v 13). Its intention is metaphorical: the slaughter was as cruel as if someone had taken an iron-toothed threshing machine used on grain threshing floors to free the grain for winnowing, and run it over helpless people instead. The effect is imagistic, bringing to mind visions of a shamelessly brutal conquest.

Yahweh's determination to punish the Arameans is expressed via the laconic 1 c sg negated hiphil verb with object suffix, לא אשיבנו. Literally this would mean something like "I will not take it back," the "it" referring implicitly to the nation mentioned (Barré, "The Meaning of *lᵉ ʾšybnw*"). In theory, Yahweh's wrath could always be restrained or delayed, even when it was well deserved, because of his ever-present mercy (cf. Jonah 4:2; 1 Kgs 21:28; 2 Kgs 22:19–20). But this is not such an instance. The crimes are too evident, too flagrant, and restoration of the implicit covenant with the nation mentioned must be refused.

4 Hazael of Damascus seized power over the Aramean coalition by assassinating Ben-Hadad (II?), as 2 Kgs 8:7–15 describes. Later, Hazael's son assumed the name Ben-Hadad (III?) upon acceding to the throne. Ben-Hadad means "son of (the god) Hadad" and was a royal throne name used by several Aramean rulers, the exact number of which is hard to determine from the limited sources available. (See B. Mazar, "The Aramean Empire and Its Relations with Israel," *BA* 25 [1962] 98–120; and M. Haran, "Observations," *IEJ* 18 [1968] 201–12.) The point of the parallelism in v 4 is, however, clear: Hazael and Ben-Hadad are both kings, perhaps even father and son in this instance; and thus God's punishment will extend even to the geographical-political heart of the nation, the fortified royal strongholds (אַרְמְנוֹת). These fortifications, an object of national pride (cf. 6:8), were apparently kings' citadels, massive masonry structures either surrounding or else abutting the palace. Built to withstand enemy attack, they would be like straw to Yahweh's fire (אֵשׁ). Destruction by fire is a type of covenant curse (no. 10; cf. Deut 32:22) with two particular connotations: fire was associated with destruction in warfare (cf. Deut 16:13; Josh 6:24; 8:8; 11:9) and with divine wrath (e.g., Gen 19:24; Exod 24:17; Num 11:1–3). In Holy War, the חרם, the accursed material devoted to destruction, was either killed, if alive, or burned, if flammable (Deut 7:25–26; 12:3; Num 31:10; Judg 1:8).

Judgment by fire constitutes a prominent theme in Amos (cf. also 5:6; 7:4). In the present complex of eight oracles, only the final one, concerning Israel, mentions no fire—not because it would have been inappropriate in Israel's case, but because fire is a synecdoche for divine destruction via warfare in these oracles. The detailed description of Israel's defeat (2:13–16) obviates the need there for a summarizing image. In all eight oracles, Yahweh himself will be the agent of destruction and defeat for the rebellious nations. None will withstand his punishment, symbolized by fire in seven of the eight oracles.

5 That the punishment the Arameans may expect will come via war (curse type 3) is further made evident in the references to breaking Damascus' gate-bar (the huge timber and / or metal bar used to lock the gates in defense); cutting off rulers (the hiphil of כרת routinely refers to destroying or annihilating, and often via warfare; cf. Josh 23:4; Judg 4:24; etc.); and exile (curse type 13). The deposition and exile of the nation's leadership (curse type 13a) implies here a complete conquest (cf. Hos 13:10–11) and therewith an end to a dynasty (1 Kgs 14:14; 21:21). In other words, Aram will not merely lose a war. It will be crushed and conquered, its kingship killed, and its people deported—all by Yahweh, working through unspecified intermediary nations in fulfillment of the curses of his implicit international covenant.

Aside from Damascus and Aram, three place names are mentioned in the verse. The location of the Valley of Aven (בקעת אוֹן) or even its original vocalization (G has Ων) is not certain. Eissfeldt's attempted identification of the place with the city of the cult center Baalbek, north of Damascus ("Die ältesten Bezeugungen von Baalbek als Kultstätte," *Forschungen und Fortschritte* 12 [1936] 51–53), is unconvincing, since the place appears to be a region— perhaps the area called בקעת לבנון "Valley of Lebanon" in Josh 11:17, as the parallelism with Beth-eden suggests. Beth-eden (בת־עדן) is the Bit-adini known mainly from Assyrian historical records, a city-state area located between the Euphrates and the Balikh rivers, actually to the north of Aram proper. It is also called simply Eden in the OT (2 Kgs 19:12; Ezek 27:23). The mention of Aven and Beth-eden reflects the reality of an amalgamation of regions confederated in the mid-eighth century, and all ripe targets for Assyrian conquest. Kir was Aram's country of origin (Amos 9:7) in eastern Mesopotamia just as Egypt was for Israel. And just as Egypt stands symbolically for captivity to Israel (Deut 28:68; Hos 7:16 et al.) so Kir would, in a sort of reversal of history, be Aram's place of reentry into oppression. Their accomplishments as a people will be undone; they will revert to their obscure, subjugated origins as a punishment for their crimes against Gilead.

6–8 The oracle against Philistia employs the same format as the one preceding it, the region in question now shifting from the northeast of Israel to the southwest. The Philistine cities will be destroyed in war, their leadership killed, and their population annihilated. The specific crime cited as evidence of their general covenant rebellion was the capture, enslavement, and sale of the population of some town or small region, including all the men, women, and children rather than merely the soldiers (from the use of שלמה). Probably in an isolated border raid at a time of Israelite or Judean vulnerability (e.g., in the days of Jehoahaz; 2 Kgs 13:7) and probably against some part of Israel or Judah, both of which bordered Philistia on the west, the Philistines took the occasion to gain wealth by treating human beings merely as a commodity. The Mosaic law required the death penalty for precisely this kind of kidnapping and selling into slavery (Exod 21:16), and it was surely recognized internationally as a cruelty, no matter how frequently it may have been practiced in biblical times (cf. I. Mendelsohn, *Slavery in the Ancient Near East* [New York: Oxford, 1949]).

The Edomites, to whom the impressed slaves were sold in this instance, may have used them for their own commerce, which included mining, shipping, and of course farming, but may also have simply resold them elsewhere (see N. K. Gottwald, *All the Kingdoms of the Earth* [New York: Harper and Row, 1964] 94–114). But these slaves, sold to foreigners, were still human beings, in God's image (cf. Exod 23:9). The technique of the transaction is unimportant in the oracle; what is unforgivable is such misuse and abuse of helpless people for the profit of the mighty. This theme is reflected in one way or another in all eight oracles in the present passage, and in Amos as a whole.

The chosen poetic format admits a single place name, Gaza, to be mentioned first and necessarily relegates Ashdod, Ashkelon, and Ekron to later positions. Gaza, the southernmost city of the Philistine pentapolis, may also have been the most prominent at this time, especially commercially. Gath, the most inland Philistine city, is not mentioned at all, probably because it was severely weakened from its conquest by Hazael (2 Kgs 12:18) and by this time was under the control of Ashdod or even Judah (cf. 2 Chr 11:8). In other prophetic oracles against the Philistines, mention of Gath is likewise omitted (Jer 25:20; Zeph 2:4; Zech 9:5–7), indicating that after the ninth century it was probably not independent.

9–10 The location shifts again, to the powerfully defended maritime city-state of Tyre on the Phoenician coast, northwest of Israel. It, too, will fall to Yahweh's punishment by fire. Amos is obviously moving from one compass point to another (northeast to southwest, and now northwest; the next three oracles all concern southeast nations). Recognition of this pattern obviates the thinly based suggestions that the Tyre oracle is a secondary late addition to the group.

Tyre was a slave-trading nation, and this oracle echoes the Philistia oracle before it (the oracles echo each other in many ways; several are linked to one another by multiple "catchwords"). Tyre, particularly powerful in the eighth century and thereafter (cf. Ezek 26–28), gained wealth and influence as the hub of a far-flung trading empire, its ocean-going ships ranging the Mediterranean Sea. This is the first OT mention of Tyre's involvement in the slave trade, a dehumanizing business for which it became notorious (Joel 3:6; Ezek 27:13). Again, Edom served as the middleman in the transaction (cf. Joel 3:8 for a similar arrangement), which involved, presumably, the captured population of some town and district in Israel, though this is unspecified.

The "brotherhood treaty" (ברית אחים) Tyre did not honor (lit. "remembered" זכר; cf. Exod 2:24; 6:5; Lev 26:42, 45) is a term unattested elsewhere, and apparently was Amos' way of summarizing the lengthy cooperative relationship that had existed between the Phoenicians and the Israelites, specifically mentioned in reference to David (2 Sam 5:11), Solomon (1 Kgs 5:1, 11), and Ahab (1 Kgs 16:31). Because Jacob and Esau were literally "brother" nations, some commentators have been inclined to see "brotherhood treaty" as a reference to Edom's historic relationship to Israel; but a Tyrian treaty is clearly meant, since Tyre is the subject of לא זכר "did not remember," and uninvolved parties do not "honor" covenants.

Tyre is the only city-state mentioned alone in the eight oracles. This may imply that other Phoenician regions do not share its guilt in these crimes. But more likely it simply results from the exigencies of the three-couplet format employed here, which says all that needs saying for the purposes of Amos' audience.

11–12 Amos begins completion of his chiastic coverage of the compass points surrounding Judah and Israel by turning attention now to Edom, in the extreme southeast, and its two major cities. Teman was Edom's southernmost major city and / or region and Bozrah its northernmost city / region. (Samaria was both a city and a region.) Both lay along the ancient King's Highway running from Damascus to the Gulf of Aqaba, and between them lay the bulk of Edom proper.

It was by the King's Highway that the Israelites under Moses had first sought to pass through Edom peacefully and had been opposed "with the sword" (בחרב; Num 20:14–21; esp. vv 18, 20). The present oracle appears to refer back even to that pre-conquest event (and the extensive Edomite-Israelite hostility that followed it thereafter) in the references to the suppression of compassion toward the previously oppressed Israelites (Num 20:15) and Edom's long history of anger and wrath against Israel. In connection with events in the time of Saul (1 Sam 14:47), David (2 Sam 8:12–14), Solomon (1 Kgs 11:14–25), Jehoram (2 Kgs 8:20–21), Amaziah (2 Kgs 14:7–10), and Amos' contemporary Uzziah (2 Kgs 14:22), the OT mentions Edomite-Israelite enmity. Indeed, as 2 Kgs 8:22 notes, Edom and Israel were constant enemies after the accession of Jehoram (853–841) through the time of the Babylonian conquest in the early sixth century and thereafter (cf. Isa 34:5–17; Joel 3:19; Jer 49:7–22; Ps 137:7; Obad; Lam 4:21–22; Mal 1:2–5). Documenting Edom's "multiple crimes" up to their own day was not hard at all for Amos' own audience or for those who learned from his oracles in later centuries.

Edom was truly a "brother" (אח) to Israel (Gen 25:24–26; cf. Deut 2:4; 23:7). Foretelling the eventual enmity of the two nations descended from Isaac's sons, Gen 25:23 also predicts Edom's subjection to Israel, as was normally the case historically; the reverse never occurred. The punishment for Edom is also fire, curse type no. 10, as in the preceding oracles.

13–15 The Ammonites (בני עמון) occupied a hardscrabble territory east of the Jordan, on the fringes of the desert, bordering on Gilead's east and south. Their only major city was Rabbah, located on the King's Highway where it met the upper Jabbok River, the location of modern Amman, Jordan. They, too, had a long history of brutal enmity toward Israel, represented in synecdochic fashion by reference to their ripping open Gilead's pregnant women (בקעם הרות), an atrocity that served as a cliche in the ancient Near East and beyond for the terrors of merciless warfare (in effect, curse type 12a; cf. 2 Kgs 8:12; Hos 13:16; and H. Schmökel, *Ur, Assur und Babylon* [Stuttgart: J. Kilpper, 1955] 114). The Ammonites (they are only rarely called "Ammon" in the OT perhaps because they were less territorially confederated than most other Palestinian nations) had since the days of the Judges often fought Israel to capture parts of fertile Gilead to increase their own area (Judg 3:12–14; 10:7–9, 17; 11:4–33; 1 Sam 11:1–11; 14:47; 2 Sam 8:12; 10:1–11:1; 2 Chr 20:1–30; 24:26). By Amos' time, Ammon was firmly under Israelite control (2 Kgs 14:25). Thus the "multiple crimes" of the Ammonites likely refers to a long history of·past crimes, and one need not postulate a theoretical early eighth-century Ammonite-Israelite border raid (e.g., after Israel was weakened by Hazael of Damascus) as the basis for God's judgment.

The connection of divine fire (curse type 10) with warfare (curse type 3) is nowhere more evident than in the present oracle. The language is more specific and graphic than in any other oracle except that about Israel (i.e., 2:13–15). The actual setting or kindling of the fire (והצתי) as opposed to simply *sending* fire, the enemy group-attack shout ("war cry" תרועה), the "day of battle" (יום מלחמה), and the two words for the furious, powerful wind / gale (סער and סופה) combine vividly to depict the horrible, loud, disorienting storm of war that will topple Ammon's royalty (king) and government (he and his officials) and remove them into (Babylonian?) exile. Twice "day" (יום) is mentioned: "day of battle" and "day of the storm." This is the vocabulary of the divine sovereign's all-powerful intervention (see D. K. Stuart, "The Sovereign's Day of Conquest," *BASOR* 221 [1976] 159–64), and its connection with words used commonly to denote theophany (סער: Ps 83:16[15]; Isa 29:6; Jer 23:19; סופה: Prov 10:25; Isa 66:15; Nah 1:3; cf. Isa 29:6 for סער, סופה and אש, "fire" together) leaves no doubt that Yahweh himself will be in control of Ammon's destruction in war. Amos' prophecy came to pass. Crushed by the Assyrians, Ammon, under a new dynasty, paid very heavy tribute during the seventh century as an Assyrian vassal state. It collapsed as an independent nation under Babylonian attack and was largely depopulated in the sixth century (G. M. Landes, "Ammon," *IDB*, 1:111–13), according to the word of Yahweh (cf. Jer 49:1–6; Ezek 21:18; 25:1–7; Amos 1:13–15; Zeph 2:8–11).

2:1–3 Moab was a brother nation of Ammon (Gen 19:36–38) and was located east of the Dead Sea, largely between the Arnon River and the Brook Zered. To the south lay Edom. Between the two nations, along the Zered, border fortifications had been built, testimony to the historic enmity between Moab and Edom (see N. Glueck, *Explorations in Eastern Palestine II*, AASOR 15 [New Haven: American Schools of Oriental Research, 1934–35] 104–6). This sixth oracle cites as the paradigmatic atrocity a particularly furious sort of vengeance: burning skeletal remains so as to prevent resurrection. The act is based on the doctrine, reflected widely in the religions of non-Israelite Palestinian nations, that the original body's remains would be fleshed out and enlivened at the time of a general resurrection of the dead (Ezek 37:1–4; 1 Cor 15:35–54; see E. Meyers, "Secondary Burials in Palestine," *BA* 33 [1970] 2–29; R. E. Cooley, "Gathered to His People: A Study of a Dothan Family Tomb," *The Living and Active Word of God: Studies in Honor of Samuel J. Schultz*, ed. M. Inch and R. Youngblood [Winona Lake, IN: Eisenbrauns, 1983] 47–58). To burn someone's bones, i.e., desiccated bodily remains, was an attempt to prevent—at least symbolically—the opportunity for that person to participate in the resurrection, thus to wish for him or her eternal death. The Bible attributes no efficacy to such acts of sympathetic magic; but the Moabites and Edomites probably did regard a proper burial as an essential guarantee of eternal life. In some past military clash (cf. 2 Kgs 3) the Moabites had captured an Edomite king and burned his bones "to lime" (לשׂיד), i.e., to a powdery ash. Perhaps they scattered this ash as well (cf. 2 Kgs 23:4–6) in order to make the potential of resurrectional reconstitution even less likely. This was, at any rate, an example of all-out vengeful war. Brother hated brother intensely and acted out the hatred.

The punishment for such international injustice was consuming fire and warfare and the exile of the royalty and government leadership—the same punishment in essence meted out to Ammon in the preceding oracle. The tumult (שׁאון), war cry (תרועה), and horn (שׁופר; the bugle of ancient warfare) all suggest the onslaught of the enemy. The word ruler (שׁופט) is used merely as a synonym for "king," a typical poetic usage (Ps 2:10; Prov 8:16, etc.) for the term.

The mention of Kerioth rather than any of the other Moabite cities relates probably to its role as a cult center for the god Chemosh, as mentioned in the Moabite Stone (Mesha Stele; *ANET*, 320).

4–5 Having completed denunciation of the southeastern nations, Amos' compound oracle shifts geographically to the center. Many in Amos' northern audience must have taken perverse delight in hearing Judah denounced for its apostasy from the Mosaic law, since Judeans had accused the Israelites of such things in the past (e.g., 2 Chr 13:5–12; but cf. 1 Kgs 14:22–24; 2 Kgs 17:19). Members of the audience may also have assumed that this oracle, with its longest-yet, sweeping specification of Judah's crimes, was the climax of the foreign oracles. After all, foreign oracles did not usually include the homeland! Judah was indeed a foreign nation from the Israelite viewpoint (cf. 2 Sam 3:1; 1 Kgs 12:19; 15:6–7, 32; 2 Kgs 16:5).

The authenticity of the Judah oracle has been doubted by many critical scholars for one or more of the following reasons: (1) Amos was authorized to speak only to Israel, not Judah (absurd on its surface in the present compound oracle); (2) the Judah oracle is anti-climactic (just the contrary); (3) it is shorter than four of the oracles (along with two others); (4) its indictment is general and does not mention specific crimes against *people* (the very genius of this oracle); and (5) it is deuteronomistic in vocabulary (relevant only if virtually all of Deuteronomy is a fabrication *de novo* of the seventh century and therefore spurious in light of the frequent vocabulary sharing of Deuteronomy and Jeremiah, Isaiah, Hosea, etc.).

A special value of the Judah oracle lies in its expanded citation of evidence, as a prelude to the greatly expanded evidence of guilt presented in the Israel oracle. Covenant disobedience is the problem, including heterodoxy in a nation whose capital is supposed to be the center of the worship of the one true God (Deut 12). In the case of Judah, where Yahweh's law (תורה) and statutes (חקים) cover a full range of personal, social, and religious behavior, God's word hardly need cite a misdeed even a pagan would recognize as an atrocity, as the previous oracles do. Here, in the instance of a nation favored with the actual stipulations of Yahweh's own national covenant, the standards are explicit and not just implicit. The interests of brevity are thus best served not by mentioning a border-war cruelty, but by an indictment that even more severely and generally condemns Judah: the twofold indictment of (1) general lawbreaking and (2) idolatry (following after "fakes" כזבים). Similar to the other oracles, a specific recent breakdown in obedience is not the issue; rather, a long history of infidelity to Yahweh is meant, signified here by the involvement of "their ancestors" (אבותם). The crimes are "multiple"—chronically characteristic. The problem has been, historically, disobedience (מאס) and apostasy (תעה), not merely a single occasion of either one. Thus Judah, too, must be destroyed in warfare by the divinely appointed fire (cf. 2 Kgs 25:9).

6–8 Yahweh's judgment will not be limited to nations whose destruction would be welcome news to the people of Israel. The eighth and final oracle includes yet another *foreign* nation. Israel herself, guilty among the other Syro-Palestinian criminal nations, is placed at the climactic point in the compound of oracles and is excoriated in far more detail than any of them.

The crimes listed in vv 6–8 all relate to social justice within Israel, in distinction to the first six oracles, which cite international atrocities, and the penultimate Judah oracle, which mentions general covenant-breaking and idolatry. Israel's crimes include (1) sale of the poor into Israelite slavery (v 6b); (2) oppression of the poor (v 7a); (3) sexual abuse (v 7b); and (4) exploitation of needy debtors (v 8). These crimes are not famous historical events. They are the daily practices of Amos' contemporaries, observable throughout Israel, and evidence of the rife injustice by which Israel has condemned itself to rejection by Yahweh as a foreign people (implicitly, curse type no. 1).

6 The "righteous" (צדיק) and the "needy" (אביון) are mentioned in parallel, not because they are strictly synonymous, but with the effect of associating them: "the righteous needy." These people, not guilty of any wrongdoing under the law, were being sold into slavery. The reference to "sandals" (נעלים) probably indicates hyperbolically the ridiculously low prices for which they were sold (מכר, a routine business transaction) but may also allude to the symbolic sandal-transfer that sealed property exchanges in early times in Israel (cf. Deut 25:9–10; Ruth 4:8; R. deVaux *Ancient Israel* [New York: McGraw-Hill, 1961] 169). In the OT any actual mention of the sandal-transfer procedure is associated with *people* construed as property (Ps 60:8 is not an instance of the same practice), but judging from Ruth 4:8 this may be merely accidental. Slavery was legal and regulated carefully and benignly in Israelite covenantal stipulations (Exod 21:2–11, 20–21, 26–27; Deut 15:12–18; 23:15–16). What Yahweh denounces through Amos is not benevolent slavery, but some kind of legal impression-indenture in which corrupt courts aided the unethical rich by making available slave labor to them. Poor people who lost rigged civil or criminal court cases were fined heavily. Unable to pay, they were then sold into slavery. The court and the buyer profited, but the covenant was violated (Exod 23:7). Justice was denied to the poor.

7 By reason of the meter (10:7 original syllable count, appropriate to the context), the visibly long first line of the couplet that begins v 7 is to be retained. Again, an element of hyperbole adds stress to the tragic social injustice practiced by Amos' contemporaries: the oppressed poor (דלים / עניים) are "stepped on" by the rich, and their progress impeded. The "turn-aside of the road" (יטו . . . דרך) literally expressed here refers elsewhere to hindering access or progress (cf. Exod 23:6; Isa 29:21) and probably also connotes denial of legal justice (cf. the similar expression in Prov 17:23). Thus v 7a expands upon and generalizes beyond the specific sort of exploitation alluded to in v 6b.

V 7b may refer to making a female slave (one meaning of נערה) a concubine of a father and son, in violation of Exod 21:8, but more likely refers to any practice of sexual adulteration (cf. Deut 22:30), made all the more odious by the possibility that it may be involuntary on the part of the woman. Yahweh's holiness demands that marriage be the context for sexual intercourse, and denies to related pairs the right to have sex with the same person (Lev 18:8, 15, 17; 20:10–20; Deut 27:20). Sexual purity is a part of holiness (Lev 20:7, 26). Profaning Yahweh's "holy name" can be accomplished by sexual immorality (cf. Lev 18:21, following a long list of sex laws) and is a way of expressing covenant disobedience via violation of taboos.

8 It was religious people who were exploiting the poor! The oracle conveys this artistically by describing the hypocritical enjoyment of the gains of oppression at places of worship. The wordings "every altar" (כל־מזבח) and "their god" (אלהיהם) clearly imply heterodox worship, though Yahweh, alone or syncretistically, may have been an object of this worship at the covenantally illegal multiple shrines.

The instances of oppression cited here represent the exploitation of people who are indebted beyond their ability to repay immediately. For example, the covenant provided in some cases for temporary—daylight—possession of an outer garment as collateral for a loan (בגדים חבולים "garments taken in pledge," cf. Exod 22:25–27) but denied it in other cases, such as that of the "widow," i.e., an abjectly needy person (Deut 24:17). But Israelites were stretching out (נטה, hiphil), i.e., bedding down for the night, on such garments, clearly violating the law. Moreover, fining (ענש) was to be employed according to the law as a vehicle for guaranteeing *restitution* (e.g., Exod 21:19, 30–32; 22:14, 15, 17; Deut 22:19), not as a means of enriching leaders who here have taken wine as payment-in-kind and debauched themselves thereby. Lengthy festive and drinking bouts at temples were characteristic of Canaanite, not Israelite, religion (Judg 9:27; Neh 1:4–9; cf. Isa 5:22–23). An orthodox Nehemiah would later protect the poor against these very sorts of oppressive people (Neh 5:1–12).

9–12 A historical retrospective establishes that Israel's chronic, essential character has been to ignore Yahweh's grace and to reject his laws. All of the other individual oracles in the passage presume a long history ("multiple crimes") of guilt. The present oracle describes such a long history in Israel's case, by suggestive allusions to its ungratefulness and its tendency to do the exact opposite of what Yahweh wanted.

9 Who is the God whose laws the people have scorned? He is the one who, in the holy war of conquest, "destroyed" (שמד, hiphil; cf. Josh 7:12; 11:20) the original inhabitants of the land so that Israel could possess it. Amorite is virtually a synonym for Canaanite in many places in the OT. In Deuteronomy it reflects especially the mountain-dwelling and Transjordanian Canaanites, i.e., the largest and most established of the natives in the promised land (e.g., Deut 1:4, 7, 19, 20; 3:9; 31:4). It was *their* long history of iniquity (Gen 15:16) that provided, in part, one function of the conquest: extermination of a corrupt culture. They were strong (Num 13:28, 31–33) and well entrenched, like great trees (cedars and oaks being the most massive of the native trees). But Yahweh completely ("above and below," cf. Isa 37:31; *ANET* 3:509) defeated them. In the context, these words may have struck Amos' audience as a prelude to how they too would be defeated for despising the sovereignty of the God who had done all this on their behalf.

10 The identity of Israelites was shaped especially by two factors: (1) they were a people rescued from Egyptian slavery, and (2) they were a people given a homeland by divine grace (cf. Judg 6:8–10; 1 Sam 12:8). Their time in the wilderness was certainly not always pleasant, but it was a time of direct leading and protection by their God (Deut 2:7). Yahweh had done so very much for them, yet they had not appreciated it (cf. Hos 2:8), as the following verses make explicit. The verse has the ring of covenant prologue language (Exod 20:2; Deut 5:6), a fact surely not lost on Amos' audience.

11–12 Emphasis on Israel's long history of disobedience continues by going beyond the time of direct leading of Yahweh in the exodus, wilderness wanderings, and conquest mentioned in the previous verse to his indirect leading via prophets and Nazirites, right up to Amos' day. God's guidance, regardless of how mediated, had been constant through Israel's history. And Israel, especially when it became secure, rejected that guidance rather constantly.

Complacent affluence was a main reason. Yahweh had faithfully honored his original covenant promises of blessing in the conquered land (Deut 28:1–13), and by the time of Jeroboam II Israel enjoyed freedom (2 Kgs 14:25, 27–28) and prosperity (Hos 2:10–15). They therefore felt secure in enticing or seducing the Nazirites to break their vows and in compelling the prophets to abandon their speaking for Yahweh.

Both men and women could be prophets and Nazirites. The fact that נביאים "prophets" and נזירים "Nazirites" are used as a parallel pair in v 11 may result from the purposeful avoidance of כהנים "priests" in light of the full corruption of the Northern priesthood (1 Kgs 12:31–32). Since Moses, the virtually unbroken succession of prophetic witness had not prevented the nation from sinking into degeneracy—to the point that the word of God was often scorned (2 Kgs 2:23) or prohibited (Amos 7:10–17). Prophets, called of God and representing him to the people, held a clearly recognized office; thus the demand for acknowledgment in v 11: "Is that not so, Israelites?"

Nazirites were consecrated (נזיר) agents of God among his people, zealous to see his will carried out. They vowed not to cut their hair as a mark of separation, abstinence from wine as a mark of self-denial, and avoidance of the dead as a mark of purity (Num 6:1–21). Men and women, slave and free, could be Nazirites, though the OT mentions only two males, Samson (Judg 13:5–7; 16:17) and Samuel (1 Sam 1:11, G; 1:22, 25; 2:20) as free Nazirites, both of whom were specially chosen by God before birth as life-long Nazirites. But even though God himself had appointed (קוּם, hiphil; cf. Deut 18:18) these called and consecrated ones, Israel's reaction was to ignore and reject them. While prophets were sometimes actually forbidden to prophesy (7:16), more often they were probably simply squelched by rejection. Forcing Nazirites to drink wine might have occurred as a cruel, vandalistic means of defiling them. But the language may also, hyperbolically, intend to connote that a climate of disinterest in orthodoxy and discrimination against serious religious living simply quenched a practice that the law provided for.

13–16 What judgment will actually come to Israel as a result of her long history of disobedience? She will be utterly defeated. That is her punishment. An impressionistic collage of panic and ineffectiveness is presented, from bogging down (v 13) to running away (v 16). No reference to deposing kings or burning royal fortifications is found here: the language is more personal, more specific, involving various sorts of soldiers and civilians in their total inability to withstand Yahweh's attacking enemy forces. The scene painted recalls the helplessness curses (type 19), as, for example, in Lev 26:36–39. Yahweh still speaks in the first person in continuity with the preceding sections of the compound oracle, but there the verbs are future, in contrast to those in the past tense in vv 9–12.

13 The *hapax legomenon* מֵעִיק has often been identified with Ugaritic *ʿqq* "tear" and Arabic *ʿaqqa* "split." From this tenuous connection a number of commentators have constructed a prediction of an earthquake as the underlying terror of vv 12–16, causing all the confusion and flight. But the verb more likely means "bog down," exactly what a heavily loaded cart sometimes does. This section deals with staying put, voluntarily or involuntarily, when running is desirable; and with running, voluntarily or involuntarily, when standing firm is desirable. So "bogging down" (KB) fits the context perfectly. Israelites will be frozen with fear when the attack comes.

14 The helplessness of two civilian (and / or military) types and one military type is described: Fast runners will be paralyzed; powerful people will become athetoid; soldiers will be defenseless!

15 The helplessness of two military types and one civilian (and / or military) type is described: Archers and riders (רֹכֵב הַסּוּס; possibly meaning horseback riders but, grammatically, likely signifying charioteers) will lose their prowess from fear. The archer, not standing his ground, will be unable to shoot accurately. The charioteer, instead of attacking, will try to ride away but will fail even to do that. Runners, who are not a class of warriors, will gain nothing from their swiftness.

16 Confusion will prevail everywhere in Israel on the day when Yahweh attacks. The stoutest soldiers will drop weapons and armor (עָרוֹם here means naked in the sense of "stripped down," cf. 1 Sam 19:24) and simply run from battle. This verse does not contradict the statements in vv 14 and 15 that there will be no escape from destruction. To flee in battle is to open oneself up to being overtaken and slaughtered (cf. Josh 7:5; 8:24; Judg 4:16; 2 Chr 13:16, 17), not to get away safely. This picture of pandemonium in defeat reflects curse type 4 (e.g., Lev 26:36).

Explanation

Most of what the prophets wrote fits broadly into three categories: (1) evidence that the divine covenant has been violated; (2) announcement of the imposition of sanctions as a result; and (3) announcement of restoration blessings to follow the sanction punishments, thus preserving the continuity of God's faithfulness to his covenant in spite of the people's unfaithfulness.

In Amos 1:3–2:16 evidence of eight nations' infidelity to Yahweh's implicit (or explicit) covenant is portrayed by citation of examples of knowing disobedience. In the first six instances atrocities improper from any reasonable human perspective constitute the sampling of evidence. In the latter two, Judah and Israel are shown to have violated their own explicit covenantal commitments.

In each case, then, the sanction punishments are announced. The divine judge will not restore (שוב, hiphil) rejected vassals. Amos the messenger is announcing to eight nations the punishment that awaits them at the hands of the One whose law they have broken. The judgment sentence is the same for each: defeat and destruction in war, as symbolized by fire. Citizenries and kings will both be affected. Yahweh himself will superintend the process.

No mention is made of restoration blessings in the present pericope. In Amos such blessings are concentrated at the end of the book. In what way, then, can such ancient predictions of judgment executed long ago have meaning for Christians? The answer lies especially in the concern for the rights and needs of people—particularly, helpless people—in each oracle. Even the Judah oracle by reason of its attack on idolatry, which is a materialistic, dehumanizing system (cf. J. Gray, "Idolatry," *IDB* 2:676–77; *NBD*, 551–53), fits the pattern of divine outrage at the exploitation, abuse, and oppression of fellow human beings for one's own personal power or profit. This Christians must be warned about and warn themselves about. If one's neighbor had been truly loved as oneself in Amos' day, the words of Amos 1:3–2:16 would need not have been delivered.

Covenantal Accountability   (3:1–2)

Bibliography

Huffmon, H. "The Treaty Background of Hebrew *YĀDAᶜ*." *BASOR* 181 (1966) 31–37. **Schmidt, W.** "Die deuteronomistische Redaktion des Amosbuches." *ZAW* 77 (1965) 168–93. **Sinclair, L. A.** "The Courtroom Motif in the Book of Amos." *JBL* 85 (1966) 351–53. **Vriezen, T. C.** "Erwägungen zu Amos 3:2." In *Archäologie und Altes Testament. FS K. Galling,* ed. A. Kuschke and E. Kutsch. Tübingen: J. C. B. Mohr, 1970. 255–58.

Translation

3:1 *Listen to this word that Yahweh has spoken against you, Israelites,*[a] *against the whole family I brought up from Egypt:*

> 2 *I have known*[a] *only you*
> *Of all the families of the earth.*
> *Therefore I will punish you*
> *For all your sins.*

Notes

1.a. G (οἶκος Ἰσραηλ) reflects בית ישראל "house of Israel," which could conceivably have been the original reading.

2.a. Or "chosen," since ידע can denote covenantal commitment and not merely cognitive perception.

Form / Structure / Setting

A short oracle, perhaps delivered by Amos originally in connection with other oracles—e.g., those that follow it—serves as a kind of introduction to the lengthy collection of judgments against Israel in chaps. 3–6 and possibly even through 9:10.

The entire oracle may be prose; v 1 is unquestionably so, and v 2, being purely synthetic in parallelism, if parallelistic at all, has a rather prosaic word order and contains the (prosaic) article once and prosaic particle את twice. As we have arranged it, however, the original vocalization would have resulted in fourteen syllables in each couplet, possible evidence of poetic structure.

This sort of oracle is often called a proclamation ("listen to this word . . .") though it hardly differs from a messenger speech or judgment sentence (the על־כן "therefore" of v 2b is reminiscent of the transition from evidence to verdict in covenant lawsuits). Nothing in the oracle helps determine its date or provenance.

Comment

1 The introductory formula of summons to listen (cf. Gen 4:23; 49:2; Exod 18:19; Deut 4:1; 6:4; etc.) denotes that an important message is coming. A principle, an issue, a teaching, or a truth is about to be revealed. Israel, God's historic people, is addressed—not merely the ten northern tribes of the northern monarchy, but the whole family (כל־המשפחה) of the exodus. Throughout the OT, reminders of the exodus deliverance serve as reminders of Israel's covenantal relationship to Yahweh. Israel is who she is because of the exodus. She became Yahweh's nation as a result of it. The teaching that follows therefore applies in general to Israel, North and South, viewed as a historical continuum in the typical covenantal manner (cf. Deut 4:25–31).

2 In 1:3–2:16 eight nations' punishments, including those of Israel and Judah, follow squarely from their conscious disobedience to propriety. Does God now assert through Amos a contrary theology—that Israel will undergo punishment merely because she is his covenant people and not because of any wrong she has done? Hardly. This saying, like many proverbial and prophetic sayings (such as 3:3–8), is elliptical. The full logic is assumed, not stated. In overt form, far less effective, of course, as a warning, the logic would be: (a) You and I are uniquely covenantally bound; (b) by the terms of our covenant it is your responsibility to obey and mine to punish you if you do not; and (c) I—no one else—am therefore the one to punish you for your sins. The last phrase of the oracle, "for all your sins" (את כל־עונתיכם), makes explicit the fact that here, too, punishment is based on iniquity committed. The point of the oracle, then, is less to make a statement about the *reasons* for punishment than about the *agent* of punishment.

ידע "know" has a rich range of meaning: know, observe, realize, notice, find out, learn, recognize, perceive, care about, be acquainted with, have sex with, understand, have insight into, and even select or choose (on the latter, cf. Gen 18:19; Jer 2:8; 1 Sam 2:12). Here it means in effect to be "specially related to." "All the families of the earth" (מכל משפחות האדמה) is an old phrase (cf. Gen 12:3; 28:14) referring to the great variety of ethnic-national groups among humankind. From all these, Israel alone (רק) is Yahweh's particular covenant people. "Punish" (פקד) is used in the OT routinely in connection with Yahweh's punishing non-Israelite nations; there is no emphasis here on something that Yahweh does to Israel that he does not do to other peoples.

Explanation

The oracle stresses not Israel's covenantal accountability, but Yahweh's. He *must* punish Israel for their sins. This was a concept which the average Israelite of Amos' time apparently found hard to understand (cf. 5:18–20). A God should protect and benefit his nation at all times, should he not? Why would a God want to harm his own people who worshiped him regularly (5:21–23)? Much of Amos' ministry was devoted to dispelling this folly. One emphasis of the preceding oracles (1:3–2:16) was on Yahweh's direct involvement in the punishments for the nations. A central argument of the following oracle (3:3–8) is that Israel's disasters are not some accident, but Yahweh's doing. Amos had to preach an aspect of religion that people did not want to hear.

Similar tendencies prevail widely in the church, and often have: Sinners cannot really help themselves, can they? Aren't they products of their environment and upbringing? How can a good God reject anyone? Won't he give everyone a second chance? Isn't God's main concern that everyone should be happy? And so on. It isn't biblical, but it seems so reasonable. This is an aspect of our religion that many people still do not want to hear.

A List of Inseparables   (3:3–8)

Bibliography

Baumgartner, W. "Amos 3:3–8." *ZAW* 33 (1913) 78–80. **Boyle, M. O.** "The Covenant Lawsuit of the Prophet Amos 3:1–4:13." *VT* 21 (1971) 338–62. **Daiches, S.** "Amos

III:3–8." *ExpTim* 6 (1914–15) 237. **Eichrodt, W.** "Die Vollmacht des Amos: Zu einer schwierigen Stelle im Amosbuch." In *FS W. Zimmerli,* ed. H. Donner et al. Göttingen: Vandenhoeck & Ruprecht, 1977. 124–51. **Gitay, Y.** "A Study of Amos's Art of Speech: A Rhetorical Analysis of Amos 3:1–15." *CBQ* 42 (1980) 293–309. **Holwerda, B.** "Da exegese van Amos 3, 3–8." . . . *Begonnen habbende van Mozes* . . . . Terneuzen: D. H. Littoij, 1953. **Junker, H.** "*Leo rugiit, quis non timebit? Deus locutus est, quis non prophetabit?:* Eine textkritische und exegetische Untersuchung über Amos 3:3–8." *TTZ* 59 (1950) 4–13. **Mittmann, S.** "Gestalt und Gehalt einer prophetischen Selbstrechtfertigung (Am 3:3–8)." *TQ* 151 (1971) 134–45. **Mulder, M. J.** "Ein Vorschlag zur Übersetzung von Amos iii 6b." *VT* 34 (1984) 106–8. **Overholt, T. W.** "Commanding the Prophets: Amos and the Problem of Prophetic Authority." *CBQ* 41 (1979) 517–32. **Pfeifer, G.** "Unausweichliche Konsequenzen: Denkformenanalyse von Amos iii: 3–8." *VT* 33 (1983) 341–47. **Schenker, A.** "Steht der Prophet unter dem Zwang zu weissagen, oder steht Israel vor der Evidenz der Weisung Gottes in der Weissagung des Propheten? Zur Interpretation von Amos 3,3–8." *BZ* 30 (1986) 250–56. **Shapiro, D.** "The Seven Questions of Amos." *Tradition* 20 (1982) 327–31. **Thomas, D. W.** "Note on נועדו in Amos 3:3." *JTS* 7 (1956) 69–70.

Translation

3:3 *Do two people travel together*
Without having met? [a]

4 *Does a lion roar in the forest*
Without having any prey?

Does a young lion cry out from his lair [a]
Without having caught something?

5 *Does a bird fall into a ground trap*
If the snare has not been set?

Does a trap rise up off the ground
If it has not caught anything?

6 *If a trumpet sounds in a city* [a]
Do not the people tremble?

If there is a disaster [b] *in a city*
Has not Yahweh caused it?

7 *Indeed, the Lord Yahweh does not do something unless he reveals his counsel to his servants the prophets.*

8 *The lion has roared!*
Who is not afraid?

The Lord Yahweh has spoken!
Who will not prophesy?

Notes

3.a. The reading in G (γνωρίσωσιν ἑαυτούς) is usually thought to reflect a niph of ידע in the G *Vorlage*. But יעד, niph, can mean "meet" (Exod 25:22; 30:6), and G may have recognized that here, even if not elsewhere.

4.a. On the metrical problems of ממענתו, see Stuart, *SEHM,* 211, n. 10.

6.a. Here a G minuscule (534) reads πολέμῳ "battle" rather than "city," presumably the result of an inner-Greek corruption.

6.b. On this meaning of רעה, cf. *Comment,* Jonah 1:2.

Form / Structure / Setting

The passage appears to be a unity, separate from the preceding and following material in Amos as evidenced by its largely interrogative, inferential format. Three subsections are visible: vv 3–6, poetry, in which the focus is on certain natural associations of a cause and effect variety; v 7, prose, in which the concern is the natural association of event and prophetic interpretation thereof (this verse provides a transition to the third section, whose topic is related); and v 8, poetry, in which the import is the necessity to prophesy. In each subsection, things that are inseparable—either as they occur in mundane life or as they relate to the special circumstances of prophecy—are listed. The emphasis appears to fall less on causality than on association. In each case, A goes with B.

The passage is obviously didactic and appears also to be a disputation in which Amos' (or any prophet's) necessity to prophesy (e.g., about disaster Yahweh has caused) is defended. What would occasion such a defense? The answer requires at least the assumption that somewhere in an Israelite city some sort of disaster(s) had occurred, known to Amos' audience (v 6b). Perhaps not even a single specific disaster was in view, as long as the principle could be accepted (cf. 4:6–11). Additionally the answer requires the knowledge that Israelites of Amos' day were mainly complacent rather than on edge. This is confirmed by passages such as 3:13–4:3; 5:18; 6:1–7, etc. Amos' contemporaries were simply ignoring the signs of the times and probably pressuring him not to prophesy (2:12; 7:12–16). Thus the necessity for the present disputation.

The timing and location are impossible to recover. Attempts to relate the passage chronologically to Amaziah's attacks on Amos (7:10, 12, 16) are only conjectural.

Comment

3–6 Amos' audience is asked seven questions. The first concerns the behavior of individuals; the next two concern lions as hunters; the next two concern snaring birds; the final two concern events in cities. The answer to the first six is clearly no. But the answer to the seventh—also but not clearly no—is the really important answer. The particular structure of each question, including the order in which the related circumstances are mentioned, is irrelevant to the impact.

3 Travel is a commonplace event, but strangers travel apart from one another. People would not be seen travelling jointly (יחדו) unless they had met (יעד, niphal), as anyone in Amos' audience would readily acknowledge.

4 The two questions in v 4 are similar. Lion (אריה) in 4a and young lion (כפיר) in 4b are normal parallel terms whose differences are insignificant. Indeed, the two couplets are "externally" parallel synonymously to each other, and thus "from his lair" in 4b, though metrically unwelcome, complements semantically "in the forest" in 4a. Lions hunt very quietly and roar only after taking prey. This, too, Amos' audience would admit as obvious.

5 The processes for trapping and snaring birds are generally well known, though there is uncertainty as to the exact meanings of פַּח (here: "trap") and מוֹקֵשׁ (here: "snare"). The point, however, of the two questions in this verse is easy to understand. Bird traps are set off by birds, not by nothing.

6 The scene shifts from intercity to inner city. Everyone knew the significance of blowing a שׁוֹפָר in a city. It was the means of alarm (cf. Hos 5:8) and usually warned of an enemy attack.

With the second couplet of v 6 comes the real point of Amos' inspired apologetic. Clearly the cause of disaster (רָעָה) in a city was not self-evident to Amos' audience, even though it should have been had they been aware enough of Yahweh's purposes. People who hoped that Yahweh would bring only help and never harm were forgetting that his covenant provided for curses as well as blessings. In effect Amos' seventh question could be paraphrased: "Do you really think that Yahweh would never punish you even if you deserve it?" Or, "When I prophesy disaster from Yahweh, am I not doing exactly what I ought?"

7 A straightforward prose declaration both clarifies the issue addressed dramatically in the seven poetic questions of vv 3–6 and generalizes it in principle. It also provides an effective transition to the combination declarationquestion format of v 8. There are no good grounds—only bad presuppositional ones—for excising this subsection of the passage as inauthentic.

The declaration goes beyond establishing that Yahweh can be the author of disaster. It establishes also that when Yahweh does such things he tells his prophets. The focus is upon legitimate prophetic authority, not upon prophetic autonomy. What prophets say comes from Yahweh; it is his סוֹד "counsel" and is therefore absolutely true. It is not that Yahweh cannot act without the help of prophets or that he is *obliged* to share his knowledge with them. Rather, consistent with other prophetical (Jer 7:25; 23:18, 22; 26:5; 35:15; 44:4) and historical (2 Kgs 17:13, 23; 21:10; 24:2) emphases on Yahweh's "servants the prophets," this verse states simply that the prophets carry a message not their own. Yahweh does explain his own actions and does use the prophets as his spokespersons. But he is hardly dependent on them. Two NT parallels are helpful: though God has chosen them, Abraham's children have no cause for boasting (Matt 3:9); God will be praised, yet those who do the praising have no reason to think themselves essential (Luke 19:40).

8 The first couplet of v 8 appears to be a double-entendre, referring literally to fear of lions and metaphorically to fear of the Lord. Yahweh's voice is compared in the OT both to the sound of thunder (e.g., Ps 29) and a lion's roar (Amos 1:2; Jer 25:30). It may even have actually sounded that way to the prophets, sometimes or always. OT descriptions of the sound of Yahweh's speaking audibly always imply a loud, roaring sound. (On the wording in 1 Kgs 19:12, frequently mistranslated "still, small voice" or the like, see J. Lust, *VT* 25 [1975] 110–15.)

The true prophet cannot ignore Yahweh's voice any more than sensible people can ignore the roar of a lion. If Yahweh has spoken to someone, can that person be expected not to prophesy (לֹא יִנָּבֵא)? To be chosen is to be obliged, as Jonah, for example, learned the hard way.

Moreover, rejection of Amos' prophecies meant rejection of Yahweh. If people were offended by what Amos preached, he was not to be blamed.

His reaction to Yahweh's revelation was inevitable and proper: he repeated it. Amos' hard words were not his own, but Yahweh's through him.

Explanation

The acts of Yahweh constitute the ultimate concern of the passage. The inseparables of the first subsection, vv 3–6, lead to a conclusion: a city's disaster is Yahweh's doing. The second subsection, v 7, makes clear that Yahweh's actions are not undertaken without prophetic explanation. The third subsection, v 8, insists that Yahweh's revelation requires repeating. Thus the logic of the passage as a whole: Yahweh has caused this disaster, has revealed it to Amos, and Amos must proclaim it. Amos' words are an eloquent defense of the necessity of doomsaying to a people wanting to hear only soothing news.

A parallel responsibility rests appropriately on those who are called to proclaim the good news of Christ: ". . . I am compelled to preach. Woe to me if I do not preach the gospel" (1 Cor 9:16).

The Annihilation of the Opulent   (3:9–4:3)

Bibliography

Barstad, H. M. "Die Basankühe in Amos 4:1." *VT* 25 (1975) 286–97. **Beebe, H. K.** "Ancient Palestinian Dwellings." *BA* 31 (1968) 38–58. **Boyle, M. O.** "The Covenant Lawsuit of the Prophet Amos 3:1–4:13." *VT* 21 (1971) 338–62. **Cohen, A.** *"Śēn."* *BMik* 23 (1978) 237–38. [Heb.] **Driver, G. R.** "Babylonian and Hebrew Notes." *WO* 2, 1 (1954) 19–26. ———. "Difficult Words in the Hebrew Prophets." In *Studies in Old Testament Prophecy Presented to T. H. Robinson,* ed. H. H. Rowley. Edinburgh: T. & T. Clark, 1950. 52–72. **Freedman, D. N.,** and **F. I. Andersen.** "Harmon in Amos 4:3." *BASOR* 198 (1970) 41. **Gese, H.** "Kleine Beiträge zum Verständnis des Amosbuches." *VT* 12 (1962) 417–38. **Glanzman, G. S.** "Two Notes: Am 3:15 and Os 11:8–9." *CBQ* 23 (1961) 227–33. **Glueck, J.** "The Verb *PRṢ* in the Bible and in the Qumran Literature." *RQ* 5 (1964–65) 123–27. **Jacobs, P.** "'Cows of Bashan'—A Note on the Interpretation of Amos 4:1." *JBL* 104 (1985) 109–10. **Loretz, O.** "Vergleich und Kommentar in Amos 3:12." *BZ* 20 (1976) 122–25. **Lurie, B. Z.** "[Amos 4:2b]." *BMik* 12, 2 (30) (1966–67) 6–11. [Heb.] **Mittmann, S.** "Amos 3, 12–15 und das Bett der Samarier." *ZDPV* 92 (1976) 149–67. **Moeller, H.** "Ambiguity at Amos 3:12." *BT* 15 (1964) 31–34. **Parrot, A.** *Samaria: The Capital of the Kingdom of Israel.* Tr. S. H. Hooke. New York: Philosophical Library, 1958. **Paul, S. M.** "Amos iii 15–Winter and Summer Mansions." *VT* 28 (1978) 358–59. ———. "Fishing Imagery in Amos 4:2." *JBL* 97 (1978) 183–90. **Pelser, H.** "Amos 3:11—A Communication." *Studies in the Books of Hosea and Amos OTWSA* 7, 8 (1964–65) 153–56. **Pfeifer, G.** "Die Denkform des Propheten Amos (iii 9–11)." *VT* 34 (1984) 476–81. **Rabinowitz, I.** "The Crux at Amos 3, 12." *VT* 11 (1961) 228–31. **Reider, J.** "דמשק in Amos 3, 12." *JBL* 67 (1948) 245–48. **Rinaldi, G.** "Due note ad Amos." *RSO* 28 (1953) 149–52. **Sawyer, J.** "Those Priests in Damascus." *ASTI* 8 (1970–71) 123–30. **Schwantes, S.** "Notes on Amos 4:2b." *ZAW* 79 (1967) 82–83. **Tucker, G. M.** "Prophetic Speech." *Int* 32 (1978) 31–45. **Vesco, J. L.** "Amos de Teqoa, defenseur de l'homme." *RB* 87 (1980) 481–543. **Watts, J. D. W.** "A Critical Analysis of Amos 4:1 ff." SBLASP (1972) 489–500. **Williams, A. J.** "A Further Suggestion about Amos iv 1–3." *VT* 29 (1979) 206–11. **Zolli, E.** "Amos 4:2b." *Antonianum* 30 (1955) 188–89.

Translation

Futility of royal fortifications

3:9 *Announce it at the royal fortifications*[a] *in Assyria*[b]
And at the royal fortifications[a] *in the land*[c] *of Egypt.*

Say: Assemble yourselves at Mount[d] *Samaria*
And see the great terror[e] *inside it, and the oppression*[f] *in its midst.*

10 *They do not know how to do right—Oracle of Yahweh—*
Those who store up violence and destruction in their royal fortifications.

11 *Therefore this is what the Lord*[a] *Yahweh said:*

An adversary[b] *will surround*[c] *the land*
And will bring down[d] *your defenses from you,*
And your royal fortifications will be plundered.

No rescue for the rich

12 *This is what Yahweh said:*

As a shepherd rescues from a lion's mouth a couple of leg bones or part of an ear, so will the Israelites who live in Samaria be "rescued"—just[a] *some luxurious bedding*[b] *here,*[a] *some fine couch fabric*[c] *there.*[a]

General demolition of the splendorous

13 *Listen and testify against the house of Jacob*
—Oracle of the Lord Yahweh, God of the Armies—

14 *For when I punish Israel for its sins,*
I will punish the altars of Bethel.
The horns of the altar will be cut off and fall to the ground.

15 *I will strike the winter house along with the summer house.*
The houses of ivory will perish,
And the mansions[a] *will be no more.*
                    —Oracle of Yahweh

The fate of Samaria's wealthy women

4:1 *Listen to this word,*
You Bashan cows on Mount Samaria,

Who oppress the poor
And crush the needy.

Who say to their[a] *masters,*[b]
"Go get us something to drink."
2 *The Lord*[a] *Yahweh has sworn by his holiness*
That days are coming for you[b]

*When they will pick you up*ᶜ *with hooks,*ᵈ
*Your remains*ᵉ *with fishing pikes.*ᶠ

³*You will be taken out*ᵃ *through the gaping holes,*ᵇ *each woman straight ahead,*ᶜ
*And will be thrown*ᵈ *to Harmon.*ᵉ

Notes

9.a. G χώραις reads ארצות "lands" rather than ארמנות "fortifications" here and in the parallel line, as well as in vv 10, 11; and 6:8. Did G's *Vorlage* somewhat systematically alter ארמנות?

9.b. Since Assyria is normally used in parallel to Egypt, and Ashdod never is, we read with G ἐν ᾿Ασσυρίοις "in Assyria."

9.c. G understandably omits a third reference to "lands."

9.d. Reading the sg with G, as supported by the succeeding sgs.

9.e. מהומה has several possible translations, as the variety among the versions attests. Here "terror."

9.f. Taking the pl to be an abstract pl.

11.a. אדוני "Lord" has no reflex in either Syr or the Sahidic Coptic, slight evidence at best against its authenticity.

11.b. צר was taken as "narrowness" (צַר) by Tg, σ', θ'; as a form of the verb צרר "to be afflicted" by Vg (*tribulator*); and as the n.loc. Tyre (צֹר) by G, α'; all reflecting less-than-likely options in light of the context.

11.c. Reading יְסוֹבֵב "will surround" with Syr (*nhdrjh*) and probably Tg (*tqph*) and Vg (*circuietur* "will be surrounded"), both of the latter being passives, yet confirming consonantal MT.

11.d. Tg and Vg read passives here as well, but in doing so still probably witness to consonantal MT.

12.a. The translation of ב...וב, highly idiomatic in the passage, cannot be literal.

12.b. Assuming פֵּאָה III "luxury," though פֵּאָה II "piece, part" is equally possible; the ambiguity may have been quite intentional.

12.c. Wolff's detailed review (196) of the options for this *hapax legomenon* phrase still fails to sustain his emendation to באמשת "at the headboard." Because of the frequent attacks on conspicuous luxury in Amos, דמשק can surely mean "damask," i.e., fine fabric.

15.a. Or "many (other) houses / buildings," as G, Vg, and Tg chose to render the ambiguous Heb. which encompasses both meanings of רבים. The often proposed emendation of רבים to הבנים "ebony" in order to parallel "ivory" above is inventive but unconvincing.

4:1.a. The passage mixes masc and fem forms and 2d and 3d person forms; an emendation to the 2 fem pl poss suff is therefore not necessary.

1.b. Or possibly "to their upper-class husbands" if a contrast with בעל is envisioned in the use of אדון here.

2.a. אדוני "Lord" is missing in G and Syr and may be secondary here.

2.b. Though the masc suffix is used, the women are still in focus. See n. 4:1.a. above.

2.c. The 3 m sg piel is used here with indefinite subject, i.e., "they."

2.d. The versions generally seem to read the pl of צנה II, "shields," though צ (butchering?) hook is more likely the word in question.

2.e. Or possibly "Your posterity / offspring."

2.f. G translates 2bβ quite differently, taking סירות as "kettles," reading דוגה as דלקה "set fire to" (so Wolff, 204, n. j) and by other constructions not easily explicable.

3.a. Assuming that the G passive ἐξενεχθήσεσθε "you will be taken out" reflects an originally intended vocalization תֵּצֶאנָה or the like.

3.b. פרצים "gaping holes" is apparently used adverbially here.

3.c. Or "all in a row," though the parallel usage in Josh 6:5, 20 is determinative.

3.d. G's passive form ἀπορριφήσεσθε "you will be taken out" probably correctly reflects a hoph vocalization of the Heb.

3.e. G εἰς τὸ ὄρος τὸ Ρεμμαν "to Mt. Rimmon" reads הר הרמונה or possibly ההר הרמון. If (Mount) Hermon is meant, an emendation to חרמונה would be required.

Form / Structure / Setting

The passage contains four oracles against Samaria: 3:9–11; 3:12; 3:13–15; 4:1–3. Are the four independent of one another, or are they subsections of an integrated whole? The latter option is the more likely for the following reasons: (1) Each describes a related aspect of Samaria's degenerate wealthy style, the four thus functioning harmoniously and in a complementary manner to depict the range of Samaria's covenant infidelity. (2) Each concludes with a brief Pentateuchal covenant curse that is graphically portrayed. (3) Each directly quotes Yahweh with overt reference to his being quoted. (4) Each assumes the coming defeat of the capital by a foreign enemy. (5) Each associates Samaria with complacent high living, in an ironic or even mocking tone. (6) Each is composed in parallelistic prose.

There are, of course, differences. For example, 3:12 is more obviously prose than the other three oracles, and it alone does not begin with a plural imperative from the root שׁמע "hear" (leading some, not unreasonably, to consider it part of the conclusion to 3:9–11). And only 3:13–15 employs first-person verb forms. But the evidence for connection outweighs that for theoretical isolation.

The passage is perhaps best identified as a partial covenant lawsuit form, with overtones of the disputation form and the messenger form. Each oracle includes evidence of Samaria's guilt before Yahweh's law and a judgment sentence against the population or some part thereof. The plural summonses to witness (against) Israel's sins in 3:9, 13 are covenant lawsuit features. Yet the repeated emphasis on citation of Yahweh's words (3:10, 11, 12, 13, 15; 4:1, 2) has the ring of a messenger speech. And the mockery of Samaria's splendid living reminds one of a disputation. So the form can hardly be rigidly classified.

The meter is highly irregular throughout. No run of balanced couplets or triplets is to be found. Some verses seem mostly or entirely to be prose (3:10, 12, 13, 14; 4:3), and others are apparently parallelistic prose or free verse. Yet each oracle shows structural balance or "parallelism" within most of its sentences, as e.g., in 3:12 where two parts of a (sheep) body are compared to two parts of Samaria's finery.

Because of the direct address to Samaritans in 3:11; 4:1–3 and our knowledge from 7:10–17 that Amos hardly avoided confrontation, it would seem likely that the setting for this four-part, compound oracle was Samaria. But since the prophetic books are replete with direct address to distant places (cf. Assyria and Egypt in 3:9), it is almost never certain that Yahweh's word about and to a place was preached at that place. Likewise, we cannot tell when in Amos' career these words were spoken. Certainly they may have been among those sayings that infuriated Jeroboam II and Amaziah, among others (7:10, 12).

Comment

9 God gives his word as if to emissaries who are to invite the leadership of nations who do not know him or keep his law to witness the corrupt reign of terror within his own people. The superpowers Egypt and Assyria, both known in the eighth century and earlier for their callous imperialism and subjugation of helpless peoples (Deut 6:12; Hos 7:8–11; 9:3; Jonah 3:8; Isa 10:5–11; Mic 5:6), have nothing on Israel. Royal fortifications (ארמנות) were impressive—multistoried, multichambered buildings in which the leisure class (royalty and nobility) of class-structured ancient societies lived and "worked" comfortably. Even people long used to living off the labor of others would be shocked to see the level of exploitation practiced in Samaria. They are invited to see Samaria's "great terror" (מהומת רבות). The term מהומה normally construed with רב or a similar adjective first appears in Deuteronomy and often refers to the panicked confusion of war (e.g., Deut 7:23; 28:20; 1 Sam 5:9; Isa 22:5), and thus, as the very opposite of "peace" or "safety" (cf. 2 Chr 15:5), it implies conditions in which no one is secure from the violence at the disposal of those in power. "Oppression" (עשוקים) straightforwardly connotes control by the relatively powerful of the relatively powerless, i.e., subjugation (cf. Eccl 4:1; Jer 22:3). Samaria in Amos' day was a city whose great wealth was controlled by and for an upper-class few and in which the exploited masses were kept in check by fear.

10 Those leaders responsible for Samaria's style were so habituated to their reign of oppression that they did not know what "right" (נכחה, which means simply what is just, honest, decent, and proper just as *right* does in English) was. In other words, Samaritan society had over the years so thoroughly departed from the standards of the Mosaic covenant, standards of which Amos was a divinely appointed enforcer, that its favored citizens generally would not know what those standards were. The standards adopted instead were the amoral Canaanite-Palestinian ones that allowed people to live selfishly and splendorously, to exploit others, to increase their holdings without limits, and to engage in virtually any personal or sensual pleasures. The Canaanites effectively had no covenantal demands on their personal or social morality and were religiously legitimate so long as they merely faithfully worshiped via the sacrificial system and financially supported the cult.

The oracle metaphorically portrays these people's treasures and expensive possessions (cf. vv 12, 15) as violence and destruction (חמס ושד). These two words occur often together in the OT prophets virtually in hendiadys as a shorthand description of the general breakdown of conditions in society (Jer 6:7; 20:8; Isa 60:18; Ezek 45:9, Hab 1:3; 2:17) and in contrast to such concepts as justice and righteousness. חמס connotes violence against people, including assault and bloodshed (cf. Job 16:17; Jer 51:35; Hab 2:8; Ezek 7:23), while שד is associated more often, though not exclusively, with violence to property (Hos 10:14; Mic 2:4; Obad 5). Together the two words cover the spectrum of abuse against people and their property. The treasures of the royal fortifications, the costly furnishings and the obscene profits of the wealthy nobility, are in God's eyes not assets but proof upon proof of horrible crimes committed against the innocent by degenerates displaying not even a basic sense of right and wrong.

11 Covenant punishments must be unleashed against such a city. The oracle announces the fulfillment of at least three specific Pentateuchal curse types, any of which might also be subsumed under curse type 3: war and its ravages (cf. esp. Deut 28:52, ". . . until the high fortified walls in which you trust fall down."). They are (1) the prediction of enemy occupation of the land (type 5; cf. Deut 28:47–57); (2) the destruction of the (fortified) cities (type 9b; cf. also the use of ירד "come down" in Deut 28:43, and עו "strength" in Lev 26:19, "I will break down the *strength* of your pride"); and (3) loss of possessions/impoverishment (cf. Deut 28:31), curse type 17. One may also detect the flavor of a futility curse here (type 15) in that the very things trusted to defend will provide no defense at all.

12 The emphasis shifts slightly from the folly of trusting in fortifications to the folly of trusting in wealth. Violent death will be the end of those who gained their conspicuous wealth by violence. The verse, assuming its state of preservation allows it to be translated accurately (see textual notes), describes a fate which fulfills covenantal curse type 24, the curse of death and destruction (cf. Deut 4:26; 28:20; 29:20) and perhaps also the curses of decimation (type 12, Lev 26:21–22; Deut 28:62; 32:36) and desolation (type 9, Lev 26:32–35; Deut 28:51). The three types are, of course, similar and interrelated. The great capital city and its population will be so destroyed that only fragments of its once proud wealth will be findable. There is a mocking, scornful tone to this denunciation of those who so enjoyed their luxury and finery. While most Israelites slept on simple mats and sat on the ground, Samaria's opulent oligarchy indulged their expensive tastes in furniture that the average citizen could never afford.

13 The subject of the plural imperatives "listen" and "testify" (שמעו והעידו) is not indicated. Of the various specific possibilities (the prophets in general, the foreign national leaders of 3:9, Amos alone, the citizenry of Israel) none really fits the context. Rather, the purpose of the language associated with court proceedings is simply to bring the hearer to an awareness of the covenant lawsuit motif. The nation is on trial, and Yahweh is the speaker summoning witnesses to consider the evidence against it and to hear his verdict. By using the term בית יעקב "house of Jacob," Yahweh reminds the Samaritans that they are not merely a cosmopolitan eighth-century political entity, but are in reality part of the continuum that began with the partiarchs (cf. 5:15; 6:8; 7:2, 5, 9, 16; 8:7) and as such are a people under the bond of a divine covenant. An appeal to people's origins is one effective way of getting their attention in their present degeneracy and thus is used widely by the OT prophets and NT apostles (being perhaps Paul's most common corrective technique).

The hearer / reader is reminded that Yahweh is the speaker twice in these verses (13 and 15), here via the expanded titulary "Lord Yahweh, God of the (heavenly) Armies," used nowhere else in Amos.

14 The evidence of Samaria's guilt is intermixed with the divine judgment sentence. The use of פקד twice reflects covenantal language (Deut 5:9; Lev 18:25, etc.), though this word with its many meanings (count, appoint, attend to, etc.) most often means "punish" in the prophetic books. What has Israel done? It has generally committed "sins" (פשעים), meaning any number of covenant violations over the years and across the land. But its leading sin is represented by Bethel. That there are *altars at Bethel* says it all. Israel worships via idolatry (1 Kgs 12:28–30; Hos 13:2) in violation of the Mosaic covenant

(Exod 20:3, 4) at an illegal place (Deut 12; Hos 4:15). For this the punishment will be destruction of the cult (curse type 2; cf. Lev 26:31, "I will lay waste your sanctuaries . . .").

15 Bethel's altars merely served those who traveled to them, especially from Samaria (cf. 7:13). If the house of worship must be destroyed, so too must the house of the worshiper (curse type 9; could it be that Lev 26:31, which mentions in parallel the desolation of sanctuaries and cities, stands behind the present oracle's similar ordering?). The verse contains two pairings (winter house . . . summer house; houses of ivory . . . mansions) which involve four times the word בית "house," thus echoing its use in v 13 (house of Jacob) and v 14 where בית is contained in the name Bethel, "house of God." Like the ארמנות "royal fortifications," Israel's great religious and secular houses constituted monuments to the nation's corruption. Yahweh will strike (הכה, cf. Lev 26:24; Deut 28:22, 27, 28, 35) them so that they perish (אבד, cf. Lev 26:38; Deut 4:26; 28:20, 22; 30:18). On "houses of ivory," cf. 6:4; 1 Kgs 22:39; Ps 45:8; and A. Parrot, *Samaria*, (New York: Philosophical Library, 1958).

4:1 The final individual unit of the compound oracle attacks the haughty women of Samaria, much like Isaiah's later oracle against the vain women of Jerusalem (Isa 3:16–4:1), which also is composed in a mixed prose / poetry style. Samaria's leading women are likened metaphorically to fat cows (פרות הבשן). The large Transjordan region of Bashan was known for the size of its cattle (Deut 32:14; Ezek 39:18; Ps 22:12) and its rich pasturage (Mic 7:14; Jer 50:19). It is probably on the allegory beginning in Deut 32:13 that the present oracle is based: the fattened animal rebels against its master and must be punished by deprivation and destruction (i.e., curse type 12, with type 12b being applied ironically here metaphorically rather than literally).

Such women are guilty of irresponsibility in two social directions: toward inferiors and toward superiors. The poor and needy (אביונים . . . דלים, a standard parallel pair for society's dependent people) they oppress / crush, i.e., abuse and misuse for their own personal profit and power. Then, from their masters (אדניהם) i.e., husbands, they demand the household service that, according to normal practice, they themselves should be providing. They are, in effect, arrogantly dominating their families (cf. 1 Tim 3:11, which speaks of the same sort of domineering on the part of women). The reference to "drink" (ונשתה, cf. 2:8; Prov 4:17; 31:4–5) adds to an impression of irresponsibility and callousness on the part of these women.

2 The absolute inevitability of death and destruction (curse type 24, cf. Deut 28:20, "destroyed and come to sudden ruin"; Deut 32:35, "Young men and young women will perish," etc.) is sealed by Yahweh's swearing an oath "by his holiness" (בקדשו), an expression known from the context of Ps 89:35 to represent divine determination to enforce a covenant (cf. also Heb 6:13–20; 7:20–22). Reference to the "days . . . coming" (ימים באים, cf. Jer 7:32; 9:24; 16:14) signals a new era when woeful destruction shall quickly replace selfish complacency (cf. Deut 4:25–26).

The oracle identifies the punishment awaiting Samaria's cruel *grandes dames:* a blend of horrible death (reflecting curse types 22, denial of burial, and

24, death) and exile (v 3, below). Such a blending is common in the Pentateuchal curses, where death takes some of the covenant-breakers, exile takes others, and both fates take yet others (e.g., Deut 28:63; Lev 26:38). Here a kind of exile of the dead combines the two curse types. The scene has something of the flavor of Lev 26:30, "I will . . . pile your dead bodies on the lifeless forms of your idols. . . ."

3 The thoroughly conquered city of Samaria will have so many gaps or holes (פרצים) broken through its perimeter wall that one could exit virtually in any direction. Josh 6:5, 20 describes how the crumbling of Jericho's walls allowed the Israelites to rush into the city "straight ahead" (איש נגדו), exactly parallel to the present איש נגדה. The dead bodies of the once proud Samaritan women will be picked up like so much meat, taken straight out of the city by the nearest breach in the wall, and thrown (שלך) away. Since שלך, hophal, is used elsewhere in connection both with exile (Jer 22:28) and the casting away of corpses (Isa 34:3; Ezek 16:5; and esp. Jer 14:16), it is conceivable that the present verse makes both a literal and a metaphorical prediction, i.e., both exile (curse type 13) and death are envisioned. The identity of the *hapax legomenon* "Harmon" remains a mystery. Suggested emendations include ארמון "royal fortification," Rimmon (cf. Judg 20:45, 47), ערמות "naked," and החרמתנה "devoted to destruction," as well as the ancient versions' options (n.3.e.). Apparently the women's bodies are to be thrown either a long distance (Mount Hermon?) or to a dumpsite, but there is no way of telling.

Explanation

Throughout the four units of this compound oracle, Samaria's present leisure and luxury is contrasted to its coming horrors. A city of pleasure seekers will see its wealth stolen, its comforts ruined, its cult annihilated and its people captured, killed, and exiled. In the enforcement of his covenant against those who have so thoroughly scorned it as to have forgotten how to live decently (3:10), Yahweh will show no mercy. "Every sort of . . . disaster" (Deut 28:61) will come upon a city whose nobility undoubtedly thought that disaster was for other people and other times. Women, as fully as men, are held responsible when Yahweh's special people, the poor, are mistreated. Samaria's sins are many. Its punishment will be severe. The city of high living will die.

Past Punishments Only a Sampling (4:4–13)

Bibliography

Berg, W. *Die sogenannten Hymnenfragmente im Amosbuch.* Bern: Lang, 1974. **Botterweck, G. J.** "Zur Authentizität des Buches Amos." *BZ* n.f. 2 (1958) 176–89. **Boyle, M. O.**

"The Covenant Lawsuit of the Prophet Amos 3:1–4:13." *VT* 21 (1971) 338–62. **Brueg-gemann, W.** "Amos 4:4–13 and Israel's Covenant Worship." *VT* 15 (1965) 1–15. **Carny, P.** "Doxologies: A Scientific Myth." *Hebrew Studies* 18 (1977) 149–59. **Crenshaw, J. L.** "A Liturgy of Wasted Opportunity: Amos 4:6–12." *Semitics* 1 (1970) 27–37. ———. "Amos and the Theophanic Tradition." *ZAW* 80 (1968) 203–15. **Crüsemann, F.** *Studien zur Formgeschichte von Hymnus und Danklied in Israel.* WMANT 32. Neukirchen-Vluyn: Neukirchener Verlag, 1969. 97–106. **Fensham, F. C.** "Common Trends in Curses of the Near Eastern Treaties and *Kudurru* Inscriptions Compared with Maledictions of Amos and Isaiah." *ZAW* 75 (1963) 155–75. **Foresti, F.** "Funzione semantica dei brani participiali di Amos: 4, 13; 5, 8s; 9, 5s." *Bib* 62 (1981) 169–84. **Galling, K.** "Bethel und Gilgal." *ZDPV* 66 (1943) 140–55; 67 (1944–45) 21–43. **Gaster, T. H.** "An Ancient Hymn in the Prophecies of Amos." *Journal of the Manchester Egyptian and Oriental Society* 19 (1935) 23–26. **Horst, F.** "Die Doxologien im Amosbuch." *ZAW* 47 (1929) 45–54. **Koch, K.** "Die Rolle der hymnischen Abschnitte in der Komposition des Amos-Buches." *ZAW* 86 (1974) 504–37. **McCullough, W.** "Some Suggestions about Amos." *JBL* 72 (1953) 247–54. **Muilenburg, J.** "The Linguistic and Rhetorical Usages of the Particle כי in the Old Testament." *HUCA* 32 (1961) 135–60. **Nishizu, T.** "Amos 4:4–5: A Post-Exilic Redaction." *Nanzan Shingaku* 6 (Feb. 1983) 1–21. [Japanese] **Ramsey, G.** "Amos 4:12—A New Perspective." *JBL* 89 (1976) 187–91. **Rudolph, W.** "Amos 4:6–13." In *Wort—Gebot—Glaube: Beiträge zur Theologie des Alten Testaments.* FS W. Eichrodt. Ed. J. J. Stamm et al. ATANT 59. Zurich: Zwingli, 1970. **Watts, J. D. W.** "A Critical Analysis of Amos 4:1ff." Society of Biblical Literature, 1972, SBLASP (1972) 489–500. ———. "An Old Hymn Preserved in the Book of Amos." *JNES* 15 (1956) 33–39. ———. *Vision and Prophecy in Amos.* Grand Rapids: Eerdmans, 1958. 51–67. **Weiser, A.** "Zu Amos 4:6–13." *ZAW* 46 (1928) 49–59. **Youngblood, R.** לקראת in Amos 4:12." *JBL* 90 (1971) 98.

Translation

A sarcastic call to illegal worship

4:4 *Come to Bethel and rebel,*

> *To Gilgal and rebel even more!*
> *Bring your sacrifices every morning*
> *And your tithes every three days.*

> 5 *Burn* [a] *a thanksgiving offering of leavened bread;*
> *Announce loudly free will offerings,* [b]
> *For this is what you love, Israelites!*
> > *—Oracle of the Lord Yahweh*

Curses already fulfilled as warnings:

Famine

6 *I even gave* [a] *you empty mouths* [b] *in all your cities and a lack of food in all your towns.* [c] *But you did not return to me.*
> *—Oracle of Yahweh*

Drought

7 *I even withheld rain from you for three months prior to the harvest. (I would cause it* [a] *to rain on one city, yet prevent it from raining on another. One field*

would get rain, while a field on which no rain fell would dry up. [8]*Two or three cities would stagger*[a] *over to another city to get water to drink, but could not get enough.) But you did not return to me.*

                                        —*Oracle of Yahweh*

Agricultural disaster

[9]*I attacked you with blight and mildew.*[a]
When your gardens and vineyards increased,

Locusts would devour[b] *your fig trees and olive trees.*
But you did not return to me.

                                        —*Oracle of Yahweh*

Pestilence and war

[10]*I sent plagues*[a] *among you as it was in Egypt.*
I killed your young men with the sword and your horses were captured;[b]
I caused the stench of your camps to rise right into your nostrils.[c]
But you did not return to me.

                                        —*Oracle of Yahweh*

The fate of the cities of the plain

[11]*I overthrew some*[a] *of you as God overthrew Sodom and Gomorrah so that you were like a log pulled away from the conflagration. But you did not return to me.*

                                        —*Oracle of Yahweh*

The worst yet to come

[12]*Therefore this is what I will do to you, Israel,*
Because this is what I have already been[a] *doing to you.*
Prepare to meet[b] *your God, Israel,* [13]*for he is:*

Hymn Fragment No. 1

The Shaper[a] *of the mountains*[b] *and the creator of the wind,*
Who reveals to human beings what his plan[c] *is,*

The one who turns the dawn into[d] *darkness*
And walks the earth's heights.
Yahweh God of the Armies is his name.

Notes

5.a. On the use of the inf abs as a substitute for virtually any finite verb in a series, see GKC, 113z; Joüon, 123x; or T. O. Lambdin, *Introduction to Biblical Hebrew* (New York: Scribners 1971), 158–59.

5.b. Syr *wndrw ndrʾ* apparently read ר instead of ב in נדבות "freewill offerings."

6.a. G δώσω "will give" assumes a prophetic perfect, i.e., a prediction, technically likely only if virtually all the impfs in vv 7, 9, etc. are repointed so as to be unconverted.

6.b. Lit., "cleanness of teeth," i.e., lack of food. Here the versions translate the idiom literally and uncomprehendingly, with G even translating γομφιασμὸν ὀδόντων, "toothaches."

6.c. I.e., any place where people lived; not (small) towns as opposed to (larger) cities.

7.a. Here and following in vv 7 and 8, G makes the verbs fut (so also Vg in part), taking the oracle as prediction rather than retrospective.

8.a. G συναθροισθήσονται "shall be gathered" read נעד rather than נדע "stagger." The metathesization may well have preceded G.

9.a. G has πυρώσει "fever" or possibly "parching" for שדפון "blight," and ἰκτέρῳ "blight" or possibly "yellowing / jaundice" for ירקון "mildew," both of which are merely interpretive and still support MT.

9.b. G attests to הרבות "devour" even in its use of a finite verb form ἐπληθύνατε, as do σ' θ' Vg Tg. The common emendation to the hiph of חרב is quite unnecessary since part of the flavor of the statement is that of a futility curse. See *Comment.*

10.a. דבר "plague" is collective here. G θάνατον "death" is simply interpretive, as in Lev 26:25, Deut 28:21, etc.

10.b. Lit., "along with the capture of your horses."

10.c. Thus rendering the *waw* intensive before באפכם "into your nostrils" (GKC, 154a).

11.a. Assuming that ב here has its force "among" and is not merely a prepositional accompaniment of the verb.

12.a. The recognition that the impf of עשה is used here with its past durative value, as frequently in the passage already, and in purposeful contrast to its use as a fut in the first half of the verse, obviates any consideration of repetitiousness.

12.b. G ἐπικαλεῖσθαι "to call on" either took לקראת as if from קרא, or had only לקרא in its *Vorlage*, or else assumed that the normal value, "to meet," was not sufficiently stern in a judgment oracle.

13.a. G renders the initial line in the 1st person (ἐγὼστερεῶν) to conform with v 12.

13.b. G reads βροντήν (= רעם "thunder") instead of "mountains," inexplicable unless G's Heb. text was already garbled.

13.c. G χριστὸν αὐτοῦ "his anointed," i.e., משיחו for מה־שחו "what his plan is" reflects an already corrupt Heb. text. Tg מא עובדוהי read מעשהו "his work" also from a corruption.

13.d. G (καὶ) and some MT MSS read "dawn *and* darkness," quite possibly the original wording ("maker of dawn and darkness").

Form / Structure / Setting

Is 4:4–13 a unity, or is it three (vv 4–5; 6–11; 12–13) or four (dividing vv 12 and 13) separate oracles? The arguments against unity are based on a purported lack of connectedness between the sections. But an interconnectedness can surely be demonstrated (cf. Wolff, 211–15): (1) The entire passage addresses Israel directly. (2) Yahweh is the speaker throughout. This is obvious in vv 6–12, and is hardly less likely in vv 4–5 and 13 simply because of a lack of first person pronominal forms. (3) The list of fulfilled curses in vv 6–11 requires a basis for the punishment of the past, which is Israel's illegal worship (vv 4–5), and also requires a concluding judgment sentence (vv 12–13) since past punishments are little threat to anyone. (4) Verse 12 leaves unexplained how awesome "meeting" God will be; it requires v 13, which tells that the one to be encountered will be terrible indeed. (5) The surprisingly consistent use of נאם יהוה "oracle of Yahweh" or similar formula to conclude successive sections (vv 5, 6, 8, 9, 10, 11) and the parallel impact of the mention of the divine name at the end of v 13 ties together the various parts. The focus of the entire oracle is a true, direct encounter with none other than the omnipotent Yahweh. (6) A connection between vv 4–5 and vv 12–13 is to be discerned in the contrast between false and true meeting with God. Worship is, in part, encounter with God. What the Israelites improperly sought by worshiping at Gilgal and Bethel (v 4) they will genuinely get, although in a way they would never have chosen, when Yahweh reveals himself to them (v 13). (7) The use of וגם אני ("I even . . .") in v 6 is probably—though not unquestionably—evidence of linkage to the preceding.

V 13, by reason of its cadenced employment of participial clauses, has been recognized by scholars since H. Schmidt (*Der Prophet Amos* [Tübingen, 1917]) as hymnic in style (see esp. Watts, "An Old Hymn"). Indeed, 4:13, 5:8, and 9:5–6 may each be fragments of an early Yahwistic hymn otherwise unknown, and excerpted as an effective means of reminding Amos' audience of old truths about their God. (For a contrary view, cf. Carny, "Doxologies.")

The curse motifs in vv 6–11 are, predictably, very closely tied to the Mosaic curses in Leviticus and Deuteronomy. On the individual types and their vocabulary affinities with Lev 26 and Deut 28, see *Comment* (Wolff, 213, provides a table of shared vocabulary which is useful except for its impression that Amos 4 is somehow unusual in its dependency on Pentateuchal curse language.)

The use of לכן "therefore" in v 12 reminds one of the covenant lawsuit form in which לכן introduces judgment sentences (cf. Hos 2:4–17). In the present oracle, there is a summons of sorts (vv 4–5), evidence of covenant crimes (esp. פשע v. 4), and announcement of punishment (v 12)—all lawsuit motifs. And yet the oracle is especially didactic in tone, so much so that J. Begrich ("Die Priesterliche Tora," *Werden und Wesen des Alten Testaments*, ed. P. Volz et al., BZAW 66 [Berlin: De Gruyter, 1936], 63–88) identified it as a prophetic parody of a priestly Torah (legal instruction). Such an identification might be more compelling if there actually existed conclusive data as to what priestly Torahs contained.

While one can imagine Amos speaking these words to pilgrims headed out of Samaria to the shrines at Bethel and Gilgal, so could Amos' audience imagine themselves en route. Thus it cannot be determined where the oracle was actually delivered or when Amos delivered it.

The passage mixes prose and poetry. Vv 4–5, 13 are clearly poetic. Vv 9 and 12 might be poetic, or else simply repetitively-structured prose. The remainder of the passage appears to be prose. Such a mixing of prose and poetry in a single oracle (called by some a "prose poem") is characteristic of Amos, as also of the prophets in general.

Comment

4 Amos' sarcastic invitation to rebel (פשע, Amos' only use of the root as a verb) may well have been designed to parody Israelite priests and / or Levites at the two great northern sanctuaries (Begrich, "Die Priesterliche Tora," *Werden und Wesen*, 63–88). Both sites had venerable histories as worship centers. Bethel, about 18 km. north of Jerusalem, was inaugurated as a sanctuary by Jacob (Gen 28:17–22) and served as a worship center after the conquest (Judg 20:18). Samuel judged there (1 Sam 7:16). Jeroboam I made it a rival of Jerusalem—the "temple of the kingdom" (Amos 7:13)—in open violation of the Mosaic law (1 Kgs 12). Gilgal, on the edge of Jericho, was the first central sanctuary after the conquest (Josh 4:19–5:15), the site of Saul's anointing as king (1 Sam 11), and, by the eighth century, apparently a substitute for Dan as a Northern pilgrimage site (cf. Hos 12:11).

But Jerusalem antedated them both as regards the worship of Yahweh (Gen 14:18–20) and alone was the legitimate sanctuary of the covenant (Deut

12). The Israelites' פשע "rebellion" was probably of three aspects: (1) they worshiped at an improper locale; (2) they worshiped in an improper manner (via illegitimate priests, idols, etc.; cf. 1 Kgs 12:28–33); and (3) they substituted worship for righteous behavior (cf. the surrounding oracles, esp. 5:21–27).

Typical pilgrimages of the day may have lasted at least three days. Sacrifices (זבחים), i.e., the slaughtering of animals, were made on the first morning after arrival, and tithes (מעשרות) given on the third. Amos exaggerates the practice to "every day" and every "third day," as if the Israelites were doing nothing but making pilgrimages. Even such intense worship was odious to Yahweh. In the context, the pronouns "your" (כם-) on "worship" and "tithes" suggest that they were not really acceptable to Yahweh.

5 "Burn" (קטר, here piel) refers to any offering by fire and is sometimes found as a parallel to זבח "sacrifice" (e.g., Hos 4:13; cf. Lev 17:5, 6). The oracle thus describes not a different sacrificial process from that of v 4, but an elaboration thereof. The thanksgiving offering (תודה) and the free will offering (נדבה) were both voluntary, beyond-the-call-of-duty sacrifices (Lev 7:12–18) and were subcategories of the peace offering. The Israelites made a point ("announce loudly") of going beyond the expected minimum. They sacrificed with a real intensity, but it was in fact simply an intensifying of their sin (cf. Hos 13:2). The grammar of v 5a makes חמץ "leaven" the object of קטר "burn." Amos therefore indicts an unwitting violation of the sacrificial laws in the burning of leaven (contrary to Lev 2:11; cf. 6:14–17). Leavened bread was part of the peace offerings (Lev 7:13), but it was not to be burned.

Using the covenantal term אהב "love / be loyal to" (cf. G. Wallis, "אהב," *TDOT*, 1:104–16), Amos reveals Israel's true love. They do not really love Yahweh or neighbor as the covenantal relationship demands (Deut 6:5; Lev 19:18). What they love is the sacrificial system with its reward for procedure and donation and its excuse for other social and religious failures.

6 Since the days of Moses, the Israelites had been told that covenantal punishments were intended not only to be retributive, but also to force the nation to return to Yahweh (Deut 4:29–31; 30:1–10; cf. Hos 2:4–17; 14:2; Isa 10:20–27; Jer 32:30–42, etc.). Through Amos God delivers a litany of failed warnings to Israel (cf. the similar warning in Isa 9:8–10:11). No particular instance of famine (Pentateuchal curse type 7) is necessarily in focus. כל (literally "all") can also mean "all sorts of" without specificity as to time and place. Hard times should have impelled Israel to repentance, but they refused to "return to" (שוב עד) Yahweh. The expression comes from Deut 4:30 (cf. Hos 14:2) and is a synonym for שוב אל, a standard expression for turning from idolatry and polytheism (cf. Deut 4:28) to orthodox faithfulness to Yahweh (see W. L. Holladay, *The Root ŠÛBH in the Old Testament* [Leiden: E. J. Brill, 1958] 116–21).

7–8 Drought (curse type 6a; cf. Lev 26:19; Deut 28:22–24)—widespread, long-enduring ("three months"), erratically localized, and frustrating—had produced no repentance either. Amos' vocabulary, specifically the words גשם "rain," המטיר "cause to rain," שבע "get enough," comes straight from the covenant sanction passages listed above, as Wolff's list (213) demonstrates. (On weather as a covenant sanction sample warning / punishment, see T. Longman, "1 Sam 12:16–19: Divine Omnipotence or Covenant curse?" *WTJ* 45 (1983) 168–71; cf. also Ezek 38:22.)

9 The third reminiscence mentions three types of curse fulfillments experienced by the Israelites as a combination warning-invitation to conversion. "Blight and Mildew" (שדפון וירקון; Deut 28:22; cf. 1 Kgs 8:37) stand as a synecdoche for crop diseases in general (type 6c). "Locusts" (גזם) stand for crop pests in general (type 6b; cf. Deut 28:39–42). The mention of "vineyards" (כרמיכם; cf. Deut 28:39) and "olive trees" (זיתיכם; cf. Deut 28:40), among others, planted and brought to maximum yield and then devoured by pests before providing food for those who tended them, is a kind of futility curse (type 15; cf. esp. Deut 28:30, 39, 40).

10 The fourth section describes the warning punishments of pestilence (type 8) and war (type 3), linked together as in Lev 26:25 and in the lengthy description of the miseries of the siege in Deut 28:49–57. The vocabulary, including the piel of שלח "send," the reference to Egypt, and the mention of the "sword" (חרב) is derived in part directly from the Mosaic law curse passages. War is hopeless when Yahweh will not even allow one's soldiers to be healthy or confident (cf. 2:13–16; 2 Kgs 19:35–36). Death and destructive defeat by enemies in war are classic curse motifs. Israel should have recognized such horrible events (as in 2:3, 6, 13, etc.) as dire warnings. But they took no heed.

11 The most extreme historical destruction known to ancient Israelites was the total obliteration of the cities of the plain (Gen 19). It figured in the Mosaic curses in Deut 28:23 as a metaphor of what Yahweh's judgment against apostate Israel would be like (curse type 23). The curse types of the present oracle increase progressively in severity, from famine (relatively cyclical and not uncommon) to miraculous divine destruction. The Israelites ought to have viewed themselves as fortunate to be alive ("a log pulled away from the conflagration"), as was the family of Lot (Gen 19:29). But whatever the actual disasters the verse alludes to (for example, earthquakes and resulting fires), they had no effect on the stubborn infidelity of the Israelites of Amos' day.

12 The past miseries, selective and occasional, had been purposeful samples of divine wrath. These sorts of things Yahweh had "already been doing" (אעשה) as warnings. Since the warnings had produced no repentance while there was still time for conversion, Yahweh's loyalty to his covenant responsibilities now demanded a full unleashing of the sanctions. What sanctions to unleash? None other than what the covenant specified: i.e., the twenty-seven types. The punishments to come would be identical in character to some of the punishments already happening in limited, constrained ways. Therefore God says, "This is what (כה) I will do (אעשה) to you." The difference, of course, is that the limits will be removed. A paraphrase might be: "You will now experience not these few, isolated miseries, but the full range of miseries they represent, all at once, everywhere, affecting everyone." Or, more simply, "You haven't seen anything yet."

. The wording לקראת אלהיך "to meet your God" appears to reflect intentionally Exod 19:17, where the same expression describes the awesome theophanic encounter at Sinai, with its potential for death (v 21). It may also, however, have a conscious connection to the oft-repeated קרי "(hostile) encounter" of Lev 26 (vv 21, 23, 24, 27, 28, 40, 41). (On הכון "prepare" as related to preparation for war, cf. Ezek 38:7. On the likelihood that 12c begins the hymnic excerpt continued in v 13, see Watts, "An Old Hymn.")

13 Yahweh is indeed one to be feared. He has the power to destroy all adversaries, including Israel, not merely because he is influential among the gods (as polytheistic Israelites of the day probably considered him) but because he is *the* creator and sustainer. He is "shaper" (יוֹצֵר), creator (בֹּרֵא), revealer (מַגִּיד), maker (עֹשֶׂה), and walker / treader (דֹּרֵךְ), i.e., in control of everything and everyone. The created order answers to him.

The identity of "your God" in 12c (the morphologically ambiguous plural may even have connoted "your gods" to some in Amos' audience) is specified in 13b: "Yahweh God of the Armies." The armies in question are the "heavenly armies," i.e., "principalities and powers" (Eph 6:12), the various angelic and demonic spirits and forces. Yahweh rules them all (cf. Ps 82) and so is called God of the Armies (cf. B. N. Wambarq, *L'epithète divine Jahwé Sebaôt* [Paris: de Brouer, 1947]).

This doxology, as it is often called (v 13, with or without 12c), closely connects Yahweh's sovereignty over natural forces with his sovereignty over humans. "Wind" (רוּחַ) may also be translated "spirit" or "breath" (cf. Ezek 37:1–14), and thus, almost chiastically, this conclusion to the oracle reminds Amos' audience of who holds their very lives in the balance. Yahweh's plan (שֵׂחוֹ) is surely a reference to the divine will and law, which, because it is possessed by human beings through revelation, makes them fully accountable for their actions.

Explanation

Sarcastically calling Israelites to their covenantally illegal worship, Amos reminds them of the hard times and disasters they have repeatedly known. He preached in a time of relative prosperity to people who were apparently quite satisfied that their approach to life, centered on cultic rather than covenantal obligation, was working well for them. But their era had not been problem-free, and their fertility religion had not always proved its worth (cf. 1 Kgs 17:1; Deut 28:23–24). Yet stubborn people saw no hint whatever in these natural disasters that their God was giving them a taste of wrath to come in recompense for their apostasy. Israel's love of the cultic reward-for-sacrifice system (v 5) was so great that they saw no reason to return to the strictures of the Sinai covenant. A variety of early unleashings of covenant punishments made no difference to them. Now they were headed for a hostile encounter with the One with all power, whose punishments would constitute more—much more, horribly more—of the same.

A Lament for Fallen Israel   (5:1–17)

Bibliography

Amsler, S. "Amos, prophète de la onzieme heure." *TZ* 21 (1965) 318–28. **Benson, A.** " 'From the Mouth of the Lion': The Messianism of Amos." *CBQ* 19 (1957) 199–212. **Berridge, J.** "Zur Intention der Botschaft des Propheten Amos: Exegetische

Überlegungen zu Am 5." *TZ* 32 (1976) 321–40. **Blau, J.** "Über Homonyme und angeblich Homonyme Wurzeln II." *VT* 7 (1957) 98–102. **Brin, G.** "The Formula X-ימי and X-יום." *ZAW* 93 (1981) 183–96. **Crenshaw, J. L.** "The Influence of the Wise upon Amos: The 'Doxologies of Amos' and Job 5:9–16; 9:5–10." *ZAW* 79 (1967) 42–52. **Dahood, M.** "Hebrew-Ugaritic Lexicography IX." *Bib* 52 (1971) 337–56 (esp. 340). **Driver, G. R.** "Two Astronomical Passages in the OT." *JTS* n.s. 4 (1953) 208–12. **Fenton, T.** "Ugaritica-Biblica." *UF* 1 (1969) 65–70. **Fohrer, G.** "Prophetie und Magie." *ZAW* 78 (1966) 25–47. **Gaster, T. H.** "An Ancient Hymn in the Prophecies of Amos." *JMEOS* 19 (1935) 23–26. **Gese, H.** "Kleine Beiträge zum Verständnis des Amos Buches." *VT* 12 (1962) 432–36. **Glück, J. J.** "Three Notes on the Book of Amos." *OTWSA* 7–8 (1966) 155–221. **Hauan, M.** "The Background and Meaning of Amos 5:17b." *HTR* 79 (1986) 337–48. **Hesse, F.** "Amos 5:4–6, 14 f." *ZAW* 68 (1956) 1–17. **Horst, F.** "Die Doxologien in Amosbuch." *ZAW* 47 (1929) 45–54. **Jackson, J.** "Amos 5,13 Contextually Understood." *ZAW* 98 (1986) 434–35. **Luria, B. Z.** "Who Calls the Waters of the Sea and Spills Them on the Face of the Earth (Amos 5:8, 9:6)." *BMik* 30 (1984/85) 259–62. [Heb.] **Lust, J.** "Remarks on the Redaction of Amos vv 4–6, 14–15." *Remembering All The Way . . .* Oudtestamentische Studiën 21. Leiden: E. J. Brill, 1981. **McCullough, W. S.** "Some Suggestions about Amos." *JBL* 72 (1953) 248. **Neubauer, K.** "Erwägungen zu Amos 5:4–15." *ZAW* 78 (1966) 292–316. **Rector, L. J.** "Israel's Rejected Worship: An Exegesis of Amos 5." *ResQ* 21 (1978) 161–75. **Ruiz, G.** "Amos 5:13: ¿prudencia en la denuncia profetica?" *CB* 30 (1973) 347–52. **Schmidt, W.** "Suchet den Herrn, so werdet ihr Leben." In *Ex Orbe Religionem I: Festschrift für G. Widengren,* ed. J. Bergman et al. Leiden: E. J. Brill, 1972. 127–40. **Speier, S.** "Bemerkungen zu Amos." *VT* 3 (1953) 305–410. **Stuart, D.** *Studies in Early Hebrew Meter.* HSM 13. Missoula, MT: Scholars Press, 1976. 187–99, 202–5. **Tangberg, K. Arvid.** "Var Israels 'Klassiske' profeter botspredikanter?" *TTKi* 50 (1979) 93–105. **Tromp, N. J.** "Amos 5:1–17: Toward a Stylistic and Rhetorical Analysis." *OTS* 23 (1984) 56–84. **Vriezen, T. C.** "Note on the Text of Amos 5:7." *VT* 4 (1954) 215–16. **Waard, J. de.** "The Chiastic Structure of Amos v. 1–17." *VT* 27 (1977) 170–77. **Watts, John D. W.** "Note on the Text of Amos 5:7." *VT* 4 (1954) 215–16. ———. *Vision and Prophecy in Amos.* Grand Rapids: Eerdmans, 1958. 54–57. **Wicke, D.** "Two Perspectives (Amos 5:1–17)." *CurTM* 13 (1986) 89–96. **Zalcman, L.** "Astronomical Allusions in Amos." *JBL* 100 (1981) 53–58.

Translation

⁵:¹ *Listen to this* ª *word which I am crying out* ᵇ *against* ᶜ *you as a lament, family of Israel:*

Description of tragedy

² *Fallen, never to rise again, is virgin Israel,* ª
Abandoned on her own land, with no one to help her up.

³ *For this is what the Lord Yahweh said:*
The city which ª *marches out as a company* ᵇ *will reclaim only a platoon.* ᶜ
That which marches out as a platoon ᶜ *will reclaim only a squad* ᵈ *of the family of Israel.*

A call to react

⁴ *For this is what Yahweh said to the family of Israel:*
Seek me and live!

⁵ *Don't seek Bethel;*
Don't go to Gilgal;
Don't travel to Beersheba! ª

Because Gilgal will surely go into exile,
And Bethel will become trouble.[b]

[6] *Seek Yahweh and live,*
Lest he progress like a fire against the family of Joseph
And consume Bethel,[a] *with no one to quench it.*

Direct address to the fallen

[7] *You*[a] *who turn justice upside down*[b]
And cast righteousness to the ground[c]—

[8] *The one who made the Pleiades and Orion,*[a]
Who turns darkness to dawn
And darkens day into night,

Who summons the sea's waters
And pours them out on the earth.
Yahweh[b] *is his name!*

[9] *Who causes destruction*[a] *to stream over*[b] *the stronghold,*
Indeed he will bring[c] *destruction to the fortified city*—

[10] *Who hate the person who reproves in the gate,*
And abhor the person who tells the truth.[a]

[11] *Therefore:*
Because when you get a judgment[a] *against the poor*
You take from him the produce[b] *of his field,*

You have built houses out of specially-cut stone,
But will not live in them.

You have planted lush vineyards
But will not drink their wine.

[12] *For I am aware of the frequency*[a] *of your crimes*
And the severity of your sins—

Persecutors of the righteous, bribe takers,
Who reject the claims of the needy[b] *at the gate!*

[13] *Therefore:*
The thoughtful person will wail[a] *then,*
For it will be a terrible time.

A call to react

[14] *Seek good and not evil so that you may live, for then Yahweh, the God of the armies, will be with you—just as you have said.*
[15] [a]*Hate evil! Love good! Establish*[a] *justice in the gate! Perhaps Yahweh, the God of the armies, will have mercy on Joseph's remnant.*

Summons to mourning

[15] *Therefore:*
This is what Yahweh said,
The God of the armies, the Lord[a]*:*

In all the streets there will be wailing.
In all the squares they will be saying, "Oh, no! Oh, no!"—

They will summon the farmhand to mourning
As well as the professional mourners to ᵇ *wailing.*

¹⁷ *There will be wailing in all the vineyards,*
For I will cross right through you, Yahweh said.

Notes

1.a. G has τὸν λόγον κυρίου τοῦτον "this word of Yahweh," which might well represent the original wording.

1.b-c. The use of נשא in contexts mentioning speech can imply loudness. The על is ambiguous, meaning either "over" or "against." The oracle contains as much judgment as lament, and these words need not be translated simply "raise . . . over."

2.a. Tg reads בנתא חדא כנשתא דישראל "a daughter of Israel's congregation," probably an attempt to make sense of a text which read בת ילת "young daughter" rather than בתולת "virgin."

3.a. G Syr Tg Vg all translate logically rather than literally: "The city out of which. . . ."

3.b,c,d. The terms indicate military units, not exact decimal-system numbers. Cf. G. Mendenhall, "The Census Lists of Numbers 1 and 26," *JBL* 77 (1958) 52–66.

5.a. Wolff's suggestion (*Joel and Amos*, 225, n.1), following A. von Gall and others, that the line mentioning Beersheba is a later addition since it has no counterpart in 5b fails to understand that there is no meaningful, effective way to pun or alliterate on the name Beersheba without destroying the staccato meter of 5b, and it also misses the progression of three cities, two cities, one city in vv 5 and 6.

5.b. For purposes of alliteration and punning, the city names are treated as masculines, contrary to typical practice.

6.a. G τῷ οἴκῳ Ἰσραηλ "[for] the house of Israel" read לבית ישראל, which in light of Hos 10:15 might have been original. But MT, supported by the versions otherwise, represents the somewhat more likely *lectio difficilior* rather than the result of a haplogr.

7.a. The article is used as a vocative. Since the lament begins at v 2 and not here, the oft-proposed emendation of ה to הוי in 5:18 and 6:1, where laments *do* begin and where הוי is expected, is obviated.

7.b. Reading with G (εἰς ὕψος) which represents, presumably, למעלה, lit., "upwards." Justice is turned "up" and righteousness "down" in the couplet.

7.c. G supports MT, but via a misinterpretation so that v 7 reads: "Yahweh is the one who gives judgment on high, and has established justice on the earth."

8.a. G (ποιῶν πάντα καὶ μετασκευάζων "Who makes all things and changes [them]") must have had either a text very different from MT or an inability to decipher these terms for constellations it elsewhere rendered properly.

8.b. G adds ὁ θεὸς ὁ παντοκράτωρ, i.e., אלהי צבאות "God of the armies," perhaps under the influence of v 14.

9.a. Since H. Oort's "De profeet Amos," *TT* 14 (1880), שד has often been emended to שבר "devastation" so as to avoid repetition in the parallelism, but without MS support otherwise.

9.b. On this meaning, see M. Dahood, "Hebrew-Ugaritic Lexicography IX," 340.

9.c. G ἐπάγων reflects יביא "bring" rather than יבוא "come."

10.a. Or, "the person who is a spokesman for the blameless." The Heb. is genuinely ambiguous, and probably purposely so.

11.a. MT בושסכם is an unknown form of unknown meaning, and probably a corruption. The versions offer no solution and no suggested emendation has been convincing. Our translation is also speculative. It guesses that, in light of the legal context, a form such as בשפטבם "judgment" may have been original.

11.b. The alternate possibility, "tax," seems less likely in the context. Taxation is no sin; wholesale impoverishment of debtors is.

12.a. Lit., "many."

12.b. Lit., "turn aside" (the need . . .).

13.a. Surely דמם II "wail" is more likely here than דמם I "keep still."

15.a-a. Some G MSS have these verbs in the 1 c pl pf, apparently because כאשר אמרתם "just as you have said" in v 14 was misinterpreted as introducing a quote.

16.a. Some G MSS omit any reflex of אדני "Lord." These may conceivably reflect a more original text than does MT.

16.b. The placement of the prep is unusual, although the sense is clear enough.

Form / Structure / Setting

There is every reason to consider 5:1–17 a unit. It begins with the announcement of a lament / elegy (קינה) for the nation in v 1 and ends with a graphic portrayal of the nation at mourning. The preceding judgment oracle ending in 4:13 and the following woe oracle (beginning in 5:18 with הוי "woe," a term which does not occur in and need not be restored to the present pericope) are identifiably distinct pericopes.

Moreover, it contains the characteristic features of a funerary lament, albeit adapted to the judgment purpose (cf. Ezek 19:1–14; Jer 9:16–23; Isa 14:4–21; etc.). By comparison to the oldest full elegy in the OT, the lament of David over Saul and Jonathan in 2 Sam 1:19–27 (see D. Stuart, *SEHM*, 187–95, on the structure and translation of that lament), and other OT laments, one can discern the following components: (1) a description of the tragedy (Amos 5:2–3; cf. 2 Sam 1:19, 23, 25, 27); (2) a call to react (Amos 5:4–6, 14–15; cf. 2 Sam 1:20), which may be addressed in any of a number of ways to the survivors of the tragedy; (3) some sort of direct address to the fallen (Amos 5:7–13; cf. 2 Sam 1:26); and (4) a summons to mourning (Amos 5:16–17, and introductorily v 1; cf. 2 Sam 1:21, where the very mountains are called to mourn!). In other words, in spite of its several unique interests, the present passage has throughout the style and tone an ancient Israelite would readily recognize as that of a funeral song.

Among the factors that make this song special are its frequent quotations of Yahweh's word (vv 3, 4–6, 16–17; and in the first person, vv 4b and 12), its threefold use of כי "for" (vv 3, 4, 5) followed by a threefold use of לכן "therefore" (vv 11, 13, 16), and its heavy distribution of eschatological language—covering both punishment and restoration—and its incorporation of a hymnic element (v 8 and perhaps also v 9), all of which serve to interweave the theme of divine judgment into the lament. We have here more than a mere elegy. It is a judgment elegy, artfully crafted—a prophetic dirge for Israel in which Yahweh speaks to and against Israel as well.

Vv 14 and 15, the second call to react, appear to be prose, as does, of course, the introduction (v 1). Otherwise the poetry is of a quite mixed meter. Perhaps the most striking portion structurally is the first call to react, vv 4 –6. There, via an admixture of *breve* and *longum* poetry (see *SEHM*, 12–13), a semi-chiastic descending pattern is observed, i.e., Bethel, Gilgal, Beersheba :: Gilgal, Bethel :: Bethel. This reminds one of the descent from three-verse triple acrostic to two-verse single acrostic to one-verse implicit [*sic*] acrostic in the final three chapters of Lamentations.

We know the setting of none of Amos' oracles except for 7:10–17. As a guess, however, one can imagine the present oracle spoken in Samaria in light of its address to heterodox pilgrims (v 5) who would presumably be based in Samaria (cf. 7:13), its national perspective, its allusion to impressive wealth on the part of the audience (v 11), and its assumption of the audience's familiarity with particularly impressive fortifications (v 9). The date is not discernible.

Comment

1 The speaker in v 1 is either Amos or Yahweh. Is Yahweh singing a mourning song (קינה) over his people (בית ישראל "family of Israel"; cf. the laments over Tyre and Egypt in Ezek 26–28 and 32)? Or is it Amos, who sings for his people an elegy on the analogy of David's dirge for Saul and Jonathan (2 Sam 1:19–27) or, later, Jeremiah's dirge for Josiah (2 Chr 35:25)? The answer is probably either or both, as long as it is remembered that the prophet is a spokesperson for God, not an author in the typical sense. The summons to "listen" is simply an attention-getting device. Such imperatives occur in blessing poems (Gen 49:2), prophetic messenger speeches, wisdom instructions, etc. The present formulation is much like that of 3:1, with the added element of the קינה. Mourning songs were a part of Israel's culture; mourning through music was a usual practice then (cf. also Matt 9:23) as in Christian funerals today. But Amos' wording is somewhat ambiguous. This is a lament על Israel, and על can mean either "over" (cf. נשא קינה על "raise a lament over" in Jer 7:29; Ezek 26:17) or "against." The following content shows that the present lament is no eulogy.

2 Lament vocabulary and themes pervade v 2. The verbs in the past tense portray Israel's demise as already a completed act in God's plan, thus a subject of lamentation in the present. The use of the verb נפל "fall" recalls not only David's employment of the term in his laments for Saul and Jonathan (2 Sam 1:19, 25, 27) and Abner (2 Sam 3:34), but suggests a war context, as v 3 makes clear; i.e., "fallen" means "fallen in battle" (cf. also Lev 26:36). Israel is seen as lying mortally wounded on her own land—humiliated by an invader, not valiantly slain while on a conquest. Israel is here the virgin (the fem sg construct indicates apposition, not possession), the young unfulfilled nation cut off in its prime, like "daughter Zion" in Isa 1:8; 10:32 or Jephthah's daughter in Judg 11:38–40. She has no one to raise her up (מקימה), i.e., help restore her to health. The tragedy of her helplessness and loneliness in death in contrast to her past potential (cf. 2 Sam 1:21, 23–26) is a focus of this prosodic obituary. The covenant curses of death and destruction (type 24) and the ravages of war (type 3) are proleptically envisioned. And possibly in view is curse type 22, denial of burial (cf. Deut 28:26), in light of the reference to abandonment (נטשא), though the term may also reflect Deut 32:15 with the tables turned: God—the only one who could help her up—has abandoned Israel (curse type 1; cf. Deut 31:18; 32:30).

3 The decimation curse of Deut 28:62 (type 12) warns: "You who were as numerous as the stars of the sky will be left but few in number." After the "messenger formula" ("this is what Yahweh said") introduced by "for," identifying the present verse as part of the lament and specifically linking it to Israel's defeat in battle (v 2), come a couplet and triplet composed in four- and five-syllable *breve* meter, emphasizing the severity of the coming military disaster (cf. also the war curses of type 3, as in Lev 26:17, 37; Deut 28:25). Ancient Israel's military unit were named by multiples of ten ("tens," "fifties," "hundreds," "thousands"; cf. 1 Sam 10:19; 17:18; 18:13; 22:7, 2 Sam 18:1), even though, as DeVaux (*Ancient Israel*, 216) points out, the actual numbers were "far smaller" than the literal unit names would indicate (cf. also n. 3.b,c,d. above). The impact is clear: troops marching out (יצא) to battle would be marching to their deaths. Israel was doomed to be slaughtered by her enemies.

How, then, can hope for life be held out to the "family of Israel" (בית ישראל)? All sorts of explanations for this sudden shift from doom to hope have been proposed, from the suggestion that Amos is using sarcasm (see A. Weiser, *Die Prophetie des Amos*) to the suggestion that Amos' audience in vv 5–7 is no longer the wicked city folk but the rural righteous (A. Alt, *Kleine Schriften* 2 [Munich: C. K. Beck, 1953] 269–70). Attention to the structure of the lament, however, coupled with an appreciation of the consistency of the orthodox prophetic eschatology, provides the rationale. V 4 begins the call to react, the part of the lament where the audience is addressed directly and adjured to conform their actions in some way to the severity of the loss being lamented (as in 2 Sam 1:20, 21, 24). In the present passage this call takes on a grand scope. God invited a reaction: the choice between himself and mere cultic activity. It is not the process of religion but the person of God that Israel must seek (דרש, cf. the religious connotations of this term in Gen 25:22; Exod 18:15; Ps 34:5; 77:3; and esp. Ps 78:34). Their sanctuaries will be destroyed; their Savior will not. Moreover, the unpredictable admixture of promise and punishment is an empirically observable feature of OT prophecy. The audience is not left to hear only their nation's doom. Its future restoration—of those who will indeed turn to Yahweh—is assured. In the midst of the worst disaster the faithful can still look toward true life (cf. Hab 2:4; and Hos 6:1–3, *comment*). To live (חיה) is a basic restoration blessing (cf. Deut 30:6; Ezek 37:14) essential to all the others. To "seek" Yahweh (cf. Deut 4:29, where בקש, a synonym of דרש, is used) is what leads to the ability to live.

5 In the clever construction of vv 5–6 Bethel is mentioned three times, Gilgal twice, and Beersheba once (cf. notes 5.a. and 6.a.), i.e., roughly in the order of their significance to Amos' audience. All three were sites of great religious-historical significance from Israel's past. Bethel, named by Jacob (Gen 28:19), was turned by Jeroboam I (931–910) into the North's preeminent worship center as a substitute for Jerusalem in the Israelite cult (1 Kgs 12:26–33). Gilgal, the first promised land encampment in the conquest, was a worship center since Joshua circumcised the conquest generation there (Josh 5:2–12). Beersheba, associated with Abraham (Gen 22:19), Isaac (Gen 26:23), and Jacob (Gen 46:1–5), was, in spite of its southern Judean location, a popular pilgrimage spot for northerners (cf. 8:14; 2 Kgs 23:8).

All three represented covenant infidelity, even if all were more-or-less Yahwistic cult centers, because Jerusalem alone was the valid site for worship (Deut 12; 1 Kgs 9:3; 2 Chr 13:9–11). These three northern centers—or any others—could not give Israel the life it needed. Using an alliteration of *g* and *l* sounds (*gilgal galoh yigleh*, "Gilgal will surely go into exile") and irony (substituting אוֶן "trouble" for אֵל "God" in Bethel; cf. Hosea's Beth-awen in Hos 4:15; 5:8; 10:5), the poem warns of the miseries to come for those shrines. Exile (curse type 13) and general horror (type 4), not the saving of life, will be their fate. This rejection of the false cult (curse type 2) could hardly be more dramatically stated.

6 A triplet concludes this subsection of the lament. Its introductory line דִּרְשׁוּ אֶת־יהוה וִחְיוּ "seek Yahweh and live" closely parallels v 4b, reinforcing the urgent message that life is possible only by a true return to Yahweh. The next line expands the warnings from the destruction of illegal sanctuaries to the destruction of the whole "family of Joseph" (בֵּית יוֹסֵף). This term can designate only the two tribes of Ephraim and Manasseh; "house of Joseph" neatly covers both sanctuaries. Beersheba, geographically part of another nation, cannot logically be included in a prediction of doom for Israel, so is not mentioned here.

Destruction by fire is, of course, a covenant curse (type 10; cf. Deut 4:24, "Yahweh your God is a consuming fire . . ."). When Yahweh himself burns through the apostate nation in judgment, Bethel, mentioned one last time in accordance with its prominence, will be destroyed. This fire is not just from Yahweh; metaphorically, it *is* Yahweh. Who could hope to extinguish (מְכַבֶּה) such a conflagration? The third line of the triplet is already longer than the first two eight-syllable lines. Emending MT's Bethel to בֵּית ‹יִשְׂרָ›אֵל "House of Israel" on the basis of the easy reading in G, as commonly proposed, would worsen, not improve, the otherwise well-structured prosody.

7 In a typical lament, the direct address to the fallen would be complementary (cf. 2 Sam 1:19, 26). But this is no typical lament. Here, instead, an excoriation is leveled against those over whom doom is predicted. Emendation of ה, the definite article "the," to הוֹי "woe" at the outset of the verse is therefore gratuitous (cf. also 6:13).

The Israelites have thrown justice (מִשְׁפָּט) upwards (see note 7.b.) and righteousness (צְדָקָה) downward: the chiastic 9:9 couplet artistically calumniates the general rejection of practices represented by two terms so commonly used in the OT to summarize what the covenant demands (cf. 5:24; 6:12). מִשְׁפָּט represents proper legal behavior, fairness in court, societal justice, etc. צְדָקָה is "rightness," as well as "innocence," including the qualities of decency, generosity, and piety. The two terms overlap somewhat in their ranges of meaning and are used widely throughout the OT.

8 Another fragment of an old Yahwistic hymn (cf. 4:13; 9:5, 6; Watts, "An Old Hymn") suddenly appears in Amos' lament. Its words may have been made to fit the lament melody (the mixed meter of the context offers little clue) or else represented a surprise shift in tune as well as topic. Amos almost certainly was singing the lament to its original audience (on prophets as musicians, see Exod 15:1; Deut 31:30; 1 Sam 10:5; 2 Kgs 3:15; Isa 5: 1–7). By including in it an old hymn—one they may have sung many times themselves and one which shares a key vocabulary word with what Amos has just said (הָפַךְ, translated "cast" in v 7 and "turns" in v 8)—the prophet reminds his audience that Yahweh can be a changer and a destroyer as well as a comforter. Yahweh put constellations in the heavens where none were before (cf. Job 9:9; 38:31). He changes dark to light and vice versa. He takes water out of the sea and puts it on earth (i.e., storms, floods, etc.; cf. 9:6).

The hymn fragment, recognizable by its predicate participles (cf. 4:13; *Comment*) and its refrain (יהוה שמו "Yahweh is his name"), serves well the purposes of the ironic lament: it reinforces the point that Yahweh can come in judgment, not just in aid, and can stand against, not just for, his people. Its insertion by the prophet into the lament has a sort of shock value for those who complacently were perverting justice (vv 7, 10).

9 This verse may be textually corrupt, but its essential intent is discernible. As a kind of departure from and initial comment on the hymnic fragment in v 8 (cf. 9:7, which carries on from 9:5–6 to concretize the hymn's destruction language vis-à-vis Israel), its points out that Yahweh's destructive powers extend to the very fortifications his people have been depending on for their security.

10 Resuming the excoriation of injustice begun in v 7, v 10 adds a personal focus. Disregard for justice is in fact a hatred of people, and not just the needy (v 11) but those who honestly and decently plead the cause of the needy or decide in their favor. A resentment of the truth characterizes the unjust. The "person who reproves" (מוכיח) is the elder in the jury that renders a verdict (cf. Prov 24:23–25; Isa 29:21). The "person who tells the truth" (דבר תמים) is the upright witness. (On these terms, cf. I. Seeligmann, "Zur Terminologie für das Gerichtsverfahren im Wortschatz des biblischen Hebräisch," in *FS W. Baumgartner,* VTSup 16 [Leiden: E. J. Brill, 1967] 251–78.) "In the gate" (בשער) refers to the location of most court proceedings: at the broad, multi-chambered gate area designed as part of city fortifications but used routinely for official legal business (cf. Ruth 4:1–11; Deut 22:15; 25:7; Job 5:4; 31:21).

11 A futility curse (type 15) introduced by the divine-judgment sentence indicator לכן "therefore" (cf. Hos 2:8, 11, 16; etc.) and further specifying the "legal crimes" of the unjust—using the courts to defraud poor people— fits well the lament context. The song generally bewails Israel's coming defeat in war (vv 2–3; 16–17). Closely related to the war-theme curses of occupation and oppression by the enemy (type 5) are the futility curses. They predict that what one has toiled for, another (i.e., implicitly the conquering enemy) will enjoy. The present curse, indicating ultimate frustration for house-builders and vineyard-planters, appears to be based very closely on Deut 28:30 (cf. also 28:39). Yet the curse is especially appropriate in another way: it turns the tables precisely on those who had been getting rich at the expense of the poor. Others will now get rich at *their* expense.

12 It is in the nature of laments to describe those being elegized. The present elegy is of course ironic, critical of its subjects. Again the theme is the wickedness of the legal system in Israel. This topic, false justice, began in v 7, following the initial indictment of false religion in vv 4–6. The lament attacks criminals (פשע) and sinners (חטאת). Who are they? They are the corrupt elders, jurists at the court trials. Consciously, purposely, Israelite leading citizens were persecuting the righteous (or "innocent" צדיק) by taking bribe money either for declaring poor peoples' cases against the rich to be without merit, or by ruling in favor of rich plaintiffs or defendants against poor plaintiffs or defendants (cf. Exod 23:6–8; 1 Sam 12:3; Isa 10:2; 29:21; Mal 3:5). Such a direct covenant violation (cf. Exod 23:1–8; Deut 16:18–20) is heinous. But Yahweh, who is surely the speaker here, knows it (ידעתי). Naturally, those who paid the bribes were also guilty. But the focus is on the jurists, trusted to be impartial, yet scurrilously the opposite. Amos places great emphasis on the court system in Israel. When it has become corrupted, punishment must ensue.

13 And it will! Again the judgment-sentence indicator לכן "therefore" introduces a curse, the general curse of fear / terror / horror (type 4): "it will be a terrible time" (היא עת רעה). So great will be the horror, the thoughtful person (משכיל; cf. Prov 10:5, 19; 17:2) will then either wail (דמם II; see *n.* 13.a.) or be stunned to silence (דמם I).

14–15 How should godly people respond when in the midst of an ungodly society about to be punished by the Creator? They must make a conscious choice to convert from evil to good, so that the covenant restoration blessings may apply to their "remnant" (שארית, v 15; cf. Isa 1:2). The chronological perspective envisioned for Israel (here again, "Joseph"; cf. v 6) is that of blessing, curse, blessing—in that order (cf. Deut 4:21–31). After being blessed in the land, Israel sinned. Then came the punishments announced by Amos in fulfillment of the covenant curses. Then and only then could blessings come again. After the "terrible time" (v 13), those remaining from the ravages of war and captivity could once again enjoy God's mercy (restoration blessing type 1; cf. Deut 4:31; 30:3) if they would seek (דרש, cf. its use in Deut 4:29 and vv 4b and 6a above) Yahweh.

Vv 14 and 15 seem to be more prose than poetry. Amos may have stopped singing at this point in order to render a blunt, colloquial assessment of his nation's only hope for the future. A presumption of the support of Yahweh against Israel's foes was apparently current (כאשר אמרתם "just as you have said"). The people took Yahweh for granted. But Amos' challenge insists that Yahweh's support will be available only to a converted nation, one which will, as both v 14 and v 15 emphasize, reject evil (רע) and do good (טוב), especially as evidence in cleaning out legal corruption (v 15). As Mays (*Amos,* 100) says, "In Amos' theological vocabulary, 'good' is the middle term between Yahweh and justice . . . the gradient in the sequence runs from *Yahweh* through *good* to *justice.* . . . One cannot speak of morality versus religion or ethics versus faith as though they were alternatives." To seek Yahweh is to do good. That is what was required for Israel to live again.

16–17 The lament concludes with an elaborate summons to mourning, introduced by לכן "therefore" (cf vv 11, 13) and by another full, formal mention of Yahweh's name and title. Clearly this is the climax of the song, and the form is again poetic (mainly 7:7 meter). When Israel experiences Yahweh's wrath (v 17), death and destruction (curse type 24) will be the result. Everywhere one will see grief: in the cities ("streets / squares") and in the countryside ("farmers" / vineyards). With not enough professional mourners to go around, even farmhands will be required to bewail the losses, so great will be the slaughter, so many the dead.

Three times in these two verses the term מספד "wailing" is used. Additionally, אבל "mourning," נהי "mourning," and הוי "Oh, no" (an actual funerary cry of misery) are employed to suggest how widespread the bitter, tragic weeping for the dead will be as burial after burial takes place throughout the land.

In v 17 Yahweh warns that he will "cross right through" (עבר ל) Israel. In 7:8 and 8:2, however, עבר ל means "pass by" or "spare." Used with various prepositions, עבר has a wide variety of nuances, from "abandon" (a possible translation here, reflecting curse type 1) to "slice." For the present expression, Lev 26:6, which depicts the "sword" crossing right through (in that context, ב is the preposition) the land, probably provides the linguistic backdrop. Perhaps the people of the Northern Kingdom were in their conversations (v 14b) expressing the hope that "Yahweh, God of the armies," would spare them from the rising Assyrian threat. The lament ends by reminding them that "Yahweh, God of the armies," would do no such thing.

Explanation

By a proleptic funerary lament, God revealed through Amos the end of the Northern Kingdom. The defeat and destruction wrought by the Assyrians in 722 was indeed devastating (2 Kgs 17:5, 18, 20, 23). The lament is artfully composed, modeled generally on a presumably classical format, which included descriptions of the tragedy, call to react, direct address to the fallen, and a summons to mourning. Worked into this framework are evidences of Israel's covenant violations, indications of her coming punishment bolstered by a fragment of an old hymn, and promises of her eventual restoration.

Israel's national guilt included two types of misbehavior mentioned explicitly: the counter-culture, i.e., worshiping at illegal sanctuaries, and exploitation of the poor by the legal system (cf. Isa 1:10–26, which likewise describes the judicial system and provides a call for repentance in order to secure future blessing). The coming punishments center on death and destruction and miseries related thereto. The second of three Yahwistic hymn fragments in the book (vv 8–9) reminds the audience that their national God is fully capable of destruction, not just of blessing (cf. v 14).

Perhaps the most fascinating features of the passage for the Christian are the restoration promises found in the two calls to react (vv 4–6, 14–15), which contain invitations to seek "Yahweh" (v 4), i.e., "good" (v 14), so that life may be the result. Surely Jesus' claim to be "the life" (John 10:10; 14:6) and the promise of life in the father (Col 3:3; cf. Eph. 4:18) represent the ultimate referents of such promises to a nation about to be destroyed. And surely the Christian has no less responsibility to love good and hate evil, as Rom 12:9, which virtually quotes Amos 5:14, reminds us. Upright, fair behavior in society is no less a responsibility of the believer and no less necessary to orthodox faith and worship now than it should have been in Amos' day.

The Woeful Day of Yahweh (5:18-27)

Bibliography

Clifford, R. J. "The Use of Hôy in the Prophets." *CBQ* 28 (1966) 458–64. **Dobbie, R.** "Amos 5:25." *Transactions of the Glasgow University Oriental Society* 17 (1959) 62–64. **Erlandsson, S.** "Amos 5:25–27 et crux interpretum." *SEÅ* 33 (1968) 76–82. **Gerstenberger, E.** "The Woe-oracles of the Prophets." *JBL* 81 (1962) 249–63. **Gevirtz, S.** "A New Look at an Old Crux: Amos 5:26." *JBL* 87 (1968) 267–76. **Herrmann, S.** *Die prophetischen Heilserwartungen im Alten Testament.* BWANT 85. Stuttgart: W. Kohlhammer, 1965. **Hertzberg, H. W.** "Die prophetische Kritik am Kult." *TLZ* 75 (1950) 219–26. **Hirota, K.** "An Interpretation of Amos 5:18–20." *Kirisutokyo Gaku* (Christian Studies) n.s. 20. Tokyo: St. Paul's / Rikkyo Univ, 1978. **Hirschberg, H. H.** "Some Additional Arabic Etymologies in Old Testament Lexicography." *VT* 11 (1961) 373–85. **Hoffmann, Y.** "The Day of the Lord as a Concept and a Term in the Prophetic Literature." *ZAW* 93 (1981) 37–50. **Hyatt, J. P.** *The Prophetic Criticism of Israelite Worship.* Cincinnati: Hebrew Union College, 1963. ———. "The Translation and Meaning of Amos 5: 23–24." *ZAW* 68 (1956) 17–24. **Isbell, C. D.** "Another Look at Amos 5:26." *JBL* 97 (1978) 97–99. **Janzen, W.** *Mourning Cry and Woe Oracles.* BZAW 125. New York: DeGruyter, 1972. **Junker, H.** "Amos und die 'opferlose Mosezeit.'" *TG* 27 (1935) 686–95. **Leewen, C. van.** "The Prophecy of the *yōm YHWH* in Amos 5:18–20." *Language and Meaning: Studies in Hebrew Language and Biblical Exegesis.* OTS 19: Leiden: E. J. Brill, 1974. 113–34. **Osswald, E.** "Zur Abgrenzung alttestamentlicher Predigtperikopen." *Wort und Welt: Festgabe für E. Hertzsch.* Berlin: Evangelische Verlangsanstalt, 1968. 243–50. **Osten-Sacken, P. von der** "Die Bücher der Tora als Hütte der Gemeinde: Amos 5:26 f in der Damaskusschrift." *ZAW* 91 (1979) 423–35. **Sacon, K. K.** "Amos 5:21–27—An Exegetical Study." In *FS Masao Sekine,* ed. S. Arai. Tokyo: Yamamoto Shoten, 1972. 278–99. (Japanese.) **Schmidt, N.** "On the Text and Interpretation of Amos 5:25–27." *JBL* 13 (1894) 1–15. **Schunck, K.** "Strukturlinien in der Entwicklung der Vorstellung vom 'Tag Jahwes.'" *VT* 14 (1964) 319–30. **Sekine, Masao.** "Das Problem der Kultpolemik bei den Propheten." *EVt* 28 (1968) 605–9. **Semen, P.** "Sensul expresiei 'Iom Iahve'—'Ziua Domnukii' la profetii VT." *Studii Teologice* 30 (1978) 149–61. **Smelik, K. A. D.** "The Meaning of Amos v 18–20." *VT* 36 (1986) 246–48. **Speiser, E. A.** "Note on Amos 5:26." *BASOR* 108 (1947) 5–6. **Wanke, Gunther.** "אוֹי und הוֹי." *ZAW* 78 (1966) 215–18. **Watts, J. D. W.** "Amos' Eschatology." *Vision and Prophecy in Amos.* Grand Rapids: Eerdmans, 1958. 68–84. **Weiss, M.** "The Origins of the 'Day of the Lord'—Reconsidered." *HUCA* 37 (1966) 29–72. **Williams, J. G.** "Irony and Lament: Clues to Prophetic Consciousness." Semeia 8 (1977) 51–74. ———. "The Alas-Oracles of the Eighth Century Prophets." *HUCA* 38 (1967) 75–91. **Würthwein, E.** "Amos 5:21–27." *TLZ* 72 (1947) 143–52.

Translation

The real nature of the Day of Yahweh

5:18 *Woe to you* [a] *who are wishing for the Day of Yahweh!*
Why do you have this attitude about the Day of Yahweh?
It is darkness, not light.

19 *Just as if someone were running away from a lion, and a bear came upon him—but he made it home and rested his hand on the wall—and then a snake bit him!* [a]

²⁰*Is not the Day of Yahweh darkness, not light; gloom with no brightness to
it?*^a

Rejection of the cult: injustice

²¹*I hate, I reject*^a *your festivals.*
I will not approve^b *your assemblies.*

²²*Even if you bring me burnt offerings*^a
And grain offerings, I will not accept them.
I will have no regard for your communion meals of fattened cattle.

²³*Get the noise of your songs away from me.*
I will not listen to the music of your harps.^a

²⁴*But let justice roll on like water,*
Righteousness like a stream that runs year-round.

Rejection of the cult: idolatry

²⁵*Did you bring me sacrifices and grain offerings*
For the forty years in the wilderness, family of Israel?^a

²⁶*Did you carry Sakkuth*^a *your "king"?*
And Kaiwan,^b *your idol, the star,*^c
Your gods which you made for yourselves?

The ultimate judgment: exile

²⁷*I will exile you past Damascus,*
Said Yahweh, whose name is the God of the armies.

Notes

18.a. Direct address is implicit, but not explicit, in the Heb. text.

19.a. Alternatively, two events may be described: escaping from a lion only to meet a bear,
and, separately, assuming a posture of rest only to be bitten by a snake.

20.a. *Contra* Wolff (253–54, n. e.), G does link all of v 20 as a single, related, interrogative.

21.a. Or, "I completely reject" or the like, the two Heb. verbs functioning in hendiadys.

21.b. Lit., "smell." In the OT, this old *terminus technicus* simply means to approve a sacrifice.

22.a. G rightly recognized that v 22 is a conditional sentence and that its initial clause does
not link to v 21 (Wolff, 259, n. c.).

23.a. In v 23 the verbs and pronominal forms are singular. This stylistic shift, confirmed by
the versions, may be occasioned by the logic: festival musicians are a small class of people.
"You" (pl) has been referring to all Israel.

25.a. Here some G MSS add λέγει κύριος "says the Lord," i.e., נאם יהוה, "oracle of Yahweh,"
though such additions are probably secondary.

26.a. G takes consonantal MT as "the tent of Molech," reflecting a *Vorlage* without the pl
possessive suffix on מלך. The vocalization סַכּוּת "sakkuth" is based on the Akkadian as opposed
to MT.

26.b. G ραιφαν must surely be an inner-Greek corruption of καιφαν "Kaifan." Akkadian *kayyamān*
is the Mesopotamian reflex for our vocalization.

26.c. MT vocalized כוכב as in construct; if this is correct, translate "the star of your gods. . . ."

Form / Structure / Setting

The present passage is a "woe oracle," an announcement of judgment
beginning with הוֹי ("woe / alas!") followed by a participle designating those
on whom the judgment will come (המתאוים). In this regard it is typical (see

Gerstenberger, "The Woe-oracles," 249–63); covenant violations are placed
in evidence, and the judgment sentence is pronounced. Woe oracles have
little to do with laments even though the word הוֹי derives from funerary
lament contexts (Clifford, "The Use of הוֹי" *CBQ* 28 [1966] 458–64; Janzen,
Mourning Cry and Woe Oracles). Woe oracles say in effect, "You are in trouble. Here's why and here's what will happen to you." Thus 5:18–27 has a
very different style and format from the lament / elegy of the previous
pericope.

In 6:1 a new passage begins, as evidenced by a new הוֹי directed at the
capitals of Judah and Israel respectively. But is 5:18–27 therefore a unit, or
should vv 18–20 be divided from the rest? If vv 18–20, third person in style
and prosaic rather than poetic, are considered an introduction to the first-
person poetic judgment sentences which begin in v 21, the structural unity
of the entire passage is evident. The "Day of Yahweh" announcement in vv
18–20 leaves unspecified the reason *why* Israel's expectations of deliverance
on that day are so completely incorrect. Those reasons come only with vv
21–27. If vv 18–20 are isolated from what follows, the only woe they announce
is a day without sunshine. The reference to the inescapability of the coming
trouble (v 19) still warrants a clarification of what that trouble will be. Only
from vv 21–27 does Amos' audience learn that divine rejection and exile
will constitute the long-awaited day. The overall passage is functionally unified,
even though its individual components may be clearly demarcated.

Because of the references to religious festivals and worship in vv 21–23
and 25–26, the site for this section of Amos' preaching has often been posited
as Bethel. But this is speculative. Somewhat less speculative may be a date
between 745 and 740 for the original delivery of the oracle. Seeking deliverance
via Yahweh's Day (see *Comment*) would be especially understandable in a populace frightened by Assyrian expansion. In Amos' times, this would have been
likely only after Tiglath-Pileser III (745–727) began his imperial expansionism.
Uzziah's death (740) provides the probable *terminus ad quem* for Amos' ministry.
Thus the half decade from 745 to 740 ought to be considered a possible
time frame for the present oracle's first hearing.

Comment

18 The Day of Yahweh (יוֹם יהוה) probably had its origins in the widespread ancient concept that a true sovereign could win his wars in a single
day (D. Stuart, "The Sovereign's Day of Conquest," *BASOR* 221 [1976] 159–
64). The "Day of Yahweh" meant to those who hoped or wished for it
(המתאוים) a time when Yahweh would intervene militarily to demolish his
foes on behalf of his people. The fact that Amos would announce woe (הוֹי)
to such people must have been quite surprising inasmuch as Israelites felt
themselves Yahweh's people if anyone was, and those likely to merit his rescue
if anyone would. But by saying that his audience will find Yahweh's Day to
be just the opposite of their expectation, and by chiding them for having
had an incorrect appreciation of the situation, Amos implicitly reveals that
God's people and God's enemy are one (cf. 3:2), i.e., that they have been
rejected by their God, as vv 21–27 will make clear. The rhetorical question

("Why do you have this attitude. . . ?") finds an immediate answer ("It is darkness . . .") and a second, reinforcing answer in v 20. Such blunt repetition was necessitated by the incredulity of the recipients. Like the student who receives an "F" for a paper he thought was brilliant, or the employee fired after doing what he thought was excellent work, or the person whose spouse suddenly announces that he or she wants a divorce when the marriage seemed to be going so well, the Israelites were undoubtedly stunned by such a reversal of their expectations.

19 Instead of rescue, the Day will bring inescapable disaster. There will be no refuge, no defense. Any deliverance will be illusionary. One way or another, Yahweh's judgment will be unavoidably felt. The situation portrayed in the verse is almost comic, but its intent is a deadly serious warning. Since harm from wild animals is a covenant curse (type 11; cf. Ezek. 14:21), those words may well have pointed toward more than merely their use for the sake of the present simile.

20 Darkness (חשך) and gloom (אפל) are both frequently used as metaphors for trouble, distress, misery, and even death in the OT (חשך: 1 Sam 2:9; Job 5:14; Ps 35:6; Prov 2:13; Isa 5:30; 49:9; אפל: Ps 91:6; Job 3:6). The realm of the dead is sometimes depicted as a land of darkness (e.g., Job 10:22, "where even the light is like darkness"). Deut 28:29, in a helplessness curse (type 19), says of those who have incurred God's wrath, "At midday you will grope around like a blind man in the dark" (אפלא, a cognate of אפל). Could anything God revealed through Amos be clearer? The Northern Kingdom was awaiting devastation, not deliverance.

21 In the prophets, the citation of wrongdoing usually precedes the announcement of a punishment. In the present oracle, the order is somewhat reversed. Not until vv 24–26 does the hearer / reader learn the charges against Israel. This continues the pattern set in vv 18–20 of placing priority on getting the Israelites to realize that their whole preconception about their relation to Yahweh was incorrect. Lev 26:31 warns the covenant people that if they break Yahweh's laws, "I will lay waste your sanctuaries and I will not approve [רוח, hiphil] the pleasing aroma of your offerings" (curse type 2). The festivals (חגים) and the assemblies (עצרת) are terms used here in parallel to denote the three yearly pilgrimage celebrations (Exod 23:15–18; 34:22–25; Deut 16:10–16) as well as any other occasions (sabbaths, new moon festivals, etc.; cf. 8:5; Hos 2:11; Neh 10:33) for gathering to eat and worship. Such worship Yahweh now rejects, for reasons yet to be mentioned, in the same way he rejected the nonsense of the Canaanite cult (cf. Deut 12:31, "detestable things Yahweh hates").

22 Whereas v 21 mentions the feast aspect of the Northern cult, v 22 specifically mentions the sacrifices. The traditional triad of burnt offerings (עלות, cf. Lev 1), grain offerings (מנחות, cf. Lev 2) and the communion meal (שלם, cf. Lev 3) are all now objectionable. God's refusal to "accept" (רצה) sacrifices any longer reflects also the language of Leviticus in regard to proper / improper offerings (Lev 19:5–7).

23 Yahweh has already rejected the cult's feasts and its sacrifices. Here he rejects even its praise. Vocal and instrumental music were integral to worship in OT time (Ps 150; Ezra 2:65; 1 Chr 15:16–24; 2 Chr 5:13; 23:13;

Isa 5:12; Dan 3:5–15). But now Israel's God will neither look at (נבט, hiphil, v 22) or listen to (שמע) his people's worship (cf. Deut. 31:17, 18; 32:20).

24 Israel's God requires regular, consistent keeping of the covenant. Sacrifices and other elements of worship (vv 22, 23) constituted occasional, intermittent righteousness and were rejected because they were not complemented by proper living in general. A society truly in harmony with Yahweh's will must practice justice (משפט) and righteousness (צדקה; on this standard combination, cf. 5:7; 6:12) routinely: always and everywhere. It is in the nature of a covenant that it cannot be kept merely now and again. For example, no one can say, "I keep my marriage covenant; I commit adultery only every few days and the rest of the time am completely faithful to my spouse." Likewise the Israelite's implicit argument was ludicrous: "I keep Yahweh's covenant. I misuse and abuse others only some of the time and otherwise faithfully worship Yahweh."

Canaanite cultic religion allowed people to be personally immoral and unethical; they could still be right with the gods if they merely supported the cult enthusiastically. Yahweh's covenant denied his people any such option (cf. Matt 7:21–23). Justice and righteousness cannot stop and start like a wilderness wadi that flows with water only during the rainy seasons and otherwise is just a dry stream bed. They must instead continue night and day, all year, like the נחל איתן (lit., "strong stream") that never goes dry.

25 Because Israel was directly led by and dependent upon Yahweh during the post-exodus wanderings, the wilderness era constituted a sort of benchmark against which the nation's current relationship to its God could be measured (cf. Deut 2:7; Hos 2:16–17; Jer 2:2, 6). The forty years in the wilderness were hardly trouble-free or sinless (cf. Deut 1:26–40; Num 16, etc.), but they did at least provide for a true closeness between Yahweh and his people. During the desert experience, neither slaughtered sacrifices (זבחים) nor grain offerings (מנחות; contra Wolff, 265, the word is used here in its usual sense, cf. v 22) were usually given. The sacrificial system was essentially predesigned for a coming era of normal food production (Exod 34:23–24; Num 15:2; 18:24–27; cf. P. C. Craigie, *Deuteronomy* [Grand Rapids: Eerdmans, 1976], 218) in a landed, settled situation. Though it began in an inaugural manner during the first year's encampment at Sinai (e.g., Lev 9:8–24), sacrificing and its association with the three yearly festivals became regular only after the conquest. God's point via the rhetorical question "Did you bring. . . ?" is simply that offerings are not really what make his people right with him. In the absence of a regular sacrificial program, the people were still convenantally his during the forty years in the wilderness. Israel's assumption that sacrifices were the *sine qua non* of their religion was mistaken.

26 But the significant fault of the Israelites was not their presumptuous abuse of the sacrificial system. It was their outright rejection of Yahweh's covenant via idolatry. Thus the wilderness continues in v 26 as a paradigm of relative propriety compared to the degenerate practices of Amos' day. This contrast between the orthodoxy of the wilderness era and the idolatry of the settled era is also made, twice over, in Jer 2:2–8. Here, specifically, two astral deities are described as "carried" around, as idols, probably atop standards (cf. *ANEP*, figs. 305, 535) and presumably as part of the pagan

worship which has pervaded the North under the influence of admiration
for Assyrian ways at least as early as the time of Ahab (874–853 B.C.) and
the days of Shalmaneser III (859–824 B.C.) to whom Israel had payed tribute.

The worship of such idols is, in fact, silly because they are simply human
products, made by or for (ל עשה; cf. 1 Kgs 14:9; 2 Kgs 17:29–30; Hos 8:6)
humans. Amos' contemporaries probably thought themselves quite sophisti-
cated in comparison to the ancient wilderness generation. But how sophisti-
cated can any group be who worships what their own hands have made (cf.
Isa 40:18–20; 41:22–24; Acts 7:41)?

The Damascus Document from Qumran (CD 7:17–19), based on a faulty
exegesis of a faulty text, interprets v 26 as a promise of deliverance: "I will
exile Sakkuth your king and Kaiwan, your images. . . ." Lines 15–19 actually
reinterpret Sakkuth as סוכת "booth of (your king)," (cf. Amos 9:11) in a
manner defying interpretational rules, and thus of no help in the exegesis
of v 26.

27 The oracle concludes by announcing the imminent fulfillment of the
curse of exile (type 13a; cf. Deut 29:28, "uprooted them from their land
and thrust them into another land"). "Past Damascus" (מהלאה לדמשק) recalls
Deut 30:4, "banished to the most distant land under the heavens." Damascus,
north northeast of Israel, provided a kind of compass point for the direction
the exile would actually take: north, then east, following the arc of the fertile
crescent and its main roads into Assyrian territory. There can be no doubt
that Amos' words imply the Assyrian captivity of Israel, fulfilled a few decades
later (722). Again Yahweh's "full title," God of the Armies (אלהי צבאות), is
employed (cf. 4:13; 5:14, 15, 16).

Explanation

Amos revealed that the Day of Yahweh—in the contemporaneous popular
hope, a day of deliverance from Israel's enemies—would instead be a day in
which Israel would be conquered and exiled by and among its enemies. Why
should Yahweh punish rather than rescue his people? Because they were
faithful to him only selectively. They observed certain procedural aspects of
his covenant, but "neglected the weightier matters of the Law" (Matt 23:23).
Intermittent, occasional righteousness (vv 21–24) is really no righteousness
at all. Partial, limited righteousness (keeping sacrifices while keeping idols,
vv 25, 26) is no true righteousness either. True covenant keeping goes beyond
special, discrete acts of devotion to steadfast loyalty (Matt 7:21–23). It does
not tolerate an admixture of devotions (cf. Acts 7:41–43, 51).

The First Shall Be First   (6:1–7)

Bibliography

Clifford, R. "The Use of *Hôy* in the Prophets." *CBQ* 28 (1966) 458–64. **Dahmen, U.**
"Zur Text- und Literarkritik von Am 6,6a." *BN* 31 (1986) 7–10. **Dahood, M.** *"NĀDĀ*

'to Hurl' in Ex 15, 16." *Bib* 43 (1962) 248–49. **Daiches, S.** "Amos VI:5." *ExpTim* 6 (1914–15) 521–22. **Eissfeldt, O.** "Etymologische und archäologische Erklärungen alttestamentlicher Wörter." *OrAnt* 5 (1966) 165–76. **Elhorst, H.** "Amos 6:5." *ZAW* 35 (1915) 62–63. **Freedman, D. N.** "But Did King David Invent Musical Instruments?" *Bible Review* 1 (1985) 48–51. **Holladay, W. L.** "Amos 6:1bβ: A Suggested Solution." *VT* 22 (1972) 107–10. **Iwry, S.** "New Evidence for Belomancy in Ancient Palestine and Phoenicia." *JAOS* 81 (1961) 27–34. **Pope, M.** "Notes on the Rephaim Texts from Ugarit." *Essays on the Ancient Near East in Memory of J. J. Finkelstein.* Hamden: Connecticut Academy of Arts and Sciences, 1977. **Wanke, G.** "אוי und הוי." *ZAW* 78 (1966) 215–18. **Williams, J.** "The Atlas-Oracles of the Eighth-Century Prophets." *HUCA* 38 (1967) 75–91. **Wolff, H. W.** "Form-Criticism of the 'Woe-Cries.' " *Hosea*, 242–45.

Translation

Announcement / summons to mourning

6:1 *Woe to those comfortable in Zion,*
And who feel secure on Mount Samaria,

Preeminent persons of the leading nation,
To whom the family of Israel come!

Call to react / direct address to the fallen

2 *Travel to Calneh and take a look;*
Go from there to the great Hamath [a]*;*
Then go down to Gath of the Philistines.

Are you [b] *better than these kingdoms?*
Is their territory larger than yours?

Description of the tragedy

3 *Those who are forecasting* [a] *a bad day*
And divining [b] *a harmful week,* [c]

4 *Who sleep on ivoried beds*
And are sprawled out on their couches,

Who eat lambs picked [a] *from the flock*
And young bulls selected [a] *from the fattening-pen,*

5 *Who improvise to the sound of the harp, like David,* [a]
Who invent for themselves all sorts of [b] *songs,*

6 *Who drink from basins of wine*
And anoint themselves with first-quality oils,
And are not bothered by the ruin of Joseph;

7 *Therefore now:*
They will go into exile at the front of the exiles;
The celebrating of those sprawled out will cease. [a]

Notes

2.a. MT vocalizes חמת "Hamath" as the constr (cf. Joüon, *Grammaire*, 131 n.), though syntactically this is hardly a necessity.

2.b. Or possibly "they," in which case "these kingdoms" would refer to Israel and Judah.

3.a,b. MT מנדים probably reflects Akkadian *nadû*, to "(fore)cast." Likewise נגע, hiphil, has the sense of "produce via divination."

3.c. Vocalizing שֶׁבֶת rather than שָׁבָה "seat." On notes 3.a,b,c., cf. Dahood, "*NĀDÂ*," 248–249; and Iwry, "New Evidence," 27–34.

4.a. This sense is implicit in the context. The food is "choice" food.

5.a. Counted syllabically, the meter suggests that כדוד "like David" ends v 5a rather than begins v 5b.

5.b. MT is not impossible. However, making up songs in one's idle time seems far more likely in the context than designing musical instruments; thus we vocalize כָּל "all" rather than כְּלֵי "instruments of."

7.a. The Heb. is much more alliterative than the translation can suggest.

Form / Structure / Setting

Two themes dominate the passage: self-indulgence and self-confidence. These are reflected both in v 1 ("comfortable . . . secure . . . preeminent") and v 7 ("at the front . . . celebration . . . sprawled out"). Verse 1 announces the woe, and v 7 provides the punishments in fulfillment of covenant curses (see *Comment*). The passage is clearly self-contained and rhetorically unified. It follows to a substantial degree the structure expected in funerary laments (cf. 5:1–17). In this connection, the second-person plural speech of v 2 makes the most sense as a combination of direct address to the fallen and call to react, rather than either a quote placed on the lips of the complacent nobles (E. Sellin, J. C. Mays) or a later interpolation. The passage is entirely poetic, in mixed *longum* meter with a predominance of synonymous parallelism.

It cannot be dated precisely, except that since Calneh, Hamath, and Gath all came under Assyrian control via the Western campaigns of Tiglath-Pileser III between 738–734 B.C., the references in v 2 predate 738 B.C. (Properly understood, v 2 does not imply that these city-states had already fallen to Assyria.) The reference to Gath, a region under Judean domination from about 800 until 734 B.C., obviates the suggestions that somehow "Zion" does not belong in v 1. While the woe oracle centers on Israel as evidenced by the explicit reference to "Joseph" (cf 5:15), it certainly seeks to condemn south and north alike for the materialistic decadence of their leading citizens.

Comment

1 Amos, like his eighth-century contemporaries Hosea, Isaiah, and Micah, was given a message which at points involved both Judah and Israel. The present oracle speaks of Zion, i.e., Jerusalem, even before it mentions Samaria, perhaps because to be "comfortable in Zion" (השאננים בציון) had a ring of decadence to it beyond what being "secure on Mount Samaria" (בהר שמרון בטחים) would connote. Jerusalem enjoyed a long history as a sacred place (Gen 14:18; Gen 22; etc.) compared to Samaria, which had been founded only a century and a quarter by Amos' time, and which had no comparable religious traditions associated with it. Both Jerusalem and Samaria were crown property, separately obtained (2 Sam 5:6–9; 1 Kgs 16:24) and governed outside of the tribal traditions and administration. As these capitals grew in importance with the fortunes of their respective nations, they became centers of conspicuous wealth as well as of substantial political

power. Association with the monarchy, whether by birth, marriage, or employment, or even proximity, afforded the opportunity for gaining wealth and prestige, but at the risk of abandoning the old original values of the covenant. With regard to Samaria, Amos' primary audience, her leading citizens undoubtedly enjoyed respect and even adulation. Those in government had the power, for example, to assign tax liabilities, to control public works projects, and to influence the distribution of wealth obtained both externally and internally. "The family of Israel," i.e., people from all over the country, came to them as the preeminent people of the "leading nation" (ראשית הגוים), which in that region Israel indeed was by now. Jeroboam II had, by God's design, even subdued Syria, Israel's often more powerful rival to the north (2 Kgs 14:25). And yet to this prestigious, materially powerful group Amos sings a funerary lament.

2 Leading Samaritans and Jerusalemites may have thought themselves important, but the oracle reminds them that they were no better or no worse than nearby nations whom they had subjugated. Calneh and Hamath were Aramean city-states under Israelite influence and were perhaps often mentioned together because they were major cities of eastern Syria (cf. Isa 10:9). Gath, one of the five major Philistine cities, was at this time under Judahite control (and thus is not mentioned in 1:6–8). It is not necessary to emend "their" to "your" and vice versa at the end of the verse. The two rhetorical questions Amos' oracle poses make the point of equality between those nations and Israel (and, implicitly, Judah). Israel / Judah is no better than they, and they are no more impressive than Israel / Judah. Nations have no right to give themselves priority as Israel had done. By thinking themselves first among the nations, the Israelites had gravely misinterpreted their situation in respect to Yahweh.

3 The description of the tragedy of Israel's decadence begins with an excoriation of two kinds of sins, both apparently frequent enough to constitute an appropriate characterization of the style of life in Samaria. (Awareness of Judah now recedes, though nothing in the remaining verses would not apply to Jerusalemite society as well.) These sins are practice of the occult (Lev 19:26, 31; Deut 18:10–11) and laziness (Prov 25:14–16). The rich were able to avoid work because of their wealth. They apparently justified this lazy behavior at least sometimes by claiming that divination told them to stay at home for a period of time ("a bad day . . . a harmful week"). As with some modern horoscopes, ancient predictions of doom could be avoided by an individual's not venturing forth at all (cf. Prov 22:13).

4 The idle rich lay around the house a lot and ate the finest foods. Their "ivoried beds" (מטות שן) were couches whose wooden frames were inlaid with ivory decorations (J. W. and G. M. Crowfoot, *Early Ivories from Samaria* [London: Palestine Exploration Fund, 1938]; *ANEP*, figs. 125–32; R. Barnett, *A Catalogue of Nimrud Ivories and Other Examples of Ancient Near Eastern Ivories* [London: Trustees of the British Museum, 1957]).

Many Israelites probably ate meat as infrequently as three times a year—only at the festivals (Deut 12:17–18) and even less often if they were poor. By contrast, the leading citizens could command choice meats, and all they wanted, so excessive was their selfishly gotten wealth (cf. 2:8; 5:11).

5 These people were living like royalty. The reference to David, rather than being a late interpolation as some have suggested, adds to the flavor of high living in an idle lifestyle. Even prior to his becoming king, David was a member of a leading Judahite family and was therefore able to indulge his musical talents. With plenty of time on their hands, the urban upper classes of Amos' day could also improvise and create music, their output rivaling that of the past master.

6 Amos' words caricature debauchery and wastefulness. Instead of drinking their wine from a cup (כוס; cf. 2 Sam 12:3; Prov 23:31; Jer 25:17; etc), these folk were drinking straight out of the storage basins! (On מזרק "basin," see A. Honeyman, "The Pottery Vessels of the Old Testament," *PEQ* 71 [1939] 76–90; cf. 1 Kgs 7:40). Anointing was a common practice of personal hygiene, since oil kills lice. But demanding the highest quality of refined oil (ראשית שמנים) for this purpose was simply an excess. And all the while, the ruin (שבר; cf. the use of the root in Lev 26:13, 19, 26) of Joseph (Ephraim) as guaranteed by the covenant curses (esp. type 9, desolation; cf. Lev 26: 31–35; Deut 29:23) was coming closer.

7 Again לכן ("therefore") introduces the judgment sentence concluding the lament (cf. 5:11, 13, 16). Twice already the passage has featured the word ראשית ("first, leading," vv 1 and 16) in connection with the preeminent citizens of Samaria and Jerusalem. These leaders will now lead the nation into exile, at their "front" (ראש). Thus the major covenant curse of exile (type 13) is to be fulfilled against them. The concluding line of the oracle is alliterative: סר מזרה סרוחים, *sar mizrah seruhim* lit., "the celebrating (-house) of those sprawled out will turn aside." Alliteration makes statements memorable. Amos' audience is left with the clear message that the present high living simply will not be allowed to last. Though מרזח can mean funerary celebrating or the place thereof (as in Jer 16:5), it also refers to general revelry, particularly that involving extremes of feasting, drinking, etc. (P. Miller, "The *Mrzh* Text," *The Claremont Ras Shamra Tablets,* ed. L. Fisher, AnOr 48 [Rome: Pontifical Biblical Institute, 1971]; M. Pope, *Song of Songs,* AB 7C [Garden City, NY: Doubleday, 1977] 214–29; O. Eissfeldt, *Etymologische . . . OrAnt* 5 [1966] 165–76).

Explanation

Yahweh would not tolerate the dissolute luxury that prevailed among the Israelite urban rich, both North and South, in the mid-eighth century B.C. Such conspicuous degeneracy witnessed to exploitation of the poor, unconcern for moral and spiritual values and practices, and an outright lack of fear of God. Jesus' severe warning that no one can serve both God and wealth, in part because one's heart will always pay attention to one's treasure (Matt 6:19–24), did not represent a pronouncement without precedent. To fall prey often to materialism is a serious enough fault; to give oneself over to materialistic hedonism is an outrageous offense. Those whom God through Amos excoriated in this passage had gained the world, but they would lose their very lives (cf. Luke 9:25). Since the royalty, nobility, and leading citizens were presumably taken captive first, i.e., prior to the general citizenry, by both the Assyrians and the Babylonians (cf. 2 Kgs 24:11–16; 25:11–12, 18–

21; *ANET*, 284–85; 2 Chr 36:5–7; Jer 24), there came eventually a literal fulfillment of the warning that the first among the people would be the first of the exiles.

Complete Defeat to Come   (6:8–14)

Bibliography

Ahlstrom, G. W. "King Josiah and the *dwd* of Amos vi.10." *JSS* 26 (1981) 7–9. **Childs, B.** *Memory and Tradition in Israel.* SBT 37. London: SCM, 1962. 11–13. **Dahood, M.** "Amos 6, 8 *meta'eb.*" *Bib* 59 (1978) 265–66. ———. "Can One Plough without Oxen? (Amos 6:12). A Study of *ba-* and *'al.*" In *The Bible World: Essays in Honor of C. H. Gordon,* ed. G. Rendsburg et al. New York: KTAV, 1980, 13–23. **Driver, G. R.** "A Hebrew Burial Custom." *ZAW* 66 (1955) 314–15. **Felsenthal, B.** "Zur Bibel und Grammatik." In *Semitic Studies in Memory of Rev. Dr. Alexander Kohut,* ed. G. A. Kohut. Berlin; 1897. 133–37. **Lang, B.** "The Social Organization of Peasant Poverty in Biblical Israel." *JSOT* 24 (1982) 47–63. **Loffreda, S.** *Ge'on Ya'cob.* Diss. Rome: Antonianum, 1962. **Metzger, M.** "Lodebar und der *tell el-mghannije.*" *ZDPV* 76 (1960) 97–102. **Soggin, J. A.** "Amos 6:13–14 und 1:3 auf dem Hintergrund der Beziehungen zwischen Israel und Damaskas im 9. und 8. Jahrhundert." *Near Eastern Studies in Honor of W. F. Albright.* Ed. H. Goedicke. Baltimore: Johns Hopkins Press, 1971. 433–41.

Translation

The extent of coming destruction

6:8 *The Lord[a] Yahweh has sworn by himself:[a]*
I abhor[b] Jacob's pride,

I destest his royal fortifications.
I will hand over the city and all it contains.

9 *Even if there are only ten men left in a single house, they will die.[a]*
10 *And when someone's relatives on his father's and mother's sides[a] pick him up to take[b] his remains outside the house, one of them will say to whoever is in the back part of the house, "Is anyone else still with you?" and he will say "No one," and then he will say,[c] "Hush! For we mustn't mention the name of Yahweh."[d]*

11 *Indeed, Yahweh is giving the command:[a]*
He will pound the large house into pieces,
And the small house into bits.

Perversions and punishment

12 *Do horses run with[a] a rock formation?*
Is it plowed[b] with oxen[c]?

Yet you have turned justice into a poison weed[d]
And the fruit of righteousness into a bitter plant,[e]

¹³*You who rejoice about Lo-Debar,*ᵃ
Who say, "Isn't it by our strength
*That we took Karnaim*ᵇ *for ourselves?"*

The extent of coming defeat

¹⁴*For I am raising up against you, family of Israel,*ᵃ *a nation who will oppress*
*you from Lebo-Hamath*ᵇ *to the Wadi Arabah.*

Notes

8.a. G omits any reflex of both אדני "Lord" and צבאות . . . נאם "Oracle of Yahweh, God of the Armies," suggesting that both are secondary. In 8:7 אדני is missing in MT as well.

8.b. MT מתאב "desire" appears to be a late mistake for מתעב "abhor," which we read with the full range of ancient versions.

9.a. G adds καὶ ὑπολειφθήσονται οἱ κατάλοιποι "but a remnant will be left behind" and reads the 3 masc sg suffixes in the beginning of v 10 as pls ("they," "their"). A single word such as נשארו, a corruption of a dittogr of נשא "pick up," could account for all of G's abnormalities. Alternatively, MT may simply be haplographic.

10.a. The Heb. terms דוד and מסרף may indicate relatives on both sides of an individual's parental lineage whose responsibility it would have been to bury the deceased. However, a meaning for מסרף as "mother's relative" or the like (so Mays, following T. H. Robinson and G. R. Driver) is admittedly speculative.

10.b. G has καὶ παραβιῶνται "and they try hard" before the inf, which may represent פרץ or a similar Heb. word in G's *vorlage*.

10.c. Lit., just "he will say."

10.d. Or, "Yahweh must not be mentioned by name" or the like.

11.a. On the proper rendering of the הנה clause, cf. T. O. Lambdin, *Introduction to Biblical Hebrew* (New York: Scribner, 1971), 168–71.

12.a. The meaning of רוצב may certainly be "run on / over" (as in Joel 2:9) but probably also meant "run (laden) with" (cf. the similar construction in 2 Chr 30:6).

12.b. Lit., "Can (one) plow it."

12.c. It is unnecessary to emend בקרים "oxen" to בקר ים to get "plow the sea with oxen," once it is recognized that the rock formation (סלע) is the "immovable object" in both halves of the couplet. Gᴬ "will they refrain from neighing at mares" is idiosyncratic, to say the least.

12.d. "Poison weed" is preferable to "poison" in light of the surrounding fruit motif.

12.e. Or "wormwood," a specific bitter plant which may not have been the only referent of לענה.

13.a. G ὁ Vg take לא דבר lit. as "nothing" or "no word," but in the context, the attested place name Lo-Debar (cf. Josh 13:26; 2 Sam 9:4, 5; 17:27) is more likely.

13.b. G Vg again translate lit. "horns."

14.a. Again (cf n. 8.a) G does not contain the oracle formulary ("oracle . . . Armies"), which is probably unoriginal.

14.b. G misconstrues לבא חמת "Lebo-Hamath" but thereby also confirms its authenticity textually.

Form / Structure / Setting

The unity of 6:8–14 is not obvious and is probably ultimately unprovable. Clearly 6:7 ends the previous woe oracle, and 6:8 opens a new oracle with Yahweh's own oath. And just as clearly, 7:1 constitutes the beginning of a new oracle based on visions. But what links vv 8–14, in which v 8 and vv 11–13 are poetic but the remainder prose? The answer is: an overall thematic consistency. The passage begins, ends, and concentrates on the well-deserved military defeat that Yahweh will impose upon Israel. Its structure is vaguely chiastic in that vv 8–10 and v 14 address the coming destruction, while vv 12–13 concentrate on the guilt of Israel, as evidenced both in its social injustice and in its arrogance (but cf. also "Jacob's pride" in v 8). The nearness and inevitability of total defeat are what the passage addresses. It is Yahweh's own doing and he promises to make it all happen. Verses 8–11 emphasize the disaster awaiting Israel via city scenes, in conformity with those pentateuchal desolation curses that focus on cities and towns (type 9b; cf. Lev 26:31, 33: "I will turn your cities into ruins . . . your cities will lie in ruins . . ."), while v 14 corresponds quite closely to the desolation curses that describe the general wasting of the land and its occupation by others (type 9c, as in Lev 26:32: "I will lay waste the land so that your enemies who live there will be appalled; cf. Deut 30:1; also enemy occupation / oppression curses, type 5, such as Lev 26:16–17; Deut 28:33; 32:21). In form, the passage is perhaps best labeled a compound curse-fulfillment announcement, or more simply, a judgment oracle.

The setting cannot be determined with any accuracy. Virtually any small or large group in virtually any small or large place in Israel could have constituted the original audience of these words of doom. There appears rather extensive detail about the horrors of war and its aftermath in vv 9–10, but that can hardly imply a date late in Amos' career, i.e., as close as possible to the Assyrian conquest, since far more extensive descriptions are found already in the Mosaic era paradigmatic source, Deut 28. It could be and has been argued that v 14 envisions Assyria as a renewed superpower, something that developed in fact only after 745 and the ascending of Tiglath-Pileser III. But the oppressor nation is not at all specified in v 14, and its language is modeled on Pentateuchal precedents.

Synonymous parallelism dominates the poetic portions, by about a two-to-one ratio over synthetic parallelism. The meter is mixed and does not appear to contain any unusual patterns. It is conceivable that בית "house / family," found in vv 9, 10, 11, 14, functions as a sort of linking term or catchword within the oracle. But its frequency can also be explained in vv 9–11 by the fact that the main structures in cities (v 8) are houses; and in v 14 the word occurs in an already standard expression, בית ישראל "family of Israel," so common as not likely to be thought of in connection with the vocabulary of the earlier verses by Amos' original hearers / readers.

Comment

8 The expression נשבע יהוה "Yahweh has sworn" occurs here for the second of its three times (4:2; 8:7; cf. Jer 22:5). Each time divine punishment of the disobedient nation is the topic. "Jacob's pride" (גאון יעקב, cf. 8:7) seems to be used at least loosely in synonymous parallelism with ארמנתיו "his royal fortifications" in the quatrain, suggesting that גאון, usually also translatable as "arrogance," involves military self-confidence. This is confirmed explicitly in v 13. On "royal fortifications," cf. 1:4, etc. Jacob's trust (on Amos' use of Jacob, cf. 3:13; 7:2, 5; 8:7; 9:8) in his own might implies a lack of trust in Yahweh, which in turn deserves the rejection / anger (curse type 1) implied in the verbs תאב "abhor" and שנא "hate, detest." Yahweh's anger will be made manifest in handing over "the city" (עיר). This could connote Samaria, but more likely is a collective: "each city / all cities" (cf. 5:3).

9 The reference to "ten men" (עשרה אנשים) and a "single house" (בית אחד) probably has nothing to do with overcrowding during a seige, but rather to the aftermath of decimation (curse type 12; cf. Lev 26:22, 36; Deut 4:27; 28:62). In a particular town, the traditional minimum of ten men (cf. the *minyan* of Jewish worship), the smallest fighting unit (cf. 5:3), would be all that would remain of the prior population. Of the prior buildings, only a single house would be left standing. And then, as if to add insult to injury, even the ten men would die. Compare Deut 32:36, "and no one is left, either slave or free."

10 Verse 10's tragic little story does not necessarily take place in the same house mentioned in v 9. The exact identity of those who claim the body (see note 10.a.) and the survivor hiding in the house are not very important to the message. Of greater significance in this laconic account is the imperative הס "Hush!" or "Silence!" which in some other contexts is associated with the imminent arrival of Yahweh (Hab 2:20; Zech 2:17; and esp. Zeph 1:7, in which silence at the arrival of the Day of Yahweh is enjoined). The point would seem to be that after the awful slaughter wrought by Yahweh, the few harried, terrified survivors will not be able to stand any further miseries and so will want to avoid "mention" (הזכיר) of Yahweh. Since the speaker already uses Yahweh's name, the issue cannot be prohibition of mere oral formulation, but must concern calling on Yahweh (cf. הזכיר in Isa 48:1) in prayers of lamentation or the like. Yahweh will have become foe, not friend. Survivors will want him to stay away, not come back. These are in effect the punishments of anger / rejection (type 1; cf., e.g., Deut 31:17) and terror (type 4; cf., e.g., Deut 28:66–67 and Deut 32:25, "In their homes, terror will reign").

11 "Command" (מצוה) would seem in the context to connote instructions in connection with warfare and even the destruction of the enemy (cf. Josh 11:20). But the human agency of destruction is unimportant, because God himself will see what it happens. For a similar participial construction in which "command" precedes his action, cf. 9:9 and Jer 34:22. Here, specifically, total desolation (curse type 9b) is expressed by the smashing of all buildings, large and small. No implication can be drawn from the language that palaces, the hovels of the poor, or any other particular structures are envisioned; nor can רסיסים "pieces" and בקעים "bits" be convincingly construed to suggest an earthquake as the means of Yahweh's wrath. Vengeful demolition by enemy hordes, for example, is just as likely intended here.

12 It is inappropriate and absurd to think that a horse could run while bearing a rock formation (or else run over one; cf. n. 11.a.) or that oxen could plow it. Because such actions are completely the opposite of what is proper, they serve as an analogy, on the principle of *reductio ad absurdum,* for what Israel has done. Israel had made justice and righteousness, here depicted metaphorically as food, into things to be avoided rather than eaten. The people have no taste for justice any more. To them it is odious when it should be sweet and desirable. Their attitude toward proper behavior and values is the exact opposite of what it ought to be. The style of the verse is that of wisdom interrogation, in which the reality of a situation is manifest via questions and statements of fact (cf. 3:3–6).

13 V 13 speaks of pride, self-confidence, and ignoring Yahweh, the stance of a people who have fallen into the reversed priorities described in v 12. The plural forms שמחים "rejoice" and אמרים "say" are not specific as to person, but in the context of vv 12 and 14 are perhaps best construed in the second person ("You who"). The verse thus functions in part transitionally, to move the topic back to war, the subject on which the pericope begins (v 8) and on which it concludes. It was obviously military victories, and decisive ones at that, that resulted in the capture of the two cities mentioned. Lo-Debar (spelled variously in Josh 13:26; 2 Sam 9:4–5; 2 Sam 17:27) was an important border town in Gilead, about three miles east of the Jordan and twelve miles south of the Sea of Galilee. Karnaim was much further north and east, over halfway from Samaria to Damascus. Both cities had come under Syrian (Aramean) domination in the ninth century, and both were recaptured by Jeroboam II in campaigns that God himself had caused to prosper (cf. 2 Kgs 14:25–28) but which Israel saw as evidence of her own greatness. Jeroboam II had actually extended Israel's control even far north of Damascus to Lebo-Hamath in the Valley of Lebanon (see *MBA*, 89) and to Hamath itself (2 Kgs 14:28), and the extent of this hegemony is alluded to in the following verse.

14 To a nation revelling in its power and influence comes a prediction of oppression! In the latter part of Jeroboam's reign (i.e., the years round 765–753) Assyria, Egypt, Syria, and all other nations of the region were relatively impotent militarily and diplomatically (cf. M. Noth, *The History of Israel*, 248–53; J. Bright, *A History of Israel*, 237–42). Within this vacuum Israel's prowess appeared impressive, but God promised a rapid reversal of the status quo in terms of the Pentateuchal curses of oppression and occupation by an enemy (type 5). Lebo-Hamath represented Israel's northernmost boundary at this time, and the Wadi Arabah (presumably the Brook Zered, or Wadi el-Qelt, at the south end of the Dead Sea) its southernmost boundary. These dimensions for the nation agree precisely with 2 Kgs 14:25. Thus the emphasis, like that of vv 8–11, is on *total* defeat. No one will escape, no territory will remain free. The oppressor nation, not yet on the horizon, would turn out to be Assyria, the agent of God's punishment (2 Kgs 17:20).

Explanation

Within about three decades, the nationwide destruction and defeat prophesied in 6:8–14 took place. The pericope links the coming horrors of war, however, not so much to world developments as to Israel's sin. Once again the attention of the hearer / reader is focused by Amos on the need for justice / righteousness and on Israel's complacency and arrogance (cf. 2:6–8; 4:1; 5:7; 5:10–15, 24; 6:1–6). The whole order of things was wrong. The society had adopted values and habits that were utter folly in light of its covenantal obligations to Yahweh—as foolish as trying to plow a ledge with oxen. The country's "pride" in its fortifications (v 8) and recent military success (v 13) represented a horrible misappraisal of reality. What was really needed was a realization that doom was coming, that the conquerors would be conquered, that the extensive territory of the nation would be extensively subdued by the enemy yet unnamed and popularly unexpected.

The reversal of expectations is a common theme in Amos (cf. 1:2; 2:9; 3:2; 3:12; 4:1–3; 5:3; 5:13; 5:18–23). Here, too, the prophet announces reversals, predicting a pitiful, whimpering ending to a great nation's boastful confidence.

Visions of Doom and an Official Response (7:1–8:3)

Bibliography

Ackroyd, P. R. "A Judgment Narrative between Kings and Chronicles? An Approach to Amos 7:9–17." *Canon and Authority.* Ed. G. W. Coats and B. O. Long. Philadelphia: Fortress, 1977. 71–87. ———. "Amos 7:14." *ExpTim* 68 (1956–57) 94. **Bartina, S.** "Viendo los higos de los sicomoros (Am 7:14)." *EstBib* 25 (1966) 349–54. **Baumgartner, W.** "Die Etymologie von Hebräischen *keˡlûb korb.*" *TZ* 7 (1951) 77–78. **Bjørndalen, A. J.** "Erwägungen zur Zukunft des Amazja und Israels nach der Überlieferung Amos 7, 10–17." *Werden und Wirken des Alten Testament.* Göttingen: Vandenhoeck & Ruprecht, 1980. ———. "Zu den Zeitstufen der Zitatformel כה אמר im Botenverkehr." *ZAW* 86 (1974) 393–403. **Brueggemann, W.** "Amos' Intercessory Formula." *VT* 19 (1969) 386–99. **Brunet, G.** "La vision de l'étain: réinterprétation d'Amos VII: 7–9." *VT* 16 (1966) 387–95. **Cohen, S.** "Amos *Was* a Navi." *HUCA* 32 (1961) 175–78. **Condamin, A.** "Le prétendu 'fil à plomb' de la vision d'Amos." *RB* 9 (1900) 586–94. **Danell, G.** "Var Amos verkligen en nabi?" *SEÅ* 16 (1951) 7–20. **Driver, G.** "Amos 7:14." *ExpTim* 67 (1955–56) 91–92. ———. "לֹא: Affirmation by Exclamatory Negation." *JANESCU* 5 (1973) 107–14. **Erlandsson, S.** "Nagra exempla pa waw explicativum." *SEÅ* 41–42 (1976–77) 69–76. **Gunneweg, A.** "Erwägungen zu Amos 7:14." *ZTK* 57 (1960) 1–16. **Hillers, D. R.** "Amos 7:4 and Ancient Parallels." *CBQ* 26 (1964) 221–25. **Hoffman, Y.** "Did Amos Regard Himself as a *nābî?*" *VT* 27 (1977) 209–12. **Holladay, W. L.** "Once More, ˣⁿnak = 'tin.' Amos 7:7–8." *VT* 20 (1970) 492–94. **Hoonacker, A. van.** "Le sens de la protestation d'Amos 7:14–15." *ETL* 18 (1941) 65–67. **Horst, F.** "Die Visionsschilderungen der alttestamentlichen Propheten." *EvT* 20 (1960) 193–205. **Junker, H.** "Text und Bedeutung der Vision Amos 7:7–9." *Bib* 17 (1936) 359–64. **Kapelrud, A.** "Profeten Amos og hans yrke." *NorTT* 59 (1958) 76–79. **Keimer, L.** "Eine Bemerkung zu Amos 7:14." *Bib* 8 (1927) 441–44. **Landsberger, B.** "Tin and Lead—The Adventures of Two Vocables." *JNES* 24 (1965) 285–96. **Lehming, S.** "Erwägungen zu Amos." *ZTK* 55 (1958) 145–69. **Limburg, J.** "Amos 7:4: A Judgment with Fire?" *CBQ* 35 (1973) 346–49. **Loewenstamm, S.** "כלוב קיץ (A remark on the Typology of the Prophetic Vision [Amos 8:1–3])." *Tarbiz* 34 (1964–65) 319–22. [Heb.; English summary.] **Loretz, O.** "Die Berufung der Propheten Amos (7, 14–15)." *UF* 6 (1974) 487–88. **MacCormack, J.** "Amos 7:14." *ExpTim* 67 (1955–56) 318. **Mackenzie, H. S.** "The Plumb-Line (Amos 7:8)." *ExpTim* 60 (1948–49) 159. **Madden, R., Wheeler, T., and Muhly, J. D.** "Tin in the Ancient Near East: Old Questions and New Finds." *Expedition* 19 (1977) 45–47. **Mallau, H.** "Las reacciones frente a los mensajes proféticos y propósito de Amos 7:10–17." *RivB* 34 (1972) 33–39. **Morgenstern, J.** "Amos Studies I." *HUCA* 11 (1936) 68–130. **Ouellette, J.** "Le mur d'étain dans Amos VII, 7–9." *RB* 80 (1973) 321–31. **Overholt, T.** "Commanding the Prophets: Amos and the Problem of Prophetic Authority." *CBQ* 41 (1979) 517–32. **Pfeifer, G.** Die Ausweisung eines lästigen Ausländers Amos 7:10–17." *ZAW* 96 (1984) 112–18. **Power, E.** "Note to Amos 7:1." *Bib* 8 (1927) 87–92. **Rahtjen, B.** "A Critical Note on Amos 8:1–2." *JBL* 83 (1964) 416–17. **Richardson, H. N.** "A Critical Note on Amos 7:14." *JBL* 85 (1966) 89. **Rinaldi, G.** "אנך (Amos 7, 7s)." *BibOr* 4 (1962) 83–84. **Roberts, J.** "A Note on Amos 7:14 and Its Context." *ResQ* 8 (1965) 175–78. **Rost, L.** "Zu Amos 7:10–17." *Festgabe für Theodor Zahn.* Leipzig, 1928. 229–36. **Rowley, H. H.** "Was Amos a Nabi?" In *Theologische Studien und Kritiken: FS Otto Eissfeldt zum 60. Geburtstag,* ed. J. Fück. Halle: Niemeyer, 1947. 191–98. **Schmid, H.** " 'Nicht Prophet bin ich, noch Prophetensohn': Zur Erklärung von Amos 7:14a." *Judaica* 23 (1967) 68–74. **Schult, H.** "Amos 7:15a und die Legitimation des Aussenseiters." *Probleme biblischer Theologie.* Ed. H. W. Wolff. München: Kaiser, 1971. 462–78. **Segert, S.** "Zur Bedeutung des Wortes *nōqēd.*" *Hebräische Wortforschung: FS zum 80. Geburtstag von Walter Baumgartner.* Ed. B. Hartmann et al. Leiden: E. J. Brill, 1967. 279–83. **Selms, A. van.** "Isaac in Amos." *OTSWA* 7–8 (1966) 157–65. **Smend, R.** "Das Nein des Amos." *EvT* 23 (1963) 404–23. **Spiegel, S.** "Amos vs. Amaziah." *The Jewish Expression.* Ed. J. Goldin. New Haven: Yale University Press, 1976. 38–65. **Talmon, S.** "The Gezer Calendar and the Seasonal Cycle of Ancient Canaan." *JAOS* 83 (1963) 177–87. **Treu, U.** "Amos 7:14, Schenute und Physiologus." *NT* 10 (1968) 234–40. **Tsumura, D. T.** "Ugaritic Contributions to Hebrew Lexicography." *Studies in Language and Literature.* Tsukuba: Institute of Literature and Linguistics, University of Tsukuba, 1976. [Japanese.] **Tucker, G.** "Prophetic Authenticity: A Form-Critical Study of Amos 7:10–17." *Int* 27 (1973) 423–34. **Vogt, E.** "Waw explicative in Amos 7:14." *ExpTim* 68 (1956–57) 301–2. **Waitz, Y.** "Amos: Sheep Breeder, Cattle Breeder, and Sycamore Fig Slitter." *BMik* 13 (1968) 141–44. [Heb.] **Werner, H.** "Der Visionsstrophenzyklus (7, 1–9; 8, 1–3; 9, 1–4)." *Amos.* Göttingen: Vandenhoeck & Ruprecht, 1969. 129–45. **Wolff, H. W.** "The Irresistible Word (Amos)." *CurTM* 10 (1983) 4–13. **Wright, S. L.** "O homem de Deus e o homem do rei." *RevT* 2 (1986) 37–42. **Wright, T.** "Amos and the 'Sycamore Fig.' " *VT* 26 (1976) 362–68. **Zaccagnini, C.** "Patterns of Mobility Among Ancient Near Eastern Craftsmen." *JNES* 42 (1983) 245–64. **Zalcman, L.** "Piercing the Darkness at Bôqēr." *VT* 30 (1980) 252–55. **Zevit, Z.** "A Misunderstanding at Bethel, Amos 7:12–17." *VT* 25 (1975) 783–90. ———. "Expressing Denial in Biblical Hebrew and Mishnaic Hebrew, and Amos." *VT* 29 (1979) 505–8. **Zimmerli, W.** "Vom Prophetenwort zum Prophetenbuch." *TLZ* 104 (1979) 481–96. **Ziv, Y.** *"boqer uboles šiqmim—betekoa'?"* *BMik* 28 (1982 / 83) 49–53.

Translation, Notes, and *Comment* sections will follow in smaller subsections.

Form / Structure / Setting

This section of Amos appears to be a discourse unit containing five distinguishable subunits: four vision-dialogue oracles; and the dialogue account of official reaction to the content of one of them together with Amos' rejoinder. Here for the first time in the book we encounter prophetic material in which Amos mentions himself, as well as the only biographical (or autobiographical) narrative about the prophet.

The passage is quite carefully structured. The following schema presents the salient features:

7:1–3	Vision 1 (locusts)	a. Yahweh initiates vision b. Amos sees, intercedes c. Yahweh responds, relents
7:4–6	Vision 2 (fire)	a. Yahweh initiates vision b. Amos sees, intercedes c. Yahweh responds, relents
7:7–9	Vision 3 (tin)	a. Yahweh initiates vision b. Yahweh interrogates Amos c. Amos answers d. Yahweh explains
7:10–17	Official reaction and prophet's response	a. Amaziah's report to the king b. Amaziah's ultimatum c. Amos' response
8:1–3	Vision 4 (summer fruit)	a. Yahweh initiates vision b. Yahweh interrogates Amos c. Amos answers d. Yahweh explains

At a glance it may be seen that the first and second vision-dialogues are identical in format, as are the third and fourth. Does not the biographical narrative of 7:10–17, then, interrupt the sequence of visions, which otherwise would neatly progress from two visions of punishment not carried out to two visions of punishment certain to come? Indeed it does, though not in an unwelcome manner. For the events described in the narrative were occasioned in part precisely by the wording of the Yahweh's explanation at the end of the third vision-dialogue and thus belong nowhere else thematically or conceivably even chronologically (see below).

Each of the four vision-dialogues has the same introductory formula, כה הראני אדני יהוה "This is what the Lord Yahweh showed me." Each introduces the vision itself by הנה (untranslatable; the equivalent of a colon [:]), and each contains a dialogue between the prophet and God. The only other vision in the book (9:1–6) is of an entirely different sort. Thus the four vision-dialogues, in spite of the differences between the first pair and second pair, are closely related. Additionally, an important progression is evident from the first two to the latter two. In the first two (both entirely prose) Amos is shown proposed covenant punishments (locusts, type 6b; and fire, type 10) which his intercession forestays. In the last two, however, (both partly poetic) Amos sees objects, tin and summer fruit, which in themselves have no significance but serve as paronomastic mnemonic devices related to Israel's coming doom.

From the progression of the four together, reinforced by the impact of 7:10–17, comes the inescapable conclusion that Israel must be destroyed and must be exiled. The notion may be spared certain particular horrors, but terminal punishment is inevitable.

Although 8:1–3 contains the expression ביום ההוה (v 3: "At that time / in that day"), which thematically influences chap. 8 (cf. vv 9, 11, 13), it is clear that this vision-dialogue concludes a pericope rather than introduces one. In 8:4 Amos returns to the topic of social injustice in a demonstrably new passage. Prose dominates 7:1–8:3. Only 7:9, 16, 17 and 8:3 contain poetry, with synonymous and synthetic parallelisms about equally represented. No short (*breve*) meter is found. Thus the third and fourth vision-dialogues share with the biographical narrative they surround the format of prose at the outset, poetry at the conclusion.

Although the precise dating cannot be known, the relative date and location of at least some of Amos' preaching is fixed by the specificity of 7:10–17, with a certainty unparalleled elsewhere in the book. V 13 confirms that Amos preached at least sometimes, if not usually, at Bethel, the main—and official—sanctuary of the North, and that the sorts of messages contained in 7:1–8:3 were characteristic of what he had apparently been preaching for some time (esp. "all his words," v 10). This does not allow us to conclude that his prophecies are arranged chronologically in the book or to estimate on how many separate occasions he may have prophesied during visits to the North or over what period of time his preaching there was undertaken.

Nevertheless, much can be inferred about Amos' personal situation, particularly from Amaziah's words. Amos' preaching must have had considerable currency in Israel, because his direct attack by name on King Jeroboam (7:9) was taken very seriously. He was apparently well known as a Judean native, but in light of vv 14–15 he may have wrongly been considered a typical professional prophet by some. His preaching was regarded by Amaziah as a program for revolt (v 10), yet Amos seems to have enjoyed the sort of diplomatic immunity generally accorded to prophets in both Israel and Judah (on this practice, see D. M. Scholer, "Your Fathers Killed the Prophets," Th.D. diss., Harvard Univ., 1982) so that while Amaziah can freely rail against him, he does not go so far as to have him arrested or forcibly deported. Finally, some features of Amos' call can be discerned in vv 14–15, including a brief quote from or summation of his inaugural revelation to become a prophet, elsewhere unattested.

Several options for the ordering of the four visions and their relation to 7:10–17 must be considered. (1) The four visions would have taken place over a substantial time period (months or years) with the activities described in 7:10–17 following the third vision, just as the material is ordered canonically. The fourth vision (8:1–3) would then have come as a confirmation of the validity of Amos' call and message, since Amaziah's attempt to squelch Amos would obviously have failed. (2) The four visions could have occurred together, or at least without any intervening revelations to Amos, with the events described in 7:10–17 having occurred thereafter. In that case 7:10–17 would be considered as located thematically, since Amaziah's response correlates so closely with 7:9, but not strictly chronologically. (3) Amos could have delivered these oracles at various times and places, interspersed with other oracles, and not necessarily in the order they presently appear. In that case 7:10–17 would not have represented so much a specific response to 7:9, but rather generally a response to Amos' doomsaying. (4) The ordering of the four visions may correspond to their actual delivery, but 7:10–17 is a story that occurred because of the general character of Amos' preaching, its inclusion in the present pericope being occasioned, on the catchword principle, by the mention of Jeroboam.

Although it would be impossible to prove one of these options—or others

that can be conceived of—we judge that option (1) is the most likely. Amos'
preaching must have irritated many people in northern Israel for years. But
the straw that broke the camel's back would have been his inspired condemnation of Jeroboam II by name (7:9) in the third vision. Such a personalized
denunciation of a single king and his family (cf. Hos 1:4, which narrows the
attack only to an entire dynasty), coupled with terminology well known from
the Mosaic covenant curses to refer to conquest, destruction, and exile, could
indeed have occasioned the events surrounding Amaziah's denunciation. The
linkage of חרב "sword" and Jeroboam in 7:9 and 7:11 is likely not accidental.
Amaziah's message to Jeroboam was probably a direct result of the prior
oracle. So in 8:1–3 God confirms to Amos and Israel that the destruction
predicted in the third vision will indeed occur. Perhaps it is as a response to
Amaziah's mention of the היכל "temple" in 7:13 that 8:3 depicts the destruction
even of the temple (picking up also part of 7:9).

Since the narrative parts of 7:10–17 describe Amos in the third person,
in contrast to the rest of the book, there is some reason to consider their
composition the work of a disciple rather than of Amos, but how near to or
far from the events that composition took place cannot be known.

Translation (7:1–6)

A locust swarm

¹*This is what [   ]ᵃ Yahweh showed me. He was forming*ᵇ *a swarm of
locusts when the late planting was beginning to come up—the late planting after
the king's mowing.*ᶜ ²*It seemed as if they would completely devour the earth's vegetation. I said, "Lord Yahweh, forgive! How can Jacob survive?*ᵃ *He is so small!"*
³*Yahweh changed his mind about this. "It will not happen," Yahweh said.*

Fire

⁴*This is what [   ]ᵃ Yahweh showed me. He was calling for a rain of
fire.*ᵇ *It devoured the great deep and would have devoured*ᶜ *the fields.*ᵈ ⁵*I said,
"Lord Yahweh, Stop!*ᵃ *How can Jacob survive? He is so small!"* ⁶*Yahweh changed
his mind about this as well. "It will not happen," [   ]ᵃ Yahweh said.*

Notes

1.a. Since most G texts do not reflect אדני "Lord," it is likely that its presence in MT derives
from a late conflation.

1.b. Only Vg read the participle יצר; G Syr and Tg all read the nominal יֶצֶר.

1.c. G reads βροῦχος εἷς Γωγ ὁ βασιλεύς "one larva Gog the king." Having already understood
יצר as "offspring" (ἐπιγονή), the G translator was apparently primed to reconstrue the consonantal
MT, which may itself already have contained אחד "one" instead of אחר "after" and a corruption
of גזי "mowing" to גוג "Gog."

2.a. G reads τίς ἀναστήσει τὸν Ιακωβ "Who will lift Jacob up," taking קום יָקִים as קִים hiph; this
is grammatically a more common construction than MT, though the latter is paralleled, e.g., in
Ruth 3:16.

4.a. G texts do not reflect אדני "Lord" strongly; cf. n. 1.a.

4.b. MT "contention / lawsuit of fire" represents an early corruption followed dutifully by
the ancient versions. Simply respacing the consonants yields רבב אש "rain of fire." Cf. D. R.
Hillers, "Amos 7:4 and Ancient Parallels," 221–25.

4.c. Or, conceivably, "devoured," though a subjunctive translation seems more appropriate for the converted pf here.

4.d. Lit., "plot(s)." G^BV add κυρίου "of Yahweh" perhaps via vertical dittogr.

5.a. Tg adds "Now leave for the guilty a remnant of the house of Jacob" (כען לחובי שארא דבית יעכב), an elaborate expansion on MT's single word "forgive" in v 2.

6.a. Again, the evidence from G suggests that אדני "Lord" is a late addition.

Comment

1 Since ראה, hiphil, can mean "reveal," "inform," as well as "make visible" (2 Kgs 8:13; Jer 38:21; Ps 71:20; 85:8), this vision and the others that follow it do not emphasize visual over auditory phenomena. Thus the conversations in vv 2 and 3 are also part of what Yahweh "showed" Amos, not merely the locust swarm (cf. the similar practice in Mari prophecies: e.g., *ANET*, 623–24, text b). Locusts are grasshoppers whose eggs hatch in ideal spring moisture conditions and whose shells turn brown rather than green from larval friction as they swarm in great numbers. They represented an unstoppable agricultural disaster in ancient times (curse type 6b; Deut 28:38, 42; cf. Exod 10:12–15; Joel 1; Amos 4:9). The locusts Amos saw came at the time of the second grain and hay growth (לקש), during April following the "latter rain." The fruit of the second planting was reserved for the farmers themselves, and without it they and their livestock would starve until the next harvest. If the text can be trusted, the first planting apparently represented the kings' claim in Jeroboam's time, though there is no other evidence of this (1 Kgs 18:5, routinely cited as evidence, has nothing to do with an annual royal mowing).

2. Because the locusts were so numerous—and not presumably because they had already begun to eat—Amos foresaw a country devoid of vegetation (cf. Deut 28:42), i.e., a devastated Israel where neither man nor animals could stay alive. He is clearly in the divine presence and is allowed to understand Yahweh's planning. Prophets often saw the future and reported on it; here Amos learns even the *potential* future. He stands as a mediator in a position to make intercession for his people. His petition begins with אדני יהוה "Lord Yahweh," a compound title typically found in prayers and supplications (2 Sam 7:18–28 six times; Josh 7:7; Judg 6:22; Jer 1:6; Ezek 4:14). The terseness of Amos' actual plea for deliverance, סלח "forgive," is not unusual. Judging from the more than sixty lament psalms in the Psalter, once an individual's or a group's distress was evident to a sovereign, a brief request for help was adequate (Ps 3:7a; 4:1; 12:1a; 13:3). Although the purpose of lament psalms is appeal to God, the appeal is virtually always shorter than the description of the danger or affliction, a ratio analogous to that of Amos' visions.

Surprisingly Amos calls Israel "Jacob." His purpose is probably to personify the nation in terms of an individual who cannot survive (יקום) without a harvest, rather than to allude to something in the patriarchal history. Little (קטן) Jacob seems to stand before Yahweh like the little people—the poor and needy—before the wealthy and powerful (as in 2:6–8; 4:1; 5:11, etc.).

3 Yahweh's response constitutes a genuine reversal of divine intent. The scriptures consistently witness to the possibility that God may choose to do something he had not planned, or not to do something he had planned, in response to human appeal (Gen 18:22–32; Num 14:11–20; Josh 7:6–13; 2 Kgs 22:19–20; Jer 18:1–10; Jonah 3:10; Joel 2:13, 14). Theologies portraying God as inflexible are hardly biblical.

The niphal of נחם with על indicates a change of mind, confirmed by Yahweh's promise to Amos, לא תהיה "It will not happen." The fem sg verb form conforms to זאת "this," which is itself a fem sg, the typical number and gender for summarizing abstracts. The total devastation of Israel's plant life by locust plague was no longer to occur.

4 The description of the second vision parallels the first in format. In v 1 Yahweh was "forming" (יצר); here he is "calling" (קרא). A רבב אש "rain of fire" (see note 4.a.) would be recognized by Amos' audience as a well-known curse (type 10; cf. Deut 32:22, "A fire has been kindled by my wrath, one that burns to Sheol below. It will devour the earth and its harvests and set on fire the foundations of the mountains"). Since the "foundations of the mountains" are sometimes visualized as being rooted in the depths of the sea (Jonah 2:6; Ps 46:2), as are the "foundations" of the earth (2 Sam 22; Ps 18:16; Prov 8:29; cf. Mic 6:1–2), the image of fire devouring the "deep" (תהום) therefore fits closely the depiction in Deut 32:22: fields and sea are devoured in both descriptions.

5–6 Amos again utters a one-word plea; this time חדל־נא "stop!" There is no special significance to this phrasing; it is another simple, straightforward request. And again Amos repeats the point that such terror would annihilate "Jacob." Yahweh's response is identical to that recorded in v 3. This as well (גם־היא) will not occur.

Translation (7:7–9)

Tin

⁷ *This is what* ⟨Yahweh⟩ᵃ *showed me:*ᵇ *He was standing on a tin*ᶜ *wall and he had some tin*ᶜ *in his hand.* ⁸ *Yahweh said to me, "What do you see, Amos?" I said, "Tin."* ⟨Yahweh⟩ᵃ *said, "I am going to put tin [moaning]*ᵇ *within my people Israel. I will no longer pass him by."*

⁹ *The high places*ᵃ *of Isaac will be destroyed.*
The sanctuaries of Israel will be desolated.
*I will rise up with a sword*ᵇ *against Jeroboam's family.*

Notes

7.a. Reading with the main evidence for G; MT is garbled, having lost יהוה "Yahweh," perhaps because of the proximity of the similar והנה.
7.b. Heb והנה is represented by the colon.
7.c. On the meaning of אנך "tin," see *Comment*.
8.a. Reading again with the bulk of good G evidence.
8.b. See *Comment*.
9.a. Or "shrines."
9.b. Or "in war."

Comment

7 Although the text of v 7 is considerably more corrupt than is the case in the first verses of the corresponding visions (7:1, 4; 8:1), the evident consistency of format among the four visions allows for a relatively confident reconstruction. There is no need to question the presence of אֲנָךְ "tin" twice in the verse. Amos carefully repeats it to prepare the hearer / reader for the coming paronomasia with אֲנַק / אֲנָה, just as he twice mentions קַיץ "summer fruit" in 8:1–2 in preparation for the pun on קֵץ "end" in 8:3.

Unfortunately, אֲנָךְ has been widely mistranslated as "plumbline." This definition was never more than a guess. Because Akkadian *anāku* can refer to either "tin" or "lead," and since lead is often used as a plummet for squaring walls, אֲנָךְ has seemed a synecdoche for "plumbline." But the Hebrew for "plummet" is מִשְׁקֹלֶת (2 Kgs 21:13; Isa 28:17) and for the "line" that holds it, קָו (Isa 28:17). Thus אֲנָךְ, used only here in the OT, clearly means simply "tin" (see esp. Holladay, "Once More, ᵃnak = 'tin,'" 492–95; Landsberger, "Tin and Lead—The Adventures of Two Vocables," 285–96; Ouellette, "Le mur d'étain dans Amos VII, 7–9," 321–31).

This is not the sort of literal punishment vision detailed in vv 1–6. This vision and its complement in 8:1–3 attach no importance to what is actually seen: the play on words is the real issue. Thus what Amos sees is in one sense ridiculous. It is hard to imagine what a tin wall would look like and what shape the tin in Yahweh's hand would take. Indeed, as v 8 makes plain, Amos made no issue of seeing Yahweh at all, only the tin. (Wolff [292–300] argues that we should understand the text to indicate that Amos merely saw "someone" in these visions, the "he" of "he was standing" in v 7, for example, is not referring to Yahweh.)

8 Amos saw what he was supposed to see: אֲנָךְ "tin." Yet a third time the word is mentioned, and on this occasion it has the prominence of a one-word reply to a question. In the visions of vv 1–6, Amos spoke sentences. Here he says only," אֲנָךְ."

The hearer / reader is now ready for the paronomasia. אֲנָךְ sounds almost exactly like אֲנַק "moaning," a term used sometimes by the prophets in connection with coming punishment miseries (Jer 51:52; Ezek 26:15; cf. the metathesized cognate נְאַק, e.g., in Ezek 30:24), and very close to אֲנָה, which also indicates "moaning" or "groaning" and is also used similarly to depict coming distress in destruction (Isa 24:7; Joel 1:18; cf. Isa 35:10). The exact pronunciation of אֲנָךְ in northern Israel in Amos' day is uncertain. It was probably either ᵃnōk or ʾanāk. The former would have sounded roughly like an inf constr; the latter like a 3 masc sg pf, or possibly a noun on the *qatāl* pattern. Since the verbs אֲנַק and אֲנָה both have corresponding nouns on the *qatalāh* pattern (אֲנָקָה, אֲנָחָה), it may have been one of the verb forms that the paronomasia was based on.

This time Yahweh will not change his mind (cf. vv 3, 6). "Moaning" implies the agony of defeat and destruction (cf. the passages cited above in Isa, Jer, Ezek, and Joel). Israel will not escape again.

9 Now comes an announcement in poetic triplet form of the punishment from which Yahweh will *not* relent. The fulfillments of two types of curses are announced: desolation of sanctuaries (type 9a, as in Lev 26:30–31 with which it shares the words שָׁמֵם "be destroyed," בָּמָה "high places," and מִקְדָּשׁ "sanctuary") and the destruction of the royalty. The latter echoes mainly type 9b ("Yahweh will drive . . . the king . . . to a nation unknown") but also suggests the loss-of-family curses (type 18, e.g., Deut 32:25, "the sword will make them childless"). In general, the "sword" (חרב) is a punishment evidencing covenant infidelity (Lev 26:25).

Since חָרֵב "to be desolate" at the end of the second line and חֶרֶב "sword" at the end of the third line of this triplet share the same consonants, it is evident that Amos has employed a kind of anastasis in linking the lines. The pattern of the triplet is also shaped by the three proper names in its three respective lines: Isaac, Israel, Jeroboam. Since Isaac's history is intimately linked with Beersheba (Gen 26:23, 33), and worship at this Southern sanctuary has already been attacked by Amos (5:5), Beersheba may be the referent for "the high places of Isaac." Wherever they are located, north or south, the counter-cultus pilgrimage sites will be destroyed.

Translation (7:10–17)

10 *Amaziah the priest of Bethel sent word to Jeroboam, king of Israel. "Amos has launched a conspiracy against you in the very heart of Israel.*[a] *The land cannot contain everything he is saying! For here is what he said: 'Jeroboam will die by the sword and Israel will definitely be exiled from her native land.' "*

12 *To Amos, Amaziah said, "Seer, leave this instant*[a] *for Judah! Earn your living*[b] *there, and do your prophesying there.* 13 *But don't do any more prophesying at Bethel, because it is a royal sanctuary, a state temple."*

14 *Amos answered Amaziah: "No! I am a prophet,*[a] *though I am not a professional prophet*[b] *because I am a livestock breeder*[c] *and a sycamore fig slitter.* 15 *But Yahweh took me away from the flocks and Yahweh told me, 'Prophesy to my people Israel.'* 16 *Now listen to Yahweh's word, you who say*

'Do not prophesy against Israel,
Do not preach against the family of Isaac.'

17 *Therefore here is what Yahweh has said:*

'Your wife will become a prostitute in the city,
And your sons and daughters will fall by the sword.

Your land will be divided up by a measuring line,
And you yourself will die in an unclean land.

Israel will definitely be exiled from its native land!' "

Notes

10.a. Lit., "in the midst of the house of Israel."
12.a. Lit., "Go, flee for yourself."
12.b. Lit., "Eat bread." On the idiomatic usage of אכל לחם "eat bread"; cf. Gen 3:19 and KB[3], 44–45.
14.a. Or, "I am not a prophet." See *Comment*. The earliest G texts have the verb ἤμην "I was not (a prophet)," a reasonable translation of the verbless clause, thus comporting with MT. See also Z. Zevit, "Expressing Denial," 505–508.
14.b. Lit., "son / student of a prophet," or "member of a prophetic guild," or the like.
14.c. Or "herdsman." See *Comment*.

Comment

10 Here begins the only biographical section of the book. This section (vv 10–17) is structured simply: Amaziah's complaint to Jeroboam (vv

10–11), Amaziah's attack on Amos (vv 12–13), Amos' stubborn reply (vv 14–17). It appears that Amaziah was at this time the chief priest at Bethel. If he were simply *a* priest there, the Hebrew would read כהן לבית־אל "a priest of Bethel" or the like. He appealed to the king not simply because Bethel was a royal sanctuary frequented by the monarchy, but also because in ancient Israel kings controlled the religion to a substantial degree (see R. deVaux, *Ancient Israel,* 113–14).

Amaziah's report probably took the form of an official letter, much longer than the quotes appearing here. However the letter may have opened, one imagines that the conspiracy charge appeared early in the body. It was certainly worded to arouse the king to action in that it presumptuously accuses Amos of קשר "conspiracy," a highly political word. The Jehu dynasty, of which Jeroboam was the final substantial member, ended in 753 B.C. with the assassination of Zechariah, Jeroboam's son (2 Kgs 15:8–12). That violence and the political turmoil that followed (2 Kgs 15:13–16) did not likely emerge *de novo,* but must have been long building toward its outburst. Just as opposition built toward Saul, David, Solomon, Manasseh, and other long-reigning kings toward the end of their tenures, opposition to Jeroboam II can hardly have been nonexistent by this time (the 750s?). Accordingly, Amaziah chose a loaded term to describe Amos' activity—"conspiracy"—one that Jeroboam could hardly ignore. He also stressed that this conspiracy was not a peripheral one, but open and central. And he further portrayed it as based virtually on the constant preaching of Amos. Amaziah's hyperbolic accusation that Amos is saying so much that the land cannot contain (כול, hiphil; cf. Jer 10:10) it portrays Amos' verbal attacks as coming like a flood.

Was Amos actually a conspirator, preaching in support of a movement of political rebellion? Certainly not. What Amaziah did see correctly, however, was the political implications of God's word *through* Amos.

11 Amaziah cites in summary fashion two aspects of Amos' preaching bound to get Jeroboam's notice: the death of the king himself in war and the exile of the nation. Since exile is accomplished only after military conquest by an enemy, the latter is automatically implied.

There is no record that Amos actually predicted that Jeroboam would die in war or by any other sort of violence (בחרב "by the sword"). Thus Amaziah was undoubtedly without foundation in virtually accusing Amos of death threats against the king. Jeroboam probably died a peaceful death (2 Kgs 14:29 is ambiguous). Clearly, however, Amos had several times prophesied the exile of Israel (5:5; 5:27; 6:8, etc.) and had done so in Samaria itself (6:7). Indeed, the prediction of exile as Amaziah cites it Amos stubbornly repeats in 7:17.

12 Many northerners, being relatively more cosmopolitan than southerners (see A. Alt, "Das Königtum in den Reichen Israel und Juda," *Kleine Schriften II* [Munich; Beck'sche Verlagsbuchhandlung, 1935] 116–34), undoubtedly regarded Judah as "the sticks" and dismissed out of hand its more conservative religion (cf. 2 Chr 13). Amaziah, a non-Aaronic priest (1 Kgs 12:31, 32) at a heterodox sanctuary, certainly had a vested interest in seeing Amos back in Judah where his attacks would not make Israelite officials nervous.

Amaziah appears to be speaking on his own. He invokes no royal authorization to send Amos home; probably none ever came. (A king could not risk appearing petty and insecure by responding officially to prophetic threats, cf. 1 Kgs 22:8; Jer 36:23, 24.) The priests' words to Amos are revealing. He calls him חזה "seer," presumably because it was the vision of vv 7–9 that had proved to be the last straw in offensiveness. The term חזה was an honorable one (even in Mic 3:7, *contra* Wolff, *Hosea*, 311) in ancient Israel (e.g., 2 Sam 24:11; 2 Kgs 17:13; Isa 30:10) and was no insult to Amos. An insult was implied, however, in the demand that Amos leave Israel immediately (ברח־לך) and earn his living (אכל לחם) in Judah. It is doubtful that Amaziah was trying to protect Amos by urging him to "flee" (ברח), i.e., from potential danger, to the safety of his homeland. The probably derogatory "earn your living there" confirms this. The priest is insinuating that Amos preached at Bethel because the remuneration was better there than in Judah. Prophets certainly were supported by donations (1 Sam 9:7–9; Mic 3:5, 11) and the profitability of religion made it worthwhile to pay handsomely for priesthoods (2 Chr 13:9). Amos' response in v 14 indicates that Amaziah was treating Amos according to his own standards.

13 By what authority does Amaziah seek to dismiss Amos from Bethel? By the authority of Jeroboam II. The tradition of monarchical control of religion was quite strong in the north (1 Kgs 12:26–33; 16:26, 30–33; 18:4, 19; cf. also above, v 10). This was one reason orthodox prophets so frequently attacked the monarchy when the nation was unfaithful to the covenant. Amaziah describes Bethel via a hendiadys: מקדש מלך "a royal sanctuary" is essentially equivalent to בית ממלכה "a state temple." Indeed, Amaziah's prose is synonymously parallelistic here, in part perhaps because his charge to Amos is formal and public. Amaziah's self-interest is undoubtedly reflected in the description of Bethel as an official site. The high priest of a sanctuary was its administrator; Amaziah thus in effect claimed governmental authority to dismiss Amos.

14 The first part of Amos' response is grammatically ambiguous and has thus engendered considerable scholarly discussion. לא נביא אנכי ולא בן נביא אנכי can conceivably mean any of the following: "I am neither a prophet nor a professional prophet (or member of a prophetic guild)"; "I am indeed [vocalizing לא as לוא] a prophet and indeed a professional prophet"; "I am indeed a prophet but not a professional prophet"; "No, I am a prophet and, indeed, a professional prophet." (There are theoretically other possibilities, though none is plausible.) The full context of Amos' protestation makes most convincing the translation: "No, I am a prophet though I am not a professional prophet." Amos could hardly deny being a נביא "prophet." He speaks of his own prophesying (נבא, niphal) favorably in the next verse (see also 3:8 and perhaps 2:12). Moreover, his concern to specify his employment indicates a determination to avoid being thought of as a בן נביא "professional prophet" / "member of a prophetic guild," i.e., one who had trained to be a prophet and supported himself / herself thereby. (See 1 Kgs 20:25; 2 Kgs 2:3, 4:1, etc., and Richardson, "A Critical Note," 89.) Thus Amos claims the prophetic office, while at the same time denying Amaziah's insinuation that he is in it for the money.

Amos claims professionally to be a בוקר "livestock breeder" / "cattleman" and a בולס "fig slitter." There is some uncertainty about the precise meaning of these terms, particularly בוקר, and it has also been suggested that Amos uses them not literally but as self-effacing terms (e.g., "Shucks, I'm just a country farmer") to indicate that Amaziah has nothing to fear from him. The evidence suggests, however, that Amos intends to identify himself as one who had no financial reason to prophesy at Bethel or anywhere else. Amos may even have been an agribusiness specialist (see P. Craigie, "Amos the *nōqēd* in the Light of Ugaritic," *SR* 11/1 [1982] 28–33). The contention that Amos' words cannot be taken literally because figs are difficult to grow in Tekoa is irrelevant if Amos is understood to be a traveling consultant / specialist. Fig slitting is the process of making a small cut in figs early in their maturation so as to produce a sweeter, softer final fruit. In his travels Amos probably performed this service. If a בוקר was something other than a common cowherd, as seems likely, it also may have been an occupation in the interest of which he traveled in the North.

15 Amos describes his call—the only mention of it in the book aside from 3:8—in terms also applied to King David's call. In 2 Sam 7:8 and Ps 78:70, "taking away from the flock" (לקח . . . צאן) is the terminology applied to David's being chosen king. Since the offices of king and prophet were legitimately only by divine election (Deut 17:15; 18:15) and since David and Amos were both involved in sheep raising, it is quite possible that Amos consciously intended for Amaziah to see the similarity. Israelites had once accepted a Judean as their king, recognizing his divine appointment (2 Sam 5:1–3).

Amos likewise claimed divine appointment to *his* office. Using covenantal language again associated with the story of David (עמי ישראל "my people Israel," cf. 2 Sam 5:2), Amos summarizes his call to prophesy not just in Judah but to the entire covenant people, north and south. Yahweh had called him to prophesy (הנבא) to them all.

16 Amaziah was therefore actually asking Amos to disobey Yahweh! Used to controlling cult prophets and priests who were mainly sycophants to the government (e.g., 1 Kgs 22:6), Amaziah presumed he had a right to address a prophet in the way he had. But his heterodox orientation had led him to ignore the Mosaic covenant's demands. Amos now turns his attention to Amaziah, who has clearly opposed the will of Yahweh. The synonymous poetic couplet that characterizes Amaziah's prohibition is not likely a direct quote of Amaziah, but Amos' inspired way of portraying Amaziah. The paralleling of ישראל "Israel" by יצחק "Isaac" cleverly reinforces Amos' assertion that all Israel, North and South, was Yahweh's domain and the proper territory of his true prophets. "Israel" ambiguously referred either to all Israel or just to Northern Israel. But "the family of Isaac" (בית יצחק) had to include Judah as well. In that sense Amos accused Amaziah of forbidding him to prophesy—period.

17 Amaziah was one of the long line of suppressors of legitimate prophecy, including the Pharaoh of the exodus, Jeroboam I, Jezebel, Ahab, Hananiah, etc. It should not be surprising that his fate was to be a severe one (cf. 1 Kgs 13:26; Jer 28:16). A prophet's denunciation of a priest is hardly without parallel (cf. 1 Sam 2:27–36; Jer 20:1–6; Hos 5:1, etc.). Here the terms of

the denunciation involve four curses against Amaziah, followed by the restatement of what Amos had been preaching: *Israel will definitely be exiled from its
native land,* a truth the priest of Bethel could not suppress.

The curses fit standard types. In the first couplet, for one's wife to
תזנה בעיר "become a prostitute in the city" and for one's children to die
by the sword are graphic ways of portraying curse type 18, loss of family
(esp. Deut 28:30, "another will take her and ravish her," and Deut 32:25,
"the sword will make them childless"; cf. Deut 28:41). Such curses are generic,
not specific. Amaziah surely understood them to mean that in the coming
exile he might be separated from his wife, who without support would have
to turn to prostitution to stay alive, and from his children, who might well
be killed in the conquest. The wording אדמתך "your land" undoubtedly
indicates Israel, not any property Amaziah might own (more likely indicated
by שדה "field"). An "unclean land" (אדמה טמאה) where Amaziah would
die in exile—i.e., never return from—is another way (appropriate to a priest
for whom "cleanness" was a preoccupation) of describing foreign territory
(cf. Hos 9:3). Dividing the land with a חבל "measuring line" reflects curse
type 5, occupation by enemies (e.g., Lev 26:32). Exile is type 13, as in Lev
26:38–39 ("you will perish among the nations . . . those . . . left will waste
away in the land of their enemies").

Amos has used אדמה "land" three times in this short oracle stressing the
inevitability of Israel's exile. Neither a threat from the monarchy or from
the clergy could change anything: their land was being taken from the Israelites, and Amos would not stop preaching that message.

Translation (8:1–3)

Summer fruit

¹ *This is what [   ]ᵃ Yahweh showed me: a basket of summer fruit.*ᵇ ² *He said,*ᵃ
*"What do you see, Amos?" I said, "A basket of summer fruit." Yahweh said to me,
"The 'end'ᵇ has come for my people Israel. I will no longer pass him by.* ³ *They
will wail*ᵃ *the temple songs at that time"—oracle of [   ]ᵇ Yahweh. "They*ᶜ *will
throw the corpses*ᵈ *into big piles everywhere. Hush!"*

Notes

1.a. אדני "Lord" was not originally present, as reflected by its absence in the best MSS
of G.

1.b. G reads ἄγγος ἰξευτοῦ "fowler's basket," either taking כלוב as "birdcage" (cf. Jer 5:27)
and associating קיץ "summer fruit" with עיט "large bird," or else by reading from a text that
had כלוב מוקש "fowler's basket" or the like (cf. מוקש in 3:5). α′ σ′ θ′ all correct toward MT.

2.a. Syr adds the equivalent of "to me," presumably under the influence of 7:8. G supports
MT.

2.b. קץ "end" is a word play with קיץ "summer fruit" above. See *Comment* below.

3.a. Taking ילל "wail," hiph, as transitive; cf. Isa 52:5. שירות songs may also be the subj of
the verb ("songs shall turn to wailing"), or the original may have been שרות "female singers of
the temple will wail."

3.b. See 1.a.

3.c. Taking the 3 masc sg as having the indefinite subj "they."

3.d. פגר "corpse" is collective here; cf. 1 Sam 17:46; Nah 3:3.

Comment

1 The introductory wording is the same as that of the three previous visions (7:1; 7:4; 7:7). The new element is the thing seen, a קיץ כלוב "basket of summer fruit." As with the third vision, there is no significance to the thing seen other than in the sound of one word: קיץ. A basket of summer fruit is merely a harvesting basket used by workers to hold the קיץ (any tree fruit, such as figs or olives that would ripen for the fall harvest). The basket was presumably of typical woven-wicker construction (as a birdcage would also be; cf. Jer 5:27). Yahweh used the sight of it, filled with its fruit, to lead to the conversation that would reveal the essence of the vision.

2 The wording of this part of the conversation is, again, routine. (On the pattern of repetition, see *Comment*, 7:7.) As with the "tin" vision in 7:7–9, the focus immediately shifts from what is seen to what it sounds like. As אנך "tin" sounded like אנק / אנח "moan," so קיץ "summer fruit" sounds like קץ "end." While the words have different roots (קיץ and קצץ, respectively), in the north in Amos' time they were both pronounced identically—*qēs*— since diphthongs had contracted in Israelite by this time (cf. קץ in the Gezer Calendar; see F. M. Cross and D. N. Freedman, *Early Hebrew Orthography* [New Haven: American Oriental Society, 1952]). On the use of קץ "end" in judgment or death contexts, cf. Ps 39:5; Lam 4:18; Ezek 7:2; etc. This vision, like the third, predicts destruction to be fulfilled, not deferred as in the first two visions. Israel's death / destruction represents curse type 24 (e.g., Deut 4:26; 28:20–22; 30:15; 31:17; 32:25; etc.).

3 Two scenes indicating death / destruction are provided synechdochically in portraying the coming disaster. Wailing (ילל, cf. Jer 4:8; Ezek 21:17; Mic 1:8; Zeph 1:11; etc.) the temple songs (שירות היכל) indicates in ironic style that death and destruction will reach the heart of the nation's religion: its temple(s). One function of this wording, of course, is as an allusion to Amaziah's attaching importance to the Bethel temple (7:13); thus Amos' prophecy "answers" Amaziah's claims at least obliquely. It is also possible that היכל here means "palace" and that it is the royalty (also 7:13) that this wording alludes to.

The description of piling up corpses (פגר) "everywhere" (בכל־מקום) likewise signals widespread death in Israel (cf. Jer 16:4). The final word, הס "Hush!" already seen in 6:10 (q.v.), indicates the solemn, fearful circumstances of the coming time of disaster.

Explanation

Amos 7:1–8:3 is the account of four prophetic visions and the story of the official opposition that was aroused particularly by the wording of the third vision. In the first two visions (7:1–3; 7:4–5), coming disasters revealed to Amos are canceled by the prophet's intercession. Yahweh shows himself merciful and compassionate, willing to change his mind about intended harm (cf. Exod 34:6; Joel 2:13; Jonah 4:2; etc.), unwilling utterly to destroy his covenant people (Deut 4:27–31).

The third and fourth visions (7:7–9; 8:1–3) revolve on the sound of spoken words that suggest punishments certain to be carried out: "moaning" and the "end" for Israel—not a total obliteration of the people, but a severe conquest, exile, and loss of life.

Even the biographical section in 7:10–17 is strongly oracular in nature, confirming and detailing Amos' revelations of Israel's coming exile. This brief story is particularly intriguing because it tells the story of an attempt by a religious official to stifle the preaching of a prophet whose message was unpleasant, embarrassing, and even threatening to the religious and governmental establishment. From a purely human point of view, the priest Amaziah's actions were reasonable. He wanted to silence Amos, a prophet not (officially at least) welcome in the region where he had been preaching, whose doomsaying was critical of persons not using their power to bring Israelite society back into conformity with the Sinai covenant.

But in trying to silence a prophet, one may actually be trying to silence God. Some in NT times, whose "fathers killed the prophets" (Luke 11:48), similarly thought that they could silence Jesus, John the Baptist, Paul, and many others, not having learned from the story of Amaziah and Amos. Indeed, religion may nearly always seek peacefulness and harmony above the truth that God demands justice and faithfulness and has appointed a day when he will judge the world. Ignorance is not bliss. Refusal to consider the reality of God's wrath against evil amounts to willingness to condone evil.

Was Amos too hard on Amaziah? Not at all. The priest who wanted to protect his king and countrymen from hearing predictions of their doom would inevitably be unable to escape the effects of that doom himself. Amos' negative message was not just sentiment; it was God's word. Amaziah, along with his fellow Israelites, had to experience the penalty of ignoring or opposing it.

Hypocrisy: Punishments Fitting the Crime (8:4–14)

Bibliography

Ackroyd, P. "The Meaning of Hebrew דור Considered." *JSS* 13 (1968) 4–10. **Bartina, S.** " 'Vivit Potentia Beer-Šeba!' (Amos 8:14)." *VD* 34 (1956) 202–10. **Bewer, J.** "Critical Notes on Amos 2:7 and 8:4." *AJSL* 19 (1903) 116–17. **Dahood, M.** "Ugaritic-Hebrew Lexicography IX." *Bib* 52 (1971) 337–56. **Givati, M.** "The *Shabbat* of the Prophet Amos." *BMik* 22, 2 (69) (1977) 278–79. [Heb.] **Gölz, F.** "Vom Biblischen Sinn des Sabbat." *Tbü* 9 (1978) 243–56. **Haag, E.** "Das Schweigen Gottes. Ein Wort des Propheten Amos (Am 8, 11s)." *BibLeb* 10 (1969) 157–64. **Halevy, B.** When Will the New Moon Be Gone? *BMik* 21 (1975) 333–46, 493. [Heb.] **Lang, B.** "Sklaven und Unfreie im Buch Amos (ii 6, viii 6)." *VT* 31 (1981) 482–86. **Morgenstern, J.** "The Loss of Words at the Ends of Lines in Manuscripts of Biblical Poetry." *HUCA* 25 (1954) 41–83. **Muraokao, T.** "Is the Septuagint Amos 8, 12–9, 10 a Separate Unit?" *VT* 20 (1970)

496–500. **Neuberg, F.** "An Unrecognized Meaning of Hebrew DÔR." *JNES* 9 (1950) 215–17. **Rusche, H.** "Wenn Gott sein Wort entzieht. Meditation zu Amos 8:11–12." *BibLeb* 10 (1969) 219–21. **Scott, R. B. Y.** "Weights and Measures of the Bible." *BA* 22 (1959) 22–40. **Szwarc, U.** "Głód Slowa Bozego Analiza Egzegetycno-Teologiczna Tekstu Am 8, 11–12." *Roczniki Teol.-Kanoniczne* 28 (1981) 35–47.

Translation

Hypocrisy in financial practices

8:4 *Listen to this, you who trample* [a] *on the poor,*
Eliminating [b] *the oppressed people of the land,* [5] *saying,*

"When will the New Moon be over [a] *so that we can sell grain,* [b]
And the Sabbath, so that we can put wheat on sale,

So that we can shrink the ephah and increase the shekel,
And cheat with inaccurate scales;

[6] *So that we can buy poor people for money,* [a]
A needy person for a pair of sandals,
And sell the sweepings in with [b] *the wheat?"* [cd]

Certainty of punishment

[7] *Yahweh has sworn by Jacob's pride,*
I will never forget [a] *all their deeds.*

Varieties of punishment

[8] *Will not the earth shake on account of this,*
And everyone who lives in it mourn,

And all of it rise like the Nile [a]
[ ] [b] *And sink* [c] *like the Nile of Egypt?*

[9] *At that time—oracle of* [ ] [a] *Yahweh—*
I will make the sun go down at noon
And darken the earth in broad daylight.

[10] *I will turn your festivals into mourning*
And all your songs into lamentation.

I will cause every waist to have sackcloth around it
And every head to be shaved bald. [a]

I will make it [b] *like mourning for an only son*
And its end like the end of [c] *an awful day.*

Hunger and thirst

[11] *The time is coming—oracle of* [ ] [a] *Yahweh—*
When I will send a famine unto the land;
Not a famine of food or a thirst for water,
But rather of hearing Yahweh's word. [b]

¹² *They will stagger from sea*ª *to sea*
And wander from north to east,
*Seeking*ᵇ *Yahweh's word; but they will not find it.*

¹³ *At that time attractive young women will drop unconscious,*
*As will strong*ª *young men, from thirst.*

¹⁴ *Those who swear by Samaria's shame*ª
And say, "As your god lives, Dan!"
*And, "As your power*ᵇ *lives, Beersheba!"*
Will fall and never rise again.

Notes

4.a. See 2:7.a. G (ἐκτρίβοντες "who grind down") supports MT.

4.b. The verb שבת "bring to an end / eliminate" is used purposely as a link to the next verse. The Heb. construction is inf with *lamedh* (לשבית) to indicate purpose. G's participial translation (καταδυναστεύοντες "tyrannizing") reflects a concern for syntactic coordination, not a different text from MT.

5.a. Or possibly, "When . . . come." See B. Halevy, "When Will the New Moon Be Gone?" 333–46, 493.

5.b. *Contra* Wolff (*Amos*, 321–22, n.f), there is no paronomasia present merely because שבר "grain" and השביר "sell grain" have the same root.

6.a. The usual translation for כסף "silver" needlessly suggests that a particular metal is desired.

6.b. Lit. "wheat sweepings we can sell as wheat."

6.c. Assuming that the quote continues to this point, rather than leaving off at 5.b. (cf. *NIV*).

6.d. The entire line "And sell . . . wheat?" belongs here metrically as part of a 6:7:6 triplet and would *not* fit metrically, as some have suggested, after 5a.

7.a. Lit., "If I forget . . . ," a typical oath formula aposiopesis.

8.a. MT כאר "like the light" is a simple miscopy omitting the *yodh*. The versions support כיאר "like the Nile."

8.b. MT ונגרשה "and will be stirred up" (גרש II) is reflected only in late G evidence. With some Heb. MSS, it should be deleted as an (unmetrical) gloss.

8.c. Reading with MT *Qere* ונשקעה "and sink."

9.a. Omitting אדני "Lord" with the best G evidence.

10.a. Lit., "I will put sackcloth . . . waist and baldness . . . head."

10.b. I.e., that time / day conceived abstractly via the fem sg.

10.c. Supplying "the end of" to the elliptical comparative.

11.a. See n. 9.a.

11.b. Reading the sg, דבר, with some Heb. MSS and the versions. MT must have resulted from a dittogr of the י of יהוה.

12.a. G ὕδατα "waters" simply vocalized MT alternatively (מָיִם).

12.b. Lit., "in order to seek." Cf. the similar infinitival construction in v 4.

13.a. Implied in בחורים "young man."

14.a. The occasional suggestion that אשמת "shame" is to be vocalized אֲשִׁימָת. "Ashimat" (a form of the deity mentioned in 2 Kgs 17:30) does not adequately appreciate the contrast with גאון יעקב "Jacob's pride" in v 7.

14.b. Taking דרך in analogy to its Ugaritic cognate (see Dahood, "Ugaritic-Hebrew Lexicography IX," 337–56; and Bartina, "Vivit Potentia Beer-Šeba," 202–10).

Form / Structure / Setting

The recognition that 8:4–14 is a unity depends especially on the observation that prophetic judgment oracles do not normally exist apart from indictments. That is, God rarely announces punishment for covenant-breaking without providing some sort of evidence or reminder of how the covenant has been broken. Prophetic restoration promises are not predicated upon Israel's good behavior (cf. 9:11–12, 13–15), but judgment oracles are nearly always predicated on Israel's bad behavior.

From the present passage, vv 9–10, vv 11–12, and vv 13–14 are often isolated as three distinct oracles of doom appended to vv 4–8 because of their similar subject matter. These latter oracles all begin with some form of יוֹם ("day" / "time") in formulae associated with oracles introducing coming events (as in 9:11, 13), such as ימים באים ("the time is coming," v 11) or ביום ההוא ("at that time," vv 9, 13). But if isolated from vv 4–8, vv 9–10 and vv 11–12 at least lack mention of covenant crimes. Vv 13–14, however, contain an indictment as well as a punishment prediction and could therefore be considered isolatable. Yet once vv 9–10 and 11–12 are joined to vv 4–8, vv 13–14 rather naturally join as well, especially by reason of their "thirst" imagery following on vv 11–12.

There are other factors linking the remainder of the chapter with vv 4–8. The entire section is concerned with religious hypocrisy. It is strict Sabbath-keepers who are cheating Israel's poor (v 4). Those indicted celebrate religious festivals (v 10) with their favorite songs (such as the Yahwistic hymn already excerpted by Amos in 4:13 and 5:8?). One of their punishments will be a removal of Yahweh's word (vv 11, 12). And syncretism is rampant (v 14). Thus "all their deeds" (v 7) are the selfish practices of people whose observance of religion is limited to worship procedures and does not extend to societal relationships (cf. 5:21–24).

The passage is structured somewhat concentrically in that the indictments (vv 4–6, 14) largely surround the predictions of doom. The initial imperative שמעו זאת "listen to this" covers all of the passage and has its closest parallel in 3:13, although 3:1; 4:1; and 5:1 are similar.

The passage can be dated confidently to the time prior to Tiglath-Pileser's invasion in 733 B.C., arguing from silence that no reflection of Assyrian domination or annexation can be found. Moreover, a date during Jeroboam's reign (cf. 1:1) is reasonable, especially in light of the evident wealth of the upper class at the expense of the poor that is associated with the time of Jeroboam II, and the reference to Dan as an existing sanctuary (v 14). The freedom to travel to Beersheba (v 14) also suggests a time when the Northern Kingdom was as dominant as it had been prior to 753. The wording gives no hint of a specific location for the original preaching of this oracle.

Comment

4 Sadly, Israel's society had developed two economic tiers during the eighth century B.C. At the expense of an increasingly impoverished large lower class, and in violation of the Mosaic covenant (Exod 23:6; Lev 19:10, 13, 15; 25:25–53; Deut 15:7–11; 24:12–22), a monied upper class had emerged (cf. 4:1–3; 6:1–7). Its members included profiteers, business persons who felt free to take advantage of tacit government policy that favored the rich and paid no heed to the interests of the poor. Such people were "trampling" (שׁאף), i.e., exploiting, the poor, with the result (thus the hiphil infinitive

לשבית) that increasingly needy people were apparently dying of starvation, selling themselves into slavery, suffering ill health and other maladies of malnourishment and lack of proper clothing and shelter, etc. There is no suggestion here that the exploiters were *trying* to kill off the impoverished. The infinitive with ל can certainly have such a force, but logic suggests that people would not seek to eliminate their source of income. The net result, nevertheless, was a tragic crime ultimately against Yahweh himself. For it should be remembered that though Israel was *ethnically* Yahweh's people, the poor were *economically* his special people (Pss 14:6; 140:12; 1 Sam 2:8; Isa 61:1).

5 The verse describes Israelite business people who are apparently strict in their observation of Sabbath and New Moon, but eager to be able to cheat their customers once business can resume. In this way they "trample" (v 4) on the poor.

The New Moon festival (חדש) was a Mosaic covenant holiday (Num 10:10; 28:11) faithfully celebrated over the years by Israelites (1 Sam 20:24–25; 2 Kgs 4:23; Isa 1:13; Hos 2:11). The Law more explicitly forbade marketing on the Sabbath (Exod 20:8; 23:12; 34:21; Deut 5:12–15; cf. Neh 13:15–22) because it involved work, and continuous work—even when voluntary—is an unhealthful oppression. But exploitive profits were so good that sellers could hardly stand to take holidays off.

The grain (שבר) and wheat (בר) together signified food produce in general (cf. Gen 42:2–3), not merely certain grains. It was especially foodstuffs that a nonfarm urban populace would pay almost any price for (see below, *Explanation*). The three descriptions of how sellers were unfairly increasing their profits reflect typical covenant language and, as in the Pentateuch, are undoubtedly meant to be suggestive of yet others unmentioned: (1) shrinking the איפה "ephah," the standard unit of bulk measure (half bushel) by using smaller than proper containers; (2) overweighting the שקל "shekel," the standard weight (⅖ ounce), so that the buyer thought he was getting more than he really was when he saw his grain weighed in the scales against the shekel; and (3) rigging up inaccurate scales (מאזני מרמה). Such practices were forbidden in the Law (e.g., Lev 19:35–36; Deut 25:13–15), attacked by the prophets (e.g., Mic 6:10; Ezek 45:9–12), and condemned in the wisdom writings (Prov 11:1; 16:11; 20:23; Job 31:6).

6 The first two lines of the triplet comprising this verse recall 2:6b. There the selling of the poor into slavery was condemned. Here the buying of them is condemned. The purchasers are those who have profited at the expense of the poor and can now buy them as slaves at low prices (נעלים "a pair of sandals"), in effect using the very money the poor had paid them to purchase overpriced food. To such hypocrites, people are commodities to be used for one's advantage. If they are desperate enough to pay for the מפל "sweepings— contaminated grain from the bins and wagons—why not mix that in with the grain and sell it too? Buy anything, sell anything—who's to stop you?

7 Yahweh. He won't *ever* (לנצח, cf. Ps 74:19) forget (שכח) anything that they have done (כל מעשיהם). The poor have a determined protector in Yahweh (Ps 82; Isa 11:4; Deut 24:14–15).

An oath was a means of committing oneself irrevocably to a course of action (Gen 21:23–24; Judg 21:1, 7, 18; 1 Kgs 1:13; etc.; Yahweh takes more oaths than any other OT figure). Twice before in Amos, Yahweh's oath affirms the certainty of his announced intent: in 4:2 he swears (שבע, Niphal) by his קדש "holiness"; in 6:8 בנפשו "by himself." But what does it mean for him to swear by גאון יעקב "Jacob's pride"? In 6:8 this term refers narrowly to the nation's invincibility. In Ps 47:5 it clearly refers more generally to the entire land of Israel. גאון יעקב must here also represent the land of Israel in some way. For Yahweh to swear "by" (ב) Israel is analogous to a person's swearing by a valuable possession (Isa 62:8; cf. Matt 5:34–36). The linguistic connection of "swearing" with the "promised" (also שבע, niphal) land is so strong as to be almost an idiom of Hebrew covenantal language (cf. Gen 50:24; Exod 13:5, 11; Num 11:12; Deut 1:8; 6:10; 8:1; 10:11; 28:11; 30:20; 31:7; etc.). Thus Yahweh here "swears by" the "sworn land," *Israel's* most precious possession—Yahweh's great gift to them.

8 That land will be a death trap for its inhabitants. Via a rhetorical question, the hearer / reader receives a prediction of death and destruction (curse type 24; cf. Deut 28:20; 30:15) with some of the overtones of generalized disaster (type 25; cf. Deut 29:19; 31:17). The mourning (אבל) will be for the dead, not merely because the land shakes. The Nile was well known to rise and sink annually, sometimes causing great harm through excessive flooding and demonstrating God's control of the elements. Judging from the similar wording in the hymnic fragment in 9:5–6, the present verse must be seen as an allusion to the truth expressed in the hymn, that Yahweh has the power to destroy. The attribution to this passage in Amos of earthquake imagery is only speculative, overly influenced by 1:1.

9 ביום ההוא "At that time" introduces events certain to come but in the indefinite future. In typical prophetic parlance via a synonymous parallelism, Yahweh pronounces the sudden, daytime darkness to come. Similar language is found elsewhere in Amos (esp. 5:18) and the prophets (e.g., Isa 8:22; Joel 2:2; Zeph 1:15). It fits specifically with the curses of category 19 (helplessness / stumbling) and is particularly close to Deut 28:29 ("At midday you will grope about like a blindman in the dark") with which it shares vocabulary and on which it may be based.

10 As a whole, v 10 announces fatal destruction (curse type 24). The emphasis is heavy upon the coming mourning (אבל) and lamentation (קינה), expressed in a variety of ways. There is here also an overtone of the futility curse (type 15) which predicts frustration of an intention (e.g., festivals ending up in mourning, songs in lamentation). So great will be the decimation of the people, such grief will be universal. Every waist will wear שק "sackcloth," the rough hair garment worn to deny the flesh at a time of grief (Isa 22:12; Joel 1:8, 13; Jonah 3:5), and every head will be shaved, a practice intended symbolically to disfigure and thus to show empathy with those in the sad situation of having lost loved ones (cf. Job 1:20; Deut 21:12–13; Jer 41:5; 48:37).

Mourning an only son (אבל יחיד) is always a bitter experience, and perhaps especially in a society where children represented the hope of a family for posterity and provision for one's old age (cf. Jer 6:26; Zech 12:10). A "bitter day" (יום מר) is one that ends in hopelessness. (On מר as the virtual equivalent of "tragedy," cf. 1 Sam 15:32; Ruth 1:20; Eccl 7:26; Isa 38:17).

11–12 The emphasis now shifts to a prediction of the punishment of anger / rejection by Yahweh (type 1; cf. Deut 31:17, 18; 32:20). Incorporated into this punishment is the curse motif of starvation / famine (type 7; cf. Lev 26: 26–29), here used metaphorically with Yahweh's word as the "food and drink," though apparently intended more literally in v 13.

These verses describe dramatically the complete absence of דבר יהוה "Yahweh's word." "From sea to sea" (מים עד־ים) usually refers to the extremes of the earth (Ps 72:8; Zech 9:10) but here must mean "from the Dead Sea (south) to the Mediterranean (west)," so that the mention of the other directions—north and east—in 12a completes the compass, saying in effect that people will wander / stagger "everywhere" without success.

And what is "Yahweh's word"? Is it the Mosaic Law? Is it prophetic revelation? Since prophetic revelation is based in and on the Law, the best answer is *both*. The human need for God's word is well established in the Pentateuch (e.g., Deut 8:3). Absence of that word is one of the agonies of the exile (Deut 4:28; 32:21; Hos 3:4). Note, however, that the covenant curses never envision a *permanent* famine for knowledge of Yahweh, but a temporary one until his wrath is fully spent (Lev 26:44–45; Deut 4:29–31; 30:1–3).

13 Because ביום ההוא "at that time" normally functions stylistically to introduce new oracles or sections thereof (see above), here it provides enough of a break from vv 11–12 that the present mention of צמא "thirst" must probably be taken as a *literal* starvation / famine prediction (type 7). This is confirmed by the ending of v 14: "They will fall and never rise again." The severity of the coming drought / famine is underlined by the identity of those who will faint dead away—not merely the old and frail or vulnerable infants, but healthy, robust young women (בתולת not properly "virgins" here) and young men (בחורים).

14 By a rapid transition of logic quite typical of OT prophecy, the focus broadens from the youthful to all Israelites whose religion distorts or abandons orthodoxy. As in v 4, the apostates' own words are cited in condemnation of them. Amos mentions three oaths (the latter two containing the standard חי "as . . . lives" formula) by three kinds of religious symbols. First is אשמת שמרון "Samaria's shame," an obvious contrast to "Jacob's pride" in Yahweh's oath in v 7. Of the many referents proposed for "Samaria's shame," only two are serious possibilities: the golden bull at Bethel or the Baal-Asherah idols at Samaria itself (cf. 1 Kgs 16:32–33; note also the linking of אשם "shame" / "guilt" with Baal worship in Hos 13:1). Since Bethel functioned as Samaria's official sanctuary (7:13) and paralleled Dan and Beersheba as a worship center, its idol cannot be excluded as the intended referent. But since אשמת בית־אל "Bethel's shame" would be easy enough to say and metrically interchangeable with אשמת שמרון "Samaria's shame," one sees no reason for referring to the Bethel worship by such a circumlocution. Thus it is likely that "Samaria's shame" refers to the Baal-Asherah idols at Samaria, and that, in addition, the Israelites had habituated themselves to swearing by the golden bull at Dan and the דוד "power" at Beersheba (Beersheba's דוד was apparently some sort of syncretized Yahweh).

To swear by a god is to commit oneself to that god as a true being, sovereign and capable of enforcing the oath. Swearing binds a person by promise, believing that the god sworn by will see that the oath is kept.

The hypocrisy of these people—deeply religious and yet disgustingly selfish—violates the covenant. Yahweh cannot be worshiped jointly with other gods, or displaced from his position as sole God, or represented via idols (Exod 20:3–5, 23; Deut 3:15–24). Their punishment must be death and destruction (curse type 24): they will "fall" (נפל, used often of death, as in 1 Sam 4:10, or even of political collapse, as in Isa 3:8) not to rise again. The employment of the converted perfect (ונפלו) rather than the imperfect seems occasioned more by the parallelism, especially with ואמרו "and say," than by any grammatical motivation.

Explanation

God originally intended a relatively egalitarian economic life for his people in Canaan. Tribes, clans, families, and individuals all had land or access to it to farm for themselves, enjoying the fruit of their industry. The book of Joshua records at length the important capture and allotment of the land "sworn" (Amos 8:7) to all the people. The covenant emphasized in many ways the necessity of equal access to land and continuity of land possession for successive generations within families (Num 26:53–56; 33:53–54; 36: 1–12). This was designated in part to prevent the few from controlling the many by controlling agricultural production—the very problem that has engendered most wars of revolution around the world since 1900. When a few people control most of the land, social injustice is virtually inevitable because of the natural role greed plays in fallen human nature.

As Israel became increasingly urbanized in the ninth and eighth centuries B.C., fewer people enjoyed the economic autonomy of owning and farming their own land. Coinage increasingly replaced bartering, and buying food in the cities replaced growing it personally. The increasingly powerful upper class secured more and more land for themselves, particularly by foreclosing mercilessly on loans to poor farmers (2:6–8; 5:12; Isa 5:8; Exod 22:24) and by ignoring the covenant's gleaning laws (e.g., Lev 19:9–10; Deut 24: 19–21), Jubilee laws (Lev 25; 27), etc. They were thus in a position to control market costs, at least in the cities, by holding back produce until the price rose to their satisfaction. What could a poor city dweller or nonlanded country peasant do about it? Frequent shopping was necessary for laborers paid daily, and day laboring was the common practice. Such persons could hardly travel around the countryside each morning or evening comparison shopping. So they paid what they had to and took what was sold them—overpriced, falsely weighed, contaminated as it was. Who sold it to them? Devotedly religious hypocrites!

Because of this, the future was to be a future of punishment—that Yahweh promised (v 7). Death and destruction, divine rejection and abandonment, famine (vv 9–13), and general upheaval (v 8) would serve to requite the exploiters. Their various idols and worship systems could not save them (v 14) and indeed were a cause of their demise.

No Escape from the Almighty's Wrath (9:1–10)

Bibliography

Erlenmeyer, M. H. "Über Philister und Kerter." *Or* 29 (1960) 121–50. **Flurival, E.** "Le jour du jugement (Amos 9:7–15)." *BVC* 8 (1954–55) 61–75. **Gese, H.** "Das Problem von Amos 9:7." *FS E. Würthwein,* 1979. 33–38. **Herrmann, W.** "Jahwes Triumph über Mot." *UF* 11 (1979) 371–77. **Hoffman, H.** "Zur Echtheitsfrage von Amos 9:9f." *ZAW* 82 (1970) 121–22. **Horst, F.** "Die Visionsschilderungen der Alttestamentlichen Propheten." *EvT* 20 (1960) 193–205. **Joüon, P.** "Notes de lexicography hébraique." *Bib* 7 (1926) 165–68. **Nagah, R.** "Are You Not Like the Ethiopians to Me (Amos 9:7)?" *BMik* 27 (1981 / 82) 174–82. [Heb.] **Ouellette, J.** "The Shaking of the Thresholds in Amos 9:1." *HUCA* 43 (1972) 23–27. **Reider, J.** "'Amos 9:9' in 'Contributions to the Scriptural Text.'" *HUCA* 24 (1952) 96. **Terrien, S.** "Amos and Wisdom." In *Israel's Prophetic Heritage: Essays in Honor of James Muilenburg,* ed. B. Anderson. New York: Harper, 1962. 108–15. **Turner, P.** "Two Septuagintalisms with ΣΤΗΡΙΖΕΙΝ." *VT* 28 (1978) 481–82. **Vogels, W.** "Invitation à revenir à l'alliance et universalisme en Amos 9, 7." *VT* 22 (1972) 223–39. **Volz, P.** "Zu Am 9:9." *ZAW* 38 (1919–20) 105–11. **Wainwright, G.** "Caphtor-Cappadocia." *VT* 6 (1956) 199–210. **Weimar, P.** "Der Schluss des Amos-Buches. Ein Beitrag zur Redaktionsgeschichte des Amos-Buches." *BN* 16 (1981) 60–100.

Translation

No escape

9:1 *I saw the Lord standing by the altar. He said:*
"Strike the pillar top [a] *so that the thresholds shake.*

Cut them off at the head—all of them!
Those who are left I will kill with the sword.

Not one of them will escape,
Not one of them will get away!

2 *If they dig down into Sheol,*
My hand will take them from there.

If they go up to heaven,
I will bring them down from there.

3 *If they hide on top of Carmel,*
I will hunt them down and take them from there.

> *If they hide from me at the bottom of the ocean,*[a]
> *I will command the serpent to bite them there.*[b]

> [4] *If they go into exile in front of their enemies,*
> *I will command the sword to slay them there.*

> *I will fix my gaze*[a] *on them*
> *For harm and not for benefit.*

Hymn refrain

> [5] *The Lord, Yahweh of the Armies,*
> *Who touches the earth so that it crumbles,*[a]
> *And all who live in it mourn,*

> *And all of it rises like the Nile*
> *And sinks like the Nile of Egypt;*

> [6] *Who builds his upper chamber*[a] *in heaven,*
> *And has founded his storeroom*[b] *on the earth;*

> *Who summons the sea's waters*
> *And pours them out on the earth—*
> *Yahweh*[c] *is his name!*

Application to Israel

[7] *Aren't you just like the Nubians in relation to me, Israelites?* —*Oracle of Yahweh.*[a] *Didn't I bring up Israel out of the land of Egypt, and the Philistines from Crete,*[b] *and Aram from Kir?*

[8] *The eyes of the Lord Yahweh are on the sinful kingdom, and I will destroy it from the face of the earth. However, I will not completely destroy the family of Jacob.* —*Oracle of Yahweh.* [9] *Indeed, I will give the command and I will shake the family of Israel in among all the nations*[a] *as if shaken in a sieve, but not a pebble*[b] *will fall to the ground.* [10] *All the sinners of my people will die by the sword, those who say, No harm will come near*[a] *us or affect us.*[b]

Notes

1.a. G (ἱλαστήριον) read כפרת "mercy seat" probably because its *Vorlage* already has metathesized the ת and ר of כפתר.

3.a. G εἰς τὰ βάθη "into the depths," though pl supports MT.

3.b. G ἐκεῖ "there" supports only שם, suggesting that MT's משם is the result of dittogr of the *mem* from הים "the sea."

4.a. Lit., "my eye." G is pl (ὀφθαλμούς) but still attests to consonantal MT.

5.a. "Crumble" is preferable to "totter" and similar translations in that מוג basically connotes deterioration from vertical to horizontal ("melt," "droop," etc.).

6.a. Reading the sg with G (ἀνάβασιν αὐτοῦ, lit., "his ascent") against MT and Wadi Murabba'at Text XII (88) 8:16 which have the pl מעלותו "his upper chambers."

6.b. אגדה is a difficult word, lit. meaning something like "cluster," thus here "storeroom." G ἐπαγγελίαν "promise" apparently took אגדה as a noun from נגד, hiph, which means to "declare" / "proclaim" in 4:13.

6.c. G MSS add ὁ θεὸς ὁ παντοκράτωρ "God Almighty," or simply παντοκράτωρ "Almighty," perhaps from 5:8.

7.a. G⁶² and G¹⁴⁷ lack λέγει κύριος (נאם יהוה "oracle of Yahweh") probably via haplogr.

7.b. G Καππαδοκία "Cappadocia" represents another tradition of the meaning of כפתר, properly "Crete," as it also does in Deut 2:23 (and as α' and σ' do in Jer 47:4). It is not entirely clear whether כפתר denoted Crete, Cilicia / Cappadocia (the Turkish coastal area north of Cyprus), or both.

9.a. Some G MSS do not contain a translation of הגוים "the nations," though its presence is logical and certainly not intrusive in the passage.

9.b. Reading "pebble" for the rare צרור, with α' (ψηφίον) Tg (אבן) and Vg (*lapillus*) against G σύντριμμα "fragment."

10.a. Vocalizing תגש as a niph rather than the hiph (MT) which would mean "bring near."

10.b. Vocalizing קדם as a piel; the hiph (MT) would mean something like "bring opposite" or the like. (It is unattested otherwise.)

Form / Structure / Setting

Rarely has 9:1–10 been considered a unit. 9:1–4 describes Amos' fifth vision, and vv 5–6, taken from an old Yahwistic hymn, are often understood as purposely and originally appended as a conclusion to vv 1–4. But vv 7–8 seem to most commentators to belong to a new section, sometimes linked to the remainder of chap. 9 because of its "remnant" emphasis (8b), sometimes linked only to vv 9–10 because of its judgment emphasis (8a), and sometimes (e.g., Mays, *Hosea*) treated as a self-contained unit.

Nevertheless, several factors point toward the unity of this material. First, the repetition of כפתר is important. In v 1 it denotes the capital of the (temple) pillar; in v 7 the isle of Crete. This repetition appears to be more than accidental or the sort of catchword by which disparate oracles are juxtaposed editorially, judging from the precedent of the homophonic word recall devices in the two previous visions (7:7–9; 8:1–3). The כפתר of v 8 intentionally echoes the כפתר of v 1, though much more distantly and subtly than, for example, קץ echoes קיץ "summer fruit" in 8:1–2. Beyond this, one notes that the imperative structure in v 1 (הך "strike!"; בצע "cut off") is echoed by the emphasis on "command" (צוה) in v 9. Moreover, the Nubian / Egyptian allusions of v 7 depend partly on the hymn's reference to Egypt in v 5 (hardly a gloss), and vv 7–10 complete the point made by the inclusion of the hymn by emphasizing that Israel, too, can be subject to the powerful control of God, like other nations are. Additionally, the theme of complacency appears in both vv 4 and 10. In v 4 Yahweh emphasizes that, contrary to popular expectation, his purposes for Israel are harm, not benefit (lit., "bad, not good"). This same concept agains surfaces in v 10, where disaster meets those who foresee no disaster.

In a more general sense, vv 7–10 are to be linked with vv 1–6 because they continue the judgment theme of vv 1–6—and specify it—without an obvious break. Eschatological promise language begins immediately in v 11, and there a new section of hope toward Israel's restoration commences. Once it is recognized that vv 7–10 elaborate especially on the judgment language of the hymnic fragment in vv 5–6, which is in turn a purposeful conclusion to the vision of vv 1–4, the unit of vv 1–10 becomes viable.

The vision that launches this pericope differs considerably from its four predecessors in 7:1–8:3. Aside from 9:1a its content is not specifically visionary at all (though this is in fact the pattern of most prophetic visions, whose emphasis is usually on *audition* rather than *vision*). There is no dialogue, no interrogation, no divine response to the prophet's comments, no description of how the prophet is caused to see something. Instead, one notes the prominent position played by Yahweh's lengthy first-person monologue throughout, with the purposeful exception of vv 5–6, and the initial imperatives (v 1). This vision-judgment oracle thus goes slightly beyond the others in order (1) to diminish Amos' role, as if to emphasize the finality of the coming judgment by implying that intercession or even dialogue would now be pointless; and (2) to stress the fact, by repetition of the demolition commands in v 1, that the process of destruction is virtually underway, in contrast to the relatively stoppable destruction of the punishments foreseen in 7:1–9 or indefinitely projected into the future as in 8:3 (ביום ההוא "in that day"). The fourth vision (8:1–3) told simply that the end was near; here we see it portrayed.

Does this portrayal of the inescapability of the coming wrath mean that the present passage is from a time relatively late in Amos' program of preaching? Perhaps, but the evidence is too meager for a definite answer. And what of the location? Was Amos in the Bethel temple seeing Yahweh on *its* altar? Was he in Jerusalem at the Solomonic temple? Or was he simply seeing a vision of Yahweh on some unspecified altar? Each of these options has merit, and it is especially tempting to link this prophecy with the literal destruction of the Bethel sanctuary by Josiah in 622 B.C. (2 Kgs 23:15–16). In the final analysis, however, the vision seems as easily symbolic as literal, especially in light of the four symbolic visions that precede it. One simply cannot, therefore, be sure of any particular *locus* for the present oracle, and none is required for its impact on either the original or the modern audience.

Vv 1–6 are poetry; vv 7–10 prose. The prose expands and comments on the poetry, which is quite repetitive in style in vv 2–4 and typically characterized by participial forms in the hymnic fragment of vv 5–6.

Comment

1 The one whom Amos saw standing on (נצב על; cf. 7:7) the altar is here called אדני "Lord" rather than the more usual Yahweh. This happens to allow the name Yahweh to stand out more forcefully in the hymnic excerpt (vv 5, 7) where it is emphasized, but the use of אדני may also reflect a concern to protect the technical invisibility of God (1 John 4:12; Judg 13:22; cf 7:7 where אדני is questionable textually). The presence of the altar implies a sanctuary, possibly that at Bethel. With the first sentence the vision per se is complete: God immediately begins to speak the first-person judgment announcement that forms the essential content of the passage.

The pillar top (כפתר) was the capital of a support pillar; the singular "pillar top" is certainly used collectively—the entire sanctuary was to be destroyed. Pillars were major, visible support / decorative features of all iron-age temples (Y. Aharoni, *The Archaeology of the Land of Israel* [Philadelphia: Westminster, 1982] 120–35; *IDB*, 534–68), and their destruction indicated full-scale demolition. The thresholds (ספים) were the cut-stone bases for the door posts (cf. Isa 6:4). Together, pillar top and threshold indicate a "top to bottom" destruction. All (כלם) pillars were to be razed. The blows of demolition would shake the earth, and the collapse of the building presumably would kill worshipers and priests inside and around it (cf. Judg 16:29–30). This may indicate that, at Bethel, worship and the feasting connected with it were conducted in part *inside* the temple building in the Canaanite fashion (cf. Judg 9:27, 46, 49; deVaux, *Ancient Israel*, 438–56; 282–83; Neh 13:6–9) rather than outside in the court in the orthodox Israelite fashion. At any rate, people not harmed by the collapse of the temple were to be killed (curse type 24).

2   The merism of heaven and hell is used several times in the OT to indicate the total area of God's control, there being no place his sovereignty does not extend (e.g., Ps 139:7–8; cf. Amarna letter 264:1, trans.: "Whether we ascend to the heavens or descend to the nether-world [*arṣiti*] our head is in your hands" in J. A. Knudtzon, *Die El-Amarna Tafeln*, 2 vols. [Leipzig, 1907–15]). Sheol (שאול) is the term used variously for the realm of the dead, or netherworld, visualized for convenience as beneath the earth (*TWOT*, 2303–4). On the ability of God's wrath to pursue the wicked even to Sheol, cf. Deut 32:22, "A fire has been kindled by my wrath, one that burns to Sheol below." Helplessness curses (type 19) are echoed in this picture of no escape. Compare Deut 28:29, "no one to rescue you" and 32:39, "no one can deliver from my hand."

3   Two further examples of geographical extremities, which might be thought to offer protection from a human foe but not from Yahweh, are given. Carmel was a high, densely forested peak overlooking the Mediterranean, popularly considered in Israel as Baal property (1 Kgs 18:17–36). And in popular imagery, the bottom of the ocean was horribly distant from the areas of human reach (cf. Jonah 2:6–7). But Yahweh could easily catch people on Carmel or simply order the "serpent" (נחש), i.e., a great denizen of the deep (*NBD*, 1165) to extinguish their life deep in the ocean. The prevailing curse motif here is still simply death (type 24).

4   Even the slavery of exile (curse type 13) would offer no protection against death. In the covenant curses, both conquest and exile bring death: "you will be destroyed. Yahweh will scatter you among the nations and only a few of you will survive" (Deut 4:26–27). Neither the original Mosaic curses nor Amos' prophecy envisions total annihilation of all Israelites via conquest and exile. (See below, *Explanation*.) For Yahweh to look upon his people "for harm" (לרעה) implies his rejection of them, on the analogy of curse type 1 (Lev 26:17, 24, 28, 41; Deut 31:17–18; 32:19–20). To "fix one's gaze on" (שם עינים על) is usually a sign of favor (Gen 44:21; Jer 24:6). Here, however, its purpose is for harm (לרעה).

5   As J. D. W. Watts ("An Old Hymn" *JNES* 15 [1956] 33–34) and others have convincingly demonstrated, vv 5–6 constitute the third and final excerpt (cf. 4:13; 5:8–9) in Amos of a probably well-known Yahwistic hymn extolling Yahweh's power over nature and, by implication, over human events. It appears that Amos was inspired to employ parts of this hymn in order to teach that Yahweh could use his power *against* Israel as well as for it. The hymn provided a point of departure for Amos' message. In effect he says: "That hymn you love shows how Yahweh controls the universe and metes out his judgment among the nations. But you have wrongly assumed that this judgment would always benefit you and harm others. Now you must realize that *you* also deserve the wrath of which the hymn speaks."

Amos often mentions "Yahweh, God of the Armies" (יהוה אלהי צבאות, as in 3:13; 6:14). The hymn in its own metrical integrity has simply "Yahweh of the Armies." The "armies" (צבאות) are the heavenly host—all the angels and forces at his disposal. Yahweh's power is sampled in earthquakes (on the parallelism of מוג "crumble" with רעש "shake" in v 1, cf. Nah 1:5). Such natural disasters can cause a whole population to "mourn" (אבל; cf. 1:2; 8:8). The well-known annual rising and sinking of the Nile provided in the hymn—whose composer and date are unknown—a simile for the undulation of the land in an earthquake. This part of the hymn, then, emphasizes Yahweh's power over earthquakes.

6 Some interpreters have taken v 6 to portray Yahweh's power in bringing beneficial rains; more likely the point is that Yahweh can cause storms, tides, floods, etc. Verse 6 begins by emphasizing Yahweh's creation: he is the builder (בונה) and founder (יסד) of heaven and earth. The particular metaphors for heaven and earth, מעלת (n. 6.a) and אגדה (probably "upper room" and "storeroom"), seem to liken creation to a house or palace. The point is clear enough: Heaven and earth are Yahweh's handiwork and domain in which all elements are subject to him. What he made he controls. Again, the refrain "Yahweh is his name" concludes the fragment (cf. 5:8).

Since 5:8b and 9:6b are identical, one or the other (usually 9:5b) has sometimes been identified as a copyist's expansion. But in light of Amos' parallel use of that part of the hymn found in 9:5b already in 8:8b, it is more likely that he has either cited the same part of the hymn once again, or that the hymn itself contained such a repetition (cf. Ps 107:8, 15, 21, 31).

7 As the hymn fragment in 5:8 was incorporated within a larger lament oracle, the hymn fragment of 9:6 is likewise a sort of pivot for material before and after. The prose statements of vv 7–10, in which Yahweh once again speaks in the first person, go on to specify just how Israel can be the object of Yahweh's destruction rather than protection.

Two rhetorical questions place Israel squarely *among* the nations, following on the hymn, in the sense that they are no different from Egypt, which Yahweh subdued in the Exodus, and are no more exempt from his power than the Nile, which he subdues yearly. The Nubians (כשיים) were the black tribes in Africa south of the second cataract of the Nile, i.e., a distant, relatively obscure people. Yet Yahweh says that Israel is no more privileged than they. So the Israelites had an exodus? The Philistines and Aramaeans did too—and Yahweh caused it. Since the Philistines and Arameans were both hated enemies of the Israelites (cf. 1:6–8; 1:3–5), these questions clearly link Israel with those peoples they thought Yahweh would protect them against. While Crete's location is well known, Kir's is not. Each, like Egypt (v 5), was the original home of a people. Israel is merely on a par with its hated neighbors.

8 "I will fix my gaze on them" in v 4 is echoed here in "The eyes of the Lord Yahweh are on" (עיני אדני יהוה ב). The term (ה)ממלכה החטאה "the sinful kingdom" is unique to Amos. Does it denote the North alone or *all* Israel? In favor of the latter option is the presence in this albeit prose passage of an antithetical parallelism with בית יעקב "family of Jacob." Elsewhere "Jacob" can denote Israel as a whole (8:7). And the context can be construed to concern all Israel, the entire group that participated in the exodus (v 7).

But on grammatical grounds the presence of the article, unmistakable from its inclusion with the adjective חטאה "sinful" (regardless of the pointing of בממלכה "on the kingdom"), probably sets the reference in a different context. That is, the sinful kingdom must be the one Amos was preaching to: (northern) Israel. Death and destruction (curse type 24) will be their fate.

That destruction will not be total, however, as v 8b insists. Here enters the theme of the escape of a remnant, so clearly promised in the Mosaic covenant (Lev 26:44; Deut 4:31; 30:3; 32:36–43) and so strongly reaffirmed by the pre-exilic prophets (e.g., Hos 2:1–2 [1:10–11]; Joel 2:18–19; Mic 2:12–13; Isa 11:10–11). God's plan for his people envisioned their destruction as a nation and their exile, but explicitly avoided their total annihilation.

9–10 Kernels of grain will fall through the sieve (כברה, a *hapax legomenon* in the OT), but the pebbles (צרור) will not. The pebbles are the impurities, trapped for disposal. The sinners of Israel are like the pebbles—none will be allowed to fall through to mix in once again with the good grain and pollute it.

The sifting spoken of in these verses will include "all the nations" (כל־הגוים). A time of general political upheaval (such as that of the Assyrian invasions of the 730s and 720s B.C.) will catch Israel, too, and provide the context for God's judgment. To die "by the sword" (בחרב) fits the covenant curse language of war and its ravages (type 3; Lev 26:25, "I will bring the sword upon you"; cf. Lev 26:33; Deut 32:24, 41, 42).

The complacency of Amos' Israel, as evidenced in their hope that "no harm" (רעה) would ever affect them (10b), was still present. Here again he must remind them that their expectations are inaccurate (cf. 5:8–10).

Explanation

This final judgment oracle in Amos does not so much introduce new information about the character of Israel's coming punishments (death, destruction, and exile) as it does stress the inevitability of that judgment. Its concern is both with certainty and extent—certainty that the judgment cannot be avoided and an extent that involves everyone, not just some subsection of the population or territory. In this regard it fittingly stands at the end of all the other judgment oracles, though the order of its composition in relation to the others cannot be known.

Yahweh himself initiates the demolition of Israel, starting at a sanctuary that he orders razed as a symbol of his rejection of Israel's cultus. In the dramatic portrayal of his power to punish (vv 1–4), virtually no quarter is given. No one can escape. The final of three fragments in the book from the old Yahwistic hymn, presumably well known to Amos' audience, buttresses the point of the present oracle by emphasizing the total power of Yahweh to control and destroy at will (vv 5–6). Israel is then brought down to size in the concluding, prose portion of the oracle (vv 7–10) by being equated with other nations in deserving death.

Language guaranteeing universal eligibility for punishment pervades the passage: "cut off . . . all of them"; "not one . . . will escape"; "not one . . . will get away" (v 1); "all . . . mourn"; "all . . . rise like the Nile" (v 5); "all the nations" (v 9); "all the sinners . . . will die" (v 10). It is fraught with images of universality in Yahweh's control of all spaces (vv 2–4), all nature (vv 5–6), and all nations (vv 7–10). He controls all and has total power; none can escape from his judgment.

But not all will die. Like Zephaniah's prophecy, which begins by predicting total destruction (1:1–3, 18) and goes on to describe the role of a remnant that will not be destroyed (2:3, 9), this prophecy portrays broadly the coming wrath and then more narrowly the escape of a remnant. There is no true contradiction here any more than there is a true contradiction in an English sentence containing the word *except*. Exceptions are usually stated after, rather than prior to, the general case.

An inevitable destruction by an all-powerful God leaving only a remnant— this, sadly, was Israel's immediate future according to the word of the Lord via Amos.

Restoration, Rebuilding, Replanting (9:11–15)

Bibliography

Braun, M. "James' Use of Amos at the Jerusalem Council: Steps Toward a Possible Solution of the Textual and Theological Problems." *JETS* 20 (1977) 113–21. **Deibner, B.,** and **H. Schult.** "Edom in alttestament Texten der Makkabäerzeit." *Dielheimer Blätter zum Alten Testament* 8 (1975) 11–17. **Greenwood, D.** "On the Jewish Hope for a Restored Northern Kingdom." *ZAW* 88 (1976) 376–85. **Haller, M.** "Edom im Urteil der Propheten." In *Vom Alten Testament: FS Karl Marti*, ed. K. Budde. *BZAW* 41 (1925) 109–17. **Herrmann, W.** "Jahwes Triumph über Mot." *UF* 11 (1979) 371–77. **Kaiser, W.** "The Davidic Promise and the Inclusion of the Gentiles (Amos 9:9–15 and Acts 15: 13–18): A Test Passage for Theological Systems." *JETS* 20 (1977) 97–111. **Kellermann, U.** "Der Amosschluss als Stimme deuteronomistischer Heilshoffnung." *EvT* 29 (1969) 169–83. **Mauchline, J.** "Implicit Signs of a Persistent Belief in the Davidic Empire [in the Prophetic Books]." *VT* 20 (1970) 287–303. **Münchow, C.** "Ethik und Eschatologie in der frühjudischen Apokalyptic und bei Paulus: Ein Beitrag zum Verständnis der Apokalyptik unk deren Rezeption in den paulinischen Briefen." Diss. Berlin/DDR 1977. *TLZ* 103 (1978) 459–61. **Richardson, H. N.** "SKT (Amos 9:11): 'Booth' or 'Succoth'?" *JBL* 92 (1973) 375–81. **Turner, P.** "ʾ*Anoikodomein* and Intra-Septuagintal Borrowing." *VT* 27 (1977) 492–93. **Weiss, M.** "These Days and the Days to Come According to Amos 9:13." *EI* 14 (1978) 69–73. [Heb.]

Translation

Power over enemies

9:11 *At that time I will raise up*
David's Succoth,[a] *which is fallen down.*[b]

I will wall up its[c] *broken-through places,*
Raise up its[d] *ruins,*
Build it as in the days of old.

[12] *So that they may possess*[a] *Edom's*[b] *remnant,*
And all the nations called by my name.
                        —*Oracle of Yahweh, who will do this.*

Agricultural bounty

[13] *The time is coming—oracle of Yahweh—*
When the plowman will catch up to the reaper,
And the grape treader to the sower of seed,

The mountains will drip with grape juice,
And all the hills will flow with it.

Return and repossession of the land

[14] *I will release my people Israel from captivity,*[a]
And they will rebuild the ruined cities and live in them.

They will plant vineyards and drink their wine;
They will make gardens and eat their fruit.

[15] *I will plant them in their own land so that they will never again be uprooted*
from their land which I have given them, said Yahweh, your God.[a]

Notes

11.a. Vocalizing סֻכּוֹת "Succoth," the city name. See *Comment.*

11.b. The present ptcp may indicate past time, but here more likely describes present (Amos' day) reality.

11.c. Reading the fem. sg suffix with G. MT's pl suffix represents a conformity to the reading סֻכֹּת "huts."

11.d. Reading the fem sg suffix with G. MT makes the ruins David's own, with its 3 masc sg suffix.

12.a. G ἐκζητήσωσιν "they will seek" must have had ידרשו instead of יירשו "they may possess" in its Heb. *Vorlage,* the second *yodh* having looked (easily enough) like a *daleth* and being miscopied thereby.

12.b. G τῶν ἀνθρώπων "of men" read in its *Vorlage* אדם rather than אדום "Edom"; especially in light of the parallelism with כל הגוים "all the nations," "humankind" would not be impossible here.

14.a. Or "I will restore my people's fortunes." The Heb. שוב שבות is ambiguous and seems to take various nuances depending on the context.

15.a. G ὁ θεὸς ὁ παντοκράτωρ = אלהי צבאות "God of the Armies" probably reflects a Heb. *Vorlage* conformed to several similar earlier appellations of Yahweh (3:13; 4:13; 5:14, 15, 16, 27; 9:5).

Form / Structure / Setting

The book concludes with a restoration blessing oracle. It has three subsections: a promise of power over enemies (vv 11–12, restoration blessing type 9); a promise of agricultural bounty (v 13, type 5); and a promise of return and repossession (vv 14–15, type 7). Verse 15 reads like prose rather than poetry and would appear to be a prose conclusion to an otherwise poetic oracle (9:1–10).

Restoration blessing oracles do not usually predicate blessings on good behavior, in contrast to judgment oracles, which normally predicate punishment on a history of covenant disobedience, at least some instance of which is specifically mentioned. Like the initial creation and blessing of Israel, its restoration blessings are wholly the product of Yahweh's grace, requiring nothing but a willingness to turn again to him and to be obedient (Deut 4:29–30; 30:1–3). In accordance with this fact—that Israel cannot really make its own restoration happen—restoration blessings tend to begin rather simply and even abruptly. Amos 9:11–15 is no exception. With only ביום ההוא "at that time," the attention of the hearer / reader is suddenly shifted to the distant future, when the miseries immediately awaiting the disobedient nation will be past and when Yahweh's ultimate, always-intended benefits can be poured out on his people in a more permanent, stable way than was ever possible before.

The oracle is genuinely from Amos. It reflects standard covenantal eschatology long held prior to his day by orthodox Israelites. Watts (*Vision and Prophecy in Amos*, 25–26), Maag (*Text, Wortschatz und Begriffswelt des Buches Amos*, 247–51), and Reventlow (*Das Amt des Propheten bei Amos*, 90–94) are among recent commentators supporting the oracle's authenticity. To their observations may be added the evidence of the *defective* spellings of the proper names סכת "Succoth" (v 11) and אדם "Edom" (v 12). Both words lack the *mater lectionis waw*, which originated in internal positions about 700 b.c. and became common internally by the sixth century (F. M. Cross and D. N. Freedman, *Early Hebrew Orthography* [New Haven: American Oriental Society, 1951] 54–57). The fact that MT misunderstood סכת as "hut / booth" and G misunderstood אדם as "man" suggests that the true values were long lost because of their early (pre-700 b.c.) orthographic origin.

A fairly common, though erroneous, assumption among scholars has been that prophetic interest in Edom is a post-exilic phenomenon. In fact, Edom was one of Israel's enemies at all periods since the conquest (Num 20), including the days of Saul (1 Sam 14:47) and David (2 Sam 8:11–14). Amos already addressed Edomite war atrocities prior to his own time (1:11–12) and had good reason to address the subject of the restoration of Israel in terms of power over Edom (see *Comment* on vv 11–12).

About half the oracle is cast in synonymous parallelism; the remainder—save for v 15's prose—in so-called antithetical parallelism. The placement of two triplets (11b, 13a) appears to be without significance.

The notion of an Israelite exile apart from any consideration of a Judean exile is already attested explicitly in 4:2–3; 5:11, 27; 6:7; 7:11, 17; 9:4; and further in Hosea. Thus nothing in Amos 9:14–15 need be seen as reflecting a later or a southern origin. Moreover, nothing in the oracle hints at the place or time of its initial delivery. Restoration promises reassure the faithful that Yahweh's punishments do not imply his total rejection of his people, and such reassurance was undoubtedly welcome at many points throughout Amos' ministry.

Comment

11 Succoth, modern Tel Deir ʿAlla, stood at a major crossroads on the
east side of the Jordan Valley, opposite the Ephraimite heartland of Israel.
The city figured prominently in Jacob's travels (Gen 33:17) and in the military
campaigns of Gideon (Judg 8:5–16) and especially David, who used Succoth
virtually as a Transjordan military headquarters (Richardson, "SKT," 375–
81). From Succoth, David successfully dominated (united) Israel's neighbors
to the east and south. In Amos' time Succoth lay in ruins, presumably having
been destroyed by the armies of Hazael of Syria (2 Kgs 10:32–33). Shortly
after Amos' time, about 730 B.C., the entire Gilead region was annexed
by the Assyrians, never again to be part of Israel—or Judah. This accounts
for its lack of prominence in the minds of later scribes who mistook
סכת for "hut of," even though huts hardly have multiple פרצים "broken
through places," הריסות "ruins," or significance from ימי עולם "days
of old."

Succoth, for its role as the staging area from which David subdued Israel's
enemies, is strongly associated with David's victories, including those over
Edom (Ps 60:8–11 = 108:8–11). Its rebuilding would herald the return of
Israel to power vis-à-vis its neighbors, in the restoration period prophesied
by Amos. The issue here is not the rebuilding of Succoth per se, but *David's*
Succoth, as a metonymy for the kind of supremacy of God's reign through
his people once enjoyed in Israel's past golden era.

Reunification (restoration blessing type 8; cf. Deut 30:3, 14) is associated
frequently in the prophets with David, the great leader who had first truly
united North and South (Hosea 3:5; Isa 9:7; Jer 33:17; Ezek 37:24). Thus
in the restoration, a *new* David would shepherd Israel (Mic 5:2–6).

12 Edom was a particularly bitter and constant foe throughout most of
Israelite history (Exod 15:15; Num 20; Judg 11:17–18; 1 Sam 14:47; 2 Sam
8:14; 1 Kgs 11:14–16; 2 Kgs 3; 8:20; 14:7–10). In the parallelism of v 12,
however, "Edom" is not used strictly for its own sake, but rather as a synecdoche
for the phrase "all the nations" (כל הגוים) which parallels it. In the context,
"called by my name" (אשר נקרא שמי) means in effect "which I control."
Thus in the restoration, God's people will "possess" (ירש), i.e., have control
over those nations once their enemies, in fulfillment of the restoration blessing
of power over enemies (type 9; Deut 30:7; cf. Lev 26:36–39, of which the
restoration blessing provides a reversal).

13 Next come two images of agricultural bounty (restoration blessing
type 5; cf. Lev 26:42; Deut 30:9), hyperbolically conveying the idea that in
the restoration harvests will be more than ample. The reaper (קצר) will still
be cutting the stalks of grain when the plowman (חורש) gets started turning
the earth over for the next planting. And the grape treader (דרך ענבים)
and sower of seed (משך הזרע) will get in each other's way. In other words,
the harvests will be so abundant that harvesters will still be trying after many
months to finish collecting one crop when it will already be time to plant
the next one. Barley and wheat are ripe in Palestine by early May; grapes
by early September. Ploughing begins in October, followed immediately by

sowing. These times will virtually blend together in the almost constant harvesting of the eschatological age, restoring the original promise of such bounty (cf. Lev 26:5, on which this wording is perhaps based).

The enormous quantities of the grape harvest—always an important crop in ancient Israel—are suggested by the image of grape juice everywhere, dripping and flowing from the hills where the grapes were grown (cf. Joel 3:18). A comparable modern expression would be: "You'll be up to your ears in grape juice." These images are purposeful exaggerations, intended by their extremity to assure the lack of want the new age will bring.

14 The oracle ends with a description of events that constitute a fulfillment of the restoration promise of return and repossession of the land (type 7; cf. Deut 30:3–5). As in the Pentateuchal promises, Yahweh is the agent of this reversal: Israel does not make its own way to restoration. The theme of rebuilding "ruined cities" (ערים נשמות) has already appeared in connection with Succoth (v 11). Here it is extended to a general rebuilding in a land whose structures have been razed in war.

Likewise, the Israelites of the new age will be able to engage simply—there is no exaggerative language this time—in normal agriculture, doing what they love, independent and able to pursue their occupations in peace. A basic enjoyment of the fruit of one's labor is a favorite prophetic way to express the serenity of the restoration (e.g., Isa 37:30; 65:21–22; Jer 29:5, 28; Ezek 34:27; 36:10, 33; Zech 8:12).

15 The concluding prose verse simply, directly, and unequivocally promises a permanent reoccupation of the promised land. "Their own land" (אדמתם) indicates the ground itself—not the overall territory (see this vocabulary in Deut 28–32, *passim*). People will once again inherit the tillable soil as was done after the conquest (Josh 13–20). Somewhat like the promise that no second flood would ever destroy people (Gen 8:21), this promise guarantees that no second exile / captivity would occur. Once the payment for sin is made (Lev 26:43; Isa 40:2), there is no danger that a similar price will be exacted again.

The verse concludes by stressing that the land is a gift (אשר נתתי "which I have given them"). Yahweh is the hero, the prime mover in the events. Israel can never really earn its rescue and restitution.

Explanation

The final oracle in Amos promises that some time in the indefinite future ("at that time") a key Davidic Transjordan military headquarters (Succoth) will be rebuilt so as to help Israel subdue "all the nations." More than ample harvest will be brought in, and Israelites will be brought back from exile and settled again in Canaan—this time permanently, enjoying securely the benefits of their labors. All this will be accomplished by Yahweh's grace.

But what are the actual referents for these divine predictions? Are all these descriptions of the future fulfilled in the return and rebuilding (and its aftermath) led initially by Sheshbazzar (Ezra 1:1–11) just over two hundred years after Amos spoke about them on God's behalf? Are they yet to be fulfilled? Is the modern state of Israel what is envisioned here? Or is this passage mainly a description of the church?

The answer hinges on (1) an appreciation of how this sort of promise oracle relates to all others within its context—i.e., the covenant restoration promises; and (2) an appreciation of how the promises of the old covenant come to actual fruition in the new. First, covenant restoration promises invariably assume their fulfillment in a new and different age. The greatness of that age is suggested by exaggerative language that often outstrips (e.g., Mic 4:1; Hos 14:5–7) but always at least equals the exaggerative language of the original promises concerning Israel's occupation of the land. Additionally, such promises relate to the experience of a *new* people, redeemed from the stock of the old. (Here in v 12, the typical term שאר/שארית "remnant" is applied only to Edom [cf. 1:8, 5:15] but elsewhere to Israel, e.g., Isa 11:16; Jer 23:3; Mic 2:12.) And most importantly, this new people must be one that has the characteristics also applied to them by other restoration promises: far greater population numerically than ancient Israel (promise type 4), orthodoxy (type 3), reunification (type 8), etc. In other words, the restoration promises in effect come as a package in the Pentateuch. The group that fulfills them, however conceived, must fulfill all—not just some. In terms of orthodoxy, at least, modern Israel fails as the referent for these promises. With respect to population increase and possession of the nations, ancient resettled Judah under Persian rule fails. The church fails, in part, on the "landedness" criteria, though it surely can claim "harvests" of a different, more important sort (Matt 9:37–38; 13:30–39; John 4:35; Gal 5:22; Rev 14:15).

Here the NT explanations become essential. In the NT one finds that the remnant of Israel has been transformed into the Christian "remnant" (κατάλειμμα, Rom 9:27; λεῖμμα, Rom 11:5); and thus in its orthodoxy, vast population, etc., that remnant inherits the "gifts and call" of God (Rom 11:29). An actual physical return from exile involved a small group, mainly fifth- and sixth-century B.C. Judeans. They are the "landed" ones of vv 14–15. But from them, through Christ, came ultimately the church. The referent for these promises is thus a continuum including all faithful believers from the exile through modern times and into the future—in some ways an amorphous group, but in every way the "Israel of God" (Gal 6:16).

There is one aspect of the promises of the present oracle yet partly unfulfilled: the possession of "all the nations" (v 12). As the passage insists via its first-person verbs, it is God who causes this prediction to come to pass (cf. Acts 15:15–21, where the G version of vv 11–12 is quoted in full). Whatever one may say about present-day fulfillments, there is also an eschatological sense to this promise, even for us: the reign of Christ over "all the nations" (Rev 12:5, etc.—πάντα τὰ ἔθνη being the equivalent of כל־הגוים).

Obadiah

Bibliography

COMMENTARIES AND BOOKS

(See also the listing of books and commentaries on several minor prophets, p. xxv.)

Aalders, G. C. *Obadja en Jona.* Kampen. Kok, 1958. **Bachmann, J.** *Der Prophet Obadja.* Berlin, 1982. **Caspari, C. P.** *Der Prophet Obadja.* Leipzig, 1842. **Coggins, R. J.** and **S. P. Re'emi.** *Nahum, Obadiah, Esther.* International Theological Commentary. Grand Rapids: Eerdmans, 1985. **Cresson, B. C.** *Israel and Edom: A Study of the Anti-Edom Bias in Old Testament Religion.* Diss. Duke University, 1963. **Deissler, A.** "Abdias." In *Les petits prophètes.* La Sainte Bible 8:1. Paris, 1961. **Eaton, J. H.** *Obadiah, Nahum, Habakkuk, Zephaniah.* Torch Bible Commentaries. London, 1961. **Fichtner, J.** *Obadja Jona, Micha.* Stuttgarter Bibelhefte. Stuttgart, 1957. **Frey, H.** *Das Buch der Kirche in der Weltwende. Die kleinen nachexilischen Propheten.* Die Botschaft des Alten Testament 24. Stuttgart, 1948. 190–203. **Gaebelein, R. E.** *The Servant and the Dove: Obadiah and Jonah, Their Messages and Their Work.* New York, 1946. **Goldman, S.** *Obadjah.* SBB. London and Bournemouth, 1948. **Keller, C. A.** *Abdias.* In Jacob, E. et al. *Osée, Joël, Amos, Abdias, Jonas.* Commentaire de l'Ancien Testament XIa. Neuchâtel: Delachaux et Niestlé, 1965. 251–62. **Kellermann, U.** *Israel und Edom: Studien zum Edomhass Israels in 6.–4. Jahrhundert vor Chr.* Münster, 1975. **Kutal, B.** *Liber Prophetarum Amos et Abdiae.* Olmütz, 1933. **Lanchester, H. C. O.** *Obadiah and Jonah.* Cambridge: Cambridge UP, 1918. **Marti, K.** *Der Prophet Obadja.* HSAT 2. Tübingen, 1923. 47–49. **Peckham, G. A.** *An Introduction to the Study of Obadiah.* Chicago, 1910. **Scharbert, J.** *Die Propheten Israels um 600 v. Chr.* Köln, 1967. **Schüngel-Straumann, H.** *Israel, und die andern? Zefania, Nahum, Habakuk, Obadja, Jona.* Stuttgarter Kleiner Kommentar. AT 15. Stuttgart: KBW, 1975. **Seydel, C. A. W.** *Vaticinium Obadjae.* Diss. Leipzig, 1869. **Thompson, J. A.** "Obadiah." *IB* 6:855–67. **Theis, J.** *Die Weissagung des Abdias.* Trier, 1917. **Trinquet, J.** *Habaquq / Abdias / Joël.* La Sainte Bible de Jérusalem. Paris, 1953. **Veldcamp, H.** *Het Gezicht van Obadja.* Kampen, 1957. **Wade, G. W.** *The Books of the Prophets Micah, Obadiah, Joel and Jonah.* Westminster Commentaries. London, 1925. **Watts, J. D. W.** *Obadiah: A Critical Exegetical Commentary.* Grand Rapids: Eerdmans, 1969. **Wolff, H. W.** *Dodekapropheton 3: Obadja und Jona.* BKAT XIV, 3. Neukirchen-Vluyn: Neukirchener Verlag, 1977.

Introduction

PAST SCHOLARSHIP ON OBADIAH

Because it is in itself an entire book of the OT, Obadiah has been paid far more attention than any other OT oracle against Edom. Most treatments of the book have given detailed consideration to (1) its historical setting, not specified in the book itself; (2) its literary integrity, particularly with regard to the relationship of vv 15–21 or vv 19–21 to the rest of the chapter, and the interrelationship of Obad 1–6 with Jer 49:9–16. No consensus has been reached on these issues, however.

Since C. P. Caspari's 1842 commentary on Obadiah the book has been

Obadiah

most often dated to the early part of the Judean exile. Earlier, Calvin decided for this date as well. Wellhausen, Bewer, and others dated the book to the late fifth century on the assumption that vv 2–9 represented a *vaticinium ex eventu* of Nabatean destruction of Edom in the early fifth century, rather than a genuine prediction. Harrison, following Torrey, prefers a date around 450 B.C., just before the Nabatean incursions. L. Allen, Eissfeldt, Edelkoort, G. A. Smith, and others argue forcefully for an exilic date, however, averring that vv 2–9 are clearly a predictive threat and not a description of events past. A date in the ninth century, related to events of ca. 850 B.C. as described in 2 Kgs 8:20–22 (2 Chr 21:8–10) was advanced by Keil, Orelli, Young, Sellin, Theis, and others. This very early date has the supposed advantage of comporting roughly with the canonical order of the Book of the Twelve, which by this theory appears to be intended as chronological in some way by its compiler. The Minor Prophets can be shown to be somewhat chronologically ordered. However, it is noteworthy that the Septuagint gives a different order from the Masoretic text. The ordering basis for the Twelve is likely to have been both thematic and catchword-oriented as well as chronological, with more demonstrably early books toward the beginning than toward the end of the Twelve (see *General Introduction*).

The unity of Obadiah has been defended by many scholars (Theis, Edelkoort, Allen, Harrison, etc.), in some cases on the basis that its structure shows it to be a prophecy designed for cultic use (Bič, Watts, and Wolff). Many others, by contrast, judge it to be a composite. Wellhausen, Rudolph, and Weiser, for example, see three fragments: vv 2–14, 15b; vv 15a, 16–18; vv 19–21. Robinson and Fohrer count about a half-dozen, while Eissfeldt finds only two (vv 1–14, 15b; vv 15a, 16–21), Brockington likewise (vv 1–18, 19–21). Complicating the analysis of Obadiah's literary unity is the question of its dependence on Jer 49 or vice versa. Naturally, those scholars who date Obadiah to the ninth century assign it priority over Jer 49; and those who date it to the fifth century usually do the opposite. For those who consider Obadiah close in date to Jer 49 (itself often dated to Jehoiakim's fourth year, thus prior to Jerusalem's fall in 586) the question is more acute. Caspari, Keil, van Hoonacker, Rudolph, and others have argued at length for the priority of Obadiah. Wellhausen, Bewer, Bonnard, and others have argued for the priority of Jer 49. Wolff and Allen see both as dependent on an early common anti-Edomite oral prophetic tradition, a stance most likely to be accurate in our opinion.

It is clear, then, that in the case of Obadiah a number of key introductory issues are very much debated. As a rule, scholarly debate on a portion of scripture increases in inverse proportion to the data available to decide the relevant questions. It must be admitted that we simply do not possess enough information to be able to settle certain issues about Obadiah and must therefore hold many positions tentatively.

DATE

A date for the composition of Obadiah can be established only in terms of likelihood, rather than certainty. There is a single question to be asked in this regard: What era does the apparent situation and perspective of the prophecy most likely reflect? A ninth-century date is difficult to sustain because of the paucity of information about the supposed occasion, the Edomite revolt against Jehoram (2 Kgs 8:20–22). Similarly, we know little about the fifth-century Nabatean conquest of Edom, which is at any rate the fulfillment of what is *predicted* in Obadiah rather than a thing narrated as a past event. It is the exilic period, particularly the early exile (580s or shortly thereafter) that meets the criterion best. Most importantly, four other OT passages from the same early sixth-century period reflect the same sort of situation and perspective found in Obadiah: Ps 137:7; Lam 4:18–22; Ezek 25:12–14; 35:1–15. These parallels echo the furious resentment expressed in Obadiah at the way the Edomites took advantage of Jerusalem's subjugation by the Babylonians. They also display an anticipation of the reversal of the (then) present painful circumstances of Judah. 1 Esd 4:45 claims that "the Edomites burned the temple when Judah was devastated by the Chaldeans," but this second-century B.C. (?) source contains much that is spurious. We know for sure only that the Edomites somehow aided and abetted the Babylonian conquest of 588–586 B.C., and profited from it, perhaps almost entirely by taking southern Judean land. The exact extent of their involvement with Babylon against Judah is not clear in Obadiah or any other trustworthy source.

EDOM IN BIBLICAL HISTORY

Israel had no shortage of enemies during its history as a nation in Canaan. Egypt, Assyria, and Babylon, the Fertile Crescent's three great powers in Old Testament times, were often actual or potential enemies of Israel. The smaller neighboring states of Aram, Philistia, Moab, Ammon, Phoenicia (Tyre and Sidon), and Edom were similarly enemies rather than allies at most times. Edom in particular was tenaciously and rather constantly hostile from beginning, i.e., after the exodus, to end, i.e., after the exile. This factor would itself be enough to cause such a small nation to receive such regular, even prominent mention in prophetic oracles against foreign nations. But Edom's prominence as an enemy was additionally noteworthy because of its historical position as a brother nation to Israel (Gen 25). There are, then, at least three factors that made Edom so prominent among Israel's enemies that it could sometimes function virtually as a paradigm for all of them: (1) the sheer chronological length of its enmity as alluded to in Ezek 35:5; (2) the consistency and intensity of its enmity (as in Obad 10–14); (3) the "treasonous" nature of its enmity (as in Amos 1:11). No other nation quite shared these characteristics.

This does not mean that anti-Edomite prophetic oracles stand out for their intensity or length, or the like. Prophetic pronouncements against Nineveh are just as bitterly worded, those against Tyre are just as graphically styled, and so on. Interestingly, however, of the ancient non-superpowers (i.e., leaving aside Egypt, Assyria, and Babylon) Edom is the subject of more separate oracles against foreign nations (seven) and more brief or passing hostile references (four) in the prophetical books than any other nation. The following list demonstrates the distribution of genuine foreign nation oracles in the prophets. While more sheer space is devoted to oracles against Moab or Tyre, for example, Edom is paid attention in a somewhat wider distribution.

Prophetic Oracles against Foreign Nations

Major Prophets	Minor Prophets	Short/Incidental
Assyria		
Isa 10:15–19	Mic 5:5–6	Jonah 3:4
Isa 14:24–27	Nah	Zech 10:11
Isa 37:21–35	Zeph 2:13–15	Isa 10:25
		Isa 30:31
Ammon		
Jer 49:1–6	Amos 1:13–15	Isa 11:14
Ezek 25:1–7	Zeph 2:8–11 (with Moab)	Jer 25:21
Arabia		
Isa 21:13–17		Jer 25:24
Jer 49:28–32 (with Hazor)		
Aram-Damascus		
Isa 17	Amos 1:3–5	Isa 7:7
Jer 49:23–27	Zech 9:1–2	Isa 8:4
Babylon		
Isa 13:1–22 Isa 47	Hab 2:4–20	
Isa 14:3–23 Jer 50, 51		
Isa 21:1–10		
Cush		
Isa 18	Zeph 2:12	
Isa 20 (with Egypt)		
Edom		
Isa 21:11–12 Ezek 35	Amos 1:11–12	Joel 4:19 [3:19]
Jer 49:7–22	Obad	Isa 11:14
Ezek 25:12–14	Mal 1:2–5	Jer 25:21
		Lam 4:21
Egypt		
Isa 19 Ezek 29, 30, 31,		Joel 4:19 [3:19]
32		Zech 10:11
Isa 20 (with Cush)		Zech 14:18–19
Jer 46		
Elam		
Jer 49:34–39		
Moab		
Isa 15, 16	Amos 2:1–3	Isa 11:14
Jer 48	Zeph 2:8–11 (with Ammon)	Jer 25:21
Ezek 25:8–11		

Prophetic Oracles against Foreign Nations

Major Prophets	Minor Prophets	Short/Incidental
Philistia		
Isa 14:28–32	Amos 1:6–8	Obad 19
Jer 47	Zeph 2:4–7	Isa 11:14
Ezek 25:15–17	Zech 9:2–8	Jer 25:20
Tyre (and Sidon)		
Isa 23 (with Sidon)		
Ezek 26, 27	Joel 4:4–8 [3:4–8]	
Ezek 28 (vv 20–23	Amos 1:9–10	Jer 25:22 (with
with Sidon)		Sidon)
Against the Nations in General		
Isa 10:12–14	Joel 4:9–16 [3:9–16]	
Isa 24	Mic 7:8–17	
Isa 34	Hag 2:20–22	
Isa 63:1–16	Zeph 1:2–3	
Jer 25:15–38	Zech 12:1–9	
Ezek 38, 39	Zech 14:12–19	

Daniel's prophecies on Media and Persia (etc.) are not included in this listing because of their atypical style.

Israel's little neighbor nation Edom, obscure on the world scene in terms of population and political influence, was nevertheless prominently represented in prophetic oracles. It should not be surprising, therefore, to find Edom the focus of a little book of the OT, somewhat in parallel to the way in which the greater nation of Assyria is the focus of the larger book of Nahum.

AUTHORSHIP

Nothing is known about Obadiah, and even the precise form of his name is uncertain. The Masoretic vocalization is עֹבַדְיָה "worshiper of Yahweh," but the Septuagint has Αβδιου and the Latin Vulgate *Abdias*, reflecting a slightly different Hebrew original, עַבְדְיָה "servant of Yahweh." The two options reflect perhaps bi-forms of the same name, comparable to Bert and Burt or Beth and Betty. The name Obadiah (following the MT vocalization) was apparently quite common in the OT era. Thirteen different Obadiahs are mentioned in the Old Testament from Davidic to post-exilic times. Additionally, the name Obed, which six different OT figures bear, including David's grandfather, is probably merely a hypocoristicon of Obadiah. Thus the author's name in its various forms is virtually as common as any other in the Bible, and not likely a symbolic or allegorical name.

In the Babylonian Talmud (*Sanh.* 39b) the author of Obadiah is identified as the Obadiah who was the palace administrator of King Ahab (1 Kgs 18:3–16), an ally of Elijah and protector of persecuted Yahwistic prophets in Israel.

Jerome also mentions this tradition, which predictably arose because this Obadiah is the one about whom most is said in the OT. Because of the suspicion that it is unlikely that a Northern ninth-century royal official would be inspired to prophesy exclusively about sixth-century Judean-Edomite relations, this traditional identification has routinely been rejected. It would probably never have arisen except for (1) the strong interest of the Talmudic writers in supplying authorship details for all parts of the OT, in combination with (2) the complete paucity of solid information about the author of the book of Obadiah.

Working inductively solely from the content and style of the book itself, one can speculate that Obadiah was a sixth-century Judean prophet, perhaps with formal prophetic training, who might well have preached his oracle in Jerusalem, whether or not he lived there. His awareness of traditional anti-Edomite prophetic language (as evidenced in the parallels with Jer 49) and the quality of his poetic expression do not prove him to be a professional prophet, but merely a gifted one. He may have been, like Amos, a nonprofessional to whom God imparted the necessary talent, aside from any formal training. We cannot tell whether he had cultic connections or not, or particular liturgical interests, since these are not clearly evidenced in the book. He is quite unknown to us except via his prophecy.

TEXT

The book's Hebrew text appears to contain a rather average number of corruptions for a chapter of OT poetry. By reason of the extensive parallels with Jer 49 it is possible in the verses involved (1–5) to achieve a somewhat higher level of certainty in reconstructing the original than would otherwise be possible. As is typically the case in the prophetical books, one must use the Septuagint with caution since the greater ambiguity of unvocalized poetry tended apparently to baffle the Alexandrian translators far more frequently than did, for example, prose narrative. G remains, however, the primary source among the ancient versions from which corrections to MT may be adduced.

Notable among necessary corrections to MT are: (v 4) תשׂים "you make," for MT שׂים "is made"; (v 6) נחפשׂ, singular, "destroyed," for MT נחפשׂו, plural; (v 13) *tišlāḥannāh,* the singular energic form of "lay (hands) on" for MT *tišlaḥnāh,* feminine plural; (v 17) מורישׁיהם "those who dispossessed them," for MT מורשׁיהם "their possessions"; (v 19) הר "mountain," for MT שׂדה "fields / land of"; and (v 20) ירשׁו "will possess," for MT אשׁר "which."

It has often been concluded that vv 15a and 15b are reversed from their original order in MT, since 15a is thought best placed as the beginning of the Day of Yahweh section of the prophecy (15a, 16–21). By this theory 15b provides a needed conclusion, i.e., judgment, for the crimes mentioned in vv 10–14. It is certainly true that v 15a begins the Day of Yahweh section. It is equally true, however, that v 15b is properly located in MT, since it shares in the ironic reversal theme central to the final section (vv 15–21) of the book and since the *entire* final section provides a fully adequate response to the crimes of Edom enumerated through v 14. The impetus to place v

15a with 16–21 and v 15b with 10–14 derives largely from the atomistic perspective that the Day of Yahweh section is self-contained, without close connection to the earlier part of the prophecy. A more holistic analysis of the book finds the emendation unnecessary.

THE MESSAGE

Prophetic oracles against foreign nations, though full of the language of doom, are also implicitly messages of hope for God's people. Such oracles look forward to a time when the predicted demise of the nation under attack will open the way for the restored, purified Israel to blossom once again as the flower of all God's plantings.

Obadiah's message fits this pattern and in some ways even typifies it. Its emphasis on the Day of Yahweh, the decisive time of God's sovereign intervention against his foes to establish his will, is by no means a common element in oracles against foreign nations. But it has the same purpose as in oracles against Israel and / or Judah: to reassure the righteous that those who oppose the Lord will meet their end, while the righteous, who have been oppressed, will be both preserved and exalted.

In Obadiah the Edomites, who have seized Judean lands in the wake of Babylon's elimination of Judean military and political powers, are excoriated for their enmity to Yahweh and his people. The fate of the Edomites, like that of other nations that occupied Israelite territory, is sealed. They will die out as a sovereign people and the Israelites will repossess the promised land under Yahweh's blessing. The present incapacitation of God's people may provide a temporary hope for Edom. But the eventual and final fate of Edom is the fate of all the wicked—death. And the eventual and final reward of God's people is life abundant. This is what Obadiah's words meant to his original audience and what they should as well mean to us.

Edom and the Future of Israel   (1–21)

Bibliography

Abel, F. M. "L'expédition des Grecs à pétra en 312 avant Jésus-Christ." *RB* 46 (1937) 373–91. **Ackroyd, P.** "Recent Foreign Theological Literature: The Old Testament." *ExpTim* 91 (1979) 8–13. **Aharoni, Y.** "Three Hebrew Ostraca from Arad." *BASOR* 197 (1970) 16–42. **Albright, W. F.** "Dedan." *Geschichte und Altes Testament (Alt FS,* BHT 16. Tübingen: Mohr, 1953. 1–12. ———. "Ostracon No. 6043 from Ezion Geber." *BASOR* 82 (1941) 11–15. **Alexandre, Jean.** "Abdias / Ovadia." *ETR* 54 (1979) 610–18. **Alt, A.** "Judas Nachbarn zur Zeit Nehemias." *Palastinajahrbuch* 31 (1931) 94–111. (Reprinted in *Kleine Schriften zur Geschichte des Volkes Israel, II.* Munich: Beck, 1953. 346–62.) **Arroyo, M. A.** "El profeta Abdias." *CB* 11 (1954) 32–33. **Bartlett, J.** "The Brotherhood of Edom." *JSOT* 2 (1977) 2–27. ———. "The Land of Seir and the Brotherhood of Edom." *JTS* 20 (1969) 1–20. ———. "The Moabites and Edomites."

In *Peoples of Old Testament Times,* ed. D. J. Wiseman. Oxford: Clarendon, 1973. 229–58. ———. "The Rise and Fall of the Kingdom of Edom." *PEQ* 104 (1972) 26–37. **Beit-Arieah, I.,** and **B. Cresson.** "An Edomite Ostracon from Horvat 'Uza." *Tel Aviv* 12 (1985) 96–101. **Bekel, H.** "Ein vorexilisches Orakel über Edom in der Klagestrophe—die gemeinsame Quelle von Obadja 1–9 und Jeremiah 49:7–22." *TSK* 80 (1907) 315–43. **Bič, M.** "Ein verkanntes Thronbesteigungsfestorakel im A.T." *ArOr* 19 (1951) 568–79. ———. "Zur Problematik des Buches Obadja." Congress Volume, Copenhagen, 1953. VTSup 1 (1953) 11–25. **Bonnard, E.** "Abdias." *DBSup* 8. 693–701. **Box, B.** "Edom: Who Can Bring Me Down." *BibIll* 12 (1986) 41–50. **Brawer, A.** "The Name Obadiah—Its Punctuation and Explanation." *BMik* 18, 3 (54) (1972–73) 418–27. (Heb.) **Brownlee, W. H.** "The Aftermath of the Fall of Judah According to Ezekiel." *JBL* 89 (1970) 393–404. **Cannon, W.** "Israel and Edom. The Oracle of Obadiah." *Theology* 15 (1927) 129–40, 191–200. **Condamin, A.** "L'unité d'Abdias." *RB* 9 (1900) 261–68. **Coughenour, R.** "A View of Value from a Servant of Yahweh." *RefR* 24 (1970s) 119–23. **Cresson, B. C.** "The Condemnation of Edom in Postexilic Judaism." *Studies in Honor of W. F. Stinespring.* 1972. 125–48. **Cross, F. M.** "An Aramaic Inscription from Daskyleion." *BASOR* 184 (1966) 7–10. ———. "Heshbon Ostracon II." *AUSS* 11 (1973) 126–31. **Davies, G.** "A New Solution to a Crux in Obadiah 7." *VT* 27 (1977) 484–87. **Delitzsch, F.** "Wann weissagte Obadja?" *Zeitschrift für die lutherische Theologie und Kirche* 12 (1851) 91–102. **Dick, Michael B.** "A Syntactic Study of the Book of Obadiah." *Semitics* 9 (1984) 1–29. **Diebner, B.,** and **H. Schult.** "Edom in alttestamentlichen Texten der Makkabäerzeit." *Dielheimer Blätter zum AT* 8 (1975) 11–17. **Dumbrell, W.** "The Tell el-Maskhūta Bowls and the 'Kingdom' of Qedar in the Persian Period." *BASOR* 203 (1971) 33–44. **Edelkoort, A.** "De profetie van Obadja." *NedTTs* 1 (1946/47) 276–93. **Fohrer, G.** "Der Tag Jhwhs." *EI* 16 (1982) 43–50. ———. "Die Sprüche Obadjas." In *Studia Biblica et Semitica: FS T. C. Vriezen,* ed. W. van Unnik and A. van der Woude. Wageningen: Veeman en Zonen, 1966. 81–93. **Freeman, A.** "The Obadiah Problem." Diss. Southern Baptist Seminary. Louisville, KY, 1950. **Gilse, J. van.** "Tijdbepaling der profetie Obadja." *Nieuw Theologisch Tijdschrift* (1913) 293–313. **Glueck, N.** "The Boundaries of Edom." *HUCA* 11 (1936) 141–57. ———. "Tell el-Kheleifeh Inscriptions." In *Near Eastern Studies in Honor of William Foxwell Albright,* ed. H. Goedicke. Baltimore: Johns Hopkins, 1971. 225–42. **Gray, J.** "The Diaspora of Israel and Judah in Obadiah 20." *ZAW* 65 (1953) 53–59. **Grimme, H.** "Der Untergang Edoms." *Die Welt als Geschichte* 3 (1937) 452–63. **Halévy, J.** "Le livre d'Obadia." *RevSém* (1907) 165–83. **Haller, Max.** "Edom in Urteil der Propheten." *Marti Festschrift,* BZAW 41. Giessen: Topelmann, 1925. 109–17. **Hanfmann, G.,** and **J. Waldbaum.** "New Excavations at Sardis and Some Problems of Western Anatolian Archaeology." In *Near Eastern Archaeology in the Twentieth Century* (Glueck FS), ed. J. Sanders. Garden City: Doubleday, 1970. 307–26. **Isopescul, S. O.** "Historische-kritische Einleitung zur Weissagung des Abdia." *WZKM* (1913) 141–62. ———. "Übersetzung und Auslegung des Buches Abdias." *WZKM* (1914) 149–81. **Kornfeld, W.** "Die judäische Diaspora in Ab. 20." In *André Robert Festschrift.* Paris, 1957. 180–86. **Lillie, J.** "Obadiah—A Celebration of God's Kingdom." *CurTM* 6 (1979) 18–22. **Lipínski, E.** "Obadiah 20." *VT* 23 (1973) 368–70. **Loewinger, S.** "Esau dans Abd. 6." *RÉJ* 110 (1951) 93s. **Luciani, F.** "Il verbo bō' in Abd. 13." *RivB* 31 (1983) 209–11. **Luria, B. Z.** *The Book of Obadiah and the Prophecies Concerning Edom.* Publications of the Israeli Society for Biblical Research, 26. Jerusalem: Kiriath-Sefer, 1972. **Maag, V.** "Jacob-Esau-Edom." *TZ* 13 (1957) 418–29. **Maier, Johann.** "'Siehe, ich mach(t)e dich klein unter den Völkern . . .'; zum rabbinischen Assoziationshorizont von Obadja 2." In *Kunden des Wortes, Beiträge zur Theologie der Propheten, Josef Schreiner zum 60* (Schreiner FS), ed. Lothar Ruppert. Würzburg: Echter, 1982. 203–216. **McCarter, P.** "Obadiah 7 and the Fall of Edom." *BASOR* 221 (1976) 87–91. **Mazar, A.** "Edomite Pottery at the End of the Iron Age." *IEJ* 35 (1985) 253–69. **Menenga, G.** "Obscure Obadiah and His Message." *Reformed Revue* (1959) 24–43. **Meyers, J.** "Edom and Judah in the Sixth-Fifth Centuries B.C." In *Near Eastern Studies in Honor of William Foxwell Albright*, ed. H. Goedicke. Baltimore: Johns Hopkins, 1971. 377–392. **Morton, W.** "Umm el Biyara." *BA* 19 (1956) 26–36. **Muilenburg, J.** "Obadiah, Book of." *IDB* 3:578–79. **Naveh, J.** "The Scripts of Two Ostraca from Elah." *BASOR* 183 (1966) 27–30. **Neiman, D.** "Sefarad: The Name of Spain." *JNES* 22 (1963) 128–32. **Ogden, G.** "Prophetic Oracles Against Foreign Nations and Psalms of Communal Lament: The Relationship of Psalm 137 to Jeremiah 49:7–22 and Obadiah." *JSOT* 24 (1982) 89–97. **Olávarri, E.** "Cronologia y estructura literaria del oráculo escatológico de Abdias." *EstBib* 22 (1963) 303–13. **Ottoson, M.** "Sarafand / Sarepta and Its Phoenician Background." *Qad* 13 (1980) 122–26 (Heb.). **Rinaldi, J. M.** "In librum Abdiae." *VD* 19 (1939) 148–54, 174–79, 201–6. **Robinson, T. (H.)** "The Structure of the Book of Obadiah." *JTS* 17 (1916) 402–8. **Rudolph, W.** "Obadja." *ZAW* 49 (1931) 222–31. **Sauer, J.** "Transjordan in the Bronze and Iron Ages: A Critique of Glueck's Synthesis." *BASOR* 263 (1986) 1–26. **Smith, J.** "The Structure of Obadiah." *AJSL* 22 (1906) 131–38. **Starcky, J.** "The Nabataeans: A Historical Sketch." *BA* 18 (1955) 84–106. **Wehrle, Josef.** "Prophetie und Textanalyse; die Komposition Obadja 1–21, interpretiert auf der Basis textlinguistischer und semiotischer Konzeptionen." Diss. Freiburg, 1981. **Weimar, P.** "Obadja, Eine redaktionskritische Analyse." *BN* 27 (1985) 35–99. **Weinburg, K.** "Biblische Motive in Stifters Abdias." *Emuna-Horizonte* 7, 1 (1972) 32–8. **Wolfers, D.** "Is Job After All Jewish?" *DD* 14 (1985) 39–44. **Wolff, H.** "Obadja—ein Kultprophet als Interpret." *EvT* 37 (1977) 273–84.

Translation

Heading

[1] *Obadiah's Revelation.*[a]

Introduction

This is what the Lord Yahweh said about[b] *Edom.*

Edom's coming defeat

We[c] *have heard a message from Yahweh,*
An envoy was sent[d] *among the nations.*
"Rise, let us rise against her[e] *in battle!"*

[2] *I will make you small among the nations.*
[a] *You will be thoroughly*[a] *despised.*

[3] *The pride of your mind has deceived you,*
Dwellers in crevices of rock, whose[a] *home is the height.*[b]
Who think to yourself, "Who can bring me down to the ground?"

[4] *Even if you soar high like an eagle,*
Even if you[a] *make your nest among the stars,*
I will bring you down from there. —Oracle of Yahweh.

[5] *If thieves came to you,*
If marauders at night,
How could you be destroyed?[a]
Wouldn't they steal only enough for themselves?

If grape gatherers came to you,
Wouldn't they leave gleanings?

⁶*How has*^a *Esau been searched through?*
His treasures ransacked?^b

⁷*They have pushed you to your border,*
All your allies have deceived you,

Your confederates have prevailed against you
Your comrades^a *have been setting a trap under you,*
^b*Without your knowing it.*^b

⁸*Will I not at that time   —oracle of Yahweh—*
Destroy the wise men from Edom
And understanding from the mountains of Esau?

⁹*Your soldiers will be terrified, Teman,*
So that everyone will be cut off from the mountains of Esau.

Edom's crimes against Judah

Because of the slaughter,^a ¹⁰*because of the violence done to your brother Jacob*
Shame will cover you and you will be cut off forever.

¹¹*At the time when you stood aside*
At the time when strangers captured his possessions,^a

And foreigners entered his gates,^b
And cast lots for Jerusalem,
You, too, were like one of them.

¹²*Do not*^a *gloat in your brother's*^b *time,*^c *in the time*^c *of his misfortune.*
Do not rejoice at the Judeans in the time^c *of their ruin.*
Do not boast in the time^c *of distress!*

¹³*Do not enter my people's gate in the time of their calamity.*^a
Do not gloat like the others^b *over his trouble in the time of his calamity*
Do not lay hands^c *on his possessions in the time of his calamity!*^d

¹⁴*Do not stand at the crossroads*^a *to cut off his fugitives.*
Do not hand over his survivors in the time of distress!

The Day of Yahweh: Restoration of Israel's sovereignty

¹⁵*For the Day of Yahweh is near, against all the nations.*
Just as you have done, it will be done to you.
Your deeds will return on your own head.

¹⁶*For just as you drank on my holy mountain,*
All the nations will drink continually.^a
They will drink and swallow, and become as if they had never been.

¹⁷*On Mount Zion will be deliverance. It will be a holy place.*
The family of Jacob will dispossess those who dispossessed^a *them.*
¹⁸*The family of Jacob will be a fire,*
The family of Joseph a flame.

The family of Esau will become stubble.
They will burn them and consume them.
There will be no survivors for the family of Esau,
    For Yahweh has spoken.

19 The people of the Negeb will possess the mountains of Esau,
The people of the Shephelah the area of the Philistines.

They will possess the mountains [a] of Ephraim and the lands of Samaria
And the people of Benjamin . . . Gilead. [b]

20 The exiles [a] of these possessions belonging to the Israelites
Will possess [b] the Canaanites as far as Zarephath.

The exiles of Jerusalem who are in Sepharad
Will possess the cities of the Negeb.

21 Those who have been rescued [a] will go up to Mount Zion
to rule over the mountains of Esau
And to Yahweh will belong the kingdom.

Notes

1.a. On this meaning of חָזוֹן, cf. Isa 1:1; Ezek 7:26; Nah 1:1; Hab 2:2; Prov 29:18.
1.b. On לְ as "about," cf. Jer 49:7.
1.c. G ἤκουσα "I have heard" and the parallel in Jer 49:14 suggest that שָׁמַעְתִּי "I have heard" may have been more original. Alternatively, G's *Vorlage* may have been corrupted in conformation to Jer 49:14.
1.d. The "defective" orthography in MT prompted the piel pf vocalization שֻׁלַּח "was sent." שָׁלוּחַ, qal pass ptcp, as in Jer 49:14, is equally likely to be original.
1.e. Here Edom is construed as fem, in contrast to the rest of the prophecy, but consistent with Jer 49:16. G[L] ἐπ᾽ αὐτόν "against him," requires the possibility of a masc original.
2.a.-a. For אַתָּה מְאֹד "You will be thoroughly," Jer 49:15 has בָּאָדָם "among humankind," more normal to the canons of synonymous parallelism (cf. "among the nations") but not provably more original. The difference from Jer 49:15 proves that G, which supports MT here, is not simply parroting Jer 49 whenever possible.
3.a. The shift to a 3 m sg suff is not abnormal after the vocative (G-K 144 p.).
3.b. G ὑψῶν and Vg suggest vocalizing מֵרִים "on high," but MT מְרוֹם "height," is confirmed by Jer 49:16.
4.a. The versions strongly support תָּשִׂים, 2 m sg impf, rather than MT's שִׂים (pass ptcp or inf abs). Cf., however, the related Num 24:21, which has שִׂים, like MT.
5.a. This clause and both clauses in v 6 are usually taken as declarative (How!) but are more naturally construed as interrogatives, obviating the frequent suggestions that one or more of them is out of place.
6.a. Since the versions have a sg verb here, MT's pl נֶחְפְּשׂוּ would appear to be a copy error under the influence of the following plural נִבְעוּ.
6.b. See 5.a.
7.a. Since לחם, qal, can mean "to fight," and the suff can conceivably be construed to refer to those one fights (along) with, "comrades-in-arms" might be a reasonable translation. However, since לחם "eat" can indicate association / comradeship in certain idioms (cf. Prov 23:6) and most of the versions, "comrades" is also appropriate.
7.b.-b. Lit., "There is not understanding in / of him / it." In light of the idiom ... בְּ / בִּין / ... בְּ הֵבִין "to understand," בּוֹ probably refers to the trap (מָזוֹר).
9.a. Following G Syr Vg, which join מִקֶּטֶל "because of the slaughter" with the first clause in v 10, adding also the copula ("slaughter and . . .").

11.a. חִיל can also mean "wealth," "strength," "army," or even"fortifications" (Watts, *Obadiah*, 53), and so has a richer range than "possessions" conveys.

11.b. Or "gate." Consonantal MT שערו is ambiguous as to plurality, as MT's primitive Kethib-Qere method of indicating textual discrepancy suggests here.

12.a. Or "you should not" or, conceivably, "you should not have . . . ," though אל with the imperfect is most naturally translated "Do not . . . ."

12.b. The double-triplet structure of vv 12 and 13 is so repetitious, with יום "time of" ending each line, that the presence of יום *here* is suspect, and "gloat over your brother" might be the more original wording.

12.c. Lit., "day"; also in v 13.

13.a. G πόνων αὐτῶν might also reflect אונם "their misery" or the like; but see 13.d.

13.b. Lit., "you also."

13.c. Reading the "energic" תִּשְׁלַחְנָה "do not lay hands" rather than MT's fem pl. On the absence of יד "hand" in the expression, cf. 2 Sam 6:6; Ps 18:17. No emendation is required.

13.d. G ἀπωλείας might reflect an original אבד, "destruction," unless the G translator simply sought a variety for the line endings in v 13 in parallel to the variety of v 12.

14.a. In Nah 3:1 פרק means "plunder," "division of spoil." Therefore it could also mean here, its only other use in the OT, the division of slaves taken from those who escaped the destruction of Jerusalem.

16.a. Many medieval Heb. MSS have סביב "all around" (cf. Zech 12:2) but the versions support MT.

17.a. Reading with G Syr Tg Vg and Murabbaat MSS 88 מורישיהם, instead of MT מורשיהם "their possessions."

19.a. G τὸ ὄρος suggests an original הר "mountains of" instead of MT שדה "lands / fields of."

19.b. The grammar and poetic structure of the second couplet are odd, suggesting textual corruption. See *Comment*.

20.a. Or "army." The text is possibly corrupt here, however.

20.b. The consistent parallel structure makes it clear that ירשו "will possess" was original, and that MT אשר is a miscopy.

21.a. Reading the hoph ptcp מוּשָׁעִים "those who have been rescued," with G, *a'*, *θ'*, Syr rather than MT "saviors."

Form / Structure / Setting

There is little disagreement among those who have analyzed the structure of Obadiah that vv 1–18 are poetic. Vv 19–21 are often judged to be prose, though their parallelism, as evidenced in the translation above, would seem to offer no barrier to their being construed as poetry. In general, there is every reason to consider Obadiah a unity; a self-contained prophetic oracle with a single topic, the denunciation of Edom vis-à-vis Israel. (See also *Introduction*.)

Prophetic oracles against foreign nations take many forms, but frequently include: (1) identification of the enemy nation to be denounced (here v 1; cf. Isa 19:1; Jer 49:1; Ezek 28:21); (2) warning to the enemy nation of its coming doom, often including direct address (here mainly vv 2–18; cf. esp. Isa 19, esp. vv 11–12; Jer 49, esp. vv 3–5; Ezek 28:22–23); (3) mention or description of Yahweh's decisive intervention and punishment of the enemy nation (here and in Isa 19; Jer 49; Ezek 28:23–26; passim); and (4) a prediction of Israel's coming ascendency relative to the enemy nation (here vv 17–21; cf. Isa 19:17, 24–25; Jer 49:3c; Ezek 28:24–26).

Ironic reversal also characterizes some oracles against foreign nations, in that, for example, the oppressor nation will receive back the very sort of

behavior it had been manifesting. In Obadiah, vv 7–8, 11, and especially v
15 reflect this, in a manner comparable to Joel 4:4–8 [3:4–8], Jer 51:49, etc.
Synthetic parallelism dominates the book, but predominantly synonymous
couplets are found in vv 5–8, 14, and 18; and predominantly synonymous
triplets in vv 12 and 13. A notable aspect of the poetic structure is the frequency
of triplets. There are twelve, among sixteen couplets, so that an individual
poetic line is statistically more likely to be found within a triplet (thirty-six
lines total) than within a couplet (thirty-two lines total). Though the distribution
of triplets is typically unpredictable and presumably insignificant, the sheer
number of triplets is remarkably high, comparable to only a few other OT
prophetical passages such as Jer 51:25–58.

The overwhelming preponderance of *longum* (*l*) over *breve* (*b*) meter is
typical. In vv 5 and 6 *b* : *b* meter predominates; otherwise *l* : *l* or *l* : *l* : *l* meter
is uniform throughout.

More than one cogent analysis of the structure of the book has been offered.
For example, Watts outlines the book as follows: superscription (1a); audition
("Rise to battle!", 1b-c); first announcement of judgment (2–4); second announcement of judgment (5–10); indictment and deprecation (11–14); theological explanation (15–16); vision of conditions to follow (17–21) [*Obadiah*
and *ISBE*, rev. ed., 574–75]. J. Muilenburg's analysis is modestly different
(*IDB*, 578–79). Vv 2–10 are titled "divine judgment on Edom" (with subdivisions as follows: her pride brought low, vv 2–4; destruction, pillage, abandonment, vv 5–7; the day of her shame, vv 8–10). Vv 11–14, 15b are titled "the
day of her treachery" (subdivisions: Edom's aloofness when Jerusalem fell,
v 11; her evil gloating over Judah's distress, v 12; her invasion of Jerusalem,
v 13; her support of the Babylonians, v 14; judgment, v 15b). His final section,
vv 15a, 16–21, is titled "the Day of Yahweh" (subdivisions: the reversal of
fate, 15a, 16–18; the lands repossessed, 19–21).

Our own analysis is somewhat different still, but should be viewed as an
alternative to rather than a rejection of others' constructions, both because
the book's clear thematic emphases are not in doubt, and because its logical
unity would be evident under any of a variety of superimposed outlines.
The book by our view may be outlined as follows:

A. Heading (v 1a)
B. Introduction (v 1b)
C. Edom's coming defeat (vv 1b–9b)
D. Edom's crimes against Judah (vv 9b–14)
E. The Day of Yahweh: restoration of Israel's sovereignty (vv 15–21)

Yahweh is quoted often (vv 1, 2, 4, 8, 13?, 16) in a manner quite consistent
with OT prophetical books in which a prophet's words come directly from
God. This is characteristic as well of the oracle against Edom in Jer 49:7–
22, in which vv 9 and 14–16 are almost identical with Obad 1–4 and 5.

This overlap of Obad 1–5 with parts of Jer 49 raises the typical question
in such cases: which came first? And as virtually always in such cases the
answer must be that there is no sure way to tell. Obadiah may have borrowed
some of Jeremiah's phrasing, or vice versa. Or both or either of them may

have borrowed independently from some earlier lengthy oracles as they were inspired to do so. The fact that Jeremiah and Obadiah place their shared blocks of text in reverse order and at different relative points in their oracles would suggest that neither was deliberately parroting the other but that each composed his oracle partly from traditional lines of poetry already in circulation in Judah. (On the fact that ancient poetry was not creative in the same way that much modern poetry is, see S. B. Lord, *The Singer of Tales* [Boston: Atheneum, 1968] 3–67.) The correspondence between Obadiah and Jer 49 may for convenience be summarized via the following side-by-side placement.

וציר בגוים שלח	שמועה שמענו מאת־יהוה	Obad 1b
" " " "	שמעתי " "	Jer 49:14a
---- למלחמה	קומו ונקומה עליה	Obad 1c
וקומו למלחמה	התקבצו ובאו "	Jer 49:14b
בזוי אתה מאד	-- הנה קטן נתתיך בגוים	Obad 2
" באדם ---	כי " " " "	Jer 49:15
--- ----	זדון לבך השיאך	Obad 3a
זדון לבך	תפלצתך השיא אתך	Jer 49:16a
מרום שבתו ----	שכני בחגוי סלע	Obad 3b
תפשי " גבעה	" " הסלע	Jer 49:16b
מי יורדני ארץ	אמר בלבו	Obad 3c
--- ------ --	---- ---	Jer 49:16
ואם בין כוכבים שים קנך	אם תגביה כנשר	Obad 4a
" --- ------ --- ---	כי " "	Jer 49:16c
נאם יהוה	משם אורידך	Obad 4b
" "	" "	Jer 49:16c cont'd.
אם שודדי לילה	אם גנבים באו לך	Obad 5a
בלילה ----- --	-- --- " "	Jer 49:9b
הלוא יגנבו דים	איך נדמיתה	Obad 5b
" השחיתו ----	------ ---	Jer 49:9b cont'd.
הלוא ישאירו עללות	אם בצרים באו לך	Obad 5c
לא " "	" " " "	Jer 49:9a

This placement ignores minor orthographic variations (e.g., שלח in Obad 1b and שלוח in Jer 49:14a) in what are otherwise obviously identical words. There are sixty-two word groups in this portion of Obadiah. Thirty-four of

them (55%) are found identically in the parallel in Jeremiah 49. Another
six (10%) are almost identical (e.g., Obad 1b שמענו "we have heard," vs. Jer
49:14a שמעתי "I heard"). Thus roughly two-thirds of the wordings are nearly
identical, a proportion impossible to imagine having occurred accidentally
in a passage of this length. Several commentators, following T. H. Robinson,
have concluded that the Obadiah wording is the more original, but that the
Jeremiah wording is the better preserved. In neither case, however, can we
be confident of any assertions about originality or preservation. Both passages
are probably independent compositions that select from commonly known
wordings. For example, Obadiah constructed a triplet in 4a, while Jeremiah
constructed a couplet (49:16c), "leaving out" several words. Where Jeremiah
constructed a couplet in 49:16a, Obadiah constructed only a single line by
"leaving out" several words and placing subject and predicate in a different
order (3a). Obadiah then made that single line the first line of a triplet that
shares its final two lines largely but not exactly with Jer 49:16b. And so on.
Accordingly, the text of Jer 49 may be used with profit to elucidate Obadiah
where the two overlap, but cannot be used to restore the text of Obadiah,
except where it can be proved by other means that something has been lost
from Obadiah in the process of transmission.

The book is probably best dated to the period shortly after the fall of
Jerusalem to the Babylonians in 586 B.C. On this dating and the history of
Edomite relations with Israel and Judah, see the *Introduction* above.

Comment

1 The simple heading matches the brevity of the book (cf. Joel, Habakkuk,
Malachi) and, like Isa 1:1, Mic 1:1, Nah 1:1, the heading uses חזון "revelation"
to describe its contents. Introductions of prophetic books take various forms.
Ten give relative chronological information in some way. Obadiah and five
others (Joel, Jonah, Nahum, Habakkuk, Malachi) are entirely undated. The
Obadiah introduction is unique in employing the compound אדני יהוה "Lord
Yahweh," a divine title not used elsewhere in the book, nor at all often in
the prophets except for Ezekiel and Amos, where it is very common. The
fact that Obadiah follows Amos in canonical order may be due to nothing
more than linkage on the basis of this "catchword."

The remainder of v 1 (called the "audition" by Watts) is a poetic triplet
that reports on the gist of a messenger speech summoning the nations in
general to military attack against Edom. The call for battle is rather typical
in style (cf. Isa 21:5; Jer 6:4–5; 49:14, 28, 31; Joel 3:9–13; Mic 4:13; see R.
Bach, *Die Aufforderungen zur Flucht und zum Kampf in Alttestamentlichen Prophetenspruch*, WMANT 9, [Neukirchen: Neukirchener Verlag, 1962] 62–65). Implicit
in the mention of "nations" (plural) is the common notion that Yahweh controls
all the world's states and peoples. Thus Edom's arrogance against Judah (vv
3–4, 12), foolishly exercised on the assumption that Judah had no allies, will
be dashed in disappointment when all turn against Edom (cf. vv 6–7, 15).

2 Edom's coming judgment is summarized at the outset. It will become
a nation vastly reduced in size and influence, and will be condemned by
other nations. Two curse types (see *General Introduction*) are thus to be fulfilled

in Edom's future: decimation (no. 12; cf. Lev 26:22, 36; Deut 4:27; 28:62) and dishonor / degradation (no. 16; cf. Deut 28:25, 27, 43, 44). Note that the curse categories announced for Israel in the pentateuchal sanctions may be applied to her enemies in oracles against foreign nations, in accordance with the restoration blessing of power for Israel over her enemies (restoration blessing type 9; cf. Deut 30:7, "Yahweh your God will put all these curses on your enemies").

In a fashion also typical of oracles against foreign nations, Yahweh speaks directly to Edom in the first person, and uses the "prophetic perfect" "I have made you / I will make you" to emphasize that the punishment is virtually accomplished already.

3 Edom's arrogance is mocked by a taunt in a manner typical of foreign nation oracles (especially those of Ezekiel: Ezek 27:3; 28:2, 17; 29:3; 31:2; 32:2; cf. Isa 37:23, 29; Hab 2:4, 5). The nation has fooled itself into thinking it is great, in part because of its rock location (*sela*ᶜ [סלע "rock"] is a pun on the name of Edom's capital, Sela). In ancient times height was always a very significant military advantage, and Sela's location on the Umm el-Biyara plateau, surrounded by steep cliffs and approachable only via the well-defended southeast slope, gave it great confidence.

4 Since Yahweh's power is unlimited, it does not matter how high-set and well defended Edom might be. It will fall. In addition to Sela, Edom's main cities of Teman and Bozrah, as well as the nascent fortress city of Petra nearby Sela, were located in nearly impenetrable high rock formations reached only by narrow, vulnerable gorges in each instance. Nevertheless, Yahweh had already shown Sela vulnerable in the successful campaign of Amaziah against the Edomites ca. 775 B.C. (2 Kgs 14:7). Sela may well have remained in Judahite control until either the Egyptian attack of 605 on Jerusalem, or the Babylonian attack of 598 B.C. On the metaphorical portrayal of strength and freedom by mention of the eagle, cf. Exod 19:4; 2 Sam 1:23; Ps 103:5; Isa 40:31; Lam 4:19; Hos 8:1; etc.

5 Two conditional interrogatives comprise v 5. Both are rhetorical questions designed to focus attention on the completeness of Edom's coming loss by contrasting to it theoretical instances of partial loss. Thieves can only take what they can carry away. Grape harvesters do not have time to do a perfect job of picking every grape (typically the case in any ancient or modern harvest, since most crop ripening occurs so rapidly that overly careful picking of the first part of the crop would allow the rest to spoil). But Edom will be stripped bare, when, as vv 6–9 say, it is defeated and despoiled in war.

6 Full-blown despoiling, thorough and leisurely on the part of the victors, will bleed from Edom all possessions of significance. The term Esau is used here for Edom, as often throughout the entire book (vv 8, 9, 18, 19, 21) a usage otherwise confined to Deut 2, Jer 49, Josh 24, Mal 1, and Genesis. Edom, the more common term for the nation, as opposed to the eponymous ancestor Esau, predominates otherwise in the OT, as also in the introduction (v 1) and by reason of pride of place in v 8.

7 Edom was a weak country militarily, its small population and its limited agricultural wealth precluding powerful armed forces. Therefore its ability to attack Judah's Negeb and help plunder Jerusalem had depended on its obsequious alliance with more powerful states, especially Babylon. The prophet's ironic reversal language continues here with a set of predictions, again in the prophetic perfect, looking forward to Edom's betrayal at the hands of those in whom it trusted and from whose strength it prospered. "Deceived" (השיא) and "trapped" (מזור), the nation will not have realized what was coming "without knowing it" (אין תבונה בו). This punishment represents a fulfillment of helplessness curses such as Deut 28:29, ". . . You will be robbed and oppressed with no one to rescue you."

8 The reason for this ignorance is that Yahweh will have intervened to eliminate good decision-making from Edom, by destroying its wise men along with the rest of its population. Essentially without leadership, the people will be helpless (curse type 19; cf. Lev 26:37; Deut 28:29). The "mountains of Esau" (הר עשו) are mentioned here only in simple synonymous parallelism with "Edom," as similarly in v 9 below, not because the wise men had fled to the mountains or the like.

9 Teman, possibly modern Tawilan (N. Glueck, *The Other Side of the Jordan* [Cambridge, MA: ASOR, 1970] 25–26), was a major city in northern Edom named after a grandson of Esau (Gen 36:11; 1 Chr 1:36). It is mentioned prominently in connection with Edom (Jer 49:7; Ezek 25:13; Amos 1:12) and was the home of some early Edomite chieftains (Gen 36:15, 34, 42) as well as Job's "comforter" Eliphaz, though there is no evidence that Teman was in fact Edom's capital. Obadiah's contemporary Habakkuk includes Teman among Yahweh's conquests in his poem about the deliverance march from the south (Hab 3:3). Sela was already mentioned in Obad 3, and Bozrah, Edom's other major city, is not mentioned in the book. Inclusion of Teman's soldiers is enough to suggest that if they are afraid (curse type 4; cf. Lev 26:36–37) the nation as a whole ("mountains of Esau") will be destroyed (curse type 24).

10 In this portion of the prophecy, the attention turns to Edom's crimes against Judah. The last word group of v 9 (מקטל "because of the slaughter") and the first of v 10 (מחמס "because of the violence") already point to some sort of armed conflict, but not necessarily a direct Edomite attack on Judah. In the remainder of the poem, the Edomites are charged with supporting the plunder of Judah (v 11), advantaging themselves at Judah's expense (v 12), plundering Jerusalem and perhaps other cities (v 13), and taking Judean prisoners from escapees (v 14), but not specifically with having any military role in the attack on Judah, which was a strictly Babylonian enterprise. For their profiteering from the Babylonian invasion, however, they themselves will be "cut off" (כרת) and subject to "shame" (בושה), essentially the same fates that the Judeans have recently experienced (vv 11–14). Here for the first time the theme of Edomite-Israelite kinship is brought forward (also vv 12, 17, 18) by the words "your brother Jacob" (cf. Gen 25:21–30).

11 This brother, however, acted like a stranger ("like one of them" כאחד מהם), offering no help when the enemy captured and despoiled Jerusalem. Of course, given the long enmity of Edom and Israel / Judah one could hardly expect Edom to rush to Judah's aid against Babylon, but that is not the point of the indictment. Rather, Edom is castigated for comfortably biding its time while the Babylonians carved up Jerusalem as the Edomites could never have done, in anticipation of moving in like vultures for the city's leftovers (v 13) and attacking Jerusalemite refugees headed south (v 14). In other words, Edom profited handsomely from its apparent policy of nonopposition to and indeed support for Babylon in 586 (or 598) B.C., since Babylon then did Edom's dirty work.

12 Now begins a series of eight prohibitions in the typical syntactical style that indicates not a general prohibition (לֹא "not" + imperfect) but a specific, individual-circumstance prohibition (אַל "do not" + imperfect). The two triplets that constitute vv 12–13 are composed in a highly stylized synonymous form, with the epiphoric בְּיוֹם "in the time of" repeating along with אַל "do not" all six times, and included a seventh time at the end of v 14. In v 12 it is Edomite gloating / rejoicing / boasting that is decried, both because it is wrong and because it cannot last (v 15). Here the Judeans (בְּנֵי יְהוּדָה) are identified as the group affected by misfortune / ruin / distress (curse type 25), and this specificity helps date the book to the Babylonian conquest of the early sixth century, Israel already having fallen to Assyria in 722 B.C.

13 The middle line of v 13's triplet speaks again of gloating (רָאָה בְ . . .) over Judah's calamity, but the first and third lines add a warning about plundering. In all likelihood Edomites did not enter Jerusalem (if ever) until long after the city was picked over and largely abandoned by the Babylonian armies. But Edomites may well have despoiled numbers of Judean towns too small and too numerous for the Babylonians to plunder systematically. Jerusalem fell in the first month of 586 B.C. after a two-year siege (2 Kgs 25:1–8). It is not impossible that even during the siege of 588–86, when Babylonian troops were concentrated at Jerusalem, Edomite parties were looting unprotected southern sites. Stylistically, epiphora again characterizes the triplet, in the repeated wording "in the time of their / his calamity" (בְּיוֹם אֵידוֹ / ם).

14 It has sometimes been theorized that the statement about cutting off (Judean) fugitives in this verse refers to an Edomite refusal to give sanctuary to Zedekiah and the Judean army fleeing from Jerusalem just prior to the fall of the city (2 Kgs 25:4–6). Since the king and his army fled northeastward toward Jericho this reconstruction would seem unlikely. That Jerusalem's siege and fall presented the Edomites a long-sought opportunity for both occupation of parts of Judah and also capture of civilians and / or detached Judean soldiers heading away from Babylonian forces can hardly be doubted, however. Moreover, the subsequent exile of Judah's leadership (2 Kgs 25:11–12) meant that little resistance to Edomite raids and even permanent settlement in Judah could be offered. The bitter denunciations of Edom's actions after 586 imply that Edom took full advantage of these options (Ps 137:7; Lam 4:21–22). On the image of "standing by the road to intercept fugitives," cf. Jer 48:19; Judg 12:5; Lam 4:12–19 (the latter possibly referring in part to Edomite activity in light of its proximity to vv 21–22).

15 The oracle now enters a new section which sets in overall context the predictions of doom against Edom: the Day of Yahweh is coming! This great day of Yahweh's sovereign intervention militarily and politically, long expected by the prophets (cf. Amos 5:18–20; Isa 13:6–13; Jer 46:10; Zeph 3:8; cf. G. von Rad, "The Origin of the Concept of the Day of the Lord,"

JSS 4 [1959] 97–108; D. Stuart, "The Sovereign's Day of Conquest," *BASOR*
221 [1976] 159–64), will be the occasion for Edom's defeat. Edom's fate is
not isolated but is caught up in a general judgment action "against all the
nations" (עַל־כָּל הַגּוֹיִם) which, like all proper judgments, will reverse evil
and establish good on a worldwide scale (cf. Isa 13:11, also within a foreign-
nation oracle). Thus what Edom deserves it will get, much in the manner of
lex talionis (cf. Lev 24:20; Deut 19:21), the punishment fitting the crime precisely. The very things Edom had done to others, thus incurring God's wrath
(as also in Joel 3:4–8, etc.), will now be done to Edom. The opportunistic
attacker and spoiler will itself be attacked and despoiled.

16 This triplet builds analogically on the contrast of drinking and drunkenness. Drinking may be pleasant, refreshing, desirable. Drunkenness is excessive, destructive, even potentially fatal. The Edomites had figuratively drunk
at Jerusalem ("my holy mountain," הַר קָדְשִׁי; cf. Isa 11:9; Ezek 20:40) in
exultant victory when Jerusalem fell to Babylon in 586 B.C. Edomites probably
did not plunder Jerusalem itself, but their seizing of Judean territory and
their plunder of southeast Judean cities is symbolized by the reference to
drinking. Now, however, *all* the nations (cf. v 15), including Edom, will drink
continually as Yahweh in effect gets them ever drunker until they die in a
stupor ("become as if they had never been"). On this theme of the nations'
drinking their punishment, see, e.g., Isa 51:17–23; Jer 25:15–29; Ezek 23:31–
34; Hab 2:16.

17 Although Edom's mountain fastnesses will have been breached and
destroyed, Judah's mountain sanctuary ("holy place," קֹדֶשׁ) will be a place
of perpetual escape (פְּלֵיטָה) from harm. It will also belong once again exclusively to Israel, "the family of Jacob." Any Edomites and any other foreign
occupiers and interlopers, who pushed Israelites out of the city, will themselves
be driven off. In effect all of Jerusalem, not just the temple area, will become
a holy place where only righteous people, by reason of God's regulations of
purity, are entitled to dwell (cf. Lev 21:11–23; Num 19:20). On Israel's homeland in general and Jerusalem in particular as God's sanctuary, cf. Exod
15:17; Ps 78:69.

18 Destruction by fire is a divine punishment (type 10; cf. Deut 28:24;
32:22) and the Israelites are here depicted metaphorically as its means of
application. In the first couplet, thoroughly synonymous, Joseph, Jacob's most
prominent son, parallels Jacob via "list" parallelism (see S. Geller, *Parallelism
in Early Biblical Poetry*, HSM 20 [Missoula, MT: Scholars Press, 1979] 35,
301–5) rather than as a means of emphasizing the northern tribes.

The triplet that concludes the verse identifies the object of the fire, Esau,
and stresses the completeness of its destruction, like burned-up stubble (קַשׁ)
and without survivors (שָׂרִיד). The interjection כִּי יְהוָה דִּבֵּר "For Yahweh
has spoken" cannot be judged a statement of closure as if v 19 began a new
section, since its placement internally in oracles is routine (e.g., Isa 1:2; Jer
13:15).

19 Repossession of the promised land is a basic sort of restoration promise
(type 7; cf. Deut 30:3–5). The remaining verses of the book are concerned
with retaking the land. In the first couplet of v 19, the predictions of repossess-
sion involve the capture of Edomite territory by Negebite Judeans, whose

territory had been encroached on by "Esau," and repossession of the western inland lowlands (Shephelah), long in Philistine hands, by the Israelites who lived there.

The second couplet looks forward to a general repossession of the north-central hill country (Ephraim . . . Samaria) and, depending on the state of the text, of the Transjordan territory of Gilead by Benjamites. This latter claim is odd, contrasting with any sort of traditional tribal territorial claim (cf. Josh 18:11–28), and thus the text is suspect. More likely the original said something about Israelites gaining back parts of Benjamin and Gilead, long incorporated into Assyrian and then Babylonian administrative districts (2 Kgs 17:24).

20 Whereas v 19 may refer either to returned exiles or to those oppressed but not deported, v 20 clearly concentrates on the blessings awaiting returnees, who will in general reoccupy the promised land (Canaan) to its ideal extreme limits. Zarephath, just south of Sidon, was at this time part of Phoenician territory, but the prediction of Israelite control so far north on the coastal plain fulfills the original northwest border assignment (Joshua 19:28, "greater Sidon"; cf. 1 Kgs 17:9, "Zarephath of Sidon") achieved only in David's reign. Zarephath was traditionally inhabited by at least some Israelites, judging from 1 Kgs 17:7–24.

The second couplet encourages hope that Jerusalemites exiled to Sepharad will return to occupy southern Judah. Sepharad's location is a matter of speculation (see D. Neiman, "Sefarad: The Name of Spain," *JNES* 22 [1963] 128–32). The likely site, however, is Assyrian "Saparda" / Persian "Sparda," a country south of Lake Urmia, north and west of Media (*NBD*, 1160). In other words, exiled Judeans will come from even beyond the far reaches of the Babylonian empire, miraculously brought back by Yahweh, driving the Edomites out of their encroachments!

21 The prophecy's concluding triplet makes three points: (1) Jerusalem will again be the center of refuge and prosperity for the exiles; (2) Jerusalem (as the capital of Judah) will control a subdued Edom in the restoration era; (3) Yahweh will be acknowledged supreme. The third point is worthy of special comment. Israelite / Judean heterodoxy saw Yahweh as merely one god among many (2 Kgs 23:4–15; Ezek 8:6–16). Obadiah envisions the day when such polytheistic error will have been removed and pure acknowledgment of Yahweh as God alone will prevail (cf. Isa 49:26; 54:10).

Explanation

The Edomites played such a consistently adversarial role in Israel's history that the prophetic literary category of "oracles against foreign nations" was bound to include predictions of judgments against Edom. Edom, indeed, becomes in the OT a kind of metonymy for "hostile nations." Israel's estranged brother nation opposed its kin at every possible point from the time of the exodus (Num 20:14–21) until the Babylonian conquest of Judah and Jerusalem, which it welcomed and abetted. Therefore, though Edom and Israel were not intrinsic enemies (Deut 23:7–8), Edomite crimes against God's people could not go unpunished. Edom's self-aggrandizement at the expense of Judean territory in the wake of Judah's 586 B.C. collapse was particularly galling. Obadiah's message about Edom follows generally the lines of other oracles against Edom, which themselves are rather typical of such oracles in general. It predicts Edom's conquest as a result of its offenses, and looks forward to the era when a resurgent Israel will be resettled and exalted and Edom put in its place under Jerusalem's sovereignty. The currently helpless Judeans, now unable to prevent Edomite crimes against them, will then subdue Edom and, with God's help and in loyalty to his covenant, reap the blessings of the new age.

Obadiah's message, like all prophecies touching on the new age, has a Christian implication. Though it is surely about Israel and Edom, it is at the same time, more generally, about God's people and the worldly powers opposed to God. It may be objected that such an interpretation involves the redefinition of terms (Israel = God's people; Edom = the world). To understand these terms and their synonyms on such a plane has ample justification biblically. By way of analogy, what Luke's gospel conveys by Jesus' references to the βασιλεία "kingdom" is conveyed instead in the book of Acts by the term ἐκκλησία "church." Or, what the OT normally indicates by ישׂראל "Israel" Paul routinely connotes by ἐκκλησία "church." "Babylon" can mean "Rome" (e.g., Rev 18:2, 10, 21), "Egypt" can stand for foreign captivity in general (Deut 28:68), "Jerusalem" is equated with "heaven" (e.g., Heb 12:22), "exile" with earthly trials (1 Pet 1:17), etc.

The Christian, therefore, will see in Obadiah's prophecy not merely a description of certain political realities and hopes from the sixth century B.C. in Palestine, but also the more general reality and hope of God's intervention on behalf of his people to rescue them from helplessness in the face of mortal danger, and to guarantee them a bright future of reward for their faithfulness (1 Pet 4:12–14). The success of earthly powers arrayed against God's purposes can be only temporary, and the ultimate victory of God's people is assured.

Jonah

Jonah

Bibliography

COMMENTARIES

Aalders, G. C. *Obadja en Jona.* Kampen: Kok, 1958. **Ackroyd, P. R.** *I & II Chronicles, Ezra, Nehemiah, Ruth, Jonah, I & II Maccabees.* Mowbray's Mini Commentaries 7. Oxford: Mowbrays, 1970. **Ahl, R.** *Fragender Glaube. Jeremia-Koheleth-Jona.* Meitinger Kleinschriften, 30. Freising: Kyrios, 1973. **Allen, Leslie C.** *The Books of Joel, Obadiah, Jonah and Micah.* NICOT 5. Grand Rapids: Eerdmans, 1975. **Arbuckle, N.** "Jonah." *The New Catholic Commentary on Holy Scripture.* London / New York. 705–7. **Banks, W. L.** *Jonah: The Reluctant Prophet.* Everyman's Bible Commentary Series. Chicago: Moody Press, 1966. **Bird, T. E.** *The Book of Jonah.* Westminster Version of the Sacred Scriptures. London / New York: Longmans, Green and Co., 1938. **Brockington, L. H.** "Jonah." *PCB.* 626–29. **Cohn, G. H.** *Das Buch Jona im Lichte der biblischen Erzählkunst.* Assen: Van Gorcum, 1969. **Deissler, A.,** and **M. Delcor.** *Les petits prophètes I: Osée, Jonas.* Paris: Letouzey & Ane, 1961–64. **Delcor, M.** "Jonas." *Les petits prophètes 8.1.* La Sainte Bible, 1961. **Dollar, J.** *Das Buch Jona.* Vienna and Leipzig: 1912. **Duval, Y.-M.** *Le Livre de Jonas dans la litterature chrétienne grecque et latine, sources et influence du Commentaire sur Jonas de saint Jerome.* Paris: Études augustiniennes, 1973. ———, ed., *Jerome. Commentaire sur Jonas.* Sources Chrétiennes 323. Paris: Éditions du Cerf, 1985. **Feuillet, A.** *Le livre de Jonas.* Paris: Éditions du Cerf, 1966. **Fichtner, J.** *Obadja, Jona, Micha.* Stuttgarter Bibelhelfte. Stuttgart, Calwer, 1957. **Fretheim, T. E.** *The Message of Jonah: A Theological Commentary.* Minneapolis: Augsburg, 1977. **Glaze, A. J., Jr.** "Jonah." *Broadman Bible Commentary.* Ed. C. J. Allen. Nashville: Broadman Press, 1972. 152–82. **Jacob, E., C.-A. Keller,** and **S. Amsler.** *Osee, Joël, Abdias, Jonas, Amos.* Neuchâtel: Delachaux et Niestlé, 1965. **Knight, G. A. F.** *Ruth and Jonah.* London: SCM Press, 1966. **Licht, J.** "Liber Jonae." *Encyclopaedia Biblica Institutum Bialik* 3 (1968) 608–13. **Livings, H.** *Jonah.* Leeds: John Paul the Preacher's Press, 1974. **Loretz, O.** *Gotteswort und menschliche Erfahrung: eine Auslegung der Bücher Jona, Rut, Hohelied und Qohelet.* Freiburg: Herder, 1963. **Martin, H.** *The Prophet Jonah: His Character and Mission to Nineveh.* The Geneva Series of Commentaries. London: Banner of Truth Trust, 1958. **McGowran, J. C.** "Jonah." *The Jerome Biblical Commentary.* Ed. R. Brown et al. Englewood Cliffs, NJ: Prentice Hall, 1968. 1:633–37. **Myers, J. M.** *The Book of Jonah.* Richmond, VA: Knox, 1959. **Naastepad, T. J. M.** *Jona: Verklaring van een Bijbelgedeelte.* Kampen: Kok, 1975. **Nishimura, T.** *Yona-sho chukai* [A Commentary on the Book of Jonah]. Tokyo: Nippon Kirisutokyōdan Shuppankyoku, 1975. **Perowne, T. T.** *Obadiah and Jonah.* Cambridge: Cambridge UP, 1883. **Rinaldi, G.** *I Profeti minori: Osea; Giole; Abdia; Giona.* La Sacra Bibbia. Rome: Marietti, 1960. **Robinson, D. W. B.** "Jonah." *NBC Revised.* Ed. D. Guthrie et al. London / Grand Rapids: Intervarsity / Eerdmans, 1970. 746–51. **Rudolph, W.** *Jona.* Tr. K. Galling. Tübingen: Mohr, 1970. ———. *Joel, Amos, Obadja, Jona.* KAT 13.2. Gütersloh: Mohn, 1971. **Schüngel-Straumann, H.** *Israel, und die andern? Zefanja, Nahum, Habakuk, Obadja, Jona.* Stuttgarter kleiner Kommentar: AT 15. Stuttgart: Verlag Katholisches Bibelwerk, 1975. **Smart, J. D.** and **W. Scarlett.** *The Book of Jonah.* IB 6:869–94. **Tatford, F. A.** *A Prophet Who Deserted: An Exposition of the Book of Jonah.* Twentieth Century Series. Eastbourne: Prophetic Witness, 1974. **Vanoni, G.** *Das Buch Jona: literar- und formkritische Untersuchung.* ArbTextSprAT 1. St. Ottilien: Eos-Verlag, 1978. **Velltuti-Zati, D.** *Il sacro libro di Giona.* Siena: 1916. **Verger, A.** and **A. M. Raggi.** "Giona." *Bibliotheca Sanctorum.* Instituto Giovanni XXIII nella Pontificia Universita lateranese 6. Rome, 1965. **Wade, G. W.** *The Books of the Prophets Micah,*

Obadiah, Joel and Jonah. Westminster Commentaries. London: Methuen and Co., 1925. **Watts, J. D. W.** *The Books of Joel, Obadiah, Jonah, Nahum, Habakkuk, and Zephaniah.* The Cambridge Bible Commentary. Cambridge: Cambridge University Press, 1975. **Weiser, A.** *Die Propheten Hosea, Joel, Amos, Obadja, Jona, Micha, übersetzt und erklärt.* ATD 24. Göttingen: Vandenhoeck & Ruprecht, 1974. **Wolff, H. W.** *Obadja und Jona.* BKAT 14 / 3. Neukirchen-Vluyn: Neukirchener Verlag, 1977. Eng. trans. Hermeneia, 1986.

BOOKS AND DISSERTATIONS

Aalders, G. C. *The Problem of the Book of Jonah.* London: Tyndale, 1948. **Abraham, A.** *Die Schiffsterminologie des Alten Testament.* 1914. **Allenbach, J.** *La figure de Jonas aux trois premiers siècles.* Diss. Strasbourg, 1970. **Andersen, F. I.,** and **A. D. Forbes.** *A Linguistic Concordance of Ruth and Jonah.* The Computer Bible 9. Wooster, OH: Biblical Research Associates, 1976. **Bacharach, J.** *Jonah Ben ʾAmittai wᵉEliyahu.* Jerusalem, 1959. **Barsotti, D.** *Meditazione sul libro di Giona.* Bibbia e liturgia 7. Brescia: Querinova, 1967. **Ben-Chorin, S.** *Die Antwort des Jona: Zum Gestaltwandel Israels.* Hamburg, 1956, ²1966. **Bergant, D.** *What Are They Saying about Wisdom Literature?* New York: Paulist Press, 1984. **Bickerman, E. J.** *Four Strange Books of the Bible.* New York, 1967. 1–49. **Bird, T. E.** *The Book of Jonah.* Westminster Version of the Sacred Scriptures. London, 1938. **Bowers, R. H.** *The Legend of Jonah.* The Hague: Martinus Nijhoff, 1971. **Bull, G. T.** *The City and the Sign: An Interpretation of the Book of Jonah.* Grand Rapids: Baker, 1972. **Cagneaux, J.** *Critique du language chez les prophètes d'Israël.* Paris: Éditions du Cerf, 1976. **Canto, R.** *Sapienciales y midras.* Madrid: Euramerica, 1966. **Cohn, G. H.** *Das Buch Jona im Lichte der biblischen Erzählkunst.* SSN 12. Assen: 1965. **DeHann, M. R.** *Jonah, Fact or Fiction?* Grand Rapids: Zondervan, 1957. **Duval, Y. M.** *Le livre de Jonas dans la littérature chrétienne grecque et latine.* Paris, 1973. **Edwards, R. A.** *The Sign of Jonah in the Theology of the Evangelists and Q.* SBT 2.18. London: SCM, 1971. **Ellul, J.** *The Judgment of Jonah.* Tr. G. W. Bromiley. Grand Rapids: Eerdmans, 1971. **Erbt, W.** *Elia, Elisa, Jona.* Leipzig, 1907. **Erlich, A. B.** *Randglossen zur hebräischen Bibel: textkritisches, sprachliches und sachliches.* Vol 5. Hildesheim: G. Olms, 1968. **Exbrayat, I.** *Témoinage et contestation. L'acualité du livre de Jonas.* Lausanne: Ligne pour la lecture de la Bible, 1977. **Fairbairn, P.** *Jonah: His Life, Character and Mission.* Grand Rapids: Kregel, 1964. **Fáj, A.** *Jonas-tema a vilagirada-lomban.* Rome, 1977. **Friedrichsen P.** *Kritische Übersicht der verschiedenen Ansichten von dem Buche Jonas nebst einem neuen Versuch über dasselbe.* 2d ed. Leipzig, 1841. **Fretheim, T.** *The Message of Jonah.* Minneapolis: Augsburg, 1977. **Good, E. M.** *Irony in the Old Testament.* Sheffield: Almond Press, 1981. 39–55. **Gordis, R.** *The Word and the Book: Studies in Biblical Language and Literature.* New York: KTAV, 1976. **Grotein, S. D.** *Omanut has-sippor bam-miqra.* Jerusalem: Jewish Agency, 1956. **Gunkel, H.** *Ausgewählte Psalmen.* Göttingen, 1904. 239–46. **Harder, B.** *Erlebnisse eines Sehers.* Gladbeck, 1955. **Hart-Davies, D. E.** *Jonah: Prophet and Patriot.* London: C. J. Thynne and Jarvis, 1925. **Hay, W. C.** *The Wideness of God's Mercy. A Study in the Book of Jonah.* Books of the Bible Series 6. Edinburgh, 1952. **Hillis, D. W.** *Jonah Speaks Again: A Dimension Guide on the Book of Jonah.* Grand Rapids: Baker, 1973. **Hoffman, P.** *Jonastegnet.* Profeti og profeter 1. Fredericia: Lohse, 1972. **Jeremias, J.** *Die Reue Gottes.* BibS 65. Neukirchen-Vluyn: Neukirchener Verlag, 1975. 98–107. **Jochurns, H.** *Von den Herrn geruten: die Botschaft des Propheten Jona* Aktuelle Fragen 21. Wuppertal: Verlag und Schriftmission der Evangelische Gesellschaft für Deutschland, 1971. **Kennedy, J. H.** *Studies in the Book of Jonah.* Nashville: Broadman, 1958. **Knight, G. A. F.** *Ruth and Jonah: The Gospel in the Old Testament.* London: SCM Press, 1966. **Levine, E.** *The Aramaic Version of Jonah.* Jerusalem: Jerusalem Academic Press, 1975. **Licht, J.** *Storytelling in the Bible.* Jerusalem: Magnes, 1978. **Limburg, J.** "Amazing Grace." *Old Stories for a New Time.* Atlanta: John Knox, 1983. **Lowy, M.** *Über das*

Buch Jona. 1892. **Magonet, J.** *Form and Meaning: Studies in Literary Techniques in the Book of Jonah.* Bern / Frankfurt: Herbert Lang / Peter Lang, 1976. **Maillot, A.** *Jonas ou les farces de Dieu.* Neuchâtel: Delachaux et Niestlé. **Marcus, J. O.** *Prophet Jonah.* Tr. A. P. Slabey. Medford, WI: V. Uhri, 1975. **Martin, A. D.** *The Prophet Jonah: The Book and the Sign.* London / New York: Longmans, Green and Co., 1926. **Mayer, F.** *Der Grund der Propheten. Vol. II: Betrachtungen über die Propheten Jona, Micha und Maleachi.* Metzingen: Ernst Franz, 1974. **Nishimura, T.** *A Thematic Study of the Book of Jonah.* In *FS M. Sekine,* ed. S. Arai. Tokyo: Yamamoto Shoten, 1976. 260–77. **Olivier, J.** *Les metamorphoses de Jonas.* Paris: Éditions du Cerf, 1968. **Parrot, A.** *Ninive et l'AT.* Neuchâtel, 1953. **Pytel, J.** *L'hospitalité dans l'Écriture Sainte.* Diss. Academie Theologie Catholicae. 1975. **Rad, G. von.** *Der Prophet Jona.* Nürnberg: 1950. [= *Gottes Wirken in Israel.* Vorträge zum Alten Testament. Neukirchen-Vluyn: Neukirchener Verlag, 1974. 65–78.] **Ronner, M.** *Das Buch Jona: Eine Auslegung.* Zürich, 1947. **Rosenthal, A.** *Das Buch Jonah metrisch übersetzt.* 1889. **Schmidt, H.** *Jona, eine Untersuchung zur vergleichenden Religionsgeschichte.* FRLANT 9. Göttingen, 1907. **Schmidt, L.** *De Deo: Studien zur Literarkritik und Theologie des Buches Jona, des Gesprächs zwischen Abraham und Jahwe in Gen. 18, 22 ff. und Hiob 1.* BZAW 143. Berlin / New York: DeGruyter, 1976. **Sessole, P.** *La salvezza dei popoli nel libro di Giona: Studio sul particolarismo ed univeralism salvifico.* Diss. Pontifical University Urbaniana, 1977. **Simpson, W.** *The Jonah Legend.* 1899. **Snaith, N.** *The Book of Jonah.* London, 1945. ———. *Notes on the Hebrew Text of Jonah.* London, 1945. **Somda Metwole, J. B.** *Le message du livre de Jonas á la lumie du genre littéraire.* Rome: G. Bernini, 1974. **Steffen, U.** *Das Mysterium von Tod und Auferstehung: Formen und Wandlungen des Jona-motivs.* Göttingen: Vandenhoeck & Ruprecht, 1963. **Stollberg, L.** *Jona.* Diss. Halle, 1927. **Tandrup, H.** *Der Prophet Jona.* Berlin, 1960. **Trible, P.** *Studies in the Book of Jonah.* Diss. Columbia University, 1963. **Ungern-Sternberg, R. F. von.** *Der Tag der Gerichtes Gottes: Die Propheten Habakuk, Zephania, Jona, Nahum.* Botschaft des AT 23 / 4. Stuttgart: Calwer Verlag, 1960. **Vanoni, G.** *Das Buch Jona. Literar- und formkritische Untersuchung.* Münchener Universitätsschriften. ArbTextSprAT 7. St. Ottilien: Eos Verlag, 1978. **Vawter, B.** *Job & Jonah: Questioning the Hidden God.* New York: Paulist Press, 1983. **Weinreb, F.** *Das Buch Jonah. Der Sinn des Buches Jonah nach der ältesten jüdischen Überlieferung.* Zürich: Origo Verlag, 1970. **Wittchow, H.** *Gott bietet Schach—und es gibt kein Remis: Jona, unser Zeitgenosse.* Linienbuch 21. Wuppertal: R. Brockhaus, 1971. **Witzenrath, H.** *Das Buch Jona. Eine literaturwissenschaftliche Untersuchung.* ArbTextSprAT 6. St. Ottilien: Eos Verlag, 1978. **Wolf, B.** *Die Geschichte des Propheten Jona.* 1897. **Wolff, H. W.** *Die Bibel—Gotteswort oder Menschenwort? Dargestellt am Buch Jona.* Neukirchen-Vluyn: Neukirchener Verlag, 1959. ———. *Jonah: Church in Revolt.* St. Louis: Clayton Publishing House, 1978. ———. *Studien zum Jonabuch.* BSt 47. Neukirchen-Vluyn: Neukirchener Verlag, 1975. **Wright, W.** *Jonah in Chaldean, Syriac, Aethiopic and Arabic.* London, 1857. **Zimmerman, F.** *Biblical Books Translated from the Aramaic.* New York: KTAV, 1975.

ARTICLES

Abel, F. M. "Le culte de Jonas en Palestine." *JPOS* 12 (1922) 175–83. **Abramowitz, C.** *"Maftir Jonah."* DD 14 (1985) 3–10. **Abramsky, S.** "Jonah's Alienation and Return." *BMik* 24 (1979) 370–95. [Heb.] ———. "Jonah ben 'Amittai." *Gazith* 17 (1959) 5–10. **Ackerman, J. S.** "Satire and Symbolism in the Song of Jonah." In *Tradition and Transformation.* 1981. 213–46. **Ackroyd, P. R.** "Recent Foreign Theological Literature: The Old Testament." *ExpTim* 91 (1979) 8–13. **Alexander, T. D.** "Jonah and Genre." *TynB* 36 (1985) 35–59. **Allenbach, J.** "La figure de Jonas dans les textes preconstantiniens ou l'histoire de l'exégèse au secours de l'iconographie." In *La Bible et les Pères,* ed. A. Benoit. Paris, 1971. 97–112. **Alonso Diaz, J.** "Dificultades que plantea la interpretacion de la narración de Jonas." *EstBib* 18 (1959) 357–74. ———. "Paralelos entre la narración del libro de Jonás y la parábola del Hijo Pródigo." *Bib* 40 (1959) 632–40. **Alonso, J.** "Lección Teológica del Libro de Jonás." *Miscelánea Antonio Perez Goyena. Estudios Eclesiásticos* 35 (1960) 79–83. **Andrew, M. E.** "Gattung and Intention of the Book of Jonah." *Orita* 1 (1967) 13–18, 75–85. **Avan-Selms, A.** "Some Geographical Remarks on Jonah." *OTWSA* 14 (1971) 83–92. **Aviezer, N.** "The Book of Jonah: An Ethical Confrontation between God and Prophet." *DD* 14 (1985) 11–15, 50. **Bacher, S.** "The Book of Jonah—The Author vs. His Hero." *BMik* 28 (1982 / 83) 39–43. [Heb.] **Badini, G.** "La lecture des livres d'Osée et de Jonas au cours secondaire. Opportunité et methode." *Lumen Vitae* 20 (1965) 674–90. **Bardtke, H.** "Der Erweckungsgedanke in der exilisch-nachexilischen Literatur des Alten Testaments." *ZAW* Beiheft 77 (1958) 9–24. **Barilier, R.** "Jonas lu pour aujourd'hui." *RR* 32 (1981) 49–87. **Ben-Yosef, I. A.** "Jonas and the Fish as a Folk Motif." *Semitics* 7 (1980) 102–17. **Berlin, A.** "A Rejoinder to J. A. Miles, Jr., with Some Observations on the Nature of Prophecy." *JQR* 66 (1975) 227–35. **Bickerman, E. J.** "Les deux erreurs du prophète Jonas." *RHPR* 45 (1965) 232–64. **Biser, E.** "Zum frühchristlichen Verständnis des Buches Jona." *BK* 16 (1961) 19–21. **Blank, S.** "The Dawn of Our Responsibility." In *Prophetic Thought*, ed. S. Blank. Cincinnati: Hebrew Union College Press, 1977. 35–43. ———. " 'Doest Thou Well To Be Angry?' A Study in Self-Pity." *HUCA* 26 (1955) 29–41. **Böhme, W.** "Die Komposition des Buches Jona." *ZAW* 7 (1887) 224–84. **Boman, T.** "Jahve og Elohim i Jonaboken." *NorTT* 37 (1936) 159–64. **Bonner, C.** "The Story of Jonah on a Magical Amulet." *HTR* 41 (1948) 31–37. **Bratsiotis, P. I.** "Ionas." *TEE* 7 (1965) 96–98. **Brenner, A.** "The Language of Jonah as an Index of Its Date." *BMik* 24 (1979) 396–405. [Heb.] **Budde, K.** "Vermutungen zum 'Midrasch des Buches der Könige.' " *ZAW* 12 (1892) 37–151. [On Jonah, pp. 40–43.] **Burrows, M.** "The Literary Category of the Book of Jonah." *Translating and Understanding the Old Testament: Essays in Honor of H. G. May*, ed. H. T. Frank and W. L. Reed. New York: Harper, 1970. 80–107. **Carlsen, B. H.** "Jonah in Judeo-Persian." *Acta Iranica* 12 (1977) 13–26. **Cazeaux, J.** "Littérature ancienne et recherché de 'structures.' " *Revue des Études Augustiniennes* 18 (1972) 287–92. **Cheyne, T. K.** "Jonah." *Encyclopedia Biblica* (1901) 2565–71. **Childs, B.** "The Canonical Shape of the Book of Jonah." In *Biblical and Near Eastern Studies: Essays in Honor of William Sanford LaSor*, ed. G. Tuttle. Grand Rapids: Eerdmans, 1978. ———. "Jonah: A Study in Old Testament Hermeneutics." *SJT* 11 (1958) 53–61. **Christensen, D.** "Andrzej Panufnik and the Structure of the Book of Jonah: Icons, Music and Literary Art." *JETS* 28 (1985) 133–40. **Cintas, P.** "Tarsis—Tartessos—Gades." *Sem* 16 (1966) 5–37. **Clements, R.** "The Purpose of the Book of Jonah." *VTSup* 28 (1975) 16–28. **Cohen, A. D.** "The Tragedy of Jonah." *Judaism* 21 (1972) 164–75. **Criado, R.** "Jonas." *EBib* 4 (1965) 580–89. **Cummings, C.** "Jonah and the Ninevites." *TBT* 21 (1983) 369–75. **Daube, D.** "Jonah: A Reminiscence." *JJS* 35 (1984) 36–43. **Deed, D. M.** "Jonah." *Scr* (1968) 26–31. **dell'Oca, R.** "El Libro de Jonas." *RevistB* 26 (1964) 129–39. **Dickstra, F. N. M.** "Jonah and Patience: The Psychology of a Prophet." *EnglSt* 55 (1974) 205–17. **Dijkema, F.** "Het Boek Jona." *Nieuw Theologisch Tijdschrift* 25 (1936) 338–47. **Döller, J.** "Verumstellungen im Buche Jona." *Katholik* 35 (1907) 313–17. **Driver, G. R.** "Linguistic and Textual Problems: Minor Prophets II, III." *JTS* 39 (1938) 260–73, 393–405. ———. "Hebrew Notes on Prophets and Proverbs." *JTS* 41 (1940) 162–75. **Duhm, B.** "Anmerkungen zu den Zwölf Propheten." *ZAW* 31 (1911) 81–93, 175–78, 184–88, 200–204. **Duval, Y. M.** "S. Augustin et le Commentaire sur Jonas de S. Jerome." *Revue des Études Augustiniennes* 12 (1966) 9–40. **Eissfeldt, O.** "Amos und Jona in volkstümlicher Überlieferung." *Kleine Schriften zum Alten Testament 4*. Berlin: Evangelische Verlagsanstalt, 1968, 137–42. **Elata-Alster, G.,** and **R. Salmon.** "Eastward and Westward: The Movement of Prophecy and History in the Book of Jonah." *DD* 13 (1984) 16–27. **Ellul, J.** "Le livre de Jonas." *Foi et vie* (1952) 81–84. **Emmerson, G. I.** "Another Look at the Book of Jonah." *ExpTim* 88 (1976) 86–88. **Eybers, J. H.** "The Purpose of the Book of

Jonah." *Theologia Evangelica* 4 (1971) 211–22. **Fáj, A.** "La soluzione logica della falsa profezia di Giona." *BibOr* 18 (1976) 141–49. ———. "The Stoic Features of the 'Book of Jonah.' " *AION* 34 (1974) 309–45. **Feuillet, A.** "Le livre de Jonas." In *Études d'exégèse et de théologie biblique.* Paris, 1975. 395–433. ———. "Les sources du livre de Jonas." *RB* 54 (1947) 161–86. ———. "Le sense du livre de Jonas." *RB* 54 (1947) 340–61. **Fränkel, L.** " 'And His Mercy Rules Over All His Works.' On the Meaning of the Book of Jonah." *Ma'yanot* 9 (1967) 193–207. [Heb.] **Fransen, I.** "Le livre de Jonas." *BVC* 40 (1961) 33–39. **Frantzen, P.** "Das 'Zeichen des Jonas.' " *TG* 67 (1967) 61–66. **Fredman, N.** "Jonah and Nineveh: The Tragedy of Jonah." *DD* 12 (1983) 4–14. **Fretheim, T.** "Jonah and Theodicy." *ZAW* 90 (1978) 227–37. **Garcia Cordero, M.** "El libro de Jonás, una novela didáctica?" *CB* 16 (1959) 214–20. **Garitte, G.** "Las version arménienne du sermon de S. Ephrem sur Jonas." *Revue des Études Arméniennes* 6 (1969) 23–43. **Gemser, B.** "Die Humor van die OuT." *Hervormde Teologiese Studies* 8 (1951) 49–63. **Gevaryahu, H.** "The Universalism of the Book of Jonah." *DD* 10 (1981) 20–27. **Glasson, T.** "Nahum and Jonah." *ExpTim* 81 (1969–70) 54–55. **Glück, J. J.** "A Linguistic Criterion of the Book of Jonah." *OTWSA* 10 (1967) 34–41. **Goiten, S. D.** "Some Observations on Jonah." *JPOS* 17 (1937) 63–77. **Goldberg, A.** "Jonas in der jüdischen Schriftauslegung." *BK* 17 (1962) 17–18. **Goldbrunner, J.** "Die Nacht-meerfahrt des Jona—Tiefenpsychologische Erwägungen zu Jona und seinem Fisch." *BK* 27 (1972) 68–70. **Goldman, M.** "Was the Book of Jonah Originally Written in Aramaic?" *AusBR* 3 (1953) 49–50. **Goodhart, S.** "Prophecy, Sacrifice and Repentance in the Book of Jonah." *Semeia* 33 (1985) 43–63. **Grünewald, H. J.** "Das Buch Jona." *Udim* 2 (1971) 69–82. **Guilmin, S.** "Jona." *ETR* 61 (1986) 189–93. **Gunkel, H.** "Jonabuch." RGG² 3:366–69. **Haller, E.** "Die Erzählung von dem Propheten Jona." *Theologische Existenz heute* 65 (1958) 5–54. **Halpern, B.** and **R. E. Friedman.** "Composition and Paronomasia in the Book of Jonah." *Hebrew Annual Review* 4 (1980) 79–92. **Hart-Davies, D.** "The Book of Jonah in the Light of Assyrian Archeology." *Journal of the Transactions of the Victoria Institute* 67 (1937) 230–49. **Hauser, A. J.** "Jonah: In Pursuit of the Dove." *JBL* 104 (1985) 21–27. **Heemrood, J.** "Jonas und die Heiden." *Das Heilige Land* 12 (1959) 33–35. **Helberg, J. L.** "Is Jonah in His Failure a Representative of the Prophets?" *OTWSA* 10 (1967) 41–51. **Hernandel, C.** "Temas inciaticos en el libro de Jonas." *Anales Valentinos* 1, ext. (1975) 271–86. **Herrman, L.** "L'Histoire de Jonas et l'antiquité?" *Grazer Beiträge* 1 (1973) 149–55. **Heuschen, J.** "L'interprétation du livre de Jonas." *Revue Ecclésiastique Liège* 35 (1948) 141–59. **Holbert, J.** "'Deliverance Belongs to Yahweh!': Satire in the Book of Jonah." *JSOT* 21 (1981) 59–81. **Howston, J.** "The Sign of Jonah." *SJT* 15 (1962) 288–304. **Jansen, H. L.** "Har Jonaboken en enhetlig opbygning en en bestemt hovedtendens?" *NorTT* 37 (1936) 145–58. **Jensen, P.** "Das Jonas-Problem." *Deutsche Literaturzeitung* 28 (1907) 2629–36. **Jepsen, A.** "Anmerkungen zum Buche Jona." *Wort—Gebot—Glaube.* FS W. Eichrodt. Zürich: Zwingli Verlag, 1970. 297–305. ———. "Kleine Beiträge zum Zwölfprophetenbuch." *ZAW* 56 (1938) 85–100. **Jeremias, J.** "Ionas." *TDNT* 3:406–10. **Junker, H.** "Die Erforschung der literarischen Arten und ihre Bedeutung für die Auslegung der Hl. Schrift." *TTZ* 13 (1964) 129–44. ———. "Die religiöse Bedeutung des Buches Jona." *Pastoralblätter* 41 (1940) 108–14. **Kaiser, O.** "Wirklichkeit, Möglichkeit und Vorurteil: Ein Beitrag zum Verständnis des Buches Jona." *EvT* 33 (1973) 91–103. **Keller, C.** "Jonas. Le portrait d'un prophète." *TZ* 21 (1965) 329–40. **Kidner, F. D.** "The Distribution of Divine Names in Jonah." *Tyndale Bulletin* 21 (1970) 126–28. **Knoch, O.** "Das Zeichen des Jonas." *BK* 17 (1962) 15–16. **Kohler, K.** "The Original Form of the Book of Jonah." *Theological Review* 16 (1879) 139–44. **Komlós, O.** "Jonah Legends." In *Études orientales presenté à Paul Hirschler.* Paris, 1950. 41–61. **Kopp, C.** "Das Jonagrab in Maschhad." *Das Heilige Land* 92 (1960) 17–21. **Korman, E.** "The Prophet Jonah and the Destruction of Nineveh." *Morijah* 13.1 (1972) 51–58. [Heb.] **Kraeling, E.** "The Evolution of the Story of Jonah." In *Hommages à André Dupont-Sommer*, ed. A. Cacquot and M. Philonenko. Paris: Adrien-Maisonneuve, 1971. 305–18. **Kriel, J.** "Jonah—The Story of a Whale or a Whale of a Story?" *Theologia Evangelica* 18 (1985) 9–17. **Kuhl, C.** "Die Wiederaufnahme—ein literarkritisches Prinzip?" *ZAW* 64 (1952) 1–11. **Lacocque, P.-E.** "Desacralizing Life and Its Mystery: The Jonah Complex Revisited." *Journal of Psychology and Theology* 10 (1982) 113-19. **Lamb, F. J.** "The Book of Jonah." *BSac* 81 (1924) 152–69. **Landes, G. M.** "Jonah." *IDBSup*, 488–91. ———. "Jonah—A Mashal?" In *Israelite Wisdom: Theological and Literary Essays in Honor of Samuel Terrien*, ed. J. G. Gammie et al. Missoula, MT: Scholars Press, 1978. ———. "Linguistic Criteria and the Date of the Book of Jonah." *Eretz-Israel* 16 (1982) 147–70. ———. "The Canonical Approach to Introducing the Old Testament: Prodigy and Problems." *JSOT* 16 (1980) 32–39. ———. "The Kerygma of the Book of Jonah." *Int* 21 (1967) 3–31. **Lawrence, M.** "Ships, Monsters and Jonah." *AJA* 66 (1962) 289–96. **Levine, E.** "Jonah as a Philosophical Book." *ZAW* 96 (1984) 235–45. **Loewen, J. A.** "Some Figures of Speech in Hosea." *BT* 33 (1982) 238–42. **Loretz, O.** "Herkunft und Sinn der Jonaerzählung." *BZ* 5 (1961) 18–29. ———. "Roman und Kurzgeschichte in Israel." In *Wort und Botschaft*, ed. J. Schreiner. Würzburg: Echter Verlag, 1967, 290–307. **Lourido Diaz, R.** "Misericordia divina y universalismo en el libro de Jonas." *Miscelanea de Estudios Arabes y Hebreos Granada* 11.2 (1965) 43–56. **Magnus, P.** "The Book of Jonah." *Hibbert Journal* 16 (1917 / 18) 429–42. **Magonet, J.** "Jüdisch-theologische Beobachtungen zum Buch Jonas." *BibLeb* 13 (1972) 153–72. **Martin-Achard, R.** "Israël et les nations." *Cahiers Théologiques* 42 (1959) 45–48. **Mather, J.** "The Comic Art of the Book of Jonah." *Soundings* 65 (1982) 280–91. **Mayr, J.** "Jonas in Bauche des Fisches." *TPQ* 85 (1932) 829–32. **Merli, D.** "Il segno di Giona." *BibOr* 14 (1972) 61–77. **Merrill, E.** "The Sign of Jonah." *JETS* 23 (1980) 23–30. **Miles, J. A.** "Laughing at the Bible: Jonah as Parody." *JQR* 65 (1974) 168–81. **Monleon, J. de.** "Preface au livre de Jonas." *Itinéraires* 62 (1962) 152. ———. "Suite à l'histoire de Jonas." *Itinéraires* 90 (1965) 110–26. **Mora, V.** "Jonas." *Cahiers Évangile* 36 (1981) 64. **More, J.** "The Prophet Jonah: The Story of an Intrapsychic Process." *American Imago* 27.1 (1970) 3–11. **Morrison, J. H.** "The Missionary Prophet." *ExpTim* 49 (1937–38) 487–89. **Mowinckel, S.** "Efterskrift til pastor Th. Bomans artikkel." *NorTT* 37 (1936) 164–68. **Mozley, F. W.** "Proof of the Historical Truth of the Book of Jonah." *BSac* 81 (1924) 170–200. **Nishimura, T.** "The Conflict of Two Motifs in the Book of Jonah: The Limitation of Prophecy and the Challenge of Wisdom." *Annual of the Japanese Bible Institute* 9 (1983) 3–23. [Japanese.] **Nowell, I.** "The Book of Jonah: Repentance of Conversion." *TBT* 21 (1983) 363–68. **Nüchtern, P.** "Das Buch Jona im evang. Religionsunterricht der fortführenden Schulen." *Deutches Pfarrerblätter Detmold* 66 (1966) 253–56. ———. "Das Buch Jona—seine Botschaft und seine Verwendung im Religionsunterricht." *Das evangelische Erzieher* 18 (1966) 143–56. **Parmentier, R.** "Les mésaventures du Pasteur Jonas." *ETR* 53 (1978) 244–51. **Parrot, A.** "Ninive und das AT." *Bibel und Archäologie* 1 (1955) 111–69. **Payne, D.** "Jonah from the Perspective of Its Audience." *JSOT* 13 (1979) 3–12. **Peifer, C.** "Jonah and Jesus: The Prophet as Sign." *TBT* 21 (1983) 377–83. **Perelmuter, H. G.** "Jonah—Astronaut or Aquanaut?" *TBT* 23 (1985) 259–60. **Pesch, R.** "Zur konzentrischen Struktur von Jona 1." *Bib* 47 (1966) 577–81. **Piser, D.** "The Book of Jonah: An Interpretation." *Central Conference of American Rabbis Journal* 23.1 (1976) 75–81. **Porten, B.** "Baalshamem and the Date of the Book of Jonah." In *De la Torah au Messie. Études d'exégèse et d'herméneutique bibliques offertes à Henri Cazelles*, ed. M. Carrez et al. Paris: Desclée, 1981. **Powers, J.** "Jonah the Dove." *TBT* 23 (1985) 253–58. **Prout, E.** "Beyond Jonah to God." *ResQ* 25 (1982) 139–42. **Qimron, E.** "The Language of Jonah as an Index of the Date of Its Composition." *BMik* 25 (1980) 181–82. [Heb.] **Rofé, A.** "Classes in the Prophetical Stories: Didactic Legend and Parable." *VTSup* 26 (1974) 153–64. **Rosen, R. B.** "The Flight of Jonah." *Shma'tin* 12.43 (1974) 10–14. **Rosenberg, J.** "Jonah and the Prophetic Vocation." *Response* 8 (1974) 23–26. **Rudolph, W.** "Jona." In *Archäologie und Altes Testament. FS K. Galling.*

Tübingen: J. C. B. Mohr, 1970. 233–39. **Russ, R.** "Jona in der Predigt—Exegetisch-homiletische Überlegungen. *BK* 27 (1972) 76–80. **Ryan, P. J.** "Jonah and the Ninevites: The Salvation of Non-Christians according to some Twentieth Century Theologians." *Ghana Bulletin of Theology* 4 (1975) 21–29. **Sauer, A. R., J. Mayer,** and **W. Danker.** "Jonah: Fishin' or Mission." *CurTM* 1 (1974) 43–49. **Schierse, F. J.** "Jona und die Bekehrung Nineves—Die Frage nach der Historizität der Gestalt Jonas." *BK* 27 (1972) 71–72. **Schildenberger, J. B.** "Der Sinn des Buches Jonas." *Erbe und Auftrag* 38 (1962) 93–102. **Schmidt, H.** "Absicht und Entstehungszeit des Buches Jona." *TSK* 79 (1906) 180–99. ———. "Die Komposition des Buches Jona." *ZAW* 25 (1905) 285–310. **Schreiner, J.** "Eigenart, Aufbau, Inhalt und Botschaft des Buches Jonas." *BK* 17 (1962) 8–14. **Schreiner, S.** "Das Buch Jona—ein kritisches Resümee der Geschichte Israels." *Theologische Versuche* 9 (1977) 37–45. **Scott, R. B. Y.** "The Sign of Jonah." *Int* 19 (1965) 16–25. **Segert, S.** "Syntax and Style in the Book of Jonah: Six Simple Approaches to Their Analysis." In *Prophecy: Essays Presented to Georg Fohrer.* 1980. 121–30. **Segre, A.** "Jona, il libro del pentimento." *Rassegna mensile di Israel* 41 (1975) 389–407. (= Miscellanea lateranense, 1975, 254–74) **Shazar, Z.** "The Book of Jonah." *DD* 1 (1972) 4–11. **Shimura, M.** "The Book of Jonah: Its Literary Structure and Theme." *Shingaku* 44 (1982) 141–73. [Japanese.] **Sievers, E.** "Alttestamentliche Miszellen. 2. Die Form des Jonabuches." *Berichte über die Verhandlungen der Sächsischen Akademie der Wissenschaften zu Leipzig, philologische-historische Klasse* 57 (1905) 35–45. **Smart, J.** "Jonah." *IB* 6:869–94. **Soggin, J. A.** "Il 'segno di Giona' nel libro del Profeta Giona." *Lateranum* 48 (1982) 70–74. **Soleh, A.** "The Story of Jonah's Reflective Adventures." *BMik* 24 (1979) 406–20. **Sousek, Z.** "Ninive, Tarsis, a Jonás." *KrR* 32 (1965) 147–48. **Stanton, G. B.** "The Prophet Jonah and His Message." *BSac* 108 (1951) 237–49, 363–76. **Steinmann, J.** "Le livre de la consolation d'Israel." *Lectio divina* 28 (1960) 286–90. **Stek, J. H.** "The Message of the Book of Jonah." *Calvin Theological Journal* 4 (1969) 23–50. **Stendebach, F. J.** "Novelle oder Geschichte?—Die literarische Gattung des Büchleins Jona." *BK* 27 (1972) 66–67. **Stenzel, M.** "Zum Vulgatatext des Canticum Jonae." *Bib* 33 (1952) 356–62. **Stommel, E.** "Zum Problem der frühchristlichen Jonadarstellungen." *JAC* 1 (1958) 112–15. **Sweet, A. M.** "A Theology of Healing." *TBT* 20 (1982) 145–49. **Thoma, A.** "Die Entstehung des Büchleins Jona." *TSK* 84 (1911) 479–502. **Trépanier, B.** "The Story of Jonas." *CBQ* 13 (1951) 8–16. **Unattributed [A Group from Rennes, France].** "An Approach to the Book of Jonah: Suggestions and Questions." *Semeia* 15 (1979) 85–96. **Vaccari, A.** "Il genere letterario del libro di Giona in recenti publicazioni." *Divinitas* 6 (1962) 231–52. **Vischer, W.** "L'evangelo secondo il profeta Giona." *Protestantismo* 16 (1961) 193–204. ———. "L'évangile selon Saint Jonas." *ETR* 50 (1975) 161–73. **Volck, W.** "Jona, Prophet." *Realencyklopädie für protestantische Theologie und Kirche* 9 (1901) 338–40. **Vycichil, W.** "Jonas und der Walfisch." *Muséon* 69 (1956) 183–86. **Weidner, E. F.** "Das Archiv des Mannu–Ki–Assur." *AfO* 6 (1940) 8–46. **Weimar, P.** "Jonapsalm und Jonaerzählung." *BZ* 28 (1984) 43. **Weiss, R.** "On the Book of Jonah." *Mahanaim* 60 (1962) 45–48. [Heb.] ———. "Where Shall I Flee from Your Presence?" *Oroth* 49 (1963) 28–33. [Heb.] **West, M.** "Irony in the Book of Jonah: Audience Identification with the Hero." *Perspectives in Religious Studies* 11 (1984) 233–42. **Wiesmann, H.** "Einige Bemerkungen zum Buche Jona." *Katholik* 38 (1908) 111–25. **Wilson, A. J.** "The Sign of the Prophet Jonah and Its Modern Confirmations." *Princeton Theological Review* 25 (1927) 630–42. **Wilson, R. D.** "The Authenticity of Jonah." *Princeton Theological Review* 16 (1918) 280–98, 430–56. **Winckler, H.** "Zum Buche Jona." *Altorientalische Forschungen* 2.2 (1900) 260–65. **Wiseman, D.** "Jonah's Nineveh." *Tyndale Bulletin* 30 (1979) 29–51. **Wolfe, R. E.** "The Editing of the Twelve." *ZAW* 53 (1935) 90–129. **Wolff, H. W.** "Jonabuch." *RGG*³ 3:853–55. ———. "Jonah—A Drama in Fine Art." *CurTM* 3 (1976) 4–7. ———. "Jonah—The Messenger Who Grumbled." *CurTM* 3 (1976) 141–50. ———. "Jonah—The Messenger Who Obeyed." *CurTM* 3 (1976) 86–97. ———. "Jonah—the Reluctant Messenger." *CurTM* 3 (1976) 8–19. **Wright, A.** "The Literary Genre Midrash." *CBQ* 28 (1966) 105–38, 417–57.

Wrigley, J. E. "An Old Testament Ecumenical Message." *TBT* 25 (1966) 1763–69. **Youtie, H. C.** "A Codex of Jonah: Berl. Sept 18—P.S.I. X, 1164." *HTR* 38 (1945) 195–97. **Ziegler, J.** "Studien zur Verwertung der LXX in Zwölfprophetenbuch." *ZAW* 60 (1944) 107–31. **Zimmerman, D.** "The Story about the Man Jonah." *Nib Hakwrutsah* 12 (1964) 706–14. **Zyl, A. H. van.** "The Preaching of the Book of Jonah." *OTWSA* 14 (1971) 92–104.

Introduction

JONAH THE PROPHET

The person Jonah is one of the best remembered biblical characters. People otherwise largely ignorant of the scripture's content have heard about Jonah and the "whale." In this impression, two significant issues are rather accurately hinted at: (1) the person of Jonah and his *personal* experience are central to the message of the book that bears his name, as contrasted to, for example, Samuel or Amos; (2) the book is written *about* Jonah biographically, rather than reflecting primarily the message he preached, as contrasted to all other OT prophetic books (see also below, *Form and Structure*).

Outside of the book that bears his name, Jonah is mentioned in the OT only once, in 2 Kgs 14:25, which summarizes his prophecies concerning the re-expansion of (northern) Israel under King Jeroboam II (793–753), into territory held for some time by Syria, but traditionally part of Israel's promised land. He is identified as a citizen of Gath-Hepher (a city of moderate size within the tribal borders of Zebulun, probably best identified with Khirbet ez-Zurra, three miles northeast of Nazareth).

His name means "Dove" or "Pigeon" in Hebrew, but there is no evidence whatever that this name bears any special significance in the book (e.g., allegorical), any more than the name of Moses' wife (Zipporah, i.e., "Birdie") does in Exodus, or than Simon Peter's father (Jonah) does in Matt 16:17. Bible names, in general, are only rarely symbolic. From the book of Jonah itself it is evident that Jonah was an ardent nationalist, pro-Israel and anti-foreign; at least, anti-Assyrian. The book also reveals, implicitly, that he was a dedicated, disciplined, strong-willed prophet; a poet (on the authenticity of the psalm in 2:3–10[2–9], see below) as all Israelite prophets presumably were, and also capable of being peevish and stubborn, even against God. But these personal traits are learned about only as the book progresses. At the outset, nothing is known of Jonah other than the barest facts: he is the son of someone named Amittai (of whom nothing is known); he is the Jonah who is a prophet; and God has called him to preach to Nineveh. The story is thus self-contained. It is not necessary to know much of anything about Jonah's life otherwise to appreciate the story. His past and future are not essential to the book's development.

AUTHORSHIP

The book of Jonah is short and sufficiently unified in theme and style (with the possible exception of the psalm in chap. 2; see below) so as to be rather clearly the work of a single author, commonly called the narrator.

Earlier attempts such as those by K. Köhler (*Theological Review* 16 [1879] 139–44), W. Böhme (*ZAW* 7 [1887] 224–84), H. Winckler (*Zum Buche Jona*, 260–65), and H. Schmidt (*ZAW* 25 [1905] 285–310) to argue that Jonah, like the Pentateuch, had a history of composite authorship and / or elaborate editing, were never convincing.

Of the single narrator, however, we know next to nothing. Solely on the basis of the use of היה "to be" in the past tense in describing Nineveh in 3:3, it has usually been assumed that the narrator had to be someone living after 612, i.e., after Nineveh fell to the Babylonians and was destroyed. This dating depends upon taking the sentence in question to read, in essence, "Nineveh was a city . . . ," i.e., is a city no longer from the perspective of the narrator and his or her audience. However, if the sentence emphasizes the *type* of city Nineveh was at the time Jonah visited it, rather than the fact that it was simply a city at all, the matter may be considered differently. That is, we must ask whether the narrator's object in 3:3 may not be to point out that Nineveh "then" was more important than it is "now," i.e., in the narrator's lifetime. This would be possible if, for example, (1) Nineveh was no longer the royal residence at the time of the composition of the story; or (2) Nineveh had ceased to be "important to God" (גדולה לאלהים) if that is indeed the sense of the unusual Hebrew wording. Thus even the relative distance of the narrator from the story is impossible to fix with certainty. Besides this, the Hebrew narrative style calls for the past tense regardless of proximity to the events. Thus the importance of the verb in 3:3 is easily overrated.

Could the narrator have been Jonah himself? This is possible, but highly unlikely in that the story is so consistently critical of Jonah. It is, indeed, an exposé of his hypocrisy and inconsistency, and ends with a portrayal of his almost childish stubbornness against the point God makes via the object lesson of the plant. A contrite Jonah, later—perhaps years later than the events described in the book—might have chosen magnanimously to characterize himself this vividly and even embarrassingly as dead wrong in his former attitudes; but it is far more likely that a third party is responsible for the story as we have it. Jonah's public image does not fare at all well in the book. Where else in the Scriptures (or any ancient literature, for that matter) does an author of a narrative so thoroughly deprecate himself or herself?

DATE AND SETTING

The actual composition of the book is not datable except within the broadest boundaries (*ca.* 750–250 B.C.) simply because there are no certain indicators in it of date. The considerations most seriously cited as relevant to the issue of dating are four: (1) the supposed Aramaisms in the language, such as בשלמי "on whose account?" in 1:7 and 1:12; (2) the possible dependence of certain motifs or theological considerations on the book of Jeremiah; (3) the close verbal connections with Joel 2; (4) the supposedly erroneous identification of Nineveh as the actual royal capital of Assyria in Jonah's time.

On the fourth consideration, see below. Of the other three, nos. (1) and (2) do not prove decisive after careful analysis. "Aramaisms" have increasingly disappeared, to be replaced by "Northwest Semitisms." That is, the vast majority of words and phrases once thought to be native only to Imperial Aramaic (and therefore, when found in the OT, proof of a date later than 587 B.C.) have now been found to belong to a far wider provenance in date and language grouping. So many "Aramaisms" have turned up in Ugaritic texts—which cannot be later than 1200 B.C.—that the arguments from silence on which such identifications are made can now be dismissed as spurious. Indeed, none of the total of seven Aramaisms variously identified in the book fits for certain the criteria necessary to constitute a "genuine" Aramaism according to O. Loretz (*BZ* 5 [1961] 19–22).

As to the possible dependence of Jonah on Jeremiah, it must be stated that the evidence is both minimal and ambiguous. The book of Jonah reminds its audience that God is willing to adjust his plans for a nation according to that nation's attitudes and actions before him, a concept expressed propositionally in Jer 18:7–8. But sharing of concepts is not the same as a dependency of concepts. The widespread tendency of biblical scholars to think only in terms of the lineal generation of ideas (i.e., if two parts of the Bible say roughly the same thing, one part must have preceded and influenced the other part) has never had merit. The similarity of Jonah and Jeremiah is far more cogently attributable to the univocal nature of divine revelation throughout the Scripture than to a borrowing from Jeremiah on the part of the book of Jonah.

The connections of Jonah and Joel must be evaluated in much the same way; though here the issue centers on the sharing of two virtually exact wordings (part of Jonah 3:9 and Joel 2:14; part of Jonah 4:2 and Joel 2:13). A frequent conclusion has been to relegate Jonah to a dependency on Joel, even though the opposite could as easily be true (a careful argument that Joel quotes from Jonah is presented by J. Magonet, *Form and Structure,* 77–79) or both could draw upon a common source for their similar wordings. It could even be the case, after all, that the prophet Joel was the anonymous narrator of the book of Jonah. There simply is not enough evidence either to prove or to disprove such speculations.

CANONIZATION

Because Jonah is so different in form from the other prophetical books, the reasons for its placement in the prophetic canon of fifteen are often debated. No less a scholar than Karl Budde actually suggested that Jonah was included among the Minor Prophets simply to bring their number to twelve (*ZAW* 12 [1892] 40–43). While his suggestion is hardly tenable, it reflects the almost uniform judgment of scholars that the Jonah story is closer in type to the stories of the prophets—particularly of Elijah and Elisha—in the book of Kings than it is to the prophetic works. Several suggestions have been advanced as to the placement of Jonah as a midrash on one or another of the prophets. E. König ("Jonah," *A Dictionary of the Bible* II, 1899) opined that Jonah is a midrash on Obadiah 1; R. Coote that it is a midrash on Amos (*Amos Among the Prophets* [Philadelphia: Fortress, 1981]) and others that it is a midrash on Joel 2:13–14.

In fact, the placement of Jonah among the prophets probably resulted from a simple combination of its length, date, and subject. Self-contained and brief, it fit easily with the latter prophets, as the similar Elisha-Elijah stories, except by being stripped from their context and perhaps condensed, could *not* easily do. Early in date (at least in Jewish tradition and quite probably in fact) it was sufficiently early that it was not relegated to the Writings (as was Daniel for example, a book later joined with the prophets in the Septuagintal, Latin, and subsequent canonical orderings). Its subject matter was the call and preaching of a prophet, a concern not entirely removed in some aspects from a book like Haggai or even Amos (chap. 7) even though the ratio of biography to quoted revelation is reversed in Jonah. Jonah is actually atypical of the prophetical books only in *quantity;* as regards quality (i.e., categories rather than percentages) there is little in Jonah that is not represented to some degree elsewhere in the prophetic corpus.

MESSAGE AND PURPOSE

On one level, the message of Jonah may be boiled down to a warning to the hearer / reader: "Don't be like Jonah." Throughout the book Jonah displays a readiness to receive mercy and blessing himself and a stubborn reluctance to see his enemies, the Assyrians, receive the same. But the point of the story goes somewhat beyond teaching the audience to love their enemies. It also places great emphasis upon the character and power of God. God's servants cannot expect (1) to oppose him and get away with it; or (2) that he will somehow be unfaithful to his own character of patience, forgiveness, and an eagerness to forestay harm. The book, in other words, is about Jonah, but it is also about God. Jonah hopes all along that somehow God won't turn out to be consistent with his own well-known character (4:2). But God *is* consistent throughout, in contrast to Jonah's hypocritical inconsistency. What happens to Nineveh and to Jonah happens precisely because of what God is like. The audience of the book is thus invited implicitly to revise their understanding of what God is like, if they have indeed shared Jonah's selfish views.

In ancient Judaism the book served as a bulwark against the narrow particularism that allowed Jews to think they alone were worthy of God's blessing while other peoples were not. To a more modern reader the message may be seen in light of Jesus' own teaching about forgiveness: it is the sinners, not the righteous, who most often may recognize their need for forgiveness and do something about it (Matt 12:41; cf. Luke 15:10). No one should oppose God's mercy in receiving sinners into the Kingdom.

At one time it was popular to assume that Jonah was written as a kind of universalistic treatise against the rigid, narrow reformist views of Ezra and Nehemiah. This view rightly lost favor on two accounts. First, the book is hardly universalistic. The fact that God should be concerned for Assyrians and be moved by their repentance is not the equivalent of saying that all people are God's chosen people or that the fate of all nations will ultimately be the same—i.e., salvation. The book nowhere implies that the Ninevites somehow became, as it were, God's chosen nation by reason of their occasion of repentance at Jonah's preaching. Second, the predominant concerns of Ezra and Nehemiah were the restoration of pentateuchal ritual practices, the security of Jerusalem, the elimination of foreign influences, and the prevention of mixed marriages. The fact that Jonah addresses none of these topics, even indirectly, means that it probably would never have occurred to the ancient Jews of the mid-fifth century B.C. that Jonah somehow was an attack on Ezra and Nehemiah. If this then was the purpose of the book, the author has kept that purpose so well hidden that it is undiscoverable.

The double question in 4:4 and 4:9 (לְךָ חָרָה הַהֵיטֵב "What right do you have to be angry?") is unmistakably the key to the book's central message. The climax of the story comes here—not with the repentance of the Ninevites in chap. 3 or at any other point—when God challenges Jonah to recognize how wrong he has been in his bitter nationalism, and how right God has been to show compassion toward the plight of the Assyrians in Nineveh.

Every hearer / reader may have some Jonah in him or her. All need to reflect on the questions God asks, including the final, specific, "Should I not spare Nineveh?" (4:11). Anyone who replies "Why is that such an important question?" has not understood the message. Anyone who replies "No!" has not believed it.

FORM AND STRUCTURE

Jonah is a prophetic narrative. It is paralleled in some ways by the prophetic narratives in the books of Kings, but with a significant difference: in those narratives considerable emphasis is placed on the prophet's faithfulness to God's call, and God's approval and blessing. In Jonah, however, the prophet is portrayed in a distinctly negative light, as one whose entire approach to fulfilling God's call is incorrect. Whereas Elijah, for example, was a prophet who powerfully proclaimed the word of God against great odds (1 Kgs 18, 19), Jonah was a prophet who ran from God's word when its implications were unpleasant to him.

All biblical narratives are didactic to some degree; but in the case of the book of Jonah, the narrator has carefully shaped the story by selectivity, summarization, and even minor chronological rearrangement (see *Comment*, 4:5), for an obviously didactic purpose. There is a flashback (4:5–11) and a "flash forward" (1:16). Large blocks of time are passed over rapidly (the long trip from Palestine to Nineveh) while brief moments (Jonah's prayer in chap. 2; the conversation between God and Jonah in chap. 4) are given detailed attention. The focus shifts from Jonah onto others (to the sailors in chap. 1; to the Ninevites, including the king, in chap. 3) and back again. And so on. The narrative techniques are by no means unique to the book of Jonah, but they are somewhat uniquely centered on building to the didactic purpose of the book, which is fully unveiled in the divine speeches in chap. 4 (vv 4, 10–11). Thus the book of Jonah must be described not simply as a prophetic narrative, but as a *didactic* prophetic narrative.

Additionally, Jonah is *sensational* literature. That is, the book is clearly composed with a high concentration of elements designed to arouse the imagination and emotion of the audience (the storm at sea, the fish story, the plant story, etc.). In this sense Jonah resembles the accounts in the early chapters of Daniel, and the miracle stories in the accounts of Elisha's ministry (mainly in 2 Kgs 2–7). On the historicity of sensational literature, see below.

As sensational, didactic, prophetic narrative the book shares features with those genres of literature known as parable and allegory, but it is not correct to identify it with either of these. "Parable" is variously defined; but strictly speaking, a parable is invariably brief (not four chapters in length, in other words) normally having: a single scene but at most two or three (as in the parable of the lost son in Luke 15); elements of comparison to people or things outside the story who are the *real* focus; and some sort of a "shock" or punch line which draws the hearer up short as it teaches a lesson, the reader seeing himself or herself in the story. Moreover, true parables also have anonymous figures as their characters. The book of Jonah borders on some of these characteristics of parable, but actually manifests none of them exactly. And most significantly, parables are obviously *fictional*. Though the reader or hearer may choose to conclude upon reflection that the book of Jonah is fictional, the story is by no means *obviously* fictional. Indeed, it is our position, in concert with the traditional view, that the book is not fictional at all.

Nor is Jonah an allegory. An allegory is a kind of extended analogy, sometimes including extended metaphors, in which the meaning of the story is not to be found in the concepts and actions presented, but in concepts and actions outside the story, to which the story points analogically. It would be an unusual allegory indeed that waited to the end (the fourth chapter in the case of Jonah) to reveal the point of its hero's actions. Allegories are distinctly constructed so as to point beyond themselves at each stage. The figures in an allegory are patently symbolic and fictional, and the audience must realize this at once if the allegory is to be effective. Jonah does not fit this pattern, either.

Jonah is also not midrash. Midrashic literature functions as commentary upon particular biblical texts, and may include illustration as well as propositional explanation. Midrash is patently didactic, but by no means is all didactic literature, including narrative, to be identified as midrashic. The Bible contains two references to midrashim, both in 2 Chronicles. Mention is made in 2 Chr 13:22 of "the Midrash of the Prophet Iddo" and in 2 Chr 24:27 "the Midrash of the Book of Kings." Both of these must have contained stories, but it is an unwarranted conclusion to assume that they were composed of nothing but stories. Probably they included commentary and other expansions upon the historical narratives they reproduced, though little can be known for certain about their content. For Jonah to be convincingly identified as a midrash, it would need to be demonstrated that the story was composed to serve as an illustrative explanation of something taught elsewhere in the OT. Not only can this never be done convincingly in light of the lack of data relevant to the task. it would be virtually the reverse of a typical biblical period midrash. The early midrashim we do know about are characterized by analytical discussion of stories, laws, or other "primary" material. By its nature Jonah appears far more likely to be not the midrash but the primary material, so that any midrash would be secondary, i.e., a discussion of the truth contained in Jonah. Attempts to relate Jonah in a midrashic manner to Joel 2:13, 14 or to Amos (Coote, *Amos Among the Prophets*) have therefore remained speculative.

STYLE

A relatively simple vocabulary prevails throughout the book, something to be expected if the inspired narrator did not wish the didactic impact of the story to be missed at any point by reason of the intrusion of an overly complex style. Two vocabulary words have been selected by the narrator and used at various points in the story, each according to two aspects of their wide ranges of meaning: גדול "great," etc., and רעה "bad," etc. Capitalizing upon two nuances of each of these words is an effective unifying device, providing diversity (in meaning) while at the same time maintaining consistency (in form).

The adjective גדול "great" appears fourteen times. It has the meaning great or large (in size or extent) eight times (1:4 [twice], 10, 12, 16, 2:1 [1:17]. 4:1, 6). However, it has the meaning "important" (or, according to one's translation preference, "key / chief / major") six times (1:2; 3:2, 3, 5, 7; 4:11) either in reference to the "important" city of Nineveh or the "important" people in the city, i.e., its nobles or leaders. The pattern of distribution of these two meanings is not mathematical, but is governed by the flow of events in the story, and thus is somewhat random. It is especially significant for the understanding of the story to see that the emphasis placed on Nineveh is not primarily in terms of its physical size but its *importance* to God. The reference to Nineveh's population in 4:11 notwithstanding, the basic issue goes beyond Nineveh's sheer bulk to its intrinsic value to God.

This value becomes evident partly in the usage of רעה. The word is used, in connection with Nineveh, to describe the *troubles* the city is having, not merely its evil ways. To fail to recognize this sense of רעה is to fail, for example, to see an early (1:2) adumbration of God's compassionate concern for the city. God is as concerned about Nineveh's miseries as he is angry at its evils, and the book's audience did not have to wait until the end of chap. 3 to gain a sense of that fact.

In total, the word רעה appears nine times in the book. In only two instances does it mean "evil" (as the adjective), 3:8 and 3:10. In the other seven occasions of its occurrence it means "trouble" or a closely synonymous word (e.g., "disaster," "misery," "difficulty," "harm," depending on translation preference, in 1:2, 7, 8; 3:10; 4:1, 2, 6). The *problems* of the Assyrians in Nineveh move God to commission Jonah to preach there; did Jonah ignore this meaning of רעה and instead hear only what he wanted to hear—that the *evils* of the Ninevites occasioned his mission? Hardly, for then he might not have fled. Jonah, too understood from the start the meaning "trouble" for רעה in 1:2, just as the hearer / reader ought to, in spite of the nearly uniform mistranslation of the term in modern English versions.

Many attempts have been made to find significance in the usage patterns of several other words used frequently in the book (recently, e.g., Trible, *Studies* [1963], and Magonet, *Form and Meaning* [1976]) but these have proved

less than entirely convincing, the "patterns" turning out ultimately to reflect
the flow of the story rather than demonstrating either a conscious or unconscious structuring of the story according to its vocabulary. The different divine
names (Yahweh, Elohim, ha-Elohim, Yahweh-Elohim) also do not appear to
be distributed in a way that makes a point or affects the impact of the story,
attempts to prove such an impact to the contrary notwithstanding. The names
vary, for the most part according to who is addressing the deity (generally,
the pagans use Elohim, Jonah uses Yahweh) and the exceptions to this pattern
are not easily explained according to any didactic motif (for a contrary view
see Magonet, *Form and Meaning*, 33–38).

As sensational didactic historical narrative, Jonah shares a certain style
with the Elijah-Elisha stories, the stories in the early chapters of Daniel, parts
of Ruth and Esther, and other OT portions as well (e.g., Exod 4:24–26;
Num 12; Judg 14–16). This style emphasizes the vivid, which is highly selective,
and involves the audience emotionally. It works to the advantage of the narrator, whose points can be made to an alert, interested, even captivated audience.
In spite of its selectivity, the style does not represent either exaggeration or
literary degradation. Jonah is not a sentimental story, nor is it humorous. It
is told straightforwardly, without embellishment but with an emphasis, by
reason of selection, on those events in Jonah's experience which are particularly
engaging of the imagination. Effective narrative writing stimulates the visual
imagination. If a hearer or reader cannot visualize a scene *at each point*, some
of the capturing of attention, and therefore impact, is lost. Jonah is quite
"scenic" in this sense—so much so that J. D. W. Watts (*Jonah, Cambridge
Bible Commentary*, 72–97) finds considerable merit in dividing the story according to its shifting "scenes."

UNITY AND INTEGRITY

The psalm in Jonah 2:3–10 [2–9] has been the only part of the book
seriously considered an interpolation. The psalm has been judged a later
addition usually on one or more of the following three grounds: (1) it may
be excised without disrupting the story; (2) it is inappropriate, being a thanksgiving psalm when a lament is called for; (3) it does not relate smoothly to
the rest of the story either in style, vocabulary, theology, or overall impact.

Each of these objections to the appropriateness of the psalm raises questions.
The ability to excise part of a literary work without doing damage to the
remainder depends entirely on how one analyzes both the remainder and
the part being excised. In fact, most such excisions do only minor damage—
so that the longer the piece from which the excision is made, and the shorter
or more self-contained the excision, the less it is missed. An ability to excise
does not equal, however, a warrant to excise. Any narrative, and most literary
pieces composed segmentally (as most literary works are), can suffer the loss
of certain segments and still remain perfectly coherent. One could easily
delete ten or twenty percent of any of the Gospels and still retain a logical,
comprehensible whole. The same could be done for the Psalms, or Deuteronomy, or Isaiah, or for that matter, the American Declaration of Independence.
They all contain segments which are not so essential to the flow of the whole
that their excision would render the remainder incoherent. To take another

example, our historical controls are such that we are assured of the integrity of Abraham Lincoln's Gettysburg address. Yet the words "by the people and for the people" could easily be eliminated without leaving the remainder unclear. Excisability is never a legitimate indication of lack of integrity in a literary work. In the case of the psalm of Jonah, the same principle applies, though we will argue below that the excision of the psalm is possible only when the story is actually misunderstood to some degree.

Should not the psalm be a lament, rather than an expression of thanksgiving? B. W. Anderson (*Out of the Depths* [Philadelphia: Westminster Press, 1974] 84) states the case typically: ". . . the psalm is obviously out of place in its present context. In the belly of a fish a cry for help (that is, a lament) would be appropriate, but not a thanksgiving for deliverance already experienced!" The trouble with this view is, of course, that the fish is precisely a vehicle of rescue in the story. Once Jonah is inside the belly of the fish he has been delivered from drowning. A lament psalm would be appropriate only while he was still sinking in the Mediterranean. He *has* already experienced deliverance, and a thanksgiving psalm is the only sort appropriate to his situation.

The relation of the content of the psalm to the content of the rest of the story is the only truly debatable issue. Style and vocabulary do not match up, as they should not. The style and vocabulary of Hebrew psalms are precisely what differentiate them from Hebrew prose. The language is generalized, so as to maximize applicability; the style is formalized so as to fit the meter, tune, and function of the genre. As psalms go, the psalm of Jonah is the closest one can get to a psalm composed specifically for the events Jonah experienced while still remaining a true psalm, i.e., general and pan-temporal (see also *Comment*, 2:3–10).

It is in the area of theology and overall impact that the psalm, upon careful examination, turns out to be genuinely integral—non-excisable—within the context of the overall message of the book. The full case has been argued convincingly by G. M. Landes (*Int* 21 [1967] 3–31). Landes' lengthy argument may be summarized briefly as follows. First, divine deliverance is a central theme in Jonah, and the psalm directly and vividly contributes to the reinforcement of this theme. Second, without the psalm, Jonah's attitude of gratefulness for his own deliverance is nowhere noted explicitly. It cannot then later serve as a contrast to his resentment at the deliverance of Nineveh. Third, when the component parts of the psalm are analyzed in detail, it becomes clear that "the psalm as it now stands is in the proper position, of an appropriate type, and agrees quite harmoniously with the situation of Jonah in the narrative, both in terms of his physical and psychological portrayal."

This does not mean, of course, that the narrator of the book composed the psalm in connection with composing the book (the least likely option) or that Jonah composed it new for the occasion. Jonah, a trained poet (as the prophets were), may have chosen the psalm from among his mental repertoire as the most fitting he could offer. Or he may have "composed" it in the sense of compiling it from segments of thanksgiving psalms already extant (judging from the considerable parallels to parts of the psalm in the Psalter proper). But it does mean that questions about the book's integrity vis-à-vis the psalm have convincing answers. Without the psalm, the story really would be impoverished, leaving the reader with the impression of a more consistent, highly principled Jonah than the story intends to convey.

HISTORICITY

One can appreciate the story of Jonah whether or not it represents actual historical events. The answer to the key question, "What right do you have to be angry?" (4:4, 9) is still "None!" even if the account is entirely or essentially fictional. But the issue of historicity has implications beyond the formal didactic function of the narrative. If the events described in the book actually happened, the audience's existential identification with the characters and circumstances is invariably heightened. People act more surely upon what they believe to be true in fact, than merely what they consider likely in theory. It is one thing to conclude that "Jonah is a story which illustrates the principle that we ought to allow God the right to show compassion to those whom we might think do not deserve it." It is quite another to conclude that "the ancient Israelite Jonah was a northern prophet who had to learn the hard way a lesson we ought to learn less stubbornly: our God has shown himself decisively to be a God of compassion and forgiveness—and not just toward us!" If it really happened, it is really serious. If this is the way God works in history, then a less narrow attitude toward our enemies is not just an "ought," it is a must; it is not simply a narrator's desire, it is God's enforceable revelation.

It is important to note that there is ample evidence to support the historicity of the book, and surprisingly little to undermine it. The style, as noted above, is neutral; sensationalism can never be equivocated with a lack of factuality. A true story may be told in a host of ways, from dull to sensational, as may a false story, as may a fictional story. Style is largely irrelevant to factuality; guilt by association (sensational equals fictional) is an inadequate basis for rejecting historicity. The usual mustering of "improbabilities," moreover, is hardly adequate to suggest a lack of historicity. Miraculous events are chronicled in various places throughout the Bible. One can reject these on the basis of a systematic anti-supernaturalist bias, but one cannot single out Jonah in this regard. The argument that "miracles can't happen, therefore they don't" is a subjective, not an objective, basis for discounting the factuality of the miracle narratives in Jonah.

As to the improbability of a general repentance in Nineveh itself, this must now be tempered by the recognition that our historical evidence preserves the fact that things were not going well at all for the Ninevites at approximately the time Jonah served as a prophet (the first half of the eighth century). Military and diplomatic losses internationally were coupled with famine and popular uprisings domestically during the time of Aššur-dān III (773–756 B.C.), for example. In addition, both an earthquake and an eclipse, dreaded major omens to the Assyrians, were experienced concurrent to these other problems. A weak, shaky monarchy reeling from domestic and international turmoil could well have welcomed the chance to solidify its acceptance by a suspicious populace, already set on edge by the prevailing problems, via the sort of royal proclamation preserved (in part?) in 3:7–9.

But did Nineveh have a "king" (3:6, 7)? Does the expression מלך נינוה

"King of Nineveh" make sense? The assumptions that the phrase "King of Nineveh" reflected a lack of understanding of the Assyrian Empire (analogous to speaking of "the King of London" [W. Neil, "Jonah," *IDB* 2:966]) and a befuddled historical memory (since Nineveh could not have been the capital of Assyria in Jonah's time) have been central objections to the book's historicity. The answers to the questions raised require an appreciation of two facts: (1) "King of Nineveh" is a perfectly simple, comprehensible phrase in the context of the book; and (2) it is entirely possible that an Assyrian king would be present in Nineveh early in the eighth century B.C. whether or not Nineveh was technically the "capital" (a modern notion, largely) of the Assyrian empire.

Regarding the first problem, the evidence for OT usage is actually quite varied, and there are ample parallels for the term "King of Nineveh." It should be noted that sometimes a king may be designated "King of X" where X has as its most normal meaning a territory actually larger than that part which the king rules. Thus Cushan-Rishathaim is called "King of Aram-Naharaim" in Judg 3:8, 10 even though his rule surely was not so extensive. He was at most king of a small part of Aram-Naharaim. A similar usage appears in Gen 14:1, 9. More significantly for the wording in Jonah 3:7, it was also common for a king to be designated by only one city within the region he ruled. In Deut 1:4; 3:2; 4:46, etc., Sihon is called "King of the Amorites." But in Deut 2:24, 26, 30, etc., Sihon is called "King of Heshbon." Jabin is called "King of Canaan / the Canaanites" in Judg 4:2, 23, 24, etc., but "King of Hazor" in Judg 4:17. A king could be associated, in other words, with a capital or main city within his empire, as well as with the empire itself (cf. 2 Sam 8:5; 1 Kgs 11:23, etc., where Hadadezer's kingship is associated with "Zobah" though his control extended considerably further).

Perhaps the closest OT parallel to "King of Nineveh" is found in 1 Kgs 21:1, where Ahab is called מלך שמרון "King of Samaria" in contrast to "King of Israel," the title used for him routinely elsewhere. If Ahab can be called "King of Samaria" in the OT there can surely be no valid objection to calling Aššur-dan III (or whoever was the king who responded to Jonah's preaching) "King of Nineveh" in Jonah 3:6. The common later OT usage "King of Babylon," by reason of being ambiguous, cannot be proved to provide a parallel to "King of Nineveh" since it is impossible in each case to tell whether the city or empire is envisioned by the term.

It is most probable that the narrator of Jonah chose "King of Nineveh" over "King of Assyria" (מלך אשור) simply because the story focuses on Nineveh per se rather than on the empire as a whole. However, since it clearly remained an option in OT narrative to speak of a king in terms of his capital or chief city, as the examples above illustrate, we cannot rule out the possibility that "King of Nineveh" was chosen according to this normal, not infrequent, idiom by a narrator and for an audience who would have considered it nothing other than a routine sort of option, as the writer (and presumably, audience) of 1 Kgs 21:1 did in the case of "King of Samaria."

But how could there be a king in Nineveh in Jonah's time? Did not Nineveh become the actual capital of the Assyrian empire only in the time of Sennacherib (705–682 B.C.) as is commonly alleged? In fact, Nineveh may well have been at least an alternate capital, if not the capital of Assyria throughout much of the first half of the eighth century B.C. We know, for example, that Shalmaneser I (1275–1246 B.C.) began an expansion of the city and that by the time of Tiglath-Pileser I (1114–1076 B.C.) Nineveh had become an alternative royal residence to both Assur and Calah. Thereafter, a palace of some sort appears to have been established in the city, and used by various kings, including Ashurnasirpal II (883–859 B.C.), before Jonah's time; and by Sargon II (722–705 B.C.), after Jonah's time. It is therefore quite likely that Nineveh functioned as a royal residence, even if not the capital technically, during most of the eighth century B.C. (cf. R. C. Thompson and R. W. Hutchinson, *A Century of Exploration at Nineveh* [London: Lusack & Co., 1929]; A. Parrot, *Nineveh and the Old Testament*, (tr. B. E. Hooke [London: SCM, 1955]). Our knowledge of the affairs of the weak kings of Assyria between the latter years of Adad-nirari III (811–784 B.C.) and Tiglath-Pileser III (745–728 B.C.) is spotty. It is probable, however, that each of these kings (Shalmaneser IV [783–774 B.C.], Aššur-dan III [773–756 B.C.] and Aššur-nirari V [755–746 B.C.]) ruled at least part of the time from Nineveh. Aššur-dān III shifted his residence at least once, and possibly more (see 3:6, 7, *Comment*). Thus, regardless of whether the ancient Assyrians thought of "capitals" in the same way that moderns do, it is clear that Nineveh became at least *de facto* the chief city of the neo-Assyrian Empire and host to royalty during much of that period. There is therefore nothing in the phrase "King of Nineveh" (3:6) that can be demonstrated spurious historically.

SOURCES FOR THE STORY

As a vehicle for divine revelation, the narrator of the book would hardly have been dependent exclusively on human sources for the details of the story. Yet virtually all the data from which the story is constructed could have been supplied by two sources: Jonah and the sailors. Any of the sailors, whose ship eventually returned to safety, would have been an adequate source for information on what happened while Jonah was asleep (1:5) and after he was thrown overboard (1:15, 16). Every other detail used in the book could have come from Jonah himself, who had ample opportunity to observe and inquire about, in and around Nineveh, those events which he may not himself have actually witnessed (e.g., the king's actions in 3:6, if in fact Jonah did not appear in person before the king). Indeed, Jonah could have been a source for the details in 1:5 and 1:15, 16. What had happened while he was asleep on board ship (1:5) would likely have been relayed to him after he awakened, if it were not still continuing in part, as 1:6 implies.

As a significant Northern prophet, Jonah was hardly an obscure personage. News of his rescue at sea, his trip to Nineveh, and his eventual return would surely have spread widely in his later years, possibly occasioning a meeting between one or more of the sailors and Jonah. In fact, if they heard that Jonah were actually alive, one wonders how the sailors could have failed to search him out. A narrator, therefore, who made contact with Jonah alone might then have possessed ample source(s) for the book eventually produced. Jonah could, of course, have told the story defensively, i.e., from his own point of view and not so self-critically as the book tells it. It would have been more probably the narrator than Jonah himself who centered so often on Jonah's improper attitudes and actions.

Jonah's travel to Nineveh is closely paralleled by the missions of Elijah to Sidon and Elisha to Syria. Further, all three prophets' stories include a rather large concentration of miracles. It may be speculated that the narrator of Jonah followed a pattern—and perhaps a style—already proved effective in the Elijah-Elisha stories in 1 Kgs 17–19 and 2 Kgs 2–9. In none of these cases would it have been necessary for the narrator to be an eyewitness to the events; the prophets themselves would have provided an adequate source for the raw materials from which the finished stories were constructed.

TEXT

The text of Jonah is remarkably well preserved. Variants are few and do not display any sort of fixed pattern. Even the Targum is only mildly expansionistic, in contrast to its substantial tendency toward commentary and explanation present in other books of the Minor Prophets.

THE IMPORTANCE OF JONAH 4:2

By including in the story Jonah's admission of the fact that he had fled from God because he knew God was compassionate, the narrator effectively silences all speculation about Jonah's motives. Regardless of any other religious or political notions Jonah may have had, it is evident that he hated the fact that Yahweh was truly consistent in being merciful and patient—that is, consistent *among* the nations as well as *within* Israel. "What is God really like?" is thus a more important question in this book than the question "What was Jonah really like?" About the latter question one may speculate; about the former question the book leaves no doubt: he is a God of grace of whom it is hopeless—indeed, hypocritical—to expect a display of grace only to his own people. It was God's grace that Jonah resented so violently; except, of course, when he was the recipient.

But the famous confession which Jonah recited (4:2) places no limit on divine grace. The wording does not restrict to any person or group God's forgiveness and willingness to reconsider bringing harm. Jonah wanted discriminatory limits on God's grace. But he knew all along, as all Israelites and Christians should know, that God will be bound by no such limits. Jonah had made up his mind that Nineveh ought to be destroyed. Yahweh had not.

Jonah Rebels against Yahweh's Revelation (1:1–3)

Bibliography

Abramowitz, H. *"Maftir Yonah."* BMik 28 (1982 / 83) 326–29. **Cross, F. M.** "An Interpretation of the Nora Stone." *BASOR* 208 (1972) 13–19. **Galling, K.** "Der Weg der

Phöniker nach Tarsis." *ZDPV* 88 (1972) 1–18, 140–81. **Garbini, G.** "Tarsis e Gen 10, 4." BibOr 6 (1964) 13–19. **Goitein, S. D.** "Some Observations on Jonah." *JPOS* 17 (1937) 63–77. **Gordon, C. H.** "The Wine-Dark Sea." *JNES* 37 (1978) 51–52. **Sasson, J.** "On Jonah's Two Missions." *Henoch* 6 (1984) 23–29. **Smitten, W. H. In der.** "Zu Jona 1, 2." *ZAW* 84 (1972) 95. **Weiss, M.** "Einiges über die Bauformen des Erzählens in der Bibel." *VT* 13 (1963) 456–75.

Translation

Yahweh's command

¹:¹ *Yahweh's word came to Jonah, the son of Amittai, as follows:* ² *"Go to the important city,* ᵃ *Nineveh, and speak against* ᵇ *it, for* ᶜ *their trouble* ᵈ *is of concern to me."* ᵉ

Jonah's flight

³ *But Jonah set out to flee out to sea,* ᵃ *away from Yahweh. He went down to Joppa, found there a ship which was going out to sea,* ᵃ *and paid for passage on it.* ᵇ *He went down inside it to go with them out to sea,* ᵃ *away from Yahweh.*

Notes

2.a. On this translation of העיר הגדולה, see *Comment*. The word גדול can also mean "big," "great," "key," "chief," etc.

2.b. G(v) reads ἐν αὐτῇ "in it" rather than "against it." The rendering of עליה in this manner is less likely a translational freedom than evidence of an original בה though either explanation is possible.

2.c. Or, "that their evil . . ." if כי is taken as a relative; in that case, v 2b becomes a summary of the content of Jonah's message rather than the reason for it, and רעה must mean "evil." Syntactically, however, this alternative is unlikely.

2.d. G appears to paraphrase (ἡ κραυγὴ τῆς κακίας αὐτῆς: "the cry of its evil") perhaps on the basis of similar expressions employing the notion of "cry" (צעקה) in Gen 18:20, 21; Exod 3:7, 9; etc. It is conceivable, though hardly likely, that קול "sound" or צעקת "cry" has dropped from MT by haplogr. On the definition of רעה as "trouble," see *Comment*.

2.e. Lit., "has come up before me." Cf. Gen 4:10; 18:21; 1 Sam 5:12; Lam 1:22.

3.a. On the meaning of תרשיש, see *Comment*.

3.b. Lit., "its fare."

Form / Structure / Setting

The book of Jonah begins with a converted apocopated imperfect verb (ויהי) usually thought to indicate the continuation of a narrative, rather than the beginning of a passage or book. Some translations even begin the book with the word "And" as if it were clearly an excerpt from a larger work. Though it is possible to regard the book in theory as an excerpt, there is nothing in this verb form to prove it. Joshua, Judges, 1 Samuel, Ruth, Esther, and [the Septuagint of] Lamentations all begin with the same converted imperfect verb form of היה (lit., "It happened that . . ."). A case could conceivably be made that Ruth, Ezra, Esther, and Jonah were excerpted from larger collections; and Joshua, Judges, and 1 Samuel are clearly part of a larger work, the so-called Deuteronomic history. In the face of a complete lack of any other evidence of excerption, however, it is best to assume that a book like Jonah is self-contained. Accordingly, וַיְהִי is for Jonah the functional equivalent of "Once upon a time . . ." i.e., a simple stylized formula for opening a narrative. The Elijah story begins abruptly in 1 Kgs 17, for example, with וַיֹּאמֶר "And [Elijah] said. . . ." Major narratives obviously do not require elaborate introductions in the Hebrew tradition. Moreover, the fact that the first sentence of the book should begin with a *waw* is hardly surprising, in that the vast majority of all independent clauses in Hebrew narrative begin likewise. The *waw* is virtually the equivalent of capitalization at the beginning of English sentences.

In keeping with the overall form of the book as didactic historical narrative, the introduction strives to be brief and simple. It presents the facts essential to a comprehension of the situation of Jonah with an absolute minimum of detail. The reason for the brevity is probably twofold: (1) the narrative itself is self-explanatory to the extent that an elaborate introduction would, if anything, hinder the didactic effectiveness of the story; (2) OT prophetic narratives in general are rather terse. In the Deuteronomic history, for example, precious little about Elijah (1 Kgs 17:1), Elisha (1 Kgs 19:19), Isaiah (2 Kgs 19:2), or Huldah (2 Kgs 22:14) can be learned from the bare-bones introductions given in the narratives about them. Even less can be learned about some prophets of whom no narrative makes mention (e.g., Obadiah, Habakkuk). More generally, it may be noted that introductions to biblical narratives of virtually any kind do not tend to dwell in detail upon matters of origin, lineage, or early life. When such details are given (as, e.g., sparsely in Gen 11:27–29 about Abraham) they are thus flagged for special attention. The Jonah story, however, like most stories about prophets, would gain nothing in its impact by a more elaborate introduction.

The structure of this crisp introduction may be described by a simple two-part outline:

Yahweh's command (vv 1–2)
Jonah's response: flight (v 3).

The introduction already gives evidence of the overall movement of the book. It is to be a story about Yahweh and Jonah. Though other characters as well as places and events will figure in the story, the focus will remain upon Yahweh and Jonah: What one wants the other does not always do.

The setting of the command in v 2 is not specified inasmuch as it is hardly necessary to the story, though it may be conjectured to have been Samaria. Though Jonah was originally from Gath-Hepher, he probably carried on his prophetic activity in and around Samaria. Surely the prophetic activity for which he is noted in 2 Kgs 14:25, i.e., oracle(s) encouraging Jeroboam II in his campaigns to expand the borders of Israel, would have been performed in the court of Jeroboam in the capital. The fact that he chose to sail from Joppa, a port city relatively near Samaria (and even nearer Jerusalem) as opposed to a more northern port like Dor, for example, closer to Gath-Hepher, also suggests that we are to assume that he was somewhere in south-central Israel when Yahweh's word came to him.

The date of our story is virtually impossible to establish beyond rather wide limits. Jeroboam II ruled 793–753 B.C. (cf. 2 Kgs 14:23). But there exist virtually no data whereby his campaigns of expansion may be fixed chronologically. Amos 6:13 contains a reference to the recapture in Gilead of Lo-debar and Karnaim, but this in fact could have taken place anytime during Jeroboam's reign.

Knowing that Jonah ben-Amittai prophesied during the reign of Jeroboam, therefore, still leaves more than a century as the span of time in which the events described by the book of Jonah could have occurred. On the one hand, 2 Kgs 14:25 could allude to the prophecy of an aged Jonah given to a new king in 793 B.C. Suppose, for example, that Jonah were 70 when Jeroboam came to power in 793 B.C., and 20 when God's word came to him as described in Jonah 1:1. That would allow Jonah's visit to Nineveh to be dated as early as 843 B.C. On the other hand, suppose Jonah were 20 when he prophesied late in the reign of Jeroboam, as virtually a contemporary of Hosea (perhaps in 755 B.C.) and 70 when he visited Nineveh. That would date the events of the book of Jonah as late as 705 B.C.—when Israel was already fully under Assyrian domination and no longer an independent nation. The reference to "the King of Nineveh" in 3:6 (q.v.) may, however, help date Jonah's experience; as we shall argue, Aššur-dān III (773–756 B.C.) was a king of Assyria whose capital, at least part of the time, was probably Nineveh, and whose circumstances may have provided the occasion for Yahweh's initial command to Jonah.

The size of Nineveh is of no help in dating the book (see *Comment* on 1:2). Nineveh was destroyed by the Babylonians in 612 B.C., long after Jonah had departed from the scene. It was a "large" city and an "important" one (depending on how one takes גדולה) for many centuries prior to Jonah's day, being already famed for its size according to one way of reading Gen 10:12. Nothing about Joppa, sea-going ships, or any other detail here or later in the book helps any further to fix the date.

Comment

1   The story begins with the mention of two essential facts: (1) Yahweh's word was given; (2) it was given to a particular prophet, Jonah, son of Amittai. The style of the introductory sentence is more that of prophetic narrative than the typical title to a prophetic book (cf. 1 Kgs 17:8; Jer 1:4; Hag 1:3, or even Gen 15:1). The connection of דבר יהוה "the word of Yahweh" and היה (in this idiom, "to come") is found similarly, however, in the titles of four of the minor prophets (Hos 1:1; Joel 1:1; Mic 1:1; Zeph 1:1), so that Jonah 1:1 can hardly be presumed to be something other than a prophetical book at its outset. This wording . . . ויהי דבר יהוה or a variation of it is used in connection with a prophet's receipt of a divine oracle 112 times in the OT (O. Grether, *Name und Wort Gottes in Alten Testament*. BZAW 64 [Giessen: A. Töpelmann, 1934] 67–68). It is a standard way to describe a revelation and therefore has no special overtone or aura.

The name of Jonah, may, however, have evoked a reaction from many of those who first heard or read this story. As the narrator of 2 Kgs 14:25 takes pains to mention, Jonah, son of Amittai, the prophet from Gath-Hepher, had been the one whom God used to proclaim his decision to bless Israel (i.e., the Northern Kingdom) under Jeroboam II by allowing it to expand its borders substantially. The days of Jeroboam became days of great prosperity and national pride. Both Hosea and Amos had attacked Jeroboam and Israel with oracles of doom for the religious syncretism and social injustice which accompanied that period of prosperity. But from Jonah, perhaps, no such criticism was heard. Accordingly, though the inference is based on an argument from silence and is thus speculative, one may wonder whether Jonah was not more or less a loyalist prophet in Israel. That is, in announcing his plans to bless a heterodox, covenantally disobedient nation during the reign of Jeroboam, God appears to have chosen a nationalistic northern prophet who adopted no critical stance toward the policies and practices of the monarchy, at least so far as we can know. 2 Kgs 14:23–29 is hardly uncritical of Jeroboam, but it is certainly not critical of Jonah, who is called Yahweh's "servant" (עֶבֶד). The oppression of Israel by foreign military conquest is given as the reason for Yahweh's intervention (vv 26–27) in a summation the wording of which is patently similar to language used to summarize interventions of deliverance in the book of Judges. Just as God could rescue his undeserving apostate people by the hand of a not very exemplary judge (Jephthah, Gideon, Samson, etc.) or Judahite king (2 Kgs 20) so he could announce via a prophet, Jonah, his intention to rescue undeserving Israel via the apostate Jeroboam II. A chauvinistic, even jingoistic prophet could serve God's purpose of proclamation as well as anyone else.

Jonah is identified only by his name and that of his father, Amittai. It is unlikely that any allegorical significance can be attached to either name. Jonah (יוֹנָה) means "dove," and is one of many Hebrew names in the OT based on animals. Amittai (אֲמִתַּי) means "truth." The -ay is a Hebrew hypocoristic ending, not unlike the -y on English "Billy" (for parallels in both cases see M. Noth, *Die Israelitische Personennamen* [Stuttgart: Kohlhammer, 1928]). Any suggestion that these names are symbolic would require two kinds of evidence: (1) It would need to be shown that "Dove, son of Truth" somehow captures the essence of or conveys some message about Jonah's personality. It does not. (2) It would need to be shown that the prior reference in 2 Kgs 14:25 also used the names symbolically. It does not. The function of v 1, then, is simply to state the fact that Jonah, identified as the known northern prophet, received a revelation from Yahweh.

2 The content of the message from Yahweh is an imperative followed by an explanation of that imperative. Jonah is told not only that his assignment involved going to Nineveh and speaking against it, but is given two bits of information about the reason for his commission: Nineveh is a chief or capital city, and Yahweh has taken notice of some calamity that has occurred there.

The wording of the divine command is, again, standard. The clause קוּם לֵךְ אֶל־ (lit., "Get up and go to . . .") appears, for example, in 1 Kgs 17:9 ("Get up and go to Zarephath . . .") as an imperative to Elijah (cf. Jer 13:6, "Get up and go to the Euphrates . . ."; קוּם לֵךְ פְּרָתָה). Jonah will receive the identical command again in 3:2 ("Go to the important city, Nineveh, to speak against it") at which time he will finally obey it.

A special aspect of this message is the distance Jonah must go to deliver it. Implied in such a command is the concept that Yahweh's sovereignty is a world-wide one, and that violation of his will by any nation can bring his wrath. The notion of the universal reign of Israel's national God and potential for the outpouring of his judgment on any nation or city is not new here. It is virtually pan-biblical. From the flood story to the story of Sodom and Gomorrah to the involvement of Elijah with Aram to the international oracles of Amos and other prophets against foreign nations to the Revelation, one finds evidence of God's covenant with all humankind in addition to his special covenant with Israel.

Nineveh's importance and its difficulties both receive attention in the brief divine speech to Jonah. The phrase we have translated "the important city, Nineveh" (נינוה העיר הגדולה) occurs here the first of three times (also 3:2 and 4:11). Its significance rather than its size is emphasized further in 3:3 (where either its circumference or diameter has usually been thought described) and in 4:11 with reference to its large population of humans and animals. But size is not the issue here. The term גדול in Hebrew, usually translated "great," can also mean not only "large" (its most basic sense) but also "important," "chief," or "leading" (Gen 39:9; 2 Kgs 10:6; Lev 21:10) and thus in connection with a city, "capital." In Assyrian times (i.e., the eighth and seventh centuries B.C.), certain phrases in OT Hebrew seem to reflect Assyrian usage in connection with the terms for leadership. For example, in Hos 5:13 and 10:6 the Assyrian king is called מלכי רב (not מלך ירב; see *Comment*), probably an actual transliteration of the Assyrian term for "chief king," i.e., emperor. The Assyrian term, usually transliterated *malku rabu*, was almost surely pronounced *malkᵉ rab*, the case endings having long since dropped from Assyrian, the *shewa* being a neutral, epenthetic sound following a doubly closed syllable (cf. J. Hyatt, *The Treatment of Final Vowels in Early Neo-Babylonian*, Yos 23 [New Haven: Yale, 1941]). One wonders, therefore, if העיר הגדולה might not be in effect a Hebrew calque of the Assyrian *ālu rabu*, "important city," or "capital." As an analogy, consider the similar pattern, המלך הגדול (2 Kgs 18:19, 28; par. Isa 36:4, 13) which appears to be a Hebrew calque of the Assyrian *malk(u)*, *rab(u)*, i.e., the "chief king" or emperor.

Moreover, Hebrew constructions in which a determined noun is modified by the determined adjective גדול (i.e., "*the* great _____") may often be construed as implying a kind of singular, specific greatness. Examples of this construction include "the great river" (הנהר הגדול, i.e., the Euphrates (e.g., Deut 1:7); "the great sea" (הים הגדול), i.e., the Mediterranean (e.g., Josh 1:4); "the great priest" (הכהן הגדול), i.e., the chief priest (e.g., Lev 21:10); "the great men" (האנשים הגדולים), i.e., the chieftains (e.g., Jer 52:15); and perhaps "this key city" (לעיר הגדולה הזאת), i.e., "this capital city" (?) Jer 22:8. Note that "*a* great _____" would simply mean a large or major _____; the determination of the noun and adjective is required for the sense "chief," or in the case of a city, "capital."

An Amarna letter from Abimilki, King of Tyre (*ca.* 1375 B.C.), provides perhaps the closest West Semitic extra-biblical parallel to העיר הגדולה. Abimilki writes to the Pharaoh, "Behold, I protect Tyre, the capital city (*ᵘʳᵘSurri uru ra-bi-tu;* note the West Semitic feminine adjective) for the king my lord . . ." (EA 147:61–63). It appears that Abimilki purposely aggrandizes the status of his city, making it out to be *the* important city, or capital of the district, so as to impress the Pharaoh with the importance of rescuing it from its enemies.

In light of the above, we conclude that there is reason to believe the phrase העיר הגדולה would have meant to Jonah and to the readers of this book in ancient Israel more than simply "the great city of Nineveh" or "that large city, Nineveh." The term "capital" may perhaps be *too* strong and specific a translation in English, but in light of the reference to Nineveh's "king" in 3:6 it is perhaps a closer approximation of the singularity suggested by the Hebrew phrase than are the renderings in most translations. We thus cautiously render "important" for גדולה here and in 3:6.

As noted in the *Introduction*, the term רעה has a range of meaning which includes and / or overlaps with several English words. It has usually been assumed that one of the two English words "evil" or "wickedness" (e.g., "their *evil* has come up before me") is best employed to translate רעה in 1:2. But the rich ambiguity of the term is not adequately noticed by such a translation. In fact, Jonah could have understood "evil," but even more likely understood "trouble," or "calamity" or "difficulty" as the meaning of רעה here in Yahweh's command. He may even have been uncertain as to which of the meanings Yahweh intended. Was he being asked to preach against Nineveh because Yahweh intended to judge the city for its evil; or was he to preach against it in the sense of providing an explanation of why Yahweh had allowed some sort of evil, i.e., "trouble," to befall it? Jonah's message in 3:4 (q.v.) allows for this, according to the following logic: Nineveh was an *evil* (רעה) city which had suffered *misfortune* (רעה). God's compassion had been aroused by the misfortune. Instead of simply destroying the city for its evil, he would give it a chance to repent so as to remove the misfortune. Jonah would announce the chance.

Nineveh's "trouble" (רעה) is left unspecified. But the reason for it is clear. The city's evil ways (3:10) are excoriated at length in Nahum (esp. 2:11–12; 3:1, 19). As in Nahum, the intent is surely to suggest the cruelties of *Assyria* as a whole—not simply the capital city. Nineveh thus stands as a synecdoche for the brutally oppressive Assyrian empire itself. Nineveh's (Assyria's) "unceasing evil" (Nah 3:19) was so notorious that the narration hardly needed elaboration on this score.

The clause "is of concern to me" (עלתה . . . לפני) literally reads "has come up before me." In the OT it functions idiomatically rather than literally (cf. Gen 4:10; 18:21; Lam 1:22, etc.) as a means of expressing the fact that a situation is extreme enough to gain the special attention of God. It implies nothing about God's relative cognitive abilities. Yahweh thus announces to Jonah that his interest in the situation has been aroused to the point that he has chosen to do something about it.

Jonah is told to "speak against" (קרא עליה) Nineveh, i.e., denounce it. To a prophet such a command could have meant little else than to warn that God was about to enforce his covenant by enacting its sanctions, or curses. Yahweh, God of the whole earth, has the prerogative to punish evil wherever it is found. But Jonah would also recognize—as would the hearers / readers of this story in ancient Israel—that to give advance warning of the imposition of covenant sanctions was to open the door to the possibility of repentance. The term "preach against" by itself probably does not imply that God will *guarantee* the Ninevites a chance to repent, but it leaves open the question. In light of the capsulization of Jonah's words found in 3:4 ("In forty days Nineveh will be overthrown"), however, it is clear that he understood Yahweh to be commissioning a warning rather than an irrevocable announcement of immediate destruction. One must of course note that this quotation may well be an abbreviation or summation of the words Yahweh gave to Jonah. The vast majority of biblical narratives give the impression that conversations are summarized rather than presented verbatim.

3 Jonah went, all right, but not to Nineveh. Instead he made his plan to flee by sea away from (מלפני) Yahweh. Nineveh was to the east. The sea, that is, the Mediterranean, was to the west. If the expression מלפני יהוה were to be taken literally, it would make little sense. If Yahweh, Lord of all the earth, could superintend matters as distant to the east as was Nineveh, how could Jonah expect to get away merely by traveling an equal distance west? In fact, however, the expression is simply idiomatic, with the meaning that he wanted to get elsewhere, where Yahweh was not worshiped, i.e., "away from Israel" (cf. Gen 4:16; 1 Sam 26:19–20; 2 Kgs 5:17; 13:23; 17:20, 23; Jer 23:39). Jonah's attempt to flee is not entirely illogical, no matter how ultimately unsuccessful it may have been. His reasoning was probably a standard one: since Israelites never heard Yahweh's word except through Israelite prophets, they probably assumed, perhaps even unconsciously, that Yahweh revealed himself only to Israel. The OT contains numerous examples of native Israelite prophets who deliver oracles for or against foreign nations, but only a single example of a foreign prophet delivering any oracles at all *by Yahweh* to Israel, i.e., Balaam. Balaam, however, was summoned to travel to the place in Moab where Israel was (Num 22:6, 11, 37), and probably thought he had to be near enough to see the Israelites to curse them (Num 22:41; 23:9, 13; 24:2, 11; so also with the Amalekites, Num 24:20 and the Kenites, Num 24:21). It would have apparently been irregular prior to the exile to receive an oracle from Yahweh, Israel's God, elsewhere than in Israel. Prophets of Yahweh could and did travel to other locations to deliver oracles received from Yahweh. Later, Ezekiel and Daniel would prophesy in Babylon while God's people were in exile there, and Jeremiah would prophesy in Egypt (Jer 43:8–44:30) accompanying God's people there somewhat involuntarily. But even these prophets received God's word in the context of the believing community. Jonah, the ardent nationalist, therefore, attempted to flee to a place where no fellow believers would be found, hoping that this would help insure that God's word would not come to him again. If he stayed in Israel, he could expect to hear more from Yahweh, but if he left, he might hear nothing further.

It is interesting in this connection to note that ברח "flee" is the verb used by Balak to send Balaam back home to Aram where he could prophesy no more on behalf of Israel (Num 24:11; cf. Amos 7:12) but this correspondence may be merely coincidental.

Jonah sought to flee on the open sea (תרשישה). The term תרשיש, usually rendered as a place name, Tarshish, has been the subject of much misunderstanding. In fact the word probably had two common meanings. First, as a place name derived from the more basic meaning "sea" it was applied to several different coastal areas in the Mediterranean, including the Greek Tartessos on the southwest of Spain (Herodotus I, 163 and IV, 152; cf. Gen 10:4), Carthage (Ezek 27 and Isa 23 in G) and Sardinia (see Cross, *BASOR* 208 [1972] 14–16, where "Tarshish" seems to be Nora). All such sites were apparently centers of metal mining and / or smelting to and from which large sea-going freighters carried metal products to various ports around the Mediterranean (Ezek 27:12; Jer 10:9). Other OT references appear to equate Tarshish in effect with distant Mediterranean coastlands (Isa 23:6, 10; 66:19). As a place name, therefore, "Tarshish" was apparently at least as common in ancient times as the analogous "Portland" is today.

Second, it had the more basic meaning "open sea," or the like. This is where the expression "ships of the open sea" אניות תרשיש or better "ocean-going ships" originated (e.g., Isa 23:1). Thus the Aramaic (Targum) consistently translates תרשיש as בימא "in / on the sea" in Jonah 1:3. Jerome in his commentary on Jonah also noted, at least in the case of the first occurrence of תרשיש, that *mare* ("sea") appeared to be the intended meaning; and in his commentary on Isa 2:16 he states that "Hebrew scholars" define תרשיש as "sea." In *Targum Onkelos*, the gem called תרשיש in Exod 28:20 and 39:13 is rendered כרום ימא, "the color of the sea." C. H. Gordon (*JNES* 37 [1978] 51–52) provides a convincing argument for the definition "open sea," as originating from a color (loosely "wine-dark" or "wine-red," cognate to the archaic poetic תירוש "wine" or "fruit-of-the-vine"). Whatever the etymology, however, it is most likely that the term in Jonah does not designate a place name, but rather the sea itself.

The port Jonah chose to embark from was Joppa, a small harbor town on the Palestine coast known as Yepu in the Amarna letters (early 14th century B.C.) and Yapu in neo-Assyrian inscriptions. It was never annexed by Israel during OT times, but became Judean only under Jonathan (*ca.* 148 B.C.; cf. 1 Macc 10:76). Accordingly, Jonah chose a port where the people he might meet, and the ships he could hire, were not likely to be Israelite. Once in Joppa he was already partly "away from Yahweh" as he apparently conceived it. That Israelites knew about Joppa and its contacts with distant parts is evident from its mention in 2 Chr 2:15 [16]; Josh 19:46; Ezra 3:7 as a port through which goods bound for Israel sometimes flowed. Of course, those who sailed ships from Joppa were hardly likely to have been worshipers of Yahweh, and this fact is important for the proper appreciation of the sailors' actions described later in the chapter.

The remainder of the verse explains largely without embellishment that the initial phase of Jonah's plan succeeded. He found the kind of ship he needed, i.e., an ocean-going ship, and one preparing to go (בוא). The verb בוא may mean, as here twice, "go" rather than its more usual "come" as long as it is modified as to direction or distance (cf. Gen 45:17; Num 32:6; 1 Sam 22:5; Isa 22:15; 47:5; Ezek 3:4). The text says that Jonah will go "with them" (עמהם), i.e., the sailors implicitly being the referent. Twice also the verb ירד "to go down" is used. But no special significance can be attached to this. To go down to the coast from higher elevations and to go down into the compartments of a ship from its upper deck are both normal, logical idioms. The story employs a simple vocabulary throughout (see *Introduction*).

At the very end of the verse the phrase תרשישה מלפני יהוה "on the open sea, away from Yahweh" is repeated. The narrator thereby efficiently makes absolutely clear to the hearer / reader the purpose of Jonah's trip. This purpose will, of course, be thwarted by Yahweh's intervention.

Explanation

In this brief introduction to the book the reader learns three central things: (1) who Jonah was; (2) what Yahweh wanted him to do; (3) Jonah's response. Thus are introduced the main characters of the story, i.e., Jonah and God; and the situation around which the story revolves, i.e., Jonah's unwillingness to carry out a divine commission which he finds odious.

If this sense of the word רעה is correct in this context, it provides an overt statement as to why Jonah found Yahweh's word so objectionable that he sought to flee from further contact with the God he had been serving as a prophet. Thus Jonah's motivation is suggested, long before his own explanation in 4:2. For it is implicit in the message he received that Yahweh had not closed the door on the possibility of sparing Nineveh. Jonah, like any other orthodox Israelite, would of course have known that, hateful though the prospect may have been to him. Through Moses the covenant blessings and curses were held before Israel. Obedience meant blessing; disobedience meant curse. For God to send prophets to remind people of their responsibilities before his covenant—national or universal—was an act of grace in itself. The description Jonah gives of God in 4:2, i.e., that God is gracious, merciful, patient, loyal, and willing to change his plan, is, as Jonah says, something he knew all along. The Israelites of Jonah's day knew this, as did all Israelites since God rescued them from bondage in Egypt, and as do we. Indeed, so did the Ninevites (3:9). God's word is always to be understood within the context of his nature. Knowing God affects the parameters of meaning one assigns to his word. Thus implicitly God's command to Jonah to "speak against" Nineveh had to be understood in light of the possibility that God might thereby bring good, rather than evil, to the city.

A second implicit reality in the introduction comes from the twice-stated phrase "out to sea, away from Yahweh." The hearer / reader cannot miss the implication that Jonah hopes to avoid further revelatory contact with Israel's God by going someplace where there are no Israelites. The rest of the words in v 3 are necessary to describe the scene. Their order, contrary to several recent attempts to see significance in the (accidentally) chiastic structure of the verse, is not really important. The repetition of the motive of Jonah is. He does not want to preach against Nineveh, to give them any chance of repentance, and he thinks he has a chance to avoid a restatement of the divine call by fleeing. It will not work, of course. The divine call will come again exactly as it did at first (3:2).

It is debatable whether Jonah really thought his flight would work. Presumably he knew that Yahweh's power was hardly limited to Israel proper. If God could be found in heaven and Sheol, and "in the distant reaches of the sea" (Ps 139:8–9), physical escape would be impossible. But Jonah was well aware that there were plenty of other prophets around. His day was a golden age for prophets. Is it not possible that he said to himself, "God has determined to give Assyria a chance. But if so, at least one of the other prophets ought to mediate his word. For me to do it goes against all I've stood for. If I withdraw from my people and exile myself in distant parts, surely God will appoint another prophet. Surely he'll prefer a willing prophet to me now (cf. Exod 4:13). And I won't have to see something I've worked against all my life come to pass."

In other words, Jonah's flight was probably not motivated by any thought that he was an essential cog in the wheel of revelation, and that God's plan would be thwarted by his flight. Rather, he simply wanted no part of something so horrible as mercy shown to a brutal, oppressing, enemy nation.

We do not have any other record in scripture of a prophet who disobeyed God's call. Amos expressed the normal response: "The Lord God has spoken, Who can but prophesy?" (3:8). Jeremiah agonized over some of his oracles (Jer 20:7–18). Isaiah at first felt unqualified for his commission (Isa 6:5). But unless some of the false prophets, of whom we have frequent mention in the OT, had become false prophets after initially resisting a true call— and of this we have no hint—Jonah does represent an anomaly. He actually disobeyed God's word, so deep was his hatred for a nation whom God loved, and his resentment that God would do something good for a people who had done so much that was bad.

Storm and Sacrifice at Sea (1:4–16)

Bibliography

Abramsky, S. "About Casting Lots in Order to Catch a Sinner." *BMik* 26 (1981) 231–66. **Allen, L. C.** *The Greek Chronicles.* VTSup 27. Leiden: E. J. Brill, 1974. 81. **Andrews, D. K.** "Yahweh the God of the Heavens." *The Seed of Wisdom, FS T. J. Meek,* ed. W. S. McCullough. Toronto: University Press, 1964. 45–57. **Avineri, I.** "The Peshitta Translation of Jonah 1." *BMik* 30 (1984 / 85) 419–21. [Heb.] **Freedman, D. N.** "Jonah 1:4b." *JBL* 77 (1958) 161–62. **Horwitz, W. J.** "Another Interpretation of Jonah 1:12." *VT* 23 (1973) 370–72. **Hurvitz, A.** "The History of a Legal Formula, *kol ʾašer hapeṣ ʿaśah.*" *VT* 32 (1982) 257–67. **Lang, B.** "Glaubensbekenntnisse im Alten und Neuen Testament." *Concilium* 14 (1978) 499–503. **Lindblom, J.** "Lot-Casting in the OT." *VT* 12 (1962) 164–78. **Pesch, R.** "Zur konzentrischen Struktur von Jona 1." *Bib* 47 (1966) 577–81. **Wachsman, S.** "Nautical Archaeological Inspection by the Israel Department of Antiquities and Museums." *Bulletin of the Anglo-Israel Archaeological Society* (1984–85) 24–29. **Weiss, M.** "Weiteres über die Bauformen des Erzählens in der Bibel." *Bib* 46 (1965) 181–206.

Translation

The storm begins

⁴*But Yahweh threw a great wind* ᵃ *at the sea. There was then* ᵇ *a great storm on the sea and the ship seemed* ᶜ *about to break apart.* ⁵*The sailors were afraid.*

They each called out to his god, and threw the cargo[a] *which was on the ship into the sea, to make it lighter for them.*

Jonah found out

As for Jonah, he had[b] *gone down into a remote place below deck*[c] *to lie down, and had fallen into a deep sleep.*[d] [6]*The captain came to him and said to him, "What are you doing in a deep sleep? Get up! Call on* your *god! Maybe the god*[a] *will consider us, and we won't perish."* [7]*They said to each other, "Let's cast lots*[a] *in order to find out who is to blame for our trouble."*[b] *They cast lots and the lot fell on Jonah.* [8]*So they said to him, "Tell us,* [a]*who is to blame for our bad situation?*[a] *What is your occupation? Where do you come from? What is your country? What nationality are you?"* [9]*He said to them, "I am a Hebrew.*[a] *I believe in*[b] *Yahweh, the God of Heaven, who made the sea and the land."* [10]*The men were very afraid and said to him, "What have you done!"*[a] (*Indeed,*[b] *the men knew that he was fleeing from Yahweh,* [c]*because he had told them.*[c])

A means of calming the storm

[11]*They said to him, "What should we do to you so that the sea will become calm for us?" since the sea was becoming even more*[a] *stormy.* [12]*He said to them, "Pick me up and throw me into the sea, and the sea will become calm for you. I know that I am to blame for this great storm which has come to you."*

[13]*The men tried to row*[a] *back to land, but they could not because the sea was growing even more stormy*[b] *on them.* [14]*So they called to Yahweh and said, "O Yahweh, please don't let us perish on account of this man's life,*[a] *and don't hold us accountable for killing an innocent person.*[c] *For you, Yahweh, have done as you wanted."*[d] [15]*They picked up Jonah and threw him into the sea, and the sea stopped raging.*

Coda: the sailors' belief

[16]*As a result,*[a] *the men really believed in*[b] *Yahweh. They sacrificed to Yahweh and made vows to him.*

Notes

4.a. G and T[c] omit any correspondent to MT גדולה "great," suggesting that it is secondary.

4.b. The *waw*-conversive narrative style implies a relatedness of the events.

4.c. The meaning of חשבה (piel) is not certain. Freedman (*JBL* 77 [1958] 161–62) on the basis of G ἐκινδύνευε suggests emending to a form of חוב (cf. Dan 11:24) vocalized חָבָה, the *shin* of MT being a secondary accretion from the following להשבר. Syr and Tg both use a form of בעה "to be about to." The passive (pual; חֻשְּׁבָה, *huššᵉbā*) is also possible. The translation "seemed" comes as close as any word to expressing the active sense called for by the piel of MT in the context, assuming the MT pointing to be accurate.

5.a. Lit., "vessels," "stuff."

5.b. Logically, the pluperfect tense is more appropriate to the chronology of the story than the simple pf ("went") would be. The Heb. pf ירד allows for either sense.

5.c. Lit., "far reaches of the decked vessel," i.e., the lowest part of the hold. A pun on ירכתי צפון "far reaches of the north" (cf. Ps 48:3 [2]; Isa 14:13; Ezek 38:6) is possible but far from certain.

5.d. By רדם the narrator signifies not simply sound sleep but a special state of depressed or hypnotic sleep. Cf. Gen. 2:21.

6.a. Or, "God." The Heb. האלהים is ambiguous. The article may signify *the* god in question, or simply accompany "God" without implying reference to one god among many.

7.a. Or, "dice." See *Comment.*

7.b. Or, "calamity," "difficulty," etc.

8.a.-a. The entire clause is omitted in G^{BSV} and some MT MSS. T^{MSS} translates as if למה rather than למי were present: "Tell us now for what reason (בדיל מא) this bad situation has come upon us." The clause is a virtual doublet from the verse above, but genuinely reflects the logic of the sailors. An excellent brief summary of the translation options is presented by L. C. Allen (209, n. 31).

9.a. G δοῦλος κυρίου stems from a misreading of עברי as . . . י עבד and compensatory scribal insertion of the remainder of the divine name perhaps under the influence of 2 Kgs 14:25. Cf. Allen, *The Greek Chronicles,* 81. Since Jonah's worship of / belief in Yahweh is immediately stated next, the context supports MT.

9.b. Lit., "fear," i.e., "worship," "serve," "believe in," etc.

10.a. The sailors' remark is an exclamation, not a true interrogative.

10.b. The force of כי in the context is to introduce a parenthetical explanation.

10.c.-c. The clause כי הגיד להם "because he (had) told them" is often thought secondary on stylistic grounds; but its presence is contextually more necessary than any other part of the parenthetical statement, since the remainder is left unexplained without it.

11.a. The connotation of הלך in the ptcp when appended to another ptcp is increase or progression.

13.a. Lit., "dig through," perhaps signifying hard rowing, though this is not certain.

13.b. See n. 11.a.

14.b. I.e., "for taking this man's life."

14.c. Lit., "Do not put innocent blood on us."

14.d. Or "For you are Yahweh. You have done as you wanted."

16.a. See n. 4.b.

16.b. Or "feared," "worshiped," etc. See *Comment.*

Form / Structure / Setting

The narrative of 1:4–16 is unified and coherent. The storm, which God causes suddenly to appear, functions as the catalyst for the rest of the action described in this pericope. This correspondence of storm and resulting action aboard ship may be described by the following four-part outline:

a. Storm begins: Sailors rush to prevent sinking, vv 4–5a.
b. Storm continues: Jonah discovered to be at fault, vv 5b–10.
c. Storm worsens: Jonah "sacrificed" to calm the sea, vv 11–15.
d. Storm over: Sailors, later, demonstrate belief, v 16.

The narrative of Jonah has sometimes been explicated by arrangement in scenes (most effectively by Watts, 72–97). By this approach all of vv 4–16 constitute a single scene, in which there is a progression of events, somewhat as we have outlined it. It is likely, however, that v 16, if not a separate scene of its own, is at least a coda to the shipboard scene portrayed in vv 4–15. Verse 16 describes what the sailors did after rowing back to shore. It is unlikely that the narrator expected the audience to believe that after throwing both cargo and a passenger overboard, the sailors had carefully saved out some animals (cf. v 5) to sacrifice to Yahweh. Accordingly v 16 may be best understood as an internal postscript (coda) confirming that the sailors genuinely believed in Yahweh (though hardly in a monotheistic manner) as a result of the miraculous, sudden appearance and subsidence of the storm. They demonstrated the belief by sacrifices and vows somewhere at a Yahwistic temple or shrine on shore, such as Jerusalem, after returning to port.

The storm dominates events. It is Yahweh's proof that he controls Jonah's fate, even outside the bounds of Canaan. As the storm worsens, so the action changes. The action is described with minimal detail, in rather simple vocabulary (though not *simplistic* vocabulary). Events move quickly and crisply to their completion. Conversation is summarized (e.g., the reference to what Jonah had already told the crew in the parenthetical statement of v 10), and data which might satisfy the curiosity (e.g., how long they had been at sea, how far they were from land, how long the storm lasted, etc.), but not contribute to an appreciation of the didactic function, are omitted.

Implicitly, the reference to an attempt to row back to land (v 13) must mean that the ship was not far out to sea when God began the storm. Therefore the intent of the inspired narrator was probably to suggest that the events described in vv 4–16 took place rather soon after Jonah's boarding the ship. One reasonable, though hardly provable, reconstruction of the events would place Jonah in the hold of the ship, deep in a depressed sleep, even *before* the ship set out to sea. The ship would then have not been long at sea when God produced the unexpected windstorm, completely unpredictable and therefore especially frightening on what might have been an otherwise fine day for sailing. Experienced sailors could hardly fail to infer, in that religious age, that a sudden storm, while still in view of land, on an otherwise fair day, was supernatural in origin. It may also be speculated that the ship either followed the coast in its voyage, or was near to landing somewhere in the Mediterranean at the time the storm came upon them. The semi-coastal voyage of the ship in Acts 27 (esp. vv 3–17) may provide a parallel of sorts. There is ultimately no way to decide such a question since the data are sparse.

Some of the words of the pericope are notable both for their repetition here and in other parts of the book. The following terms stand out in the Hebrew text for their frequency: גדול "great"; טול, hiphil "throw"; ירא "believe, fear"; קרא "call on"; על "against," etc. Three of these terms may be proleptic of future points. The word גדול echoes the great fish in 2:1 and the great city of Nineveh in 3:2, etc. The Ninevites call (קרא) on Yahweh (3:8) just as Jonah called on him from the fish (2:3). And Jonah preaches against (על) Nineveh as commanded a second time (3:2).

Upon careful analysis, however, it becomes evident that there is no special didactic significance to the simple repetition of vocabulary here or anywhere else in the book. The words טול and ירא, for example, do not appear again though they are so prominent in 1:4–16. If the narrator had desired to make vocabulary connections throughout the book, it would have been easy to have the Ninevites believe / fear (ירא) rather than "be convinced" (אמן; 3:5). Moreover, certain words like אמר "say," תרשיש "open sea," סער "storm," and ים "sea" require repetition in light of the events of the story, their frequency of occurrence being therefore unavoidable.

A full discussion of words repeated in Jonah is given in Magonet, *Form and Meaning*, 13–38, including a charting of the distribution by chapters on p. 14. The net result is overinterpretation. In Magonet's analysis (and those of similar studies) the book of Jonah ceases to be a simple narrative and becomes a complex vocabulary puzzle whose solution or even existence would never have occurred to any hearer or reader until the advent of the current fascination with complex rhetorical analysis. Magonet's patterns (hardly consistent) are of the type one would find in any narrative of a few chapters' length where sets of actions are described in simple terms.

Most of the repetition of vocabulary that does exist in this chapter and in the book as a whole is due to a single factor: the desire for simplicity. The narrator obviously has no lofty stylistic designs, but wishes the story to have its impact via the actual events themselves rather than by any obtrusive language. The simpler the language, the broader the audience, and the more effective the impact. Simplicity in this case requires a relatively limited vocabulary.

Several attempts have been made to discern an elaborate (usually chiastic) structure to the narrative in vv 4–16. Fretheim (*The Message of Jonah,* 73–79), for example, posits an ABCCBA ordering to the material, in which the individual events group into three main categories: (1) a narrative framework in which hurling of wind (v 4) parallels the hurling of Jonah (v 15) and the sailor's appeal to their gods (v 5a) is paralleled by their fear to Yahweh (v 16); (2) a narrative segment in which the captain's words, dealings with Jonah, and views about God (vv 5b–6) parallel the sailors' words, dealings with Jonah, and views about God (vv 13–14); (3) a dialog in which Jonah is determined the cause of the storm and responds (vv 7–9) paralleled by the same sort of development in vv 10–12.

This analysis and others like it are forced. There *are* patterns and structures in the book but they are not deliberately this elaborate. The correspondences within vv 4–16 result almost entirely from normal narrative requirements of consistency and coherence, rather than any elaborate attempt by the narrator to inform the hearer / reader of anything via the structure alone.

Comment

4 The developing emergency at sea is described succinctly, in three simple statements denoting three consecutive and related events. Yahweh caused a wind, which caused a storm, which caused the ship to be in danger of sinking. This danger provides the conditions under which most of the remaining action takes place, through v 15 at least. The words leave no doubt that the storm is Yahweh's doing. In the rapid flow of the narrative the storm unmistakably represents an intervention and therefore judgment on Jonah's flight, thus our translation "But" for the ו (adversative *waw*) which begins the verse. The use of the verb טול, hiphil ("throw") to convey metaphorically Yahweh's control and origination of the wind is notable. In the same way that one would throw a spear (1 Sam 18:11) or cargo (Jonah 1:5) or Jonah himself (1:15), Yahweh threw the wind at the sea around the ship. There was no way that this storm could be considered by the story's audience a coincidence. Yahweh's control of wind and sea is a theme expressed relatively often in the OT, often metaphorically as here (e.g., Exod 10:13–19; 14–15; Num 11:31; Job 26:12; Ps 89:9; Ps 135:7; Isa 50:2; Jer 49:32–36; Amos 4:13; Nah 1:4; cf. Mark 4:37–39).

5 The frenzy of the sailors, terrified, crying out to their gods and hurling the cargo overboard, contrasts sharply with Jonah's state. He remains asleep.

The sailors' hectic moves would have taken some time. There was presumably plenty of cargo on board to retrieve from the hold and throw overboard (cf. Ezek 27:25: ". . . ocean-going ships . . . filled with heavy cargo . . ."), and time had obviously been consumed in the sailors' prayers as well. Yet all the while, as the ship reeled, the waves pounded, and the wind shrieked, Jonah continued in his deep sleep (וירדם) as the pluperfect of the translation is intended to indicate. *Where* he was sleeping, i.e., "in the far reaches of the decked ship" (ירכתי הספינה) is significant in that it resulted in a delay for the crew in determining the cause of the miraculous storm. Were Jonah awake on deck, he might have volunteered the reason earlier. It is not clear, at any rate, where the crew and passengers on ocean-going ships slept. Perhaps the "far reaches of the hold" contained chambers of sorts for passengers. Not a great deal is known about the construction of a ספינה. The word is used here alone in the Hebrew OT, though commonly in its Aramaic and Arabic cognates. The root רדם, used with either the verb or the noun (תרדמה), indicates a special state of deep or hypnotic sleep, from which wakefulness would hardly be automatic. Adam's deep sleep (Gen 2:21) allowed for surgery. Jonah's deep sleep therefore can hardly be evidence that he was uncaring or irresponsible, as the rest of the narrative makes clear, but rather that he was "out cold." What would bring on such a condition? Depression is the most likely cause, though the narrative hardly provides enough data for a decision on the issue. Blankness, listlessness, and sleepiness (sometimes bordering on narcolepsy) are extremely common symptoms of physiological depression. That depression should have followed upon a prophet's decision to end his career and exile himself from his home and country is hardly surprising. It is also possible, however, that we are to assume that the special deep sleep is actually divinely produced (cf. BDB, 922). But what purpose this serves in Yahweh's rebuke of Jonah is then left unanswered.

6 In the course of their frequent trips to the hold for cargo, the sailors had eventually come upon Jonah, hidden away and asleep, perhaps even in a passenger chamber. Probably having no authority themselves to do anything to a passenger, they reported this incongruity to the captain, who did not hesitate to go to wake Jonah up. The captain's words, "What are you doing in a deep sleep?" (מה לך נרדם) do not indicate a judgmental attitude, though they may possibly indicate surprise. The captain's speech is in its entirety typical of brief summations of discourse in narrative; its seeming rudeness is only a reflection of modern expectations of lengthy dialog of a sort not found often in ancient literature. Similarly the apparently abrupt speech of the Levite to his dying or dead concubine in Judg 19:28, "Get up, let's go," proves on examination to be simply an abridgment. Here too, a probably respectful, though urgent speech from the captain is abridged so as not to intrude upon the action. The narrator provides once again the bare essentials, but little more.

The first words ascribed to the captain, קום קרא "Get up! Call . . . ," contain the two verbs God had used in summoning Jonah to preach against Nineveh in v 2. Should we discern here a purposeful, ironic connection? "Jonah must have thought he was having a nightmare. These were the very words with which God had disturbed his pleasant life a few days before" (Allen, 208).

It is hard to be sure. The use of קוּם in the imperative is so typically idiomatic that the hearer / reader could hardly think it significant that it is repeated. As for קרא, the connection might have been evident; but this verb, too, has so many common nuances (call, speak, read, cry out, etc.) that it is not certain that a comparison to the usage in v 2 could really be obvious to the audience.

The captain is, of course, a polytheist and probably a syncretist. There are many gods and goddesses in his belief system. Most inhabitants of Palestine at this time believed in three kinds of gods: personal gods, whom one would worship in connection with individual concerns; family gods, worshiped by all the members of a clan; and national gods, worshiped as the guardians and motivators of an entire nation. For the captain to urge Jonah to "call on *your* God" may reflect his presumption that Jonah, a stranger, is bound to have a god different from the others on board. But more likely, it simply reflects the captain's certainty that everyone has a personal god on whom he would call in time of calamity, and whether or not Jonah's personal god was unique among those on board or not, it should be appealed to. Generally, nationality and religion went together in OT times. Since Jonah was not one of their number, he might just provide the religious complementation the crisis called for!

The captain's hope is that Jonah's God will "consider" (יתעשׁת) their peril and do something about the storm. The verb עשׁת, unique here in the OT, seems to connote "think favorably" or the like, judging from the versions; the cognate in OT Aramaic, however, connotes only "think" or "plan" (Dan 6:4). The captain's main concern is to get the attention of some god, somewhere. The gods could and did ignore people. They were not constantly watchful over their worshipers (cf. 1 Kgs 18:26, 27, 29) as was Yahweh (Ps 121:3, 4).

7 The sailors decide on a strategy of divination, and use it to determine that Jonah is the source of their problem. It is evident to them that the storm represents a divine punishment. Someone among those on board ship has done something to offend a god, and casting lots (גורלות) will let them know (ונדעה) who that person is.

Lots were probably dice, their sides alternately light or dark in color (thus the "lights" and "darks" or Urim and Thummin, אורים ותמים, of Exod 28:30, etc., dice kept ready in the high priest's ephod for discerning Yahweh's will). At several significant points in OT history, these lots had been employed in a process of elimination, for which they were designed: Josh 7:16–18 (implicitly); 1 Sam 10:20–21; 14:40–42. Lots were used commonly in decision making, especially in the division of land (cf. Ps 16:6), probably accompanied by a prayer for God to guide the outcome (cf. Acts 1:24–26). A mild sort of confidence is expressed for this method of divination in Prov 16:33: "From one's bosom the lot is cast, but from Yahweh is its every judgment." This proverb seems to assert through its admittedly laconic wording that lot casting does not in itself have automatic validity, but that it may accurately provide the thrower with knowledge if Yahweh makes it do so. This appears to be the sense of the disciples in Acts 1:24–26, at any rate.

The casting of the lots probably was interpreted as follows. Two dark sides up meant "No." Two light sides up meant "Yes." A light and a dark meant "Throw again." Using this system, the sailors eliminated others on ship until Jonah was left. The narrator tells us nothing about Jonah's thoughts or feelings during the divination process, since Jonah's perspective on the matter is not in focus. But God evidently chose to cause the lots to work according to plan, for they fell on Jonah.

8 The five questions pressed hurriedly on Jonah while the storm still howls are not mere idle conversation-starters. The first question is the most crucial. Its answer is not obvious. The crew quite naturally wonders if somehow *they* might have done some wrong deserving of this calamity. Have they offended Jonah? Are they helping him do something wrong? Is it guilt by association? Or is Jonah alone to blame? Are they transporting someone who has committed a great crime? Or is someone else, whom Jonah knows or is associated with, the source of the problem? The sometimes suggested translation ". . . since you are to blame for our bad situation" is not truly reflective of the Hebrew syntax (see n. 8.a-a.). They are still genuinely wondering why the lot fell on Jonah and what it means for them. The crew is also desperate to know exactly who Jonah is, because they now know only that he is somehow the focus of the problem. Until they know his identity, they can hardly expect to know, for example, which god he has offended, and how. Thus the sailors pepper him with urgent questions. His occupation, once they know it, will tell them much. If he were a priest, or a prophet, or an executioner, or an idol-maker, or had any one of many other religiously sensitive occupations, part of the answer might already be realized. Jonah does not answer this question directly, but not necessarily because he is trying to be evasive (see v 9, *Comment*). Rather, it is likely that the questions mentioned merely summarize a whole series of actual questions, the gist of which is communicated by the rapid-fire recounting of five of them. The final three questions all concern Jonah's origin. The answer to those also would have religious significance, since one's national god was usually the most important divinity in one's life at this point in history. The ancients believed in three kinds of gods: personal, family, and national. But the world increasingly organized itself by empires and nations (in contrast, for example, to the relative isolation of the city-state system that had prevailed in Palestine in most of the second millennium B.C.). By Jonah's time, people's personal destinies became inextricably linked with their national destinies, and national gods functioned increasingly as personal gods, at least in Palestine.

Moreover, the crew certainly had reason to suspect that Jonah was a Palestinian of some sort, since the ship sailed from a Palestinian port, and Jonah presumably spoke and dressed like a Palestinian. If he had been Greek, or Egyptian, or Assyrian, for example, his fluency in the sailor's native Canaanite (the broad dialect of Philista, Israel, Judah, Edom, Moab, Phoenicia, etc.) would have been less likely and his foreign accent more evident, to mention nothing of his dress. What they wanted to know specifically, then, was which of the Palestinian nations he was from. Each had a national god. That would tell them at least which god he was likely to "fear" (cf. 1 Kgs 11:5–7).

9 Jonah replies forthrightly. His answer is for the most part a standard one. He identifies himself as a "Hebrew" (עברי), a term apparently used rather commonly by Israelites in explaining themselves to foreigners (cf. Gen

40:15; Exod 1:19). "Hebrew" in legal portions distinguishes Israelites from non-Israelites (e.g., Exod 21:2; Deut 15:12). It is obvious to Jonah that the sailors also want to know his religion, so he declares that he "believes in" (ירא; the terms "fear" or "worship" might also be used in translation) Yahweh. Would not this be obvious? Would not all Hebrews believe in Yahweh? Not necessarily! A prophet, of all people, would be keenly aware that outright Baal worship was not uncommon in Israel (Hos 2:19 [17]; 11:2; 2 Kgs 17:16, etc.). If this part of Jonah's life is dated early in the eighth century, the influence of Baalism might not have been as pervasive as it was at the end of Jeroboam II's reign, or in the reigns of his successors. But Jehu's anti-Baal reforms in 842 B.C. did not likely last even through the reign of Jehoahaz (814–798 B.C.). The Asherah idol he allowed to be worshiped (2 Kgs 13:6) was evidence for Baal worship, in all probability, since Asherah was Baal's consort. Her possible role as Yahweh's consort is speculative.

The epithet "God of Heaven" (אלהי השמים) was a convenient way for the Israelites to describe Yahweh's identity to syncretistic, polytheistic foreigners. The sounds in the name Yahweh meant little to non-Israelites. This was an age in which hundreds of different deities were worshiped in various areas of the fertile crescent and Mediterranean. Later, in the Persian period, the Jews in foreign lands would be well served by this convenient application of an old (Gen 24:3, 7) title. It answered the question "Yahweh—what's he god of?" very nicely and simply, while having the additional merit of implicitly suggesting that Yahweh was at least chief of all the gods. To the Sumerians and Babylonians, for example, Anu was the god of heaven, the progenitor and at least titulary ruler of all the gods, since their dwelling place was heaven. The "God of Heaven" was logically the supreme deity. We find the term thus commonly used after the exile (2 Chr 36:23; Ezra 1:2; Neh 1:4, 5; 2:4) by Jews and Persians (in their dealings with Jews) alike. The term had its reflex also in Aramaic (אלה שמיא; e.g., Dan 2:18; Ezra 5:11; 7:12). The formulation had a parallel as well in the name of the Canaanite-Phoenician deity Baʿal-šamēm (O. Eissfeldt, *"Baʿalšamēm und Yahweh,"* ZAW 57 [1939] 1–31 = *Kleine Schriften* 2:171–98).

Jonah adds to his confession of belief / worship a universalistic claim for Yahweh, one highly apropos in light of the present circumstances at sea. The designation of Yahweh as the one "who made the sea and the land" has the ring of an Israelite credal confession, and indeed a credal formula of this kind might have its basis or reflection in such hymnody as Ps 95:5 ("The sea is his, for he made it; and his hands formed the land"; cf. Ps 135:7; Exod 10:13–19; 14–15; Num 11:31; Isa 50:2; Jer 49:32–36; Amos 4:13; Job 26:12). It has often been suggested that Jonah's words are purposely cast by the narrator so as to be ironic. But this does not bear up under scrutiny. Jonah by this point knows all about the suddenness of the storm, and has seen God control the lots. He cannot fail to recognize that his attempt at flight has proved futile. If he has not already told, he is beginning to tell the sailors that he has been fleeing Yahweh (v 10). It is time to give up and to confess everything. His confession of faith, therefore, can hardly be understood as a mindless rote recitation of a credal formula by which he unwittingly condemns himself. Rather, it is an open admission that his God is all-powerful,

and his will inescapable. Jonah has resigned himself to being punished by
the God he could not outrun, the universal Yahweh. The idea that the storm
may be stopped by his death (v 12) is probably already in his mind.

10 The attention shifts immediately to the sailors' reaction. Jonah has
now confessed all to them. The pieces of the puzzle have been completely
fit together. The storm is indeed a divine judgment of a most serious sort:
the God Yahweh is punishing one of his prophets who has disobeyed his
word. And the crew is caught in the process! It is no wonder that they were
very afraid (ויראו יראה גדולה) and exclaimed "What have you done!"
(מה זאת עשית). A paraphrase of their words would be: "Oh, no! You've
done that!?" or even "How could you!?" These were religious Canaanite
sailors. They knew how serious Jonah's actions were, and they did not like
the fact that he had chosen their vessel as his means of flight. The storm
was cause enough for fear. Now to be associated with this disobedient prophet,
even innocently! It was like being tied up to a person who was calling for
lightning to strike him dead.

The parenthetical statement in the second half of the verse summarizes
for the hearer / reader what several lines of conversation might be required
to convey, i.e., that the sailors had found out Jonah's story. They now know,
in effect, just as much as the hearer / reader does at this point in the story.

11 Jonah has told them what has caused their trouble and therefore he
may know the solution for it. The sailors are not Yahwists, and certainly
not prophets. Jonah is both the guilty party and the expert here. At most,
they might think they know what Baal, for example, would require in such
a situation; but this situation stems from *Yahweh's* punishment of a person,
so Jonah is the only one who can tell them what Yahweh would require to
turn aside his wrath. They ask him what to do. There must be some punishment
of Jonah which they can instigate that will stop the storm. The sea was churning
ever higher, so the lightening of the ship by throwing cargo overboard had
only bought time; it had not really gotten them out of danger. The Hebrew
הלך וסער "becoming even more stormy" alerts the reader to the fact that
those words are spoken anxiously in a situation which is ever more desperate.

12 Jonah's reply is blunt and shocking. They must kill him. The death
penalty is the penalty he deserves—nothing short of it. Jonah is hardly suggesting that he be sacrificed to the sea, as if the sea were an independent judge
or even a deity. Rather, the sea is evidently Yahweh's device for punishment;
so if the crew will throw Jonah to the sea, it will do the work Yahweh intended
it to do, and the sailors can have peace. The sailors are of course innocent.
Jonah knows that Yahweh is hardly out to punish them (cf. Deut 24:16).
He resignedly offers his own life in this way so that theirs may be spared.
Let Yahweh complete his judgment.

To this point, Jonah may not have admitted in so many words what he
now asserts categorically: "I know that I am to blame for this great storm
which has come on you." It is hard to imagine, however, that the gist of his
words, as summarized in v 10b, "Indeed the men knew that he was fleeing
from Yahweh, because he had told them," had not already made this clear
to the crew. The force of Jonah's words at this point in the narrative therefore
might be: "I know that I *alone* am to blame . . .", though the Hebrew (בשלי)
is ambiguous as to emphasis.

Moreover, nowhere does the story suggest that Jonah did not heretofore recognize his guilt. There is no evidence of "nonchalant indifference" (L. C. Allen, 211) suddenly now displaced by a genuine realization of sin. Jonah, when he was awakened, may have initially wondered in his own mind whether the storm represented Yahweh's punishment for his flight, or had some other purpose, or was merely coincidental. But there is no reason to suspect that Jonah did not realize how wrong his actions were. His words, therefore, firmly connect the storm with his flight, so that if there were any doubt in *his* mind previously of whether the storm really was sent by Yahweh—the crew having no doubt by now at all—that doubt is gone and the crew's recourse is clear. Jonah must be thrown overboard.

13 The crew, however, did not want to throw Jonah to the sea. That is evident not by their words, but by their actions, succinctly described by the narrator. They tried instead to row (or "pull hard," see n. 13.a.) to land. Why? The answer comes in v 14; they fear that the same Yahweh who has sought to punish Jonah for *his* misdeed by the storm will turn to punish *them* if they murder Jonah. He may have commissioned the storm to do his will, but he had not commissioned *them* to do it. But as the sea got even *more* stormy (הולך וסער, as in v 11) their attempt to make it to land had to be abandoned.

Here it is evident that the ship was either not yet so far from port that it was out of sight of land, or else following a coastal route which kept within sight of land. The sailors desperately wanted to get Jonah off the ship, but did not want to accomplish this by causing his death themselves. To put him ashore was their decision, probably arrived at after further frantic discussion. But Yahweh controlled events. He kept the sea riled all the more. The crew could hardly change what Yahweh had planned. Their attempt to short-cut God's will, revealed by the guilty prophet himself, would necessarily fail. Getting to shore was soon no longer an option.

14 The great fear of the crew is evident in their plea. They decide to do as Jonah suggests, but they cannot be sure such a dire action will not bring divine wrath upon them, too. Jonah might be wrong. He is, after all, an outlaw prophet of a god they do not otherwise worship. So they pray to Yahweh themselves, beseeching him to accept their role in Jonah's death. What they are afraid of is blood-guilt. In the ancient Semitic world, people could not be put to death without a trial and a determination of guilt, any more than would be possible in modern times. The sailors plead that they might not perish (אבד; cf. the use of this verb by the captain in v 6). They already fear perishing from the storm. Now they must also fear perishing from sin. They are acting in desperation, without giving Jonah a trial.

On a strictly human plane, Jonah's death thus would require avenging. Any relative of his might feel honor bound to seek the death of the sailors if the word got out how Jonah died (cf. 2 Sam 14:7). As regards the divine will, Jonah's God Yahweh might hold the sailors accountable for Jonah's death. The shedding of "innocent blood" (דם נקיא) was a terribly serious crime. Deut 21:1–9 prescribes the practice for absolving the guilt of an unsolved murder from the nation of Israel as a whole. The formula for the prayer in Deut 21:8, ". . . Do not hold your people accountable for the blood of an innocent person," is quite similar to the wording in Jonah 1:14. The idiom in Hebrew is נתן דם נקיא "to hold accountable for the blood of an innocent person." Jer 26:15 provides another parallel to the sailor's concern. Jeremiah, a prophet, warns that if he is killed, the officials and indeed the whole citizenry of Jerusalem will answer to God for it. Shedding innocent blood is murder.

The sailors express in the closing sentence of their prayer the belief that they are carrying out Yahweh's will. "You, Yahweh, have done as you wanted" (אתה יהוה כאשר חפצת עשית) reflects not a general evaluation of Yahweh's power to carry out his will, but a specific identification that their act is a fulfillment of Yahweh's desire. Yahweh wanted Jonah killed, they reason. He is accomplishing this now. They will help him do what he wants. The storm provided the divine verdict and showed the penalty.

15 Jonah's words were accurate once again. The sailors' actions produced immediately the desired result. The sea had raged because of God's wrath at Jonah's disobedient flight. The sailors "threw" him (טול, hiphil) into the sea just as Yahweh "had thrown" (טול, hiphil) the wind at the sea to bring about the tempest in the first place, and as they "had thrown" (טול, hiphil) the cargo overboard. No special point is made by the frequency of the verb form. Indeed the very opposite is the case. A simple vocabulary word describes all three simple acts. The hearer / reader may not draw any special conclusions from the words employed.

The sailors' prayer was also answered. Yahweh delivered them, and no further threat was seen. From their point of view, presumably, Jonah had now met the fate Yahweh had destined. Jonah was not in fact innocent (v 14) but very much guilty. They had done the right thing and Yahweh had spared them.

16 Verse 16 is best considered a post-script of sorts, i.e., a coda. It does not seem to describe anything that the sailors did immediately after the storm stopped, but rather relates to the audience the fact that the events the sailors had witnessed were so awesome as to have made a profound and lasting impression on them. Three statements indicate this. The first is the narrator's summary statement that they "really believed" (ויראו יראה גדולה, lit., "feared greatly"). This would hardly mean to the ancient audience that the crew had been converted to monotheistic Yahwism. They had, however, been so convinced that Yahweh really could do "as he wanted" (v 14) that they added Yahweh to the god(s) they already believed in. Their belief, of course, was not limited simply to the notion that Yahweh existed. That was a rather automatic assumption of the syncretism they practiced. Rather they believed in Yahweh in the genuine sense of active response. Yahweh had become a God to be served and feared, a God whom they no longer were willing to ignore.

Thus the second statement that they "sacrificed" (זבח) to Yahweh. This could hardly have occurred on board the ship, denuded of its cargo. The transportation of edible animals on ocean-going ships was as infrequent in ancient times as in modern. The sacrifice would have taken place on shore, for another simple reason. In all the religions of the ancient Near East, as far as the evidence is known, sacrifices took place at shrines or temples. One could not simply sacrifice wherever one felt like it. Usually, a shrine was thought consecrated or established by the appearance or self-revelation of a god there, though the Israelite patriarchs at least evidently broke this tradition and built altars to worship God whenever they sojourned. At any rate, the sailors in all likelihood went to an already established Yahwistic shrine or temple to offer their sacrifices of gratitude (in effect, thank offerings; cf. Lev 7:11–21) for deliverance. Where did they go? Assuming that the ship's home port, not just a port of call, was Joppa, the sailors might even have made a pilgrimage to Jerusalem itself, the central shrine and only legitimate worship center of all Israel. The relative syncretism which flourished in Jerusalem during most of the eighth century would have allowed for the worship of outsiders like the sailors. Most likely, however, the sailors would have gone to any of the large number of heterodox Yahwistic shrines which dotted the landscape of both Judah and Israel (e.g., 2 Kgs 14:4; 15:4; cf. Hos 4:13; 2 Kgs 16:2–4) and offered their sacrifices to Yahweh there. Such sacrifices were hardly orthodox, but that is not the narrator's point. The sailors responded to their deliverance in the way they knew how; just as the Ninevites would later plead for deliverance in the way they knew how (3:5).

The final statement of the narrator tells us that the sailors made vows (נדרים) to Yahweh. These vows were almost certainly nothing other than promises to bring yet more sacrifices to Yahweh in the future. Sacrifices are sometimes linked in poetic parallelism with the notion of making good on vows (e.g., Pss 76:11; 116:17–18). Deut 12:6, 11 mentions "vows" (נדרים), sacrifices which fulfill past promises to sacrifice. The mention of the vows confirms to the audience that the sailors' fear of Yahweh was not short-lived. Just as Jonah's own prayer would promise to offer sacrifices as a payment on the promises to do so (2:10), the sailors took very seriously their newfound commitment to Yahweh, Jonah's God. Yahweh was a God not to be trifled with. He had killed Jonah (as far as the sailors knew) for disobeying his word!

Explanation

While Jonah and the crew of the ship he took from Joppa are the focal points for the part of the story told in 1:4–16, God is the one who controls the events. It was God's command to his prophet that evoked Jonah's futile response of flight in the first place. It was God who hurled his wind at the sea to produce the life-threatening storm. God caused the lots to designate Jonah to the crew as the source of their distress, and God calmed the sea suddenly when Jonah was thrown overboard. Imagine being one of the sailors when the empty ship arrived back at port in Joppa. When the others proposed worshiping as a group at a shrine of Yahweh to show their lasting gratitude, would it be easy to say "Not me—some other time, perhaps"? What had happened to the sailors was probably the most awesome and shocking experience of their lives. Could they ever forget what they had seen Yahweh, Jonah's God, do?

For Jonah these events were hardly less grave. We do not know anything for sure about his experience of obedience to Yahweh before this point. If our story takes place prior to his prophetic service described in summary fashion in 2 Kgs 14:25, this may be Jonah's first encounter with Yahweh's word, and an occasion to learn that when

The Lord Yahweh has spoken
Who can not prophesy? (Amos 3:8)

If, on the other hand, Jonah's call to preach against Nineveh came after an already distinguished career of pro-nationalist mediation of Yahweh's word, one can understand all the more readily how galling this particular word from Yahweh seemed to Jonah. Regardless of the timing in Jonah's life, his actual attitude, made clear from the rest of the story, was that he could not stand the thought of preaching a message that might somehow give warning to a people he so justly hated for their evil (cf. Nah 3:4–7).

To be a prophet was not necessarily to be a great theologian. God chooses whom he will, whether trained professional specialist or not (cf. Amos 7:14–15) to proclaim his word. Jonah may have thought his desperate run from God's call might succeed. He may have assumed it would fail but decided—irrationally—to try it anyway. His flight may have been carefully planned, or it may have been hastily undertaken. He may have thought of it as permanent or as merely temporary. Regardless of the actual details, unknowable as they are, the simple fact remains: Jonah chose disobedience over obedience because the former was less odious to him than the latter.

Aboard ship, after he is awakened to face the storm with the others, Jonah still resists the will of Yahweh. He does not, after all, suggest that the sailors try to row back to shore so that he might now contritely fulfill the command of his God, having learned his lesson. That is *their* idea. His solution is death. He would rather face it than participate in a process that would possibly spare Nineveh. He would even die so that the sailors might be spared, but would not preach so that Nineveh might be. The contrast is evident in the way the story is told. The sailors are willing to do whatever Yahweh wants, as soon as they can find it out. Jonah already knows exactly what Yahweh wants, but tries to escape it. He would rather live in exile, or even die, than bring favor to Assyrians. What God wants, Jonah cannot stand to be part of.

The events of the passage progress in such a way that knowledge unfolds as the storm grows in intensity. This is not an especially intrusive framework, however. It is more the natural consequence of the discourses and decisions which come quickly in the face of the brute fact of the life-threatening storm. The storm changes everything. It ruins the voyage of the ship, brings Jonah's flight to an end, and disproves decisively the thought that one can escape from Yahweh—as both Jonah and the sailors come to realize. It shows that Yahweh is in control of land and sea (v 15) and thus surely the circumstances of people whether on land or sea. God's control over and use of nature is an evident biblical theme which finds its portrayal in Jonah in the storm, the fish (2:1, 10), the vine (4:6), the worm (4:7), and the east wind (4:8).

In this regard it is useful to note the connection between the present passage and many others which speak of God's control of the sea (e.g., Ezek 28:2; Dan 7:2; Nah 1:4; Hab 3:8; Hag 2:6; Ps 89:9). Two NT passages contain striking parallels to this part of the Jonah story. Acts 27:13–44 tells the story of the storm encountered by the ship on which Paul was traveling to Rome. While no attempt is made to suggest that God caused the storm, it is evident that its timing was in his control as Paul virtually said (v 24). On that occasion, too, desperation was evident (vv 19, 20, 30, 33) and a single servant of God on board ship held the key to its fate (v 24). God was in control. Things would happen as he ordained.

Matt 8:23–27 likewise describes a storm over which only God could have control. Jesus slept through part of that one, just as Jonah did through his. The disciples appeared as afraid (v 25) as the crewmen aboard Jonah's ship had been. Jesus showed himself master of the elements by rebuking the wind and waves (v 26). The amazement of the others on ship paralleled that of the amazement of the sailors who saw the storm abate after throwing Jonah into the sea. The lessons of both texts are similar. The Lord—Yahweh or Jesus—is sovereign. He commands. All else and all others must obey.

Jonah Rescued by Yahweh's Grace (2:1–11)

Bibliography

Anderson, B. W. *Out of the Depths.* Philadelphia: Westminster Press, 1974. 77–95. **Auffret, P.** "'Pivot Pattern': Nouveaux Examples." *VT* 28 (1978) 103–110. **Bader, G.** "Das Gebet Jonas. Eine Meditation." *ZTK* 70 (1973) 162–205. **Batto, B.** "Red Sea or Reed Sea?" *BAR* 10 (1984) 56–63. **Bauer, J. B.** "Drei Tage." *Bib* 39 (1958) 354–58. **Christensen, D.** "The Song of Jonah: A Metrical Analysis." *JBL* 104 (1985) 217–31. **Cross, F. M.** "Studies in the Structure of Hebrew Verse: The Prosody of the Psalm of Jonah." In *The Quest for the Kingdom of God: Studies in Honor of George E. Mendenhall*, ed. H. B. Huffmon et al. Winona Lake, IN: Eisenbrauns, 1983. ———. and **D. N. Freedman.** *Early Hebrew Orthography.* AOS 36. New Haven: American Oriental Society, 1952. **Culley, R. C.** *Oral Formulaic Language in the Biblical Psalms.* Toronto: University of Toronto Press, 1967. **Gevirtz, S.** *Patterns in the Early Poetry of Israel.* SAOC 32. Chicago: University of Chicago Press, 1963. **Johnson, A. R.** "Jonah 2:3–10: A Study in Cultic Fantasy." In *Studies in Old Testament Prophecy: FS T. H. Robinson*, ed. H. H. Rowley. Edinburgh: T. & T. Clark, 1950. 82–102. **Landes, G. M.** "The Kerygma of the Book of Jonah." *Int* 21 (1967) 3–31. ———. "The 'Three Days and Three Nights' Motif in Jonah 2:1." *JBL* 86 (1967) 446–50. **Nötscher, F.** "Zur Auferstehung nach drei Tagen." BBB 17 (1962) 231–36. **Pope, M. H.** "The Word שחת in Job 9:31." *JBL* 83 (1964) 269–78. **Seydl, E.** "Das Jonalied." *ZTK* 24 (1900) 187–93. **Stenzel, M.** "Altlateinische Canticatexte im Dodekapropheton." *ZNW* 46 (1955) 31–60. **Walsh, J.** "Jonah 2,3–10: A Rhetorical Critical Study." *Bib* 63 (1982) 219–29. **Westhuizen, J. P. van der.** "Assonance in Biblical and Babylonian Hymns of Praise." *Semitics* 7 (1980) 81–101. **Whitley, C. F.** "The Semantic Range of *Hesed*." *Bib* 62 (1981) 519–26. **Wilson, R. D.** "מנה, 'To Appoint' in the Old Testament." *Princeton Theological Review* 16 (1918) 645–54.

Translation

God's surprise

1 [1:17]*But Yahweh designated*[a] *a large fish to swallow Jonah. Jonah was inside*[b] *the fish for*[c] *three days and*[c] *three nights.*

Jonah's prayer of thanksgiving

2 [1] *So Jonah prayed to Yahweh his God from inside the fish.*
3 [2] *He said:*

> I called in my distress
> To Yahweh,[a] and he responded to me.
>
> From the belly of Sheol I cried out;
> You heard my voice.

4 [3] *You had*[a] *thrown me* $\begin{cases} \text{into the deep}^{\text{b}} \\ \text{into the heart of the seas}^{\text{b}} \end{cases}$

> So that the current surrounded me.
>
> All your breakers and billows
> Passed right over me.

5 [4] *I thought,*[a] *"I have been driven*
> Out of your sight.
>
> How[b] can I again look
> Upon your holy temple?"

6 [5] *Water enveloped me to my throat;*[a]
> The deep surrounded me,
> Seaweed[b] was wrapped around my head.

7 [6] *To the bases*[a] *of the mountains I descended;*
> The underworld's[b] bars were shut behind[c] me forever.
>
> But you brought my life up from the pit,[d]
> Yahweh, my God.

8 [7] *As I was losing consciousness,*[a]
> I remembered Yahweh.
>
> My prayer came to you,
> To your holy temple.

9 [8] *Those who give attention to the empty nothings*[a]
> Abandon their loyalty.[b]

10 [9] *But I with a voice of thanksgiving*
> Will sacrifice to you.
>
> That which I have vowed I will carry out.
> Salvation belongs to Yahweh!

Jonah suddenly on land

11 [10] *Yahweh spoke to the fish so that it vomited Jonah onto the land.*

Notes

1.a. The piel of מנה may also carry the senses "allot," "provide," "appoint," and "offer." The converted imperfect may also be translated as a pluperfect, i.e., "had appointed," which would be especially appropriate to bring the reader back to the ocean and the focus on Jonah, from the coda about the sailors' faith.

1.b. Or "in the belly / stomach of."

1.c-c. Co^s and L^c omit the reference to the days, probably because it seemed logical to the translators or copyists of those MSS that inside a fish there is only "night."

3.a. G reads τὸν θεόν μου, i.e., אלהי "my God," perhaps under the influence of אלהיו "his God" in 2:2 [1] and אלהיך "your God" in 1:6. Jonah's prayer is surely a "J" psalm (cf. vv 7, 8, 10), however, and MT יהוה "Yahweh" ought therefore to be retained.

4.a. The pluperfect is the appropriate tense in light of the logic of the chronology of events.

4.b-b. "Into the deep" (מצולה) and "into the heart of the seas" בלבב ימים are most likely alternate formulas, i.e., alternate poetic wordings equally valid, both of which were technically "original," and both of which have been transmitted along with the psalm. Grammar and meter suggest that either one or the other, but not both, was actually sung on any one occasion when the song was heard. For other examples of alternate formulas see D. Stuart, *Studies in Early Hebrew Meter*, 171–86.

5.a. "I said" is much less likely, since the suppliant's words refer more to his experience than to any public declarations. In both prose and poetic contexts, אמר commonly means "think," often connoting a false assumption (cf., e.g., Gen 44:28; Eccl 8:17).

5.b. θ' (πῶς) can only have been reading אֵיך "how" rather than אַך "surely" in the text before him. Though his is the only versional evidence for אֵיך, the parallelism of the verse commends its restoration. The asseverative "surely" is intrusive in the context, though not provably unoriginal.

6.a. Or, the phrase עד־נפש here "to my throat" may conceivably have the sense "threatening my life" or the like. On נפש as "throat," cf. Ps 69:2 [1]; Isa 5:14, and Dahood, *Psalms III*, 212.

6.b. G ἐσχάτη took סוף as סוף "end," an illogical reading in the context. Tg ים דסוף "Reed Sea" and a' ἐρυθρα "red (sea)" fail to recognize the generic meaning of סוף "seaweed," thus rendering according to its geographical associations from Exodus.

7.a. MT קצבי from קצב "shape" may have the secondary meaning "base" or "foundation." The alternatives, i.e., emendations of MT, are not attractive.

7.b. "Underworld" as one meaning of ארץ is fairly common in the case of Ugaritic and Hebrew poetry. Cf. M. Dahood, *Psalms III*, AB 17 (Garden City: Doubleday, 1970) 28, n. 11, 353–54, n. 7; and W. L. Holladay, "ᵓERES—'Underworld,'" *VT* 19 (1969) 123–24.

7.c. The translation "shut behind" is an extension of the meaning of בעדי, "behind," "around."

7.d. Or "grave."

8.a. This is the apparent meaning of the idiom ("to lose consciousness," עטף, hithp plus נפש).

9.a. Or "worthless idols" or the like. The literal translation helps capture some of the derogatory flavor of this special term of contempt for idols.

9.b. Or "covenant loyalty," i.e., covenant obedience.

Form / Structure / Setting

It is evident that a new pericope begins at 2:1 [1:17] and ends with 2:11 [10]. Most of the characters of the previous passage, i.e., the sailors; and the locations of the action (on board ship for vv 4–15 and, later, on land for v 16) are changed. Now the focus shifts to Jonah and the fish—though God remains the one who determines the course of events, as throughout the book. After 2:11 [10], the command of 3:1–3a, echoing the original call of 1:1–3, begins a new pericope, in a new location (land) with a new purpose (the completion of the original intention of Yahweh through Jonah).

If one thinks of the passage 2:1–11 [1:17–2:10] in terms of a scene, that scene is played with Jonah in the Mediterranean Sea without a ship, yet in a divinely appointed, highly unique conveyance. For all but a fraction of the time, he is in the dark, inside something that has swallowed him and therefore kept him from drowning. Alone with his thoughts, as it were, he prays the psalm which constitutes the bulk of the passage.

From the sailors' sacrifices and vows of 1:16 the hearer / reader must return to Jonah in 2:1 [1:17]. It is almost as if the passage should begin: "Meanwhile . . ." as indeed Allen renders it (Allen, 213). The narrator accomplishes this transition to a focus on Jonah by first focusing briefly on Yahweh. Yahweh is the subject of the first sentence, in 2:1a [1:17a], and then, in v 1b, Jonah becomes the subject.

The passage is a narrative within which is sandwiched a poem. The prose contexts of vv 1–2 [1:17–2:1] and v 11 [10] constitute a sort of inclusio within which the psalm prayed by Jonah is set as a central component. Biblical Hebrew prose narratives often incorporate poetry in this way. All the narrative books in the Pentateuch and former prophets—and to this group may be added 1 and 2 Chronicles—employ similar occasional use of poems, usually especially memorable poems associated with an individual person or event, as a minority part of a story which is otherwise conveyed via prose. Aside from the obvious benefits of variety and a ring of archaic authenticity generated by the inclusion of such poetic materials, the inspired author also increases the effectiveness of the narrative's message by including a poem that "says it all." In the same way that modern historical writing often quotes verbatim materials—especially speeches of key characters—which give the reader a sampling of the actual words spoken in given critically important situations, so biblical historical narrative writers could employ either excerpts or the entire text of significant poetic documents. Luke, of course, did this sort of thing with prose speeches and poems in the NT, and Paul cites a poem with good effect in an epistolary context (Col 2:6–11). The NT writers, moreover, frequently cite verbatim bits of OT texts relevant to their argumentation.

It must be remembered, then, that the occasional citation of poems in prose contexts is an aspect of normal OT narrative style. A failure to recognize this fact has allowed for a widespread tendency to excise the psalm from the book of Jonah as a late interpolation. The decision to question the authenticity of the psalm is made on one or more of three bases: (1) the fact that the psalm may be neatly excised from the book without loss of continuity; (2) the supposed lack of correspondence of topics in the psalm to topics in the rest of the book; (3) the inappropriateness of a thanksgiving psalm in a context of misery. None of these arguments has merit (cf. *Introduction*).

First, excisability has never been a legitimate criterion for questioning the integrity of a pericope. Inability to excise a pericope without affecting the coherence of the context is a valid argument *for* integrity; but the opposite is not a valid argument *against* integrity. With diligence, one can find at least some part of virtually *any* document, ancient or modern, that is not actually required for the sensible flow of logic, and which would not therefore be "missed" in the strict sense if it were not present. The vast majority of all literary portions which *could* be eliminated are not interpolations but original to the texts they are contained in. A confusion of possibility with probability has resulted in a tendency in biblical literary criticism to think that what *could* be an interpolation *must* be an interpolation. The psalm of Jonah could be an interpolation; but the potential that this is so is not evidence thereof. Very few literary works contain the minimum that may be said. Nearly all have room for abridgment. The potential for abridgment is therefore a common feature of literary works rather than an indication that the works themselves contain secondary expansions. On this basis, then, an empirical approach to the psalm must retain it in the book as original.

As to the lack of correspondence of topics in the psalm to topics in the rest of the book, two points must be made. (1) With the exception of historical hymns and one notable lament (Ps 137) there simply are very few psalms whose content clearly binds them to particular historical circumstances. It is in the nature of psalms to be general in applicability, even to the point of being virtually pan-historical and pan-cultural. They are composed not for a particular moment, but for all moments. Their popularity among believers in all ages reflects this non-specific nature. Thanksgiving psalms are particularly non-specific. The reader simply cannot tell what actual circumstances the speaker in the psalm has been delivered from, because the psalm is written to be useful by all who pray its words in *all* situations of thankfulness. Thus a psalm so specific in wording as to apply directly and uniquely to Jonah's rescue would be an anomaly in ancient Israel—an overly specific psalm, useless except to Jonah! If such a psalm had existed, which is doubtful, it would never have been included in a narrative about Jonah. What good would it do the hearer / reader?

(2) Within the stringent limitations set by the fact that thanksgiving psalms are general in their applicability, the psalm of Jonah is as closely related thematically to the rest of the book as a psalm of its type could be. Landes (*Int* 21 [1967] 3–31) has argued persuasively that the psalm is integral to the entire book and therefore in all likelihood original. "[If] the Jonah psalm [is] . . . the work of a scribe who was not the author of the prose stories . . . he was no less sensitive to the form, structure and content of the book than the original author himself. When, as we think, it is just as plausible that the initial author of Jonah knew of and used the psalm, this raises the question of whether it is even necessary to introduce the figure of a secondary interpolator." A summary of the interrelationships one finds between the psalm and events otherwise described in the book may best be presented in outline form.

The Psalm		*The Book as a Whole*	
v 3 [2]	Jonah in distress	1:4–15	The plight at sea; 4:29 (flashback at distressing nature of divine call)
	Jonah's prayer to Yahweh	4:2	Jonah's second prayer
	The "belly" of Sheol	2:1	The "inside" of the fish
	Yahweh responds to Jonah	2:1, 11 [1:17, 2:10]	The fish as deliverance
v 4 [3]	Thrown into the deep, etc.	1:12, 15	Jonah thrown overboard

v 5 [4]	Driven from Yahweh's sight, etc.	1:3	"away from Yahweh"
v 6 [5]	Water, the deep, sea-weed, etc.	1:12, 15	(as above)
v 7 [6]	Descent to death	1:12–15; 4:3, 8:	Jonah's wish for death
	Rescue by Yahweh	2:1, 11 [1:17, 10]	(as above); cf. 4:2 the mercy of Yahweh
v 8 [7]	Remembering Yahweh and praying to him	2:1 [1:17]	Jonah prayed "to Yahweh, his God."
vv 9–10 [8–9]	Attack on idolatry, vow to sacrifice	1:16	Idolatrous sailors' sacrifice to Yahweh;
		3:5–10	Nineveh's repentance
v 10b [9b]	Salvation belongs to Yahweh	2:1, 11 [1:17; 10] 3:10; 4:11	Jonah saved Nineveh saved by Yahweh's grace

It is obvious from a glance at this list of correspondences that the outline of the book is hardly governed by the content of the psalm. And some of the correspondences are far more direct and obvious than others. But there is no significant component of the psalm which lacks some sort of recognizable affinity with some theme or event elsewhere in the book. In this sense the psalm Jonah prayed was obviously highly appropriate to his overall situation.

(3) The psalm itself is a parade example of the thanksgiving psalm category. Thanksgiving psalms frequently display a five-part structure, as described here:

Thanksgiving Psalm Structure	*Jonah 2:3–10 [2–9]*
Introduction to the psalm	v 3 [2]
Description of past distress	vv 4–7a [3–6a]
Appeal to God for help	v 8 [7]
Reference to the rescue God provided	v 7b [6b]
Vow of praise and/or testimonial	vv 9–10 [8–9]

In the book of Jonah, the fish God designated rescued Jonah from death. Left in the sea, he would surely have drowned. Swallowed by the fish, he was preserved alive. As time passed, inside the fish, Jonah came to have a change of heart, at least as regards Yahweh's faithfulness to him personally. He had assumed that Yahweh wanted him dead; now he found himself alive and breathing. As the hours went by he began to realize that he had been spared. The psalm functions as eloquent testimony to that fact. It is therefore appropriate to the context, rather than "out of place in its present context" (Anderson, *Out of the Depths*, 84).

What would be lacking if the psalm were not present in the book? Four things would be missed. (1) The partial change of heart experienced by Jonah that caused him to be willing to obey the command of God when it came to him a second time (3:1) would be left unexpressed. The psalm covers this ground especially via the vow (vv 9–10 [8–9]). (2) The attention to Jonah's lasting thankfulness at his rescue would be virtually eliminated. The psalm is the only element in the book which explicitly conveys his realization that to him personally Yahweh has shown the sort of mercy he will also show to Nineveh. (3) The nature of Jonah's sojourn in the fish would be left unstated. The hearer / reader learns—albeit implicitly—that Jonah is in the fish thinking, learning, and alert, rather than unconscious or in agony, because of the psalm. The fact that he was well enough to pray this psalm (or possibly even to compose it; see below) says a considerable amount about his mental and physical state inside the fish. (4) A major theological thrust of the book would be weakened. As Landes argues, the psalm captures part of the essence of the book's message: that Yahweh is a merciful God, a God of love who desires to forgive rather than punish (cf. 4:2). Through the psalm the wayward Jonah confesses Yahweh's undeserved rescue. In contrast to the psalm, he cannot abide Yahweh's undeserved rescue of the Ninevites. The psalm provides the focal statement of Yahweh's concern for individuals in need of favor (cf. 4:11).

Far from being extraneous, therefore, the psalm is actually pivotal. The hypocrisy of Jonah's attitude in chap. 4 is muddled without the psalm. The psalm celebrates Yahweh's deliverance (cf. Exod 15; Judg 5), and thus fixes an ironic contrast: Jonah's obedience (3:3) is won by mercy; but Jonah cannot abide the thought that Nineveh's obedience could be won the same way! Jonah cannot fail existentially to appreciate God's strategy in dealing with the Assyrians. He just can't stand it, because his hate for them is so great.

Nothing in the psalm or the prose inclusio gives any sure indication as to the date, provenance, or authorship. There are no exclusively late or early features, no certain indications of dialect. A possible indication of dialect and date is the presumed defective (i.e., vowelless) spelling of אֵך "How?" in 2:5b [4b]. That is, if the poem were already committed to writing by the eighth or seventh century B.C., prior to the widespread use of *matres lectiones* (prior to the generalized spelling אֵיךְ, cf. Cross and Freedman, *Early Hebrew Orthography*, 59), the preservation of the spelling אֵך, later misunderstood by the Masoretes as אַךְ, could be explained. But the lack of the *yodh* could also reflect haplography; or the word could actually be אַךְ "surely" in spite of the intrusiveness of a declaration of assurance at that point in the psalm. The psalm simply cannot be dated on the basis of internal evidence.

Even a firmly established eighth-century date for the psalm (and no dating method can fix poetic dates so precisely) would hardly prove that Jonah was the author. As to authorship, there are four theoretical possibilities: (1) The psalm existed prior to Jonah's experience. He knew it, and prayed it inside the fish because it seemed to him an appropriate psalm to express his own thanksgiving for being kept alive. (2) Jonah composed the psalm while inside the fish. Most, if not all, Israelite prophets were trained musical poets who knew and used the techniques of oral formulaic composition and could "create" psalms of various types (cf. S. Gevirtz, *Patterns in the Early Poetry of Israel*, 1–14; A. B. Lord, *The Singer of Tales* [Cambridge: Harvard U. Press, 1969]

13–29; R. C. Culley, *Formulaic Language,* passim). Drawing upon known images, themes, styles, and vocabulary, they composed and recomposed poems with ease. (3) The psalm was composed apart from the book, at whatever date, and secondarily, inserted into the book after the prose portion was complete. (4) The psalm was composed by a later redactor specifically for the purpose of insertion into the book.

These final two options are obviated, as Landes argues (*Int* 21 [1967] 3–31) by the fact that the psalm fits so well within the book. An authoritative answer to the question of date and authorship can never be given. An empirical approach, however, would not question the integrity of chap. 2 and authenticity of the psalm without strong evidence for rejecting either. The evidence is weak, not strong; the psalm should therefore be considered authentic, and an integral part of the entire story of Jonah.

Comment

2:1 [1:17]   Again only the bare details of the story are told, and much that might satisfy curiosity is omitted. That God should have planned to rescue Jonah in this extraordinary, utterly surprising way comes as sudden news to the hearer / reader. The length of the coda in 1:16 is just enough to suggest that Jonah was surely dead by this time, his body entombed in the deep sea. But he had not died at all! A fish swallowed him! And the fish did not swallow him in order to eat him, but to shelter him.

The wording of the first sentence is precise. Yahweh is in control; the fish simply does what it is told (cf. 2:11 [10]). The verb מנה piel "designate; specify; appoint" does not imply that God had long in advance created a special type of fish or modified an existing one so that it could keep a person alive for seventy-two hours (cf. Wilson, *Princeton Theological Review* 16 [1918] 645–54). The story does not specify what kind of fish it was, how Jonah could have lived inside it, or the answers to any other such queries. Yahweh can easily toss the wind around to make a storm when he wants to. Miraculously rescuing someone from drowning via a fish is no great feat, either. But it is not, also, a feat to be described analytically. A miracle is a divine act beyond human replication or explanation. The numerous attempts made in the past to identify the sort of fish that could have kept Jonah alive in it are misguided. How would even Jonah himself have known? Can we assume that he caught a glimpse of it as it turned back to sea after vomiting him out on shore (v 11 [10])? How much could he have understood of what had happened to him when he was swallowed? These questions have no answer. To ask them is to ignore the way the story is told. What sorts of fish people can live inside is not an interest of the scripture.

Significance must be attached to the assertion that Jonah remained inside the fish for "three days and three nights" (שלשה ימים ושלשה לילות). The mention of both days and nights as descriptions of duration may well have a double force. Idiomatically it would seem to stress the duration of the time, i.e., "three *full* days" as "forty days and forty nights" does in Gen 7:4, 12(17). But beyond this, there may have been a sort of popular notion or cliché of expression in ancient times that the journey from the land of the living to Sheol (or vice versa) took three full days. Landes (*JBL* 86 [1967]

446–50) marshals convincing evidence to demonstrate that the Sheol journey motif is probably behind the author's choice of words as a purposeful echo of the reference to the Underworld in the psalm (v 7 [6]). In other words, instead of reporting simply that Jonah was in the fish for "three days" before reaching land, the author expresses the duration by a wording which suggests all the more strongly to the hearer / reader that the fish represented actual divine rescue back from the Underworld, i.e., death. A modern example of this sort of mode of expression might be constructed as follows: An avalanche has buried a mountain climber under several feet of snow. Rescuers dig him out alive. One of them later comments: "He's lucky to be alive. We thought he was six feet under." The phrase "six feet under" can have its own literal sense. But it can also, as above, be a cliché for "dead and buried." In the same way, "three days and three nights" probably connoted something on the order of "all the way back from Sheol" in addition to its literal meaning, and thus for the narrator's purposes it constituted a felicitous choice of words.

2 [1] Where Jonah's prayer was made, and to whom, is important for the narrator to mention. It would have been unavoidable to mention that Jonah prayed, lest the psalm suddenly intrude without introduction. But in addition, we are reminded that Yahweh was still, as ever, Jonah's God. Everything that had happened so far could only further convince Jonah of what he had always known: that Yahweh could do as he wished (1:14b) and would not be dissuaded from it (4:2). Jonah's flight and the circumstances that followed in no way contravened Jonah's faith. That remained as strong as ever. But in addition, Jonah now had at least some time to think. The events on board ship after his being awakened by the captain had been frantic, resulting finally in his being thrown off the pitching deck through the howling wind into the churning sea. He had begun to drown, sinking into the water. But something had enclosed him—he may have guessed or sensed it to be a fish or perhaps not known for sure what it was. At any rate, as the hours went by it became evident that he was not going to die. He felt himself safe, no matter how uncomfortable he may have been. His ability to pray thankfully from inside the fish implies, at least, that the situation there was less than entirely painful or panicky.

3 [2] The first element in Jonah's thanksgiving psalm is the summary of the answered prayer, i.e., the reason for his thankfulness. This is the introduction to the psalm (see *Form / Structure / Setting*). It is comprised of two couplets, between which an external (overall) synonymous parallelism is evident. Both couplets, then, report the same thing: the speaker appealed to Yahweh from a situation of mortal peril, and was rescued.

The words are general in their application. Anyone delivered from any sort of danger—illness, accident, war, etc.—might pray such a prayer. If Jonah chose an already existing psalm, he picked one which fit his situation without being composed exclusively for it. And if he himself was the composer, the same holds true. Psalmists composed with a wide audience in mind. The language of psalms is not normally specific to any time or place.

The term "belly" (בטן) is the one word in v 3 [2] which links rather directly to Jonah's situation. Interestingly, the prose portion of the book does not employ the word, using instead "inside" (במעי) for Jonah's location in the fish. The phrase "belly of Sheol" (בטן שאול) is unique here in the OT, though "the belly of El" is figuratively alluded to in Job 20:15. The psalm, by employing the phrase "belly of Sheol," shows its intended use for serious, life-threatening situations. Jonah himself was, of course, as good as dead once he was thrown off the ship. The psalm refers to a plea ("I called"; "I cried out") but none is otherwise mentioned of Jonah. He may, of course, have prayed desperately for help as he started to drown. But the psalm need not reflect anything Jonah himself did. It would be composed in traditional style and wording to apply normally to people who *did* pray and receive Yahweh's aid.

The verse does indicate rescue. "Responded to me" (ויענני) and "heard my voice" (שמעת קולי) are both idioms for more than just auditory sensation; they connote the gracious accession of God to the suppliant's situation, not simply receipt of his or her words. Employing literary clichés typical of thanksgiving psalms, Jonah's psalm actually concentrates not on what he said but on the fact that, from the trouble he was in, God mercifully delivered him.

4 [3]   The two couplets which comprise v 4 [3] begin the description of past distress, via sea, the metaphor for life-threatening suffering around which the psalm is constructed. Other OT psalms employ the imagery of drowning in the sea to express the trials of the suppliant (e.g., Pss 88:8 [7]; 69:1–2, 14–15). Ps 42:8 [7], indeed, contains a set of verbal formulas identical to the second half of this verse of Jonah's psalm (כל משבריך וגליך עלי עברו; "all your breakers and billows passed right over me"). It must be noted, however, that Jonah's psalm, alone in the OT, uses deep-water imagery consistently and dominantly. In all other cases, such imagery constitutes only a minority of the metaphorical stock of a psalm (see *Introduction*).

Notable here is the use of the verb שלך, hiphil (ותשלכני) rather than טול, hiphil, as in the prose portion, for "throw." The psalm obviously is not merely an expansion on the vocabulary used elsewhere, but has its own internal consistency and style. From the point of view of the choice of vocabulary, then, the psalm here is thematically *interrelated* rather than verbally *interdependent* with the rest of the book.

Jonah's psalm continues in this verse the theme of the brush with death begun in v 3 [2]. It was a mortal danger that Yahweh had caused ("*you* threw me"). Yahweh had almost done away with him before the rescue by the fish. Jonah had pronounced his own death sentence (1:12) and the sailors had carried it out.

5 [4]   A presumed rejection by God is the theme of the two couplets in this verse. The psalm's language captures Jonah's situation strikingly. Contrary to fact, Jonah thought (אמר; see n. 5.a) that this was the end of his life. The punishment for his flight, drowning, he thought guaranteed his death. The phrase "out of your sight" (מנגד עיניך) and the notion of being distant from God's temple are essentially metaphorical rather than literal. That is, they connote the separation of death. In the land of the living, according to the metaphor, one can be in Yahweh's sight or presence (i.e., worshiping at or "looking upon" his temple), but in the land of the dead this is impossible. There, people are simply cut off from Yahweh, and he from them (cf. Pss 88:5, 10–12; 115:17). No more worship or praise is possible; death ends that opportunity. The words of v 5 [4] are, therefore, constructed neither to describe Jonah's past regret at having run away from Palestine nor a technical analysis of the possibility of conscious thought in Sheol. They are part of a stereotyped language which effectively describes death's finality. Jonah thought, as in general some suppliants thought who prayed this kind of psalm, that he had been dying.

6 [5] The deep-sea drowning metaphor is expanded to depict the physical sensation of being trapped, down in the ocean, unable to breathe, water everywhere. This is a vivid, powerful metaphor for the sensation of dying, and it happens also to be the sort of thing that literally did happen to Jonah. We do not know, of course, how much time went by and how deep Jonah may have sunk below the surface between the time he was thrown from the ship and the time he was swallowed by the large fish. The psalm employs hyperbolically graphic language because it is in the nature of such psalms to do so. Jonah's situation *was* serious; the psalm appropriately reflects that urgency by its vivid images of lack of air (water at the throat), water everywhere (the surrounding deep), and entrapment (seaweed about the head).

7a [6a] The first couplet of v 7 [6] concludes the description of Jonah's distress. While the couplet contains "synthetic" rather than synonymous parallelism, its point is singular: Jonah presumed himself to be dead. The psalm is composed on the same assumption. The "bases (?) of the mountains" (קצבי הרים) and "bars (בריחיה) of the Underworld" are both expressions which have a background in ancient Near Eastern and OT imagery relating to death (cf. Johnson, *Studies in OT Prophecy*, 87–89). The NT usage πύλαι ᾅδου "gates of Hades" in Matt 16:18 borrows on the latter metaphor. The distance from the land of the living represented by arrival at the bases of the mountains and the fact that the Underworld's bars prevented one from returning back to life once dead are metaphors for the finality of death. God's prophet thought himself dead for sure.

7b [6b] "Pit" (שחת) signifies the grave or realm of the dead, often in the OT (cf. Pope, *JBL* 83 [1964] 269–78). The words of the psalm metaphorically describe *rescue* from death itself. Jonah's situation is that which the psalm describes. He was not simply spared from serious risk. He was actually snatched up from the grave, as it were. The direct address to Yahweh, which dominates the psalm, is in evidence here as well. Jonah calls Yahweh "my God" (cf. v. 2 [1]) stressing again his single devotion to Yahweh and to no other.

8 [7] Yahweh's wrath as seen in the storm at sea must not be allowed to distract from the reality of Yahweh's grace in rescuing Jonah. In the psalm, this grace is expressed in several ways; in this verse, the aspect of Yahweh's willingness to hear the prayer of a suppliant in severe distress receives attention. Because the psalm is cast in standardized thanksgiving psalm wording, it is not possible to infer here, either, from "I remembered Yahweh / My prayer came to you . . ." that Jonah prayed for deliverance as he was thrown into the water, and therefore Yahweh responded. The prose portion contains no accounts of any prayers made by Jonah. The way the story is told Yahweh makes things happen so that Jonah must do his bidding; Jonah does not initiate his own (partial) change of heart, Yahweh does. Accordingly the psalm here should not be read to imply that Jonah appealed for mercy in a prayer unrecorded in the prose account between 1:16 and 2:1.

The temple ("your holy temple," היכל קדשך) was the prime locus of the worshiper's contact with Yahweh (cf. *Comment* 1:16). For the suppliant's prayer to "come" there implies nothing about the limitations of Yahweh's residence.

Here the temple is simply a "B" word in the elements of synonymous parallelism to the "A" word, "you."

9 [8]   The psalmist lauds Yahweh's power to save (cf. also v 10b [9b]) by a contrastive denunciation of the uselessness of idolatry. How foolish are those who seek help in life via the הבלי שוא, "the empty nothings!" But idols represent not only ineffectiveness; worshiping them also shows a lack of faith in Yahweh. For any Israelite to trust in idol worship was a violation of the covenant. Covenant loyalty (חסד) was a mutual obligation both of God, the initiator of the covenant (Exod 20:6, etc.), and of the Israelites to whom the covenant was given. Accordingly, one who broke the covenant's first commandment by having other gods had "abandoned" (עזב) his or her loyalty to Yahweh.

10 [9]   In the psalm, loyalty to Yahweh finds expression also in the concern to praise and worship him. This is, of course, exactly the motivation which the sailors felt so keenly (1:16). One cannot simply bask in the relief from distress which God provides. One must respond to grace! Worshipers in ancient Israel may well have recited the praise / sacrifice portions of thanksgiving psalms as they presented to the priest their offerings for the worship sacrifices (here, v 10a [9a]). But they also could promise not to make their thanksgiving sacrifice a single event (v 10b [9b]). By vowing to continue to return thanks to God on future occasions of temple sacrifice ("that which I have vowed I will carry out"), they extended the period of their gratefulness. They gave willingly in the present, and then pledged to give again in the future. Thus the sacrifices of thanksgiving for deliverance could be made on an installment basis, as it were, thereby multiplying the magnitude of the total thanksgiving gift in parallel to the magnitude of the gratefulness for Yahweh's merciful rescue.

The final ejaculation of praise, ישועתה ליהוה "Salvation belongs to Yahweh," honors Yahweh in at least two ways. First, it extols his work as Savior, reflecting what he has done for the one offering the prayer of thanksgiving. Additionally, it implicitly extols Yahweh's position as *sole* Savior. Though it is brief and technically elliptical, there can be little doubt that this final declaration means, in comport with v 9 [8], that salvation belongs to Yahweh in contrast to belonging to any other god, or coming from any other source.

But is not a third sense also inherent in these words? Can they not also connote that Yahweh is in charge of salvation, i.e., that he decides whom he will save and how? Salvation is his area of authority. In it, he alone makes the decisions. This latter sense is important for the Jonah story, since one function of the psalm is to voice Jonah's own gratefulness for undeserved rescue, thereby exposing the inconsistency of his unwillingness that Nineveh should experience the same gratefulness, however undeserved. Jonah cannot decide whom Yahweh ought to save or not. Salvation is Yahweh's to offer. He has offered it to Jonah, who has gladly accepted it with all his heart. Moreover, he is free to offer it to Nineveh!

11 [10]   The prose part of the story resumes. While Jonah had been thinking and praying, the fish had been swimming. Its actions were determined by Yahweh, however, so that after the three days were completed, the fish was ready to discharge its unusual cargo. It did so at Yahweh's command. "Vomited" is indeed the action described by ויקא; the fish had swallowed

(בלע, v 1 [1:17]) Jonah, not simply taken him in its mouth. Suddenly expelled from his delivering shelter of three days, Jonah found himself out in the open, on land. He was, in all likelihood, back in Palestine proper, whence he had fled. His plan to evade Yahweh had simply not worked. Yahweh had seen to that.

Explanation

Jonah deserved death, not deliverance. And yet Yahweh graciously delivered him by special intervention so that Jonah could not but recognize the greatness of Yahweh's compassion, praise him for it, and recognize his reliance on Yahweh alone (cf. 2 Cor 1:9, 10).

The peripeteia of chap. 2 serves well the narrator's purpose for the book as a whole. Jonah's circumstances prepare the reader for the circumstances of Nineveh in chap. 3. Nineveh also deserves death, not deliverance. Nineveh also was graciously delivered by Yahweh's special intervention, for which the Ninevites had every reason to be grateful. Indeed, the Ninevites took Yahweh's word to heart as soon as they heard it; Jonah had resisted it. The mercy God now shows Jonah in spite of his direct, specific disobedience obviates Jonah's right to resent the same sort of mercy being shown the Assyrians in spite of their general, long-standing disobedience. Once the hearer / reader has been brought through the content of the second chapter, and especially the profound gratitude expressed in the psalm, he or she cannot then fail to be struck by the irony of Jonah's attitude in chap. 4. The first-time hearer / reader does not yet know what will happen to Nineveh, but is virtually "primed" for what actually does happen, and for the ability to see how hypocritical Jonah's attitude really is.

The psalm is crucial to the development of this contrast between Jonah's attitude toward his own deliverance and his attitude toward Nineveh's deliverance. The main purpose of the book is to teach Israelites that God loves other nations than their own; or, in fact, to teach us that he loves other nations than *our* own. In service of this purpose, Jonah stands for most Israelites—or most of us—as he represents the typical attitude people tend to have toward nations they have no reason to love themselves. The psalm was of a common type. Israelites, and later Jews, were intimately familiar with thanksgiving songs, and would recognize them instantly. Ancient hearer / readers probably needed no more than a line or two of Jonah's psalm in chap. 2 to see immediately that Jonah had realized himself to be rescued from his own "sentence" of death. They knew already from the story that Jonah was guilty of disobedience, that he was cast to the sea, that a fish which Yahweh had prepared had swallowed Jonah, and that he was still inside it. For Jonah, then, to begin to speak—and then to sing a thanksgiving psalm—made it very clear that Yahweh had spared him, and that he (as well as the reader) knew it. With all its overtones of deep, emotional gratitude, of heartfelt thanks for deliverance, housed in the form Israelites knew so well to be employed by people joyously grateful for their own escape from danger, the psalm both rationally and emotively involved the hearer / reader in the comparison (yet to be completed) between Jonah and Nineveh. In its overall context the chapter, of which the psalm is the major part, shows Jonah's relative selfishness.

By including the unique and memorable mention of the big fish, and the psalm, which by reason of its poetic nature stands out from the rest of the book, the narrator plants in the mind of the hearer / reader certain impressions which are not forgotten when the material in chaps. 3 and 4 is heard or read.

God is sovereign in this chapter, as elsewhere in the book. He designates the fish (v 1 [1:17]). He effects by it the rescue celebrated in the psalm Jonah prays. He tells the fish to put Jonah ashore (v 11 [10]). Neither Jonah nor the fish has had any control over events. And God has used his sovereignty to rescue a disobedient prophet! He will accomplish what he intends (cf. 1:14) and his intention, it is becoming clear, is that Jonah should be taught a lesson about grace. If Jonah himself experienced deliverance from a deserved death, maybe then he will have some ability to commiserate with the citizens of the city and nation to whom he has been called to preach.

This chapter is, in a way, the happiest part of the story. Full of rescue and thanksgiving, miracle and praise, it allows Jonah to see that God's determination to do good can mercifully benefit even those who deserve punishment. Consider only what the hearer / reader knows about the story so far, this time without reference to the remainder of the events as described in chaps. 3 and 4. Jonah has tried to disobey Yahweh's word and yet has failed to get away from it. He has been committed to death yet has survived it. He was in an impossible predicament and has been rescued by completely unexpected, serendipitous means. Will not good now come? Will not the story end happily, with an obedient prophet, grateful to God for sparing his own life, preaching faithfully to Nineveh as it should have been all along? The story so far allows for just such an ending, and therefore the actual (contrary) ending is effectively highlighted. Jonah's stubborn resentment expressed in chap. 4 is all the more a warning to the audience not to do likewise. As a parable highlights by contrast an attitude or a practice so that the hearer, if he too shares that attitude or practice, is caught short by it, so Jonah's situation does the same for the audience. He had every reason to empathize with Nineveh now. That he would later fail to be concerned for their situation is its own indictment on his stubborn, narrow nationalism.

Death is what Jonah deserved. It is in one sense the ultimate covenant punishment (Lev 26:16, 30, 38, 39; Deut 28:21, 26, 61; etc.). Jonah had not wanted the sailors to die, so he had volunteered to be killed so that they might be spared. They had not violated the covenant—he had. He, like those disgusting Ninevites, was now a covenant transgressor. Yet he had been allowed to live on to praise, to sacrifice, and to vow further worship of his God. And Nineveh?

A Second Beginning   (3:1–3a)

Bibliography

Alonso Díaz, J. "Paralelos entre la narración del libro de Jonás y la parábola del Hijo Pródigo." *Bib* 40 (1959) 632–40. **Ellul, J.** *The Judgment of Jonah.* Tr. G. W. Bromiley.

Grand Rapids: Eerdmans, 1971. 69–89. **Jepsen, A.** "Anmerkungen zum Buche Jona." In *Wort-Gebot-Glaube: FS Walther Eichrodt.* Zürich: Zwingli Verlag, 1970. 297–306. **Sasson, J.** "On Jonah's Two Missions." *Henoch* 6 (1984) 23–29.

Translation

^{1} *Yahweh's word came to Jonah a second time:* ^{2} *"Go to Nineveh, the important city,*[a] *and speak to it the speech*[b] *which I will say*[c] *to you.* ^{3} *So Jonah went to Nineveh as Yahweh had said.*

Notes

2.a. Or, "the great city," or "capital city." Cf. n. 1:2.a.

2.b. G translates κήρυγμα, i.e., "proclamation" for this *hapax legomenon.* Whether קריאה had such an official ring to it or not is impossible to tell. At any rate, G frequently renders קרא by κηρύσσω.

2.c. Or "am saying / telling." The tense may be either present or future.

Form / Structure / Setting

With the beginning of chap. 3, the prose narrative which was resumed in 2:11 takes up a new subject: the commission Yahweh had originally given to Jonah he now gives again. The narrative is thus resumptive in nature. The hearer / reader finds in vv 1–3a a wording which largely repeats and therefore consciously echoes the wording of 1:1–3. Such a "new beginning" is best treated as a separate pericope rather than merely as an appendage to the rescue story of chap. 2. In v 3b the description of Nineveh shifts the focus once again, this time to Jonah's preaching in Assyria itself. Thus 3:1–3a constitutes a pericope in itself.

If one considers the book in terms of scenes ("Act III, Scene 1" [Watts, 87–88]), the present passage also stands out somewhat from its context. Before, Jonah was at sea, either aboard ship or inside the fish. Now he is back in Palestine, hearing Yahweh's word there a second time (שנית). Immediately afterward he will be in Nineveh, carrying out the command to speak Yahweh's word in a new scene set out partly by the description of Nineveh's size and significance.

The passage of time was not a concern of the narrator, since such a detail would contribute virtually nothing to the story's message. While the juxtaposition of events may give the impression that God spoke again to Jonah immediately after he had been vomited onto land by the fish, there is actually nothing other than silence to prove that a considerable amount of time had not passed. The terse style could hide the fact that perhaps several months had gone by between Jonah's deliverance from drowning and his renewed commission to preach in Nineveh. (Several *weeks* certainly must pass between 3:3a and 3:4, for example.) Or as little as a few days may be involved in all that has taken place in the book up to 3:3a. Just as there is no word in the story about Jonah's trip to Nineveh, there is also no word about Jonah's personal circumstances immediately prior to that trip.

Comment

1 Where אמתי בן "son of Amittai" stood in 1:1, שנית "a second time"
stands in 3:1. Otherwise the verses are identical. If one has listened or read
carefully, there can be no doubt that the story is, as it were, starting over.
Once again Jonah has heard the word of Yahweh. Jonah is back where it all
started. His attempted flight had no effect.

2 Nothing essential has changed in the divine command except that the
mention of Nineveh's trouble in 1:2 is now no longer necessary, and more
attention is paid to the fact that Jonah must obediently preach exactly what
he is given to say. If anything, this new injunction ("speak to it the speech
which I will say to you") reminds Jonah that he has no option but to obey.
The style of the command is terse *figura etymologica* (like that of וייראו יראה
"and they feared a fear" in 1:10, 16, etc.; cf. Jepsen, *Wort-Gebot-Glaube*, 298).
Jonah has already learned that he cannot escape Yahweh's call to Nineveh.
Now he is reminded that he cannot hope to influence or adjust the message
Yahweh will give him. He must resign himself to the fact that Yahweh is
concerned for Nineveh.

It is important to note that he still does not know for sure whether or
not God will spare the city. Concern does not equal a guarantee of grace.
The same technical ambiguity found in 1:2 prevails here also. The content
of the speech (קריאה) itself is left unspecified. Neither Jonah nor the hearer /
reader knows yet—regardless of how strong their suspicions may be—if the
city will actually be punished or destroyed. We find out in 3:4 that the speech
he must give is indeed richly ambiguous, requiring a precise wording. Jonah,
in other words, is here commanded to say *exactly* and *only* what Yahweh will
tell him to say. He is held to a tight leash in terms of his verbal freedom.

3a This time Jonah obeyed. We know nothing of how soon he left, how
the trip went, when he arrived in Nineveh, or any such detail. We know
only that he had learned his lesson about trying to avoid the call of Yahweh.
That his "change of heart" was at best partial we learn in retrospect from
chap. 4. At present we can assume only that he recognized the futility of
further disobedience to his God and would attempt no further rebellion, at
least in terms of his actions (cf. Alonso Díaz, *Bib* 40 [1959] 632–40).

Explanation

The function of the brief pericope found in 3:1–3a is both resumptive
and transitional. God had accomplished his will in Jonah's life even after
Jonah's attempted rebellion. He had taught Jonah both that God's will cannot
be ignored and, as well, that he was a God of compassion whose will included
forgiveness and rescue.

Now begins a new segment of the Jonah story. Yahweh's command came
to him again. It demanded faithful obedience. Jonah had to do as he was
told. And he did. Jonah may have been hoping that although Yahweh rescued
him from sure death, he would not so rescue the Assyrians. He may, on the
other hand, have been quite pessimistic, afraid that his enemies, the Ninevites,
would get off lightly. We are not told what he thought, however, because

what he thought is not important yet. That he was required to obey is what is important. Nineveh, the hated city, was to hear Yahweh's word of warning, delivered by an authentic prophet, and thereby be given at least a theoretical chance to repent. Whether Jonah liked it or not, he went. And there is nothing here to suggest that Jonah liked it any more this time than the first.

Preaching and Repentance at Nineveh   (3:3b–10)

Bibliography

Christensen, D. "Anticipatory Paranomasia in Jonah 3:7–8 and Genesis 37:2." *RB* 90 (1983) 261–63. **Crenshaw, J. L.** "The Expression *mi yodea*ᶜ in the Hebrew Bible." *VT* 36 (1986) 274–88. **Derousseaux, L.** "Dieu aime tous les hommes (Jon 3)." *AsSeign* 34 (1973) 20–25. **Fáj, A.** "The Stoic Features of the Book of Jonah." *AION* 34 (1974) 309–45. **Feuillet, A.** "Les sources du livre de Jonas." *RB* 54 (1947) 161–86. **Good, E. M.** *Irony in the Old Testament.* Philadelphia: Westminster Press, 1965. **Jeremias, J.** *Die Reue Gottes.* BibS 65 (1975) 98–109. **Kutsch, E.** " 'Trauerbräuche' und 'Selbstminderungsriten' im Alten Testament." *Theologische Studien Zurich* 78 (1965) 25–42. **Madhloum, T.** "Excavations at Nineveh." *Sumer* 23 (1967) 76–82. **Ogden, G. S.** "Time, and the Verb היה, in O.T. Prose." *VT* 21 (1971) 451–69. **Parrot, A.** *Nineveh and the Old Testament.* Tr. B. E. Hooke. New York: Philosophical Library, 1955. **Peifer, C.** "Sackcloth and Ashes: Jonah 3:6–8." *TBT* 21 (1983) 386–87. **Pinches, T. G.** *The Old Testament in the Light of the Historical Records and Legends of Assyria and Babylonia.* London: SPCK, 1902. **Pritchard, J. B.** *Gibeon, Where the Sun Stood Still.* Princeton, NJ: Princeton University Press, 1962. **Schaumberger, I.** "Das Bussedikt des Königs von Ninive bei Jona 3,7.8 in Keilschriftlicher Beleuchtung." *Miscellanea Biblica* 2 (1934) 123–34. **Thomas, D. W.** "A Consideration of Some Unusual Ways of Expressing the Superlative in Hebrew." *VT* 3 (1953) 210–24. **Thompson, R. C.** and **R. W. Hutchinson.** *A Century of Exploration at Nineveh.* London: Luzack, 1929. **Winckler, H.** "Zum Buche Jona." *Altorientalische Forschungen* 2.2 (1900) 260–65. **Wiseman, D. J.** "Jonah's Nineveh." *TynB* 30 (1979) 29–51.

Translation

Jonah's first day of preaching at Nineveh

³ᵇ *Now, Nineveh* ᵃ *was* ᵇ *a city important* ᶜ *to God,* ᵈ *requiring a three-day visit.* ᵉ ⁴ *Jonah had only begun going into the city on the first day of the visit* ᵃ *and spoke as follows: "In forty more days,* ᵇ *Nineveh will be overthrown."*

The Ninevites' repentance and the king's decree

⁵ *And the people* ᵃ *of Nineveh believed God! They called for a fast, and put on sackcloth—from the most important to the most obscure of them.* ⁶ *The word touched even* ᵃ *the King of Nineveh. He got up from his throne, stripped off his royal robe,* ᵇ *put on sackcloth, and sat in ashes.* ⁷ *He had them announce in Nineveh: "By the*

decree of the king and his nobles: No human or animal, herd or flock, can taste anything, graze, or drink any water. ⁸*Both humans and animals must put on sackcloth and call on God with all their might. Everyone must give up*[a] *his or her evil practices and frequent*[b] *violence.* ⁹*Who knows? the god*[a] *may change his mind*[b] *and turn away from his anger, so that we will not perish."*

Coda: God's forgiveness

¹⁰*When God*[a] *saw what they did, that they gave up their evil practices, he changed his mind about the harm he had said he would cause them and did not do it.*

Notes

3.a. The verb follows נינוה, "Nineveh," which is therefore emphasized, especially following the *waw*.

3.b. Or "is" since היה can be used to indicate a condition which began in the past and continues in the present, e.g., Isa 49:5, "my God *is* (היה) my strength." (Cf. Ogden, *VT* 21 [1971] 453.)

3.c. The Hebrew word גדול is also used in the sense of "important" in Josh 10:2; see *Comment* and cf. 1:2.

3.d. It is also possible that "to God" is an idiomatic way of saying "(important) even by divine standards," i.e., "extraordinarily important." Similar expressions occur in Gen 10:9; Ps 36:7; 80:11 [10]. Cf. D. W. Thomas, *VT* 3 (1953) 210–24. We think, however, that the literal meaning is the more likely here.

3.e. Lit., "visit of three days," a nominal phrase asyndetically juxtaposed to the preceding. The term מהלך appears to have a range of meaning requiring more than one equivalent word in English. It is here possible that the phrase מהלך שלשת ימים means simply "three days' travel" as a description of the width of Nineveh, but this is not the most likely meaning. See *Comment*.

4.a. Cf. 3.e.

4.b. Or, "there are still forty days before . . ." In either translation, the point of the wording is to allow time for repentance.

5.a. Heb. אנשי is used here in contrast to animals, not women, and thus means "people of," not "men of."

6.a. The usual translations render on the order of: "Word (had) reached the King of Nineveh." But יגע is simply not used this way (i.e., to express the travel of news) in the OT. The king was touched / moved / affected by Jonah's prophecy. Cf. Job 4:5; Jer 51:9; Wiseman, *TynB* 30 (1979) 44. The pluperfect would be required only if the king were the one who "called for" the fast in v 5.

6.b. Heb. אדרת "royal robe" may also mean simply "fine clothing" or "formal robe" or the like; cf. Josh 7:21.

8.a. Lit., "turn from."

8.b. Lit., "violence which is in their hands," connoting regularity or frequency.

9.a. As in 1:6, it appears that the polytheistic speaker intends to single out one god among many, rather than speaking of "God" as if there were only one. But האלהים in Heb. is ambiguous; it may also be translated simply "God."

9.b. Lit., "turn and change his mind." "Change the mind" is often the sense of נחם, niph, though "to be sorry" and "to relent" are also appropriate translations.

10.a. Or, possibly "the God," if the article is understood to continue to represent the perspective of the Ninevites, for whom Yahweh was only one god among many.

Form / Structure / Setting

A new scene begins with 3:3b. Jonah has arrived at Nineveh and is no longer in Palestine or on the sea. The topic of the pericope is his message and the response in Nineveh. The passage concludes with God's response to the Ninevites. Chap. 4 will concern itself with a new topic: Jonah's response to God's response, and a new scene: Jonah is back in view, the people of Nineveh are not.

The passage continues the narrative of the book by apprising the hearer / reader of three events: Jonah did finally preach to Nineveh (vv 3–4); the Ninevites repented—from royalty to animals (vv 5–9); and God then spared the city (v 10). The proclamation of "the king and the nobles" (vv 7–9) represents a central focus of the passage. In it God, the mover and master of all the events in the book, also occupies the position of effective power. The decree mentions God twice, as the one the people must call upon and one who has the authority to stay judgment if the sincerity of the people is evident.

In keeping with the rest of the book, the passage in 3:3b–10 contains a substantial amount of visualizable action: Jonah's travels and preaching in the great city, the change from regular clothing to sackcloth, the announcing of the decree, the fasting from food, etc. Again the style is simple and terse. The narrator provides always enough to clarify the central theme—God's grace toward the enemy—but leaves most details unspoken.

The narrative bears no hint of humor. The common but fallacious notion that the book is intended to amuse has no support in the words themselves. The reference to the involvement of animals in the appeal to God, mentioned in the royal decree (vv 7–8), is certainly not funny. It is the language of severity; it demonstrates the urgency of the situation in Nineveh rather than any awkward choices on the part of the king and his nobles.

The word *Elohim* ("God," אלהים) is employed five times in the passage (vv 3b, 5, 8, 9, 10) whereas Yahweh (יהוה) is not used. In the case of the royal decree, i.e., the usages in vv 8 and 9, the reason is obvious: what would an Assyrian king and the citizens of Nineveh know about Yahweh? In 3:3b the term לאלהים "to God" is something that could conceivably have contained the name *Yahweh* rather than *Elohim;* but if the idiom "extraordinarily" is intended, *Yahweh* could not be substituted for *Elohim* in that instance. However, the narrator provides the term *Elohim* also in vv 5 and 10, where the previous reasons clearly do not apply. It has sometimes been suggested that the hearer / reader is supposed to imagine him / herself in the position of the Ninevites, for whom the more neutral term was more appropriate than "Yahweh." If so, why did the narrator have the sailors sacrifice "to Yahweh" instead of "to God" in 1:16? The answer must be that the sailors knew "Yahweh" as the God Jonah dealt with; the Ninevites did not. Jonah is not quoted as mentioning Yahweh in v 3b, and the omission can be no accident. His message was probably delivered in the name of "God." The narrator picks up on this fact and thereby subtly identifies "God" with "Yahweh." To the monotheistic narrator as well as the monotheistic hearer / reader, the terms are, in fact, interchangeable (see *Comment*).

There is something of the flavor of the Genesis narratives about Sodom and Gomorrah in this part of the Jonah story, particularly in the use of הפך "overthrow" (v 4), and in the charge of "violence" (חמס, v 8) against the city. In addition, the fear of "God" displayed by the Ninevites comports with the general fear of God on the part of pagans mentioned in some of the Genesis narratives (e.g., Gen 20:11; 39:9; 42:18; cf. Y. Kaufmann, *The Religion of Israel*, tr. M. Greenberg [Chicago: University Press, 1960] 283; L. C. Allen, 176). But there are also connections in form to the Elijah-Elisha stories and other OT literature, so that the form of the present passage cannot be linked fixedly with any single OT narrative genre.

Once Jonah delivers the divine message to Nineveh (v 4) he is not mentioned further in the passage. The attention (and the scene, to a degree) shifts to the citizenry of Nineveh, and particularly to the king, and their relationship to God. Jonah's relationship to God, the more dominant theme in the book as a whole, returns as the subject of chap. 4.

It is, of course, not possible from the few details given about Nineveh to date the passage—or the story—with certainty beyond the general limits afforded by the knowledge that Jonah prophesied for Jeroboam II (793–753). If the text named "the King of Nineveh" the date would be known; but it does not. Moreover, we cannot be absolutely certain that "the King of Nineveh" means "the king whose capital was Nineveh," especially if ויגע in v 6 is to be translated "reached," as is common, rather than "touched" as we have taken it. If "reached" is the sense of נגע here, it could suggest that the "king" is an Assyrian emperor not physically present in the city, though still, of course, its king. So technically, any of several Assyrian kings of the eighth century could be the king during whose reign Nineveh's "trouble" (רעה) moved God to compassion.

However, many factors point to the possibility that Aššur-dān III (773–756 B.C.) or one of the other weak eighth-century predecessors of Tiglath-Pileser III might have been the king who responded so concertedly to Jonah's message to the city. Shocked and threatened by military encroachments, major unfavorable omens, and riots, a king like Aššur-dān would surely have been far more open to the possibility that Jonah's preaching was divinely ordained and authoritative. The populace of Nineveh, spooked by the disasters known to have occurred during this king's reign, could well have responded positively to Jonah's call for repentance, and the king would, in his weakened position, be hard-pressed not to follow the people's lead (see 3:6–9, *Comment*). Thus, if a speculation as to the date of the (brief) Ninevite repentance be allowed, the year 758 B.C. would not be improbable.

Comment

3b The narrator includes here a rare bit of detail. Nineveh's importance (or conceivably, size; see below) is described by two unusual descriptive formulations: the city is גדולה לאלהים "important to God" (or possibly, "extraordinarily important") and it is מהלך שלשת ימים "requiring a three-day visit," lit., "visit / journey of three days." The terms are both difficult to translate with certainty, because *as phrases*, both are *hapax legomena* in OT Hebrew. The majority of commentaries and translations have understood these phrases to apply to the physical size of Nineveh, i.e., "an extraordinarily large city, three days' journey (in breadth)" or the like. This understanding of the two expressions may be correct, but there is much to suggest that it is not. From Josh 10:2 ("Gibeon was an *important* city like one of the royal cities" [NIV]) it is evident that (ה)גדול could be used in connection with a city to indicate significance rather than size. Gibeon was in fact physically rather small, being less than two and one-half acres in extent (see Pritchard, *Gibeon,* 10), a size that is surely not "great" as compared to other ancient Canaanite / Israelite cities. In light of the usage already established in 1:2, גדול can certainly connote importance as well as physical size, yet we must not too readily assume that גדול, used in two different ways in the book (see *Introduction*) should mean "important" *here.* It could as well mean "large," and in that sense relate to the emphasis placed upon its population in 4:11. But population also correlates with importance just as well as with size. And the emphasis of the book is upon Nineveh's relationship to God. As we have already noted, between 3:3b and 3:10, the word אלהים "God" is used instead of יהוה "Yahweh." Whatever the reason for this, it is obvious that if one takes לאלהים in this verse in its most basic, literal sense, the meaning "to God" is the result. Indeed, there is no reason to resort to a special idiom to explain לאלהים in this case and not in the case of באלהים in v 5. The term באלהים in v 5 means simply "in God." Here, as long as גדולה is understood to mean "important" rather than simply "large," לאלהים may best be translated simply "to God." Alternatively, translate "extraordinarily important," but not "extraordinarily large."

The point is that Nineveh was a city God was concerned for, one that was by no means insignificant to him. Nineveh's physical size may have figured prominently in its importance, as may have its population, but there is no ground for assuming that size per se is the issue in 3:3b. In this connection the meaning of מהלך "visit" has often been distorted. As Wiseman (*TynB* 30 [1979] 36–37) points out, the term מהלך can hardly refer to "a linear measure denoting a length of road or journey" here in Jonah, if at all in the OT. In Neh 2:6 the word surely means "visit," since the king could hardly be concerned for the distance from Babylon to Jerusalem, which was well known. Thus his question, "How long will your (מהלך) be?" refers to the length *in time* of Nehemiah's sojourn away from Babylon, not how far the two cities were apart. Other usages of מהלך (e.g., as "passageway" in Ezek 42:4 and Zech 3:7) are less determinative for the present usage of the word.

What then would be the point of the narrator's nominal phrase מהלך שלשת ימים "a visit of three days"? It is quite possible that the issue at hand is what Wiseman calls "the ancient oriental practice of hospitality whereby the first day is for arrival, the second for the primary purpose of the visit and the third for return" (*TynB* 30 [1979] 38). Wiseman outlines the relevant Mesopotamian evidence for political as well as prophetic visits of "men from one city-state entering another for specialist advice" (42–43). He concludes: "There is therefore no difficulty in a prophet being received by the leaders of the city (3:5), though he would probably have had to establish his *bona fides* first" (44). Accordingly, Nineveh was undoubtedly a place Jonah, like any other "emissary," had to enter and leave according to accepted protocol. The story of course does not provide us with the details of how this was done. But we may assume that his first and third days involved meetings and explanations, perhaps even formal hearings. He may even have presented gifts to city officials upon his arrival, as was the custom in the case of official state visits, though his contacts may have been less formal and less high-level. The popular notion that Jonah, virtually unnoticed (except, as some have argued, for his skin stained or bleached by digestive juices!) wandered into Nineveh casually and then, at various stages of his trip, suddenly began shouting his message, would be far from a realistic portrayal of the events—and would have seemed as strange to the ancient hearer / reader as to the modern one. Rather, the narrator's point is that Nineveh was a "three-day visit city," a major diplomatic center of the ancient world, a city where a formal protocol was observed by official visitors, whose business could not easily be accomplished hastily, as if it were a small town. Another explanation is also to be considered. A prophet might reach the populace of a small town with a word from God in a very short time. But in a major city, a prophet would have to travel to various sections, speaking to different crowds, over a period of time. "A three-day visit (city)" could imply simply that Nineveh's population and importance made it necessary for Jonah to preach there for at least three days, to be sure that God's message had been really heard by the bulk of the populace. One of these meanings must lie behind the nominal phrase מהלך שלשת ימים, used adjectivally to modify נינוה.

4 Jonah began to preach his message as soon as it was feasible to do so. Of course, if the great size of Nineveh were in view, the narrator might be making the point that Jonah did *not* begin to preach immediately, but went far enough into the city to be somewhere "downtown" before he preached. That is, he did not merely deliver his warning *pro forma* at the city limits. However, if the three-day visit protocol is in view, as we have argued, the logic is even more evident. Jonah, already on the first day, sounded all the warning he would ever need to sound against Nineveh.

Does the narrator actually intend for us to understand that Jonah preached *only* that first day? Why does he make the point that his preaching began then, and not mention the other days (or distances)? The answer is simple: the people of Nineveh "beat him to it." They repented before he could even get into the full task of preaching to them. According to the usual expectation of ancient protocol, Jonah would have preached widely throughout the city on the second and third day to all who would listen. Only then would he depart, the full visit being complete. On the first day he would not have had the opportunity yet to see the king, if protocol were followed. And the full impact of his mission would hardly be felt until the third day, when everyone had heard, from the least to the greatest, and the formal requirements of bringing important concerns to the attention of an important city would be obliged. But all this was short-circuited by the eager response of the Ninevites. Jonah was just beginning to warm up, just starting the process, and they were already believing God *en masse* (v 5). Thus the mention of the first day of the visit and the silence about the other days eloquently makes the narrator's point. Jonah only had to start to go (ויחל לבוא) into the city with his message that first day. The Ninevites needed only that initial word, so ready were they to turn from their evil practices. Jonah's words reached eager ears right away. And the Ninevites themselves repeated the message all over the city until it touched even the king (v 6). Three days of preaching by Jonah himself would not even be needed. Like the Hebrew women who gave birth before the midwives could arrive (Exod 1:19), the Ninevites responded to God's message almost before the preacher could finish his speech!

Nor would forty days of warning be needed. Jonah preached the words Yahweh had given him, "In forty more days Nineveh will be overthrown (נהפך)." In Assyrian the full sentence would be rendered *adi arbât ūmē ninua innabak*, as simple and as ambiguous as the Hebrew. The ambiguities would be threefold. First, as this word was passed around among the populace, it would not automatically be clear whether Jonah had warned only the enclosed city (*alninua*) or the entire district (*ninuaki*) that it would be overthrown by God. Second, the people might wonder whether the mention of "forty days" was to allow time for repentance, or simply to assure that the divine judgment was not far off. Third, by nature Heb. הפך / Assyrian *abāku* carries a certain ambiguity. The term can signify an overthrow, a judgment, a turning upside down, a reversal, a change, a deposing of royalty, or a change of heart (Wiseman, *TynB* 30 [1979] 49). In other words, Jonah's words in Assyrian, just as in Hebrew, could mean both "In forty more days Nineveh will be overthrown" and "In forty more days Nineveh will have a change of heart" (cf. Good, *Irony in the OT,* 48–49). It must be remembered that these words are not what Jonah composed, but are exactly what Yahweh told him to say (3:2). The alert hearer / reader who would catch the ambiguity would begin to sense what 3:5 then reports.

Jonah's message mentioned "forty days." In spite of its potential ambiguity, this must have seemed to many Ninevites to be an invitation to repentance, giving hope that they and their city or land might not be destroyed. "Forty" (ארבעים) is a term which is often used in the sense of "a good many" or "dozens." It does not necessarily connote a literal forty, i.e., one more than thirty-nine (cf. Num 13:25; Josh 4:13; Judg 3:11; 5:8; 13:1; etc.). Its association with time for purging, in the OT at least (e.g., the wandering in the wilderness for forty years which eliminated the unfaithful; the forty days of rain which began the flood and thus eliminated the wicked; the forty years of Egypt's desolation prior to its restoration, in Ezek 29:11–16, etc.), and at least once with fasting (Deut 9:18, 25; cf. Matt 4:2) might reflect a similar association elsewhere in the ancient Near East (cf. also 1 Kgs 19:8; Exod 24:18; Num 13:25). To the original Israelite / Judean audience the multiple implications of "forty" would be heard; to Jonah they would be evident, and apparently the point was not lost on the Ninevites, either.

5 Swiftly and sincerely the people of wicked but important Nineveh believed Jonah's warning and began to act upon it. Already on the first day (v 4a) of the three (v 3) and of the forty (v 4b) people were ceasing eating and were changing into sackcloth, the mourning garb of the ancient Near East. Everyone took part, from the nobility to the poor. This response of faith and penitence was city-wide in its scope.

The narrator describes the repentance simply. It follows a rather logical and therefore commonly attested order in the OT in which (a) a threat of harm is followed by (b) repentance, and then (c) by God's decision not to bring about the harm after all (cf. 1 Sam 7:3–14; Ezra 8:21–23; Jer 36:3; Joel 2:11–29; for Assyrian parallels, cf. Schaumberger, *Miscellanea Biblica* 2 [1934] 123–34).

The sailors had shown a similar eagerness to believe God (1:16). God's threat was not announced devoid of the possibility of forgiveness. Jeremiah 18:7–8 provides a prophetic paradigm for the implicit conditionality of warning oracles:

> If at any time I declare concerning a nation or a kingdom that I will pluck up, break down, and destroy it, and if that nation, about which I have spoken, turns from its evil (רעה) I will change my mind about the harm (רעה) I intended to do it.

So the Ninevites understood that they still had a chance, and acted accordingly. Corporate fasting was probably rare in ancient times. But a popular call for generalized fasting does have a parallel in the situation of Jerusalem in Jehoiakim's time (604 B.C.) described in Jer 36:9.

6 Jeremiah 36:9–31 makes clear that Jehoiakim of Jerusalem was notably unmoved by Jeremiah's words and therefore was denounced for his obstinance. But his pagan predecessor, the king of Nineveh, acted quite differently. Though as the despot of a vast empire he might be expected, of all people, to remain aloof from the vicissitudes of popular religious trends, in this case "even" (נגע אל) he was affected. And even he donned sackcloth and left the throne to sit humbly in ashes in the Semitic posture of mourning and penitence. The emperor of the Assyrian empire abjectly appealed for mercy from the God on whose authority a vassal Israelite prophet had preached!

The predictable and understandable conclusion of many modern commentators has been that all of this is patently fictional. There are three main reasons for skepticism: (1) no Assyrian historical records lend support to this unusual event; (2) it is unlikely in the extreme that an emperor and a great city would act this way; (3) the entire account is full of obvious exaggeration which may have didactic value, but hardly any historical reliability.

The conclusion that the book, or this part of it, is fictional will have to be established on other grounds, however, since the three arguments listed above do not stand close examination. The silence of official Assyrian records on the preaching of Jonah per se is quite understandable. It was hardly incumbent upon archivists to keep lists of visiting prophets! Moreover, official records tend to be as sycophantic toward the royalty as possible. The bluntly negative evaluation of kings and officials in the OT is quite unique in ancient Near Eastern historiography. As to Assyrian records of the fast, see v 7 below. What condition, then, could produce such fear and repentance, indeed, even the initial willingness to listen to a foreign prophet's warning? We may never know for sure, since we cannot date the book precisely. But several reasonable possibilities exist. First we must note the fact that the king was affected by Jonah's message. (Did Jonah have an official audience with someone in the court that first day, as formal diplomatic custom would have allowed?) From the evidence of Assyrian omen texts, we may posit at least four situations which could move a king to action of the sort described in Jonah: (1) invasion of the land by an enemy; (2) a total solar eclipse; (3) famine conjoined with an epidemic; (4) a severe flood. Any of these could appear to be an evidence of divine wrath, predisposing an Assyrian king to look for deliverance lest his own position of authority be threatened (Wiseman, *TynB* 30 [1979] 44). If Jonah, in God's timing, arrived at Nineveh during or immediately following one of these disasters (רעות), the reaction of the king—and citizenry—to the message God gave him would be far more believable than has otherwise been thought. A prophet like Jonah coming as it were out of nowhere and speaking in the name of "God" (or even "Yahweh" which the Assyrians would have then rendered generally as *il[u]*, "God") might, at the time of a substantial national crisis of a sort thought to be characteristic of God's disfavor, have an impact far beyond anything imaginable under normal conditions.

Invasion would not seem to be the issue here for Nineveh proper since there exists no evidence of any serious threat to Nineveh itself until 614 B.C., when the Babylonians began their long and ultimately successful conquest of Assyria and its empire. The fact that parts of the empire (e.g., Carchemish) had fallen already to the Urartians may, however, have engendered a sense among the populace that the military might of Assyria was failing (see below). A total solar eclipse is an even more substantial possibility. Just such an event occurred in the tenth year of the Assyrian King Aššur-dān III (773–756), on June 15, 763 B.C. Aššur-dān III was, of course, a contemporary of Jeroboam II of Israel (793–753), during whose reign Jonah ben Amittai prophesied in the north (2 Kgs 14:25). For this to have occurred at the very same time the nation of Urartu was expanding its empire at the expense of Assyria cannot have been fortuitous for the confidence of the population. The Urartian King Argishti I forced repeated Assyrian retreats on the weak Assyrian kings Shalmaneser IV (783–774) and Aššur-dān III. Moreover, Argishti's successor Sarduri II (755–735) continued to dominate Assyria in border wars throughout the reign of Aššur-dān's successor Aššur-nirari V (755–746). Sometime during the years 760–750, major Assyrian possessions such as Commagene, Melitene, and even Carchemish were lost to Urartu. One could argue that a great, successful emperor like Tiglath-Pileser III (745–728) would be unlikely to have cared one whit about Jonah's warnings. But what of a weak monarch such as Aššur-dān III, whose hold on the empire's territories was shaky, whose personal power might therefore be waning, and who had just experienced the awesome religious terror of a total solar eclipse? How might he react to the blunt warning of a prophet who had traveled to Nineveh from the opposite end of the Fertile Crescent and arrived at a time of paramount trouble (רעה)? It must be remembered that an Assyrian king, as a syncretist, would hardly wish automatically to deny the validity of any god or any prophet. And does not an outsider often command far more respect than those with whom one regularly deals—even in the case of prophets and other clergy (cf. Melchizedek and Abraham, Gen 14:17–24; Moses and Pharaoh, Exod 5–14; Balaam and Balak, Num 22–24; the Levite from Bethlehem and the Danites, Judg 17–18; etc.)? Wiseman provides translations of some of the relevant conditional warnings from the actual Nineveh versions of the *Enuma Anu Enlil* omen texts. These texts give predictions of what sorts of events may be expected to follow a solar eclipse, including: "the King will be deposed and killed and a worthless fellow seize the throne"; "the King will die, rain from heaven will flood the land. There will be famine"; "a deity will strike the King and fire consume the land"; "the city walls will be destroyed" (*TynB*

30 [1979] 46). Kings of the Assyrians took such omens seriously. They had substantial correspondence with prophets about them (A. L. Oppenheim, "Divination and Celestial Observation in the Late Assyrian Empire," *Centaurus* 4 [1969] 97–135) and in some cases even abandoned the throne to a substitute King of Nineveh (!) until the danger would pass (W. G. Lambert, *AfO* 18 [1957] 288–89; *AfO* 19 [1960] 199; S. Parpola, *Letters from Assyrian Scholars*, AOAT 5.1 [1970] nos. 26–30). Wiseman points out that solar eclipse omen texts mention not only the king, but animals, and the land as a whole, in their specifications of those on whom the divine wrath indicated in the eclipse might fall. This, of course, comports remarkably with the decree issued by the king (3:7, 8).

An earthquake would also constitute an event predisposing a king to worry about his security. Earthquakes (*rībū*) were, in Assyrian religion, evidence of divine wrath. Assyrian kings required reports on earthquakes to be made to the royal court. Of special interest for the study of Jonah is a record of an earthquake in the month of Siwan in the reign of an Aššur-dān. It cannot be deduced from the text whether this is Aššur-dān III, the contemporary of Jeroboam II, or not (Wiseman, *TynB* 30 [1979] 48). If it *were* the same Aššur-dān during whose reign a solar eclipse also occurred, his readiness to resort to sackcloth and ashes might be even more understandable.

Famine also, especially if accompanied by an epidemic of any sort, could, according to the omen texts, indicate divine displeasure and therefore tend to produce a climate in which repentance was possible. The general fasting prescribed in the king's decree (v 7) may even have proved remarkably convenient if, in fact, food supply was already a problem. Flooding, which tends to contaminate water supplies and thus cause disease as well as interrupt food production, may also have brought on famines, in light of the significance given to floods in the omen texts. Whatever the possible cause, the Assyrian eponym lists for the years of Aššur-dān III's reign (773–756) contain several references to famine (Assyrian *mutanu*) either lasting from 765 to 759 B.C. or at least recurring during that seven-year period (whether the famine was constant or intermittent is not clear from the eponym lists; cf. Wiseman, *TynB* 30 [1979] 50). The result was a succession of rebellions against Aššur-dān III's leadership in various cities in Assyria until 758 B.C. when peace again prevailed, and Aššur-dān III moved to Gozan temporarily.

There is, of course, absolutely no way to identify with confidence the king mentioned in Jonah 3:6. On the other hand, a king such as Aššur-dān III, during whose reign an agonizing confluence of omens and disasters (eclipse, earthquake (?), famine, rioting) had occurred, whose capital (or at least common residence) may have been Nineveh, though this cannot be proved, and who was beset by international problems including continuing military failures against Urartu, was certainly the sort of king (among others) who might well have been predisposed to receive Jonah's message sincerely as a chance for respite from his troubles. The Ninevites of the time of Aššur-dān were certainly no strangers to "trouble" (רעה; 1:2)!

7–8 The king's decree calls for extreme fasting—even to abstinence from water—and general penitence, i.e, wearing sackcloth and praying for mercy. What Jonah was afraid might happen was happening in the most extreme manner. The Ninevites, led by their king, were turning with all their might to repentance. Jonah's message had certainly been well received!

The leadership of the king comes in response to the people's initiation of fasting and mourning. The king's decree adds impetus and official sanction to what is already well under way. Sovereigns, though hardly always the initiators of major civil movements, must usually take charge of and give direction to a popular action if they wish not to be perceived as opposing the populace. It is noteworthy that the decree is issued in the name of the king *and* his nobles. The practice of royal consultation with advisors was common in Assyria as elsewhere; but jointly issuing decrees was not. As a result the wording has sometimes been thought to reflect a later Persian practice. Alternatively, if the Assyrian king at this time was truly weak, his authority to govern being in some doubt in parts of the nation, or if his reign followed an interregnum during which government by consensus had been necessary (cf. Wisemen, *TynB* 30 [1979] 51), the decision to include "his nobles" (גדליו) in the decree becomes understandable. It may also be that the wording reflects a genuine consensus, clearly and intentionally bringing the powers that be into conformity with the people. A king grasping at straws might well be willing to modify a claim to sole authority in such a case.

Fasting and uncomfortable dress represented self-denial to the ancient Semites. By overtly eschewing normal comforts and making themselves physically miserable they sought to show the genuineness of their prayers for mercy. The decree adds the prescription that the animals must, as well, be involved. In Persian times and later, animals were sometimes made part of the mourning process (Herodotus ix.24; Plutarch, *Alexander* 72; Jdt 4:10) but the practice is unknown otherwise among the Assyrians. While this aspect of the king's decree may be somewhat hyperbolic, i.e., intending to stress how complete the penitence should be, the close interrelationship of humans and animals in ancient times may itself account for their being mentioned together here (cf. 4:11). The generalized language of mourning which *is* found in some Assyrian decrees is of the type found in Jonah. Wiseman cites two examples. The first is from a royal Assyrian decree received in Gozan by the governor there, Mannu-kī-Aššur, who began his governorship in 793 B.C. and who therefore may have been a contemporary of Aššur-dān III:

> Decree of the King. You and all the people, your land, your meadows will mourn and pray for three days before the god Adad and repent. You will perform the purification rites so that there may be rest.

A royal letter of uncertain date contains this reference to generalized penitence: ". . . this mourning in the month Siwan concerns all the people in the land" (for both decrees see *TynB* 30 [1979] 51). While the latter mourning period may have been closer to the "forty days" of Jonah's message, the three-day mourning of the former is probably more nearly representative of what the Assyrians actually did. Although people and animals can survive without food for weeks on end, to survive without water for more than a few days is difficult. Accordingly, the decree to abstain even from water would appear to contemplate a short, intense period of penitence rather than one of extended duration. Such a provision might have proved especially convenient, of course, if some of the water supplies were already unusable, temporarily, because of flooding. The Ninevite response to Jonah's message in the form of a severe generalized fast parallels the first-day response (v 4). The point the narrator makes by including these materials is evident: God's word is being heard and taken seriously at all levels (מגדולים ועד קטנים "from the greatest to the least" v 5). The decree acknowledges, moreover, that the people's misbehavior on a general scale is the basis for the divine wrath. This is not so astounding an admission as it might seem, since throughout the ancient world people assumed that disasters were caused by divinities displeased with the humans who worshiped them. The decree intends, therefore, to couple a short-term penance of discomfort with a long-term reform from "evil practices" (דרך רעה, indicating general immoral behavior) and "frequent violence" (חמס אשר בכף, indicating especially social injustice). The decree would be virtually unenforceable as law. It would depend on voluntary cooperation in any quarter where fasting and mourning were not already under way. The sincere willingness of the people of Nineveh as a whole, therefore, was still required in spite of the decree's severity. What God saw (v 10) would have to be genuine. The people could not continue in sin and expect a ritual of self-denial to exonerate them.

9 There was real hope. True repentance and reform could work. But "the gods" were considered sovereignly independent to the Assyrians and other ancient Near Easterners just as Yahweh was sovereign over Israel. No god could be made to act; the gods responded according to their sovereign will. "The god" in whose name Jonah preached could have been identified by the syncretistic Ninevites with any of dozens of deities in their pantheon. Alternatively, Jonah may simply have mentioned "God," and so the Ninevites left the deity unspecified. Even more likely as the reason for the use of האלהים "the god" in the Hebrew rendering of the decree is the fact that Jonah preached exactly the warning that Yahweh had given him (cf. 3:3), "In forty more days, Nineveh will be overthrown," thus mentioning no god at all *explicitly*. The Ninevites then assumed that one of their gods—it is ultimately immaterial which one they may have thought it to be, or if they found it necessary to make such an identification—was planning to compound their recent troubles by bringing disaster to the city.

The first four words of the Hebrew of v 9 (מי יודע ישוב ונחם "Who knows? He may change his mind") are found in the same order in Joel 2:14. This may reflect a coincidence, a dependence in either direction (Magonet [*Form and Meaning*, 77–79] argues convincingly for the priority of Jonah rather than Joel), or a mutual dependence on something in ancient Israelite liturgies or prophetic language which became popular enough to be used twice in the OT, including in a rendering of an Assyrian edict. At any rate, Joel 2:12–14 is closely related to the Jonah story through its emphasis on the possibility of repentance on the part of a truly sinful people, if the repentance is genuine, and its portrayal of God as patient and merciful (Jonah 4:2).

The king's decree captures what Jonah resentfully understood all along: God can forgive anybody, even a (self-) important city famous for its wickedness, which had oppressed Jonah's own people. It was that possibility—that God would actually be true to his forgiving nature and spare Nineveh—that the Ninevites now grasped toward.

10 In the overall progression of the story, Jonah may not yet know for certain what the hearer / reader is now let in on. Jonah may not know, indeed, of many of the events which took place as described in vv 5–9. He is out of the picture at this point, even though he had surely seen the beginnings of repentance before he left the city (4:6) and had presumably spent the full three days' visit Nineveh's importance required. And he must have been aware of the king's decree (which although undated, must have followed the first day of Jonah's visit soon enough to have caused Jonah's pessimism as recorded in 4:1).

But we are now told that God was everything Jonah feared (4:2) and the sinful city hoped. As a result of the genuine repentance of the people ("they gave up their evil practices," שבו מדרכם הרעה) God relented, simply and fully, of his original plan to punish them. The warning נהפך "shall be over-thrown" (v 4) had now become null and void by reason of the compassion of Yahweh. The Ninevites would not, of course, know this for sure until the forty days had passed without incident. Thus the verse appears to function somewhat in the manner of 1:16, as a coda, describing a result that endured on into the indefinite future from the point of view of the narrator.

What God did was to change his mind in accordance with what he revealed of himself elsewhere in Scripture. The statement in Joel 2:12–14 about the potential of divine "repentance" has already been mentioned. Jer 18:7–10 is the *locus classicus* of the OT teaching on the contingency of prophetic warning. As v 8 says, "if that nation I warned turns from its evil (רעה) then I will relent (נחם) of the trouble / harm I had intended to do to it."

Jonah's words of warning to Nineveh had never been certain predictions of doom. They had contained an implicit contingency on the order of that described in Jer 18:8. And when Nineveh repented, God relented. Nothing catastrophic happened to the city after all. However widespread was the repentance, however long it lasted, it was enough. Jonah's mission had had a wonderful effect! It is only too bad that Jonah would not think so—or would he? The answer to that the hearer / reader will be given immediately (4:1).

Explanation

"Who knows?" (מי יודע), the poignant question asked in the royal decree (v 9) and echoed in Joel 2:14, expresses the theological issue around which the chapter revolves: contingency and divine sovereignty. Jonah is not certain what will result from his finally preaching in Nineveh the words God has given him. Jonah can hope for the destruction of the city, but cannot surely expect it (cf. 4:5). God alone will decide its fate. The citizens of Nineveh can believe and repent, but sincerity alone cannot control what God is free to do for them or against them. They can hope for deliverance, but cannot surely expect it (v 9). The hearer / reader does not know what will happen either. Then, in v 10, comes the answer to the suspense generated already in 1:2. Nineveh's repentance was acceptable to God. He spared the city. None, after all, perished. God alone knew the answer to the question "who knows?"

That God should choose to make his own actions contingent—at least in part—upon human actions is no limitation of his sovereignty. Having first decided to place the option of obedience and disobedience before nations, his holding them responsible for their actions automatically involves a sort of contingency. He promises blessing if they repent, punishment if not (cf. Jer 18:7–10). But this hardly makes God dependent on the nations; it rather makes them dependent on him, as is the point of the lesson at the potter's house in Jer 18:1–11, and the point of the mourning decree in Jonah 3:5–9. God holds all the right, all the power, and all the authority.

A message of the book of Jonah is that God does not exercise his power arbitrarily and discriminatorily. Jonah, the nationalist, wants God to bless Israel and harm all its enemies. His own actions, showing respect and concern for the sailors in chap. 1 and the plant in chap. 4, are, of course, evidence of the inconsistency of his own position. But God is patient, "not wanting anyone to perish, but everyone to come to repentance" (2 Pet 3:9), and "wants all people to be saved and to come to a knowledge of the truth" (1 Tim 2:4). He manifests his sovereignty not in stubbornness but in grace; not in narrow particularism but in a willingness to forgive *any* people. There is, however, a contingency. The book of Jonah does not teach a naïve, lowest-common-denominator universalism. Only genuine repentance can result in forgiveness. God's threat is not to be taken lightly. His warning is as severe as the Ninevites took it to be.

An implicit, yet impossible-to-ignore comparison permeates the chapter; i.e., a comparison between Israel and Assyria. Yahweh's mercy to his "own" people, Israel, is well known. Neither Jonah, nor the narrator, nor the hearer / reader could block out of memory the stories of divine mercy shown to Israel when it deserved otherwise, but was granted pardon upon appeal (e.g., Exod 32:7–14, in which v 14 contains phraseology not unlike that found in Jonah 3:10). But here, the pagan Assyrians of Nineveh repent as fully and heartily as any Israelites ever did! The chosen people had not yet in their history (i.e., to the mid-eighth century B.C.) repented so sincerely. Only later, in the days of Ezra (Ezra 10:1–17) and Nehemiah (Neh 9:1–3) do we read of appeals for mercy quite so self-abnegating. Even the revivals of Hezekiah (2 Kgs 18:1–8) and Josiah (2 Kgs 22:11–23:3) lack some of the earnestness and popular impetus—at least as they are described—that the narrator has attributed to the Assyrian turn from sin. The Ninevite repentance became justly famous as an example of a turn toward righteousness by a people undeserving otherwise of mercy.

Excursus: The Sign of Jonah (Matt 12:39–41; Luke 11:29–32)

Jesus spoke of the "sign of Jonah" not only in reference to the three days and nights Jonah spent inside the fish (the emphasis given the "sign" in Matt 12:40) but also apparently in reference to Jonah's appearance as a visiting prophet giving warning to an evil people (the emphasis given the "sign" in Matt 12:41 and Luke 11:30, 32). In the latter instance, Jonah was a type of Christ, and the Ninevites were a type of the Jews of Jesus' day, or even people of any disbelieving generation who then take to heart a message from God. This is the sense upon which chap. 3 of Jonah concentrates. Jonah was a sign to the Ninevites as a prophet, not as a survivor of drowning. At least as the story is narrated, there is no evidence whatever that anyone in Nineveh knew about the rescue at sea via the fish. What the Ninevites believe in is *God*—not Jonah. His authority comes from his message, not his experiences. This is the point of the "sign" in Matt 12:41 and Luke 11:30, 32. It is Jesus' message, because it bears divine authority, that people must believe—not any particular "proof." The Ninevites, likewise, showed real faith by believing in God without an overwhelming, doubt-dispelling miraculous guarantee that Jonah was God's emissary. They recognized the message, not the messenger, as truthful, and acted upon it.

Eventually, Nineveh became again a nation famous for its evil. It is clear that the city-wide repentance need not have been (and certainly was not) permanent in order for God to forgive the city. What the people showed was genuine contrition *at one point,* which was enough for God to unleash his waiting grace and bind his waiting wrath. Biblical descriptions of the effects of repentance seem to presume that an act of general repentance is relevant to a single generation (cf., e.g., Deut 4:9 compared to 4:25). Later generations (the definition of "generation" in this case being any group with a new mindset, not necessarily a group twenty years later) will be responsible for their *own* repentance. A later generation of unrepentant Ninevites was destroyed (in 611 B.C.).

Repentance and faith do not necessarily equal conversion. The Ninevites to whom Jonah preached did not become monotheistic Yahwists. They remained, by all accounts, the same polytheistic, syncretistic pantheists they had been all along. It is almost certain that they considered Jonah a representative of *a* god, one of their own deities. As syncretists they would identify virtually any foreign god with one of their own. Their theology may have been woefully inadequate, but their actions and faith were true evidence of repentance. It was on that evidence that God acted.

The king's actions of contrition and his genuine fear of God are usually thought ridiculously improbable on the part of an Assyrian king. But in the same way that Hezekiah donned sackcloth and sought God's help upon hearing the Assyrian challenge delivered by the Rabshakeh outside the walls of Jerusalem in 701 B.C. (2 Kgs 19:1), a wearied, harassed king such as Aššur-dān III of Assyria could well have sought divine help for the many tragedies and miseries he faced, upon hearing a potentially hopeful word of warning from a prophet who had come a long way to deliver it. Jonah's reluctant mission had succeeded against all his own hopes. God did indeed love more than just Israel. He loved—to Jonah's horror—the Assyrians.

God Teaches Jonah about Anger and Compassion (4:1–11)

Bibliography

Blank, S. H. "'Doest Thou Well to Be Angry?' A Study in Self-Pity." *HUCA* 26 (1955) 29–41. **Bojorge, H.** "Los significados posibles de *lehaṣṣil* en Jonas 4,6." *Stromata* 26

(1970) 77–87. **Boman, T.** "Jahve og Elohim i Jonaboken." *NorTT* 37 (1936) 159–68.
Brekelmans, C. "Some Translation Problems, Judges v29, Psalm cxx 7, Jona iv 4,9."
OTS 15 (1969) 170–76. **Brongers, H. A.** "Bemerkungen zum Gebrauch des adverbialen
weʿattāh im alten Testament." *VT* 15 (1965) 289–99. **Daube, D.** "Death as a Release
in the Bible." *Donum Gratulorium Ethelbert Stauffer.* Leiden: E. J. Brill, 1962. 82–104.
Davies, G. I. "The Uses of *rʿʿ* Qal and the Meaning of Jonah IV 1." *VT* 27 (1977)
105–110. **Glueck, N.** *Hesed in the Bible.* Tr. A. Gottschalk. Cincinnati: Hebrew Union
College Press, 1967. **Gruber, M.** "Was Cain Angry or Depressed? Background of a
Biblical Murder." *BAR* 6 (1980) 34–36. **Heschel, A.** *The Prophets.* Vol. 2. New York:
Harper and Row, 1962. 59–78. **Kaiser, O.** "Wirklichkeit, Möglichkeit und Vorurteil:
Ein Beitrag zum Verständnis des Buches Jona." *EvT* 33 (1973) 91–103. **Kidner,
F. D.** "The Distribution of Divine Names in Jonah." *TynB* 21 (1970) 126–28. **Lohfink,
N.** "Jona ging zur Stadt hinaus (Jon 4,5)." *BZ* NF 5 (1961) 185–203. **Möllerfeld, J.**
"'Du bist ein gnädiger und barmherziger Gott' (Jonas 4,2)." *Geist und Leben* 33 (1960)
324–33. **Rad, G. von.** *The Message of the Prophets.* Tr. D. M. G. Stalker. New York:
Harper and Row, 1965. ———. *Der Prophet Jona.* Nürnberg: Laetare-Verlag, 1950.
Also in *God at Work in Israel.* Tr. J. H. Marks. Nashville: Abingdon, 1980. 58–70.
Robinson, B. "Jonah's Qiqayon Plant." *ZAW* 97 (1985) 390–403. **Sakenfeld, K. D.**
The Meaning of Hesed in the Hebrew Bible. HSM 17. Missoula, MT: Scholars Press,
1978. **Smudi, Y.** "Jonah's Gourd." *BMik* 28 (1982 / 83) 44–48. [Heb.] **Weimar, P.**
"Jon 4,5: Beobachtungen zur Entstehung der Jonaerzählung." *BN* 18 (1982) 86–109.
Weiss, R. "Where Shall I Flee from Your Presence?" *Oroth* 49 (1963) 28–33. [Heb.]
Wilson, R. D. "'To Appoint' in the O.T." *Princeton Theological Review* 16 (1918) 645–
54.

Translation

Jonah's anger and God's reply

[1] *This was absolutely disgusting*[a] *to Jonah, and he became angry.* [2] *He prayed
to Yahweh: "This, O Yahweh, is exactly what I said*[a] *when I was back in my own
country. That is why I fled, earlier, on the open sea.*[b] *I knew that you were a God
who is gracious, compassionate, patient, firmly loyal,*[c] *and one who decides against
disaster.*[d] [3] *So, Yahweh, take my life from me. I would rather be dead than alive."*[a]

[4] *Yahweh said, "What right do you have to be angry?"*[a]

Coda: an object lesson from God

[5] *When Jonah had left*[a] *the city, he had situated*[a] *himself on the east of the city.
There he made for himself a shelter and stayed under it until he might see what
would happen to the city.* [6] *Yahweh God designated a climbing gourd*[a] *to grow up
over Jonah to shade his head and to relieve*[b] *his trouble.*[c] *Jonah was absolutely
delighted with the climbing gourd.* [7] *But the next day, at sunrise, God*[a] *designated
a worm to attack the climbing gourd so that it shriveled.* [8] *As the sun rose, God
designated a withering*[a] *wind from the east, and the sun beat down*[b] *on Jonah's
head so that he was overcome, and wanted to die. He said "I would rather be
dead than alive."*[c]

[9] *God said to Jonah, "What right do you have to be angry about the climbing
gourd?"*

He said, "I have the right! I'm so angry I could die!"[a]

¹⁰ *Yahweh said, "You are so concerned about the climbing gourd which you did not have to lift a finger to grow,*ᵃ *which came up overnight and died overnight.* ¹¹ *Should not I*ᵃ *be concerned about Nineveh, the important city which has in it more than*ᵇ *a hundred twenty thousand people who do not know their right hand from their left, as well as a large number of animals?"*

Notes

1.a. Lit., "It was / became wrong to Jonah as a great wrong." The Heb. employs paronomasia between the verb רעע "be evil, disgusting" and the noun רעה "wrong," the latter word being used in yet another sense here in chap. 4 (see *Introduction*).

2.a. Lit., "Is this not what I said . . . ," an idiomatic way of stressing that it was exactly what he said (i.e., to himself, not necessarily publicly).

2.b. Cf. 1:3.

2.c. The basic sense of חסד is loyalty; thus רב־חסד, lit., "great of loyalty," would mean approximately "firmly loyal." Cf. Sackenfeld, *Hesed;* and Glueck, *Hesed in the Bible.*

2.d. Or "trouble." Again רעה is employed in one of its many shades of meaning in the book.

3.a. Lit., "my death (is) better than my life."

4.a. Or, possibly, "Does it do any good for you to be angry?" The question is hardly neutral but is meant to correct Jonah forcefully.

5.a. The verbs are presumably to be construed as pluperfect in this verse, thereafter reverting to simple perfects in light of the fact that vv 5–10 obviously constitute a flashback.

6.a. The exact botanical designation of קיקיון is not known. It may be the *rinicus communis*, i.e., castor-oil plant, or possibly a cucumber. It may also refer generally to a class, i.e., "gourd."

6.b. The verb הציל "relieve" may be intended as a paronomasia with צל "shade."

6.c. Heb. רעה again.

7.a. The Heb. has the article (האלהים) yet would be awkwardly translated "the God," even though this was possible in 1:6 and 3:9.

8.a. The meaning of חרישית is not certain. The versions provide translations on the order of either "scorching" or "silent," the latter being the basis for our "withering." Emendations to either חריפית "sharp," "scorching," or חרירית ("hot") have been proposed. A single Dead Sea Scroll (1QH 7:4, 5) usage (בזעף חרישית; "in a blasting (?) storm") is not entirely helpful in pinpointing the definition. "Searing" or "enervating" may also be possible.

8.b. Lit., "attacked" (cf. v 7) or "hit."

8.c. Cf. n. 3.a.

9.a. Or, "I'll be angry until the day I die!" The Heb. עד־מות, lit., "until death," is ambiguous.

10.a. Lit., "Which you did not toil over and did not grow."

11.a. The special use of אני "I" with 1 indicates stress.

11.b. On the use of הרבה, the hiphil inf constr with מן, cf. Judg 18:26b; 1 Kgs 5:10.

Form / Structure / Setting

Although 4:1 describes the reaction of Jonah to Yahweh's decision to spare the city, which preceded immediately in 3:10, there is no reason to conclude that any part of chap. 4 should be linked as a literary unit with chap. 3. With chap. 4 another emphasis begins, that of the reaction of Jonah to the display of divine mercy on Israel's enemies. Previously the book chronicled Jonah's attempt to avoid any part in a process he expected might result in benefit for the Assyrians. Now that it has happened, we find out just how odious the result is to him. The focus of chap. 3 was on the Ninevites and their appeal. The focus of chap. 4 shifts to Jonah's reaction and the lessons he learns from Yahweh. No mention was made of Jonah in the previous pericope (3:3b–10). Now he is the central human character once again.

The pericope known as chap. 4 contains two divisions, vv 1–4, in which Jonah pours out his bitter frustration to God, and vv 5–11, in which the object lesson of the climbing gourd exposes Jonah's narrowness. Both occur in the aftermath of Jonah's preaching; the former when Jonah is absolutely sure that the city will not be punished, the latter while the "forty days" are yet in progress and Jonah is still hoping for harm to come to Nineveh. In this regard vv 5–11 function as a concluding coda, being a flashback to a time when the outcome of the Ninevites' attempt at repentance was not yet evident.

The form of the pericope is vivid (or sensational) historical narrative, continuing the didactic style which characterizes the book as a whole. There is a rather heavy concentration of dialog in the chapter. And for the first time, Jonah and God converse with one another, i.e., back and forth. This method of narration allows the hearer / reader actually to learn firsthand rather than guess at Jonah's own self-expressed ideas and attitudes, selfish and inconsistent as they are, as well as God's reasons for his actions in contradiction to Jonah's wishes. All is finally explained to the hearer / reader, so that the book ends leaving no doubt as to its message: God has every right to show mercy to all nations and peoples and we (like Jonah) have no right at all to think that some are intrinsically less deserving than others of this mercy.

The structure of the passage may be outlined as follows:

Jonah's Anger and God's Reply	vv 1–4
Narrative Introduction	v 1
Jonah's Confession and Dissatisfaction with Yahweh	v 2
Jonah's Desire to Die	v 3
Yahweh's Corrective Reply	v 4
Coda: An Object Lesson from God	vv 5–11
The Story of the Gourd	vv 5–7
Jonah's Desire to Die	v 8
Yahweh's Corrective Reply	v 9a
Jonah's Stubbornness and Yahweh's Explanation	vv 10–11

Each of the two major sections of the passage begins with a narrative introduction, setting the scene, and proceeds to a dialog in which Jonah converses with God. Each ends with a brief divine speech correcting Jonah's (and the hearer / reader's) improper attitudes toward the fact of Nineveh's release from destruction.

Repeated verbatim and clearly pivotal for the chapter as well as the entire book is Yahweh's question: "What right do you have to be angry?" This question constitutes the rhetorical conclusion to the first section, in v 4. As the narrator has constructed the passage, the audience is invited to keep that question in mind, while the narrator "flashes back" to the event he has chosen as a coda to conclude the book, the story of the gourd. In this sense the second section (vv 5–11) may be understood as a kind of expansion on that question. It, too, contains the same question ("What right have you to be angry . . . ," הֵיטֵב חָרָה לָךְ) now applied specifically to Jonah's anger about the gourd's demise. Jonah's answer, "(I) have the right!" (הֵיטֵב) and his following protestation of being angry enough to die, are his final words in the book. By this arrangement the audience is left with a choice: to copy Jonah's "embarrassing and ridiculous" (von Rad, *The Message*, 269) hatred of his enemies, or to see the world as God sees it, a world greatly in need of mercy.

The book thus ends at a point which chronologically came earlier than what is described in 4:1–4, but which logically provides a concluding challenge to the hearer / reader. The didactic power of chap. 4 is enhanced by this non-chronological flashback arrangement, as was the case with the flashforward codas in 1:16 and 3:10. The material in 4:1–4 must be understood to follow after the forty days of waiting are up, Jonah's prayer being occasioned by his conclusion that Yahweh had indeed spared the city, as 3:10 informs the audience. The story of the gourd, however, takes place after the completion of Jonah's preaching in the city but before the divine decision described in 3:10 is known to Jonah. V 5 therefore mentions "the city" (העיר) three times, so as to draw the reader back in time to the point where Jonah had just left the city itself, before he could know for certain the outcome of his warning. Both sections of the passage in chap. 4, accordingly, are to be understood as set outside the city to the east, though the setting of vv 1–4 is otherwise not provided.

Jonah chose a spot on the east of the city (v 5) to build his shelter, not because of anything about the geography of the environs of Nineveh that would make such a location advantageous but because the east was where he ended up after traveling through the city. Coming from the west, he would have entered at the west. Completing his task, he would find himself at the east, and from there would go out to watch. The environs of Nineveh, like those of many ancient Mesopotamian cities, were relatively bleak. Outside the city, Jonah would have had access to plenty of stones to build his shelter, and perhaps some poor-quality brush not already taken for firewood but little else. The gourd described in v 6 would indeed have been very welcome to him, roofing materials of any sort being in short supply.

The pattern of the divine names employed in the passage appears to be a random one. Yahweh is used four times, exclusively, in the first section (vv 1–4). In the remaining section, Yahweh is used once (v 10), Elohim is used once (v 9) without the article and once (v 7) with it, and Yahweh-Elohim is used once (v 6). The latter constitutes the only use in the book of this compound divine name common elsewhere in the OT. Attempts to see special significance in the variation of divine names have not been convincing, both because the names do not correspond in usage to any changes or developments in the story, and because nothing more significant than purposeful variation in the interest of good style can be shown to account for the diversity.

Comment

1 Any doubt remaining in the audience's minds about the true nature of Jonah's original motive for flight is dispelled by the blunt assertion in v 1 that Jonah was infuriated that God should spare Nineveh. The language employed in the Hebrew (וירע אל־יונה רעת גדולה), lit., "It became evil / wrong to Jonah as a great evil / wrong," contains both the verbal root רעע

"to be evil / wrong" and the nominal / adjectival root רעה "evil / wrong," in paronomasia, the clause thus expressing Jonah's dissatisfaction about as strongly as would be possible to say it in Hebrew. Here רעה is used in a nuance closely related to "trouble," i.e., that of something "wrong" or "awful," i.e., objectionable to Jonah. The verb רעע itself is the subject of a play of sorts, since it can hardly be forgotten when its opposite in meaning טוב, hiphil "to be right, to have right," is used by God in v 4. Jonah hated what God had done. It made him furious. If this is shocking, it is supposed to be so. The narrator carefully tells the story according to his inspired purpose, which is to arouse the audience to disassociate itself from Jonah's narrow nationalism. Though Jonah hardly comes across as a hero anywhere in the book, he appears especially selfish, petty, temperamental, and even downright foolish in chap. 4.

He had hoped, right to the end (v 5), that God would somehow destroy Nineveh. He now found it loathsome that Yahweh could have let the forty days go by without doing anything. Nothing had happened. The city had gone back to its business. Obviously Yahweh had decided not to overthrow hated Nineveh. He had accepted the prayers of these oppressors, these international outlaws! In the same way he had once spared the Israelites, his own covenant people (Exod 32), he now had spared Assyrians, the very enemies of his own people. How could Yahweh do such a thing?

2 In fact, Jonah knew very well how Yahweh could do what he had done. He had always known it, but had not wanted to face it. Thus his prayer bemoaned the fact that he was afraid all along that Yahweh would prove to be the sort of God that the OT in various places says he is. The narrator now reveals fully, by citing Jonah's prayer, the motivation for Jonah's flight in chap. 1. This had been left unexpressed throughout the book, not to keep the audience in the dark but to highlight the inner conflict Jonah felt, thereby helping the hearer / reader to feel the didactic impact of the story.

Jonah did not want Yahweh to do what was right and proper according to his merciful nature. Instead of showing to Assyria the kind of undeserving favor he had granted to Israel, he should punish the Assyrians without giving them any chance to repent. The book's audience is hardly exempt from such thinking. It is always easier to assume that God is with us more than he is with our enemies. In war, how can God be on the side of the foe? Whether it was the time of the Assyrian Empire, the Babylonian Empire, or the Persian Empire (etc.) those Israelites who heard or read the story of Jonah were all people who chafed under subjugation by a foreign power. Their natural tendency would be to presume that God was with them and not with their oppressors. But they could not confine God to serving their own interest! Jonah's resentment at having his fears come true strikes at the complacency of the audience. In his "own country" (אדמתי) Jonah would have found many kindred minds, people who would rather endure the wrath of God themselves than see the kindness of God shown to their enemies. Jonah tells us in his own words why he fled when he first received the prophetic assignment to preach in Nineveh. He wanted nothing to do with bringing benefit to the Assyrians. Jonah thus argues with God, complaining at God's goodness! The hearer / reader is forced to recoil from this sort of attitude so blatantly

and honestly admitted by the prophet. Jonah's approach is wrong—and therefore the hearer / reader's approach, if similar, is wrong, too.

Further digging his own grave verbally, Jonah cites an ancient formulation,
virtually a creed, about Yahweh's grace ("Yahweh is gracious, compassionate,
patient," etc.). This list of divine attributes, minus the contextually important
reference to deciding against disaster (נחם על־הרעה) is first found in the
OT in Exod 34:6 and thereafter occurs in Num 14:18; Pss 86:15; 103:8;
145:8; Nah 1:3; Neh 9:17. The wording Jonah uses, which includes the
phrase נחם על־הרעה, highly appropriate to the situation of Nineveh, is found
verbatim in Joel 2:13. Since the first four words of Joel 2:14 also appear in
the book of Jonah (3:9) the possibility of either a dependency (in one direction
or the other) or a commonality of some sort between Joel and Jonah cannot
be ignored. The evidence, however, is again too scant to be decisive. At any
rate, by citing this ancient formulation, Jonah confesses eloquently that hoping
to see Nineveh destroyed even after he has preached there (4:5) he was
actually expecting God to suppress his own natural inclination to show mercy
wherever possible. It was not simply the case that Jonah could not bring
himself to appreciate Nineveh. Rather, to a shocking extent, he could not
stand God!

3 Jonah had thought his life would end when he asked the sailors to
throw him overboard (1:12). It had not ended, because God had mercifully
rescued him from drowning via the fish. Now he asks Yahweh himself to
end his life. The ardent nationalist could not abide the fact that Yahweh
had mercifully rescued Nineveh. Rescue was all right for Jonah, but not for
that important enemy city. A world in which God forgives even Israel's enemies
is a world Jonah does not wish to live in. He asks for death in a straightforward
way, reminiscent of Elijah's request to die in 1 Kgs 19:4. Death would at
least remove him from his present anguish (cf. Daube, *Donum Gratulorium,*
97–98). He would actually rather die than live, and emphasizes this with a
sentence that will be quoted again in the flashback (v 8).

The verse begins with the Hebrew ועתה "So . . . ," an element that often
introduced the central point of a prayer, letter, or speech following the preamble (cf. Gen 44:33; Isa 5:3, 5; Brongers, *"weʿattāh* im AT," *VT* 15 [1965] 296–
97) upon which the point is based. In this structure, Jonah's request for
death is formally predicated on the fact that Yahweh is a merciful God. Jonah
would prefer death to serving this patient, forgiving Yahweh, the God who
refuses to limit his grace just to Israel.

4 Yahweh responded incisively with a rhetorical question which both condemned Jonah's attitude and at the same time struck home to the audience.
"What right do you have to be angry?", three simple words in the Hebrew
(ההיטב חרה לך), conclude the section forcefully and serve the didactic point
of the narrator admirably. Jonah is angry, but without merit.

Note that Yahweh ignored Jonah's request to die. It was a stupid request,
voiced out of frustration and pettiness, and Yahweh did not honor it with a
response. The heart of the issue was not Jonah's status, but his narrow attitude.
Could Jonah then provide any logical rejoinder to Yahweh's question? Of
course not. His own confession in v 3 has condemned him. If Yahweh is a
forgiving God, and Jonah is his servant, what right indeed does he have to

be angry at what Yahweh has done for Nineveh? It is upon this question
that the coda which concludes the book is based, the flashback serving to
heighten and expand the divine challenge to Jonah, and to the audience as
well.

5 With v 5 the narrator commences a flashback to a point at which Jonah
was still not certain of the outcome of his warning the city. Jonah remained
both stubborn and inconsistent to the end: stubborn in his opposition to
God's evident concern for the enemy, but inconsistent in that he was perfectly
happy to be the beneficiary of God's concern himself. For didactic purposes,
it is advantageous for the audience to be left at the end of the book with
their freshest memory being that of the one incident which, more forcefully
than any other, shows Jonah to be wrong and God to be right. Thus the
narrator has selected the story of the gourd, placed it as the climax of the
book, in the position of a coda, and thus masterfully accomplished his inspired
purpose.

The verbs which begin the verse (ויצא "had left" and וישב "had situated
himself") are therefore almost certainly pluperfect in meaning. (For a review
of the positions taken on the question of the chronological position of vv 4–
11, see L. C. Allen, 231, n. 16.) The last words chronologically in the book
are those of God in v 4; v 5 is resumptive, but not chronologically, of those
words, "What right do you have to be angry?" The story which begins with
v 5 shows that Jonah has no right at all, regardless of his own protestation
to the contrary.

We are to presume that Jonah started his preaching on the west of Nineveh,
and continuing through the city, was at the eastern side when he exited.
From there he had gone to a place some distance outside, in a spot within
sight of the city but otherwise unspecified in the narrative. Because he wanted
to see "what would happen to the city," i.e., he still hoped that he might be
able to witness a Sodom-Gomorrah style destruction, he constructed a temporary shelter. The word used here, סכה, is that used of the Israelite shelters
in the feast of Booths (Tabernacles), i.e., a simple hut for shade (cf. Lev
23:40–42). Because "forty days" (3:4) can be an imprecise term, Jonah probably
had to wait a month and a half or so. But he was hardly one to shrink from
a challenge. Personal fear had had nothing to do with any of his past actions.
So he constructed a crude shelter and settled down to wait for the doom—
hopefully spectacular—that Yahweh would bring upon Nineveh.

6 Timber was scarce then, as now, in Mesopotamia. It was an expensive,
imported item. Jonah's shelter was undoubtedly built from the common materials available to him: stones and / or clay. A true roof for his shelter would
have required wooden beams. Jonah used instead, we may assume, what
branches he could find from brush and / or trees in the area not already
claimed for firewood. His shelter, in other words, almost certainly did not
have much of a roof to it, i.e., nothing like the roofs that the Israelites could
build in their vineyards during the grape and olive harvests. Where Jonah
got water and purchased food during this time of waiting is insignificant to
the story; travelers and visitors near cities in all ages have usually managed
to find food and water. The issue here is Jonah's protection from the sun, a
major concern to anyone in the ancient Near East living in the open during
the daytime.

Yahweh God (the term Elohim compounded with Yahweh is used uniquely here in the book, probably simply for variety, though it is a common combination in many places in the OT) intervened to show concern for Jonah, by designating a gourd to give him shade. The word "designate" (מנה) is that used of God's provision of the fish already in 2:1. Here again God has specially acted on Jonah's behalf. The audience cannot miss the comparison. The narrator also mentions that the gourd "relieved Jonah's troubles," using רעה in another nuance of "trouble," that of personal discomfort. The entire term הציל מרעה "to relieve trouble," "deliver from harm" is almost certainly intended as a sort of *double entendre* since it would apply to what God has already decided to do for Nineveh, as well as to what he is now doing for Jonah. Jonah's "trouble" in this case was simply his physical discomfort. He could hardly have chosen to stay in a city about to be demolished; but living outside in the wilderness was no happy alternative.

The text says literally that "Jonah rejoiced with a great joy at the climbing gourd." His actions betrayed his inconsistency. The gourd suddenly appeared and grew very quickly (v 10). Jonah could hardly miss the point that this, too, was a merciful gift to him from God. But such gifts were fine with him only as long as they were not also given to his enemies, i.e., the enemies of his people. A general rejoicing in Nineveh over deliverance from divine wrath would infuriate Jonah. But personally, his own special good fortune resulting from an act of pure divine grace was a great delight. The gourd was a wonderful relief! Its thick, wide leaves gave him cool shade. The Hebrew word הציל "relieve," "deliver" is so close to הצל "to provide shade" as to be, in all probability, a further evidence of paronomasia on the part of the narrator.

7 The climbing gourd had given only one full day of shade: just enough for Jonah to appreciate its great worth to him during his stubborn vigil. But God's purpose in the gourd was to teach Jonah something about concern and compassion, so God "designated" (וימן, as before) "a worm" (תולעת), the genus of which is unspecified, to kill the gourd plant by eating away the root or stem. Any speculation about the exact nature of the gourd, how fast such plants can grow, or the nature of the worm and how fast such worms may eat is useless. The fact that the rinicus (castor-oil plant) is easily killed even by slight damage to its stem should have some weight in the identification of the plant, but attempts to explain the mechanics of miracles are usually doomed to failure. As was the case with the fish, the climbing gourd and worm did a special, abnormal task at Yahweh's bidding, and that is all the hearer / reader is told about them. Cut through, the gourd died and shriveled, its leaves no longer providing shade for the top of Jonah's hut and therefore the top of his head.

8 The day the gourd died was not to be a normal day by any means. Again God specially designated (וימן) an element of nature to affect Jonah. It was the wind once more (cf. 1:14), this time an east wind so hot and / or debilitating (see n. 8.a.) that it robbed Jonah of all comfort. This wind may have been that sort called elsewhere the scirocco, i.e., constant hot air so full of positive ions that it affects the levels of serotonin and other brain neurotransmitters, causing exhaustion, depression, feelings of unreality, and, occasionally, bizarre behavior. In some Moslem countries, the punishment for a crime committed while the scirocco is blowing may be reduced at judicial

discretion, so strongly does the prolonged hot wind affect thinking and actions.

To this God added a cloudless sky so that the sun beat down (lit., "attacked," נכה, the same verb used to describe the action of the worm on the gourd) on Jonah. Such weather, oppressive in the extreme at least where Jonah's shelter was located, caused Jonah to experience sunstroke / heat prostration, the common symptoms of which are physical weakness and mental anguish or depression. (The verb translated "overcome," עלף, hithpael, is used in Amos 8:13 to describe the desperate weakness caused by prolonged thirst.)

Jonah then uttered a plea for death, the same plea he stubbornly repeated later, as the audience already knows from v 4. His words, echoing those of Elijah in a despondent state on Mt. Horeb / Sinai (1 Kgs 19:4), are the words of a suffering prophet. Like Jeremiah (Jer 20:7–18) or Moses (Num 11:10–15) or Elijah, he apparently really believed he was enduring misery for a proper cause. He wanted to see Nineveh's destruction through to the end on behalf of his people Israel, and yet the circumstances were so hard that he could not stand them. He still did not comprehend how wrong he was. From his point of view, everything had gone wrong for him, and he simply couldn't stand it anymore.

9 God then intervened verbally, because the incident of the climbing gourd was planned not as a harassment, but as an object lesson to teach Jonah something about the inconsistency of his own position over against that of God. God began his question with the same wording which constituted his previous question (v 4), "What right do you have to be angry?" (ההיטב חרה לך), though here he added: "about the gourd." This question about the right to be angry is central to the whole book, and crucial to the narrator's point in telling the story as he has. What right do we have to demand that God should favor us and not others? By reducing the question to the particular issue of the gourd, God focused the question in a way that would cause Jonah to condemn himself by his own words. Jonah did just that.

His reply to God could not be more appropriate to the point God will make. Jonah insisted in the strongest terms possible that the gourd was important to him. It was significant in his eyes! He loved it! It delighted him! Now that it is dead, he is furious. He feels enough anger at the loss of that plant to prefer death to life.

In the argument, God now has him where he wants him. Of his own free will Jonah has declared a plant to be eminently worthy to live, a thing of great concern to himself. He has expressed outrage that the plant has been annihilated. It is horribly wrong that the gourd has been struck down!

10–11 So how can it be right that Nineveh should be struck down? If it was not right for the gourd how can it be right for Nineveh? Jonah could give no good answer to that question, even if he tried. The book ends with an explanation from Yahweh himself, a clear and convincing argument against Jonah's (and the audience's) narrow particularism.

Yahweh's speech focuses on concern (חוס). Jonah's delight, anger, disappointment, frustration, and the other emotions he may have experienced in connection with the gourd are all aspects of concern. Likewise, the various "emotions" Yahweh may have felt toward Nineveh can be summarized by the statement that he had concern for it. In other words, Yahweh was only doing for Nineveh what Jonah had insisted *he* had the right to do for a plant. The verb חוס can mean both to be worried about, to be concerned about, and also to show active concern for, i.e., even "to spare" (usually with על) as in 1 Sam 24:11 and Ezek 24:14. Yahweh thus almost certainly declared by these words not only his right to feel concerned about but also his right to intervene for the benefit of Nineveh.

Additionally, the divine speech contrasts the worth of the gourd with that of Nineveh. The gourd was only a plant. Jonah invested no effort in it, and it lived only a day. Nineveh, however, was the important city (העיר הגדולה, cf. 1:2, etc.) of its day, a city of enormous population. (On the population of Nineveh, probably cited as a round figure [Rudolph, *Jona*, 368, n. 15], i.e., a dozen myriads, cf. Wiseman, *TynB* 30 [1979] 35–42, the most detailed recent treatment of the question.) Can there be any doubt which is the more important, the more deserving of concern?

But there is more. The speech goes on to point out that the people of Nineveh "do not know their right hand from their left," an idiomatic expression for a lack of knowledge, and / or innocence. The precise sense of the expression is hard to isolate. It does not seem to refer to infants per se (the closest OT parallel construction being Isa 7:15–16) as if the total population were so huge that just the infants alone were more than 100,000 in number. The first two words, ידע בין ("know the difference between"), occur in the OT otherwise only in 2 Sam 19:36 [35], where they clearly indicate an inability to discriminate ("between what is good and what is not"). An expression in Deut 1:39 (ידע טוב ורע "knowing good and evil"), sometimes cited in connection with Jonah 4:11, is actually a different idiom, essentially the same as is used in Gen 2:17 in the phrase "tree of knowledge of good and evil," i.e., "all sorts of knowledge" (good and evil being polarities which express totality in the Semitic merism).

This "lack of knowledge" displayed by the people of Nineveh probably means therefore that they could not make the kind of decision that would give them relief from the trouble (רעה) that had come to Yahweh's attention (1:2). The full expression ("who do not know their right hand from their left") might even be translated "helpless" or "pitiful" in keeping with Yahweh's announced intention to show the Ninevites concern in their plight. This is a profound point in light of the assumption of Jonah, and quite probably most ancient Israelites, that the people of Nineveh would surely be fully responsible in every sense for whatever miseries may have befallen them. It is *not* likely that Yahweh's words are to be interpreted as implying that the Ninevites are morally innocent, e.g., that they bear no guilt for their many crimes detailed in Nahum and other OT prophetical books. The people themselves acknowledge by their penitence that they have done wrong (3:5), and the royal decree categorically so states (3:8). Rather, these Assyrians are "innocent" and undiscerning in another sense: they are trapped by their troubles, not knowing how to escape them. Their troubles may not have necessarily been the result of any particular sin they have committed, especially since in other times they prospered while equally as evil. For most of its history, in other words, Assyria's fortunes were no more linked to its faithfulness to divine law than were Israel's fortunes. In the long run, sin against God was the cause for Assyria's destruction (Zeph 2:15) just as for Israel's (2 Kgs 17), but in the short run, i.e., at virtually any given point prior to the final destruction of these nations, they were not subject to punishments which correlated directly with the intensity of their sins (cf. 2 Kgs 17:14). Nineveh got away with a great deal of evil before Jonah's visit, and it would do so again for another century and a half until its downfall in 611 B.C. Here, in spite of its sinfulness, the miseries the city has endured have moved Yahweh to provide a means of escape. Jonah's preaching had set two options before the people of Nineveh: repent and find relief, or continue to sin arrogantly and be totally overthrown. Yahweh offered this choice out of pure grace, to a people who had known no other course than sin, and who could be rescued from their present difficulties (cf. *Comment* 3:6, 7) only by divine fiat.

The mention of animals at the very end of the book has often either puzzled or misled commentators. It has been thought to represent a final humorous twist, especially because the previous reference to animals, in sackcloth (3:8), as well as the reference to animal life in general in the book (the fish and the worm) are thought to be somehow humorous. On the other hand, it is possible to make too much of the status of animals, as if they were being declared here to be virtually equal to human beings, important as animals—especially cattle—are considered in the OT. The reference to animals, rather, makes a simple point: God would have every right to spare Nineveh if only because of the dumb animals in it! They *alone* would be worth more by any accounting than was the gourd Jonah had become so attached to. If it was unfair in Jonah's thinking that the poor innocent gourd should die, how could he relish the death of countless cattle just because it was Assyrians who happened to be their owners?

It is possible of course, that the animals are mentioned because animals are *ipso facto* innocent and also lack intellectual prowess. Thereby Jonah and the audience would understand that the Ninevites, likewise, are innocent and stupid. But a more likely reason for the mention of animals is that they constitute the middle point in the worth scale upon which the argument of Yahweh is based. That is, the people of Nineveh are of enormous worth. They are human beings (אדם), and they are the citizens of the most important city of their day. The animals (בהמה) in turn are of less worth, but still significant in the economy of any nation or city. (In the ancient world, possession of cattle, like slaves, was a measure of personal worth; e.g., Gen 12:16; 32:5; Job 1:3; 42:12.) The gourd, on the other hand, is of minor worth. Compared to many animals, a single small plant would hardly be of great significance by any method of reasoning. But compared to many people, a plant is insignificant indeed. Jonah has furiously argued for the worth of a one-day-old plant (v 9b). He can have no good argument, then, against the worth of Nineveh, with all its people and animals.

Explanation

"What right do you have to be angry?" constitutes the challenge of chap. 4 for the hearer / reader. God's question to Jonah in vv 4 and 9 is God's challenge to the book's audience as well. The answer to the question is not complex, though it may be quite unpleasant to those who have always expected God to take sides among the nations of the world in their rivalries and wars: God does what is right by reason of the fact that it is his nature to do so (v 2) as Jonah admits; no one therefore can rightfully be angry that God should act according to his own nature.

Nineveh ought to have been spared, its rampant sinfulness past and future notwithstanding. The Ninevites may have been spiritually incompetent (v 11), lacking Israel's history of revelation in word and mighty deed. They may, according to human terms, have deserved all the misery they had been enduring, and wholesale destruction besides. These idolaters (idolatry being plainly stupid in OT terms; cf. Isa 44:9–20; Hos 13:2) may have had a completely objectionable theology and a record of disgusting behavior, but they had believed God's word when it was preached to them (3:5) and God had accepted their earnest penitence (3:10), temporary though its results may have been.

What God did *was* right. Nineveh had great intrinsic worth in spite of its many objectionable characteristics. It had worth by reason of being the important city of its day, by reason of containing a large human population, or even by reason of its many cattle. No one—certainly not Jonah who argued vehemently for the great worth in a single plant—could have the right to doubt the propriety of God's finding worth in Nineveh. Yet Jonah hated the whole business enough to die. He had resisted God's will in this connection once already, unto death, as it were (1:12). Stubborn and unrepentant himself to the end, he could not abide seeing God show compassion and grace to the enemies of his people, Israel. Jonah was sincere, dedicated, honest, and even courageous. He was principled, too, though his principles were badly askew. In chap. 4 the pettiness and ultimate inconsistency of his position is shown for what it is. He had accepted and even hymned God's merciful deliverance for himself (2:3–10) and had shown that he knew what it was to feel deep concern for something that of itself may not have actually earned any such concern (4:10). But he would rather die (4:3) than see Yahweh do likewise.

The fish was a gift to Jonah. It delivered him from death. He certainly did not deserve that deliverance. The climbing gourd was also a gift to Jonah. He had done nothing to earn it (4:10). Why then cannot God, in the same sort of way, give Nineveh something it does not deserve, has not earned? What right does Jonah have to be angry? What right have we to be angry that God should bless people, groups, institutions, nations who have done nothing to deserve such blessing? Can we ever rightly resent—let alone denounce—the grace of God shown to any of the world's nations or peoples, oppressed or oppressor, peace-loving or war-making? What sense is there in the common, tacit assumption that *our* only nation is *his* only nation?

The "weightier matters" of the law include mercy (Matt 22:23). We who have had mercy shown to us must, of all people, be willing to show mercy in return (Matt 18:33). Jonah knew all along that God was gracious, compassionate, faithful, and loyal and that he decided against bringing death whenever he could find cause to relent from it (cf. Gen 18:21–33; Exod 32:11–14). Yet any Christian is capable, at least secretly, of Jonah's stance. Many Christians have taken it openly: praying against rather than for their enemies, taking delight in the misfortunes of the ungodly, whether individual, corporate, or national. But no Christian ought to take Jonah's stance. Jonah said "I have the right!" But he did not.

Index of Authors Cited

Index of Selected Subjects

Index of Biblical Texts

[Listings are for the *Hebrew* coordinates where these differ from English, and primarily for those verse references whose location would not be obvious from the *Contents*.]

A. Old Testament

B. Apocrypha

C. New Testament

Index of Hebrew Words